LIPSEY&CHRYSTAL
ECONOMICS

13TH EDITION

OXFORD

UNIVERSITY PRESS

OXFORD
UNIVERSITY PRESS

Great Clarendon Street, Oxford OX2 6DP,
United Kingdom

Oxford University Press is a department of the University of Oxford.
It furthers the University's objective of excellence in research, scholarship,
and education by publishing worldwide. Oxford is a registered trade mark of
Oxford University Press in the UK and in certain other countries

Tenth edition 2004
Eleventh edition 2007
Twelfth edition 2011
Impression: 1

Published in the United States of America by Oxford University Press
198 Madison Avenue, New York, NY 10016, United States of America

British Library Cataloguing in Publication Data
Data available

Library of Congress Control Number: 2014959010

ISBN 978–0–19–967683–5

Printed in Great Britain by Bell & Bain Ltd., Glasgow

OUTLINE CONTENTS

DETAILED CONTENTS

MICROECONOMICS

PART ONE MARKETS AND CONSUMERS

PART TWO MARKETS AND FIRMS

MACROECONOMICS

WHY STUDY ECONOMICS?

Some of you may already be excited by the prospect of studying economics, but others among you will answer the question posed in the heading with 'It was part of my course of study, so I had no choice'. To both the reluctant conscripts and the willing volunteers we offer hope and encouragement.

Economics studies topics that are highly relevant both to decision-making in most jobs that you are likely to do in life and to understanding many of the most pressing issues facing today's world—free markets versus government intervention, resource exhaustion, pollution and environmental degradation, climate change, the revolution in digital communications media, government taxes and spending, employment, unemployment and recessions, inflation, income inequality in advanced nations, rapid growth in some of the world's emerging economies, and stagnation among many of the world's poorest nations. Thus, economics is both a preparation for taking day-to-day decisions in a firm or other organization, and training in how to understand many of the 'big issues' of our time.

One of the most important events in the first three-quarters of the twentieth century was the rise of communism. One of the most important events in the last quarter of that century was communism's fall. The century-long battle between free markets and government planning as alternatives for organizing economic activity had been settled in almost all countries with a degree of decisiveness that is rare for great social issues. Understanding why market-oriented capitalist economies perform so much better than fully planned or highly government controlled economies is a core issue in economics. Economic theories are expressly designed to help us understand the successes (and, where they occur, the failures) of free-market economies.

The triumph of market-oriented economies suggests that income- and wealth-creating activities are usually best accomplished through the efforts of private citizens operating in largely unregulated markets. But this is not the end of the story, for at least three fundamental reasons.

First, although market economies certainly work better than fully planned economies, they do not work perfectly. One of today's great social issues is how best to allocate the responsibilities of government, leaving it to do what it can do best and leaving free markets to do what they can do best. Economists ask: 'What are the important roles that governments can play in improving the functioning of a basically market-oriented economy?' During the three decades or so up to 2007 the consensus was moving in favour of more market freedom. However, the global financial crisis of 2007–8 raised questions about the extent to which markets can be left alone. Substantial reforms of banking and financial market regulation have been introduced since the crisis, but there is also an ongoing debate in official and academic circles about the regulatory policies needed to avoid, or at least mitigate, any future crises in the financial system—crises that can have ramifications far beyond the bounds of the financial system, spreading to have an adverse effect on the entire economy.

Secondly, market economies produce severe short-term cycles as well as long-term growth. Long-term growth has raised the living standards of the ordinary working person from the horrors and degradations described by Charles Dickens in the nineteenth century to those of the property-owning workers of today, whose living standards are higher than those of 99.9 per cent of all the people of all classes who ever lived on Earth. Yet capitalist growth is uneven growth, because economic activity cycles around its rising trend. In recessions, unemployment is high and living standards typically stand still or even fall temporarily. Although each cycle tends to leave living standards higher than all previous cycles, the ups and downs of uneven market-driven growth can be upsetting to those affected by it. During the 1990s and 2000s it appeared that the authorities had learned to avoid major cycles in activity, but the recession of 2008–9 made clear that sharp downturns can still occur, that these are costly in terms of lost output and employment, and that governments have only limited power to moderate their effects.

Thirdly, capitalist growth is unequal growth. Although most people agree that it is desirable to create higher incomes and wealth, they also care about how these are distributed among all citizens. Poverty for a minority in the midst of plenty for the majority has always been a problem in wealthy countries—just as poverty for the majority and plenty for the minority has always been a problem for poor countries. A recent phenomenon in some of the richest countries has been rapidly rising real incomes for the few very best off while the average worker sees little or no real income rise. We ask: 'What are the sources of these distributional shifts and can governments do anything to affect the income and wealth distributions that market economies create?'

Economists have been in the forefront of analysing, explaining, and, where appropriate, offering solutions to all of the issues mentioned above—and many more. They have often succeeded in these tasks, mainly because economics has a core of useful theories that explain how markets work and evaluate their performance. Although some economic analysis is extremely abstract, and sometimes even economists wonder about its value, the basic core of economic theory that is the secret of the subject's success can be understood by anyone who is willing to make the effort. This basic theory has an excellent record in illuminating issues in ways that lead to both deeper understanding and useful policy recommendations.

When you start to read this book, you are setting out on the study of a subject that, as the above discussion suggests, is highly relevant to understanding and improving the world in which we live. Approached in the right way, your study will be an adventure. The basic theory must be mastered. Whether or not you find this effort fun in itself, you will find surprisingly early in your studies that theories can be used to understand many practical issues. The world is complex, and fully understanding its economic aspects requires much more economic theory than can be packed into one elementary textbook. But mastery of the subject to the level of this one book will contribute greatly to your understanding of many important issues and many of the policies directed at dealing with them. It will also provide you with a toolbox that will prove useful in the world of work, whatever occupation you eventually enter.

Good luck and good studying!

RICHARD LIPSEY and ALEC CHRYSTAL
Vancouver, BC, and Cambridge, England
August 2014

NEW TO THIS EDITION:

- Fully revised chapter on fiscal and monetary policy brings students up to date with key real policy questions that have parallels in most major economies.

- Greater coverage of quantitative easing and fiscal retrenchment enables students to understand current macro policy dilemmas.

- A wholly new chapter deals with new expectations for a stable inflation rate, helping students to understand policy choices and areas where conventional analysis does not reflect reality.

- An innovative macro section which teaches the theory as explaining three actual inflationary regimes: firstly, the gold standard and Bretton Woods in which the inflation expectations were firmly anchored at, or close to, zero are covered by the basic macro that everyone must learn; secondly, the period of ragged inflation which is covered by the standard extensions to cover inflation expectations; thirdly, the period of inflation targeting from 1992 to today, which provides the context for the new chapter developing the variations of the basic model which are appropriate to a world in which inflation is successfully targeted at a low and fully expected rate.

- A new chapter on risk and financial crises explains the role of risk in the economic system and why the financial system is prone to occasional crises.

HOW TO USE THIS BOOK

This book is enriched with learning features designed to help you develop the knowledge and skills you need to study economics. This guided tour shows you how to use your textbook fully and get the most out of your study.

Learning objectives

Each chapter opens with a bulleted list of learning objectives outlining the main concepts and ideas you will encounter in this part of the text. These serve as helpful signposts for learning and allow you to clearly track your progress and revision.

Boxes

125 boxes found throughout the book give you practical illustrations of the theory described in the main body of the text. They include real-life examples and empirical demonstrations as well as more detailed explanations of key points, all to ensure that you fully grasp core economic theory.

Key terms

Key terms are printed in bold the first time they appear in the text to alert you to each new concept. These terms are then compiled and defined in the glossary at the end of the book.

CASE STUDIES

1. Game theory for real

The global video games market exceeded revenue
billion in 2013 and was expected by cons
Gartner[14] to exceed $110 billion in 2015.

The biggest segment in this market by reven
video game consoles, estimated to be worth $55 b
2015, up from $37 billion in 2012. A surprising
of this vast market is that it is completely domin
three players: Microsoft with its Xbox, Sony with

Case studies

All chapters, except Chapter 1, conclude with a
minimum of two topical case studies. These cases
will help you to contextualize your understanding of core chapter themes and encourage you to
apply your learning to real-life situations.

SUMMARY

■ International trade normally requires the exchange of
the currency of one country for that of another. The
major exception is trade within the eurozone. The
exchange rate between two currencies is the amount of
one currency that must be paid in order to obtain one
unit of another currency.

The market for foreign exchange

■ The demand for pounds arises from UK exports of goods
and services, income payments from overseas, capital
inflows, and the desire of foreign governments to use
sterling assets as part of their reserves.

End-of-chapter summaries

At the end of each chapter, the key points and
concepts are summarized to help fix them in your
mind. This feature reinforces your understanding
of the material you have just covered and are an
excellent revision tool.

TOPICS FOR REVIEW

■ Effect of a rise in the price level on the *IS* and *LM* curves
■ The real money effect
■ The wealth effect
■ The balance-of-payments effect
■ The derivation of the *AD* curve
■ Causes of demand shocks
■ The SRAS curve, definition and slope
■ What causes the *SRAS* curve to shift

Topics for review

Each chapter ends with a list of topics for review
which prompt you to evaluate your understanding of these subjects. They will prove very helpful
when you come to revision.

QUESTIONS

1. Your local authority undoubtedly provides a police
   station, a fire brigade, and a public library.
   a) What are the market imperfections, if any, that
      each of these seeks to correct?
   b) Which of these are closest to being public goods?
   c) Which are furthest from being public goods?
   d) What would happen if governments were
      prevented from offering these services?
2. Not counting the ones mentioned in the text, list
   some goods and services that are:

   a) non-rivalrous but excludable

End-of-chapter questions

Problem-solving exercises and essay-type questions at the end of each chapter help you to
develop your analytical skills. Use them to test
what you have learned so far before moving on
to the next chapter, or as a basis for group discussion or further revision.

HOW TO USE THE ONLINE RESOURCE CENTRE

The Online Resource Centre which accompanies this book provides students with ready-to-use learning resources. They are free of charge and are designed to maximise the learning experience. www.oxfordtextbooks.co.uk/orc/lipsey13e

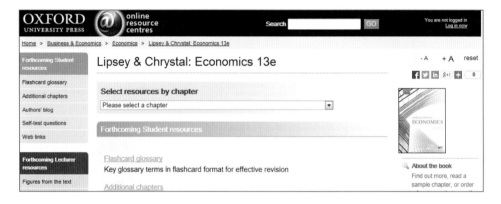

FOR STUDENTS

Self-test questions

A suite of questions for each chapter in the book allows you to test your knowledge of the key themes in the text.

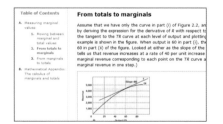

Interactive chapters

Additional course material is provided in an interactive format to assist and support your learning.

Web links

A selection of regularly updated web links, chosen by the authors with comments that explain their value allows, you to conduct further research on those topics that are of particular interest to you.

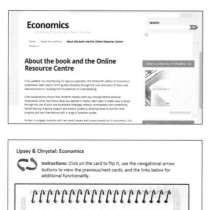

Author blog

Visit the authors' blog to read further discussions of current economic issues.

Flashcard glossary

The key glossary terms from the text are presented in an interactive format to help you remember and revise important concepts

FOR LECTURERS

PowerPoint slides

A suite of PowerPoint slides is provided for use in lecture presentations. Arranged by chapter theme, the slides may also be used as handouts in class and can be easily adapted to suit your teaching style.

Test bank

A suite of test questions is provided which you can use for assessment purposes.

Instructor's manual

This comprehensive guide for instructors provides you with further discussion of the core themes in each chapter as well as the answers to all of the questions set in the textbook.

Figures from the text

You can download all of the figures found in the textbook electronically and you can use them to support student learning.

VLE cartridge

The VLE cartridge allows you to fully integrate the book's online resources with your own teaching materials. By enabling you to import all the material at once it provides you with the ability to customize the resources and allows students access to all of the course content within your institution's Virtual Learning Environment.

ABOUT DASHBOARD
SIMPLE. MOBILE. INFORMATIVE.

Dashboard is a cloud-based online assessment and revision tool. It comes pre-loaded with self-test questions for students, a homework course if your module leader has adopted Dashboard, and additional resources as listed below.

For further information on how to access your Dashboard course, visit: www.oxfordtextbooks.co.uk/dashboard/

SIMPLE: With a highly intuitive design, it will take you less than 15 minutes to learn and master the system.

MOBILE: You can access Dashboard from every major platform and device connected to the internet, whether that's a computer, tablet or smartphone.

INFORMATIVE: Your assignment and assessment results are automatically graded, giving your instructor a clear view of the class's understanding of the course content.

FOR STUDENTS

Self-test questions
A suite of questions for each chapter in the book allows you to test your knowledge of the key themes in the text. These consist of a mix of multiple-choice, short-answer and problem-based questions.

Assignments
If your module leader has adopted Dashboard, they will be able to assign test questions to you, so they can check your progress.

Interactive chapters
Additional course material is provided in an interactive format to assist and support your learning.

Web links

A selection of regularly updated web links chosen by the authors with comments which explain their value allows you to conduct further research on those topics that are of particular interest to you.

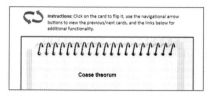

Flashcard glossary

The key glossary terms from the text are presented in an interactive format to help you remember and revise important concepts.

FOR LECTURERS

Pre-loaded homework assignments and test bank

A pre-loaded homework course structured around the book is available, supported by a test bank containing a wealth of additional multiple-choice questions. Your students can follow the pre-loaded course, or you can customize it, allowing you to add questions from the test bank or from your existing materials to meet your specific teaching needs.

Gradebook

Dashboard will automatically grade the homework assignments.

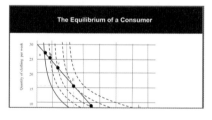

PowerPoint slides

A suite of PowerPoint slides is provided for use in lecture presentations. Arranged by chapter theme, the slides may also be used as handouts in class and can be easily adapted to suit your teaching style.

Instructor's manual

This comprehensive guide for instructors provides you with further discussion of the core themes in each chapter as well as the answers to all of the questions set in the textbook.

Figures from the text

You can download all of the figures found in the textbook electronically and can use them to support student learning.

APPROACHES TO STUDYING ECONOMICS

You need to study a book on economics in a different way from how you would study a book on, say, history or English literature. Economic theory has a logical structure that builds on itself from stage to stage. Thus, if you understand some concept or theory only imperfectly, you will run into increasing difficulty when, in subsequent chapters, this concept or theory is taken for granted and built upon. Because of its logical structure, quite long chains of reasoning are encountered; if A then B; if B then C; if C then D; and if D then E. Each step in the argument may seem simple enough, but the cumulative effect of several steps, one on top of the other, may be bewildering on first encounter. Thus when, having followed the argument step by step, you encounter the statement 'It is now obvious that if A then E', it may not seem at all obvious to you. This is a problem that everyone encounters with chains of reasoning. The only way to deal with it is to follow the argument through several times. Eventually, as the reasoning becomes familiar, it will become obvious that *if A then E*.

Economics has its own technical language or jargon. At first you may feel that you are merely being asked to put complicated names to commonsense ideas. To some extent this is true. It is a necessary step, however, because loose thinking about vaguely formed ideas is a quick route to error in economics. Furthermore, when you begin to put several ideas together to see what follows from them, jargon—a clearly defined term to refer to each idea—becomes a necessary part of your equipment.

A book on economics is to be worked at, and understood step by step. It is usually a good procedure to read a chapter quickly in order to see the general run of the argument, and at this stage you might omit the captions to the figures. You then need to re-read the chapter carefully, making sure that the argument is understood step by step. On this reading, you *must* study the captions to all the figures carefully. If you do not understand the captions, you have not understood the economics. You should not be discouraged if, occasionally at this stage, you find yourself spending quite a bit of time on only a few pages.

A pencil and paper are valuable adjuncts to your reading. Difficult arguments should be followed by building up your own diagram while the argument unfolds, rather than relying on the printed diagram, which is complete from the beginning. Numerical examples can be invented to illustrate general propositions.

In short, the technical vocabulary aside, you must seek to *understand* economics, not to memorize it. Theories, principles, and concepts are always turning up in slightly unfamiliar guises. If you have understood your economics, this poses no problem; if you have merely memorized it, it spells disaster.

Email us

Economics is a subject about which one never stops learning. We are grateful to many users—students and teachers—who have taken the trouble to email us pointing out possible errors, making comments, and offering suggestions. We hope that readers will continue to teach us with as many further comments and criticisms as they have in the past. We try to acknowledge every such communication.

OUTLINES FOR SHORT OR MODULAR COURSES

This book provides a comprehensive coverage of basic economics suitable for a full one-year course. We have, however, designed the text to be flexible enough to cover shorter courses. To illustrate, we give our suggestions for the chapter content of several shorter courses.

A short Introduction to Economics course (20 weeks)

Chapters 1–14 for basic micro, and 15–25 for basic macro

An Introduction to Microeconomics course (one semester)

Chapters 1–14

An Introduction to Macroeconomics course (one semester)

Chapters 1 and 15–25. (Alternatively, for a course with a growth emphasis include Chapter 26; for a course with an international emphasis, the key chapters are 24 and 27, with addition of our web-based material on developing countries.)

ACKNOWLEDGEMENTS

Finally we wish to say a word of thanks to some people who have helped make this book possible. In our office, Joanna Lipsey-Ouimet has been tireless in dealing with the manuscript and the art. At the OUP, we are indebted to Sarah Iles for guiding the project for most of its gestation. Francesca Mitchell and Lien Vanmarsnille have helped in tidying up the manuscript and getting it into production. This edition has also benefited from many students, especially Cass undergraduates, who have pointed out mistakes or unclear passages in the previous edition. We would also like to thank Helen Stedman for her diligent proof reading. The usual disclaimer of course holds here: for all remaining shortcomings and mistakes, the authors may blame each other, but readers should blame us both.

R.G.L.
K.A.C.

MICRO
ECONOMICS

PART **ONE**

MARKETS AND CONSUMERS

ECONOMIC ISSUES AND CONCEPTS

A modern economy produces millions of goods and services for people to choose from. It provides jobs for most people who want to work. It allows us to travel and communicate easily with anybody anywhere in the world. It produces growth in the total output available for citizens to consume. Yet nobody has sat down and planned how all this will work. Its workings have evolved as a response to economic forces interacting with individuals and institutions. Our main tasks in this book are to study how such an economy works, why it does not always work well, and what can be done to improve its performance where that is needed.

This book is divided into two main parts. Microeconomics studies how and why basic resources are transformed by producers into all the many goods and services that modern consumers want. Macroeconomics studies the amount of activity in the economy as a whole and the role of governments in trying to influence that activity. Chapters 2–14 are about microeconomics, while Chapters 15–27 are about macroeconomics.

This introductory chapter provides a broad context for the study of microeconomics, but we also discuss the important links between microeconomics and macroeconomics that have become topical as a result of the financial crisis of 2007–8. It is intended as an introduction for those of you who are immediately going to study microeconomics further, and as providing essential basic micro information for those readers who are going on to study macro now. For you, Chapter 15 provides the main introduction to macroeconomics.

In the present chapter you will learn:

- that a modern market economy uses price signals to solve the complex problems involved in producing all the goods and services that people want;
- how economics studies the choice between competing demands for scarce resources;
- how production, employment, and consumption decisions interact;
- that the market economy usually delivers outcomes desired by consumers;
- that governments sometimes intervene when markets fail to produce results that are regarded as desirable.

The complexity of the modern economy

If you want a pint of milk, you go to the shop and buy it. The shop owner is just one part of a complex supply chain that makes this milk available when you want it. When the shop owner needs more milk, she orders it from the distributor, who in turn gets it from the bottling plant, which in its turn gets it from the dairy farmer. The dairy farmer buys cattle feed and electric milking machines, and gets power to run all his equipment by putting a plug into a wall socket where the electricity is supplied as he needs it. The milking machines are made from parts manufactured in several different parts of the world, while these in their turn are made from materials mined and refined in a dozen or more different countries.

As it is with the milk you drink, so it is with everything else that you buy. When you go to the appropriate shop, what you want is normally in stock. Those who make these products find that all the required components and materials are available when needed—even though these things typically come from many different parts of the world and are made by people who have no direct dealings with each other. The economy is so good at delivering what we want when we want it that we only tend to notice when it goes wrong.

The sales and purchases in which you are involved are only a small part of the amazingly complex set of transactions that take place every day in a modern society. Shipments arrive daily at our seaports and airports. These include raw materials, such as iron ore and logs, parts, such as computer chips and circuit boards, tools, such as screwdrivers and digging equipment, perishables, such as fresh flowers and fruits, and all kinds of manufactured goods, such as washing machines and TV sets. Rail and road shippers receive and dispatch these goods to thousands of different destinations. Some go directly to consumers. Others are used by domestic firms as inputs into the manufacture of their own products—of which some will be sold in the home market and some exported. Box 1.1 reports on a project that illustrates that the modern economy is able to deliver complex products at remarkably low prices.

Most people who want to work have a job. By working they earn incomes, which they then spend on the goods and services that they, and other workers, produce. Some people own businesses that employ workers to assist in making and selling their products. Business owners earn part of their income as profit from their enterprises, though they may also pay themselves some salary as managers if they work in their own firms.

Some activity takes place in the public sector in which the services produced are provided free to consumers, and where wages and salaries are paid for by the government out of general taxation. Public sector workers then spend their incomes on a wide range of goods, just as other types of workers do.

Self-organization

Economics as a subject began when thoughtful observers asked themselves how such a complex set of transactions is organized. Who coordinates the vast array of production, employment, and consumption decisions? Who makes sure that all the activities fit together, providing jobs to produce the goods and services that people want and delivering those things to where they are wanted?

The answer is: no one!

The great insight of the early economists was that an economy based on free-market transactions is self-organizing.

By following their own self-interest, doing what seems best and most profitable for themselves, and responding to the incentives of prices set on open markets, people produce a spontaneous social order. In that order, literally thousands of millions of transactions and activities fit together to produce the things that people want within the constraints set by the resources that are available to the nation.

Box 1.1 Toasting the complexity of a modern economy

A good example of how the modern economy delivers very complex products at low prices is provided by a project conducted by Thomas Thwaites,[1] a London-based design student, who set out to make a simple toaster from scratch. His comparator was a basic two-slice toaster available on sale at Asda in 2010 for £4.47 (but was £3.94 when he started the project). Much more sophisticated toasters were on sale at the same time in high street stores for anything from £10 to around £50.

Thwaites started by taking the Asda version apart. He found that it had 404 separate components made of many different materials. He then set about collecting the raw materials to construct components for a toaster of his own making. For him this meant not just buying finished components like wire and screws, but rather getting the ore necessary for metal parts and converting this into refined metal before moulding it into the needed parts.

It took him nine months of his time and £1187.54 of his own money to construct from scratch a device that would toast a piece of bread. This sum excludes the value of his own time, which would have increased the costs substantially even if he had only paid himself the minimum wage.

His product worked far less well and looked much less attractive than the basic Asda model!

The message we take from this is that the modern world economy does a remarkable job of delivering complex products that consumers want at low prices. Key elements of how it does this include a high degree of specialization in production, large volumes of specific outputs that reduce costs per unit, mechanization of routine tasks that save labour time, and globalization of supply chains which means that components can be bought from their cheapest source. All of these ideas and other parts of the story will be developed in the following chapters. Just bear in mind how expensive and difficult it would be to make your own iPad, mobile phone, laptop, or TV, yet the modern economy provides these at prices that many can afford. It is easy to take this for granted but it is actually a remarkable achievement.

[1] Thomas Thwaites, The Toaster Project, New York: Princeton Architectural Press, 2011. See also: <http://www.metropolismag.com/story/20100317/the-cost-of-convenience> and <http://www. thetoasterproject.org>

The great Scottish economist and political philosopher Adam Smith, who was the first to develop this insight fully, put it this way:

It is not from the benevolence of the butcher, the brewer, or the baker, that we expect our dinner, but from their regard to their own interest. We address ourselves, not to their humanity but to their self-love, and never talk to them of our own necessities but of their advantages. Nobody but a beggar chuses to depend chiefly upon the benevolence of his fellow-citizens. (Smith 1776, pages 26–7 of 1976 edn)

Smith is not saying that benevolence is unimportant—indeed, he praises it in many passages. He is saying, however, that the massive number of economic interactions that characterize any economy cannot all be motivated by benevolence. Although benevolence does motivate some of our actions, such as when we donate to earthquake, famine, and tsunami relief funds, the majority of our everyday actions are motivated by self-interest. The individual pursuit of self-interest is, therefore, the main behavioural incentive that drives a market economy to behave as it does.

Efficient organization

That a market economy is self-organizing is beyond question, but how efficient the results of that organization are is much debated. Another great insight, which was hinted at by Smith and fully developed over the next century and a half, was that this spontaneously generated social order is relatively efficient. Loosely speaking (we will be more precise later), efficiency means that the resources available to a nation are organized to produce the maximum possible total output of the types of goods and services that people wish to consume.

An economy organized by free markets behaves almost as if some power had guided it. This does not literally mean that a supernatural presence runs economic affairs. Instead, it refers to the relatively efficient order that emerges spontaneously out of many independent decisions made by those who make, sell, and buy goods and services. The key to explaining this market behaviour is that these people all respond to the same set of prices, which are determined in markets that reflect the overall conditions of scarcity or plenty. Much of economics is devoted to understanding how this market outcome is generated, and to assessing the efficiency of that outcome.

A planned alternative

A century after Adam Smith, another great economist and political philosopher, Karl Marx, argued that although this market system would produce high total output, it would distribute that output in such a way that, over time, the rich would get richer and the poor poorer. Others took up this line of thinking and argued that when societies became rich enough, they should dispense with the spontaneous social order. They should then replace it by a consciously created system, called a command economy, or communism, in which the government plans all of the economic transactions and, in so doing, creates a more equal and just distribution of the total output.

Beginning with the USSR, the governments of many nations established systems in which conscious government central planning largely replaced the spontaneous order of the free market. For much of the twentieth century two systems—the centrally planned and the market—competed with each other for the favour of undecided governments. Then, within the last two decades of the century, governments of one communist country after another abandoned their central planning apparatus. More and more economic transactions and activities were then left to the market. Seldom has a great social issue been settled with such conclusiveness. Box 1.2 discusses some important issues that arise when economists use their analysis to give economic advice to policy-makers.

Marx was right about many things, including the importance of technological change in raising living standards over the centuries. Where the Marxists were wrong, however, was in believing that the market could be replaced by central planning as a way of organizing all of a nation's economic activities. The task was far too complex and led to inefficiencies and waste, while not satisfying many of the needs of consumers.

In contrast with the failures of command economies, the performance of the free-market price system has generally been impressive. One theme of this book is the success of the market—how the price system works to coordinate with relative efficiency the decentralized decisions made by millions of private consumers and producers. However, this does not mean that doing things better implies doing things perfectly. Another theme of this book is market failure—how and why the unaided market economy can fail to produce socially desirable outcomes.

In short, economists seek to understand how well the market economy works and identify where governments may need to intervene to correct specific aspects of market failure.

Main characteristics of market economies

What then are the main characteristics of market economies that produce this spontaneous self-organization?

• Individuals pursue their own self-interest, buying and selling what seems best for themselves and their families.

• People respond to incentives. Other things being equal, sellers seek high prices while buyers seek low prices.

Box 1.2 Economic advice: positive and normative statements

Economists give advice on a wide variety of topics. If you read a newspaper, watch television news, or listen to commentaries on the radio you will often notice some economist's opinions being reported. Perhaps it is on the prospects for unemployment, inflation, or interest rates, on some new tax, or on the case for privatization or regulation of an industry.

Advice comes in two broad types: normative and positive. A commentator might advise that the government ought to try harder to reduce unemployment or to preserve the environment. This is normative advice. He or she may be using their expert knowledge to come to conclusions about the costs of various unemployment-reducing or environment-saving schemes, but when it is said that the government *ought* to do something, this involves making judgments about the value of the various things that the government could do with its limited resources. Advice that depends on a value judgment is normative—it tells others what they ought to do.

Another type of advice is illustrated by the statement 'If the government wants to reduce unemployment, then this is an effective way of doing so'. This is positive advice. It does not rely on a judgment about the value of reducing unemployment. Instead the adviser is saying, '*If* this is what you want to do, *then* here are ways of doing it'.

It is difficult to have a rational discussion of issues if positive and normative issues are confused. Much of the success of modern science depends on the ability of scientists to separate their views on *what does*, or *might*, *happen* in the world, from their views on *what they would like to happen*. For example, until the eighteenth century almost everyone believed that the Earth was only a few thousand years old. Evidence then began to accumulate that the Earth was thousands of millions of years old. This evidence was hard for most people to accept since it ran counter to a literal reading of many religious texts. Many did not want to believe the evidence. Nevertheless, scientists, many of whom were religious, continued their research because they refused to allow their feelings about what they wanted to believe affect their search for the truth. Eventually, scientists came to accept that the Earth is about 4,500 million years old.

Distinguishing what is true from what we would like to be, or what we feel ought to be, true depends to a great extent on being able to distinguish between positive and normative statements.

Normative statements depend on value judgments. They involve issues of personal opinion, which cannot be settled by recourse to facts. In contrast, **positive statements** do not involve value judgments. They are statements about what is, was, or will be; that is, statements that are about matters of fact.

Table 1.1 **Positive and normative statements**

Positive	Normative
A. Higher interest rates cause people to save more	G. People should save more
B. High income tax rates discourage effort	H. Governments should tax the rich to help the poor
C. High taxes on cigarettes discourage smoking	I. Smoking should be discouraged
D. Road-use charges would increase traffic	J. The tax system should be used to reduce traffic
E. People are more worried about inflation than unemployment	K. Technical change is a bad thing because it puts some people out of work
F. The burning of fossil fuels is causing global warming	L. Governments should do more to reduce carbon emissions in order to save the planet from global warming

All six statements listed in Table 1.1 as positive assert things about the nature of the world in which we live. In contrast, the six statements listed as normative require value judgments.

Notice two things about the positive/normative distinction. First, positive statements need not be true. Statement D is almost certainly false. Yet it is positive, not normative. Secondly, the inclusion of a value judgment in a statement does not necessarily make the statement normative. Statement E is about the preferences that people hold; that is, about their value judgments. We could, however, check to see if people really do worry more about inflation than unemployment. We can observe their answers to survey questions, and we can observe how they vote for parties that give different priority to these objectives. There is no need to introduce a value judgment in order to check the validity of the statement itself.

You can decide for yourself why each of the other statements is either positive or normative. Remember to apply the two tests.

1) Is the statement only about actual or alleged facts? If so, it is positive.

2) Are value judgments necessary to assess the truth of the statement? If so, it is normative.

- Most prices are set in open markets in which suppliers compete to sell to potential buyers.

- People earn their incomes by selling their services to those who wish to use them—their labour services—or by selling things they have produced, or by selling the services of the property that they own.

- All of these activities are governed by a legal framework largely created, administered, and enforced by the state.

Resources and scarcity

All the issues discussed so far would not matter much if we lived in an economy of plenty, where there was enough of everything for everybody. But instead we live in a world of scarcity. Most of us want better food, clothing, housing, schooling, holidays, hospital care, and entertainment. But there is not enough to go around. Even the richest economy can only produce a small fraction of the goods and services that people would like to have if everything was free. Hence economics is concerned with the problem of choice under conditions of scarcity. We cannot have everything we want, so we must choose what we will and will not have.

At this stage, it is helpful to clarify a few terms and concepts that you will use in studying economics.

Kinds of resource

An economy's resources can be divided into four main categories:

- All those gifts of nature, such as land, forests, minerals, etc., are commonly called natural resources and called by economists **land**, for short.

- All human resources, mental and physical, both inherited and acquired, which economists call **labour**.

- All those man-made aids to further production, such as tools, machinery, and factories, which are used in the process of making other goods and services rather than being consumed for their own sake. Economists call these **capital**.

- Those who take risks by introducing new products and new ways of making old products. They develop new businesses and forms of employment and are called **entrepreneurs** or **innovators**. The resource they provide is **entrepreneurship**.

Traditionally, these resources have been called **factors of production** but we shall more frequently refer to them just as different types of input into the production process. Part 3 of this book focuses explicitly on **resource allocation**; that is, why are resources drawn into one activity rather than another—why do some people work in agriculture, others in manufacturing, and yet others in services, for example?

Ownership of resources

Private property is a key institution of a market economy. Individuals own the majority of the nation's resources. They also own the goods that they produce and the things that they buy. Some assets are owned by the state—roads, schools, public buildings, etc.—but most are, and must be, in private hands. People cannot make contracts to buy and sell what is not theirs. So without private ownership the market economy cannot function.

Kinds of production

The resources of the economy are used in a production process to make **goods** that are tangible, in that they have a physical existence, such as cars, cans of beans, and shoes, and **services** that are intangible, such as haircuts, TV programmes, car maintenance, and telephone calls. Throughout this book we use the term 'goods' to cover both goods and services, unless we explicitly make a distinction between the two.

A nation's total output of all goods and services over one year is called its gross domestic product or **GDP** for short. The act of making goods and services is called **production**, and the act of using up these goods and services to satisfy wants is called **consumption**. Anyone who makes goods or provides services is called a **producer**, and anyone who consumes them to satisfy his or her wants is called a consumer.

Choice and opportunity cost

You might want a mobile phone so that you can call your friends or an iPod so that you can listen to your favourite music. Your parents might have a car to get them to work or to visit your grandparents at the weekend. In general, people value specific goods and services because they help them to satisfy their needs. Goods and services are thus regarded as a means to an end, the satisfaction of wants. Because no economy can produce enough goods and services to satisfy all of its citizens' wants, choices must be made.

Most of us have only a specific amount of income that we can spend. If we want to have more of one thing, then we must have less of something else. For example, suppose that a friend of yours is considering whether to go out and have a few drinks with friends. The cost of these extra drinks could be measured as the money cost of so much per pint of beer or glass of juice. A more revealing way of looking at the cost, however, is in terms of what other consumption this person must forgo in order to obtain the drinks. Suppose that he or she decides to give up going to the cinema and use the money instead to buy the drinks. If the price of one drink is, say, one-third of the price of a cinema seat, then the cost of three drinks is one cinema visit; put the other way around, the cost of one cinema visit is three drinks.

Now think of the same problem at the level of a whole society. If the government decides to build more roads and finds the required money by building fewer schools, then the cost of the new roads can be expressed as so many schools per hundred miles of road.

Opportunity cost is a measure of costs expressed as alternatives given up, rather than in terms of money. If some course of action is adopted, there are typically many alternatives that could have been satisfied instead. For example, once the government has decided on its total spending for any given year, this provides it with an aggregate resource constraint and it must then decide how to allocate that spending between various competing parts of the public sector, such as health, education, and the police. So it could be, for example, that if the government decides that it wants to hire 1,000 extra police it will have to reduce spending on education and 900 fewer teachers can be afforded. So the opportunity cost of 1,000 police would be 900 teachers.

Of course it would not necessarily have to be the education budget that was cut. It could have been the health budget or the defence budget or some other part of the public sector. Indeed, it might be a little bit cut off all the other spending components. The point is that, for any given aggregate resource constraint, if you want more of one thing you have to give up some of something else. The something else given up is the opportunity cost of what is obtained.

The concept of opportunity cost highlights the choices that must be made by measuring the cost of anything that is chosen in terms of the alternative that could have been chosen instead.

The production-possibility boundary

All the things that governments provide, such as schools, national defence, and roads, are produced in what is called the **public sector**. Everything else, including all the goods and services that consumers buy, is produced in the **private sector**. How should the nation's productive resources be divided between these two sectors? To

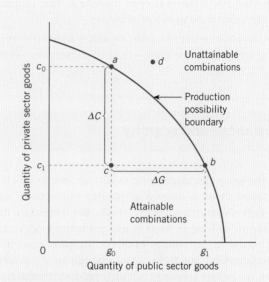

Figure 1.1 A production-possibility boundary

The negatively sloped boundary shows the combinations that are just attainable when all of the society's resources are efficiently employed. The quantity of public sector goods produced is measured along the horizontal axis, and the quantity of private sector goods is along the vertical axis. Any point on the diagram indicates some amount of each kind of good produced. The production-possibility boundary separates the blue-shaded attainable combinations, such as a, b, and c, from unattainable combinations, such as d. It is negatively sloped because, in a fully employed economy, more of one good can be produced only if resources are freed by producing less of other goods. Moving from point a (whose coordinates are c_0 and g_0) to point b (whose coordinates are c_1 and g_1) implies producing an additional amount of public sector goods, indicated by ΔG in the figure, at an opportunity cost of a reduction in private sector goods by the amount indicated by ΔC. Points a and b represent efficient uses of society's resources. Point c represents either an inefficient use of resources or a failure to use all the resources that are available.

illustrate this choice we put all the goods and services that governments provide into one group called 'public sector goods'. The rest are provided by non-government organizations and we call these 'private sector goods'. The balance between public and private provision is determined through the political process by government tax and spending policies. Higher public provision requires higher taxes, and higher taxes reduce private consumption[2].

The choices that each country must make are illustrated in Figure 1.1. The horizontal axis measures the quantity of public sector goods, while the vertical axis measures the quantity of private sector goods. The curve on the figure shows all those combinations of public and private goods

---

[2] If the public provision is financed by borrowing rather than by taxes, this merely postpones the need to raise taxes until a later date.

that can be produced if all the nation's resources are fully employed. It is called a **production-possibility boundary**. Points outside the boundary show combinations that cannot be obtained because there are not enough resources to produce them. Points on the boundary are just obtainable; they are the combinations that can just be produced using all the available supplies of resources.

Choice, scarcity, and opportunity cost illustrated

A single country's production-possibility boundary illustrates three concepts that we have already discussed: scarcity, choice, and opportunity cost. Scarcity is shown by the unattainable combinations beyond the boundary. There are some things that we just cannot have. Choice arises because of the need to select one of the attainable points on or inside the boundary. No economy can be at more than one point at one time. Any combination of public sector and private sector goods that is within the blue shaded area is achievable and anything outside is not. Opportunity cost is shown by the negative slope of the boundary. As the economy moves along that boundary, more of one type of good is being obtained at the cost of fewer of the other types.

Increasing opportunity cost

The production-possibility boundary of Figure 1.1 is drawn with a slope that gets steeper as one moves along it from left to right. The increasing slope indicates increasing opportunity cost as more and more private goods have to be given up for each additional unit of public goods. Start, for example, at the vertical axis where all production is of private sector goods. A small increase in the production of public goods moves the economy along a fairly flat part of the curve, indicating a small reduction in the production of private sector goods. But the loss of private goods gets greater (for each additional unit of public goods) as we move further along the boundary.
The figure can also be used to illustrate another three important economic issues.

Three key issues

What should be produced

How should scarce resources be allocated between the various possible kinds of production? Where to locate on the country's production-possibility boundary is the graphical representation of this key question. Each point on the boundary indicates a specific combination of the possible outputs. Alternative points indicate different allocations of the country's resources, producing different combinations of outputs.

Efficient production

If an economy is located inside its boundary more of everything could be produced. There are two main reasons

why an economy may produce inside its production boundary. First, some of its resources may be unemployed. Putting them back to work would raise production of some goods without having to lower the production of anything else. Secondly, although its resources are fully employed, some of them may be inefficiently employed. If they could be used more efficiently, the production of some goods could be increased without having to produce less of anything else. We will have much more to say about inefficient uses of resources in later chapters.

These two possibilities help to reveal the source of opportunity cost.

If all of the country's resources are fully employed, and none is employed inefficiently, then more of one good can be produced only by taking resources away from the production of another good.

The lost production of the other good is the opportunity cost of the first.

Economic growth

There is one other way an economy can get more of everything without having less of anything. If the economy's capacity to produce goods is increasing through time, the production-possibility boundary will be moving outwards over time, as illustrated in Figure 1.2. More of all goods can then be produced. This is what economic growth has accomplished from one decade to the next for the last several hundred years—and sporadically before then,

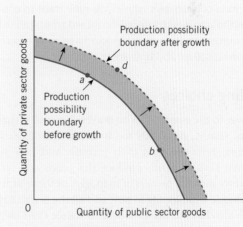

Figure 1.2 The effect of economic growth on the production–possibility boundary

Economic growth shifts the production-possibility boundary outward, allowing more of all commodities to be produced. Before growth in productive capacity points *a* and *b* were on the production-possibility boundary and point *d* was an unattainable combination. After growth point *d* becomes attainable, as do all points within the dark blue band.

Box 1.3 The terminology of production possibilities

We have used the term 'production-possibility boundary'. 'Boundary' emphasizes that the points on the line are maximum points. It is always possible to produce at points inside the line by not employing some factors of production, or by using them inefficiently. Two other terms, 'frontier' and 'curve', are often used instead of 'boundary'.

The words 'production possibility' emphasize the alternative possibilities available to a society. However, the term 'transformation' is often used instead. The idea behind the term 'transformation' is that society can, in effect, 'transform' one product into another by moving resources from the production of one product into the production of the other. Speaking of transforming one product into another involves the idea of opportunity cost. Of course, one good is not literally transformed into another but, by moving

resources from producing one type of good to producing another, quantities of the first type of good are sacrificed to gain quantities of the second type.

You can make up six terms by combining the following words:

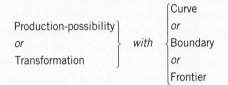

All six terms mean the same thing. All six are commonly used.

back to the beginning of history. We will study this growth later in the book. In the meantime, we merely note that in the long term growth is driven by technological change. Over the years we learn to make existing products better and more cheaply, and also to make many new products

that satisfy old needs in new ways and others that create altogether new needs.

Box 1.3 deals with some of the sometimes confusing terminology that surrounds the concept of the production-possibility boundary.

Who makes the choices and how

In the previous section we discussed the production possibilities for a country as a whole. We now want to consider how the actual outcome is determined among all the possible outcomes. Economic choices have to be made, but who makes them and how are they made?

Spending choices

The answer to the question 'Who makes choices?' is that we all do. That is, everybody has to decide how to earn their living, how to spend their income, and how to invest their savings. Firms produce the goods and services that we buy, the owners or managers of those firms have to decide what inputs to buy, and all the firms they buy from also have to decide where to source their own inputs.

Hence, the outcome for the economy as a whole is the result of millions of individual decisions made by all the economically active population. To be 'economically active' in this sense you only have to spend even the smallest amount of money on some product, as you are then influencing what is produced. Thus, economic outcomes are driven by the buying and selling decisions of

individuals[3] and firms. Later we shall also discuss the role of the government.

Maximizing decisions

The most important characteristic that economists assume about how individuals and firms take their decisions is that everyone tries to do as well as possible for themselves. In the jargon of economics, they are assumed to be *maximizers*. When individuals decide how much of their labour services to sell to producers and how many products to buy from them, they are assumed to make choices designed to maximize their well-being. When managers of firms decide how many inputs to buy from individuals and other firms, and how many of their own products to make and sell to them, they are assumed to be seeking to maximize their profits.

Marginal decisions

Individuals and firms make most of their choices *at the margin*. When you enter a shop to buy a newspaper and a pint

---

[3] We often refer to the basic decision-making unit for individual people as the 'household'. The term 'consumer' is also widely used, and official data sometimes refers to the 'personal sector'.

of milk, you are deciding to buy one more newspaper and one more pint of milk this week. You do not have to decide which product to spend your entire income on, and neither do you have to decide what to spend your income on next week or next year. You can, and do, decide to spread your spending around and to make these decisions incrementally (more or less) one at a time. Today you could buy two newspapers and a half-pint of milk. Tomorrow you might buy one newspaper, six eggs, and two pints of milk. These are marginal decisions—decisions to buy a bit more or a bit less. These decisions are made sequentially, not all at once.

Individuals and firms are constantly taking marginal decisions about whether to buy or produce a bit more or a bit less of the things that they consume or make. These decisions are assumed to be taken in order to achieve the most desirable outcome; that is, to maximize some objective.

Production choices

Managers of businesses decide what to produce and how to produce it. Some products, like haircuts, are quite simple to produce. But some other production processes are very complex. A typical car manufacturer assembles a product out of thousands of individual components. It makes some of these components itself. Most are subcontracted to other parts manufacturers, and many of the major parts manufacturers subcontract some of their work out to smaller suppliers. This kind of production displays two characteristics noted two centuries ago by Adam Smith, and one that is more recent. These are specialization, the division of labour, and globalization.

Specialization

In ancient hunter–gatherer societies, and in modern subsistence economies, most people made most of the things they need for themselves. However, from the time (about 10,000 years ago) that people first engaged in settled agriculture and some began to live in towns, people have specialized in doing particular jobs. Farmers, carpenters, soldiers, and priests had some of the earliest specialized occupations. The allocation of different jobs to different people is known as **specialization of labour**, or the **division of labour**. There are two fundamental reasons why specialization is extraordinarily efficient compared with self-sufficiency.

First, individual abilities differ, and specialization allows each person to do what he or she can do relatively well while leaving everything else to be done by others. This is one of the most fundamental principles in economics. It is called the principle of **comparative advantage**, and a much fuller discussion is found in Chapter 27 where the principle is applied to international trade.

The second reason is that people's abilities change when they specialize. A person who concentrates on one activity becomes better at it than a jack-of-all-trades. This is called **learning by doing**. Learning by doing is very important in many jobs today where complex tasks are required.

The division of labour

Throughout history, most workers who specialized in making some product made the whole of that product. Over the past several hundred years, many technical advances in methods of production have made it efficient to organize agriculture and manufacturing into large-scale firms organized around a division of labour. There is job specialization within the production process of a particular product. Few people work alone to make a whole product. Instead, most individuals specialize in making one bit of the final product, which is the outcome of the contributions of the labours of many specialist workers and machines. This is obviously true of most manufactured products such as cars, TV sets, and washing machines, which have many components, and many individuals play different roles in the assembly process. It is also true of most service industries where individuals work in teams to deliver a complex product.

Globalization

Market economies constantly change, largely as a result of the development of new products and new technologies. One important recent development is referred to as **globalization**. Globalized trade is not new—it has been around for hundreds, and in some areas thousands, of years. Since the Industrial Revolution, the usual pattern was manufactured goods being sent from Europe, and later from North America, to the rest of the world, with raw materials and primary products[4] being sent back in return. What is new in the last few decades is the globalization of manufacturing, and in particular the rapid growth of manufacturing, mainly in China, but also in India and some of the countries of Southeast Asia.

Two major causes of globalization are the rapid reduction in transportation costs and the revolution in information technology. Firstly, the cost of moving products around the world fell greatly in the second half of the twentieth century owing to air travel, containerization, and the greatly increased size of ships. Secondly, our ability to transmit and to analyse data has been increasing dramatically over the past fifty years, while the costs of doing so have been decreasing equally dramatically. For example,

---

[4] In an older usage products were divided into primary, secondary, and tertiary products. This division is no longer used, but the term 'primary products' remains in use to cover raw materials and agricultural goods.

today £1,000 or so buys a powerful computer that fits into a briefcase and has the same computing power as one that in 1970 cost £5 million and filled a large room.

This revolution in information and communication technology (ICT) has made it possible to coordinate economic transactions around the world in ways that were difficult and costly fifty years ago and quite impossible a hundred years ago. This, combined with falling costs of transport, has allowed manufacturing activities to be decentralized. Fifty years ago, if a car was to be assembled in Longbridge, all the parts had to be made nearby. Today it is possible to make parts anywhere in the world and get them to Longbridge exactly when they are required. As a result, manufacturing, which was formerly concentrated in the advanced industrial countries of Europe and North America, now takes place all over the world. A typical CD player, TV set, or car contains components made in literally dozens of different countries. Cars, for example, are made up of tyres, wheel hubs, windows, seats, computers, clocks, CD players, speedometers, petrol gauges, locks, doors, handles, pistons, gears, distributors, wiper blades, brakes, brake liners, switches, steering wheels, etc., and we have not even started listing the components of the engine. All of these can be made by different suppliers that may be in different parts of the world, the general rule being that production of each item takes place where it is cheapest to do so because the costs of transport to the point of assembly are so low as to be almost irrelevant. We still know where a product is assembled, but it is becoming increasingly difficult to say where it is made.

Also, many *markets* are globalizing. For example, as some fashions have become universal, we can see the same designer jeans, brand labels, and fast food outlets in virtually all big cities. Many *corporations* are globalized, as more and more of them become what the UN calls **transnationals**, but which are also known as **multinationals**. These are massive firms with a physical presence in many countries—McDonald's restaurants are as visible in Paris or Beijing as in London or New York. Many other brands are also virtually universal, such as Coca Cola, Kellogg, Heinz, Nestlé, Guinness, Toyota, Mercedes, BMW, Dell, Starbucks, Apple, Sony, Gucci, and Gap.

The pros and cons of globalization have recently been a subject of great controversy (which we elaborate in several places in later chapters). Notice, however, that globalization is not the only game in town. Globalization has affected financial markets and manufacturing, but an ever-increasing proportion of employment is in service industries, many of which, by the nature of the product, are very local. How far, for example, would you be prepared to travel for an evening meal, a haircut, a concert, or a trip to the theatre? Most people shop in their local town and visit their local doctor and local hospital,

though in cases of highly specialized needs some purchase products on the internet from anywhere in the world and others will travel great distances to consult a Harley Street specialist or a US medical expert at the Mayo Clinic. Having said that, it is also important to note that globalization is spreading rapidly in the service industries. When you seek advice on some problem with one of your electronic devices, such as your computer or iPhone, you are more likely to receive it in an Indian or a Philippine accent than an English one. Many firms centralize their bookkeeping and billing in one country, often Switzerland. Many US medical clinics send their data records each evening to Ireland where the accounts are kept and returned each morning. Digitalized data on such things as fingerprints allow police located anywhere in the world to access information collected anywhere else in the world. Computerized operations allow physicians located in key medical centres to operate on patients located in distant places. Many university degrees and professional qualifications can now be gained through distance learning without ever seeing the bricks and mortar of the granting institutions. And so on for a growing number of service operations.

Markets and money

People who specialize in doing only one thing, whether they are factory workers or computer programmers, must satisfy most of their needs by consuming goods and services produced by other people. In early societies, exchange of products took place by simple mutual agreement between neighbours. In the course of time, however, trading became centred on particular gathering places called *markets*. For example, the French markets or trade fairs of Champagne were well known throughout Europe as early as the eleventh century. Even now, many towns have regular market days. For economists, however, the term 'market' has a much broader meaning. We use the term **market economy** to refer to a society in which people specialize in productive activities and meet most of their material wants through voluntarily agreed exchanges. Most employed people, for example, work for a single employer (at any one time) and buy goods and services in a wide range of outlets (such as shops and restaurants, or by phone and internet, etc.).

Specialization must be accompanied by trade. People who produce only one thing must trade most of it to obtain all the other things they require.

Early trading was by means of **barter**; the trading of goods directly for other goods. But barter is costly in terms of time spent searching out satisfactory exchanges. If a farmer has wheat but wants a hammer, he must find someone who has a hammer and wants wheat. Thus a successful barter transaction requires what is called a *double coincidence of wants*.

Money eliminates the restrictive system of barter by separating the transactions involved in the exchange of products. If a farmer has wheat and wants a hammer, she does not have to find someone who has a hammer and wants wheat. She merely has to find someone who wants wheat. The farmer takes money in exchange. Then she finds a person who wishes to trade a hammer and gives up the money for the hammer.

The existence of 'money' greatly expands the possibilities of specialization and trade.

Consumer sovereignty

Many individuals may feel that most power over economic outcomes is in the hands of firms, especially big firms. However, if consumers will not buy a product, it does not pay to produce it. No business can survive for long if it makes things that nobody wants to buy. If a firm sees an opportunity to satisfy some unsatisfied need, it will develop a product to fill this gap. Even if a need is already satisfied by some product, firms have an incentive to develop products that better satisfy the same need or satisfy it more cheaply. In this, and in many other ways, consumers drive much economic activity, even though the production itself is done by firms. Because these firms are motivated by profits, they respond to (and try to anticipate) consumers' preferences as these are revealed by their purchases in the marketplace.

Box 1.4 provides a discussion of some important methodological issues that arise in economics.

Box 1.4 Economic theories

Economists seek to understand how the economy works and to make predictions about the consequences of certain changes that are either natural, such as a crop failure, or policy-induced, such as a tax on petrol. To do such things they construct economic theories, many of which you will study throughout this book. First, the things with which the theory is concerned, called its variables, must be carefully defined. Then, assumptions are made about how these variables behave and about other things that may affect them. The implications of these assumptions are then derived. This may be done verbally, geometrically, or mathematically, with the choice between these methods depending on the degree of complexity of the assumptions. These implications are the theory's predictions: if so and so happens, then so and so will follow. For example, if a tax is placed on white bread, its price will rise and the quantity produced and consumed will fall (as consumers switch to alternative products).

A theory is tested by confronting its predictions with the facts, often called empirical observations. If the facts agree with the theory's predictions, the theory has passed the test and is said to be consistent with the facts. If the theory continues to pass the test, it will be found useful, but it can never be regarded as conclusively proved to be true as there is always the possibility that conflicting facts will be observed in the future. If the facts disagree with the theory's predictions, the theory has failed to pass the test. If the theory fails the test in enough cases, it will be regarded as refuted and will be abandoned.

It is possible to develop theories that have no testable implications. Such theories are empty of empirical content since they are consistent with all possible states of the world. To have empirical content—that is, to be useful in understanding the world in one way or another—a theory must make predictions that are at least capable of being contradicted by evidence.

There is debate among economists as to whether a theory's assumption should be subject to empirical testing as well as its predictions. In his essay 'The methodology of positive economics', the Nobel Prize winning economist Milton Friedman argued that only the predictions of a theory should be subject to testing, and if a theory passes the test, it does not matter how unrealistic, or otherwise counterfactual, its assumptions are. In his book *The Methodology of Economics: or How Economists Explain*, Mark Blaug, one of the twentieth century's greatest methodologists, criticized the license that Friedman's 'methodology of positive economics' gave economists to make any and all unrealistic assumptions, provided only that their theories yielded verifiable implications.

Blaug made many arguments against Friedman's position, a few of which follow. Firstly, Friedman failed to note the important requirement that assumptions that are patently counterfactual should be robust in the sense that they can be relaxed without seriously altering the theory's predictions. Secondly, since one of the key purposes of behavioural assumptions is to link a theory's predictions to observable behaviour, the view of the extreme irrelevance of assumptions implies that it does not make sense to ask which of the assumptions is causing the trouble if a theory that seemed to accord with the facts no longer does so. Thirdly, if a theory that makes empirically correct predictions includes an empirically false assumption, it is

(continued)

Box 1.4 *continued*

interesting to ask why this is so. Perhaps the empirically incorrect assumption is unnecessary and can be stripped away. Perhaps there is a second incorrect assumption that cancels out the effect of the first, in which case it surely is worth knowing this. Finally, Friedman's discussion did not recognize the several different senses in which assumptions are used in economics and the different implicit ways in which they should be assessed. Some assumptions merely give the circumstances under which the theory is meant to apply, in which case it is not relevant to criticize the theory because such assumptions are 'unrealistic'. Other assumptions give the behaviour that is driving the results of the theory, in which case we gain by knowing if such assumptions are right or wrong. For example, if some of the predictions of a theory that assumes that all sellers are motivated by altruism rather than self-interest passes some tests, we would still not put much faith in it since we have other evidence that this behavioural assumption is wrong.

The Online Resource Centre contains a further discussion of the role of assumptions and 'models' in the construction of economic theories.

Government and the market economy

We have just explained how the interaction of firms and consumers through markets determines what is produced. We now discuss the role of governments in the economy. In order to put this in context we first consider what alternatives there may be to a free-market economy. There are four main types of economic system.

Traditional systems

A **traditional economic system** is one in which behaviour is based primarily on tradition, custom, and habit. Young men follow their fathers' occupations—typically, farming, hunting, fishing, and tool-making. Women do what their mothers did—typically cooking, mending, and fieldwork. There are few changes in the pattern of production from year to year, other than those imposed by the vagaries of nature. The techniques of production also follow traditional patterns, except when the effects of an occasional new invention are felt. The concept of private property is often not well defined, and property is frequently held in common, such as common grazing land. Finally, production is allocated between the members of society according to long-established traditions. In short, the answers to the economic questions of what to produce, how to produce, and how to distribute are determined by what has happened in the past. Such a system works best in an unchanging environment. Under static conditions, a system that does not continually require people to make choices can prove effective in meeting economic and social needs.

Traditional systems were common in earlier times. The feudal system under which most people lived in medieval Europe was a largely traditional society. Today only a few small, isolated, self-sufficient communities still retain mainly traditional systems; examples can be found in a few of the most isolated parts of the Canadian Arctic, the Himalayas, the Amazon jungle, and isolated parts of Papua New Guinea.

Command systems

We have already seen that in command systems some central authority determines economic behaviour. It makes most of the necessary decisions on what to produce, how to produce it, and who gets it. Because centralized decision-makers usually lay down elaborate and complex plans for the behaviour that they wish to impose, the terms command economy and **centrally planned economy** are usually used synonymously.

The sheer quantity of data required for the central planning of an entire economy is enormous, and the task of analysing it to produce a fully integrated plan can hardly be exaggerated, even in the age of computers. Moreover, the plan must be a rolling process, continually changing to take account not only of current data but also of future trends in labour supplies, technological developments, and people's tastes for various goods and services. This involves the planners in the notoriously difficult business of forecasting the future.

Three decades or so ago, over one-third of the world's population lived in countries that relied heavily on central planning to deal with the basic economic questions. Today the number of such countries is small. Even in countries where central planning is the official system, as in China, rapidly increasing amounts of market determination are being accepted and encouraged.

Pure market systems

Earlier in this chapter we discussed the basics of a free-market economy. Millions of consumers decide what products to buy and in what quantities. A large number of firms produce those products and buy the inputs that are needed to make them. Individual decisions collectively determine the economy's allocation of resources between competing uses and the distribution of its output among individual citizens.

In a **pure market economy** all of these decisions, without exception, are made by buyers and sellers acting through unhindered markets. The state provides the legal structure and external defence but, beyond that, markets determine all resource allocation and income distribution.

Mixed systems

Fully traditional, fully centrally controlled, and fully free-market economies are useful concepts for studying the basic principles of resource allocation. When we look in detail at any real economy, however, we discover that its economic behaviour is the result of some mixture of central control and market determination, with a certain amount of traditional behaviour as well. The term **mixed economy** refers to an economy in which both free markets and governments have significant effects on the allocation of resources and the distribution of income.

In practice, every economy is a mixed economy in the sense that it combines significant elements of all three systems—traditional, command, and market—in determining economic behaviour.

The proportions of the mixture of free-market determination and government control vary from economy to economy and over time. There is more free-market determination in the UK and the USA than in France and South Korea. There is more free-market determination in the UK today than there was forty years ago. The mix also varies from sector to sector within any one economy. For example, European agricultural markets have a substantial amount of government control. Under market determination, the average size of a farm would be much larger and agricultural prices much lower than they now are. In contrast, the markets for information and computer technologies are largely free from government intervention. Even the economies closest to free markets have a significant role for government, so it appears that there is no real alternative to a mixed system with major reliance on markets but also with a substantial government presence in many aspects of the economy.

Government in the modern mixed economy

Modern market economies in advanced industrial countries are based primarily on market transactions between people who voluntarily decide whether or not to transact. Private individuals have the right to buy and sell what they wish, to accept or refuse work that is offered to them, and to move to where they want when they want. But governments create the legal framework that governs transactions.

Key institutions are private property and freedom of contract, both of which must be maintained by active government policies. The government creates laws of ownership and contract, and then provides the courts to enforce these laws. Governments are also responsible for provision of a stable-valued money that is the measuring rod for all prices.

In modern mixed economies governments go well beyond these important basic functions. They intervene in market transactions to correct what are called 'market failures'. These are identifiable situations in which free markets do not work well. For example, natural resources such as fishing grounds and common pastureland tend to be overexploited to the point of destruction under free-market conditions. Some products, called **public goods**, are not provided at all by markets because, once produced, no one can be prevented from using them. Therefore their use cannot be restricted to those who are willing to pay for them. Defence and law and order are public goods. In other cases, private agents impose costs called **externalities** on others by their economic activities, such as when factories pollute the air and rivers. The public is harmed but has no part in the producers' decisions about what to make and how to make it. These are some of the reasons why free markets sometimes fail to function in desirable ways. They explain why citizens wish governments to intervene and alter the outcome that would result from leaving everything to the market.

There are also some products, like health and education, that could be provided through the market, but which governments have decided should be provided by the state and (in some cases) free of charge. These are not pure public goods, but many countries' governments have decided that at least some minimum provision must be available to all, at least at some basic level, so this cannot be left to the market. These are sometimes referred to as **merit goods**.

The **distribution of income** indicates how the nation's total income is distributed among its citizens. This is largely determined by the price that each type of resource input can command and by how evenly the endowments of these resources are distributed. It could be thought that labour is equally endowed to individuals, because each person has only one body. However, talents are not equally endowed and people acquire varying skill levels. Ownership of land and other property varies considerably between people.

There are important equity (or fairness) issues that arise from letting free markets determine people's incomes. Some people lose their jobs because firms are reorganizing in the face of new technologies. Others may keep their jobs, but the market values their services so poorly that they face economic hardship. The old and the chronically ill may suffer if their past circumstances did not allow them to save enough to support themselves. For many reasons of this sort we accept government intervention to redistribute income by taking something from the 'haves' and giving it to the 'have-nots'. Almost everyone accepts that there should be some redistribution of incomes. Care must be taken, however, not to kill the goose that lays the golden egg. Taking too much from the haves risks eliminating their incentive to work hard and produce income, some of which is to be redistributed to the have-nots.

Macro and micro roles of government

So far we have been discussing the intervention by government in specific markets on a permanent basis. There is another important role for government in the context of managing the economy in order to ensure that aggregate activity is at as high a level as is sustainable and inflation is avoided. The worldwide recession of 2008–9, which followed from the financial crisis of 2007–8, highlights the importance of the role of the central authorities in **stabilization policy** (see Chapter 15 onwards).

The standard tools of stabilization are monetary and fiscal policies. The former works by influencing the money supply, interest rates, or exchange rates, while the latter works through taxation and government spending.

There has never been a strict separation between macro and micro policies, but in the two decades prior to 2007 there had been a broad consensus that the micro interventions of governments in the market should be kept to a minimum and that macro policy should concentrate on controlling inflation and keeping real activity as close to its sustainable trend level as possible. However, the widespread collapses of financial institutions, many of which had to be bailed out by governments (and some taken into state ownership), have led to an active debate about whether the role of government needs to be extended on a permanent basis. Box 1.5 discusses the underlying issues further.

It is unlikely that governments will wish to keep major financial institutions in state ownership, but it is highly likely that there will be much greater state intervention in the form of tighter regulation of financial market activity.

Box 1.5 Government and the market

The 2007–8 world financial crisis and the subsequent recession has reopened old debates about the role of government at both the level of managing the economy as a whole (macroeconomics), and the level of intervention in specific markets (microeconomics), especially financial markets.

At the macroeconomic level, the debate has been characterized as between Keynesians[5] and monetarists, or between Keynesians and classical economists. The Keynesians advocate active use of government spending and taxes (and/or interest rates) to control the level of activity in the economy, while the others see the economy as self-stabilizing and thus oppose active management by governments.

The micro level debate is also between those who see markets working well on their own and those who emphasize the imperfections of markets and recommend various types of correction for 'market failure'. We discuss this further in Chapter 13.

The links between the micro and the macro approaches to these questions are well brought out by the following extract from a report by a UN Commission of Financial Experts chaired by Nobel Prize winner Joseph Stiglitz that was set up to investigate the implications of the recent financial crisis.

Part of the explanation for the current crisis may be found in the underlying economic fundamentals. Another is in the economic theories that motivated the financial and economic policies that produced the crisis. ... These same economic doctrines—the belief that economic agents are rational, that governments are inherently less informed and less motivated by sound economic principles and therefore their interventions are likely to distort market allocations, and that markets are efficient and stable, with a strong ability to absorb shocks—also affects macroeconomic policies.

One of the most important lessons of the Great Depression was that markets are not self-correcting and that government intervention is required at the macroeconomic level to ensure recovery and a return to full employment. In

[5] They are followers of British economist John Maynard Keynes (1883–1946).

Box 1.5 *continued*

the aftermath of the Great Depression, governments introduced policies that provided automatic stabilizers for aggregate demand and implemented discretionary policy frameworks to reduce economic instability. But as the Great Depression and earlier panics and crises faded from memory, confidence in the self-stabilizing nature of the market returned.

The fact that the world recovered so quickly from financial crises such as the East Asia crisis of 1997–8 and the global liquidity crisis of August 1998 induced false confidence in the self-correcting nature of market processes. While the recovery was due to public policies, it was credited to market processes. More generally, the historical role for government intervention in recovery and stability was forgotten. ('The Stiglitz Report: reforming the international monetary and financial systems in the wake of the financial crisis', New York: New Press, 2010)

This issue is a recurring question throughout this book. The micro aspects are mainly discussed in Chapters 2–14 and the macro questions are covered from Chapter 15 onwards. However, the micro and macro questions can both be stated in the same words: what can be left to the market and what is the appropriate role of government intervention?

Direct regulation of private sector firms interferes in the market behaviour of these firms. The reason this is necessary is that large financial institutions, especially banks, have a unique role as guardians of people's savings and as central players in the payments system. If a major bank were to close for business at short notice, it would stop a lot of other economic activity at the same time. This means that there is systemic risk and some of these banks have been considered 'too big to fail'.

Thus, while much activity can be left to the market, the government has to intervene to prevent major adverse events, such as a bank collapse, from bringing down many other parts of the economy with it, and so causing a major recession. We discuss the financial crisis in more detail later. However, the point to take from this discussion is that views about the appropriate role of government in the market economy are influenced by both microeconomic and macroeconomic considerations.

Conclusion

Economics is about how all the goods and services that we want to buy are produced and how we earn the income to pay for them. It also studies how the production and employment system can go wrong and what can be done to fix it. In particular, economics highlights specific areas in which the economy can go wrong and policies that can be followed by governments in order to make improvements to the outcome.

SUMMARY

The complexity of the modern economy

- A market economy is self-organizing in the sense that when individuals act independently to pursue their own self-interest, responding to prices set on open markets, they produce coordinated and relatively efficient economic outcomes.

Resources and scarcity

- Scarcity is a fundamental problem faced by all economies because not enough resources—land, labour, capital, and entrepreneurship—are available to produce all the goods and services that people would like to consume. Scarcity makes it necessary to choose among alternative possibilities: what products should be produced and in what quantities.

- The concept of opportunity cost highlights scarcity and choice by measuring the cost of obtaining a unit of one product in terms of the number of units of other products that could have been obtained instead.

- A production-possibility boundary shows all the combinations of goods that can be produced by an economy whose resources are fully employed. Movement from one point to another on the boundary shows a shift in the amounts of goods being produced, which requires a reallocation of resources.

Who makes choices and how

■ Economic choices are made by individuals and firms.

■ Modern economies are based on the specialization and division of labour, which necessitate the exchange of goods and services.

■ Exchange takes place in markets and is facilitated by the use of money.

■ Markets work to coordinate millions of individual, decentralized decisions.

Government and the market economy

■ Three pure types of economy can be distinguished: traditional, command, and free market.

■ In practice, all economies are mixed economies in that their economic behaviour responds to mixes of tradition, government command, and price incentives.

■ Governments play an important part in modern mixed economies. They create and enforce important background institutions such as private property. They intervene in an attempt to increase economic efficiency by correcting situations where markets do not effectively perform their coordinating functions. They also redistribute income and wealth in the interests of equity.

■ The role of the government is also influenced by the need to ensure that the economy as a whole avoids inflation and recessions.

TOPICS FOR REVIEW

■ Kinds of resource

■ Self-organization

■ Goods and services

■ Scarcity, choice, and opportunity cost

■ Production–possibility boundary

■ Resource allocation

■ Growth in productive capacity

■ Specialization and the division of labour

■ Command, traditional, market, and mixed economic systems

■ Positive and normative statements

QUESTIONS

1 Write down a list of all the economic activities that contribute to each of the following: a) delivering the evening news bulletin to your television or radio, b) providing cotton shirts on sale in your local high street stores, and c) providing a hamburger in a local fast-food restaurant.

2 What is the opportunity cost to you of each of the following: a) studying at weekends, b) doing charity work on two evenings of the week, and c) working in paid employment during every vacation?

3 List some of the choices you make on a daily basis in terms of how you spend your time and how you spend your money.

4 Make a list of all the different goods and services you typically buy in a normal week. In how many different markets does this suggest that a typical individual trades on a regular basis?

5 Explain the concept of opportunity cost and discuss how it relates to the problem of choice between scarce alternatives.

6 Outline the differences between traditional, command, and market economies and explain why the former two have been superseded.

7 In what ways does money facilitate specialization and the division of labour?

8 Why do governments have a role in a market economy? (Revisit this question once you have studied Chapters 13 and 14.)

9 Economics used to be known as the 'dismal science' because it pointed out that choices had to be made between scarce alternatives. Assess the prospects of scarcity being eliminated in the foreseeable future.

10 Which of the following statements are positive and which are normative?

   a) The health of poor people is worse than the health of rich people.

   b) Economic growth in sub-Saharan Africa is affected by the AIDS epidemic.

c) Rich countries should provide medicine more cheaply to Africa.

d) Protectionist policies in rich countries are hurting poor countries and should be abolished.

11 Which one of the following is not a positive statement?

a) If the price of oil rises people will make fewer journeys by car.

b) There would be less pollution if more people used public transport rather than driving to work.

c) If petrol was cheaper there would be more traffic and this would make the roads more congested.

d) People should use public transport more in order to reduce congestion.

12 Which one of the following is not a normative statement?

a) People should be made to pay for non-essential surgery in the NHS in order to divert resources to essential life-saving operations.

b) All treatment in NHS hospitals should be free for those who need it.

c) Government spending on the NHS has exceeded its targets in the budget.

d) Prescriptions should only be free for the over-sixties who cannot afford to pay.

CHAPTER 2

DEMAND AND SUPPLY

Why does the price of computers keep falling while train fares keep rising? This is a question about how markets work and what factors influence the outcomes. To answer it we need to understand how markets function. This is one of the most important topics in economics. You will see that we can go a long way in understanding how markets work with some very simple tools.

In particular, you will learn:

● Who are the participants in markets and what motivates them.

● What are the main factors that influence how much of a product consumers wish to buy.

● What are the main factors that influence how much producers wish to sell.

● How consumers and producers interact to determine the market price.

● While demand and supply forces are present in all markets, many different institutional structures also affect market outcomes.

Growers of crops come to a town to sell their produce in farmers' markets. High street stores stock a wide range of goods for individuals to buy. Commodity markets determine worldwide prices for products such as oil, copper, and wheat. Potential buyers or renters of housing units deal with sellers of houses or landlords in housing markets. Workers sell their services to employers in labour markets. Indeed, a market exists whenever buyers and sellers exchange goods or services—usually for money.

Markets do not necessarily happen in one place. There is a separate housing market in each town and city, while there is a single market for some skilled labour (for example, university lecturers in physics) throughout the country. The stock market and the foreign exchange market operate globally using computers and telephones. The book market works partly through bookshops and partly by internet and mail order.

Our aim is to help you understand all of these different types of market. We start by focusing on a market in which there are many buyers and many sellers. (Markets with a few, or even just one, of either or both buyers and sellers are considered in later chapters.) Buyers of goods and services for consumption, also called *demanders* or consumers, are households or just individuals. The suppliers of those goods or services, often called *producers*, are firms. The product whose markets we choose to analyse is a good that has a physical existence, so it has to be grown or made

by the producing firm. Anyone who makes decisions relevant to our theory is called an **agent**. To make the study of their behaviour more manageable, we deal with just three types of agent: consumers, firms, and government. In this chapter you will encounter consumers as demanders and firms as suppliers. In a later chapter, when we study the labour market, you will find individuals supplying and firms demanding. Governments also play a role in some markets as either producers or demanders. They can also intervene in markets by taxing transactions (with a sales tax, value-added tax, or excise tax) or by imposing regulations that impose maximum or minimum prices. In this chapter and the next few we ignore the potential role of governments, but we look closely at this in Chapters 13 and 14.

Box 2.1 provides an example of a real product, tea, which is typical of the type of goods whose markets we will be studying first. We will return to this example as a case study at the end of this chapter, but for now notice how the balance between demand and supply forces is key to any market, and that in markets for agricultural products abnormal weather conditions are often a key short-term influence. Note also that this is about wholesale tea prices and not about the price of a box of PG Tips teabags, though the wholesale and retail markets are connected. How demand and supply interact to determine the market price is what we are about to explain.

Box 2.1 Tea prices to soar after droughts

Tea is a typical example of an agricultural commodity whose price can be understood using demand and supply analysis. This box's title was a headline in a newspaper in 2009. It reflected the fact that there had been adverse weather conditions in India and Kenya and this had led to reduced tea crops. Official estimates were that demand was then running ahead of production (supply) and thus it was expected that wholesale prices of tea would rise.

According to IMF data[1], from 2003 until the end of 2007 tea prices had fluctuated in the range of 170 to 250 US cents per kilo, but the weather disruptions referred to above (combined with internal conflict in Kenya) reduced supply to such an extent that the price rose to over 300 US

cents per kilo by the summer of 2008. In late 2008, the banking collapse and world recession led to a sharp fall in demand and the price dropped back to around 220 US cents per kilo. However, in late 2009 demand recovered while production did not and prices rose to over 360 US cents per kilo. However, the deteriorating weather conditions appeared to be sustained (possibly due to longer-term climate change) and the price remained high until the end of 2012.

Prices declined again in 2013, but we postpone an explanation of this until later in this chapter. The key point to take from this example is that market prices are the result of the interaction of demand and supply forces. Understanding how this all works is the main object of this chapter and much of the first half of this book.

[1] *International Financial Statistics* database.

Demand

Individuals and motives

In formulating our demand theory, the consumers are all assumed to be adult individuals who earn income, and they spend this income purchasing various goods and services.[2]

Most economic theories assume that each individual consumer seeks maximum *satisfaction*, or *well-being*, or *utility*, as the concept is variously called. The consumer is assumed to 'maximize utility' within the limits set by his or her available resources. Utility is hard to measure directly, but we only need to assume that typical consumers know what they like, and make spending choices that give them as much personal satisfaction as possible. We discuss utility in more detail in Chapter 4.

The nature of demand

The amount of a product that consumers wish to purchase is called the **quantity demanded**. Notice two important things about this concept. First, quantity demanded is a *desired* quantity. It is how much consumers *wish* to purchase *given the resources at their command*,

not necessarily how much they actually succeed in purchasing. We use phrases such as **quantity actually purchased** or **quantity actually bought and sold** to distinguish actual purchases from quantity demanded. Secondly, note that quantity demanded is a *flow*. We are concerned not with a single isolated purchase, but with a continuous flow of purchases. Therefore we must express demand as so much per period of time—for example, 1 million oranges *per day*, or 7 million oranges *per week*, or 365 million oranges *per year*. The important distinction between stocks and flows is discussed in Box 2.2.

The concept of demand as a flow appears to raise difficulties when we deal with the purchases of durable consumer goods (often called consumer durables). It makes obvious sense to talk about a person consuming oranges at the rate of thirty per month, but what can we say of a consumer who buys a new television set every five years? This apparent difficulty disappears if we measure the demand for the *services* provided by the consumer durable. Thus, at the rate of a new set every five years, the television purchaser is using the service (viewing TV programmes) at the rate of 1/60th of a set per month. For most purposes, however, we will be interested in the same question that television manufacturers want to know, which is: how many new TV sets are bought in total per period by consumers as a whole?

[2] When real-world data are studied, the spending unit analysed is often not the individual consumer but the household. A household is defined as all the people who live under one roof and who make joint financial decisions or are subject to others who make such decisions for them. For purposes of developing our analysis of markets, however, we view consumers as individuals.

Box 2.2 Stocks and flows

Economics makes extensive use of both stock and flow variables and it is important not to confuse the two. A *flow variable* has a time dimension; it is so much per unit of time. The quantity of free-range eggs purchased in Glasgow is a flow variable. Being told that the number purchased was 2,000 dozen eggs conveys no useful information unless we are also told the period of time over which these purchases occurred. For example, 2,000 dozen per hour would indicate an active market in eggs, while 2,000 dozen per month would indicate a sluggish market.

A *stock variable* has no time dimension; it is just so much. Thus, the number of eggs in an egg producer's warehouse—for example, 20,000 dozen eggs—is a stock variable. All those eggs are there at one time, and they remain there until something happens to change the stock held by the producer. The stock variable is just a number, not a rate of flow of so much per day or per month.

Economic theories use both flow variables and stock variables, and it takes a little practice to keep them straight. The amount of income earned is a flow—so much per year or per month or per hour. The amount of a consumer's spending is also a flow—so much spent per week or per month. In contrast, the amount of money in your bank account is a stock—just so many pounds sterling. The key test for a variable being a flow is that a time dimension is required to give it meaning. Other variables are neither stocks nor flows; they are just numbers, (e.g. the price of eggs).

The determinants of quantity demanded: the demand function

Five main variables are assumed to influence the quantity of each product that is demanded by each individual consumer:

(1) the price of the product;

(2) the prices of other products;

(3) the consumer's income and wealth;

(4) the consumer's tastes;

(5) various individual-specific and environmental factors.

This list is conveniently summarized in what is called a **demand function**:

$$q_n^d = D(p_n, p_1, \ldots, p_{n-1}, Y, S).$$

The term q_n^d stands for the quantity that the consumer demands per time period (possibly a week or a month) of some product, which we call 'product n'. The term p_n stands for the price of this product, while $p_1, \ldots, p_{n-1}$ is a shorthand notation for the prices of all other products. The term Y is the consumer's income. The term S stands for a host of factors that will vary from individual to individual, such as age, number of children, place of residence (e.g. big city, small town, country), and other assets (e.g. car owners will demand petrol, while non-car owners will demand train tickets). There are also some environmental factors that will affect demand patterns, such as the state of the weather and the time of year. Although these factors matter in real markets, they are not central to our current analysis. Finally, the precise way in which demand is affected by the variables listed earlier is determined by the tastes of the consumer.

The demand function is just a shorthand way of saying that quantity demanded, which is on the left-hand side, is assumed to depend on the variables that are listed on the right-hand side. The form of the function determines the nature of that dependence.[3]

We will not be able to understand the separate influences of each of the above variables if we ask what happens when all of them change at once. To avoid this difficulty, we consider the influence of the variables one at a time. To do this, we use a device that is frequently employed in economic theory. We assume that all except one of the variables on the right-hand side of the demand function are held constant. Then we allow this one variable, say p_n, to change and see how the quantity demanded (q_n^d) changes. We are then studying the effect of changes in one influence on quantity demanded, *assuming that all other influences remain unchanged*, or, as economists are fond of putting it, **ceteris paribus** (which means 'other things being equal' or 'holding other things constant').

We can do the same for each of the other variables in turn, and in this way we can come to understand the effect of each variable. Once this is done, we can combine the separate influences of each variable to discover what will happen when several variables change at the same time—as they often do in practice.

Demand and price

We are interested in developing a theory of how products are priced. To do this, we hold all other influences constant and ask: 'How will the quantity of a product demanded vary as its own price varies?'

---

[3] The 'form of the function' refers to the precise quantitative relation between the variables on the right-hand side of the equation and the variable on the left. For example $y = f(X)$ is a general function stating that Y is related to X, while $Y = 2 + 3X$ is a form of that function indicating a specific relation between these two variables.

A basic economic hypothesis is that the lower the price of a product, the larger the quantity that will be demanded, other things being equal.

This negative relationship between the price of a product and quantity demanded is sometimes referred to as the **law of demand**. Why might this law be true? A major reason is that there is usually more than one product that will satisfy any given desire or need. Hunger may be satisfied by meat or vegetables; a desire for green vegetables may be satisfied by broccoli or spinach. The need to keep warm at night may be satisfied by several woollen blankets, or one electric blanket, or a sheet and a lot of oil burned in the boiler. The desire for a holiday may be satisfied by a trip to the Scottish Highlands or to the Swiss Alps, the need to get there by a plane, a bus, a car, or a train, and so on. Name any general desire or need, and there will usually be several different products that will contribute to its satisfaction.

Now consider what happens when we vary the price of one product, holding all other potential variables constant.

First, suppose the price of the product rises. The product then becomes a more expensive way of satisfying a want. Some consumers will stop buying it altogether, others will buy smaller amounts, still others may continue to buy the same amount, but no rational consumer will buy more of it. (Do not forget the important qualification 'other things being equal'. Of course she might buy more if there was some offsetting change in something else, such as her health, which affects what she would like to buy.) Because many consumers will switch wholly, or partially, to other products to satisfy the same want, less will be bought of the product whose price has risen. For example, as meat becomes more expensive, consumers may switch some of their spending to meat substitutes; they may also forgo meat at some meals and eat less meat at others.

Secondly, let the price of a product fall. This makes the product a cheaper method of satisfying any given want. Consumers will buy more of it and less of other similar products whose prices have not fallen. These other products have become expensive *relative to* the product in question. For example, when a bumper tomato harvest drives prices down, shoppers buy more tomatoes and fewer other salad ingredients, which have now become relatively more expensive than tomatoes.

The demand schedule and the demand curve

An individual's demand

A **demand schedule** is one way of showing the relationship between quantity demanded and price. It is a numerical tabulation that shows the quantity that will be demanded at some selected prices.

Table 2.1 **Alice's demand schedule for eggs**

Reference letter	Price (£ per dozen)	Quantity demanded (dozen per month)
a	0.50	7.0
b	1.00	5.0
c	1.50	3.5
d	2.00	2.5
e	2.50	1.5
f	3.00	1.0

The table shows the quantity of eggs that Alice demands at each selected price, other things being equal. For example, at a price of £1.00 per dozen she demands 5 dozen per month, while at a price of £2.50 per dozen she demands only 1.5 dozen.

Table 2.1 shows one consumer's demand schedule for eggs. Alice often eats boiled eggs for breakfast and, as she lives on her own, she often finds omelettes a convenient evening meal. But she does not have a lot of money, so she keeps an eye on the price of eggs when she does her weekly supermarket shopping. The table shows the quantity of eggs that she wishes to buy each month at six selected prices. For example, at a price of £1.50 per dozen Alice demands 3.5 dozen per month. For easy reference each of the price–quantity combinations in the table is given a letter.

Next we plot the data from Table 2.1 in Figure 2.1, with price on the vertical and quantity on the horizontal axis.[4] The smooth curve drawn through these points is called the demand curve, even though it may often be drawn as a straight line. It shows the quantity that Alice would like to buy at every possible price; its *negative slope* indicates that the quantity demanded increases as the price falls.

A single point on the demand curve indicates a single price–quantity relationship. *The whole demand curve shows the complete relationship between quantity demanded and*

[4] Readers trained in other disciplines often wonder why economists plot demand curves with price on the vertical axis. The normal convention, which puts the independent variable (the variable that does the explaining) on the horizontal axis and the dependent variable (the variable that is explained) on the vertical axis, calls for price to be plotted on the horizontal axis and quantity on the vertical axis. The axis reversal—now enshrined by a century of usage—arose as follows. The analysis of the competitive market that we use today stems from the French economist Leon Walras (1834–1910), in whose theory *quantity* was the dependent variable. However, graphical analysis in economics was popularized by the English economist Alfred Marshall (1842–1924), in whose theory *price* was the dependent variable. Economists continue to use Walras's theory and Marshall's graphical representation, and thus draw the diagram with the independent and dependent variables reversed—to the everlasting confusion of readers trained in other disciplines. In virtually every other type of graph in economics the axes are labelled conventionally, with the dependent variable on the vertical axis.

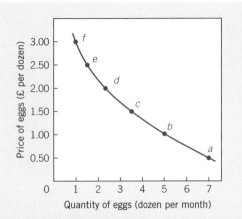

Figure 2.1 Alice's demand curve

This curve relates the price of a commodity to the amount that Alice wishes to purchase. Each point on the figure relates to a row in Table 2.1. For example, when the price is £3.00, 1 dozen are bought per month (point *f*), while when the price is £0.50, 7 dozen are bought (point *a*).

price. Economists often speak of the conditions of demand in a particular market as 'given' or 'known'. When they do so they are referring not just to the particular quantity that is being demanded at the moment (i.e. not just to a particular point on the demand curve) but to the whole demand curve. The whole demand curve remains in one place as long as all variables other than the price of the product itself remain unchanged.

The market demand curve

So far we have discussed how the quantity of a product demanded by one consumer depends on the product's price, other things being equal. To explain market behaviour, we need to know the total demand of all consumers. To obtain a market demand schedule, we sum the quantities demanded by each consumer at a particular price to obtain the total quantity demanded at that price. We repeat the process for each price to obtain a schedule of total, or market, demand at all possible prices. A graph of this schedule is called the *market demand curve.*

To avoid unnecessary complication, Figure 2.2 illustrates the summation graphically for only two consumers, Sarah and William. The figure illustrates the proposition that the market demand curve is the horizontal sum of the demand curves of *all* the individuals who buy in the market.

In practice, our knowledge of market demand is usually derived by observing total quantities of sales directly. The derivation of market demand curves by summing individual curves is a theoretical operation. We do it to understand the relation between curves for individual consumers and market curves.

In Table 2.2 we assume that we have data for the market demand for eggs. The schedule tells us the total quantity that will be demanded by all buyers of that product at selected market prices. The data are plotted in Figure 2.3, and the curve drawn through these points is the market demand curve.

Market demand: a recap

We now summarize what we have learned about demand.

The total quantity demanded depends on the price of the product being sold, on the prices of all other products, on the incomes of the individuals buying in that market, and on their tastes. The market demand curve relates the total quantity demanded to the product's own price, on the assumption that all other prices, total income, tastes, and all other environmental factors are held constant.

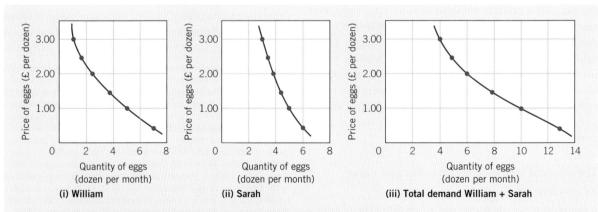

(i) William   **(ii) Sarah**   **(iii) Total demand William + Sarah**

Figure 2.2 The relation between individual and market demand curves

The market demand curve is the horizontal sum of the demand curves of all consumers in the market. The figure illustrates aggregation over two individuals, William and Sarah. For example, at a price of £2.00 per dozen William purchases 2.4 dozen and Sarah purchases 3.6 dozen, and together they purchase 6 dozen.

Table 2.2 **A market demand schedule for eggs**

Reference letter	Price (£ per dozen)	Quantity demanded ('000 dozen per month)
U	0.50	110.0
V	1.00	90.0
W	1.50	77.5
X	2.00	67.5
Y	2.50	62.5
Z	3.00	60.0

The table shows the quantity of eggs that would be demanded by all consumers at selected prices, ceteris paribus. For example, row *W* indicates that, if the price of eggs were £1.50 per dozen, consumers would want to purchase 77,500 dozen per month.

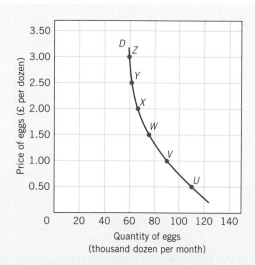

Figure 2.3 **A market demand curve for eggs**
The negative slope of the curve indicates that quantity demanded increases as price falls. The six points correspond to the six price–quantity combinations shown in Table 2.2. The curve drawn through all the points and labelled *D* is the demand curve.

Shifts in the demand curve

The demand schedule and the demand curve are constructed on the assumption of ceteris paribus (other things held constant). But what if other things change, as surely they must? What, for example, if consumers find themselves with more income? If they spend their extra income, they will buy additional quantities of many products *even though market prices are unchanged*, as shown in Table 2.3. But if consumers increase their purchases of any product whose price has not changed, the new purchases cannot be represented by the original demand curve. The rise in consumer income *shifts* the demand curve to the right, as shown in Figure 2.4. This shift illustrates the operation of an important general rule.

A demand curve shifts to a new position in response to a change in any of the variables that were held constant when the original curve was drawn.

Any change that increases the quantity of a product consumers wish to buy at each price will shift the demand curve to the right, and any change that decreases the quantity consumers wish to buy at each price will shift the demand curve to the left.

Changes in other prices

We saw that demand curves have negative slopes because the lower a product's price, the cheaper it becomes relative to other products that can satisfy the same needs. Those other products are called **substitutes**. A product becomes

Table 2.3 **Two alternative market demand schedules for eggs**

(1)	Price of eggs (£ per dozen) (2)	Quantity of eggs demanded at original level of personal income ('000 dozen per month) (3)	Quantity of eggs demanded when personal income rises to new level ('000 dozen per month) (4)	(5)
U	0.50	110.0	140.0	U'
V	1.00	90.0	116.0	V'
W	1.50	77.5	100.8	W'
X	2.00	67.5	90.0	X'
Y	2.50	62.5	81.3	Y'
Z	3.00	60.0	78.0	Z'

An increase in total consumers' income increases the quantity demanded at each price. When income rises, quantity demanded at a price of £1.50 per dozen rises from 77,500 dozen per month to 100,000 dozen per month. A similar rise occurs at every other price. Thus the demand schedule relating columns (2) and (3) is replaced by the one relating columns (2) and (4). The graphical representations of these two schedules are labelled D_0 and D_1 in Figure 2.4.

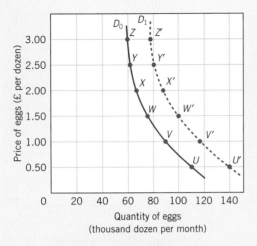

Figure 2.4 Two demand curves for eggs

The rightward shift in the demand curve from D_0 to D_1 indicates an increase in the quantity demanded at each price. The lettered points correspond to those in Table 2.3. When the curve shifts from D_0 to D_1, more is demanded at each price and a higher price is paid for each quantity. For example, at price £1.50 quantity demanded rises from 77,500 dozen (point W) to 100,000 dozen (point W'), while the quantity of 90,000 dozen, which was formerly bought at a price of £1.00 (point V), will be bought at a price of £2.00 after the shift (point X').

cheaper relative to its substitutes if its own price falls. This also happens if the substitute's price rises. For example, eggs can become cheap relative to pizzas either because the price of eggs falls or because the price of pizzas rises. Either change will increase the amount of eggs that consumers are prepared to buy. For example, Alice may eat more omelettes and fewer pizzas whenever she wants a quick meal.

A rise in the price of a product's substitute shifts the demand curve for the product to the right. More will be purchased at each price.

Thus, a rise in the price of pizzas may shift the demand curve for eggs from D_0 to D_1 in Figure 2.4, just as a rise in income did.

Products that tend to be used jointly with each other are called **complements**. Cars and petrol are complements; so are golf clubs and golf balls, bacon and eggs, electric cookers and electricity, an aeroplane trip to Austria and tickets on the ski lifts at St Anton. Since complements tend to be consumed together, a fall in the price of either will increase the demand for both. For example, a fall in the price of cars which causes more people to become car owners will, ceteris paribus, increase the demand for petrol.

A fall in the price of one product that is complementary to a second product will shift the second product's demand curve to the right. More will be purchased at each price.

Changes in total income

If consumers receive more income, they can be expected to purchase more of most products even though product prices remain the same. Such a shift is illustrated in Table 2.3 and Figure 2.4. A product whose demand increases when income increases is called a **normal good**.

A rise in consumers' incomes shifts the demand curve for normal products to the right, indicating that more will be demanded at each possible price.

For a few products, called **inferior goods**, a rise in consumers' income leads them to reduce their purchases (because they can now afford to switch to a more expensive, but superior, substitute).

A rise in income will shift the demand for inferior goods to the left, indicating that less will be demanded at each price.

The distribution of income

If total income and all other determinants of demand are held constant while the distribution of income changes (i.e. some become richer and others become poorer), the demands for normal goods will rise for consumers gaining income and fall for consumers losing income. If both gainers and losers buy a good in similar proportions, these changes will tend to cancel out. However, this will not always be the case.

When the distribution of income changes, demand will rise for those goods favoured by those gaining income and fall for those goods favoured by those losing income.

Individual characteristics

Changes in the characteristics of the individuals who make up the market will cause demand curves to shift. For example, a reduction in the typical number of children per family, as happened in the twentieth century, will reduce the demands for the things used by children at home or in childcare. If the number of retired people increases, there will be a rise in the demand for goods consumed during leisure times.

Environmental factors

Demand for some products is different at different times of year. Some of this is due to weather; for example, demand for electricity is higher in the winter when days are short and the weather is cold,[5] and demand for cold lager and ice cream is higher in the summer during hot weather. Other variations may be due to traditions associated with annual festivals, such as buying presents at

---

[5] In some hot countries, demand for electricity may be even greater in summer than in winter owing to the use of air-conditioners.

Box 2.3 Weather matters

Other things than price and incomes do influence demand, and sellers have to keep abreast of these non-economic causes—which have distinct economic effects.

A newspaper article quotes a person responsible for getting groceries to the stores at the right time and in the right quantities on the effects of a sudden turn in the weather from cold to hot: 'The trigger point is 80 degrees, especially if it is sustained for more than three days. For products such as ice cream, soft drinks, and salads sales can rise by between 70 per cent and 225 per cent on a big change in temperature'. As a result of a sudden upturn in the weather he had recently had to organize another million cases of soft drinks and additional lorry loads of salad and other fast-selling products 'if the shelves [were] not to be bare by lunchtime'.

Here are some of the ways in which the article said the weather affects UK demand.

- Drink sales respond immediately to temperature change.

- After two days of good weather we might think about buying a bike, but it has to be nice for more than a week before we start buying suntan lotion.

- Curiously, hot weather increases the sales of plain coleslaw much more than coleslaw with pineapple.

- Soft drink sales depend not only on heat but also on humidity.

- Rain and mild temperatures suit insurers best—we drive less and so have fewer and less serious prangs.

- Builders like storms—they interrupt work but generate huge business volumes repairing and replacing roofs.

- Every one degree colder adds 4 per cent to gas demand and increases electricity demand by about 5,000 megawatts—enough to supply the whole of Sheffield.

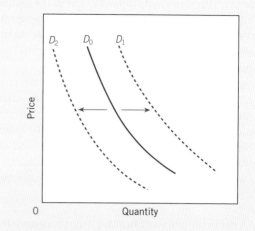

Figure 2.5 Shifts in the demand curve

A shift in the demand curve from D_0 to D_1 indicates an increase in demand; a shift from D_0 to D_2 indicates a decrease in demand. An increase in demand can be caused by a rise in the price of a substitute, a fall in the price of a complement, a rise in income, a redistribution of income towards groups who favour the commodity, or a change in tastes that favours the commodity. A decrease in demand can be caused by a fall in the price of a substitute, a rise in the price of a complement, a fall in income, a redistribution of income away from groups who favour the commodity, or a change in tastes that disfavours the commodity.

forces—things that lie outside the theory, affecting demand, sometimes greatly, but not themselves being explained by the theory. Box 2.3 illustrates the major influence that weather can exert on demand.

Changes in tastes

If there is a change in tastes in favour of a product, more will be demanded at each price, causing the demand curve to shift to the right. In contrast, if there is a change in tastes away from a product, less will be demanded at each price, causing the entire demand curve to shift to the left.

Figure 2.5 summarizes our discussion of the causes of shifts in the demand curve. Notice that, since we are generalizing beyond our example of eggs, we have relabelled our axes 'price' and 'quantity', dropping the qualification 'of eggs'. The term *quantity* should be understood to mean quantity per period in whatever units the goods are measured. The term *price* should be understood to mean the price measured in pounds per unit of quantity for the same product.

Movements along demand curves versus shifts

Suppose that you read in today's newspaper that carrot prices have soared because more carrots are being demanded, perhaps following a report that carrot consumption gives protection against some disease. Then tomorrow you read that the rising price of carrots is greatly reducing the typical consumer's demand for carrots as shoppers switch to potatoes, courgettes, and peas. The two statements appear to contradict each other. The first associates a rising price with a rising demand; the second associates a rising price with a declining demand. Can both statements be true? The answer is that they can be, because they refer to different things. The first refers to a *shift* in the demand curve; the second refers to a movement *along* a demand curve in response to a change in price.

Consider first the statement that the increase in the price of carrots has been caused by an increased demand for carrots. This statement refers to a shift in the demand curve for carrots. In this case, the demand curve must have shifted to the right, indicating more carrots demanded at each price. As we will see later in this chapter, this shift will increase the price of carrots.

Now consider the statement that fewer carrots are being bought because carrots have become more expensive. This refers to a movement along a given demand curve and reflects a change between two specific quantities being bought, one before the price rose and one afterwards.

So what lay behind the two stories might have been something like the following.

1. A rise in the perceived health-giving properties shifts the demand curve for carrots to the right as more and more are demanded at each price. This in turn is raising the price of carrots (for reasons we shall soon study in detail). This was the first newspaper story.

2. The rising price of carrots is causing each individual consumer to cut back on his or her purchase of carrots. This causes a movement upward to the left along any particular demand curve for carrots. This was the second newspaper story.

To prevent the type of confusion caused by our two newspaper stories, economists have developed a specific vocabulary to distinguish shifts of curves from movements along curves. **Demand** refers to one *whole* demand curve. **Change in demand** refers to a *shift* in the whole curve; that is, a change in the amount that will be bought at *every* price.

An increase in demand means that the whole demand curve has shifted to the right; a decrease in demand means that the whole demand curve has shifted to the left.

Any one point on a demand curve represents a specific amount being bought at a specified price. Therefore it represents a particular quantity demanded. A movement along a demand curve is referred to as a **change in the quantity demanded**.

A movement down a demand curve is called an increase (or a rise) in the quantity demanded; a movement up the demand curve is called a decrease (or a fall) in the quantity demanded.

To illustrate this terminology, look again at Table 2.3. First, at the original level of income, a decrease in price from £2.00 to £1.50 increases *the quantity demanded* from 67,500 to 77,500 dozen a month. Secondly, the increase in average consumer income *increases demand* from what is shown in column (3) to what is shown in column (4). The same contrast is shown in Figure 2.4, where a fall in price from £2.00 to £1.50 increases the quantity demanded from the quantity shown by point X to the quantity shown by point W. An increase in total consumers' income increases demand from curve D_0 to curve D_1.

Supply

We now look at the supply side of markets. The suppliers are **firms**, which are in business to make the goods and services that consumers want to buy.

Firms' motives

Economic theory gives firms several attributes.

First, each firm is assumed to make consistent decisions, as though it was run by a single individual decision-maker. This allows the firm to be treated as the agent on the production or supply side of product markets, just as the consumer is treated as the individual unit of behaviour on the consumption or demand side.

Secondly, firms hire workers and invest capital and entrepreneurial talent in order to produce goods and services that consumers wish to buy. (There are some markets in which firms sell to other firms, or the government, and in the labour market individuals sell their services to firms. But here we focus on consumer goods markets for simplicity.)

Thirdly, firms are assumed to make their decisions with a single goal in mind: to make as much profit as possible. This goal of *profit maximization* is analogous to the consumer's goal of utility maximization.

The nature of supply

The amount of a product that firms are able and willing to offer for sale is called the **quantity supplied**. Supply is a desired flow: how much firms are willing to sell per period of time, not how much they actually sell.

Here, we make a start on analysis of supply, establishing only what is necessary for a theory of price. In later chapters we study the behaviour of individual firms, and then aggregate individual behaviour to obtain the behaviour of market supply. For our present purposes, however, it is sufficient to go directly to market supply, the aggregate behaviour of all the firms in a particular market.

The determinants of quantity supplied: the supply function

Three major determinants of the quantity supplied in a particular market are:

(1) the price of the product;

(2) the prices of inputs to production;

(3) the state of technology.

This list can be summarized in a **supply function**:

$$q_n^s = S(p_n, F_1, ..., F_m)$$

where q_n^s is the quantity supplied of product n, p_n is the price of that product, $F_1, ..., F_m$ is shorthand for the prices of all inputs into production, and the state of technology determines the form of the function S. (Recall, once again, that the form of the function refers to the precise quantitative relation between the variables on the right-hand side of the equation and the one on the left.)

Supply and price

For a simple theory of price, we need to know how quantity supplied varies with a product's own price, all other things being held constant. Therefore we are only concerned with the ceteris paribus relationship $q_n^s = S(p_n)$; that is, between the quantity firms wish to supply and the price of the product itself. We will have much to say in later chapters about this relationship. For the moment, it is sufficient to state the hypothesis that, holding other things constant, *the quantity of any product that firms will produce and offer for sale is positively related to the product's own price, rising when the price rises and falling when the price falls.*

In Chapter 5 we link this hypothesis to the profit-maximizing behaviour of firms. In the meantime, all we need to note is that the basic reason behind this relationship is the way in which costs are assumed to behave as output changes. The cost of increasing output by another unit is assumed to be higher, the higher is the existing rate of output. So, for example, if the firm is already producing 100 units per week, the cost of increasing output to 101 units per week might be £1, while if 200 units were already being produced, the cost of increasing output to 201 units might be £2. Clearly, the firm will not find it profitable to increase output if it cannot at least cover the additional costs that are incurred. As the price of the product rises, the firm can cover the rising costs of more and more additional units of output. As a result, higher

Table 2.4 A market supply schedule for eggs

Reference letter	Price (£ per dozen)	Quantity supplied ('000 dozen per month)
u	0.50	5.0
v	1.00	46.0
w	1.50	77.5
x	2.00	100.0
y	2.50	115.0
z	3.00	122.5

The table shows the quantities that producers wish to sell at various prices, ceteris paribus. For example, row *y* indicates that if the price were £2.50 per dozen, producers would wish to sell 115,000 dozen eggs per month.

and higher prices are needed to induce firms to make successive increases in output. The result is a positive association between market price and the firm's output. This assumed relationship is discussed in much more detail in in Chapter 5.

The **supply schedule** given in Table 2.4 is analogous to the demand schedule in Table 2.2. It records the quantity that all producers wish to produce and sell at a number of alternative prices, rather than the quantity consumers wish to buy.

The six points corresponding to the six price–quantity combinations shown in Table 2.4 are plotted in Figure 2.6. The curve drawn through the six points is a **supply curve** for eggs. It shows the quantity produced and offered for sale at each price.[6]

The supply curve in Figure 2.6 has a positive slope. This is a graphical expression of the following assumption.

The market price and the quantity supplied are positively related to each other.

Shifts in the supply curve

A shift in the supply curve means that, at each price, a different quantity is supplied. An increase in the supply at each price is illustrated in Table 2.5 and plotted in Figure 2.7. This change appears as a rightward shift in the supply curve. A decrease in the supply at each price causes a leftward shift.

There is an important general rule for supply curve shifts similar to the one stated earlier for demand curves.

---

[6] Since we are not considering individual firms in this chapter, all supply curves are market curves showing the aggregate behaviour of the firms in the market. Where that is obvious from the context, the adjective 'market' is usually omitted.

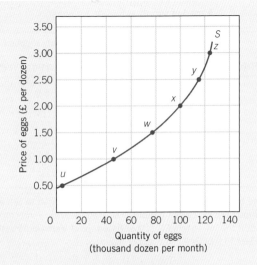

Figure 2.6 A supply curve for eggs

This supply curve relates quantity of eggs supplied to the price of eggs; its positive slope indicates that quantity supplied increases as price increases. The six points correspond to the price–quantity combinations shown in Table 2.4. The curve drawn through these points, labelled S, is the supply curve.

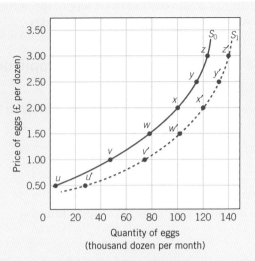

Figure 2.7 Two supply curves for eggs

The rightward shift in the supply curve from S_0 to S_1 indicates an increase in the quantity supplied at each price. For example, at the price of £1.00 the quantity supplied rises from 46,000 dozen to 76,000 dozen per month.

When there is a change in any of the variables (other than the product's own price) that affects the amount of a product that firms are willing to produce and sell, the whole supply curve for that product will shift.

The major possible causes of such shifts are summarized in the caption to Figure 2.8 and are considered briefly in the next two sections.

Prices of inputs

All things that a firm uses to produce its outputs—such as, in the case of an egg producer, chicken feed, labour, and egg-sorting machines—are called the firm's *inputs*. Other things being equal, the higher the price of any input used to make a product, the less will be the profit from making

Table 2.5 Two alternative market supply schedules for eggs

	Price of eggs (£ per dozen)	Original quantity supplied ('000 dozen per month)	New quantity supplied ('000 dozen per month)	
(1)	(2)	(3)	(4)	(5)
u	0.50	5.0	28.0	u'
v	1.00	46.0	76.0	v'
w	1.50	77.5	102.0	w'
x	2.00	100.0	120.0	x'
y	2.50	115.0	132.0	y'
z	3.00	122.5	140.0	z'

An increase in supply means that a larger quantity is supplied at each price. For example, the quantity that is supplied at £2.50 per dozen rises from 115,000 dozen to 132,000 dozen per month. A similar rise occurs at every price. Thus the supply schedule relating columns (2) and (3) is replaced by the one relating columns (2) and (4).

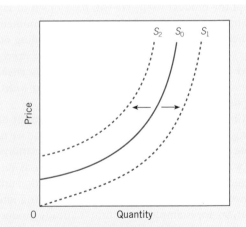
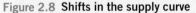

Figure 2.8 Shifts in the supply curve

A shift in the supply curve from S_0 to S_1 indicates an increase in supply; a shift from S_0 to S_2 indicates a decrease in supply. An increase in supply can be caused by improvements in technology or decreases in the costs of inputs that are important in producing the commodity. A decrease in supply can be caused by increases in the costs of inputs that are important in producing the commodity or by changes in technology that increase the costs of production (although such changes are rare).

that product. Thus the higher the price of any input used by a firm, the lower will be the amount that the firm will produce and offer for sale at any given price of the product.

A rise in the price of any input shifts the supply curve to the left, indicating that less will be supplied at any given price; a fall in the price of inputs shifts the supply curve to the right.

Technology

At any time, what is produced and how it is produced depend on the technologies in use. Over time, knowledge and production technologies change, and so do the quantities of individual products that can be supplied.

A technological change that decreases costs will increase the profits earned at any given price of the product. Since increased profitability leads to increased production, this change shifts the supply curve to the right,

indicating an increased willingness to produce the product and offer it for sale at each possible price.

Movements along supply curves versus shifts

As with demand, it is essential to distinguish between a movement along the supply curve (caused by a change in the product's own price) and a shift of the whole curve (caused by a change in something other than the product's own price). We adopt the same terminology as with demand: **quantity supplied** refers to a particular quantity actually supplied at a particular price of the product, and **supply** refers to the whole relationship between price and quantity supplied. Thus, when we speak of an *increase* or a *decrease in supply*, we are referring to shifts in the supply curve such as the ones illustrated in Figures 2.7 and 2.8. When we speak of a *change in the quantity supplied*, we mean a movement from one point on the supply curve to another point on the same curve.

The determination of price

So far we have considered demand and supply separately. We now outline how demand and supply interact to determine price?

The concept of a market

For the present purposes a **market** can be defined as an area over which buyers and sellers negotiate the exchange of some product or related group of products. It must be possible, therefore, for buyers and sellers to communicate with each other and to make meaningful transactions over the whole market. Some markets are local, such as the farmers' market in a county town, while others cover the entire world, such as the market for petroleum or wheat. In recent times, the technology of computers has greatly increased the number of world markets. For example, many commodities are advertised for sale to a worldwide audience on eBay.

Individual markets differ in the degree of competition among the various buyers and sellers. In the next few chapters we will confine ourselves to markets in which the number of buyers and sellers is sufficiently large that no single one of them has any appreciable influence on price. This is a very rough definition of what economists call *perfectly competitive markets*. Starting in Chapter 7, we will consider the behaviour of markets that do not meet this competitive requirement.

The graphical analysis of a market

Table 2.6 brings together the demand and supply schedules from Tables 2.2 and 2.4. Figure 2.9 shows both the

demand and the supply curves on a single graph; the six points on the demand curve are labelled with uppercase letters, while the six points on the supply curve are labelled with lowercase letters, with each letter referring to a common price on both curves.

Quantity supplied and quantity demanded at various prices

Consider first the point at which the two curves in Figure 2.9 intersect. Both the figure and Table 2.6 show that when the market price is £1.50, the quantity demanded is 77,500 dozen, and the quantity supplied is the same. At that price consumers wish to buy exactly the same amount as producers wish to sell. Provided that the demand curve is negatively sloped and the supply curve positively sloped throughout their entire ranges, there will be no other price at which the quantity demanded equals the quantity supplied.

Now consider prices below £1.50. At these prices consumers' desired purchases exceed producers' desired sales. It is easily seen that at all prices below £1.50 the quantity demanded exceeds the quantity supplied. Furthermore, the lower the price, the larger is the excess of the one over the other. The amount by which the quantity demanded exceeds the quantity supplied is called the **excess demand**, which is defined as quantity demanded *minus* quantity supplied ($q^d - q^s$). This is shown in the last column of Table 2.6.

Finally, consider prices higher than £1.50. At these prices consumers wish to buy less than producers wish to sell. Thus, quantity supplied exceeds quantity demanded.

Table 2.6 Demand and supply schedules for eggs and equilibrium price

Price per dozen (£)	Quantity demanded ('000 dozen per month)	Quantity supplied ('000 dozen per month)	Excess demand (quantity demanded minus quantity supplied) ('000 dozen per month)
0.50	110.0	5.0	105.0
1.00	90.0	46.0	44.0
1.50	77.5	77.5	0.0
2.00	67.5	100.0	−32.5
2.50	62.5	115.0	−52.5
3.00	60.0	122.5	−62.5

Equilibrium occurs where quantity demanded equals quantity supplied so that there is neither excess demand nor excess supply. These schedules are repeated from Tables 2.2 and 2.4. The equilibrium price is £1.50. For lower prices there is excess demand; for higher prices there is excess supply, which is shown as negative excess demand.

It is easily seen, and again you should check a few examples, that for any price above £1.50 quantity supplied exceeds quantity demanded. Furthermore, the higher the price, the larger is the excess of the one over the other. In this case there is negative excess demand ($q^d - q^s < 0$). This is also shown in the last column of Table 2.6.

Negative excess demand is usually referred to as **excess supply**, which measures the amount by which supply exceeds demand ($q^s - q^d$).

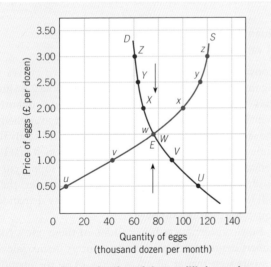

Figure 2.9 Determination of the equilibrium price of eggs

The equilibrium price corresponds to the intersection of the demand and supply curves. Point E indicates the equilibrium. At a price of £1.50 per dozen quantity demanded (point W) equals quantity supplied (point w). At prices above equilibrium there is excess supply and downward pressure on price. At prices below equilibrium there is excess demand and upward pressure on price. The pressures on price are represented by the vertical arrows.

Changes in price when quantity demanded does not equal quantity supplied

Whenever there is excess demand, consumers are unable to buy all they wish to buy; whenever there is excess supply, firms are unable to sell all they wish to sell. In both cases some agents will not be able to do what they would like to do. How will they react?

There is a key driving force in markets, which is called the **law of price adjustment** (not to be confused with the *law of demand* that we introduced earlier, which says that demand curves have a negative slope). This law predicts what will happen to the price in a competitive market when there is either excess demand or excess supply.

When supply exceeds demand, the market price will fall. When demand exceeds supply, the market price will rise.

Excess supply means that producers cannot sell all that they wish to sell at the current price. They may then begin to offer to sell at lower prices, such as through clearance sales or discounts. If purchasers observe the glut of unsold output they may begin to offer lower prices. For either or both of these reasons, the price in the market will fall.

If, at the current price, consumers are unable to buy as much as they would like to buy, they may offer higher prices in an effort to get more of the available supply for themselves. Suppliers are unable to produce a greater quantity of the product in the short run, but they can ask higher prices for the quantities that they are producing, and will make more profit if they do so. For either or both of these reasons, prices will rise.

This law of price adjustment makes considerable sense and conforms to common experiences of how markets work—shortages of any product tend to lead to price rises, while gluts tend to lead to price falls. Most importantly, it implies that prices will move towards the level at which demand and supply will be equal.

This is a necessary condition for the market to exhibit *stability*. Whenever the current price is not the one that equates demand and supply, the law of price adjustment ensures that the price will move towards the market-clearing price rather than away from it. Thus, it is not enough that there exists a price for which demand is equal to supply. Stability of the market also requires some mechanism to return the price to the market-clearing level whenever it is away from that point. The combination of a negatively sloped demand curve and a positively sloped supply curve with the law of price adjustment will guarantee a stable market, as long as any market in this product exists (that is, the demand and supply curves intersect at some positive price and quantity).

The equilibrium price

In our hypothetical example, for any price of eggs above £1.50 the price will fall, while for any price below £1.50 the price will rise. At a price of £1.50 there is neither excess demand associated with a shortage, nor excess supply associated with a glut; the quantity supplied is equal to the quantity demanded. Once supply and demand are equal, there is no tendency for the price to change because suppliers are just able to sell all that they want and

demanders are just able to buy all that they want. Nobody has any incentive to change the price.

The price of £1.50, where the supply and demand curves intersect, is the price towards which the actual market price will tend. It is called the **equilibrium price**: the price at which quantity demanded equals quantity supplied. The amount that is bought and sold at the equilibrium price is called the **equilibrium quantity**. The term 'equilibrium' means a state of balance; it occurs when desired purchases equal desired sales and there are no forces tending to make anything change. Box 2.4 discusses the implications of inflation for our interpretation of market price.

When quantity demanded equals quantity supplied, we say that the market is in **equilibrium**. When quantity demanded does not equal quantity supplied we say that the market is in **disequilibrium**.

Summary

We have now developed one of the most famous and powerful theories in all of economics, and it is worth summarizing what we have done.

Assumptions concerning a competitive market

- **The law of demand: demand curves have negative slopes throughout their entire range.**

Box 2.4 **Prices in periods of inflation**

Up to now we have developed the theory of the prices of individual products under the assumption that all other prices remain constant. Does this mean that the theory is inapplicable during an inflationary period when almost all prices are rising? Fortunately, the answer is no.

We have mentioned several times that what matters for demand and supply is the price of the product in question relative to the prices of other products. The price of the product expressed in money terms is called its money price; the price of a product expressed in relation to other prices is called its relative price.

In an inflationary world changes in a product's relative price can be measured by changes in the product's own price relative to changes in the average of all other prices, which is called the *general price level*. If, during a period when the general price level rose by 40 per cent, the price of oranges rose by 60 per cent, the price of oranges rose relative to the price level as a whole. Oranges became *relatively* expensive. However, if the price of oranges had risen by only 30 per cent when the general price level had risen by 40 per cent, their relative price would have fallen. Although the money price of oranges rose, oranges became *relatively* cheap.

In Lewis Carroll's famous story *Through the Looking-Glass*, Alice finds a country where everyone has to run in

order to stay still. So it is with inflation. A product's price must rise as fast as the general level of prices just to keep its relative price constant.

It has been convenient in this chapter to analyse a change in a particular price in the context of a constant price level. However, the analysis is easily extended to an inflationary period. Any force that raises the price of one product when other prices remain constant will, given general inflation, raise the price of that product relative to the average of all other prices. Consider the example of a change in tastes in favour of eggs that would raise their price by 20 per cent when other prices were constant. However, if the general price level goes up by 10 per cent, then the price of eggs will rise by 32 per cent.[7] In each case the price of eggs rises 20 per cent *relative to the average of all prices*.

In price theory, whenever we talk of a change in the price of one product, we mean a change *relative* to the general price level.

---

[7] Let the price level be 100 in the first case and 110 in the second. Let the price of eggs be 120 in the first case and *x* in the second. To preserve the same relative price, we need *x* such that $120/100 = x/110$, which makes $x = 132$.

- The theory of supply: supply curves have positive slopes throughout their entire range.

- The law of price adjustment: prices rise when demand exceeds supply, and fall if supply exceeds demand. They remain unchanged when demand and supply are equal.

Implications

- There is no more than one price at which quantity demanded equals quantity supplied: equilibrium is unique.

- Only at the equilibrium price will the market price remain constant.

- The market is stable in the sense that forces exist to move the price towards its market-clearing level.

Collectively these forces are sometimes known as the *laws of demand and supply*.

The predictions of demand and supply analysis

Earlier in this chapter, we studied shifts in demand and supply curves. Recall that a rightward shift in the relevant curve means that more is demanded or supplied *at each market price*, while a leftward shift means that less is demanded or supplied *at each market price*. How does a shift in either curve affect price and quantity?

The answers to this question are the predictions of our supply and demand theory. We wish to see what happens when an initial position of equilibrium is upset by some shift in either the demand or the supply curve, and a new equilibrium position is then established. This will enable us to derive predictions about what will happen in any market when something changes and this is why we study economics—so that we can anticipate what will happen in specific markets when some change happens.

To discover the effects of the demand and supply shifts that we wish to study, we use the method known as **comparative statics**. We start from a position of equilibrium and then introduce the change to be studied. The new equilibrium position is determined and compared with the original one. The differences between the two positions of equilibrium must result from the change that was introduced, for everything else has been held constant.

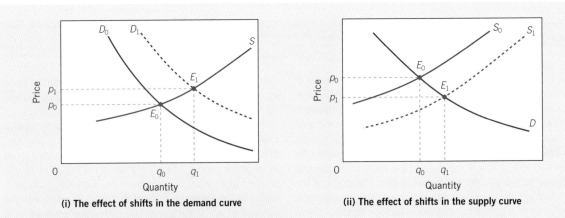

| (i) The effect of shifts in the demand curve | (ii) The effect of shifts in the supply curve |

Figure 2.10 **The predictions of demand and supply theory**

The predicted effects on equilibrium price and quantity of shifts in either demand or supply are as follows.

An increase in demand. In part (i) assume that the original demand and supply curves are D_0 and S, which intersect to produce equilibrium at E_0, with a price of p_0 and a quantity of q_0. An increase in demand shifts the demand curve to D_1, taking the new equilibrium to E_1. Price rises to p_1 and quantity rises to q_1.

A decrease in demand. In part (i) assume that the original demand and supply curves are D_1 and S, which intersect to produce equilibrium at E_1, with a price of p_1 and a quantity of q_1. A decrease in demand shifts the demand curve to D_0, taking the new equilibrium to E_0. Price falls to p_0 and quantity falls to q_0.

An increase in supply. In part (ii) assume that the original demand and supply curves are D and S_0, which intersect to produce an equilibrium at E_0, with a price of p_0 and a quantity of q_0. An increase in supply shifts the supply curve to S_1, taking the new equilibrium to E_1. Price falls to p_1 and quantity rises to q_1.

A decrease in supply. In part (ii) assume that the original demand and supply curves are D and S_1, which intersect to produce an equilibrium at E_1, with a price of p_1 and a quantity of q_1. A decrease in supply shifts the supply curve to S_0, taking the new equilibrium to E_0. Price rises to p_0 and quantity falls to q_0.

The four main predictions of demand and supply are derived in Figure 2.10. The analysis of that figure generalizes our specific discussion about eggs. Because it is intended to apply to any product whose price is determined by the forces of demand and supply and not the decisions of specific individual agents, the horizontal axis is simply labelled 'quantity' and the vertical axis 'price'.

The predictions of supply and demand theory are as follows.

1. A rise in the demand for a product (a rightward shift of the demand curve) causes an increase in both the equilibrium price and the equilibrium quantity bought and sold.

2. A fall in the demand for a product (a leftward shift of the demand curve) causes a decrease in both the equilibrium price and the equilibrium quantity bought and sold.

3. A rise in the supply of a product (a rightward shift of the supply curve) causes a decrease in the equilibrium price and an increase in the equilibrium quantity bought and sold.

4. A fall in the supply of a product (a leftward shift of the supply curve) causes an increase in the equilibrium price and a decrease in the equilibrium quantity bought and sold.

In Figures 2.5 and 2.8 we summarized the many events that cause demand and supply curves to shift. Using the four predictions derived in Figure 2.10, we can understand the link between these events and changes in market prices and quantities. To take one example, a rise in the price of butter will lead to an increase in both the price of margarine and the quantity bought. This is because a rise in the price of one product causes a rightward shift in the demand curves for its substitutes, and prediction 1 tells us that such a shift causes price and quantity to increase.

The theory of the determination of price by demand and supply is beautiful in its simplicity and yet powerful in its range of applications. Box 2.5 gives some simple applications of demand and supply to real market events.

Box 2.5 Demand and supply: what really happens

Here are examples of newspaper headlines or extracts that illustrate how demand and supply shifts are relevant to explaining what is happening to price and/or output of a specific product. As an exercise, you should draw a demand and supply curve and then shift the relevant curve in each case to see how the theory explains the outcome.

- OPEC countries once again fail to agree on output quotas. Output soars and prices plummet.

- Oil prices fall as world GDP growth declines sharply.

- Drought in Australia forces up the price of wool.

- The price of cashew kernels has fallen nearly 6 per cent in 10 months as Vietnam has begun to challenge India and Brazil, the world's two largest exporters.

- How deep is the art market's recession? In today's unforgiving economic climate, the sales of contemporary, impressionist, and modern works of art took hits at this week's auctions. Sales totalled just under £60 million compared with £500 million just one year ago. Many paintings on offer went unsold, and those that did sell went for well under their predicted price.

- Coffee prices at the London Commodity Exchange staged another spectacular rise, putting them above their level at the start of the year. The president of the Association of Coffee Producing Countries said that the supply shortages that are underpinning prices would last quite some time.

- Increased demand for macadamia nuts causes price to rise above competing nuts. A major producer now plans to double the size of its orchards during the next five years.

- World steel prices fell as China's increased production capacity came on stream just as world demand fell owing to the financial crisis.

- The price of oats surged 40 per cent in a week as torrential rains in Canada left fields unplanted, raising fears of lower supply of key agricultural commodities.

But are markets really like that?

As we built up our analysis of markets in this chapter, you might have been saying to yourself: 'This is all very well in theory but the markets I know about are not like that'. There is one important respect in which you would be absolutely correct. But we now want to persuade you that the doubts you might have about this analysis are not a real problem. Demand and supply analysis is applicable to many more markets than you might think if you just looked at those prices that react continually to changes in either demand or supply.

Administered prices and auction prices

One important worry that you may have when reading the analysis of markets is that most of the markets in which consumers operate, including you and us, do not work in the way we describe. For example, if you wish to attend your local cinema for a peak-time showing of a much-hyped film you may find queues outside the cinema to buy tickets. There may be more people who want to go at that time than the number of seats available for sale. According to our theory, this means that there is an excess demand and so the price of cinema seats should rise until enough people are discouraged and all those left in the queue are just able to obtain a seat.

Of course, this does not happen. What actually happens is that the cinema continues to sell tickets at its existing prices until it has sold all the seats and it then puts up a notice saying: 'sold out' or 'house full'.

Similarly, if you go into your local supermarket or department store, you will find the prices of all the goods clearly labelled. You can buy as much of each product as you like at the price set by the store, but the price does not change according to how many people are buying the product on a particular day. If some product is very popular the store will run out and the shelf will be empty, but the store does not adjust the price to ensure that there is just enough supply to meet the demand.

To go further we have to understand that market institutions vary with product and participants. Let us think about different ways in which prices are set and then we shall try to give some reasons for these differences.

The prices that most obviously fit our theory are referred to as **flexible price** or **auction prices**, as they adjust on a continuous basis to equate demand and supply. Prices in the foreign exchange market, the markets for petroleum, minerals, and grains are flexible as they can change minute by minute while the market is open. Prices that are set by the supplier, who then just waits to see how much of the product sells at that price, are known as **administered prices** or **fixed prices**. Most consumer goods and services are sold at administered prices.

Demand and supply theory is also applicable to many administered prices

Although prices in most retail outlets are set by the retailer, this does not mean that these prices do not adjust to market forces over time. On any particular day we find that all products have a specific price ticket on them. However, this price may be different from day to day or week to week. The price that the farmer gets from the wholesaler is much more flexible from day to day than the price that the retailer charges consumers. If, for example, bad weather leads to a poor potato crop, then the price that supermarkets have to pay to their wholesalers for potatoes will go up and this will be reflected in the prices they mark on potatoes in their stores. Thus, these prices do reflect the interaction of demand and supply in the wider marketplace for potatoes. Although they do not change in the supermarket from hour to hour to reflect local variations in demand and supply, they do change over time to reflect the underlying conditions of the overall production of and demand for the goods in question. For example, fresh strawberries sell at very different prices in mid-winter than in mid-summer. In the summer they are locally grown, but in winter they will have been flown in from the other side of the world.

Even within a supermarket that sets prices on all its produce there will be times when they mark down prices in order to get rid of stock. This may be as it approaches its sell-by date, or if they have new lines arriving the next day. Department stores often have sales at lower prices in order to get rid of stock that has not sold and to make room for new products. When the costs of producing such durable consumer goods as TV sets and refrigerators rise or fall, their prices follow, even if there is a substantial interval between the two sets of changes. However, in all these cases, the supplier is still setting a price and then (in effect) saying: 'Take it or leave it at this price'.

Why are most retail prices administered?

If administered prices do eventually respond to reflect demand and supply conditions, why are they set at a fixed price in the first place? The answer is that this is a more efficient way to organize a retail marketplace. Auction markets work well where all the potential buyers can be assembled in one place (the auction room), or are connected by communication equipment (telephones or computers), so that they can simultaneously bid for the product. The price is set so that the highest bidder gets the goods, and all the goods available are sold.

Imagine the chaos, however, if all the people who shop in your local supermarket have to turn up at the same time and make bids for their weekly shopping basket. This is clearly not feasible. Imagine also what the checkout queues would be like if every shopper had to negotiate the price of each item in their shopping trolley as they check it out. Again, this would be a very time-consuming way of shopping. There have been some attempts to organize some retail markets by collecting bids through the internet, such as via eBay. However, it seems unlikely that this form of shopping is going to replace the supermarket and the department store any time soon.

Mixed pricing

Some markets do have a mixture of administered prices and a degree of price negotiation. This is efficient because these are usually markets for items that are large and ones that you do not buy very often. Cars, for example, have 'list prices' but there is usually some leeway for negotiation about the price of the car itself, about the extras it includes, or about the trade-in price of your old car. When new models are introduced, stocks of the old models may be sold off at lower than the original list price. Houses also are typically listed at an 'asking price' but there is some negotiation around this price, and if several people are chasing the same house there may be what amounts to an auction where the house goes to the highest bidder. Indeed, in Scotland a sealed-bid auction system is the norm. Bidders have to enter a written bid on the same day without knowing what others have bid, and the highest bidder gets the property.

Many manufactured goods are put on sale in shops at a fixed price. But these prices are influenced by supply factors such as costs of production, and the rent and wages paid by the retailer. Demand influences will certainly affect the price. A very popular item that the retailer is finding hard to get may have its ticket price raised, while unsold items will be marked down for clearance at some stage. Clothing and other fashion items also typically stay on sale for a period at a fixed price but are then sold off in clearance sales to make way for new fashions or new styles. Indeed, while most clothes retailers have 'sales' around twice a year, many also have permanent racks of discounted items within their store. A similar example is wine shops that regularly have 'bin end' sales of unwanted stock to make space for their new stock.

So far the discussion has concerned administered prices of retailers who sell to consumers. Although demand and cost conditions will also exert considerable influence on the producers of the goods that end up in shops and also the many services that exist in a modern economy, we need to know more than is contained in the theory of competitive markets that we have just developed to understand the pricing and output decisions of most of these producers. These decisions will be the topic of Chapters 6, 7, and 8.

Summary

The theory of price determination by demand and supply is useful in understanding the working of many different types of market, but some care is needed. The theory works more or less exactly as described in markets where prices are set impersonally by market forces and adjust more or less continually in response to changes in demand and supply. Agricultural commodities at the wholesale level, raw materials, such as iron ore and crude petroleum, and many other similar products fall into this group, as do markets for foreign exchange and company shares. Although most retailers sell at administered prices, these change as the prices that they pay their

suppliers change. Thus, the price of food stuffs will change from week to week, or even day to day, as the wholesale prices that the supermarkets must pay their suppliers change. So variations in demand and supply do explain variations in prices—sometimes immediately and sometimes with lags that depend on such things as who is setting prices and how often it is efficient for these to be changed, and sometimes we need to know more than is contained in the theory of competitive markets to understand pricing and output decisions of those who actually make the goods and services that are eventually sold to consumers .

Relationships between different markets

Although each of the individual markets referred to above is distinct, all are interrelated and we need to see why.

The separation of individual markets

Markets are separated from each other in three main ways: by the product sold, by natural economic barriers, and by barriers created by governments. One example of each type of separation is given in the following.

1. The market for men's shirts is different from the market for refrigerators because different products are sold in each.

2. The market for cement in the UK is distinct from the market for cement in the western USA. The costs of transporting cement are so high that UK purchasers would not buy American cement even if its market price in the western USA was much lower than its market price in the UK.

3. The market for textiles used to be separated between many countries because government-imposed trade restrictions severely limited the amount that firms in one country could sell to consumers in another or the prices at which they could sell.

Because markets are distinct we can use demand and supply analysis to study the behaviour of markets one at a time.

The interlinking of individual markets

Although all markets are to some extent separated, most are also interrelated. Consider again the three causes of market separation: different products, spatial separation, and government intervention. Firstly, the markets for different kinds of product are interrelated because all products compete for consumers' income. Thus, if consumers spend more in one market, they will have less to spend in other markets. Secondly, the geographical separation of markets for similar products depends on transport costs.

Products whose transport costs are high relative to their production costs tend to be produced and sold in geographically distinct markets. Products whose transport costs are low relative to their production costs tend to be sold in what amounts to one world market. But whatever the transport costs, there will be some price differential at which it will pay someone to buy in the low-priced market and ship to the high-priced one. Thus, there is always some potential link between geographically distinct markets, even when shipping costs are high. Thirdly, markets are often separated by policy-induced barriers, such as tariffs (which are taxes paid when goods come into a country from abroad). Although high tariffs tend to

separate markets, they do not do so completely. If price differences become large enough, it will pay buyers in the high-price market to import from the low-price market and producers in the low-price market to export to the high-price one, even though they have to pay the tariff as a result.

Because markets are interrelated we must treat them as a single interrelated system for many purposes. *General equilibrium analysis* studies markets as a single interrelated system in which individual demands and supplies depend on all prices, and what happens in any one market will affect many other markets—and in principle could affect all other markets.

CASE STUDIES

1. A storm in a tea cup

In Box 2.1 we introduced the wholesale tea market. The central theme of this story was that adverse weather conditions were affecting crops and the supply shortage was expected to lead to higher prices. Supply had also been adversely affected by 'political unrest' in Kenya. The other key datum in the story was that consumption had been rising at a faster rate than production. In other words, demand was rising relative to supply. Figure 2.11 shows the wholesale price of tea. The chart shows clearly the rising price of tea in 2008 which can be explained by the excess demand reported.

Box 2.1 also explained the fall in the price of tea in the later months of 2008. Almost all commodity prices fell in the final

quarter of 2008 owing to the recession in most major countries, associated with a collapse in industrial production, world trade, and consumer demand. Against this background the fall in tea prices was relatively modest; for example, the price of crude oil fell from over $140 per barrel to around $40 per barrel at the same time as the tea price fell from $3.22 per kilo to $2.28 per kilo.

The drought conditions in many producing countries were the main driver of sharply rising tea prices in 2009. Production appeared to be recovering in 2010 and the price dropped back into its earlier range. However, the respite was temporary and it became clear that the drought conditions of 2008–9 were far from temporary. Industry analysts started to talk about the implications of longer-term climate change for tea-growing areas.

The best tea grows on cool hillsides at around 1,000 feet above sea level. However, climate change has meant that the weather has become too hot and dry in some traditionally successful production areas, such as Assam. Moving to higher ground takes time as tea plants take between four and twelve years to seed, while plants grown from cuttings do not give crops for at least three years. This means that it takes some time to move production to cooler higher ground. This combination of lower production in old plantations and slowness to expand in new areas helps explain why supply remained restricted between 2010 and the end of 2012.

So what explains the price reductions in 2013? There seem to be two main elements to this. The first is that greater supply finally came on stream in response to the high tea prices of 2010–12. The second is that economic disruption in Egypt and the civil war in Syria led to a sharp fall in demand in two important tea-drinking nations.

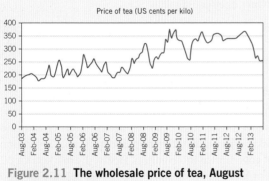

Figure 2.11 The wholesale price of tea, August 2003–July 2013

Source: IMF, *International Financial Statistics* database

The central message conveyed by this example is that by studying the determinants of demand and supply in a specific market we can explain the main movements of the prices in that market.

A common feature of the markets for many agricultural products is that that they normally have fairly stable demand conditions, as demand for food is not very sensitive to either income or price changes (though major wars and recessions can have an impact), while supply can be vulnerable to extreme weather conditions and can thus involve sudden adverse supply shifts. In the case of tea, climate change has been the recent problem. We shall see in the next chapter another example, coffee, where supply is vulnerable to abnormally harsh winters in the main producing countries.

In contrast with markets for agricultural products, markets for metals tend to be characterized by stable supply conditions and demand that varies with the business cycle. The following case study provides supporting evidence for this statement.

2. Keeping the lid on the tin

Figure 2.12 shows the price of tin from August 1993 to August 2013. The price was fairly flat for a decade, though there was a slight rise in the first half of the 1990s as the world came out of recession, and there was a dip between 2000 and 2003 during the post-millennium slowdown. These price variations would look significant if drawn on a larger scale but they are dwarfed by the subsequent price swings.

Tin is mined in most of the continents of the world even though it is relatively rare as an element in the Earth's crust. Production facilities take time to build, but once in place they can produce at steady levels until the area is exhausted. As most mining is underground it is not subject to adverse weather conditions, and as many countries have tin mines the market is not normally much affected by production problems in any one country. These factors explain the stable price of tin over the decade from 1994, when there was a balanced growth of both demand and supply.

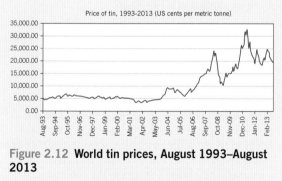

Figure 2.12 World tin prices, August 1993–August 2013

Source: IMF, *International Financial Statistics* database

So what happened next? Tin is an input into many manufactured products. It is used in the production of bronze, pewter, and die-casting alloys, and in modern engineering to make tungsten more machinable. The largest uses for tin are for the production of solders and for tin plating (providing a coating for many iron and steel products). The demand for tin soared in 2006–8 as demand soared for the products in which tin is an input. These include aircraft, ships, trains, white goods (washing machines, dishwashers, tumble driers, refrigerators), cars, commercial buildings and housing. The demand growth was worldwide, but the biggest single contributor over this period was China whose output was growing at around 10 per cent a year in real terms.

Speculative purchases by investment institutions probably also helped boost the price of tin during the first half of 2008. These institutions did not want tin for their own use, but at the time they thought that prices were likely to continue rising. They could buy a tin contract in the present and sell it later at a higher price (if they were right and prices did rise) without ever taking delivery of the tin itself. Of course, if prices fell they would lose money, so this was a risky thing to do. However, some institutions specialize in taking such bets and being quick to sell if the price moves against them.

In any event, the boom in tin prices burst in the late summer of 2008, at around the same time as many other commodity and asset prices collapsed. This collapse was linked to the worldwide recession that set in during the latter half of 2008. This price fall came from the realization that world demand was falling, and so production would fall and demand for industrial commodities would also fall.

From the spring of 2009 the world economy recovered strongly and with it so did the demand for tin. Added to the previous uses of tin this time around was the surge in demand for tablet computers which swept the world. The tin price was driven even higher than in 2008. Indeed, the price went so high in 2010 that many producers looked actively into reopening old mines and existing producers tried to expand their production capacity. Accordingly, supply increased somewhat and the price fell below its 2010 peak.

Thus the 2006–9 tin price boom and bust can be explained very simply by a strong rightward shift in the demand curve combined with a positively sloped supply curve (due to the rise in the cost of producing tin as the rate of extraction rises) followed by a sharp leftward shift in the demand curve. The 2009–11 boom can also be attributed to a sharp rightward shift in the demand curve, and the subsequent moderation of price can be thought of as the result of a modest rightward shift of the supply curve as new production capacity came on stream.

The movements in demand are explained by the boom and bust in world activity, or what we will call after Chapter 15 the world *business cycle*. Metal prices tend to be pro-cyclical (they rise in a boom and fall in a slump) as demand for the metal is high when industrial production is high and vice versa. The price of tin clearly fits this pattern.

Conclusion

In many of the markets in which we are interested, the analysis of how demand and supply interact to determine the market-clearing price is an essential tool. All the more detailed analyses that we are going to do between now and Chapter 14 is designed to build a fuller and fuller understanding of the forces affecting different types of market and market structure, and the motives and behaviour of market participants. But we have already gone a long way towards an understanding of how markets work.

SUMMARY

- The decision-taking units in economic theory are called agents. They are (a) individuals, for demand in goods markets and for supply in labour markets, (b) firms, for supply in goods markets and demand in labour and capital markets, and (c) governments, for supply of some goods and for regulation and control of the private sector. Given the resources at their command, each individual is assumed to maximize his or her satisfaction, and each firm is assumed to maximize its profit.

Demand

- An individual consumer's demand curve shows the relation between the price of a product and the quantity of that product the consumer wishes to purchase per period of time. It is drawn from the assumption that all other prices, income, and tastes remain constant. Its negative slope indicates that the lower the price of the product, the more the consumer wishes to purchase.

- The market demand curve is the horizontal sum of the demand curves of all the individual consumers. The demand curve for a normal good shifts to the right when the price of a substitute rises, when the price of a complement falls, when total income rises, when the distribution of income changes in favour of those with large demands for the product, and when tastes change in favour of the product. It shifts to the left with the opposite changes.

- A movement along a demand curve indicates a change in quantity demanded in response to a change in the product's own price; a shift in a demand curve indicates a change in the quantity demanded at each price in response to a change in one of the conditions held constant along a demand curve.

Supply

- The supply curve for a product shows the relationship between its price and the quantity that producers wish to produce and offer for sale per period of time. It is

drawn on the assumption that all other forces that influence quantity supplied remain constant, and its usual positive slope indicates that the higher the price, the more producers wish to sell. A supply curve shifts in response to changes in the prices of the inputs used by producers, and to changes in technology. The shift represents a change in the amount supplied at each price. A movement along a supply curve indicates that a different quantity is being supplied in response to a change in the product's own price.

The determination of price

- At the equilibrium price the quantity demanded equals the quantity supplied. Graphically, equilibrium occurs where the demand and supply curves intersect. At any price below equilibrium there will be excess demand and price will tend to rise; at any price above equilibrium there will be excess supply and price will tend to fall.

- A rise in demand raises both equilibrium price and quantity; a fall in demand lowers both. A rise in supply raises equilibrium quantity but lowers equilibrium price; a fall in supply lowers equilibrium quantity but raises equilibrium price.

But are markets really like that?

- Most retail markets do not have prices adjusting continuously to changes in demand and supply. Prices are set at a specific level and shoppers can buy as much as they want at this price. Prices are administered by the seller.

- Even administered prices do adjust to demand and supply forces, but it would not be efficient for these prices to be set either by auction or by negotiation, or to change every minute. Price changes do happen in response to persistent changes in the conditions affecting both demand and supply, but they do not do so instantaneously.

TOPICS FOR REVIEW

- Quantity demanded and the demand function
- The demand schedule and the demand curve for an individual and for the market
- The law of demand
- Shifts in the demand curve and movements along the curve
- Substitutes and complements
- Quantity supplied and the supply function

- The supply schedule and the supply curve
- Shifts in the supply curve and movements along the curve
- Excess demand and excess supply
- Equilibrium and disequilibrium prices
- The law of price adjustment
- Auction prices and administered prices

QUESTIONS

1 What is the equilibrium market price and quantity for each of the following pairs of demand and supply curves:

  i. Demand: $p = £100 - 2q$; supply: $p = £0 + 3q$
  ii. Demand: $p = £100 - 2q$; supply: $q = 30$
  iii. Demand: $p = £100$; supply: $p = £20 + 5q$

2 Use demand and supply curves to analyse what is happening in each of the following situations.

- The price of coffee has risen because of a frost in Brazil reducing the coffee crop.
- A fall in air fares from the UK has raised demand for hotel rooms on the Spanish coast.
- Further falls in chip prices have led to a reduction in the price of laptop computers.
- An exceptionally cold winter in North America has led to a higher price of oil.
- A disease in British beef has necessitated the slaughter of large numbers of cattle.

3 List the 'markets' in which you regularly buy goods or services. How are the price and quantity determined during your transaction? Do these prices change on a day to day basis or only infrequently? If prices do not adjust continually, what happens when there is an excess demand or supply?

4 Outline the main determinants of quantity demanded and quantity supplied, and explain how these interact to determine the market price.

5 Explain the main differences between administered prices and auction prices, and discuss which markets are most suitable for these two different mechanisms.

6 Outline the conditions that are required to achieve equality between demand and supply at a market-clearing price.

7 Explain the effect on market price and quantity in the market for mobile phones of each of the following: consumer incomes rise; technical improvements reduce production costs; the price of fixed-line calls falls sharply.

8 Suppose that the world price of cocoa rose by 20% last year and the quantity supplied (and demanded) fell by 5%. Which one of the following could explain this?

  a) There was an increase in supply from a new producer country.
  b) Incomes in the main consuming countries rose strongly.
  c) The price of coffee, which is a substitute, fell.
  d) There was a reduction in supply of cocoa on world markets due to civil unrest in the Ivory Coast (one of the main producers of cocoa).
  e) There was a reduction in supply of coffee on world markets due to an early frost in Brazil.

9 Suppose that the price of takeaway pizzas has risen sharply owing to a rise in the world price of wheat. What will happen to the demand curve for takeaway Chinese meals, assuming that these are substitutes for pizzas. Choose one answer.

  a) It will become flatter.
  b) It will become steeper.
  c) It will shift to the left.
  d) It will shift to the right.
  e) The demand curve will not move but the supply curve will shift to the left.

10 Suppose that the world price of coffee fell by 10%
last year and the quantity purchased fell by 5%.
Which one of the following could explain this?

a) There was a rise in supply from a producer
country, but no change in demand conditions.

b) Demand for coffee rose owing to higher incomes in
consumer countries.

c) The price of tea rose and tea is a substitute for
coffee.

d) There was a reduction in supply of coffee owing to
bad weather in the main producing countries and
price elasticity of demand is –0.5.

e) There was a reduction in demand owing to a
recession in the main consumer countries.

CHAPTER 3

ELASTICITY OF DEMAND AND SUPPLY

In this chapter we continue to study how markets work. In particular, we develop some very important concepts that will help you better understand markets. The key points to learn are:

- How the sensitivity of quantity demanded to a change in price is measured by the elasticity of demand and what factors influence it.
- How elasticity is measured at a point or over a range.
- How income elasticity is measured and how it varies with different types of goods.
- How elasticity of supply is measured and what it tells us about conditions of production.
- Some of the difficulties that arise in trying to estimate various elasticities from sales data.

The demand and supply analysis of the previous chapter helps us to understand the direction in which price and quantity would change in response to shifts in demand or supply. In most real-world situations economists and business analysts are not going to get away with saying things like: 'If we raise our price sales will fall' or 'If incomes rise this year our demand will increase'. The question they need to answer is: 'By how much?' Fortunately, tools exist to help them, and you, to answer this question in the many different circumstances in which it may be asked. These tools measure the responses of the quantity demanded and the quantity supplied to changes in the variables that determine them, particularly prices and incomes.

To illustrate why we want to have these measures, consider the effects of a new government tax intended to reduce emissions of greenhouse gases by taxing each litre of petrol that is refined. This will shift the supply curve of petrol to the left because less will be offered at each price, or equivalently any specific quantity will only be offered at a higher price. If the demand for petrol is as shown in part (i) of Figure 3.1, the effect of the government's policy will be to increase petrol prices slightly, while greatly reducing the quantity refined and consumed. However, if the demand is as shown in part (ii) of Figure 3.1, the effect

of the policy will be to increase petrol prices greatly, but to reduce petrol production and consumption by only a small amount. If the purpose of the tax is to reduce the amount that is produced and consumed, then the policy will be a great success when the demand curve is similar to the one shown in part (i), but a failure when the demand curve is similar to that shown in part (ii). However, if the main purpose of the tax is to achieve a large increase in tax revenue, the policy will be a failure when demand is as shown in part (i) but a great success when demand is as shown in part (ii).

This example shows that it is often not enough to know whether quantity rises or falls in response to some change. It is important to know by how much. To measure this we use the concept of *elasticity*.

Box 3.1 contains a real report of events in the world markets for two commodities, coffee and sugar. The central event in both markets is a rise in price in response to a supply shortage. We return to both these cases later in the chapter, but we introduce them at this stage to alert readers to the fact that understanding the concept of elasticity will help a great deal in understanding developments in real-world markets. We will only be able to spell out the relevance of elasticity to these markets once we have explained the concept in more detail.

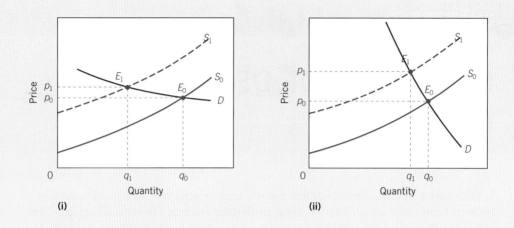

Figure 3.1 The effect of the shape of the demand curve

The flatter the demand curve, ceteris paribus, the less the change in price and the greater the change in quantity. Both parts of the figure are drawn on the same scale. Both show the same initial equilibrium price p_0 and quantity q_0, the same shift of the supply curve from S_0 to S_1, and a new equilibrium at p_1 and q_1. In part (i) the effect of the shift in supply is a slight rise in the price and a large fall in quantity. In part (ii) the effect of the identical shift in the supply curve is a large rise in the price and a relatively small fall in quantity.

Box 3.1 Real markets that elasticity will help understand

The following is an extract from a report by the World Bank relating to events in two important markets, the world wholesale markets for coffee and sugar. We will return to these examples later in the chapter to explain how the concept of elasticity is important in understanding these markets.

*The World Bank's beverage price index (comprised of coffee, cocoa, and tea) is down 36 percent since its February 2011 record high. The earlier surge (and recent decline) in beverages reflects mostly **coffee** prices—specifically, arabica—which reached $6/kg in 2011, the highest nominal level ever. The increase in arabica reflected a shortfall in production in Colombia, the world's second-largest arabica supplier after Brazil. However, as Colombian production recovered partially, and coffee companies began using more robusta in their blends, arabica prices declined and are now hovering at half their early 2011 highs. Global coffee output reached 145 million bags in 2012, up from 137 million bags in 2011. Furthermore, Brazil, the world's top*

coffee supplier, is expected to have a bumper crop in 2013–14 (April–March), currently estimated at almost 47 million bags. Coffee supplies from Vietnam (the world's largest robusta supplier), Colombia, and Indonesia are also expected to be large.

***Sugar** prices have been weakening as well and are down 16 percent since a year ago and nearly 40 percent below their 2011 peak. The sugar market now faces a large surplus. Global sugar production exceeded 182 million tons in 2012, up from 173 million tons in 2011 while consumption in both years averaged 163 million tons. Good crops in South America (especially Brazil) and Asia have contributed to the surplus. Brazil, world's top sugar supplier, in an attempt to boost prices, announced a tax credit to ethanol producers; the announcement failed to support prices, though.*

(Source: *Global Economic Prospects: Commodity Market Review*, World Bank, July 2013)

Demand elasticity

In the first part of this chapter we deal with quantity demanded and start by considering its response to changes in a product's own price.

Price elasticity of demand

In Figure 3.1, we were able to compare the responsiveness of quantity demanded along the two demand curves because they were drawn on the same scale. But you should not try to compare two curves without making sure that the scales are the same. Also, you must not leap to conclusions about responsiveness of quantity demanded on the basis of the apparent steepness of a single curve. The hazards of so doing are illustrated in Figure 3.2. Both parts of the figure plot the same demand curve, but the choice of scale on the 'quantity' and 'price' axes serves to make one curve look steep and the other flat.

Measuring the responsiveness of demand to price

We wish to get a measure of responsiveness that is independent of the units in which we measure our quantities and prices as well as the way we draw our graphs; to do this we deal in percentage changes. A given percentage change in the amount of petrol purchased will be the same whether we measure it in gallons or litres. Similarly, although we cannot easily compare the absolute changes in kilos of carrots and barrels of oil, we can compare their two percentage changes.

These considerations lead us to the concept of the **price elasticity of demand**, which is defined as the percentage change in quantity demanded *divided by* the percentage change in price that brought it about.[1] This elasticity is usually symbolized by the lower-case Greek letter eta (η):

$$\eta = \frac{\text{percentage change in quantity demanded}}{\text{percentage change in price}} \qquad (3.1)$$

Many different elasticities are used in economics. To distinguish η from the others, the full term 'price elasticity of demand' can be used. Since η is by far the most commonly used elasticity, economists often drop the adjective 'price' and refer to it merely as *elasticity of demand*, or sometimes just *elasticity*. However, when more than one

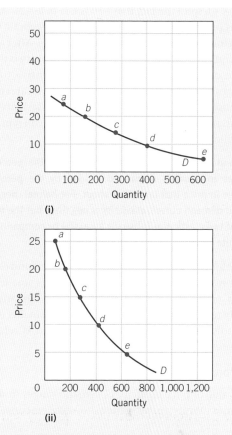

(i)

(ii)

Figure 3.2 One demand curve drawn on two different scales

Suitable choice of scale can make any demand curve appear steep or flat. Parts (i) and (ii) plot the same demand curve. Because the same distance on the quantity axes stands for twice as much in part (ii) as in part (i), and the same distance on the price axes stands for half as much, the curve is steeper when plotted in graph (ii) than when plotted in graph (i).

kind of elasticity could be involved, η should be given its full title.

The sign of the measure

Because of the negative slope of the demand curve, price and quantity will always change in opposite directions. One change will be positive and the other negative, making the measured elasticity of demand negative. This would pose no problem except for two unfortunate habits of economists. First, either by carelessness or design, the minus sign is often dropped and elasticity is reported as a positive number. Secondly, it is almost universal practice

---

[1] Elasticity is an example of what mathematicians call a *pure number*, which is a number whose value is independent of the units in which it is calculated. Slope, $\Delta p/\Delta q$, is not a pure number. For example, if price is measured in pence, $\Delta p/\Delta q$ will be 100 times as large as $\Delta p/\Delta q$ along the same demand curve where price is measured in pounds sterling.

ı comparing two elasticities to compare their absolute, not their algebraic, values.[2] For example, if product X has an elasticity of −2 while product Y has an elasticity of −10, economists will say that Y has a greater elasticity than X (despite the fact that −10 is *less than* −2). As long as it is understood that absolute and not algebraic values are being compared, this usage is acceptable. After all, the demand curve with the larger absolute elasticity *is* the one where quantity demanded is more responsive to price changes. For example, an elasticity of −10 indicates greater response of quantity to price than does an elasticity of −2.

This need not cause confusion so long as you remember the following.

Demand elasticity is measured by a ratio: the percentage change in quantity demanded divided by the percentage change in price that brought it about. For normal, negatively sloped demand curves, elasticity is negative, but the relative size of two elasticities is usually assessed by comparing their absolute values.

Table 3.1 shows the calculation of two demand elasticities, one that is quite large and one that is smaller. The larger elasticity indicates that quantity demanded is highly responsive to a change in price. The smaller elasticity indicates that the quantity demanded is relatively unresponsive to a change in price.

Interpreting price elasticity

The value of price elasticity of demand ranges from zero to minus infinity. In this section, however, we concentrate on absolute values, and so ask by how much the absolute value *exceeds zero*.

Elasticity is zero if quantity demanded is unchanged when price changes, namely when quantity demanded does not respond to a price change. A demand curve of zero elasticity is shown as curve D_1 in Figure 3.3. It is said to be *perfectly* or *completely* inelastic.

As long as there is some positive response of quantity demanded to a change in price, the absolute value of elasticity will exceed zero. The greater the response, the larger the elasticity. Whenever this value is less than one, however, the percentage change in quantity is less than the percentage change in price and demand is said to be **inelastic.**

When elasticity is equal to one, the two percentage changes are equal to each other. This case, which is called **unit elasticity,** is the boundary between elastic and inelastic demands. A demand curve having unit elasticity over its whole range is shown as D_3 in Figure 3.3.

When the percentage change in quantity demanded exceeds the percentage change in price, the elasticity of demand is greater than one and demand is said to be **elastic.** When elasticity is infinitely large, there exists some small price reduction that will raise quantity demanded from zero to infinity. Above the critical price, consumers will buy nothing. At the critical price, they will buy all that they can obtain (an infinite amount, if it were available). The graph of a demand curve with infinite price elasticity is shown as D_2 in Figure 3.3. Such a demand curve is said to be *perfectly* or *completely elastic*. (This unlikely looking case will turn out to be important later when we study the demand for the output of a single firm with many competitors all producing an identical product.)

Table 3.1 Calculation of two demand elasticities

	Original	New	% change	Elasticity
Good A				
Quantity	100	95	−5%	$\frac{-5}{10} = -0.5$
Price	£1	£1.10	10%	
Good B				
Quantity	200	140	−30%	$\frac{-30}{20} = -1.5$
Price	£5	£6	20%	

Elasticity is calculated by dividing the percentage change in quantity by the percentage change in price. With good A, a rise in price of 10p on £1, or 10 per cent, causes a fall in quantity of 5 units from 100, or 5 per cent. Dividing the 5 per cent reduction in quantity by the 10 per cent increase in price gives an elasticity of −0.5. With good B, a 30 per cent fall in quantity is caused by a 20 per cent rise in price, making elasticity −1.5.

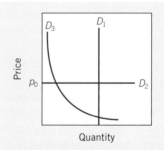

Figure 3.3 Three constant-elasticity demand curves

Each curve has a constant elasticity. D_1 has *zero elasticity*: the quantity demanded does not change at all when price changes. D_2 has *infinite elasticity at the price p_0*: a small price increase from p_0 decreases quantity demanded from an indefinitely large amount to zero. D_3 has *unit elasticity*: a given percentage increase in price brings an equal percentage decrease in quantity demanded at all points on the curve; it is a rectangular hyperbola for which price *times* quantity is a constant.

---

[2] The absolute value is the magnitude without the sign. Thus, for example, −3 is smaller in algebraic value than 2 but larger in absolute value.

Box 3.2 summarizes the discussion of this and subsequent sections. The terminology in the table is important, and it is worth becoming familiar with it at some stage, but you may want to come back to it once you have read the rest of the chapter.

Elasticity and total spending

How does consumers' total spending on a specific product react when the price of the product is changed? The total spending of the product's buyers is equal to the money received by the product's sellers plus any taxes that the government levies on the product. For simplicity, we ignore any taxes, so that sellers' receipts are equal to buyers' spending.

A simple example can be used to show that buyers' total spending and sellers' receipts may rise or fall in response to a decrease in price. Suppose 100 units of a product are being sold for £1 each. The price is then cut to £0.90. If the quantity sold rises to 110, the total spent falls from £100 to £99. But if quantity sold rises to 120, total spending rises from £100 to £108.

The change in total spending brought about by a change in price is directly related to the elasticity of demand. If elasticity is less than unity (so demand is inelastic), the percentage change in price will exceed the percentage change in quantity. The price change will then be the more influential of the two changes, so that total spending will change in the same direction as the price changes, rising as price rises and falling as price falls. However, if elasticity exceeds unity (demand is elastic), the percentage change in quantity will exceed the percentage change in price. The quantity change will then be the more influential change, so that the total amount spent will change in the same direction as quantity changes (that is, in the opposite direction to the change in price).

Box 3.2 The terminology of elasticity

TERM	SYMBOL	NUMERICAL MEASURE OF ELASTICITY	VERBAL DESCRIPTION
Price elasticity of demand (supply)	η (ε_s)		
Perfectly or completely inelastic		Zero	Quantity demanded (supplied) does not change as price changes
Inelastic		Greater than zero, less than one	Quantity demanded (supplied) changes by a smaller percentage than does price
Unit elasticity		One	Quantity demanded (supplied) changes by exactly the same percentage as does price
Elastic		Greater than one, but less than infinity	Quantity demanded (supplied) changes by a larger percentage than does price
Perfectly, completely, or infinitely elastic		Infinity	Purchasers (sellers) are prepared to buy (sell) all they can at some price and none at all at a higher (lower) price
Income elasticity of demand	η_y		
Inferior good		Negative	Quantity demanded decreases as income increases
Normal good		Positive	Quantity demanded increases as income increases:
Income-inelastic		Less than one	less than in proportion to income increase
Income-elastic		Greater than one	more than in proportion to income increase
Cross-elasticity of demand	η_{xy}		
Substitute		Positive	Quantity demanded of some good and the price of a substitute are positively related
Complement		Negative	Quantity demanded of some good and the price of a complement are negatively related

1. When elasticity of demand exceeds unity (demand is elastic), a fall in price increases total spending on the good and a rise in price reduces it.

2. When elasticity is less than unity (demand is inelastic), a fall in price reduces total spending on the good and a rise in price increases it.

3. When elasticity of demand is unity, a rise or a fall in price leaves total spending on the good unaffected.[3]

You can check points 1 and 2 above for yourself using the example in Table 3.1. Calculate what happens to total spending on the product when price changes in each case. In the case of good *A*, whose demand is inelastic, you will see that a rise in price raises total spending (and thus also the revenue of sellers). In contrast, the rise in the price of good *B*, whose demand is elastic, lowers total spending (and sellers' revenue).

Some complications

We now need to look a little more closely at the elasticity measure. Let us first write out in symbols the definition that we have been using, which is percentage change in quantity divided by percentage change in price:

$$\eta = \frac{(\Delta q/q)\times 100}{(\Delta p/p)\times 100}$$

We can cancel out the 100s and multiply the numerator and denominator by $p/\Delta p$ to get

$$\eta = (\Delta q/q) \times (p/\Delta p).$$

Since it does not matter in which order we do our multiplication (i.e. $q \times \Delta p = \Delta p \times q$), we can reverse the order of the two terms in the denominator and write

$$\eta = (\Delta q/\Delta p) \times (p/q). \tag{3.2}$$

We have now split elasticity into two parts: $\Delta q/\Delta p$, the ratio of the *change* in quantity to the change in price, which is related to the slope of the demand curve, and p/q, which is the ratio of the *level* of the price to the quantity at which we make our measurement.

Figure 3.4 shows a straight-line demand curve. If we wish to measure the elasticity at a point, we take our *p* and *q* at that point and consider a price change, taking us to another point, and measure our Δp and Δq between those

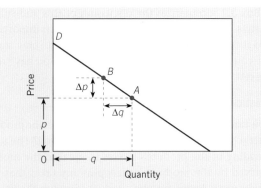

Figure 3.4 Elasticity on a linear demand curve

Elasticity depends on the slope of the demand curve and the point at which the measurement is made. Starting at point *A* and moving to point *B*, the ratio $\Delta p/\Delta q$ is the slope of the line, while its reciprocal $\Delta q/\Delta p$ is the first term in the percentage definition of elasticity. The second term is p/q, which is the ratio of the coordinates of point *A*. Since the slope $\Delta p/\Delta q$ is constant, it is clear that the elasticity along the curve varies with the ratio p/q, which is zero where the curve intersects the quantity axis and 'infinity' where it intersects the price axis.

two points. The slope of the straight line joining the two points is $\Delta p/\Delta q$. However, the term in eqn (3.2) is $\Delta q/\Delta p$, which is the reciprocal of $\Delta p/\Delta q$. (This involves just turning the ratio upside down. For example, the reciprocal of 2/3 is 3/2, and the reciprocal of a whole number is its inverse: the reciprocal of 4 is ¼.) Thus, the first term in the elasticity formula (3.2) is the reciprocal of the slope of the straight line joining the two price–quantity positions under consideration. The second term is the ratio of price to quantity at the point where elasticity is measured.

Now we can use the expression in eqn (3.2) to discover a number of things about our elasticity measure.

First, the elasticity of a negatively sloped straight-line demand curve varies from infinity at the price axis to zero at the quantity axis. A straight line has a constant slope, so that the ratio $\Delta p/\Delta q$ is the same anywhere on the line. Therefore its reciprocal $\Delta q/\Delta p$ must also be constant. We can now infer the changes in η by inspecting changes in the ratio p/q as we move along the demand curve. At the price axis $q = 0$ and p/q is undefined. However, if we let q approach zero, without ever quite reaching it, we see that the ratio p/q becomes very large. Thus, elasticity increases without limit as q approaches zero. Loosely, we say that elasticity is infinity when q is zero. Now move the point at which elasticity is being measured down the demand curve. As this happens, p falls and q rises steadily; thus the ratio p/q is falling steadily, so that η is also falling. At the q axis the price is zero, so the ratio p/q is zero. Thus, elasticity is zero.

Secondly, with a straight-line demand curve the elasticity measured from any point (p, q), according to eqn (3.2),

---

[3] Algebraically, total spending is price *times* quantity. If, for example, the equilibrium price and quantity are p_1 and q_1, then total spending is p_1q_1. On a demand curve diagram price per unit is given by a vertical distance and quantity by a horizontal distance. It follows that on such a diagram total spending is given by the *area* of a rectangle, the length of whose sides represent price and quantity. Total revenue (receipts) to the supplier and total spending by consumers are identical in these examples.

is independent of the direction and magnitude of the change in price and quantity. This follows immediately from the fact that the slope of a straight line is a constant. If we start from some point (p, q) and then change price, the ratio $\Delta q/\Delta p$ will be the same whatever the direction or the size of the change in p.

Our third point takes us back to the beginning of this chapter, where we warned against judging elasticity from the apparent shape of a demand curve. We often want to compare elasticities of two different demand curves, but we have just seen that the elasticity of a straight-line demand curve varies as we move along it. So how can we compare two numbers both of which are ranging from zero to infinity for every straight line demand curve? Fortunately, if two demand curves intersect, their elasticity can be compared *at the point of intersection* merely by comparing the slopes of the two curves. The steeper curve is the less elastic. Figure 3.5 shows two intersecting curves and proves that the steeper curve is less elastic than the flatter curve when elasticity is measured at the point where the two curves intersect. The intuitive reason is that at the point of intersection p and q are common to both curves, so all that differs in the elasticity formula is their relative slopes. This is a valuable result which we will use many times in later chapters.

Measured at the point of intersection of two demand curves, the steeper curve has the lower elasticity.

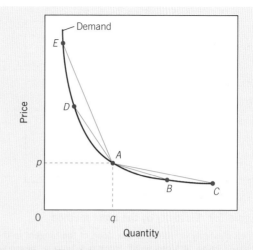

Figure 3.6 **Elasticity on a non-linear demand curve**
Elasticity measured from one point on a non-linear demand curve and using the percentage formula varies with the direction and magnitude of the change being considered. Elasticity is to be measured from point A, so the ratio p/q is given. The ratio $\Delta p/\Delta q$ is the slope of the line joining point A to the point reached on the curve after the price has changed. The smallest ratio occurs when the change is to point C and the highest ratio when it is to point E. Since the term $\Delta q/\Delta p$ in the elasticity formula is the reciprocal of this slope, measured elasticity is largest when the change is to point C and smallest when it is to point E.

The fourth point is that when eqn (3.2) is applied to a non-linear demand curve, the elasticity measured at any one point varies with the direction and magnitude of the change in price and quantity. Figure 3.6 shows a non-linear demand curve with elasticity being measured at one point. The figure makes it apparent that the ratio $\Delta q/\Delta p$, and hence the elasticity, will vary according to the size and the direction of the price change. This result is very inconvenient. It happens because the ratio $\Delta q/\Delta p$ gives the average reaction of q to a change in p over a section of the demand curve, and, depending on the range that we take, the average reaction will be different.

A more precise measure

The measure defined in eqn (3.2) gives the elasticity over some range, or *arc*, of the demand curve. This measure is sometimes used in empirical work where elasticity is measured between two observed price–quantity situations. In theoretical work, however, it is normal to use a concept that gives a unique measure of the elasticity at each specific point on the demand curve. Instead of using the changes in price (Δp) and quantity (Δq) over some range of the curve, this elasticity measure uses the concept of how quantity is *tending* to change as price changes at each specific point on the curve.

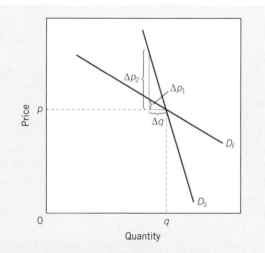

Figure 3.5 **Two intersecting demand curves**
At the point of intersection of two demand curves, the steeper curve has the lower elasticity. At the point of intersection p and q are common to both curves, and hence the ratio p/q is the same. Therefore elasticity varies only with $\Delta q/\Delta p$. The absolute value of the slope of the steeper curve, $\Delta p_2/\Delta q$, is larger than the absolute value of the slope $\Delta p_1/\Delta q$ of the flatter curve. Thus, the absolute value of the ratio $\Delta q/\Delta p_2$ on the steeper curve is smaller than the ratio $\Delta q/\Delta p_1$ on the flatter curve, so that elasticity is lower.

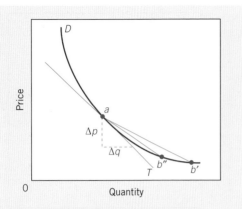

Figure 3.7 Elasticity by the exact method

When elasticity is related to the slope of the tangent to the demand curve at some point, there is a unique measured value of elasticity at that point. In this method the ratio $\Delta q / \Delta p$ is taken as the reciprocal of the slope of the line that is tangent to point a. Thus, there is only one measured elasticity at point a. It is p/q multiplied by $\Delta q/\Delta p$ measured along the tangent T. There is no averaging of changes in p and q in this measure because only one point on the curve is used.

If we wish to measure the elasticity in this way, we need to know the reaction of quantity to a change in price at each point on the curve, not over some range on the curve. We use the symbol dq/dp to refer to this concept and define it as *the reciprocal of the slope of the straight line (i.e. $\Delta q/\Delta p$) that is tangent to the demand curve at the point in question.* Figure 3.7 illustrates the use of this measure to calculate the elasticity of demand at the point a. It is the ratio p/q (as it has been in all previous measures) now multiplied by the ratio $\Delta q/\Delta p$ measured along the straight line that is tangent to the curve at a.[4] This definition can now be written as

$$\eta = (dq/dp) \times (p/q). \qquad (3.3)$$

This elasticity measure is the one normally used in economic theory. Elasticity measured by the percentage formula $(\Delta q/\Delta p)(p/q)$ can be regarded as an approximation to this expression. It is obvious from inspecting Figure 3.7 that the elasticity measured from $(\Delta q/\Delta p)(p/q)$ will come closer and closer to that measured by (dq/dp) (p/q), the smaller the price change used to calculate the value of $\Delta q/\Delta p$. Thus, if we consider the percentage definition of elasticity as an approximation to the precise definition, the approximation improves as the size of Δp diminishes. Box 3.3 further investigates some of the properties of the percentage definition and shows a practical way of avoiding some of its undesirable aspects.

----

[4] Although the expression dq/dp, as we have defined it, is the differential calculus concept of the derivative of quantity with respect to price at the point (p, q), you can understand the concept without knowing calculus.

What determines elasticity of demand?

The main determinant of elasticity is the availability of substitutes. Some products, such as margarine, cabbage, Coca Cola, and the Ford Fiesta, have quite close substitutes—butter, other green vegetables, Pepsi, and the Vauxhall Corsa. When the price of any one of these products changes, *the prices of the substitutes remaining constant,* consumers will to some extent substitute one product for another. When the price falls, consumers buy more of the product and less of its substitutes. When the price rises, consumers buy less of the product and more of its substitutes. More broadly defined products, such as all foods, all clothing, cigarettes, and petrol, have few if any satisfactory substitutes. A rise in their price can be expected to cause a smaller fall in quantity demanded than would be the case if close substitutes were available.

A product with close substitutes tends to have an elastic demand; one with no close substitutes tends to have an inelastic demand.

Closeness of substitutes—and thus measured elasticity—depends both on how the product is defined and on the time period under consideration. This is explored in the following sections. One common misconception about demand elasticity is discussed in Box 3.4.

Definition of the product

There is no substitute for food; it is a necessity of life. Thus, for food taken as a whole demand is inelastic over a large price range. However, it does not follow that any one food—say Weetabix or Heinz tomato soup—is a necessity in the same sense. Each of these has close substitutes, such as Kellogg's Cornflakes and Campbell's tomato soup. Individual food products can have quite elastic demands, and they frequently do.

Durable goods provide a similar example. Durables as a whole have less elastic demands than individual durable goods. For example, after a rise in the price of TV sets, some consumers might replace their personal computer or their hi-fi system instead of buying a new TV. Thus, although their purchases of TV sets fall, their total purchases of durables fall by much less.

Because many specific manufactured goods have close substitutes, they tend to have price-elastic demands. A particular Marks & Spencer own-brand raincoat could be expected to be price elastic, but all clothing taken together will be inelastic. This is because it is easy to substitute a Marks & Spencer raincoat with a John Lewis or Selfridges raincoat, but you have to wear something in the winter and you cannot avoid wearing clothing altogether when its price in general rises relative to, say, the price of food.

Box 3.3 Measuring elasticity over a range

We have seen that the percentage formula gives different answers for the elasticity at any point on a non-linear demand curve depending on the size and the direction of the change being considered. Many textbooks just give the percentage elasticity formula, without warning the reader about this property. Inquisitive students usually discover this property with a shock the first time they try to calculate some elasticities from numerical data.

One common way in which students discover the problem is when they try to calculate the elasticity on a unit-elasticity curve. Using the percentage formula the answer never comes out to be 1. For example, the demand curve

$$p = £100/q \qquad \text{(i)}$$

is a unit-elastic curve because expenditure pq remains constant at £100 whatever the price. But if you substitute any two prices into the above equation and calculate the elasticity according to the percentage formula, you will never get an answer of 1, whatever two prices you take. For example, the equation tells us that if price rises from £2 to £3, quantity falls from 50 to 33.3. If we take the original price as £2, we have a price change of 50 per cent and a quantity change of −33.3 per cent, making an elasticity of −0.667. If we take the original price as £3, the elasticity comes out to be −1.5.

This is unsatisfactory. The problem can be avoided when measuring elasticity between two separate points on the curve by taking p and q as the average values between the two points. This measure has two convenient properties. First, it is independent of the direction of the change and, secondly, it gives a value of unity for any point on a demand curve whose true value is unity.

In the above example the average p is £2.50 and the average q is 41.667. This makes the percentage change in price 40 per cent ($(1/2.5) \times 100$) and the percentage change in quantity also 40 per cent ($(16.667/41.667) \times 100$). So elasticity is correctly measured as 1. Whatever two prices you put into eqn (i), you will always get a value of unity for the elasticity, provided that you use the average of the two prices and of the two quantities when calculating the elasticity. Readers who enjoy playing with algebra can have fun proving this proposition.*

The best approximation to the correct measure when elasticity is measured between two separate points on a demand curve is obtained by defining p and q as the average of the prices and quantities at the two points on the curve.

This is the best way to measure elasticities given readings from any two points on a curve when that is all that is known. As we have seen in the text, for theoretical purposes the way out of the problem is to measure the ratio $\Delta q/\Delta p$ as the slope of the tangent to one point on the curve rather than between two points on the curve. To do this we need to know a portion of the demand curve around the point in question.

In practice economists do not usually estimate elasticity on the basis of only one observation. It is more common to report an elasticity measure that is valued at the mean of two p and q data points. This is analogous to the averaging we suggest here.

* What you need to prove is that

$$\frac{q_2 - q_1}{p_2 - p_1} \cdot \frac{(p_1 + p_2)/2}{(q_1 + q_2)/2} = 1$$

Any one of a group of related products will tend to have an elastic demand, even though the demand for the group as a whole may be inelastic.

Long-run and short-run elasticity of demand

Because it takes time to adjust fully to some price changes, a demand that is inelastic in the short run may prove elastic when enough time has passed. For example, before the first OPEC oil price shocks of the early 1970s, the demand for petrol was thought to be highly inelastic because of the absence of satisfactory substitutes. But the large price increases over the 1970s led to the development of smaller, more fuel-efficient cars and to less driving. The elasticity of demand for petrol was measured as −0.6 soon after the price rose. However, when the first five years of quantity adjustment had been allowed for the elasticity had become −1.2.

For many products the response of quantity demanded to a given price change, and thus the measured price elasticity of demand, will tend to be greater the longer the time span considered.

The different quantity responses can be shown by different demand curves. Every demand curve shows the response of consumer demand to a change in price. For products such as cornflakes and ties, the full response occurs quickly and there is little reason to worry about longer-term effects. Therefore a single demand curve will suffice for these products. Other products are typically used in connection with highly durable appliances or machines. A change in price of, say, electricity or petrol may not have its major effect until the stock of appliances and machines using these products has been adjusted. This adjustment may take a long time, making it useful to identify two kinds of demand curve for such products. A *short-run demand*

Box 3.4 Elasticity and income

It is often argued that the demand for a product will be more inelastic the smaller the proportion of income spent on it. The argument runs as follows. When only a small proportion of income is spent on some product, consumers will hardly notice a price rise. Hence, they will not react strongly to price changes one way or the other.

The most commonly quoted example of this alleged phenomenon is salt. However, salt is a poor example for the argument being advanced. Although it does take up a very small part of consumers' total expenditure, it also has few close substitutes. Consider another product, say one type of mint. These mints no doubt account for only a small portion of the total expenditure of mint suckers, but there are many close substitutes—other types of mints and other sucking sweets. The makers of Polo mints, for example, know that if they raise Polo prices greatly, mint suckers will switch to other brands of mint and to other types of sucking sweets. Thus, they face an elastic demand for their product.

Similar considerations apply to any one brand of matches. If the makers of Swan Vesta matches raise their prices significantly, people will switch to other brands of matches rather than pay the higher price.

What this discussion shows is that *goods with close substitutes will tend to have elastic demands whether they account for a large or a small part of consumers' incomes.*

However, there is another aspect of the influence of income. To see this, consider any good that has an inelastic demand. A rise in its price causes more to be spent on it. If consumers spend more on that product, they must spend less on all others taken as a group. But the higher the proportion of income spent on the product, the less likely they are to spend more on it when its price rises. After all, if a consumer spends all of his or her income on potatoes, demand must have unit elasticity. As price rises, purchases must then fall in proportion since the consumer has only a given income to spend. Thus, *for a good to have a highly inelastic demand it must have few good substitutes, and it must not take up too large a proportion of consumers' total expenditure.*

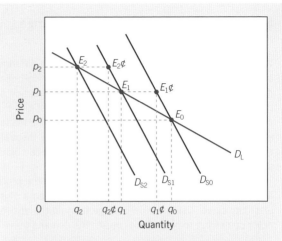

Figure 3.8 Short-run and long-run demand curves

This long-run demand curve is more elastic than the short-run curves. D_L is the long-run demand curve showing the quantity that will be bought after consumers become fully adjusted to each given price. Through each point on D_L there is a short-run demand curve. It shows the quantities that will be bought at each price when consumers are fully adjusted to the price at which that particular short-run curve intersects the long-run curve. So, at every other point on the short-run curve consumers are not fully adjusted to the price they face, possibly because they have an inappropriate stock of durable goods. When consumers are fully adjusted to price p_0, they are at point E_0 consuming q_0. Short-run variations in price then move them along the short-run demand curve D_{S0}. Similarly, when they are fully adjusted to price p_1, they are at E_1 and short-run price variations move them along D_{S1}. The line D_{S2} shows short-run variations in demand when consumers are fully adjusted to price p_2.

curve shows the response of quantity demanded to a change in price, *given* the existing quantities of the durable goods that use the product, and *given* existing supplies of substitute products. A different short-run demand curve will exist for each such structure of durable goods and substitute products. The *long-run demand curve* shows the response of quantity demanded to a change in price after enough time has passed to allow all adjustments to be made.

The relation between long-run and short-run demand curves is shown in Figure 3.8. Assume, for example, that there is a large rise in the price of electricity. The initial

response will be along the short-run demand curve. There will be some fall in quantity demanded, but the percentage drop will be less than the percentage rise in price, making short-run demand inelastic. Over time, however, many people will replace their existing electric cookers with gas cookers as they wear out. New homes will be equipped with gas rather than electric appliances more often than they would have been before the price rise. After further time, some factories will switch to relatively cheaper sources of power. When all these types of long-run adaptation have been made, the demand for electricity will have fallen a great deal. Indeed, over this longer period of time, the percentage reduction in quantity demanded may exceed the percentage increase in price. If so, the long-run demand for electricity will be elastic.

The long-run demand curve for a product that is used in conjunction with durable products will tend to be substantially more elastic than any of the short-run demand curves.

It should not be concluded that long-run elasticities always exceed their short-run value. Estimates of demand for automobiles themselves suggest that the long-run price elasticity of demand may be as low as –0.2, while the short-run elasticity is of the order of –1.2 to –1.4.[5] This evidence comes from the United States where having a car is essential, especially for those living in rural areas, so demand is not very sensitive to price in the long run. However, it is usually easy to postpone buying a new car for some time, so higher prices do reduce spending on cars more than in proportion to the rise in price over the first several months after a price rise. The demand for the cars of one specific maker is even more price elastic in the short run. Chevrolet, for example, was estimated to face a short-run price elasticity of –4 if it were to raise its own price while other producers held their prices constant.

Durable goods may have a higher price elasticity of demand in the short run than in the long run, as it is possible to post-pone the purchase of a replacement for some time.

These insights will prove valuable in several of the chapters that follow.

Other demand elasticities

So far we have discussed *price elasticity of demand*, the response of the quantity demanded to a change in the product's own price. The concept of demand elasticity can be broadened to measure the response to changes in *any* of the variables that influence demand. How much, for example, do changes in income and the prices of other products affect quantity demanded?

Income elasticity

Economic growth has raised the real income of the average citizen of Europe and North America quite dramatically over the past two centuries. At low levels of income, most money is spent on such basics as food, clothing, and shelter. As income rises an increasing proportion of expenditure tends to fall on manufactured goods, particularly such durables as cars, TV sets, and refrigerators. At yet higher levels of income more and more of any additional income goes to services such as foreign travel, entertainment, and education.

The responsiveness of demand for a product to changes in income is termed **income elasticity of demand**, and is defined as

$$\eta_y = \frac{\text{percentage change in quantity demanded}}{\text{percentage change in income}}.$$

For most products, increases in income lead to increases in quantity demanded, and therefore income elasticity is positive. If the resulting percentage change in quantity demanded is larger than the percentage increase in

income, η_y will exceed unity. The product's demand is then said to be **income-elastic**. If the percentage change in quantity demanded is smaller than the percentage change in income, η_y will be less than unity. The product's demand is then said to be **income-inelastic**. In the boundary case, the percentage changes in income and quantity demanded are equal, making η_y unity. The product is said to have a *unit income elasticity of demand*.

While virtually all observed price elasticities are negative, income elasticities are observed to be both positive and negative.

We have already encountered the link between income changes and demand in Chapter 2. We argued that a change in income would shift the demand curve for a product. If a rise in income causes more of it to be demanded (other things being equal) so that the demand curve shifts rightward, as it does with most products, we call it a *normal good*. If a rise in income causes less of it to be demanded, which means a leftward shift in the product's demand curve, we call it an *inferior good*. So normal goods are those that have positive income elasticities, while inferior goods are those that have negative income elasticities. Finally, the boundary case between normal and inferior goods occurs when a rise in income leaves quantity demanded unchanged, so that income elasticity is zero.

The important terminology of income elasticity is sum-marized in Figure 3.9 and Box 3.2. It is worth spending a bit of time familiarizing yourself with this terminology. Figure 3.9 illustrates all possible reactions by showing a product whose income elasticity goes from zero to positive to nega-tive. No specific good is likely to show a pattern exactly like this. Most goods will have a positive income elasticity at all levels of income—people demand more as they get richer. (It should be obvious that no good can have a negative income elasticity at *all* levels of income.) A graph that directly relates quantity demanded to income, such as Figure 3.9, is called an *Engel curve* after Ernst Engel (1821–96), the German econ-omist who used this device to display the relationship between household income and spending on necessities.

Income elasticities may be larger in the long run than in the short run, just as many price elasticities are. This is because people may take time to adjust spending patterns as their resources change over time. You may, for example, get a pay rise this year, but not buy a bigger car until it is clear that your income has reached a sustainable higher level or your current car is sufficiently depreciated. This explains why one study found that the income elasticity of fuel demand is between 1.1 and 1.3 in the long run, and between 0.35 and 0.55 in the short run.

Cross-elasticity

The responsiveness of quantity demanded for one prod-uct to changes in the prices of other products is often of

---

[5] See <http://www.mackinac.org/article.aspx?ID=1247>.

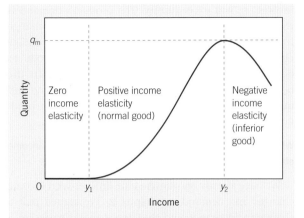

Figure 3.9 The relation between quantity demanded and income

Normal goods have positive income elasticities; inferior goods have negative elasticities. Nothing is demanded at income less than y_1, so for incomes below y_1 income elasticity is zero. Between incomes of y_1 and y_2, quantity demanded rises as income rises, making income elasticity positive. As income rises above y_2, quantity demanded falls from its peak at q_m, making income elasticity negative.

considerable interest. Producers of, say, beans and other meat substitutes find the demands for their products rising when cattle shortages force the price of beef up. Producers of large cars find their sales falling when the price of petrol rises dramatically.

The responsiveness of demand for one product to changes in the price of another product is called **cross-elasticity of demand.** It is defined as

$$\eta_{xy} = \frac{\text{percentage change in quantity demanded of product } x}{\text{percentage change in price of product } y}$$

Cross-elasticity can vary from minus infinity to plus infinity. Complementary goods have negative cross-elasticities and substitute goods have positive cross-elasticities.

Mobile phones and the calls that can be made on them, for example, are complements. A fall in the price of calls causes an increase in the demand for both handsets and calls. Thus, changes in the price of calls and in the quantity of handsets demanded will have opposite signs—price of calls goes down and demand for handsets goes up. In contrast, mobile calls and fixed-line calls are substitutes: a fall in the price of mobile calls increases the quantity of mobile calls made but reduces the quantity demanded of fixed-line calls. Therefore changes in the price of mobile calls and in the quantity of fixed-line calls demanded will have the same sign. The terminology of cross-elasticity is also summarized in Box 3.2.

Box 3.5 provides some examples of the importance of taking elasticity into account when making many practical decisions.

Box 3.5 Elasticity matters

Elasticities may seem rather boring concepts to learn about and to calculate. But they are powerful tools. Practical people who scorn theory ignore elasticity considerations at their peril. Here are a few cautionary tales.

• Not long ago the treasurer of a professional association introduced a motion at the annual meeting 'to increase membership fees by 10 per cent so as to increase our revenues by 10 per cent'. You could have told them that they were optimistically assuming that the elasticity of demand for membership was zero. If the elasticity differed at all from zero, revenues would rise by less than 10 per cent. If the elasticity proved to be greater than unity, they would actually suffer a loss of revenue as a result of the rise in fees.

• A local bus company raised its prices by 10 per cent in an attempt to cover increased costs. It was pleased to see its revenues rise by 5 per cent. The next year it confidently raised its prices again and was surprised and dismayed to find that its revenues fell by 2 per cent. The manager was reported in the local press as saying, 'It is hard to do business when our customers are so erratic'. You could have told him that there was nothing erratic about the customers'

behaviour. The manager was unreasonably assuming that the elasticity of demand for bus rides was constant over the whole relevant range. All that happened was that the second increase took fares into the range where the market demand curve was elastic.

• Many countries have recently experienced water shortages and some have decided to install water meters and pricing by usage in order to reduce demand from households. However, the evidence later emerged that domestic water consumption has a very low price elasticity of demand. For internal use this figure could be as low as –0.04. If this number is correct a 10 per cent rise in water prices would only lower domestic usage by less than half of one per cent. Water providers may have slightly better luck in lowering external usage (for the garden and car washing) as the price elasticity for this is significantly higher at –0.3. This is still inelastic, but a 10 per cent rise in price would achieve a 3 per cent cut in usage. Thus, pricing would not be an effective way of reducing demand in the case of water, but it may generate enough revenue to justify investing in new supply capacity.

Supply elasticity

We have seen that elasticity of demand measures the response of quantity demanded to changes in any of the variables that affect it. Similarly, elasticity of supply measures the response of quantity supplied to changes in any of the variables that influence it. Because we wish to focus on the product's own price as a variable influencing its supply, we will be mainly concerned with *price elasticity of supply*. The usual practice is to drop the adjective 'price', referring to 'elasticity of supply' or 'supply elasticity' whenever there is no ambiguity in this usage.

Supply elasticities are important in economics. Our treatment is brief for two reasons: first, much of what has been said about demand elasticity carries over to the case of supply elasticity and does not need repeating; secondly, we will have more to say about the determinants of supply elasticity later in this book when we have looked more closely at the production decisions of firms.

A definition

The **price elasticity of supply** is defined as the percentage change in quantity supplied divided by the percentage change in price that brought it about. Letting the lower-case Greek letter epsilon, ε, stand for this measure, its formula is

$$\varepsilon_s = \frac{\text{percentage change in quantity supplied}}{\text{percentage change in price}}$$

Supply elasticity is a measure of the degree of responsiveness of quantity supplied to changes in the product's own price.

Since supply curves normally have positive slopes, supply elasticity is normally positive.

Interpreting supply elasticity

Figure 3.10 illustrates three cases of supply elasticity. The case of zero elasticity is one in which the quantity supplied does not change as price changes. This would be the case, for example, if suppliers persisted in producing a given quantity and dumping it on the market for whatever it would bring. Infinite elasticity occurs at some price if nothing is supplied at lower prices but an indefinitely large amount will be supplied at that price. Any straight-line supply curve drawn through the origin, such as the one shown in part (iii) of Figure 3.10, has an elasticity of unity. The reason is that, for any positively sloped straight line, the ratio of p/q at any point on the line is equal to the ratio $\Delta p/\Delta q$ that defines the slope of the line. Thus, in the expression $(\Delta q/\Delta p)(p/q)$ the two ratios are equal, so the product is unity.

The case of unit supply elasticity illustrates that the warning given earlier for demand applies equally to supply. Do not confuse geometric steepness of supply curves with elasticity. Since *any* straight-line supply curve that passes through the origin has an elasticity of unity, it follows that there is no simple correspondence between geometrical steepness and supply elasticity. The reason is that varying steepness (when the scales on both axes are unchanged) reflects varying *absolute* changes, while elasticity depends on *percentage* changes. The terminology of supply elasticity is summarized in Box 3.2.

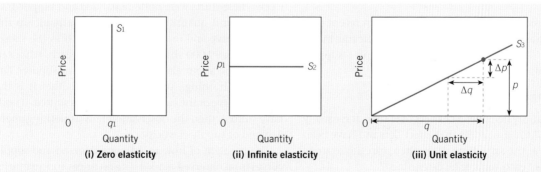

Figure 3.10 Three constant-elasticity supply curves

All three curves have constant elasticity. Curve S_1 has a *zero elasticity*, since the same quantity, q_1, is supplied whatever the price. Curve S_2 has an *infinite elasticity at price p_1*; nothing at all will be supplied at any price below p_1, while an indefinitely large quantity will be supplied at the price of p_1. Curve S_3, as well as all other straight lines through the origin, has a *unit elasticity*, indicating that the percentage change in quantity equals the percentage change in price between any two points on the curve.

What determines elasticity of supply?

What determines the response of producers to a change in the price of the product that they supply? First, the size of the response depends in part on how easily producers can shift from the production of other products to the one whose price has risen. If agricultural land and labour can be readily shifted from one crop to another, the supply of any one crop will be more elastic than otherwise. Here also, as with demand, length of time for response is critical. It may be difficult to change quantities supplied in response to a price increase in a matter of weeks or months, but easy to do so over a period of years. An obvious example concerns the planting cycle of crops. Also, new oilfields can be discovered, wells drilled, and pipelines built over a period of years, but not in a few months. Thus, the elasticity of supply of oil is much greater over five years than over one year, and greater over one year than over one month. Secondly, elasticity is strongly influenced by how costs respond to output changes. This issue will be looked at in more detail in later chapters.

Measurement of demand and supply

Much of what economists do to earn a living uses measurements of demand and supply elasticities. Will a fare increase help to ease the deficit of London Underground or the Panama Canal? The answer requires knowledge of price elasticity of demand. The United Nations Food and Agriculture Organization (FAO) and producers' co-operatives use income elasticities of demand to predict future changes in demand for food. Over the past decade, many industries have estimated their products' cross-elasticities of demand with petroleum in order to predict the effects of sharply changing petroleum prices. Members of the Organization of Petroleum Exporting Countries (OPEC) may wish to know supply elasticities in non-member countries in order to predict the reaction to price increases manipulated by OPEC. The methods for obtaining this information are dealt with in econometrics courses.[6] We now discuss solutions to two of the most troubling problems concerning demand measurement.

Problems of demand measurement

The explosion of knowledge of elasticities in recent decades came about when econometricians overcame major problems in measuring demand (and supply) relationships.

Everything is changing at once

When quantity demanded changes over time, it is usually because *all* the influences that affect demand have been changing at the same time. How, then, can the separate influence of each variable be determined?

What, for example, is to be made of the observation that the quantity of butter consumed per capita rose by 10 per cent over a period in which average consumer income rose by 5 per cent, the price of butter fell by 3 per cent, and the price of margarine rose by 4 per cent? How much of the change is due to income elasticity of demand, how much to price elasticity, and how much to the cross-elasticity between butter and margarine? If this is all we know, the question cannot be answered. However, if there are many observations showing, say, quantity demanded, income, price of butter, and price of margarine every month for four or five years, it is possible to discover the separate influence of each of the variables. The standard technique for doing so is called *multiple regression analysis*.

Separating the influences of demand and supply

A second set of problems concerns the separate estimation of demand and supply curves. We do not observe directly what people wish to buy and what producers wish to sell at each possible price. Rather, we see what they do buy and what they do sell. So, in any specific market we observe a price and quantity that is a point on both the supply and demand curve. For example, UK retailers might sell 100,000 white shirts at £30 each in a particular week. These shirts were both demanded and supplied, so the price and quantity combination is a point on the demand curve and on the supply curve. If in the subsequent week 90,000 shirts are sold at £32 each, what can we conclude about elasticity of demand or supply? The answer is 'nothing', unless we know whether it is the demand curve or the supply curve that has shifted. If both have shifted, then the observation tells us nothing about demand or supply elasticity.

The problem of how to estimate demand and supply curves from observed market data on prices and quantities actually traded is called the **identification problem**.

---

[6] Econometrics is the application of statistical methods to measurement and testing in economics.

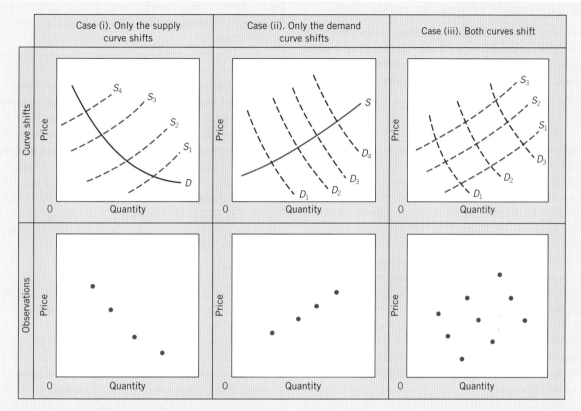

Figure 3.11 The identification problem
Observations on prices and quantities are sufficient to identify the slope of one of the curves only when it is stationary while the other shifts. In each case the curves in the top row shift randomly from one numbered position to another, generating the observations shown by the points in the corresponding bottom row. In case (i) the observations trace out the shape of the demand curve. In case (ii) they trace out the supply curve. In case (iii) neither curve can be identified from the observed prices and quantities.

To illustrate the problem, we assume in Figure 3.11 that all situations observed in the real world are equilibrium ones, in the sense that they are produced by the intersection of demand and supply curves. The first two parts of the figure show cases where only one curve shifts. Observations made on prices and quantities then trace out the curve that has not shifted. However, the third part of the figure shows that when both curves are shifting, observations of prices and quantities are not sufficient to identify the slope of either curve.

The identification problem is surmountable. The key to identifying the demand and supply curves separately is to bring in variables other than price, and then to relate demand to one set and supply to *some other* set. For example, supply of the product might be related not only to the price of the product but also to its cost of production, and demand might be related not only to the price of the product but also to consumers' incomes. Provided that these other variables change sufficiently, it is possible to determine the relation between quantity supplied and price as

well as the relation between quantity demanded and price. The details of how this is done will be found in a course on econometrics.

Econometricians allow for the identification problem when estimating demand curves. In more popular discussions, however, the problem is sometimes ignored. Whenever you see an argument such as 'We know that the foreign elasticity of demand must be very low because the price of whisky rose by 10 per cent last year while whisky exports hardly changed at all', you should ask if the author has really identified the demand curve. If the rise in price was due to a rise in foreign demand for whisky, we may actually have discovered that the short-run *supply curve* of whisky is very inelastic (since whisky takes several years to manufacture). The general proposition to keep in mind is:

Unless we know that one curve has shifted while the other has not, price and quantity data alone are insufficient to reveal anything about the shape of either the demand or the supply curve.

Measurements of specific elasticities

The solution of the statistical problems associated with demand measurement has led to a large accumulation of data on demand elasticities. The value of these data to the applied economist shows the usefulness of demand theory.

Price elasticities

Much of the early work on demand measurement concentrated on the agricultural sector. Large fluctuations in agricultural prices provided both the incentives to study this sector and the data on which to base estimates of price elasticities of demand. Nobel Laureate Professor Richard Stone in the United Kingdom (1913–91) and Professor Henry Schultz (1893–1938) in the United States did much of the pioneering work. Many agricultural research centres extended their work and even today are making new estimates of the price elasticities of foodstuffs. The resulting data mostly confirm the existence of low price elasticities for food products as a whole, as well as for many individual products. The policy pay-off of this knowledge in terms of understanding agricultural problems has been enormous; it represents an early triumph of empirical work in economics.

Although the importance of the agricultural problem led early investigators to concentrate on the demand for foodstuffs, modern studies have expanded to include virtually the whole range of products on which consumers spend their incomes. The demands for consumer durables such as cars, radios, refrigerators, TV sets, and houses are of particular interest because they constitute a large fraction of total demand, and because they can vary markedly from one year to the next. A durable product can usually be made to last for another year; thus purchases can be postponed with greater ease than can purchases of non-durables such as food and services. If enough consumers decide simultaneously to postpone purchases of durables, even for six months, the effect on the economy can be substantial. This means that demand for durables is typically more price elastic in the short run than it is in the long run. Specific numbers for the case of cars were mentioned earlier in the chapter.

Durables as a whole have an inelastic demand, especially in the long run, while many individual brands of durable have elastic demands. This is another example of the general proposition that the broader the category, the fewer the close substitutes and hence the lower the elasticity. Indeed, whether durable or non-durable, many specific manufactured goods have close substitutes, and studies show that they tend to have price-elastic demands. This is why many firms try to build strong brands so that consumers of their product remain loyal. It helps them to raise price without losing substantial market share.

Table 3.2 shows some measures of price elasticity for food products.

Notice that all the price elasticities shown in Table 3.2 are negative, and staples like potatoes and eggs have relatively low price elasticities. What is not clear from the table is that, within the categories shown in the table, the elasticity for a subset of that category can be much higher than for the product class as a whole. Carcass meats, for example, have a price elasticity of –0.69, but the price elasticity for lamb is –1.29, for pork it is –0.82, and for bacon it is –0.78. This indicates that different carcass meats are closer substitutes for each other than are other foods for carcass meats as a whole.

Income elasticities

Table 3.2 also shows some measured income elasticities for the United Kingdom. Note the low income elasticities for all of the food products. The income elasticity for food as a whole (not shown in the table) is estimated at 0.2, which says that for every 1 per cent increase in incomes there is only a 0.2 per cent increase in spending on food. Notice, however, that all the estimates in the table except one show a positive income elasticity. Eggs have a negative income elasticity, but this number is not significantly different from zero, so we should not conclude from this that eggs are an inferior good. The

Table 3.2 Price and income elasticities of UK food items

	Price elasticity	Income elasticity
Milk and cream	–0.36	0.05
Cheese	–0.35	0.23
Carcass meats	–0.69	0.2
Fresh fish	–0.69	0.27
Eggs	–0.28	–0.01
Fresh green vegetables	–0.66	0.27
Fresh potatoes	–0.12	0.09
Fresh fruit	–0.29	0.3
Fruit juices	–0.55	0.45
Bread	–0.4	0.12
Beverages	–0.37	0.1

Source: Expenditure and Food Survey, DEFRA, 2002. Available on <http://www.defra.gov.uk>. Data for price elasticities are for 1988–2000, and data for income elasticities are for 1998–2000. Estimates are derived from panel data (i.e. cross-section data for several periods of time).

only clear estimate of an inferior good among food products (not shown in the table but from the same source) is margarine, which has an estimated income elasticity of –0.37.

One implication of a low income elasticity of demand for food is that poorer households tend to spend a higher proportion of their incomes on food than richer households. In 2012, for example, the poorest 20 per cent of UK households spent 16.6 per cent of their income on food, while the proportion spent for all households was only 11.6 per cent.

Cross-elasticities

Cross-elasticities are much harder to estimate as there are many more of them. Each product has only one own-price elasticity and one income elasticity but it has a (potential) cross-elasticity with every other product. The source for Table 3.2 does report estimates of cross-elasticities for the same food products, but most of them are insignificant. One that is not, however, is the positive cross-elasticity of bread and cheese (0.34), which indicates that bread and cheese are substitutes.

Though hard to measure, the concept of cross-elasticity is important. In many countries monopoly is illegal. Measurement of cross-elasticities has helped courts to decide on the allegation that a monopoly exists. To illustrate, assume that the competition authority of a particular country brings a suit against a company for buying up all the firms making aluminium cable, claiming that the company has created a monopoly of the product. The company replies that it needs to own all the firms in order to compete efficiently against the several firms producing copper cable. It argues that these two products are such close substitutes that the firms producing each are in intense competition with each other, so that the sole producer of aluminium cable cannot be said to have an effective monopoly over the market for cable. Measurement of cross-elasticity can be decisive in such a case. A cross-elasticity of 10, for example, would support the company by showing that the two products were such close substitutes that a monopoly of either would not be an effective monopoly of the cable market. A cross-elasticity of 0.5, on the other hand, would support the contention that the monopoly of aluminium cable *was* a monopoly over a complete market.

Other evidence

UK evidence on food is supported by that from other countries. Estimates from the United States suggest that the price elasticity of demand for salt is –0.1 and that for coffee is –0.25 (see source in footnote 5), while that for fish eaten at home is –0.6 (very similar to the UK figure in

Table 3.2). Higher elasticities were found in the US for movie visits (–0.9) and for owner-occupied housing (–1.2),[7] while some relative luxuries like restaurant meals had a much higher elasticity (–2.3) and that for foreign travel (–4.0) was higher still. Clearly people have to eat, but they do not have to eat out. Similarly, in a big country like the United States it is easy to take a vacation at home rather than indulge in an overseas trip when the relative price of the latter rises.

Elasticities and economic growth

One of the most interesting constants in the behaviour of elasticities is the tendency for both income and price elasticities of demand for food to fall as nations become richer after a certain minimum income has been achieved. In very poor countries where people literally do not have enough to eat, most of any extra income is spent on additional foods, making the income elasticity very high. For countries that are even slightly richer the situation is different. Over the decades, economic growth has been increasing the real incomes of many countries throughout the world. As this happens the demand for foodstuffs increases, but at a slower and slower rate. At the same time the demand becomes less and less sensitive to price fluctuations. For example, the price elasticity of demand for food is only about –0.1 in the United States, the country with the highest per capita income. As we go down the income scale, price elasticities rise in absolute size, being about –0.3 in the United Kingdom, –0.45 in Israel, –0.55 in Peru, and around –0.7 in India. Over the same income range, income elasticities also rise as income falls. They go from about 0.15 in the United States, 0.2 in the United Kingdom, 0.5 in Israel, and 0.65 in Peru to almost 0.8 in India.

Other variables

Research shows that demand is often influenced by a wide variety of socioeconomic factors—family size, age, religion, geographical location, type of employment, wealth, and income expectations—not included in the traditional theory of demand. Although significant, the total contribution of all these factors to changes in demand tends to be small. Typically, less than 30 per cent of the variations in demand are accounted for by these 'other' factors and a much higher proportion is explained by the traditional variables of current prices and incomes.

[7] Note that the United States has a healthy market in rental properties in most areas, so owner-occupied housing does not have a low price elasticity there, as it might if it were an essential item of spending, like food.

Why the measurement of demand is important

The empirical measurements of demand elasticity help to provide the theory of price with empirical content. If we knew *nothing* about demand elasticities, all of the exercises we have gone through in previous chapters would have very little application to the real world. As time goes by, further evidence accumulates, and economists are far beyond merely wondering if demand curves have negative slopes. Not only do we now know the approximate shape of many demand curves, but we also have information about how demand curves shift. Our knowledge of demand relations increases significantly every year.

This knowledge has two general uses. First, in our study of economics it helps us to understand much more about how individual markets and the market economy work. This is helpful for understanding the world around us, and it helps inform debates about whether, for example, the market outcome can be trusted or whether government should intervene. Secondly, those of you who work in business after you have finished in college will find that your employer is competing with other firms in some markets and you will be expected to suggest ways in which the firm can be more successful. This will require you to build a detailed knowledge of the markets in which your firm operates, so that you can analyse issues like pricing of existing products and potential impact of new products.

CASE STUDIES

1. The coffee market

Judging from the large number of Starbucks and Costa Coffee outlets in most high streets, airports, and railway stations you might think that the market for coffee is booming. So it is for the final product, whether your preference be for a tall skinny latte or a machiatto grande. However, this is not the entire truth in the wholesale market for coffee beans. There are two main varieties of coffee bean; arabica and robusta,[8] and their prices tend to move together, so we focus on arabica which provides over 70 per cent of consumption.

Figure 3.12 shows the price of arabica coffee beans in US cents per kilogram weight from January 1960 to August 2013. The long-term price history shows a nearly flat long-run trend with, if anything, a slight downward drift (at least between the mid-1970s and around 2003). This means that the real price of coffee (relative to other consumer goods whose prices in money terms have generally risen over time) was clearly trending downwards. Also, there are several episodes of a sharp upward jump in the price. The price of coffee beans fell to a historic low level in late 2001 and early 2002. It recovered somewhat in the mid-2000s, but then had another strong upward spike that peaked in early 2011 (as discussed in Box 3.1). The price low (in 2002) was the lowest price of coffee in real terms (i.e. adjusted for inflation) in the last hundred years, and the lowest price in money terms since the early

1970s. Between 2011 and 2013 the price more than halved. So how can we explain this price behaviour?

We start by explaining the downward trend in price (with occasional sharp upward spikes) between the mid-1970s and 2002–3.[9]

Demand for coffee grew over time, but only slowly. The World Bank has estimated that the worldwide income elasticity of demand for coffee was about 0.6 up to the mid-1990s, and that this figure falls as per capita income rises. For example, in the United States, which has the highest per capita income in the world, the income elasticity is estimated to be close to zero. This means that demand rises at a slower rate than incomes in the coffee-importing countries. An income elasticity of demand of 0.6, for example, means that a 10 per cent increase in (real) incomes would lead to a 6 per cent increase in demand for coffee (other things being equal). An annual trend growth rate of about 2 per cent (such as is the case for the United Kingdom) would imply a growth in demand for coffee of about 1.2 per cent per annum.[10]

---

[8] Robusta is cheaper than arabica and is largely used to make instant coffee and coffee flavouring rather being consumed by the serious coffee connoisseurs

[9] Note that we are analysing wholesale demand for coffee beans here and not demand for prepared coffee-based drinks in retail outlets, which has a different market.

[10] This is assuming an income elasticity of demand of 0.6, though it could be lower (or higher).

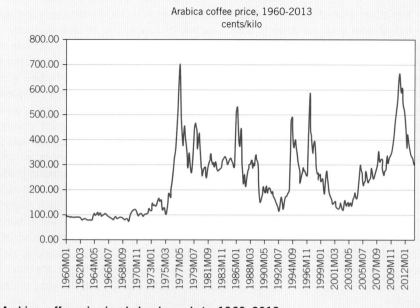

Arabica coffee price, 1960-2013
cents/kilo

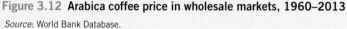

Figure 3.12 Arabica coffee price in wholesale markets, 1960–2013

Source: World Bank Database.

On the supply side there was a steady increase in output capacity as traditional coffee-producing countries, such as Brazil, expanded their capacity and newer suppliers such as Vietnam also became big producers. The excess of supply over demand led to growing stocks of coffee beans in consuming countries. When stocks are already high, consumer countries become increasingly unwilling to accumulate more, so only a fall in price can discourage further excess supply. However, the World Bank also estimates that supply elasticities are very low in the short term, which means that despite sharp falls in prices, the quantity supplied falls only slightly. Hence, unless there is a crop failure (typically due to bad weather) in a major producing country such as Brazil (as happened in 1977, 1986, 1994, and 1997) the prospects were for coffee prices to stay low. And since demand is inelastic, the lower is the price the lower are the incomes of producers.

The report quoted in Box 3.1 explains the 2011 spike in prices as being a result of adverse weather conditions in Colombia, but this came on top of a period of strong demand growth driven by China and India and some other fast-growing countries. The sharp price falls between 2011 and 2013 were clearly linked to a strong recovery in production from Colombia and other major producers such as Brazil, so that supply again ran ahead of demand.

Low prices do little to encourage an increase in quantity demanded in consumer countries as the own-price elasticity of demand is also low. We reported earlier a figure of

−0.25 for the price elasticity of demand for coffee in the United States. When there is a supply disruption due to bad weather, the low value of the price elasticity of demand means that prices have to rise a long way to reduce demand sufficiently to cope with the lower supply, hence the occasional very large spikes in the price.

In summary, the demand curve for coffee is shifting to the right as income increases, but only slowly[11] (owing to a low income elasticity), and the curve is fairly steep (owing to a low price elasticity). The supply curve, however, has been shifting more quickly to the right over time (owing to new production methods and greater planting). This means that prices have tended to fall in normal times, but then rise sharply in abnormal times, such as when there is a crop failure in a major producer country, perhaps due to bad weather. When growth in supply is not greater than growth in demand, the price will tend to stabilize.

This is a good illustration of the interaction of demand and supply forces. There are other elements to the story, which should not be totally ignored, but we do not have the space to discuss fully here. First, a low coffee price causes severe problems for many of the world's poorest countries—coffee provides 76 per cent of export revenue for Burundi, 68 per cent for Ethiopia, 62 per cent for Rwanda, and 60 per cent

---

[11] Demand temporarily grew more strongly in the mid-2000s as coffee became more fashionable in some rapidly growing countries, like China.

for Uganda. Secondly, much of the recent growth in capacity has been in 'sun grown' plantations, which have no tree cover (as the forests have been cut down to provide the space) and use chemicals to enhance yields. The plantations can produce high yields quickly, but environmental groups argue that they are bad for the environment as they do not use the tree cover of traditional 'shade grown' coffee plantations and this is harmful to bird life (as well as involving destruction of forests). Thirdly, the (relatively) low coffee price of the early 2000s was particularly harmful to the traditional 'shade grown' producers of Central America who have not been covering costs and so have cut output (but not enough to affect the price significantly) and suffered lower prices, and therefore have dramatically reduced incomes. They were doing much better when the price was high in 2011 but will have been very worried in 2013 that the price was heading sharply down again.

2. One lump or two?

Box 3.1 reported that sugar prices were also falling sharply after 2011. We shall see there are major differences in the drivers of sugar prices as compared with coffee, but there is one obvious common feature in recent years and that has been that an excess of supply over demand has been driving down the price.

As with coffee and many other food commodities, sugar has a low price and income elasticity. The price elasticity is not as low as for coffee. UK estimates are for a value of

−0.79 and this is probably because there are closer substitutes (artificial sweeteners) for sugar than there are for coffee. However, the income elasticity of demand for sugar is extremely low. The UK estimate is that it is zero, which means that demand for sugar (for food consumption) does not grow at all as income grows. This is not likely to be true for all countries, especially less developed countries. For example, there is evidence of a positive income elasticity of demand among consumers in fast-growing countries such as India and China.

As we have seen, coffee prices are affected by occasional adverse weather conditions in producing countries that generate large swings in price. Weather does matter for sugar as well, but not so much. Sugar is produced in hot climates from sugar cane and in temperate climates from sugar beet, and both can be grown in a much greater variety of soil and weather conditions. Hence, sugar supplies are not often subjected to the major adverse shocks that can affect coffee and therefore prices are much less volatile.

Two other important influences affect sugar prices. First, there is a major alternative use for sugar in addition to its role as a food sweetener. It can be converted into ethanol that is a substitute for petrol. This means that there are clear links between sugar prices and oil prices. High oil prices tend to raise demand for ethanol (as a petrol substitute) and this tends to raise sugar prices. Secondly, sugar producers in the EU and the United States have been protected by domestic agricultural support policies. This has the effect of stabilizing domestic prices in

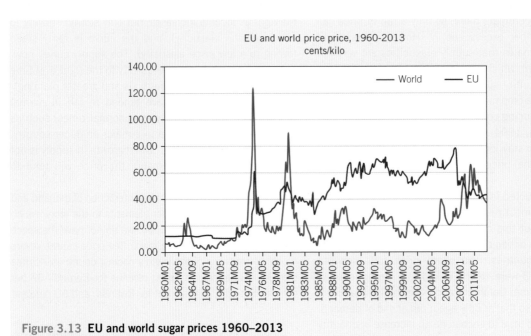

Figure 3.13 EU and world sugar prices 1960–2013

Source: World Bank Database

the EU and the United States and restricting access of outside producers to these markets. The EU has been lowering its barriers to sugar imports since 2006, and this has brought the EU price much closer to the world price.

Figure 3.13 shows the wholesale price of sugar in the EU and in the world market. The surges in the prices of sugar in 1973–4 and 1980 coincided with the major oil price hikes that occurred at that time. Prices in the 1990s were broadly flat but with a mild downward trend, as increasing supply more than kept up with slowly growing demand. From about 2002 there was an upward trend in prices as oil prices rose and there was growing demand for biofuels, and sugar production was shifted into ethanol production, especially in Brazil. It is notable that the EU price was consistently maintained at a level well above world prices, though that gap shrunk sharply after 2006 as EU import barriers were lowered. The story in Box 3.1 explains how downward pressures on prices in 2012–13 came from an excess of supply over demand.

3. Keeping up with The Times

In most real-world cases many things are changing at the same time. This example is rare in the sense that only one price changed while those of all the close substitutes remained constant. For this reason it's worth going back a few years to see how it all worked out. In September 1993 the owners of *The Times* newspaper unilaterally lowered its price by one-third. Initially, all the major competing newspapers kept their prices constant and carried on as if nothing had happened. Only later did a price war break out.

Table 3.3 provides price and sales figures for the four major national broadsheet[12] newspapers—*The Times*, the *Guardian*, the *Daily Telegraph*, and the *Independent*. Since consumers' average incomes changed only slightly over the period and newspapers have a low income elasticity, we would expect total sales to have remained constant, unless there had been a major change in taste over the period in question. The data suggests that tastes did not change significantly, since the combined sales of all the newspapers held constant at around 2.5 million copies daily. Hence, the existing suppliers were fighting for a share of a stable market. If one gained more customers, it had to be at the expense of rival suppliers.

Observed price elasticities

Table 3.3 shows us that a 40 per cent price reduction of the price of *The Times* led to a 17.5 per cent increase in its sales.[13] This indicates a price elasticity of demand for *The Times* of –0.44 (calculated as percentage change in quantity divided by percentage change in price or 17.5/–40). As a result, the daily sales revenue of *The Times* fell from £169,576 (376,836 × £0.45) to £134,689 (448,962 × £0.30). Only if the price elasticity had been greater than unity would total revenue have increased.

The competing papers suffered, and the *Independent* suffered most, with a 15.2 per cent loss of sales. This would

[12] We continue to refer to them as 'broadsheets' even though three of the four have changed their format.

[13] Note that we are measuring the price and quantity (*P* and *Q*) used in our elasticity calculations as the midpoint between the initial price and quantity and the ultimate price and quantity. The reasons for doing it this way are explained in Box 3.3. Use of the midpoint as the base applies to all calculations in this section.

Table 3.3 **Changes in the demand for newspapers**

	Price		Average daily sales		Percentage change	
	Pre-Sept. '93	Post-Sept. '93	Pre-Sept. '93	Post-Sept. '93	Price	Sales
The Times	45p	30p	376,836	448,962	–40.0	+17.5
Guardian	45p	45p	420,154	401,705	0.0	–4.5
Daily Telegraph	45p	45p	1,037,375	1,017,326	0.0	–1.95
Independent	50p	50p	362,099	311,046	0.0	–15.2
			2,196,464	2,179,039		

***The Times* led but no one followed**. The table shows the fall in the price of *The Times* and the less than proportionate increase in sales. It also shows the constant prices of the other papers, with declining sales as they lost readers to *The Times*. Percentage changes in the last two columns are calculated from the initial position, but calculations of elasticity in the text are made at the midpoint between the initial and ultimate position.

Source: Audit Bureau of Circulation. The sales figures are daily average circulation for September 1992 to February 1993 and for September 1993 to February 1994.

suggest that the *Independent* was the closest substitute for *The Times*. The cross-elasticity of demand implied by these figures was −15.2/−40 = 0.38. (This is positive as both the sales and the price changes were negative.) The cross-elasticity for the *Guardian* was −4.5/−40 = 0.11, and the cross-elasticity for the *Daily Telegraph* was −1.95/−40 = 0.05.

Applying demand and supply

The theory of demand and supply developed in Chapter 2 assumes that there are many buyers and many sellers, each one of whom must accept the price that is determined by overall demand and supply. Newspapers fit this theory on the demand side, since there are tens of thousands of buyers, each of whom can do nothing to affect the price. On the supply side, however, there are only a few newspapers and each sets the price of its own product. In the terminology of Chapter 2, it is an administered price. However, we can handle the supply side if we note that each newspaper sells all the copies that are demanded at the price that it sets. Graphically, this is shown by a horizontal supply curve at each newspaper's fixed price. The elasticity of supply is effectively infinite at the set price. (Of course this does not mean the newspaper would supply an infinite number of copies, only that they will supply all that is demanded at the price they set.)

Figure 3.14 illustrates the effect of the price cut on both *The Times* and the *Independent*. Notice that, since each newspaper is a distinct product, there is no industry supply curve for newspapers. Each supplier simply sets a price and lets demand determine its sales.

Rival newspapers may not have followed *The Times* in cutting prices because they believed that their demands would prove as inelastic as those of *The Times*. If so, they would have lost more revenue by cutting their prices than they did by leaving prices unchanged. As it was, the *Independent* suffered a daily loss of revenue of a little over £25,000 (just over 50,000 sales at 50p each).

The puzzle is why *The Times* persisted with its price drop even though it lost sales revenue. One possibility is that the increased circulation led to an increase in advertising revenue. Newspapers' advertising rates are related to their circulation. If *The Times* increased its advertising revenue by more than about £35,000, the price reduction would have increased its profit.

The *Independent* was known to be in financial difficulty, and it is possible that the managers of *The Times* thought that their price cut might force the *Independent* out of business—a strategy sometimes referred to as **predatory pricing**. Had it succeeded, a high proportion of *Independent* readers would have moved over to *The Times*, since the cross-elasticities show that the *Independent* was the closest substitute for *The Times*. A third possibility is that its managers expected that *The Times*' demand elasticity would increase over time sufficiently to compensate for the price cut. Indeed, *The Times* did continue to increase its market share beyond the period studied in Table 3.3. In June 1994 the *Telegraph* reacted to *The Times*' growing market share by cutting its price, and the *Independent* followed. *The Times* responded to this by cutting its own price still further, although prices settled down at slightly higher levels soon after. To some extent this third explanation has proved correct. By July 1998 *The Times*' price

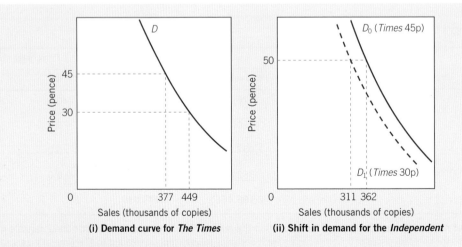

Figure 3.14 Demand for *The Times* and the *Independent*
A cut in the price of The Times shifted the *Independent*'s demand curve to the left. Part (i) shows the price cut for *The Times*. When its price was lowered from 45p to 30p, sales rose from 377,000 to 449,000 copies per day. Part (ii) shows the shift in demand for the *Independent* as a result of the fall in the price of *The Times*. At a constant price of 50p sales fell from 362,000 to 311,000.

was 35p while the *Guardian*, *Telegraph*, and *Independent* were at 45p. *The Times'* sales were around 800,000, almost double what they had been just after the first gains following the outbreak of the price war. In contrast, the *Independent*'s sales were 210,000, less than 60 per cent of what they were just before the price war began.

These relative positions stayed more or less unchanged for the next five years. However, between 2002 and 2006 there was a significant decline in the market for this group of newspapers, no doubt mainly as a result of the growth of the internet and 24-hour news TV channels. The nature of competition seems to have changed as a result. Price competition took a back seat as *The Times* raised its price to that of the *Guardian*, the *Independent*, and the *Telegraph*. The *Independent* introduced a new tabloid format followed by *The Times* and *Guardian*. The big loser in this new style of war was the *Telegraph* whose average daily sales fell markedly.

The aggressive pricing strategy adopted by *The Times* in the early 1990s does appear to have had a very long-lasting effect on the sales pattern of UK newspapers. The changes in sale patterns established in the mid-1990s were still evident a decade later, even though the price war was clearly over.[14]

Since that time, the newspaper market has faced a continual threat from new technologies. As hardcopy sales declined steadily, newspapers switched their promotion efforts into apps for tablets, such as the iPad, and mobile phones. Linked to these new systems for delivering newspaper content were subscription deals that gave cheaper hard copies and free content download (including videos).

In August 2013, *The Times* was doing best with hardcopy sales holding up at around 400,000 per day. But *Telegraph* sales had declined to around 550,000, the *Guardian* to 190,000, and the *Independent* to about 70,000.

In short, price competition has ceased to be the main story about how newspapers compete. Instead, it is competition via technical innovation in content delivery that has become of primary importance.

---

[14] In January 2014, *The Times* and the *Telegraph* were priced at £1.20, while the *Independent* and the *Guardian* were £1.40.

Conclusion

Demand and supply analysis is an essential tool for understanding how markets work and the concept of elasticity is an important addition to this. It enables us to quantify our understanding and thus helps in answering questions such as: What will happen in this market if such and such occurs? Price elasticity, for example, enables us to predict how much the quantity demanded of a product will fall if we raise its price, and income elasticity enables us to say how much demand for a product will rise as consumer incomes rise.

Elasticity may seem like an abstract and difficult concept at first, but after repeated use it will become straightforward and easy to apply. You will find yourself using it frequently throughout your career.

SUMMARY

Demand elasticity

- Elasticity of demand (also called price elasticity of demand) is defined as the percentage change in quantity divided by the percentage change in price that brought it about.
- When the percentage change in quantity is less than the percentage change in price, demand is inelastic and a fall in price lowers the total amount spent on the product. When the percentage change in quantity is greater than the percentage change in price, demand is elastic and a fall in price raises total spending on the product.

- A more precise measure that gives a unique value for elasticity at any point on any demand curve replaces $\Delta q / \Delta p$ measured between two points on the curve with $\Delta q / \Delta p$ measured along the tangent to the curve at the point in question (symbolized by dq/dp).
- The main determinant of the price elasticity of demand is the availability of substitutes for the product. Any one of a group of close substitutes will have a more elastic demand than the group as a whole.
- The reaction of demand to a change in price is often different depending on how much time has elapsed.

(i) The demands for ordinary goods that are bought often and consumed quickly tend to adjust quickly to any price change and so there is no need to distinguish a short- and a long-run elasticity.

(ii) Goods that are complementary with durables that have long lives, as is petrol with cars or electricity with most household appliances, tend to take a long time to adjust fully to a price change because the durables with which they are consumed are long-lived. This makes the price elasticity of the complementary good (e.g. petrol and electricity) lower in the short run than in the long run.

(iii) Durables themselves often show the reverse reaction with elasticities being higher in the short run than in the long run because it is easier to postpone a purchase for a while than indefinitely.

■ Income elasticity is the percentage change in quantity demanded divided by the percentage change in income that brought it about. The income elasticity of demand for a product will usually change as income changes in the long run.

■ Cross-elasticity is the percentage change in quantity demanded divided by the percentage change in the price of some other product that brought it about.

Products that are substitutes for one another have positive cross-elasticities; products that are complements to one another have negative cross-elasticities.

Supply elasticity

■ Elasticity of supply measures the ratio of the percentage change in the quantity supplied of a product to the percentage change in its price.

■ A commodity's elasticity of supply depends on how easy it is to shift resources into the production of that commodity and how the costs of producing the commodity vary as its production varies.

Measurement of demand and supply

■ Over the years, economists have measured many price, income, and cross-elasticities of demand. Being able to do so requires the use of statistical techniques to measure the separate influences of each of several variables when all are changing at once. It also requires a solution of the identification problem, which means measuring the separate shapes of the demand and supply curves. This cannot be done from price and quantity data alone.

TOPICS FOR REVIEW

■ Price, income, and cross-elasticity of demand

■ Zero, inelastic, unitary, elastic, and infinitely elastic demand

■ The relation between price elasticity and changes in total expenditure

■ Determinants of demand elasticity

■ Income elasticities for normal and inferior goods

■ Cross-elasticities between substitutes and complements

■ Long- and short-run elasticity of demand

■ Elasticity of supply and its determinants.

QUESTIONS

1 Calculate the elasticity of demand for the demand curve $P = 100 - 5Q$ at each of the following price and quantity levels:

$P = 90$ and $Q = 2$
$P = 50$ and $Q = 10$
$P = 5$ and $Q = 19$.

2 Calculate the elasticity of supply for the supply curve $P = 10 + 3Q$ at each of the following price and quantity levels:

$P = 25$ and $Q = 5$
$P = 40$ and $Q = 10$
$P = 70$ and $Q = 20$.

3 In one particular month 1.2 million kilos of potatoes are sold at £1.20 per kilo. In the next month 1.5

million kilos are sold at £1.40 per kilo. Which of the following explanations is consistent with this observation (there may be more than one or none at all).

a) The price of carrots has risen and carrots are a close substitute for potatoes.

b) The price of fish has risen and fish is a complement to potatoes.

c) Bad weather has reduced the potato crop.

d) Consumer incomes have risen and potatoes are an inferior good.

e) Newspapers have reported that potatoes have health-giving properties, and this has generated a shift of tastes towards potatoes.

4 A Brand X tablet computer sold 10 million units at £400 each last year. It is known that the price elasticity of demand is –2.0 (calculated at the latest price and quantity that is quoted here). What would sales be this year if there are no other changes affecting demand and the price per unit is raised to £420?

    a) 11 million.
    b) 9 million.
    c) 9.5 million.
    d) 10.5 million.

5 Brand Z sold 2 million of its widgets at £20 each last year. This year it reduced its price to £18 and sold 2.4 million widgets. Assuming that there were no other changes affecting the market, what is the price elasticity of demand?

    a) –1
    b) –0.5
    c) –4
    d) –2

6 Suggest products that you think might have the following patterns of elasticity of demand:

    a) high income elasticity, high price elasticity;
    b) high income elasticity, low price elasticity;
    c) low income elasticity; low price elasticity;
    d) low income elasticity, high price elasticity.

7 Define the elasticity of demand and explain why this concept should be of interest to anyone in business who has a choice to make about the price at which to sell their products.

8 Why is demand likely to be more elastic in the long run than in the short run?

9 Outline the main determinants of demand and supply elasticity.

10 What is the identification problem? How does it affect the interpretation of observed price and quantity changes, and what does it imply that we need to know before we can say whether any specific price and quantity change contains information about either demand or supply elasticity?

11 Explain the concept of income elasticity. Why does the income elasticity of demand for food tend to be low in rich countries? Give examples of types of goods and services the demand for which you would expect to have a high income elasticity in rich countries? How would the last answer differ in poorer countries?

CHAPTER 4

CONSUMER CHOICE: INDIFFERENCE THEORY

In this chapter we look more closely at the determinants of consumer demand. In particular, we discuss the concept of utility and use it to gain insights into how consumers allocate their spending. We first explain some key insights that were achieved by thinking about utility when we assume it can be measured. We then outline the approach which does not require utility to be measurable but yields many similar insights into the determinants of demand.

In particular, you will learn that:

- The theory of consumer choice assumes that consumers wish to maximize their overall satisfaction.
- Consumers will achieve this goal when the marginal utility per pound spent is equal for all products purchased.
- A theory of demand can be built by focusing on bundles of goods between which the consumer is indifferent.
- Indifference curves show combinations of goods that give the same level of satisfaction.
- A budget constraint shows what the consumer could buy with a given income.
- A consumer optimizes by moving to the highest indifference curve that is available with a given budget constraint.
- The consumer's response to a price change can be decomposed into an income and a substitution effect.
- For a good to have a positively sloped demand curve it is necessary (but not sufficient) that it be an inferior good.

In this chapter we will first explain some important insights that come from early analyses of utility in the nineteenth century. We then explain how modern economics uses indifference curves to develop a theory of consumer choice. We show how indifference curves can be used to describe consumers' tastes and then introduce a budget line to describe the consumption possibilities open to a consumer who has a given income. After that, we show how consumers reach equilibrium by consuming the bundle that allows them to reach the highest possible level of satisfaction. We can then see how consumers alter their behaviour when either income or prices change, and go on to derive the negative slope of the demand curve.

This approach to consumer behaviour has two great advantages. First, it allows us to distinguish between two effects of a change in price, called the income and the substitution effects. This distinction has important practical applications. Secondly, it allows us to understand the rare but interesting exception to the prediction that all demand curves are negatively sloped, which arises with a so-called Giffen good.

All of the theories in this chapter use the basic assumption that consumers are motivated to make themselves as well off as they can, or, as economists like to put it, to maximize their satisfaction, or utility.

Early insights

All units of the same product are identical—for example, one tin of Heinz baked beans is the same as another tin of Heinz baked beans—but the satisfaction that a consumer gets from each unit of a product in not the same. If you are hungry you will get great satisfaction from a good meal, but you will not get the same satisfaction from having a second identical meal immediately. This suggests that the satisfaction that people get from consuming a unit of any product varies according to how many of this product they have already.

Economists and philosophers thinking about consumer choice and satisfaction in the nineteenth century developed the concept of utility and therefore were sometimes called *utilitarians*.[1] But the big breakthrough for economics came in the 1870s with what is known as the *marginal revolution*, which gave birth to *neoclassical economics*.[2]

For a long time it was thought that utility could not be measured, and hence that utility theory was based on unverifiable concepts. Recently, however, there has been a boom in empirical studies based on measures of 'happiness', a concept that is closely related to utility. Box 4.1 discusses some of the key results of these happiness studies, and a case study at the end of this chapter returns to the topic of happiness and utility.

---

[1] Leading members of the utilitarian school were Jeremy Bentham (1748–1832), James Mill (1773–1836), and John Stuart Mill (1806–1873).
[2] Key contributors to the marginal revolution were the English economist William Stanley Jevons (1835–82), the Austrian Carl Menger (1841–1910), and the Swiss Leon Walras (1834–1910).

Box 4.1 Happiness and utility: why the Danes are smiling

In the past decade or so there has been an upsurge in studies by economists and psychologists of the happiness of people in various countries. We have used the term 'utility' to describe the level of satisfaction or personal well-being perceived by individuals in response to their personal consumption patterns. So are happiness and utility related? We return to this question in the case study at the end of the chapter. Here we highlight results of work that measures happiness by use of large surveys of opinion.

How the nations ranked on happiness

1st – Denmark
2nd – Switzerland
3rd – Austria
4th – Iceland
5th –The Bahamas
23rd – United States
41st – United Kingdom
90th – Japan
178th – Burundi

Adrian White of the University of Leicester used a survey of 80,000 people to produce a map of world happiness. Denmark was measured as the happiest nation on Earth while Burundi was the unhappiest. The UK ranked 41st.

The United Nations now produces an annual *World Happiness Report*[3] which encourages policy-makers to think about the happiness of citizens as well as their material well being.

Most people agree that societies should foster the happiness of their citizens. The US Founding Fathers recognized the inalienable right to the pursuit of happiness. British philosophers talked about the greatest good for the greatest number. Bhutan has famously adopted the goal of Gross National Happiness rather than Gross National Product. China champions a harmonious society.

Yet most people probably believe that happiness is in the eye of the beholder, an individual's choice, something to be pursued individually rather than as a matter of national policy. Happiness seems far too subjective, too vague, to serve as a touchstone for a nation's goals, much less its policy content. That indeed has been the traditional view. Yet the evidence is changing this view rapidly.

A generation of studies by psychologists, economists, pollsters, sociologists, and others has shown that happiness, though indeed a subjective experience, can be objectively measured, assessed, correlated with observable brain functions, and related to the characteristics of an individual and the society. Asking people whether they are happy, or satisfied with their lives, offers important information about the society. It can signal underlying crises or hidden strengths. It can suggest the need for change.

(World Happiness Report, *United Nations, 2012, p. 6*)

For the time being let us note that utility relates to the satisfaction received from the consumption of specific goods and services while happiness is one's overall state of well-being. For the rest of this chapter we focus on the former but return to the latter in the first case study at the end of the chapter.

---

[3] See <http://unsdsn.org/happiness/>

Marginal and total utility

What we want to think about first is how an individual consumer's satisfaction changes as he or she alters the amount consumed of a single product. The satisfaction a consumer receives from consuming that product is called *utility*. **Total utility** refers to the *total satisfaction* derived from all the units of that product consumed. **Marginal utility** refers to the *change in satisfaction* resulting from consuming one unit more or one unit less of that product over some specified time period. For example, the total utility of consuming 14 cups of coffee a week is the sum total satisfaction provided by all 14 cups of coffee. The marginal utility of the fourteenth cup of coffee consumed is the addition to total satisfaction provided by consuming that extra cup. Or put another way, the marginal utility of the fourteenth cup is the addition to total utility gained from consuming 14 cups of coffee per week rather than 13.

Diminishing marginal utility

A basic assumption of utility theory, which is sometimes called the *law of diminishing marginal utility*, is as follows.

The marginal utility generated by additional units of any product diminishes as an individual consumes more of it, holding constant the consumption of all other products.

The way in which most of us use water provides a good example of diminishing marginal utility. We consume it in many forms: tap water, soft drinks, bottled water, or water flavoured with such things as tea leaves and coffee grounds. Whatever the form in which we consume it, water is necessary to our very existence. Anyone denied water will not survive very long. So we value the minimum of water needed to sustain life as much as we value life itself. Therefore we would be willing to pay quite a lot if this were the only way to obtain the amount of water needed to stay alive. Thus, the total utility of that much water is extremely high, as is the marginal utility of the first few units drunk. More than this bare minimum will be drunk, but the marginal utility of successive amounts of water drunk over any period of time will decline steadily. Furthermore, water has many uses other than for drinking. A fairly high marginal utility will be attached to some minimum quantity for bathing, but much more than this minimum will be used only for more frequent baths or showers. The last weekly gallon used for washing is likely to have a low marginal utility. Again, some small quantity of water is necessary for tooth brushing, but many people leave the water running while they brush. The water going down the drain between wetting and rinsing the brush surely has a low utility. When all the many uses of water by the modern consumer are considered (washing machines, dishwashers, lawn sprinklers, car washing, etc.), it is certain that the marginal utility of the last, say, 10 per cent of all units consumed is very low and falling, even though the total utility of all the units consumed is extremely high.

Maximizing utility

We can now ask: What does diminishing marginal utility imply for the way a consumer who has a given income will allocate spending in order to maximize total utility? How should a consumer allocate his or her income in order to get the greatest possible satisfaction, or total utility, from that spending?

If all products had the same price, the answer would be easy. A consumer should simply allocate spending so that the marginal utility of all products was the same. If the marginal utility of all products were not equal then total utility could be increased by a different spending pattern. For example, if one product had a higher marginal utility than the others, then spending should be reallocated so as to buy more of this product, and less of all others that have lower marginal utilities. By buying more, its marginal utility would fall. Only when the last unit of all products bought gives the same satisfaction is the consumer getting the greatest possible total utility from his or her spending pattern.

How does this work if products have different prices? Again, the same principles apply but now the best a consumer can do is to rearrange spending until the last unit of satisfaction per pound spent on each product is the same. For example, suppose that a consumer is deciding to allocate income between going to football matches and going to the cinema and that tickets to football cost £45 while a cinema ticket costs £15. If a consumer gets more than three times as much extra satisfaction from another football match as another movie then off to more football matches he or she as a maximizer would go. This consumer will be maximizing total utility from his or her income only when the last match attended just generates extra utility that is three times that generated by the last movie.

To maximize utility consumers must allocate spending between products so that equal utility is derived from the last unit of money spent on each.[4]

The conditions for maximizing utility can be stated more generally. Denote the marginal utility of the last unit of product X by MU_X and its price by p_X. Let MU_Y and

---

[4] By the 'last unit' we do not mean money spent over successive time periods. Instead we are talking about buying more or fewer units at one point in time; that is, alternative allocations of spending over a given period of time.

p_Y refer, respectively, to the marginal utility of a second product, Y, and its price. The marginal utility per pound spent on X will be MU_X/p_X. For example, if the last unit adds 30 units to utility and costs £2, its marginal utility per pound is 30/2 = 15.

The condition required for any consumer to maximize utility is that the following relationship should hold for all pairs of products:

$$MU_X/p_X = MU_Y/p_Y. \qquad (4.1)$$

This merely says in symbols what we earlier said in words. Consumers who are maximizing their utility will allocate spending so that the utilities gained from the last pound spent on both products are equal.

This is the fundamental equation of utility theory. Each consumer demands each good up to the point at which the marginal utility per pound spent on it is the same as the marginal utility of a pound spent on each other good. When this condition is met, the consumer cannot shift a pound of spending from one product to another and increase total utility.

Consumers choose quantities not prices

If we rearrange the terms in eqn (4.1), we can gain additional insight into consumer behaviour:[5]

$$MU_X/MU_Y = p_X/p_Y. \qquad (4.2)$$

The right-hand side of this equation states the relative price of the two goods. It is determined by the market and is beyond the control of individual consumers, who react to these market prices but are powerless to change them. The left-hand side of the equation states the relative contribution of the two goods to add to satisfaction if a little more or a little less of either of them were consumed, a choice that is available.

If the two sides of eqn (4.2) are not equal, the consumer can increase total satisfaction by changing the spending pattern. Assume, for example, that the price of a unit of X is twice the price of a unit of Y ($p_X/p_Y = 2$), while the marginal utility of a unit of X is three times that of a unit of Y ($MU_X/MU_Y = 3$). Under these conditions, it pays to buy more X and less Y. For example, reducing purchases of Y by two units frees enough purchasing power to buy a unit of X. Since one extra unit of X bought yields 1.5 times the satisfaction of two units of Y forgone, the switch is worth making. What about a further switch of X for Y? As the consumer buys more X and less Y, the marginal utility of X falls and the marginal utility of Y rises. In this example the consumer will go on

rearranging purchases—reducing Y consumption and increasing X consumption—until the marginal utility of X is only twice that of Y. At this point, total satisfaction cannot be further increased by rearranging purchases between the two products.

Think about what the utility maximizing consumer is doing. She is faced with a set of prices that cannot be changed. She responds to these prices and maximizes satisfaction by adjusting the things that can be changed—the quantities of the various goods purchased—until eqn (4.2) is satisfied for all pairs of products.

We see this sort of equation frequently in economics—one side representing the choices the outside world presents to decision-takers and the other side representing the effect of those choices. It shows the equilibrium position reached when decision-takers have made the best adjustment they can to the factors that constrain their choices.

When they enter the market, all consumers face the same set of market prices. When they are fully adjusted to these prices, each one of them will have identical ratios of their marginal utilities for each pair of goods. Of course, a rich consumer may consume more of each product than a poor consumer and get more *total utility* from them. However, the rich and the poor consumer (and every other consumer who is maximizing utility) will adjust their relative purchases of each product so that the relative *marginal utilities* are the same for all. Thus, if the price of X is twice the price of Y, each consumer will purchase X and Y to the point at which his or her marginal utility of X is twice the marginal utility of Y. However, consumers with different tastes will derive different marginal utilities from their consumption of the various commodities. Therefore they will consume differing relative quantities of products. But all will have declining marginal utilities for each commodity and hence, when they have maximized their utility, the ratios of their marginal utilities will be the same for all of them.

A very important insight can be derived from this analysis. It is that marginal not average values are what matter for maximization. We will return to this idea in subsequent chapters when we see that marginal values are also important for the profit-maximizing behaviour of firms. Box 4.2 reinforces just how important marginal utility is as a concept in that it helps explain what used to be known as the **paradox of value**. The key point to notice from this is that because consumers adjust their marginal utilities to them, market prices reflect marginal utilities of various products and not total or average utilities. Hence, market prices are not a measure of the total value to society of one good or service compared with that of some other good or service.

---

[5] This is done by multiplying both sides of the equation by p_X/MU_Y.

Box 4.2 The paradox of value

Early thinkers about the economy struggled with the problem of what determines the relative prices of products. They encountered the *paradox of value*: many essential products without which we could not live, such as water, have relatively low prices. On the other hand, some luxury products, such as diamonds, have relatively high prices even though we could easily survive without them. Does it not seem odd they asked, that water, which is so important to us, has such a low market value, while diamonds, which are much less important, have a much higher market value? It took a long time to resolve this apparent paradox, so it is not surprising that, even today, similar confusions about the determinants of market values persist and cloud many policy discussions.

The key to resolving the 'paradox' lies in the distinction between total and marginal utility. We have already seen in this chapter that a utility-maximizing consumer will adjust his or her spending pattern so that the marginal utility per pound spent is equal for all products. It follows that the value consumers place on the last unit consumed of any product, its marginal utility, is equal in equilibrium to the product's price.

Three related concepts matter for the utility that a consumer gets from some quantity of a product. Marginal utility is what he gets from consuming the last unit. Total utility is what he gets from the total amount consumed. **Consumers' surplus**, discussed in Box 4.3, is the utility that he gets over and above what he pays.

Now look at the total amount spent to purchase the product—the price paid for it multiplied by the quantity bought and sold—which we can call its total market value or sale value. The figure shows the markets for two goods, one for which total market value is a very small fraction of its total utility and another for which total market value is a much higher fraction of total utility.

The resolution of the paradox of value is that a good that is very plentiful, such as water, will have a low price. Therefore it will be consumed to the point where all purchasers place a low value on the last unit consumed, whether or not they place a high value on their total consumption of the product; that is, marginal utility will be low whatever the value of total utility. On the other hand, a product that is relatively scarce will have a high market price. Therefore consumption will stop at a point at which consumers place a high value on the last unit consumed whatever value they place on their total consumption of the good; that is, marginal utility will be high whatever the value of total utility.

This analysis leads to an important conclusion:

The market price of a product depends on demand and supply. Hence, no paradox is involved when a product on which consumers place a high total utility sells for a low price, and hence has only a low total market value (i.e. a low amount spent on it).

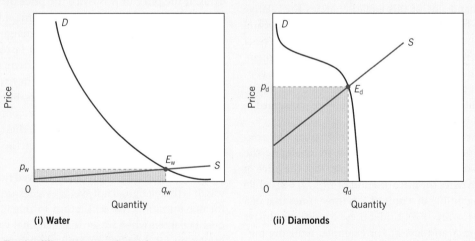

(i) Water   (ii) Diamonds

Total utility versus market value

The market value of the amount of some commodity bears no necessary relation to the total utility that consumers derive from that amount. The total utility that consumers derive from water, as shown by the area under the demand curve in part (i), is great—indeed, we cannot possibly show the curve for very small quantities, because people would pay all they had rather than be deprived completely of water. The total utility that consumers derive from diamonds is shown by the area under the demand curve in part (ii). This is less than the total utility derived from water. The supply curve of diamonds makes diamonds scarce and keeps their price high. Thus, when equilibrium is at E_d, the total market value of diamonds sold, indicated by the blue area of $p_d q_d$, is high. The supply curve of water makes water plentiful and low in price. Thus, when equilibrium is at E_w, the total market value of water consumed, indicated by the blue area of $p_w q_w$, is low.

Implication of marginal utility theory for demand curves

The assumption that all products exhibit diminishing marginal utility has a simple implication for demand curves: they are all negatively sloped. The reason is that if consumers were already maximizing utility and the price of one product fell, in order to restore eqn (4.2) consumers would have to buy more of the product whose price had fallen and less of all other products. In the twentieth century economists moved away from relying upon the assumption of diminishing marginal utility as a key building block in their theory of demand. The reason is that it was harder to take the theory much further without being able to measure utility, which seemed impossible at the time. However, considerable progress was made without the need to measure utility. All that was needed was to assume that consumers could rank alternative bundles of products in order of preference without necessarily being able to say by *how much* they preferred one to another.

We now outline this modern approach to consumer choice. In it, the two key insights that we have just discussed remain valid:

1. Marginal comparisons are what matter for consumer choice and eqns (4.1) and (4.2) remain valid as optimization conditions for consumers whether or not utility is assumed to be measurable.

2. The demand for a product at any particular market price depends on the marginal utility that consumers get from consuming the last unit of it, not the total utility they get from consuming all of it.

Box 4.3 outlines a concept known as consumers' surplus that is related to diminishing marginal utility.

Box 4.3 Consumers' surplus

The negative slope of the demand curve has an interesting consequence:

All consumers pay less than they would be willing to pay for the total amount of any product that they consume.

The difference between the maximum they would be willing to pay —which is the value of the total utility that they derive from consuming the product—and what they do pay—which is their total spending on that product—is called consumers' surplus.

This concept is important and deserves further elaboration. The table gives hypothetical data for the weekly consumption of milk by one consumer, Ms Green. The second column, labelled 'Total utility', gives the total value she places on consumption of so many glasses per week (when the alternative is zero). The third column, labelled 'Marginal utility', gives the amount she would pay to add the last glass indicated to weekly consumption. Thus, for example, the marginal utility of £0.80 listed against four glasses gives the value Ms Green places on increasing consumption from three to four glasses. It is the difference between the total utilities she attaches to consumption levels of three and four glasses per week.

Consumers' surplus on each unit consumed is the difference between the market price and the maximum price the consumer would pay to obtain that unit. The table shows the value that Ms Green puts on successive glasses of milk consumed each week. As long as she is willing to pay more than the market price for any glass, she obtains a consumer's surplus when she buys it. The marginal glass of milk is the eighth. This is the one she values at just the market price and on which she earns no consumer's surplus.

(i) Consumer's surplus

(1)	(2)	(3)	(4)
Glasses of milk consumed per week	Total utility	Marginal utility	Consumer's surplus on each glass if milk costs £0.30 per glass
1	£3.00	£3.00	£2.70
2	4.50	1.50	1.20
3	5.50	1.00	0.70
4	6.30	0.80	0.50
5	6.90	0.60	0.30
6	7.40	0.50	0.20
7	7.80	0.40	0.10
8	8.10	0.30	0.00
9	8.35	0.25	—
10	8.55	0.20	—

If Ms Green is faced with a market price of £0.30, she will maximize total utility by consuming eight glasses per week because she values the eighth glass just at the market price, while valuing all earlier glasses at higher amounts. Because she values the first glass at £3.00 but gets it for £0.30, she makes a 'profit' of £2.70 on that glass; that is, she gets £3.00 worth of satisfaction for £0.30. Between her £1.50 valuation of the second glass and what she has to pay for it, she clears a 'profit' of £1.20. She clears £0.70 on the

(continued)

Box 4.3 *continued*

third glass, and so on. These 'profits', which are called her consumer's surpluses on each unit, are shown in the final column of the table. The total surplus is £5.70 per week. In the table, we calculate Ms Green's surplus by summing the surpluses on each glass. However, we arrive at the same total by first summing the maximum that Ms Green would pay for all the glasses bought (which is £8.10 in this case) and then subtracting the £2.40 that she does pay.

The value placed by each consumer on his or her total consumption of some product can be estimated in at least two ways. The valuation that the consumer places on each successive unit may be summed, or the consumer may be asked the maximum that he or she would pay to consume the amount in question if the alternative were to have none. While other consumers would put different numerical values into the table, diminishing marginal utility implies that the figures in the final column would be declining for each person. Since a consumer will go on buying further units until the value placed on the last unit equals the market price, it follows that there will be a consumers' surplus on every unit consumed except the last.

The data in columns (1) and (3) of the table give Ms Green's demand curve for milk. It is her demand curve because she will go on buying glasses of milk as long as she values each glass at least as much as the market price she must pay for it. When the market price is £3.00 per glass she will buy only one glass, when it is £1.50 she will buy two glasses, and so on. The total consumption value is the area below her demand curve, and consumers' surplus is that part of the area that lies above the price line. This is shown in Figure (i).

Figure (ii) shows that the same relationship holds for the smooth market demand curve which indicates the total amount all consumers would buy at each price.[6]

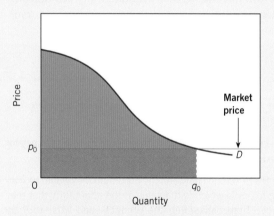

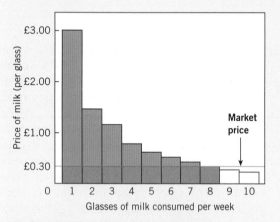

(i) Consumer's surplus for an individual

Consumer's surplus is the sum of the extra valuations placed on each unit above the market price paid for each. This figure is based on the data in Table (i). Ms Green pays the pink area for the eight glasses of milk she consumes per week when the market price is £0.30 a glass. The total value she places on these eight glasses of milk is the entire shaded area (pink and blue). Hence her consumer's surplus is the blue area.

(ii) Consumers' surplus for the market

Total consumers' surplus is the area under the demand curve and above the price line. The area under the demand curve shows the total valuation that consumers place on all units consumed. For example, the total value that consumers place on q_0 units is the entire area shaded pink and blue under the demand curve up to q_0. At a market price of p_0 the amount paid for q_0 units is the pink area. Hence consumers' surplus is the blue area.

[6] Figure (i) is a bar chart because we allowed the consumer to vary her consumption only in discrete units, one at a time. Had we allowed her to vary her consumption continuously, we could have traced out a continuous curve for Ms Green similar to the one shown in Figure (ii).

Consumer optimization without measurable utility

The basic assumption about consumer *motivation* does not change between this and the previous section. Consumers are assumed to maximize their satisfaction by allocating a given budget between the various goods and services that they wish to buy. Each consumer may be aware of exactly how much satisfaction is delivered by each of the goods consumed (though we do not need to assume so). However, the key difference in this section is that in explaining the consumer's behaviour, we do not need to know *how much* satisfaction he or she derives from consuming each product. Nor indeed does the consumer need to know this. All that is needed is that each consumer can order any two bundles of goods by saying which gives more satisfaction and hence is the preferred bundle. Faced with a choice between many bundles, the maximizing consumer will then choose the one with the highest rank order of preference—and hence is the most preferred of all available bundles.[7]

First, we ask how we can find the consumer's equilibrium allocation of spending in this new framework. Once that is done, we will be able to study consumers' responses to changes in such things as prices and incomes.

The consumer's preferences

In the analysis that we are about to develop, the consumer's tastes or preferences, as they are variously called, are shown by indifference curves.

A single indifference curve

We start by deriving a single indifference curve. To do this we give an imaginary consumer, Kevin, some quantity of each of two products, say 18 units of clothing (*C*) and 10 units of food (*F*). This bundle is plotted as point *b* in Figure 4.1. Now think about the alternative combinations of these two products in the two shaded areas created by drawing vertical and horizontal lines through *b*. Would Kevin prefer the bundles of goods in these two shaded areas? To help answer this, we introduce our first assumption about tastes:

Assumption 1. **Other things being equal, the consumer always prefers more of any one product to less of that same product.**

This allows us to rank the bundles of goods represented by the two shaded areas in Figure 4.1. Combinations on the edges of this space to the northeast of point *b* all have more of one good and no less of the other, while points inside this area represent bundles containing more of both goods. Thus, all points in this space, apart from *b* itself, will be preferred to *b*. By similar logic all points to the southwest of *b* represent either fewer of both goods or fewer of at least one and no more of the other. These points will all be inferior for the consumer as they deliver a lower level of satisfaction.

But what about bundles that have more of some products and less of others? At point *b*, Kevin consumes 18 units of clothing and 10 units of food. Let us ask how

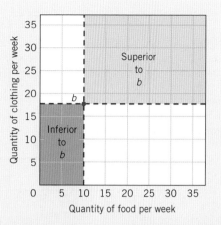

Figure 4.1 Some consumption bundles compared
According to assumption 1, bundle *b* is superior to bundles that have less of both goods and inferior to all bundles that have more of both. All points in the dark blue area are regarded as inferior to bundle *b* because they contain less of both commodities (except on the dashed boundaries, where they have less of one and the same amount of the other).

much extra clothing we would have to give him to make him equally satisfied if we took away one unit of food. The answer might be that 20 units of clothing and 9 units of food would leave Kevin just as satisfied as with the initial combination. If we do this again, taking away another unit of food, there will be some further increase in clothing that could just compensate. Table 4.1 shows that when we have taken away 5 units of food, Kevin would require 30 units of clothing to leave him feeling just as satisfied as at point *b*. This is also illustrated by point *a* in Figure 4.2. These combinations of fewer units of food and increased quantities of clothing that leave Kevin just as satisfied trace out the line segment from *b* to *a* in the figure.

Starting again at point *b*, we can now move in the opposite direction and ask how much extra food would Kevin need to leave him equally satisfied as we take successive units of clothing away from him? The answer to this question traces out the line through points *c*, *d*, *e*, and *f*.

By construction, the curved line drawn out in Figure 4.2 shows combinations of clothing and food, all of which give Kevin the same level of satisfaction. He is indifferent between all of the different bundles of goods represented by that line (some specific combinations of which are listed in Table 4.1). For this reason this red line is called an **indifference curve**. The line joining points *a*–*f* in Figure 4.2 is one indifference curve.

An indifference curve shows combinations of products that yield the same satisfaction to the consumer. Thus, a consumer is indifferent between the combinations indicated by any two points on one indifference curve.

---

[7] This approach was originally due to the Italian economist Vilfredo Pareto (1848–1923). It was introduced to the English-speaking world (and greatly elaborated) by two British economists, John Hicks (1904–89) and R.G.D. Allen (1906–83).

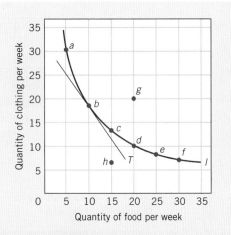

Figure 4.2 An indifference curve

The indifference curve shows combinations of food and cloth-ing that yield equal satisfaction and among which the con-sumer is indifferent. Points *a* to *f* are plotted from Table 4.2 and an indifference curve is drawn through them. Compared with any point on the curve, point *g* is superior while point *h* is inferior. The slope of the tangent *T* gives the marginal rate of substitution at point *b*. Moving down the curve from *b* to *f*, the slope of the tangent flattens, showing that the more food and the less clothing Kevin has, the less willing he will be to sacrifice further clothing to get more food.

Points above and to the right of the indifference curve in Figure 4.2 show combinations of food and clothing that Kevin would prefer to combinations indicated by points on the curve. Consider, for example, the combination of 20*F* and 20*C*, which is represented by point *g* in the figure. Although it might not be obvious that this bundle is pre-ferred to bundle *a* (which has more clothing but less food), assumption 1 tells us that *g* is preferred to bundle *c*, because *g* has more clothing *and* more food than *c*. Inspection of the graph shows that *any* point above the curve will be obvi-ously superior to *some* points on the curve in the sense that

Table 4.1 Bundles conferring equal satisfaction

Bundle	Clothing	Food
a	30	5
b	18	10
c	13	15
d	10	20
e	8	25
f	7	30

Since each of these bundles gives Kevin equal satisfaction, he is indifferent between them. None of the bundles contains more food *and* more clothing than any of the other bundles. Therefore Kevin's assumed indifference among these bundles is not in conflict with the assumption that more is preferred to less of each product.

it will contain both more food and more clothing than those points on the curve. But since all points on the curve are equally valuable in Kevin's eyes, any point above the curve must, therefore, be superior to *all* points on the curve. By a similar argument, points such as *h*, which are below and to the left of the curve, represent bundles of goods that Kevin regards as inferior to all bundles on the curve. These comparisons are summarized in Figure 4.3.

Diminishing marginal rate of substitution

What is the shape of a typical indifference curve? To answer this we need a second assumption:

Assumption 2. **The less of one product that is presently being used by a consumer, the smaller the amount of it that the consumer will be willing to forgo in order to increase consump-tion of a second product.**

This is called the assumption of a **diminishing mar-ginal rate of substitution**. The *rate of substitution* tells how much more of one product we need to compensate for successive lost units of the other. The *diminishing* of this rate of substitution may seem intuitively akin to diminish-ing marginal utility; however, for the latter we hold con-sumption of all but one good constant, while here we have more of one good compensating for less of the other.[8]

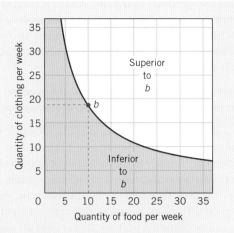
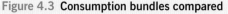

Figure 4.3 Consumption bundles compared

The indifference curve allows any bundle such as *b* to be compared with all others. Kevin regards all bundles in the blue area as inferior to *b* and all bundles in the white area as superior to *b*. The indifference curve is the boundary between these two areas. All points on the curve yield equal satisfac-tion, and therefore Kevin is indifferent among them.

....

[8] Diminishing marginal utility implies a diminishing marginal rate of substitution but not the reverse since the former is a stronger assumption than the latter. In other words, if we could measure all utilities we could tell which combinations you would prefer to other combinations, but being able to order these combination does not imply that we can measure how much utility each would give you.

Diminishing marginal rate of substitution is illustrated in Table 4.2, which is based on the example of food and clothing shown in Table 4.1. As we move down the table through points *a* to *f*, Kevin has bundles with fewer and fewer units of clothing and more and more food. In accordance with the hypothesis of diminishing marginal rate of substitution, he is willing to give up smaller and smaller amounts of clothing to further increase his consumption of food by one unit. When Kevin moves from *c* to *d*, for example, the table tells us that he is prepared to give up 0.6 units of clothing to get a further unit of food. When he moves from *e* to *f*, he will give up only 0.2 units.

The geometrical expression of this hypothesis is found in the shape of the indifference curve. Look closely, for example, at the slope of the curve in Figure 4.2. Its negative slope indicates that if Kevin is to have fewer units of one product, he must have more of the other to compensate. A diminishing marginal rate of substitution is shown by the curve being convex viewed from the origin: moving down the curve to the right, its slope gets flatter and flatter. The absolute value of the slope of the curve is the marginal rate of substitution, the rate at which the consumer is willing to reduce his consumption of the product plotted on the vertical axis in order to increase his consumption of the product plotted on the horizontal axis.

The slope of the indifference curve at any point is measured by the slope of the tangent to the curve at that point. The slope of tangent *T* drawn to the curve at point *b* shows the marginal rate of substitution at that point. It can be seen that, moving down the curve to the right, the slope

of the tangent gets flatter and flatter and hence the marginal rate of substitution is diminishing.[9]

The indifference map

So far, we have constructed only a single indifference curve. However, there must be a similar curve passing through any of the other points in Figure 4.2, in addition to those points on the single curve drawn. Starting at another point, such as *g*, and going through the same exercise there will be other combinations that will yield Kevin equal satisfaction. If the line joining all of *these* combinations is drawn, another indifference curve will be constructed. This exercise can be repeated many times, generating a new indifference curve each time.

It follows from the comparisons given in Figure 4.3 that the further away any indifference curve is from the origin, the higher is the level of satisfaction given by the consumption bundles that it indicates. We refer to a curve that confers a higher level of satisfaction as a *higher curve*.

A set of indifference curves is called an **indifference map**. An example is shown in Figure 4.4. It specifies Kevin's tastes by showing his complete ordering of preferences between different bundles of these two products, and it shows his rate of substitution between them at each specific point. When economists say that a consumer's tastes are *given*, they do not mean merely that

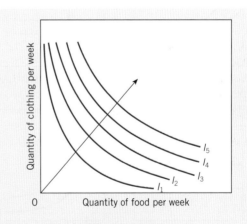

Figure 4.4 An indifference map

A set of indifference curves is called an indifference map. The further the curve is from the origin, the higher is the level of satisfaction it represents. If Kevin moves along the arrow, he is climbing a 'utility mountain', moving to ever higher utility levels and crossing ever higher equal-utility contours, which we call indifference curves.

Table 4.2 Diminishing marginal rate of substitution

Movement	Change in clothing (1)	Change in food (2)	Marginal rate of substitution (3)
From *a* to *b*	−12	5	2.4
From *b* to *c*	−5	5	1.0
From *c* to *d*	−3	5	0.6
From *d* to *e*	−2	5	0.4
From *e* to *f*	−1	5	0.2

The marginal rate of substitution measures the amount of one product a consumer must be given to compensate for giving up one unit of the other. This table is based on the data in Table 4.1. When Kevin moves from *a* to *b*, he gives up 12 units of clothing and gains 5 units of food, a rate of substitution of 12/5 or 2.4 units of clothing sacrificed per unit of food gained. When he moves from *b* to *c*, he sacrifices 5 units of clothing and gains 5 of food (a rate of substitution of 1 unit of clothing for each unit of food). Note that the marginal rate of substitution (MRS) is the absolute value of the ratio of ΔC to ΔF. Since these two changes always have opposite signs, the MRS is obtained by multiplying this ratio by −1.

---

[9] Table 4.2 calculates the rate of substitution between distinct points on the indifference curve. Strictly speaking, these are the incremental rates of substitution between the two points. Geometrically, the slope of the chord joining the two points gives this incremental rate. The marginal rate refers to the slope of the curve at a single point and is given by the slope of the tangent to the curve at that point. Similar issues arose in Chapter 3 for the measurement of elasticity.

the consumer's current consumption pattern is given; rather, they mean that the consumer's entire indifference map is given.

Of course, there must be an indifference curve through *every* point in Figure 4.4. To graph them, we only show a few, but all are there. Thus, as Kevin moves upwards to the right starting from the origin, his utility is rising continuously. As he follows a route such as the one shown by the arrow, consuming ever more of both products, he can be thought of as climbing a continuous utility mountain. We show this 'mountain' by selecting a few equal-utility contours, labelled I_1 to I_5. But every point between each of the contours shown must also have a curve of equal utility passing through it. Thus, an indifference map is really like

the continuous surface of one half of a cone, rather than a set of discrete lines.

In indifference theory we do not need to make any assumptions about how big the difference is between the level of satisfaction on one indifference curve and the next—that is, we do not need to assume that utility can be quantified. Instead, all we assume is that the utility attached to I_5 exceeds that attached to I_4, which in turn exceeds the utility attached to I_3, and so on. We can say that the consumer is climbing a utility mountain as he moves along the arrow starting from the origin, but we do not need to know if the mountain is gentle or steep.

Box 4.4 shows some possible shapes of indifference curves that correspond to specific taste patterns.

Box 4.4 Shapes of indifference curves

Any taste pattern can be illustrated with indifference curves. This box shows a few examples that will help you to understand how indifference curves work. In each case the curve labelled I_2 indicates a higher utility than the curve labelled I_1.

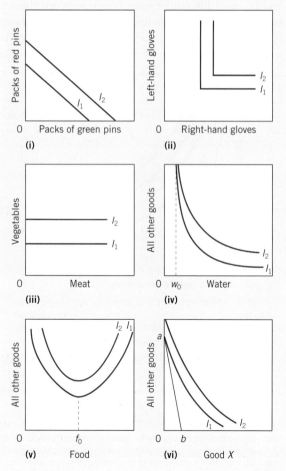

Perfect substitutes: part (i) Drawing pins that came in red packages of 100 would be perfect substitutes for identical pins that came in green packages of 100 for a colour-blind consumer. He would be willing to substitute one type of package for the other at a rate of one for one. The indifference curves would thus be a set of parallel lines with a slope of −1, as shown in part (i) of the figure. *Indifference curves for perfect substitutes are straight lines whose slopes indicate the rate at which one good can be substituted for the other.*

Perfect complements: part (ii) Left- and right-hand gloves are perfect complements, since one of them is of no use without the other. This gives rise to the indifference curves shown in part (ii) of the figure. There is no rate at which any consumer will substitute one kind of glove for the other when she starts with equal numbers of each. *Indifference curves for perfect complements are 'L-shaped'.*

A good that gives zero utility: part (iii) When a good gives no satisfaction at all, a person would be unwilling to sacrifice even the smallest amount of other goods to obtain any quantity of the good in question. Such would be the case for meat for a vegetarian consumer, whose indifference curves are horizontal straight lines. *Indifference curves for a product yielding zero satisfaction are parallel to that product's axis.*

An absolute necessity: part (iv) There is some minimum quantity of water, w_0, that is necessary to sustain life. As consumption of water falls towards w_0, increasingly large amounts of other goods are necessary to persuade the consumer to cut down on his water consumption. Thus, each indifference curve becomes steeper and steeper as it approaches w_0, and the marginal rate of substitution increases. *The marginal rate of substitution for an absolute necessity approaches infinity as consumption falls towards the amount that is absolutely necessary.*

Box 4.4 *continued*

A good that confers a negative utility after some level of consumption: part (v) Beyond some point, further consumption of many foods and beverages, films, plays, or cricket matches would reduce satisfaction. Figure (v) shows a consumer who is *forced* to eat more and more food. At the amount f_0 she has all the food she could possibly want. Beyond f_0 her indifference curves have positive slopes, indicating that she gets *negative* value from consuming the extra food and so would be willing to sacrifice some amount of other products to avoid consuming it. *When, beyond some level of consumption, the consumer's utility is reduced by further consumption, the indifference curves have positive slopes.*

This case does not arise if the consumer can dispose of the extra unwanted units at no cost. The indifference curves then become horizontal.

A good that is not consumed: part (vi) Typically, a consumer will consume only one or two of all of the available types of cars, TV sets, dishwashers, or tennis rackets. If a consumer is in equilibrium consuming a zero amount of say, green peas, she is in what is called a *corner solution* (as shown in part (vi) of the figure by the budget line *ab* and the curve I_1). *When a good is not consumed, the indifference curve cuts the axis of the non-consumed good with a slope flatter than the budget line.*

The choices available to the consumer

An indifference map tells us what any consumer *would like* to do—reach the highest possible indifference curve, that is, be as high up the utility mountain as possible. To see what that consumer *can* do, we need another construction called the budget line.

We start by considering a single consumer, Jane, who is allocating the whole of her money income between two goods, called food and clothing.[10]

The budget line

The **budget line** shows all those combinations of the goods that are just obtainable given Jane's income and the prices of the products that she buys.[11]

Assume initially that Jane's income is £120 per week, the price of food is £2 per unit, and the price of clothing is £4 per unit. As in the earlier discussion, we denote food by F and clothing by C. Thus, for example, a bundle containing 20 units of food and 10 units of clothing is written as $20F$ and $10C$. Table 4.3 lists a few of the bundles of food and clothing available to Jane, while the blue line running from z to w in Figure 4.5 shows all the possible bundles that she could buy with her income. At point w, for example, Jane is spending all her income to buy $60F$ and

Table 4.3 **Data for Jane's budget line**

Quantity of food	Value of food	Quantity of clothing	Value of clothing	Total spending
60	£120	0	£0	£120
50	100	5	20	120
40	80	10	40	120
30	60	15	60	120
20	40	20	80	120
10	20	25	100	120
0	0	30	120	120

The table shows combinations of food and clothing available to Jane when her income is £120 and she faces prices of £4 for clothing and £2 for food. Any row indicates a bundle of food and clothing that exactly exhausts Jane's income.

no clothing, while a point z indicates that she is spending all her income to buy $30C$ and no food. Points on the line between z and w indicate how much Jane could buy of both products.

The slope of the budget line

Marked on Figure 4.5 as points x and y are two of the specific spending combinations from Table 4.3. It is clear from the figure that the absolute value of the slope of the budget line measures the ratio of the change in C to the change in F as we move along the line. This ratio, $\Delta C/\Delta F$, is 0.5 in our present example (10/20).

How does the slope of the budget line relate to the prices of the two goods? This question is easily answered if we remember that all points on the budget line represent bundles of goods that just exhaust Jane's whole income. It follows that when she moves from one point on the budget line to another, the change in expenditure on C must be

---

[10] These assumptions are not as restrictive as they seem at first. Although just two goods are used, so that the analysis can be handled graphically, the argument can easily be generalized to any number of goods with the use of mathematics. Savings are ignored because we are interested in the allocation of expenditure among commodities for current consumption. Saving and borrowing can be allowed for, but doing so affects none of the results in which we are interested here.

[11] A budget line is analogous to the production–possibility boundary shown in Figure 1.1 in Chapter 1. The budget line shows the combinations of commodities available to one consumer given her income and prices, while the production possibility curve shows the combination of commodities available to the whole society given its supplies of resources and techniques of production.

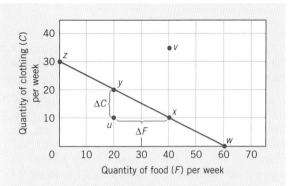

Figure 4.5 Jane's budget line

The budget line shows the quantities of goods available to Jane, given her money income and the price of the goods she buys. With an income of £120 a week and prices of £2 per unit for food and £4 per unit of clothing, the coloured line is Jane's budget line showing all combinations of F and C that are obtainable. Bundle u (10C and 20F) does not use all of her income. Bundle v (35C and 40F) requires more than her present income. If Jane moves from point y (20F and 20C) to point x (40F and 10C), she consumes 20 more F and 10 fewer C. These amounts are indicated by ΔF and ΔC in the figure. Thus, the opportunity cost of each unit of F added to consumption is 10/20 = 0.5 units of clothing forgone. This is the absolute value of ΔC/ΔF, which is the slope of the budget line zw in the figure.

of equal value, but opposite in sign, to the change in expenditure on F. Letting ΔC and ΔF stand for the changes in the quantities of clothing and food, respectively, and p_c and p_f stand for the money prices of clothing and food, respectively, we can write this relation as follows:

$$\Delta C p_c = - \Delta F p_f.$$

There is nothing difficult in this. All it says is that if any amount more is spent on one product, the same amount less must be spent on the other. A given income imposes this discipline on any consumer.

If we divide this equation through, first by ΔF and then by p_c, we get the following:

$$\Delta C/\Delta F = - p_f/p_c.$$

Therefore the slope of the budget line is the negative of the ratio of the two prices (with the price of the good that is plotted on the horizontal axis appearing in the numerator).

Notice that the slope of the budget line depends only on the ratio of the two prices, not on their absolute values. To check this, consider an example. If clothing costs £4 and food costs £2, then Jane must forgo 0.5 units of clothing in order to be able to purchase one more unit of food. If clothing costs £8 and food costs £4, Jane must still forgo 0.5 units of clothing to be able to purchase one more unit

of food. As long as the price of clothing is twice the price of food, Jane must forgo half a unit of clothing in order to be able to purchase one more unit of food.

More generally, the amount of clothing that must be given up to obtain another unit of food depends only on *the ratio of* their two prices. If we take the money price of food and divide it by the money price of clothing, we have the opportunity cost of food in terms of clothing (the quantity of clothing that must be forgone in order to be able to purchase one more unit of food). This can be written:

p_f/p_c = opportunity cost of food in terms of clothing.

It is apparent that changing both money prices in the same proportion leaves the ratio p_f/p_c unchanged.

What money prices do is to determine how far out from the origin the budget line lies for any given level of money income. The lower are the money prices of the two goods for any given relative price, the further out from the origin is the budget line, indicating that more of both goods can be consumed.

This discussion helps to clarify the distinction between money prices and relative prices. Both p_f and p_c are money prices, while the ratio p_f/p_c is a relative price.

The consumer's equilibrium

The budget line tells us what each consumer *can* do: he can select any consumption bundle on or below the line, but not above it. This means that he can only spend within the limits of his given income. To see what each consumer *wants* to do, we introduce our third assumption:

Assumption 3. **Consumers seek to maximize total satisfaction, which means reaching the highest possible indifference curve.**

We have now developed representations of a consumer's tastes and available choices. Figure 4.6 brings together the budget line and the indifference curves for another consumer, Paul. Any point on the budget line can be attained. Which one will Paul actually choose?

Would Paul choose to consume 25 units of food and no clothing, as he could do with his income? Might he instead choose to consume 30 units of clothing and no food? The answer is no in both cases. By moving away from either of these combinations he can move to a higher indifference curve. Indeed, he can get to higher and higher indifference curves by moving along the budget line from each of the corners into the middle until he reaches the point E, where the line is just touching (i.e. is tangent to) the highest possible indifference curve. When Paul is at this point of tangency between the indifference curve and the budget line, he cannot reach a higher indifference curve by varying the bundle consumed. Any move from this point that remains within the

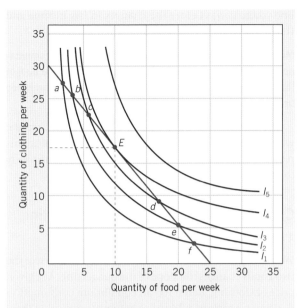

Figure 4.6 The equilibrium of a consumer

Equilibrium occurs at *E*, where an indifference curve is tangent to the budget line. Paul has an income of £150 a week and faces prices of £5 a unit for clothing and £6 a unit for food. A bundle of clothing and food indicated by point *a* is attainable, but by moving along the budget line to points such as *b* and *c*, higher indifference curves can be reached. At *E*, where the indifference curve I_4 is tangent to the budget line, Paul cannot reach a higher curve by moving along the budget line. If he did alter his consumption bundle by moving from *E* to *d*, for example, he would move to the lower indifference curve I_3 and thus to a lower level of satisfaction.

budget constraint will lead him to a lower indifference curve and thus lower his satisfaction.

Satisfaction is maximized at the point where an indifference curve is tangent to a budget line. At that point, the slope of the indifference curve, which measures the consumer's marginal rate of substitution, is equal to the slope of the budget line, which measures the opportunity cost of one good in terms of the other as determined by market prices.

Notice that Paul is presented with market prices that he cannot change. He adjusts to these prices by choosing a bundle of goods such that, at the margin, his own relative valuation of the two goods conforms to the relative valuations given by the market. Paul's relative valuation is given by the slope of his indifference curve, while the market's relative valuation is given by the slope of his budget line.

When Paul has chosen the consumption bundle that maximizes his satisfaction, he will go on consuming that bundle unless something changes. Thus, the consumer is in equilibrium.

It is also worth noting that the equilibrium position we have just derived has the same characteristics as the one the utilitarians discovered which is expressed in eqns (4.1) and (4.2). The price ratio p_x/p_y is the slope of the budget line in Figure 4.6. The slope of each indifference curve, which we have called the *marginal rate of substitution*, is the ratio of the marginal utilities of the two products, MU_x/MU_y, and so where the budget line is tangent to the highest possible indifference curve (i.e. where the consumer is maximizing utility) it will also be true that $MU_x/MU_y = p_x/p_y$.

The consumer's response to price and income changes

How do consumers change their spending patterns when there is a change in goods prices or available income? To answer this, we take another hypothetical consumer called Karen. Her tastes are given, and this is represented by her indifference map. We first show that changes in her income and the prices she faces can be represented as a shift in the budget line. We then investigate the change in spending induced by price and income changes.

Parallel shifts in the budget line

A change in money income

A change in Karen's money income will, other things being equal, shift her budget line. For example, if income rises, Karen will be able to buy more of both goods. Therefore her budget line will shift out parallel to itself to

indicate this expansion in her consumption possibilities. (The fact that it will be a parallel shift is established by our demonstration in the previous section that the slope of the budget line depends only on the relative price of the two products.)

A change in the consumer's income shifts the budget line parallel to itself, outwards when income rises and inwards when income falls.

The effect of income changes is shown in Figure 4.7. For each level of income, there is an equilibrium position at which an indifference curve is tangent to the relevant budget line. Each such equilibrium position means that Karen is doing as well as she possibly can for that level of income. If we join up all the points of equilibrium, we trace out what is called her **income–consumption line**.

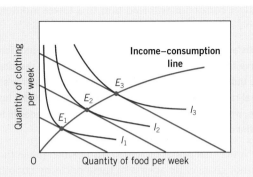

Figure 4.7 An income–consumption line

This line shows how Karen's purchases react to changes in income with relative prices held constant. Increases in income shift the budget line out parallel to itself, moving the equilibrium from E_1 to E_2 to E_3. The blue income–consumption line joins all these points of equilibrium.

This line shows how the consumption bundle changes as income changes, with prices held constant.[12]

A proportionate change in all prices

If all prices are cut in half, Karen can buy twice as much of both products. This causes the same shift in the budget line as when Karen's income doubles with prices held constant. On the other hand, a doubling of all prices will cause her budget line to shift inwards in exactly the same way as if her money income had halved with prices held constant. This illustrates a general result.

An equal proportionate change in all money prices, with money income held constant, shifts the budget line parallel to itself, towards the origin when prices rise and away from the origin when prices fall.

From this point on the analysis is the same as in the previous section, since changing money prices proportionately has the identical effect to changing money income.

Offsetting changes in money prices and money incomes

The results in the last two sections suggest that we can have offsetting changes in money prices and money incomes. Consider a doubling of money income that shifts Karen's budget line outwards. Let this be accompanied by a doubling of all money prices that shifts her budget line inwards. The net effect is to leave her budget line where it was before the changes in her income and the market prices. This illustrates a general result.

Multiplying money income by some constant, λ, and simultaneously multiplying all money prices by λ, leaves the budget line unaffected and hence leaves consumer purchases unaffected.

The symbol λ is the lower-case Greek letter lambda, which is often used for some constant multiple. This result is sometimes referred to as the *homogeneity condition*.

Changes in the slope of the budget line

A change in relative prices

We already know that a change in the relative price of the two goods changes the slope of the budget line. At a given price of clothing, Karen has an equilibrium consumption position for each possible price of food. Connecting these positions traces out a **price–consumption line**, as shown in Figure 4.8. Notice that, as the relative prices of food and clothing change, the relative quantities of food and clothing purchased also change. In particular, as the price of food falls, Karen buys more food.

Real and money income

The preceding analysis allows us to look deeper into the important distinction between two concepts of income. **Money income** measures a consumer's income in terms

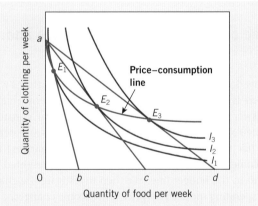

Figure 4.8 The price–consumption line

This line shows how a consumer's purchases react to a change in one price with money income and other prices held constant. Decreases in the price of food (with her money income and the price of clothing constant) pivot Karen's budget line from *ab* to *ac* to *ad*. Her equilibrium position moves from E_1 to E_2 to E_3. The blue price–consumption line joins all such equilibrium points.

---

[12] The income–consumption line can be used to derive the curve relating quantity demanded to income. This is done by plotting the quantity of one of the goods consumed at the equilibrium position against the level of money income that determined the position of the budget line. Repeating this for each level of income produces the required curve.

Box 4.5 Relative prices and inflation

Allocation of resources: the importance of relative prices

Price theory shows why the allocation of resources depends on the structure of relative prices. If the money value of all prices, incomes, debts, and credits were doubled, there would, according to our theory, be no noticeable effects. We have already seen that doubling money income and all money prices leaves each consumer's budget line unchanged. So, according to the theory of consumer behaviour, the combination of these changes gives the consumer no incentive to vary any purchases. As far as producers are concerned, if the prices of all outputs and inputs double, the relative profitabilities of alternative lines of production will be unchanged. Thus, producers will have no incentive to alter production rates so as to produce more of some things and fewer of others. The same set of relative prices and real incomes would exist, and there would be no incentive for any reallocation of resources. The economy would function as before.

In contrast, a change in *relative* prices will cause resources to be reallocated. Consumers will buy more of the relatively cheaper products and less of the relatively more expensive ones, and producers will increase production of those products whose prices have risen relatively, and reduce production of those whose prices have fallen relatively (since the latter will be relatively less profitable lines of production).

The theory of price and resource allocation is a theory of relative, not absolute, prices.

Inflation and deflation: the importance of absolute prices

The average level of all money prices is called the general price level, or more usually just the **price level**. If all money prices double, we say that the price level has doubled. An ongoing increase in the price level is called **inflation**; a decrease is called **deflation**. If a rise in all money prices and incomes has little or no effect on the allocation of resources, it may seem surprising that so much concern is expressed over inflation. Clearly, people who spend all their incomes, and whose money incomes go up at the same rate as money prices, lose nothing from inflation. Their real income is unaffected.

Inflation, while having no effect on consumers whose incomes rise at the same rate as prices, does nonetheless have many serious consequences. These arise mainly because all prices do not rise at the same rate and some assets are denominated in money terms and hence their value falls as the price level rises. These consequences are studied in detail later in this book.

When the price level is constant a change in one money price necessarily changes that price *relative* to the average of all other prices. However, the theory extends to situations in which the price level is changing. Under inflationary conditions, whenever shifts in demand or supply require a change in a product's relative price, its price rises *faster* (its relative price rising) or *slower* (its relative price falling) than the general price level is rising. Explaining this each time can be cumbersome. Therefore it is simpler to deal with relative prices in a theoretical setting in which the price level is constant. However, it is important to realize that even though we develop the theory in this way, it is not limited to such situations. The propositions we develop can be applied to changing price levels merely by making explicit what is always implicit; in the theory of relative prices, 'rise' or 'fall' *always* means rise or fall *relative to the average of all other prices*.

---

of some monetary unit; for example, so many pounds sterling or so many dollars. **Real income** measures the *purchasing power* of the consumer's money income. A rise in money income of *x* per cent combined with an *x* per cent rise in all money prices leaves a consumer's purchasing power, and hence his or her real income, unchanged.

When we speak of the real value of a certain amount of money, we are referring to the goods and services that can be bought with the money—that is, to the purchasing power of the money.

Box 4.5 discusses the importance of relative prices and the problems created by inflation.

The consumer's demand curve

We now establish the link between the above analysis of indifference curves and budget constraints, and the consumer's demand curve. To derive the consumer's demand curve for any product, we need to depart from the world of two products. We are now interested in what happens to the consumer's demand for some product, say petrol, as the price of that product changes, *all other prices being held constant*. We can do this simply with the tools developed so far by simply making the bundle of 'all other goods' take the place of the second product.

Derivation of the demand curve

In part (i) of Figure 4.9 a new type of indifference map is plotted in which the horizontal axis measures litres of petrol and the vertical axis measures the value of all other goods consumed. We have, in effect, used *everything but petrol* as the second product. The indifference curves now give the rate at which another hypothetical consumer, Philip, is prepared to substitute petrol for money (which allows him to buy all other goods).

The derivation of a demand curve is illustrated in part (ii) of Figure 4.9. For a given income each price of petrol gives rise to a particular budget line and a particular spending choice. Plotting the quantity of petrol that Philip consumes for the specific budget line at any given price yields one point on his demand curve. Each other

possible price yields a different point. The resulting price–quantity combinations trace out Philip's whole demand curve.

The slope of the demand curve

The price–consumption line in part (i) of Figure 4.9 indicates that as price decreases, the quantity of petrol demanded increases. For many important purposes it is useful to divide this change into two parts called the *income effect* and the *substitution effect*.

Income and substitution effects

The separation of these two effects according to indifference theory is shown in Figure 4.10. We can think of it as occurring in the following way. After the price of the good has fallen, we reduce money income *until the original indifference curve can just be obtained*. Philip is now on his original indifference curve but facing the new set of relative prices. His response is defined as the **substitution effect**: the response

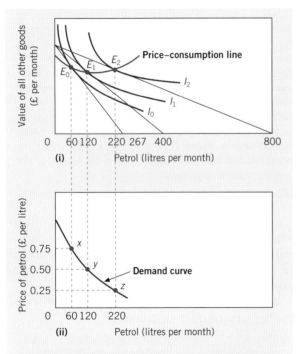

(i)

(ii)

Figure 4.9 Derivation of an individual's demand curve

The points on a price–consumption line provide the information needed to draw a demand curve. In part (i) Philip has an income of £200 per month and alternatively faces prices of £0.75, £0.50, and £0.25 per litre of petrol, choosing positions E_0, E_1, and E_2. The information for the number of litres he demands at each price is then plotted in part (ii) to yield his demand curve. The three points *x*, *y*, and *z* in (ii) correspond to the three equilibrium positions E_0, E_1, and E_2 in (i).

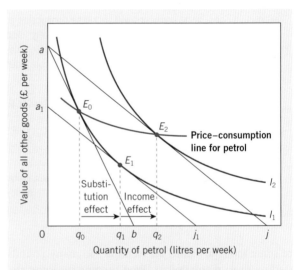

Figure 4.10 The income and substitution effects

The substitution effect is defined by sliding the budget line around a fixed indifference curve; the income effect is defined by a parallel shift of the budget line. The original budget line is *ab* and a fall in the price of petrol takes it to *aj*. The original equilibrium is at E_0 with q_0 of petrol consumed, and the final equilibrium is at E_2 with q_2 of petrol consumed. To remove the income effect, imagine reducing Philip's income until he is just able to attain his original indifference curve at the new price. We do this by shifting the line *aj* to a parallel line nearer the origin until it just touches the indifference curve that passes through E_0. The intermediate point E_1 divides the quantity change into a substitution effect, $q_1 - q_0$, and an income effect, $q_2 - q_1$. The point E_1 can also be obtained by sliding the original budget line *ab* around the indifference curve until its slope reflects the new relative prices.

of quantity demanded to a change in relative price, real income being held constant (meaning staying on the original indifference curve). Then, to measure the income effect, we restore money income. Philip's response to this is defined as the **income effect**: the response of quantity demanded to a change in real income, relative prices held constant.

Box 4.6 explains an alternative method of isolating the income and substitution effects.

In Figure 4.10 the income and substitution effects work in the same direction, both tending to increase quantity demanded when price falls. Is this necessarily the case? The answer is no. It follows from the convex shape of indifference curves that the substitution effect is always in the same direction: more is consumed of a product whose relative price has fallen. However, the income effect can be in either direction: it can lead to more or less being consumed of a product whose price has fallen. The direction of the income effect depends on the distinction between normal and inferior goods.

The slope of the demand curve for a normal good

For a normal good an increase in any consumer's real income, arising from a decrease in the price of the product, leads to increased consumption, reinforcing the substitution effect. Because quantity demanded increases, the demand curve has a negative slope.[13] This is the case illustrated in Figure 4.9.

The slope of the demand curve for an inferior good

Figure 4.11 shows indifference curves for inferior goods. The income effect is negative in each part of the diagram. This follows from the nature of an inferior good: as income rises, other things being equal, less of the good is consumed. In each case the substitution effect serves to increase the quantity demanded as price decreases and is offset to some degree by the negative income effect. The final result depends on the relative strengths of the two effects. In part (i) the negative income effect only partially offsets the substitution effect, and thus quantity demanded increases as a result of the price decrease, though not as much as for a normal good. This is the typical pattern for

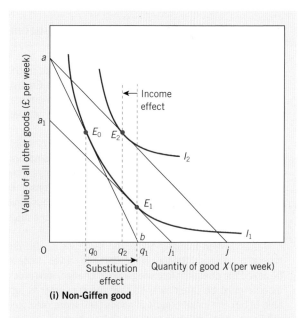

(i) Non-Giffen good

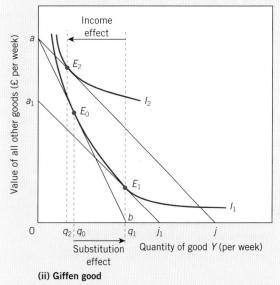

(ii) Giffen good

Figure 4.11 Income and substitution effects for inferior goods

A large enough negative income effect can outweigh the substitution effect and lead to a decrease in consumption in response to a fall in price. In each part of the diagram Philip is in equilibrium at E_0, consuming a quantity q_0 of the good in question. The price then decreases and the budget line shifts to aj, with a new equilibrium at E_2 and quantity consumed q_2. In each case the substitution effect increases consumption from q_0 to q_1. In (i) there is a negative income effect of $q_1 - q_2$. Because this is less than the substitution effect, the latter dominates, so good X has a normal negatively sloped demand curve. In (ii) the negative income effect $q_1 - q_2$ is larger than the substitution effect, and quantity consumed actually decreases. Good Y is a Giffen good.

---

[13] A possible exception to this arises from the *endowment income effect*. This arises in some situations in which the consumer has an initial endowment of goods and may choose to be a net seller of some goods. If the price of these goods rises, the consumer has a higher income and thus can buy more of all normal goods, including the goods for which he or she is a net seller. As one example suppose the price of haircuts rises (all other prices remaining constant). For most consumers we would predict that the quantity demanded of haircuts would fall. However, hairdressers are now richer, so for them the price rise has generated a positive rather than a negative income effect. So for hairdressers the income effect goes the other way, such that their income rises as the price of haircuts rises.

Box 4.6 The Slutsky decomposition of income and substitution effects

The discussion of income and substitution effects in the text is based upon the analysis developed by the English Nobel Laureate Sir John Hicks (1904–1989). An alternative approach was developed by the Russian mathematician Evgeny Slutsky (1880–1948).

Hicks' decomposition was derived in the context of developing the concept of indifference curves, so it was natural for him to ask the question: following a price change, how much income must be taken way in order that the consumer can return to the original indifference curve and thus have the same level of utility or satisfaction as prior to the price change?

Slutsky, when thinking about the same issue, did not have at his disposal the tool of indifference curves. Instead he asked the question: following a price change, how much income must be taken away so that the consumer is just able to buy the initial bundle of goods (and therefore could not be any worse off than in the initial position)?

The figure illustrates the difference between these two approaches. There is a fall in the price of good 1 holding the price of good 2 constant. The initial consumption point is at A, and after the price fall the consumption point is at B.

As we saw in the discussion of Figure 4.10, Hicks' decomposition generates an income compensation that returns the consumer to the original indifference curve I_1 following the fall of price of good 1 and the associated shift of the budget constraint from P_1 to P_2. This is achieved by shifting the new budget line P_2 towards the origin until it is just tangent to the original indifference curve. Thus, the Hicks substitution

effect takes the consumer from point A to point C, and the income effect takes her from C to B.

To find the Slutsky decomposition we shift the new budget constraint inwards parallel to its new position until it just passes through the original consumption bundle at point A. If the consumer had faced this budget constraint with the original level of disposable income but at the new relative prices, she would have chosen to be at point D that is on indifference curve I_2 and thus is at a higher utility level than the initial position.

Because these methods answer slightly different questions, they have different uses. The Slutsky compensation is useful in applied work because it is easy to calculate the change in income needed to compensate for a change in price. The Hicks compensation is useful for theoretical welfare comparisons because it tells us the income change that leaves the consumer *feeling* just as well off as before, but it is difficult to calculate in practice. Therefore the choice of method should depend on the purpose to which it is put.

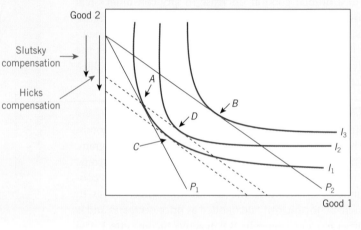

---

inferior goods, and it also leads to negatively sloped demand curves, usually relatively inelastic ones.

The slope of the demand curve for a Giffen good

In part (ii) the negative income effect outweighs the substitution effect and thus leads to a positively sloped demand curve. This possibility is referred to as a **Giffen good** after the Victorian economist Sir Robert Giffen (1837–1910), who is reputed to have documented a case of such a curve. We now show how this case can be analysed using indifference curves. For the Giffen good to occur, the good must be inferior. But that is not enough; the change in price must have a negative income effect *strong enough* to more than offset the substitution effect. These circumstances are unusual because strong

inferiority is rarely found. Such goods, if they ever existed, would tend to disappear from use as consumers get richer. Most goods are normal goods. A positively sloped market demand curve is thus a possible rare exception to the general rule that demand curves have negative slopes.

Equivalent and compensating variations

There are further concepts associated with the income effect of a price change that are commonly used in economics. These are known as **equivalent variation** and **compensating variation**.

Equivalent variation

The equivalent variation is the answer to the question: if we had given the consumer a sum of money instead of a

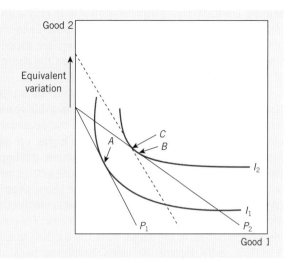

Figure 4.12 Equivalent variation of income

The equivalent variation is the change in income that leaves the consumer just as well off as some specific change in the price of a good. The consumer is initially at point A on budget line P_1. The price of good 1 falls, the budget line shifts to P_2, and the consumer shifts her spending pattern to B, which is on a higher indifference curve. The equivalent variation in income is given by the size of the parallel shift in the original budget line that would have taken the consumer to the level of utility indicated by the higher indifference curve (that is achieved after the fall in the price of good 1.) The equivalent income variation would have generated consumption point C as the optimal choice, but the consumer is indifferent between points B and C.

lower price of one product, how much extra income would have made her feel just as well off? This is illustrated in Figure 4.12. It is calculated by shifting the original budget line outwards parallel to itself until it just touches the new indifference curve achieved after a price fall of one good.

Compensating variation

This works backwards rather than forwards. It is the same as the income effect shown in Figure 4.10, and is measured by the distance a–a_1 in that figure. It is the amount of income that has to be taken away from the consumer following a price fall of one good in order to return her to the initial indifference curve and thus leave her feeling just as well off as before.

The difference between these two effects is whether the income adjustment is made relative to the consumption bundle chosen at the original prices or that chosen at the new prices.

CASE STUDIES

1. Happiness, utility, and well-being

At one time it was believed that it was not possible to measure tastes or satisfaction, only to infer them by observing what people did. If people chose A over B they must have done so because it made them happier to have A rather than B. However, modern psychologists have measured tastes and happiness in a range of ways from asking people directly to measuring their brain impulses. This has led them to suggest many new conclusions about what makes people happy.

A key assumption in economics is that anything that increases an individual's income, other things being equal, will raise his or her utility, roughly making him or her happier. By extension, then, anything that increases a country's national income will make its citizens happier on average.

The happiness literature questions both of these assumptions. On the individual level, researchers point out that people gain much satisfaction from a favourable comparison of what they have relative to what their 'reference group' has, rather than from the absolute amount they themselves have. For example, experiments show that faced with a choice between all of a firm's employees getting no rise in pay next year and the subject getting a 2 per cent rise while everyone else in the firm gets a 5 per cent rise, most subjects chose the former alternative. They care more about how they fare relative to others in their firm than how they fare absolutely. On another comparison, however, subjects faced with the choice of (1) you get two weeks vacation and others in the firm get one week and (2) you get four weeks vacation while all the others get eight, most subjects chose the second alternative. This suggests that people are more rivalrous with respect to income than to leisure and other amenities.

This research suggests that one's happiness depends on how well one is doing in relation to one's reference group, which may not be everyone. In one dramatic example, winners of the silver medal in the Olympics tend to be less happy than winners of the bronze medal. Silver winners are sadly saying something like 'With only a tiny improvement in my performance, I would have been the gold medallist', while bronze medal winners are happily saying something like 'Look, I am better than the dozens of competitors who got no medal'.

On the national level, although income and consumption has increased dramatically over the last 50 years, happiness researchers find that people in the developed countries are on average no happier. The higher up the income scale any individual is at any one time, the happier he or she tends to be. But when everyone gets richer, as happens with economic growth over the years, people on average become no happier, at least after some threshold income that is around US $15,000 per year. For people with incomes in the range from US $1,000 to US $15,000, extra income increases happiness because they can get more of the essentials and simple luxuries of life. But above that figure, extra income and the extra consumption that it allows seem to bring no increase in measured happiness. For per capita national incomes in that higher range, which includes all the developed countries, there is no correlation between income and measured happiness. For example, people in countries with per capita incomes substantially higher than New Zealand are happier in Iceland, Denmark, and the Netherlands, and less happy in Italy, Japan, and Germany.

Happiness researchers suggest that one reason for this apparently perverse result is that people adjust quickly to what they have. An increment in real income, such as a bigger house and most other increments to their 'living standards', makes them feel happier for a while but it soon becomes customary and their happiness reverts to what it was, depending mainly on comparisons with others, and not the absolute level of their consumption. This is known as *habituation*. An individual who is promoted or wins the lottery is very happy when it happens, but he or she gets used to it and will not be quite so ecstatic a few months later. This person may be permanently better off in terms of material possessions but the boost to happiness does not last (or at least not much).

There are big international differences in happiness across countries as we saw in Box 4.1 at the beginning of this chapter. In 50 countries in a recent study, 80 per cent of the differences could be explained by six factors, where (+) and (−) indicate, respectively, a positive and negative correlation with happiness: the divorce rate (−), the unemployment rate (−), the level of trust (+), a variable that has a been falling steadily in the United States and the United Kingdom but rising in continental Europe over the last few decades, membership of non-religious organizations (+), a variable that has been falling dramatically in many developed countries in the last few decades, quality of government (+), and belief in a God (+).

Some of the things that increase national efficiency seem to lead to less rather than greater happiness. Here are just a few examples.

Labour mobility: Crime is lower when people trust each other. And people trust each other more if fewer people are moving house and the community is more homogeneous. So violence tends to be high and happiness low where residential mobility is high, and where there are concentrations of newcomers (not necessarily from other nations). Therefore periods of labour mobility may increase economic efficiency but lower happiness.

Performance-related pay: Individual differences in receipts from performance pay tend to lead to happiness reducing comparisons even if they raise efficiency by making people work harder.

Monetary incentives: When fines were charged for parents who were late picking up their children from child-care centres, lateness was much more frequent than when there was only a general admonition to try to be on time because the parents' lateness made the attendants late in getting home to their own families.

Trust often matters more than monetary and other incentives: Staff who were told to work eight hours a day but to come and go as they wished tended to work more than those who were controlled by a strict time clock. Staff given a statuary allotment of sick leave tended to take more such leave that those who were just told to take sick leave but only when absolutely necessary.

Does happiness research upset the assumptions of unlimited wants and that economic growth brings increased well-being?

As we have seen, happiness research suggests that more does not always make people happier. Some worry that this observation upsets two of economics' basic assumptions: (1) that wants are unlimited, and (2) that economic growth makes us better off in some definable sense.

First, consider the assumption of unlimited wants. This assumption implies that, given a choice between two bundles of goods and services, one with more of everything than the other, people will choose the larger bundle. It follows that to obtain the larger bundle rather than the small one people will be willing to sacrifice an amount of money as long as it is less than the difference in their valuation of the two bundles. The unlimited wants assumption is just a formalization of this behaviour. Operationally, it means that within any currently achievable amount, people would be willing to pay something to obtain more rather than less or, in other words, more than is available today would be consumed if it were available at a lower price than rules today. The key difference that matters here is the difference between having more goods and services and having more happiness. It is a matter of common experience that we sometimes make choices that we end up regretting: we may go to a movie that we find distressing; we may go on a tour we regret because of our dislike for our fellow passengers; we may make a marriage that starts out looking wonderful but ends in disaster. Similarly, there is nothing inconsistent with making choices that result in a higher income only to find that the new way of life yields less happiness than the simpler ways that we abandoned when our incomes rose. But most people would still opt for the higher income if they could choose.

Next, consider whether there is a conflict between the happiness research result that growth does not necessarily make us happier and the conclusion that growth makes us better off in some definable ways. It is clear that in many ways we are better off objectively than our forebears. Consider just a few measurable examples. People living a century ago did not have modern dental and medical equipment, penicillin, bypass operations, organ transplants, safe births, control of genetically transmitted diseases, opportunities for fast and cheap worldwide travel, affordable universities, central heating, air conditioning, and food of great variety free from ptomaine and botulism. Detergents, washing machines, electric stoves, vacuum cleaners, refrigerators, dishwashers, and a host of other labour-saving household products have eliminated the endless drudgery that was the lot of most housewives until well into the twentieth century. Also, robot-operated computer-controlled modern factories have largely replaced the noisy dangerous factories that spewed coal smoke over the surrounding countryside until less than a hundred years ago. The technological change that drives economic growth in the long run has also eliminated or controlled the terrible diseases that maimed, crippled, and killed—plague, tuberculosis, cholera, dysentery, smallpox, and leprosy, to mention only the most common. In 1700, average European life expectancy was about 30 years. In 1900, death from botulism and ptomaine poisoning from contaminated food was common. Chemical additives virtually eliminated these killers and allow us to live long enough to worry about the long-run cancer-causing effects of some of these additives. Now they are being replaced by safer preservatives.

It is clear from this partial list that the technological changes that drive long-run economic growth have made people better off in many measurable ways. Nonetheless, it has not necessarily made people happier. The key here is that being better off than previous generations is different from being happier than previous generations. One of the main reasons is that people have no direct experience of what it would have been like to live 100 years ago. There is little doubt that if today's people were transferred back to 1900 in the same relative income position they would be made less happy and would eagerly accept being transferred

back to the present. But this is not a comparison that they actually make. For example, you probably do not say 'Gosh I am happy that I have running water in my home'. Instead, you take for granted the tap water that was the source of enormous happiness to those who were first able to abandon the trip outside to draw water from a well. Similar comments apply to such things as indoor flush toilets compared with dry toilets located in outhouses, to word-processing packages compared with typewriters. and to talking movies and TV shows compared with music-hall performances. Instead, people are more likely to judge their happiness relative to their neighbours' living standards, accepting without thought all the technological advances that have made them better off than their ancestors.

There are three different concepts—(1) want satisfaction, (2) happiness, and (3) objectively measurable changes that almost everyone would agree are improvements—and these three measures often change in different directions.

When we compare most people with their counterparts in previous generations we find that they have more wants satisfied in the sense that they consume more goods and services, yet many are less happy although they are almost all better off in many definable ways.

We conclude that recent evidence from happiness research does not invalidate the utility-based analysis that we developed earlier in this chapter. Utility theory helps us understand the allocation of a particular income between alternative consumption bundles in a specific period, but it does not imply that having more of everything will always make the average person permanently happier.

2. Income and substitution effects in practice

Although they sound highly abstract and 'theoretical' when first encountered, the income and substitution effects turn out to be useful tools. They help us to deal with many problems, such as: Do high rates of income tax act as disincentives to work? Would cutting the rate of income tax increase the amount of work people do? Would raising the wage rate of workers in some industry lead to a reduction in absenteeism?

Such questions frequently face decision-takers and they are often surprised at the results that the market produces. For example, many years ago the National Coal Board, which used to run the UK coal industry, raised miners' wages in an attempt to boost coal production and was surprised to find miners working fewer rather than more hours. In several countries increases in rates of income tax (within a moderate, not a confiscatory, range) have been found to be associated with people working more hours rather than fewer even though they earn less after-tax income for each hour worked; at other times reductions in tax rates seem to have caused people to work less even though they earn more after-tax income for each hour worked. The surprise in all these cases was the same. Intuition suggests that if you pay people more they will work more. Experience shows that the result is sometimes the opposite: more pay, less work; less pay, more work.

The explanation of this surprising behaviour lies in distinguishing the income effect from the substitution effect of a change in the reward for work.

Think of Luke starting with an endowment of 24 hours per day and deciding to consume some of it as 'leisure' (including sleeping time) and to trade the rest for income by working. If Luke works 9 hours a day at an after-tax rate of £10 per hour, he is consuming 15 hours a day of leisure and trading the other 9 hours for £90 worth of income that can be used to buy goods and services.

Now, let the after-tax wage rate rise to £12 an hour, either because the wage rate rises or because the rate of personal income tax falls to produce that increase in after-tax earnings. Luke's response to this change will have an income and a substitution component.

The substitution effect works the way intuition suggested: more wages, more work. Gaining income is now cheaper in terms of the leisure Luke must sacrifice. At the new wage rate 1/12 of an hour (i.e. 5 minutes) of work earns Luke £1 worth of income, whereas before it took 1/10 of an hour (6 minutes). Looked at the other way around, consuming leisure is now more expensive per amount of income that Luke must give up. An extra hour of leisure consumed requires sacrificing £12 of income instead of £10. The substitution effect leads to an increased consumption of the thing whose relative price has fallen—everything that income can buy in this case—and a reduced consumption of the thing whose relative price has risen—leisure.

So far so good. The surprise lies in the income effect. The rise in the after-tax wage rate has an income effect in the sense that Luke can have more goods *and* more leisure. For example, he could consume an extra hour of leisure by cutting his hours worked from nine to eight while at the same time raising his income from £90 a day (9 hours @ £10) to £96 a day (8 hours @ £12). The income effect leads him to consume more goods and more leisure—that is, to work fewer hours.

Only if the substitution effect is strong enough to overcome the income effect will the rise in the wage rate induce Luke to work more. If the substitution effect is strong enough, Luke might, for example, work 9.5 hours instead of 9 hours and increase his income from £90 to £114 a day. However, this means choosing this combination of income and leisure in preference to all combinations that give more income and more leisure, such as 8.5 hours of work (down from 9 hours) and £105 of income (up from £90).

So, we should not be surprised if increases in the after-tax hourly wage lead to less work; this merely means that the income effect is stronger than the substitution effect.

The above analysis helps to explain why employers separate higher overtime rates from normal rates of pay. If the normal rate of pay is increased, the income effect is quite large, whereas if only the overtime rate is raised, the income effect is much smaller but the substitution effect is unchanged. In the above example, raising the normal wage rate from £10 to £12 increases Luke's income by £18 if he continues to work an unchanged 9 hours a day. But introducing an overtime rate has an income effect only in so far as overtime hours are already being worked. If, in the previous example, the employer introduced a £15 hourly rate for work of over 9 hours a day, the income effect would be zero; Luke must work more in order to gain any benefit from the higher overtime rate.

3. Experimental economics and the concern for fairness

In the past decade or so economists and other scientists have cooperated in designing experiments to determine how people actually respond to various choices. This line of enquiry has provided evidence that individuals do not invariably maximize their own utility with no regard for what others around them are doing. The following extract summarizes the results of one such experiment.

Imagine that somebody offers you $100. All you have to do is agree with some other anonymous person on how to share the sum. The rules are strict. The two of you are in separate rooms and cannot exchange information. A coin toss decides which of you will propose how to share the money. Suppose that you are the proposer. You can make a single offer of how to split the sum, and the other person—the responder—can say yes or no. The responder also knows the rules and the total amount of money at stake. If her answer is yes, the deal goes ahead. If her answer is no, neither of you gets anything. In both cases, the game is over and will not be repeated. What will you do?'

Instinctively, many people feel they should offer 50 per cent, because such a division is 'fair' and therefore likely to be accepted. More daring people, however, think they might get away with offering somewhat less than half of the sum.

Before making a decision, you should ask yourself what you would do if you were the responder. The only thing you can do as the responder is say yes or no to a given amount of money. If the offer were 10 per cent, would you take $10 and let someone walk away with $90, or would you rather have nothing at all? What if the offer were only 1 per cent? Isn't $1 better than no dollars? And remember, haggling is strictly forbidden. Just one offer by the proposer: the responder can take it or leave it.

So what will you offer?

According to utility maximizing theory you should keep the majority of the money for yourself and offer a very small amount to the responder. After all, her alternative is to get nothing. So, if she is a maximizer, she will accept any offer greater than zero. But this is not what happens in such experiments!

Instead, two thirds of the offers are between 40 and 50 per cent of the total sum. Only four in 100 people offer less than 20 per cent. Also more than half of all responders reject offers that are less than 20 per cent.

The motive of the person making the offer may be mixed. On the one hand, he may be concerned with what he thinks is fair. On the other hand, he may know that very small offers are likely to be refused because the responder will react strongly to what she perceives as an unfair offer.

But the motivation of the responder is not so complicated. She either accepts or rejects whatever offer she receives. According to maximization theory, there is a puzzle here: why should anyone reject an offer as 'too small'? The responder has just two choices: take what is offered or receive nothing at all. The only rational option for a maximizing individual is to accept any offer. Even $1 is better than nothing. A maximizing proposer who is also sure that the responder is also a maximizer will therefore make the smallest possible offer. In response, the responder will accept any offer greater than zero. The predictions of maximizing theory are clear on this one: offer as little as possible and accept anything positive, no matter how meagre.

The resolution of the puzzle in the case of both players is that they care about fairness almost as much as they care about doing as well as they can for themselves.

The scenario just described, called the Ultimatum Game, belongs to a small but rapidly expanding field called experimental economics. ... For a long time, theoretical economists postulated a being called homo economicus—a rational individual relentlessly bent on maximizing a purely selfish reward. But the lesson from the Ultimatum Game and similar experiments is that real people are a cross-breed of homo economicus and homo emoticons, *a complicated hybrid species that can be ruled as much by emotion as by cold logic and selfishness ...*

Centuries ago philosophers such as David Hume and Jean-Jacques Rousseau emphasized the crucial role of 'human nature' in social interactions. Theoretical economists, in contrast, long preferred to study the selfish homo economicus. They theorized about how an isolated individual—Robinson Crusoe on some desert island—would choose among different bundles of commodities. We are, however, not Robinson Crusoes. Our ancestors' line has been social for hundreds of millions of years. And in social interactions, our preferences turn out to be far from selfish.

(Karl Sigmund, Ernst Fehr, and Martin A. Nowak 'The economics of fair play', *Scientific American*, January, 2002, pages 82–7.)

In other experiments very young children, and, yes, even chimpanzees, are shown to be motivated by considerations of fairness. Children as young as one year old watch puppet shows in which puppet one behaves unhelpfully to puppet three while puppet two is helpful to puppet three. Then, when asked to chose puppet one or two as a present, by almost a ten to one margin they chose the kind puppet over the unhelpful one. In another experiment, one chimpanzee allows another to eat his banana when the experimenter takes the banana away from him, but gets extremely angry when the other chimp steals the banana. The outcome is the same: the chimp loses his banana, but his actions show that how this happens matter strongly to him.

The preceding cases do not imply that the assumption that individuals maximize their own utility or self-interest is useless. In everyday decisions, such as how many potatoes or holidays in Switzerland to buy, self-interest explains behaviour quite well. But the self-interest assumption is not applicable to many forms of group behaviour. We care about others as well as ourselves, and we also care about what others think of us. This often affects our behaviour, altering it from what a purely selfish individual would do.[14]

Conclusion

The demand curves for most products have negative slopes. Knowledge of the precise nature of the demand curve for a product is obviously important for firms who want to be able to predict the likely quantity demanded at various prices. An understanding of demand is also important for policy-makers who wish to impose taxes, intervene in markets in other ways, or predict the effects of sudden shortages of such things as food or energy. For economists, an understanding of demand is one important step along the road to understanding the detailed workings of a market economy.

---

[14] For a fascinating discussion of the wider implications of altruistic behaviour, see Nigel Barber, *Kindness in a Cruel World: The Evolution of Altruism*, New York: Prometheus Books, 2004.

SUMMARY

Early insights

■ Consumers maximize their utility where the ratio of marginal utility to price is equal for all products.

■ The paradox of value can be resolved when it is realized that consumers relate their marginal utilities not their total utilities to market prices.

Consumer optimization without measurable utility

■ Indifference theory assumes only that individuals can order alternative consumption bundles, saying which bundles are preferred to which but not by how much.

■ A single indifference curve shows combinations of products that give the consumer equal satisfaction and among which he or she is therefore indifferent. An indifference map is a set of indifference curves.

■ The basic assumption about tastes in indifference curve theory is that of a diminishing marginal rate of substitution: the less of one good and the more of another good the consumer has, the less willing he or she will be to give up some of the first good to get more of the second. This implies that indifference curves are negatively sloped and convex to the origin.

■ While indifference curves describe the consumer's tastes and therefore refer to what he or she *would like* to purchase, the budget line describes what the consumer *can* purchase.

■ Each maximizing consumer achieves an equilibrium at the point at which an indifference curve is tangent to his or her budget line.

How the consumer responds to changes

■ The income–consumption line shows how quantity consumed changes as income changes with relative prices constant.

■ The price–consumption line shows how quantity consumed changes as relative prices change. The consumer will normally consume more of the product whose relative price falls.

■ The price–consumption line, relating the purchases of one particular product to all other products, contains the same information as an ordinary demand curve. The horizontal axis measures quantity, and the slope of the budget line measures price. Transferring this information to a diagram whose axes represent price and quantity leads to a conventional demand curve.

The consumer's demand curve

■ A change in price of one product, all other prices and money income constant, changes both relative price and the real incomes of those who consume it. The effect of changes on consumption is measured by the substitution effect and the income effect.

■ Demand curves for normal goods have negative slopes because both income and substitution effects work in the same direction, with a decrease in price leading to increased consumption.

■ A decrease in price of an inferior good leads to more consumption via the substitution effect and less consumption via the income effect. In the exceptional case of a Giffen good, the income effect more than offsets the substitution effect, causing the product's demand curve to have a positive slope.

TOPICS FOR REVIEW

■ Marginal and total utility

■ The paradox of value

■ An indifference curve and an indifference map

■ Slope of an indifference curve and diminishing marginal rate of substitution

■ Budget line

■ Absolute and relative prices, and the slope of the budget line

■ Response of a consumer to changes in income and prices

■ Derivation of the demand curve from indifference curves

■ Income and substitution effects

■ Hicks and Slutsky decomposition

■ Normal goods, inferior goods, and Giffen goods

■ Equivalent and compensating variations of income.

QUESTIONS

1 Suppose that a consumer's disposable income is £200 per week and she has a choice between spending this on meals or on concerts. Concerts are £10 each and meals are £20 each. List the possible combinations of meals and concerts that could be bought with the income.

2 Using the same information as in question 1, the price of meals now falls to £10. What combinations of meals and concerts can now be purchased with the same income?

3 Assuming that (facing the prices in question 1) the consumer chose to consume 10 concerts and 5 meals per week, what change in income would leave the consumer still just able to consume this same combination of meals and concerts while facing the prices set in question 2? Would you expect this consumer to purchase the same combination of meals and concerts as before, if faced by the new prices but with this lower amount of income?

4 Which of the following statements is true (there may be more than one or none)? If the price of good X rises holding all other prices and income constant:

a) The substitution effect alone will make a consumer buy more of X if X is inferior.

b) The income effect alone will make a consumer buy more of X if it is a normal good.

c) The income effect alone will make a consumer buy less of X if it is an inferior good.

d) The substitution effect will make a consumer buy less of X and it is irrelevant whether X is a normal or inferior good.

e) The consumer will buy less of good X unless it is an inferior good, in which case she would always buy more.

5 Which one of the following correctly describes the relationship between the income effect and the substitution effect on demand for a normal good whose price has risen (assuming that consumers have a fixed income and constant preferences)?

a) A rise in the price of the product leads to a fall in quantity demanded through the substitution effect and it is a normal good so the income effect also leads to lower demand.

b) A rise in the price of the product leads to a fall in quantity demanded through the substitution effect and it is a normal good so the income effect increases demand and the overall effect on demand is ambiguous.

c) A rise in the price of the product leads to rise in quantity demanded through the substitution effect and the income effect also leads to an increased demand.

d) A rise in the price of the product leads to a fall in quantity demanded through the substitution effect. The income effect leads to an increase in demand, which is smaller than the substitution effect so demand still falls.

e) A rise in the price of the product leads to a fall in quantity demanded through the substitution effect and it is a normal good so the income effect leads to higher demand and this outweighs the substitution effect.

6 A positively sloped demand curve can only arise in which one of the following circumstances:

a) A rise in the price of the product leads to a fall in quantity demanded through the substitution effect and it is a normal good so the income effect also leads to lower demand.

b) A rise in the price of the product leads to a fall in quantity demanded through the substitution effect and it is a luxury good so the income effect is very strong.

c) A rise in the price of the product leads to a fall in quantity demanded through the substitution effect. The product is an inferior good and the income effect leads to an increased demand but the income effect is smaller than the substitution effect.

d) A rise in the price of the product leads to a fall in quantity demanded through the substitution effect. The product is an inferior good, and the income effect leads to an increase in demand, which is bigger than the substitution effect.

e) A fall in the price of the product leads to a fall in quantity demanded through the substitution effect and it is a normal good so the income effect also leads to lower demand.

7 Explain the difference between the income effect and substitution effect of a price change.

8 What is a Giffen good? Explain using indifference curves how it could arise.

9 'Indifference curve analysis is not much use because it only tells us that demand curves slope down except when they don't.' Discuss.

10 A company that normally pays its workers £400 per week in money, decides to pay them instead with £400 worth of a specific good. Assume that there is no second-hand market in these goods, so they cannot be sold for cash, but also assume that the workers would have chosen to consume some of these goods anyway. Using budget constraints and indifference curves, analyse whether the workers are likely to be just as happy with this arrangement as they were when they received their wages in money.

PART **TWO**

MARKETS AND FIRMS

CHAPTER 5

THE COST STRUCTURE OF FIRMS

In the previous two chapters we looked closely at the determinants of demand, and saw how interaction of demand and supply affects the market price. We now start the task of understanding the influences on supply in more detail. The most important suppliers in the economy are firms, and we concentrate on them in this chapter.[1] In the following three chapters we shall see that firms' options are affected by the market structure in which they operate. They also have to make supply decisions in the light of their costs of production. In this chapter we focus on the structure of costs, before analysing firms' profit-maximizing behaviour in subsequent chapters.

In particular, you will learn that:

- The production function relates physical quantities of inputs to the quantity of output.
- Cost curves show the money cost of producing various levels of output.
- In the short run some inputs are fixed while in the long run all inputs can be varied.
- When a firm has a fixed input, all of which must be used all of the time, we say the use of that input is indivisible. The resulting short-run average variable cost curve is U-shaped because when some inputs are held constant the law of diminishing returns applies to those that are allowed to vary.
- When a firm has a fixed input, some of which can be left idle, we say that the use of that input is divisible. The resulting short-run average variable cost curve is horizontal up to capacity output.
- The long-run cost curve can take on various shapes depending on the scale effects when all inputs are allowed to vary at once.
- Costs in the very long run are altered by technical change.
- There is a difference between economists' measure of profit and accountants' measure of profit.
- For economists, profit is the difference between total cost and total revenue, where total cost includes the opportunity cost of owners' capital.

We first explain what we mean by a firm and what we assume about firms' goals. Then, in order to identify the most profitable level of production for a firm, we need to see how its costs vary with its output. This we do in three sections of this chapter. The first of these deals with the short run, when a firm can vary only some of its inputs and output is governed by the famous 'law of diminishing returns'. The next part deals with the long run, when the firm can alter all of its inputs. Here, we pay special attention to scale economies, where increases in total output lead to reductions in the cost of producing each unit of output. Then, we discuss how firms alter their production capabilities by research and development, in response to such economic signals as rising costs of particular inputs. Finally, we discuss an important issue relating to measurement of profit.

[1] Government agencies and enterprises, and not-for-profit organizations, also supply goods and services but in this chapter we concentrate on the most important suppliers, profit-seeking firms.

Costs, revenues, and profit maximization

The firm is the most important agent in the economy that makes decisions about production of the specific goods or services in which it specializes.

Firms in theory

In Chapter 2 we defined the firm as the unit that takes decisions with respect to the production and sale of goods and services. This theoretical concept of the firm includes all types of business organization. It also covers the whole variety of business sizes and methods of financing, from the single inventor operating in his garage and financed by whatever he can extract from a reluctant bank manager, to vast undertakings with many thousands of shareholders and customers.

To theorize about the firm we make two key assumptions.[2] First, all firms are profit maximizers, seeking to make as much profit for their owners as is possible. Secondly, each firm can be regarded as a single consistent decision-taking unit.

The desire to maximize profits is assumed to motivate all decisions taken within a firm, and such decisions are assumed to be unaffected by the peculiarities of the people taking the decisions and by the organizational structure in which they work.

These assumptions allow us to ignore the firm's internal organization and its financial structure. They also allow us to derive predictions about the behaviour of firms. To do this, we first study the choices open to the firm, establishing the effect that each choice would have on the firm's profits. We then predict that the firm will select the alternative that produces the largest profit.

We must now define a little more precisely the concepts of production and profit maximization that we need for our analysis of the firm.

Production

In order to produce the goods or services that it sells, each firm needs inputs. Hundreds of inputs enter into the production of any specific output. Among the many inputs entering into car production, for example, are sheet steel, rubber, spark plugs, electricity, the work space of the factory, machinists, cost accountants, spray-painting machines, forklift trucks, painters, and managers. These inputs can be grouped into four broad classes: (1) inputs to the car firm that are outputs of some other firm, such as spark plugs, electricity, and sheet steel; (2) inputs provided directly by nature, such as land and air; (3) efforts of people, such as the services of workers and managers; (4) the use of plant and machines.

The items that make up the first class of inputs, goods and services produced by other firms, are called **intermediate products**. These appear as inputs only because different firms are involved at different stages of production. For example, one firm mines iron ore and sells it to a steel manufacturer. Iron ore is an intermediate product—an output of the mining firm and an input for the steel plant. The output of the steel maker is then an input for the car manufacturer. Box 5.1 contains an example of the range of components that make up an airliner.

If all the production of each product was done by a single firm, there would be no intermediate inputs. In this case, or if we merely view the chain of each good's production as a whole, all production can be accounted for by the services listed as items (2)–(4) earlier in this section. These were first discussed in Chapter 1, as the gifts of nature, such as soil and raw materials, called *land* (item 2), physical and mental efforts provided by people, called *labour* (item 3), and the services of factories, machines, and other man-made aids to production, called *capital* (item 4). These are traditionally called *factors of production*, though we mainly refer to them more simply as *inputs*.

The **production function** relates inputs to outputs. It describes the technological relation between the inputs that a firm uses and the output that it produces. A production function is written as

$$q = \psi(f_1, ..., f_m) \tag{5.1}$$

where q is the quantity of output of some good or service and $f_1, ..., f_m$ are the quantities of m different inputs used in its production, with everything being expressed as rates per period of time. The Greek letter ψ tells us that q is a function of the fs; that is, the fs determine q.

When using the production function, remember that it relates flows of inputs to flows of outputs: so many units *per period of time*. For example, if it is said that production rises from 100 to 101 units, this does not mean that 100 units are produced this month and 1 unit next month. Rather it means that the rate of production has risen from 100 units *each month* to 101 units *each month*.

Profit-maximizing output

To develop a theory of supply, we need to determine the level of output that will maximize a firm's profit, to which

---

[2] The approach is known as the *neoclassical theory* of the firm.

Box 5.1 Dreaming of nuts and bolts

In 2011 the Boeing 787 Deamliner entered service three years later than was originally planned. There were several problems encountered in developing this new plane. The body of the aircraft was designed to be made of new carbon-fibre composite materials that would be more fuel efficient. The 787 would be lighter than the previous generation of planes but at least as strong. In order to achieve this innovative specification, the work was farmed out to many different companies around the world. This led to many coordination problems that contributed to delays.

The most surprising problem encountered was a shortage of nuts and bolts. Previous designs of planes had involved around 50,000 fasteners within each plane and there was no difficulty in getting those manufactured at low unit cost.

However, the Dreamliner only needed small numbers of non-standard fastenings. Potential suppliers set very high prices for these as they could not reap any cost reductions from large-scale production. Complicated lathes had to be set up and this made the cost very high. Indeed, the potential production runs were so small that few suppliers would tender for the work.

Even after the 787 went into service it continued to have technical problems. One was fires caused by faulty batteries; another was when some body panels fell off in flight.

Teething problems linked to using highly innovative technologies are not unusual, but it is a surprise that even the basic nuts and bolts caused production difficulties.

---

we give the symbol π (the lower-case Greek letter pi). This is the difference between the revenue, R, that each firm derives from the sale of its output and the cost, C, of producing that output:

$$\pi = R - C.$$

Thus, what happens to profit as output varies depends on what happens to revenue and costs. In the rest of this chapter we analyse how input costs vary with output. This analysis is common to all firms, irrespective of the market structure in which they operate. In the chapters that follow we consider how revenue varies with output. Costs and revenues are then combined to determine the profit-maximizing equilibrium for firms in various market situations. The resulting theory can then be used to predict the outcome of changes in such things as demand, costs, taxes, and subsidies. This may seem like quite a long route to get to a theory of supply, *and it is*, but the pay-off when you get there is in being able to understand a big part of the working of a market economy.

We start with inputs. Suppose that a firm wishes to increase its rate of output. To do so, it must increase the use of at least some of its inputs. For the rest of this chapter, we consider a very simple example relating to the production of some manufactured product. However, the approach is the same for any product. Even in service industries, for example, there will be various inputs that are combined to produce the output. A haircut requires the labour of a hairdresser (or barber) plus the services of a chair, shop space, scissors, dryers, basins, mirrors, electricity, hair spray, etc. Virtually any business you can think of involves the combination of human effort (labour), some equipment or tools (capital), and some materials (intermediate inputs).

To keep things as simple as possible, we analyse a hypothetical firm which has only two inputs. The first is labour, to which we give the symbol L. The second is capital, to which we give the symbol K. This means that we are ignoring land and all intermediate inputs[3] and dealing with the simplified version of the production function introduced earlier in this chapter:

$$q = \psi(L, K) \tag{5.2}$$

where q is quantity of output per period of time, L is labour employed in production (measured as worker hours per period—ten men working an eight-hour day is eighty worker hours per day), and K is units of capital services used (measured as machine-hours per period). The Greek letter ψ again stands for the relationship that links the inputs to the outputs; here it links K and L to q.

A firm cannot vary all of its inputs with equal speed. It can usually vary labour at short notice, but time is needed to install more machinery or buildings. To capture the fact that different inputs cannot be varied with the same ease, we abstract from the more complicated nature of real decisions and think of each firm as making three distinct types of decision. These are (1) how best to employ its existing plant and equipment, (2) what new plant, equipment, and production processes to select using currently available technology, and (3) what to do about encouraging the development of new technology. The first set of decisions is said to be made over the *short run*, the second over the *long run*, and the third over the *very long run*.

---

[3] Nothing is lost by this simplification, as it is easy to generalize our results to the case of multiple inputs at a later stage.

Costs in the short run when the fixed input is indivisible

The **short run** is defined as the period of time over which some inputs, sometimes called **fixed factors** or *fixed inputs*, are fixed in quantity.[4] The input that is fixed in the short run is usually capital (such as plant and equipment). The inputs that can be varied in the short run are called *variable inputs*, or **variable factors**. What matters for the analysis is that at least one significant input is fixed in quantity—it cannot be increased. We can gain much understanding of how costs vary in the short run if we start with the strong assumption that all of the fixed input must be used all of the time. In this case, we say that the use of the fixed input is *indivisible*, and for simplicity we just refer to the 'indivisible fixed input'. Later we will consider what changes are needed when some of the fixed input can be left idle or unused in the short run. Here we say that the use of the fixed input is *divisible*, and for simplicity we just refer to the 'divisible fixed input'. The short run is not of the same real-time duration in all industries. In the electric power industry, for example, it takes three or more years to build new power stations, so an unforeseen increase in demand must be served as well as possible with the existing capital equipment for several years. At the other end of the scale, a machine shop can acquire new equipment in a few weeks, and thus the short run is correspondingly short. The length of the short run is influenced by technological considerations such as how quickly equipment can be manufactured and installed. These things may also be influenced to some extent by the price the firm is willing to pay to increase its capacity quickly.

Short-run variations in input

In the short run we are concerned with what happens to output and costs as more, or less, of the variable input is set to work with a given quantity of the fixed input. In the simplified production function given above, we assume that capital is fixed and labour is variable. Our firm starts with a fixed amount of capital equipment. It then contemplates using various amounts of labour to work with it. Table 5.1 shows three different ways of looking at how output varies with the quantity of the variable input. We now need to define some terms.

---

[4] 'Factors' in this context refers to *factors of production* which are the resource inputs of the economy, such as land, labour, and capital, not the common usage of the term to mean items of influence. As noted above, we shall mostly refer to factors of production as 'inputs', as this is a more familiar terminology for most readers.

Table 5.1 Total, average, and marginal products in the short run

Quantity of labour (L) (1)	Total product (TP) (2)	Average product (AP) (3)	Marginal product (MP) (4)
1	43	43	43
2	160	80	117
3	351	117	191
4	600	150	249
5	875	175	275
6	1,152	192	277
7	1,372	196	220
8	1,536	192	164
9	1,656	184	120
10	1,750	175	94
11	1,815	165	65
12	1,860	155	45

The relation of output to changes in the quantity of the variable input can be looked at in three different ways. Capital is assumed to be fixed at 10 units. As the quantity of labour increases, the rate of total output increases, as shown in column (2). The average product in column (3) is found by dividing the total product in column (2) by the labour requirement shown in the corresponding row of column (1). The marginal product is positioned between the rows because it refers to the change in output from one level of labour input to another.

Total product (TP) means just what it says: the total amount produced during some period of time by all the inputs that the firm is using at that time. If all but one of the inputs is held constant, the total product will change as the variable input is changed. This variation is illustrated in column (2) of Table 5.1, which gives a total product schedule. Figure 5.1(i) shows such a schedule graphically. (The shape of the curve will be discussed shortly.)

Average product (AP) is the total product *per unit* of the variable input, which is labour in the present illustration:

$$AP = TP/L.$$

Average product is shown in column (3) of Table 5.1. Notice that as more of the variable input is used, average product first rises and then falls. We argue below that this is one likely pattern, but other patterns are possible. The point where average product reaches a maximum is called the *point of diminishing average returns*. In the table,

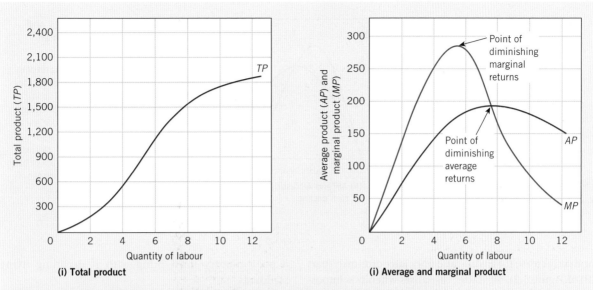

Figure 5.1 Total, average, and marginal product curves with an indivisible fixed input

Total product (*TP*), average product (*AP*), and marginal product (*MP*) curves often have these shapes. The curves are plotted from the data in Table 5.1. In part (i) the *TP* curve shows the total product steadily rising, first at an increasing rate and then at a decreasing rate. This causes both the average and the marginal product curves in part (ii) to rise at first and then decline. Where *AP* reaches its maximum, *MP* = *AP*.

average product reaches a maximum when 7 units of labour are employed.

Marginal product (*MP*) is the change in total product resulting from the use of one more (or one less) unit of the variable input:[5]

$$MP = \Delta TP/\Delta L$$

where ΔTP stands for the change in the total product and ΔL stands for the change in labour input that caused TP to change.

Computed values of the marginal product appear in column (4) of Table 5.1. Marginal product in the example reaches a maximum between $L = 5$ and $L = 6$ and thereafter declines. The level of output where marginal product reaches a maximum is called the *point of diminishing marginal returns*.

Figure 5.1(ii) shows the average and marginal product curves plotted from the data in Table 5.1. Notice, first, that *MP* reaches its maximum at a lower level of L

than does *AP*, and, secondly, that $MP = AP$ when AP is a maximum. These relations are discussed in more detail below.

Finally, bear in mind that the schedules of Table 5.1, and the curves of Figure 5.1, all assume a specified quantity of the fixed input that is fully used at all times. If the quantity of capital had been, say, 14 units instead of the 10 that were assumed, there would be a different set of total, average, and marginal product curves. The reason is that if any specified amount of labour has more capital to work with, it can produce more output. Its total, average, and marginal products will be greater.

The law of diminishing returns

We now consider the variations in output that result from applying different amounts of a variable input to a given quantity of a fixed input. These variations are the subject of a famous hypothesis called the **law of diminishing returns**.

The law of diminishing returns states that if increasing quantities of a variable input are applied to a given quantity of a fixed input, the marginal product and the average product of the variable input will eventually decrease.

The law of diminishing returns is consistent with marginal and average product curves that decline over the whole range of output (as illustrated in part (i) Figure 5.2),

----

[5] Strictly speaking, the text defines what is called 'incremental product'—that is, the rate of change of output associated with a discrete change in an input. Marginal product refers to the rate at which output is tending to vary as input varies at a particular output. Students familiar with calculus will recognize the marginal product as the partial derivative of the total product with respect to the variable input. In symbols, $MP = \partial q/\partial L$. In the text we refer only to finite changes ΔL and ΔTP, but the phrase 'a change of one unit' should read 'a very small change'.

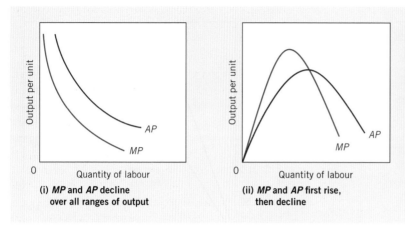

Figure 5.2 Alternative average and marginal product curves with an indivisible fixed input

According to the law of diminishing returns, average and marginal product must eventually decline as output increases. The law of diminishing returns permits the average and marginal product curves to decline at all positive levels of output, as shown in part (i). The law also allows the average and marginal products to rise over an initial range of output and then decline, as shown in part (ii).

or that increase for a while and only later diminish (part (ii) of Figure 5.2). The latter case arises when it is impossible to use the fixed input efficiently with only a small quantity of the variable input (if, say, one man was trying to farm 1,000 acres). In this case increasing the quantity of the variable input makes possible more efficient division of labour, so that the addition of another unit of the variable input would make all units more productive than they were previously. According to the hypothesis of diminishing returns, the scope for such economies must eventually disappear, and sooner or later the marginal and average products of additional workers must decline.

Notice that when various amounts of labour are applied to a fixed quantity of capital, the proportion in which the two types of input are used is being varied.

The law of diminishing returns is also called the 'law of variable proportions', because it predicts the consequences of varying the proportions in which input types are used.

The common sense of diminishing marginal product is that the fixed input limits the amount of additional output that can be obtained by adding more of the variable input. Were it not for the law of diminishing returns, there would be no need to fear that rapid population growth will cause food shortages in poorer countries. If the marginal product of additional workers who were employed on a fixed quantity of land was constant, then a country's food production could be expanded in proportion to the increase in population merely by keeping the same proportion of the population on farms. As it is, diminishing returns means an inexorable decline in the marginal product of each additional labourer as an expanding population is applied, with static techniques, to a fixed supply of agricultural land. Thus, unless there is a continual improvement in the techniques of production, a population increase among subsistence farmers in

a poor country must bring with it declining living standards.[6]

The relation between marginal and average product curves

Notice that in Figure 5.2(ii) the *MP* curve cuts the *AP* curve at the latter's maximum point. It is important to understand why. The key is that the average product curve slopes upward as long as the marginal product curve is above it; it makes no difference whether the marginal curve is itself sloping upwards or downwards. The common sense of this relation is that if an additional worker is to raise the average product of all workers, the worker's addition to total output must be greater than the average output of all existing workers. It is immaterial whether his contribution to output is greater or less than the contribution of the worker hired immediately before him; all that matters is that his contribution to output exceeds the average output of *all* the workers hired before him. Since *AP* slopes upwards or downwards depending on whether *MP* is above or below *AP*, it follows that *MP* must equal *AP* at the highest point on the *AP* curve.

This relationship between marginal and average values is a mathematical one that is thus not restricted to economics. A cricketer, for example, will raise his batting average if his next score is above his current average, and he will lower his average if his next score is below the current average.

---

[6] This has not happened everywhere in the world because rapid technological advances have increased productivity in agriculture faster than the increase in population. However, in many poorer countries farmers subsist mainly on what they themselves grow, and they use relatively static techniques. For them, rising population in combination with the law of diminishing returns means declining output per person and hence declining living standards.

Short-run variations in cost

We have now seen how output varies with changes in just one of the inputs in the short run with a fixed amount of the other being used. By costing these inputs, we can discover how the cost of production changes as output varies. For the time being we consider firms that are not in a position to influence the prices of their inputs, so they take the prices of these inputs as given.

We now define cost concepts that are closely related to the product concepts introduced earlier.

Total cost (*TC*) means just what it says. It is the total cost of producing any given rate of output. Total cost is divided into two parts: total fixed costs (*TFC*) and total variable costs (*TVC*). **Fixed costs** are those costs that do not vary with output; they will be the same if output is one unit or one million units. These costs are also often referred to as *overhead costs* or *unavoidable costs*. All of those costs that vary positively with output, rising as more is produced and falling as less is produced, are called **variable costs**. In our present example, since labour is the variable input, the cost of labour would be a variable cost. Variable costs are often referred to as *direct costs* or *avoidable costs*. The latter term is used because the costs can be avoided by not hiring any of the variable input.

Average total cost (*ATC*) is the total cost of producing any given output divided by the number of units produced—that is, the cost per unit. *ATC* may be divided into **average fixed costs** (*AFC*) and **average variable costs** (*AVC*) in just the same way as total costs were divided.

Marginal cost (*MC*) is the increase in total cost resulting from raising the rate of production by one unit. The marginal cost of the tenth unit, for example, is the change in total cost when the rate of production is increased from nine to ten units per period.

These three measures of cost are merely different ways of looking at a single phenomenon, and they are mathematically interrelated.[7] Which we use depends on the task in hand.

Short-run cost curves

The relationships just outlined are most easily understood if we show them as cost curves. To illustrate how this is done, we take the production relationships in Table 5.1 and assume that the price of labour is £20 per unit (worker hours) and the price of capital is £10 per unit (machine hours). In Table 5.2 we present the cost schedules computed for these values. Figure 5.3(i) shows the total cost curves; Figure 5.3(ii) plots the marginal and average cost curves that are derived in Table 5.2.[8]

How cost varies with output

Since total fixed cost (*TFC*) does not vary with output, average fixed cost (*TFC/q*) is negatively related to output, while marginal fixed cost is zero. In contrast, variable cost is positively related to output, since to produce more requires more of the variable input. However, average variable cost may be negatively or positively related to output. Marginal variable cost is always positive, indicating that it always costs something to increase output, but, as we will soon see, marginal cost may rise or fall as output rises.

Notice that the marginal cost curve cuts the *ATC* and *AVC* curves at their lowest points. This is another example of the relation (discussed above) between a marginal and an average value. For example, the *ATC* curve slopes downwards as long as the marginal cost curve is below it; it makes no difference whether the marginal cost curve itself is sloping upwards or downwards.

In Figure 5.3 the average variable cost curve reaches a minimum and then rises. With fixed input prices, when average product per worker is at a maximum, average variable cost is at a minimum. The common sense is that each new worker adds the same amount to cost but a different amount to output, and when output per worker is rising the cost per unit of output must be falling, and vice versa.

Short-run *AVC* curves are often drawn U-shaped. This reflects the assumptions (1) that average productivity is increasing when output is low, but (2) that average productivity eventually begins to fall fast enough to cause average variable cost to increase.

The law of diminishing returns implies eventually increasing marginal and average variable cost.

The definition of capacity

The output that corresponds to the minimum short-run average total cost is very often called **capacity**. Capacity in this sense is not an upper limit on what can be produced, as you can see by looking again at Table 5.2. In the example, capacity output is between 1,536 and 1,656 units, but higher outputs can be achieved. A firm producing *below capacity* is producing at a rate of output less than the one for which average total cost is a minimum. A firm producing *above capacity* is producing more than this amount. Thus it is incurring costs per unit of output that are higher than the minimum achievable.

---

[7] Mathematically, average total cost is total cost divided by output while marginal cost is the first derivative of total cost with respect to output.

[8] The calculation here involves discrete changes, while calculating marginal values requires very small changes. Thus, we are producing an approximation calculated over a specific range to the true marginal value which is calculated at a single point.

Table 5.2 Variation of costs with capital fixed and labour variable

Inputs		Output (q) (3)	Total cost			Average cost			Marginal cost (MC)[d] (10)
Capital (1)	Labour (L) (2)		Fixed (TFC) (4)	Variable (TVC) (5)	Total (TC) (6)	Fixed (AFC)[a] (7)	Variable (AVC)[b] (8)	Total (ATC)[c] (9)	
10	1	43	£100	£20	£120	£2.326	£0.465	£2.791	£0.465
10	2	160	100	40	140	0.625	0.250	0.875	0.171
10	3	351	100	60	160	0.285	0.171	0.456	0.105
10	4	600	100	80	180	0.167	0.133	0.300	0.080
10	5	875	100	100	200	0.114	0.114	0.228	0.073
10	6	1,152	100	120	220	0.087	0.104	0.191	0.072
10	7	1,372	100	140	240	0.073	0.102	0.175	0.091
10	8	1,536	100	160	260	0.065	0.104	0.169	0.122
10	9	1,656	100	180	280	0.060	0.109	0.169	0.167
10	10	1,750	100	200	300	0.057	0.114	0.171	0.213
10	11	1,815	100	220	320	0.055	0.121	0.176	0.308
10	12	1,860	100	240	340	0.054	0.129	0.183	0.444

The relation of cost to the rate of output can be looked at in several different ways. These cost schedules are computed from the product curves of Table 5.1, given the price of capital of £10 per unit and the price of labour of £20 per unit. Marginal cost (in column (10)) is positioned between the other rows because it refers to the *change* in cost divided by the *change* in output that brought it about. Marginal cost is calculated by dividing the increase in costs by the increase in output when one additional unit of labour is used. This gives the increase in cost per unit of output over that range of output. For example, the *MC* of £0.08 is the increase in total cost of £20 (from £160 to £180) divided by the 249 unit increase in output (from 351 to 600). This tells us that when output goes from 351 to 600 (because labour inputs go from 3 to 4), the increase in costs is £0.08 per unit of output. In constructing a graph, marginal costs should be plotted midway in the interval over which they are computed. The *MC* of £0.08 would thus be plotted at output 475.5.

[a] Col. (4) ÷ col. (3).   [c] Col. (6) ÷ col. (3) = col. (7) + col. (8).
[b] Col. (5) ÷ col. (3).   [d] Change in col. (5) from one row to the next ÷ corresponding change in col. (3).

A family of short-run cost curves

A short-run cost curve shows how costs vary with output for a given quantity of the fixed input—say a given size of fully used plant. A small plant for manufacturing nuts and bolts will have its own short-run cost curve. A medium-sized and a very large plant will each have their own short-run cost curves. If a firm expands by replacing its small plant with a medium-sized plant, it will move from one short-run cost curve to another.

There is a different short-run cost curve for each quantity of the fixed input.

We now discuss the shape of short-run cost curves when firms can operate with some capital idle, a situation that many firms find themselves in much of the time.

Costs in the short run when the fixed input is divisible

Ever since economists began measuring the cost curves of manufacturing firms many years ago, they have reported constant short-run marginal and average variable costs up to capacity output for many manufacturing firms. The evidence is now clear that in most manufacturing, and in many service industries, cost curves are shaped like the average and marginal cost curves shown in Figure 5.4, with a long flat portion and a rising section only after capacity output has been achieved. For such a cost curve, there is a large range of output over which marginal and average variable costs are constant and equal to each other.

Why are many cost curves saucer-shaped like this rather than being U-shaped? The U-shape of the short-run cost curve that we have developed earlier is predicted by the

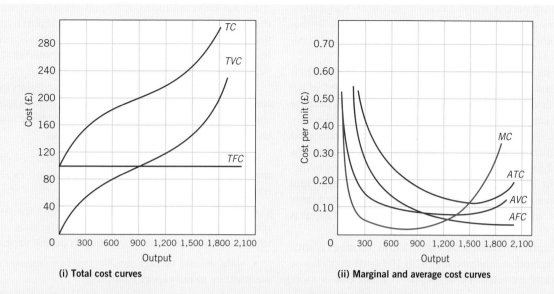

(i) Total cost curves **(ii) Marginal and average cost curves**

Figure 5.3 Total cost, average cost, and marginal cost curves with an indivisible fixed input

Total cost (*TC*), average cost (*AC*), and marginal cost (*MC*) curves often have the shapes shown here. These curves are plotted from Table 5.2. Total fixed cost does not vary with output. Total variable cost and the total of all costs (*TC* = *TVC* + *TFC*) rise with output, first at a decreasing rate and then at an increasing rate. The total cost curves in (i) give rise to the average and marginal curves in (ii). Average fixed cost (*AFC*) declines as output increases. Average variable cost (*AVC*) and average total cost (*ATC*) fall and then rise as output increases. Marginal cost (*MC*) does the same, intersecting the *ATC* and *AVC* curves at their minimum points. Capacity output is at the minimum point of the *ATC* curve, which is an output of 1,500 in this example.

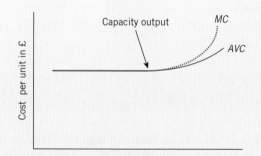

Figure 5.4 Short-run cost curves when the fixed input is divisible

When the fixed input is divisible marginal and average costs are constant up to full capacity output. When the fixed input is divisible, the ratio of fixed to variable input can be held constant up to full capacity output. Thus the short-run marginal and average variable costs do not vary with output as shown by the horizontal portion of the curves in the figure. Once full capacity output is reached, the fixed input is fully employed and further increases in output cause marginal and average variable costs to rise as more of the variable input is applied to the maximum available amount of the fixed input.

law of diminishing returns whenever a variable amount of one input, say labour, is applied to a fixed amount of a second input, say capital. However, this is not what happens when many firms vary their outputs in the short run. Even though the firm's plant and equipment are fixed in the short run so that *no more* than what exists is available, it is usually possible to use less than this amount. In this case, we say that the fixed input is divisible

Consider, as a simple example, a factory that consists of ten sewing machines in a shed, each of which has a productive capacity of twenty units per day when operated by one operator for one shift. If 200 units per day are required, all ten machines would be operated by ten workers on a normal shift. If demand falls to 180, one operator could be laid off. However, there is no need to have the nine remaining operators dashing about trying to work ten machines. Clearly, one machine could be 'laid off' as well, leaving constant the ratio of *employed* labour to *employed* machines.

Production could go from twenty all the way to 200 units per day without any change in the proportions in which the employed inputs are used. In this case, we would expect the factory to have constant marginal and average variable costs from twenty to 200 units per day. Only beyond

200 units per day would it begin to encounter rising costs, because production would have to be extended by overtime and other means of combining more labour with the maximum available supply of ten machines.

In such a case, the fixed input is *divisible*. There is then no need to depart from the most efficient ratio of *labour used* to *capital used* as production is decreased because some capital can be left unemployed as fewer workers are hired. The *divisibility* of the fixed input means that diminishing returns does not apply, because variations in output below full capacity are accomplished by reducing the input of both labour and capital. Both marginal and average variable costs are then constant over a large range, up to the point at which all of the fixed input is used.[9]

A similar situation occurs when a firm has many plants. For example, a manufacturer with 10 plants may choose to reduce its output by temporarily closing one or more plants while operating the rest at normal capacity output. Another firm can choose to put its factory on short time, working six hours a day or four days a week, thus reducing its use of both capital and labour. In such cases the *firm's* short-run variable costs tend to be constant over a large range of output because there is no need to depart from the optimal combination of labour and capital in the plants that are kept in operation.

----

[9] Let K stand for the amount of capital used by the firm and K_0 for the fixed amount available in the short run. In the case of indivisible capital considered earlier, the constraint governing the use of capital is $K = K_0$, while in the present case of divisible capital the constraint is $K \leq K_0$.

Similar cost conditions occur in some modern service industries in which there are no significant inputs that are fixed in the short run. In these cases their capital consists mainly of rented accommodation and computers that can be bought off the shelf at a moment's notice.

We can now briefly consider how the main points made earlier for the case of an indivisible fixed input apply to the present case of a divisible fixed input. We consider each of the headings of the previous section.

- Short-run variations in output encounter constant marginal and average variable costs up to full capacity output.

- This is because up to full capacity output the law of diminishing returns does not apply as the uses of all inputs are varied in equal proportion as output varies.

- Marginal and average variable costs are constant and identical up to full capacity output.

- Thus, as shown in Figure 5.4, the marginal and average cost curves of firms in this situation are horizontal up to capacity but then rise, just like those for firms with an indivisible fixed input.

- Capacity occurs at the point at which the fixed input is fully employed and beyond which the short-run marginal and average variable cost curves take on a positive slope.

- There is a family of short-run cost curves, just as there is for firms with an indivisible fixed input, only the shape of each curve is different with a horizontal portion instead of a negatively sloped portion below full capacity output.

Costs in the long run

In the short run, with only one input variable and an indivisible fixed input, there is only one way to produce a given output—adjusting the use of the variable input. Thus, once the firm has decided on a rate of output, there is only one technically possible way of achieving it.

In contrast, in the long run all inputs can be varied. The firm must decide on both a level of output *and* the best input mix to produce that output. Specifically, this means that firms in the long run must choose the nature and amount of plant and equipment, as well as the size of their labour force.

Long-run decisions are risky because the firm must anticipate what methods of production will be efficient, not only today, but also for many years in the future when the costs of labour and raw materials will no doubt

have changed. The decisions are also risky because the firm must estimate how much output it will want to produce. Is the industry to which it belongs growing or declining? Will new products emerge to render its existing products less useful than an extrapolation of past sales suggests?

Profit maximization and cost minimization

In making this choice, the profit-maximizing firm will wish to avoid being technically inefficient, which means using more of *all* inputs than is necessary. Being technically efficient is not enough, however. To be economically efficient, the firm must choose, from among the many technically efficient options, the one that produces a given level of output at the lowest possible cost. This implication of the hypothesis of profit maximization is called **cost minimization**: from the alternatives open to it, the profit-maximizing firm will choose the least costly way of producing whatever specific output it chooses.

Choice of input mix

If it is possible to substitute one input for another in such a way that output remains constant while total cost falls, the firm is not using the least-cost combination of inputs. The firm should then substitute one input for another input. Such cost-reducing substitutions are always possible whenever the marginal product of one input per £1 spent on it is greater than the marginal product of the other input per £1 spent on it. The firm has not minimized its costs as long as these two magnitudes are unequal. For example, if an extra £1 spent on labour adds more to output than an extra £1 spent on capital, the firm can reduce costs by spending less on capital and more on labour.

If we use K to represent capital, L to represent labour, and P_K and P_L to represent the prices of a unit of each, the necessary condition for cost minimization is as follows:

$$MP_K/P_K = MP_L/P_L. \qquad (5.3)$$

Whenever the two sides of eqn (5.3) are unequal, there are possibilities for input substitutions that will reduce costs.

To see why this equation must be satisfied if costs of production are to be minimized, consider a situation where the equation is not satisfied. Suppose, for example, that the marginal product of capital is 20 and its price is £2, making the left-hand side of eqn (5.3) equal to 10. Suppose that the marginal product of labour is 32 and its price is £8, making the right-hand side of eqn (5.3) equal to 4. Thus, the last £1 spent on capital adds 10 units to output, whereas the last £1 spent on labour adds only 4 units to output. In such a case the firm could maintain its output level and reduce costs by using £2.50 less of labour and spending £1.00 more on capital. Making such a substitution of capital for labour would leave output unchanged and reduce costs by £1.50. Thus, the original position was not cost minimizing.[10]

We can take a different look at cost minimization by multiplying eqn (5.3) by P_K/MP_L to obtain:

$$MP_K/MP_L = P_K/P_L. \qquad (5.4)$$

[10] The illustration in this paragraph assumes that the marginal products do not change when expenditure changes by a small amount.

The ratio of the marginal products on the left-hand side of the equation compares the contribution to output of the last unit of capital and the last unit of labour. If the ratio is 4, this means that one unit more of capital will add four times as much to output as one unit more of labour. The right-hand side of the equation shows how the cost of one unit more of capital compares with the cost of one unit more of labour. If the ratio is also 4, the firm cannot reduce costs by substituting capital for labour or vice versa. Now suppose that the ratio on the right-hand side of the equation is 2. Capital, which is four times as productive as labour, is now only twice as expensive. It will pay the firm to switch to a method of production that uses more capital and less labour. However, if the ratio on the right-hand side is 6 (or *any* number more than 4), it will pay to switch to a method of production that uses more labour and less capital.

We have seen that when the ratio MP_K/MP_L exceeds the ratio P_K/P_L, the profit-maximizing firm will substitute capital for labour. This substitution is measured by changes in the **capital/labour ratio**, which is the amount of capital per worker. So, if the firm uses £1m worth of capital and employs 100 workers, its capital–labour ratio is 10,000 (1,000,000/100), indicating that there is £10,000 worth of capital for each worker.

How far does the firm go in making this substitution? There is a limit, because the law of diminishing returns tells us that as the firm uses more capital, the marginal product of capital falls, and as it uses less labour, the marginal product of labour rises. Thus, the ratio MP_K/MP_L falls. When it reaches 2, the firm does not need to substitute further. The ratio of the marginal products is equal to the ratio of the prices.

Equation (5.4) shows how the firm can adjust the elements over which it has control (the quantities of inputs used, and thus the marginal products of those inputs) according to the market prices of the inputs.

Long-run equilibrium of the firm

The firm will have achieved its equilibrium capital/labour ratio when there is no further opportunity for cost-reducing substitutions. This occurs when the marginal product per pound spent on each input is the same (eqn (5.3)) or, equivalently, when the ratio of the marginal products of inputs is equal to the ratio of their prices (eqn (5.4)).

The principle of substitution

Suppose that a firm is meeting the cost-minimizing conditions shown in eqns (5.3) and (5.4) and that the cost of labour increases, while the cost of capital remains unchanged. The least-cost method of producing any output will now use less labour and more capital than was required to produce the same output before the factor prices changed.

Methods of production will change if the relative prices of inputs change. Relatively more of the cheaper input and relatively less of the more expensive input will be used.

This is called the **principle of substitution**, and it follows from the assumptions that firms minimize their costs and that the inputs can be substituted for each other.

The principle of substitution plays a central role in resource allocation, because it relates to the way in which individual firms respond over the long run to changes in relative input prices that are caused by the changing relative scarcities of factors of production in the economy as a whole. When some resource becomes scarcer to the economy as a whole, its price will tend to rise. This motivates individual firms to use less of that input. When some other input becomes more plentiful to the economy as a whole, its price will tend to fall. This motivates individual firms to use more of it. Firms need never know the relative national scarcities of the various factors of production. As long as relative prices reflect relative scarcities, firms will tend to substitute plentiful inputs for scarce inputs. They do this through their own cost-minimizing responses to the changes in the prices of their inputs.

Box 5.2 discusses the broader significance of the principle of substitution.

The long-run cost curve

When all inputs can be varied, there is a least-cost method of producing each possible level of output. Thus, with given input prices, there is a minimum achievable cost for each level of output; if this cost is expressed as a quantity per unit of output, we obtain the long-run average cost of producing each level of output. When this least-cost method of producing each output is plotted on a graph, the result is called a **long-run average cost curve** (*LRAC*). Figure 5.5 shows one such curve. Fortunately, since all costs are variable in the long run we do not need to distinguish between firms that have divisible and indivisible inputs that are fixed in the short run

This cost curve is determined by the industry's current technology and by the prices of the inputs. It is a 'boundary' in the sense that points below it are unattainable; however, points on the curve are attainable if sufficient time elapses for all inputs to be adjusted. To move from one point on the *LRAC* curve to another requires an adjustment in all inputs, which may, for example, require building a larger and more elaborate factory.

Box 5.2 **The economy-wide significance of the principle of substitution**

In free markets, relative input prices reflect the relative scarcities (in relation to demand) of different inputs. Abundant inputs have prices that are low relative to the prices of those that are scarce. Firms seeking their own private profit and responding to relative input prices will be led to make lavish use of the inputs with which the whole country is plentifully endowed, and to be frugal in their use of the inputs that are in scarce supply.

For example, a country with a great deal of land and a small population will experience a low price for its plentiful land and a high price for its scarce labour. Firms producing agricultural goods will tend to make lavish use of the cheap land and economize on the expensive labour. In contrast, a small country with a large population will have expensive land and relatively cheap labour. Firms producing agricultural goods will tend to economize on land by using a great deal of labour per unit of land.

Some time ago, construction workers' wages rose sharply relative to the wages of factory labour and the cost of machinery. In response, builders shifted from onsite construction to panelization, a method of building that uses standardized modules and is now in universal use. The wiring, plumbing, insulation, and painting of these standardized modules are all done at the factory. The bulk of the factory work is performed by machinery and by assembly-line workers whose wages are significantly less than those of onsite construction workers.

These are examples of the price system operating as an automatic control mechanism. No single firm need be aware of national resource surpluses and scarcities. Since these are reflected in relative market prices, individual firms that never look beyond their own private profits are led to economize on inputs that are scarce in the nation as a whole. Therefore we should not be surprised to discover that methods of producing the same product differ in different countries. In Europe, where labour is highly skilled and very expensive, a manufacturer may use very elaborate equipment to economize on labour. In China, where labour has been abundant and capital scarce, a much less mechanized method of production may have been appropriate, though this is changing as real wages in China rise.

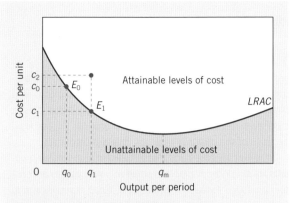

Figure 5.5 A long-run average cost curve

The long-run average cost (*LRAC*) curve is the boundary between attainable and unattainable levels of cost. Since the lowest attainable cost of producing q_0 is c_0 per unit, the point E_0 is on the *LRAC* curve. Suppose that a firm producing at E_0 desires to increase output to q_1. In the short run it will not be able to vary all inputs, and thus unit costs above c_1, say c_2, must be accepted. In the long run a plant that is the optimal size for producing output q_1 can be built and costs of c_1 can be attained. At output q_m the firm attains its lowest possible per-unit cost of production for the given technology and input prices.

The *LRAC* curve is the boundary between cost levels that are attainable, with known technology and given input prices, and those that are unattainable.

Just as the short-run cost curves discussed earlier in this chapter are derived from the *production function* describing the physical relationship between inputs and output, so is the *LRAC* curve. The difference is that in deriving the *LRAC* curve there are no fixed inputs, so all inputs are treated as variable. Because all input costs are variable in the long run, we do not need to distinguish between average variable cost (*AVC*), average fixed cost (*AFC*), and average total cost (*ATC*), as we did in the short run. In the long run, there is only one long-run average cost (*LRAC*) for any given set of input prices.

The shape of the long-run average cost curve

As the firm varies its output, average cost may vary for two distinct reasons. First, the prices of its inputs may change. Secondly, the physical relationship between its inputs and outputs may change. To separate these two effects we assume for the moment that all input prices remain constant.

Now look at the *LRAC* curve shown in Figure 5.5. This curve is often described as U-shaped, although empirical studies suggest it is often 'saucer-shaped'.

Decreasing costs

Over the range of output from zero to q_m, the firm has falling long-run average costs: an expansion of output permits a reduction of costs per unit of output. Technologies with this property are said to exhibit **economies of scale**. (Of course, when output is increased, such economies of scale will be realized only after enough time has elapsed to allow changes to be made in all inputs.) Recall that the prices of inputs are assumed to be constant for the moment. Thus the decline in long-run average cost must occur because output is increasing *more than* in proportion to inputs as the scale of the firm's production expands. Over this range of output, the decreasing-cost firm is often said to enjoy long-run **increasing returns**, or *increasing returns to scale*. This is an extremely important phenomenon, and its sources are discussed in the next section. Output q_m is called the **minimum efficient scale**, defined as the lowest level of output at which all scale economies are exploited.

Box 5.3 gives some evidence of sources of economies of scale in the electronics industry and we discuss economies of scale in electricity supply in the first case study at the end of this chapter.

Increasing costs

Over the range of outputs greater than q_m, the firm encounters rising long-run unit costs. An expansion in production, even after sufficient time has elapsed for all adjustments to be made, will then be accompanied by a rise in average costs per unit of output. Since input prices are still assumed to be constant, the firm's output must be increasing *less than* in proportion to the increase in inputs. When this happens, the increasing cost firm is said to encounter long-run **decreasing returns**. Decreasing returns imply that the firm suffers some diseconomy of scale. As its scale of operations increases, diseconomies are encountered that increase its per-unit cost of production.

These diseconomies may be associated with the difficulties of managing and controlling an enterprise as its size increases. For example, planning problems do not necessarily vary in direct proportion to size. At first there may be scale economies as the firm grows, but sooner or later planning and coordination problems may multiply more than in proportion to the growth in size. If so, management costs per unit of output will rise. Another source of scale diseconomies concerns the possible alienation of the labour force as firm size increases. Also, providing appropriate supervision becomes difficult as more and more tiers of supervisors and middle managers come between the person at the top and the workers on the shop floor. Control of middle-range managers may also

Box 5.3 Economies of scale in the electronics industry

Many manufacturing industries exhibit economies of scale over some range of production. The following is an extract from an industry source in the electronics industry:

Economies of scale in electronics production

... how can they sell a PC Keyboard for $15?

The PC industry typifies the economies of scale rule. The quantities in which most PC components are produced are so awesome that the final price to the user drops far below the off-the-shelf price of the individual chips, connectors, and other hardware.

The large number of units produced means that the Research and Development cost amortization is very low—an extra thousand dollars spent on design costs is not terribly important in the greater scheme of things, indeed if it can save fifty cents on production costs it is well worthwhile.

In contrast, some of our clients are start-up companies (where the volumes are initially quite low), and many are companies targeting niche markets. We also design circuitry for companies producing many thousands of units, the point is that different rules apply dependent on the expected volume of production.

It would be difficult to push the cost of producing an ordinary 4 function pocket calculator below $50 if the production quantity was small—say 200 pcs in each run. That is assuming that there was a suitable ready-made plastic case available. We can buy a calculator for $5 (or less) because of the quantity in which they are produced.

In many cases the parts that are used in high-volume products are simply unavailable in small volumes, as they are custom produced for each manufacturer. Good examples would be the plastic case used in a calculator, the LCD display, and the calculator IC (integrated circuit or chip) itself ...

A realistic development path for a start-up company will usually involve designing a low-volume high-price version of their product first, and then moving to high-volume designs as the market matures. This is only possible where there is some demand even when the price is high. Fortunately, high technology products usually exhibit [such] demand—for instance there was a market for facsimile machines even when they cost well over $10,000 each.

Source: Airborn Electronics, <http://www.airborn.com.au/method/volume.html>

---

become more difficult. As the firm becomes larger, managers may begin to pursue their own goals rather than devote all of their efforts to making profits for the firm. (This is the principal–agent problem, which is discussed in detail in Chapter 10.)

Constant costs

In Figure 5.5 the firm's long-run average cost falls until output reaches q_m and rises thereafter. The firm is encountering increasing returns to scale for outputs up to q_m and decreasing returns for higher outputs. Another possibility should be noted. The firms might encounter constant returns to scale over part or all of its possible range of outputs. Over the range of output that constant returns to scale are encountered, the firm's *LRAC* curve is horizontal at the minimum points on each possible short-run *ATC* curves. The firm's long-run average costs per unit of output do not change as its output changes. Because input prices are assumed to be fixed, the firm's output must be increasing *exactly in proportion to* the increase in inputs. A firm in this situation is said to be encountering **constant returns**.

Box 5.4 discusses the sources of economies of scale. It also discusses **economies of scope**, which are reductions in average costs that come from producing more than one

product in the same firm. That these economies are almost universal in manufacturing is shown by the fact that almost no manufacturing firms produce a single product; instead, they produce a whole range of more or less related products. Scope economies are also found in many service industries where firms also produce a range of related services.

Sources of increasing returns

Whenever a firm finds that it can increase its output per unit of input, that firm is enjoying economies of large-scale production. These economies are important, and wherever they exist they encourage large plants and/or large firms. Three important sources of scale economies are geometrical relationships, one-time costs, and the technology of large-scale production.

Geometric relationships

One important source of scale economies lies in the geometry of our three-dimensional world. To illustrate how geometry matters, consider a firm that wishes to store liquid. The firm is interested in the *volume* of storage space. However, the amount of material required to build the container is related to the *area* of its surface. When the size

Box 5.4 Economies of scale and scope

Economies of scale

Economies of scale arise whenever the average cost of production of a product falls as the numbers produced rise. Some of these economies may be due to factors *internal* to the firm. For example, when books were printed usinga metal type face it would be expensive to set up the type, so the first book in the print run would have a high cost but the average cost would fall as larger numbers were printed. Similarly, any production process with a high fixed cost of setting up but a lower marginal cost of production would exhibit economies of scale. Products with high research and development (R&D) costs also fall into this category.

Economies of scale that are *external* to the firm can arise when firms in an industry are supported by a network of related suppliers. The auto industry, for example, traditionally had a number of assembly plants in the same area and a host of components suppliers (such as suppliers of tyres, windscreens, and electrical components). Each of the component suppliers made inputs for more than one car maker, so economies of scale in components manufacture would be passed on in lower input costs for all the car manufacturers.

Diseconomies of scale can also arise when firms get too large and complex to manage efficiently. Such firms then become unprofitable and/or lose their market share. Some go out of business while others are taken over and restructured.

Economies of scope

Economies of scope arise when average costs fall because of the production of more than one product by the same firm. Banks, for example, sell loans, deposits, mortgages, pensions, and life insurance, all from the same branch. The fixed costs of maintaining the branch (and paying the staff) are spread between all of these different products. Indeed, virtually all retailers sell a variety of products from each shop. Most manufacturers are multi-product firms, and this suggests that some of their input costs can be shared across the different products.

Diseconomies of scope can also arise if firms are trying to do too many unrelated activities, but this is when they should bring in management consultants who will tell them to dispose of the product lines that contribute least to the value of the business.

We return to the subject of increasing returns industries in Chapter 11.

---

of a container is increased, the storage capacity, which is determined by its volume, increases faster than its surface area.[11] This is a genuine case of increasing returns—the output, in terms of storage capacity, increases proportionately more than the increase in the costs of the required construction materials. Another of the many other similar effects concerns smelters. The heat loss is proportional to the smelter surface area, while the amount of ore smelted depends on its volume. Thus, there is a scale economy in heat needed per tonne of ore smelted as smelters get larger. In practice, however, the size of the smelter is limited by the need to deliver a smooth flow of air to all of the molten ore.

One-time costs

A second source of increasing returns consists of inputs that do not have to be increased as the output of a product is increased, even in the long run. For example, the

R&D costs to design a new generation of aeroplanes, or a more powerful computer, have to be incurred only once for each product. Hence, they are independent of the scale at which the product is subsequently produced. Even if the product's *production costs* increase in proportion to output in the long run, average total costs, including *product development costs*, will fall as the scale of output rises. The influence of such once and for all costs is that, other things being equal, they cause average total costs to be falling over the entire range of output.[12]

The technology of large-scale production

A third and very important source lies in technology. Large-scale production can use more specialized and highly efficient machinery than smaller-scale production. It can also lead to more specialization of human tasks, with a resulting increase in human efficiency.

---

[11] For example, consider a cubic container with metal sides, bottom, and lid, all of which measure 1 m by 1 m. To build this container, 6 m^2 of metal is required (six sides, each 1 m^2), and it will hold 1 m^3 of gas or liquid. Now increase all of the lengths of each of the container's sides to 2 m. Now 24 m^2 of metal is required (six sides, each 4 m^2), and the container will hold 8 m^3 of gas or liquid (2 m × 2 m × 2 m). So increasing the amount of metal in the container's walls fourfold has the effect of increasing its capacity eightfold.

[12] This phenomenon is popularly referred to as 'spreading one's overhead'. It is similar to what happens in the short run when average fixed costs fall with output. The difference is that fixed short-run production costs are variable long-run production costs. If the firm increases its scale of output for some product, it will incur more capital costs in the long run as a larger plant is built. However, its costs of developing that product are not affected.

Even the most casual observation of the differences in production techniques used in large and small plants will show that larger plants use greater specialization. These differences arise because large specialized equipment is useful only when the volume of output that the firm can sell justifies employment of that equipment. For example, assembly-line techniques, body-stamping machinery, and multiple-boring engine block machines in car production are economically efficient only when individual operations are repeated thousands of times. Use of elaborate harvesting equipment (which combines many individual tasks that would otherwise be done by hand and by tractor) provides the least-cost method of production on a big farm but not on a few acres. Typically, as the level of planned output increases, capital is substituted for labour and complex machines are substituted for simpler ones. Robotics is a contemporary example. Electronic devices can handle huge numbers of operations quickly, but unless the level of production requires such a large volume of operations, robotics or other forms of automation will not provide the least-cost method of production.

Until very recently large-scale production meant mass production, sometimes referred to as 'Fordism', a system that was introduced early in the twentieth century. It was based on a very detailed division of jobs, often on a production line, in which each person did one repetitive task in cooperation with very specialized machinery (called dedicated machinery). In this technology size was very important. Very high rates of output were required in order to reap all the scale economies available to this type of production.

In the later decades of the twentieth century production technology was revolutionized by *flexible manufacturing*. This is a much less specialized type of production in which workers do many tasks in cooperation with machinery that is also less specialized. One of its most important characteristics is its ability to achieve maximum efficiency with low average costs at much smaller rates of output than are required for mass production techniques.

Sources of decreasing returns

If there were no sources of decreasing returns there would be nothing that limited size except the extent of the market. Larger firms would always be lower cost producers than smaller firms, and competition would tend to produce one firm in each industry—a monopoly. Fortunately, there are many reasons why increasing returns are limited and eventually disappear as the volume of production gets larger and larger.

If all the dimensions of a bridge are altered in the proportion λ, its structural strength is altered by $1/\lambda$ and its

weight is altered by λ^3. In other words, bridges and many other structures exhibit diminishing returns in the sense that as their size and the amount of materials used in their construction is increased, their strength increases less than in proportion. This structural relation is one of the most important sources of diminishing returns that limits the extent to which other sources of increasing returns can be exploited by building larger versions of some generic capital good.

In many cases the limits of the technology in use dictate that returns will diminish if the technology is required to perform beyond its physical limitations. For example, early means of providing air to smelters were quite limited in their capacity. Thus, if smelters were built too large, the pumps could not deliver enough air to the whole interior. This limited the extent to which the scale effects concerning area and volume could be exploited. Later, when better pumps were designed, smelters could be built larger but, again, if size was expanded beyond the capacity of the newer pumps to deliver enough air to the interior of the smelter, diminishing returns were encountered

The relationship between long-run and short-run costs

The short-run cost curves and the long-run cost curves are all derived from the same production function. Each curve assumes given prices for all inputs. In the long run all inputs can be varied; in the short run some must remain fixed. The long-run average cost (*LRAC*) curve shows the lowest cost of producing any output when all inputs are variable. Each short-run average total cost (*SRATC*) curve shows the lowest cost of producing any output when one or more factors are held constant at some specific level. No short-run average total cost curve can fall below the long-run average total cost curve, because the latter represents the lowest attainable cost for each possible output. Because we are now considering the relation between the long run and the short run, it is necessary once again to distinguish between firms whose fixed capital is indivisible and those whose fixed capital is divisible

The LRAC when the fixed input is indivisible and scale effects exist

As the level of output is changed, a different-sized plant will be required to achieve the lowest attainable cost. This is shown in Figure 5.6, where the *SRATC* curve lies above the *LRATC* curve at all outputs except q_0. As we observed earlier in this chapter, a short-run cost curve such as the *SRATC* curve shown in Figure 5.6 is one of many such curves. Each curve shows how costs vary as output is varied from a base output, holding the fixed input at the quantity most appropriate to that output. Figure 5.7 shows a family of short-run average total cost

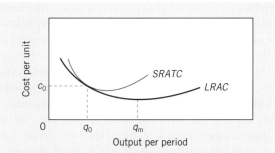

Figure 5.6 Long-run average cost and short-run average total cost curves

The short-run average total cost (*SRATC*) curve is tangent to the long-run average cost (*LRAC*) curve at the output for which the quantity of the fixed input is optimal. The curves *SRATC* and *LRAC* coincide at output q_0, where the fixed plant is optimal for that level of output. For all other outputs there is too little or too much plant and equipment, and *SRATC* lies above *LRAC*. If some output other than q_0 is to be sustained, costs can be reduced to the level of the long-run curve when sufficient time has elapsed to adjust the size of the firm's fixed capital. The output q_m is the lowest point on the firm's long-run average cost curve. It is called the firm's *minimum efficient scale* (**MES**), and it is the output at which long-run costs are minimized.

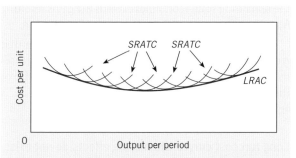

Figure 5.7 The envelope long-run average cost curve

For every point on the long-run average cost (*LRAC*) curve there is an associated short-run average total cost (*SRATC*) curve tangent to that point. Each short-run curve shows how costs vary if output varies, with the fixed input held constant at the level that is optimal for the output at the point of tangency. As a result, each *SRATC* curve touches the *LRAC* curve at one point and lies above it at all other points. This makes the *LRAC* curve the envelope of the *SRATC* curves.

curves along with a single long-run average cost curve. The long-run average cost curve is sometimes called an **envelope** because it encloses a series of short-run average total cost curves by being tangent to them. Each *SRATC* curve *is tangent to* the long-run average cost curve at the level of output for which the quantity of the fixed input is optimal, and lies above it for all other levels of output.

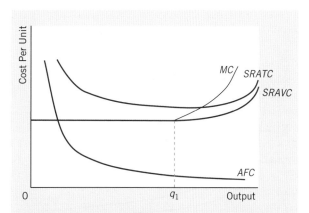

Figure 5.8 Short-run cost curves when the fixed input is divisible

Average variable and marginal cost are constant up to capacity output while the average fixed cost is shown by a rectangular hyperbola. Up to capacity output, q_1 in the figure, average total cost is the fixed cost per unit displaced upward by the constant amount of average variable cost. Above capacity average variable and marginal costs are rising and so average total cost rises more steeply than it would have done if the average cost had been constant.

The LRAC when the fixed factor is divisible and scale effects exist

When the fixed input is divisible, the SRAC curve is horizontal up to capacity, as shown in in Figure 5.4. Figure 5.8 repeats the curves in that figure and adds the average fixed cost and average total cost curves. Since fixed costs are by definition constant as output varies, the curve is a rectangular hyperbola ($AFC = F^*/q$, where F^* is the given fixed cost and q is output). Since the *SRAVC* curve is horizontal up to capacity output, the *SRATC* curve, which is the vertical sum of the *SRAFC* and *SRAVC* curves, is a hyperbola with the *SRAVC* curve as its base up to capacity output.

Now consider a larger plant when economies of scale exist over the relevant range of outputs. This is shown in Figure 5.9. Because of the scale economies, the new larger plant has lower average variable costs by the amount Δc. Because it is a larger plant, it will have higher fixed costs and a higher capacity output. Because the average fixed cost curve is hyperbolic for all plants up to their capacity, their average total cost curves must always lie either above or below each other at any level of output up to the capacity of the plants. They cannot intersect below capacity as they do in Figure 5.7. The difference lies in the fact that with the indivisible fixed input, the average variable cost curve is U-shaped so that the average total cost curve, which is the vertical addition of a rectangular hyperbola and a U-shaped curve, is itself U-shaped. But when the fixed input is divisible, all plants have average

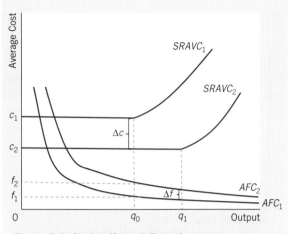

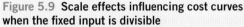

Figure 5.9 Scale effects influencing cost curves when the fixed input is divisible

The larger plant's *SRAVC* curve lies above while its *ATC* curve lies below those for the smaller plant. $SRAVC_1$ and AFC_1 are the average variable and fixed cost curves for the smaller plant. $SRAVC_2$ and AFC_2 are the similar curves for the larger plant. The capacity outputs are q_1 for the smaller plant and q_2 for the larger plant. The average total cost curve for each plant is the vertical sum of its *SRAVC* and *AFC* curves. These are not shown in the diagram but the curve for the larger plant will be below that for the smaller plant if the saving in variable cost, Δc, exceeds the extra fixed cost Δf of the larger plant. (If the *SRATC* curve for the larger plant lies below the *SRATC* curve for the smaller plant at output q_1 it must also do so at q_2 since the curve for the smaller plant begins to rise faster than it would if it were a simple hyperbola because the plant's *SRAC* curve is positively sloped after q_1.)

total costs that are a rectangular hyperbola below full capacity output and only differ by the constant value of average variable cost. Two rectangular hyperbolas that are just vertical displacements of each other cannot intersect. As a result we can compare the total costs of the two plants at the capacity output of the smaller plant. The new larger plant has lower average variable costs by Δc and higher average fixed costs by Δf and so will have lower average total costs as long as $\Delta c > \Delta f$, that is, as long as it decreases average variable costs by more than it increases average fixed costs evaluated at the capacity output of the smaller plant.[13]

Now assume that, as in Figure 5.7, there are scale economies up to some level of output and then scale diseconomies

---

[13] The average total cost up to capacity output is $c_1 + f_1$ for the smaller firm and $c_2 + f_2$ for the larger firm, where c stand for variable cost and f for fixed costs. The larger firm will have lower total cost than the smaller firm if $c_2 + f_2 < c_1 + f_1$. Transposing some of the terms yields $f_2 - f_1 < c_1 - c_2$, which states that the large firm's reduction in variable costs must exceed the increase in fixed costs, all evaluated at the capacity output of the smaller firm.

after that. As output is increased over the range of increasing returns to scale, the successive Δcs will become smaller while the successive Δfs may rise or stay the same, depending on how much higher the fixed costs of the larger plant are compared with those of the smaller one. Sooner or later, a point will come at which Δc will still be positive but just equal to Δf. Beyond this point average total costs will increase as plant size is further increased. So the optimal least-cost size of plant occurs when $\Delta c = \Delta f$ and the short-run average total cost curve for a plant of that size will lie below those or *all* larger and smaller plants over the whole range of outputs.

Notice several things about this discussion of long run costs when scale effects exist.

1. In both the cases of an indivisible and a divisible fixed input there is a unique size of plant at which the average total costs of production are minimized.

2. If a lower output is required in the case of an indivisible input, a smaller plant will be built, while in the case of a divisible input the least-cost plant will be built and under-used by producing on the horizontal short-run average cost curve at less than capacity.

3. When the least-cost plant is used, the physical scale economies indicated by Δc are not fully exhausted. It is just that the increase in cost for building a larger plant to exploit the remaining scale economies exceeds the gains resulting from the reduction in the variable costs of production.

4. It follows that any technological improvement that reduces the cost of building the larger facility or increases its efficiency, and thus lowers Δf, will increase the size of the least-cost plant up to the new point at which Δc is again equal to Δf.

Long run cost curves when scale effects do not exist

When an industry encounters constant returns to scale, all plants, whatever their size, have the same costs at the least-cost point of operation. Thus, the long-run average total cost curve is horizontal. In the case of an indivisible factor the short-run cost curves are U-shaped and tangential to the long-run curve as before, except that the long-run curve is now a horizontal line and not U-shaped as shown in Figure 5.7.

Now consider that case of a divisible fixed factor. Since we have constant returns to scale, altering the size of a production facility increases both total fixed costs and total variable costs in proportion to the new capacity when the facility is operating at that capacity. Hence the *AFC* and the *SRAVC* are the same at each plant's capacity output. So instead of having U-shaped *SRATC* curves tangent to a horizontal LRATC curve in the case of an indivisible fixed factor, all *SRATC* curves coincide with the *LRATC* curve up to the plant's capacity.

Shifts in cost curves

The cost curves derived so far show how cost varies with output, given constant input prices and fixed technology. Changes in input prices will cause the entire family of short-run and long-run average cost curves to shift. If a firm has to pay more for any input that it uses, the cost of producing each level of output will rise; if the firm has to pay less for any input that it uses, the cost of producing each level of output will fall.

A rise in input prices shifts the family of short-run and long-run average cost curves upward. A fall in input prices, or a technological advance, shifts the entire family of average cost curves downward. This is true for the cases of both divisible and indivisible fixed inputs

Although input prices usually change gradually, sometimes they change suddenly and drastically. In 2006 crude oil prices reached around $70 per barrel, which was a big increase on the $20–30 price range it had been at in 2002–4. However, the boom of 2006–8 saw the oil price rise even higher to around $140 in July 2008. This bubble burst, and by January 2009 oil was trading at around $40 per barrel. However, as the world economy recovered from the financial crisis of 2007–8 the price of oil rose again. In June 2014 it was around $110 per barrel but by the end of the year it had fallen to nearly $50. These price swings mean big shifts in the input costs of firms and thus big shifts in firms' average and marginal cost curves.

The very long run: endogenous technical change

In the long run profit-maximizing firms do the best they can to produce known products with the techniques and the resources currently available. This means being *on*, rather than above, their long-run cost curves. In the very long run, production techniques change. This means that the production function itself alters so that the same inputs produce more output. This in turn causes long-run cost curves to shift.

The decrease in costs that can be achieved by choosing from among the available inputs, known techniques, and alternative levels of output is necessarily limited. In contrast, improvements by invention and innovation are potentially limitless. Hence, sustained growth in living standards is critically linked to *technological change*, which allows the same output to be produced with fewer inputs and, hence, more output to be produced with society's limited amount of resources. Technological change was once thought to be mainly a random process, brought about by inventions made by ingenious individuals and eccentric scientists working in garages and scientific laboratories. However, research over the past few decades has shown that this is an incorrect view.

Changes in technology are endogenous to the economic system. They occur mainly because inventors and innovators see the opportunity to make profits from their activities. These may be in the invention of wholly new products, new production processes, or new forms of organizing economic activity. Sometimes these occur because of changes in economic signals, such as changes in input prices, the composition of the

population, or the needs of consumers, and sometimes just because it is anticipated that something new will find a profitable niche in the economy.[14]

In our discussion of long-run demand curves in Chapter 2 we looked at just such technological changes in response to rising relative prices when we spoke of the development of smaller, more fuel-efficient cars in the wake of rising petrol prices. Similarly, much of the move to substitute capital for labour in manufacturing, transportation, communications, mining, and agriculture in response to rising wage rates has taken the form of inventing new labour-saving methods of production. In contrast, the invention of the machines that mechanized agriculture in the late nineteenth and early twentieth centuries were not in response to a rise in the wages of agricultural workers, but the realization that new mechanical methods would significantly reduce the costs of farming by replacing much farm labour with machines.

Most microeconomic theory analyses only the short- and long-run responses of the firm to various changes. In the short run, firms can change price and output within the confines of fixed plant and equipment. In the long run, they can change all inputs but within the confines of fixed technology. Such an analysis is incomplete whenever technological change is an endogenous response to economic signals. Consider, for example, a rise in the price of an

[14] For an explanation of the incorporation of endogenous technical change into economics see David Warsh, *Knowledge and the Wealth of Nations*, New York and London, Norton, 2006.

important input in one country. In the short run, firms that use the input will cut back production in response to the rise in costs. In the long run, they will substitute other inputs for the one whose price has risen. When all adjustments have been made, however, firms still find themselves at a cost disadvantage compared with competitors in other countries who have not suffered the rise in the price of their inputs. In the very long run, the domestic firms may engage in research and development designed to reduce further the use of the newly expensive inputs. If the firms succeed, they may develop processes that allow them to reduce costs below those of their competitors in other countries who did not suffer the increased input prices and so did not have the same incentive to innovate.

Modern research into induced technological development has documented many such instances. As a result, the response of firms to changes in such economic signals as output prices and input costs must be studied in three steps:

(1) the short-run response that changes the variable input;

(2) the long-run response that consists of adjusting *all* inputs;

(3) the R&D response in which firms seek to innovate their way out of difficulties caused by reductions in their product prices and/or increases in their input prices.

Studies that ignore the third set of responses ignore what are often the most important effects, once several years have elapsed.

In this context it is interesting to note that flexible manufacturing, which revolutionized production in most industrialized countries in the latter part of the twentieth century, was first developed by the Japanese car producers in response to a scale disadvantage. They were unable to reach the efficient scale of production when they were selling only in their small protected home market. In response, they innovated their way out of these difficulties. They developed techniques that allowed them to produce a superior product at lower prices than their American and European competitors and so turned a long-run disadvantage into a very-long-run advantage.

The definition of profit in economics

Before we move on to discussing the profit-maximizing behaviour of firms in the next three chapters, we need to clarify an important issue relating to a difference between the measurement of profit as used in economics and that used by accountants and managers.

Costs and profits

In the real world, firms arrive at what they call profits by taking the revenues they obtain from selling their output and deducting all the costs associated with their inputs, including depreciation of their own capital. When all costs have been correctly deducted the resulting 'profits' are the return to owners' capital.

In economic theory the concepts of costs and profits differ from that used by actual firms because economists count the opportunity cost of the owner's capital as part of the firm's costs. This opportunity cost is not just the depreciation of the capital, but also includes an estimate of what the capital, and any other special advantages owned by the firm, could have earned in their best alternative uses. When this larger set of costs is deducted from revenues, the remainder is called **pure profit** or **economic profit**, or, where there is no room for ambiguity, just profit.

The owners' opportunity cost of the financial capital that they have tied up in their firm can be divided into two parts. The first part can be determined by asking what could be earned by lending the capital to someone else in a riskless loan. For example, the firm could have purchased a government bond, which has no significant risk of default. Suppose the return on this is 4 per cent per annum. This rate is called the pure return, or risk-free rate of return on capital. It is clearly an opportunity cost, since the firm could close down operations, lend out its money, and earn a 4 per cent return. To determine the second part, ask what the firm could earn in addition to this amount by lending its money to another firm where risk of default was equal to the firm's own risk of loss. Say this is an additional 5 per cent. This is called the *risk premium* and it is clearly also a cost. If the firm does not expect to earn this much in its own operations, it could close down and lend its money out to some other equal-risk use earning 9 per cent (4 per cent pure return plus 5 per cent risk premium).[15]

Tables 5.3 and 5.4 compare the concepts of cost and profit as used by firms in practice and in economic analysis.

Table 5.3 Profit and loss account for XYZ Company for the year ending 31 December 2016

Expenditure		Income
Variable costs		
Wages	£200,000	Revenue from sales £1,000,000
Materials	300,000	
Other	100,000	
Total VC	600,000	
Fixed costs		
Rent	50,000	
Managerial salaries	60,000	
Interest on loans	90,000	
Depreciation allowance	50,000	
Total FC	250,000	
Total costs	850,000	
Profit		150,000

The profit and loss account shows profits as defined by the firm. The table gives a simplified version of a real profit and loss statement. The total revenue earned by the firm, minus what it regards as costs, yields profits. (Note that costs are divided into those that vary with output, called variable costs, and those that do not, called fixed costs. This distinction was discussed earlier in this chapter.)

Table 5.4 Calculation of pure profits

Profit as reported by the firm	£150,000
Opportunity cost of capital	
Pure return on the firm's capital	− 100,000
Risk premium	− 40,000
Pure or economic profit	10,000

The economist's definition of profit deducts the opportunity cost of capital. To arrive at the economist's definition of profit, the opportunity cost of capital—the return on a riskless investment plus any risk premium—must be deducted from the firm's definition of profit. What is left is pure profit.

What firms call profit is the return to the owners' capital. In economic theory we deduct from this profit figure the imputed opportunity cost of the owners' capital (and any marketable special advantages owned by the firm) to obtain pure or economic profits.

Since there are two different concepts it would be better if two different terms were used to denote them. But we are stuck with the fact that economists use a slightly different definition of 'profit' from that used by firms and accountants. When there is any possibility of confusion, we speak of economic or pure profit. It is the standard usage in economic theory to use the word 'profit' to mean the return to the firm over and above all costs including the opportunity cost of capital (the pure risk-free return *and* the risk premium).[16]

The relevance of this to our earlier analysis of costs is that the fixed costs of firms are assumed in economics to include the normal cost of capital (that is what we have just called the *opportunity cost of capital*). This cost is always included in our measures of total cost and of average total cost, such as shown in Figure 5.3 and 5.7. However, the cost of capital does not affect short-run marginal costs and average variable costs as the level of capital is fixed for these cases.

Neither of the two alternative definitions of profits is better or worse than the other. Instead, each is appropriate for different purposes. Firms are interested in the return to their owners and seek to maximize this, which is what they call profit. They must also conform to tax laws and accounting standards, which define profit this way. In contrast, in economics we are interested in how profits affect resource allocation and the definition we use is best for that purpose.[17]

Profits and resource allocation

When resources are valued by the opportunity cost principle, their costs show how much these resources would earn if used elsewhere in the economy. If the revenues of all the firms in some industry exceed opportunity cost, the firms in that industry will be earning pure profits—that is, the returns will be higher than in other industries with comparable risks. Thus, the owners of resources will want to move into this industry, because the earnings potentially available to them are greater there than in alternative

---

[15] A firm may also own a valuable patent or a highly desirable location, or a popular brand name such as Gucci, Rolex, Polo, or Porsche. Each of these involves an opportunity cost to the firm in production (even if it was acquired free), because if the firm did not choose to use the special advantage itself, it could sell or lease it to others. Therefore the firm must impute a charge to itself for using the special advantage.

[16] An alternative terminology avoids the potential confusion arising from using the same term to refer to two different things. You may encounter it elsewhere, since it is still used in some elementary textbooks—but seldom in more advanced theory. This terminology calls the opportunity cost of capital *normal profit*. Any excess of revenue over normal profits is then called *supernormal profit*.

[17] Note that any activity that maximizes one concept of profit also maximizes the other. The only difference is that by subtracting the opportunity cost of capital from the firm's concept of profit, economists make positive or negative pure profit the signal for resources to enter or leave an industry.

activities. If, in some other industry, firms are incurring economic losses, some or all of this industry's inputs will earn higher rewards by moving to new activities.

Profits and losses as defined in economic theory play a crucial signalling role in the workings of a free-market system.

Positive profits in an industry are the signal that resources can profitably be moved into the industry. Losses are the signal that the resources can profitably be moved elsewhere. Only if there are zero economic profits is there no incentive for resources to move into or out of an industry.

CASE STUDIES

1. Economies of scale in the electricity industry

In the 1940s, 1950s, and 1960s major economies of scale in electricity generation in the United Kingdom came from the use of larger and larger generators: from 30 MW (= 30,000 kilowatt) generating sets in 1948 to 100 MW sets in 1956, 200 MW sets in 1959, and 500 MW sets in 1966.

Since the 1970s there has been little increase in the size of generators, with the largest now being installed at 660 MW. Furthermore, total generating capacity was about the same in 2013 as it had been in the early 1980s. Energy demand did grow between 1985 and 2005 but it declined after that to the levels of the early 1980s. Output had grown over this period but production had become less energy intensive.

Despite the absence of further economies in the size of generators after 1970, and the levelling off in overall capacity after 1980, methods of gaining scale economies were still being found. The new method was to reduce the *number* of power stations, with each station having several generators. As a result, the average capacity of each power station has continued to rise significantly, bringing a different type of economy of scale. The number of power stations fell from 233 in 1965 to 174 in 1978 to 78 in 1987. The average capacity of these stations rose from 147 MW in 1965 to 324 MW in 1974 to 671 MW in 1987.

Costs were also reduced by exploring economies of scale in bulk transmission of electricity. The 'Supergrid' of 400 kV (= 400,000 volts) transmission lines that was built in the 1960s replaced three lines operating at 275 kV and eighteen lines operating at 132 kV, without a corresponding increase in costs.

Economies of scale have allowed the industry to cope with rising *real* prices of its main inputs—coal and labour—without raising the real price of electricity. During the 1960s the real price of oil, the major alternative fuel, was falling owing to the increasing exploitation of

economies of scale in oil tankers delivering crude oil from the Middle East. In response, the UK electricity industry was able to reduce the real price of electricity for a while, which is one of the reasons why electricity was adopted more and more widely in preference to other fuels. Higher oil prices in the 2000s led to greater use of gas-fired power stations and a decline in the use of oil.

Privatization at the end of the 1980s did not change the cost structure of the industry immediately, partly because producers were locked into three-year contracts to buy coal. After this period shifts were made to cheaper imported coal and, where new capacity was required, to the adoption of the cheaper technology of combined cycle gas turbines (CCGTs). There are mild economies of scale with current technology (in 2013) as size increases from 240 to 500 MW, but bigger generators (which are typically around 700 MW) do not deliver significant further scale economies.

Strictly speaking, scale economies refer to the effects of increasing output *along* a negatively sloped *LRAC* curve as a result of rising output within the confines of known technology, while changes in technological knowledge *shift* the *LRAC* curve. As this example shows, the two forces usually become mixed in most real-world applications. The rise in demand for electricity in the three decades of the 1950s, 1960s, and 1970s required an increase in output. The rise in output made the use of higher capacity equipment possible and thus provided an incentive for the development of such equipment. No fundamental new knowledge was required, but the details of the technology of larger generators had to be developed through research rather than being taken from already existing blueprints.

Competitive forces continue to put pressure on producers to reduce costs. The main pressures now are on cutting costs through productivity gains rather than exploiting further economies of even-larger-scale production of individual plants and distribution systems. However, current pressures now relate to the environmental impact of power production, especially coal-, gas-, and oil-fired stations. The current policy debate is whether to invest in a new generation of nuclear power stations, whether carbon-capture technologies can make conventional power stations sufficiently environmentally friendly, or whether some renewable energy sources, such as wind, wave, solar power, or biofuels can produce sufficient power at affordable cost.

2. Endogenous materials design: a new industrial revolution?

A new industrial revolution has been in progress in the past two decades or so. It is the 'materials revolution'. Throughout history, an important source of technological advancement has been the development of new materials. Indeed, we label stages of history by the materials that were used—the Stone Age, the Bronze Age, and the Iron Age. Many key twentieth century advances in manufacturing would not have been possible without materials such as steel and hydrocarbons. Today, important technical progress is built upon polymers, composites, and ceramics.

Previous materials advances were usually the outcome of a process of trial and error—Edison allegedly tried many thousands of different materials and designs before he 'invented' the light bulb. Today, however, scientists are able to use knowledge of the microstructure of matter, combined with advanced computing power, to design the materials to be used in production simultaneously with the engineering of production itself. This is having profound effects on the design of most new products and processes.

One example of new materials technology can be found in sports equipment. When Björn Borg won the Wimbledon tennis tournament five times in the late 1970s he played with a wooden racket. Jimmy Connors won it in 1982 playing with an aluminium alloy racket. Andy Murray, the 2013 men's singles champion, played with a new type of racket—a product of the materials revolution. The frame material of a modern racket is most commonly made from graphite and fibreglass, and sometimes also other materials such as titanium and kevlar, mixed with a plastic resin. The stiffness and cost of composite frames varies depending on the exact mix of materials and can be adjusted to meet the needs of individual players. Golf clubs, skis, and surfboards are also examples of new materials in sports equipment.

The Boeing 787 Dreamliner which came into service in 2011 (discussed in Box 5.1) is another example of the application of new materials. The wings and body of this plane are made of a carbon composite material that is light but also strong. The Airbus A380 also incorporated new materials, as do many modern cars, trains, and bikes. New materials are also hitting the kitchen in frying pans, baking trays, and oven liners.

The latest phase in the materials revolution is associated with *nanotechnology*. This involves working with materials at the atomic or molecular level. It is named after the nanometre, which is one billionth of a metre. Nanotechnology is relatively new, but it is already having significant applications in the creation of new products in medicine, electronics, textiles, mechanical engineering, energy supply and use, and agriculture. You may even own a pair of nano sunglasses!

Conclusion

Cost structures are central to understanding what is produced, by how many firms, and with what combinations of inputs. Firms have incentives to make their products as cheaply as possible and to be on a continual search for ways to be more efficient. So understanding costs structures and how they may vary with scale, new technologies, and over time is fundamental to the analysis of modern entreprises. In the next few chapters we build on this foundation by adding another important dimension, which is the market structure within which firms operate. Cost structures can influence the market structure that emerges, but the latter adds an extra dimension to the product and pricing strategies that firms need to pursue.

SUMMARY

Costs, revenues, and profit maximization

- Firms are assumed to maximize their profits.
- The production function relates quantities of inputs to quantities of outputs.
- Profit is the difference between total cost and total revenue.

Costs in the short run

- When the fixed input is indivisible short-run variations in output are subject to the law of diminishing returns: equal increments of the variable input sooner or later produce smaller and smaller additions to total output and, eventually, a reduction in average output per unit of variable input. The same is true when a divisible fixed input is fully employed and more is being produced by applying more units of the variable factor to the given amount of the fixed factor.
- With an indivisible fixed input, short-run average and marginal cost curves are U-shaped, the rising portion reflecting diminishing average and marginal returns. The marginal cost curve intersects the average cost curve at the latter's minimum point, which is called the firm's capacity output. With a divisible fixed input the short-run average and marginal cost curves are horizontal up to capacity output.
- There is a family of short-run average and marginal cost curves, one for each amount of the fixed input.

Costs in the long run

- In the long run, the firm can adjust all inputs to minimize the cost of producing any given level of output.
- Cost minimization requires that the ratio of an input's marginal product to its price be the same for all inputs.
- The principle of substitution states that when relative input prices change, firms will substitute relatively cheaper inputs for relatively more expensive ones.
- With an indivisible fixed input, long-run average cost curves are U-shaped, indicating decreasing average

costs (increasing returns to scale) followed by increasing average costs (decreasing returns to scale).

- With an indivisible fixed input, the long-run average cost curve is the envelope of the family of short-run cost curves, all of which shift when input prices shift.
- With a divisible fixed input and scale economies the long run average cost curve is the short-run average total cost curve of the firm with the lowest short-run costs.
- With constant returns to scale the long-run average total cost curve is a horizontal straight line. This line is the locus of lowest points on the short-run average cost curves when the fixed factor is divisible. The line is the average variable cost curve displaced upwards by the amount of average capital costs at capacity output (where 'capital cost' refers to the cost of the factor that was fixed in the short-run).

The very long run

- In the very long run, innovations introduce new methods of production that alter the production function.
- These innovations often occur in response to changes in economic incentives such as variations in the prices of inputs and outputs. They cause cost curves to shift downwards.

The definition of profit in economics

- In addition to what firms count as their costs, economists include the imputed opportunity costs of owners' capital. This includes the pure return, what could be earned on a riskless investment, and a risk premium (what could be earned over the pure return on an equally risky investment). Pure or economic profits are the difference between revenues and all these costs.
- Pure profits play a key role in resource allocation. Positive pure profits attract resources into an industry; negative pure profits induce resources to move elsewhere.

TOPICS FOR REVIEW

- The production function
- The short, long, and very long runs
- The law of diminishing returns
- Short-run average, marginal, fixed, and total costs
- Conditions for long-run cost minimization
- The principle of substitution

- Indivisible and divisible fixed inputs
- The long-run cost curves
- Constant, increasing, and decreasing long-run costs
- Invention and innovation in the very long run
- Imputed costs
- Alternative definitions of profits.

QUESTIONS

1 The following series of scores in successive innings is made by a batsman in cricket: 10, 20, 50, 60, 80, 100, 100, 100, 70, 50, 0, 10, 20, 0. Calculate the cumulative total of runs scored after each innings and the average score after each innings. Each successive score tells us the marginal score. Say what happens to the average when the marginal score is above the previous average and what happens to the average when the marginal score is below the average. Notice that these relationships between marginal and average values are not purely applicable to economics.

2 Suppose that the production function is $Q = 20(K^{0.5} L^{0.5})$ and the value of capital is 100. Calculate the total product for the following values of labour input: 1, 5, 10, 20, 40, 50, 80, 100, 150, 200. Calculate the average product at each of these levels of output. How does marginal product vary over this range of output?

3 Here are data for total production costs of a manufacturing firm at various levels of output.

Output (units)	Total cost (£)
0	1,000
20	1,200
40	1,300
60	1,380
100	1,600
200	2,300
300	3,200
400	4,300
500	5,650
1,000	13,650

a) Calculate average variable cost (AVC), average total cost (ATC), and average fixed cost (AFC). (*Hint*: fixed costs have to be incurred even when output is zero and do not vary with the production level in the short run.)

b) Calculate marginal or incremental cost over each production range for which data are given.

c) [You may attempt this and subsequent parts now but you could also return to them after reading Chapter 6.] If this firm can sell as much as it wants at a price of £11, what is its profit-maximizing output?

d) How much profit is made?

e) At output levels shown in the table immediately on either side of the profit-maximizing output, what is the level of profit?

4 Using the production function $Q = 20(K^{0.5} L^{0.5})$, where K is machine-hours per week, L is worker-hours week, and Q is output per week, calculate five different combinations of capital and labour that will generate each of the following levels of output: 20, 100, 1,000, 2,000.

5 Suppose that capital is £10 per machine-hour and labour is £5 per worker-hour. What would be the cost-minimizing combination of capital and labour that could be used to produce each of the four levels of output listed in question 4?

6 Holding capital constant at 100, and varying labour input accordingly, calculate the short-run average cost of producing the levels of output listed in Question 4 (and using the input prices set out in Question 5). Repeat the exercise for the following levels of capital: 16, 25, 36, 49, 64, 81?

7 Which one of the following is true about the relationship between marginal cost and average variable cost (AVC).

a) If marginal cost is rising then AVC is rising.

b) If marginal cost is constant then AVC is falling.

c) If marginal cost is above AVC then AVC must be rising.

d) If marginal cost is above AVC then AVC must be falling.

e) If marginal cost is below AVC then marginal cost must be rising.

8 Explain the difference between economists' and accountants' definition of profit.

9 What is the law of diminishing returns, and what does it imply about the likely shape of short-run cost curves? In what circumstances might the law not apply to short-run variations in costs. Why?

10 Explain the differences between economies of scale, constant returns to scale, and diminishing returns to scale.

CHAPTER 6

PERFECT COMPETITION

In Chapter 5 we studied what determines a firm's costs and how these costs vary with the firm's output. In this and the next two chapters, we build on what we have learned about costs to study how the structure of the markets in which firms operate affects what they do. This market structure depends on the number of firms that operate in the industry and on the nature of the product that they make and sell.

In this chapter we study a market structure called perfect competition in which all firms produce an identical product and there are so many firms that no one of them can affect the market price by varying its own output. Since each firm can sell as much as it wants at the going price, its sales revenue is proportional to its output. For example, doubling the amount produced and sold at any constant price doubles sales revenue.

In Chapter 7 we study market structures in which there is only one large firm, and in Chapter 8 we study intermediate cases in which a number of firms produce a range of products that are variants of one generic product type, such as breakfast cereal or toothpaste. In both of these cases firms can influence the price of their product by varying the amount that they offer for sale. When the price of a firm's product changes as the amount produced changes, the relationship between production and revenue is more complicated than when firms face a market price that they cannot alter as they do in perfect competition.

Our first main task in this chapter is to derive the supply curve for a perfectly competitive industry. To do this we ask two questions. First, what determines the amount of output that each firm will supply? Secondly, what does this tell us about the relation between market price and the total amount supplied by all the firms in an industry? We then go on to study how such an industry reacts to various forces that affect it, including changes in demand and costs. We also ask if the behaviour we have discovered serves the interests of consumers as well as those of firms.

In this chapter you will learn that:

- The impact of the product market on firms' price and output choices is determined by the nature of the product and the market structure in which they operate.

- In perfect competition firms produce a homogeneous product and are price takers.

- All profit-maximizing firms choose their output to equate marginal cost and marginal revenue.

- Under perfect competition marginal cost will equal the market price, and so the supply curve of firms is determined by the marginal cost curve.

- The long-run supply curve of a competitive industry may be positively sloped, horizontal, or negatively sloped, depending on how input prices are affected by the industry's expansion.

- Perfect competition maximizes the benefit that consumers receive from the output of the product in question.

Market structure and firm behaviour

The degree to which firms can influence the price of their product through their own actions depends upon market structure, a concept that needs discussion at the outset.

Does Shell compete with BP in the sale of petrol? Does HSBC Bank compete with Barclays? Does a wheat farmer from Essex compete with a wheat farmer from Somerset? If we use the ordinary meaning of the word 'compete', the answer to the first two questions is plainly yes, and the answer to the third is no.

Shell and BP both advertise extensively to persuade car drivers to buy *their* products. Gimmicks such as new mileage-stretching additives and free airmiles are used to tempt drivers to buy one brand of petrol rather than another. Most town centres in England and Wales not only have Barclays and HSBC banks but also others such as Lloyds, NatWest, and Santander. In Scotland the choices look different, but many of the institutions are linked. For example, Royal Bank of Scotland owns NatWest, and HBOS, formed from a merger between the Bank of Scotland and the Halifax, was then taken over by Lloyds. Banks all provide similar services but work hard to attract business from each other. For example, they often offer incentives for students to open bank accounts in the hope that they will stay with that bank for life. If one bank is very successful in attracting business, it will do so at the expense of its rival banks.

In the wheat market, however, there is nothing that the Essex farmer can do to affect either the sales or the profits of the Somerset farmer, and the sales and profits of the Somerset farm have no effect on those of the Essex farm.

To understand who is competing with whom and in what sense, it is useful to distinguish between the behaviour of individual firms and the *type of market* in which they operate.

Market structure and behaviour

The term **market structure** refers to the type of market in which firms operate. Markets can be distinguished by the number of firms in the market and the type of product that they sell.

Competitive market structure

In the theory of the firm and industry we define the competitiveness of a market as depending on individual firms' power to influence market prices. According to this definition, the less power an individual firm has to influence the market in which it sells its product, the more competitive that market is.

The extreme form of competitive structure occurs when each firm has zero market power. In such a case many firms sell an identical product and each must accept the price set by the forces of market demand and market supply. The firms can sell as much as they choose at the prevailing market price but have no power to influence that price.

This extreme is called a *perfectly competitive market structure*. (Usually the term 'structure' is dropped and economists speak of a *perfectly competitive market*.) In it, there is no need for individual firms to compete actively with one another, since one firm's ability to sell its product does not depend on the behaviour of any other firm. For example, Essex and Somerset wheat farmers operate in a perfectly competitive market over which they have no power. The price of wheat is set in world markets and there are thousands of suppliers to that market in many different countries.[1]

Box 6.1 explains how the market for a product like chocolate can have different levels, some of which are close to perfect competition and others that are dominated by a few large firms and are thus what economists call *oligopolistic*. An **oligopoly** is a market in which a small number of large suppliers compete head to head and thus have to be aware of what rivals are up to. We discuss this market structure in Chapter 8. Retail markets for chocolate bars and chocolate confectionary are dominated by a few big producers, while the market for cocoa beans is perfectly competitive as there are a large number of very small suppliers, none of whom can affect the prices they receive.

Competitive behaviour

In everyday language the term 'competitive behaviour' refers to the degree to which individual firms actively compete with one another. For example, Shell and BP certainly engage in competitive behaviour. Both companies also have some real power over their market. Either firm could raise its price of petrol at the pumps and still continue to attract customers. Each has the power to decide, within limits set by buyers' tastes and the prices of competing products, the price that people will pay for their petrol and oil. So although they actively compete with each other, they do so in a market that does not have a perfectly competitive structure.

---

[1] Of course government agencies may intervene to influence the price, such as in the EU Common Agricultural Policy, but this does not change the fact that individual farmers are price takers.

Box 6.1 Chocolate assortment

The British eat a lot of chocolate. Average annual consumption per person is over 10 kilograms.[2] Germans and Swiss eat a comparable amount, but the Japanese and Chinese eat very little. The worldwide sales of chocolate in 2012 were worth over $105 billion, which is larger than the annual national income of nearly 100 countries in the world including, for example, Serbia, Croatia, and Kenya.

So where does the chocolate come from? The simple answer is that it grows on trees, or at least the cocoa bean does and this is the main ingredient (to which is often added milk, sugar, and other sweeteners). The chocolate that we buy in the form of snack bars, chocolate confectionery, and drinking chocolate is almost all manufactured by one of a small number of very large global firms. The names should mostly be familiar: Mars, Nestlé, Kraft (owner of Cadbury), Hershey, and Ferrero are among the biggest. These brands dominate the market in Europe and North America, and each firm produces a wide range of different chocolate products. All these firms have

considerable market share and market power. This means that they have some discretion over the prices they choose to set, but they also have to watch what their key competitors are up to. However, these big firms buy their cocoa on the world wholesale market and the supply side of this market is very different.

Ninety per cent of the world's cocoa is grown on five million small farms that are between one and five hectares in size. None of these farms has a distinctive brand name, and they all sell an identical product into the world wholesale market (sometimes via a government-owned purchasing agency which then sells on the world market). Each farmer has to accept the price on offer and can do nothing to affect it. At the same time, each farmer can sell as much as he or she can produce at the prevailing market price. This is an example of a perfectly competitive market structure, in which each producer is a price taker and cannot influence the market price.

As it is with chocolate, so also is it with many other primary agricultural commodities. Perfect competition for those who grow the crop but not for those who convert the crop into the finished consumer product. We return to the cocoa market in the case study at the end of this chapter.

[2] <http://www.divinechocolate.com/uk/about-us/research-resources/resources/chocolate-facts>

In contrast, Essex and Somerset wheat farmers do not engage in competitive behaviour because the only way they can affect their revenues is by changing their outputs of (or their costs of producing) wheat.

Behaviour versus structure

The distinction that we have just made explains why firms in perfectly competitive markets (e.g. the Essex and Somerset wheat farmers) do not compete actively with each other, whereas firms that do compete actively with each other (e.g. Shell and BP) do not operate in perfectly competitive markets.

The significance of market structure

The firms that make a product, or a closely related set of products, constitute an **industry**. The market demand curve for any particular product is the demand curve facing the *industry*.

When firms take their production and sales decisions, they need to know what quantity they can sell at various prices. Therefore their concern is not with the *market* demand curve for the whole industry, but rather with the demand curve for their own output. If a firm's managers can estimate the demand curve that their own firm faces,

they know the sales that their firm can make and the revenue it will earn at each possible price. If they also know their costs of production, they can calculate the profits that would be associated with each rate of output. With this information, they can choose the output that maximizes their profits.

The structure of the market in which a firm operates determines the relationship between the market demand curve for the product and the demand curve facing each individual firm in that industry. To reduce the analysis of market structure to manageable proportions, we analyse four theoretical market structures. These are perfect competition, monopoly, monopolistic competition, and oligopoly. Monopoly and perfect competition lie at the two extremes of market structure. In monopoly the industry contains only one firm, which therefore can set its price without concern about how competing firms in the industry will react (since there are none). In perfect competition there are so many firms in the industry that no one of them has any power to influence the market price for its product. Many real markets are somewhere in between these extreme cases. Perfect competition will be dealt with in the rest of this chapter; the other market structures will be dealt with in the two chapters that follow.

Perfectly competitive markets

The perfectly competitive market structure—usually referred to simply as *perfect competition*—applies directly to a number of real-world markets. It also provides an important benchmark for comparison with other market structures.

Assumptions of perfect competition

Our analysis of **perfect competition** is built on a number of key assumptions relating to the firm and to the industry.

- **Assumption 1.** All the firms in the industry sell an identical or **homogeneous product**.
- **Assumption 2.** Buyers of the product are well informed about the characteristics of the product being sold and the prices charged by each firm.
- **Assumption 3.** When each firm is operating at its normal capacity, its output is a small fraction of the industry's total output.
- **Assumption 4.** Each firm is a **price taker.** This means that each firm can alter its output without significantly affecting the market price of its product. Each firm must passively accept the existing market price, but it can sell as much as it wants at that price.[3]
- **Assumption 5.** There is *freedom of entry and exit* meaning that any new firm is free to enter the industry and start producing if it so wishes, and any existing firm is free to cease production and leave the industry.

The difference between the wheat farmers that we considered earlier and Shell is in *degree of market power*. Each firm that is producing wheat is an insignificant part of the whole market and thus has no power to influence the price of wheat. The oil company does have power to influence the price of petrol because its own sales represent a significant part of the total sales of petrol, even though all the firms in the industry sell a product that is close to homogeneous.[4] Box 6.2 explores further the reasons why each wheat-producing firm finds the price of wheat to be beyond its influence.

A perfectly competitive market is one in which individual firms have zero market power.

Demand and revenue for a firm in perfect competition

A major distinction between firms operating in perfectly competitive markets and firms operating in any other type of market is the shape of the firm's own demand curve.

In perfect competition each firm faces a demand curve that is horizontal, because variations in the firm's output have no noticeable effect on price so that the firm can sell all it wishes to sell at that price.

The horizontal (perfectly elastic) demand curve does not mean that the firm could actually sell an infinite amount at the going price. What it does mean is that the variations in output *that it will normally be possible for the firm to make* will leave price virtually unchanged because they have only a negligible effect on the industry's total output. Figure 6.1 contrasts the demand curve for the product of a competitive industry with the demand curve facing a single firm in that industry.

To study the revenues that each firm receives from the sales of its products, we use total, average, and marginal revenue. These are the revenue counterparts of total, average, and marginal cost that we considered in Chapter 5.

Total revenue (*TR*) is the total amount received by the seller from the sale of a product. If q units are sold at a price of p pounds each, $TR = p \times q$.[5]

Average revenue (*AR*) is the amount of revenue per unit sold. This is equal to the market price of the product.

Marginal revenue (*MR*), sometimes called *incremental revenue*, is the change in a firm's total revenue resulting from the sale of one extra unit. Whenever output changes by more than one unit, the change in revenue must be divided by the change in output to calculate marginal revenue. For example, if an increase in output of three units per month is accompanied by an increase in revenue of £1,500, the marginal revenue resulting from the sale of *one extra unit* per month is £1,500/3, or £500.[6]

---

[3] To emphasize its importance, we identify price taking as a separate assumption, although strictly speaking it is implied by the first three assumptions.

[4] Even homogeneous commodities come in different types—for example, different varieties of wheat or coffee bean. Any firm may produce more than one variety, but across firms each type and grade of a commodity is the same (e.g. super unleaded petrol or number one grade durum wheat).

[5] Four common ways of indicating that two variables such as p and q are to be multiplied together are $p \cdot q$, $p \times q$, $(p)(q)$, and pq.

[6] Because we use discrete changes in the text, we are, strictly speaking, using incremental revenues, $\Delta TR/\Delta q$. Marginal revenue is defined geometrically as the slope of the tangent to the total revenue curve at the point in question. For those readers who know some calculus, it is the first derivative of total revenue with respect to output, dTR/dq. For small changes, incremental revenue can be regarded as an approximation of marginal revenue, as we do in the text.

Box 6.2 Demand under perfect competition: firm and industry

Because all products have negatively sloped market demand curves, *any* increase in the industry's output will cause *some* fall in the market price. However, the calculations given in this box show that any conceivable increase that one wheat farm could make in its output has such a negligible effect on the industry's price that the farmer correctly ignores it.

The calculations given below arrive at the elasticity of demand facing one wheat farmer in two steps. Step 1 shows that a 200 per cent variation in the farm's output leads to only a very small percentage variation in the world price. Thus, as step 2 shows, the elasticity of demand for the farm's product is very high: −71,429!

Although the arithmetic used in reaching these measures is unimportant, understanding why the wheat farmer is a price taker in these circumstances is vital.

Here is the argument that the calculations summarize. The market elasticity of demand for wheat is approximately −0.25. This means that if the quantity of wheat supplied in the world increased by 1 per cent, the price would have to fall by 4 per cent to induce the world's wheat buyers to purchase the extra wheat.

Even huge farms produce a very small fraction of the total world crop. In a recent year, one large farm produced 1,750 metric tonnes of wheat; this was only 0.00035 per cent of the world production of 500 million metric tonnes. Suppose that the farmer decided in one year to produce nothing and in another year managed to produce twice the normal output of 1,750 metric tonnes; this is an extremely large variation in one farm's output. The increase in output from zero to 3,500 metric tonnes represents a 200 per cent variation measured around the farm's average output of 1,750 metric tonnes. Yet the percentage increase in world output is only (3,500/500,000,000) × 100 = 0.0007 per cent. The calculations show that this increase would lead to a decrease in the world price of 0.0028 per cent (2.8p in £1,000) and give the farm's own demand curve an elasticity of over

−71,000. This is an enormous elasticity of demand. The farm would have to increase its output by over 71,000 per cent to bring about a 1 per cent decrease in the price of wheat. Therefore it is not surprising that the farmer regards the price of wheat as unaffected by any change in output that his one farm could conceivably make. To all intents and purposes, the wheat-producing firm faces a perfectly elastic demand curve for its product—*it is a price taker.*

We will now proceed with the calculation of the firm's elasticity of demand (η_f) from market elasticity of demand (η_m), given the following figures:

World elasticity of demand (η_m) = −0.25

World output = 500,000,000 metric tonnes.

A large farm with an average output of 1,750 metric tonnes varies its output between 0 and 3,500 tonnes. The variation of 3,500 tonnes represents 200 per cent of the farm's average output of 1,750 metric tonnes. This causes world output to vary by only (3,500/500,000,000) × 100 = 0.0007 per cent.

Step 1: Find the percentage change in world price. We know that the market elasticity is −0.25. This means that the percentage change in quantity must be one-quarter as big as the percentage change in price. Put the other way around, the percentage change in price must be four times as large as the percentage change in quantity. We have just seen that world quantity changes by 0.0007 per cent, so world price must change by 0.0007 × 4 = 0.0028 per cent.

Step 2: Find the firm's elasticity of demand. This is the percentage change in its *own output* divided by the resulting percentage change in the world price. This is 200 per cent divided by 0.0028 per cent. Clearly, the percentage change in quantity vastly exceeds the percentage change in price, making elasticity very high. Its precise value is (minus) 200/0.0028 or (minus) 2,000,000/28, which is −71,429.

To illustrate each of these revenue concepts, consider a firm that is selling an agricultural product in a perfectly competitive market at a price of £3 per tonne. Because every tonne brings in £3, the average revenue per tonne sold is clearly £3. Furthermore, because each *additional* tonne sold brings in £3, the marginal revenue of an extra tonne sold is also £3. Table 6.1 shows calculations of these revenue concepts for a range of outputs between 10 and 13 tonnes.

The important point illustrated in Table 6.1 is that as long as the market price is unaffected by the amount the firm sells, its marginal revenue is equal to its average revenue (which is *always* equal to the price at which the output is sold). Graphically, as shown in part (i) of

Figure 6.2, average revenue and marginal revenue are the same horizontal line drawn at the level of market price. Because the firm can sell any quantity it chooses at this price, the horizontal line is also the *firm's demand curve*; it shows that any quantity the firm chooses to sell will be associated with this same market price.

If the market price is unaffected by variations in the firm's output, the firm's demand curve, its average revenue curve, and its marginal revenue curve all coincide in the same horizontal line.

This result can be stated in a slightly different way, which turns out to be important for our later work.

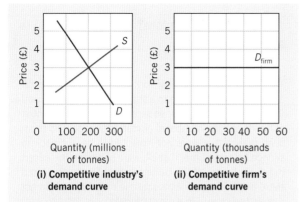

(i) Competitive industry's demand curve

(ii) Competitive firm's demand curve

Figure 6.1 **The demand curve for a competitive industry and for one firm**

The industry's demand curve is negatively sloped; the firm's demand curve is virtually horizontal. Notice the difference in the quantities shown on the horizontal scale in each part of the figure. The competitive industry has output of 200 million tonnes when the price is £3. The individual firm takes that market price as given and considers producing up to, say, 60,000 tonnes. The firm's demand curve in part (ii) is horizontal because any change in output that this one firm could manage would leave price virtually unchanged at £3.

Table 6.1 **Revenue concepts for a price-taking firm**

Quantity sold (units) (q)	Price (p)	TR = p × q	AR = TR/q	MR = ΔTR/Δq
10	£3.00	£30.00	£3.00	
11	3.00	33.00	3.00	£3.00
12	3.00	36.00	3.00	3.00
13	3.00	39.00	3.00	3.00

When price is fixed, average revenue, marginal revenue, and price are all equal to each other. The table shows the calculation of total revenue (*TR*), average revenue (*AR*), and marginal revenue (*MR*) when market price is £3.00 and the firm varies its quantity over the range from 10 to 13 units. Marginal revenue is positioned between the rows because it represents the change in total revenue in response to a change in quantity. For example, when sales rise from 11 to 12 units, revenue rises from £33 to £36, making marginal revenue (36–33)/(12–11) = £3 per unit.

For a firm in perfect competition, price equals marginal revenue.

This means, of course, that total revenue rises in direct proportion to output, as shown in part (ii) of Figure 6.2.

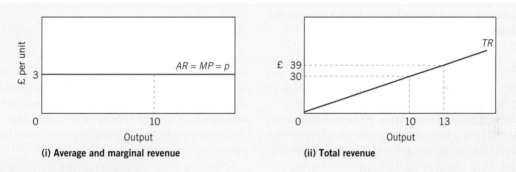

(i) Average and marginal revenue

(ii) Total revenue

Figure 6.2 **Revenue curve for a firm**

The demand curve for a perfectly competitive firm is a horizontal straight line. The graph shows the data in Table 6.1. Because price does not change, neither marginal nor average revenue varies with output—both are equal to price. When price is constant, total revenue is a straight line through the origin whose positive slope is the price per unit.

Short-run equilibrium

The next step is to combine information about the firm's costs and revenues to determine the level of output that will maximize its profits. We have just seen how the revenue of each price-taking firm varies with its output. In the short run, the firm has one or more fixed inputs, such as its plant and machinery, and the only way in which it can change its output is by altering its variable inputs such as labour. In effect, the firm has to choose where it wants

to be on its short-run cost curve (the curve we derived in Chapter 5).

In Chapter 5 we distinguished between firms whose fixed input was divisible and those whose fixed input was indivisible. Fortunately, both types of firms behave in similar ways when they are price takers. As a result, we can do all the analysis in this chapter for the first type of firm, those with indivisible fixed inputs.

Near the end of the chapter we will consider how this relates to the behaviour of firms with divisible fixed inputs.

Rules for all profit-maximizing firms

We start by stating three rules that apply to *all* profit-maximizing firms, whether or not they operate in perfectly competitive markets.

Should the firm produce at all?

The firm always has the option of producing nothing. If it exercises this option, it will have an operating loss that is equal to its fixed costs. If it decides to produce, it will add the variable cost of production to its costs and the income from the sale of its product to its revenue. Therefore, it will be worthwhile for the firm to produce as long as it can find some level of output for which revenue exceeds variable cost. However, if its revenue is less than its variable cost at *every* level of output, the firm will actually lose more by producing than by not producing.

Rule 1. A firm should not produce at all if, for *all* levels of output, the total variable cost of producing that output exceeds the total revenue derived from selling it or, equivalently, if the average variable cost of producing the output exceeds the price at which it can be sold.

The shutdown price

The sale price at which the firm can just cover its average variable cost when producing at its most profitable level of output is called the **shutdown price** or **break-even price**. At that price it is indifferent between producing and not producing. At any price below it, the firm will shut down. Such a price is shown in part (i) of Figure 6.6. At a price of £2 the firm can just cover its average variable cost by producing q_0 units. Any other output would not produce enough revenue to cover variable costs. For any price below £2 there is no output at which variable costs can be covered. Thus the price of £2 in part (i) is the shutdown price.

Box 6.3 deals with an interesting case of what to do with some parts of a firm's production facilities when their variable costs cannot be covered.

How much should the firm produce?

If a firm decides that (according to rule 1) production is worth undertaking, it must decide how much to produce. Common sense dictates that, on a unit-by-unit basis, if any unit of production adds more to revenue than it does to cost, producing and selling that unit will increase profits. However, if any unit adds more to cost than it does to revenue, producing and selling that unit will decrease

The terrorist attack on New York's World Trade Center on 11 September 2001 led to a sharp downturn in demand for air travel. Many airlines soon reduced their number of flights and the number of aircraft in service. Two thousand planes that were not expected to be put back in service for some time, if at all, were parked in the desert in the southwest of the United States. They were stored there as the dry air means that the metal planes do not rust as they would in a moist climate.

Airlines could consider selling their unwanted planes, but the second-hand value is very low when most other airlines have excess capacity at the same time. The planes that are 'parked' tend to be older models and planes that have already had many years of service. Eventually, decisions have to be taken about whether each plane can be sold, whether it will be put back into service, or whether it will be broken up for the value of the spare parts that can be stripped out. This decision will clearly be based on whether the average variable cost of running (and restoring) an old plane will be less than the average variable cost of running other planes in the fleet, which in turn remains less than the average total cost of buying new planes.

profits. Using the terminology introduced earlier, a unit of production raises profits if the marginal revenue obtained from selling it exceeds the marginal cost of producing it; it lowers profits if the marginal revenue obtained from selling it is less than the marginal cost of producing it.

Now, let a firm with some existing rate of output consider increasing or decreasing that output. If a further unit of production will increase the firm's profits, the firm should expand its output. However, if the last unit produced reduces profits, the firm should contract its output. From this it follows that the only time the firm should leave its output unaltered is when the last unit produced adds the same amount to costs as it does to revenue. These results yield the following rule.

Rule 2. Whenever it is profitable for the firm to produce some output, it should produce the output at which marginal revenue equals marginal cost.

Maximization not minimization

Figure 6.3 shows that it is possible to fulfil rule 2 and yet have profits at a minimum. Rule 3 is needed to distinguish minimum-profit from maximum-profit positions:

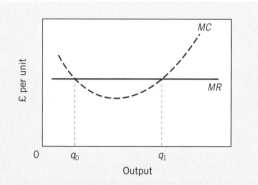

Figure 6.3 Two outputs where marginal cost equals marginal revenue

The equality of marginal cost and marginal revenue is necessary, but not sufficient, for profit maximization. $MC = MR$ at outputs q_0 and q_1. Output q_0 is a minimum-profit position because a change of output in either direction would increase profit: for outputs below q_0 marginal cost exceeds marginal revenue and profits can be increased by *reducing* output, while for outputs above q_0 marginal revenue exceeds marginal cost and profits can be increased by *increasing* output. Output q_1 is a maximum-profit position, since at outputs just below it marginal revenue exceeds marginal cost and profit can be increased by *increasing* output towards q_1, while at outputs just above it marginal cost exceeds marginal revenue and profit can be increased by *reducing* output towards q_1.

Rule 3. An output where marginal cost equals marginal revenue may be either profit maximizing or profit minimizing. Profit maximization requires that marginal cost be less than marginal revenue at slightly lower outputs and that marginal cost exceed marginal revenue at slightly higher outputs.

The geometric implication of this condition is that at the profit-maximizing output, the marginal cost curve should intersect the marginal revenue curve from below. This ensures that MC is less than MR to the left of the profit-maximizing output and greater than MR to the right of the profit-maximizing output.

The optimum output

These three rules determine the output that will be chosen by any firm that maximizes its profits in the short run. This output is called the firm's **profit-maximizing output**, and sometimes its **optimum output**.

• The firm's optimum output is zero if total revenue is less than total variable cost at all levels of output; the optimum output is positive if there is any output for which total revenue equals or exceeds total variable cost.

• When the firm's optimum output is positive, it is where marginal cost equals marginal revenue.

• If output is reduced slightly from the optimum level, marginal cost must be less than marginal revenue; if output is increased slightly from the optimum level, marginal cost must exceed marginal revenue.

Rule 2 applied to price-taking firms

Rule 2 tells us that any profit-maximizing firm that produces at all will produce at the point where marginal cost equals marginal revenue. However, we have already seen that for price-taking firms marginal revenue is the market price. Combining these two results gives an important conclusion.

A firm that is operating in a perfectly competitive market will produce the output that equates its marginal cost of production with the market price of its product (as long as price exceeds average variable cost).

In a perfectly competitive industry the market determines the price at which the firm sells its product. The firm then produces the output that maximizes its profits. This is the output for which price equals marginal cost.

When the firm has reached a position where its profits are maximized, it has no incentive to change its output because it is doing as well as it can do given the market situation. Therefore, unless prices or costs change, the firm will continue to produce that output. The firm is in *short-run equilibrium*, as illustrated in Figure 6.4. (The long run is considered later in this chapter.) In summary:

In a perfectly competitive market each firm is a price taker and a quantity adjuster. It pursues its goal of profit maximization by producing the output that equates its short-run marginal cost with the price of its product that is determined by the market.

Figure 6.4 shows the equilibrium of the firm using average cost and revenue curves. We can, if we wish, show the same equilibrium using total cost and revenue curves. Figure 6.5 combines the total cost curve first drawn in Figure 5.3 with the total revenue curve first shown in Figure 6.2. It shows the profit-maximizing output as the output with the largest positive difference between total revenue and total cost. This must, of course, be the same output as we located in Figure 6.4 by equating marginal cost and marginal revenue.

Short-run supply curves

We have seen that in a perfectly competitive market the firm responds to a price that is set by the forces of demand and supply. By adjusting the quantity it produces in response to the current market price, the firm helps to determine the market supply. The link between the behaviour of the firm and the behaviour of the

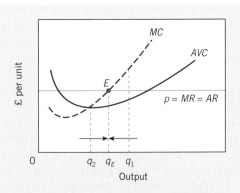

Figure 6.4 The short-run equilibrium of a firm in perfect competition

The firm chooses the output for which $p = MC$ above the level of AVC. When price equals marginal cost, as at output q_E, the firm loses profits if it either increases or decreases its output. At any point left of q_E, say q_2, price is greater than the marginal cost, and it pays to increase output (as indicated by the left-hand arrow). At any point to the right of q_E, say q_1, price is less than the marginal cost, and it pays to reduce output (as indicated by the right-hand arrow).

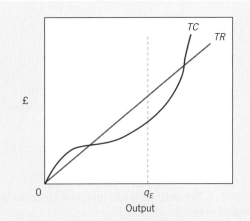

Figure 6.5 Total cost and revenue curves

The firm chooses the output for which the gap between the total revenue and the total cost curves is the largest. At each output the vertical distance between the TR and TC curves shows by how much total revenue exceeds or falls short of total cost. In the figure the gap is largest at output q_E, which is thus the profit-maximizing output.

competitive market is provided by the *industry supply curve*, which is also called the *market supply curve*.

The supply curve for one firm

The firm's supply curve is derived in part (i) of Figure 6.6, which shows a firm's marginal cost curve and four alternative prices. The horizontal line at each price is the firm's demand curve when the market price is at that level. The firm's marginal cost curve gives the marginal cost corresponding to each level of output. We require a supply curve that shows the quantity that the firm will supply at each price. For prices below average variable

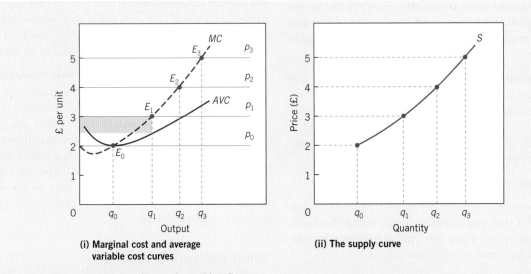

(i) Marginal cost and average variable cost curves

(ii) The supply curve

Figure 6.6 The supply curve for a price-taking firm

For a price-taking firm the supply curve has the same shape as its *MC* curve above the level of *AVC*. The point E_0, where price p_0 equals *AVC*, is the shutdown point. As price rises from £2 to £3 to £4 to £5, the firm increases its production from q_0 to q_1 to q_2 to q_3. If, for example, price were £3, the firm would produce output q_1 and be earning the contribution to fixed costs shown by the shaded rectangle. The firm's supply curve is shown in part (ii). It relates market price to the quantity the firm will produce and offer for sale. It has the same shape as the firm's *MC* curve for all prices above *AVC*.

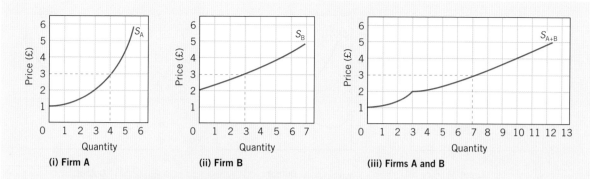

Figure 6.7 The supply curve for a group of firms

The industry supply curve is the horizontal sum of the supply curves of each of the firms in the industry. At a price of £3 firm *A* would supply 4 units and firm *B* would supply 3 units. Together, as shown in part (iii), they would supply 7 units. In this example, because firm *B* does not enter the market at prices below £2, the supply curve S_{A+B} is identical to S_A up to price £2 and is the sum of S_A and S_B above £2.

cost, the firm will supply zero units (rule 1). For prices above average variable cost, the firm will equate price and marginal cost (rule 2, modified by the proposition that $MR = p$ in perfect competition). This leads to the following conclusion.

In perfect competition the firm's supply curve is its marginal cost curve for those levels of output for which marginal cost is above average variable cost.

The supply curve of an industry

To illustrate what is involved, Figure 6.7 shows the derivation of an industry supply curve for an industry containing only two firms. The general result is as follows:

In perfect competition the industry supply curve is the horizontal sum of the marginal cost curves of all firms in the industry (above the level of average variable cost).

The reason for summing the marginal cost curves is that each firm's marginal cost curve shows how much it will supply at each given market price, and the industry supply curve is the sum of what each firm will supply. The reason for the qualification 'above the level of average variable cost' is that, as rule 1 shows, the firm will not produce at all if price is less than its average variable cost.

This supply curve, based on the short-run marginal cost curves of all the firms in the industry, is the industry's supply curve that was first encountered in Chapter 2. We have now established the profit-maximizing behaviour of individual firms that lies behind that curve. It is sometimes called a **short-run supply curve** because it is based on the short-run profit-maximizing behaviour of all the firms in the industry. This distinguishes it from a *long-run supply curve*, which relates quantity supplied to the price

that rules in long-run equilibrium when there are no fixed inputs (which we study later in this chapter).

Short-run equilibrium price

The price of a product sold in a perfectly competitive market is determined by the interaction of the industry's short-run supply curve and the market demand curve. Although no one firm can influence the market price significantly, the collective actions of all firms in the industry (as shown by the industry supply curve) and the collective actions of consumers (as shown by the market demand curve) together determine the equilibrium price. This occurs at the point where the market demand curve and the industry supply curve intersect.

At the equilibrium price each firm is producing and selling a quantity for which its marginal cost equals price. Given their fixed inputs, all firms are maximizing their profits and so have no incentive to alter output in the short run. Because total quantity demanded equals total quantity supplied, there is no reason for market price to change. Thus the market and all the firms in the industry are in short-run equilibrium.

Short-run profitability of the firm

We know that when an industry is in short-run equilibrium, each firm is maximizing its profits. However, we do not know *how large* these profits are. It is one thing to know that a firm is doing as well as it can, given its particular circumstances; it is another thing to know how well it is doing.

Figure 6.8 shows three possible positions for a firm in short-run equilibrium. In all cases the firm is maximizing

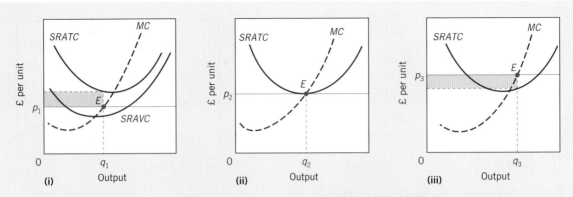

Figure 6.8 Alternative short-run equilibrium positions for a firm in perfect competition

When it is in short-run equilibrium, a competitive firm may be suffering losses, breaking even, or making profits. The diagram shows a firm with given costs faced with three alternative prices, p_1, p_2, and p_3. In each part E is the point at which $MC = MR =$ price. Since in all three cases price exceeds AVC, the firm is in short-run equilibrium. In part (i) price is p_1. Because price is below average total cost, the firm is suffering losses shown by the blue area. Because price exceeds average variable cost, the firm continues to produce in the short run. Because price is less than ATC, the firm will not replace its capital as it wears out. In part (ii) price is p_2 and the firm is just covering its total costs. It will replace its capital as it wears out since its revenue is covering the full opportunity cost of its capital. In part (iii) price is p_3 and the firm is earning pure profits in excess of all its costs, as shown by the blue area. As in part (ii) the firm will replace its capital as it wears out.

its profits by producing where price equals marginal cost, but the size of the profits is different in each case. In part (i) the firm is suffering losses. In part (ii) it is just covering all of its costs—it is just breaking even. In part (iii) it is making pure profits because average revenue exceeds average total cost. In part (i) we could say that the firm is minimizing its losses rather than maximizing its profits, but both statements mean the same thing. In all three cases the firm is doing as well as it can, given its costs and the market price.

Long-run equilibrium

In perfect competition, the forces that produce long-run equilibrium of the industry are created by the entry and exit of firms. The incentive for entry or exit comes from the existence of profits or losses.

The effect of entry and exit

Firms in *short-run equilibrium* may be making profits, suffering losses, or just breaking even. Because costs include the opportunity cost of capital, firms that are just breaking even are doing as well as they could do by investing their capital elsewhere. Thus there will be no incentive for such firms to leave the industry. Similarly, if new entrants expect just to break even, there will be no incentive for firms to enter the industry, because they can earn the same return on their capital elsewhere in the economy. However, if existing firms are earning revenues in excess of all costs, including the opportunity cost of capital, new capital will enter the industry attracted by these profits. If

existing firms are suffering losses, capital will leave the industry because a better return can be obtained elsewhere in the economy. This process of entry and exit is an important driver of the dynamics of a market economy, so it is worth looking at in a little more detail.

An entry-attracting price

First, suppose that all firms in a competitive industry are in the position of the firm shown in part (iii) of Figure 6.8. Attracted by the profitability of existing firms, new firms will enter the industry. If, for example, in response to the high profits that the 100 existing firms are making, 20 new firms enter, the market supply curve that formerly added up the outputs of 100 firms at each price must now add up the outputs of 120 firms. At any price, more will be supplied because there are more producers.

With an unchanged market demand curve, this shift in the short-run industry supply curve means that the previous equilibrium price will no longer prevail. The

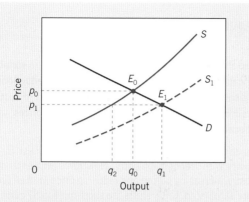

Figure 6.9 New entrants shift the supply curve

The supply curve shifts to the right and the equilibrium price falls. The entry of new firms shifts the supply curve to S_1, the equilibrium price falls from p_0 to p_1, and output rises from q_0 to q_1. Before entry only q_2 would have been produced at this price. The extra output is supplied by the new firms.

increase in supply will lower the equilibrium price, and both new and old firms will have to adjust their output to this new price. This is illustrated in Figure 6.9. New firms will continue to enter, and the equilibrium price will continue to fall, until all firms in the industry are just covering their total costs. Firms will then be in the position of the firm shown in part (ii) of Figure 6.8, which is called a *zero-profit equilibrium*.

Profits in a competitive industry create an incentive for the entry of new firms; the industry will expand, pushing the price down until profits fall to zero.

An exit-inducing price

Now suppose that the firms in the industry are in the position of the firm shown in part (i) of Figure 6.8. Although the firms are covering their variable costs, the return on their capital is less than the opportunity cost of capital. They are not covering their total costs. This is a signal for the exit of firms. Old plants and equipment will not be replaced as they wear out. As a result, the industry's short-run supply curve shifts leftwards and the market price rises. Firms will continue to exit, and the market price will continue to rise, until the remaining firms can cover their total costs—that is, until they are all in the zero-profit equilibrium illustrated in part (ii) of Figure 6.8. The exit of firms then ceases.

Losses in a competitive industry create an incentive for the exit of firms; the industry will contract, driving the market price up until the remaining firms are just covering their total costs.

The break-even price

Firms exit an industry when they are making losses and enter when attracted by positive profits. There is no further entry or exit when firms are just covering all their costs. This means that:

The long-run equilibrium of a competitive industry occurs when firms are earning zero profits.

The firm in part (ii) of Figure 6.8 is in a zero-profit long-run equilibrium. For that firm, the price p_0 is its shutdown or break-even price. It is the price at which all costs, including the opportunity cost of capital, are being covered. The firm is just willing to stay in the industry. It has no incentive to leave, nor do other firms have an incentive to enter.

Profit seeking generates movement of resources between different industries. Freedom of entry combined with profit seeking tends to push profit towards zero in any industry, whether or not it is perfectly competitive.

Box 6.4 uses the theory just developed to investigate the costs and benefits of changes in input prices.

Marginal and intramarginal firms

If firms have an incentive to exit from an industry, which ones will leave? Here it is useful to distinguish marginal from intramarginal firms. The marginal firm is just covering its full costs and would exit if price fell by even a small amount. The intramarginal firm is earning profits and would require a larger fall in price to persuade it to exit. In the pure abstract model of perfect competition, however, all firms are marginal firms in long-run equilibrium. All firms have access to the same technology, and therefore all will have identical cost curves when enough time has passed for full adjustment of all capital to be made. Thus, in long-run industry equilibrium all firms are in position (ii) in Figure 6.8. If price falls below p_2 in that figure, all firms wish to withdraw. Exit must then be by some contrived process, such as random lot, since there is nothing in the theory to explain who will exit first.

In real-world situations firms are not identical, since technology changes continually and different firms have different histories. A firm that has recently replaced its capital is likely to have more efficient lower-cost plant, and hence lower cost curves, than a firm whose capital is ageing. The details of each practical case will then determine the identity of the marginal firm that will exit first when price falls. As one example, assume that all firms have identical costs and differ only in the date at which they entered the industry. In this case, the firm whose capital comes up for replacement first will be the marginal firm. It will exit first

Box 6.4 Who benefits and loses from changes in input costs?

A fall in the cost of production causes a downward shift in each firm's marginal cost curve. As a result the short-run supply curve, which is the sum of the individual firms' marginal cost curves, shifts downwards. This leads to a higher output and a lower price. However, the price will fall by less than the fall in costs, while profits will now be earned because of the lower costs of production. These changes are shown in the figure.

A fall in costs in a competitive industry leads to a fall in price, an increase in output, and the emergence of profits. In part (i) the original demand and supply curves of D and S_0 intersect at E_0 to yield a price and quantity of p_0 and q_0. When each firm's production costs fall, the supply curve—which is the sum of the marginal cost curves of all firms in the industry—shifts downwards by the amount of the fall in costs, to S_1. If price fell by the full amount that costs had fallen, price would become p_2. Instead, price falls to p_1 while quantity rises to q_1, at the new equilibrium E_1.

In part (ii) the typical firm is shown in equilibrium at price p_0 with cost curves $SRATC_0$ and MC_0. The cost curves then shift to $SRATC_1$ and MC_1. The firm would be willing to produce output q_0 at price p_2. Instead, price falls only to p_1, and the firm increases its output to q_1. At this price–quantity combination it earns profits shown by the shaded area.

In the short run under perfect competition a fall in variable cost causes price to fall, but by less than the reduction in marginal cost. Thus the benefit of the reduction in cost is shared between consumers, in terms of lower prices, and producers, in terms of profits.

In the long run, however, profits cannot persist in an industry with freedom of entry. New firms will enter the industry, increasing output and reducing price until all profits are eliminated. Entry shifts the short-run supply curve to the right. Now each firm, old and new, just covers its total costs by producing at the minimum point on its average total cost curve.

Under perfect competition all of the benefits of lower costs are passed on to consumers in terms of higher output and lower prices in the long run.

The case of a rise in costs is just the reverse. In the short run the effects will be shared between consumers, in terms of higher prices, and producers, in terms of losses. In the long run, however, firms will leave the industry until those remaining can cover all their costs. Therefore the long-run effects of higher costs are fully borne by consumers in terms of lower output and higher prices.

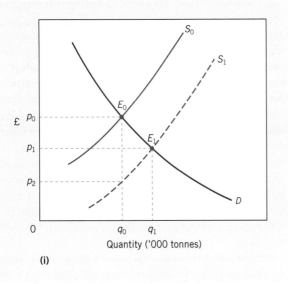

(i)

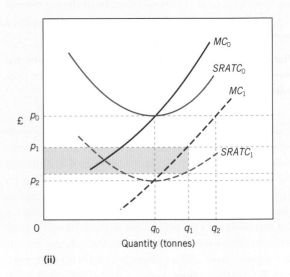

(ii)

because it will be the first to confront the long-run decision about replacing its capital in a situation where no firms are covering long-run opportunity costs.

Box 6.5 shows how the theory can be used to understand some of the effects of technological changes that lower production costs.

The effect of making capital a variable input

Consider the position of the firms and the industry when both are in long-run equilibrium. There is no change that any firm could make over the short or long run that would

Box 6.5 The effects of changing technology

A once-and-for-all change

To see the effects of a single advance in an industry's production technology, let the industry start in long-run equilibrium where each firm is earning zero profits. Some technological development in the industry's production process now lowers the production costs of newly built plants. In this case, as with many technological changes, old production facilities cannot use the technology because it must be embodied in new plant and equipment. Since initially the price was just equal to the average total cost for the existing plants, new plants will be able to earn profits and they will be built immediately. But this expansion in capacity shifts the industry's short-run supply curve to the right and drives price down.

The expansion in capacity and the fall in price will continue until price is equal to the average total cost of the new plants. At this price old plants will not be covering their long-run costs. However, as long as price exceeds their average variable cost, they will continue in production. As the outmoded plants wear out, they will gradually disappear. Eventually a new long-run equilibrium will be established in which all plants use the new technology. Output will be larger, price will be lower, and the new plants will be just covering their total costs.

Ongoing changes

Now ask what happens in a competitive industry in which this type of technological change occurs more or less continuously. Plants built in any one year will tend to have lower costs than plants built in any previous year. The figure illustrates such an industry. Plant 1 is the oldest plant in operation. It is just covering its average variable costs, and it will close down when price falls below p_0. Plant 2 is of intermediate age. It is covering its variable costs and earning some contribution towards its fixed costs, as shown by the shaded area in part (ii). Plant 3 is the newest plant with the lowest costs. It is fully covering its fixed costs as shown by the dark shaded area in (iii). It is also making additional profits

(shown by the light shaded area) which will offset the losses it expects to suffer later, when firms with newer technology enter the industry.

Such an industry typically has a number of interesting characteristics.

First, plants in operation will be of many different ages and at different levels of efficiency. This is dramatically illustrated by the variety of types and vintages of generator found in any long-established electricity industry. Critics who observe the continued use of older less efficient plants and urge that the industry be modernized miss the point of economic efficiency. If the plant is already there, it can be operated profitably as long as it can cover its variable costs.

A second characteristic of such an industry is that price will be governed by the minimum average total cost of the most efficient plants. Entry will continue until plants of the latest vintage are just expected to cover the opportunity cost of their capital over their lifetimes. This means that new plants must earn pure profits when they enter to balance the losses they expect later in life when newer firms with superior technologies enter the industry. The benefits of the new technology are passed on to consumers, because all units of the product, whether produced by new or old plants, are sold at a price that is related solely to the average total costs of the new plants. Owners of older plants find their returns over variable costs falling steadily as increasingly efficient plants drive the price down.

A third characteristic is that old plants will be discarded when the price falls below their average total costs. This may occur well before the plants are physically worn out. In industries with continuous technical progress, capital is usually discarded because it is economically obsolete, not because it has physically worn out. This illustrates the economic meaning of 'obsolete'.

Old capital is obsolete when its average variable cost exceeds the average total cost of new capital.

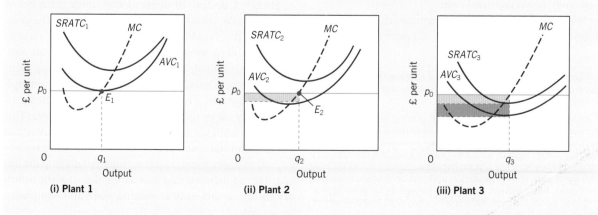

(i) Plant 1   (ii) Plant 2   (iii) Plant 3

increase its profits. This requirement can be stated as three distinct conditions.

1. *No firm wants to vary the output of its existing plants.* Short-run marginal cost (*SRMC*) is equal to price.

2. *Profits earned by existing plants are zero.* This implies that short-run *ATC* is equal to price—that is, firms are in the position of the firm in Figure 6.8(ii).

3. *No firm could earn profits by building a plant of a different size.* This implies that each existing firm must be producing at the lowest point on its long-run average cost curve.

We have already seen why the first two conditions must hold. The reasoning behind the third condition is shown in Figure 6.10. Although the firm with the average cost curve $SRATC_0$ is in short-run equilibrium, it is not in long-run equilibrium because its *LRAC* curve lies below the market price at some higher levels of output.[7] Therefore the firm can increase its profits by building a plant of larger size, thereby lowering its average total costs. Since the firm is a price taker, this change will increase its profits.

A price-taking firm is in long-run equilibrium only when it is producing at the minimum point on its *LRAC* curve.

All three of the preceding conditions are satisfied when each firm in the industry is in the position shown in Figure 6.10 by the short-run cost curve $SRATC*$.[8]

Long-run response to a change in demand

What will happen if demand for the product increases? Price will rise to equate demand with the industry's short-run supply. Each firm will expand output until its short-run marginal cost once again equals price. Each firm will earn profits as a result of the rise in price, and the profits will induce new firms to enter the industry. This will shift the short-run supply curve to the right and force down the price. Entry will continue until all firms are once again just covering average total costs.

What if demand falls? The industry starts with firms in long-run equilibrium, as shown in Figure 6.10, and the

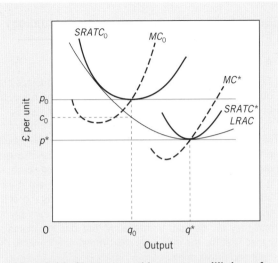

Figure 6.10 Short-run and long-run equilibrium of a firm in perfect competition

A perfectly competitive firm that is not at the minimum point on its *LRAC* curve cannot be in long-run equilibrium. The firm's existing plant has short-run cost curves $SRATC_0$ and MC_0 while market price is p_0. The firm produces q_0, where MC_0 equals price and total costs are just being covered. Although the firm is in short-run equilibrium, it can earn profits by building a larger plant and so moving downwards along its *LRAC* curve. Thus the firm cannot be in long-run equilibrium at any output below $q*$ because average total costs can be reduced by building a larger plant. If all firms do this, industry output will increase and price will fall until long-run equilibrium is reached at price $p*$. Each firm is then in short-run equilibrium with a plant whose average cost curve is $SRATC*$ and whose short-run marginal cost curve, $MC*$, intersects the price line $p*$ at an output of $q*$. Because the *LRAC* curve lies above $p*$ everywhere except at $q*$, the firm has no incentive to move to another point on its *LRAC* curve by altering the size of its plant. The output $q*$ is the firm's minimum efficient scale.

market demand curve shifts left and price falls. There are two possible consequences.

First, the decline in demand may force price below *ATC* but leave it above *AVC*. Firms are then in the position shown in Figure 6.8(i). They can cover their variable costs and earn some return on their capital, so they remain in production for as long as their existing plant and equipment lasts. However, exit will occur as old capital wears out and is not replaced. As firms exit, the short-run supply curve shifts left and market price rises. This continues until the remaining firms in the industry can cover their total costs. At this point, it will pay to replace capital as it wears out, and the industry will stop declining. This adjustment may take a long time, for the industry shrinks in size only as existing plant and equipment wears out.

---

[7] Because all inputs are variable in the long run, no distinction is needed between variable and fixed costs. There is only one long-run average cost curve.

[8] The text discussion implies that all existing firms and all new entrants face identical *LRAC* curves. This means that all firms face the same set of input prices and use the same technology. We are in the long run, where technological knowledge is given and constant, and where all firms have had a chance to adjust their capital to the best that is available. This is a theoretical construction designed to analyse tendencies. In any industry in which technological change is ongoing, full long-run equilibrium will never be established and a variety of technologies will be used by different firms at each point in time.

The second possibility is that the decline in demand is large enough to push price below the level of *AVC*. Now firms cannot even cover their variable costs, and some will shut down immediately. Reduction in capital devoted to production in the industry occurs rapidly because some existing capacity is scrapped or shifted to other uses. The decline in the number of firms reduces supply and raises the equilibrium price. Once the price rises enough to allow the remaining firms to cover their variable costs, the rapid withdrawal of capital ceases. Further exit occurs more slowly, as described in the previous paragraph.

Entry of new capital into a profitable industry can take place only as fast as new plants can be built and new equipment installed. Exit of existing capital from an unprofitable industry with losses will occur very quickly when price is less than average variable cost, but only at the rate at which old plant and equipment wear out when price exceeds average variable cost.

Box 6.6 applies what we have just learned to the case of declining industries.

The long-run industry supply curve

Possible adjustments of the industry to the kind of changes in demand just discussed are shown by the **long-run industry supply (*LRS*) curve**. This curve shows the relationship between equilibrium market price and the output that firms will be willing to supply after all desired entry or exit has occurred.

The long-run supply curve shows the quantity supplied at each market price in long-run equilibrium—that is, after all demand-induced changes have occurred and the incentives for exit and entry have been eliminated.

For given input prices, the long-run supply curve of a competitive industry will be horizontal. But when induced changes in input prices are considered, it is possible for the *LRS* curve to be positively or negatively sloped. The various cases are illustrated in Figure 6.11.

In Figure 6.11(i) the long-run supply curve is horizontal. This indicates that, given time, the industry will adjust its size to provide whatever quantity is demanded at a constant price. That price is set by the minimum point of the firms' long-run average cost curves. An industry with a horizontal long-run supply curve is said to be a *constant-cost industry*.

This case occurs when a change in the size of the industry leaves the long-run cost curves of existing firms unchanged, which requires that the industry's input prices do not change as the whole industry's output expands or contracts. Since all firms are assumed to have access to the same technology and face the same input

---

Box 6.6 Declining industries

What happens when a competitive industry begins to suffer losses because the demand for its output begins to decline? The market price will begin to fall, and firms that were previously covering average total costs will no longer be able to do so. They find themselves in the position shown in part (i) of Figure 6.8. Firms suffer losses instead of breaking even; the signal for the exit of capital is given, but exit takes time.

The economically efficient response to a steadily declining demand is to continue to operate with existing equipment as long as its variable costs of production can be covered. As equipment becomes obsolete because it cannot cover even its variable cost, it will not be replaced unless the new equipment can cover its total cost. As a result the capacity of the industry will shrink. If demand keeps declining, capacity must keep shrinking.

Declining industries typically give a depressing impression. Revenues are below long-run total costs, and as a result new equipment is not brought in to replace old equipment as it wears out. Thus the average age of equipment in use rises steadily. An observer, seeing the industry's plight, is likely to blame it on the old equipment.

The antiquated equipment in a declining industry is often the effect rather than the cause of the industry's decline.

Governments are often tempted to support declining industries because they are worried about the resulting job losses. However, experience suggests that propping up genuinely declining industries only delays their demise—at significant national cost. When the government finally withdraws its support, the decline is usually more abrupt and hence more difficult to adjust to than it would have been had the industry been allowed to decline gradually under the market force of steadily declining demand.

Once governments recognize the decay of certain industries and the collapse of certain firms as an inevitable aspect of economic growth, a more effective response is to provide temporary income support and retraining schemes that cushion the impacts of change. These can moderate the effects on the incomes of workers who lose their jobs and make it easier for them to transfer to expanding industries. Intervention that is intended to increase mobility while reducing its social and personal costs is a viable long-run policy. In contrast, trying to freeze the existing industrial structure by shoring up a declining industry is not viable in the long run.

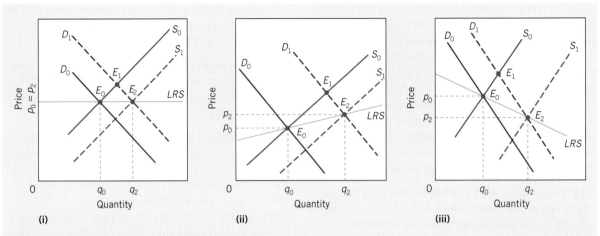

Figure 6.11 Long-run industry supply curves

The long-run industry supply curve may be horizontal, or positively or negatively sloped. In all three parts the initial curves are at D_0 and S_0, yielding equilibrium at E_0 with price p_0 and quantity q_0. A rise in demand shifts the demand curve to D_1, taking the short-run equilibrium to E_1. New firms now enter the industry, shifting the short-run supply curve outwards and pushing price down until pure profits are no longer being earned. At this point the supply curve is S_1 and the new equilibrium is E_2 with price at p_2 and quantity q_2. In part (i) price returns to its original level, making the long-run supply curve horizontal. In part (ii) profits are eliminated before price falls to its original level, giving the *LRS* curve a positive slope. In part (iii) the price falls below its original level before profits return to normal, giving the *LRS* curve a negative slope.

prices, all firms have identical cost curves. Under these circumstances the long-run equilibrium with price equal to minimum long-run average total cost of each and every firm can be re-established after a change in demand only when price returns to its original level.

Changing input prices and rising long-run supply curves

When an industry expands its output it needs more inputs. The increase in demand for these inputs may bid up their prices.[9]

If costs rise with increasing levels of industry output, so too must the price at which the producers are able to cover their costs. As the industry expands, the short-run supply curve shifts outwards but the firms' *SRATC* curves shift upward because of rising input prices. The expansion of the industry comes to a halt when price is equal to minimum *LRAC* for existing firms. This must occur at a higher price than ruled before the expansion began, as illustrated in Figure 6.11(ii). A competitive industry with rising long-run supply prices is often called a *rising-cost industry*.

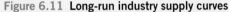

[9] In a fully employed economy the expansion of one industry implies the contraction of some other industry. What happens to input prices depends on the proportions in which the expanding and the contracting industries use the inputs. The relative price of the input used intensively by the expanding industry will rise, causing the costs of the expanding industry to rise relative to those of the contracting industry. In a two-sector, two-input model a rising long-run industry supply curve is normal because of the effect that changes in industry outputs have on relative input prices.

Can the long-run supply curve be negatively sloped?

So far we have suggested that the long-run supply curve may be horizontal or positively sloped. Could it ever be negatively sloped, thereby indicating that higher outputs are associated with lower prices in long-run equilibrium?

It is tempting to answer 'yes', because of the opportunities of more efficient scales of operation using greater mechanization and more effective specialization of labour. But this answer would not be correct for perfectly competitive industries because each firm in long-run equilibrium must already be at the lowest point on its *LRAC* curve. If a firm could lower its costs by building a larger more mechanized plant, it would be profitable to do so without waiting for an increase in demand. Since any single firm can sell all it wishes at the going market price, it will be profitable to expand the scale of its operations as long as its *LRAC* is falling.

The scale economies that we have just considered are within the control of the firm; they are said to be **internal economies**. However, a perfectly competitive industry might have falling long-run costs if industries that supply its inputs have increasing returns to scale. Such effects are outside the control of the perfectly competitive firm and are called **external economies**. Whenever expansion of an industry leads to a fall in the prices of some of its inputs, the firms will find their cost curves shifting downwards as they expand their outputs.

As an illustration of how the expansion of one industry could cause the prices of some of its inputs to fall, consider the early stages of the growth of the car industry. As the output of cars increased, the industry's demand for tyres grew considerably. This increased the demand for rubber and tended to raise its price, but it also provided the opportunity for tyre manufacturers to build larger plants which exploited some of the economies available in tyre production. These economies were large enough to offset any input-price increases, and tyre prices charged to car manufacturers fell. Thus, car costs fell, because of lower prices of an important input. This case is illustrated in part (iii) of Figure 6.11. An industry that has a negatively sloped long-run supply curve is often called a *falling-cost industry*.

Notice that although the economies were external to the car industry, they were internal to the tyre industry. However, if the tyre industry had been perfectly competitive, all its scale economies would already have been exploited. So this is a case of a perfectly competitive industry that uses an input produced by a non-perfectly-competitive industry, whose own scale economies have not yet been fully exploited because demand is insufficient. Another example is provided by perfectly competitive agricultural industries, which buy their farm machinery from the farm implement industry, which is dominated by a few large firms.

Can perfectly competitive industries have unexploited scale economies?

The key to answering this question lies in the size of the firm relative to the size of the market.

A perfectly competitive firm will not be in equilibrium on the falling part of *LRAC*—if price is given and costs can be reduced by increasing the scale of output, profits can be increased by doing so. Thus, firms will grow in size until all scale economies are exhausted. Provided that the output that yields the minimum *LRAC* for each firm is small relative to the industry's total output, the industry will contain a large number of firms and will remain competitive. However, if reaching the minimum *LRAC* makes firms so large that each one has significant market power,

they will cease to be price takers and perfect competition will also cease to exist. Indeed, scale economies may exist over such a large range that one firm's *LRAC* is still falling when it serves the entire market. That firm will then grow until it monopolizes the entire market. This case, which economists call a *natural* monopoly, is considered further in Chapter 13.

A necessary condition for a long-run perfectly competitive equilibrium is that any scale economies that are within the firm's control should be exhausted at a level of output that is small relative to the whole industry's output.

Firms with a divisible fixed input

Figure 5.8 in Chapter 5 shows a firm with a constant average variable and marginal cost up to 'capacity output'. If the firm is a profit maximizer, it will behave in perfectly competitive markets just as does a firm with an indivisible fixed input. It will maximize profits by equating marginal costs with price and will continue to produce as long as price is not less than its average variable costs. The only difference from a firm with an indivisible fixed input is that its *SRAVC* curve is horizontal rather than upward sloping for outputs below q_i.

If there are no significant differences between the behaviours of two types of firm, one may reasonably ask why we took all the trouble to distinguish them in the preceding chapter on costs? The answer is that the technologies of the divisible and indivisible factors are different, and it is important to know if these make a difference in actual behaviour. We have seen that under perfect competition the difference in fixed costs makes no difference to the behaviour of profit-maximizing firms. Later we will see that it does make a difference in some aspects of the behaviour of firms that face negatively sloped demand curves for their products. Some of these differences will be seen in the next few chapters, but the most important ones do not show up until one we cover macroeconomics, especially in Chapter 22.

The allocative efficiency of perfect competition

We saw in Chapter 1 that resources are allocated by markets in which people make independent decisions motivated by self-interest. Under certain conditions this market outcome is *optimal* or *efficient*. (These two words mean the same thing in this context.) Resources are efficiently allocated if there is no other allocation that would allow someone to be made better off while no one else was made worse off. To put this statement the other

way around, resources are *inefficiently* allocated if the allocation could be changed in such a way as to make at least one person better off while making no one else worse off. For example, if resources could be reallocated so as to make fewer hats and more shoes, and someone was made better off by the change while no one was made worse off, the current allocation cannot be efficient.

It can be shown that a perfectly competitive economy would allocate its resources efficiently. However, a number of other conditions also need to be fulfilled, as we shall see in Chapter 13. In the meantime, we will show one way in which the tendency for perfect competition to produce an optimal allocation of resources can be established. We do this using the concepts of consumers' and producers' surplus.

We first introduced the idea of consumers' surplus in Box 4.3 in Chapter 4. **Consumers' surplus** is the difference between the total value that consumers place on all the units consumed of some product and the payment that they actually make for the purchase of that product. This surplus arises because each consumer, who has a negatively sloped demand curve for each product, would be prepared to pay more for the first unit of a product consumed than for the second, and a decreasing amount for each subsequent unit. Take, for example, my demand for visits to the movies each month. If tickets cost £30, I would go once per month (and £30 is the value I place on that first visit). At £20 I would go twice per month (and still value the first visit at £30 and the second visit at £20) and at £10 I might go three times per month (valuing the first visit at £30, the second at £20, and the third at £10). If the market price is £10, then I will go to the movies three times a month and pay £30 for these visits (three tickets at £10 each). But I will value these visits at £60 (£30 for the first visit, £20 for the second visit, and £10 for the third visit). This is because I would have been prepared to pay £30 for the first visit but only had to pay £10, and I would have been prepared to pay £20 for the second visit but only had to pay £10, and so on. Thus, the value of my consumer surplus from purchases of movie tickets is £30 per month (the £60 of value that I place on these visits minus the £30 I actually paid at £10 per ticket).

Put another way, consumers pay the same amount for each unit that they purchase but, given diminishing marginal utility, they value every unit that they purchase at more than that price—with the exception only of the last marginal unit, which they value at just the price they pay for it. The difference is the consumers' surplus, which is positive for each unit purchased, except for the last unit where the value they get is just equal to the price that they pay.

For consumers in general, the total value that they place on the amount they consume of a specific product is the area under the demand curve, which represents the summation of all the marginal valuations they place on each successive unit consumed. What they pay is the area representing the price multiplied by the quantity consumed. The difference between these two is shown in Figure 6.12 as consumers' surplus.

Producers' surplus is analogous to consumers' surplus. It occurs because all units of each firm's output are sold at

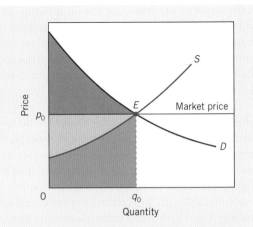
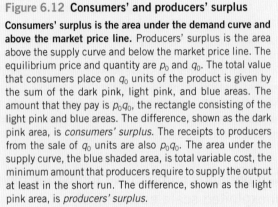

Figure 6.12 Consumers' and producers' surplus

Consumers' surplus is the area under the demand curve and above the market price line. Producers' surplus is the area above the supply curve and below the market price line. The equilibrium price and quantity are p_0 and q_0. The total value that consumers place on q_0 units of the product is given by the sum of the dark pink, light pink, and blue areas. The amount that they pay is p_0q_0, the rectangle consisting of the light pink and blue areas. The difference, shown as the dark pink area, is *consumers' surplus*. The receipts to producers from the sale of q_0 units are also p_0q_0. The area under the supply curve, the blue shaded area, is total variable cost, the minimum amount that producers require to supply the output at least in the short run. The difference, shown as the light pink area, is *producers' surplus*.

the single market price, while, given a rising supply curve, the marginal cost of all but the last unit is less than the market price. **Producers' surplus** is defined as the amount that producers are paid for a product less the total variable cost of production. The total variable cost of producing any output is shown by the area under the supply curve up to that output, which represents the summation of the marginal costs of producing each unit of output.[10] Thus, producers' surplus, which is shown in Figure 6.12, is the area between the supply curve and the market price line. (All firms are either directly or indirectly owned by people, so producers' surplus is really owners' surplus.)

If the total of consumers' and producers' surplus is not maximized, the industry's output could be altered to increase that total. The additional surplus could then be used to make some people better off without making any others worse off.

[10] The area under a marginal cost curve up to any output is the total variable cost of producing that output. Graphically, taking the area under a marginal cost curve is equivalent to summing all the marginal costs to get total variable cost. Similarly, summing the area under the demand curve yields the total amount that consumers would be willing to pay if offered each unit one at a time, i.e. the total valuation that they place on all the units.

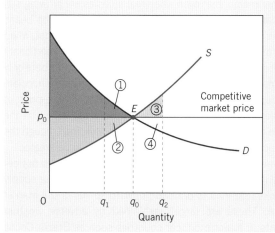

Figure 6.13 The allocative efficiency of perfect competition

Competitive equilibrium is allocatively efficient because it maximizes the sum of consumers' and producers' surplus. At the competitive equilibrium E consumers' surplus is the dark pink area above the price line, while producers' surplus is the light pink area below the price line. Reducing the output to q_1 but keeping price at p_0 lowers consumers' surplus by area 1 and lowers producers' surplus by area 2. If producers are forced to produce output q_2 and to sell it to consumers, who are in turn forced to buy it at price p_0, producers' surplus is reduced by area 3 (the amount by which variable costs exceed revenue on those units), while consumers' surplus is reduced by area 4 (the amount by which expenditure exceeds consumers' satisfactions on those units). Only at the competitive output, q_0, is the sum of the two surpluses maximized.

Allocative efficiency occurs where the sum of consumers' and producers' surplus is maximized.

The allocatively efficient output occurs under perfect competition where the demand curve intersects the supply curve—that is, at the point of equilibrium in a competitive market. This is shown graphically in Figure 6.13. For any output that is less than the competitive output, the demand curve lies above the supply curve, which means that the value consumers put on the last unit of production exceeds its marginal cost of production. Suppose, for example, that an additional pair of shoes costs £60 to make but is valued by consumers at £70. If the shoes are sold at any price between £60 and £70, both producers and consumers gain; there is £10 of potential surplus to be divided between the two. In contrast, the last unit produced and sold at competitive equilibrium adds nothing to either consumers' or producers' surplus. This is because consumers value it at exactly its market price, and it adds the full amount of the market price to producers' costs.

If production were pushed beyond the competitive equilibrium, the sum of the two surpluses would fall. Assume, for example, that firms were forced to produce and sell further units of output at the competitive market price and that consumers were forced to buy these extra units at that price. (Neither group would do so voluntarily.) Firms would lose producers' surplus on those extra units because their marginal costs of producing them would be above the price that they received for them. Purchasers would lose consumers' surplus because the valuation that they placed on these extra units, as shown by the demand curve, would be less than the price that they would have to pay.

The sum of producers' and consumers' surplus is maximized when a perfectly competitive industry is in equilibrium with demand equal to supply. The resulting level of output is allocatively efficient.

CASE STUDIES

The markets that best fit the assumptions of perfect competition are those for primary commodities. These are homogeneous products, they typically sell on world markets, and each individual supplier is small in the sense that each one cannot influence the world market price by acting alone. In Chapter 3 we discussed some features of the market for coffee beans, which at the level of individual coffee farmers fits into our classification of a perfectly competitive market. We now look at two others, the markets for cocoa beans and the market for copper.

1. Cocoa: 'the food of the gods'[11]

Cocoa beans are the main natural material used to make chocolate, and the links between the markets for chocolate and cocoa were raised in Box 6.1. Cocoa beans grow on trees that require a tropical climate and substantial

---

[11] This is the name given to cocoa by the Spanish conquistadors when they first came across it in South America around 500 years ago. We are grateful to Juan Berg for this information.

rainfall. They require the shade of other trees, but once matured a cocoa tree will bear fruit for up to a hundred years or so. The plant is a native of South America but its cultivation spread to Africa and Asia. In the 1970s cocoa production was concentrated in Côte d'Ivoire, Ghana, Nigeria, and Brazil, but a high world market price encouraged entry for other producer countries such as Indonesia and Malaysia. In 2013, these six countries plus Ecuador, Cameroon, and the Dominican Republic accounted for over 90 per cent of the world market supply.

While there are eight major producing countries, within these countries production is fragmented into a mixture of medium-sized estates and small farms. In some cases, such as Ghana, the national government has created a marketing board to buy the beans from domestic farmers (and guarantee a price each year to these farmers). In other cases, private agents buy from the farmers and then sell in the world market. But in all cases the farmers themselves are price takers and are unable to influence the price that they receive each year.

Figure 6.14 shows the world price of cocoa beans between September 1983 and September 2013. The world market price reached an all-time high of around $4.40 per kilogram in the late 1970s as growing world demand hit a limited supply, and this encouraged a significant increase in planting. The result of this was that supply growth outstripped demand growth for much of the 1980s and 1990s. This supply increase helped to reduce the price. On several occasions the world price fell below $1.00 per kg.

As with many food products the demand side of the cocoa market is dominated by two important economic characteristics: a low income elasticity and a low price elasticity. The former means that even when real incomes are growing significantly in consumer countries, demand for cocoa beans grows only very slowly. Low price elasticity means that, when the price falls, this encourages a less than proportionate increase in quantity demanded. Cocoa beans contribute only a small component of the total cost of finished chocolate products, so, for example, a significant fall in the price of wholesale cocoa beans will have a very small effect on the price of a half-pound box of Cadbury's Milk Tray, though the impact on prices of dark chocolate is likely to be greater.

One characteristic of the coffee market that is noticeable in Figure 3.12 is that there are occasional big supply shocks that lead to dramatic upward spikes in the market price. These are largely explained by adverse weather events in major producer countries such as Brazil. Cocoa is not subject to such adverse weather events. This is because, while cocoa and coffee are both grown in tropical regions, coffee is grown in cooler locations on higher ground that can be subjected to unseasonal frosts.

There was a clear price spike in the cocoa market in 2002 which was caused by a reduction in supply due to a civil war in Côte d'Ivoire, the largest producer country. The price spike in 2007–8 is harder to explain, but it does seem to be due to crop failures in the main African producing countries combined with buoyant demand in consuming countries. The even bigger price spike that came in 2010 took the cocoa price to a thirty-year high. This was caused by political disruption in Côte d'Ivoire. The incumbent president lost an election but refused to stand down and the country came to a standstill. By early 2011 the crisis was over, production had recovered, and the world price fell by around 30 per cent.

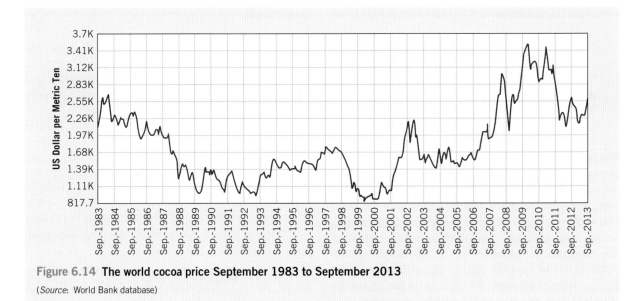

Figure 6.14 The world cocoa price September 1983 to September 2013

(*Source*: World Bank database)

It is easy to imagine the main decisions that cocoa farmers have to make. The first decision is made when deciding to go into the business of growing cocoa trees. How much land should be devoted to this crop? When the world price is high, it is likely that this would encourage new planting. Once the trees are planted, it takes three to five years for them to bear a crop and they can produce for at least another 25 years. Once planted, the fertility of the trees determines the size of the crop and then it is up to world market conditions to determine what the crop will be worth. When prices are low it is hard to shift the land into other uses. The farm could be sold, but would not fetch much if covered in low-value-producing cocoa trees. Alternatively, the cocoa trees and the surrounding shade-giving trees could be chopped down and the land converted to another use. However, this is expensive, hard to reverse, and alternative crops may be few and just as low yielding. Hence, in the short-term, a typical cocoa farmer has little choice but to live as best he or she can off whatever revenue the crop from their existing trees generates each year. This is not a perfect world, but it is one example of perfect competition at work. The world market price is determined by the global interaction of demand and supply, and each producer has to accept whatever price is so determined.

2. Copper

Archaeological evidence demonstrates that copper was one of the first metals used by humans and was used at least 10,000 years ago for items such as coins and ornaments in western Asia. During the prehistoric Chalcolithic Period (derived from chalkos, the Greek word for copper), man discovered how to extract and use copper to produce ornaments and implements. As early as the 4th to 3rd millennium BC, workers extracted copper from Spain's Huelva region.

The discovery that copper, when alloyed with tin, produces bronze, led to the Bronze Age, c. 2,500 BC. Israel's Timna Valley provided copper to the Pharaohs (an Egyptian papyrus records the use of copper to treat infections and to sterilize water). Cyprus supplied much of the Phoenician, Greek and Roman needs for copper. 'Copper' is derived from the Latin Cyprium, literally Cyprian metal. The Greeks of Aristotle's era were familiar with brass as a valued copper alloy. In South America, the pre-columbian Maya, Aztec and Inca civilizations exploited copper, in addition to gold and silver.

During the Middle Ages, copper and bronze works flourished in China, India and Japan. The discoveries and inventions relating to electricity and magnetism of the late 18th and early 19th centuries by scientists such as Ampere, Faraday and Ohm, and the products manufactured from copper, helped launch the Industrial Revolution and propel copper into a new era.

Today, copper continues to serve society's needs. Although copper has been in use for at least 10,000 years, innovative applications for copper are still being developed as evidenced by the development of the copper chip by the semi-conductors industry.

(Source: World Copper Factbook 2013, International Copper Study Group, Lisbon.)

The copper market shares some characteristics with the tin market that we discussed in the case study at the end of Chapter 2. They are both metals that are inputs into industries in the major countries of the world. In common with other markets that have a perfectly competitive structure, there is a homogenous product and the world price is determined in the aggregate by the interaction of demand and supply. In the cases of both copper and tin (as compared to coffee and cocoa) it is less obvious that all the assumptions of perfect competition are satisfied because there some very large producers in these markets. However, in both cases the world market is so large compared to the output of even the largest firms that each firm is a price taker. Also both copper and tin can be produced in many different parts of the world.

Figure 6.15 shows world copper prices since 1983. As copper is an input into virtually all construction projects, demand tends to rise when there is a construction boom in the main consuming countries. Thus, demand was high in the late 1980s and the mid-1990s. In a period of slack demand, such as the mid-1980s and 1998–2002, there is an excess of production over final demand that leads to a big build-up of stocks. Rundowns of stocks in periods of high demand help to moderate the resulting price rises. This feature of the copper market, that inventories are built up when demand is low and run down when it is high, serves to moderate price fluctuations and makes this market rather different from that of a perishable commodity. However, it does not violate the assumptions of perfect competition because all that is required is that individual producers know about the price fluctuations and prefer to maintain production and build up stocks when they perceive that demand is low and to sell these off when they perceive that demand is high.

In 2003, world copper demand started to grow faster than new production could be brought online and accumulated inventories of copper ran down rapidly. This demand growth came largely from the rapid growth in demand for construction in China, India, and other Asian countries. By 2004 stocks reached historically low levels and prices started to rise sharply from $3000 per tonne to $8000 in 2006. This boom in demand relative to supply kept the price high until the financial crisis of 2008 led to a collapse of asset and commodity prices globally. Demand started to recover strongly in 2009 as confidence returned, and reached an all-time high in

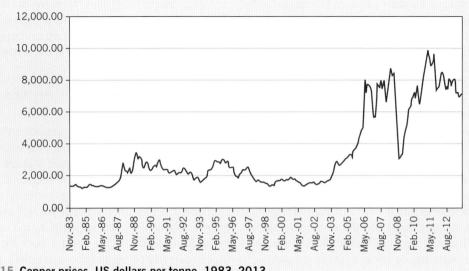

Figure 6.15 **Copper prices, US dollars per tonne, 1983–2013**

Source: World Bank database

mid-2011. Prices moderated in late 2011 but remained well above the levels that applied before 2005. Demand remained robust relative to supply but growth in Europe became weak and China's growth appeared to be moderating. For individual firms, the choices posed by the market in which they operate fit well with the perfect competition model. They take the world market price as beyond their control and then have to decide how much to produce. Firms in this industry own mines or mining rights, but extracting the metal is expensive as it is found deep underground and much labour and machinery are required to recover the ore. Production has increasing marginal costs even in existing mines. Opening up new mines has high marginal costs and considerable time must pass before sales can increase. Hence, when prices are low firms cut back on their production and cease operation in specific mines that do not cover average variable costs. (This is similar to the decision by airline operators to park their planes when demand is low, discussed in Box 6.3.) When the price is high, firms expand production up to the point where marginal cost is equal to price. They may also investigate the opening up of new mines. In general they will go ahead with such investment decisions if the expected extra revenue exceeds the extra cost. (The precise calculation involved in such an investment decision is discussed in Chapter 11.)

As the world price is given, the main incentive for profit-maximizing firms is to seek ways of reducing their costs of production. This means looking for improved extraction technology, hiring more productive workers, or reducing costs of management and distribution. The perfect competition model is more than adequate to help us understand the context of these decisions.

A worrying and dangerous consequence of the high price of copper from 2006 onwards was an increase in theft as the following two extracts indicate.

In March, a Port of Houston security guard was arrested for giving his friends and families access to the port, where they allegedly stole more than 22,000 pounds of copper. Meanwhile in 2008, thieves posing as utility workers in Florida stole more than $1 million worth of copper cables installed below the city streets. In particular thieves are targeting the energy, transportation, communications, agriculture, and water sectors as they are the most lucrative. These industries have facilities that house large quantities of copper components and often lack security measures to prevent theft making them appealing targets.

Law enforcement officials are keen to stop these robberies as they often disrupt electricity and communications networks and are expensive to replace. The Department of Energy estimates that in 2007 US electrical utilities spent nearly $1 billion annually to repair the disruptions made by copper wire theft.

(Source: <http://www.homelandsecuritynewswire.com/dhs-warns-copper-thefts-rise>)

Copper thieves are threatening US critical infrastructure by targeting electrical substations, cellular towers, telephone land lines, railroads, water wells, construction sites, and vacant homes for lucrative profits. Copper thefts from these targets have increased since 2006; and they are currently disrupting the flow   of electricity, telecommunications, transportation, water supply, heating, and security and emergency services, and present a risk to both public safety and national security.

• According to open-source reporting, on 4 April 2008, five tornado warning sirens in the Jackson, Mississippi, area did not warn residents of an approaching tornado because copper thieves had stripped the sirens of copper wiring, thus rendering them inoperable.

• According to open-source reporting, on 20 March 2008, nearly 4,000 residents in Polk County, Florida, were left without power after copper wire was stripped

from an active transformer at a Tampa Electric Company (TECO) power facility. Monetary losses to TECO were approximately $500,000.

• According to agricultural industry reporting, as of March 2007, farmers in Pinal County, Arizona, were experiencing a copper theft epidemic as perpetrators stripped copper from their water irrigation wells and pumps resulting in the loss of crops and high replacement costs. Pinal County's infrastructure loss due to copper theft was $10 million.

(Source: <http://www.fbi.gov/stats-services/publications/copper-thefts>)

Conclusion

Perfect competition is a special case that only exists in a few sectors where the product is homogeneous and there are so many buyers and sellers that no one of them can influence the market price by altering the amount that he or she buys or sells. This applies to primary commodity industries but it does not apply to most of the goods and services purchased by consumers. The bread and washing powder in Sainsbury's and Tesco may be identical but supermarkets are not operating under perfect competition as they have some power over their prices, and their brands do differentiate what is the same generic product. Most other consumer products are even more affected by brands and actual product differentiation. Hence, the perfect competition model is not directly applicable to most markets for consumers' goods and services. But along with many primary products, the theory of perfect competition does apply to many financial markets. Government bonds, the shares and bonds issued by private firms, and foreign exchange are all sold in markets that come close to being perfectly competitive. Most of those who buy and sell in these markets

can do nothing to affect the going price but instead can buy or sell as much as they want at the market price. However, when governments issue bonds they know that the amount they offer for sale will influence the price to some extent. But when these bonds are bought and sold subsequently by investors in the private sector, these agents can do little to affect price. Occasionally, there are a few operators in these markets who are large enough to affect the price. Also what is being sold is part of an existing a stock of assets, not a flow of current production. Nonetheless most of the time the price in these markets behaves just as predicted by the theory of perfect competition.

Indeed, the model of perfect competition gives us some key insights into the working of any market economy. It gives us a simple example within which to understand the principles of profit maximization. It highlights the incentive role played by profits in driving entry and exit of firms. Finally, it provides the benchmark for the optimal allocation of resources. All of these insights have a pay-off in later chapters.

SUMMARY

Market structure and firm behaviour

■ Competitive *behaviour* refers to the extent to which individual firms compete with each other to sell their products. Competitive *market structure* refers to the power that individual firms have over the market—perfect competition occurs where firms have no market power and hence no need to react to each other.

Elements of the theory of perfect competition

■ The theory of perfect competition is based on the following assumptions: firms sell a homogeneous

product; customers are well informed; each of the industry's many firms is a price taker; firms are free to enter or leave the industry.

Short-run equilibrium

■ Any firm maximizes profits by producing the output where its marginal cost curve intersects the marginal revenue curve from below—or by producing nothing if average variable cost exceeds price at all possible outputs.

■ A perfectly competitive firm is a quantity adjuster, facing a perfectly elastic demand curve at the given market price and maximizing profits by choosing the output that equates its marginal cost to price.

■ The supply curve of a firm in perfect competition is its marginal cost curve, and the supply curve of a perfectly competitive industry is the horizontal sum of the marginal cost curves of all its firms. The intersection of this curve with the market demand curve for the industry's product determines market price.

Long-run equilibrium

■ Long-run industry equilibrium requires that each individual firm be producing at the minimum point of its *LRAC* curve and be making zero profits.

■ The long-run industry supply curve for a perfectly competitive industry may be (i) positively sloped, if input prices are driven up by the industry's expansion, (ii) horizontal, if plants can be replicated and input prices remain constant, or (iii) negatively sloped, if some other industry that is not perfectly competitive produces an input under conditions of falling long-run costs.

The allocative efficiency of perfect competition

■ Perfect competition produces an optimal allocation of resources because it maximizes the sum of consumers' and producers' surplus by producing equilibrium where marginal cost equals price.

TOPICS FOR REVIEW

■ Competitive behaviour and competitive market structure

■ Behavioural rules for the profit-maximizing firm

■ Price taking and a horizontal demand curve

■ Average revenue, marginal revenue, and price under perfect competition

■ Relation of the industry supply curve to its firms' marginal cost curves

■ The role of entry and exit in achieving long-run equilibrium

■ Exhaustion of scale economies in perfectly competitive long-run equilibrium.

QUESTIONS

1 A firm sells its products at £15 each. Calculate its total, average, and marginal revenue at sales levels of 100, 500, and 10,000.

2 Suppose that total fixed costs of the firm in Question 1 are £300 and total variable costs for production levels between 100 units of output and 108 units of outputs are:

$$100 = £1,000$$
$$101 = £1,010$$
$$102 = £1,021$$
$$103 = £1,033$$
$$104 = £1,046$$
$$105 = £1,060$$
$$106 = £1,075$$
$$107 = £1,091$$
$$108 = £1,108$$

What is the profit-maximizing level of output, given a sale price of £15 as in Question 1?

3 Calculate the average variable cost and the average total cost associated with the output levels in Question 2. How much profit is made at the profit-maximizing level of output? How much profit would be made at the two higher and two lower levels of output? What would be the profit-maximizing output and profit at a sales price of £12?

4 Which of the following observed facts about an industry are inconsistent with its being perfectly competitive?

a) Different firms use different methods of production.
b) The industry's product is extensively advertised by a trade association.
c) Individual firms devote a large fraction of their sales receipts to advertising their own product brands.
d) There are twenty-four firms in the industry.
e) All firms made economic profits in 2010.
f) All firms are charging the same price.

5 A firm can sell its products for £500 each in a perfectly competitive output market. Its total cost of production for the production range of 4,000 units to 4,005 units per month is as follows

Units produced	4,000	4,001	4,002	4,003	4,004	4,005
Total cost	£800,000	£800,380	£800,780	£801,260	£801,780	£802,600

What is the profit-maximizing level of production?

a) 4,001
b) 4,002
c) 4,003
d) 4,004
e) 4,005

6 A firm can sell its products for £50 each in a perfectly competitive output market. Its total cost of production for the production range of 1,500 units to 1,505 units is given below:

Units produced	1,500	1,501	1,502	1,503	1,504	1,505
Total cost	£64,300	£64,340	£64,388	£64,437	£64,489	£64,550

What is the profit-maximizing level of production?

a) 1,501
b) 1,502
c) 1,503
d) 1,504
e) 1,505

7 What are the three rules of profit maximization? Explain these rules in the context of a firm that is in a perfectly competitive market structure.

8 Suppose that all of the potentially arable land in some country is currently being used for growing either wheat or barley. Both crop markets are in equilibrium. Discuss exactly how decentralized competitive markets would respond to shift resources following a report that barley helps to reduce cancer risk.

9 Why would the existence of entry barriers make it unlikely that an industry would be perfectly competitive? What types of entry barriers do you think are important in practice? How can the existence of economies of scale affect the degree of competitiveness in a market?

10 How does technical progress affect the equilibrium of a firm and of the perfectly competitive industry in which it operates? Why do some industries decline while others grow? At what point should firms quit a declining industry?

11 What factors determine the shape of the long-run supply curve of an industry?

12 What is allocative efficiency? Why is the outcome under perfect competition allocatively efficient?

CHAPTER 7

MONOPOLY

How does a firm choose its profit-maximizing output when it is the only producer of some product and so faces the negatively sloped market demand curve for that product? What price would this firm set? Does a monopolist have unlimited power to exploit consumers by charging them whatever price it pleases? These are some of the questions that we address in this chapter.

In particular, you will learn that:

- A monopolist sets marginal cost equal to marginal revenue, but marginal cost is less than price.
- If a perfectly competitive industry were monopolized and its costs were unaffected by the change, output would be reduced.
- Pure profits can exist in the long run under monopoly, but only to the extent that there are effective barriers to the entry of other firms.
- These profits can be increased for a monopolist if it is possible to charge different prices to different customers or in separate markets.
- Cartels can increase profits when previously competitive firms collude, but individual members of a cartel have an incentive to cheat.

Monopoly is at the opposite extreme from perfect competition. A **monopoly** occurs when one firm, called a monopolist or a monopoly firm, produces an industry's entire output. In contrast with perfectly competitive firms, which are price takers, a monopolist sets the market price.

As in the previous chapter, it is convenient to conduct the main analysis for a monopoly firm with an indivisible fixed input and at the end ask what difference there is if the firm has a divisible fixed input. In the first part of this chapter we show that when a monopoly firm must charge a single price for its output, it will produce less, charge a higher price, and earn greater profits than firms operating under perfect competition. Next, we explain why all monopoly firms have an incentive to charge different prices to different classes of user or for different units sold to the same user. We also see that monopoly profits provide a strong incentive for new firms to enter the industry and that this will happen unless there are effective barriers to entry, of either a natural or a man-made variety. In the final part of the

chapter we analyse how groups of firms can band together to form a cartel that raises profits by acting as if they were a single monopoly. Box 7.1 highlights a case where a monopoly owed its existence to government-imposed legal restrictions that have now been lifted. In the case studies at the end of the chapter we discuss other examples.

In Chapter 13 we discuss further the public policy issues posed by monopoly. Because a monopoly, and any other firm that faces a negatively sloped demand curve, produces less and charges more than the socially optimal output and price, there would be a social gain in altering behaviour in such an industry. Yet most industries that have one or a small number of firms do so because scale economies dictate that large firms are more efficient than smaller firms. In such cases perfect competition is not sustainable in a free market. Therefore one public policy issue is how to move price and output towards the socially optimal points in situations in which this cannot be done by market forces alone operating to produce the perfectly competitive result.

Box 7.1 Losing at monopoly

Many monopolies have existed in the past, but they are becoming harder to find. Some were created and protected by government regulation; others were an (almost) inevitable result of available technology. There has been a monopoly in postal services in most major countries for much of the past two centuries, but the picture has changed in the last decade. One reason why governments have long been concerned about having a reliable postal service is because they have wanted to ensure that messages (including tax demands and military conscription) can be guaranteed to be delivered to all residents. A US postal service was mandated in the US constitution (in the 1790s).

The Royal Mail (and its predecessor service which dates back to 1516) had a monopoly of letter delivery in the United Kingdom for over three hundred years, but this was ended in 2006. Many other countries have recently abolished their postal monopoly, including New Zealand, Sweden, Germany, and the Netherlands. In 2008, the EU Commission announced plans to abolish all postal monopolies in the Europen Union by 2013. The US Postal Service still has a legal monopoly over letter delivery, but it does have competition from companies like United Parcel Service and Federal Express in parcel delivery.

Most postal services were at one time owned by national governments, but that has also been changing. The UK's Royal Mail was privatized in October 2013 in the wake of several European countries doing the same thing, but the Post Office, which runs a network of retail outlets, remains in public ownership.

Though in private ownership and no longer a monopoly, Royal Mail continues to be regulated (by Ofcom). It has to maintain a universal service guarantee, which means that it will deliver six days of the week to all parts of the country. It is also subject to price caps on some of its products, but the services affected were reduced from 80 per cent of its revenue generation to 10 per cent in 2012.

However big the regulatory and ownership changes that have affected postal services, an even bigger impact has been felt from the massive and rapid growth of digital communications technologies, such as emails and texts. UK letter delivery volumes peaked in 2004 and have been declining ever since. Hence, the ending of postal monopolies has not just been a product of governments changing the rules but rather it has been the result of the arrival of a major new technology which could not have been dreamed of even 50 years ago. While letter deliveries have declined, parcel deliveries have grown for a related reason—online retailing and the delivery needs that result.

Other industries where monopolies have existed in the United Kingdom include railways, coal extraction, steel making, gas and electricity generation, and telephones. These were under state ownership from the 1940s until the 1980s when the businesses were split up and privatized. Once privatized they were still regulated to ensure that they did not exploit consumers (in ways we discuss below) and greater competition was stimulated (by, for example, assisting purchases from other providers). Technological advances also helped to break down monopolies. For example, BT still owns the majority of fixed telephone lines to houses and businesses that were once the source of its monopoly in the provision of UK telephone services, but ways were found to enable other suppliers access to these lines, and then along came mobile phones! This is discussed further in the first case study at the end of this chapter.

A single-price monopolist

We first analyse the price and output decision of a monopoly firm that charges a single price for its product. The firm's profits, like those of all firms, will depend on the relationship between its production costs and its sales revenues.

Cost and revenue in the short run

In Chapter 5, we saw that firms with an indivisible fixed input had U-shaped short-run cost curves. Since the conditions of cost are the same no matter what type of market the firm sells its product in, we can assume that monopoly firms with this type of fixed input also have U-shaped short-run cost curves.

Because the monopoly firm is the only firm in its industry, there is no distinction between the market demand curve and the demand curve facing a single firm, as there is in perfect competition. Thus the monopoly firm faces a negatively sloping market demand curve and can set its own price. However, this negatively sloped market demand curve presents the monopoly firm with a trade-off: sales can be increased only if price is reduced, or, to put the same point the other way around, price can be increased only if sales are reduced.

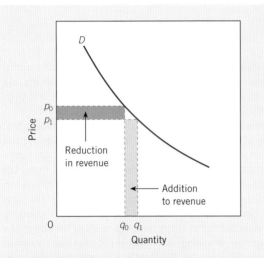

Figure 7.1 The effect on revenue of an increase in quantity sold

Because the demand curve has a negative slope, marginal revenue is less than price. A reduction of price from p_0 to p_1 increases sales by one unit from q_0 to q_1 units. The revenue from the extra unit sold is shown as the light blue area. But to sell this unit, it is necessary to reduce the price on each of the q_0 units previously sold. The loss in revenue is shown as the dark blue area. Marginal revenue of the extra unit is equal to the *difference* between the two areas.

Average and marginal revenue

When the monopoly firm charges the same price for all units sold, average revenue per unit is identical to price. Thus the market demand curve is also the firm's *average revenue curve*. But unlike the firms in perfect competition the monopoly firm's demand curve is not its marginal revenue curve, which shows the change in total revenue resulting from the sale of an additional (or marginal) unit of production. Because its demand curve is negatively sloped, the monopoly firm must lower the price that it charges on *all* units in order to sell an *extra* unit.

It follows that the addition to its revenue resulting from the sale of an extra unit is less than the price that it receives for that unit (less by the amount that it loses as a result of cutting the price on all the units that it was selling already).

The monopoly firm's marginal revenue is less than the price at which it sells its output.

This proposition is illustrated in Figure 7.1.

To clarify these relationships we use a numerical example of a specific straight-line demand curve. Some points on this curve are shown in tabular form in Table 7.1, while the whole curve is shown in Figure 7.2. Notice in the table that the change in total revenue associated with a change of £0.10 in price is recorded between the rows corresponding to three different prices. The data show what happens when the price is changed from the value shown in one row to the value shown in the adjacent row.

Table 7.1 Total, average, and marginal revenue

Price $p = AR$	Quantity q	Total revenue $TR = p \times q$	Marginal revenue $MR = \Delta TR/\Delta q$
£9.10	9	£81.90	
9.00	10	90.00	£8.10
8.90	11	97.90	7.90

Marginal revenue is less than price because price must be lowered to sell an extra unit. The marginal revenue of the 11th unit is the total revenue when 11 units are sold minus the total revenue when 10 units are sold. This is £7.90, which is less than the price of £8.90 at which all 11 units are sold. Marginal revenue is the £8.90 gained from selling the extra unit at £8.90 minus £0.10 lost on each of the 10 units already being sold when their price falls from £9.00 to £8.90.

Notice also from Figure 7.2 that when price is reduced, starting from £10, total revenue rises at first and then falls. The maximum total revenue is reached in this example at a price of £5. Since marginal revenue is the change in total revenue resulting from the sale of one more unit of output, marginal revenue is positive over the range where total revenue is increasing, and is negative where total revenue is falling.[1]

The proposition that marginal revenue is always *less than* average revenue, which is illustrated numerically in Table 7.1 and graphically in Figure 7.2, provides an important contrast with perfect competition. Recall that in perfect competition the firm's marginal revenue from selling an extra unit of output is *equal to* the price at which that unit is sold. The reason for the difference is not difficult to understand. The perfectly competitive firm is a price taker; it can sell all it wants at the given market price. The monopoly firm faces a negatively sloped demand curve; it must reduce the market price in order to increase its sales.

Marginal revenue and elasticity

In Chapter 3 we discussed the relationship between the elasticity of the market demand curve and the total revenue derived from selling the product. Figure 7.2 summarizes this earlier discussion for a linear demand curve and extends it to cover marginal revenue.

Over the range in which the demand curve is elastic, total revenue rises as more units are sold; therefore marginal revenue must be positive. Over the range in which the demand curve is inelastic, total revenue falls as more units are sold; therefore marginal revenue must be negative.

---

[1] Notice that the marginal revenue shown in Table 7.1 is obtained by subtracting the total revenue associated with one price from the total revenue associated with another, lower, price and then apportioning the change in revenue among the extra units sold. In symbols, it is $\Delta TR/\Delta q$.

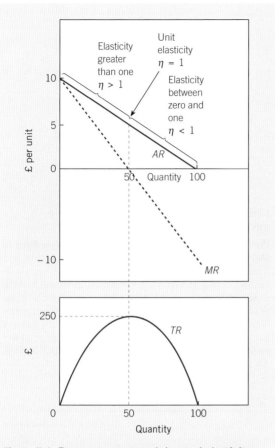

Figure 7.2 Revenue curves and demand elasticity

Rising *TR*, positive *MR*, and elastic demand all go together, as do falling *TR*, negative *MR*, and inelastic demand. In this example, for outputs from 0 to 50 marginal revenue is positive, elasticity is greater than unity, and total revenue is rising. For outputs from 50 to 100 marginal revenue is negative, elasticity is less than unity, and total revenue is falling. (All elasticities refer to absolute, not algebraic, values.)

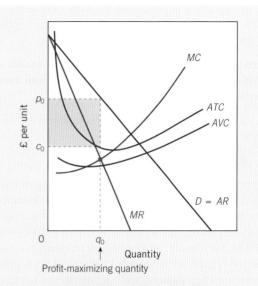

Figure 7.3 The equilibrium of a monopoly

The monopoly maximizes its profits by producing where marginal cost equals marginal revenue. The monopoly produces the output q_0 for which marginal revenue equals marginal revenue (rule 2). At this output the price of p_0, which is determined by the demand curve, exceeds the average variable cost (rule 1). Total profits are the profits per unit of $p_0 - c_0$ multiplied by the output of q_0, which is the blue area.

Short-run monopoly equilibrium

To show the profit-maximizing equilibrium of a monopoly firm, we bring together information about its revenues and its costs and then apply two rules developed in Chapter 6. First, the firm should not produce at all unless there is some level of output for which price is at least equal to average variable cost. Secondly, if the firm does produce, its output should be set at the point where marginal cost equals marginal revenue. At this point, marginal cost should be rising relative to marginal revenue, so that if any additional units were to be produced they would add more to cost than to revenue, and so would reduce profit.

When the monopoly firm equates marginal cost with marginal revenue, it produces an outcome such as that shown in Figure 7.3. The profit-maximizing output is the level at which marginal cost equals marginal revenue. The point on the demand curve vertically above that output is the price at which that output can be sold, as this is the price that demanders are willing pay for that quantity. (We normally think of this the other way round: at price p_0 demanders would choose to buy quantity q_0.)

We have explained the monopolist's decision as if it were taken in two steps: set the quantity that is determined by *MC* equals *MR*, and then see what price can be charged for that quantity. This is not how it works in practice, as the position of *MR* is itself determined by the demand curve. So what is really happening is that the monopolist is choosing price and quantity simultaneously from the interaction of cost and demand conditions. The monopolist is solving the following problem: given the constraints of costs and demand, what is the profit-maximizing combination of price and quantity that can be achieved? The answer to this question is the same whichever way we look at it: set marginal cost equal to marginal revenue and then determine the price to be charged, or determine the price–quantity combination that maximizes profit.

An important characteristic of the outcome under monopoly is that the market price of the product exceeds the marginal cost of producing it. In the next section we discuss why this may be regarded as a less than optimal outcome.

When the monopoly firm is in profit-maximizing equilibrium, equating marginal revenue with marginal cost, both are less than the price it charges for its output.

This is because the firm's marginal revenue curve is always below the demand curve.

Elasticity of demand for a monopolist

The relationship between elasticity and revenue discussed earlier has an interesting implication for the monopoly firm. Because marginal cost is always greater than zero, a profit-maximizing monopoly (which must produce where $MR = MC$) will always produce where marginal revenue is positive—that is, where demand is elastic. If the firm were producing where demand was inelastic, it could reduce its output, thereby driving up the price sufficiently to increase its total revenue while reducing its total costs and hence increasing its profits. No such restriction applies in perfect competition. Each firm faces a perfectly elastic demand curve whatever the elasticity of the market demand curve at the market price. So the aggregate market equilibrium can occur where the market demand curve is either elastic or inelastic.

Monopoly profits

The fact that a monopoly firm produces the output that maximizes its profits tells us nothing about how large these profits will be, or even whether there will be any profits at all. Figure 7.4 illustrates this by showing three alternative average total cost curves: one where the monopoly firm can earn pure profits, one where it can just cover its costs, and one where it makes losses at any level of output.

No supply curve for a monopoly

In perfect competition the industry short-run supply curve depends only on the marginal cost curves of the individual firms. This is true because, under perfect competition, profit-maximizing firms equate marginal cost with price. Given marginal costs, it is possible to know how much will be produced at each price. In contrast, a monopoly firm's output is not solely determined by its marginal cost. Let us see why.

As with all profit-maximizing firms, the monopolist equates marginal cost to marginal revenue, but marginal revenue does not equal price. Hence, the monopolist does *not* equate marginal cost to price. In order to know the amount produced at any given price, we need to know the market demand curve as well as the marginal cost curve. Under these circumstances, it is possible for different demand conditions to cause the same output to be sold at

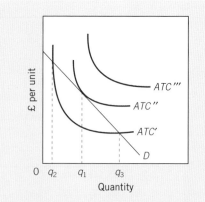

Figure 7.4 Alternative profit possibilities for a monopolist

Profit maximization means only that the monopoly is doing as well as it can do. The figure shows one demand curve and three alternative cost curves. With the curve ATC''' there is no positive output at which the monopolist can avoid making losses. With the curve ATC'' the monopolist covers all costs at output q_1, where the ATC curve is tangent to the D curve. With the curve ATC' profits can be made by producing at any output between q_2 and q_3. (The profit-maximizing output will be some point between q_2 and q_3, where $MR = MC$, which is not shown on the diagram.)

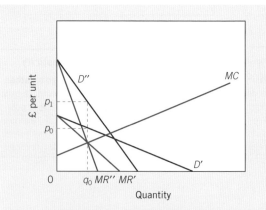

Figure 7.5 No supply curve under monopoly

There is no unique relation between price and the quantity sold. The demand curves D' and D'' both have marginal revenue curves that intersect the marginal cost curve at output q_0. But because the demand curves are different, q_0 is sold at p_0 when the demand curve is D', and at p_1 when the demand curve is D''.

different prices. This is illustrated in Figure 7.5 by an example in which two monopolists facing the same marginal cost curves but different demand curves sell identical outputs at different prices. An important conclusion follows from this.

For a monopoly firm there is no unique relationship between market price and quantity supplied.

Box 7.2 Demand for once-off production

An interesting case of monopoly pricing occurs with 'limited editions'. These are sometimes works of art, such as lithographs, prints, etchings, or woodcuts by famous artists. But limited editions are also produced of everything from cars to T-shirts and briar pipes. In 2001 the Singer Company offered a limited edition gold coloured sewing machine with a 22k gold badge, to commemorate the 150th anniversary of the invention of the original machine. Our favourite example, however, is a limited edition model of a prize-winning goat called Mostyn Minival: 'A beautifully crafted limited edition of 100, each individually numbered. £110 for members and £120 for non-members'.

Do you want a new case for your iPad? If so try:

The Limited Edition Black and Lime Brown Case for the Apple iPad is beautifully designed and is a form fitting case made from the best caterina leather. The Mamut Suela case comes in stylish brown textured leather on the outside and a softer smooth leather interior. The iPad fits into the case from the opening at the top and is held snuggly in place for everyday use. When the front of the Vaja case is not in use, it has been designed so it can be attached to the back of the iPad for convenience. The case allows you to fully access all of the iPads ports and features without having to remove your iPad from the case. There is access to the headphone jack, power button, volume keys, connector and speaker. This gives you 100% control over your iPad whenever you need it ...[2]

If this is not exclusive enough for you try filling it with a gold-plated iPad, limited edition of course: '*Every machine is Gold dipped in 24ct Gold four times to ensure thickness and shine. This is then polished to create a mirror finish which looks both stylish and expensive.*'[3]

A recent internet search (in November 2013) for 'limited edition offer' produced around 240,000 hits.[4] This suggests that limited edition offers are a popular marketing tool. They are a way of appearing to add value to products,

especially collectibles, by creating an image of restricted supply, which may make the product seem unusual and therefore more valuable in future, or more exclusive as a fashion item.

So what is the economics of all this? The normal demand curve is for a repeated flow of purchases, period after period. In the case of limited editions, the demand is for a stock to be produced once only. The smaller the total number of items produced, the more people value each item and the higher the price that can be charged. This gives rise to a negatively sloped demand curve.

If producers know the curve exactly and know their marginal cost of production, choosing the profit-maximizing price–quantity combination is simple. They equate marginal cost with marginal revenue. But since limited edition production and sales are not repeated period after period, producers have no chance to learn the shape of the demand curve. They must guess on the basis of the sales of earlier, more or less similar, limited editions. If they set the price too low, they will sell all their output but not at its profit-maximizing price. If they set the price too high, they will be left with unsold output, which they must destroy or readvertise at considerable expense. Most importantly perhaps, the limited edition promotion is a way of creating a demand for something that would have very little intrinsic demand in the absence of scarcity value. Selling art work is a hard job for all but the most famous artists, but at least if the work is rare it has a chance of having some market value in the future. We do not expect many readers to make their living out of making models of champion goats ... why not try something even more unusual!

---

[2] <http://www.mobilefun.co.uk/vaja-limited-edition-mamut-suela-leather-ipad-case-p25841.htm>

[3] <http://www.crystalrocked.com/store/index.php/shop/gold-plating/newipad-24ct-gold.html>

[4] This is the result if the phrase is put in quotation marks so that the words have to appear in that exact order.

Firm and industry

Because the monopolist is the only producer in an industry, there is no need for separate analysis of the firm and the industry, as is necessary with perfect competition. The monopoly firm *is* the industry. Thus, the short-run profit-maximizing position of the firm, as shown in Figure 7.3, is also the short-run equilibrium of the industry.

Box 7.2 deals with an interesting variation of monopoly theory, the pricing of limited editions.

A multi-plant monopoly

So far we have implicitly assumed that the monopoly firm produces all of its output in a single plant. The analysis can easily be extended to a multi-plant monopolist. Assume, for example, that the firm has two plants. How will it allocate production between them? The answer is that any given output will be allocated between the two plants so as to equate their marginal costs. Assume, for example, that plant *A* was producing 30 units per week at a marginal cost of £20, while plant *B* was producing

25 units at a marginal cost of £17. Plant *A's* production could be reduced by one unit, saving £20 in cost, while plant *B's* production was increased by one unit, adding £17 to cost. Overall output is held constant while costs are reduced by £3. The generalization is that whenever two plants are producing at different marginal costs, the total cost of producing their combined output can be reduced by reallocating production from the plant with the higher marginal cost to the plant with the lower marginal cost.

A multi-plant profit-maximizing monopoly firm will always operate its plants so that their marginal costs are equal.

It is worth noting that the message that a multi-plant firm should equate marginal cost in each plant does not just apply to a monopoly—it applies to *any* firm. For any given output and any market structure, if the firm is not equating the marginal cost of production of an identical product between plants, it is not maximizing profit. It could reduce total cost for the same output by rearranging production between its plants.

How does the multi-plant monopoly firm determine its overall marginal cost? Assume, for example, that both plants are operating at a marginal cost of £10 per unit and one is producing 14 units per week while the other is producing 16. The firm's overall output is 30 units at a marginal cost of £10. This illustrates the following general proposition:

The monopoly firm's marginal cost curve is the horizontal sum of the marginal cost curves of its individual plants.

It follows that the analysis in this chapter applies to any monopolist, no matter how many plants it operates. The marginal cost curve we use is merely the sum of the marginal cost curves of all the plants. In the special case in which there is only one plant, the *firm's MC* curve is that *plant's MC* curve.

The allocative inefficiency of monopoly

We showed in Chapter 6 that the perfectly competitive equilibrium maximizes the sum of consumers' and producers' surpluses by equating marginal cost with the product's price. Output under monopoly is lower and so must result in a smaller total of consumers' and producers' surpluses than if it produced where marginal cost was equal to price.

When the monopoly maximizes its profits it chooses an output where marginal cost is less than price. As a result, consumers' surplus is less than it would be if the output were raised until marginal cost equalled price. In this way, the monopoly firm gains at the expense of consumers. However, this is not the whole story.

When the output between the level that equates marginal cost with marginal revenue and the level that equates marginal cost with price is not produced, consumers lose more surplus than the monopolist gains. Thus there is a net loss of surplus for society as a whole. This loss of surplus is called the *deadweight loss of monopoly*. It is illustrated in Figure 7.6.

It follows that there is a conflict between the private interest of the monopoly producer and the public interest of all the nation's consumers. This creates a rational case for government intervention to prevent the formation of monopolies if possible, and, if that is not possible, to control their behaviour. Box 7.3 points out that the concept of allocative efficiency used here is a static one and that in a dynamic world things may look different.

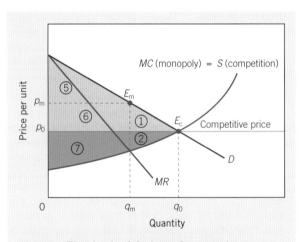

Figure 7.6 The deadweight loss of monopoly

Monopoly is allocatively inefficient because it does not maximize the sum of consumers' and producers' surpluses. At the perfectly competitive equilibrium E_c consumers' surplus is the sum of the pink shaded areas 1, 5, and 6. When the industry is monopolized, price rises to p_m and consumers' surplus falls to area 5. Consumers lose area 1 because that output is not produced, and they lose area 6 because the price rise has transferred it to the monopolist. Producers' surplus in a competitive equilibrium is the sum of the blue areas 7 and 2. When the market is monopolized and price rises to p_m, the surplus area 2 is lost because the output is not produced. However, the monopolist gains area 6 from consumers. Area 6 is known to be greater than area 2 because p_m maximizes profits. Thus, areas 1 and 2 are lost to society. They represent the deadweight loss resulting from monopoly and account for its allocative inefficiency.

Box 7.3 Statics and dynamics in the theory of monopoly

Notice two important things about the discussion of the allocative inefficiency of monopoly. First, the analysis is about situations in which the firm is in a static equilibrium, fully adjusted to *unchanging* cost and demand structures. Second, the analysis applies to all firms that face negatively sloped demand curves for their products. This includes firms that have no direct competitors, monopolists, firms that we will study in the next chapter, which have only a few competitors, called oligopolists, and firms that have many competitors but sell differentiated products, called monopolistic competitors. In all these cases, price will exceed marginal cost in equilibrium.

Since the great majority of all production occurs under one or another of these three categories, should we be concerned that the economy is permeated with static inefficiencies? The answer is 'no' because the analysis does not take into account effects on economic growth. Over the long term, what happens to our living standards depends critically on economic growth, which is driven primarily by technological change. A major competitive tool kit of firms that are in active competition with each other is the development of new technologies that will give them an advantage over

their competitors. As a result, over the past two centuries the new technologies that have transformed our living standards and changed society from being predominantly rural to being predominantly urban have come from firms that face negatively sloped demand curves rather than from firms in perfect competition facing horizontal demand curves. Furthermore, the very profits that look socially undesirable in static theory have provided both the incentive for making, and the source of funds for financing, the R&D that firms must engage in if they are to succeed against actual or potential competitors by inventing and introducing new technologies.

So what looks inefficient and undesirable from a static point of view often turns out to be efficient and desirable from a dynamic-growth-centred point of view.

Note, however, that this argument applies to firms that fear actual or potential competition, but not to monopolies that are so entrenched that they have nothing to fear from potential entrants. In such cases their profits may serve no social function and society would be better off if the firm was induced to price its products at, or at least close to, marginal cost.

A multi-price monopolist: price discrimination

So far in this chapter we have assumed that the monopoly firm charges the same price for every unit of its product, no matter where or to whom it sells that product. We now show that a monopoly firm will also find it profitable to sell different units of the same product at different prices whenever it gets the opportunity.[5]

Raw milk is often sold at one price when it is to be used as fluid milk but at a lower price when it is to be used to make ice cream or cheese. Doctors in private practice often charge for their services according to the incomes of their patients. Cinemas often have lower admission prices for children and pensioners than for adults. Railways charge different rates per tonne per kilometre for different products. Electricity producers sell electricity at one rate to homes and at a lower rate to firms. Airlines often charge less to people who stay over a Saturday night than to those who come and go within the week.

Price discrimination occurs when a seller charges different prices for different units of the same product

for reasons not associated with differences in cost. Not all price *differences* represent price *discrimination*. Quantity discounts, differences between wholesale and retail prices, and prices that vary with the time of day or the season of the year may not represent price discrimination, because the same product sold at a different time, in a different place, or in different quantities may have different costs. If an electric power company has unused capacity at certain times of the day, it may be cheaper for the company to provide service at those hours than at peak demand hours. If price differences reflect cost differences, they are not discriminatory. In contrast, when a price difference is based on different buyers' valuations of the same product, price discrimination does occur.

Some forms of price discrimination may be illegal or contrary to regulations in an industry. We make no moral judgments about whether price discrimination is a good or a bad thing. The analysis is merely designed to show that a firm that has some market power has an incentive to segment its market and charge a different price in each segment if it can.

---

[5] Because this practice is also prevalent in markets that contain a few large firms, called *oligopolistic* markets, the range of examples quoted covers both types of market structure.

Why price discrimination is profitable

Why should it be profitable for a firm to sell some units of its output at a price that is well below the price that it receives for other units of its output? Persistent price discrimination is profitable either because different buyers are willing to pay different amounts for the same product or because one buyer is willing to pay different amounts for different units of the same product. The basic point about price discrimination is that, in either of these circumstances, sellers may be able to capture some of the consumers' surplus that would otherwise go to buyers.

Discrimination between units of output

Let us revisit the example we used in Chapter 6 where one of us expressed a demand for cinema visits per month such that there would be one visit if the entry price was £30, two visits if it were £20, and three visits if it were £10. At a market price of £10 per visit, he would go three times per month and would have a value of consumer surplus of £30 (because the first visit would have been undertaken at an entry price of £30 but only £10 was charged, and the second visit would have been undertaken at an entry price of £20 but again only £10 was charged, and so the surplus for this consumer on the first visit was £20 and on the second visit £10).

Perfect price discrimination occurs when the firm obtains the entire consumers' surplus. In this example, the managers of the cinema could increase their revenue if they charged £30 for the first visit, £20 for the second visit, and £10 for the third visit, thereby increasing total revenue by £30 and converting what had previously been a surplus benefit to the movie buff into profit for the cinema. Of course, achieving a pricing structure that is able to distinguish how many times each customer has visited each month is not easy, but the point we are making here is that if each unit sold could be separately priced then the seller could increase total revenue by extracting some or all of the consumers' surplus.

Box 7.4 offers another example of how pricing incentives such 'buy-one-get-one-free' can easily be understood in this context.

Discrimination between buyers in one market

If different buyers have different demand curves for some commodity, a monopoly producer can profitably discriminate by charging more to those with a higher demand for

---

Box 7.4 BOGOF or rip off?

Have you ever wondered why it is so common to see retailers making promotions of the form buy-one-get-one-free (BOGOF), three-for-the-price-of-two, or buy-one-get-another-50%-off? Wouldn't it be simpler just to cut the price of the product for every single unit? Yes it would be simpler, but it would not be so profitable for the seller. The reason is that this is a form of price discrimination between different units of the product sold and it increases the profit of the retailer. To see this, suppose that a supermarket chain can source punnets of strawberries at an average unit cost of £1, so the marginal cost is also £1, and there is a contract with suppliers to take 1 million per week in the summer season. Thus total cost per week is £1 million. Suppose also that the sales manager estimates that the demand curve is such that they could sell 250,000 if they price the strawberries at £3, they could sell 500,000 at £2, and the whole million at £1.10. The last price is the only one of these that generates a profit and this would be £100,000 (10p each on a million punnets). So what promotional deals could improve on this?

At a price of £3 they will have a total revenue of £750,000, lose £250,000 on the deal, and waste 750,000 punnets of strawberries which will be unsold. But suppose instead they say 'price £3 buy-one-get-one free'. Demand will increase substantially as the average price has fallen to £1.50.

Suppose, sales in packs of two now go to 800,000. Revenue rises to £1.2 million and the profit is £200,000 which is double the best outcome with single product pricing.

Let us now try another strategy. Set the price of the first one at £2 and the second one 50 per cent off. This could well lead to all 1 million strawberry punnets being sold, as consumers perceive that they are paying only £1 for the second punnet. The average price received is £1.50 and this yields a total profit of £500,000 (£1.5 million minus £1 million) which is far better than we can achieve with single product pricing at any possible price.

There may be an even better pricing strategy, but what is best in general depends on the demand curve. However, the key point is that splitting the pricing between the first unit and subsequent units is a way of retailers mopping up some of the consumer surplus and thus increasing their profit. This works because consumers will buy a much larger quantity if the second unit is cheaper than the first (or it could be the third unit that is cheaper). The strategy provides what consumers want (as they feel they are getting a good deal) and is profitable as long as the average price of the units sold to customers exceeds the average unit cost of the products to retailers. For any given margin between unit revenue and cost, profit increases with volumes sold.

the commodity and less to those with a lower demand. We illustrate with a simple example.

Think of the demand curve in a market that is made up of individual buyers, each of whom has indicated the maximum price that he or she is prepared to pay for the single unit each wishes to purchase. Suppose, for the sake of simplicity, that there are only four buyers, the first of whom is prepared to pay any price up to £4, the second of whom is prepared to pay £3, the third £2, and the fourth £1. Suppose that the product has a marginal cost of production of £1 per unit for all units. If the selling firm is limited to a single price, it will maximize its profits by charging £3, thereby selling two units and earning profits of £4. If the seller can discriminate among each of the buyers, it could charge the first buyer £4 and the second £3, thus increasing its profits from the first two units to £5. Moreover, it could also sell the third unit for £2, thus increasing its profits to £6. It would be indifferent about selling a fourth unit because the price would just cover marginal cost.

Discrimination between markets

Many monopoly firms sell in two different markets. A firm might be the only seller in a tariff-protected home market, while being a price taker in foreign markets where there is more competition. The firm would then equate its marginal cost to the price in the foreign market, as does any perfect competitor. But in the domestic market it would equate marginal costs to marginal revenue, as does any monopolist. As a result, it would charge a higher price on sales in the home market than on sales abroad. This case is elaborated in the appendix to this chapter.

Price discrimination more generally

One reason that demand curves have a negative slope is because different units are valued differently by consumers. If tastes or incomes differ, the same unit will be valued differently by different individuals. These facts, combined with a single price for a product, are what give rise to consumers' surplus.

The ability to charge multiple prices gives a seller the opportunity to capture some (or, in the extreme case, all) of the consumers' surplus.

The larger the number of different prices that can be charged, the greater is the firm's ability to increase its revenue at the expense of consumers.

It follows that if a selling firm is able to discriminate through price, it can increase revenues received (and thus also profits) from the sale of any given quantity. However, price discrimination is not always possible, even if there are no legal barriers to its use.

When is price discrimination possible?

Discrimination between units of output sold to the same buyer requires that the seller be able to keep track of the units that a buyer consumes in each period. Thus, the tenth unit purchased by a given buyer in a given month can be sold at a price that is different from the fifth unit *only* if the seller can keep track of who buys what. This can be done by an electricity company through its meter readings or by a magazine publisher by distinguishing between renewals and new subscriptions. It can also be done by distributing certificates or coupons that allow, for example, a car wash at a reduced price on a return visit.

Discrimination between buyers is possible only if the buyers who face the low price cannot resell the goods to the buyers who face the high price. Even though the local butcher might like to charge the banker twice as much for buying steak as he charges the taxi driver, he cannot usually succeed in doing so. The banker can always shop for meat in the supermarket, where her occupation is not known. Even if the butcher and the supermarket agreed to charge her twice as much, she could hire someone to shop for her. However, the surgeon may succeed in discriminating (especially if other reputable surgeons do the same) because it will not do the banker much good to hire the taxi driver to have her operation for her.

Price discrimination is possible if the seller can either distinguish individual units bought by a single buyer or separate buyers into classes such that resale between classes is impossible.

The ability to prevent resale tends to be associated with the character of the product or the ability to classify buyers into readily identifiable groups. Services are less easily resold than goods; goods that require installation by the manufacturer (e.g. heavy equipment) are less easily resold than movable goods such as household appliances.

Of course, it is not enough to be able to separate different buyers or different units into separate classes. The seller must also be able to control the supply going to each group. There is no point, for example, in asking more than the competitive price from some buyers if they can simply go to other firms who sell the good at the competitive price.

Transportation costs, tariff barriers, and import quotas separate classes of buyers geographically and may make discrimination possible.

Consequences of price discrimination

A monopoly firm that is able to discriminate between two markets will allocate its output between those two markets so as to equate the marginal revenues in the two.

If this is not done, total revenue can always be increased by reducing sales by one unit in the market with the lower marginal revenue and raising sales by one unit in the market with the higher marginal revenue. This reallocation of sales raises total revenue by the difference between the two marginal revenues. If the demand curves are different in the two markets, having the same marginal revenues means charging different prices.

Two important consequences of price discrimination follow from this result.

Proposition 1. **For any given level of output the most profitable system of discriminatory prices will provide higher total revenue to the firm than the profit-maximizing single price.**

Remember that a monopolist with the power to discriminate could produce exactly the same quantity as a single-price monopolist and charge everyone the same price. Therefore it need never receive *less* revenue, and it can do better if it can raise the price on even one unit sold, as long as the price need not be lowered on any other.

Proposition 2. **Output under price discrimination will generally be larger than under a single-price monopoly.**

Remember that a monopoly firm that must charge a single price for a product will produce less than would all the firms in a perfectly competitive industry because it knows that selling more depresses its price. Price discrimination allows the firm to avoid this disincentive. To the extent that the firm can sell its output in separate blocks, it can sell another block without spoiling the market for the block that is already being sold. In the case of perfect price discrimination, in which every unit of output is sold at a different price, the profit-maximizing monopolist will produce every unit for which the price charged is greater than or equal to its marginal cost. Therefore it will produce at a level of output where marginal cost equals price, which is the socially optimal level of output.

Figure 7.7 illustrates the output-expanding effects of price discrimination. It shows a case in which a monopoly firm has maximized profits selling at a single price. The firm then finds that it can isolate a group of potential buyers who were unwilling to purchase at the monopoly price. Perhaps it forms a buying club from which members of the first group are excluded. A lower price can be used to attract the new group of buyers without having to lower the price charged to its original customers. As long as the new price exceeds the marginal cost of producing the extra output, the monopoly firm adds to its profits. But consumers' surplus is also increased, since a new group of buyers is now in the market. So both the monopolist and consumers earn additional surplus.

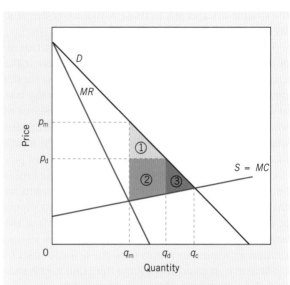

Figure 7.7 A price-discriminating monopolist
Price discrimination reduces the deadweight loss of monopoly. Initially the monopolist produces output q_m where $MC = MR$ instead of the competitive output q_c where MC equals demand (which is consumers' marginal utility). The deadweight loss is the sum of the three blue shaded areas labelled 1, 2, and 3. A second group of consumers is then isolated from the first. This group, who would buy nothing at the original price of p_m, will buy an amount that would increase total output to q_d at a price of p_d. The monopoly firm's profits now rise by the shaded area 2, which is the difference between its cost curve and the price p_d that is charged to the new group who buy the amount between q_m and q_d. Consumers' surplus rises by the shaded area 1 and total deadweight loss falls to the shaded area 3.

Normative aspects of price discrimination

There are two quite separate issues involved in evaluating any particular example of price discrimination. The first concerns the effect of discrimination on the level of output. Discrimination usually results in a higher output than would occur if a single price were charged. As we saw in Figure 7.7, price discrimination tends to reduce the deadweight loss of monopoly and therefore leads to a more efficient allocation of resources than does a single-price monopoly.

Often, however, it is the effect on income distribution that accounts for people's strong emotional reactions to price discrimination. Compared with perfect competition, price discrimination transfers income from buyers to sellers. When buyers are poor and sellers are rich, this may seem undesirable. However, some cases are more complex. For example, doctors in countries with market-based medical systems often vary their charges with their patients' incomes. This enables them to serve their poorer patients in ways that they could not if they had to charge everyone a single price for their services. Another example is the prevalent practice of giving discounts to old-age pensioners or airline passengers who stay on over a weekend. These practices often allow lower-income consumers to buy a product that they would be unable to afford if it were sold at the single price that maximized the producers' profits.

Box 7.5 outlines some interesting cases of price discrimination.

Box 7.5 Examples of price discrimination

The principle of charging different customers different prices has been around for a very long time. The earliest example we have come across is from the Egyptian kingdom of Rameses the Great in the period 1304–1237 BC. (We are grateful to Professor Arie Melnik of Haifa University for this example.) In what is now southern Lebanon the Egyptians maintained a toll road on an important route across a range of hills. There were other routes, but they were considerably more tortuous than this one. The servant of the Egyptian ruler sent to administer this toll road found that he had some discretion over pricing. He wrote to his employers asking for guidelines on charges. The reply came back: 'Charge what the traffic will bear'. So famous is this instruction that the phrase has become something of a cliché. It is based upon the insight, set out in the text, that setting different prices increases revenue. In practice the discriminating monopolist charges each traveller the maximum that he or she would be prepared to pay to use the road.

Here are two more examples from transport. The first shows price discrimination in action. The second shows that problems can arise when price discrimination does not occur.

Air fares

In February 2006 a standard economy fare on British Airways from London Heathrow to Rome was £618.40. This fare permitted return the same day or within a week. However, if you stayed over Saturday night and were prepared to fly from Gatwick you could go for £123.90! This difference for the same class of fare on the same planes discriminates between the business traveller and the tourist. Such discrimination was profitable because the elasticities of demand for these two types of travel are different, being lower for business than for leisure travel. However, by June 2009 the discrimination on this route and many other short-haul routes had been dramatically reduced. This happened as a result of low-cost airlines such as EasyJet and Ryanair taking growing market share by undercutting the higher of these fares. All airlines had a cheap class of fares to compete with the low-cost airlines head on. For example, you could get a fare of around £200 return to Rome with a range of airlines at short notice. But you could do even better than that if you were prepared to book well ahead of time. Nonetheless, in November 2013 a standard BA return from London Heathrow was £574 if you returned before the weekend but was £312 if you returned after the weekend, so the discrimination between business and leisure travellers remains.

Price discrimination also applies in long-haul flights such as transatlantic flights, but this practice has not been affected by low-cost competition. In early 2006 a standard economy return fare between London and Chicago on the major airlines (such as British Airways, United, and American) cost around £1,040. However, the fare with the same carriers if booked fourteen days in advance for a stay of at least seven days was around £330. The fare structure was similar in November 2013. A BA economy fare from London Heathrow to Chicago would cost £1,708 if you return within the week but £505 if you stay over the weekend.[6] These substantial differences reflect a segmentation of the market between business travellers, who presumably get their fares paid by their company, and tourists who are paying out of their own pocket. Business people do not want to use up more time than is necessary on a business trip, as the opportunity cost of their time is high, so the seven-day minimum (or having to stay over Saturday night) keeps them from taking advantage of the low fare. Also, there are restrictions on entry into this market, so low-cost airlines have so far been unable to break in.

British Rail

This case illustrates the problems that arise when segmentation is not allowed even though both producers and consumers could be better off if it were. Some years ago British Rail (the nationalized industry that once operated all British railways) was not allowed to charge different prices to passengers travelling on different lines. In the interest of equity, a fixed fare per passenger mile was laid down by government and had to be charged on all lines whatever the density of their passenger traffic and whatever the elasticity of demand for their services. In the interests of economy, branch lines were closed down when they could not cover their costs. This meant that some lines closed even though the users preferred rail transport to any of the available alternatives, and the strength of their preferences was such that they would voluntarily have paid a price sufficient for the line to cover its costs. Nonetheless the lines were closed because it was thought inequitable to charge passengers on one line more than passengers on other lines.

Since privatization of the railways in the 1990s differential pricing has been permitted. For example, train companies such as the operators of the Gatwick Express were able to charge higher prices for trips from London Victoria to Gatwick Airport than were being charged by other companies running on the same route—the only difference being a non-stop journey.

---

[6] These fares were for a booking made only one week in advance, so better deals may have been available with some planning.

Monopoly firms with a divisible fixed input

The major difference between firms with an indivisible and a divisible fixed input lies in how price and quantity vary as demand fluctuates, as it does, for example, over the business cycle. As shown in Figure 7.8, how the output fluctuations of the two types of firms compare depends on the nature of their marginal costs over the range of the demand fluctuations. The firm with the divisible fixed input, call it Firm 1, alters output until its constant marginal cost is equal to the new marginal revenue. The monopoly firm with the indivisible fixed input, call it Firm 2, does the same, and how its output fluctuations compare with those of Firm 1 depends on how its marginal cost responds over the range of fluctuations. We show two possible cases: one with a positively sloped marginal cost, and the other with a negatively sloped marginal cost. Both these cases are equally plausible. The indivisible fixed input means that diminishing returns are more likely to have set in. However, if this is a falling marginal cost industry, this could explain why we have a monopoly in this market.

If the marginal cost curve is negatively sloped, the output fluctuations resulting from demand fluctuations will be larger than those for Firm 1. If, on the other hand, Firm 2's marginal cost curve is positively sloped over the range of possible demand fluctuations, its fluctuations in output will be smaller than those of Firm 1.

The absolute impact on price fluctuations will depend on the specific slopes of the MC curves and the size of the demand shift, but what can be said is that when demand falls the price set by a firm with a positively sloped MC curve will be lower than that for one with a horizontal MC curve, which in turn is lower than that for a firm with a negatively sloped MC curve. When demand rises, the price will be highest for the firm with a positively sloped demand curve, and lowest for the firm with the negatively sloped MC curve, while Firm 1 with the horizontal MC curve has a price in between these two.

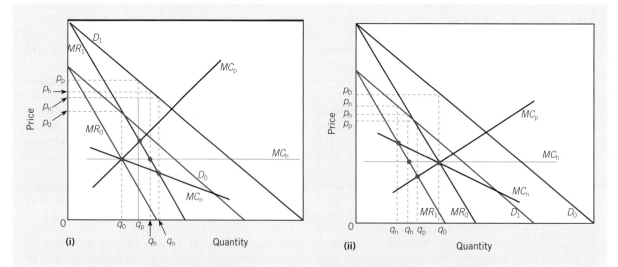

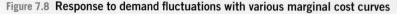

Figure 7.8 Response to demand fluctuations with various marginal cost curves

Quantity fluctuations depend on the slope of the *MC* curve. The case of a horizontal *MC* curve is compared with both positively and negatively sloped *MC* curves. All three initial equilibrium positions give the same quanty, q_0 and price p_0, when the marginal revenue curve is MC_0 and the demand curve is D_0 in both parts (i) and (ii). Firm 1's marginal cost curve, MC_h, is horizontal up to capacity because its fixed input is divisible. MC_n is the negatively sloped marginal cost curve and MC_p is the positively sloped marginal cost curve.

In part (i) demand increases from D_0 to D_1 with a corresponding shift in MR from MR_0 to MR_1. The output at which Firm 1's MC_h equals MR rises from q_0 and q_h. There are two alternative MC curves for Firm 2 that has an indivisible fixed input. With the positively sloped curve MC_p its quantity rises from q_0 and q_p, less than does that of Firm 1. With a negatively sloped curve MC_n, its quantity rises from q_0 and q_n, more than does that of Firm 1. Price ends up highest for the firm with the positively sloped marginal cost curve and lowest with the firm with the negatively sloped curve. Firm 1 is between these two outcomes.

In part (ii) demand decreases from D_0 to D_1 with a corresponding shift in MR from MR_0 to MR_1. The output at which MC_h equals MR falls from q_0 and q_h. There are two alternative MC curves for Firm 2 which has an indivisible fixed input. With the positively sloped curve MC_p its quantity falls from q_0 and q_p, less than does that of Firm 1. With a negatively sloped curve MC_n, its quantity falls from q_0 and q_n, more than does that of Firm 1. Price ends up lowest for the firm with the positively sloped marginal cost curve and highest for the case of the negatively sloped marginal costs curve, with the horizontal marginal cost curve in between these two.

Long-run monopoly equilibrium

In all industries, including those that are both monopolized and those that are perfectly competitive, profits and losses provide incentives for entry and exit.

If a profit-maximizing monopoly firm is suffering losses in the short run, it will continue to operate as long as it can cover its variable costs. In the long run, however, it will leave the industry unless it can find a scale of operations at which its full opportunity costs can be covered.

If the monopoly firm is making profits, other firms will wish to enter the industry in order to earn more than the opportunity cost of their capital. If such entry occurs, the equilibrium position shown in Figure 7.3 will change, and the firm will cease to be a monopolist.

Entry barriers

Impediments that prevent entry are called **entry barriers**; they may be either natural or created.

If a monopoly firm's profits are to persist in the long run, effective entry barriers must prevent the entry of new firms into the industry.

Barriers determined by technology

Natural barriers most commonly arise as a result of economies of scale. When the long-run average cost curve is negatively sloped over a large range of output, big firms have significantly lower average total costs than small firms.

You will recall from Chapter 6 that perfectly competitive firms cannot be in long-run equilibrium on the negatively sloped segment of their long-run average cost curve (see Figure 6.10).

Now suppose that an industry's technology is such that any firm's minimum achievable average cost is £10, which is reached at an output of 10,000 units per week. Further, assume that at a price of £10 the total quantity demanded is 11,000 units per week. Under these circumstances only one firm can operate at or near its minimum costs.

A **natural monopoly** occurs when, given the industry's current technology, the demand conditions allow no more than one firm to cover its current production costs while producing at the minimum point of its long-run cost curve. In a natural monopoly, there is no price at which two firms can both sell enough to cover their total costs.

Another type of technologically determined natural monopoly arises from *set-up cost*. If a firm could be catapulted fully grown into the market, it might be able to compete effectively with the existing monopolist. However, the cost to the new firm of entering the market, developing its products, and establishing such things as its brand image and its dealer network may be so large that entry would be unprofitable.

The theory outlined so far deals with natural monopolies since if the market contained two firms with the same costs as those shown for one firm in the diagrams used so far, there would be no price at which both firms could sell enough to cover their costs.

Policy-created barriers

Many entry barriers are created by conscious government action and therefore are officially condoned. In these cases one firm's costs may be such that many firms could exist in the industry, making it more competitive were it not for the barriers. For example, each of the firm's plants may have a cost-minimizing level of output that is well below the market demand for the product. So each plant could be separately owned were it not for the entry barriers.

Patent laws, for instance, may prevent entry by conferring on the patent holder the sole legal right to produce a particular product for a specific period of time. Also, firms may be granted a charter or a franchise that prohibits competition by law. Regulation and licensing of firms, often in service industries, can restrict entry severely. For example, the 1979 Banking Act required all banks in the UK to be authorized by the Bank of England. The 1986 Financial Services Act required all sellers of investment products to be authorized by the Securities and Investment Board (SIB) or some other recognized regulatory body. Regulation and authorization of all financial firms, including banks, was formally transferred to the Financial Services Authority (FSA) in December 2001.

It was announced in 2010 that the FSA itself was to be abolished and oversight of financial regulation be returned to the Bank of England. This was implemented in 2013 when the Bank of England took over responsibility for prudential regulation of banks and other major financial institutions, while the Financial Conduct Authority (FCA) was set up to regulate market conduct and many small financial institutions[7]. The intention of this reform was to make financial regulation more effective, following the problems revealed by the financial crisis of 2007–8.

Other barriers can be created by the firm or firms already in the market. In extreme cases the threat of force or sabotage can deter entry. The most obvious entry barriers of this

---

[7] The FCA took formal responsibility for its tasks in the spring of 2014.

type are encountered in the production and sale of illegal goods and services, where operation outside the law makes available an array of illegal but potent barriers to new entrants. The drug trade is a current example. In contrast, legitimate firms must use legal tactics such as those that are intended to increase a new entrant's set-up costs. Examples are the threat of price cutting, designed to impose unsustainable losses on a new entrant, and heavy brand-name advertising. (These and other created entry barriers will be discussed in much more detail in Chapter 8.)

The significance of entry barriers

Because there are no entry barriers in perfect competition, profits cannot persist in the long run.

Profits attract entry, and entry erodes profits.

In monopoly, however, profits can persist in the long run whenever there are effective barriers to entry.

Entry barriers frustrate the adjustment mechanism that would otherwise push profits towards zero in the long run.

'Creative destruction'

In the very long run, technology changes. New ways of producing old products are invented, and new products are created to satisfy both familiar and new wants. This has important implications for entry. A monopoly that succeeds in preventing the entry of new firms capable of producing its current product will sooner or later find its barriers circumvented by innovations. One firm may be able to use new processes that avoid some patent or other barrier that the monopolist relies on to bar entry of competing firms. Another firm may compete by producing a new product which, although somewhat different, still satisfies the same need as the monopoly firm's product. Yet another firm might get around a natural monopoly by inventing a technology that produces the good at a much lower cost

than the existing monopoly firm's technology. (The cost curve may be lowered throughout its range and/or the minimum level of costs may be reached at a lower output than previously.) The new technology may subsequently allow several firms to enter the market and still cover costs.

Joseph Schumpeter (1883–1950) argued that entry barriers were not a serious problem in the very long run. According to Schumpeter, the possibility of obtaining monopoly profits provides a major incentive for people to risk their money by financing inventions and innovations. The large short-run profits of a monopoly encourage others to try to capture some of these profits for themselves. If a frontal attack on the monopolist's barriers to entry is not possible, the barriers will be circumvented by such means as the development of similar products against which the monopolist will not have entry protection.

Schumpeter called the replacement of an existing monopoly by one or more new entrants through the invention of new products or new production techniques the *process of creative destruction*. He argued that this process precludes the very long run persistence of barriers to entry into industries that earn large profits.

It is worth noting that the same argument applies to an oligopolistic industry with a few firms of the sort we will consider in the next chapter. If they are making profits and succeed in barring entry, new firms may circumvent the entry barriers by inventing new technologies in the very long run.

The presence of potentially large profits in a monopolistic industry creates incentives for development of new technologies that break down entry barriers and eliminate monopolies.

The first case study at the end of the chapter gives some examples of this process at work. Two obvious examples have been the breaking of the monopoly of fixed-line telephone providers as a result of mobile phone technology, and the breaking of the letter post monopoly by faxes and emails.

Cartels as monopolies

Until this point in our discussion, a monopoly has meant that there is only one firm in an industry. A second way in which a monopoly can arise is for the firms in an industry to agree to cooperate with one another—to behave as if they were a single seller—in order to maximize joint profits by eliminating competition among themselves. Such a group of firms is called a **cartel**, or sometimes just a producers' association. A cartel that includes *all* firms in the industry can behave in the same way as a single-firm monopoly that owned all of these firms. The firms can

agree among themselves to restrict their total output to the level that maximizes their joint profits.[8] Of course, most governments legislate to make anticompetitive practices

----

[8] In this chapter we deal with the simple case in which *all* of the firms in a perfectly competitive industry form a cartel in order to act as if they were a monopoly. Cartels are sometimes formed by a group of firms (or countries) that account for a significant part, but not all, of the total supply of some commodity. The most famous example of this type is OPEC, and we discuss this further in the case study at the end of this chapter.

illegal, but it still helps to understand the incentives facing firms. Also, governments cannot do much when other governments form the cartel, as in the case of the Organization of Petroleum Exporting Countries (OPEC) discussed in the case study at the end of this chapter.

Cocoa producers in West Africa, farmers in the European Union, coffee growers in Brazil, oil producers, taxi drivers in many cities, and labour unions throughout the world have all sought to obtain, through collective action, some of the benefits of departing from the price-taking aspects of perfect competition. In all of these cases the sellers were so numerous that each one had no individual market power. Acting individually each had to accept the market price that was determined by forces beyond its control. Acting collectively, they were able to influence prices by restricting supply. Cases of this sort are worth studying because they occur frequently and in various guises.

The effects of cartelization

Perfectly competitive firms take the market price as given and increase their output until their marginal cost equals price. In contrast, a monopoly firm knows that increasing its output will depress the market price. Taking account of this, the monopolist increases its output only until marginal revenue is equal to marginal cost. All the firms in an industry can achieve the same result by grouping together into what is called a cartel to take collective action to reduce output and drive up price. They can agree to restrict industry output to the level that maximizes their joint profits (where the industry's marginal cost is equal to the industry's marginal revenue). One way to do this is to establish a quota for each firm's output. Suppose that a cartel is formed in what was a perfectly competitive industry and that the joint profit-maximizing output is two-thirds of the perfectly competitive output. When the cartel is formed, each firm could be given a quota equal to two-thirds of its competitive output.

The effect of cartelizing a perfectly competitive industry and reducing its output through production quotas is shown in Figure 7.9(i).

It always pays the producers in a perfectly competitive industry to enter into an output-restricting agreement (at least so long as it is legal).

Problems facing cartels

Cartels encounter two characteristic problems. The first is ensuring that members follow the behaviour that will maximize the industry's *joint* profits, and the second is preventing these profits from being eroded by the entry of new firms.

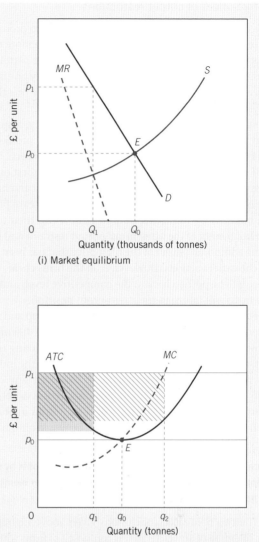

(i) Market equilibrium

(ii) Firm equilibrium

Figure 7.9 Conflicting forces affecting cartels

Cooperation leads to the monopoly price, but individual self-interest leads to production in excess of the monopoly output. Market conditions are shown in part (i), and the situation of a typical firm is shown in part (ii). (Note the change of scale between the two graphs.) Initially the market is in competitive equilibrium, with price p_0 and quantity Q_0. The individual firm is producing output q_0 and is just covering its total costs. The cartel is formed and then enforces quotas on individual firms that are sufficient to reduce the industry's output to Q_1, the output that maximizes the joint profits of the cartel members. Price rises to p_1. The typical firm's quota is q_1. The firm's profits rise from zero to the amount shown by the grey area in part (ii). However, once price is raised to p_1 the individual firm would like to increase output to q_2, where marginal cost is equal to the price set by the cartel. This would allow the firm to earn profits shown by the blue hatched area. If all firms violate their quotas, industry output will exceed Q_1, the price will drop towards p_0, and the profits earned by all firms will fall.

Enforcement of output restrictions

The managers of any cartel want the industry to produce its profit-maximizing output. Their job is made more difficult if individual firms either stay out of the cartel or enter and then cheat on their output quotas. Any one firm has an incentive to do just this: to be either the one that stays out of the organization or the one that enters and then cheats on its output quota. For simplicity, assume that all firms enter the cartel, so enforcement problems are concerned strictly with cheating by its members.

If Firm X is the only firm to cheat, it is in the best of all possible situations. All other firms restrict output and hold the industry price near its monopoly level. They earn profits, but only by restricting output. Firm X can then reap the full benefit of the other firms' output restraint and sell some additional output at the high price that has been set by the cartel's actions. However, if all the firms cheat, the price will be pushed back to the competitive level, and all the firms will return to their zero-profit position.

This conflict between the interests of the group and the interests of the individual firm creates the cartel's dilemma. Provided that enough firms cooperate in restricting output, all firms are better off than they would be if the industry remained perfectly competitive. However, any one firm is even better off if it remains outside the cartel, or joins it and then cheats by exceeding its output quota. If all firms act on this incentive, all will be worse off than if they had joined the cartel and restricted output.

Each individual cartel member can increase its profits by violating the output restrictions, provided that the other members do not violate theirs.

The two bold-faced conclusions given above highlight the dilemma of any cartel that is composed of firms which, acting individually, would be price takers—whether it be OPEC or a local producers' association. Each firm is better off if the cartel is effective in restricting output and so raising price. But each is even better off if everyone else cooperates while it cheats. Yet if all cheat, all will be worse off. Thus:

Cartels are often unstable because of the strong incentives for individual firms to violate the output quotas needed to enforce the monopoly price.

The conflict between the motives for cooperation and for independent action is analysed in more detail in Figure 7.9(ii).

Cartels and similar output-restricting arrangements have a long history. For example, schemes to raise farm incomes by limiting crops bear ample testimony to the accuracy of the predicted instability of cartels. In the past, industry agreements to restrict output often broke down as individual farmers exceeded their quotas. This is why most crop-restriction plans are now operated by governments rather than by private cartels. Production quotas backed by the full coercive power of the state can force monopoly behaviour on existing producers and effectively bar the entry of new ones.

Restricting entry

A cartel must not only police the behaviour of its members, but must also be able to prevent the entry of new producers. In an industry with no strong natural entry barriers, to maintain its profits in the long run it must create its own barriers. Otherwise new firms will enter and force down price until the profits disappear. Successful cartels are often able to license the firms in the industry and to control entry by restricting the number of licences. At other times the government has operated a quota system and has given it the force of law. If no one can produce without a quota and the quotas are allocated among existing producers, entry is precluded.

CASE STUDIES

1. Not so natural monopolies

There are many examples of monopolies that used to exist but only a few survive today. The example of postal monopolies was discussed in Box 7.1. There was a postal monopoly in most countries at one time, and in some countries, such as the United States, this survives today. The source of monopoly in this case has been government legal protection, usually in conjunction with government ownership. One of the main reasons for this state involvement is almost certainly to guarantee that mail will be delivered to every location in the country, however remote that might be. This helps guarantee political communication and tax collection. Hence, even where the monopoly has been ended, a requirement for universal delivery has been maintained for the ex-monopoly providers.

Monopolies were also common in public utilities such as telephones, gas, and electricity. These were often in public ownership[9] as they were regarded as *natural monopolies*.

---

[9] In Europe they tended to be in public ownership, whereas in the United States they were in private hands but subject to regulation. After privatization in the United Kingdom a number of regulators were established to ensure that remnants of monopoly were not exploited.

Moves to privatize these utilities were followed by a search for ways of introducing more competition. This became easier owing to changes in technology, illustrating the process of creative destruction discussed above. The telephone market provides a good example of this process at work.

British Telecom (later to become BT), which was part of the state-owned Post Office, used to have a monopoly of provision of UK telephone services through its network of wires to every house and office building in the country. When it was privatized in 1984 the market was split between two companies, but this duopoly was ended in the early 1990s. Originally, operators connected people by hand (by plugging wires into sockets) and later through a mechanical switching device. More recently the switching technology used computers and this enabled regulators to insist that other telephone providers should be able to compete via the BT telephone lines. Cable companies then installed their own network of higher-capacity cables in most urban areas for delivery of telephone, TV, and internet services. On top of this, wireless technology that enabled mobile phones was developed. The barriers to entry were suddenly dramatically reduced and new providers, such as Vodafone, Orange, T-Mobile, and Virgin, could become big players in the UK telephone market.

Privatization of state monopolies combined with technical innovations have permitted similar dismantling of monopolies in the energy supply industry. Monopolies in both gas and electricity supply were split up and privatized in the 1980s and ways were found of allowing consumers to buy their power from a choice of providers. This had earlier been thought impossible as duplication of power lines and gas pipes was thought to be too costly. However, as with telephone lines, ways were found to permit suppliers to feed into the same grid so that duplication of networks was unnecessary.

The one area where regional monopolies still exist is in the provision of water supplies. There are twenty-six UK companies supplying water (twelve of which also provide sewage services) but each has a monopoly of provision in a specific area to residential customers. However, these companies are closely monitored by a regulator and are expected to match the best efficiency and quality standards of others. Large business customers are able to shop around between suppliers.

2. The world over a barrel? A case study of the OPEC cartel

The behaviour of OPEC over the past several decades provides an example of the cartelization of an industry. As we shall see, OPEC did not control the whole supply side of the oil industry. However, their experience helps us understand the forces affecting cartels in general.

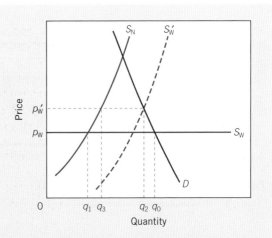

Figure 7.10 OPEC as a successful cartel

Given a rising non-OPEC supply curve of oil, OPEC could determine equilibrium price by choosing its contribution to total supply. The curve S_N represents the non-OPEC supply curve of oil. When the OPEC countries were prepared to supply all that was demanded at the world price p_W, the world supply curve was S_W. At that price production was q_1 in non-OPEC countries and $q_0 - q_1$ in OPEC countries. By fixing its production, OPEC shifted the world supply curve to S'_W, where the horizontal distance between S_N and S'_W is OPEC's production. The world price rose to p'_W. Production became q_3 in non-OPEC countries and $q_2 - q_3$ in OPEC countries. OPEC increased its oil revenues because, although sales fell, the price rose more than in proportion. Non-OPEC countries gained doubly because they were free to produce more and to sell it at the new higher world price.

Early success

In contrast with today's market, all through the twentieth century there was more capacity to produce oil than was demanded. As a result output rose until the market price was approximately equal to the marginal costs of production and distribution. In this context OPEC was formed in 1960. However, it did not attract world attention until 1973, when its members voluntarily agreed to restrict their outputs by negotiating quotas. At the time OPEC countries accounted for over half of the world's supply of crude oil and an even bigger proportion of world oil exports. So, although it was not quite a complete monopoly, the cartel had substantial market power. As a result of the output restrictions, the world price of oil nearly quadrupled within a year, from about $3 to nearly $12 a barrel. (Oil prices are customarily stated in US dollars.) The demand and supply analysis of what happened (in simplified terms) is analysed in Figure 7.10

OPEC's policy succeeded for several reasons. First, the member countries provided a significant part of the total world supply of oil. Secondly, other producing countries could not increase their outputs quickly in response to price increases. Thirdly, as Figure 7.10 shows, the world demand

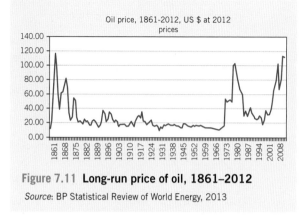

Figure 7.11 Long-run price of oil, 1861–2012

Source: BP Statistical Review of World Energy, 2013

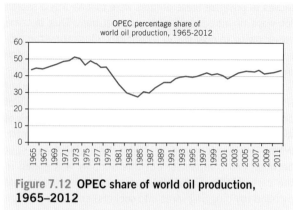

Figure 7.12 OPEC share of world oil production, 1965–2012

Source: BP Statistical Review of World Energy, 2013.

for oil proved to be highly inelastic in the short run. Data for oil prices over time are shown in Figure 7.11.

The higher prices were maintained for the remainder of the decade. As a result, OPEC countries found themselves suddenly enjoying vast wealth. The increase in their wealth was so great that the temptation to cheat, in order to gain even more, was small during the rest of the 1970s. However, by the end of the decade the OPEC countries had become used to their vast wealth and were spending more and more on arms, as well as on economic development. Eager for yet more income, they engineered a second output restriction that pushed prices from the $10–$12 range to over $30 a barrel. New income poured in, and OPEC's power to hold the oil-consuming world to ransom seemed limitless.

However, longer-term market forces were working against OPEC.

Pressure on the cartel

Monopolistic producers always face a long-run dilemma. The closer are their prices to the profit-maximizing level, the greater their short-term profits, but also the greater the incentive for market reactions that will reduce their profits in the longer term. In OPEC's case the market reactions came from both the demand and supply sides of the market.

Increasing world supply

The high prices and high profits achieved by the OPEC cartel spurred major additions to the world's oil supply by non-OPEC producers. This was, in effect, new entry and a rightward shift in the non-OPEC supply curve. In 1973 OPEC produced more than half of the world's oil; by 1979 its share was well under half, and by 1985 it was only just over a quarter (see Figure 7.12). The increased supply of non-OPEC oil tended to drive the world price down. To maintain the price, OPEC had to reduce its own output more and more.

Declining world demand

The market demand curve for oil in Figure 7.10 shows how variations in the price of oil affect purchases, holding other variables constant. Other things being equal, there was little that users could do to reduce their consumption of petroleum products in response to the price rise. Over a longer period of time, however, other things did not remain equal. A host of long-term adaptations—including smaller cars, more efficient insulation in oil-heated buildings, and more economical diesel engines—economized on petroleum products within known technology. The long-run demand curve proved to be much more elastic than the short-run demand curve. (See Figure 3.8 for an elaboration of the distinction between short- and long-run demand curves.) For example, UK demand for petroleum products fell from 107 million tonnes in 1973 to 72 million tonnes in 1981, and three decades later in 2012 it had fallen further to 67 million tonnes.

Very long run forces were also unleashed. The high price of petroleum led to a burst of scientific research to develop more petroleum-efficient technologies and alternatives to petroleum. Solar-heating technology was advanced, as was technology concerning many longer-term alternatives such as tidal power and heat from the interior of the Earth. Had the price of petroleum remained at its 1980 peak, this research would have continued at an intense pace and would have borne increasing fruit in the decades that followed.

The pressure to cheat

As world output of oil grew, OPEC output had to be reduced substantially to maintain the high prices. As a result, incomes in OPEC countries declined sharply and the instabilities inherent in any cartel began to be felt. In 1981 the cartel price was about five times as high as the 1972 price (measured in constant dollars), but production quotas were less than half of OPEC's capacity. Upset by declining incomes, OPEC producers began to violate their quotas. They met every few months to debate quotas, deplore cheating, and argue about strategy. But the agreements that were reached proved impossible to enforce, and at the end of 1985 OPEC eliminated production quotas. The price fluctuated considerably and then settled down near $18 a barrel, which was a little higher than the price before OPEC's restrictions began (allowing for inflation)—the slightly higher price being accounted for by the modest output restrictions that OPEC was still able to enforce.

More recently, OPEC got its act together again. This is not surprising as world consumption, particularly in the United States, rose and discovery of new supplies fell so that non-OPEC production levelled off, and OPEC came to have a rising share of the market. OPEC had real market power again and it used it. This time it was aided by rapidly rising demand from such growing economies as China and India, and by declining reserves of oil that could be brought online in response to high prices. In 2006–8 oil prices rose to all-time highs in money terms as a result of strong demand rather than any major additional restriction of supply, though OPEC did cut supply when prices fell sharply after the summer of 2008 (when the world economy slowed sharply owing to the impact of the financial crisis). Even more recently, changes in extraction technology for energy (especially 'fracking') have raised new doubts about the power of OPEC over energy prices, but how this all works out will have to wait for a later edition of this book.

The relevance of the OPEC experience

OPEC's experience illustrates some basic problems of output-restriction schemes.

1. Where demand is inelastic, restriction of output to below the competitive level can lead to immense profits in the short term.

However, supply is likely to increase when, as Schumpeter long ago predicted, new producers find ways of overcoming entry barriers in order to share in the large profits. Furthermore, demand is likely to decrease as new substitutes are invented and produced. These long-term adjustments limit the market power of monopolies and cartels, but only with a significant time lag.

2. Maintaining market power becomes increasingly difficult as time passes.

The closer the cartel pushes price to the monopoly level, the higher are the short-run profits, but the greater is the incentive for longer-term profit-reducing reactions from both the supply side and the demand side of the market.

3. Producers with market power face a basic trade-off between profits in the short term and profits in the longer term.

When there are many producers it is difficult to force them all to maintain the output restrictions, because each one has an incentive to cheat. This is particularly so if declining demand and increasing competition from new sources, or new products, lead to a steadily shrinking share of the market and falling profits.

4. Output restriction by voluntary agreement among several producers is difficult to maintain over any long period of time.

For a while OPEC massively exploited the non-OPEC world, but then the forces of the free market came to the rescue. Although the prospects for the near future are for rising demand for oil two forces are likely to hold the price of petroleum down for some time to come. First, concern over global warming is accelerating the move towards the use of non-fossil fuels. Second, and more important, the new technology of fracking, plus new offshore discoveries, are likely to expand supplies at faster than demand is growing for some time to come.

3. Tamiflu: a monopoly that may not last[10]

Tamiflu is an antiviral drug that was developed and patented by a US pharmaceutical company, Gilead Sciences. In 1996, Gilead signed an exclusive licensing agreement for marketing and manufacture with Roche, a Swiss pharmaceutical company. The patent and the licensing agreement run to 2016. A patent gives legal protection to the inventor of a product so that they have exclusive rights to benefit from the sale of that product for some period of time, normally 20 years. A patent, in effect, creates a legal monopoly.

In 2005, an outbreak of bird flu hit the world headlines as a virulent strain, known as the H5N1 virus, was caught by some humans who subsequently died. There was a serious concern that the virus could mutate into a form that would be transmitted from human to human and, thereby, possibly initiate a worldwide influenza pandemic. This could have been especially virulent as there was no human resistance to this strain and there was no available vaccine.

Tamiflu was only one of two known antiviral drugs with proven results at treating influenza-like conditions. In 2005 Roche's sales of Tamiflu increased by 370 per cent over 2004 and revenue rose from about $220 million to well over $1 billion as health authorities around the world bought in stocks of the drug in case of a major flu outbreak.

Clearly, this monopoly position was hugely beneficial to Roche, and to Gilead, which received a percentage on all

---

[10] This case study has drawn on an excellent project written by Cass Business School students Gintare Sribykyte, Seonghee Yang, and Lina Landelius.

sales. However, the position is nothing like as simple as portrayed in our analysis earlier in the chapter of a monopolist who sells directly to a large number of individual consumers. First, in many countries drug purchases are undertaken on behalf of government-controlled health authorities and these authorities have some power in the negotiation of prices. So the seller of a drug has to negotiate a price that is acceptable to both parties, rather than one that maximizes its own profit. Secondly, health issues are of major political concern and governments can change the law if they wish, including imposing taxes on companies, overturning patents, and compulsory purchase of a company or any of its assets. In 2003 the World Trade Organization stated that, in cases of a national health crisis, patent protection of specific drugs could be violated. Thirdly, while Roche and Gilead have a patent on Tamiflu until 2016 they cannot stop other companies developing a drug that is even more effective or a vaccine that would make Tamiflu redundant.

Hence, the problem for Roche was not as simple as just maximizing profit during the period of patent protection, given current conditions of demand and supply. Rather it had to walk a fine political line as well as an economic one. It did not want to be seen as overcharging for a drug at a time of a health crisis, as this would encourage governments to withdraw patent protection. Taiwan did just this in 2005.

A further problem was that the surge in demand initially left Roche with inadequate production capacity, and this itself led to political criticism. Roche proceeded to negotiate sublicense agreements with other producers in countries such as India and China, but this looked likely to be leading to a legal dispute with Gilead as to whether the original license agreement had been violated. In order to head off political criticism (or for entirely altruistic reasons), Roche donated five million doses of Tamiflu to the World Health Organization in 2005.

The prospects for Tamiflu looked very good in 2006 as most governments were committed to further build up of their stocks of this drug. But two major threats remained. First, it is possible that a future major influenza outbreak could lead governments to violate the patent and authorize generic copies of the drug. Secondly, it is possible (indeed quite likely) that, if there is a major outbreak of influenza in humans, a new vaccine will be developed quickly. There already exists a vaccine for the H5N1 virus, but it is not clear whether this would be the virus at the heart of human outbreak.

Another major boost to demand for Tamiflu arose in 2009 with an outbreak of a new flu virus known as swine flu (H1N1). The demand for Tamiflu grew over 400 per cent in 2009 and raised its contributions to Roche's revenue significantly. However, this surge was only temporary. While Tamiflu continued to do well in some parts of the world it contributed only 2 per cent to Roche's pharmaceutical sales in 2013. However, it seemed likely to take a big hit to sales in April 2014 when an independent report claimed that trials had shown that it was no more effective than paracetemol in treating flu viruses.

Large pharmaceutical companies are used to living in a world in which they seek to develop a 'blockbuster' drug that generates large profits for a period and then becomes unprofitable once the patent expires or a superior substitute is developed. The anti-ulcer drug Zantac was just such a product which made huge profits for Glaxo, but since the expiry of its patent it has been cheaply available in generic form.

Government policy in this area needs to tread a fine line between creating incentives for the invention of new drugs and making sure that the best treatments currently known are available and affordable for those who need them. In the drug industry, monopolies come and go under patent protection, but they never last forever. Twenty years is the maximum length under current laws, but under political pressure the window of opportunity may become much shorter, even without an adverse report on efficacy.

4. Fares fair?

In the United Kingdom the competition authorities have the task of ensuring that restrictive practices that hurt consumers do not survive. The following extract outlines the campaign by the Office for Fair Trading (OFT) to inform minicab drivers of the illegality of conspiring to fix fares.

The OFT has launched a campaign to ensure minicab operators across the UK understand competition rules.

The OFT is concerned there may be a particular lack of awareness among private hire vehicle operators of the stringent civil and criminal laws against price fixing, following a number of reports of minicab operators entering into agreements with their competitors to set prices.

In several cases competitors appear to have agreed prices in their local area on a per mile or minimum journey cost basis. The most recent report involved firms in Lancashire but the OFT has received information alleging similar practices elsewhere in the UK.

Minicabs are pre-booked, with customers able to choose a service by shopping around. The market is different to taxi services where the first available vehicle is hailed off the street and fares are usually set under separate licensing rules.

Minicab operators are being warned that individuals may face criminal liability for price-fixing, including fines and even the possibility of imprisonment. In addition businesses could be fined up to 10 per cent of their total turnover.

During the campaign the OFT is working with trade associations, the Licensed Private Hire Car Association (LPHCA), the Private Hire Board and the National Private Hire Association to spread awareness of the rules. The OFT has also written to Local Authority Trading Standards Services and taxi licensing officers informing them of these issues.

Simon Williams, Head of the OFT's Cartel and Criminal Enforcement Group, said: 'Minicab operators in some areas appear to be unaware of the importance of independent price setting. Companies are free to change their prices but must understand that the law forbids any collusion with competitors when deciding price levels'.

(Source: <http://www.oft.gov.uk/news-and-updates/press/2008/131-08#. UnOdgXDQBQg>)

This case study provides an excellent example of why totally unregulated free-market capitalism may not produce the most socially desirable results. Active intervention from the government is needed in this, and many other similar cases, to keep firms competing and so providing services and prices that give the best results for consumers.

Conclusion

A monopoly has power over the market in which it sells. Monopolies faced with a large number of consumers can force up the market price by restricting their output. As a result, monopolies are rarely left alone by government, and monopoly profits create incentives for others to

invent new products. Few monopolies, other than natural ones, last for very long, and if they do their actions are generally heavily restricted by regulation or public ownership. We discuss the response of government to monopoly further in Chapter 13.

SUMMARY

A single-price monopolist

■ A monopoly is an industry containing a single firm. The monopoly firm maximizes its profits by equating marginal cost to marginal revenue, which is less than price. Production under monopoly is less than it would be under perfect competition, where marginal cost is equated to price.

The allocative inefficiency of monopoly

■ Monopoly is allocatively inefficient. By producing less than the perfectly competitive output it transfers some consumers' surplus to its own profits and also causes deadweight loss of the surplus that would have resulted from the output that is not produced.

A multi-price monopolist

■ If a monopolist can discriminate between either different units or different customers, it will always sell more and earn greater profits than if it must charge a single price.

■ For price discrimination to be possible, the seller must be able to distinguish individual units bought by a single buyer or to separate buyers into classes between whom resale is impossible.

Long-run monopoly equilibrium

■ A monopoly can earn positive profits in the long run if there are barriers to entry. These may be man-made, such as patents or exclusive franchises, or natural, such as economies of large-scale production and large set-up costs.

Cartels as monopolies

■ The joint profits of all firms in a perfectly competitive industry can always be increased if they agree to restrict output. After agreement is in place, any one firm can increase its profits by violating the agreement. If they all do this, profits are reduced to the perfectly competitive level.

TOPICS FOR REVIEW

■ Relationship between price and marginal revenue for a monopolist

■ Relationships among marginal revenue, total revenue, and elasticity for a monopolist

■ Short- and long-run monopoly equilibrium

■ Natural and created entry barriers

■ Price discrimination among different units and different buyers

■ Individual firm versus industry profits in a cartel

QUESTIONS

1 Using the same cost information as for the firm described in Question 3 of Chapter 5, you are now given information about demand. The table shows the price at which the corresponding quantity can be sold.

Sales (units)	Price (£)
20	19.20
40	18.40
60	17.60
100	16.00
200	12.00
300	8.00
400	4.00
500	0.00
1,000	—

(You might like to know that this is a straight-line demand curve that can be expressed as $p = 20 - 0.04q$, where p is price and q is quantity sold.)

a) What is the marginal revenue for each level of sales?

b) What are the approximate profit-maximizing levels of sales and price?

c) Draw a graph showing total costs, total revenue, and profit at each level of sales.

2 Suppose now that the firm in Question 1 has constant marginal costs of £4.00 per unit (i.e. ignore previous information about costs) and that it faces two segmented

Sales (units)	Price (£)
20	9.60
40	9.20
60	8.80
100	8.00
200	6.00
300	4.00
400	2.00
500	0.00
1,000	—

markets. One has the demand curve in Question 1, and the other has the demand curve shown at the foot of the previous column.

$p = 10 - 0.02q$.

a) What quantity will the firm sell in each market?

b) What price will be charged in each market?

3 For the two demand curves listed in Questions 1 and 2, calculate the price elasticity of demand at each of the listed sales levels. What is the elasticity at the sales level that maximizes total revenue? Are there any sales levels for which demand is inelastic? What is marginal revenue at this level of sales?

4 Firms in both perfect competition and monopoly will maximize profit in the short run where (choose one answer):

a) They set $MC = MR$, MC cuts MR from above, and price exceeds average variable cost.

b) They set $AC = $ price, AC is at a minimum, and price exceeds average total cost.

c) They set $MC = MR$, MC cuts MR from below, and price exceeds average fixed cost.

d) They set $AC = AR$, AC cuts AR from below, and price exceeds average variable cost.

e) They set $MC = MR$, MC cuts MR from below, and price exceeds average variable cost.

5 A monopolist that can sell into two segmented markets that have different demand conditions will (choose one answer):

a) equate profit margins in the two markets

b) equate average revenue in the two markets

c) equate marginal revenue in the two markets

d) equate price in the two markets

e) equate average total cost in the two markets.

6 Explain why static analysis shows that monopoly is allocatively inefficient compared to perfect competition. How might dynamic considerations change this conclusion?

7 Explain how a cartel can raise the joint profit of its members. Why are cartels likely to be unstable?

8 If a firm produces an identical product in two separate plants, explain how it should decide the profit-maximizing production levels in each plant.

9 Why can a monopolist increase profit by segmenting its markets and charging different prices in each segment?

10 Explain why a profit-maximizing monopolist will never be selling on an inelastic portion of its demand curve.

Appendix: Price discrimination between two markets

Consider a monopoly firm that sells a single product in two distinct markets, *A* and *B*, with demand, marginal revenue, and cost curves as shown in Figure 7A.1. Resale among customers is impossible and a single price must be charged in each market.

What is the best price for the firm to charge in each market? The simplest way to discover this is to imagine the firm deciding how best to allocate any given total output Q^* between two markets. Since output is fixed arbitrarily at Q^*, there is nothing the monopolist can do about costs. The best thing it can do, therefore, is to maximize the revenue that it gets by selling Q^* in the two markets. *To do this it will allocate its sales between the markets until the marginal revenues are the same in each market.* Consider what would happen if the marginal revenue in market *A* exceeded the marginal revenue in market *B*. The firm could keep its overall output constant at Q^* but reallocate a unit of sales from *B* to *A*, gaining a net addition in revenue equal to the difference between the marginal revenues in the two markets. Thus, it will always pay a monopoly firm to reallocate a given total quantity between its markets as long as marginal revenues are not equal in the two markets.

If we assume that marginal cost is constant, we can determine the profit-maximizing course of action from Figure 7A.1. The *MC* curve in both parts shows the constant marginal cost. The firm's total profits are maximized by equating *MR* in each market to its constant *MC*, thus selling q_A at p_A in market *A* and q_B at p_B in market *B*.

Marginal revenue is the same in each market ($c_A = c_B$) so that the firm has its total output correctly allocated between the two markets, and marginal cost equals marginal revenue, showing that the firm would lose profits if it produced more or less total output.

Next, assume that marginal cost varies with output, being given by *MC'* in Figure 7A.2(iii). Now, we cannot just put the *MC* curve onto the diagram for each market, since the marginal cost of producing another unit for sale in market *A* will depend on how much is being produced for sale in market *B* and vice versa. To determine what overall production should be, we need to know overall marginal revenue. To find this, we merely sum the separate quantities in each market that correspond to each particular marginal revenue. For example, if the tenth unit sold in market *A* and the fifteenth unit sold in market *B* each have a marginal revenue of £1 in their separate markets, then the marginal revenue of £1 corresponds to overall sales of twenty-five units (ten units in *A* and fifteen in *B*). This example illustrates the general principle: the overall marginal revenue curve for a discriminating monopolist is the horizontal sum of the marginal revenue curves in each of its markets. This overall curve shows the marginal revenue associated with an increment to production on the assumption that sales are divided between the two markets so as to keep the two marginal revenues equal.

This overall *MR* curve is shown in Figure 7A.2(iii) and is labelled *MR'*. The firm's total profit-maximizing

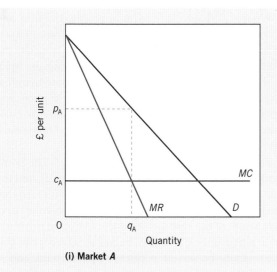

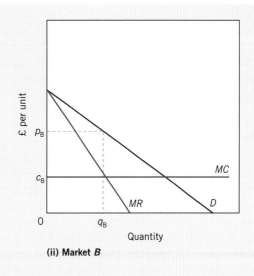

(i) Market *A*   **(ii) Market *B***

Figure 7A.1

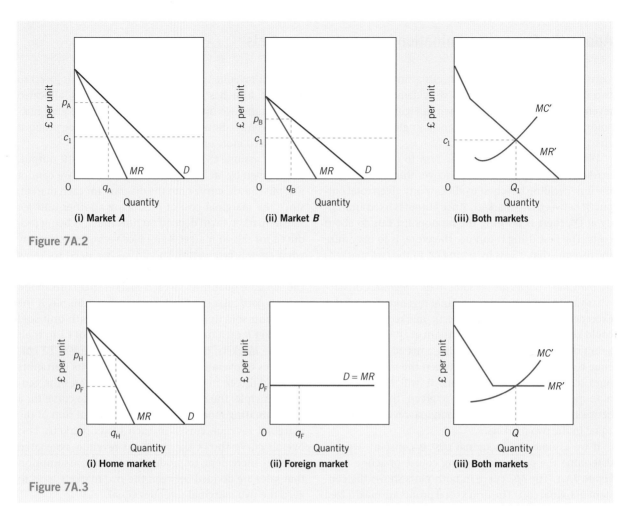

Figure 7A.2

Figure 7A.3

output is at Q_1, where MR' and MC' intersect (at a value of c_1). By construction, marginal revenue is c_1 in each market although price is different. To find the equilibrium price and quantity in each market, find the quantities q_A and q_B that correspond to this marginal revenue; then find the prices in each market that correspond to q_A and q_B. All of this is illustrated in parts (i) and (ii) of the figure.

An application

In some industries firms sell competitively on international markets while enjoying a home market that is protected from foreign competition by tariffs or import quotas. To illustrate the issues involved, consider the following extreme case. A firm is the only producer of product X in country A. There are thousands of producers of X in other countries, so that X is sold abroad under conditions of perfect competition. The government of country A grants the firm a monopoly in the home market by prohibiting imports of X. The firm is now faced with a negatively sloped

demand curve at home and a perfectly elastic demand curve abroad at the prevailing world price of X.

What will it do? To maximize profits, the firm will divide its sales between the foreign and the home markets so as to equate marginal revenues in the two. On the world market its average and marginal revenues are equal to the world price. Thus, the firm will equate marginal revenue in the home market with the world price, and since price exceeds marginal revenue at home (because the demand curve slopes downwards), price at home must exceed price abroad.

The argument is illustrated in Figure 7A.3. The home market is shown in (i), the foreign market in (ii), and the sum of the marginal revenue curves in (iii). Provided that the marginal cost curve cuts the marginal revenue curve to the right of the kink (i.e. MC does not exceed the world price when only the home market is served), the two markets will be served at prices of p_H at home and p_F abroad. The total quantity sold will be Q, of which q_H is allocated to the home market and the rest ($q_F = Q - q_H$) is sold abroad.

CHAPTER 8

IMPERFECT COMPETITION

Perfect competition and monopoly are extreme cases that do not involve active competition at all. In the former, firms have no influence over the market price, while in the latter there is only one producer. In neither case do they need to worry about what other firms are doing. So, what about the intermediate cases where firms do have some market power but also have competitors? These cases are the subject of this chapter. In particular you will learn that:

- Concentration of production varies among industries, but firms in all intermediate types of industry have some power to influence their price.
- In industries where there are many firms producing differentiated products, free entry will tend to eliminate profits in the long run.
- Where there is a small group of dominant producers (oligopoly), strategic interaction is important because one firm's sales are affected by what its rivals do.
- Insights into the choices available and the nature of outcomes in small group situations can be achieved using game theory.
- Oligopoly can be associated with pure profits in the long run if there are barriers to entry.
- Competition among firms in oligopolistic industries has been the source of many of the innovations that have contributed to the long-term growth of living standards.

Most real firms outside of agriculture and other primary product industries, operate under intermediate market structures rather than the two extremes of perfect competition and monopoly. On the one hand, they are not monopolies because their industries contain several firms, which often compete actively against each other. Firms manufacturing cars, refrigerators, TV sets, breakfast cereals, and many other consumer goods are in industries containing several close rivals, usually both foreign and domestic. Even in small towns, residents find more than one chemist, garage, hairdresser, and supermarket competing for their patronage. On the other hand, these firms do not operate in perfectly competitive markets because the number of competing firms is often small, and, even when the number is large, *the firms are not price takers*.

In this chapter, we study firm behaviour in two intermediate market structures. One, which is called monopolistic competition, is close to perfect competition with one important difference. Firms do not sell a homogeneous product. The second, called oligopoly, deals with industries that typically contain a few large firms that compete actively with each other.

Patterns of concentration in UK industry

One measure of the extent to which firms in some industries have potential market power is called a **concentration ratio**. This measures the fraction of total output in the country that is produced by some specified number of the industry's largest firms. Common types of concentration ratios cite the share of an industry's total output made by the largest three or five firms. For example, the UK five-firm concentration ratio for leather goods in 2004

Table 8.1 Concentration ratios for UK industries, 2004

	Output of largest five businesses as a percentage of the output of the sector
Dairy products	32
Sugar	99
Tobacco products	99
Textile weaving	26
Wearing apparel, dressing and dyeing of fur	14
Leather goods	30
Wood and wood products	9
Pulp, paper, and paper board	21
Publishing and printing	12
Coke, refined petroleum products, and nuclear fuel	66
Iron and steel	61
Rubber products	45
Cutlery and tools	11
Office machinery and computers	37
Radio, TV, and communication equipment	46
Furniture	5
Motor vehicles	34
Telecommunications	61
Postal and courier services	65
Electricity production and distribution	55

Source: Economic Trends, ONS, October 2006.

was 30 per cent. This means that the largest five firms in that industry accounted for 30 per cent of the domestic industry's total output.

Table 8.1 gives the latest available five-firm concentration ratios for twenty subsectors of UK industry. In many of these industries the largest five firms were too large a part of the total market to be price takers. Yet none of these industries is a single-firm monopoly. The most concentrated (by this measure) were tobacco products and sugar, where the five largest firms accounted for virtually the entire output. In furniture, however, the largest five firms only accounted for 5 per cent of the output.

Although national concentration ratios provide useful information, care must be taken in interpreting them. For example, markets often extend across national borders. Even if there was only one home producer of a product in the United Kingdom it would not have a monopoly if it was competing in the UK market against several close substitute products imported from other

countries. The globalization of competition, brought about by the falling costs of transportation and communication, has been one of the most significant developments in the world economy in recent decades. Global competition has greatly reduced the market power of home producers in domestic markets. For example, in the cigarette market the US-based company Philip Morris had about a 10 per cent share of UK sales in 2012, mainly with its Marlboro brand, but none of its cigarettes was produced in the UK. However, 85 per cent of sales in the UK tobacco market were from the various brands of just two companies—Imperial Tobacco and Japan Tobacco International.

The phenomenon of globalization in business is discussed further in Box 8.1.

The extent of competition in any market depends not just on the number of domestic producers but also on the ability of foreign producers to compete effectively in that market.

Box 8.1 Globalization of production and competition

A mere 150 years ago people and news travelled by sailing ship, so that it took months to communicate across various parts of the world. Advances in the twentieth century sped up both communications and travel. In the past several decades the pace of change in communications technology has accelerated. The world has witnessed a communications revolution that has dramatically changed the way business decisions are made and implemented.

Sixty years ago telephone links were laboriously and unreliably connected by operators; satellites were in the dreams of rocket scientists; photocopying, fax, and e-mail were completely unknown, as was the internet. Hand-delivered mail was the only way to send hard copy, and getting it to overseas destinations often took weeks. Computers were in their infancy and only accessible to an elite few academics and military scientists. Jets were just beginning to replace the much slower and less reliable propeller aircraft. Today, direct voice and video communication is available to most parts of the world at a tiny fraction of what long-distance calls cost even forty years ago, and in some cases it is completely free. The internet, faxes, satellite TV links, fast jet travel, email, cheap courier services, mobile phones, and a host of other developments have made communication that is reliable, and often instantaneous, available throughout the world.

The communications revolution of the last few decades has been a major contributor to the development of what has become known as the 'global village', three important characteristics of which are a *disintegration* of production, an increase in competition, and a decline in the power of the nation-state.

Production

The communications revolution has allowed many large international companies, known as transnational corporations (TNCs), to decentralize their production process. They are now able to locate their research and development (R&D) where the best scientists are available. They can produce various components in dozens of places, locating each activity in the country where costs are low for that type of production. They can then ship all the parts, as they are needed, to an assembly factory where the product is 'made'.

One of the most dramatic examples of globalization can be seen in two ways. The first is the emergence of China as the world's leading maker of many manufactured products (many of whose components are made in other developing countries). The second and related phenomenon is the decline of the industries producing these products—a development often referred to as de-industrialization—in the United States, the United Kingdom, and much of Western Europe.

The globalization of production has also brought employment, and rising real wages, to people in many less developed countries. At the same time, it has put less skilled labour in the developed countries under strong competitive pressures, which has been a major reason for the lack of real wage increases for this group over the past few decades.

Competition

The communications revolution has also caused an internationalization of competition in many industries. National markets are no longer protected for local producers by high costs of transportation and communication or by consumers' ignorance of similar foreign products. Walk into a local supermarket or department store today and you will have no trouble in finding products representing most of the United Nations member states.

Consumers gain by being able to choose from an enormous range of goods and services. Firms that are successful gain worldwide sales. However, firms that fall behind, even momentarily, may be wiped out by competition coming from many quarters. Global competition is fierce competition, and firms that want to survive must be fast on the uptake of their own and other people's new ideas.

Economic policy

The globalization of production, and consequently of competition, has greatly reduced the scope for individual countries to implement distinctive economic policies. Today, firms of all sorts, from large transnationals to individuals operating out of homes through computer links, can relocate production easily. So tough national policies that reduce local profitability are often self-defeating, as firms move production elsewhere.

Imperfectly competitive market structures

The market structures that we will now study are called *imperfectly competitive*. The word 'competitive' emphasizes that we are not dealing with monopoly, and the word 'imperfect' emphasizes that we are not dealing with perfect competition.

Some patterns of firm behaviour are typical of all imperfectly competitive market structures. We outline these first, before looking at specific models of imperfect competition.

Firms create their own products

If a new farmer enters the wheat industry, the full range of products that can be produced is already in existence. If he decides to produce No. 1 durum wheat, it will be the same as the No. 1 durum wheat produced by all other farmers. In contrast, if a new firm enters the computer software industry, that firm must decide on the characteristics of the new computer programs that it is to produce. It will not produce programs that are identical to those already in production. Rather, it will develop new programs, each of which will have its own distinctive characteristics. Indeed, in virtually all consumer and capital goods industries firms sell a range of differentiated products. The term **differentiated product** refers to a group of products that are similar enough to be considered variations on one generic product but dissimilar enough that they can be sold at different prices; for example, Ford and Mercedes both make cars but their models are different.

Most firms in imperfectly competitive market structures sell differentiated products. In such industries, the firm itself must decide on the characteristics of the products it will sell.

Firms choose their prices

In imperfectly competitive markets firms typically have several product lines that differ more or less from each other and from the competing product lines of other firms. Unlike perfect competition, no impersonal market sets a single price for all blue jeans, TV sets, MP3 players, mobile phones, or computer games. Instead, *each* variety of the differentiated product has a price that must be set by its maker, and then some mark-up is set by the retailer (whenever the product is sold through a retailer, rather than direct to the consumer). These are the administered prices that we discussed in Chapter 2. Having set the price, firms wait to see how much is sold at that price.

In market structures other than perfect competition, firms set their prices and then let demand determine sales. Changes in market conditions are signalled to the firm by changes in the quantity that the firm sells at its current administered price.

The changed conditions may then lead firms to change their prices, but they may decide to change their level of production instead.

Short-run price stability

In perfect competition, prices change continually in response to changes in demand and supply. In markets for differentiated products, prices often change less frequently. Prices for motor cars, computers, TV sets, and CDs are set by their manufacturers and do not change with anything like the frequency of price changes in markets for basic materials, company shares, and foreign exchange.

Because firms producing differentiated products must administer their own prices, they must decide on the *frequency* with which they change these prices.

In making this decision, two key considerations are important to the firm.

1. What is the cost of making price changes? Modern firms that sell differentiated products typically have hundreds, or even thousands, of distinct products on their price lists. Changing such a long list of administered prices involves costs. These include the costs of printing new list prices and notifying all customers, the difficulty of keeping track of frequently changing prices for purposes of accounting and billing, and the loss of customer and retailer goodwill owing to the uncertainty caused by frequent changes in prices

2. How much revenue will be lost by holding prices constant in the face of changes in market conditions? This of course depends on the magnitude of the difference between the constant price and the variable profit-maximizing price and how long that divergence persists.

The size of the disturbance to which the firm is adjusting, and the probability that the disturbance will be reversed, influences the first of the above points The more transitory are the fluctuations in demand, the higher is the cost over time of adjusting prices each time demand changes. The nature of the firm's cost structure influences the second consideration. If the firm has constant average and marginal costs, as do firms with divisible fixed inputs, on balance it will lose less by holding prices constant over fluctuations in demand than will firms with variable marginal costs. Firms with divisible fixed inputs often follow what is called *full cost pricing* rather than profit maximization. They calculate the total average cost at capacity output and add a profit mark-up. They then hold that price constant as demand varies randomly or cyclically. They may alter prices if demand changes permanently, or if costs change significantly, or if such changes are needed in order to compete with other similar firms. But they do not alter their prices in response to short-term fluctuations in their demands but instead respond by altering outputs and sales. This behaviour may be at, or at least close to, profit-maximizing behaviour for two reasons. First, if the profit-maximizing price only varies slightly in the face of random and cyclical variations in demand, the profits forgone by not changing price continuously may be small. Secondly, if the loss is smaller than all the costs associated with frequent price changes, the behaviour is profit-maximizing. If the loss is slightly higher, then, although not quite profit-maximizing, it is a much simpler and less risky procedure than trying to estimate the correct profit-maximizing prices as demands for each of the firms' products change continually. Note that firms are not given knowledge of their demand curves. They know one point on each for sure: their current price and their sales for each of the products. But if they wish to alter price, they must estimate the curve at other prices and they often do so with very imperfect information. This implies that making frequent estimates of changes in their demand curves, and acting on them, is costly over time. There is a risk of deviating significantly from the profit-maximizing price but there are also costs of too frequent price changes.

It is interesting to note in this context that retailers tend to be more flexible than manufacturers in altering prices as demand changes. For example, automobile manufacturers set a price at which they will sell each of their cars to all of their dealers. In contrast, each dealer is free to bargain with each individual customer, which allows the dealer to discriminate among individual buyers—and, as we saw in Chapter 7, profits can always be higher with some degree of price discrimination rather than always selling at one price. Also, the cost for any retailer of varying the price among purchasers is much less than when a manufacturer sets a price at which it will sell to all of its dealers. To the dealer, the cost is only the time taken in reaching individual bargains. Also the dealer's risks associated with price variations are minimal because she is not setting a price for all comers but only for the person with whom she is currently bargaining.

One recent development, the rise of internet sales, has encouraged much more price flexibility than there used to be among retailers and even some producers who sell on the net. For example, the prices of airline seats now change frequently, sometimes hourly, whereas in pre-computer days the prices were posted in a printed brochure and were changed only infrequently.

Non-price competition

Many firms spend large sums of money on advertising. They do so in an attempt both to shift the demand curve for the industry's product and also to attract customers from competing firms. Firms often offer competing standards of quality and product guarantees. Any kind of sales promotion activity undertaken by a single firm would not happen under perfect competition since each firm can sell any amount at the going market price. Any such scheme directed at competing firms in the same industry is, by definition, inconsistent with monopoly. Firms also use advertising to signal their commitment to quality and service, in order to generate customer loyalty to their brand. Again, this is something a perfect competitor would never do, and something a pure monopolist is unlikely to need to do.

Unexploited scale economies

Many firms in imperfectly competitive industries appear to be operating on the downward-sloping portions of their long-run average cost curves.[1] One reason for this is the high development costs and short product lives of many modern products. Some popular software products, for example, did not exist five years ago and will almost certainly have been superseded in five years' time. A computer program takes a lot of time and effort to write but further copies of it can be run off very cheaply. Similarly, a new drug typically requires years of R&D costs to discover and test, but it will often be inexpensive to manufacture once the formula has been discovered. In such cases, firms face steeply falling long-run average total cost curves. The more units that they sell, the lower are their fixed development costs per unit. If they were in perfect competition, these firms would go on increasing outputs and sales until rising marginal costs of production just balanced their falling average fixed costs, bringing their average total cost to a minimum. But under imperfect competition firms often face falling average total cost curves throughout each product's life. Such industries are sometimes referred to as **increasing returns industries**.

Entry prevention

Firms in many industries engage in activities that are designed to hinder the entry of new firms, thereby preventing existing pure profits from being eroded by entry. We discuss these activities in much more detail later in the chapter.

Monopolistic competition

One simple model of imperfect competition is known as monopolistic competition. Tractability of this model is achieved by limiting the form of interdependence between producers. We deal with this case first before discussing more general types of strategic interactions between firms in oligopolistic market structures.

Monopolistic competition refers to a market in which there are many firms and each sells a single differentiated

---

[1] Although this is also possible under monopoly, firms in perfect competition must, in the long run, be at the minimum point of their long-run average cost curves (see Figure 6.10).

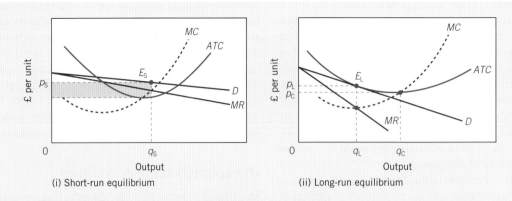

Figure 8.1 Equilibrium of a typical firm in monopolistic competition

In the short run a typical firm may make pure profits, but in the long run it will only cover its costs. In part (i) a typical monopolistically competitive firm is shown in short-run equilibrium at point E_S. Output is q_S, where $MC = MR$, price is p_S, and profits are the blue area. In part (ii) the firm is in long-run equilibrium at point E_L. Entry of new firms has pushed the existing firm's demand curve to the left until the curve is tangent to the ATC curve at output q_L. Price is p_L, and total costs are just being covered. Excess capacity is $q_C - q_L$. If the firm did produce at capacity, its costs would fall from p_L per unit of output to p_C. Note that to make the points q_L and q_C visually distinct, the demand curve in part (ii) has been drawn more steeply sloped than in part (i). The flatter demand curve of part (i) is what is expected in monopolistic competition. If it were drawn in part (ii), q_L would more realistically be closer to q_C, but the differences being illustrated by the figure would be harder to see.

product. Since each firm's product is somewhat different from those of its competitors, each faces a negatively sloped demand curve for its product.[2]

The theory

Assumptions

The theory is based on four key assumptions.

1. *Each firm produces one specific variety, or brand, of the industry's generic product.* Thus, each firm faces a demand curve that, although negatively sloped, is highly elastic because many close substitutes are sold by other firms.

2. *The industry contains so many firms that each one ignores the possible reactions of its many competitors when it makes its own price and output decisions.* Each firm makes decisions based on its own demand and cost conditions, and does not take any account of potential reactions by other firms.

3. *There is freedom of entry and exit in the industry.* If existing firms are earning profits, new firms have an incentive to enter. When they do, the demand for the industry's product must be shared among more brands.

4. *There is symmetry.* When a new firm enters the industry selling a new differentiated version of the generic product, it takes customers equally from all existing firms.

For example, a new entrant that captured 5 per cent of the existing market would do so by capturing 5 per cent of the sales of each existing firm.

Equilibrium

Short-run equilibrium

Because each firm's product has some different features from those of competitors, each firm faces a negatively sloped demand curve. But the curve is rather elastic because similar products sold by other firms provide many close substitutes. The negative slope of the demand curve provides the potential for monopoly profits in the short run, as illustrated in Figure 8.1(i).

Long-run equilibrium

Freedom of entry and exit forces profits to zero in the long run. If existing firms in the industry are earning profits, new firms will enter. Their entry will mean that the demand for the product must be shared among more and more brands. Thus, the demand curve for each existing firm's brand shifts to the left.[3] Entry continues until profits fall to zero as shown in Figure 8.1(ii).

Excess capacity

The absence of positive profits requires that each firm's demand curve be nowhere above its long-run average

---

[2] US economist Edward Chamberlin (1899–1967) was the originator of the theory of monopolistic competition. A related approach was developed by the British economist Joan Robinson (1903–83).

[3] The amount of the shift in the demand curve is determined by the *symmetry assumption*: a new entrant takes sales in equal proportion from all existing firms.

total cost curve. The absence of losses, which would cause exit, requires that each firm be able to cover its costs. Thus, average revenue must equal average total cost at some output. Together, these requirements imply that, when a monopolistically competitive industry is in long-run equilibrium, each firm will be producing where its demand curve is tangent to (i.e. just touching at one point) its average total cost curve.

Two curves that are tangent at a point have the same slope at that point. If a negatively sloped demand curve is to be tangent to the long-run average cost (*LRAC*) curve, the latter must also be negatively sloped at the point of tangency. This situation is shown in Figure 8.1(ii); the typical firm is producing an output less than the one at which its *LRAC* reaches its minimum point.

This is the **excess capacity theorem** of monopolistic competition. Each firm is producing its output at an average cost that is higher than it could achieve by producing its capacity output. In other words, each firm has *unused* or *excess* capacity. So:

The theory of monopolistic competition shows that an industry can be competitive, in the sense of containing numerous competing firms and no pure profits, and yet contain unexploited scale economies, in the sense that each firm is producing on the negatively sloped portion of its average total cost curve.

This implies that firms typically invest in capacity that is not fully utilized.

Is excess capacity wasteful?

The long-run equilibrium of a monopolistically competitive industry might seem inefficient. Production costs are not as low as they could be if firms produced at the lowest point on their average cost curves, and firms typically invest in some capacity that goes unused.

But this is not necessarily inefficient because people value diversity and are prepared to pay a price for it. For example, each brand of breakfast food, shampoo, car, and blue jeans has its sincere devotees. Increasing the number of differentiated products has two effects. First, it increases the amount of excess capacity in the production of each product, because the total demand must be divided between more products. Secondly, the increased diversity of available products will better satisfy diverse tastes.

How will consumers' satisfaction be maximized in these circumstances?

Consumers' satisfaction is maximized when the number of differentiated products is increased until the marginal gain in consumers' satisfaction from an increase in diversity equals the loss from having to produce each existing product at a higher cost.

There is no reason why the free-market process would produce exactly this optimal result; it might produce

more or less diversity than this. For this reason, among others, the prediction that large group monopolistic competition would lead to inefficiency in the use of resources is not proven—it might and it might not.

Empirical relevance

Is there any empirical relevance of the monopolistic competition model? Although product differentiation is an almost universal phenomenon in industries producing consumer goods and capital goods, the monopolistically competitive market structure is found only infrequently in practice. Although many industries produce a vast array of differentiated products, these are often produced by only a few firms. For example, a mere three firms produce most of the many breakfast cereals. Similar circumstances exist in soap powder, chemicals, cigarettes, and numerous other industries. These industries are clearly not perfectly competitive and neither are they monopolies. Are they monopolistically competitive? The answer is no, because they contain few enough firms for each to take account of the others' reactions when determining its own behaviour (thus violating the second assumption above). Furthermore, these firms often earn large profits without attracting new entry (thus violating the prediction of zero profits in the long run).

A good example of an industry that comes close to being monopolistically competitive is UK restaurants. Each competes in the 'prepared meal' market, but most individual restaurants are not critically affected by any one other. Each has a different product and entry into the market is easy. The more entry there is, the smaller the market share of the others is likely to be, but each clearly has some discretion about the prices it charges and the impact of any single restaurant on most of the others is typically tiny. There were, for example, over 100,000 catering firms registered for VAT in the UK in 2009 (some of which had many branches) and some 85,000 pubs, most of which served food. All the restaurant chains combined served no more than 14 per cent of the meal market and they faced competition from take-aways, hotels, and stand-alone restaurants. There was also competition from ready meals supplied by supermarkets. Hence, it seems that today there are large numbers of relatively small providers in this market, but each one of them has some market power as they have some discretion over the prices they set. However, restaurants have a location in space and type. As a result the symmetry assumption—that a new restaurant takes custom equally from all existing restaurants—is not strictly true. A new Chinese restaurant is likely to take more customers from other nearby Chinese restaurants than from Chinese restaurants at the other end of the city, and fewer still from a fish-and-chip shop, even if it is located nearby.

Box 8.2 The price of haircuts and the profits of hairdressers

Suppose that there are many hairdressers and freedom of entry into the industry—anyone can set up as a hairdresser. Assume that the going price for haircuts is £15 and that at this price all hairdressers believe their incomes are too low.

The hairdressers hold a meeting and decide to form a trade association. The purpose of the association is to impose a price of £25 for haircuts. What is the result?

We need to distinguish between the short-run and the long-run effects of an increase in the price of haircuts. In the short run the number of hairdressers is fixed. Thus, in the short run the answer depends only on the elasticity of the demand for their services. If demand elasticity is less than 1, total expenditure will rise and so will the incomes of hairdressers; if demand elasticity exceeds 1, the hairdressers' revenues will fall. Thus, to answer the question we need some knowledge about the size of the elasticity of demand for haircuts. Assuming it to be inelastic, hairdressers will be successful in raising incomes in the short run.

What about the long run? If hairdressers were just covering costs before the price change, they will now be earning economic profits. Hairdressing will become an attractive trade relative to others requiring equal skill and training, and there will be a flow of new entrants into the industry. As the number of hairdressers rises, the same amount of business must be shared among more and more of them, so the typical hairdresser will find business—and thus earnings—decreasing.

Profits may also be squeezed from another direction. With fewer customers coming their way, hairdressers may compete against one another for the limited number of customers. Their agreement does not allow them to compete through price cuts, but they can compete in service. They may spruce up their shops, offer their customers expensive magazines to read and a cup of coffee, and so forth. This kind of non-price competition will raise operating costs.

These changes will continue until hairdressers are just covering their opportunity costs, at which time the attraction for new entrants will vanish. The industry will settle down in a new long-run equilibrium in which individual hairdressers make incomes only as large as they did before the price rise. There will be more hairdressers than there were in the original situation, but each one will be working for a smaller fraction of the day and will be idle for a larger fraction. (The industry will have excess capacity.) Customers will have shorter waits, even at peak periods, and they will get to read a wide choice of magazines, but they will be paying £25 for haircuts.

If the association adopted the plan in order to raise the average income of hairdressers, it will have failed. It has created more jobs for hairdressers, but not a higher income for each.

The general lesson is clear: one cannot raise income by raising price above the competitive level unless one can prevent new entry or otherwise reduce the quantity of the product or service provided.

Some other retail service providers, such as hairdressers (see Box 8.2), convenience stores, and plumbers, provide other examples of markets that approximate to monopolistic competition.

While there are not many industries that even approximately fit the assumptions of monopolistic competition, there are two ways in which the model is a useful part of the tool box of economics. First, it gives a simple illustration of the dynamics of competition by which entry of new firms tends to eliminate pure profit in the long run. (For example, although some restaurants are very profitable, the

average restaurant does not make large pure profits.) Secondly, the model shows how any market with differentiated products will tend to involve excess capacity and price unequal to marginal cost. (For example, almost all of the restaurants in any city could serve many more customers than they actually serve each day.) However, this apparent inefficiency needs to be set against the benefits of more diverse choices available with product differentiation. No one would prefer a situation in which there was only one type of restaurant with a single menu and price list, even if it was cheaper than existing restaurants!

Oligopoly

Oligopoly is imperfect competition among the few; it applies to an industry which contains only a few competing firms. Each firm has enough market power to prevent it being a price taker, but each firm is subject to enough

interfirm rivalry to prevent it considering the market demand curve as its own. In most modern economies this is the dominant market structure for the production of consumer and capital goods, as well as many basic

Box 8.3 Supermarket rivalry

A good example of an oligopolistic market is provided by UK supermarkets. In the first quarter of 2014, four big firms between them occupied nearly three-quarters of the market. The biggest was Tesco with 28.6 per cent market share. Then came Asda with 17.4 per cent and Sainsbury's with 16.5 per cent. The fourth is Morrisons with 11.1 per cent. The next 20 per cent of the market is shared between only five smaller supermarkets. In size order these are the Co-op, Waitrose, Aldi, Lidl, and Iceland. Of these, Aldi and Lidl had the fastest rising market share, largely at the expense of the big four. After accounting for the share of these nine named supermarkets, there is only around five per cent of the market left for all other supermarkets and the thousand of small corner shops that sell groceries.

The big four watch each other carefully, but they are also concerned about the rising market share of Aldi and Lidl.

In September 2013, Asda cut its petrol prices sharply, hoping that those who come for petrol will also do their weekly shop. The other three responded by dropping their own petrol prices within days.

In February 2014 Tesco initiated a price war with an initial £200 million of price cuts, but Sainsbury's matched their prices and then in May 2014 Morrisons announced price cuts on 1200 everyday items.

All this indicates that each of the big four supermarkets is watching the others very carefully, even to the extent of monitoring the prices of a very wide range of products in their rivals' stores. Not only do they react very quickly to attempts by one to undercut the others, they even give explicit guarantees to customers that they will match the others' prices. These are clear signs of oligopolistic markets, and the firms involved are very open about who their main competitors are and that they are watching each other. The most recent feature of this market has been the rising market share of Lidl and Aldi, based largely on their low prices, and this has reinforced the price-cutting strategies of the big four aimed at protecting market share from new entrants as well as from each other.

---

industrial materials such as steel and aluminium. Services, however, are often produced in industries containing a larger number of firms—although product differentiation prevents them from being perfectly competitive and the absence of symmetry prevents them from being monopolistically competitive.

In contrast with a monopoly, which has *no* competitors, and with a monopolistically competitive firm, which has *many* competitors, an oligopolistic firm faces *a few* competitors. A special case of oligopoly is a **duopoly** where there are just two firms competing. Because there are only a few firms in an oligopolistic industry, each firm realizes that its competitors may respond to any move it makes. The prudent firm will take such possible responses into account. In other words, oligopolists are aware that the decisions made by the various firms in the industry affect the other firms. An example of an oligopoly, the major UK supermarkets, is discussed in Box 8.3.

This is the key difference between oligopolists on the one hand and perfect competitors, monopolistic competitors, and monopolies on the other hand. The behaviour of oligopolists is **strategic**, which means that they must take explicit account of the impact of their decisions on competing firms and of the reactions they expect from competing firms. In contrast, firms in perfect and monopolistic competition engage in **non-strategic** behaviour, which means they make decisions based on their own costs and their own demand curves without considering any possible reactions from their large number of competitors. The behaviour of a monopolist is also non-strategic. It has no competitors with whom to interact.

Oligopolistic industries are of many types. In some industries there are only a few firms, but oligopoly is also consistent with a large number of small sellers, called a 'competitive fringe', as long as a 'big few' dominate the industry's production. For example, about 500 banks operate in the United Kingdom, but the big four[4]—Barclays, Lloyds, Royal Bank of Scotland (which owns NatWest), and HSBC—dominate its retail commercial banking industry. Similarly, there are four big oil firms that dominate the UK petrol retailing business—Shell, BP, Esso, and Texaco. Forty-five per cent of retail petrol sales in 2013 were through supermarkets (see Box 8.3), but they buy their supplies from the big oil producers. In oligopolistic industries prices are typically administered. Products are usually differentiated. Firms engage in rivalrous behaviour, although the intensity of the rivalry varies greatly across industries and over time. Some aspects of this rivalrous behaviour can be analysed using the tools of economics, but it is also the subject of strategy courses in business schools and the central topic running through thousands of business management books (a sample of which can be seen in any airport bookstore). Successful captains of industry, whose memoirs often sell millions of copies, are not those who are just good at deciding where marginal cost is equal to marginal revenue. Rather, they

---

[4] There were five big retail banks until Lloyds took over HBOS in 2008 when the latter was in financial difficulties.

are those who lead a large team of managers and workers in a complex competition to develop winning products and gain market share against teams of others who are trying to do the same.

… firms jostle for advantage by price and non-price competition, undercutting and outbidding rivals in the marketplace by advertising outlays and promotional expenses, launching new differentiated products, new technical processes, new methods of marketing and new organisational forms, and even new reward structures for their employees, all for the sake of headstart profits that they know will soon be eroded.

(M. Blaug, *Economic Theory in Retrospect*, Cambridge: Cambridge University Press, 1997, page 594)

Why bigness?

Several factors explain why a few large firms dominate so many industries. Some of these factors are 'natural', and some are created by the firms themselves.

Natural causes of bigness

Economies of scale

Much manufacturing production applies the principle of the division of labour that we first studied in Chapter 1. The production of a complex product is broken up into hundreds of simple repetitive tasks. This type of division of labour is the basis of the assembly line, which revolutionized the production of many goods in the early twentieth century, and it still underlies economies of large-scale production in many industries.[5] Division of labour is, as Adam Smith observed long ago, dependent on the size of the market. If only a few units of a product can be sold each day, there is no point in dividing its production into a number of specialized tasks. So big firms have an advantage over small firms whenever there is great potential for economies based on division of labour. The larger the scale of production, the lower their average variable costs of production.

Fixed costs

It is costly to design, test, and market a new product. In technologically dynamic industries it may be a matter of only a few years before each new version is replaced by some superior version of the same basic product. Yet the fixed costs of product development must be recovered in the revenues from sales of the product. The larger the firm's sales, the lower the cost that has to be recovered from each unit sold. Consider a product that costs £1 million to develop and market. If 1 million units can

be sold before the product is replaced by a superior version, £1 of the selling price of each unit must go towards recovering the development costs. However, if the firm expects to sell 10 million units, each unit need contribute only 10 pence to these costs and the market price can be lowered accordingly. With the enormous development costs of some of today's high-tech products, firms that can sell a large volume have a distinct pricing advantage over firms that sell a smaller volume. Firms with large product development costs face downward-sloping average total cost curves even if their average variable costs are constant.

Economies of scope

Economies of scope apply to a multi-product firm because some resources of the firms can be shared between different product areas (see Box 5.5). **Economies of scope exist if production of several different products within one firm leads to the unit costs of production of each product being lower than if they had been produced in independent firms.** Such economies may arise because some functions are shared, such as marketing and distribution, or because of some common skills in the firm that can be applied to more than one product.

Where size confers a cost advantage, through economies of either scale or scope, there may be room for only a few firms, even when the total market is quite large. This cost advantage of size will dictate that the industry be an oligopoly, unless government regulation prevents the firms from growing to their efficient size.

Firm-created causes of bigness

The number of firms in an industry may be decreased while the average size of the survivors rises owing to the *strategic* behaviour of the firms themselves. Firms may grow by buying out rivals (acquisitions), or merging with them (mergers), or driving them into bankruptcy, sometimes through predatory practices. This process increases the size and market shares of the survivors and may, by reducing competitive behaviour, allow them to earn larger profit margins. But these high profits will attract new entrants unless the surviving firms can create and sustain barriers to entry. Although most firms would like to behave in this manner, it is no easy task to create effective entry barriers when natural ones do not exist. We return to entry barriers later in the chapter.

Is bigness natural or firm created?

The answer to this question is probably 'some of both'. Some industries have production in the hands of few firms because the efficient size of the firm is large relative to the overall size of the industry's market. Other industries may have more concentrated production than

---

[5] This is sometimes referred to as *Fordism*, after Henry Ford who introduced the modern assembly line method of production.

efficiency considerations would dictate because the firms are seeking enhanced market power through large size combined with entry barriers. What is debatable is the relative importance of these two forces—the one coming from the efficiencies of large scale and scope, and the other coming from the desire of firms to create market power by growing large.

Harvard economist Alfred D. Chandler Jr is a champion of the view that the major reason for the persistence of oligopolies in the manufacturing sector is the efficiency of large-scale production. His monumental work *Scale and Scope*[6] argues this case in great detail for the United States, the United Kingdom, and Germany.

The basic dilemma of oligopoly

Oligopolistic behaviour is typically *strategic* behaviour. In deciding on strategies, oligopolists face a basic dilemma between competing and cooperating.

The firms in an oligopolistic industry will make more profits as a group if they cooperate; however, any one firm may make more profits for itself if it goes it alone while the others cooperate.

This behaviour is similar to that established in Chapter 7 for the cartelization of a perfectly competitive industry.[7] However, in a perfectly competitive industry there are so many firms that it is difficult for them to reach the cooperative solution unless some central governing body is able to force the necessary behaviour on all firms. In contrast, the few firms in an oligopolistic industry will themselves recognize the possibility of cooperating to avoid the loss of profits that will result from competitive behaviour.

The cooperative solution

If the firms in an oligopolistic industry cooperate, either overtly or tacitly, to produce among themselves the monopoly output, they can maximize their joint profits. If they do this, they will reach what is called a **cooperative solution**, which is the position that a single monopoly firm would reach if it owned all the firms in the industry. Of course, explicit cooperation by firms may be forbidden by competition laws. However, even within the range of what is legal, firms can choose whether to compete aggressively or to be more passive. The more passive approach can be equivalent to tacit cooperation.

The non-cooperative equilibrium

The analysis of a cartel in Chapter 7 shows that if all the firms in an oligopolistic industry adopt the cooperative pricing and output level, it would be profitable for any one of them to cut its price or raise its output, as long as the others do not do so. However, if all do the same thing, they will be worse off as a group and may all be worse off individually. An equilibrium that is reached by firms when they proceed by calculating only their own gains, without cooperating with others, is called a **non-cooperative equilibrium** or a **Nash equilibrium**. This type of equilibrium is named after the US mathematician John Nash, who developed the concept in the 1950s and received the 1994 Nobel Prize in economics for this work.[8] It is an equilibrium in which each firm's best strategy is to maintain its present behaviour, *given the present behaviour of the other firms*.

Nash equilibrium is a concept widely used in *game theory*, which is an approach to formal modelling of strategic interaction. We outline the game theory approach next.

Oligopoly as a game

Game theory may sound trivial or humorous; after all we play 'games' for fun. However, **game theory** is a major tool in many disciplines because it is an approach to analysing rational decision-making behaviour in any interactive or conflict situation. The 'game' element arises because the outcome depends not only on the choices made by one player, but also on what other players choose to do at the same time (or subsequently). For this reason, game theory has become a branch of economic analysis that provides many insights into the real-world behaviour of economic agents in situations where there is an actual or potential conflict of interest, such as in competition among oligopolists.

In a game, agents aim to maximize their own pay-off by choosing specific actions, but the actual outcome also depends on what all other players do. The game consists of a specified interactive playing field (which in the case of firms would be the market for their product), a specification of all available courses of action, and a

---

[6] A.D. Chandler Jr, *Scale and Scope: The Dynamics of Industrial Capitalism*, Cambridge, MA: Harvard University Press, 1990.

[7] The basic reason is that when only one firm increases its output by 1 per cent, the price falls by less than when all firms do the same. Thus, when the point is reached at which profits will be *reduced* if all firms expand output together, it will still pay one firm to expand output *if* the others do not do the same.

---

[8] Nash was commemorated by Hollywood in the 2002 film of his life, *A Beautiful Mind*, starring Russell Crowe.

schedule of the pay-offs to each of the players under all possible outcomes. Players plan their own courses of action in order to maximize their expected pay-off, knowing that the other players are trying to do the same. A player's *strategy* is a complete specification of the actions to be taken in response to outcomes that are discovered as the game proceeds (though a strategy may include some random elements). One player's pay-off from choosing a strategy depends on what the other players do, but players cannot make binding agreements with each other.

Given all the players' strategies, there will be a set of possible outcomes to the game. These determine the potential pay-offs for each of the players. A specific outcome is called equilibrium if no player can take actions to improve their own pay-off while all other players continue to follow their optimal strategies.

There is a circularity to the problem that has to be solved, as, in order to select his or her best strategy, a player must know what other players will do, but they in turn are in the same position. In **normal** (or **strategic**) **form games** players choose their moves simultaneously. Whenever the choices available are discrete and finite the game can be represented in the structure of a table setting out the possible outcomes for each of the players depending on what the other players do. In an **extensive form game** players make moves in some order over time, so the analysis of the game needs a specification of the pay-offs and information at each point in time. Real business interactions are obviously more closely analogous to an extensive form game, as firms interact dynamically over time. However, whenever the precise timing of moves is not essential to the outcome, a 'game' can often be represented more simply as a normal form game.

A game that is played only once is a 'one-shot' game. Repeated games open possibilities of learning and of acting in order to punish or reward the other players. A **supergame** is a game that is repeated an infinite number of times.

Example 1

Let us think of a simple example in order to give an intuitive feel for the issues involved. Suppose that you are in your first year at university and you are planning for your summer vacation. In all the previous years of your life you have gone on a summer vacation with your parents. This year you would like to go away with your own friends rather than with your parents. However, you think that your parents will be offended if you say that you do not want to go on holiday with them—after all, they are helping to finance your education. So what do you say when your parents phone up and say that they

are booking the summer vacation and are assuming that you will come?

What happens and the pay-offs (i.e. level of happiness of all involved) depend upon what your parents' true preferences are. In one possible case, they would prefer to go on holiday without you, as they have had to have holidays that suit their children for the last 20 years or so. However, they think they should give you the option of going with them even though they hope you will say no, but they do not want to offend you.

Clearly, the best solution for everybody, which would be called the cooperative solution, is that everybody reveals their true preferences and you can agree to have separate holidays so that all end up happy. However, a likely outcome in a one-shot game is that each of you tries to avoid the really bad outcome (as you perceive it) of offending the other, so your parents ask you to join them and you agree to go. This is not as bad as everybody feeling offended, but it is inferior for everybody to the best outcome of everybody having the holiday they want. Thus, each choosing a strategy of avoiding the worst possible outcome leads to a solution, but one that is not the best that could be achieved for all concerned.

Of course, if this game were repeated for several years in a row then the preferences of each side might be revealed more clearly and the optimal solution of separate holidays might be arrived at.

The other possibility is that your parents really would prefer you to come on holiday with them while you really would prefer not to. In this situation there is no way in which you can both achieve your preferred solution. If you say no to them, they really will be upset, but if you say yes, you will not have as good a holiday as you could with your friends. Your decision will depend on how you weigh up the psychic cost of offending your parents against the loss of having a good time elsewhere.

This is obviously a rather special case and, happily, in a family situation there are other ways of communicating and solving problems where objectives conflict. However, hopefully this can give a feel for what is going on in a game structure. Individuals have a range of possible choices, but the outcomes are affected by what other players do at the same time. In business games we normally consider the potential pay-offs in terms of profit, but strategy can just as easily be based on other types of preference—such as avoiding offending your parents.

Solutions to games

The first thing to look for in a game is whether each player has a **dominant strategy**. This is a strategy that is the best response, independently of what the other players do. If each player has a dominant strategy, that player will adopt it, and the outcome of the game will be the pay-off associated with all players following their dominant strategy. *Dominated strategies* are all those other than the dominant strategy and will not be played whenever there is a dominant strategy. However, it is possible to have a game with only dominated strategies and hence no dominant strategy.

An equilibrium in which all players follow a dominant strategy is one example of what is called a **Nash equilibrium**. This is an equilibrium in which each player is doing as well as he or she can given what the other players are doing. In this situation, no player would want to change his or her strategy as it is believed that all other players would not change theirs.

We now discuss a hypothetical example to illustrate the above concepts. Box 8.4 outlines some classic interactive decision dilemmas that can be analysed in the game theory framework.

Example 2

Firms that are competing head-to-head with a small number of other firms have to decide how aggressive to be. Suppose, for example, that there are just two firms producing a similar product and that each firm has two possible strategies. One is to act aggressively by increasing output and trying to increase market share. The other is to act passively and keep producing at the current level of output which involves each firm having roughly half the market and jointly sharing the monopoly profit. The possible outcomes illustrate the relevance of game theory to oligopoly.

When game theory is applied to oligopoly, the players are firms, their game is played in the market, their strategies are their price/output decisions, and the pay-offs are their profits.

The basic dilemma of oligopolists is shown in Figure 8.2 for the case of a two-firm oligopoly. The simplified game, adopted for the purposes of illustration, allows only two strategies for *each firm*. Each firm can produce an output equal to either one-half of the monopoly output (the passive strategy) or two-thirds of the monopoly output (the aggressive strategy). Note that the passive strategy amounts to tacit cooperation while the aggressive strategy is clearly non-cooperative. This simple game is sufficient to illustrate several key propositions in the modern theory of oligopoly.

Figure 8.2 presents the *pay-off matrix*. The data in the matrix show the profits that result from the four possible combinations of strategies.

1. The passive (cooperative) solution

If both sides tacitly cooperate, *each producing* one-half of the monopoly output, they share the monopoly profits by

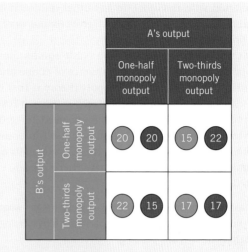

Figure 8.2 The oligopolist's dilemma: to cooperate or to compete

Cooperation to determine the overall level of output can maximize joint profits, but it leaves each firm with an incentive to alter its production. The figure gives what is called a pay-off matrix for a two-firm duopoly game. Only two levels of production are considered in order to illustrate the basic problem. A's production is indicated across the top, and its profits (measured in millions of pounds) are shown in the blue circles within each square. B's production is indicated down the left side, and its profits (in millions of pounds) are shown in the green circles within each square. For example, the top right-hand square tells us that if B produces one-half, while A produces two-thirds, of the output that a monopolist would produce, A's profits will be £22 million, while B's will be £15 million. If A and B cooperate, each produces one-half the monopoly output and earns profits of £20 million, as shown in the upper left box. In this 'cooperative solution' either firm can raise its profits by producing two-thirds of the monopoly output, provided that the other firm does not do the same. So this is not a Nash equilibrium because, given the opponents' current behaviour, each firm will want to alter its behaviour by producing a larger output. Now let A and B behave non-cooperatively. A reasons that whether B produces either one-half or two-thirds of the monopoly output, A's best output is two-thirds. B reasons similarly. They then reach the non-cooperative Nash equilibrium, where each produces two-thirds of the monopoly output, and each makes less profit than it would if the two firms cooperated.

jointly producing the output that a monopolist would produce. As a group, they cannot do better.

2. The aggressive (non-cooperative or Nash) solution

There is one Nash equilibrium in Figure 8.2. In the bottom right-hand cell, the best decision for each firm, given that the other firm is producing two-thirds of the monopoly output, is to produce two-thirds of the monopoly output itself. Between them they produce a joint output of one-and-a-third times the monopoly output. Neither firm has an incentive to depart from this position, except through cooperation with the other. In any other cell, each firm has an incentive to alter its output, *given the output of the other firm*.

This shows that the basis of a Nash equilibrium is rational decision-making in the absence of cooperation. Its particular importance in oligopoly theory is that it is the only type of equilibrium that is *self-policing*. It is self-policing in the sense that there is no need for group behaviour to enforce it. Each firm has a self-interest to maintain it because no move that it can make on its own will improve its profits, given what other firms are currently doing.

If a Nash equilibrium is established—by any means whatsoever—no firm has an incentive to depart from it by altering its own behaviour. It is self-policing.

3. Strategic behaviour

The Nash equilibrium will be attained if each firm behaves strategically by choosing its optimal strategy taking into account what the other firm may do. Let us see how this works.

Suppose that firm A reasons as follows: 'B can do one of two things. What is the best thing for me to do in each case? First, what if B produces one-half of the monopoly output? If I do the same, I receive a profit of 20, but if I produce two-thirds of the monopoly output, I receive 22. Secondly, what if B produces two-thirds of the monopoly output? If I produce one-half of the monopoly output, I receive a profit of 15, whereas if I produce two-thirds, I receive 17. Clearly, my best strategy is to produce two-thirds of the monopoly output in either case.' Aggressive behaviour is the dominant strategy.

B will reason in the same way. As a result, they end up by jointly producing one-and-a-third times the monopoly output, where each earns a profit of 17.

This type of game, where the non-cooperative equilibrium makes both players worse off than if they were able to cooperate, is like the **prisoner's dilemma** shown in Box 8.4. The important insight following from prisoner's dilemma games is that individual maximization does not always lead to the best result for the players taken as a group. In the Nash equilibrium of the prisoner's dilemma game, both players can be made better off if they cooperate and so move to the top left-hand box. But if both make individual maximizing decisions, they end up in the bottom right-hand box.

Box 8.4 Games and their applications

The 'prisoner's dilemma' game

This is the story that lies behind the name:

Two men, John and Bill, are arrested for jointly committing a crime and are interrogated separately. They know that if they both plead innocent they will get only a light sentence. However, each is told that if either protests innocence while the other admits guilt, the one who claims innocence will get a severe sentence while the other will be let off. If they both plead guilty, they will both get a medium sentence.

The table shows the pay-off matrix for that game.

		John's plea	
		Innocent	Guilty
Bill's plea	Innocent	*J* light sentence / *W* light sentence	*J* no sentence / *W* severe sentence
	Guilty	*J* severe sentence / *W* no sentence	*J* medium sentence / *W* medium sentence

John reasons as follows: 'If Bill pleads innocent, I get a light sentence if I also plead innocent, but no sentence at all if I plead guilty, so guilty is my better plea. Secondly, if Bill pleads guilty, I get a severe sentence if I plead innocent and a medium sentence if I plead guilty. So once again guilty is my preferred plea'. Bill reasons in the same way, and, as a result, they both plead guilty and get a medium sentence, whereas if they had been able to communicate, they could both have agreed to plead innocent and get off with a light sentence.

The prisoner's dilemma has many business applications as it is the classic case in which cooperation would maximize joint income, but the strategic interaction of firms is more likely to lead to the non-cooperative outcome, as in a Nash equilibrium.

Battle of the sexes

		Jane	
		Soccer	Theatre
John	Soccer	100, 200	0, 0
	Theatre	0, 0	200, 100

Imagine a situation where a husband and wife have a choice between going to the theatre and going to a soccer game. John really wants to go to soccer and Jane really

(continued)

Box 8.4 *continued*

wants to go to the theatre. Jane's pay-off is the first number in each box and John's is the second. Each would get some satisfaction from going along with the other's preferred choice but neither would be at all happy to go alone to either of the potential activities. There are two Nash equilibria in the game as set out here as both have an incentive to move from the off-diagonal outcomes. However, in a one-shot game it is not clear which of the two possible equilibria will emerge. In a repeated game the outcome may depend on who moves first and on whether they can agree to alternate outcome—theatre this time, soccer next time.

The structure of this game illustrates some business situations in which it pays to cooperate rather than compete. The choice between VHS and Betamax as a video standard shows that it does not pay to go it alone. Betamax was technically the better standard, but once VHS got to be on top in usage it paid all producers to adopt it. The same applies to cell phones, computer operating systems, and many integrated trading systems.

Zero sum game

As the name suggests a zero sum game is one in which whatever is won by one player is lost by the other. This is not the normal outcome of economic games, as in most economic interactions both parties can become better off and so there is some positive net gain to be shared out. However, the zero sum game is a frequently used reference point in economics for any interactive situation in which there is a distributional impact but no net increase in income or wealth for the participants.

A sweepstake is a zero sum game, as each player gets one horse in the race or one team in the competition and the winner takes all the stakes put in by others. Poker played among friends is a zero sum game if we only take account of the money won and lost. But if everyone enjoys playing the game irrespective of what they personally win or lose, it is a positive utility sum game. Many takeover bids are close to a zero sum game, where most of what is determined is the distribution of gains and losses between shareholders of the bidding and bid-for firms.

---

4. Breakdown of cooperation

The Nash equilibrium is attained by the strategic reasoning just outlined. However, it can be used to give an intuitive argument for why tacit cooperation tends to break down.

Assume that the cooperative position has been attained. Each firm is producing one-half of the monopoly output and each is earning a profit of 20. The data in Figure 8.2 show that if A cheats by increasing its output, its profits will increase. However, B's profits will be reduced. A's behaviour drives the industry's prices down, so B earns less from its unchanged output. Because A's cheating takes the firms away from the joint profit-maximizing monopoly output, their joint profits must fall. This means that B's profits fall by more than A's rise.

Figure 8.2 shows that similar considerations also apply to B. It is worthwhile for B to depart from the joint maximizing output, as long as A does not do so. So both A and B have an incentive to depart from the joint profit-maximizing level of output.

Finally, Figure 8.2 shows that, when either firm departs from the joint-maximizing output, the other has an incentive to do so as well. When each follows this 'selfish' strategy, they reach a non-cooperative equilibrium at which they jointly produce one-and-a-third times as much as the monopolist would. Each then has profits that are lower than with the cooperative solution.[9]

Game theory more generally

An important general result concerning games is called the **Nash Theorem**. It shows that every game with a finite number of players and a finite number of strategies will have at least one Nash equilibrium. For this to hold, however, the player's strategies must contain some random and hence unpredictable element.[10] A strategy with some random elements is referred to as a *mixed strategy*. Another problem is that there may be multiple Nash equilibria and it is not always obvious which one will arise. Finally, it is generally true that the Nash equilibrium is not the global optimum in the sense that if players could cooperate, they could all become better off.

A game theory framework can often help us understand the strategic choices available but it does not always help predict which of many possible outcomes may occur.

Nonetheless, game theory is an extremely flexible tool that has been applied to many branches of economics. Box 8.5 outlines some real-world situations that illustrate the strategic choices that firms have to make in practice.

---

[9] This is why we do not speak of the cooperative *equilibrium*. It is a solution to the problem of finding the best cooperative behaviour, but it is not an equilibrium since, once achieved, each firm has an incentive to depart from it.

[10] A random element in a game would arise if, for example, players had to roll dice or draw cards to determine some, but not all, of their actions. In the business context the equivalent is some unpredictable external events that affect the behaviour of firms in some situations.

Box 8.5 Real-world strategic games

There are many situations in which firms have to make strategic decisions about reactions to their main rival suppliers. Here are some examples.

Supermarket price wars

Major supermarket chains are in competition with each other for growth and market share in a relatively static business area—demand for food grows only slowly. They can grow by opening stores in new areas, by trying to attract customers from other stores by advertising, or by lowering prices.

Managers of supermarkets would like to run their businesses with comfortable profit margins, and in normal times there is a standard mark-up on most products that gives an adequate return on the company's capital employed. From time to time one of the major players decides that it will make a push for more customers and significantly cuts its prices on a wide range of standard products. Frequently, the rival players will cut their prices too in order to stem the loss of customers.

This may look like pure price competition. However, supermarkets are multi-product firms, and the aim of price wars is not to lose money but rather to get more customers into the store so that they will buy a range of other products on which the prices have not been cut. Of course, if other stores also cut their prices, then the price war could reduce the combined profits of all supermarkets. But it is also possible that the big players will end up better off as a result of attracting more customers from smaller grocery shops.

Here are some news media headlines relating to this issue.

Tesco and Asda fire first shots in food price war: Cheaper groceries despite soaring costs (June 2008)

Tesco to step up supermarket price war (March 2013)

Tesco to launch a supermarket price war... and this time it's real (September 2011)

Supermarket price war: Can they all be cheapest? (December 2011)

Petrol price war: Joy for motorists as supermarkets slash fuel by 6p a litre (September 2013)

Morrisons cuts price of 1,200 products in bid to win customers back (May 2014)

Airline pricing

Similar examples of aggressive price cutting can be found in the airline industry as the following headlines indicate.

Airlines launch price war cutting fares by up to 25 per cent (December 2008)

Airline price wars are back, just when carriers cannot afford them (July 2009)

Budget airline carriers set for price war as competition increases (February 2012)

Budget airline wages price war on BA and Virgin by launching £150 flights to New York from Gatwick (October 2013)

Lean season sees air fares drop, airlines brace for price war (August 2013)

It's raining airfare discounts, airlines cut prices by up to 50% (January 2014)

Behind these headlines there are some differences between supermarket price wars and those between airlines. The grocery market within a specific country is dominated by a few players and they compete head to head for market share. Their price wars are periodic but often focused on a subset of the goods they sell, such as the petrol example above. The price cuts are designed to attract customers who will buy other products while they are in the store, and if they like what they see they may come back. Airline price wars, on the other hand, are often triggered by an airline that is trying to set up from scratch or to break into a new route. They need to attract enough passengers to fly their planes at close to capacity and cover the costs of supporting the route (check-in and maintenance staff). The price wars are normally focused on popular routes where there are large numbers of potential passengers. So these price wars between airlines tend to happen on a few routes in specific parts of the world but rarely, if ever, break out into general price wars.

Dynamics of oligopolistic industries

Suppose that firms in an oligopolistic industry succeed in raising prices above long-run average total costs and earn substantial profits that are not completely eliminated by non-price competition. In the absence of significant barriers to entry, new firms will enter the industry and erode the profits of existing firms, as they do in monopolistic competition. Natural barriers to entry are an important part of the explanation of the persistence of profits in many oligopolistic industries. Among these, scale economies are probably the most important. Where such natural barriers do not exist, oligopolistic firms can earn profits in the long run only if they can create entry barriers.

Entry barriers

We have already discussed the importance of both natural and created entry barriers, and here we extend this discussion with some cases of created entry barriers that are most relevant to oligopoly.

Brand proliferation

By altering the characteristics of a differentiated product, it is possible to produce a vast array of variations on the general theme of that product. Think, for example, of cars with a little more or a little less acceleration, braking power, top speed, cornering ability, petrol mileage, and so on, compared with existing models.

Although the multiplicity of existing brands is no doubt partly a response to consumers' tastes, it also discourages the entry of new firms. For an illustrative example, consider an industry that contains three large firms, each selling one brand of cigarettes, and say that 30 per cent of all smokers change brands in a random fashion each year. If a new firm enters the industry, it can expect to pick up one-third of the smokers who change brands.[11] This would give the new firm 10 per cent (one third of 30 per cent) of the total market in the first year merely as a result of picking up its share of the random switchers, and it would keep increasing its share for some time thereafter. However, if the existing three firms have five brands each, there would be fifteen brands already available. A new firm selling one new brand could then expect to pick up only one-fifteenth of the brand switchers, giving it 2 per cent of the total market the first year, with smaller gains also in subsequent years. This is an extreme case, but it illustrates a general result:

The larger the number of differentiated products sold by existing oligopolists, the smaller the market share available to a new firm entering with a single new product.

An example of brand proliferation drawn from the alcoholic drinks industry is given in Box 8.6.

---

[11] Since there are now four brands to choose from, you might think that the new brand would pick up one-quarter of the switchers. But this is not correct because, by definition, the switcher rejects his old brand and chooses one of the others. Each switcher's choice-set therefore consists of three brands—two of the pre-existing brands and the one new brand.

Box 8.6 Brand proliferation in alcoholic drinks

Readers who drink wine or spirits will all have their favourite brand, but what you might not know is that many of the major drinks brands are owned by three big corporations: Diageo of the United Kingdom, Pernot Ricard of France, and Beam of the United States.[12]

Diageo, for example, sells a wide range of alcoholic products. For mixers they have Archers, Pimm's, and TGI Friday's. As liqueurs they sell Baileys, Sheridans, Yukon Jack, and Godiva's. Their spirit lines include Bell's, Johnnie Walker, Vat 69, and J&B scotch whisky; Bushmills Irish whiskey; Cacique, Captain Morgan, Bundaberg, Pampero, and Myers' rum; Crown Royal and Seagram's Canadian whisky; Don Julio and José Cuervo tequila; Booth's, Gordon's, and Tanqueray gin; Hennessy cognac; Smirnoff, Ciroc, Silent Sam, Popov, and Ketel One vodkas; George Dickel Tennessee whiskey; Black Haus, Goldschläger, and Rumple Minze Schnapps; and Bulleit Bourbon.

For drinkers of single malts they have Caol Ila, Cardhu, Clynelish, Cragganmore, Dalwhinnie, Glen Elgin, Glen Ord, Glenkinchie, Knockando, Lagavulin, Oban, Royal Lochnagar, and Talisker. But if you prefer beer they have Guinness, Harp lager, Kilkenny Irish beer, Smithwick's, Tusker, Windhoek lager, and Red Stripe lager. Wine drinkers are not forgotten, as Diageo owns Sterling Vineyards, Piat d'Or, Barton & Guestier, Beaulieu Vineyard, Blossom Hill, Canoe Ridge Vineyard, Acacia, Chalone, Provenance, and Rosenblum, and has distribution rights for Dom Perignon and Moët & Chandon champagne.

Its main rival in the industry, Pernod Ricard, has an almost equally impressive list of drinks brands. For example it owns Ballantine's, Chivas, Royal Salute, Clan Campbell, Something Special, Passport100, Pipers, Imperial, and Long John blended scotch whiskies; Aberlour, The Glenlivet, Glendronach, Strathisla, Longmorn, Scapa, and Tormore single malts; Jameson, Paddy, and Powers Irish whiskies; Walker Special Old, and Wisers Canadian whiskies; Wild Turkey American Bourbon; Martell, Bisquit, and Renault Cognacs; and Don Pedro, Presidente, AraratAnejo, Los Reyes, Azteca, De Oro, and Brandy Domecq brandies. Among its wine-based aperitifs and fortified wines are Ambassadeur, Bartissol, Dubonnet, Sandeman, Byrrh, and La Ina. It also owns Australian winemakers Jacob's Creek and Wyndham Estate, and New Zealand wine labels Montana, Stoneleigh, Lindauer, and Church Road. On top of this it owns Mumm and Perrier-Jouët champagnes and 20 other

---

[12] These companies between them bought up the brands previously owned by the UK company Allied Domecq and Seagrams of Canada.

(continued)

Box 8.6 *continued*

wine brands from around the world. Liqueurs in its stable include Kahlúa, Malibu, Tia Maria, Hiram Walker, Soho, Dita, Zoco, Ruavieja, and Cusenier. For vodkas it has Absolut, Level, Luksusowa, Wyborowa, Lodowa, Huzzar, and Altai. If it is gin you drink then they have Beefeater, Seagram's Gin, and Cork Dry Gin, and for rums they have Havana Club and Montilla. Of course we should not leave out the anis-based spirit brands of Ricard, Pernod, and Pastis 51 that were the original products of the company.

Beam also has an impressive portfolio of well-known brands that include Harvey's sherry, Cockburn port, Courvoisier brandy, DeKuyper liqueurs, Gilbey's gin, Jim Beam bourbon, Canada Club, Kilbeggan, and Teacher's whiskies, Laphroaig, and Ardmore single malts, Pinnacle vodka, and Sauza Techila.

The production of such a wide range of differentiated products helps to satisfy consumers' clear demand for diversity. Having this range within a single firm also has the effect of making it more difficult for a new firm to enter the industry. If the new firm wishes to compete over the whole range of differentiated products, it must enter on a massive scale. If it wishes to enter on only a small scale it faces a formidable task of establishing brand images and customer recognition with only a few products over which to spread the expenses of entry. There may also be significant economies of scope for the big drinks companies as they can share some central management skills and distribution channels for most of their products.

Advertising

Existing firms can create entry barriers by imposing significant fixed costs on new firms that enter their market. This is particularly important if the industry has only weak natural barriers to entry because the minimum efficient scale occurs at an output that is low relative to the total output of the industry.

Advertising serves the useful function of informing buyers about their alternatives, thereby making markets work more smoothly. Indeed, advertising is essential to make consumers aware of new products whether produced by existing firms or new entrants.

Nonetheless, advertising can also operate as a potent entry barrier by increasing the set-up costs of new entrants. Where heavy advertising has established strong brand images for existing products, a new firm may have to spend heavily on advertising to create its own brand images in consumers' minds. If the firm's initial sales are small, advertising costs *per unit sold* will be large, and price will have to be correspondingly high to cover those costs.

The combined use of brand proliferation and advertising as an entry barrier helps to explain one apparent paradox of business life—one firm often sells multiple brands of the same product, which compete actively against each other as well as against the products of other firms.

The soap and cigarette industries provide classic examples of this behaviour. Because quite small plants can realize all available scale economies, both industries have few natural barriers to entry. Both contain a few large firms, each of which produces an array of heavily advertised products. The numerous existing products make it harder for a new entrant to obtain a large market niche with a single new product. The heavy advertising, although it is directed against existing products, creates an entry barrier by increasing the set-up costs of a new product that seeks to gain the attention of consumers and to establish its own brand image[13].

Product innovation and new technologies

New products, some of which may be protected by patents for up to twenty years, give the inventing firms (or the firms that hold the licence to produce) a period in which they can profit. The pharmaceuticals and electronics industries provide copious examples. With them the competitive process is a race to invent the next blockbuster drug or the next communication device or the next standard software package. An example from the drugs industry is provided by Tamiflu, discussed at the end of Chapter 5. Drugs giants like Roche, Pfizer, and GlaxoSmithKline have a portfolio of products that are most profitable while under patent protection, and they are always working on finding new ones as they know that there is only a limited period during which their existing products will yield high revenues. The main competition in this world is not about cooperative or aggressive strategies relating to pricing and production of the same product. Rather, it is about seeking out new products (either by R&D or by seeking to license products invented by others) that replace the drugs of other companies or provide cures for diseases that other companies do not have a cure for.

The electronics industry is similar to the drugs industry. IBM lost out in the computer mainframe industry (which declined) as Apple invented the PC, but then IBM fought back with a new PC of its own. In turn, IBM lost out again as it was unable to stop cheaper clones of the PC sweeping the market and the key operating system was owned by

---

[13] Note that in recent decades many countries have put severe restrictions on tobacco advertising, so it is no longer true that tobacco companies can use advertising in this way. However, it also means that new entrants cannot advertise either, so the existing players remain in an entrenched position.

Microsoft (which had the protection of a patent). Apple survived as a computer supplier as result of niche devotees to its Mackintosh computer and operating system, but it hit the big time again in 2004–5 with the take-off of its iPod player of downloadable music. Many competitors emerged in the MP3 music player market, but Apple had a patent on one of the key features of its iPod, so exact imitation was not possible, at least for some time. Apple then had further innovation with its iPhone, which gave it a lead in the mobile phone market, and the iPad, which created and then took a major part of the tablet computer market.

This process is one of competition to find new technologies or new products that are sufficiently different from existing ones that they can achieve patent protection, or a window of advantage until rivals catch up. This then gives a period of time during which profit can be made on the new product and effort (and money) can be invested in looking for the next new product. It is found in many industries as diverse as those producing mobile phones, cameras, aircraft, and teaching devices.

Contestable markets and potential entry

The theory of contestable markets shows that pure profits may be eliminated even though the industry contains only a few firms and experiences no actual entry. *Potential* entry can do the job just as well as actual entry, as long as two conditions are fulfilled. First, entry must be easy to accomplish (e.g. there must be no major natural barrier to entry such as scale economies), and, secondly, existing firms must take potential entry into account when making price and output decisions.

Entry is usually costly to the entering firm. It may have to build a plant, it may have to develop new versions of the industry's differentiated product, and it may have to advertise heavily in order to call attention to its product. These and many other initial expenses are often called **sunk costs of entry**, which are defined as costs that a firm must incur to enter the market and that cannot be recovered if the firm subsequently exits.

A market in which there are no major scale economies and new firms can enter and leave without incurring any sunk costs of entry is called a perfectly **contestable market**. A market can be perfectly contestable even if the firm must pay some costs of entry, as long as these can be recovered when the firm exits. Because all markets require at least some sunk costs of entry, contestability must be understood as a variable. The lower the sunk costs of entry, the more contestable the market.

In a contestable market the existence of profits, even if they are due to transitory causes, will attract entry. Firms will enter to gain a share of these profits and will exit when the transitory situation has changed.

Consider, for example, the market for air travel on the lucrative London–Paris route. This market would become quite contestable *if* counter and loading space were easily available to new entrants at the two cities' airports. An airline that was not currently serving the cities in question could shift some of its existing planes to the market with small sunk costs of entry. Some training of personnel would be needed for them to become familiar with the route and the airport. This is a sunk cost of entry that cannot be recovered if the cities in question are no longer to be served. However, most of the airline's costs of entering the London–Paris market are not sunk costs. If it subsequently decides to leave a city, the rental of terminal space will stop, and the aeroplanes and the ground equipment can be shifted to another location. The former head of the American Civil Aeronautics Board, and architect of airline deregulation, captured this point by referring to commercial aircraft as 'marginal cost with wings'.

Sunk costs of entry constitute an entry barrier. The larger they are, the larger the profits of existing firms can be without attracting new entrants. The flip side of this coin is that firms operating in markets without large sunk costs of entry and no significant scale economies will not earn large profits. Strategic considerations will lead them to keep prices near the level that would just cover their total costs. They know that if they charge higher prices, firms will enter to capture the profits while they last and then exit.

Contestability, where it is possible, is a force that can limit the profits of existing oligopolists. Even if entry does not occur, the ease with which it could be accomplished may keep existing oligopolists from charging prices that would maximize their joint profits.

Contestability is just another example, in somewhat more refined form, of the key point that the possibility of entry is the major force preventing the exploitation of market power. Notice that the entrants do not have to be new firms. They can be domestic firms entering new domestic markets or foreign firms entering the domestic market.

Oligopoly and the functioning of the economy

Oligopoly is found in many industries and in all advanced economies. It typically occurs in industries where both perfect and monopolistic competition are made impossible by the existence of major economies of scale or scope (or both). In such industries, there is simply not enough room for a large number of firms, all operating at or near their minimum efficient scales.

Three questions are important for the evaluation of the performance of the oligopolistic market structure. First, do oligopolistic markets allocate resources very differently from perfectly competitive markets? Secondly, in their short-run and long-run price–output behaviour, where do oligopolistic firms typically settle between the extreme outcomes of earning zero profits and earning the profits that would be available to a single monopolist? Thirdly, how much do oligopolists contribute to economic growth by encouraging innovative activity? We consider each of these questions in turn.

The market mechanism under oligopoly

We have seen that under perfect competition prices are set by the impersonal forces of demand and supply, and changes in the market conditions for both inputs and outputs are signalled by changes in the prices of a firm's inputs and outputs. The market signalling system works slightly differently when prices are administered by oligopolists. Changes in prices still signal changes in market conditions for inputs. However, changes in the market conditions for outputs are typically signalled by changes in the volume of their sales at the administered prices.

Increases in costs of inputs will shift cost curves upward, and oligopolistic firms will be led to raise prices and lower outputs. Increases in demand will cause the sales of oligopolistic firms to rise. Firms will then respond by increasing output, thereby increasing the quantities of society's resources that are allocated to producing that output. They will then decide whether or not to alter their administered prices.

The market system reallocates resources in response to changes in demands and costs in roughly the same way under oligopoly as it does under perfect competition.

Profits under oligopoly

Some firms in some oligopolistic industries succeed in coming close to joint profit maximization in the short run. In other oligopolistic industries firms compete so intensely among themselves that they come close to achieving competitive prices and outputs.

In the long run, those profits that do survive competitive behaviour among existing firms will tend to attract entry. These profits will persist only in so far as entry is restricted either by natural barriers, such as large minimum efficient scales for potential entrants, or by barriers created, and successfully defended, by the existing firms.

Very long run competition

Once we allow for the effects of technological change, we need to ask which market structure is most conducive to the sort of very long run changes that we discussed in Chapter 5. These changes are the driving force of the economic growth that has so greatly raised living standards over the last two centuries. They are intimately related to Schumpeter's concept of creative destruction, which we

first encountered in our discussion of entry barriers in Chapter 7. Notice that very long run does not necessarily mean a very long time, just enough time to change technology, which in some industries is a matter of a few months.

Examples of creative destruction could fill many pages. Here are just a few. In the nineteenth century, railways began to compete with horse-drawn wagons and barges for the carriage of freight. In the twentieth century, lorries operating on newly constructed highways began competing with rail. During the 1950s and 1960s, aeroplanes began to compete seriously with lorries and rail.

The development of fax transmission and email eliminated the monopoly of the Royal Mail in delivering hardcopy (as opposed to oral) communications. Mobile phone technology and internet-based video systems (like Skype and Facetime) eliminated the monopoly of fixed-line telephone companies. In their myriad uses, computers for the home and the office have swept away the markets of many once-thriving products and services. For instance, in-store computers answer customer questions, decreasing the need for salespeople. Aided by computers, 'just in time' inventory systems greatly reduce the investment in inventories required of existing firms and new entrants alike. Computer-based flexible-manufacturing systems allow firms to switch production easily and inexpensively from one product line to another, thereby reducing the minimum scale at which each can be produced profitably. Computers are involved in book production, having replaced the author's hand- and type-written copy and the publisher's laborious page make-up procedures. One day soon the e-book or website may replace the textbook altogether. The internet and the computer have allowed distance learning to flourish so that one can take degrees in a vast number of subjects from a large number of universities worldwide, without ever setting foot in any of them—something that was totally impossible a couple of decades ago.

An important defence of oligopoly relates to this process of creative destruction. Many economists argue that intermediate market structures, such as oligopoly, lead to more innovation than would occur in either perfect competition or monopoly. Oligopolists face strong competition from existing rivals and cannot afford the more relaxed life of the monopolist. At the same time, however, oligopolistic firms expect to keep a good share of the profits that they initially earn from their innovative activity.

Here are some examples of the everyday observations that provide support for this view. Leading North American firms that operate in highly concentrated industries, such as Apple, Microsoft, Du Pont, Intel, General Electric, and 3M, have been highly innovative over many years. UK examples of innovative firms include Rolls Royce, GlaxoSmithKline, Vodafone, AstraZeneca, and BAE Systems. All of these firms operate in markets in which success depends critically on keeping products up to speed with the latest technology.

The technologies that have revolutionized agricultural production over the last century, allowing us to feed six billion people where a century ago it would have been impossible to feed two billion, have come from oligopolistic industries such as agricultural machine manufactures and biological firms such as Monsanto and public sector laboratories, while none of them came from the perfectly competitive industry of agricultural production.

CASE STUDIES

1. Game theory for real

The global video games market exceeded revenue of $90 billion in 2013 and was expected by consultancy Gartner[14] to exceed $110 billion in 2015.

The biggest segment in this market by revenue is for video game consoles, estimated to be worth $55 billion in 2015, up from $37 billion in 2012. A surprising feature of this vast market is that it is completely dominated by three players: Microsoft with its Xbox, Sony with its Playstation, and Nintendo with Wii. All three of these products were launched in the mid-2000s. Wii had the largest cumulative sales from launch up to 2013 with nearly 100 million units sold compared with 75 million for Xbox and 74 million for Playstation. However, the popularity of Wii declined such that it had only 14 per cent of the market in 2013 while Xbox had 35 per cent and Playstation had shot ahead with 51 per cent of the market in that year. All these makers launched new versions in late 2013, and early indications were that Playstation was maintaining its market-leading position, if not increasing its dominance.

Price is not a key element in competition between the console makers. Two other aspects of the product matter much more. The first is the technology; hence all three firms have been striving to develop a better technical product than the others. Wii seemed to have the edge in the late 2000s but later lost it to Playstation.

The other critical element that most helps sales is having the best games software to play on the console. There is much more open competition in the market for games software as entry into this activity is much easier, but obviously a games developer would want to write software for the console that has the biggest usership as this is most likely to sell more software. Better software supports greater console sales, and this process can be cumulative. Hence, the declining relative sales of Wii will discourage software developers and this in itself will make it less attractive to buy Wii ... and so on until a new technology shakes it all up again.

One trend evident in the software market is the growth of free games. This is presumably encouraged by the console makers as the more of these of good quality there are for a specific device, the more likely are purchases of that console.

The segment of the games market that is for other devices than consoles is also huge, expected to exceed $50 billion in 2015. Within this market there are three main segments: handheld video games, PC games, and games for mobile devices. The market for handheld games has been declining in the past two or three years, largely owing to the rapid growth of games for mobile devices such as tablets and smartphones. Clearly, this is linked to the rapid growth in ownership and use of these mobile devices, such as the iPad. For similar reasons, the market for PC games is expected to decline as relative use of PCs declines while tablet use soars.

The message from this case is that price is not the only factor, or even the most important one, that drives competitive strategy in some product markets. Technology is important but so also are the add-ons that are linked to the main product. Who would buy a games console if there was nothing to play on it?

2. Patents as entry barriers

A patent confers a monopoly right to the exclusive use of an invention for a specified period of time (twenty years in the United Kingdom). Patent laws differ from one country to another. In the United Kingdom, to be patentable an invention must be new, involve an inventive step, be capable of industrial application, and not be 'excluded'. Among exclusions are all discoveries, such as scientific theories or mathematical methods, that have no specific products as an outcome. Also excluded are works of art and literature (though these may be covered by copyright laws) and new designs that have no function other than appearance. Patents are granted for an initial four-year period, renewable annually for up to twenty years.

The benefit of patent protection is that it gives an inventor several years of monopoly trading and thus

14 <http://www.gartner.com/newsroom/2614915>

creates an incentive to invest in R&D that can generate some patentable product. As discussed earlier, drugs companies invest large sums in searching for new drugs.

Patents also have drawbacks. First, they create a tension because there are social pressures to provide a potentially life-saving drug as cheaply as possible to as many people as possible, once it has been invented. For example, there has recently been considerable pressure on Western drugs companies to provide anti-AIDS drugs to poor countries in Africa at their marginal cost of production, rather than at the monopoly price charged to the richer countries.

Secondly, the patent may hold up the spread of technology. One of the most famous examples in history is the patent protection granted to James Watt for his invention of the steam engine. This patent applied to any process using steam to drive a piston, and no one could infringe the patent until it ran out in 1800. This greatly inhibited the spread of existing engines by holding up their prices. It also held up the development of more effective engines because Watt had no faith in the potential of high-pressure engines. After his patent ran out, others showed how wrong he was by developing high-pressure engines without which steam could only be a stationary source of power. Steam engines powerful and light enough to be used for railways and ships had to be of the high-pressure variety.

Furthermore, patents only provide strong protection in a fairly narrow range of products where each version is distinctly different from its competitors—pharmaceuticals are one of the modern industries where patents work best. In many other industries firms do not even bother to prosecute believed patent violations because of the cost of legal proceedings. Rather, they rely on secrecy and a short product cycle to stay ahead of the field, so that by the time imitations come along some newer product has been developed.

Thus, patent protection has only a limited role in creating monopolies, and this is at best temporary. Perhaps a more important product protection device derives from laws relating to *trademarks* and *passing off*. For example, there is no patent protection to stop a soft drinks manufacturer making a drink identical to Coca Cola. However, this firm would not be allowed to sell this product under the Coca Cola label or sell it in red cans that might fool customers into believing that they were buying genuine Coca Cola. Here, it is the brand that has commercial value rather than the specific product itself.

3. Creative destruction—an endless process

The steel-nibbed pen eliminated the quill pen with its sharpened bird's feather nib. The fountain pen eliminated the steel pen and its accompanying inkwell. The ballpoint pen or 'biro' virtually eliminated the fountain pen. Rolling-ball and fibre-tipped pens have partly replaced the biro. Who knows what will come next in writing implements.

The hand-cranked adding machine replaced the Dickensian clerk adding up long columns of figures in his head. (This *was* an all-male occupation.) The electrically driven mechanical desk calculator eliminated the hand-cranked version. The electronic desk calculator eliminated the mechanical calculator, while the pocket calculator eliminated the slide rule (which was a device for doing calculations based on logarithms). The mainframe computer largely replaced the electronic calculator during the 1960s and 1970s (except for pocket use). In the late 1980s and early 1990s the increasingly powerful personal computer largely replaced the mainframe. A modern PC will do in a fraction of a second what the Dickensian clerk did in a week, and what a desk calculator could do in half a day.

The silent film eliminated vaudeville. The 'talkies' eliminated silent films, and colour largely eliminated black-and-white films. TV seriously reduced the demand for films (and radio) while not eliminating either of them. Satellites reduced the demand for terrestrial TV reception by offering better pictures and a more varied selection. For a while it looked as if fibre-optic cable might do the same to satellite transmission, but at the time of writing it seems that cable will be made redundant by both simpler satellite systems and technical changes in the ability to deliver fast signals (suitable for broadband internet) down telephone lines.

In the 1920s and 1930s the American supermarket threatened the small grocery store as the main shopping place for the typical family. By fighting back with assistance from the courts and the regulators, the small store was able to slow the advance of the supermarkets. But in the end the big stores were seen to offer a superior product and they pushed the small operations into the niche of the convenience store or corner shop. In the 1960s supermarkets spread throughout Britain. In the 1980s and 1990s out-of-town shopping malls and hypermarkets threatened town centre supermarkets. But by the 2000s major supermarket groups had slowed their out-of-town expansion and focused on smaller town centre 'metro' convenience stores close to where people live or work.

For long-distance passenger travel by sea the steamship eliminated the sailing vessel around the late nineteenth century. The aeroplane eliminated the ocean liner in the 1950s and 1960s. For passenger travel on land the train eliminated the stagecoach, while the bus competed with the train without eliminating it. The aeroplane wiped out the passenger train in most of North America, while leaving the bus still in a low-cost niche used mainly for short and medium distances. In Europe distances are such that bus, train, and plane all compete over many routes, while air transport dominates longer trips.

The preceding examples are all product innovations. Production processes also undergo the same type of creative destruction. The laborious hand-setting of metal type for printing was replaced by the linotype, which allowed the type to be set by a keyboard operator but still involved a costly procedure for making corrections. The linotype was swept away by computer typesetting, and many of the established printing shop operations have been replaced by desktop publishing.

Masses of assembly-line workers, operating highly specialized and inflexible machines, replaced the craftsman when Henry Ford perfected the techniques of mass production at the beginning of the twentieth century. A smaller number of less specialized flexible-manufacturing workers, operating sophisticated and less specialized machinery, have now replaced the assembly-line workers who operated the traditional factory in many industries. Many of these have now been displaced by robots, which are the main source of manual labour in assembly plants.

The list of such cases can be extended almost indefinitely, and they all illustrate the same general lesson. Creative destruction transforms the products we consume, how we make those products, and how we work. It continually sweeps away positions of high income and economic power established by firms that were in the previous wave of technological change and by those who work for them. It is an agent of dynamism in our economy—an agent of change and economic growth. But it is not without its negative side. Some firms go bust, owners lose wealth, and workers become redundant.

Conclusion

Oligopoly is an important market structure in modern economies because there are many industries in which the minimum efficient scale is simply too large to support many competing firms. The challenge to public policy is to keep oligopolists competing, rather than colluding, thus using their competitive energies to improve products and lower costs, rather than merely to erect entry barriers.

SUMMARY

Imperfectly competitive market structures

■ Firms in market structures other than perfect competition face negatively sloped demand curves and must administer their prices.

Monopolistic competition

■ In the theory of large group monopolistic competition, many firms compete to sell differentiated products. Each may make pure profits in the short run. In the long run, freedom of entry shifts its demand curve until it is tangent to the *ATC* curve, leading to excess capacity and production at average costs above the minimum possible level.

■ Not all industries with a large group of firms are monopolistically competitive within the terms of the theory. One of the main reasons is that all differentiated products are seldom if ever equally good substitutes for each other (as required by the symmetry assumption). Firms will then pay attention to the actions of other firms that produce the products that are the closest substitutes for their own.

Oligopoly

■ Oligopoly involves competition between a few rivals and the outcome for each is dependent on the behaviour of the others. In planning its production and pricing decisions, each must attempt to anticipate the reactions of the others.

■ Competitive behaviour among oligopolists may lead to a non-cooperative or Nash equilibrium. It is self-policing in the sense that no one has an incentive to depart from it unilaterally.

■ Oligopolistic profits can persist only if there are entry barriers. Natural barriers include economies of large-scale production and large fixed costs of entering the market. Artificial barriers include brand proliferation and high levels of advertising.

Oligopoly as a game

- Small group interaction can be analysed using a game theory framework, which sets out the available actions and the pay-offs under various actions.

- In a Nash equilibrium each firm is doing the best it can, given the current behaviour of its competitors.

- A cooperative solution is likely to be the one that maximizes joint profits, but each firm will typically have an incentive to cheat, and explicit cooperation between firms may be proscribed by competition laws.

Dynamics of oligopoly industries

- In qualitative terms the workings of the allocative system under oligopoly are similar (but not identical) to perfect competition.

- Oligopolistic industries appear to have contributed much more to the technological changes that underlie the long-run growth of productivity than have perfectly competitive industries or monopolies.

TOPICS FOR REVIEW

- The assumptions of monopolistic competition
- Excess capacity under monopolistic competition
- Dominant and dominated strategies in games
- Nash equilibrium
- The prisoner's dilemma

- The cooperative solution and the non-cooperative equilibrium
- Entry barriers
- Resource allocation under oligopoly

QUESTIONS

1 Consider the following pay-off matrixes for the interaction of two firms, A and X. They each have an aggressive or a passive strategy that they could adopt. The first pay-off in each pair is for A and the second is for X. In each case attempt to identify:

a) the dominant strategy for each player
b) the Nash equilibrium
c) the cooperative equilibrium.

i)

		Firm X choice	
		Aggressive	Passive
Firm A choice	Aggressive	100, 100	150, 50
	Passive	50, 150	175, 175

ii)

		Firm X choice	
		Aggressive	Passive
Firm A choice	Aggressive	100, 75	160, 60
	Passive	50, 60	110, 80

iii)

		Firm X choice	
		Aggressive	Passive
Firm A choice	Aggressive	250, 110	320, 120
	Passive	130, 160	300, 240

2 In each of the games set out in Question 1, would the outcome be likely to change if the game were repeated?

3 In monopolistic competition, which one of the following is true.

a) The outcome is the same as in perfect competition in the long run.
b) Each producer faces a downward sloping demand curve, sets $MC = MR$ and makes no profit in the long run.
c) Each producer sets marginal cost equal to price.
d) Each producer sets MC equal to price in the long run but not in the short run.
e) Each firm in the industry produces where its marginal cost is negative.

4 Explain the short-run equilibrium condition for a firm under monopolistic competition. If this is characterized by the existence of pure profit, what will happen to bring about the long-run equilibrium of the industry?

5 Give examples of barriers to entry and explain why existing firms can benefit from the creation of such barriers.

6 What is a Nash equilibrium and why is it self-policing?

7 Why do you think that non-price competition is an important factor where there is a small group of interacting competitors?

PART THREE

MARKETS FOR INPUTS

CHAPTER 9

DEMAND AND SUPPLY OF INPUTS

Up to now we have been studying markets for consumer goods where firms are the suppliers and individuals are the demanders. For this and the next two chapters we focus on the markets for the inputs that the firms use to make their outputs—mainly capital and labour (which includes all forms of effort, whether mental or physical, supplied by people to those who employ them in return for wages, salaries, bonuses or any other form of remuneration). In these markets it is firms that are typically the demanders, and the suppliers may be either other firms or individuals; for example, in labour markets firms are the demanders and individuals are the suppliers. Fortunately, we can analyse these markets with demand and supply tools just as we did for consumer goods.

How do firms decide how many people to employ? Under what circumstances will employers lay off employees and substitute machines that do the work instead? Do input prices determine the prices of final goods or is it the other way round?

In this chapter you will learn that:

- Firms' demand for inputs is derived from the demand for their output.

- Profit-maximizing firms will hire inputs up to the point where the extra cost is just equal to the extra contribution to revenue.

- Profit-maximizing firms will substitute cheaper inputs for dearer ones in the long run.

- The supply of inputs is more elastic for one specific use than for the economy as a whole.

- Economic rent is the return achieved in one use in excess of the highest available alternative return in another use.

We first study the forces that determine the demand for inputs, then the forces that determine supply, and finally how these interact in competitive markets to determine the prices of inputs.

Overview of input markets

A theory of distribution?

Markets for inputs are of interest in their own right. As employees we are interested in the market for our efforts, and firms want to understand the markets for all the inputs that they buy. The prices of certain key inputs, such as oil, have important effects on the economy as a whole. However, there is another reason for analysis of input markets, which is to understand the determinants of the distribution of income among different groups in society, hence the term *distribution theory*. A century or so ago it was realistic to think of inputs as being divided into three main groups of resources—land, labour, and capital—each of which was owned by a different class of society—landowners, workers, and capitalists. The prices determined by the market for each of these different resources then determined the division of the national income among these different classes of society. Hence, the analysis of input pricing was also a theory of income distribution among these different groups.

The distributional implications of input pricing are of interest today, but inputs are no longer associated with distinct social classes. For example, much of the nation's capital is now owned by employees' pension funds rather than by some separate class of capitalists.

The way income is distributed among different groups in society, whether among broad groups such as the owners of capital and the suppliers of labour or among narrower groups such as skilled and unskilled workers or physical and mental workers, is called the **functional distribution of income** because incomes are being divided among groups that fulfil different functions in the productive process. The distribution of income among various groups with different amounts of income, such as those who are in the top 10 per cent of all income earners versus the rest, or the gap in income between the top 20 per cent of income earners and the bottom 20 per cent, is called the size distribution of income.

The functional distribution of income refers to the share of total national income going to owners of different resources and so focuses on the source of income. The size distribution of income refers to the proportion of total income received by various income groups and so focuses on differences in the incomes of various income earners, irrespective of the source from which that income is derived.

Box 9.1 highlights the trends in real incomes and income distribution in the United Kingdom based upon household characteristics. This is an important public policy issue, as governments do not want to be seen to favour one section of the population over others. The media often create headlines such as: 'The rich are getting richer and the poor are getting poorer'. This often causes public concern about distribution issues. However, the truth is normally a bit more subtle, as the report in the Box indicates.

Box 9.1 Incomes and income distribution

The following extract from a report by the UK Institute of Fiscal Studies explains some of the recent trends in real incomes and income distribution in the United Kingdom. It highlights the improved position of pensioners, the deterioration in the relative position of young adults, and the significant growth of earnings inequality in general.

Average incomes tend to grow over time as the economy expands. Since our consistent data series began more than 50 years ago in 1961, mean household net incomes have grown by about 1.6% per year in inflation-adjusted terms. [This growth rate doubles this income measure every 45 years.] An alternative measure of 'average income' is median income, which is the income of the individual right in the middle of the income distribution. Median household net income has grown by an annual average 1.4% since 1961. However, income growth has tended to fluctuate over time. For instance, there was strong growth in the late 1990s, but weak growth between 2002 and 2007, even before the financial crisis hit.

Key findings on living standards from this year's report include:

• Average incomes in the UK fell in 2011–12. After accounting for inflation, official statistics recorded a fall of 2.8% in median household income, from £440 per week to £427 per week (both in 2011–12 prices), and a fall of 1.6% in mean household income, from £537 to £528. These latest falls came on top of large falls in 2010–11; by 2011–12, real median income was 5.8%

below its 2009–10 level and real mean income was 7.2% lower.

• This two-year fall in average incomes was preceded by a slight rise in average incomes during the recession between 2007–08 and 2009–10. Two key factors explain this pattern. First, average gross earnings were remarkably stable between 2007–08 and 2009–10 despite increases in unemployment. However, gross earnings then fell by 6.6% between 2009–10 and 2011–12. Second, while income from benefits and tax credits grew significantly between 2007–08 and 2009–10, it fell by 5.3% over the following two years. This was partly the result of discretionary increases to benefits during the recession and discretionary cuts made since. Changing inflation also played an important role. Falling inflation during the recession helped support real earnings and benefit rates, while rising inflation since has exacerbated the real-terms falls in earnings and benefits...

Changes in the economy, demographics, family structure, savings and employment behaviour over the last few decades have had important effects on the income distribution. There are now more elderly people and more single parents. Significant policy reforms have altered the way that different groups are treated by the tax and benefit system. Pensioners are much more likely to have saved through private or occupational pensions during their working lives, and entitlements to state pensions

Box 9.1 *continued*

have also increased. The labour market has changed radically too: for example, earnings inequality increased rapidly during the 1980s; lone parents are much more likely to be employed than they were 20 years ago; and the employment rates of young adults have recently been falling rapidly. Over time, these kinds of changes have dramatically altered the types of people who are relatively rich and relative poor, and the levels of inequality within different parts of the population.

Key findings in this year's report that relate to long-run changes in the distribution of income include:

• Income (measured before housing costs) is distributed much more evenly across the major family types than in decades past. Pensioners remain the lowest-income group, and working-age adults without dependent children remain the highest-income group, on average. But the gaps have closed very significantly since the late 1970s.

• The proportion of pensioners with incomes in the lowest income quintile has fallen from 47% in the late 1970s to 21% in 2011–12. Over the same period, the proportion with incomes in the highest two income quintiles has risen from 18% to 31%. This strong improvement in the relative position of pensioners has been driven mostly by higher private pension incomes for younger cohorts of pensioners, and by higher benefit receipts due to increases in benefit rates and increases in the numbers entitled to state pensions. Meanwhile,

the relative position of working-age adults without dependent children has worsened significantly since the late 1970s, at both the top and bottom of the distribution.

• Although differences in income between the major family types have narrowed since the late 1970s, there have been large rises in inequality within these family types. There are now much larger gaps between the richest and poorest individuals in families with children, and between the richest and poorest working-age adults without children. The main factor behind this is an increase in earnings inequality. The poorest pensioners have also fallen further behind middle-income pensioners, although inequality within most of the top half of the pensioner income distribution has changed little. Since 1996–97, inequality within each of these family types has generally stopped rising, except that approximately the highest-income 5% of each group have continued to 'race away'.

• Income inequality is now clearly lower among pensioners than among other adults aged 30 and above. This is a big transformation. In the late 1970s, income inequality was almost constant across the adult age distribution; and when our consistent time series began in the early 1960s, incomes were more unevenly distributed among pensioners than among any other age group.

(*Source:* Jonathan Cribb, Andrew Hood, Robert Joyce, and David Phillips, *Living Standards, Poverty and Inequality in the UK: 2013*, IFS Report R81, June 2013)

Before proceeding, one word of warning is needed. Beware of confusing the terms 'unequal' and 'inequality' with 'unjust' and 'inequitable'. For example, a completely equal distribution of the nation's income among all individuals—those who worked hard and those who loafed about on the job; those who did dangerous jobs and those in safe ones; those on whose skills we relied and those who relied on others' skills—would not satisfy many people's idea of a just distribution of income.

In any case, the analysis we develop below is designed to explain how incomes are determined, not to evaluate whether the outcome is equitable or inequitable, just or unjust. The policy implications of income inequalities and attempts by government to redistribute income are discussed in Chapter 14, and the rising rewards of top earners are dicussed in case studies at the end of Chapter 10.

The link between output and input decisions

In Chapter 5 we showed how firms' costs vary with their output and how they can achieve cost minimization by finding the least costly combination of inputs to produce any given output. In Chapter 6 we saw that firms in perfect competition decide how much to produce by equating their marginal cost to the market price. We also saw how the market supply curve interacts with the market demand curve in each goods market. This interaction determines the market price as well as the quantity that is produced and consumed.

These events in goods markets have implications for input markets. The decisions of firms on how much to produce and how to produce it imply specific demands for various quantities of inputs. These demands, together with the supplies of inputs (which are determined by the owners of resources), come together in markets for inputs.

According to the market theory of input pricing these demands and supplies together determine the quantities of the various inputs that are employed, their prices, and the incomes earned by their owners.

The above discussion shows that there is a close relationship between the production and pricing of the goods and services supplied by firms on the one hand and the pricing, employment, and incomes earned by the owners of inputs that they hire on the other hand. These are two related aspects of how the market economy determines the production of goods and services and the allocation of the nation's resources among their various possible uses. This discussion provides a brief introduction to one of the great insights of economics:

When demand and supply interact to determine the allocation of resources between various lines of production, they also determine the incomes of the owners of inputs that are used in making the outputs.

Note that this is the total incomes of all the input owners. How that income is shared among them may require further explanation.

The way this works can be summarized as follows.

1. The income of owners of different types of inputs depends on the price that is paid for these inputs and the amount that is used.

2. According to the market theory of input pricing demands and supplies in input markets determine input prices and quantities in exactly the same way that the prices and quantities of goods and services are determined in product markets.

3. All that is needed to explain input pricing is to identify the main determinants of the demand for, and supply of, various inputs (and adjust for the many changes to what would be the free market prices caused by the actions of governments, unions, the power of large firms and other market imperfections).

Figure 9.1 illustrates the market theory of input pricing by showing how in this theory competitive market forces determine the income accruing to owners of a specific input. The rest of this chapter is an elaboration of this important theme. We first study the demand for inputs, then their supply, and finally how they come together to determine input prices and quantities.

Two assumptions

We now need to make two assumptions that will underlie our analysis.

Other prices constant

In order to ensure that we are speaking of relative and not just absolute prices and quantities, we make the following assumption. When the changes studied in Figure 9.1

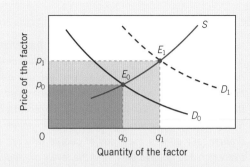

Figure 9.1 Income of owners of primary resources determined in competitive markets

The interaction of demand and supply in competitive input markets determines resource owners' equilibrium price and quantity, and hence their income. The original demand and supply curves are D_0 and S. Equilibrium is at E_0, with price p_0 and quantity employed q_0. The resource owners' incomes are shown by the dark blue area in the figure. When the demand curve shifts to D_1, equilibrium shifts to E_1, with price p_1 and quantity q_1. The resource owners' incomes rise by the amount of the light blue area.

occur, *the prices of all other inputs, the prices of all goods, and the level of national income are held constant.*[1] Under these circumstances fluctuations in an input's equilibrium price and quantity cause fluctuations (1) in the money earnings of the owners of that input, (2) in their earnings relative to owners of other inputs, and (3) in the share of national income going to those owners.

Competitive markets

In this chapter we confine ourselves to perfectly competitive markets. This means that individual firms are price takers in both output and input markets. On the one hand, they face a given price for the product they produce, and that price is both their average and marginal revenue. On the other hand, they face a given price of each input that they buy, and that price is both the average and marginal cost of the input. These input and output prices may change but they cannot be influenced by the actions of any single firm (or any single seller of inputs). Similarly, sellers of the services of inputs must also accept whatever market price currently rules for their services.

Dealing first with firms that are price takers in product and input markets allows us to study the principles of input price determination in the simplest context. Once these are understood, it is relatively easy to allow for monopolistic elements in either or both types of market. This is done in Chapter 10.

---

[1] We make these assumptions because we are interested in resource owners' relative share of total national income. These assumptions are only a simplifying device. They do not affect the generality of the conclusions.

The demand for inputs

Firms use the services of land, labour, capital, and natural resources[2] as inputs. They also use products, such as steel, plastics, and electricity, that are produced by other firms. These products are in turn made by using land, labour, capital, natural resources, and other produced inputs. If we continue following through the chain of outputs of some firms that are used as inputs by other firms, we can account for all of the economy's output in terms of inputs of the basic resources—land, labour, capital, and natural resources. The theory of input pricing applies to *all* inputs used by a firm. The logic of what we discuss below can be used to analyse any stage of the production process. Box 9.2 illustrates the complex supply chain of inputs that contribute to a typical manufactured product.

Firms require inputs not for their own sake but as a means to produce goods and services. For example, the demand for computer programmers and technicians is growing as more and more computers are used. The demand for carpenters and building materials rises and falls as the amount of housing construction rises and falls.

---

[2] Although natural resources are often included with land as a single type of resource, they have so many important special characteristics that it is sometimes worthwhile treating them as a separate type of primary input.

Thus, demand for any input is derived from the demand for the goods and services that it helps to produce; for this reason, the demand for all inputs is called a derived demand.

Derived demand provides a link between the markets for output and the markets for inputs.

Input demand in the long run

In the long run, all inputs are variable. In this case, both the substitution and the income effects contribute to the negative slope of the demand curve. We consider the case of a price reduction and leave a price rise as a simple variation, which is easy to work through for yourself.

The substitution effect

A fall in an input's price makes it less expensive relative to other inputs and more of it will tend to be used relative to those whose price has not fallen. This is true at all levels of aggregation. It is true if the price of all labour falls relative to capital, or if the price of one type of labour falls relative to other types of labour. We showed in Chapter 5 that a fall in the price of all types of labour will lead profit-maximizing

---

Box 9.2 Produced inputs and the supply chain

In this and the next few chapters we concentrate on analysing demand and supply of primary resource inputs, especially labour and capital, but most firms buy many of their inputs from other firms. For example, an HDTV manufacturer will buy in many of the components that go into its HDTVs (as illustrated in the diagram), as well as hire assembly workers, designers, marketing experts, and accountants, etc., and use its own capital and land for its factory. So why not analyse the markets for these other produced inputs?

Although we do not need to analyse the factors affecting demand for produced inputs directly, the principles that are set out in this chapter also apply just as easily to manufactured inputs as they do to labour, capital, and other inputs. Demand for produced inputs is a derived demand depending on demand for the final product. Profit-maximizing firms (as we shall see below) will buy these inputs up to the point where the extra cost of the last unit is just equal to the value of the extra output that input generates. The demand curve for produced inputs will be negatively sloped as it is for all inputs (as we can rule out the Giffen-good case that arises with consumer demand), so markets for produced inputs can be analysed with demand and supply tools just like any other market.

By focusing on demand for primary resource inputs in the text we are aggregating across the entire supply chain of produced goods and services, and focusing on the inputs for industry as a whole rather than on each link in that supply chain. We do this because we are interested in resource allocation for the economy as a whole. But analysis of each intermediate market between firms and their suppliers of produced inputs is straightforward.

Individual firms do have some issues to resolve relating to their produced inputs. First, should they buy in the input or make it for themselves? So long as quality and reliability of supply are guaranteed, the answer will be: buy from another firm if they can make the product more cheaply than we can make it ourselves. Secondly, if the product is bought in, should the firm simply set up a long-term supply contract with the input producer or should it try to buy on the market from the cheapest supplier in each period? The answer here will depend on whether this is a standardized product that is widely available at short notice, or a highly specific input that needs special skills or equipment to produce. In the latter case, a longer-term supply contract is more likely.

Box 1.4 *continued*

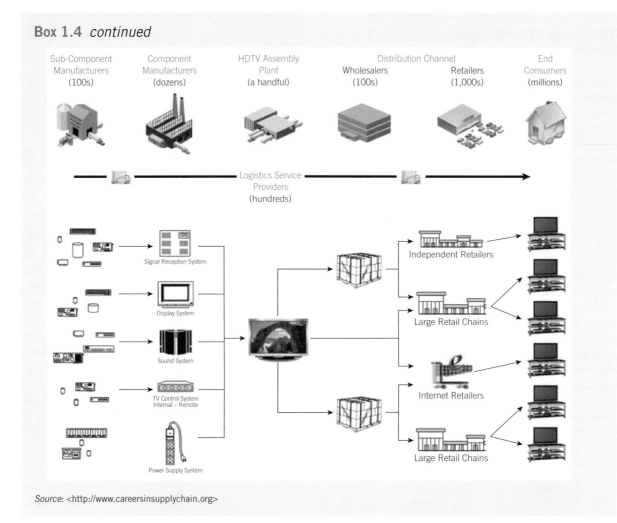

Source: <http://www.careersinsupplychain.org>

firms to substitute labour for capital. According to the principle of substitution, they will use more of the now cheaper input and less of the relatively more expensive ones. A fall in the wage of one type of labour will lead to more of that type being used as a replacement for other types of labour whose wage has not fallen. For example, some time ago the wages of building labour rose dramatically. This led builders to substitute prefabricated parts made in factories for parts made to order on the building site. Window frames, door jambs, walls, and a host of other parts of buildings that used to be custom made on the site were prefabricated to standard designs in factories where wages were much lower than those on construction sites. In effect, factory labour whose price had not risen was substituted for building labour whose price had risen.

Note, however, that in the long run technology is given and with many technologies there is little room to substitute between capital, labour, and material inputs, as even in the long run these inputs are required in fixed proportion by the technologies of many production processes. So some of the demands for any one type of input may

not change as its price varies, even in the long run. But for the rest, the argument of the previous paragraph holds: more of the relatively cheaper input and less of the relatively more expensive ones will be used when the price of one changes.

Over the very long run, technology is also variable and there will be an incentive to invent and innovate technologies that use more of a newly cheaper input and less of a more expensive one. For example, when cheaper electricity became available to rural areas a number of new technologies, such as electric milking machines, were invented thus adding to the demand for electricity. Such changes reinforce the effects that operate in the long run, making the demands for inputs more sensitive to price changes the longer the time span being considered.

The income effect

A fall in the price of one input reduces the cost of making all products that use that input. The cost curves of these products thus shift downwards, shifting the sum of the marginal cost curves—which in a competitive market is the industry supply curve. As a result more will be produced and sold. To make more output, an increase in all the inputs is required. This leads to a rise in the amount demanded of the input whose price has fallen, as well as a rise in the demand for all other inputs that cooperate with it in production. In oligopolistic and monopolistic markets the effects are more complex because there is no unique industry supply curve. But we do not expect a fall in an input price to lead to a fall in the output of products that use it, and in most cases it will lead to a rise. So once again, the quantity of any input demanded will, overall, vary inversely with its price, rising as its price falls and falling as its price rises.

Input demand in the short run

In the short run some inputs are fixed and only a few can be varied. As in previous chapters, we must now distinguish between firms whose fixed input is **indivisible** and those for whom it is **divisible**. As before we consider the case of the indivisible fixed input first. Most of what follows is applicable to both types of firm. When this discussion is completed we will note what needs to be altered for firms with a divisible fixed input.

If we think of an extreme situation in which only one input can be varied, we can derive a famous proposition that is true for each and every input as long as the firms that hire them are maximizing their profits and have an **indivisible** fixed input.

The maximizing firm

In Chapter 6 we set out the rules for the maximization of a firm's profits in the short run. When one input is fixed and indivisible and another is variable, the profit-maximizing firm increases its output until the last unit produced adds just as much to cost as to revenue—that is, until marginal cost equals marginal revenue. An equivalent way of stating that the firm maximizes profits is to say that *the firm will increase production up to the point at which the last unit of the variable input employed adds just as much to revenue as it does to cost*.

The addition to total cost resulting from employing one more unit of an input is its price. (We assume that the firm is buying its inputs in a competitive market, so the extra purchase does not affect the market price.) So, if one more worker is hired at a wage of £15 per hour, the addition to the firm's costs is £15 (and other workers' wages remain unchanged).

The amount that a unit of a variable input adds to revenue is the amount that the unit adds to total output multiplied by the change in revenue resulting from selling an extra unit of output.

In Chapter 5 we called the variable input's addition to total output its *marginal product*. When dealing with demand for inputs, we use the term **marginal physical product** (*MPP*) to avoid confusion with the revenue concepts that we also need to use.

The change in revenue resulting from selling one extra unit of output is just the price of the output, *p* (since the firm is a price taker in the market for its output). The resulting amount, which is *MPP* × *p*, is called the input's **marginal revenue product** and is given the symbol *MRP*.

For example, if the variable input's marginal physical product is two widgets per hour and the price of a widget is £7.50, then the input's marginal revenue product is £15 (£7.50 × 2).

We can now state the firm's profit maximization condition in two ways. First,

| Addition to total costs caused by hiring another unit of the variable input | = | The input's marginal revenue product (MRP) | (9.1) |

Note that if the firm is a price taker in input markets the left-hand side is just the price of a unit of the variable input, which we now call *w* (as the variable input is often labour and its price is the wage rate). Also, note that as long as the firm is a price taker in the market for its output, the right-hand side is the input's marginal physical product, *MPP*, multiplied by the price at which the output is sold, which we call *p*. We can now restate eqn (9.1) as follows:

| Price of a unit of the variable input | = | The input's marginal physical production multiplied by the product's market price | (9.2) |

and in symbols

$$w = MPP \times p. \qquad (9.2')$$

Here is an example to clarify the meaning of eqn (9.2). Suppose that the extra labour is available to the firm at a cost of £10 an hour ($w = £10$). Suppose also that employing another hour's work adds three units to output ($MPP = 3$). Suppose further that output units sell for £5 each ($p = £5$). Thus, the additional hour of input adds £15 to the firm's revenue and £10 to its costs. Hiring one worker for an extra hour brings in £5 more than it costs. *The firm will take on more of the variable input whenever its marginal revenue product exceeds its price as this adds more to revenue than to cost.*

Now suppose that the last hour of work by the variable input has a marginal physical product of one unit of output—it adds only one extra unit to output—and so adds only £5 to revenue. Clearly, the firm can increase profits by reducing its use of the input, since hiring for one hour less reduces revenues by £5 while reducing costs by £10. *The firm will hire less of the variable input whenever its marginal revenue product is less than its price.*

Finally, suppose that the last hour of labour hired has an *MPP* of two units, so that it increases revenue by £10. Now, the firm cannot increase its profits by altering its employment of the variable input in either direction. *The firm cannot increase its profits by altering employment of the variable input whenever the input's marginal revenue product equals its price.*

We are doing nothing new here. We are merely looking at the firm's profit-maximizing behaviour from the point of view of its inputs rather than its output. In Chapter 6 we analysed the firm varying its output until the marginal cost of producing the last unit of output was equal to the marginal revenue derived from selling that unit. The same profit-maximizing behaviour involves the firm varying its inputs until the marginal cost of the last input hired is just equal to the revenue derived from selling the marginal product of that extra input. These are exactly the same because the variable input is the only component of marginal cost (and its *MRP* is the same as *MR* for the firm).

The firm's demand curve for the input

It is now easy to see why in the short run with only one variable input the firm's demand curve for that input is negatively sloped. Suppose that the firm starts in equilibrium. The relationship shown in eqn (9.2) must hold, which means that that input's marginal revenue product is equated to its price. Now the price of the input falls. The unchanged marginal revenue product is now higher than the lowered price. So, it pays the firm to hire more of the input. As it hires more inputs the marginal physical product falls, and since the firm is a price taker so does the marginal revenue product. The firm goes on hiring more

of the variable input until the marginal revenue product falls to the level of the new lower price.

What this tells us is that:

In the short run with only one variable input, the firm's demand for its variable input is negatively sloped.

We now show more precisely where this demand curve comes from. Here, we explain the case where there is one variable input, and in Box 9.3 we extend the analysis to cover more than one input.

Equation (9.2′) tells us what determines the quantity of a variable input a firm will demand when faced with some specific price of the input and some specific price of its output. The firm's demand curve shows how much the firm will buy at *each* price of the variable input. To derive this curve, we start by considering the right-hand side of eqn (9.2′), which tells us that the input's marginal revenue product is composed of a physical component and a value component.

The physical component of MRP

As the quantity of the variable input used changes, output will vary. The hypothesis of diminishing returns, first discussed in Chapter 5, predicts what will happen. As the firm adds further units of the variable input to a given quantity of the fixed input, the additions to output will eventually get smaller and smaller. In other words the input's marginal physical product will decline. This is illustrated in Figure 9.2(i), which uses hypothetical data that have the same general characteristics as the data in

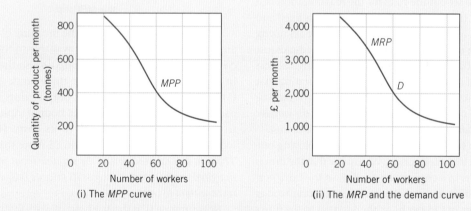

(i) The *MPP* curve

(ii) The *MRP* and the demand curve

Figure 9.2 **From marginal physical product to demand curve**

Each additional unit of the input employed adds a certain amount to total product (part (i)) and hence a certain amount to total revenue (part (ii)), and this determines the amount of the input that firms will demand at each price. Part (i) assumes data that are consistent with marginal productivity theory; it shows the addition to the firm's *output* produced by additional units of labour hired. The curve is negatively sloped because of the law of diminishing returns. Part (ii) shows the addition to the firm's *revenue* caused by the employment of each additional unit of labour. It is the marginal physical product from part (i) multiplied by the price at which that product is sold. In this case the price is assumed to be £5. (The multiplication is by market price because the firm is assumed to be a price taker in the market for its output.) Since the firm equates the price of the variable input, which in this case is labour, to the input's marginal revenue product, it follows that the *MRP* curve in part (ii) is also the demand curve for labour, showing how much will be employed at each price.

Table 5.2. The negative slope of the *MPP* curve reflects the operation of the law of diminishing returns: each unit of labour adds less to total output than the previous unit.

The value component of MRP

To convert the marginal physical product curve of Figure 9.2(i) into a curve showing the marginal revenue product of the variable input, we need to know the value of the extra physical product. As long as the firm sells its output on a competitive market, this value is simply the marginal physical product multiplied by the market price at which the firm sells its product.

This operation is illustrated in Figure 9.2(ii), which shows a marginal revenue product curve for labour on the assumption that the firm sells its product in a competitive market at a price of £5 a unit. This curve shows how much would be added to revenue by employing one more unit of the input *at each level of total employment of the input*. Notice that part (ii) of the figure is measuring money values on the vertical axis, whereas part (i) was measuring physical units of output.

Profit-maximizing firms will equate the addition to the cost of buying another unit of a variable input with the addition to revenue caused by selling the output of that unit, which we call the input's marginal revenue product, *MRP*. The *MRP* is always composed of a physical component, which is the input's *MPP*, and a value component, which is

the marginal revenue of selling those extra physical units of output. Because our firms are price takers in their output markets, the marginal revenue is just the price that they face in that market. If the firms faced a negatively sloped demand curve for their output, we know from Chapter 7 that the addition to revenue from selling further units is not the market price because marginal revenue is less than price.

From MRP to the demand curve

Equation (9.2′) states that the profit-maximizing firm will employ additional units of the input up to the point at which the *MRP* equals the price of the input. If, for example, the price of the variable input were £2,000 per month, then it would be most profitable to employ sixty workers. There is no point in employing a sixty-first, since that would add just less than £2,000 to revenue but a full £2,000 to costs. So, the profit-maximizing firm hires the quantity of the variable input that equates the marginal revenue product to the price of the variable input. Thus the curve that relates the quantity of the variable input employed to its *MRP* is also the curve that relates the quantity of the variable input the firm wishes to employ to its price.

The *MRP* curve of the variable input is the same as the demand curve for that input. The reason that both are negatively sloped is as a result of the operation of the law of diminishing returns.

The case of multiple inputs is discussed in Box 9.3.

Box 9.3 Demand for inputs where there is more than one variable input

When a firm can vary the amounts of several inputs that it uses, profit maximization requires that the last £1 it spends on each input brings in the same amount of revenue.

To see how this works out for two inputs, call their prices p_A and p_B and their marginal revenue products MRP_A and MRP_B. The amount of extra revenue per £1 spent on hiring more of input *A* is MRP_A/p_A, while the amount of extra revenue per pound spent on hiring more of input *B* is MRP_B/p_B. For example, if one more unit of *A* costs £3 and adds £6 to revenue, it yields £2 of revenue per £1 spent on it. If one more unit of *B* costs £5 and adds £10 to revenue, it too yields £2 of revenue per £1 spent on it. If the firm wants to equate these *MRP*s per pound spent on the inputs, it must set

$$\frac{MRP_A}{p_A} = \frac{MRP_B}{p_B}. \tag{1}$$

The marginal revenue product is the marginal physical product multiplied by the product's selling price. We now have three prices, two for the variable inputs and one for output. To prevent confusion, we call the output price p_S, which stands for selling price. So $MRP = MPP \times p_S$. So we can rewrite eqn (1) as

$$\frac{MPP_A(p_S)}{p_A} = \frac{(MPP_B)(p_S)}{p_B}. \tag{2}$$

If we eliminate the common p_S term, we have

$$\frac{MPP_A}{p_A} = \frac{MPP_B}{p_B}. \tag{3}$$

Equation (9.3.3) can be rewritten as follows:

$$\frac{MPP_A}{MPP_B} = \frac{p_A}{p_B}. \tag{4}$$

In eqn (4) the firm is given prices of the two inputs, and it adjusts to these by altering the quantities of the two inputs until it has the profit-maximizing amount of each. This behaviour is similar to that of the consumer described in Chapter 4. The consumer is given the prices of two commodities and she adjusts her consumption until her utility is maximized (which she does by making the ratios of the marginal utilities equal the ratio of their prices).

Profit-maximizing firms hire inputs up to the point where the ratio of the marginal products of inputs is equal to the ratio of the inputs' prices.

The industry's demand curve for an input

So far we have seen how a single firm that takes its market price as given will vary its quantity demanded for an input as that input's price changes. But when an input's price changes, and *all firms* in a competitive industry vary the amount of the input that they demand in order to vary their output, the price of the industry's product changes. That change will have repercussions on desired output and the quantity of the input demanded.

For example, a fall in carpenters' wages will reduce the cost of producing houses, thus shifting the supply curve of houses to the right. Price-taking construction firms would plan to increase construction, and hence increase the quantity of carpenters demanded, by some specific amount if the price of houses does not change. However, because the demand curve for houses is negatively sloped, the increase in output leads to a fall in the market price of houses. As a result each individual firm will increase its desired output *by less* than it had planned to do before the market price changed.

An increase in carpenters' wages has the opposite effect. The cost of producing houses rises, the supply curve shifts to the left, and the price of houses rises. As a result, the individual firm will cut its planned output and employment of inputs by less than it would have done if market price had not changed.

The industry's demand curve for an input is steeper than it would be if firms faced an unchanged product price because the reaction of market price must be allowed for.

It may be useful to summarize the argument so far.

1. In the short run, the derived demand curve for an input on the part of a *price-taking* firm will have a negative slope because of the law of diminishing returns. As more of the input is employed in response to a fall in its price, its marginal product falls. No further units will be added once its marginal revenue product falls to the input's new price.

2. An industry's short-run demand curve for an input is less elastic than suggested by point 1. As the industry expands output in response to a fall in an input's price, the price of the firm's output will fall, causing the final increase in each firm's output, and hence its demand for employment of inputs, to be less than it would be if the output price remained unchanged.

Firms whose fixed inputs are divisible

As we saw in the section 'Firms with a Divisible Fixed Input' in Chapter 6, page 141, when such a firm is operating in a perfectly competitive market, it is faced with a given market price. If that price is above its average variable cost it will produce where the marginal cost curve is positively sloped and the proportions of fixed to variable inputs are changing as output changes. Thus the previous analysis holds exactly.

The only difference occurs when the firm faces a negatively sloped demand curve, which covers most firms producing other than primary products. When the firm varies its output over any range up to capacity, it varies inputs of both the variable and the fixed input and so does not face diminishing returns. However, when the price of the firm's variable input changes, the firm's horizontal short run cost curve shifts. In response, the firm alters its output. and hence its demand for the variable input, producing more, and hence demanding more of the variable input, when the input price falls and less when it rises. So this type of firm also has a negatively sloped demand curve for the variable factor. There is, however, one difference in the determinants of electivity, which are discussed below. Because diminish returns do not apply to such firms in the short run, the first of the four determinants discussed in the next section does not apply while the other three do.

Elasticity of demand for inputs

The elasticity of demand for an input measures the *degree* of the response of the quantity demanded to a change in its price. The influences that were discussed in the preceding sections explain the *direction* of the response; that is, the quantity demanded is negatively related to price. Therefore you should not be surprised to learn that the amount of the response depends on the strength with which these influences operate. This section gives the four principles of derived demand that were first set out by the British economist Alfred Marshall (1842–1924). We state them and note the extent to which they apply in the short, long, and very long runs.

Diminishing returns

The first influence on the slope of the demand curve is the diminishing marginal productivity of an input. If marginal productivity declines rapidly as more of a variable input is employed, a fall in the input's price will not induce many more units to be employed. Conversely, if marginal productivity falls only slowly as more of a variable input is employed, there will be a large increase in quantity demanded as price falls.

The faster the marginal productivity of an input declines as its use rises, the lower is the elasticity of each firm's demand curve for the input.

For example, both labour and fertilizers are used by market gardeners who produce vegetables for sale in nearby cities. For many crops additional doses of fertilizers add significant amounts to yields over quite a wide range of fertilizer use. Although the marginal product of fertilizer does decline, it does so rather slowly as more and more fertilizer is used. In contrast, although certain amounts of labour are needed for planting, weeding, and harvesting, there is only a small range over which additional labour can be used productively. The marginal product of labour, although high for the first units, declines rapidly as more and more labour is used. Under these circumstances, market gardeners will have an elastic demand for fertilizer and an inelastic demand for labour.

This is a short-run influence that applies whenever the fixed input is being fully used, either because it is indivisible or because the firm with a divisible fixed input is producing at full capacity output. It does not apply for firms with divisible inputs who are producing at less than capacity (which requires that they face a negatively sloped demand curve for their product), as the fixed and variable inputs are used in a constant proportion.

Substitution

In the long run all inputs are variable. If one input's price rises, firms will try to substitute relatively cheaper inputs instead. For this reason, the slope of the demand curve for an input is influenced by the ease with which other inputs can be substituted for the input whose price has changed.

The greater the ease of substitution, the greater is the elasticity of demand for the input.

The ease of substitution depends on the substitutes that are available and the production technology. It is often possible to vary input proportions in surprising ways. For example, in car manufacturing and building construction glass and steel can be substituted for each other simply by varying the dimensions of the windows. Another example is that more durable parts can be substituted for repair work in the case of most manufactured goods. This is done by making the product more or less durable and more or less subject to breakdowns, and by using more or less expensive materials in its construction.

Such substitutions are not the end of the story. Manufacturing equipment is being replaced continually, and this allows more or less capital-intensive methods to be built into new factories in response to changes in input prices. Similarly, car engines that use less petrol per mile tend to be developed when the price of petrol rises significantly. Note that these are long-run and very long run effects, not strictly short-run effects when the fixed input is given. Altering the capital intensity of any

production facility is typically a very long run process requiring new technologies, while even small changes in the design of a car will require some alteration in the dies and machine tools that are part of the fixed input. Since they are long-run effects, they apply to all firms whatever the nature of the input that is fixed in the short run.

Importance of the input

Other things being equal, the larger the fraction of the total costs of producing some product that is made up of payment to a particular input, the greater is the elasticity of demand for that input.

To see this, suppose that wages account for 50 per cent of the costs of producing a good and raw materials for 15 per cent. A 10 per cent rise in the price of labour raises the cost of production by 5 per cent (10 per cent of 50 per cent), but a 10 per cent rise in the price of raw materials raises the cost of the product by only 1.5 per cent (10 per cent of 15 per cent). The larger the increase in the cost of production, the larger is the shift in the product's supply curve, and hence the larger the decreases in quantities demanded of both the product and the inputs used to produce it. This effect applies over all runs and all types of firm.

Elasticity of demand for the output

The fourth, and last, principle of derived demand is:

Other things being equal, the more elastic the demand for the product that the input helps to make, the more elastic is the demand for the input.

If an increase in the price of the product causes a large decrease in the quantity demanded—that is, if the demand for the product is elastic—there will be a large decrease in the quantity of an input needed to produce it in response to a rise in the input's price. However, if an increase in the price of a product causes only a small decrease in the quantity demanded—that is, if the demand for the product is inelastic—there will be only a small decrease in the quantity of the input required in response to a rise in its price. Once again this effect applies over all time periods and to all firms. Whatever the nature of the firm's fixed input—divisible or indivisible—a change in input costs shifts the cost curve and will lead to a change in output in both perfectly and imperfectly competitive markets.

In Box 9.4 the forces affecting the elasticity of the derived demand curves that have just been discussed are related more specifically to the market for the industry's output.

Box 9.4 The principles of derived demand

This box demonstrates two of the four principles of derived demand using demand and supply curves.

1. The larger the proportion of total costs accounted for by an input, the more elastic is the demand for it

Consider part (i) of the figure. The demand curve for the *industry's product* is D and, given the input's original price, the *industry supply curve* is S_0. Equilibrium is at E_0 with output at q_0.

Suppose that the input's price then falls. If the input accounts for a small part of the industry's total cost, each firm's marginal cost curve shifts downwards by only a small amount. So also does the industry supply curve, as illustrated by the supply curve S_1. Output expands only a small amount to q_1, which implies only a small increase in the quantity of the variable input demanded.

If the input accounts for a large part of the industry's total costs, each firm's marginal cost curve shifts downwards a great deal. So also does the industry supply curve, as illustrated by the curve S_2. Output expands greatly to q_2, which implies a large increase in the quantity of variable input demanded.

2. The more elastic the demand curve for the product, the more elastic is the demand for the input

Consider part (ii) of the figure. The original demand and supply curves for the industry's product intersect at E_0 to produce an industry output of q_0. A fall in the price of an input causes the industry's supply curve to shift downwards to S_1.

When the demand curve is relatively inelastic, as shown by the curve D_i, the industry's output increases by only a

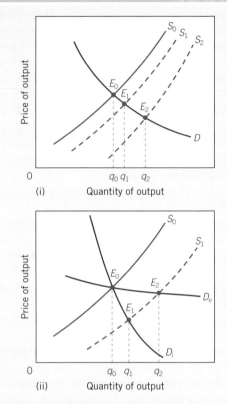

small amount to q_1. The quantity of the variable input demanded will increase by a correspondingly small amount.

When the demand curve is relatively elastic, as shown by the curve D_e, the industry's output increases by a large amount to q_2. The quantity of the variable input demanded will then increase by a correspondingly large amount.

The supply of inputs

When we consider the supply of any input, we must consider the amount supplied to the economy as a whole, to each industry and occupation, and to each firm. The elasticity of supply of an input will normally be different at each of these levels of aggregation. We start with the highest level of aggregation—the total supply of each resource input to the economy as a whole.

The total supply of resources

At any one time the total quantity of inputs of each resource is given. For example, in each country the labour force is of a certain size, there is so much arable

land available, there is so much machinery installed in factories, and there is a given supply of discovered raw materials. However, these supplies can and do change in response to both economic and non-economic forces. Sometimes the change is very gradual, as when climatic changes slowly turn arable land into desert or when a medical discovery lowers the rate of infant mortality and hence increases the rate of population growth. Sometimes the changes can be quite rapid, as when the UK discovered oil in the North Sea, or when a boom in business activity brings retired people back into the labour force, or when a rise in the price of agricultural produce encourages the draining of marshes to add to the supply of arable land.

Total supply of capital

The supply of capital in a country consists of the stock of existing machines, factories, equipment, and so on. Capital is a manufactured input, and its total quantity is in no sense fixed, although it changes only slowly. Each year the stock of capital goods is diminished by the amount that becomes physically or economically obsolete and is increased by the amount that is newly produced. The difference between these is the net addition to, or net subtraction from, the capital stock. On balance, the trend has been for the capital stock to grow from decade to decade over the past few centuries. In Chapter 11 we will discuss the determinants of investment in capital.

Total supply of land

The total area of dry land in a country is almost completely fixed, but the supply of *fertile* land is not fixed. Considerable care and effort are required to sustain the productive capacity of land. If farmers earn low incomes, they may not provide the necessary care and the land's fertility may be destroyed within a short time. In contrast, high earnings from farming may provide the incentive to increase the supply of arable land by irrigation and other forms of reclamation.

Total supply of labour

The number of people willing to work is called the *labour force*; the total number of hours they are willing to work is called the **supply of effort** or, more simply, the **supply of labour**. The supply of effort depends on three influences: the size of the population, the proportion of the population willing to work, and the number of hours worked by each individual. Each of these is partly influenced by economic forces.

Population

Populations vary in size, and these variations are influenced to some extent by economic forces. For example, there is some evidence that the birth rate and the net immigration rate (immigration minus emigration) are higher in good times than in bad. However, much of the variation in population is explained by factors outside economics.

The labour force

The proportion of the total population, or of some subgroup such as men, women, or teenagers, that is willing to work is called that group's **labour force participation rate**. This rate varies in response to many influences. One non-economic influence is change in attitudes and tastes. The substantial rise in female participation rates in the second half of the twentieth century is a case in point. One economic influence is the change in the demand for labour.

This has two distinct effects. First, if it is accompanied by a rise in earnings, it will usually lead to an increase in the proportion of the population willing to work. More married women and elderly people are willing to be in the labour force when wages are high than when they are low. For the same reasons the labour force tends to decline when earnings and employment opportunities decline. The second reason is the availability of work. In this chapter we are assuming a competitive market for labour in which everyone who wishes to work can do so because if there is an imbalance between the supply of and the demand for labour, wage rates will change until an equilibrium is restored in the labour market. In practice, wages do not vary much cyclically and pools of unemployed labour accumulate during the downturns of the business cycle. Then what is called the *discouraged worker effect* occurs as many give up looking for jobs and so leave the labour force, only to re-enter it when the demand for labour rises during the upturns of the cycle.

Hours worked

Not only does the wage rate influence the number of people in the labour force (as we observed above), it is also a major determinant of hours worked. By giving up leisure in order to work, workers obtain the incomes they need to buy goods. Therefore they can be thought of as trading leisure for goods.

A rise in the wage rate implies a change in the relative prices of goods and leisure. Goods become cheaper relative to leisure, since each hour worked buys more goods than before. The other side of the same coin is that leisure becomes more expensive, since each hour of leisure consumed is at the cost of more goods forgone.

This change in relative prices has both the income and the substitution effects that we studied in Chapter 4. The substitution effect leads the individual to consume more of the relatively cheaper goods and *less* of the relatively more expensive leisure—that is, to trade more leisure for goods. However, the income effect leads the individual to consume more goods and *more* leisure, since the rise in the wage rate makes it possible for the individual to have more of both. For example, if the wage rate rises by 10 per cent and the individual works 5 per cent fewer hours, more leisure and more goods will be consumed.

Because the income and substitution effects work in the same direction for the consumption of goods, we can be sure that a rise in the wage rate will lead to a rise in income earned and goods consumed. However, because the two effects work in opposite directions for leisure:

A rise in the wage rate leads to less leisure being consumed (more hours worked) when the substitution effect is the dominant force and to more leisure being consumed (fewer hours worked) when the income effect is the dominant force.

Box 9.5 The supply of labour

The discussion in the text can be formalized using indifference curves. The key proposition is the following.

Because a change in the wage rate has an income effect and a substitution effect that pull in opposite directions, the supply curve of labour may have a positive or a negative slope

Part (i) of the figure plots leisure (in hours) on the horizontal axis and the consumption of goods (measured in pounds) on the vertical axis. The budget line always starts at 24, indicating that everyone is endowed with 24 hours a day that may be either consumed as leisure or traded for goods by working.

At the original wage rate the individual could obtain q_a of goods by working 24 hours (i.e. the hourly wage rate is $q_a/24$). Equilibrium is at E_0, where the individual consumes l_0 of leisure and works $24 - l_0$ hours in return for q_0 of goods.

The wage rate now rises, so that q_b becomes available if 24 hours are worked (i.e. the hourly wage rate is $q_b/24$). Equilibrium shifts to E_1. Consumption of leisure falls to l_1, and

the individual works $24 - l_1$ hours in return for a consumption of q_1 goods. The rise in wages increases the hours worked.

The hourly wage rate now rises further to $q_c/24$, and equilibrium shifts to E_2. Consumption of leisure rises to l_2, whereas $24 - l_2$ hours are worked in return for an increased consumption of q_2 goods. This time, therefore, the rise in the wage rate lowers the hours worked.

Part (ii) of the figure shows the same behaviour as in part (i), using a supply curve. It plots the number of hours worked against the wage rate. At wage rates of up to w_1 the individual is not in the labour force, since no work is offered. As the wage rate rises from w_1 to w_2, more and more hours are worked so the supply curve of effort has the normal positive slope. The wage rates that result in E_0 and E_1 in part (i) of the figure lie in this range. Above w_2 the quantity of effort falls as wages rise, so that the supply curve has a negative slope. This latter case is often referred to as a *backward-bending supply curve of labour*. The wage that gives rise to equilibrium E_2 in part (i) lies in this range.

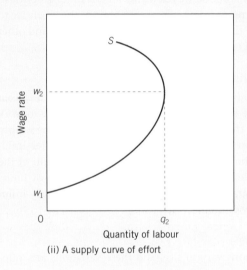

(i) Indifference curves

(ii) A supply curve of effort

Box 9.5 provides an optional analysis of these two cases using indifference curves.

The long-run evidence for high-income countries tends to show that as real hourly wage rates rise for the whole economy, people wish to reduce the number of hours worked.

The supply of inputs for a particular use

Most primary resources have many uses. A piece of land can be used to grow any one of several crops, or it can be subdivided for a housing development. A computer programmer in Oxford can work for one of several firms, for the government, or for the university. A lathe can be used

to make many different products, and it requires no adaptation when it is turned for one use or another. Plainly, it is easier for any one user to acquire more of a scarce resource than it is for all users to do so simultaneously.

One user of an input can bid resources away from another user, even though the total supply of that input may be fixed.

When we are considering the supply of an input for a particular use, the most important concept is *resource mobility*. An input that shifts easily between uses in response to small changes in incentives is said to be *mobile*. Its supply to any one of its uses will be elastic, because a small increase in the price offered will attract many units of the input from other uses. An input that does not shift easily from one use to another, even in response to large changes in remuneration, is said to be *immobile*. It will be in inelastic supply in any one of its uses, because even a large increase in the price offered will attract only a small inflow from other uses. Often a specific input may be immobile in the short run but mobile in the long run.

An important key to input mobility is time. The longer the time interval, the easier it is to convert an input from one use to another.

Consider the mobility between uses of each of the three key types of input.

Capital

Some kinds of capital equipment—lathes, lorries, and computers, for example—can be shifted easily between uses; many others are difficult to shift. A great deal of machinery is quite specific; once built, it must be used for the purpose for which it was designed, or it cannot be used at all. (It is the immobility of much fixed capital equipment that makes the exit of firms from declining industries a slow and difficult process.)

In the long run, however, capital is highly mobile. When capital goods wear out, a firm may simply replace them with identical goods, or it may exercise other options. It may buy a newly designed machine to produce the same goods, or it may buy machines to produce totally different goods. Such decisions lead to changes in the long-run allocation of a country's stock of capital between various uses.

Land

Land, which is physically the least mobile of inputs, is one of the most mobile in an economic sense. On agricultural land one crop can be harvested and a totally different crop can be planted. A farm on the outskirts of a growing city can be sold for a housing development at short notice—as long as planning permission is forthcoming. Once land is built on, its mobility is much reduced. A site on which a hotel has been built can be converted into a warehouse site, but it takes a large differential in the value of land use to make that transfer worthwhile because the hotel must be demolished.

Although land is highly mobile between alternative uses, it is completely immobile as far as location is concerned. There is only so much land within a given distance of the centre of any city, and no increase in the price paid can induce further land to be located within that distance. This locational immobility has important consequences, including high prices for desirable locations and the tendency to build tall buildings to economize on the use of scarce land, as in the centre of large cities.

Labour

Absentee landlords, while continuing to live in the place of their choice, can obtain income from land or buildings located in another part of the world. Physical capital needs to be present at the production site, but its owner need not be. However, when a worker who is employed by a firm that produces men's ties in York decides to supply labour service to a firm that produces women's shoes in Northampton, she must physically travel to Northampton.

While it is true that most people who work in manufacturing production have to attend their place of work each day, in many other cases, including many service occupations, labour services can be supplied at a distance and their product communicated to the purchaser by phone, various electronic means, couriers, or even post.

Because in both of these types of cases people who supply their services to firms have to do so under specific conditions, whether in a factory, office, or at home, the location and conditions under which they work matter to people in the way that the location and conditions under which production occurs does not directly affect the owners of land or capital.

Because the conditions under which people work matter to them, non-monetary considerations are much more important for the supply of labour than for other inputs.

People may be satisfied with, or frustrated by, the kind of work that they do, where they do it, the people with whom they do it, and the social status of their occupation. Since these considerations influence their decisions about what they will do with their labour services, they will not always move just because they could earn a higher wage.

Nevertheless, labour does move between industries, occupations, and areas in response to changes in the signals provided by wages and opportunities for employment. The ease with which movement occurs depends on many forces. For example, it is not difficult for a receptionist to shift from one company to another in order to take a job in Cheltenham instead of in Hull, but it can be difficult for a coalminer to become an editor, a model, a machinist, or a doctor within a short period of time. Workers who lack skills, training, or inclination find certain kinds of job moves to be difficult or impossible.

Some barriers to movement may be virtually insurmountable once a person's training has been completed. It may be impossible for a farmer to become a surgeon or for a lorry-driver to become a professional athlete, even if the relative wage rates change greatly. However, the *children* of farmers, doctors, lorry-drivers, and athletes, when they are deciding how much education or training to obtain, are not nearly as limited in their choices as their parents, who have already completed their education and are settled in their occupations.

In any year some people enter the labour force directly from school or further education, and others leave it through retirement or death. The turnover in the labour force owing to these causes is 3 or 4 per cent per year. Over a period of ten years the allocation of labour can change dramatically merely by directing new entrants to jobs other than the ones that were left vacant by workers who left the labour force.

The role of education in helping new entrants adapt to available jobs is important. In a society in which education is provided to all, it is possible to achieve large increases in the supply of any needed labour skill within a decade or so. These issues are discussed at greater length in the first part of Chapter 10.

The labour force as a whole is mobile, even though many individual members of it are not.

The supply of inputs to individual firms

Most firms usually employ a small proportion of the total supply of each input that they use. As a result they can usually obtain their inputs at the going market price. For example, a firm of accountants can usually augment its clerical staff by placing an advert in the local paper and paying the going rate for accounts clerks. In hiring just one more person, the firm will not affect the rate of pay earned by accounts clerks in its area. Similarly, most individual firms are price takers in markets for their inputs.

The operation of input markets

The determination of the price, quantity, and income of an input in a single perfectly competitive market poses no new problems. Figure 9.1 has already shown a competitive market for an input in which the intersection of the demand and supply curves determines the input's price and the quantity of it that is employed. As we saw at that time, the input's price times its quantity employed is its total income, and that amount divided by the total income earned by all resource owners in the economy represents that specific resource owner's share of the nation's total income. (We will study total national income and total national output (GDP) in some detail in later chapters.)

Reward differentials

If every worker were the same, if all benefits were monetary, and workers moved freely between markets, wage rates would tend to be the same in all jobs. Workers would move from low-priced to high-priced jobs. The quantity of labour supplied would diminish in occupations in which wages were low, and the resulting labour shortage would tend to force those wages up; the quantity of labour supplied would increase in occupations in which wages were high, and the resulting surplus would force wages down. The movement would continue until there were no further incentives to change occupations—that is, until wages were equalized in all uses.

As it is with labour, so it is with other types of input. If all units of capital or land were identical and moved freely between markets, all units would have the same market price in equilibrium.

In reality, of course, different units of any specific input type receive very different rewards. These differentials can be divided into two distinct types: those that exist only in disequilibrium situations, and those that persist in equilibrium.

Disequilibrium differentials lead to, and are eroded by, movements of inputs between alternative uses; equilibrium differentials are not eliminated by mobility.

Disequilibrium differentials

Some price or wage differentials reflect a temporary state of disequilibrium. They are brought about by circumstances such as the growth of one industry and the decline of another. The differentials themselves lead to reallocation of inputs, and such reallocations in turn act to eliminate the differentials, although this process may take a long time to accomplish fully.

Over the past few decades, the process of globalization—largely due to technological changes in transportation and communications—have created a global market for relatively unskilled labour. This has tended to raise wages in poorer countries where wages were extremely low, but to reduce wages in richer countries where wages, even for the unskilled, were relatively high. In so far as these low wages induce those in rich countries who would otherwise have remained unskilled to learn new skills that are in higher demand and pay higher wages, the very low wages in rich countries will have been disequilibrium wages. In so far as some cannot or will not learn the necessary skills, the low wages will persist and be equilibrium wages. In practice, the result will probably be some of both, with fewer unskilled workers but with those who remain unskilled earning lower wages than before globalization occurred. Whatever the final result, this process will take a long time to complete as younger people learn new skills and some unskilled older persons retire or otherwise leave the labour market.

The behaviour that causes the erosion of disequilibrium differentials is summarized in the assumption of the *maximization of net benefit*:[3] the owners of inputs will allocate them to uses that maximize the net benefit to themselves, taking both monetary and non-monetary rewards into consideration. If net benefits were higher in occupation A than in occupation B, inputs would move from B to A. The increased supply in A, and the lower supply in B, would drive earnings down in A and up in B until net benefits were equalized, after which no further movement would occur. This analysis gives rise to the prediction of *equal net benefit*:

In equilibrium, inputs will be allocated among alternative possible uses in such a way that the net benefits in all uses are equalized.

Although non-monetary benefits are important in explaining differences in levels of pay for labour in different occupations, they tend to be quite stable over time. As a result, monetary rewards, which vary with market conditions, lead to changes in *net benefits*.

A change in the relative price paid for the same inputs in any two activities will change the net benefits to the owner and create an incentive to shift some inputs into the activity in which relative rewards have increased.

This implies a positively sloped supply curve for an input in any particular use. When the price of an input rises in that use, more will be supplied to that use. This input supply curve (like all supply curves) can also *shift* in response to changes in other variables. For example, an improvement in the safety record in a particular occupation will shift the labour supply curve to that occupation.

Equilibrium differentials

Some price differentials persist in equilibrium without generating any forces that will eliminate them. These **equilibrium differentials** can be explained by intrinsic differences in the type and quality of inputs and, for labour, by differences in the cost of acquiring skills and by different non-monetary advantages of different occupations. These were first called *compensating differentials* by Adam Smith over two hundred years ago.

Intrinsic differences

If some inputs of the same general type have different specific characteristics, their market prices will differ. For example, if intelligence and dexterity are required to accomplish a task, intelligent and manually dextrous workers will earn more than less intelligent and less dextrous workers. If land is to be used for agricultural purposes, highly fertile land will command a higher rental value than poor land. These differences will persist even in long-run equilibrium.

Acquired differences

It takes time and money to acquire qualifications. If this did not lead to higher expected future earnings, there would be no incentive to invest the time and money. So those employers who wish to hire highly qualified people will have to pay sufficiently higher salaries to compensate for that investment. Obtaining an MBA, for example, can cost well over £60,000 in terms of fees and lost earnings. Few people would study for this qualification unless they thought it would sufficiently enhance their earnings prospects.

Non-monetary benefits

Whenever working conditions differ, workers will earn different equilibrium amounts in different occupations. The difference between a test pilot's wage and a chauffeur's wage is only partly a matter of skill; the rest is compensation to the worker for facing the higher risk of testing new planes compared with driving a car. If both were paid the same, there would be an excess supply of chauffeurs and a shortage of test pilots.

Academics commonly earn less than they could earn in the world of commerce and industry because of the substantial non-monetary advantages of academic employment, such as flexible working and long breaks from teaching, which can be devoted partly to research and partly to leisure. If chemists, for example, were paid the same in universities and industry, many chemists would prefer academic to industrial jobs. Excess demand for industrial chemists and excess supply of academic chemists would then force chemists' wages up in industry until the two types of job seemed equally attractive on balance.

The same forces account for equilibrium differences in regional earnings of otherwise identical workers.[4] People who work in remote logging or mining areas are paid

---

[3] This is just another form of 'utility' maximization and 'profit' maximization. Here, the pay-off is a mixture of financial reward and (especially in the case of labour) non-financial reward, such as status and job satisfaction.

[4] Many regional wage differences are disequilibrium phenomena where a wage in a declining industry is not yet sufficiently low to compensate for costs of moving.

more than people who do jobs requiring similar skills in large cities. Without higher pay, insufficient people would be willing to work at sometimes dangerous jobs in unattractive or remote locations.

Pay equity

The distinction between equilibrium and disequilibrium wage differentials raises an important consideration for policy. Trade unions, governments, and other bodies often have explicit policies about earnings differentials, sometimes seeking to eliminate them in the name of equity. The success of such policies depends to a great extent on the kind of differential that is being attacked. Policies that attempt to eliminate equilibrium differentials will encounter severe difficulties.

Some government legislation seeks to establish *equal pay for work of equal value*, or *pay equity*. These laws can work as intended whenever they remove pay differentials that are due to prejudice. However, they run into trouble whenever they require equal pay for jobs that have different non-monetary advantages.

To illustrate the problem, say that two jobs demand equal skills, training, and everything else that is taken into account when deciding what is work of equal value but

that, in a city with an extreme climate, one is an outside job and the other is an inside job. If some pay commission requires equal pay for both jobs, there will be a shortage of people who are willing to work outside and an excess of people who want to work inside. Employers will seek ways to attract outside workers. Higher pensions, shorter hours, longer holidays, overtime paid for but not worked, and better working conditions may be offered. If these are allowed, they will achieve the desired result but will defeat the original purpose of equalizing the monetary benefits of the inside and outside jobs. They will also cut down on the number of outside workers that employers will hire, since the total cost of an outside worker to an employer will have risen. If the authorities prevent such 'cheating', the shortage of workers for outside jobs will remain.

In Chapter 10 we discuss the effects of discrimination on wage differentials. Although discrimination is often important, it remains true that many wage differentials are a natural market consequence of supply and demand conditions that have nothing to do with inequitable treatment of different groups in society.

Policies that seek to eliminate wage differentials without considering what caused them or how they affect the supply of specific types of worker are likely to have perverse results.

Economic rent

Economic rent is one of the most important concepts in economics. The owner of an input must earn a certain amount in its present use to prevent it from moving that input to another use. This is called its **reservation price** (Alfred Marshall called it the input's *transfer earnings*). If there were no non-monetary advantages in alternative uses, the input's reservation price would equal what it could earn elsewhere (its opportunity cost). This usually holds for capital and land. However, labour gets non-monetary advantages that differ between jobs. It must earn enough in one use to equate the total benefits, monetary and non-monetary, of the two jobs.

Any excess that the owner of an input earns over its reservation price is called its **economic rent**. Economic rent is analogous to economic profit as a surplus over the opportunity cost of capital. The concept of economic rent is crucial in predicting the effects that changes in earnings have on the movement of inputs between alternative uses. However, the terminology of rent is confusing because economic rent is often called simply *rent*, which can of course also mean the full price paid to hire something, such as a house or a piece of land. How the same

term came to be used for these two different concepts is explained in Box 9.6.

How much of earnings is rent?

In most cases economic rent makes up part of the actual earnings. However, the distinction is most easily seen by examining two extreme cases. In one case all of earnings is rent; in the other none is rent.

The possibilities are illustrated in Figure 9.3. When the supply curve is perfectly inelastic (vertical), the same quantity is supplied whatever the price. Evidently, there is no minimum that the owners of this input need to be paid to keep it in its present use, since the quantity supplied does not decrease no matter how low the price goes. In this case the whole of the payment is economic rent. The price actually paid allocates the fixed supply to those who are most willing to pay for it.

When the supply curve is perfectly elastic (horizontal), none of the price paid is economic rent. If any lower price is offered, nothing whatsoever will be supplied. All units of the input will be transferred to some other use.

Box 9.6 Origin of the term 'economic rent'

In the early nineteenth century there was a public debate about the high price of wheat in England. The price was causing great hardship because bread was a major source of food for the working class. Some people argued that wheat had a high price because landlords were charging high rents to tenant farmers. In short, it was argued that the price of wheat was high because the rents of agricultural land were high. Some of those who held this view advocated restricting the rents that landlords could charge.

David Ricardo, a great British economist who was one of the originators of classical economics, argued that the situation was exactly the reverse. The price of wheat was high, he said, because there was a shortage, which was caused by the Napoleonic Wars. Because wheat was profitable to produce, there was keen competition among farmers to obtain land on which to grow wheat. This competition in turn forced up the rent of wheat land. Ricardo advocated removing the tariff so that imported wheat could come into the country, thereby increasing its supply and lowering both the price of wheat and the rent that could be charged for the land on which it was grown.

The essentials of Ricardo's argument were these. The supply of land was fixed. Land was regarded as having only one use, the growing of wheat. Nothing had to be paid to prevent land from transferring to a use other than growing wheat because it had no other use. No landowner would leave land idle as long as some return could be obtained by renting it out. Therefore, all the payment to land—that is, rent in the ordinary sense of the word—was a surplus over and above what was necessary to keep it in its present use.

Given a fixed supply of land, the price of land depended on the demand for land, which depended on the demand for wheat. *Rent*, the term for the payment for the use of land, thus became the term for a surplus payment to a resource owner over and above what is necessary to keep the resource in its present use.

Later two facts were realized. First, land often had alternative uses, and, from the point of view of any one use, part of the payment made to land would necessarily have to be paid to keep it in that use. Secondly, owners of resources other than land also often earned a surplus over and above what was necessary to keep them in their present use. For example, television stars and great athletes are in short and fairly fixed supply, and their potential earnings in other occupations are often quite moderate. However, because there is a huge demand for their services as television stars or athletes, they may receive payments greatly in excess of what is needed to keep them from transferring to other occupations. This surplus is now called *economic rent*, whether the factor is land, labour, or a piece of capital equipment.

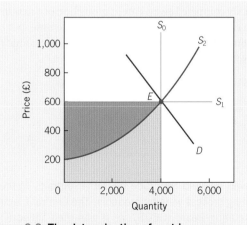

Figure 9.3 The determination of rent in resource owners' incomes

The amount of rent in earnings depends on the shape of the supply curve. A single demand curve is shown with three different supply curves. In each case the competitive equilibrium price is £600, and 4,000 units of the input are hired. The total payment (£2.4 million) is represented by the entire dark and light blue areas. When the supply curve is vertical (S_0), the whole payment is economic rent, because a decrease in price would not lead any units of the input to move elsewhere. When the supply curve is horizontal (S_1), none of the payment is rent, because even a small decrease in price offered would lead all units of the input to move elsewhere. When the supply curve is positively sloped (S_2), part of the payment is rent. Although the 4,000th unit is receiving just enough to persuade it to offer its services in this market, the 2,000th unit is earning well above what it requires to stay in this market. The aggregate of economic rents is shown by the dark blue area, and the aggregate of what each of the individual units must be paid to keep them in this market is shown by the light blue area.

The more usual situation is that of a gradually rising supply curve. A rise in the price paid for an input attracts more resources into the market in question, but the same rise provides additional economic rent to all units of the input that are already employed. We know that the extra pay that is going to the units already employed is economic rent because the owners of these units were willing to supply them at the lower price. The general result for a positively sloped supply curve is as follows.

If there is an upward shift in the demand for a specific input in some sector, its price will rise. This will attract additional inputs into that sector. It will also increase the economic rent going to all the owners of the inputs already employed in that sector.[5]

Determinants of the split

The proportion of earnings that is economic rent varies from situation to situation. We cannot point to owners of any specific resource and assert that some fixed fraction of their income is always economic rent. The proportion of their earnings that is rent depends on the alternatives that are available.

Consider first a narrowly defined use of a specific input, say the use of a worker by a particular firm. From that firm's point of view the worker will be highly mobile, since he or she could readily move to another firm in the same industry. The firm must pay the going wage or risk losing that worker. Thus, from the perspective of the *single firm* a large proportion of the payment made to a worker is needed to prevent him or her from transferring to another use.

Now consider a more broadly defined use—for example, the worker's use in an entire industry. From the industry's point of view the worker is less mobile, because it would be more difficult for him or her to gain employment quickly outside the industry. From the perspective of the particular *industry* (rather than the specific *firm* within the industry), a larger proportion of the payment to an input is economic rent.

From the even more general perspective of a particular *occupation*, mobility is likely to be less, and the proportion of earnings that is economic rent is likely to be more. The often controversial large salaries that are received by some highly specialized types of labour, such as superstar singers and professional athletes, illustrate these distinctions. These performers have a style or a talent that cannot be duplicated, whatever the training. The earnings that they receive are mostly economic rent from the viewpoint of the occupation; these performers enjoy their occupations and would pursue them for much less than the high remuneration that they actually receive. For example, Wayne Rooney would choose football over other alternatives even at a much lower salary than the £300,000 per week he was reported to be earning in 2014. However, because of Rooney's skills as a football player, most teams would pay handsomely to have him, and he is able to command a high salary from the team he does play for. From the perspective of the firm, Manchester United, most of Rooney's salary is required to keep him from switching to another team and hence is not economic rent. From the point of view of the 'football industry', however, much of his salary is economic rent. Similar arguments apply to top pop stars who may earn several million pounds from record sales and concerts but would earn much less in alternative occupations.

The notion of *rent seeking* is also commonly in use in the business world. Modern businesses are all trying to find products that give them some advantage over their rivals that generates economic profits and cannot be quickly competed away. Patent protection of a new invention can give such an advantage for some time, but reputation and brand loyalty may also create economic rents for some companies.

---

[5] In this context the term 'sector' can stand for occupation, industry, or geographical area.

CASE STUDIES

1. Electricity generation: substitution in practice

The principle of substitution has been important in the choice of fuels used to generate electricity, but it has not always worked in the same direction.

During the 1950s and 1960s increasing economies of scale in shipping crude oil from the Middle East to Western Europe made oil-based fuels more and more competitive. The relative price of fuels for industrial use fell by even more than the production cost of petrol, as it was the demand for petrol that was mainly responsible for the derived demand for crude oil. Other outputs of the oil-refining process were by-products. The Central Electricity Generating Board (CEGB), as it was then called (it has since been privatized as National Power and Powergen, and other electricity suppliers have entered the market), responded to the falling relative price of 'bunker' oil by building more and more oil-fired power stations and gradually closing down (or converting) the older coal-fired stations. From 85 per cent of electricity generated from coal and 11 per cent from oil in 1962, the CEGB steadily changed the 'mix' so that by 1971 it was generating about 65 per cent from coal and 25 per cent from oil.

Then came the 'oil shocks' of 1973 and 1979–80, when the OPEC countries dramatically raised the price of crude oil, leading to correspondingly dramatic increases in the prices of all oil products. Even though people in coal-mining saw an opportunity to raise coal prices substantially, the *relative* price of oil was significantly higher in the 1980s than it had been in the 1960s and early 1970s. The CEGB accordingly switched back to increasing reliance on coal-firing, generating around 80 per cent of its electricity from coal and only 5 per cent from oil in 1983.

Nevertheless, the electricity industry clearly retained the ability to switch back to oil rapidly if required. In 1984–5 a coal-miners' strike that lasted almost a whole year led to an amazing 41 per cent of electricity being generated from oil (with total output slightly higher than the previous year) and only 42 per cent from coal. After the strike, the figures quickly returned to their 1983 levels. However, the proportion of coal used declined in the late 1980s and 1990s owing to the growing use of natural gas and nuclear power (and environmental problems caused by the high sulphur content of British coal). By 2005 the percentages of fuels used in UK electricity generation were coal 29, nuclear 24, gas 38, oil 1, and others (including hydroelectric, wind, and imports) 8.[6] The latest figures available for 2013 show that coal had made something of a comeback in electricity generation at 35 per cent, while nuclear and gas had both declined significantly to 18.6 per cent and 28.5 per cent respectively. The biggest change though was a dramatic rise in the role of renewables at 15.5 percent, with only 2.4 per cent generated by all other fuels (including oil and imported electricity).The future composition of energy sources is highly uncertain. Natural gas supplies from the North Sea have a limited life and foreign suppliers of gas can be unreliable. Some want to build a new generation of nuclear power stations as these will generate electricity without adding to carbon emissions, while others are opposed to nuclear because of the long-term problems of waste disposal. Coal is abundant but carbon emissions are problematic. Energy prices have been very volatile in recent years, so it remains to be seen how energy production will actually evolve.

2. Employment in manufacturing

The UK used to be known as the 'workshop of the world'. The industrial revolution started in the United Kingdom and the British manufacturing sector used to be the largest source of both employment and output in the UK economy. In global terms, Britain was overtaken long ago as a centre for manufacturing, first by Germany, then the United States, and more recently by Japan and China (among others).

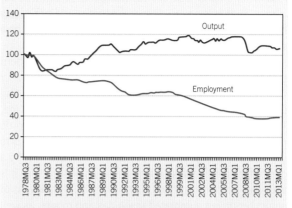

Figure 9.4 Index of UK manufacturing employment and output, 1978 Q2–2013 Q2

Source: UK National Statistics online database

Within the United Kingdom, employment in manufacturing has declined more or less continuously since the 1950s. Even in the past three decades or so, manufacturing employment has continued its decline from over 7 million jobs in the late 1970s to around 2.6 million in 2013. Many commentators have concluded that this is evidence of the terminal decline of manufacturing as an activity in the United Kingdom. However, the reality is not so simple.

It is certainly true that the share of world manufacturing made in United Kingdom has been in decline, but this decline started in the mid-1800s as other countries industrialized. It is also true that the share of manufacturing in UK GDP has been declining steadily since the Second World War, and that the share of employment in manufacturing continues to decline, as it has in most other developed industrialized countries. But a contrasting fact is that the volume of manufacturing output in the United Kingdom in 2000 Q4 was at an all-time high (see Figure 9.4 which shows an index of manufacturing output and employment with 1978 Q2 set to equal 100). That is to say that, despite its relative decline as a world player, despite the absolute fall in employment in manufacturing, and despite the relative growth of the service sector in the economy, UK manufacturing industry produced a greater volume of output in 2000 Q4 than in any previous quarter in its history.This all-time high was very close to being exceeded in the last quarter of 2007 and the first quarter of 2008, but the financial crisis struck and output fell sharply in the United Kingdom and throughout the industrial world. Thus, a key element of the UK manufacturing story is that the industry has achieved growing output over time with fewer and fewer employees. In effect, output per worker, or labour productivity, has been rising. A central

---

[6] The imported power is accessed by cable connections from France and the Republic of Ireland.

reason for this is that capital has been substituted for labour, so that many routine tasks that would previously have been performed by a line of assembly workers are now done by computerized machinery.

A major part of the story lies in the nature of modern technological change. For example, a mass production car factory in 1960 had a large number of workers operating dedicated and inflexible machinery on an assembly line. The modern car factory uses automated machines to do most of the things that these highly paid workers used to do. The paint is sprayed on at just the right moment by a computer-operated spraying machine. As with cars, so it is with many other manufacturing processes. The advent of computer-driven automated machines and robots, as well as the new method of lean production in which small groups of workers do multiple jobs has drastically reduced the labour requirement per unit of output. So output has risen while employment has fallen. (Since the freed-up labourers are available to do other jobs, the net effect is a rise in living standards as more is produced throughout the economy per unit of labour employed.)

Another part of the story is globalization. A UK-based manufacturer has to pay high real wages to UK workers, but can buy in ready-made parts or materials from other countries where wages are lower. Thus, a product that is finished in the UK may have inputs made by workers in many parts of the world.

A final part of the story relates to the restructuring of companies that has taken place since the 1980s. In the 1950s and 1960s a large manufacturing company would have groups of workers hired directly to provide virtually all of the services that it needed: catering, building mainte-nance, transport, etc. In the past two decades or so, firms have moved to focus mainly on their core activities and buy in other services needed from external firms. Thus, a large firm that has a canteen for its workers would previously have hired its own kitchen staff, but now it is most likely to have its catering provided by an external catering company. Before the change the same kitchen staff would have been classified as workers in manufacturing, but afterwards they became service sector workers in the catering industry.

Accordingly, some of the decline in manufacturing employment is due to restructuring that has changed the boundaries of the manufacturing sector, even though these services are still purchased by manufacturing firms. Some is due to the substitution of expensive domestic labour by cheaper foreign labour, and some is due to the direct sub-stitution of capital for labour in domestic production. All of these are processes that are being driven by the relative prices of inputs.

Conclusion

The key driving force of resource allocation in a market economy is that inputs are attracted into uses where they receive the highest rewards. In the case of capital and other non-human inputs the reward sought is typically financial. However, in the case of labour, financial rewards are only part of the story, as working conditions, job satisfaction, and other psychic benefits may also matter. Firms will demand inputs in relation to the value that those inputs add to output. Hence, inputs will tend to be drawn towards those industries in which they are most productive and for which output demand is highest—the demand for inputs is derived from the demand for the outputs that they help produce. Thus, there is a direct link from consumer demand for final products to demand for inputs and the rewards that the owners of those inputs receive.

SUMMARY

- The determination of prices in input markets depends on demand and supply, just as in markets for final goods and services.

- The distribution of income is determined in input markets.

- The income of owners of inputs depends on the price paid per unit of the input and the quantity used.

The demand for inputs

- The firm's decisions on how much to produce and how to produce it imply demands for inputs, which are derived from the demand for goods that they help to produce.

- A profit-maximizing firm equates an input's marginal cost to its marginal revenue product, which is its marginal physical product multiplied by the marginal revenue associated with the sale of another unit of output. When the firm is a price taker in input markets, the marginal cost of the input is its price per unit. When the firm sells its output in a competitive market, the marginal revenue product is the input's marginal physical product multiplied by the market price of the output.

A firm's demand for an input is negatively sloped in the long run because cheaper inputs will be substituted for dearer ones and a fall in an input's price leads to an increase in the output of the commodities it is used to make. It is negatively sloped in the short run because of the law of diminishing returns.

The industry's demand for an input will be more elastic: (a) the slower the marginal physical product of the input declines as more of it is used, (b) the easier it is to substitute one input for another, (c) the larger is the proportion of total variable costs accounted for by the cost of the input in question, and (d) the more elastic is the demand for the good that the input helps to make.

The supply of inputs

The total supply of land and capital is fixed at any moment but can vary over time. The total supply of labour varies with the size of the population, the participation rate, and hours worked. The latter two vary with the wage rate. A rise in the wage rate has a substitution effect which tends to induce more work, and an income effect which tends to induce less.

The supply of an input to a particular use is more elastic than its supply to the whole economy because one user can bid units away from other users. The elasticity of supply to a particular use depends on resource mobility, which tends to be greater the longer the time allowed for a reaction to take place.

The operation of input markets

Disequilibrium price differentials induce resource movements that eventually remove the differentials. Equilibrium differentials persist indefinitely.

Whenever the supply curve is positively sloped, part of the total return going to owners of a resource is needed to prevent them from transferring it to another use, and the rest is economic rent. The proportion of each depends on the potential mobility of the resource.

TOPICS FOR REVIEW

- Distribution theory
- Derived demand
- Marginal physical product
- Marginal revenue product

- Input mobility between alternative uses
- Disequilibrium and equilibrium differentials
- Equal net benefit
- Economic rent.

QUESTIONS

1 A firm making lawnmowers has an existing factory and machinery but it can vary the number of workers it hires. The following are data for total numbers of lawnmowers produced per week when hiring between 7 and 16 workers.

Workers per week	Lawnmowers produced per week
7	99
8	110
9	120
10	129
11	137
12	144
13	150
14	155
15	159
16	162

a) Calculate the marginal physical product of worker numbers 8 to 16.

b) Calculate the marginal revenue product of each worker if the lawnmowers can all be sold at £100.

c) How many workers will this firm wish to hire if it is profit-maximizing and the going wage is £500 per week?

2 Suppose that the firm has the same production relationships as in Question 1 but it faces a downward-sloping demand curve for lawnmowers. The demand curve is $P = 400 - 1Q$, (so the marginal revenue curve is $MR = 400 - 2Q$), where Q is the output of lawnmowers per week. If workers can again be hired at £500 per week, how many workers will be hired?

3 If the firm were faced with an upward-sloping supply curve of labour: $W = 300 + 20M$, where W is the wage per week and M is the number of men hired per week, and the demand conditions in Question 2 obtain, how many men will be hired?

4 A profit-maximizing firm which has a given capital stock has to decide how many workers to hire per week in the range of 128–133. The weekly wage that has to be paid to every additional worker is constant at £1,000 and the total revenue per week received after hiring the numbers of possible workers is as follows.

Workers	128	129	130	131	132	133
Total revenue	£160,150	£161,300	£162,400	£163,450	£164,400	£165,200

How many workers will be hired?

a) 129
b) 130
c) 131
d) 132
e) 133

5 A profit-maximizing firm which has a given capital stock has to decide how many workers to hire per week in the range of 8–13. The weekly wage that has to be paid to every worker is constant at £1,500 and the total revenue per week received after hiring the numbers of possible workers is as follows.

Worker	8	9	10	11	12	13
Total revenue	£16,000	£18,000	£19,800	£21,400	£22,800	£24,000

How many workers will be hired?

a) 9
b) 10
c) 12
d) 11
e) 13

6 Explain how demand for inputs is linked to the demand for the final outputs that those inputs help produce.

7 What determines the elasticity of demand for an input in one specific use and in general use?

8 Is the high price of hotel rooms in central London determined by high demand or by the scarcity of land on which hotels can be built (or something else)?

9 Rank the following occupations in terms of the likely proportion of rent (compared with transfer earnings) in typical earnings: pop stars, professional footballers, taxi drivers, computer consultants, university teachers, shop assistants, doctors.

10 What are the implications for input markets of rising demand for the following products: mobile phones, cheap flights, organic vegetables?

CHAPTER 10

THE LABOUR MARKET

Labour markets, which include all markets in which people sell their services, both mental and physical, are the most important markets for most people as this is where they find employment and earn their living. We refer to everyone who sells services in labour markets, be they carpenters, bank clerks, or university professors, as 'workers' or 'labourers', and we refer to the pay that they receive as 'wages' whether in the form of a weekly wage, a monthly salary, or bonuses and other forms of remuneration. Can labour markets be analysed just like any other market? How do we explain wide differences in pay among different occupations? How do potential employers select employees when their quality is uncertain? What incentives are there for workers to perform once in the job? These are some of the questions we address in this chapter.

In particular, you will learn that:

- Some long-lasting wage differentials arise from differences in skills and educational attainments; some arise for differences in age and sex.

- Some wage differentials arise from the type of market in which labour is sold; different wages are likely to be produced by competitive markets, where there are many buyers and sellers, monopoly markets in which unions control the supply, and markets in which there are so few employers that each has power to influence the outcome.

- The full set of characteristics of many of today's workers is hard to ascertain in advance, so labour market practices evolve to cope with information that is *imperfect,* in the sense that neither side in the labour–management bargaining process knows everything that is relevant, and with information that is *asymmetric* in the sense that one side may know more than the other.

- To deal with such issues, selection and management procedures often evolve to provide effective monitoring and incentive mechanisms.

- Workers are often paid what are called 'efficiency wages', which are wages above the minimum that would be required to hire a worker as they contain an incentive for the employee to perform well.

- Internal labour markets within firms are like tournaments in which employees compete for promotion to more senior and better-paid jobs.

The first part of the chapter is devoted to explaining wage differentials among different types of labour. These are due partly to different skills and educational attainments, partly to age and sex, and partly to the type of market in which labour services are supplied. Workers can improve upon free-market outcomes if they are organized as a single seller dealing with a large number of buyers, but they may do worse when unorganized and selling to a single buyer.

In the first part of this chapter we assume that wages are set in competitive markets. These markets clear, in the sense that neither excess demand nor excess supply persists. Theories that use this assumption can explain quite a bit about the forces that create wage differentials in the real world, because competitive markets where neither buyers nor sellers can significantly influence the price are more common in input markets than in final output markets.

But they are not the whole story since they treat labour as a homogeneous commodity, which is far from the truth.

People are heterogeneous in both their physical and mental capacities. When goods are being produced with physical labour, it is usually fairly easy to monitor the output of individual workers and discipline those who shirk on the job. Today, however, more and more employees are hired for their brain rather than their brawn and it is much more difficult to determine the contributions of such employees to the firm's success. This is partly because the employees' outputs are intangible and partly because they are members of a team in which individual contributions are hard to separate from those of the whole group. In such cases, the motives of the employee matter, especially when they do not coincide with the objectives of the firm to maximize its profits. In the final part of this chapter, we study the many institutions and practices that have evolved to deal with these modern labour-market problems.

Wage differentials

We noted in the previous chapter that if labour were homogeneous, jobs all had the same non-financial characteristics, and labour markets were perfectly competitive, every person would earn the same income in equilibrium. Disequilibrium differentials in wages would arise whenever demand or supply curves shifted. However, workers would then move from the lower-wage to the higher-wage jobs until the differentials had disappeared. In reality, some workers continue to receive low rates of pay, others receive modest but higher wages, while yet others are paid very high wages (or salaries). These are equilibrium differentials that persist if after all markets had reached equilibrium. For full-time employees who work a standard week and have no income from assets, rates of pay translate into incomes.

- *Incomes vary with the type of job.* Cleaners and casual staff in fast-food restaurants earn less than electricians and IT support staff.

- *Incomes vary with education.* Average earnings of people with university degrees exceed the average earnings of those with only A-levels, which in turn exceed the average earnings of those with only GCSEs, which exceed the average earnings of those with no qualifications at all.

- *Incomes vary with age.* Average earnings tend to rise until a person's mid-forties and fall thereafter (though this pattern varies with occupation).

- *Incomes vary with years on the job.* Generally, the longer one stays with one firm or organization, the higher the income one earns.

- *Incomes vary with sex and race.* On average, men earn more than women, and members of some minority ethnic groups earn less than members of majority groups—even when differences in education and experience are allowed for.

- *Incomes vary with the type of market in which labour sells its services.* Workers who sell their labour in markets dominated by unions often earn more than similar people who sell their labour in more competitive markets.

Box 10.1 discusses the very topical issue of reward differentials. The real incomes of many average workers fell in the five years after the 2007–8 crisis while the real earnings of the very highest paid rose substantially. We return to this issue in two case studies near the end of this chapter.

We now discuss some of the major causes of equilibrium differentials in the earnings of various types of labour.

Differentials due to basic differences: non-competing groups

More highly skilled jobs pay better wages than less highly skilled jobs. Why does a movement from the latter to the former not erode these differentials?

One obvious answer lies in human differences that are either innate or acquired so early in life as to be beyond each individual's personal control. Some people are brighter than others; some are more athletic; some are blessed with a good singing voice; others are better endowed with manual skills. People might be separated by their natural endowments of intelligence, skills, and abilities into separate groups among which no movement was possible. We would then have many *non-competing groups*. They would be selling their services in a number of *segmented labour markets*.

Figure 10.1 shows that wage differentials between any two non-competing groups arise from the positions of both the demand and the supply curves. One group will earn higher incomes than another only if its supply is low *relative to the demand for it.* It is not good enough to have a rare skill; that skill must be rare in relation to the demand for it.

Over time, wage differentials change. On the demand side, economic growth constantly alters the derived demands for many specific groups of labour, creating new differentials and eroding old ones. On the supply side, there may be exogenous shifts. For example, a new group of immigrants may alter the mix of skills available in the local market. Furthermore, human differences notwithstanding, substantial mobility among groups does

Box 10.1 Top pay rockets away

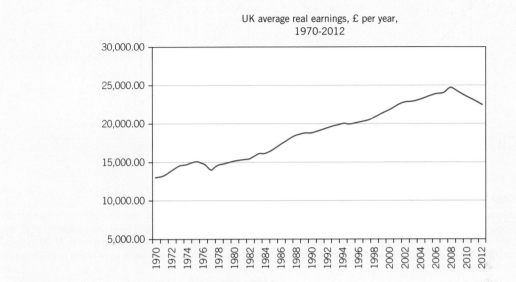

UK average real earnings, £ per year,
1970-2012

UK average real earninings, £ per year, 1970–2012

Source: Office of National Statistics

UK average real earnings grew from about £15,000 per year in 1975 to £25,000 per year in 2008 (all measured in constant 2012 prices) but then they fell for at least four years in a row. Thus the average worker was no better off in real terms in 2012 that he or she had been in 2002. The plight of the poorest workers was even worse in the United States where the 20 per cent of workers on lowest pay were no better off in 2012 than they had been 1970, while over the same period the real pay of the best paid 5 per cent had more than doubled in real terms. This is telling us two important things. First, in recent decades the earnings of ordinary workers have grown very slowly, if at all, in real terms in a number of countries. Secondly, pay of the very highest paid has risen substantially. Here are the conclusions of a recent study of top pay around the world.

We obtain three main empirical results. First, most countries experienced a sharp drop in top income shares in the first half of the twentieth century. In these countries, the fall in top income shares is often concentrated around key episodes such as the World Wars or the Great Depression …

[Second] In the second half of the twentieth century, top percentile shares experienced a U-shape pattern, with further declines during the immediate postwar decades followed by increases in recent decades. However, the degree of the U-shape varies dramatically across countries. In all *of the Western English speaking countries (in Europe, North America, and Australia and New Zealand), and in China and India, there was a substantial increase in top income shares in recent decades, with the United States leading the way both in terms of timing and magnitude of the increase. Southern European countries and Nordic countries in Europe also experience an increase in top percentile shares although less in magnitude than in English speaking countries. In contrast, Continental European countries (France, Germany, Netherlands, Switzerland) and Japan experience a very flat U-shape with either no or modest increases in top income shares in recent decades.*

Third, as was the case for the decline in the first half of the century, the increase in top income shares in recent decades has been quite concentrated with most of the gains accruing to the top percentile with much more modest gains (or even none at all) for the next 4 per cent … However, in most countries, a significant portion of the gains are due to an increase in top labor incomes, and especially wages and salaries. As a result, the fraction of labor income in the top percentile is much higher today in most countries than earlier in the twentieth century.

(Anthony B. Atkinson, Thomas Piketty, and Emmanuel Saez, 'Top incomes in the long run of history', *Journal of Economic Literature*, **49**(1), 3–71, 2011.

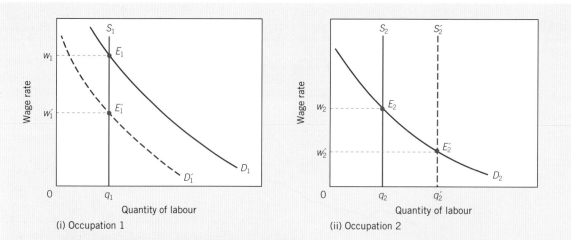

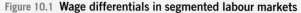

Figure 10.1 Wage differentials in segmented labour markets

When labour cannot move from one market to another, wage differentials of any size can persist. Because of basic differences in abilities the supply of labour is fixed at q_1 in occupation 1 and at q_2 in occupation 2. Demand and supply curves intersect at E_1 and E_2 to produce the high wage of w_1 in occupation 1 and the low wage of w_2 in occupation 2. A fall in demand from D_1 to D_1' in occupation 1 takes equilibrium to E_1', lowering its wage to w_1'. A rise in supply in occupation 2, to q_2', takes equilibrium to E_2', lowering its wage to w_2'.

occur—particularly in the long run, when older people with specific skills leave the labour force and young people with different skills enter.

Nonetheless, one lesson from the simple theory of non-competing groups is important.

Some income differentials arise because basic human characteristics cause the supplies of some types of labour to remain low relative to the demand for them, even in the long run.

Differentials due to human capital

The key to mobility among occupations is education. Many skills are learned rather than inherited. These can be thought of as a stock of human capital acquired by each worker.

A machine is physical capital. It requires an investment of time and money to create it, and, once built, it yields valuable services over a long period. In the same way, the acquisition of labour skills requires an investment of time and money, and, once acquired, these skills yield an increased income to their owner over a long period. Since investment in labour skills is similar to investment in physical capital, acquired skills are called **human capital**.

Because acquiring human capital is costly, the more highly skilled the job, the more it must pay if enough people are to be attracted to train for it.

The stock of skills acquired by individual workers is called human capital; investment in this capital is usually costly, and the return is higher labour productivity and hence higher earning power.

The two main ways in which human capital is acquired are through formal education and on-the-job training.

Formal education

Compulsory education provides some minimum human capital for all citizens. Some people, either through luck in the school they attend or through their own efforts, profit more from their early education than do others. Those who decide to stay in school beyond the years of compulsory education are deciding to invest voluntarily in acquiring further human capital.

Costs and benefits

The cost of further education is the income that could have been earned if the person had entered the labour force immediately after compulsory education, plus any out-of-pocket costs for such things as fees and equipment, minus any student grant or scholarship. The return is the difference between the income that would have been earned if one had left school and the income that is earned as a result of going on to higher education. (There is also a consumption return whenever higher education is something that students enjoy more than work.) These costs and benefits are analysed in Figure 10.2.

Changes in costs and benefits

If the demand for labour with low amounts of human capital falls, as it has in recent times, the earnings of such people will fall. This will lower the opportunity

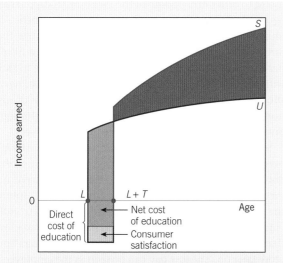
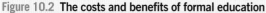

Figure 10.2 The costs and benefits of formal education

Acquiring human capital through formal education beyond minimum school-leaving age implies costs now and benefits later. Age is plotted on the horizontal axis and income earned on the vertical axis. Income is zero until age L, which is the minimum school-leaving age. After that the pink line U shows the income of a typical person who leaves school at age L and takes the relatively unskilled job for which his or her human capital is suitable. The blue line S shows the more complicated stream of payments and income receipts of someone who stays on for T years of formal training after age L. At first receipts are negative, reflecting the net out-of-pocket expenses related to attending school and university. Deducting the consumption value placed on being at school rather than at work (light pink area) yields the net cost associated with being in school. Adding this to the income that could have been earned by going directly into the labour force at age L yields the total cost of the education, which is the medium pink area. The benefit is shown by the dark pink area, representing the difference between the income earned in the skilled job that is acquired at year L + T (line S) and the income that would have been earned if the labour force had been entered at age L (line U). The investment in human capital could not possibly be worthwhile unless the dark pink benefit area exceeded the medium pink cost area. The net benefit to a particular individual depends on how much he or she discounts the more distant gain in order to compare it with the more immediate costs.

costs of staying on in school, since the earnings forgone by not going to work are reduced. A rise in unemployment will also lower the costs, because the probability of earning a steady income will be reduced, and this will reduce the expected loss from not entering the labour force early. If the demand for labour with high human capital rises, the earnings of such labour will rise. This will raise the expected return to those currently deciding whether or not to make the investment themselves.

Individual decisions

For any *given* state of these incentives, why do some people decide to acquire human capital while others do not?

First, there are differences among individuals. For reasons related to inherited abilities or early educational experience, some people at the age of eighteen correctly decide that they have a low chance of profiting from further formal education. For them, the return from such education is lower than for others who have the necessary aptitudes and inclination.

Secondly, some people have special talents for types of work that do not require further human capital. For them, the cost of acquiring more human capital is higher than it is for others; the earnings they would forgo by not entering the labour force are higher than the earnings that would be forgone by the average school-leaver. Obvious examples are pop singers and professional football players—Sir Mick Jagger did not suffer any loss of income by quitting his economics degree at the LSE and joining the Rolling Stones!

Thirdly, different people have different time-preferences. The cost of acquiring human capital is forgone income *now*, and the return is a *probability* of higher income *later*. Tastes differ. Some people put a high value on income now and are not willing to pay the cost of postponing it. Others place a higher value on income to be earned later in life and are willing to have less now in return for the chance of much more later on.

Fourthly, different people put different values on the consumption aspects of education. Those who enjoy the experience find the costs of acquiring human capital lower than those who do not. Those who would prefer to be at work rather than at school or university find the cost *increased* by the negative value they place on the educational experience.

Market forces adjust the overall costs and benefits of acquiring human capital, while individuals respond according to their varying personal evaluation of these costs and the benefits.

In the long run, decisions to acquire human capital help to erode disequilibrium differentials in incomes. Market signals change the costs and benefits of acquiring human capital in specific forms, such as skill in electronics, accountancy, law, or medicine. By reacting to these signals, young people increase the supply of high-income workers and reduce the supplies of low-income workers, thus eroding existing disequilibrium differentials. However, there are others forces, which we discuss later, that have increased differentials between the pay of high-skilled and low-skilled workers.

Another problem arises because it takes years for signals that some types of human capital are in high demand for the supply side to react. Students entering college may hear that these skills are in high demand and set about acquiring them. If they are lucky, the high demand will still be present some years later when they enter the labour market. But if they are unlucky, the demand may have diminished before they enter.

On-the-job education

Wage differentials according to age are readily observable in most firms and occupations. To a significant extent these differentials are a response to human capital acquired on the job. This type of human capital falls into two types.

Firm-specific human capital

Three examples of firm-specific information are the way in which the firm makes its decisions, how the firm's various departments interact, and how customer complaints are dealt with. As employees acquire familiarity with such internal workings of one firm, they become more valuable to that firm. But this knowledge is not of value to other firms; workers who move to similar jobs with other firms will have to learn the new firm-specific characteristics of their working environment from scratch.

Firms do not want to lose long-term employees with large amounts of firm-specific human capital since other employees will then have to be trained. But, being firm-specific, the capital is of no value to other firms. So if the firm pays its employees a wage that reflects the productivity conferred by this capital, they will have an incentive to stay in the job rather than to move to another firm where their value would initially be much less.

General human capital

If a firm trains a clerical assistant through various ranks up to becoming the PA of the managing director, able to run her office efficiently, the PA's skills will be potentially useful to other firms. Some of the PA's human capital can be acquired only through on-the-job training; hence it must be acquired within the firm. However, unlike the firm-specific capital, a PA who is paid the value of his or her marginal product has no monetary incentive to stay with the firm that taught these transferable skills, as he or she could earn the same elsewhere. The same is true of any non-firm-specific human capital acquired through on-the-job experience by any of the firm's employees.

So why would firms invest in training employees if this investment on human capital is free to walk out of the door and move to another employer? Firms have no incentive to provide training when they cannot capture the benefits themselves; rather, the benefit accrues to individual employees. One solution is to pay each worker less than his or her marginal product in the early years and more later on. The low pay can be seen as the employees' payment to the firm for helping them to acquire marketable human capital. The high pay later in life is partly a return on that capital, and partly an inducement to stay with the firm.

Human capital acquired through on-the-job experience provides a reason why earnings rise with the length of time spent with a firm. Firms tend to pay employees the value of their current marginal products for firm-specific capital, but for general human capital they pay less than the marginal products early in life and more later in life.

Box 10.2 discusses some other ways in which a firm can have a longer-term grip on the capital embodied in its employees, and some in which it cannot.

Box 10.2 The rental and purchase price of labour

If you wish to farm a piece of land, you can buy it yourself, or you can rent it for a specific period of time. If you want to set up a small business, you can buy your office and equipment, or you can rent them. The same is true for all capital and all land; a firm often has the option of either buying or renting.

Exactly the same would be true for labour if we lived in a slave society. You could buy a slave to be your assistant, or you could rent the services of either someone else's slave or a free person. Fortunately, slavery is illegal throughout most of today's world. As a result, the labour markets that we know deals only in the services of labour; we do not go to a labour market to buy a worker, only to hire his or her services.

However, you can buy the services of a worker for a long period of time. In professional sports, multi-year contracts are common, and ten-year contracts are not unknown. For example, football clubs pay a transfer fee to buy a player if he is still contracted to another club, so long as all parties agree. Publishers sometimes tie up their authors in multi-book contracts, and film and television production firms often sign up their actors on long-term contracts. In all cases of such *personal service contracts*, the person is not a slave, because his or her personal rights and liberties are protected by law. Nonetheless, the purchaser of the long-term contract is buying ownership of the person's services for an extended period of time. The price of the contract will reflect the person's expected earnings over the contract's lifetime. If the contract is transferable, the owner can sell these services for a lump sum or rent them out for some period. As with land and capital goods, the price paid for this *stock* of labour services depends on the expected rental prices over the contract period.

Another reason why rewards tend to rise with length of service is that competition tends to be strongest at the initial point of entry into the firm and to weaken thereafter, when promotions to more senior posts typically go to internal candidates (see the discussion of *internal labour* markets below). This will tend to hold wages down to competitive levels at entry points but allow them to rise above those levels for employees in more senior posts and with years of experience. This pattern does not always hold of course—in universities, for example, new faculty members are often paid more than those who have been in place for some time. This is because the university is trying to recruit the brightest and best on the market and has to pay high rates to attract them, while the existing staff have some job security (so cannot easily be fired) but might not be the strongest candidates if applying for a new job in the current market conditions.

Market solutions

The previous discussion illustrates the subtlety of market solutions to the issues posed by the human capital acquired through on-the-job experience. What may look arbitrary, or unfair, to the casual observer is often a rational response that has evolved to handle some aspect of the employment relationship—such as the fact that on-the-job training creates capital that is sometimes firm-specific and sometimes transferable, but in all cases is embodied in the employee rather than the firm itself.

To illustrate the importance of these insights, consider two jobs with equal initial requirements for being hired. One of these jobs provides on-the-job training that is mainly firm-specific, and the wage follows the time path of the employee's evolving marginal product fairly closely. The second job provides training that builds up transferable skills, and the wage paid is less than the marginal product for younger employees and greater for older ones. Now assume that government policy-makers become worried about the discrimination among workers in different jobs and introduce legislation requiring equal pay for 'work of equal value'. Both types of employee must now be paid the value of their marginal products. Firms then become reluctant to invest in training their employees to acquire transferable human capital, because it is now illegal to use a time pattern of wages that allows the firm to recover the cost of providing this capital. However fair it may appear to some, this government policy, designed to enhance equity, may not be in the interests of the workers affected by it.

Differentials due to sex and race

Aggregate statistics show that incomes vary by race and sex. More detailed studies suggest that much of these differences can be explained by such influences as amount of human capital acquired through both formal education and on-the-job experience. When these influences are taken into account, however, a core of difference remains that is consistent with discrimination based on race and sex. This is further discussed with respect to male–female earnings differentials in Box 10.3.

Some forms of discrimination make it difficult, or impossible, for particular groups to take certain jobs, even if skill and education equip them for these jobs. Until fairly recently, non-whites and women found many occupations closed to them. Even today, when overt discrimination is illegal, many feel that more subtle forms of discrimination are applied.

To the extent that such discrimination occurs, it reduces the supply of labour in the exclusive jobs—by keeping out the groups who are discriminated against. It also increases the supply in non-exclusive jobs, which are the only ones open to the groups subject to discrimination. This raises the wages in the exclusive jobs and lowers them in the non-exclusive jobs. Since discrimination prevents movement from the lower- to the higher-wage jobs, the resulting wage differences are equilibrium, not disequilibrium, differentials.

A model of labour market discrimination

To isolate the effects of discrimination, we begin by considering a non-discriminating labour market. We then introduce discrimination between two groups of equally qualified workers, group X and group Y. The analysis applies to workers who are distinguished on any grounds other than their ability, such as female and male, black and white, alien and citizen, Catholic and Protestant.

Suppose that, except for the fact that half of the people are marked with X and the other half are marked with Y, the groups are the same. Each has the same number of members, the same proportion who are educated to various levels, identical distributions of talent, and so on. Suppose also that there are two occupations. Occupation E (for elite) requires people of above-average education and skills, and occupation O (ordinary) can use anyone. If wages in the two occupations are the same, employers in occupation O will prefer to hire the above-average worker. Finally, suppose that the non-monetary advantages of the two occupations are equal.

In the absence of discrimination the wages in E occupations will be bid up above those in O occupations in order that the E jobs attract the workers of above-average skills. Both Xs and Ys of above-average skill will take the E jobs, while the others, both Xs and Ys, will have no choice but to seek O jobs. Because skills are equally distributed, each occupation will employ one-half Xs and one-half Ys.

Now discrimination enters in an extreme form. All E occupations are hereafter open only to Xs; all O

Box 10.3 Why are women paid less than men?

The figure shows the percentage gap between male and female median hourly earnings (excluding overtime) in the United Kingdom from 1997 to 2012[1]. The gap for all workers has narrowed from around 28 per cent to 20 per cent over this period. Among full-time workers the gap is smaller at just under 10 per cent in 2012, though part-time women workers are better paid than men. However, part-time wage rates are lower than full-time rates and more women work part-time than do men, which explains why the gender pay gap is greater for all types of work than for full-time work alone.

Wage discrimination can affect women (or any other group that is discriminated against) in at least two ways. They may earn less than men when doing the same job, or they may be forced into jobs that typically pay lower wages than the jobs from which they are excluded. Non-discriminatory wage differentials arise when men and women differ on average in relevant labour market characteristics. For example, men and women differ significantly in their average educational qualifications and their labour-market experience, with women typically spending somewhere between five and ten years out of the labour market raising children.

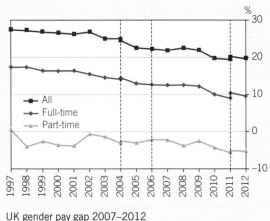

UK gender pay gap 2007–2012

Source: Office of National Statistics

Across the whole economy, the average pay of women is less than that of men. This has been known since at least the 1880s, when reliable records started. Indeed, at the Trades Union Congress of 1888 a motion was passed stating that where men and women do the same jobs they should get the same pay. However, it was 1970 before the Equal Pay Act finally legislated that pay must be the same 'for broadly similar work'.

Since 1975, when the Equal Pay Act came into effect, the pay gap has closed considerably. It continues to narrow on recent trends but a gap remains. Research published by the government in December 2001 (*The Gender Pay Gap*) authoritatively identifies the key drivers behind the gender pay gap.

It finds that the reasons for the pay gap are complex and interconnected.[2]

Key factors include:

- *Human capital differences:* i.e. differences in educational levels and work experience. Historical differences in the levels of qualifications held by men and women have contributed to the pay gap. However, women are still more likely than men to have breaks from paid work to care for children and other dependants. These breaks impact on women's level of work experience, which in turn impacts on their pay rates.

- *Part-time working:* the pay gap between men and women's part time hourly earnings and men's full-time hourly earnings is particularly large and, because so many women work part-time, this is a major contributor to the gender pay gap. Some of this gap is due to part-time workers having lower levels of qualifications and less work experience. However, it is also due to part-time work being concentrated in less well-paid occupations.

- *Travel patterns:* on average, women spend less time commuting than men. This may be because of time constraints due to balancing work and caring responsibilities. This can impact on women's pay in two ways: smaller pool of jobs to choose from and/or lots of women wanting work in the same location (i.e. near to where they live) leading to lower wages for those jobs.

- *Occupational segregation:* women's employment is highly concentrated in certain occupations (60 per cent of working women work in just 10 occupations). And those occupations which are female-dominated are often the lowest paid. In addition, women are still under-represented in the higher paid jobs within occupations—the 'glass ceiling' effect.

- *Workplace segregation:* at the level of individual workplaces, high concentrations of female employees are associated with relatively low rates of pay. And higher levels of part-time working are associated with lower rates of pay, even after other factors have been taken into account.

On a narrow interpretation the pay differentials linked to different labour market experiences are a reflection of the resulting lower marginal products. On a wider view of

---

[1] *Note*: The vertical dotted lines in the figure indicate changes in the sample used for the calculation.

[2] See <http://www.womenandequalityunit.gov.uk/pay/pay_facts.htm>

(*continued*)

Box 10.3 *continued*

discrimination, however, these different experiences are merely convenient excuses for paying women less. This wider view is given some plausibility by the fact that in Sweden, the most egalitarian country in Europe, female earnings average over 90 per cent of male earnings.

It is harder to estimate the effects of discrimination that excludes women from certain jobs and crowds them into others. However, studies suggest that if the discrimination in type of employment were eliminated, wages in occupations that are currently dominated by females

would rise by as much as 50 per cent! In contrast, wages in male-dominated jobs would fall by only a few percentage points.

Broadly, the evidence does suggest two things. First, there is almost certainly some discrimination against women remaining in labour markets today. Secondly, we have to be very careful in interpreting the raw data. The measured average differentials have to be adjusted for labour-force characteristics in order to identify any residual that is due to discrimination.

occupations are hereafter open to either Xs or Ys. The immediate effect is to reduce by 50 per cent the supply of job candidates for E occupations; candidates must now be *both* Xs and above average. The discrimination also increases the supply of applicants for O jobs by 50 per cent; this group now includes all Ys and the below-average Xs.

Wage-level effects

As shown in Figure 10.3 wages now rise in E occupations and fall in O occupations.

Discrimination, by changing supply, can decrease the wages and incomes of a group that is discriminated against.

In the longer run, further changes may occur. Notice that total employment in the E industries falls. Employers may find ways to utilize slightly below-average labour and thus lure the next best qualified Xs out of O occupations. Although this will raise O wages slightly, it will also make these occupations increasingly 'Y occupations'. If discrimination has been in effect for a sufficient length of time, Ys will learn that it does not pay to acquire above-average skills. Regardless of ability, Ys are forced by discrimination to work in unskilled jobs.

Now suppose that a long-standing discriminatory policy is reversed. Because they will have responded to discrimination by acquiring fewer skills than Xs, many Ys will be locked into the O occupations, at least for a time.

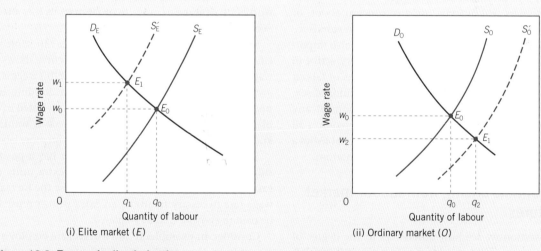

(i) Elite market (E)   (ii) Ordinary market (O)

Figure 10.3 Economic discrimination

If market E discriminates against one group and market O does not, the supply curve will shift to the left in E and to the right in O. Market E requires above-average skills, while market O requires only ordinary skills. When there is no discrimination, demands and supplies are D_E and S_E in market E, and D_O and S_O in market O. Initially the wage rate is w_0 and employment is q_0 in each market. (The actual wage in market E will be slightly higher than the wage in market O.) When all Ys are barred from E occupations, the supply curve shifts to S_E' and the wage earned by the remaining workers, all of whom are Xs, rises to w_1. Ys put out of work in the E occupations now seek work in the O occupations. The resulting shift in the supply curve to S_O' brings down the wage to w_2 in the O occupations. Because all Ys are in O occupations, they have a lower wage than many Xs. The average X wage is higher than the average Y wage.

Moreover, if both *X*s and *Y*s come to expect that *Y*s will have less education than *X*s, employers will tend to look for *X*s to fill the *E* jobs. This will reinforce the belief of *Y*s that education does not pay. This, and other kinds of subtle discrimination, can persist for a very long time, making the supply of *Y*s to *O* jobs higher than it would be in the absence of the initial discrimination, thus depressing the wages of *Y*s and poor *X*s.

The kind of discrimination that we have considered in our model is extreme. It is similar to South Africa's former apartheid system (which was eliminated by 1994), in which blacks were excluded by law from prestigious and high-paying occupations. In most Western countries labour market discrimination against a specific group usually occurs in somewhat less obvious ways. First, it may be difficult (but not impossible, as in our model) for members of the group to get employment in certain jobs. Secondly, members of groups subject to discrimination may receive lower pay for a specific kind of work than members of groups not subject to discrimination.

It is interesting to note that falling transport and communication costs over the past century have expanded firms' choice of location for the production of goods, from local markets, to national markets, to wider regional markets, and now often to global markets. This has greatly reduced the power of local prejudices to impose discriminatory employment policies on firms. If firms are unhappy about local pressures to employ one group rather than another, production can be transferred to other sites and the customers will quickly lose any concern about, or even awareness of, the nature of the far-distant workforce that makes the products they consume. It is also important to note that governments have been very active in introducing legislation that outlaws all forms of labour market discrimination, whether it be on grounds of sex, age, race, colour, disability, sexual orientation, or any other characteristics. The 2010 Equality Act requires all employers to be proactive in this regard and establishes a government agency to monitor the implementation.

Differentials arising from labour market structures

In this section we see how differences in the degree of competition can contribute to income differentials among market segments. We then go on to study unions in a little more detail.

The determination of wages without unions

When labour is supplied competitively each individual worker must take the existing wage rate as given and decide how many hours to work at that wage.[3] Each worker has a supply curve showing how many hours of work he or she will supply at each wage. The sum of these curves yields a market supply curve showing the total supply of work hours to this market as positively related to the real wage rate. The determination of wages under competitive supply can now be divided into three possible cases. The distinguishing characteristic of these cases is whether labour is bought by competitive purchasers, by a single-wage *monopsonist*, or by a *discriminating monopsonist*.

Case 1: A competitive market

We first assume that there are so many purchasers of labour services that no one of them can influence the market wage rate. Instead, each merely decides how much labour to hire at the current rate. Since both demanders and suppliers are price takers and quantity adjusters, this labour market is perfectly competitive. Demand and supply, as shown in Figure 9.1, then determine the wage rate and volume of employment.

Case 2: A single-wage monopsonist—a single purchaser

Now consider a labour market containing only a few firms. For simplicity we deal with a case in which the few purchasers form an employers' association and act as a single decision-taking unit in the labour market. In this section the single buyer is restrained to paying a single wage to all workers of one type that it employs.

When there is a single purchaser in any market, that purchaser is called a **monopsonist**. A monopsonist can offer any wage rate it chooses, and workers must either work for that wage or move to other markets (i.e. change occupation or location).

Suppose that the monopsonist decides to hire some specific quantity of labour. The labour supply curve shows the wage that it must offer. To the monopsonist this wage is the *average cost curve* of labour. However, in deciding how much labour to hire, the monopsonist is interested in the marginal cost of hiring additional workers. It wants to know how much its costs will rise if it takes on more labour.

Whenever the supply curve of labour has a positive slope, the marginal cost of employing extra units will exceed the average cost (the wage) because the increased wage rate necessary to attract an extra worker must also be paid to *everyone already employed*.

Consider an example. If 100 workers are employed at £2 per hour, then total cost is £200 and average cost per worker is £2. If an extra worker is employed and this drives the wage rate up to £2.05, then total cost becomes £207.05 (101 × £2.05); the average cost per labourer is £2.05, but the total cost has increased by £7.05 as a result of hiring one more labourer.

---

[3] In practice, the individual decision may be whether or not to work the standard working week at the going wage.

Monopsony results in a lower level of employment and a lower wage rate than when labour is purchased competitively.

The reason is that the monopsonistic purchaser is aware that, by purchasing more, it is driving up the price against itself. Therefore it will stop short of the point that is reached when the input is purchased by many different firms, none of which can exert an influence on its price.

Case 3: A discriminating monopsonist

What happens if the monopsonist can discriminate among different units of a single type of labour that it hires? By discrimination here we mean that the employer negotiates a different contract with each individual employee. We do not imply that this is related to any ethnic and gender characteristics whose impact we discussed above. As with the discriminatory monopolists that we studied in Chapter 7, the ability to discriminate has two effects.

A discriminating monopsonist will hire more labour and earn more profits than will a monopsonist who must pay the same wage to everyone.

In Figure 10.4 the monopsonist who must pay the same wage to all did not hire more labour, because doing so drove up the wage of its existing workers. For this reason the monopsonist's marginal cost of hiring labour exceeds the average cost. If the monopsonist can split its labour into groups, it can hire a second group without driving up the price of the first group. Consider the extreme case in which the monopsonist can make a separate bargain with each worker, paying just what is needed to persuade that person to accept a job. The supply curve is then the marginal cost curve of labour and the monopsonist employs the same amount of labour as would a perfectly competitive industry, but only the last worker hired gets the equivalent of the competitive wage—all others get less.

A perfectly discriminating monopsony is the extreme case. However, whenever the monopsonist can discriminate between two or more groups, employment and profits will be higher than when a single wage must be paid to all.

The determination of wages with unions

Unions affect wages and employment in two ways, depending on whether labour is hired competitively or monopsonistically.[4]

Case 4: Monopoly—a single seller

Suppose that a union enters a competitive labour market and raises the wage above its equilibrium level. By so

[4] For simplicity we deal here with only the single-wage monopsonist. Combining a union with a discriminating monopsonist complicates the analysis substantially without adding any new insights.

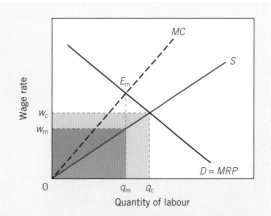

Figure 10.4 A monopsonist facing many sellers
Under monopsony employment and wages are less than under competition. The competitive wage and employment are w_c and q_c, where the demand and supply curves intersect. The monopsonist that must pay the same wage to all equates the marginal cost of hiring labour with labour's marginal revenue product, which occurs at point E_m. The firm hires q_m workers at a wage of w_m. (According to the supply curve, w_m is the wage at which q_m workers will be supplied.) Labour's income is shown by the dark pink and dark blue areas enclosed by q_m and w_m. A perfectly discriminating monopsonist can pay each worker his or her supply price, so the S curve is also its marginal cost curve. It will hire q_c labour and pay labour a total income equal to the dark and light blue areas *under* the S curve. The light pink area between w_m and w_c is now part of the monopsonist's profits, as is the dark pink area between w_m and the S curve (whereas under perfect competition both pink areas are part of labour's income).

doing, it is establishing a minimum wage below which no one will work. The industry can hire as many units of labour as are prepared to work at the union wage, but none at a lower wage. Thus, the industry (and each firm) faces a supply curve that is horizontal at the level of the union wage up to the quantity of labour willing to work at that wage.

This is shown in Figure 10.5. The intersection of this horizontal supply curve and the demand curve establishes a higher wage rate, and a lower level of employment, than would occur at the competitive equilibrium.

There will be a group of workers who would like to obtain work in the industry or occupation but cannot. Pressure from the unemployed to cut the wage rate may develop, but the union must resist this pressure if the higher wage is to be maintained.

A union can raise wages above the competitive market level, but only at the costs of lowering employment and creating an excess supply of labour with its consequent pressure for wage cutting.

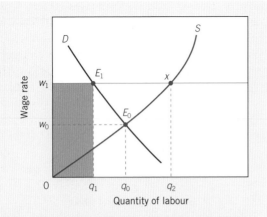

Figure 10.5 A single union facing many employers

A union that faces many employers can raise wages above the competitive level. Competitive equilibrium is at E_0. When the union sets the wage at w_1, it creates a perfectly elastic supply curve of labour up to the quantity q_2, which is the amount of labour willing to work at the wage w_1. Equilibrium is at E_1, with q_1 workers employed and $q_2 - q_1$ willing to work at the going wage rate but unable to find employment in that occupation. Labour income is shown by the blue area.

Case 5: A monopsony versus a monopoly

We now consider the effects of introducing a union into the monopsonistic labour market first illustrated in Figure 10.4.

The (single-wage) monopsonistic employers' organization now faces a monopoly union, and the two sides will settle the wage through collective bargaining. The outcome of this bargaining process will depend on the objective that each side sets and on the skill that each has in bargaining for its objective. We have seen that, left to itself, the employers' organization will set the monopsonistic wage shown in Figure 10.4.

To understand the range over which the wage may be set after the union enters the market, let us ask what the union would do if it had the power to set a wage below which its members would not work. There is now no point in the employers' holding off hiring for fear of driving the wage up, or of reducing the quantity demanded in the hope of driving the wage rate down. Here, just as in the case of a wage-setting union in a competitive market, the union presents the employer with a horizontal supply curve (up to the maximum number of workers who will accept work at the union wage). As demonstrated in Figure 10.6, the union can raise wages *and employment* above the monopsonistic level.

Because the union turns the firm into a price taker in the labour market, it can stop a firm from exercising its monopsony power and thus raise both wages and employment to the competitive level.

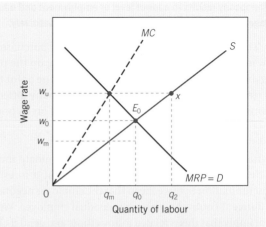

Figure 10.6 A single union facing a single employer

A union can raise both the wage and employment above their monopsonistic levels. The monopsonist facing competitively supplied labour is in the equilibrium analysed in Figure 10.4, with q_m workers employed at a wage of w_m. If a newly entering union sets its wage at w_0, the supply curve runs from w_0 to E_0 and then rises along the line S. Equilibrium is at E_0 with employment at q_0. If the union seeks a wage higher than w_0, it must accept a lower level of employment than q_0. The union can, for example, set a wage of w_u, creating a supply curve that runs from w_u to x then up the S curve. This yields the same level of employment, q_m, as when the monopsonist dominated the market, but at the much higher wage of w_u. At that wage rate there are $q_2 - q_m$ people who would like to work but who are unable to find employment in that occupation.

The union may not be content merely to neutralize the monopsonist's power. It may choose to raise wages further. If it does, the outcome will be similar to that shown in Figure 10.5. If the wage is raised above the competitive level, the employer will no longer wish to hire all the labour that is offered at that wage. The amount of employment will fall, and unemployment will develop. This is also shown in Figure 10.6. Notice, however, that the union can raise wages substantially above the competitive level before employment falls to a level as low as it was in the pre-union monopsonistic situation.

We know that the employer would like to set the monopsonistic wage and that the union would not want a wage below the competitive wage. The union may target a still higher wage depending on what trade-off it is willing to make between employment for its members and the wage that they earn. If the union is willing to accept the resulting low amount of employment, it could target a wage rate substantially higher than the competitive wage.

Simple demand and supply analysis can take us no further. As we have already observed, the actual outcome will depend on other things such as the target wage that the two sides seek to achieve, their relative bargaining skills, how each side assesses the cost of concessions, and how serious a strike would be for each.

Differentials arising from product market structures

The ability of a union to raise wages above the competitive level depends partly on the profitability of the industry in which it is operating. Some industries are highly competitive because they contain a large number of small firms and entry and exit are easy. Typically, firms in such industries will be earning enough to cover the opportunity cost of their capital, but no pure profits. A strong union might still raise wages in such an industry. This would increase costs and lead to exit until prices rose sufficiently for the remaining firms to cover their now higher costs fully. Thus the rise in wages would be accompanied by a fall in output and employment. However, even this limited gain may not be possible. If the union does not have a closed shop, new firms may enter, with lower costs achieved by hiring non-union labour. Also, if there is competition from foreign firms that do not face strong unions, the domestic industry may suffer a drastic contraction.

In other industries scale economies allow only a few firms, each one of which may earn significant profits. Government regulation that restricts competitive behaviour can also create profits over and above the opportunity cost of capital. Evidence suggests that unions can appropriate a share of these profits for their members through aggressive collective bargaining. Wages fell significantly in the UK newspaper industry after new technology gave the opportunity to break the union monopoly on print workers.

Many firms in the financial sector, such as commercial banks, investment banks, hedge funds, and asset managers, operate in oligopolistic markets and make very large profits (in normal times). Their middle and senior employees often receive much of their remuneration from bonuses. To the extent that these bonuses are based on the firm's profitability, there is an incentive to act to increase the firm's profits. But often the bonuses have been based on the volume of business, irrespective of the profitability of some lines of activity. In such cases, there is a perverse incentive to increase sales, even at the expense of profits. For example, in the build-up to the financial crisis of 2007–8 many mortgages in the United States carried low interest rates and did not generate much profit for the issuing firms. But the employees of the selling firms were paid bonuses based on the number of mortgages contracted, not current profits. The incentive was to sell as many mortgages as possible even if the purchasers were risky customers with low credit ratings. Later, these mortgages were packaged into a form of derivative known as collateralized debt obligations (*CDOs*), each one made up of the income from hundreds of different mortgages[5]. These *CDOs* were sold to others, both the public and other financial institutions, without regard for, or knowledge of, the real risks they carried. Again, the incentive of both the mortgage sales teams and those creating and selling *CDOs* was to maximize sales, not long-term profits. When higher interest rates kicked in, many mortgagees were unable to meet the higher payments and defaulted on their loans. Those who now held the *CDOs* lost a large proportion of their investments and the general panic that followed brought down several major banks.

The employees of the firms that created *CDOs* all earned very large incomes until the crash ensued, and many even after that. In competitive markets these very high incomes would have been kept down by the large number who would like to enter those high earning occupations. But the firms only hired what they needed, leaving other equally well qualified people to seek other less remunerative jobs. The high and rising incomes earned in the financial sector provide one of the major causes of the growing inequality in the distribution of incomes, particularly in the United States and the United Kingdom.

Minimum-wage laws

When unions set wages for their members, they are in effect setting a minimum wage. Governments can cause similar effects by legislating specific *minimum wages*, which define the lowest wage rates that may legally be paid. Such minimum wages are common in the United States and Canada and in some EU countries. The United Kingdom introduced a minimum wage in 1999, with a minimum wage of £3.60 an hour for adult workers and £3.00 an hour for 18–21-year olds (16- and 17-year olds were exempt at that time). In the year to October 2014 the adult rate stood at £6.31 per hour, while that for 18–21-year olds was £5.03 per hour. There was also a rate of £3.72 per hour for 16- and 17-year olds.

To the extent that minimum wages are effective, they raise the wages of employed workers. However, an effective floor price (which is what a minimum wage is) may well lead to an excess supply—in this case, unemployment. Thus, minimum wages may benefit some groups of workers while hurting others.

---

[5] This process of converting loans into a tradable security is known as *securitization*.

Analysis of the impact of a minimum wage is complicated because not all labour markets are competitive, only a small proportion of the labour force is affected by minimum wage laws, and many firms do not sell in perfectly competitive markets and so earn pure profits, some of which may be transferred to employees by such laws. Moreover, some groups in the labour force, especially youth and minorities, are affected more than is the average worker. Also, it is worth bearing in mind that labour is not a homogeneous commodity (even though much of our demand and supply analysis assumes that it is). A change in employment conditions that encourages workers to work harder or to invest in improving their skills may have effects that differ from those that would occur in a market where the 'product' is homogeneous and unchanging.

A comprehensive minimum wage

Consider a minimum wage law which, as in the United Kingdom, applies uniformly to all occupations. The occupations and the industries in which minimum wages are effective will be those paying the lowest wages. They will usually involve unskilled or, at best, semi-skilled labour. In most of them the workers will not be members of unions. Thus the market structures in which minimum wages are likely to be most effective include both those in which competitive conditions obtain and those in which employers exercise monopsony power. The effects on employment are different in the two cases.

Competitive labour markets

The consequences for employment of an effective minimum wage are unambiguous when the labour market is competitive and labour is homogeneous. By raising the wage that employers must pay, minimum wage legislation leads to a reduction in the quantity of labour that is demanded and an increase in the quantity of labour that is supplied. As a result, the actual level of employment falls, and a pool of people who would like to work in those jobs but cannot find employment is created. This does not necessarily lead to an increase in recorded unemployment because those who are unsuccessful in seeking a highly paid job can be expected to settle for a lower-paid one after some time. This situation is exactly analogous to that which arises when a union succeeds in setting a wage above the competitive equilibrium wage, as was illustrated in Figure 10.5. The excess supply of labour at the minimum wage also creates incentives for people to evade the law by working below the legal minimum wage. How much this matters depends on the elasticity of demand for the type of labour affected by these laws. For example, if the demand is quite inelastic because there is not much room to substitute other inputs for unskilled labour, the magnitude of the unemployment caused by the laws will be small.

In competitive labour markets, effective minimum wage laws raise the wages of those who remain employed but also cause some reductions in employment.

Monopsonistic labour markets

By flattening out the labour supply curve, a minimum wage law can simultaneously increase both wages and employment in monopsonistic labour markets. The circumstances in which this can happen are the same as those in which a union that is facing a monopsonistic employer succeeds in setting a wage above the wage that the employer would otherwise pay, as was shown in Figure 10.6. Of course, if the minimum wage is raised above the competitive wage, employment will start to fall, as in the union case. However, when it is set at the competitive level, the minimum wage can protect workers against monopsony power *and* lead to increases in employment.

A summary of the evidence of the impact of minimum wages in the United Kingdom and elsewhere is provided as a case study at the end of this chapter.

Heterogeneity, incentives, and monitoring costs

In the first part of this chapter we have studied the broad forces that create wage differentials among different groups of workers. For some purposes, it is a useful simplification to assume that workers of each type are identical individuals. But to understand other labour market issues, we need to recognize that no two workers are identical, while each can choose how to behave on the job. Labour market institutions evolve in subtle ways to cope with problems that arise from heterogeneity of employees and incomplete information about worker characteristics.

Individuals differ from each other. They all respond to the same incentives, but they respond differently. Given the same wage, some will work harder than others; some have more ability than others; with the same amount of effort, some produce more and get better results than others. This applies to all employees, whether working in production, design, planning, or supervision.

Asymmetric information

Firms might like to reward good workers more than indifferent workers, but it is difficult to know one from the other in many work situations. Generally, workers know more about their own effectiveness than does their employer.

Adverse selection

Adverse selection is a problem that arises most commonly in insurance markets where, faced with the same rates, high risk persons are more inclined to apply for insurance than low risk persons. The relevance to labour markets is that firms do not know all the characteristics of workers before they are hired, and they want to act in such a way as to attract 'good' workers and not 'bad'. A firm seeking to hire people usually advertises a particular job with an associated pay, or pay range. From the pool of those who meet the paper specifications, applicants are more likely to be lower-quality workers who find that wage a good bargain than higher-quality workers who know they can get as good a wage elsewhere. This would not be a problem if the employer knew as much about his prospective employees as did the employees themselves. But this is an obvious case of asymmetric information. You know more about yourself, your work habits, and your strengths and weaknesses than any potential employer.

Moral hazard

Moral hazard is defined as an adverse change of behaviour that results from an agreement or contract. A common example is an insurance-induced alteration of behaviour that makes the event insured against more likely to occur. For example, accident insurance may make a car driver act with less caution, and fire insurance may make a home owner less careful about turning off electrical appliances before going out. Thus, moral hazard arises when insurance leads people to take risks that they would avoid if they did not have an insurance policy. In the context of labour markets, the relevance of moral hazard is that some forms of labour contract may lead to the employee changing his or her behaviour in ways that are harmful to the firm. For example, if an employee was given a fixed salary for life, this individual might decide to take it easy and put in the minimum amount of effort consistent with fulfilling the contract. Thus incentives for good performance and the monitoring of the outcome become important.

Costly monitoring

It is difficult and costly for management to monitor its employees to find out how well each is contributing to the production process.

Contracts and performance monitoring

When you purchase a haircut, you have a clear idea of what you expect to get and you can accurately judge the quality of the service you receive. When a firm hires a divisional manager, it knows that it wants good work but cannot say specifically what the manager should be doing at each moment in her working day. Furthermore, it is not easy to judge how much of the division's subsequent performance is due to the manager's efforts and how much to forces beyond the manager's control.

Many modern employment situations are better thought of as an ongoing relationship rather than as the equivalent of a purchase of a specific, exactly definable labour service. Hence, employment contracts are often referred to as *relational contracts*. These contracts do not attempt to cover all of the many contingencies that could arise in a job. Instead, they set out general duties to be fulfilled in the post and leave the details to be decided by an evolving interaction between employer and employee. In many modern jobs it is not even desirable in principle to establish an exact job description because the nature of the work is continually evolving. For example, as recently as the 1980s a secretary's job involved taking handwritten notes from dictation and creating hard copy using a typewriter. Today, the same job typically involves taking draft documents already in electronic form and developing them using a word-processor or web-publishing package. Instead of typing letters and addressing envelopes, the secretary (who is now more likely to be called a PA) will be sending email messages and taking on a much wider range of organizational functions. A precise 1980 job description would have been a hindrance to necessary changes.

Under relational contracts neither employer nor employee has an exact or agreed expectation of each other's detailed behaviour.

The firm does not know the marginal product of each employee. The employees do not know precisely what they need to do to get promoted and avoid being sacked. Neither workers nor firms can make accurate decisions based upon full information.

The principal–agent problem

The management wishes to motivate employees to work in the firm's best interest, while employees often have different and conflicting motivations. Management would like to design incentive systems that motivate workers to provide the type of effort that it requires. This is known as the **principal–agent problem**. One context in which this problem arises is in the potential conflict of interest between owners of firms (shareholders), who are the principals in this context, and the managers of the firm, who are the agents. Shareholders want to maximize the value of their shares, but managers may have an incentive to overpay themselves and to empire build. Solutions to this version of the problem are generally sought by trying to align the interests of both groups by, for example, giving senior managers share options or profit-related bonuses. A similar analysis can help us to understand the relationship between senior management and all other employees. The bosses want workers to work hard and achieve production targets, but not all forms of employee behaviour can be observed or measured. So what incentives will persuade employees to buy into the goals set by senior management and behave productively?

An obvious principal–agent problem that arises with relational contracts, from the perspective of the firm, is that employees have some range of discretion about how hard they work, and they may have objectives of their own that are different from those of the employer.

The firm (the principal) cannot monitor the performance of many of its employees (the agents) accurately. It is often too costly even to try, and in many jobs it would be impossible even if money were no object. In such circumstances, the firm needs to design mechanisms that will induce its employees to act in the firm's interests. In general, unless there is costly monitoring of the agents' behaviour, the problem cannot be completely solved.

Principal–agent analysis shows that when employees have some range of discretion, their self-interested behaviour will make profits lower than in a 'perfect', frictionless world in which principals act as their own agents, or agents always do exactly what the principals want.

Many law, accountancy, and consultancy firms are partnerships. This means that the bulk of the employees (the partners) also own the firm and are jointly liable for its losses. This structure gives the partners a very strong incentive to ensure that the firm is profitable and that it does not take excessive risks. Investment banks were all partnerships at one time, but they converted into PLCs in the 1990s. With this change the partners became just employees and no longer owned the business. This is the point in time when they lost the incentive to monitor the risks of the business and started paying themselves extremely high salaries and bonuses, and a strong case can be made that this is one of the key causes of the build-up of risk in the banking system that led to the 2007–8 financial crisis.

Much labour market behaviour that seems odd at first sight has evolved to deal—more or less effectively—with the principal–agent problem. For example, people put in positions of trust are often paid much more than is needed to induce them to take these jobs. Why should principals pay their agents more than they need to pay to fill the jobs? The explanation is that agents who are paid much more than they could earn in other jobs have an incentive not to violate the trust placed in them. If they do violate the trust and are caught, they lose the premium attached to the job and are unlikely to find another such job elsewhere.

Efficiency wages

The theory of competitive markets predicts that excess supply causes price to fall until the excess supply is eliminated—that is, until demand equals supply. Often, this does not happen in labour markets. In the face of excess supply, firms do not typically cut wages, even though such a move would seem to enhance profits. Why?

Employers are worried about the quality and performance of the heterogeneous workers that they hire as well as just their price. The wage that yields the best combination of price and quality of worker is known as the **efficiency wage**.

The theory of the *efficiency wage* helps to explain why it may be optimal for firms to set wages that are permanently above the level that would clear the labour market. Efficiency wage theory applies to hiring, to productivity on the job, and to worker turnover.

Efficiency in hiring

Firms do not know the characteristics of specific workers until after they have sunk costs into hiring and training them. Good workers know who they are and are likely to have a higher reservation wage than bad workers. The reservation wage is the lowest wage at which a person is prepared to work for a particular firm. By lowering the wage that it offers, a firm will significantly lower the average ability of the workers who apply for its jobs. This tendency for a firm that pays lower wages to attract poor-quality workers is a case of adverse selection. As a result, paying lower wages can make the firm worse off.

In labour markets with informational asymmetries, where unobserved characteristics of workers are correlated with the reservation wage, it will generally be optimal for firms to pay wages that exceed their employees' reservation wages.

Productivity on the job

If wages are so low that workers are just indifferent between staying and losing their job, they are unlikely to do more than the minimum required. Workers are likely to give greater effort if they feel they are being well rewarded. Workers will then expect to be much worse off if they lose their current job, and they will be aware of a queue of good-quality workers prepared to work for the high wage. The high wage improves on-the-job efficiency.

Minimizing turnover

Many firms find that high quit rates are costly because they must invest in training their workers. Thus firms are reluctant to lower wages for existing workers, even in the face of an excess supply of labour. Workers who are already inside the company and know its work practices are worth retaining, even at premium wages. New workers, though possibly cheaper, may not be as good and will be costly to train.

Efficiency wage theory says that firms will find it advantageous to pay high enough wages that staying in their present job is a superior alternative to being laid off. This will minimize labour turnover and improve the quality of workers' effort.

When considering the supply curve of labour, we saw that high wages may induce less work from workers who can choose their hours because of an income effect that is stronger than the substitution effect (see Box 9.5). High efficiency wages give the workers a different choice, which is to work hard for a high reward or not to work at all (or, perhaps, to work in another job at the much lower average wage). By posing an all-or-nothing choice, employers alleviate the disincentive effects of high wages. Workers who do not work hard enough risk losing their high-paying job. This *potential-loss-of-income effect* reinforces the substitution effect, and for many workers encourages them to adopt the hard-work/high-pay solution—at least among those who are fortunate enough to have this choice.

Signalling

Participants in markets with asymmetric information will develop informal criteria for signalling information about some of these unseen characteristics. Employers who pay a high efficiency wage signal that they are interested in high-quality staff and are prepared to pay them well. Educational qualifications provide a signal from potential employees. Hopefully your university degrees, or higher education certificate, will indicate that you have acquired some useful knowledge and skills. However, another important function of the degree you will acquire is to convince potential employers that you are ambitious, hardworking, intelligent, and committed to self-improvement—just the kind of person that every employer is looking for! The degree creates a signal about

your personal characteristics independent of the subject of the degree. In selection situations the signal about who you are may play as important a role as what you have learned.

Internal labour markets

Most manual and other unskilled workers have little or no expectation of advancement or even of long-term employment. They are often paid an hourly rate and have little job security. In contrast, many skilled manual workers, most white-collar workers, and virtually all technical, managerial, and professional staff have a long-term employment relationship which provides a career path within the firm. Typically, there are limited entry points into the firm and most senior posts are filled by promotions from within the firm. These workers operate in what is known as an **internal labour market**, composed of a firm and its long-term employees—that is, the market is internal to the firm. Such a market has only limited connections with external labour markets and its structure reflects the needs and traditions of each specific firm. The market offers a *job ladder* for the firm's long-term employees, with most employees starting somewhere near the bottom of the ladder and working their way up throughout their career.

Pay and promotion

Firms with internal labour markets do not generally try to assess their employees' marginal productivity and then pay them accordingly. Instead, firms have a number of defined job grades with pay rates attached to the job rather than to any individual's productivity. Employees generally improve their pay by moving up the ladder of promotion. Good work in the current job has a potential pay-off more in terms of promotion prospects than in terms of dramatically increased current pay.

There are at least three reasons why internal labour markets may be more efficient than tying individuals' pay to their individual performance. First, most of the relevant jobs involve a great deal of learning. A long-term employment relationship, with a potential for promotion, creates an incentive for employees to invest in acquiring skills that will benefit the firm. These firm-specific skills will take time to acquire and will take even longer to generate a pay-off to the firm. Hence, to achieve the benefits of this learning effect, firms have to offer the prospect of both long-term employment and future promotion.

The second reason why internal labour markets may be efficient derives from efficiency wage theory. The incentives for good performance built into the efficiency wage require a long-term employment relationship. The 'good' workers are attracted to the firm by high rewards and also by a commitment on the part of firms to a high degree of employment stability and 'good prospects'. Hence, both employees and employers are likely to generate a more productive relationship via mutual longer-term commitment, rather than via temporary employment contracts and minimal mutual commitment.

The third factor supporting internal labour markets is that successful firms require long-term strategic thinking from their senior staff. The ability to take and implement long-term strategies is not something that shows up or can be tested over a short horizon. Hence, successful firms have significant numbers of senior managers who have been selected as a result of observing their performance within the company, and who have sufficient expectation of continuing employment that they are prepared to take a long-term view. A manager who does not expect to stay with a firm very long may postpone important investments, while one who sees his own future as tied to the success of the firm will want to ensure its continued survival.

The internal labour market increases the convergence of interests between the employee and the firm, thereby reducing principal–agent problems.

Tournaments

One way to think of an internal labour market is as a *tournament*. Workers enter the tournament when they join a firm on the lower rungs of the ladder. Workers at each level compete with each other to show the senior management that they are most worthy of promotion. Periodically, when a more senior job becomes vacant, someone from the grade immediately below the vacant post is chosen to progress up the ladder. As there are fewer senior jobs than junior jobs, not everybody can progress up the ladder at the same pace. The winner of the tournament is the one who reaches the post of chief executive.

In an internal labour market tournament the pay of senior executives is as much about motivating everybody in the organization as it is about paying a 'fair' compensation for the incumbent of any specific post. The £1 million salary paid to a chief executive officer (CEO) may be more important in terms of motivating junior staff to strive to rise to that exalted post than in terms of rewarding the current CEO for his efforts. Even though those who enter a golf or tennis tournament know that they cannot all win, tournaments with the greatest prize for winning still attract the best players and tend to bring out the best in them. The issue of CEO pay is discussed further in a case study at the end of this chapter.

The tournament structure of rewards has three advantages for firms. First, when a candidate is selected for promotion, only enough information is needed to make relative judgments among potential candidates. No absolute or detailed performance measures are needed. This economizes on the need to acquire costly information, which may in any case be unreliable.

The second advantage is that pay ranges are set in advance for each job, so time is not wasted on individual pay negotiations with each and every employee. An employee who wants more pay must work for a promotion, so bargaining time is saved. Equally, there is no incentive for employers to argue about performance in order to avoid having to pay bonuses.

The third advantage is that tournaments reduce the problems of asymmetric information. Employees who are chosen for promotion from within the firm will have become well known to their superiors, and so there is little uncertainty about their characteristics. Equally, employees who are promoted already know a great deal about the functioning of the company, so they can become effective in their new position more quickly than would be likely with an outsider.

The promotion path in an internal labour market can be thought of as a tournament in which higher pay rates in more senior jobs create an incentive for employees to progress up the career ladder.

Seniority and *MRP*

The incentive issues discussed above suggest that where there is a long-term relationship between firm and workers, firms will find it efficient to reward loyalty and long service. Hence, it will generally be true that longer-serving workers will get higher rewards than younger workers. The rewards for long service will come via higher wages and company pension schemes, which will naturally reward long service with a higher pension. A pension can be thought of as deferred wages.

The need to reward long service means that on average there is a cross-subsidy passing from young workers, who get less than their current marginal revenue products, to older workers, who get more. However, the young workers have the encouragement of knowing that they themselves will eventually benefit from this cross-subsidy when they themselves become older workers, provided that they stay with the firm. Thus, ceteris paribus, expectations of lifetime earnings will be the same for both groups.

CASE STUDIES

1. The impact of minimum wages

The UK introduced a statutory national minimum wage in 1999 and there has now been a considerable amount of research on its impact. The following is an extract from *Government evidence to the Low Pay Commission on the National Minimum Wage*, December 2008, that summarizes the evidence.[6]

Impact on the labour market

While UK academic research to date has not found overwhelming evidence that the adult minimum wage has reduced employment, there has not yet been time for the full impact of the recent minimum wage upratings to be seen. In addition, the minimum wage has not yet been in place through a significant economic downturn or recession. Early indications from Dickens and Draca (2005) which looked at the impact of the minimum wage increase in 2003 and Mulheirn (2008) which examined the impact of the 2006 uprating found no significant evidence of an adverse employment impact.

There has been a slight decline in the share of UK employment in low-paying sectors since 1999. However, there is no evidence that this is the result of the minimum wage and the trend also predates the introduction of NMW.

There is some evidence of a small impact of the NMW on hours worked. Over 1999–2008 total hours worked in the low-paying sectors grew around 5.6 per cent, less than the 6.5 per cent growth in the non low-paying sectors. The slight decline in the share of UK employment since 1999 in low-paying sectors partly explains the smaller growth in total hours worked but there has also been a slight fall in mean hours worked in low-paying sectors.

The evidence presented so far has been in the context of a growing labour market. There is less evidence, from both the UK and internationally, of the impact of minimum wages in periods of economic downturn ...

The evidence summarized here suggested that the UK national minimum wage had no detectable impact on adult employment, but a slightly different conclusion is reached by a study based on more recent data.

Research to date suggests that the UK National Minimum Wage (NMW) has raised the earnings of low paid workers, without significantly affecting their employment

opportunities. We re-examine existing evidence and suggest the picture is less clear cut. We explore whether the impacts of the NMW differ for workers in different size firms. Examining more recent data we investigate whether the NMW has affected the employment opportunities of low paid workers during the recession. In contrast to previous research we find some evidence to suggest that the introduction of the NMW may have had a small adverse impact on the employment opportunities of particular low paid workers, although, in line with previous research, for many low paid workers we find no impact. In general, it is not obvious that the impacts of the NMW on employment have differed over the business cycle. In comparison to other workers, low paid workers are more likely to work in smaller firms. We find that on average any potentially harmful effects of the NMW on the employment chances of low paid workers tend to be more significant amongst employees in large firms ... We do find some evidence that the NMW has led to a small reduction in employment retention amongst female part-time workers, particularly upon NMW introduction and during more recent years.

(*Richard Dickens, Rebecca Riley, and David Wilkinson, Re-examining the impact of the national minimum wage on earnings, employment and hours: the importance of recession and firm size, Report to the Low Pay Commission, January 2012*)

2. The earnings of superstars

Small groups of people in many professions are often paid extraordinarily large salaries. Wayne Rooney was reported in the 2013–14 football season to be paid around £300,000 *per week* by Manchester United, which is more than ten times greater than the *annual* average wage. In June 2009, Real Madrid signed Cristiano Ronaldo from Manchester United for a transfer fee reported to be around £80 million. He was given a six-year contract which was said to include a wage in excess of £11 million per year. Real Madrid topped this in 2013 by buying Gareth Bale from Tottenham Hotspur for around £85 million and paying a wage of £15 million per year. In 2004, David Beckham was transferred to Real Madrid from Manchester United for £25 million, and Beckham himself was reported to have earned a total income of around £17 million in 2004 alone, when all his sponsorship deals are added to what his club pays him. By 2008 Beckham was playing partly for LA Galaxy and partly for AC Milan, but was still reported to be the highest earning soccer player with annual income of around $65 million. In 2005 Michael Schumacher earned $60 million from driving Formula 1 racing cars, and the 2008 world champion, Lewis Hamilton, was given a $140 million dollar contract over five

---

[6] The full document and the literature references (not reproduced here) are available at <http://www.berr.gov.uk/files/file49192.pdf>

years by McLaren. In 2004, pop singer Robbie Williams was reported to have signed a £40 million five-record deal with EMI. TV star Oprah Winfrey earned $275 million in 2008, while in the same year pop star Madonna earned $110 million and Bruce Springsteen made $70 million, as did the group Coldplay. These rewards for pop stars and top sports stars are not new. Michael Jordan the basketball player made $100 million in 1998, Mike Tyson the boxer made $75 million in 1996, and singer/songwriter Sir Paul McCartney amassed a nearly £1 billion fortune out of his career in popular music and still had an annual income of around £25 million in 2013 even though his earliest hit records with the Beatles were in the 1960s. Top opera stars, concert soloists, and conductors also get very high rewards for their performances.

Why are superstars so highly paid? Should not market incentives encourage others to compete for these large rewards, with the end result that the massive rewards for a few would fall and be replaced by more modest rewards for the many. On the contrary, forces in the modern economy appear to be increasing the gap between superstars and the rest. There are three components to the explanation.

First, the general increase in real wealth over time has created an increase in demand for output in the sectors in which superstars perform.

Secondly, in some of these activities there is a premium to being the very best over what the merely competent can command. For example, if you are wealthy and need a lawyer or a heart surgeon, you are going to pay for the best. Someone who is good but not the best will not do. Equally, if you want your team to win the Premier League, you need the best striker in the country. Coming second is commendable but not good enough. Hence, those who are 'the best' may be only, say, 10 per cent better than a bunch behind them, but they may command a substantial wage premium just because there is no one better. (The *MRP* of being the best greatly exceeds the *MRP* of being second.)

For example, Tiger Woods, the world's number one ranked golfer for several years in a row in the 2000s, was predicted by *Forbes* magazine to pass $1 billion lifetime earnings in 2010. In 2007 alone he earned around $110 million in prize money and endorsements. However, he is only on average about two shots per 18-hole round better than a player ranked around number 100. Yet the 100th ranked player earned around $1.2 million in prize money and endorsements combined. So Tiger, who was less than 2 per cent better at golf than the 100th ranked player, earned 96 times as much. Who was the highest paid sportsman in 2013? Yes, it was Tiger Woods, who earned $78.1 million in that year alone.

Thirdly, modern communications have increased the size of the market over which stars compete. What used to be many local markets where the person who was the best in each market earned a moderately high income have become a single global market in which people compete to be the best in the world. The winners earn huge sums because they serve huge markets. TV, movie, and pop stars are the obvious examples. Why listen to a local opera company when you can listen to La Scala, Milan, or the Vienna State Opera on a CD, or the Metropolitan Opera of New York beamed live to your local cinema? Why listen to a local band when you can access the latest global music hits easily downloadable to your iPod? The marginal revenue products of top stars in both pop and classical music have been vastly increased by modern communications media that allow them to reach audiences thousands or even millions of times larger than could be reached a century ago.

In recorded music, superstars' earning powers do not necessarily end with their death. Demand for the music of all-time greats like Maria Callas, Frank Sinatra, Elvis Presley, and Billie Holiday is as great (or higher) today as it was when they were at the peak of their careers, and Michael Jackson's albums went back to the top of the charts when it was announced that he had died.

These influences go well beyond the entertainment fields. Doctors can now operate at a distance by directing robots on the site. This is just beginning to cause an increased demand for the best surgeons to operate beyond their immediate locations. Consultants of all sorts can now operate worldwide using modern communications.

3. CEO pay—fat cats or optimal incentives?

Can chief executives of large companies possibly be 'worth' their very large salaries? This was already a huge issue, but became headline news as a result of rewards of bankers (and in many cases in failing banks) revealed during the global credit crisis of 2007–9.

Multi-million dollar salaries are now common in the United States, as are salaries of £1 million or more for UK chief executives and chairmen. Some people believe that these high salaries for British and American CEOs are an inefficiency caused by the principal–agent problem. In this view, CEOs have escaped shareholders' control. Their high pay is evidence that shareholders are being ripped off. If this were the whole truth, the solution would be to give genuinely independent non-CEOs more power in setting compensation, or to give shareholders a vote on CEO pay[7]. Howerver, there are some economic reasons why high payments to CEOs are often needed for the incentives they create within the company. There are three elements to the incentive issue.

One is the tournament model of internal incentives. High pay for CEOs provides an incentive for all the workers in the firm to aspire to the top job. Hence, the pay

---

[7] There are several recent cases where shareholders have voted down a proposed reward package for a CEO.

is not justified solely by the performance of the specific incumbent CEO. Rather, it is desirable for the extra effort it motivates from those who have any serious prospects of eventually becoming CEO. For them, high CEO pay may increase loyalty and the ambition to achieve promotion.[8]

The second element is that the CEO does have to be motivated by his rewards, because there is no further promotion available. Hence, while middle-managers may be motivated partly by the prospect of moving up the promotion ladder, the CEO needs other motivation.

The third element relates to the incentives to take risks. If employees are risk averse, they will take the safe option rather than take a chance of being fired for making a risky decision that goes wrong. However, in a modern dynamic economy, firms need to be at least risk neutral, if not risk takers. This means that CEOs need an incentive to take risks in the interest of the long-term health of the company. One way to encourage them is to offer a reward if risk taking pays off, while imposing no penalty when failures occur. Just such a reward profile is offered by share options. These options become valuable if the company's shares rise in value, but carry no cost to the CEO if the options expire worthless. Share options may encourage senior executives to take risks. A significant proportion of CEO compensation does involve just such incentives. However, it is clear that the incentives to take risks can be overdone at times. This applies particularly to financial institutions that took on too many risky assets in the run up to the 2007–8 financial crisis.

One further important use of employment-contingent options to buy shares in the future is to bind managers to the firm. A young firm in a dynamic industry may not be able to pay its executives a large current salary. Thus it risks having them leave, taking their firm-specific experience with them. As well as providing an incentive to take risks, options to buy the firm's shares in the future reduce the incentive to leave for a higher-paying job. After all, the stock options become worthless when the manager leaves.

Of course, the actual rewards of top management cannot always be justified on incentive grounds. There are undoubtedly many cases where senior executives have overpaid themselves, and others where they have expropriated funds of both shareholders and pension fund members. However, there has been a general phenomenon in the United States and the United Kingdom of CEO pay rising much faster than that of average workers, and many think that this is a cause of serious concern.

4. The rich get richer and the poor stand still

The previous two case studies have focused on the pay of the rich, whether they be superstars or chief executives. We

now discuss the more general problem of the widening distribution of income which raises questions about whether the current capitalist economic system is really working for the benefit of most of the population. The problem is particularly stark in the United States, so we use data from that country to illustrate what has been happening.

Figure 10.7 shows the mean real annual incomes for quintiles of the US income distribution. Therefore it shows the poorest 20 per cent, the next poorest 20 per cent, and so on to the richest 20 per cent. It also shows the mean real income of the richest 5 per cent of the population.

Two facts stand out from this figure. First, all income groups suffered a fall in real incomes after the financial crisis, so all were worse off in 2012 than they had been in the early 2000s. Secondly, the poorest 40 per cent of the population were no better off in 2012 than they had been in the 1970s. The middle 20 per cent of the US population were no better off in real terms in 2012 than it had been at the end of the 1980s. The next 20 per cent had seen some modest growth in real incomes, but the top 20 per cent was the only section of the population to see significant real income gains. Meanwhile, the richest 5 per cent had seen their real incomes double between the 1970s and the 2000s. For the top 5 per cent, of course, this income increase was the most substantial, but we know from other data that the group within the top 5 per cent that did by far the best was the top 1 per cent (which included many superstars, CEOs, and professionals).

There are obviously some important questions to be asked about social cohesion and the very survival of a system in which all the gains from growth go to a small minority of the population. After all, the 'American dream' was built upon the expectation of continuing rising living standards of an average middle-income family. The potential long-term consequences of all the rewards going to a small elite require a much deeper analysis than we can give here and involve political science and sociology as well as economics. However, here we ask: What are the economic forces driving these huge shifts in income distribution?

Two big global forces have almost certainly played a part in this story. The first is the growth of new technologies and the second is the globalization of production and outsourcing. Technology has worked in three main ways. First, it has replaced many high-pay jobs in manufacturing with computers and machinery. It has also created a premium to the small numbers of highly educated who understand the technology, can make it work, and can develop it further when needed. Secondly, it has led to delayering in large organizations with the loss of many middle management jobs. Thirdly, cheaper communications and the internet have permitted outsourcing to cheaper locations and to offshore sources of cheaper parts and services. Globalization is linked to the last of these as the emergence of cheap manufacture in Asia, and especially China, has provided

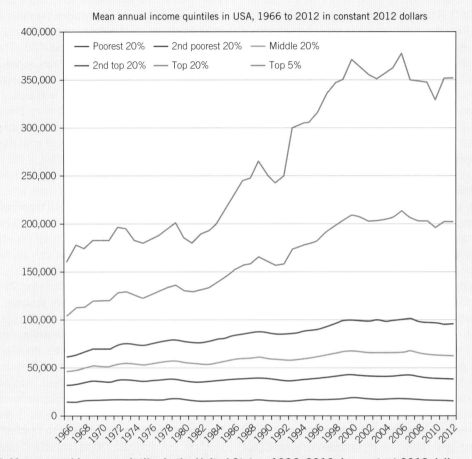

Figure 10.7 **Mean annual income quintiles in the United States, 1996–2012, in constant 2012 dollars. (Note that incomes are before tax but do include social security benefits other than those received in kind such as food stamps.)**

Source: US Bureau of Census

low-cost consumer goods but at the same time has removed domestic jobs from the manufacturing sector. Where there has been job growth in the United States, and in other western economies, it has largely been in lower-paid retail and service sector occupations, sometimes referred to as 'Mac-jobs', but even some of these have been vulnerable to 'offshoring' in the form of call centres in distant countries, such as India. Unskilled and semi-skilled workers in the poorer countries have gained from these changes, while those in developed countries have lost.

What has happened in the recent past is beyond dispute, but we cannot know if this is a temporary or longer-lasting phenomenon. The main industrial countries thrived from the spread of democracy, education, and the growing living standards of the bulk of the population. Until recently each generation has been better off than its parents and has thus felt that the system broadly has served it well. How long will citizens tolerate a situation in which the majority

stand still while a small elite wins all the prizes? Even this might work if members of the majority had a fair chance to join the elite. This was possible when a quality education was available at low cost to the majority. However, public funding squeezes and full-cost student loans are turning the tables in favour of the children of the rich elite who can afford the best private schools which also gets them access to the best universities and then to the best jobs.

All this may not look so bad when and if the industrial world returns to its pre-crisis long-term growth trends. Then it is possible that the average citizen will also get real benefits from that growth. It is also possible that corporate excesses will be brought under better control by reforms in corporate governance and more active participation of shareholders in senior executive remuneration. However, the future is uncertain and all we can say is that recent trends raise some big economic and social issues for the near future.

Conclusion

Labour is the most important input into any modern firm. A hundred years ago it was mainly the manual effort of workers that was being hired. Today, however, the majority of workers are not hired for their physical strength. Rather, they are hired for their mental skills. Today, brainpower rather than muscle power drives much of business success.

Brainpower is a much more complicated input to manage than was muscle power. The mental ability of potential new employees is difficult to assess and the effort of brain workers is hard to monitor accurately. Yet the success of a firm in the long term depends crucially upon selecting, keeping, and motivating a stock of brainpower. The institutions and practices discussed in this chapter have evolved to provide the structure within which a company's most talented employees are nurtured, motivated, and developed. However, there are some important issues raised by recent trends in the distribution of rewards in the economy.

SUMMARY

Wage differentials

- Equilibrium wage differentials can arise among jobs because (a) each requires different degrees of physical or mental abilities, (b) each requires different amounts of human capital acquired through costly formal education or on-the-job training, (c) some jobs are closed to people who could fill them as a result of discrimination, and (d) the markets for the types of workers needed in different jobs have different competitive structures.

- In perfectly competitive input markets wages are set by demand and supply, and there is no unemployment in equilibrium. In monopsonistic markets, wages and employment are less than their competitive levels, but there is no unemployment in equilibrium.

- If a union enters a perfectly competitive market, it can raise wages above the competitive level at the cost of lowering employment and creating a pool of people who would like to work at the union wage but cannot. If a union enters a monopsonistic labour market, it can raise wages *and* employment to the competitive level. If it raises wages beyond that point, employment will fall.

- Unions and professional associations can sometimes restrict the supply of labour and thereby achieve wages above the competitive equilibrium without creating a pool of unemployed.

- Minimum wage laws have a similar effect to the setting of wages by unions. If the market was monopsonistic before the minimum wage is imposed, wages *and* employment can be raised. If it was competitive, wages can be raised only at the expense of some (possibly small) reduction in employment in the affected occupation.

Heterogeneity, incentives, and monitoring costs

- Today's labour markets are complicated by the fact that brainpower is extremely heterogeneous making it hard for employers to discern the full characteristics of individual workers.

- Many employment contracts are relational contracts, which do not specify in detail what workers have to do. This creates the potential for principal–agent problems, where the hired employees act, in part, in their own interest rather than that of the employer.

- Solutions to the principal–agent problem involve some combination of incentives and monitoring.

- Most skilled, managerial, and professional workers now find themselves in internal labour markets that have some of the characteristics of a tournament. Here, the main incentive for lower- and middle-ranking staff is to achieve promotion. Higher pay generally attaches to more senior jobs, and the competition to gain promotion can be thought of as a tournament.

TOPICS FOR REVIEW

- Causes of equilibrium wage differentials
- Human capital
- Formal education and on-the-job training
- wage differentials due to departure from perfect competition on the demand and the supply sides of labour markets

- Relational contracts
- Principal–agent problems in labour markets
- Efficiency wages
- Signalling in the labour market
- Internal and tournament labour markets

QUESTIONS

1 Using the *MRP* data and supply curve of labour from the questions 1–3 of Chapter 9, calculate how many workers would be hired and what wage would be paid if the hiring firm were a profit-maximizing monopsonist.

2 How would the outcome in Question 1 differ if the monopsonist could price discriminate and pay each worker the minimum wage for which he or she would work?

3 How would the outcome in Question 1 change if a trade union was able to impose a going wage for all workers of £500 per week?

4 Adverse selection can be a problem in markets in which (choose one):

 a) the characteristics of the product are well known;

 b) there are not many products to choose from;

 c) pricing or selection strategy may generate poor-quality applicants (in case of labour) or higher than average risks (in the case of insurance);

 d) the market is affected by monopoly power;

 e) behaviour of one set of agents may change after the contract is signed.

5 Select the one answer here that does **not** apply. It may be profit enhancing to pay an efficiency wage (a wage that is higher than the minimum necessary to attract job applicants) because:

 a) the efficiency wage attracts higher quality workers;

 b) the efficiency wage gives workers an incentive to work hard and reduces monitoring costs;

 c) the efficiency wage reduces labour turnover and thus protects the value of investment in on-the-job training;

 d) the efficiency wage facilitates faster turnover of workers;

 e) the efficiency wage helps retain workers with on-the-job experience of the firm.

6 Why are wage rates not equal in different jobs even in equilibrium?

7 What are the main differences between labour markets and markets for homogeneous commodities?

8 How does the efficiency wage help to solve the problems of recruitment, monitoring, and retention?

9 In what ways is the principal–agent problem manifested in employment relationships and what measures are available to ameliorate the problem?

10 How does asymmetric information affect labour-hiring decisions and what role might signalling play in this process?

11 What is different about an internal labour market (as compared to the goods markets that we have studied earlier in this book)?

CHAPTER 11

CAPITAL, INVESTMENT, AND NEW TECHNOLOGY

After studying human inputs into production, we now turn to physical inputs. What differences are there between the firm's decision on how much capital equipment to put in place and its decision on how much labour to hire? What factors have to be taken into account in the decision to invest? How does technical change influence the way in which firms operate and how does it affect the competitive process? These are some of the questions we address in this chapter.

In particular, you will learn that:

- Physical capital differs from other variable inputs in that it is usually 'lumpy' and durable, and is often bought outright rather being hired for specific periods of time.

- In order to evaluate a potential outright investment in capital equipment, firms need to calculate if it adds net present value to the firm.

- The present value of any future income stream is what it would be worth paying today to obtain that income stream in the future.

- An investment adds net value to a firm if the present value of the income stream generated exceeds the present value of the extra costs incurred.

- Firms will invest up to the point at which the net present value of the project ceases to be positive. This is conceptually equivalent to the principle that a profit-maximizing firm will set marginal cost equal to marginal revenue.

- All investments are risky to some degree as their value relies on future income streams and the future is uncertain.

- The recent revolution in information and communication technology (ICT) has important implications for the whole economy, including the organization and behaviour of firms.

Inputs that can be replaced, either by being manufactured, as is the case with machines, or by reproducing themselves, as do plants, people, or animals, are called **renewable resources**. Inputs that cannot be replaced, such as fossil fuels, are called **non-renewable** or **exhaustible resources**. Physical capital and non-renewable resources are similar inputs in that each is a stock of valuable things that gets used up in the process of producing goods and services. They are different in that physical capital can be replaced, while non-renewable resources cannot. A new machine can always be created to replace one that wears out, but when a barrel of oil is used there is a permanent reduction in the world's total stock of oil. In this chapter we focus on renewable inputs, but we provide an extended discussion of the issues surrounding non-renewable resources in the Online Resource Centre.[1]

Capital as an input

The capital stock consists of all those produced goods that are used in the production of other goods and services. Factories, machines, tools, computers, roads, bridges, houses, and railways are a few examples. Because capital is a produced input, it is a renewable resource, though technical changes over time mean that the

---

[1] <http://www.oxfordtextbooks.co.uk/orc/lipsey13e/>

characteristics of capital change over time. Here, we are always talking about physical capital, such as machines, and not about financial capital. Clearly the two are connected, as firms often need to raise finance in order to purchase capital equipment. But our focus is on the equipment itself and not on the way in which its purchase is financed.

The pure return on capital

For a profit-maximizing firm, the decision to invest in capital will be guided by whether the extra revenue that the capital generates justifies the cost.[2] To calculate the *return on capital*, we take the receipts from the sale of the output that the capital helps to make and subtract all variable costs of production. This gives us the **gross return on capital**.[3] It is convenient to divide this gross return into four components.

1. *Depreciation* is an allowance for the decrease in the value of a capital good over time resulting from its use in production and its obsolescence. Depreciation is often assumed to occur at a constant rate.

2. The *pure return on capital* is the amount that capital could earn in a riskless investment in equilibrium. When expressed as a return per £1 worth of capital invested, the result is called the **pure rate of interest**.

3. The *risk premium* compensates the owners for the actual risks of the enterprise.

4. *Pure* or *economic profit* is the residual after all other deductions have been made from the gross return. It may be positive, negative, or zero.

The *gross return* on capital is the sum of these four items. The *net return* is the sum of the last three—that is, the gross return minus depreciation.

In a competitive economy positive and negative pure profits are a signal that resources should be reallocated, because earnings exceed opportunity costs in some lines of production and fall short of costs elsewhere. Thus economic profits are a disequilibrium phenomenon in a perfectly competitive economy .

To study the return to capital in its simplest form, consider an economy that is in a perfectly competitive equilibrium. Thus, economic profits are zero in every productive activity. This does not mean that the owners of capital get nothing; it means only that the gross return to capital does not include an element of pure profit. Thus the *equilibrium* net return on capital is composed of components 2 and 3 minus component 1.

To simplify things further at the outset, imagine a world of perfect certainty: everyone knows what the return to an existing new unit of capital will be in any of its possible uses. Since there is no risk, the gross return to capital does not include a risk premium.

We have now simplified to the point where the net return to capital is all pure return (item 2 on the above list), while the gross return is pure return plus depreciation (items 1 and 2). What determines this pure return on capital? This is the return that varies from time to time and from place to place under the influence of economic forces. Broadly speaking, it will be determined by the overall balance between saving and investment in the economy as a whole. Risk and disequilibrium differentials are then additions to that pure return.[4]

Implications of durability

Next, we consider an important issue that arises because capital is durable—a machine, a factory building, or a computer program lasts for years.[5] To see some of the implications of durability, it is helpful to think of a capital good's lifetime as being divided into short periods that we refer to as production periods, or rental periods. The present time is the current period. Future time is one, two, three, and so on, periods hence.

The durability of capital goods makes it necessary to distinguish between the capital good itself and the flow of services that it provides in a given production period. For example, a firm could rent the use of a building for some period of time, or it could buy the building outright. This distinction is just a particular instance of the general distinction between flows and stocks that we first encountered in Box 2.2 in Chapter 2. Box 11.1 shows the growth rate of the UK capital stock and of capital services for the period 1950 to 2009.

If a firm hires a piece of capital equipment for some period of time—for example, one lorry for one month—it pays a price for the privilege. If the firm buys the lorry outright, it pays a different (and higher) price for the purchase. Consider in turn each of these prices.

Rental price

The *rental price of capital* is the amount that a firm pays to obtain the services of a capital good for a specific period of time. The rental price of one week's use of a piece of

---

[2] Households and governments may have slightly different reasons to invest, but firms can be assumed to wish to maximize profits.

[3] This simplified example assumes that capital is the only fixed input.

[4] We are implicitly assuming a constant price level. Under inflationary conditions we need to distinguish the nominal return on capital, where everything is measured in nominal monetary units, from the real return, where nominal values are deflated by a price index. This distinction is discussed in Chapter 2.

[5] Labour is also durable, but the difference from the point of the view of the firm is that the firm only buys the current services of the worker and not the worker him- or herself, while the firm typically buys the durable capital good and then uses its services over time.

Box 11.1 Capital stock and capital services growth, UK 1950–2009

The growth of the capital stock and of capital services that are actually used in the period tend to move together, but they have periods of significant divergence. The difference between them is due to the fact that installed capital may lie idle or be under-utilized. The capital stock tends to grow fastest in periods when the economy is booming and firms are looking to expand, and a bigger capital stock is associated with an increase in capital services. In recessions, such as in the early 1980s, early 1990s, and 2008–9, the increase in capital stock slows down sharply and the growth of capital services also tends to slow.

There was a big divergence in these two series in the late 1990s and early 2000s when capital services growth clearly outstripped the growth of the capital stock. This is most likely to be due to the growth of the internet and other IT-related innovations which made the productivity of computers rise much faster than the stock of installed computing equipment.

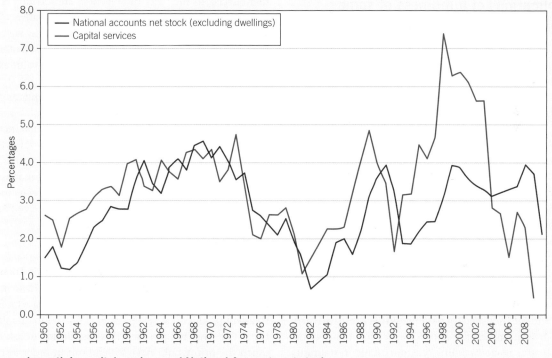

Annual growth in capital services and National Accounts net stock

Source: John Appleton and Gavin Wallis, 'Volume of capital services: new annual and quarterly estimates for 1950 to 2009', *Economic and Labour Market Review*, Office of National Statistics, May 2011.

capital is analogous to the weekly wage rate that is the price of hiring the services of labour.

Just as a profit-maximizing firm operating in competitive markets continues to hire labour until its marginal revenue product (*MRP*) equals its wage, so will the firm go on hiring capital until its *MRP* equals its rental price. Since in a competitive market all firms will face the same rental price, all firms that are in equilibrium will have the same *MRP* of each type of capital.

A capital good may also be used by the firm that owns it. In this case the firm does not pay out any rental fee. However, the rental price is the amount that the firm could charge if it leased its capital to another firm. Thus it is the *opportunity cost* to the firm of using the capital good itself. This rental price is the *implicit* price that reflects the value to the firm of the services of its own capital that it uses during the current production period.

Whether the firm pays the rental price explicitly or calculates it as an implicit cost of using its own capital, the profit-maximizing firm will employ capital up to the point where the rental price of a capital good is just equal to its marginal revenue product.

Purchase price

The price that a firm pays to buy a capital good, say a machine, is the *purchase price of capital*. When a firm buys such a machine outright, it obtains the marginal revenue product that the machine is expected to yield over its lifetime. The firm's willingness to buy the machine is, naturally enough, related to the value that it places now on this stream of *expected* receipts over future time periods and how this compares with the cost of the machine.

The term 'expected' emphasizes that the firm is usually uncertain about the prices at which it will be able to sell its outputs in the future. For simplicity, we assume that the firm knows the future *MRP*s.

Implications of lumpiness of some capital goods

While virtually all physical capital is durable, virtually all physical capital is also lumpy. This means that it cannot be divided into small units and still serve the same purpose. The Channel Tunnel, for example, would not be much use if it stopped halfway between England and France, and the Severn Bridge has to be long enough to span the river—a shorter structure would not do. Many manufacturing plants also have a minimum functional scale and/or involve pieces of equipment that are large and thus also costly.

The economic implication of lumpiness is that the option of having a bit more or a bit less is not available in investment decisions. Rather, the choice will be of an 'all or nothing' nature. For example, you either build a fifth terminal at Heathrow Airport or you make do with four. And if you do build, then it has to be of sufficiently large scale that it can handle a substantial number of large aircraft and the thousands of passengers that these will carry. This in turn implies the need for space for maintenance facilities, luggage handling, customs halls, restaurants, executive lounges, car parks, airline offices, etc. So, the facility is either of substantial size or it is not built at all, though on the drawing board you can make a marginal decision to build it a bit bigger or a bit smaller. Similar considerations apply to power dams, car factories, and most other pieces of physical capital

Once started, big investment projects, like the Channel Tunnel or the London Olympic Games complex, take a long time to complete, in some cases many years. This makes it particularly difficult to estimate the cost of the project in advance, as prices and wages may change over time and unexpected technical problems may emerge along the way. We return to this issue below when we discuss how the riskiness of a project affects the decision to invest.

For now, a key issue to notice about decisions relating to capital projects is that a central problem is how to evaluate costs and revenues from a project when they accrue at different periods of time. Most capital projects will involve up-front costs, but the revenue will be generated over some future time periods, which could be many years.

Present value of future returns

When we looked at decisions of firms on how much of a variable input to hire, we came to the conclusion that, to maximize profits, inputs should be hired up to the point where the marginal cost of the last unit of input was just equal to the value of the extra revenue generated by hiring that last unit. These values were easy to compare because they were happening at the same point in time. In investment decisions the costs and revenues are accruing at different points in time. So how can a firm compare revenue in the future with costs today? We first ask how we compare income today with income at a future period of time. This question is relevant to the issue of how to value assets as well as to the issue of how much capital firms should install. Box 11.2 discusses the valuation of brands as capital assets.

How much is an asset that generates a particular income stream in the future worth *now*? How much would someone be willing to pay now to buy the right to receive that flow of future payments? The answer is called that asset's *present value*. In general, **present value** (*PV*) refers to the value *now* of one or more payments to be received *in the future*.

Present value of a single future payment
One period hence

Let us start with the simplest possible case. How much would a firm be prepared to pay *now* to purchase an asset that will produce a single payment of £100 in one year's time? One way to approach this question is to ask how much the firm would have to lend out in order to have £100 a year from now. Suppose for the moment that the interest rate on a riskless loan (e.g. a government bond) is 5 per cent, which means that £1.00 invested today will be worth £1.05 in one year's time.[6]

If we denote this unknown amount by *PV*, we can write *PV*(1.05) = £100. (The left-hand side of this equation means *PV* multiplied by 1.05.) Thus, *PV* = £100/1.05 = £95.24. This tells us that the present value of £100, receivable in one year's time, is £95.24 when the interest rate is 5 per cent. Anyone who lends out £95.24 for one year at 5 per cent interest will get back £95.24 plus £4.76 in interest, which makes £100 in total. When we calculate this present value, the interest rate is used to *discount* (i.e. reduce to its present value) the £100 to be received one year hence. The maximum price that a firm would be

---

[6] The analysis in the rest of this chapter assumes *annual* compounding of interest.

Box 11.2 The value of a brand

Why is a Rolex watch more expensive than a similar watch that looks as good and tells the time just as well? Why are Gucci shoes more expensive than similar leather shoes from a less well-known shoemaker? Why are specific designer labels associated with higher-priced fashion items in clothing shops? This is to do with the economics of branding. Designers and manufacturers of cars, clothes, watches, and many other consumer items attempt to create a distinctive image of quality associated with their own product which creates consumer loyalty and adds value to the product that is additional to the cost of the materials that go to make it. Establishing a valuable brand is not straightforward, but it is clearly something that many producers wish to do. In part this may be achieved by advertising, which establishes a good image of the product, and perhaps gives the impression that this product is used by top media stars or sports personalities.

How to establish a good brand is a topic for business studies courses. From the perspective of economics what matters is that a good brand adds a dimension to a product for which consumers are prepared to pay. In effect, they have a taste for specific brands and are prepared to pay extra to buy the brands they know. Thus a brand is a capital asset that is of value to the firm that owns it and it can be valued just like any other capital asset.

For example, the Apple brand was valued at $185 billion in 2013. The top ten global brands and their estimated values are listed in the table in millions of $US.

Top ten most valuable global brands, 2013

		Brand	Brand value ($million)
1	Technology		185,071
2	Technology	Go gle	113,669
3	Technology	IBM	112,536
4	Fast food	M	90,256
5	Soft drinks	Coca-Cola	78,415
6	Telecoms	at&t	75,507
7	Technology	Microsoft	69,814
8	Tobacco	Marlboro	69,383
9	Credit card	VISA	56,060
10	Telecoms	CHINA MOBILE	55,368

Source: <http://www.wpp.com/~/media/Reading-Room/BrandZ/brandz_2013_top_100_report_may13.pdf>

---

willing to pay for this asset is £95.24 (assuming that the interest rate relevant to the firm is 5 per cent).

To see why, let us start by assuming that the firm is offered the asset at some other price. Say that it is offered at £98. If, instead of paying this amount for the asset, a firm lends its £98 out at 5 per cent interest, at the end of one year it would have more than the £100 that the asset will yield. (At 5 per cent interest, £98 yields £4.90 in interest, which, together with the principal, makes £102.90.) Clearly, no profit-maximizing firm would pay £98—or, by the same reasoning, any sum in excess of £95.24—for the asset. It could do better by using its funds in other ways.

Now suppose that the good is offered for sale at £90. A firm could borrow £90 to buy the asset and would pay £4.50 in interest on its loan. At the end of the year, the asset yields £100. When this is used to repay the £90 loan and the £4.50 in interest, £5.50 is left as profit to the firm. Clearly, it would be worthwhile for a profit-maximizing firm to buy the asset at a price of £90 or, by the same argument, at any price less than £95.24.

The actual present value that we have calculated depended on assuming that the interest rate was 5 per

cent. What if the interest rate is 7 per cent? At that interest rate the present value of the £100 receivable in one year's time would be £100/1.07 = £93.46.

These examples are easy to generalize. In both cases we have found the present value by dividing the sum that is receivable in the future by 1 plus the rate of interest.[7] In general, the present value of £R one year hence at an interest rate of i per year is

$$PV = \frac{R}{(1+i)}. \qquad (11.1)$$

Several periods hence

The next step is to ask what would happen if the sum were receivable at a later date. What, for example, is the present value of £100 to be received *two* years hence when the interest rate is 5 per cent? This is £100/(1.05 × 1.05) = £90.70. We can check this by seeing what would happen if £90.70 were lent out for two years. In the first year the loan would earn interest of (0.05)(£90.70) = £4.54, and

---

[7] Notice that in this type of formula the interest rate, i, is expressed as a decimal fraction; for example, 7 per cent is expressed as 0.07, so $(1 + i)$ is 1.07.

hence after one year the firm would receive £95.24. In the second year the interest would be earned on this entire amount; thus interest earned in the second year would equal (0.05)(£95.24) = £4.76. Hence, in two years the firm would have £100. (The payment of interest in the second year on the interest income earned in the first year is known as *compound interest*.)

In general, the present value of £R after t years at i per cent is

$$PV = \frac{R}{(1+i)^t}. \qquad (11.2)$$

All that this formula does is discount the sum, R, by the interest rate, i, repeatedly, once for each of the t periods that must pass until the sum becomes available. If we look at the formula, we see that the higher i or t is, the bigger is the whole term $(1 + i)^t$. However, this term appears in the denominator, so PV is *negatively* related to both i and t.

The formula $PV = R/(1 + i)^t$ shows that the present value of a given sum payable in the future will be smaller the more distant the payment date and the higher the rate of interest.

Present value of a stream of future payments

Now consider the present value of a stream of receipts that continues indefinitely[8]. At first glance that PV might seem very high, because the total amount received grows without reaching any limit as time passes. However, the analysis in the previous section suggests that people will not value the far-distant money payments very highly.

To find the PV of £100 a year, payable for ever, we ask how much you would have to invest now, at an interest rate of i per cent per year, to obtain £100 each year. This is simply iPV = £100, where i is the interest rate and PV the investment required. Dividing through by i shows the present value of the stream of £100 a year for ever to be

$$PV = \frac{£100}{i}. \qquad (11.3)$$

For example, if the interest rate were 10 per cent, the present value would be £1,000. This merely says that £1,000 invested at 10 per cent yields £100 per year, for ever. Notice that, as in the previous sections, PV is negatively related to the rate of interest: the higher the interest rate, the less is the present value of the stream of future payments.

In the text we have concentrated on finding the present value of amounts available in the future. Box 11.3 reverses the process and discusses the future value of sums available in the present.

----

[8] Some government securities, known as perpetuities, have the characteristic that they pay out a specific sum at regular intervals with no terminal (or maturity) date.

Implications for firms' desire to invest in capital

Profit-maximizing firms will want to invest in capital as long as it offers a return that is at least as good as could be achieved by investing a similar sum of money at the going market interest rate. Equivalently, if firms are borrowing the funds to finance the investment, they will want to purchase capital that offers a return in terms of revenue that exceeds the cost of the loan. Clearly, the costs of the capital and revenues that arise from using the capital will accrue at different points in time. In order to compare payments and receipts at different points in time the firm needs simply to calculate the present value of the extra revenues and deduct the present value of the costs. This gives the **net present value** (*NPV*) of the investment project.

Profit-maximizing firms should undertake any investment project for which the net present value is positive, as this means that it is increasing the present value of profits and thus adding value to the firm. On the plausible assumption that firms are faced with diminishing returns to capital, firms will invest up to the point where the net present value of investment is zero. Beyond this point, further investment is adding more to the present value of costs than to the present value of revenues, and would thus lower the value of the firm.

Notice that when firms must compare income streams at different points in time we must generalize our interpretation of the assumption that firms maximize profits. This is because it may be rational for a firm to have its costs exceed its revenues (by investing) in one period in order to make even more profit in future. Hence, when intertemporal revenue transfers are possible the objective of the firm would not be to maximize profit in one specific period, but rather to maximize the present value of all current and expected future profit streams. This is the same thing as maximizing the present value of the firm.

When considering the decision to invest, firms can be assumed to wish to maximize the present value of the firm itself. The value of the firm will increase if it undertakes projects that have a positive net present value.

Investment decisions are very important for firms so we now look in more detail at the investment decisions for profit-maximizing firms and what this implies for demand for capital.

Equilibrium of the firm

When putting a present value on future income flows, each firm will discount them at a rate that reflects its own opportunity cost of capital, often called its *internal rate of*

Box 11.3 The future value of a present sum

In the text we have concentrated on the present value of amounts to be received in the future. However, we can turn the question around and ask, 'What is the future value of an amount of money that is available in the present?'

Assume that you have £100 available to you today. What will that sum be worth next year? If you lend it out at 5 per cent, you will have £105 in one year. Letting PV stand for the sum you have now and FV for the value of the sum in the future, we have $FV = PV(1.05)$ in this case. Writing the interest rate as we have in the text, we obtain

$$FV = PV(1 + i).$$

If we divide through by $(1 + i)$, we get eqn (11.1) in the text. (In the text we denote the future value by R.)

Next, if we let the sum build up by reinvesting the interest each year, we obtain

$$FV = PV(1 + i)^t.$$

If we divide both sides by $(1 + i)^t$, we obtain eqn (11.2) in the text.

This tells us that what we did in the text is reversible. If we have an amount of money today, we can figure out what it will be worth if it is invested at compound interest for some number of future periods. Similarly, if we are going to have some amount of money at some future date, we can figure out how much we would need to invest today to get that amount at the specified date in the future.

Our argument tells us that the two sums, PV and FV, are linked by the compound interest expression $(1 + i)^t$. To go from the present to the future, we *multiply* PV by the interest expression, and to go from the future to the present we *divide* FV by the interest expression.

The so-called rule of 72 is a convenient way of going from PV to FV by finding out how long it takes for FV to become twice the size of PV at any given interest rate. According to the rule, the time it takes for any amount to double in size is given approximately by $72/100i$. So, for example, if i is 0.1 (an interest rate of 10 per cent), any present sum doubles in value in $72/10 = 7.2$ years.

---

discount. With perfect credit markets in which the firm can borrow all that it needs, the internal rate of discount will equal the market rate of interest (suitably adjusted for risk in each case). However, the evidence suggests that most firms do not face perfect capital markets and have internal rates of return that exceed market rates. Thus, when firms evaluate an internally financed investment project they will use an internal rate of discount that exceeds the relevant market rate of interest. The general points made in the text are not affected by this complication, as long as i is interpreted in each case to mean the 'appropriate rate of discount'. For the time being we make the simplifying assumption that firms face perfect capital markets so that the internal rate of discount is equal to the market rate of interest, but we discuss the appropriate discount rate further in the next section.

In adjusting to market forces, an individual firm faces a given interest rate and given purchase prices of capital goods. The firm can vary the quantity of capital that it employs, and, as a result, the marginal revenue product of its capital varies. The law of diminishing returns tells us that the more capital the firm uses, the lower will be the MRP of its capital.

The decision to purchase capital

Consider a firm that is evaluating a potential increase in its capital stock. It can borrow (and lend) money at an interest rate of, say, 10 per cent per year. The first thing the firm needs to do is to estimate the expected marginal

revenue product of the new piece of capital over its lifetime. That is, for example, the net addition to revenue generated by the extra output in each period of time made possible by installing the extra machine. Then it discounts this at the appropriate rate, 10 per cent in this example, to find the present value of that stream of receipts the machine will create.[9] Let us say it is £5,000.

The present value, by construction, tells us how much the flow of future net receipts is worth today. If the firm can buy the machine for less than the *PV of the extra revenue stream it generates*, this is a good buy. If it must pay more, the machine is not worth buying.

It is always worthwhile for a firm to buy another unit of capital whenever the present value of the stream of future *MRP*s that the capital provides exceeds its purchase price.

The size of the firm's capital stock

The *MRP* of each addition to the firm's capital stock is assumed to decline as the amount of capital is increased. The firm will go on adding to its capital stock until the

---

[9] Suppose that the machine has an *MRP* of £1,000 each period. First, suppose the machine only lasts this period. The present value is then £1,000. Next, suppose that it lasts for two periods. The *PV* is then £1,000 + £1,000/1.10 = £1,909.09. If it lasts for three periods, the *PV* is £1,000 + £1,000/1.10 + £1,000/(1.10)² = £2,735.53, and so on. Each additional period that it lasts produces an *MRP* of £1,000, but at a more and more distant date, so that the *present value* of that period's revenue gets smaller owing to heavier discounting.

present value of the flow of *MRP*s conferred by the last unit added is equal to the purchase price of that unit. The firm then has its equilibrium amount of capital.

The equilibrium capital stock of the firm is such that the present value of the stream of net income that is provided by the marginal unit of capital is equal to its purchase price.

This is yet another example of the condition that, for equilibrium, marginal cost will equal marginal revenue.

Now let the firm be in equilibrium with respect to its capital stock and ask what would cause it to buy more capital. Given the price of the machines, anything that increases the present value of the flow of income that the machines produce will have that effect. Two things will do this job. First, the *MRP*s of the capital may rise. That will happen, for example, if technological changes make capital more productive so that each unit produces more than before. (This possibility is dealt with later in this chapter.) Secondly, the interest rate may fall, causing an increase in the present value of any given stream of future *MRP*s. For example, suppose that next year's *MRP* is £1,000. This has a *PV* of £909.09 when the interest rate is 10 per cent and £952.38 when the interest rate falls to 5 per cent.

So, when the interest rate falls, the firm will wish to add to its capital stock. It will go on doing so until the decline in the *MRP*s of successive additions to its capital stock, according to the law of diminishing returns, reduces the present value of the *MRP*, at the new lower rate of interest, to the purchase price of the capital.

The size of a firm's desired capital stock increases when the rate of interest falls, and it decreases when the rate of interest rises.

This relationship is shown in Figure 11.1. It can be considered as the firm's demand curve for capital plotted against the interest rate. It shows how the desired stock of capital varies with the interest rate. (It is sometimes called the *marginal efficiency of capital curve*.)

Equilibrium for the whole economy

The term **capital stock** refers to some aggregate amount of capital. The *firm's capital stock* has an *MRP*, showing the net increase in the firm's revenue when another unit of capital is added to its existing capital stock. The *economy's capital stock* can also be thought of as having a marginal revenue product; this is the addition to total national output (GDP) that is caused by adding another unit of capital to the economy's total stock. This capital stock also has an average product, which is total output divided by the total capital stock (i.e. the amount of output per unit of capital).

The same analysis that we used for one firm in the previous section applies to the whole economy. The lower the rate of interest, the higher is the desired stock of capital that all firms will wish to hold. Such a curve is shown as the economy's demand curve in Figure 11.2.

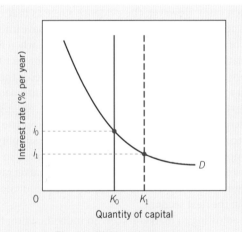

Figure 11.2 The equilibrium interest rate

In the short run the interest rate equates the demand for capital with its fixed supply. The economy's desired capital stock is negatively related to the interest rate, as shown by the curve D. In the short run, when the stock is K_0, the equilibrium interest rate is i_0. When the capital stock grows to K_1 in the long run, the equilibrium interest rate falls to i_1.

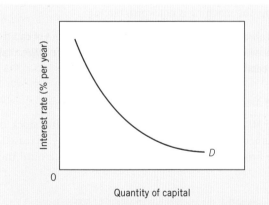

Figure 11.1 The firm's demand curve for capital

The firm's desired capital stock is negatively related to the rate of interest. The lower the interest rate, the higher is the present value of any given stream of marginal revenue products, and hence the more capital the firm will wish to use.

---

[10] We know that the central bank sets the short-term nominal interest rate; however, we are talking here about long-term real interest rates. These are normally set by market forces, and are the rates relevant for long-term investment decisions.

Short-run equilibrium

In the short run the economy's capital stock is given, but for the economy as a whole the interest rate is variable.[10] Whereas the firm reaches equilibrium by altering its capital stock, the whole economy reaches equilibrium through variations in the interest rate.

For the economy as a whole the condition that the present value of the *MRP*s should equal the price of capital goods determines the equilibrium interest rate.

Let us see how this comes about. If the price of capital were less than the present value of its stream of future *MRP*s, it would be worthwhile for all firms to borrow money to invest in capital. For the economy as a whole, however, the stock of capital cannot be changed quickly. As a result, the main effect of this demand to borrow would be to push up the interest rate until the present value of the *MRP* equals the price of a unit of capital goods. Conversely, if the price of capital is above its present value, no one would wish to borrow money to invest in capital, and the rate of interest would fall. This is also illustrated in Figure 11.2.

Accumulation of capital in the long run

In an economy with positive saving, more capital is accumulated over time and the stock of capital grows slowly. As this happens, other things being equal, the *MRP* falls. This will cause the equilibrium interest rate to fall over time, as is also shown in Figure 11.2.

Changing technology in the very long run

In the very long run technology changes. As a result the capital stock becomes more productive as the old, obsolete capital is replaced by newer, more efficient capital. This shifts the *MRP* curve rightwards because any given amount of capital will have a higher *MRP*. This in turn tends to increase the equilibrium interest rate associated with any particular size of the capital stock. This, of course, is also the equilibrium return on capital. However, the accumulation of capital moves the economy downwards to the right along any given *MRP* curve, and that tends to lower the return on capital associated

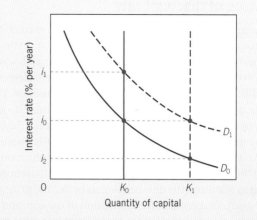

Figure 11.3 Changes in technology and the capital stock

Increases in technological knowledge and in the capital stock have opposite effects on the interest rate. The original demand curve D_0 and capital stock K_0 produce an interest rate of i_0. Technological improvements shift the desired capital stock curve to D_1 and, with a constant stock of capital, would raise the interest rate to i_1. However, the capital stock increases to K_1, which ceteris paribus would lower the interest rate to i_2. In the figure the two effects exactly offset each other, and the interest rate remains unchanged at i_0, where K_1 and D_1 intersect.

with any one *MRP* curve. The net effect on the return on capital of both of these changes may be to raise it, lower it, or leave it unchanged, as shown in Figure 11.3. The very long run effects of changing technology, combined with a growing capital stock, are studied further in Chapter 26, and we discuss some aspects of recent changes in technology in the last section of this chapter.

So we see that the income going to owners of capital is the *pure risk-free rate of return* (multiplied by the amount of capital in use), plus a risk premium, plus any pure profits or minus any pure losses. The pure return serves to allocate capital to its most productive uses. All uses that yield more than the pure rate of return (plus any necessary risk premium) will be exploited; all uses that earn less than the pure rate will not be taken up.

The investment decision

In the previous section we explained how a firm can evaluate whether or not an increase in its capital stock will increase its value. The message is that firms should undertake investment projects that have a positive net present value. This is easy to understand conceptually, but it is much harder to implement in practice. We now discuss some of the issues that inevitably arise in the practical evaluation of a potential investment project.

Choice of discount rate

Assuming that the firm faces a perfect capital market, the discount rate appropriate for appraising an investment project is the true opportunity cost of the financial capital involved as valued by this market. There are two elements to this. First, there is the pure time value of money. This is usually measured by the market rate of interest on a risk-free investment, such as a government bond. To find this figure it is necessary only to look in the daily financial press. However, even here there is slight complication in that the yield on government bonds varies with the bond's term to maturity (the number of years before the principle is repaid). This implies that calculation of the appropriate discount rate should take into account not just short-term interest rates, but also long-term rates, though for simplicity it is common to assume a single risk-free rate.

The second element of the opportunity cost of capital is the return in excess of the risk-free rate that is necessary to compensate for risk. The greater the risk associated with a project the greater should be the risk premium attached to the discount rate used in evaluating the project. It should be stressed that the opportunity cost of capital relevant to these decisions is that set by the capital markets. It is not appropriate for a firm to argue that, for example, since the money used to finance the project is generated internally, the opportunity cost of the capital is lower than it would be if borrowed externally, so a lower discount rate can be used in investment appraisal (indeed, as discussed above, given the likelihood of market imperfections, the appropriate discount rate for internally generated funds may be *above* market rates). The reason this would be an error is that the firm has the option of investing its capital in other projects via the capital markets, or of returning the money to shareholders. If it does not use the market valuation of the opportunity cost of capital in valuing its potential project, it will find that it has invested in an internal project that adds less value to the firm than could have been achieved by investing the resources elsewhere via the capital markets. Equivalently, it may accept a project as having a positive *NPV* when in fact it has a negative *NPV* when evaluated at the true opportunity cost of capital.

In practice, many firms use weighted average cost of capital (*WACC*) as a discount rate for investment appraisal purposes. This is calculated on the basis of the average interest cost on all the sources of funds raised by the firm itself, such as equity, bonds, and bank loans. This is not a correct procedure from the perspective of economic theory, as the *WACC* reflects the average cost of capital to the firm, rather than marginal cost of funds and the riskiness of the project being assessed. However, for an investment project that is about as risky as the existing business and that still has access to its various sources of funds, this may

not be a bad approximation to the true opportunity cost of capital.

Treatment of inflation

Another factor that complicates investment appraisal is inflation. The problem here is that the value of money itself changes over time, so that care has to be taken to make sure that a project is generating added value *in real terms*.

The net present value method is ideally suited to judging real added value because the assessment criterion is measured unambiguously in money values at the beginning period of the investment project. In other words, if we are making the decision in 2016, then the calculation is converted into 2016 pounds sterling. However, there are two different ways in which this can be done, and it is important that one or other approach be applied consistently.

The first approach involves using expected current money values for all cash flows—that is, the actual money values that are expected to be recorded at the time the flows accrue. These money values are then discounted back to the initial-year present values using a nominal discount rate. The nominal discount rate is the actual money value of the interest rate in the markets for the appropriate level of risk.

The second approach measures all future cash flows in terms of, say, 2016 (base-year) money and discounts these back to the present using a *real* discount rate. The real discount rate is approximately equal to the nominal rate minus the rate of inflation. The reason why this is an approximation is discussed in Box 11.4.

If applied correctly, these two methods will come up with exactly the same result. They should give identical results as they are different ways of converting future cash flows into present real values: both methods use the same numeraire of base-period money values. However, mistakes will be made if a mixture of real and nominal data slips into the same calculation, such as if nominal cash flows were discounted by the real rate of interest.

Sunk costs

There are two aspects of the problem of sunk costs, depending upon whether these costs have already been incurred or whether the expenditure is yet to be made and therefore is still an object of choice.

In the past

A common error in investment decisions is to give weight to the past and try to rescue past mistakes. This is reflected in statement such as: 'We need to spend more money on

Box 11.4 Real and nominal interest rates

If today you put £100 into a savings deposit and the bank is offering 5 per cent interest, in one year's time you will receive interest of £5. If today is 1 March 2016, the interest will be received on 28 February 2017. This 5 per cent is referred to as the *nominal rate of interest*. However, between these two dates it is likely that the purchasing power of each £1 of money will have changed. This is because of inflation, which by definition is a fall in the purchasing power of money. Inflation is typically measured by the annual percentage change in the retail price index (RPI) or the consumer price index (CPI).

If there is inflation in 2016–17, the £5 interest you receive in February 2017 will buy fewer goods and services than it would have done a year earlier. The real rate of interest is the number that tells you how much extra goods your money interest will buy you. In order to calculate the real rate of interest *ex post* you need to know what the inflation rate has been over the period in question. It is approximately true to say that the real rate of interest is the nominal rate of interest minus the rate of inflation.

We say this is 'approximate' for two reasons. First, the exact relationship between real rates, nominal rates, and inflation is:

$$(1 + r) = (1 + i)(1 + p),$$

where r is the nominal interest rate, i is the real interest rate, and p is the rate of inflation. If you multiply out the right-hand side of this equation you get $1 + i + p + ip$. Hence, the nominal rate is not exactly equal to the sum of the real interest rate and the inflation rate, because there is also the term ip. This term will be very small when both i and p are small, but not if they are large, such as when inflation is high. Secondly, the relationship is often used to apply to 'expected' interest rates. In this context, expectations may be incorrect, so that the relationship holds subject to a random error. Expected real interest rates are what matter for most investment decisions by firms, because firms are converting a purchase of physical capital today into a stream of extra output of goods in the future.

A measure of inflation expectations can be obtained by comparing the yields on nominal and index-linked government securities. The latter pay a return that compensates for actual inflation. In December 2013, a UK government indexed bond was yielding 0.9 per cent (plus whatever inflation turned out to be), while a nominal bond of similar maturity was yielding 3.6 per cent. The real interest rate is the yield on the indexed bond while the nominal rate is that on the nominal bond. The difference between the two yields suggests that inflation was expected to be around 2.7 per cent per year on average over the life of these two bonds.

---

this factory because otherwise the investment we made last year will be wasted'.

A key element of rational decision-making in this context is that sunk costs from the past do not affect the profitability of new investments. Bygones are bygones. What matters is whether incremental spending adds to present value or not. The success or failure of past investments is irrelevant to this decision.

What this implies is that decisions about the profitability of spending more on anything must be forward looking. In judging profitability the relevant question is: does the present value of the extra revenue generated exceed the present value of the extra spending incurred? If the answer is yes, then the spending will increase the value of the firm. If the answer is no, then the extra spending will decrease the value of the firm, and should not be undertaken.

This does not mean that present value techniques cannot be used to take decisions about whether or not to scrap old plant and machinery; they can. Suppose that we have a factory that is declining in efficiency, and suppose also that it has zero scrap value. The question is whether to keep it going or close it down entirely. The answer will depend solely on the present value of the extra spending

required to keep it going relative to the extra revenues that will be generated by keeping the plant operating. The original cost of the factory is irrelevant to the decision, though the scrap or resale value of the factory would be relevant if this were positive, as this would represent potential future cash flow.

Sunk costs do not influence the profitability of future investment decisions.

In the future

Until recently, economists implicitly assumed that irreversible costs that had not yet been incurred should not be treated in any special way in investment appraisal. However, important insights have been derived from option pricing theory. Box 11.5 explains what 'options' are in this context and illustrates the idea with a numerical example.

There are two key features of many real-world investment projects. The first is that there is some significant chunk of costs that is irreversible so that it cannot be recovered if it is later decided to abandon the project. The second feature is that implementation does not have to be done immediately, as it is usually possible to delay. The

Box 11.5 The option to invest

Financial options come in two types. A *call option* is the right to buy an asset at a specified price (the exercise price) within some period of time. A *put option* is the right to sell an asset at a specified price within some period of time. These options can be exercised if the buyer so wishes, but there is no obligation to do so. If the buyer is better off not exercising the option then non-exercise is OK—hence the term 'option'. The option will expire worthless. Options have some value as long as they have some time left to run and as long as there is even a faint possibility that the underlying value of the asset will exceed the exercise price of the call option, or be less than the exercise price has been placed on the put option.

Investment that firms plan to make in the future is just like the option to buy some underlying asset at some specified price. This is a call option. The value of this call option is conceptually separate from the value of the underlying asset itself. This is because the call option still allows you to back out without any further costs, whereas the investment itself incurs substantial sunk costs.

An example may help to illustrate these ideas. Suppose that a firm has a potential investment project. This project would involve an instant irreversible cost of £800 (these numbers can be thought of as millions). The revenue from the project will depend on which of two states of the world emerges in a year's time, affecting whether the output from the project sells for £150 or £50. These alternative states of the world are equally likely to arise, but only next year will it be clear what is going to happen. For simplicity, we can

assume that the revenue streams established next year will then continue at that level for ever and that the appropriate discount rate is 10 per cent.

Suppose we do the *NPV* calculation relating to an immediate investment. The expected revenue on average will be £100, so the *NPV* is –£800 plus the present value of £100 for ever. The latter sum is £1,100 (we have £100 produced instantly plus the present value of a perpetual payment £100 for ever, which is £1,000). Hence, the *NPV* is £300 (calculated as –£800 + £1,100).

However, suppose we wait and only go ahead with the project if the revenue received is £150, cancelling the project if it turns out to be £50. The present value of that alternative is £380 (calculated as half the present value of –£800 ('half' because there is a 0.5 probability of going ahead) plus half the present value of £150 in perpetuity, starting next year). Hence, the present value of waiting one year is greater than the present value of investing now. The value of the wait-and-see option today is £80. The strategy that maximizes the present value of the firm is in these circumstances to do nothing until next year.

This approach gives important insights into how uncertainty about the environment can inhibit investment. Who will win the next election? Will the price of oil go higher? Will there be a war in the Middle East? Any event that increases uncertainty about future investment returns will increase the value of the option to invest later and thus make it more likely that firms will wait and see by postponing an investment decision.

advantage of being able to delay is that more information may come along later that would help to avoid making a wrong decision.

The important idea is that some financial value should be assigned to the option to wait and see. Once the investment is undertaken, this option is killed and its value is lost. Hence, an irreversible investment should only be undertaken if the net present value is sufficiently large to compensate for the loss in value of the option.

An investment that involves significant sunk costs should only be undertaken by a profit-maximizing firm if the net present value of proceeding exceeds the value of the wait-and-see option.

One way to think about why this option must be valuable to a firm is to notice that if the investment goes ahead, the sunk costs of the project will be incurred with certainty, and there is always some probability that the project itself will lose money—that is, have a negative *NPV*. By postponing the project and perhaps cancelling it

later when new information comes along, the firm is not losing money with certainty. Hence, by exercising the option to wait and see, the firm could end up creating extra value (by not throwing money down the drain on an unprofitable project).

This analysis helps us understand why firms may require a substantial estimated *NPV* of a project before they will invest, whereas the theory set out above suggests that *any* positive *NPV* would be adequate to justify an investment.

The same idea can be applied to the close-down decision of firms. In Chapter 5 we assumed that costs were incurred in the same period as the benefits that they produced. Under these circumstances, profit-maximizing firms would close down if they were not covering their average variable costs. We are now considering situations in which costs incurred now may produce benefits in the future. As a result we need to alter this shutdown decision. The prediction of immediate close-down ignored the value of the options that the firm may have to engage in value-enhancing projects once market conditions improve. If the firm closes down irreversibly, these options would be lost. Hence, the statement about close-down decisions now needs to be modified to say that profit-maximizing firms should close down if the present value of the current and expected current losses exceeds the present value of the firm's expected present and future operations. This revision explains why other firms are often prepared to pay substantial sums to take over a firm that is currently not covering even its variable costs. Essentially, these firms are buying the investment options that the target firm owns.

New technologies[11]

So far, we have talked about capital as if investment was just a matter of adding more of the same. In reality, technical change almost always uses new capital that embodies new ways of doing things. In this section we illustrate the importance of technical change by examining the significance of the recent and ongoing revolution in information and communications technology. First, however, we need to consider growth in general and then discuss the place that *general-purpose technologies* play in the growth process.

Technologically driven growth

Long-term economic growth is driven by technological change—that is, by changes in the products that are produced, the process by which they are produced, and the ways in which productive activities are organized—what are called product, process, and organizational technologies. Although each person living in Western Europe and North America has nearly ten times as much 'real purchasing power' as did their forebears who lived 100 years ago, they consume it largely in the form of *new commodities* made with *new techniques* and *new organizations*. Those who lived at the beginning of the twentieth century could not have imagined modern dental and medical equipment, such as MRI and CAT scanners, penicillin, painkillers, bypass operations, safe births, control of genetically transmitted diseases, personal computers, compact discs, DVDs, TV sets, iPods and iPads, digital cameras, the internet, efficient automobiles, opportunities for cheap, fast worldwide travel, safe food of great variety free from ptomaine and botulism, or the elimination of endless kitchen drudgery through the use of detergents, washing machines, electric stoves, microwave ovens, vacuum cleaners, refrigerators, dishwashers, and a host of other labour-saving household products that we take for granted today. Nor could they have imagined the clean, robot-operated, computer-controlled modern factories that have largely replaced their noisy, dangerous, factories that spewed coal smoke and other pollutants over the surrounding countryside.

The point is important. Technological advance not only raises our incomes, but it also transforms our lives through the invention of new, hitherto undreamed of, things that are made in new, hitherto undreamed of, ways.

General purpose technologies

The technological changes that drive long-term economic growth range from small incremental improvements in existing technologies through to the introduction of what are called *general-purpose technologies* (GPTs). GPTs share some important common characteristics. They begin as fairly crude technologies with a limited number of uses. As they diffuse throughout the economy, they evolve into much more complex technologies with dramatic increases in their efficiency, the range of their use, the range of economic outputs that they help to produce, and the range of new product and process technologies that incorporate or otherwise depend on them.

Throughout history the most important new GPTs have had major impacts on the economic, social, and political structures, creating what may be called a series of 'new economies.' Here are some of the main ones.

- **Information and communication technologies** (ICTs): writing, printing with movable type, and the computer, which, along with several related technologies, has been driving the recent ICT revolution (see below).

- **Materials**: bronze, iron, and steel, and the current ability to create made-to-order materials invented specifically for use in newly developed products and processes.

- **Power-delivery systems**: domesticated animals, the water wheel, the steam engine, electricity, and the internal combustion engine.

- **Transportation**: the three-masted sailing ship, railways, the iron steamship, the motor vehicle, and

[11] This section draws heavily on the material in R.G. Lipsey, K.I. Carlaw, and C.T. Bekar, *Economic Tranformations: General Purpose Technologies and Long Term Economic Growth*, Oxford: Oxford University Press, 2005.

commercial aircraft (the latter two of which were enabled by the internal combustion engine).

- **Organizational technologies**: the factory system, mass production, and flexible manufacturing (or lean production, or Toyotaism, as it is variously called).

As each new GPT diffuses through the economy, it creates a research programme for entrepreneurs to apply its principles to create new processes, new forms of organization, and new products, and to improve old ones. These, in turn, create other new opportunities, and so on in a chain reaction that stretches over decades, even centuries. Note, for example, all of the myriad ways that innovators have found to use the computing power of electronic chips; how these ways have multiplied as the power and reliability of chips have increased; and how some of these ways have in turn enabled other developments, and so on in a complex linking of related innovations.

GPTs typically greatly reduce the cost of providing some good or service. Power GPTs reduced the cost of power, while information GPTs reduced the cost of creating, storing, transmitting, and analysing information.

However, it is important to note that some of the most important consequences to any new GPT depend on technological relations and not a mere change in the cost of delivering some given product of service. For example, the use of water power, the main source of non-human power for manufacturing until well into the nineteenth century, required that factories be located near fast-running water. The introduction of steam power freed manufacturing from that constraint and allowed it to locate in the industrial cities that grew up in the nineteenth century. No fall in the price of water power, even to zero, could have given rise to this transforming relocation of industry. For another example of this important point, the high power-to-weight ratio of the internal combustion engine allowed planes and small cars to be powered mechanically, which would have been impossible with steam engines, even if the price of steam power had fallen to zero.

Most GPTs require major changes in the entire structure of the economy, and often impact on social and political structures as well. For example, the change from water wheels to steam for powering manufacturing activities in the early nineteenth century allowed industry to move from the countryside to the new cities, urbanizing the United Kingdom for the first time in its history. It gave rise to a new entrepreneurial class that challenged the old aristocracy for economic and political power. It also gave rise to a landless proletariat who for the first time depended solely on their employer for economic survival.

New economies

Each of the GPTs mentioned above introduced a set of economic, social, and political transformations which could be called the creation of a 'New Economy'. Two examples from earlier ICT revolutions illustrate that what we are seeing today is not a new phenomenon.

Writing

The invention of writing around 3,500 BC caused a radical transformation of the societies of the Tigris–Euphrates valley. Written records permitted the development of sophisticated systems of taxation and public spending that were quite impossible when all records were held in human memory. The new public savings financed the world's first major irrigation works, the technology of which evolved rapidly. The area under cultivation increased and agricultural surpluses rose. The populations of the largest settlements, which typically had been measured in the hundreds for millennia, increased over the span of a mere two centuries into the tens of thousands.

Printing

In the fifteenth century the invention of printing with movable type greatly lowered the total cost of reproducing a manuscript. It also altered the ratio of variable to fixed costs: the major cost of manuscript reproduction was the variable cost of the scribe's time; the major cost of printing was the high fixed cost of typesetting, while the marginal cost of printing an extra copy was low. This new cost structure made mass communication feasible. Costs of large-scale publications fell and learning exploded. Monopolies of knowledge were upset. The results of new scientific experiments were quickly disseminated, and results were duplicated and expanded upon at a speed that would have seemed miraculous a century earlier. Mass communication helped the Protestant Revolution, since its direct appeal to the people would have been impossible without the many low-cost printed pamphlets written in the vernacular.

In the sixteenth century, the tiny Netherlands rose to become a world power. A key contributor to its success was its liberal attitude towards the technology of printing and the learning that it embodied—unlike the Islamic nations and China which suppressed it and continued with hand-copied manuscripts or wood-block reproductions for centuries. The creation of the Dutch information network, which was based on low cost reproduction of the printed word, greatly increased the economy's productive efficiency and the government's tax revenues. Between 1590 and 1620, the multinational corporation, the stock exchange, efficient year-round financial intermediation, the federal state, and a systematically drilled army all made their first appearances.

The information and communication technology (ICT) revolution

For the past few decades, the world has been living through a set of major structural adjustments associated with the so-called revolution in information and communications technologies (ICTs). Like most GPTs, the ICT revolution has roots that go a long way back in technological history. This one began with the development of commercially useful electricity in the nineteenth century. True 'tele' communications started in the 1840s with the introduction of the telegraph and its associated communications language, the Morse code. Submarine telegraphy started in 1851 with the first line from England to France. In 1866, the first commercial submarine cable came into regular use between Britain and the USA. The telephone was invented in 1876, and the wireless telegraph followed 20 years later. Wireless speech communication was first established in 1906, and in 1920 the first commercial radio station went on the air. Television first appeared in the late 1930s but was only widely available, at prices most households could afford, after 1945. Within little more than a century, the world in which news could travel no faster than humans, assisted by horses and ships, could carry it, which had existed since the dawn of time, was transformed into a world of instant worldwide communication. Never again could anything like the events of 1814 occur when the British were defeated by the Americans in the great Battle of New Orleans, a full two weeks after the Treaty of Ghent ended the war between them, but before the news reached the two armies.

The modern ICT revolution that began in the latter half of the twentieth century and is still going on today is based on a new GPT that is driven by a cluster of technologies centred around the electronic computer, but also including efficient long-distance STD telephonic communication, faxes, satellite transmissions, lasers, fibre optics, and the internet (most of which either use computers directly, or were developed with their assistance). These technologies have been changing product design, production, marketing, finance, and the organization of firms over the last several decades. By managing information flows more effectively than did the old hierarchically organized mass of middle managers, computers have caused a major reorganization in the management of firms. They have also created a wide range of new products incorporating hardcoded chips, computers, and/or software. Computers are used to design products, fly aeroplanes, drive

trains, operate machines, run buildings systems, facilitate scientific research, warn of unsafe driving practices, monitor health, and facilitate communication through the internet, e-mail, and desktop publishing.

When computers were initially introduced, they entered organization structures designed for the paper world, merely substituting for human hands and minds. Before they could really pay off, administration and production facilities had to be redesigned both physically and in their command structures. Slowly, as it was with electricity, the whole process of producing, designing, delivering, and marketing goods and services was, and still is being, reorganized along lines dominated by computing technologies.

ICT not only affects every industry and service but also every function within each industry, that is R&D, design, production, marketing, transport, and general administration. It is systemization rather than automation, integrating the various previously separate departments and functions. In design and development every industry now depends on computers. This is not just a question of Computer-Aided Design (CAD), although this is of great importance, especially in complex products, such as large buildings, chemical plants, aircraft, and ships as well as the products of the electronics industry itself. It is also a question of the accuracy, speed and volume of all kinds of calculations and access to data banks at all stages of the R&D process.

(Christopher Freeman, in Robert Mansell (ed.), *Management of Information and Communication Technologies*, London: Association of Information Management, 1994, pages 14–15.)

The current 'new economy'

The current ICT revolution is transforming many economic, social, and political relations, just as did most previous GPTs such as writing and printing. However, the term 'new economy' has been used in more than one sense in recent years, which can be a cause of confusion. During the internet bubble of the late 1990s and early 2000s, some used the term to refer to an economy in which the laws of supply and demand no longer held and there were neither business cycles nor inflations. Not many academic economists were gullible enough to believe that the ICT revolution would so alter normal economic behaviour. Others define the 'new economy' as the sector producing computing power and related things. By this supply-side definition, the 'new economy' covers only a small fraction of the whole economy. Yet others define a 'new economy' as occurring only when there is a sustained acceleration in the rate of growth of productivity. In contrast, the well-established procedure uses the term in a wider sense to refer to the social, economic, and political changes brought about by the current ICT revolution. It is an economy-wide *process*, not located in just one hi-tech *sector* any more than the new economy initiated by electricity was confined to the electricity generating sector.

Today people speak of many economies as being '*knowledge based*'. What does this mean, since knowledge has always been important in designing and producing both capital and consumers goods? The term 'knowledge-based economy' refers to the fact that today much more of most firms' capital is human rather than physical. Many firms consist of an office, some computers, and some highly trained and intelligent workers generating various services. Other firms that make goods require a highly trained workforce to design, produce, and market these goods. Compared with fifty or 100 years ago, much more of the typical firm's capital investment is in human knowledge than in physical machines. So, the higher is its ratio *human capital/physical capital* the more knowledge-based is a particular economy.

Box 11.6 shows some evidence of the potential importance of knowledge-based outputs for the economy as a whole.

We now list just a few of the many changes that have been driven by the ICT revolution since 1970. They are grouped loosely under the headings of process, product, and organizational technologies, and social and political implications, although the categories clearly overlap.

Process technologies

- Computerized robots and related technologies have transformed the modern factory and eliminated most of the high-paying low-skilled jobs that existed in the old Fordist assembly line factories.

- Computer-aided design (CAD) has revolutionized the design process and eliminated much of the need for 'learning by using', where complex products such as new aircraft had to be built before their behavioural characteristics could be fully established.

- Surgery on hips, knees, and other delicate parts of the body is more and more conducted by computer-driven robots. They have now facilitated distant surgery, permitting specialists working in major urban hospitals to operate on patients in remote parts of the world. Now, artificial limbs can be controlled by a person's thought which communicates with a computer that then issues orders to the limb with which it communicates. Now artificial limbs are being developed that allow the person to feel what is touching her, just as if it was her real arm or leg.

Box 11.6 Intangible assets matter

Capital formation is an important activity in the economy but, as we have seen in Box 11.2, it is not just physical capital, such as machines and buildings, that matter. Intellectual capital is also valuable even though it is hard to measure. Traditional measures of capital formation concentrate on physical capital, or what is generally called 'tangible capital'. However, recent research has shown that intangible capital formation is of growing significance and on some estimates has become larger than tangible capital formation.

The table lists an estimate of the growth in spending on intangible assets between 1990 and 2007. Comparable figures for tangible asset formation are given in the top row. Intangible asset formation was smaller than tangible asset formation in 1990, but by 2007 it was considerably larger.

The types of asset involved in intangibles include software, R&D, design, mineral exploration and copyrights, branding, training, and organizational developments. Of these, only software has been measured as part of capital formation in official figures and that only recently. Many of these assets are not easy to measure but they clearly add value to businesses when successful, and thus should not be ignored as enhancements to the stock of productive capital.

Year	1990	1995	2000	2007
All tangibles	67	62	87	95
Intangible category				
Software development	6	10	16	20
R&D	8	8	11	15
Design	9	12	18	22
Mineral exploration and copyrights	3	3	2	4
Branding	5	7	12	14
Training	13	16	24	32
Organisational	9	12	17	26
All intangibles	52	69	100	133

Note : Data are absolute investments figures, in £ billions, current prices. For clarity, 'Design' refers to architectural & engineering design, and financial product development

Source: J. Haskel, T. Clayton, P. Goodridge, A. Pesole, D. Barnett, G. Chamberlin, R. Jones, K. Khan, and A. Turvey, *Innovation, Knowledge Spending and Productivity Growth in the UK, Interim Report for NESTA Innovation Index Project*, London: NESTA, 2009

- Research in everything from economics to astronomy has been changed dramatically by the ability to perform complex calculations that were either impossible or prohibitively time consuming without electronic computers.

- Computer-age crime detection is much more sophisticated than it was in the past. Here, the biological and the ICT revolutions complement each other, as is so often the case with coexisting GPTs.

- Traffic control in the air and on the ground has been revolutionized in many ways, while navigation at sea is now so easy that lighthouses, the sailor's friend for several millennia, are being phased out as unnecessary since ships can determine their location to within a few yards using satellites and computers.

Product technologies

- Many goods now contain chips that allow them to do new things or old things more efficiently. New applications continue to be developed. For example, some cars are now equipped with systems that warn drivers of oncoming dangers and take over control if the driver fails to take evasive action. Self-parking cars are now a reality, soon to be followed by cars that can drive over city streets without human assistance.

- ATMs have enormously facilitated accessing one's bank account and obtaining funds in any currency in almost any part of the world.

- Email has largely replaced conventional mail, with a large increase in volume and speed of transmission, from days or weeks in the past, depending on the two locations, to seconds today.

- Computerized translation is a now a reality and will go from its present crude form to high degrees of sophistication within the lifetimes of most of us. We are witnessing the arrival of Douglas Adam's vision in *The Hitch Hiker's Guide to the Galaxy*: the ability to hear in one's own language words spoken in any other language, and to be understood in any other language while speaking one's own. The only difference is that instead of inserting a fish into one's ear, a small computer will be attached to one's body.

- Distance learning is growing by leaps and bounds, and many are enrolled in education courses where they never (or only rarely) set foot inside the institution whose courses they are studying.

- Smart buildings and factories already exist and will grow rapidly in number. Among many other things, power consumption can be adjusted continually in response to real-time price signals sent out by the electricity supply company and calculated in response to current loads.

- Electronic means of reading books are coming into increasing use. The book's blank page fills up on demand with any one of a hundred or more books stored in a chip that is housed inside the device. A touch of a button and one is reading a physics text; with another touch, a chemistry text replaces it. When you get bored with this, you can switch to where you were in a detective story.

Organizational technologies

- The management of firms has been reorganized as direct lines of communication opened up by computers eliminated the need for the old pyramidal structure in which middle managers processed and communicated information. Today's horizontally organized loose structure bears little resemblance to the management structure of the 1960s.

- Firms are increasingly disintegrating their operations. Virtually no firm in Silicon Valley, California's pioneering hi-tech sector, now produces physical products. In other industries, the main firm is increasingly becoming a coordinator of subcontractors who do everything from designing products, through manufacturing them, to distributing them.

- The e-lance economy, so-called after 'freelancers' who are connected by internet—groups of independent contractors who come together for a single job and then disperse—is growing and, incidentally, becoming difficult for authorities to track.

- Just as the first industrial revolution took work out of the home, the ICT revolution is putting much of it back, as more and more people find it increasingly convenient to do all sorts of jobs at home rather than 'in the office'.

- ICTs have been central to the globalization of trade in manufactured goods and of the market for unskilled workers. This has shifted the location of much manufacturing and allowed poorer countries to industrialize, creating new opportunities and challenges for both developed and developing nations.

- Digitalized special effects have changed the movie industry in many ways—for example, by reducing the need for shooting on location and the requirement fo myriad extras whose presence can often be produced digitally.

Political and social technologies

- The computer-enabled internet is revolutionizing everything from interpersonal relations to political activity. Facebook, Twitter, blogging, and chat rooms form the basis for new forms of community and communication, making interpersonal relations possible on a scale and complexity never seen before. For example, non-governmental organizations (NGOs) and individuals are able to organize activities to protest about a wide variety of environmental and other political issues.

- Dictators find it much harder to cut their subjects off from knowledge of what is going on in the outside world, and hence to maintain their power.

- Driven by the internet, English is becoming a lingua franca for the world and, unlike Latin in the Middle Ages, its use is not limited to the intelligentsia.

- In former times, a physical presence was required from virtually everyone providing a service. With computers, email links, and a host of other ICTs, this link between physical presence and provision has been broken in many services, with profound social and political effects on such things as place of residence and the ability to regulate and tax many activities.

Falling cost curves

Most of the firms that we have looked at in earlier chapters have been assumed to have U-shaped or horizontal marginal and average variable cost curves. Typically, many ICT firms have very large fixed costs associated with the R&D and set-up costs of creating and establishing a new technology in the ICT sector. In contrast, marginal costs of producing another unit of output are constant and very small or virtually zero. As a result, the average fixed and average total cost curves are close together and both decline throughout their whole relevant ranges. Microsoft, for example, spent a lot of money and effort developing its Windows software (and MS DOS before that), but once it existed, an extra copy could be made at virtually no cost. Similarly, modern telephone cables have a very high capacity so that once the lines are in place, the extra cost of delivering a marginal call is virtually zero.

Increasing returns tend to generate natural monopolies (discussed in Chapter 7). Such industries tend to be characterized by *winner takes all* outcomes, as new entrants find it virtually impossible to break in to an industry where an established player is selling its product at very low marginal cost. This is reinforced by the *network externalities* that arise from the adoption of common standards. For example, compatibility of computers is helpful so that they can exchange messages and software. When Microsoft Windows emerged as the standard platform, most software was developed to be compatible with it and new operating systems found it hard to break in. Similarly,

because a telephone network is more useful to any one user the more other users are on the same system, new phone companies found it hard to break into the UK telephone market while BT owned all the lines. Regulators tried to offset this advantage by insisting that BT give other companies access to the network. Later, in an example of Schumpeter's creative destruction, the new technology of mobile phones made traditional phone lines less important.

Increasing returns are not unique to ICT industries. Pharmaceuticals also have some products, such as major drugs, that incur huge costs to develop, but then can often be produced at low marginal cost. These products tend to gain a dominant position while patent protection lasts (see Chapter 7), and the companies making them hope to recoup their development cost during the patent period. Once the patent expires, such drugs are typically copied and sold by other drug companies at close to marginal cost.

It is not always the best product that obtains the winner-take-all advantage. The VHS format became the dominant standard for videotapes because it established a critical mass ahead of Betamax, even though the latter may have been a better system. But videotape formats of both types were later superseded by digital recording technologies.

The nature of competition is different in constant or falling marginal cost industries. Where costs are rising, firms are competing at the margin—a small price change or quality initiative will take a bit of business at the margin from several main rivals. Market share may rise or fall, but only a small amount at a time. However, constant or falling marginal cost industries tend to have big jumps from one dominant player to another. Companies like Intel, Microsoft, Amazon, AOL, Nokia, and Vodafone grew to be huge within less than two decades. They may disappear just as quickly if some new and better technology removes their edge. In contrast, traditional retailers, banks, and manufacturers tend to grow slowly and fade slowly. They may merge or be taken over and so lose their name, but they are rarely made redundant by the sudden appearance of a new technology.

In these and many other ways, new ICTs have already revolutionized society and will continue to do so throughout the twenty-first century. Some of these are minor while others are transforming—for example, globalization and its many ramifications, the dramatic changes in the organization of firms, the end of mass production and its associated labour and management requirements, the alternations in the political power structure, and the emergence of the civil society and its effects on the conduct of international negotiations.

CASE STUDIES

1. Taken for a ride? Taxis in New York and London

The pricing of capital assets is well illustrated by comparing the system of regulating taxicabs in London with the different one in use in New York. In 1937, the New York authorities issued 11,787 permits to operate a taxi, known as 'medallions', for $10 each and issued no additional medallions for another six decades. These medallions came to change hands for significant sums of money. A Pakistani immigrant who bought a medallion in 1981 for $30,000 is reported to have sold it in 2007 for $600,000. An auction of a small number of new medallions issued by the New York authorities in 2006 is reported to have raised an average price of $514,000. Another auction of 200 new medallions held in November 2013, after five years of no new issues, raised an average price of $1 million.

The entry restriction in New York clearly makes it worth investing a significant sum of money to be able to operate a taxi. This entry cost can be thought of as an investment in an asset that yields a positive stream of income in the future. The market clearing entry price is thus the present value of the extra income that can be earned in this occupation compared with the best alternative.

The licensing system controls both the number of taxicabs and the fares they can charge, and as a result the number of cabs is kept well below what it would be in a free-market situation. As the population increases and people earn higher incomes, the demand for the services of taxicabs rises. In a free-market fares would rise, increasing the earnings of taxi owners. The higher earnings would attract new entrants until earnings had been reduced to what could be earned in other comparable lines of activity. But regulations imply that neither of these things can happen, so existing cabs spend less time empty and hence earn more for their owners. Since investment in a taxi would now earn more than comparable other investments, investors would like to enter the industry. However, the only way to do so is to buy one of the fixed supply of medallions. So the market price of medallions is bid up. The price rises to equal the present value of the extra earnings that can be obtained by investing in a taxicab rather than other comparable lines of activity. As a result, new entrants earn only normal returns on their investment, which includes the price of the medallion. Eventually the regulating authority raises fares in response to the excess demand. If the demand proves inelastic, the gross income from operating a cab rises. But the price of the medallion is bid up correspondingly. Thus the fare increase amounts to a windfall to the current holders of medallions; it does nothing to raise the net incomes of cab operators newly entering the industry, or to make it more attractive to enter.

Most medallions were originally owned by individuals who drove their own taxi. Now many are owned by investors who hire drivers at the minimum wage to drive taxis for them. The investors pocket the surplus revenue (income above the minimum wage) and hope to benefit further from the rising value of the medallions.

This system of regulating taxis is not unique to New York. For example, one of the 1,825 existing medallions to operate a taxi in Boston was reported to cost $600,000 in 2013, and similar examples can be found in other North American cities.

In London, on the other hand, the fares of black cabs are rigidly regulated, but entry is free to anyone who can pass a set of tests.[12] The fares of minicabs are unregulated and entry is free (but they are prohibited from cruising the streets in search of fares). Periodically, black cab fares are raised in an effort to raise incomes. If demand is inelastic, incomes do rise in the short run. But this attracts new entrants, who continue to enter until each existing cab is carrying just enough fares to cover its full opportunity cost, at which price economic profits have been reduced to zero. This case is analytically identical to the case of hairdressers discussed in Box 8.2 in Chapter 8.

2. The economics of land prices and the height of skyscrapers

This case study shows that the evolution of a city over time is determined to a great extent by the size and type of buildings that the market shows to be currently most profitable. This in turn depends on both demand for the products produced in the city and the evolving technology of construction. All of these influence decisions about the installation of new capital.

The larger is a city's population, the larger is the demand for all the inputs that are required to run its industries and service its residents. One of these inputs is land. So, according to the principles of derived demand, the larger the city, the higher the demand for land on

---

[12] The main test is known as 'The Knowledge' as it involves learning street names and locations.

which to site all of its activities. A high demand for labour in the city will attract more people to come to the city. But land cannot move from one place to another. So, the higher the demand for land, the higher its rental and purchase price.

Since land in the centre of cities is a more desirable location for almost all commercial activities than land on the periphery, the demand for central land is higher than that for land on the periphery. As a result, virtually all cities show a 'rent gradient' with rents and property prices looking like a tent, highest in the centre and declining towards the edges. Figure 11.4 shows typical gradients for two cities, one larger than the other. If land were physically mobile, it would be reallocated until these gradients disappeared. Since it is immobile, the gradients persist indefinitely.

It follows that the margin between the price of land in the centre of the city and on the edges will increase as the city grows. So the margin is higher in London than in Bristol and higher in Bristol than in Shrewsbury.

What determines the height of buildings? Construction costs per square metre of usable space rise as the height of buildings rises. There are many reasons for this, including the requirements that higher buildings be stronger with more and faster lifts than smaller buildings. Profit-maximizing developers will go on adding to a building's designed height until the extra cost per square metre can

just be covered by rentals. So for any piece of land, the larger the city and the closer to the centre is its location, the higher the demand for the space it provides—thus the higher the building that can be profitably erected on it. For this reason most large cities display a profile of average height of building that is similar to their rent profile, highest in the centre and lowest at the peripheries.

Why is this predicted profile much clearer in New York than in London? The reason is that until the last half of the twentieth century, construction technology did not permit the erection of very high buildings on the clay that underlies London. In contrast, New York is largely built on rock, and for more than a hundred years technology has been adequate for the construction of very high buildings on rock. When the technology of construction improved in the last half of the twentieth century, the average height of new London buildings began to increase, just as the theory predicts.

Why, when the technology changed, did London's profile not immediately change to mimic New York's? One reason is related to sunk costs. It can take a long time for durable physical capital to exit a declining industry. Similarly, it takes a long time for old buildings to wear out and be replaced. The buildings are already there, and all the associated construction costs are sunk. They cannot be recovered by exiting. A new building must earn, over and above what the old building can earn, enough to repay the

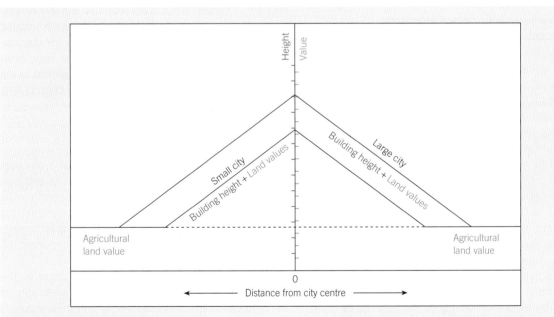

Figure 11.4 Rent and height profiles

Both land rents and building heights tend to be highest at the city centre. The figure shows two typical rent gradients for cities of two different sizes. Rents are highest at the city centre and fall towards the periphery. At the boundary between the city and the countryside, the rent that urban users can pay just equals the rent that can be paid for the same land in agricultural use. Building heights will show a similar profile, being highest at the centre and tending to fall as one moves towards the periphery.

full costs of construction. So, as the theory predicts, we see large variations in the sizes of buildings, even on the most expensive land in the centre of the city. But old buildings are eventually demolished, either because they reach the limit of their age, or because their productivity falls sufficiently below what a new building would earn on the same site. So old and new coexist, but gradually the old go and new higher buildings take their place.

A second reason is related to government regulations. Many of the older London boroughs and hamlets had long-standing restrictions on building heights. These tended to push the new higher buildings away from the very centre of the city to the nearest convenient location where these restrictions do not apply. Canary Wharf and Docklands are literally and figuratively monuments to the new construction technologies and the response of the market to economic and political forces.

3. The winner's curse

In any auction market the sale price is determined by what the highest bidder is prepared to pay. In a standard auction, the price keeps rising until all but one bidder drops out. The highest bidder, who ends up acquiring the object for sale, is often described as the 'winner'. However, the winner of an auction, especially in the context of the 'winner' of a takeover bid, may not be a winner at all.

The winner of a takeover fight has to pay a price so high that not only are the existing owners prepared to sell, but also all other bidders have dropped out. This means that the so-called winner has paid a price for the target firm that is higher than the valuation placed on it by any other party in the auction.

The winner may know something about the value of the target firm that nobody else knows. More often, however, all bidders have roughly the same information. But there is always some uncertainty about how to assess the importance of this information. The uncertainty gives rise to differences in the potential purchasers' assessments of the true value of the target firm. The auction guarantees that the winner will be the bidder with the most optimistic estimate. If the average of all the bidders' estimates is close to the true value, the firm that wins will always pay more than the true value. Fortunately for the winner, uncertainty is such that sometimes even the most optimistic estimate is less than the true value. Also, the target firm is sometimes worth more to the winner than to any other bidder. In such cases the winner really wins.

In other cases, however, the firm that wins a takeover battle does not increase the value of its own company. Indeed, in a hotly contested bidding war in which there are rival bidders and the winning bid is well above the initial bid, the successful bidder may end up paying more than

the target firm is really worth. This is why this phenomenon is known as the winner's curse.

The true winners in a takeover war may be not only the shareholders of the target company but also the rival bidders who failed to 'win'. The shareholders win because they sell their shares for more than they are really worth, at least in the opinion of most potential buyers. The losing bidders win because their rival who 'won' the auction may be saddled with a capital loss that could weaken its ability to compete in other ways.

A good example of this phenomenon is the takeover of the Crocker Bank of California by the UK's Midland Bank. This so weakened Midland that it ended up being taken over itself by HSBC. Another example is the takeover of RJR Nabisco by Kolberg Kravis Roberts (KKR) in one of the most famous (and biggest—$25 billion) takeover auctions of all time. KKR survived, but the firm's ability to raise capital for other activities was severely dented for most of the following decade.

In 2007 RBS (and a consortium of other banks) outbid Barclays to take over the Dutch bank ABN Amro for around £48 billion. In 2008, RBS would have gone bust itself if it had not received a massive capital injection from the UK government. RBS had to write off the entire cost of its share of the bid, which means that it lost every penny spent to buy this bank. The then chairman of RBS admitted later that the takeover was a 'bad mistake'.

The winner's curse applies not just to takeover bids but also to any transaction in which there is competitive bidding, such as for supply contracts which go to the lowest bidder. That bidder may have underestimated the true costs and hence may lose on the deal.

Telecom companies such as BT and Vodafone were stockmarket stars when they entered an auction for 3G telecoms licences in April 2000. They 'won' licences in the auction but at a very high price, and the companies' share prices declined dramatically in the two subsequent years. The beneficiary in this case was the UK government, which received a total revenue of £23 billion for the five licences on offer. Its earlier estimate of the likely revenue was £3 billion. BT did not learn from this experience, as their results in January 2009 were seriously worsened by £340 million losses on contracts (including one providing IT for the NHS) that it had obtained by bidding too low.

4. Graphene: material of the future

Graphene is a new material that is a product of nanotechnology (see Case Study 2 at the end of Chapter 5). It is made up of a single layer of carbon atoms that are assembled in a new way (the old way is as graphite that is used for the lead in a pencil). This material was developed by

Professor Geim and Professor Vovoselov of the University of Manchester who were awarded to 2010 Nobel Physics prize for this work.

Graphene is a substance that is extremely strong but also very light, and it is an excellent conductor of both heat and electricity. Graphene has many potential applications[13] but the most obvious of these are where the strength to weight ratio is important, such as in aircraft or packaging, including luggage. The electrical conductivity and heat transmission properties make graphene suitable for use in mobile electronic devices such as tablets and

phones, as well as in batteries, fuel cells, and solar cells. Other potentially important applications are in disease diagnosis sensors, water desalination equipment, and chemical sensors (such as those that detect explosives). Myriad other applications will no doubt emerge in due course.

Carbon is a very abundant element, found most obviously in coal, oil, and wood, but recent advances in materials science have facilitated a complete transformation of what can be done with this element. Indeed, carbon dioxide in the atmosphere is one of the main greenhouse gases associated with global warming, but perhaps carbon in one form can help solve the problems caused by carbon in another.

---

[13] See http://www.understandingnano.com/graphene-applications.html

Conclusion

Capital is an important input into production. Increases in the capital stock are central to the process of generation of productivity gains that underpin the growth of real living standards over time. All businesses that invest in new capital have to make a careful assessment of the contribution of additional capital to the value of the firm. New capital often embodies new technology, and technical change often has substantial implications for the range of employment opportunities and for the organization of firms and the economy as a whole. Recent and ongoing changes in information, communication, and materials technology are also transforming the world in which we all live and work.

SUMMARY

Capital as an input

■ Because capital goods are durable, it is necessary to distinguish between the stock of capital goods and the flow of services provided by them, and thus between their purchase price and their rental price. The linkage between them relies on the ability to assign a present value to future returns.

■ The present value of a future payment will be lower when the payment is more distant and/or the interest rate is higher.

■ Profit maximizing firms will hire capital goods up to the point at which the rental price of capital in each period equals its marginal revenue product in that period.

■ The rental price is the amount that is paid to obtain the flow of services that a capital good provides for a given period.

■ The purchase price is the amount that is paid to acquire ownership of the capital, and firms will buy capital good up to the point where their price is just equal to the present value of the future net income stream generated by the capital. This is the present value of capital's future stream of marginal revenue products.

■ A profit maximizing firm will invest in capital goods as long as the present value of the stream of future net income that is provided by another unit of capital exceeds its purchase price.

■ For a single firm and for the economy as a whole, the size of the total capital stock demanded varies negatively with the rate of interest.

The investment decision

■ A central element of an investment appraisal is the choice of discount rate. Firms should discount future cash flows at a rate that reflects the cost of funds to them and the riskiness of the project involved.

■ Present value calculations should allow for inflation appropriately.

■ Sunk costs do not affect the profitability of future investment decisions.

- The option value of an investment that has not yet been made may justify delaying the investment.

New technology

- The revolution in information and communication technologies (ICTs) has roots that go back to the nineteenth century, but it accelerated in the latter part of the twentieth century when a new general-purpose technology, the electronic computer and a few related technologies, began to transform much of the economic, social and political structure of society.

- The revolution has been associated with many new products, new production processes, and new forms of organization.

- Nonetheless, resources still move in response to price signals and profit motives.

- Two of the special features of ICT industries are increasing returns and network externalities. These generate a winner-take-all competition between firms.

TOPICS FOR REVIEW

- Rental price and purchase price of capital
- The present value of a future sum
- The net present value (*NPV*) investment criterion
- The interest rate and the capital stock
- The risk-free rate and the risk premium
- Nominal and real interest rates
- Sunk costs
- The value of option to wait-and-see

- The ICT revolution
- General purpose technologies
- Declining average total cost curves due to high costs of R&D and set-up for entry
- Network externalities
- Winner takes all
- Winner's curse

QUESTIONS

1 An extra tractor will lead to an increase in revenue for a farmer in successive years of £500, £4,000, £3,000, £3,000, and £1,000, after which the tractor is sold for £1,000. Assuming that the first revenue is treated as current, and the interest rate is 8 per cent, what is the present value of the extra income stream?

2 If a new tractor costs £10,000 in the current period, would the purchase of the tractor increase the present value of profit?

3 If the tractor could be paid for in five equal instalments of £2,000 in each of the five years, would this make the purchase of the tractor more attractive?

4 Suppose that you are offered, free of charge, one from each of the following pairs of assets:

   a) a perpetuity that pays £20,000 per year for ever, or an annuity that pays £100,000 per year for five years;

   b) an oil-drilling company that earned £100,000 after corporate taxes last year, or British government bonds that paid £100,000 in interest last year;

   c) a 1 per cent share in a new company that has invested £10 million in a new cosmetic that is thought to appeal to middle-income women or a £100,000 bond that has been issued by the same company.

What considerations would determine your choice in each case?

5 How would you go about evaluating the present value of each of the following?

   a) the existing reserves of a relatively small oil company,

   b) the total world reserves of an exhaustible natural resource with a known, completely fixed supply,

   c) a long-term bond, issued by a very unstable Third World government, that promises to pay the bearer £1,000 per year for ever,

   d) a lottery ticket that your neighbour bought for £10 that was one of a million tickets sold for a draw to be held in one year's time that will pay £2 million to the single winner.

6 If the interest rate is 6 per cent, then the net present value of a project which requires an investment of £100,000 this year and then yields £30,000 in each of the next four years is (choose one):

a) + £3,690
b) + £3,950
c) + £12,140
d) + £20,000
e) – £20,000.

7 If the interest rate is 8 per cent, then the net present value of a project which requires an investment of £100,000 this year and then yields £30,000 in each of the next four years is (choose one):

a) + £640
b) – £590
c) – £640
d) – £20,000
e) + £640.

8 List some of the ways in which increasing returns industries differ from traditional diminishing returns industries.

9 In what ways has the internet changed the education sector?

10 What threats and opportunities has digital music recording (including downloads) created for the market in recorded music?

CHAPTER 12

ECONOMICS OF RISK AND FINANCIAL CRISES

Nothing in life is certain. Economic transactions, just like everything else we do, involve some element of risk. In some cases the risk does not significantly affect what is done and can be ignored. In other cases the riskiness of the transactions seriously affects the behaviour of those involved in them. Investment, which we discussed in Chapter 11, is always risky to some degree as the future return is unknown at the time the resources are committed. Risk is also central to understanding the financial system, as borrowing and lending involve risks that need to be managed and understood. It is this impact of risk on economic choices and markets that we need to understand, as well as why the financial system is prone to occasional crises. Risk is not strictly an input into the economy, but it is a major element of much of economic and human activity.

In this chapter you will learn that:

- Diminishing marginal utility of income is sufficient to make people averse to taking risks.

- Risk-averse individuals will rationally wish to buy insurance even if it is not a fair gamble.

- Markets for insurance have to cope with problems of moral hazard—people take more risk because they are insured—and adverse selection—people who know they are most at risk are those most likely to buy insurance.

- Portfolio diversification can reduce financial risks faced by investors.

- Financial intermediaries exist in part because of their ability to spread risk.

- Financial crises can arise after periods of optimism when asset prices rise, debt increases, and speculators expect further rises in asset prices. A collapse can result when some event changes expectations sharply and investors race to sell their assets while prices fall sharply and the solvency of some financial institutions is threatened.

We first look at how risk can be characterized and measured. Then we discuss insurance and gambling, both of which involve risk. We find that there appears to be a paradox when people are willing to supply and demand both insurance and gambling activities. After resolving the apparent paradox, we look at problems that arise in markets for insurance and some other financial transactions. First, the existence of insurance may influence how people behave. Secondly, the buyers and sellers of insurance may have different amounts of information about the risks that are being insured against. Later in the chapter we consider the problems of investing in financial assets that carry different amounts and types of risk. This leads to the important issues of portfolio diversification and the management of risk by use of appropriate financial instruments. We also discuss some new insights into financial behaviour that have been associated with new work in behavioural finance. Finally, we look at the factors involved in financial crises. Box 12.1 looks at one aspect of financial risk associated with movements in stock markets.

Box 12.1 Risky financial markets

There are many types of risk, both financial and non-financial, but one form of risk is linked to asset prices. Collapses in asset prices usually happen during a financial crisis. We explain the characteristics of many financial crises in the last section of this chapter and also look at events surrounding the collapse of one UK bank in 2007. Here we want to show what happened to the major world equity markets around the time of the 2007–8 financial crisis. The figure shows data for stock market indexes in four places: S&P 500 for the United States, FTSE All-Share for the United Kingdom, Euro Stoxx for the Eurozone, and Topix for Japan. Each index is set at 100 for 2 January 2007.

All of these markets fell sharply in September 2008 at the time of the financial crisis when the US investment bank Lehman Brothers went bust and several other banks around the world had to be bailed out with government funds. All of these markets lost about half of their value between mid-2007 and early 2009. The index represents a weighted average of all companies' shares traded on that market, so many specific shares will have fallen a lot more that this average. Indeed, some shares became worthless when the company concerned went bust. Northern Rock, a British bank, was one such company, and we discuss its demise in a case study at the end of this chapter.

A notable feature of the behaviour of the stock markets shown here is that all started to recover in about March 2009, but the recovery did not last in Japan and the Euro zone. Indeed, the Topix index was as low in 2012 as its lowest point in 2009. The Eurozone stock market also was significantly depressed in 2011 and 2012 at the time of the Eurozone debt crisis (discussed in a case study at the end of Chapter 25). The Japan and Eurozone stock markets did recover in 2013, but only to levels about 40 per cent below their 2007 peaks. In contrast, UK and US stock markets reached all-time highs in 2013. The key message is that these markets are volatile so investing in shares is risky.

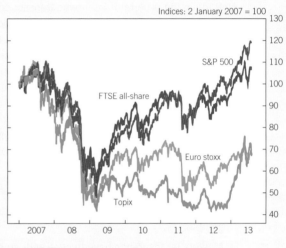

Source: Bank of England, *Inflation Report*, August 2013.

Risk and consumer choice

In Chapter 4 we studied the behaviour of consumers who were presented with choices that involve various outcomes. We asked, for example, if a consumer would prefer bundle A, containing ten units of food and five units of clothing, to bundle B, containing six units of food and twelve units of clothing. In so doing, we assumed implicitly that the bundle chosen could be obtained with certainty. What happens, however, if the consumer is faced with only a *probability* of obtaining each bundle?

This is not the type of choice that normally faces a shopper. Usually, she knows that if she pays her money she will get what she has paid for with certainty. Sometimes, however, the shopper is uncertain about the quality of the various products offered for sale. She may think that the more expensive brand X will last longer and require less maintenance than the cheaper brand Y. However, she may not, be sure of how *much* longer it will last, and how *much* less maintenance will be involved.

Other types of choice involve more serious kinds of risk. You may reduce the chance of being burgled by buying a flat in area A rather than area B or installing a burglar alarm or bars on the ground-floor windows—but by how much? Flats in one area may appreciate in value more than in another—but by how much?

Many of the principles discussed in this chapter were first developed by analysing games of chance such as roulette or coin-tossing.[1] The same principles arise in consumption and production decisions involving risk, but they can often be more easily appreciated in the context of games, such as some of those outlined in Chapter 8, where all the possible outcomes and their probabilities are known. Risk in the real world is generally more open-ended and

---

[1] The first major analysis of choices involving risk was by the Swiss mathematician Daniel Bernoulli (1700–82) in 1738. The subject was greatly advanced by the publication in 1944 of *Theory of Games and Economic Behaviour* by John von Neumann (1903–57) and Oskar Morgenstern (1902–77).

therefore more complex to analyse. This chapter gives only an intuitive overview of the issues involved.

The characterization of risk

How do people make choices when the outcome of any choice is not certain? To study this question we need two important concepts. The first is called **expected value**. This is defined as the most likely outcome if some situation is repeated over and over. The second is called the **degree of risk**. This is measured by the dispersion of possible outcomes if some situation is repeated over and over. Under certainty, there is only one possible outcome to any given choice. Thus this outcome is the expected value and the dispersion of outcomes is zero, indicating no risk. Under risk, more than one outcome is possible. Now the most likely outcome is the expected value and the spread of possible outcomes is the degree of risk.

Expected value

Suppose that two people, Tom and Jo, play a game in which a coin is tossed *once every minute*. The coin is fair in that there is an equal chance of throwing a head or a tail. The probability of throwing a head is said to be 0.5 or 1/2, and the probability of throwing a tail is also 0.5 or 1/2.[2] Tom pays Jo £1 if the result is a head, and Jo pays Tom £1 if the result is a tail.[3] If they play the game for 10 minutes, one may have a lucky run and win £10 in 10 minutes, but there is an equal chance of having an unlucky run and losing £10. However, it is much more likely that there will be some heads and some tails, so the winnings of one player and the losses of the other will be much smaller than £10. The single most likely outcome is that Tom and Jo will exactly break even. This is because there are more sequences of ten tosses that will end up with five heads and five tails than any other single combination of heads and tails. For the same reason, the two next most likely results are that Jo will win £2 (six heads and four tails) or that Jo will lose £2 (six tails and four heads). Outcomes with larger gains and larger losses are less likely. The two least likely results are Jo winning £10 or losing £10 (and vice versa for Tom).

Now consider playing the game repeatedly day after day. It is still quite possible that either player will end up winning £10 or losing £10. For example, if they have broken even after many days of play, the chance that they will now encounter ten heads in a row is the same as it was on their first ten tosses of the coin. But as they go on

playing, the average return *per minute spent playing the game* gets smaller and smaller. This return can be expressed as $(H - T)/n$, where n is the number of minutes they have spent playing the game, which is the same as the number of tosses, H is the number of heads obtained so far, and T is the number of tails. Every time the game is played, n increases by 1; the only way the numerator can increase by the same amount is if *every* toss is an H, or every toss is a T. So, if one player's sequence of losses contains a mixture of heads and tails, the average gain or loss per play will tend to decline. Indeed, it can be shown that, as they go on playing for longer and longer periods of time, so that n increases without limit, the value of $(H - T)/n$ tends to zero. This is the expected value of the game.

The expected value is the most likely outcome for a small number of tosses and the expected earnings on average per toss if the game is repeated many times—in the example above the expected value is zero.

Another way of calculating the expected value of the outcome of any game is to add up the various outcomes, each multiplied by its probability of occurrence. The coin tossing game above has two possible outcomes for each player on each toss: either he wins £1 with probability 0.5, or he loses £1 with probability 0.5. The expected value of the outcome is £1(0.5) – £1(0.5) = £0.50 – £0.50 = 0.

Degree of risk

In the above game each player stood to win £1 per toss or lose £1 per toss. If they agreed to play for 10 minutes, their maximum possible loss would be £10. Now suppose they play the same game, one toss per minute, but this time Tom pays Jo £100 for each head and Jo pays Tom £100 for each tail. The expected value of the outcome is still zero. But they each risk more if they play it for any given amount of time. There is the same chance that Jo will encounter an unlucky run of ten tails, but now she stands to lose £1,000 in this event. Clearly, there is more risk attached to the second game than to the first. Risk refers to the dispersion of the possible results that is the range of possible outcomes. In the first game the possible results from 10 minutes play are dispersed over a range running from +£10 to –£10; in the second game the possible results are dispersed over a range running from +£1,000 to –£1,000.

The degree of riskiness associated with a decision is determined by the dispersion in the possible outcomes that could result from making that choice.[4]

---

[2] These are equivalent expressions. The first, 0.5, is the ratio of the expected number of heads to the overall number of tosses. The second, 1/2, says there is one chance in two of throwing a head (since there are two equally likely outcomes on any one toss).

[3] This game is a *zero sum game*, first mentioned in Box 8.4 in Chapter 8; it is defined as any game in which the sum of the winnings and losses of all the players is always zero. In other words, what someone in the game wins, someone else in the game must have lost.

[4] In the text we approximated the degree of dispersion by the range between the two most extreme possible results. A better and more common measure is called the *variance* of the possible results, which is the average of the sum of the squares of the deviations of each possible result from the average, or most likely, result. It is also often measured by the *standard deviation*, which is the square root of the variance.

Fair and unfair games

The penny-toss game that we have considered so far is a mathematically fair game in the sense that each player has just as much chance of winning as of losing. A lottery in which all of the ticket money is paid out is also a fair game. Say, for example, that 100 lottery tickets are sold for £1 each, and a draw then determines which one of the ticket-holders wins £100. This is a fair game because each ticket-holder has one chance in 100 of winning £99 (the person's own £1 back and £99 of winnings) and 99 chances out of 100 of losing £1. To find the expected value of this gamble, we multiply the winnings of £99 by the chance of winning it (one chance in 100) and subtract the loss multiplied by the chance of losing it (99 chances in 100). This gives

$$£99(1/100) - £1(99/100) = £0.99 - £0.99 = 0.$$

A mathematically fair game is one for which the expected value of the outcome is zero.

If you play a fair game repeatedly, you may end up winning or losing, depending on the 'luck of the toss', but the *average gain or loss per play* calculated over all plays will tend towards zero as time passes.

Now consider playing the coin-tossing game under the following rules: heads we pay you £2, tails you pay us £1. The expected value of the outcome of this game to you is £2(0.5) − £1(0.5) = £1 − £0.50 = £0.50. If you play the game only once, you will either win £2 or lose £1. However, if you play it repeatedly, your average gain will tend towards £0.50 per toss. This is not a fair game. Instead, it is biased in your favour (and hence is biased *against* us). (However, it is still a zero-sum game, since your gain will always be exactly equal to our loss.)

What about the kind of lottery that typically exists? The organizers take a proportion of the ticket revenue as their profit (and perhaps for charity) and distribute the rest as prize money. Therefore, all such lotteries are not fair games. They are biased against the participants in the sense that the expected value of participating in the game is negative. (Also, they are not zero sum games because the losses of those whose tickets are not selected exceed the gains for those whose tickets are winners.)

To illustrate, take a lottery where 100 tickets are sold at £1 each. Now assume that the organizers take £50 as their profit and pay out the other £50 to the winning ticket. The expected value of a lottery ticket is now £49(1/100) − £1(99/100) = £0.49 − £0.99 = −£0.50. The negative value shows that this is not a fair game; instead, it is biased against anyone who plays it. Another way of seeing this is to ask yourself what would happen if you bought all the tickets. You would spend £100 and win back £50, thus making a loss of £50. This is a loss of £0.50 per ticket, which, we have already seen, is the expected value of each ticket. (Explain why it is irrational to buy two tickets instead of one in order to increase the chances of winning money.)

(Note that in the present context 'fair' is a descriptive term about the sign of the game's expected value; it does not refer to the game's fairness in the moral sense. For example, it might be thought that buying a lottery ticket that gives you a small chance of winning something and a much larger chance of contributing funds to the charity is very fair, as long as the pay-offs are transparent. But this is not a fair game in our sense.)

Consumers' tastes for risk

Economists distinguish three possible patterns of preference when risk is involved. Those who are **risk-neutral** will be indifferent about playing a fair game; they will willingly play one that is biased in their favour, but will not play one that is biased against them. Those who are **risk-averse** will only play games that are sufficiently biased in their favour to overcome their aversion to risk, and will be unwilling to play fair games, let alone ones that are biased against them. Finally, people who are **risk-loving** are willing to play games even when they are biased against them, the extent of the love of risk being measured by the degree of bias that a person is willing to accept. (No one would knowingly buy a ticket in a lottery in which the prize was zero, but some extreme risk-lovers might enter a lottery in which only 10 per cent of the ticket money was paid out as prize money.)

Is it just as likely that any individual will be a risk-lover as that he will be risk-averse? To answer this question, we use an assumption that is related to the discussion of diminishing marginal utility in Chapter 4.

According to the *assumption of diminishing marginal utility of income (and wealth)*, individuals get less and less satisfaction from successive equal increases in their income (and wealth).

The argument is that if you earn only £1,000 per year you will spend it on satisfying your most urgent wants. If your income is increased by £1,000, you will also spend it on quite important needs, but the additional needs will be a little less urgent than those satisfied by the first £1,000. If your income is increased progressively by £1,000 increments, needs that are less and less urgent will be satisfied by the expenditure of each additional £1,000 of income. The general idea, therefore, is that people can arrange their wants in order and will satisfy the ones that give them most utility first, and then, as their incomes increase, those that give them progressively less and less utility. It follows from this assumption that the utility each consumer will attach to successive equal increments of income will

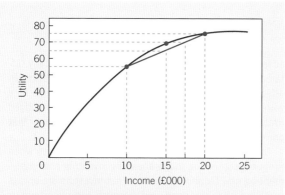

Figure 12.1 The utility of income

Diminishing marginal utility of income implies risk aversion. The curve shows the total utility attached to various incomes to be received with certainty. Amanda's utility from an income of £15,000 for certain is 70. An occupation that gives a 50 per cent chance of either £10,000 or £20,000 has an expected value of £15,000 but an expected utility of only 65. To make her accept a risky income source, its expected value would have to be £17,500 (which yields a utility of 70, as does the certain income of £15,000).

decrease steadily as income increases; put the other way around, the utility attached to successive equal reductions of income will increase steadily as income is decreased.

Figure 12.1 shows an illustrative utility curve for income for one hypothetical individual, Amanda. The curve relates any income received with certainty to the utility that Amanda derives from it.

Amanda must now choose between two different occupations. The first is an office job that pays her a definite income of £15,000 per year. The second is as a salesperson working on commission. If she is good at the job she will earn £20,000, but if she is poor at it she will earn only £10,000. She is uncertain about her sales ability and reckons that she is equally likely to be good or bad at the job. So she assigns a probability of 0.5 to each of the two possible outcomes. Thus the expected value of the income from the sales job is £15,000—that is, (0.5)(£10,000) + (0.5)(£20,000). If Amanda were risk-neutral, she would be indifferent between these two occupations, since they both yield the same expected income. But the risky alternative yields her either £5,000 more or £5,000 less than the certain one. Because of diminishing marginal utility of income, she assigns a smaller utility to £5,000 more than the office job salary than she assigns to £5,000 less than it. The graph tells us that the utility of the certain income of £15,000 is 70 while the utilities attached to £20,000 and £10,000 are 75 and 55 respectively. Although the expected incomes from the two occupations are the same, the expected utilities are not.

The sales job yields either £10,000 with a probability of 0.5 or £20,000 also with a probability of 0.5. So the expected utility associated with this job is only (55)(0.5) + (75)(0.5) = 65. So she prefers the job with the certain income of £15,000 to the job with the uncertain income that has the same expected value of £15,000. Amanda is risk-averse.[5]

A moment's reflection will show that this conclusion is independent of the particular utility values that we selected. All that it requires is diminishing marginal utility of income. This means that the addition of utility resulting from an income that is above average by some amount is less than the subtraction from utility resulting from an income that is below average by the same amount.

What would the expected value of the risky alternative have to be to leave Amanda indifferent between the two occupations? The answer is read off the curve in Figure 12.1. The expected value of the risky income needs to be £17,500 for her to obtain the same utility from the sales job as the office job offers. The difference between the actual expected value of the sales job and the expected value she would need to leave her indifferent between the risky and the riskless job measures her cost of risk. This is what we would have to give her to leave her indifferent between a certain income and an uncertain one with the same expected value.

Diminishing marginal utility of income makes utility-maximizing people risk-averse.

Box 12.2 discusses the important distinction between risk and uncertainty, a distinction that was emphasized long ago by the American economist Frank Knight in his seminal work *Risk, Uncertainty and Profit* (Boston, MA: Hart, Schaffner & Marx, 1921). In it he divided what business people count as profits into the normal return on capital in its day-to-day working, which was called normal profits, and the return for undertaking the uncertainties associated with R&D to develop and innovate new products, new processes, and new forms of organization, which was called pure profits.

---

[5] We explain here how expected income and utility vary as Amanda's probability of being good at her sales job varies. Let the probability of Amanda being good at the job be p and of her being bad at it be $1 - p$. The expected value of the income associated with the sales job is then $(£20,000)(p) + (£10,000)(1 - p) = £10,000 + £10,000p$. The expected utility is the utility attached to the high income multiplied by the probability of achieving the high income plus the utility attached to the low income multiplied by the probability of achieving the low income. In the case shown in Figure 12.1, this is $(75)(p) + 55(1 - p) = 55 + 20p$. So, as p varies between 0 and 1, the point showing the expected value of the income and the utility arising from the sales job varies along a straight line joining the two points (£10,000, 55) and (£20,000, 75). This is the straight line shown in Figure 12.1.

Box 12.2 **Risk and uncertainty**

In this chapter we depart from situations where outcomes are perfectly certain, as we considered those that are risky. The key characteristic of risky events is that they have well-defined probability distributions and expected values. For example, no one knows when or if a particular house in Britain will burn down. But we can calculate the probability that a randomly chosen one will burn down, and this allows insurance companies to sell fire insurance at a premium sufficient to allow them to pay the owners for their fire losses while still earning a profit. In a risky situation, two agents desiring the same objective, having the same information, and choosing among the same alternative actions, will make the same choice—the one that maximizes the expected value of the outcome. This means that behaviour is predictable not just when outcomes are known for certain, but when they are subject to risk.

In contrast, uncertain events have neither well-defined probability distributions nor expected values. What are the chances of a third world war breaking out in the next decade, and what are the chances of a currently unknown disease afflicting the human population in the near future? There must be some chance of both these happening but there is no scientific basis on which to calculate what that chance is. This is genuinely uncertainty.

In uncertain situations, the two agents referred to above may make different choices, neither of which can be shown ex ante to be better than the other. This means that when outcomes are subject to uncertainty one cannot predict what choices will be made. There are many such situations in which business decisions must be made under conditions of uncertainty rather than risk. One of the most important is R&D undertaken by firms to discover new products and new technologies. Much evidence has been amassed that uncertainty is pervasive in the process of creating such new products and technologies. Since invention and innovation mean doing something never done before, there is an element of genuine uncertainty in all activities directed at inventing and implementing new technologies. It is often impossible even to enumerate in advance the full set of outcomes of a particular line of research, let alone assign a probability of success to each. Time and money are often spent investigating specific research questions to discover if the alley they lead up is blind or rich in potential. As a result, massive sums are sometimes spent with no positive results, while trivial expenditures sometimes produce results of great value, often accidentally. This uncertainty is not something that arises from lack of trying; it is in the very nature of both discovering new knowledge and learning how to use it in commercially successful ways that if this was known in advance, it would not be new knowledge.

This prevalence of uncertainty in invention and innovation is important because firms compete with each other to develop new products and new production processes, and these activities require substantial investments. In making R&D expenditures directed at a major technological advances, similarly situated firms may make radically different decisions, backing different lines of investigation. In effect, each is deciding to back a different horse in a race with unknown odds. Neither firm's decisions can be judged irrational ex ante, although it will often be clear ex post that one made a better decision than the other.

One reason why there can be investment booms when firms are competing to get ahead by inventing and implementing new technologies is not that investors are always irrational or ill-informed, but because the uncertainties associated with such activities make the outcomes essentially unpredictable. Of course, firms make judgments all the time when deciding how to direct their R&D in an effort to gain competitive advantages over their rivals. But it is a matter of luck, hunch, good judgment, and intuition rather than fully rational calculations that must drive decisions made both by firms about their R&D and by investors in deciding which firms, industries, or new products to back.

This distinction between risk and uncertainty is also relevant to understanding what went wrong in the 2007–8 financial crisis. Banks, investors, and regulators were all using forms of risk assessment, including one known as value at risk (*VAR*), that estimated risks based upon volatilities and default rates over recent years. Therefore as the world went through a period of extreme stability, known as the great moderation, it looked as if risk had fallen, and this was reflected in regulatory capital requirements as well as pricing of assets (such as corporate bonds) and derivatives (such as credit default swaps). In other words, they all used an assumption that risk was measurable and that the measure could be based on the evidence of the recent past. However, they had all forgotten (or never understood) that there was also genuine uncertainty to which a probability could not be assigned, and when the unexpected happened they all came badly unstuck. What was wrong here was a complete misunderstanding of the fact that uncertainty existed and the false belief that the risk measures used were appropriate—that is, that statistical patterns in the past are a sufficient guide to what will happen next in so far as outcomes will all be drawn from the same statistical distribution.

This is the point that N.N. Taleb made in his book *The Black Swan: The Impact of the Highly Improbable* (New York: Random House, 2007). Based on knowledge of Europe alone, everybody thought all swans were white, but then Europeans found Australia and its indigenous black swans. A financial crisis on the 2008 scale had not happened in living memory, so its possibility was not in most people's calculations and few were prepared for the extreme events that followed. Some refer to this as 'tail risk', as it might be thought to happen in the extreme tails of distributions with a very low probability, but even tail risk is calculable in principle, so *uncertainty* is a better way to think about it as there is no basis on which to calculate the probability of potential outcomes.

The demand for insurance

The Smiths, who own a house valued at £200,000, estimate that there is one chance in 1,000 that it will be destroyed by fire during their period of ownership and 999 chances in 1,000 that there will be no fire. The most likely outcome is that nothing will happen at all, but there is a small chance of a really big loss. Someone offers them a mathematically fair insurance policy that avoids this big loss. The policy costs £200 to be paid now. If they buy the policy, they give up £200. However, if the disaster occurs they will be fully compensated.

So the Smiths have a choice between two alternatives.

• *Alternative A: the status quo* If they choose not to buy the policy, they have one chance in 1,000 of losing £200,000 and 999 chances out of 1,000 of losing nothing. Multiplying these possible losses of £200,000 and zero by their probabilities gives the expected value of this alternative as –£200 (i.e. –£200,000(1/1,000)+ £0(999/1,000) = –£200).

• *Alternative B: purchase the policy* In this case £200 is spent for certain but there is no chance of losing £200,000.

The insurance policy represents a fair bargain because the expected value of the status quo is equal to the certain cost of the policy. Not buying the insurance is, however, a much riskier course of action for the homeowners than buying it. If they are lucky, they save the £200 insurance premium; if they are unlucky, they lose £200,000. What should they do?

Risk-averse individuals will buy the policy. The expected value of the outcome is the same as if they did not buy the policy, but the utility values are not, given diminishing marginal utility of income. By buying the policy they give up the utility value of £200 but avoid the one chance in a thousand of losing the utility value of £200,000.

One further complication needs to be mentioned. Since insurance companies must themselves make money, they do not offer their policy-holders mathematically fair policies such as the one just described. In the above case, where the risk to the insurance company is one chance in 1,000 of losing £200,000, it would charge a premium of more than £200, possibly £220. The insurance company expects to pay out an average of £200 per policy, so the £20 per policy goes to help cover its total costs.

For the purchaser the certain total cost of buying the policy is now –£220. But the expected value of not buying remains at –£200. A risk-neutral person would not buy the policy, which requires spending £220 to avoid a situation (no insurance) whose expected value is –£200.

People with diminishing marginal utility of income are risk averse and hence willing to buy insurance that is not mathematically 'fair' because they value the reduction of risk more than they value the reduction in their expected income when they buy the policy.

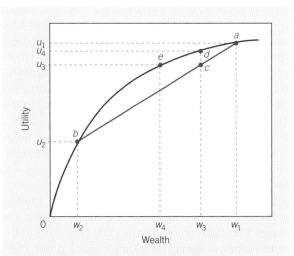

Figure 12.2 Purchasing insurance

Diminishing marginal utility of wealth makes a mathematically unfair insurance policy attractive to utility-maximizing consumers. Without insurance, the homeowners will have *either* wealth of w_1 with utility of u_1 if there is no fire (point *a*) or wealth of w_2 and utility u_2 if there is a fire (point *b*). The expected value of their wealth is w_3 with an associated utility of u_3 (point *c*). Point *c* is closer to point *a* than to point *b* because the fire is an unlikely event. A mathematically fair insurance policy would charge a premium that reduced the owners' wealth to w_3 for certain. The utility associated with w_3 achieved with certainty is u_4, which is higher than u_3. The maximum the owners would be prepared to pay for a mathematically unfair policy is the amount that would reduce their wealth to w_4. Paying that amount would make their wealth w_4 for certain (point *e*), yielding them the same utility as is associated with not buying insurance (point *c*).

Figure 12.2 shows the decision facing our homeowners. Here we deal with wealth rather than the income that we considered in Figure 12.1. Wealth is merely the present value of all current assets including any expected future income. Thus, diminishing marginal utility of either implies diminishing marginal utility of the other

The demand to gamble

We now know that diminishing marginal utility of income and wealth leads people to be risk-averse and thus to insure against losses. Why then do people gamble? Why do they buy lottery tickets, enter the football pools, and bet on horse races? These are different from insurance, where one pays money to avoid the risk of a large loss. In gambling one pays money to purchase the chance of a gain. The buyer accepts a large chance of a small loss (the purchase price of the ticket) in return for a small chance of a large gain (the pay-off to the winning tickets).

Earlier in this chapter we considered a lottery consisting of 100 tickets sold for £1 each, with a single prize of £100 going to the winning ticket. If you buy a ticket you have 99 chances out of 100 of losing £1 and one chance in 100 of winning £99. (If you win, you get your £1 back and £99 more.) This is a mathematically fair game, since the expected value of a ticket is zero (£99(1/100)– £1(99/100)). But, given diminishing marginal utility of income, the utility you get from winning £100 will be less than 100 times the utility you sacrificed by giving up £1. Thus, because the expected value of the ticket measured in money is zero, the expected value of the ticket measured in utility is negative. If you are a utility maximizer and have diminishing marginal utility of income, you would not buy the ticket.

The lottery above is a mathematically fair gamble. However, most betting games are biased against the player. The organizer of the game takes out some of the stake money to cover costs and provide a profit. Only the remainder is distributed as prize money. This is true of all private and government-run commercial gambling, including lotteries, pools, dog and horse races, and casino gambling. (The gambling games individuals play at home with each other are usually fair in the sense that the value of what is won is equal to the value of what is lost, so that the expected value of playing the game is zero—assuming all players are equally skilled at the game, or that it is one of pure chance with no skill required.)

Gambling on any event in which the organizers take a profit has a negative expected value, and thus playing such games is inconsistent with utility-maximizing risk-averse participants who are subject to diminishing marginal utility of income.

Yet we observe such behaviour every day. How can we explain it? At least five possibilities suggest themselves.

One possibility is that people have increasing marginal utilities of income, over some range of income. This could explain why they gamble on games that have negative expected values. However, it would be inconsistent with their buying insurance policies with negative expected values.[6] So this explanation would work only if there were one class of people who gambled (those with increasing marginal utility of income) and another class who bought insurance (those with decreasing marginal utility of income). The observation that there are many people who do both rules out this possibility as a general explanation.

A second possibility is that people derive utility from gambling for its own sake. Although they would not engage in gambling as a way of maximizing the money values of their income and wealth, they get pleasure out of the very act of gambling. In this sense, they are giving up some income to purchase the pleasure of gambling, just as if they purchased a ticket to obtain the pleasure of attending the theatre.

A third possibility in the case of gambling games with massive wins, such as the football pools, is that the appeal may be somewhat different. Diminishing marginal utility of increases in income may not hold for massive wins that could change one's whole lifestyle in ways that would otherwise be quite beyond the gambler's reach. It may not matter that the average player will lose money over his or her lifetime. The gamblers are sustained by the mere thought that, against all the odds, they might win a sum large enough to transform an otherwise hard life, in the same way that Cinderella's fairy godmother transformed hers. In this case the gambler may be thought of as buying hope. There is nothing irrational in this behaviour as long as the gambler realizes that the expected value of this behaviour is negative but less than the utility gained from the continued hope of a lucky big win.

A fourth possibility is that people are badly informed. They may not know the expected values of the gambles that they take. It is probably true that many people do not realize the magnitude of the negative expected value of many gambles. (The smaller the *pay-out ratio*—the ratio of money paid out to money taken in—the larger the magnitude of the negative expected value of the game.)

A fifth possibility is that people are superstitious, as many people are observed to be. They do not believe that the law of averages applies to them. They think that by choosing lucky numbers, or engaging in various rituals, they will beat the odds. These people do not care that they are playing mathematically unfair games. They believe that their personal powers will influence the results in some way or another—as those who choose what they regard as lucky numbers are observed to believe.

Recent work in psychology has developed many other insights into how people make their choices in risky situations. Indeed, this work has created a whole new field known as behavioural finance. This challenges many of the assumptions associated with the expected utility theory approach that we have been using here. Box 12.3 sets out some of the key ideas that have come out of this new field.

The supply of gambling

Why are firms willing to supply insurance and gambling deals to consumers who demand them? We first consider the easy case of gambling, and then go on to the more difficult, but also more interesting, case of insurance.

---

[6] Unless there just happened to be diminishing marginal utility of income below some person's current income level and increasing marginal utility of income above it. In which case it would be rational to insure against a significant loss of income and at the same time to gamble to attempt to achieve an increase in income (even in an unfair game).

Box 12.3 Behavioural finance

Mainstream economics and finance have typically assumed that the economy is populated with well-informed rational agents who seek to maximize their personal satisfaction or utility. The typical agent in such a world is often referred to as 'homo economicus'. The approach we have adopted in much of this book so far is in this tradition. However, empirical work in psychology has revealed many behaviour traits that differ from those to be expected in a fully informed rational agent. This work has come to be called behavioural economics or, more narrowly, behavioural finance. We refer mainly to behavioural finance here as it is obviously most applicable to understanding risky choices and interaction with financial markets. A leading researcher in this field is psychologist Daniel Kahneman (born 1934) of Princeton University who was awarded the 2002 Nobel Prize in economics[7].

A key finding in behavioural finance is that agents take decisions based on a subset of the information potentially available. This is sometimes referred to as *bounded rationality*. Kahneman and Tversky (K&T) found that decision-making can be fitted into one of two boxes. In System 1 decisions are made through intuition or guess work, and most quick decisions are made in this way. System 2 is only used for making more complete calculations closer to what we would call fully rational decisions. So, while agents are capable of making the complete calculation, they mostly do not bother.

Prospect theory is the name given to the study of what they seem to do in taking decisions. This has two main elements. The first is called *editing*, which means that agents tend to simplify or restrict the choices facing them in order to make the problem manageable. For example, when investing a windfall a person might decide to choose between the highest ten yielding shares, or between the dozen that grew fastest last year, or those tipped at the start of the year in a newspaper. These all provide simple strategies, but extensive research might produce better ones. The second is the arbitrary use of reference points as a standard to help make decisions. An example used by K&T is the taxi driver who aims to make a certain revenue each day and goes home once the target has been reached. He or she could make much more money on a rainy day when there is high demand for taxis, but instead knocks off early. On sunny days when trade is slow the driver works much longer in order to reach the target. Rational

revenue maximization would suggest: work long hours when demand is high, but stay at home or play golf when demand is low.

An important reference point for many decisions is the status quo. Losses relative to the status quo have a much stronger negative effect (on satisfaction or utility) than gains. This phenomenon is called *loss aversion*. Clearly this could be added to our explanation of why people buy insurance, but it also explains why agents are inclined to take much greater risks with money they have just gained (e.g. a capital gain on an investment or winnings on a horse race or lottery) than they would with assets they have had for some time (and thus part of their normal wealth). Investors often hang on too long to shares whose price has fallen, in the vain hope that it will recover, and gamblers who have had a losing streak on a particular day often take bigger risks on the last race of the day in the hope of making back their losses ... but end up losing even more. There are obvious potential parallels here with trading behaviour in financial markets. For example, Nick Leeson brought down Barings in 1995 by taking increasingly risky bets to try to overcome earlier losses, but ended up losing £827 million of the firm's money. There are some more recent examples of even larger losses from 'rogue traders' at other banks, but these have not (so far) driven the banks concerned into insolvency.

Another assumption of expected utility theory that is challenged by behavioural finance is that agents are selfish, so they pursue their own interest (or that of their own family) without regard to what others are doing. There are two strong bodies of evidence that support the behavioural view that real-world agents are neither selfish nor adopt behaviour that is unaffected by what others are doing or the social context. The first shows that people generally have a strong sense of fairness, so they care what is happening to others around them as well as to themselves. We have discussed this in some detail in the third case study in Chapter 4, so we will not elaborate it here. The second shows that agents' behaviour is strongly influenced by what others around them are doing. This phenomenon is known as *herding*, and it helps explain why investors often follow fads or fashions rather than fundamentals. Thus specific markets can experience speculative bubbles, such as tulip mania in Holland in the 1630s and the internet bubble in the US and UK stock markets in the late 1990s.

Finally, it is clear both that much remains to be learnt in this field and that further insights into how agents make risky choices are likely to come from many different disciplines, including psychology and other cognitive and social sciences, as well as from economics.

---

[7] Much of this work was done jointly with Amos Tversky (1937–96). For an overview of this work see 'Maps of bounded rationality: a perspective on intuitive judgment and choice', Nobel Prize Lecture, 8 December 2002. Available at <http://www.nobelprize.org/nobel_prizes/economic-sciences/laureates/2002/kahneman-lecture.html>

There is no real difficulty in understanding why firms are willing to provide such gambling opportunities as the football pools or betting on horse or dog races and the outcomes of other sporting events. If betting firms make their own odds after they know the amounts bet, they are on the right side of a mathematically unfair game from which they must win. Assume, for example, that you run a lottery and are free to take for yourself what you wish from the funds raised and then distribute the rest as prizes. You cannot lose. Similarly, bookmakers who take bets on a horse race will adjust the odds as bets are placed in order to ensure that they make a profit whichever horse wins.

Firms providing this type of gambling service sometimes have a government monopoly and sometimes are subject to competition from other firms. If there is competition, there will be pressure to keep the pay-out ratio high, provided that ticket purchasers are aware of the prizes given out by competing lotteries. If the lottery has a monopoly, there will be an optimum pay-out ratio that will maximize the profits of the firm running the game. As the pay-out ratio goes to one, profits go to zero, since all money taken in is paid out. As the pay-out ratio goes to zero, profits will also go to zero, since fewer and fewer people will be willing to bet as the size of the winnings and/or the number of winners becomes smaller.

Somewhere in between a ratio of zero and one is the optimum pay-out ratio that maximizes the profits of a monopoly firm running a lottery or other betting game.

Charitable lotteries are rather different, as the purchasers of tickets know that, even if they lose, the profit of the lottery largely goes to good causes.

The supply of insurance

In the gambling case, a bookmaker (by adjusting the odds) can decide how much to pay out after it is known how much has been taken in. Insurance is a different matter. The insurance company takes your money and agrees to pay out a certain sum if some unlucky event strikes you. Conceivably, the insurance company could have a run of bad luck in which, in the limit, all the people it insures suffer losses at the same time. Therefore the basis for profitable insurance firms is not being on the right side of an unfair game. Instead, it lies in the mathematics of what are called *pooled risks*.

Risk-pooling

To see what is involved in the pooling of risks, consider two individuals, John and Jane, who receive incomes that vary according to the toss of a coin. (Once again, the coin toss stands for any source of risk.) Each individual tosses a coin each month. If a head comes up, John gets £500; if a tail, he gets nothing. The same applies to Jane: she gets

Table 12.1 **Risk-pooling**

Coin toss	Risks are not pooled		Risks are pooled: Both get
	John gets	Jane gets	
T–T	0	0	0
T–H	0	500	250
H–T	500	0	250
H–H	500	500	500

Pooling of independent risks reduces risk. Both John and Jane toss a coin, and each gets an income of £500 if he or she tosses a head (H) and nothing for a tail (T). There are four possible results, in two of which one head and one tail occur. In the other two there are either two tails or two heads. When each accepts his or her own risks, each expects an income of £500 half the time and zero the other half. When the incomes are pooled and then split, only one combination in four gives them zero income, while half of the time they will get £250. Pooling leaves the expected value of their incomes unchanged but lowers the average amount of variation around that value.

£500 if she tosses a head and nothing if a tail comes up. The expected value of their income is £500(0.50) = £250 per month. Over a long period of time, their monthly incomes will indeed average close to £250 each. But neither of them may like the possibility of going from £500 to nothing on the toss of a coin each month. Suppose they decide to pool their incomes each month and each take half of the resulting amount. The expected value of the pooled income is £500 while the expected value of each individual income is unchanged at £250 per month.

Importantly, however, the variation from month to month in each income will be diminished. The result is shown in Table 12.1. When they were operating on their own, each income deviated from its expected value by £250 each month; in good months it was £250 above, and in bad months it was £250 below. When the two incomes are pooled, the expected value is reached whenever one is lucky and the other unlucky, which will tend to be about half the time. Only in a quarter of the outcomes will income be £250 above, and in a quarter it will it be £250 below. These two results require that both John and Jane are lucky at the same time or that both are unlucky.

If three people pool their incomes, the extreme cases of £500 each and zero each occur only when all three are lucky or unlucky at the same time. These two cases *each* occur with a probability of one chance in eight. (There is one chance in two that any one person will get a head, and (1/2)(1/2)(1/2) = 1/8 that all three will get heads at once. Similarly, there is one chance in eight that all three will toss tails at the same time.) So the extreme cases in which everyone gets *either*

£500 *or* zero occur only two times out of eight, which is one-quarter of the time. If four people pool their incomes, the extreme cases of *either* £500 *or* zero income per person will occur only with probability 2/16, which is one-eighth of the times. By the time ten people are involved, the two extreme cases will occur only twice in two raised to the tenth power (2^{10}) times,[8] which is a very small fraction indeed.

The larger the number of independent events that are pooled, the less likely is it that extreme results will occur.

The key to this proposition is that the events must be independent; the result of John's coin toss must not be in any way related to the result of Jane's. In the unpooled case, the extreme result occurs to one of them when he or she is unlucky or lucky. The probability of the extreme result is less likely when they pool their incomes because it requires that *both* be unlucky or lucky at the same time.

The same reasoning applies to all kinds of events that may be regarded as chance occurrences, as long as they are independent of each other. There is some probability that any given house in the country will burn down in any given year; let us say it is one in 1,000. An insurance company takes a premium from house-owners and offers them full compensation if their house burns down. If the company is so small that it insures only ten houses, it may be unlucky in having ten owners who just happen to be careless in the same year and burn their houses down accidentally. This is unlikely, but not impossible. A bad bit of luck over all ten houses insured would ruin the company, which could not then meet all its insured risks at the same time. But let the company be large enough to insure 100,000 houses. Now it is pooling risk over a large number, and the chances are that very close to one house in every 1,000 insured houses burning down. With 100,000 houses insured, the most likely outcome is that 100 houses will burn down. The company might be unlucky and have 110 burn down, or lucky and have only 90 burn down. But to have 200 burn down is very unlikely indeed, as long as a fire in one house is independent of a fire in another.

This requirement of independence explains why insurance policies normally exclude wars and other situations where some common cause acts on all the insured units. A war may lead to a vast number of houses being destroyed. Since the cause of the loss of one house is not independent of the cause of the loss of another, the insurance company has a high probability, should a war break out, of suffering ruinous losses.

The basic feature of insurance is the pooling of independent events, which is what makes extreme outcomes unlikely. A common cause that seriously affects all insured items in the same way defeats the principle on which insurance is based.

Therefore the typical insurance company deals with repeated events, such as fires or death, in which the probability of each insured person becoming a claimant is independent of the probability of any other person becoming a claimant.

Risk-sharing

A further practice of insurance companies allows them to extend their coverage to events that are not repeated and where the loss might be large enough to ruin any one company. Say that a famous pianist wants to insure her hands against any event that would stop her from playing the piano. The amount insured could be very large, sufficient to compensate for the loss of all the income she would earn over her lifetime if her hands stayed unharmed. The company can calculate the chances that any randomly chosen female in the population will suffer such a loss of the use of her hands. But it is not insuring the whole population. Only one person is involved. If there is no catastrophe, the company will gain its premium. If there is a catastrophe, the company will suffer a very large loss.

The trick in being able to insure the pianist, or any single person or thing where the loss would be large, lies in *risk-sharing* (or re-insurance, as it is sometimes called). One company writes a policy for the pianist and then breaks the policy up into a large number of subpolicies. Each subpolicy carries a fraction of the pay-out and earns a fraction of the premium. The company then sells the sub-policies to many different firms.

Assume, for illustration, that 100 firms each write one such primary policy—one on a pianist's hands, one on a footballer's legs, one on a rare treasure being flown to Japan for exhibit, etc. Each then breaks its primary policy up into 100 subparts and sells a part to each of the other 99 firms. Each firm ends up holding risks that are independent of each other, no one of which is large enough to threaten the firm should it give rise to a claim. This is what Lloyd's of London does. It is a syndication of a large number of insurance underwriters. Each is prepared to insure almost anything as long as a claim would not break all the firms when the risk is spread over a large number of them.[9]

We return to risk in the context of financial investments later in this chapter.

---

[9] This is also what bookmakers do when they cannot control the odds themselves. When they take bets at odds set by others, one large bet could ruin them by requiring a pay-out greater than their current assets. To avoid such risks, they lay off part of the bet with other bookmakers. In this way no one ends up holding bets that are big enough to threaten their solvency if they suffer an unlucky run of pay-outs.

Problems with insurance

Two major problems arise in insurance: these are called moral hazard and adverse selection. These problems also arise in many other markets, including those for financial assets and labour services, so the concepts have important general applications.

Moral hazard

If the contents of your home are valuable but are not insured for theft, you are likely to be careful in locking your door every time you leave and will take other sensible anti-break-in precautions. If you take out an insurance policy, you may be less careful. Say, for example, that you get ten minutes down the road and realize that you forgot to lock up. You may decide to press on, reasoning that you cannot afford the time you would lose in returning to lock up, that being visited by burglars on any particular day is unlikely, and that anyway you are insured against burglary.

The existence of the insurance policy has altered your behaviour. You take more risks, making a loss from burglary more likely than if you were uninsured. This behaviour, called **moral hazard**, is defined as an insurance-induced alteration of behaviour that makes the event insured against more likely to occur.

Moral hazard occurs in many lines of insurance. For example, people are observed to be more careless about fire prevention when they are insured than when they are not. Fire insurance is clearly socially beneficial in allowing people to pool risks, thus avoiding the chances of a large loss in return for a relatively small payment. However, there is an offsetting social loss if the very existence of fire insurance leads to more destruction by fire than would occur without it.

To deal with moral hazard insurance companies create incentives for purchasers of insurance to be careful. For example, car drivers get a no-claims bonus if they have no accident for some number of years. Many policies include an 'excess' clause, which means that the insurer will pay out the value of losses only above some amount. So, for example, a car owner might have to pay the first £100 of a damage claim and the insurer would pay the rest. Home contents policies typically require that homes are fitted with secure locks to doors and windows.

Moral hazard arises in many markets where behaviour can change after a deal has been done. For example, an employer may agree to a high salary for a star employee in expectation of outstanding performance. But the employee may decide to take the money and shirk. We discussed this issue of performance in labour markets in Chapter 10.

Adverse selection

When the person on one side of a bargain knows more about what is being bought and sold than the person on the other side, we have a situation of *asymmetric information*. This can lead to undesirable consequences.

For example, a person who is considering taking out life insurance may know more about her health than the insurance company can find out in one medical examination and a few lifestyle questions. The insurance company will quote a rate that covers the average risk for all persons in some category, such as middle-aged female non-smokers in apparent good health. Those who believe their health is better than average know they are being asked for a premium that is high relative to their individual risk. In contrast, those who know they are less healthy than the average in their group know they are being offered a bargain—insurance at a rate that is low relative to their own individual risk. As a result, a higher proportion of people who are above the average risk will insure themselves than those who are below the average risk.

Adverse selection, in the context of insurance, refers to the tendency for people who are more at risk than the average to purchase insurance and for those who are less at risk than the average to reject insurance. This occurs whenever individuals within a group that is offered a common insurance rate know which way their own risk deviates significantly from the average risk within the group. Those at high risk relative to the average are offered a bargain; those at low risk are offered expensive insurance.

This problem would be serious if all people were charged the same rate as the customer with the average risk. Young healthy non-smokers would be heavily penalized and much less inclined to take out insurance. In contrast, older smokers with chronic ailments would be subsidized and would have a strong inducement to insure themselves.

The result would be that the average risk of the group who took out insurance would rise above the average risk in the whole population. Rates would then have to be raised to cover the average risk of the insured groups, and this would provide an even stronger incentive for those who have below-average risks to be uninsured.

Insurance companies try to cope with this problem by classifying customers into different groups ranked by risk. They then charge each group a different rate based on the average risk of that group. For example, rates for theft insurance in London and other cities of the United Kingdom vary with their postal code. This certainly helps, but it is always true that there will be variations within any one group. Those who know they are more at risk than the average in their group are offered a bargain, while those who know they are less at risk than

Box 12.4 Used-car prices: the problem of 'lemons'

It is common for people to regard the large loss of value of a new car in the first year of its life as a sign that consumers are overly style conscious and will always pay a big premium for the latest in anything. The US economist George Akerlof, winner of the Nobel Prize for economics in 2001, proposed a different explanation. This was based on the proposition that the flow of services expected from a one-year-old car that is *purchased on the used-car market* would be lower than that expected from an *average* one-year-old car on the road.

Any particular model year of motor cars will include a certain proportion of 'lemons'—cars that have one or more serious defects. There were faults in their assembly, or in the parts assembled, that went undetected. Purchasers of new cars of a certain year and model take a chance on their car turning out to be a lemon. Those who are unlucky and get a lemon are more likely to resell their car than those who are lucky and get a well-functioning car. Hence the used-car market will contain a disproportionately large number of lemons for sale. Because it is difficult to identify a lemon or a badly treated used car before buying it, the purchaser is prepared to buy a used car only at a price that is low enough to offset the increased probability that it is of poor quality.

This is a rational consumer response to asymmetric knowledge between the seller of a car and its eventual buyer. It helps to explain why one-year-old cars typically sell for a discount that is somewhat larger than can be explained by the physical depreciation that occurs in one year in the *average* car of that model. The larger discount reflects the lower services that the purchaser can expect from a used car because of the higher probability that it will be a lemon.

the average are offered what is, for them, expensive insurance.

An insurance company sometimes makes a surprising offer, such as life insurance for people over fifty-five with no medical examination. When it does this, a company is consciously choosing to avoid obtaining relevant medical knowledge. This increases the degree of knowledge asymmetry between the company and the policy purchaser, and thus strengthens the tendency towards adverse selection. If the company is to earn a profit, its rates for this kind of policy will have to be set higher than the rates on otherwise equivalent policies that require a medical examination. The policy may still be a bargain for very high risk people—possibly the only way they can get life insurance. For average and low risk people the rates must be higher than they could obtain by purchasing a policy that required a medical examination.

Adverse selection also applies in banking. Banks tend to expand their lending business by merger or acquisition, rather than by organic growth. The reason is that the marginal customers obtained by attracting new business are not necessarily the ones banks want to lend to. They are riskier than average.[10] However, when one bank buys another bank it gets the whole set of that bank's existing customers. It knows their average characteristics, and it picks up good customers as well as bad.

All the large UK banks have grown up from mergers of existing banks. None of their major components is less than 150 years old. (The growth of RBS, Lloyds, Barclays, and HSBC all fit this story.)

Box 12.4 outlines a different case of moral hazard; in this case it is the sellers who know more about the product than the buyers.

Financial choices and risk

An important function of any financial system is to channel funds from one set of agents, who have money to lend, to another set of agents, who wish to borrow. Those who do this are called financial intermediaries. Savers are investing their own money in the hope of receiving an interest return on that investment. They also have to consider risk, because borrowers may default. Even if default is not likely, many forms of investment involve risks of capital gains and losses, which occur when the market value of the investment changes. Accordingly, all investors have to take into consideration not just the expected return on their investment, but also the risks involved.

---

[10] This is mainly a problem with unsecured lending. Mortgages are secured on a known property, so less risk is involved for the lender.

The analysis of risk and return as applied to finance has created a vast literature. Here we can develop only a few of the key ideas that help in understanding a wide range of financial behaviour.

Portfolio diversification

'Don't put all your eggs in one basket' is a well-known proverb which summarizes the message that there are benefits from diversification. If you carry your breakable items in several baskets there is a chance that one will be dropped, but you are unlikely to drop all your baskets on the same trip. Similarly, if you invest all your wealth in the shares of one company, there is a chance that the company will go bust and you will lose all your money. Since it is unlikely that all companies will go bust at the same time, a portfolio of shares in several companies is less risky.

This may sound like the idea of risk-pooling, which we discussed earlier in this chapter, and risk-pooling is certainly an important reason for diversification. We will use the notion of risk-pooling to explain some forms of financial behaviour, but a full understanding of portfolio diversification involves a slightly wider knowledge of the nature of risk than what is involved in coin-tossing.

The key difference between risk in the real world of finance and the risk of coin-tossing is that many of the potential outcomes are not independent of other outcomes. If you and I toss a coin, the probability of yours turning up heads is independent of the probability of my throwing a head. However, the return on an investment in, say, BP is not independent of the return on an investment in Shell. This is because these two companies both compete in the same industry. If BP does especially well in attracting new business, it may be at the expense of Shell. So high profits at BP may be associated with low profits at Shell, or vice versa. On the other hand, all oil companies might do well when oil prices are high and badly when they are low. The important matter here is that the fortunes of these two companies are not independent of each other.

The fact that the risks of individual investments may not be independent has important implications for investment allocations, or what is now called *portfolio theory*. Investments can be combined in different proportions to produce risk and return characteristics that cannot be achieved through any single investment. As a result, institutions have grown up to take advantage of the benefits of diversification.

Diversified portfolios may produce combinations of risk and return that dominate non-diversified portfolios.

This is an important statement that requires a little closer investigation. That investigation will help to identify the circumstances under which diversification is beneficial. It will also clarify what we mean by the word 'dominate'.

Table 12.2 **Combinations of risk and return**

	Situation 1	Situation 2
(i) Returns are negatively correlated		
Asset A	10%	30%
Asset B	30%	10%
(ii) Returns are positively correlated		
Asset A	10%	30%
Asset B	0%	40%

Assets differ in expected return and variability in returns. Part (i) illustrates the return on two assets in two different situations. Asset A has a high return in situation 2 and a low return in situation 1. The reverse is true for asset B. A portfolio of both assets has the same expected return but lower risk than a holding of either asset on its own. In (ii) both assets have a high return in situation 2 and a low return in situation 1. For the risk-averse investor asset A dominates asset B.

Table 12.2 sets out two simple examples. In both there are two assets that an investor can hold, and there are two possible situations which are assumed to be equally likely. Thus there is a probability of 0.5 attached to each situation and the investor has no advance knowledge of which is going to happen. The two situations might be a high exchange rate and a low exchange rate, a booming and a depressed economy, or any other alternatives that have different effects on the earnings of different assets.

Consider part (i) of the Table 12.2. In this case both assets have the same expected return (20 per cent) and the same degree of risk. (The possible range of outcomes is between 10 and 30 per cent on each asset.) If all that mattered in investment decisions were the risk and return of individual shares, the investor would be indifferent between assets A and B. Indeed, if the choice were between holding only A or only B, all investors should be indifferent (whether they were risk-averse, risk-neutral, or risk-loving) because the risk and expected return are identical for both assets. However, this is not the end of the story, because the returns on these assets are not independent. Indeed, there is a perfect negative correlation between them: when one is high the other is low, and vice versa.

What would a sensible investor do if permitted to hold some combination of the two assets? Clearly, there is no possible combination that will change the overall expected return, because it is the same on both assets. However, holding some of each asset can reduce the risk. Let the investor decide to hold half his wealth in asset A and half in asset B. His risk will then be reduced to zero, since his return will be 20 per cent whichever situation

Box 12.5 Conglomerates: not all diversification is beneficial

In the 1960s and 1970s it was fashionable to argue that the benefits of diversification would apply to all firms. Rightly or wrongly, this argument led to the build-up of several large conglomerate firms made up of a portfolio of diverse businesses in many different industries. The UK firm Hanson, for example, was a conglomerate that owned a cigarette company and a brick business in the United Kingdom and a coal mining business and a whirlpool bath manufacturer in the United States, among dozens of other operations. UK company Tomkins had about fifty different companies ranging from buns (Rank Hovis McDougall) to guns (Smith and Wesson), and including businesses like lawnmower manufacturers and car hose makers.

However, the most successful firms of the 1980s and 1990s were not conglomerates. Instead they were those who concentrated on being the leading players in one industry—for example Microsoft in software, Glaxo in pharmaceuticals, Intel in semiconductors, BP in oil, and GE in electrical engineering.

By the early years of the twenty-first century, most conglomerates had 'de-merged' their businesses into separate companies, and the argument had been accepted (at least

for the time being) that it was not efficient for specific non-financial companies to diversify. Financial analysts argue that diversification does not add value to a firm because investors can achieve their own optimal diversification either through holding a mix of different firms' shares directly or investing in mutual funds. Thus, a diversified firm is not worth any more than the sum of its parts. Indeed, diversification may create diseconomies of scope because the central management of a conglomerate cannot keep fully informed about all the different markets and industries in which it is operating. Hence the conglomerate may be worth less than the sum of its parts, and so it will have a greater market valuation if it is split up.

Thus the accepted wisdom at the time of writing is that the job of non-financial firms is to maximize the value of the firm, and this cannot be achieved by trying to run diverse businesses within one organization. Certainly the managers should try to manage the business risks that are an unavoidable part of the core business, but there is no value added by trying to run too many different types of business purely as a way of reducing the risks of the combined businesses.

---

arises. This diversified portfolio will clearly be preferred to either asset alone by risk-averse investors. The risk-neutral investor is indifferent to all combinations of A and B because they all have the same expected return, but the risk-lover may prefer not to diversify. This is because, by picking one asset alone, the risk-lover still has a chance of getting a 30 per cent return and the extra risk gives positive pleasure.

Risk-averse investors will choose the diversified portfolio, which gives them the lowest risk for a given expected rate of return, or the highest expected return for a given level of risk.

Diversification does not always reduce the riskiness of a portfolio, so we need to be clear what conditions matter. Consider the example in part (ii) of Table 12.2. As in part (i), both assets have an expected return of 20 per cent. But asset B is riskier than asset A and it has returns that are positively correlated with A's returns. Portfolio diversification does not reduce risk in this case. Risk-averse investors would invest only in asset A, while risk-lovers would invest only in asset B. Combinations of A and B are always riskier than holding A alone. Thus, we could say that for the risk-averse investor asset A *dominates* asset B, as asset B will never be held so long as asset A is available. The key difference between the example in part (ii) of Table 12.2 and that in part (i) is that in the second example returns

on the two assets are positively correlated, while in the former they are negatively correlated.[11]

The risk attached to a combination of two assets will be smaller than the sum of the individual risks if the two assets have returns that are negatively correlated.

Diversifiable and non-diversifiable risk

Not all risk can be eliminated by diversification. The specific risk associated with any one company can be diversified away by holding shares of many companies. But even if you held shares in every available traded company, you would still have some risk because the stock market as a whole tends to move up and down over time. Hence we talk about market risk and specific risk. *Market risk* is non-diversifiable, whereas *specific risk* is diversifiable through risk-pooling.

Box 12.5 discusses the issue of whether all firms should diversify the activities in order to reduce risk.

---

[11] Readers who have studied statistics will recall that if two statistical series A and B are added together, the variance of the combined series is equal to the variance of A plus the variance of B plus twice the covariance of A and B. The covariance of A and B will be negative if A and B are negatively correlated, hence the combined variance will be less than the sum of its parts.

Beta

It is now common to use a coefficient called **beta** to measure the relationship between movements in a specific company's share price and movements in the market. A share that is perfectly correlated with an index of stock market prices will have a beta of 1. A beta higher than 1 means that the share moves in the same direction as the market but with amplified fluctuations. A beta between 1 and 0 means that the share moves in the same direction as the stock market but is less volatile. A negative beta indicates that the share moves in the opposite direction to the market in general. Clearly, other things being equal, a share with a negative beta would be in high demand by investment managers, as it would reduce a portfolio's risk.

The *capital asset pricing model (CAPM)* predicts that the price of shares with higher betas must offer higher average returns in order to compensate investors for their higher risk.

For any given market condition there is a trade-off between risk and return. Investments with higher risk will be priced to offer higher expected returns than those with low risk.

Mutual funds

Many small investors do not have enough wealth to invest in the shares of enough different companies to gain the benefits of a diversified portfolio. Yet the average return on investing in shares is higher than that on safe assets, such as government bonds or bank and building society deposits. Hence there is a role for institutions which sell small investors a share in a much bigger and more diversified portfolio.

Such institutions are generally known as mutual funds. They are like clubs in which savers pool their funds and then jointly own a diversified set of investments. In the UK they are known as unit trusts and investment trusts.

Mutual funds play an important role in helping small investors to achieve international diversification. Just as diversification across UK companies can be beneficial in improving the risk–return trade-off, so international diversification can improve it still further. Small investors find it difficult and costly to buy and sell foreign shares, but mutual funds are able to access foreign markets and spread the costs over large numbers of investors. Investment opportunities for small investors are thereby greatly enhanced.

Financial intermediaries

Mutual funds are a form of financial intermediary. They take in money from savers and invest the money in company shares or bonds. Banks and building societies are also important financial intermediaries. Some other financial instruments that help companies or individuals to manage risk are discussed in Box 12.6.

The traditional building society takes in deposits from savers and makes loans (mortgages) to house purchasers. Why do savers not lend directly to house-buyers rather than through this intermediary? The building societies' costs could then be avoided and lenders and borrowers could, perhaps, get better terms. (The spread between building society deposit rates and loan rates could be split between the lender and the borrower.)

There are several reasons why both lenders and borrowers prefer not to deal with each other directly. Which of these applies to specific institutions depends on the nature of the business involved.

First, there are transaction or search costs for lenders and borrowers before they can meet. The intermediary provides a 'trading post' where depositors know they can find a willing borrower at all times and borrowers know they can find a willing lender. This applies to both banks and building societies.

Secondly, the characteristics of the loan that a saver wants to make may differ from those the ultimate borrower would be happy with. A typical saver may want to get her money back at short notice; a typical house buyer will want to borrow money for twenty or twenty-five years. The building society can make long-term loans by taking in a whole series of different short-term deposits. Banks also make long-term loans funded by deposits that can be withdrawn at short notice.

Thirdly, a typical saver could lend to no more than one or two house-buyers. Any single house may fall in value[12], or the borrower may default. A building society can spread the risk over a wide range of different borrowers and a wide range of different types of dwelling. Building societies with nationwide coverage grew up to take advantage of the fact that wide diversification of loans across different industries and regions is safer than, say, lending only to coal miners in South Yorkshire. Banks also spread their risk by making loans to many different borrowers. Hence minimizing overall risk is a central part of any financial intermediary's *raison d'être*.

A fourth reason for the existence of financial intermediaries is the provision of loans that are not secured by any asset; that is personal loans other than mortgages and some business loans.[13] In such cases the lending institutions must make judgments about who is likely to pay them back and who is not. Banks and building societies are well placed to

---

[12] Perhaps because a new motorway being built, or an uninsured house has burnt down.

[13] With a mortgage the lender takes the deeds to the house and can sell this if the borrower defaults on loan repayments. Some business loans are secured against the assets of the firm, such as its buildings or land.

Box 12.6 Derivatives: dealing with risk in financial markets

Many modern financial instruments create markets in various aspects of risk. Agents who wish to avoid or reduce risk can deal on these markets with others who are willing to accept the risk (for a price). The financial products involved can be used to change the risk characteristics of someone's underlying asset or liability position. They are often referred to as 'derivatives'.

Futures and forward contracts

Futures contracts are contracts traded in standard sizes and maturities on organized exchanges, such as the London International Financial Futures Exchange (LIFFE). They can be resold at any time up to maturity. For example, a farmer might sell his wheat crop six months before it is harvested in order to hedge against the risk of the price falling at harvest time, or a tyre manufacturer might buy rubber ahead of production needs to lock into a particularly favourable current supply price. *Forward contracts* are contracts that are typically made between a customer and a bank and are custom-made in terms of characteristics. (Hence they are said to be traded in the over-the-counter (OTC) market.) They cannot generally be resold before settlement. For example, an importer of American jeans who will have to pay the producer in dollars in nine months' time may buy the US dollars with his local currency in the forward foreign exchange market in order to avoid the risk that the dollar might appreciate in the meantime. The key characteristic of both of these types of arrangement is that they enable agents to buy, at a price agreed today, some product or asset that will be delivered and paid for at some time in the future.

Swaps

Interest rate swaps are also known as *contracts for differences*, as two parties agree to pay or receive the difference (over some future period) between two different interest rates (typically, one fixed and one floating rate). Swaps are used to manage interest rate risk. Agents who hold assets that pay a fixed interest rate or who have liabilities that pay interest at the current rate will be exposed to losses if interest rates rise, because the cost of borrowing will rise while the return on assets will not. Swapping either the fixed asset rate into a floating rate or the floating liability rate into fixed rate will reduce risk. The principle involved here is referred to as 'matching' because it creates assets and liabilities that will move up or down together.

Options

Options come in two varieties. A *call option* is the right (but not the obligation) to buy some commodity or security at a specific price called the *exercise price*. A *put option* is the right (but not the obligation) to sell some commodity or security at a specific price. With a forward or futures contract you are committed to a future transaction; with an option you have the right to go ahead, but you can walk away from the deal if you prefer. A wheat farmer who has sold his crop on the futures market must fulfil the contract. (If the size of his crop falls short of the quantity he has sold, he must buy at the market price to make up the shortfall.) However, with a put option he could choose not to deliver if the market price turned out to be much higher than the exercise price of his contract. Options thus have favourable characteristics. They limit the downside risk without limiting the upside possibility of gain. Naturally, there is a price that has to be paid for this one-way bet, which is known as the *option premium*. Those who sell options must charge a premium high enough to cover their losses when options are exercised at prices that are much better than the original market price.

do this because they will normally lend only to people with whom they have an ongoing banking relationship. They can see how much money a customer is earning because it passes through his or her account. Therefore they have better information about the creditworthiness of a potential borrower than any other potential lender could have.

Banks and building societies have superior information about the risks involved, and they are in a good position to monitor the financial progress of their customers over time.

Thus, the existence of risk is central to the need for some intermediary to play this role. The nature of the relationship between intermediaries and their customers puts them in an ideal position to monitor (and possibly control) those risks.

Financial intermediaries allow savers to find relatively safe outlets for their savings which pay a competitive rate of interest. (Financial intermediaries compete for business just like the other firms that we have discussed.) Those who wish to borrow are also able to do so in a well-developed market for loans. Such savings-and-loans markets are important for the functioning of a market economy. In particular, they enable consumers to move consumption either forwards or backwards in time, thereby greatly enhancing the range of choices available. Saving postpones consumption for the future. Borrowing permits consumption today that will be paid for in future, or the purchase of large durable product like a house or a car, the services of which will be consumed over future periods.

Financial crises

So far in this chapter we have been explaining aspects of how the financial system works in normal times. From time to time, however, things go badly wrong and financial markets crash and/or financial institutions collapse. When many financial institutions are in trouble at the same time, this is associated with a financial crisis. This section introduces the topic of financial crises, but we say more in Chapter 23, where we discuss the business cycle in general. Box 12.7 discusses some specific factor behind the global financial crisis of 2007–8, and the two case studies at the end of this chapter cover other important aspects of this crisis.

A global financial crisis erupted in Europe and North America in 2007–8 and its after-effects were still being felt in the middle of the following decade. Certainly they were still influencing major economies and government policies in 2014 when this book was being written. We will look more closely at several aspects of this financial crisis in the case studies below and in several of the following chapters. The underlying forces are the same forces that are associated with business cycles (see Chapter 23). Financial crises are not the outcome in every cycle but they are associated with the most severe downturns.

The broad pattern leading up to a crisis starts with a long period of growth and rising optimism. Confidence is high, asset prices rise, and firms and individuals borrow in expectation of further asset price rises. Banks increase lending on the assumption that those to whom they lend are solvent and able to repay. However, at some point there is a setback which makes people doubt that the boom can last. Asset prices fall and a panic can set in. Those who have borrowed on the assumption of rising asset values may find their net worth evaporates and

Box 12.7 Neither a borrower nor a lender be!

A number of specific factors contributed to the instability in the US and UK banking systems and led to the 2007–8 financial crisis. Many of these are discussed in the text, in this and later chapters, but some other important underlying influences are set out here.

At one time investment banks and many other financial firms were partnerships and their managers were also owners who cared about the long-term profits and survival of the business. They were also personally liable for the debts of the business and so had a strong incentive to monitor and control the risks being taken across the firm. When these firms became limited liability companies in the 1980s and 1990s (the timing varied between countries) the managers were no longer also owners and they were then playing with other people's money. Their perspective then became that of maximizing current returns on which their salaries and bonuses depended, even if this meant taking on bigger risks. Many of them were paid bonuses based on how much new business they had set up for their bank within a specific year, so they had an incentive to set up as many deals as possible even if some of these deals were increasingly risky (such as the securitization of mortgages as discussed in the second case study in this chapter). These deals looked profitable when first set up but banks as a whole made huge losses when the underlying value of these assets collapsed (and many banks found themselves holding large amounts of mortgage-backed securities, or were liable for those that they had created).

Financial innovations, such as the growth of derivatives and securitization (see second case study) allowed them to bundle loans together and sell them on in such a way as to confuse inventors. For example, by bundling very bad loans with a few quite good ones they could make the average look not too bad and so unload the real turkeys.

The rating agencies also had a role to play in the explosion of the mortgage-backed securities market. They were paid by the banks to rate the securities they were issuing, and thus were caught in a classic conflict of interest situation. The ratings agencies gave AAA ratings to securities that turned out to be very risky and so were really B or C (or worse). Investors bought these as they were rated as low risk and banks could use the funds raised to buy even more risky mortgages and resell those too.

Since agents selling the mortgages and the firms granting them got paid commissions and bonuses based on current sales and securitization allowed them to offload these high risk assets before the risks were obvious, the incentives were all in the wrong direction.

Thus, a central element of the recent financial crisis was the incentive structure faced by bankers themselves. How these incentive problems can be avoided in future remains a topic of active debate. One solution that has been adopted in some countries is to require bonuses to be paid in a form that cannot be spent for several years and can be clawed back if the deals upon which it was based later turn bad.

insolvencies can follow. Borrowers default on bank loans, and if the problems are widespread, banks may also fail. Spending falls as consumers and investors become cautious and so GDP falls and unemployment rises.

The United Kingdom had a boom that burst in 1990 and was followed by a recession. The recovery started in 1992 and there followed a period until the mid-2000s with generally stable growth and rising asset prices. Problems started in the United States with falls in house prices in 2006, but it was not until 2007 that serious disruption hit financial markets in the United Kingdom (see the first case study below). These took over a year to lead to the worst of the financial crisis.

In the 2007–8 financial crisis, for example, the first bank problems emerged in August 2007, but it was September 2008 when Lehman Brothers collapsed in the United States, causing a major fall in world stock markets, and both RBS and Lloyds needed substantial injections of government funds in the United Kingdom to avoid them both going bust. It was 2009 when the worst effects of this financial crisis were felt in the real economy with a major recession in many countries and a collapse in world trade.

Prior to 2007 there was a feeling in Europe and North America that the financial system was working well, and that financial crises only happened in developing of emerging economies. The events of 2007–8 and the subsequent impact on real activity have changed this perception dramatically. At the time of writing the regulatory response is still evolving. However, it is very clear that nobody is complacent any more. It is fully understood that financial crises can happen anywhere, and that when they do they are extremely costly.

CASE STUDIES

1. Holed on a rock

A sinking feeling started to come over the UK financial system in September 2007 with the troubles at Northern Rock bank. This was the first that many people knew about what was later to become a major financial crisis engulfing several large banks and other financial institutions in Europe and the United States. Northern Rock was not the cause of the problems, and as it was a small player was not in itself a significant threat to financial stability. Rather, it was a victim of a sudden change in financial market conditions that left it vulnerable and unable to carry on without state assistance.

Commercial banks are involved in maturity transformation. This means that they borrow deposits that can be withdrawn on demand, and they make longer-term loans. Their assets are longer term than their liabilities. This could cause problems if their depositors want their money back in a hurry, as banks cannot liquidate their loans quickly. This is why banks tend to manage this problem by holding liquid reserves, and they have also developed a market (the inter-bank market) through which they can lend to each other when one bank is in need of short-term funds while others have a surplus.

In the two years prior to 2007, Northern Rock had embarked upon a strategy of expanding its loans (mainly mortgages) rapidly and financing these loans by borrowing in the wholesale money markets (including the inter-bank market). Traditionally, mortgage providers had lent only out of the deposits of their own customers. The attraction of expanding in this way was that Northern Rock's management thought that the loans were safe, as the value of collateral in the form of houses would keep on rising, and that they would always be able to borrow all the funds they needed in the wholesale markets. Profitability would be assured because the interest rate they could charge on mortgages would be above the rate they would have to pay to borrow wholesale funds.

Things did not go according to plan. In the United States the Federal Reserve had raised interest rates and the US housing market had slowed after a sustained boom. House prices started to fall and assets that were securitized on mortgages (see next case study) started to fall in value. The asset-backed securities market had become so large and so many banks were involved in both issuing these assets and trading them that the wholesale money markets took fright. Banks became very cautious about lending to each other on an unsecured basis.[14]

Figure 12.3 shows what happened to interest rates in the inter-bank market in the United States, the United Kingdom, and the Eurozone. The market froze and any trades that were

---

[14] Secured lending involves the holding of some asset as security for the loan, whereas an unsecured loan can be worthless if a borrower defaults. Mortgages are a secured loan as the lender holds the deeds to the house, while inter-bank lending is typically unsecured.

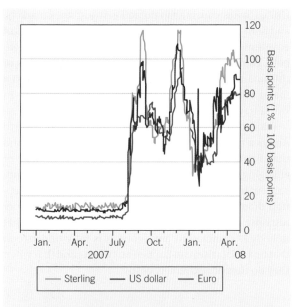

Figure 12.3 Three-month interbank rates relative to expected policy rates[a]

[a]Spread of three-month Libor to three-month overnight indexed swap (OIS) rates.

Sources: Financial Stability Report, Bank of England, April 2008; data are Bloomberg and Bank calculations.

done involved a substantial risk premium. For Northern Rock the message was simple. It could no longer borrow the funds it needed to finance its loan book. Neither could it sell off its mortgages as the appetite for mortgage-backed securities had just dried up. To make matters even worse, the UK housing market also started to turn down, so the quality of its assets (which were secured on houses) deteriorated.

Northern Rock had to turn to the UK government for help. It initially obtained an emergency loan from the Bank of England, but the publicity surrounding this only served to make customers think that the bank was in serious trouble, and queues of depositors wishing to withdraw their funds built up outside the bank. The Chancellor of the Exchequer stepped in by guaranteeing all deposits in Northern Rock and eventually taking Northern Rock into government ownership.

The possible alternatives to nationalization were: closing the bank or arranging a takeover by a stronger bank. The latter option was attempted, but no willing buyer could be found at the right price. Closing the bank would have caused severe disruption to the many savers who held deposits with Northern Rock (even though there was insurance on deposits up to £35,000[15] at the time) and it would have led to runs on other banks.

[15] This was raised to £50,000 in October 2008, and in April 2014 stood at £85,000.

There were plenty of other problems still ahead for the world's banking system before the financial crisis was over. We return to these in later chapters in the second half of this book.

2. Bankers as conjurers: securitization moves the boundaries.

Traditional commercial banking involved banks taking deposits and making loans. They paid a lower interest rate on their deposits than they charged on their loans, and this is how they made a profit. The profit margin had to be sufficient to cover their costs and cover any losses that arose from loan defaults. However, the growth of the bank was constrained by the growth of its deposit base. Without more deposits a bank could not make more loans. Individual banks could compete for deposits by offering higher interest rates, but this squeezed their profit margins and did not increase deposits as a whole.

Securitization was a financial technique that changed the constraints facing banks. They could make a bunch of loans, say mortgages, and sell off the income stream from those loans in the form of a fixed-income investment instrument like a bond. Potential buyers would be attracted by the interest stream that they could get with apparently low risk. Banks could lock in some profit on the deal and could then use the proceeds to make even more loans ... and then perhaps securitize those too. This financial innovation meant that banks could expand their loan business faster than the increase in their deposits. One estimate is that by 2007 around 25 per cent of UK bank loans were securitized.

Figure 12.4 shows the level of issuance in the global residential mortgage-backed securities market. This

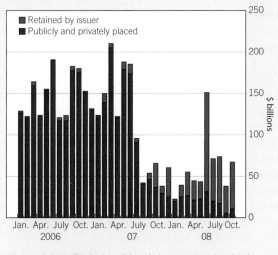

Figure 12.4 Global residential mortgage-backed securities issuance

Source: Financial Stability Review, Bank of England, October 2008

market collapsed in July 2007 and remained subdued for several years after that.

Northern Rock was caught by the collapse of the securitization market as well as by the freezing of the inter-bank market, as one of its potential sources of funding had been mortgage-backed bond sales.

Many other financial institutions found themselves in trouble when the mortgage-backed securities market imploded. The most serious phase in this crisis happened in September 2008, with the collapse of Lehman Brothers and the bail out of RBS and Lloyds by the UK government.

Conclusion

All economic activity carries some degrees of risk. Goods are produced or bought today for sale in the future. Contracts commit producers, customers, and borrowers to exchange goods and services in the future, and lenders to various actions in the future. Because the future can never be known with certainty, these essential economic activities all carry risks.

One of the triumphs of the market economy is its ability to facilitate a specialization of tasks. For a fee, specialists in risk assume the risks that others must take. In the process, they reduce the total amount of risk because of risk-sharing and their own specialized knowledge of risky situations. Insurance grew up when overseas trade became important in the post-medieval world. It allowed merchants who were specialists in markets to pass the risks of

the voyage on to insurers who were specialists in marine risks. The joint-stock company grew up in the nineteenth century as a way of allowing the accumulation of the vast amounts of capital that were needed to finance the factories of the Industrial Revolution with acceptable risks to the individual investors.

Today's specialists in risks are many and varied. They often act as financial intermediaries, standing between savers and borrowers. They facilitate complex transactions, which among other things allow many economic agents to specialize in what they can do best while allowing others to assume the risks that are inherent in these activities. But those who deal in risk and those who do not can all be taken by surprise when financial crises erupt.

SUMMARY

Risk and consumer choice

■ Many economic decisions involve risky choices, which can often be characterized by the expected value of the outcome and the degree of risk as measured by the dispersion of the possible outcomes.

■ Because those providing insurance or gambling must make profits, those who gamble or buy insurance do not take mathematically fair gambles. Diminishing marginal utility explains why people are risk-averse and therefore buy insurance policies, but it also predicts that such people would not gamble. Gambling where there is a small chance of a very large gain may be explained by the value placed on the hope (however small) of transforming one's life. Gambling where small gains and losses are involved may be explained by enjoyment of gambling in itself.

■ From the firm's point of view, providing gambling games where the odds can be set endogenously is a no-lose situation. Providing insurance is risky, but the pooling of independent risks minimizes the risk.

■ Two problems with insurance are moral hazard, where the existence of insurance alters people's behaviour in a socially costly way, and adverse selection, which arises under conditions of asymmetric information.

Financial choices and risk

■ Portfolio diversification allows investors to reduce their risk by holding a broad spectrum of financial assets. The risk reduction comes partly from the pooling of the return on assets whose risks are independent of each other, and partly from the pooling of assets whose risks are correlated with each other but of different magnitude. Optimum portfolio diversification allows investors to choose a bundle of assets that minimizes the risk on any given expected rate of return.

■ Mutual funds allow even small investors to hold highly diversified portfolios.

■ Financial intermediaries are institutions that stand between savers and borrowers. Their specialized knowledge and large volume of transactions reduce the transaction costs of matching savers and lenders and reduce risk.

Financial crises

■ Financial markets sometimes get carried away with over-optimism leading to asset price booms and associated with credit expansion.

■ Failures of financial institutions can result when asset prices collapse and defaults ensue.

■ Financial crises will have real effects and are associated with a downturn in activity.

TOPICS FOR REVIEW

■ Expected value and risk

■ Fair and unfair games

■ Attitudes to risk

■ Risk-sharing and risk-pooling

■ The demand for insurance

■ Portfolio diversification

■ The beta coefficient

■ Mutual funds

■ Financial intermediaries

DISCUSSION QUESTIONS

1 Calculate the expected return on each of the following sets of returns on an asset when each of the alternative possible outcomes has an equal chance of occurring:

a) 5%, 8%, 9%, 12%, 14%
b) 2%, 4%, 10%, 14%, 18%
c) 20%, 14%, 10%, 4%, 0%.

2 Calculate the deviation of each of the five possible alternative outcomes in (a) in Question 1 from its expected value. Square this deviation and multiply it by the probability of the outcome occurring. Add these terms together. This gives a measure of the variance of returns. Take the square root of the variance to find the standard deviation. Repeat this for (b) and (c). Rank these outcomes in terms of the standard deviation of returns.

3 Suppose that the returns in Question 1 arise in five possible states of the world and are returns on three different assets, (a), (b), and (c), which could be combined in a portfolio. The first number relates to the return on each asset in state 1, the second number to state 2, etc. Each state is equally likely to arise.

a) Calculate the expected return and standard deviation of return for a portfolio containing one-third of each asset.

b) Calculate the expected return and standard deviation for the following portfolios:
  (i)   half asset (a) and half asset (b)
  (ii) half asset (a) and half asset (c)
  (iii) half asset (b) and half asset (c).

Which combination of these assets will a risk-averse investor prefer?

4 A lottery pays one prize of £1,000,000 and sells 2,000,000 tickets for £1 each. What is the expected value of one ticket? Jo optimist decides to buy 10 tickets on the grounds that this will increase his chances of winning the big prize. What are his chances relative to those who only buy one ticket? What is the expected value of his investment in the ten tickets?

5 Why can it be rational for a consumer both to gamble and to buy insurance?

6 Explain the problems that arise from moral hazard and adverse selection in insurance or financial

markets. How can both insurance and banks deal with these problems?

7 Why does the presence of risk help explain the existence of financial intermediaries?

8 Under what circumstances is portfolio diversification beneficial for an investor?

9 Except for the aged and very poor, all medical and hospital insurance for Americans is provided by private insurance companies. In 2013 and 2012 the US Patient Protection and Affordable Care Act, popularly called Obamacare, required that all US citizens purchase medical insurance and that all insurance companies offer coverage independent of the person's health or past medical history. One of the government's major worries was that not enough young people would sign up for this insurance. What problem discussed in this chapter does this worry illustrate? What would be the effect on the insurance market if large numbers of the young did not sign up? In order to avoid this eventuality, a fine was imposed on all persons who did not carry medical insurance. What calculations would a rational utility-maximizing young person make when deciding whether to enrol in an insurance scheme or pay the fine?

PART FOUR

GOVERNMENT AND THE MARKET

CHAPTER 13

SUCCESSES AND FAILURES OF MARKETS

So far our main aims have been to understand how individual markets work, and how the market economy as a whole allocates resources between competing uses. We now ask whether market forces alone can be relied upon to deliver outcomes that are regarded as good, or even ideal. Do markets always generate efficient allocations of scarce resources? If they do not, in what circumstances do they fail to do so? Where markets fail, what alternative methods are available to deliver desired outcomes?

In particular, you will learn that:

- A perfectly competitive economy is allocatively efficient in the static sense since it operates where price equals marginal cost.[1]

- Free markets can fail to achieve the most efficient imaginable outcome for one of several possible causes of 'market failure'.

- Private markets will tend to overexploit common property resources.

- Goods that can be jointly consumed by many people simultaneously are called public goods, and they cannot be provided efficiently by the market.

- Costs and benefits of production that are external to producers cause the free-market level of production to deviate from socially acceptable outcomes, let alone the socially optimal level.

- Government policy towards competition is designed to encourage competitive practices and discourage monopoly.

In this chapter we first look at the basic functions that all governments have undertaken since the dawn of history—to provide institutions that protect the security of such things as personal safety, property, and contracts. If these functions are reasonably well performed, the free-market economy will allocate resources with relative efficiency. Indeed, an idealization of the free market, in which there is perfect competition in all markets, allocates resources optimally. We go on to see that in the real world markets fail to achieve a complete, or even a socially satisfactory, level of efficiency under a number of well-defined circumstances, including scale economies, common property resources, public goods, harmful externalities, and excessive market power. These so-called market failures provide the potential for government intervention to improve market efficiency. We see what government policies could achieve this objective under ideal circumstances. In Chapter 14 we study the role of government more broadly.

Because we are concerned here with assessing how well the economy is doing at delivering the needs of society, the issues covered in this chapter and the next are sometimes called 'welfare economics' or 'public economics'.

---

[1] We demonstrated this result in Chapter 6.

Basic functions of government

Organized governments arose shortly after the Neolithic agricultural revolution turned people from hunter–gatherers into settled farmers. An institution that has survived that long must be doing something right! Over the intervening more than 100 centuries, the functions undertaken by government have varied enormously. But through all that time the function that has not changed is to provide what is called a *legal monopoly of violence*. Violent acts can be conducted by the military and the civilian police arms of government. Also, through its judicial system, the government can deprive people of their liberty by incarcerating them or, in extreme cases, by executing them. This is a dangerous monopoly that is easily abused, as is any monopoly, but with consequences that are more serious than when monopolies act inefficiently. For these reasons satisfactory governments have systems of checks and balances designed to keep the use of their monopoly power directed to the general good rather than to the good of the individuals in a narrow government circle.

The importance of having a monopoly of violence can be seen in those countries whose governments do not have it. Somalia and Afghanistan in recent decades and China in the 1920s provide examples of countries in which individual warlords commanded armies that could not vanquish each other. Colombia provides an example of a country where, for some time, organized criminals (linked to the drugs trade) had substantial power to commit violence that the government could not control. In extreme cases, where many groups have almost equal ability to exert military violence, power struggles can create havoc with normal economic and social life. Life then becomes 'nasty, brutish, and short'—to use the words of the seventeenth-century English political philosopher Thomas Hobbes.

The importance of having checks on the arbitrary use of its monopoly by a selfish government is seen in the disasters that ensue in the many dictatorships that misuse their power. The USSR under Stalin, Uganda under Idi Amin, Nigeria under Sanni Abacha, Cambodia under Pol Pot, Liberia under Charles Taylor, Libya under Muammar Gaddafi, and Zimbabwe under Robert Mugabe are a few of the many modern-day examples.

When the government's monopoly of violence is secure and functions with reasonable restraints against its arbitrary use, citizens can safely carry on their ordinary economic and social activities.

So governments are, as they always have been, institutions to which people give the legal monopoly of violence in return for their enforcement of 'law and order'.

A related government activity is to provide security of property. Governments define and enforce property rights that give people a secure claim to the fruits of their own labour. These property rights include clear definitions and enforcement of the rights and obligations of individuals and institutions such as joint-stock companies, banks, insurance companies, and stock exchanges, as well as provisions for bankruptcy and protection against the rise and/or abuse of monopoly power over markets.

A further important function is to provide security of contract and arbitration in disputes. It is important that contracts among individuals and firms can be made binding, thereby providing the security needed to enter into the many contractual relations that are essential to a well-functioning market economy. It is also important to have independent courts through which disputes can be settled.

As the founder of British classical economics, Adam Smith, put it a long time ago:

The first duty of the sovereign [is] that of protecting the society from the violence and invasion of other independent societies … The second duty of the sovereign [is] that of protecting, as far as possible, every member of the society from the injustice or oppression of every other member of it.

Adam Smith, *The Wealth of Nations*, 1776; New York: Random House, 1937 edn., pages 653, 669)

In a modern complex economy, providing these 'minimal' government services is no simple task. Countries whose governments are not good at doing these things have seldom prospered economically.

Before proceeding to discuss specific market outcomes in detail it is important to recall that the market economy also determines the distribution of income by establishing the prices of resources (such as land, labour, and capital) that provide incomes for their owners. The income distribution that results may have characteristics that are regarded as undesirable, in that some people may have incomes on which it is impossible to live, either at all or at the minimum socially acceptable standard. Governments step in to ensure a safety net of some kind and thus to redistribute income compared with what a pure market outcome would deliver. We do not list 'unacceptable, market-determined distributions of income' as 'market failures' below because what is socially acceptable is a value judgment that is not a dimension of efficiency. We discuss the role of government in redistributing income in the following chapter.

How well do markets work?

Within a secure framework of law and order, and well-defined and enforced property rights and other essential institutions, a modern economy can function at least moderately well without further government assistance. In this section we see how and why this is so. In subsequent sections we study government functions that arise when free markets fail to produce results that are regarded as acceptable.

Box 13.1 puts in context some recent claims that the 2007–8 financial crisis and subsequent worldwide recession mark the end of 'free markets' or even the end of 'capitalism as we know it'. We discuss the lessons of this episode more fully in the first case study at the end of this chapter.

Markets, when they work reasonably well, are impressive institutions. Consumers' tastes and producers' costs help to generate price signals. These signals coordinate the separate decisions taken by millions of independent agents, all pursuing their own self-interest and needing to take no account of national priorities. In doing so, they allocate the nation's resources without conscious central direction. Furthermore, in modern market economies firms compete to get ahead of each other by producing better goods more cheaply, and in the process

Box 13.1 The end of free-market economics?

The global financial crisis of 2007–8 and the resulting recession were regarded by many as indicating both a failure of the economic system and a failure of the economics profession. The UK Prime Minister, Gordon Brown, said in his New Year message for 2009 that 2008 'would be remembered as the year in which the old era of unbridled free-market dogma was finally ushered out'. That the events raised big issues cannot be doubted, but a bit of perspective should help to put more extreme claims in context.

Debates about the role of the free market versus some form of state intervention have gone on for a long time. One version of this focused on external competition and the issue of protectionism versus free trade. In the United Kingdom this debate centred on the campaign to repeal the Corn Laws in the early nineteenth century. An even earlier debate had taken place in France in the eighteenth century where the opponents of state intervention had coined the phrase laissez faire as a slogan for those who favoured letting businesses work with minimal intervention. This idea was incorporated in Adam Smith's famous book Wealth of Nations, published in 1776. Smith explained the benefits of the 'invisible hand' of market forces and defined the appropriate, but fairly limited, role that governments should play.

The Industrial Revolution and the resulting growth of factory production was a great success of the free market system. But the benefit to workers came only gradually, while in the shorter term many business owners became very rich while the typical worker remained extremely poor and had a very harsh existence. Labour unions grew up to try to improve the lot of the workers, and several writers, including Karl Marx, developed a critique of the capitalist system which created support for much greater state intervention, including full state ownership of industry. These ideas were implemented in the Soviet Union after the 1917 Bolshevik revolution with the creation of a 'communist' system of state ownership and central planning of the economy.

The communist experiment eventually failed, and almost all former communist countries converted back to a market system at the end of the 1980s. However, even in the non-communist world, the Great Depression of the 1930s had stimulated further debate about the shortcomings of a market economy and the possible need for significant government intervention. These events, combined with the Second World War, led to much greater state participation than hitherto, and in the United Kingdom this was extended even further after the war with the nationalization of major industries, such as railways, steel, and power supply.

The case for less state intervention started to be put more frequently in the 1970s, as evidence grew of the inefficiency of state-run industries. This culminated in the wave of deregulation and privatization in the 1980s and was paralleled by the collapse of communism. It is safe to say that by the late 1990s and early 2000s the proponents of a relatively free market economy and opponents of major state interventions had won the argument. But the 2007–8 financial crisis has raised many of the old arguments about the shortcomings of a market economy. The full implications of all this are not yet clear, but what is clear is that we should not write off the market economy. It is here to stay and there is no serious alternative, even though there may be a significant role for state regulation, especially in the financial sector.

In this chapter we point out many well-known ways in which markets fail. None of these overturns the case for a market economy, but each provides a case for some form of government involvement.

generate the technological changes that have raised average living standards fairly steadily over the past two centuries or so.

The general case

The most general case in support of market economies is that they fulfil their functions better than any known alternative. We observed that this *was* so in Chapter 1, but now we have developed a deeper insight into *why* this is so.

Better information

An enormous amount of information about constantly changing market conditions is conveyed both by prices and, when these are set by producers, by the quantities that they sell. The central planners of the former Soviet Union found that generating this information by conscious planning was a massive job. For example, the Soviet authorities had to set prices for over five million items. Yet their economy was much simpler than any Western economy because the planners suppressed most of the vast range of differentiated products available to consumers in modern industrial economies.

Greater flexibility

Compared with any known alternative, the decentralized market system is more flexible and leaves more scope for personal adaptation at any moment in time. For example, if a scarcity of oil results in a rise in its price, one individual can elect to leave her heating on full and economize on her car's petrol consumption, while another may wish to do the opposite. In order to obtain the same overall reduction in consumption by non-price rationing, the government typically forces the same reduction in heating and driving on both individuals, independent of their tastes, doctor's advice, and other perceived needs.

Better adaptability

In market economies prices and quantities demanded change as conditions change. Decentralized decision-makers can react continuously to these changing signals, whereas government quotas, allocations, and rationing schemes are slower to adjust. Millions of adaptations to millions of changes in tens of thousands of markets are required every year. The Eastern European planners discovered that it is a Herculean task to anticipate these, or even to know that they had already happened, and then to plan the necessary adjustments.

Decentralization of power

The market economy decentralizes power and thus requires less coercion of individuals than do other types of economy. Governments must coerce if markets are not allowed to allocate people to jobs, and products to consumers. The power to allocate creates major opportunities for bribery, corruption, and allocation according to the tastes of the central administrators. If, at the going prices and wages, there are not enough flats or coveted jobs to go around, the bureaucrats must allocate them. Some will go to those who pay the largest bribe, some to those with religious beliefs, hairstyles, or political views that the bureaucrats like, and only the rest to those whose names come up on the waiting list.

Of course, large firms and large unions exercise substantial economic power in market economies. However, that power tends to be constrained by both the competition of other large entities and the emergence of new products and firms, and it is always less than that exercised by a powerful central government.

The efficiency of perfect competition

While they accept the general case for the superiority of the market economy just outlined, some professional economists have wanted to be more precise about just what the market economy does do well. They have attempted to do this by proving that an idealized, although in practice totally unachievable, model of the market economy (universal perfect competition) leads, in equilibrium, to an optimum, or efficient, allocation of resources. This result is often referred to as **Pareto optimality** after the great Italian economist Vilfredo Pareto (1848–1923), who studied it in great detail.

In Chapter 6 we showed that perfect competition was efficient in the sense that it maximized the sum of producers' and consumers' surplus. In Chapter 7 we showed that monopoly was not efficient in that same sense because it restricts output below what is required to maximize these surpluses. In this section we develop an alternative proof of the proposition that perfect competition leads to efficient allocation of resources. We divide our discussion into two parts. First, the meaning of efficiency and, secondly, the proof that a perfectly competitive economy leads to an efficient, or as it is usually called an optimum, allocation of resources. We make this separation because there is no debate about the meaning of efficiency, while there is great debate about the significance of the proof of the optimality of perfect competition.

The meaning of efficiency

According to the static definition of efficiency, an economy's resources are said to be allocated efficiently when it is impossible to reallocate them so as to make at least one person better off without simultaneously making another person worse off. Watch the double negative! An allocation of resources is productively *in*efficient when it is possible to make at least one person better off without making another person worse off. It is efficient when this cannot be done—for example, when the only way to make anyone better off is to make at least one other person worse off. Efficiency has two aspects, *productive efficiency* and *allocative efficiency*.

Static **productive efficiency** is defined as occurring when it is impossible to produce more of any one product without simultaneously producing less of some other product. It, in turn, has two aspects—one concerning the allocation of resources within each firm, and one concerning the allocation of resources among the firms in an industry. The first condition for productive efficiency is that each firm should produce any given output at the lowest possible cost. Any firm that is not being productively efficient is producing at a higher cost than is necessary and hence wasting resources.

The second condition for productive efficiency is that all firms producing the same homogeneous product should have the same marginal cost. This ensures that the total output of each industry is allocated among its individual firms in such a way that the total cost of producing the industry's output is minimized. If all firms' marginal costs were not the same, resources could be transferred from the firm with the highest marginal cost to the firm with lowest. The same output could then be produced, but at a lower cost.

Look again at the production-possibility frontier in Figure 1.1 in Chapter 1. An economy that is productively inefficient will be at some point inside the curve, such as point *c*. It will be possible to produce more of some goods without producing less of others.

Productive efficiency implies being on, rather than inside, the economy's production-possibility frontier.

Allocative efficiency relates to the allocation of resources among the industries that supply all the goods and services that are produced within an economy. In other words:

Allocative efficiency relates to the choice among alternative points on the production-possibility curve.

It concerns, for example, the choice between points such as *a* and *b* in Figure 1.1. Changing the allocation of resources in a productively efficient economy implies producing more of some goods and less of others. Allocative efficiency means that it is impossible, by producing a different bundle of goods (i.e. moving from one point on the production-possibility curve to another point), to make any one person better off without making at least one

other person worse off. Conversely, **allocative inefficiency** means that it is possible, by moving from one point on the production-possibility curve to another, to make at least one person better off while making no other person worse off.

How do we find the allocatively efficient point on the production-possibility curve? For example, how many shoes, dresses, and hats should be produced to achieve allocative efficiency? The answer is as follows.

The economy's allocation of resources is efficient when the marginal cost of producing each good is equal to its market price.

To understand the reasoning behind this answer, we need to look at the significance of price and marginal cost.

First, look at price. The price of any product indicates the value that each consumer places on the last unit purchased of that product. Faced with the market price of some product, the consumer goes on buying units until the last one is valued exactly at its price. Consumers' surplus arises because each consumer would be willing to pay more than the market price for all but the last unit bought. On the last unit bought (i.e. the marginal unit), however, the consumer only 'breaks even', because the valuation placed on it is just equal to its price.

Now consider marginal cost. It is the value of the resources used to produce the last unit of output. Thus, when marginal cost is equated to price, the value that consumers place on the last unit they consume is exactly equal to the value of the resources required to produce that unit of output.

Optimality

Productive efficiency can be achieved under many different market conditions. First, all profit-maximizing firms, including those in perfectly competitive industries, will wish to produce their output at the lowest possible cost. Otherwise they would not be maximizing their profits. Secondly, in most industries that produce a homogeneous product, including those in perfectly competitive industries, firms face a given world price for their product, even if there are only a few firms in any one country. If they all have access to the same technology, they will all have the same cost curves. Thus, when they equate marginal cost to price (equals marginal revenue), they end up all having identical marginal costs. However, all profit-maximizing firms that face negatively sloped demand curves for the products must set the prices for each of them. They will equate marginal cost with marginal revenue which is less than price. So these firms will not be allocatively efficient in the static sense that we are considering here.

Allocative efficiency, however, occurs only under universal perfect competition. To see that it does occur under perfect competition, suppose that the entire economy is perfectly competitive. Marginal cost will then equal price in all lines of production. The value that consumers place on the last unit of each and every commodity that they consume will be equal to the cost of producing that unit.

In a perfectly competitive economy £1 worth of resources reallocated from the production of any one product would produce £1 worth of value for consumers whatever product it was then used to produce.

To illustrate, assume that marginal cost equals price in all lines of production except blue jeans. Jeans sell for £25 but initially cost £30 to produce at the margin. If one pair of jeans fewer is produced, consumers lose the £25 of value that they place on it. But resources worth £30 are freed. If those resources move to any industry in which marginal cost equals price, they will produce £30 worth of value. Society will have gained £5 in total value and it will be possible to make someone better off by £5 worth of consumption without making anyone else worse off.

Now let the output of jeans be such that they only cost £20 to produce at the margin but still sell for £25. If one more pair of jeans is now produced, resources worth £20 will have to be withdrawn from some other line of production. But since marginal cost equals price in all other lines, only £20 worth of consumer satisfaction will be lost when these resources move. When they produce one more pair of jeans, consumers get a product they value at £25. So there is a net gain of £5 on the transfer.

Finally, let the output of jeans increase until the marginal cost of the last pair produced is equal to its £25 price. If *one pair of jeans fewer* is produced, £25 worth of value is sacrificed and the £25 worth of resources that are freed could produce £25 worth of value anywhere else in the economy. If *one more pair of jeans* is produced, the producers of jeans create £25 of value but £25 worth of value is lost when the resources are taken from some other industry. So there is no gain in reallocating resources either into or out of the production of blue jeans. The current allocation is efficient.

When marginal cost equals price in all industries it is impossible to reallocate resources between alternative lines of production and increase consumer satisfaction by making at least one person better off while making no one worse off. The economy is then allocatively efficient.

A perfectly competitive economy is allocatively efficient because it equates marginal cost to price in all lines of production and (as we saw in Chapter 6) because this maximizes the sum of producers' and consumers' surplus.

Any economy in which marginal cost does not equal price in at least some industries is not allocative efficient because consumers could be made better off by moving production from industries in which the gap between marginal cost and price was greatest to industries in which the gap was smallest.

Of course, perfectly competitive economies do not, and could not, exist in the world in which we live. Recall also that we are doing a static analysis of efficiency here (see Box 7.3) and there are large alleged benefits from deviating from perfect competition in the form of providing such things as strong incentives for innovation and diversity of choice for consumers.

How markets fail

Is the analysis of the optimality of perfect competition of any practical value? Economists are divided on the answer they give to this question. Some believe that it gives, by analogy, a defence of the price system as it works in practice.[2] Some also see it as a guide to practical policy—satisfy the conditions for an optimal allocation of resources wherever that is possible, even if they cannot be satisfied everywhere in the economy. For example, wherever firms can be influenced by the government, they should be directed to set their product prices equal to marginal cost, and whenever taxes are levied, they should be as neutral as possible in the sense of not distorting prices from what they would be under perfect competition. This is called piecemeal welfare policy advice. The problem with such piecemeal policies is that although satisfying all of the optimum conditions would raise static efficiency above what it is in any real economy, satisfying just some of them is not a sure road to improving efficiency and community welfare. The reasons for this are shown in what is called *the general theory of second best* and are discussed briefly in Box 13.2.

Yet others start by observing, as we did in Chapters 7 and 8, that firms in most lines of production have some market power over their prices because they face negatively sloped rather than perfectly elastic demand curves for their products. When firms face negatively sloped demand curves, price will exceed marginal cost in equilibrium. Thus, no real market economy has ever achieved anything even close to perfect allocative efficiency. These economists argue that, because of this, the study

---

[2] For example, R.M. Starr says that that proof of the optimality of perfect competition provides 'a significant defense of the market's resource allocation mechanism' and A. Mas-Colell, M.D. Whinston, and R.J. Green say that the proof offers 'a strong conceptual affirmation of the use of competitive markets, even for dealing with distributional issues'.

Box 13.2 **The theory of second best**

The theory of second best applies to the real world in which there are many sources—taxes on goods and labour, subsidies on production, rules and regulations—of divergence from the conditions that would establish an optimal static allocation of resources under perfect competition, called the first-best conditions. So, in the absence of any hope of achieving a first-best optimum, piecemeal theorists advocate satisfying the optimum conditions wherever possible, even if we know that we can never establish all of them.

Second-best theory upsets this policy advice by showing that in a world of many divergences from the first-best conditions, satisfying any one of them may raise or lower welfare. The proof is quite general and shows two things.

First, if a full static optimum allocation of resources does obtain and one unalterable source of divergence from the first-best conditions is introduced, it is generally desirable to depart from all the other first-best conditions to establish what is called a second-best optimum. This is the best that one can do, given the existence of the one unalterable source of divergence. For example, if one specific tax is levied on one commodity in an otherwise perfectly competitive world, it is optional to introduce a series of taxes of varying size on all the other commodities.

Secondly, if we start with the real-world case in which there are many sources of divergence from the first-best

conditions, the removal of one source of divergence to make it satisfy its first-best condition may raise or lower efficiency and welfare. For example, in our world, the removal of one commodity tax or tariff may raise or lower efficiency depending on the details of the specific situation under consideration.

Second-best optima are almost as difficult to obtain as first-best optima. What the theory shows is not what to do, but what not to do; do not assume that the removal of one source of divergence from the first-best conditions will necessarily improve efficiency or community welfare. There are no valid scientifically derivable general rules for policy that are true for all market economies, all of the time. Instead, the effect of specific policies is context-specific: any policy, such as forming a customs union with one's trading partners, can raise or lower efficiency and welfare depending on the circumstances of the particular case.

But, as noted in the text, optimality analysis is still useful whenever some specific and well-articulated objective is being sought that is less ambitious than raising the welfare of the whole community.

The box on this subject in the Online Resouce Centre contains an example that may help the reader to understand the second-best concept.[3]

---

[3] www.oxfordtextbooks.co.uk/orc/lipsey13e/

---

of the imaginary perfectly competitive economy is of no practical value.[4] Furthermore they argue that, even if it were attainable, we would not want a perfectly competitive economy because static efficiency, with its zero profits everywhere, is not consistent with the kind of inter-firm competition that brings about the technical changes that are the engine of long-term economic growth.

Other economists take a middle of the road position and argue that the conditions for efficiency are meant only as a benchmark to help in identifying sources of allocative inefficiency, called market failures. These

sources provide scope for possible government intervention designed to improve market efficiency—even if not to achieve complete efficiency. (But there are also costs of such intervention, which we consider later in this chapter.)

There can be little doubt that optimality analysis can be useful when there are more specific goals than optimizing resource allocation over the entire economy. For example. when the issue is how to obtain a specified reduction in some pollution or road congestion at the least cost, economic analysis can show how to obtain this limited optimum without appealing to any economy-wide result. We consider these actual examples later in the chapter.

There are several important circumstances under which markets fail to allocate resources with even modest efficiency, let alone achieving the optimal allocation of resources:[5]

1. Producers with excess capacity set positive prices, referred to as inefficient exclusion.

---

[4] For example, M. Blaug says 'these beautiful theorems [of the optimality of perfect competition] are mental exercises without the slightest possibility of ever being practically relevant', while W.J. Baumol says that the they are a 'fairy tale' that should be discarded. Economists who reject the relevance of economy-wide optimality provided by perfect competition still hold that optimality analysis can be useful when there are more specific goals than optimizing resource allocation over the entire economy. For example. when the issue is how to obtain a specified reduction in some pollution at the least cost, economic analysis can show how to obtain this limited optimum without appealing to any economy-wide result. We consider this actual example later in the chapter.

[5] New terms introduced in this list are explained later in this chapter.

2. There are resources that can be used by everyone but belong to no one—called common property resources.

3. Public goods exist. A public good is a good that is non-rivalrous, so your consuming it does not preclude my consuming it at the same time, and non-excludable, so I cannot prevent you from consuming it once it is produced.

4. People not party to some market bargain are nonetheless significantly affected by it, i.e. externalities exist.

5. One party to a market transaction has fuller knowledge of its consequences than is available to the other party, a situation referred to as asymmetric information.

6. Needed markets do not exist—known as missing markets.

7. Substantial market power in the hands of producers causes prices to diverge from marginal costs.

There is one other important reason why perfect competition is not attainable which is not on the above list—scale economies. Because large-scale production is efficient in many industries, there is only room in them for a few large firms and, in the limit, for only one firm. There are at least two advantages of having these large firms. First, production is more efficient with them than with many small firms who cannot reap the scale economies. Secondly, the active competition among them is the source of many new technologies that have raised living standard steadily over the decades, while the transient but large profits that they earn by temporarily getting ahead of competitors provide much of the funds needed to finance the R&D that leads to these new technologies.

Coping with the seven market failures listed above provides governments with major functions in addition to the law and order functions discussed earlier. In the rest of this chapter we study these sources of market failure and how government policies could conceivably alleviate them. In Chapter 14 we study the costs of government intervention that must be set against the possible benefits before an intervention is justified on economic grounds. This raises the question of how well government policies actually work in coping with market failures as well as in achieving all the other goals that governments set for themselves.

Rivalrous and excludable goods

Economies must allocate resources between the production and consumption of the four major classes of goods and services that are shown in Table 13.1. A good is rivalrous if no two people can consume the same unit. For example, if you buy and eat an apple, no one else can buy and eat that same apple. A good is excludable if people can be prevented from obtaining it. Excludability requires that an owner be able to exercise effective property rights over the good or service in order to determine who uses it—typically only those who pay for the privilege.

Most of the goods and services that you and I buy are rivalrous and excludable. If I buy a chocolate bar and eat it, no one else can buy and eat that bar, and the owner can prevent me from having it if I am unwilling to pay for it (unless I steal it). If an airline sells you a seat on a particular flight, it cannot let another person occupy that seat as well as you.

Obvious though these characteristics may seem, there are important classes of goods and services that lack one or both of them. Goods and services are non-rivalrous when the amount that one person consumes does not affect the amount that other people can consume. They are non-excludable when, once produced, there is no way to stop anyone from consuming them.

Rivalrousness is usually fixed once and for all by the nature of the good or service. An apple is rivalrous. If you eat it, I cannot also eat it. The viewing of a work of art is not rivalrous. We can both see it without affecting each other's enjoyment. In contrast, excludability depends on the specific circumstances and the state of technology.

What determines which is which?

Circumstances

Before the advent of GPS systems the Fastnet lighthouse guided all shipping making a landfall on southwest Ireland and there was no way to force passing ships to pay for its services. It is still useful to many, although its importance has been diminished by technological change in navigation. All passing could see the light so it is non-rivalrous (my seeing it does not stop you seeing it) and non-excludable (once lit any passer-by can see it for nothing). The New Brighton lighthouse illuminates the entrance to the River Mersey and the Port of Liverpool, and it is equally non-rivalrous and non-excludable from the perspective of the ships using the port. However, if its operators had turned it off (prior to the invention of radar

Table 13.1 **Four types of good**

	Excludable	Non-excludable
Rivalrous	*Normal goods*	*Common property*
	Apples	Fisheries
	Dresses	Common land
	TV sets	Wildlife
	Computers	Air
	A seat on an aeroplane	Streams
Non-rivalrous (up to capacity)		*Public goods*
	Art galleries	Defence
	Museums	Police
	Fenced parks	Public information
	Roads	Broadcast signals
	Bridges	Some navigation aids

The table gives examples of items in each of the four categories. Markets cope best with rivalrous excludable goods. The market can produce goods that are excludable but non-rivalrous, but their efficient use often requires a zero price. Goods that are non-excludable but rivalrous are common property resources, which are overused by free markets. Goods that are non-rivalrous and non-excludable are public goods, which will often not be produced at all by the free market.

and GPS), many ships would have passed on to another, better lit harbour entrance. In this case private owners could sell the lighthouse's services, not to passing ships, but to the port authorities who knew they needed it in order to compete with rival ports. So here there is a degree of excludability (if the port authorities do not pay, their harbour entrance does not get lit and they lose business). There is also a degree of rivalrousness in that the Port of Liverpool could have lost out if the lighthouse owner had built it elsewhere.

Technology

Early TV programmes were all broadcast openly to anyone who had a set and hence were non-rivalrous and non-excludable. But the development of satellites, encoded signals, and cable transmission allowed some forms of TV signals to be provided only to those who pay for the service. The programmes are still non-rivalrous in the sense that there is no limit to the number of people who can watch a given programme. But the new technologies made them excludable so that private companies would be willing to provide them. As another example, until recently it has been impracticable to charge tolls for the use of urban roads and exclude non-payers because of the

excessive costs involved in the many tollbooths needed to service a road in a densely populated urban area. Today, it is technically possible to implant in each car a device that tracks its location at very small cost. Fees for the use of urban roads can now be assessed and non-payers denied use of the roads or charged a fine. The London congestion charge does not use a device in cars, but it does use cameras that photograph cars entering the charge zone and a computer that checks car number plates against those who have paid the charge for that day.

Cost

In some cases it is technically possible to make a good excludable but is too costly to do so. One could put a fence around the Lake District National Park and charge hikers a fee for walking in the area, but the cost of erecting and policing the fence makes it uneconomic to exclude non-payers.

In what follows, we look at the characteristics of goods and services that fall into the four possible combinations of excludable and non-excludable and rivalrous and non-rivalrous as shown in Table 13.1.

Excludable goods

Private agents who produce goods and services for sale on the free market must be able to prohibit consumption of their output by those who will not pay for the privilege. Otherwise the producers cannot gain the revenue they need to cover their production costs.

Therefore excludability is necessary for a good to be produced by a firm for sale on the market.

Ordinary goods: excludable and rivalrous

The market works best when goods and services are rivalrous and excludable.

Private firms can produce and sell ordinary goods. Furthermore, whenever these firms are price takers they will fulfil the condition for static allocative efficiency by operating where marginal cost equals price.

Art galleries, museums, and parks: excludable but non-rivalrous

Some excludable goods and services are non-rivalrous, at least up to a large capacity constraint. This is the first reason on our list of market failures. A park with a fence around it provides an excludable service, but one person's use does not interfere with another person's use—at least until there are so many users that overcrowding becomes a serious problem. Such goods can be provided by private firms, but since the marginal cost of adding another user is zero (until capacity is reached), any admission fee that the owner charges will result in a non-optimal use of the facility. It costs nothing to add another user, but to cover their costs the providers must charge each user a fee. Thus, under private provision, price will exceed marginal cost and some people who are willing to pay more than this marginal cost but less than the current price do not use it. This market failure is called **inefficient exclusion**.

To avoid inefficient exclusions, governments often provide non-rivalrous but excludable goods and services.

The costs are then met out of taxation, and the service is provided free. Parks, art galleries, roads, and bridges often come under this category. Box 13.3 reviews the debate that arose in the early 1990s when the Conservative government in the UK reduced the grants to galleries and museums and the trustees of some felt they had little option but to levy charges for admission. The subsequent Labour government abolished admission charges, but the debate continues.

Non-excludable goods

This class provides the next two sources on our list of major market failures—those associated with common property resources and public goods.

Common property: non-excludable but rivalrous

If you catch a fish in the open ocean, I cannot catch it, so it is rivalrous. But in a free market there is no way for you to exclude me from catching it, so it is non-excludable. This is the second reason on our list of causes of market failures. A **common property resource** is one that is rivalrous but non-excludable. No one has an exclusive property right to it, and it can be used by anyone. No one owns the ocean's fish until they are caught. No one owns common grazing land. The world's international fishing grounds are common property for all fishermen, as is common grazing land for all livestock owners. If, by taking more fish, one fisherman reduces the catch of other fishermen, he does not count this as a cost, although it is a cost to society. If, by

---

Box 13.3 Pricing of galleries and museums

Art galleries, museums, fenced parks, bridges, and similar public institutions are examples of goods that are excludable—admission is easily controlled at entrances—but non-rivalrous at least up to substantial capacity. Except on crowded days, one person's use does not reduce another person's ability to use the facility. The efficient solution is to allow everyone to use the facility free of charge on non-crowded days but to charge a price on days on which the crowds make the facility's use a rivalrous activity, or when there is a special (and popular) exhibition.

The argument *against* the policy of free admission runs along the following lines. Many taxpayers who never use the facility, and do not even care that it exists, are forced to help pay for it. Many of these people may have below-average incomes and be less well educated. Therefore the free-admission policy is to a great extent a subsidy for the cultured middle classes. In times of financial stringency, those who want to use the facility should pay for it.

Whatever the reasons, in the early 1990s the Conservative government in the United Kingdom decided to curtail drastically its support for the arts. In response, many museum and gallery trustees decided that the only course open to them was to institute admission charges, although others did not. Controversy was sustained and often bitter.

Those who opposed the imposition of charges argued several points. The admission fees would lead to inefficient exclusion. Institutions that were under-used and could add

more visitors would be excluding potential users by their not insignificant charges. Those excluded would be from lower-income classes who had contributed little to the costs of operation in the past because they paid little in income tax.

There is no easy resolution of such debates. They tend to pit those who worry about equity against those who worry about efficiency. But even that is not always a clear division. It is an equity argument that those who benefit from the facilities should pay for them. But it is also an equity argument that positive admission fees should not be used to preclude the poor from taking part in an activity that has a zero marginal cost.

In 2001 the Labour government abolished admission charges. Comparing December 2001 monthly attendances with those in December 2000, and thereby controlling for seasonal influences, shows a huge increase in museum visits at the zero price. The Victoria and Albert Museum (V&A) experienced the biggest increase, with monthly visitor numbers rising from 42,600 in December 2000 to 174,000 in December 2001—an increase of 309 per cent. Similarly, though not so dramatically, the Museum of London had an 88 per cent increase, the Natural History Museum had an 82 per cent increase, and the Museums of Science and Industry in Manchester had a 75 per cent increase. However, this surge in usage did not end the debate, as many institutions found themselves squeezed by government funding cuts.

grazing her own sheep, a peasant farmer reduces the feed available for other people's goats, she does not count this as a cost. The result has been called *the tragedy of the commons*—the tendency for commonly held property to be overexploited, often to the extent of destruction.

It is socially optimal to add to a fleet that is fishing any given fishing area until the last boat increases the *value of the fleet's total catch* by as much as it costs to operate the boat. Similarly, it is optimal to add another sheep to the flock that grazes on the commons as long as the total supply of meat (and milk) is increased by as much as the cost of maintaining the extra animal. These are the sizes of fishing fleet and flock of sheep that a social planner or a private monopolist would choose.

The socially optimal exploitation of a common property resource occurs when the marginal cost of the last user equals the value of the marginal addition to total output.

However, the free market will not produce that result. Consider the fishery. Potential new entrants will judge entry to be profitable if the *value of their own catch* is equal to the costs of operating their boats. But a new entrant's catch is *partly* an addition to total catch and *partly* a reduction of the catch of other fishermen—because of congestion each new boat reduces the catch of all other boats. Thus, under competitive free entry there will be too many boats in the fleet and too many sheep on the common.

How does a potential new fisherman judge the value of entering the industry? He will expect to do about as well as the average boat. So it pays to enter, adding a new boat to the fleet, until the *average* value of the catch of a typical boat in the fleet is equal to the cost of running the newly entering boat.[6]

The free market will add users to a common property resource until the marginal cost of the last entrant equals the average output of all existing producers.

At this point, however, the *net* addition to the *total* catch brought about by the last boat will be substantially less than the cost of operating the boat, and it may even be negative.

With common property resources the level of output will be too high because each new entrant will not take account of the cost that he or she imposes on existing producers.

6 This subtle point is the same as the difference between the perfectly competitive producer and the monopolist. The monopolist knows that if it sells more, it will reduce the market value of what it is already selling. The perfect competitor must take the market price as given and so values a marginal unit of production at the market price, i.e. at the average value of all units already being sold.

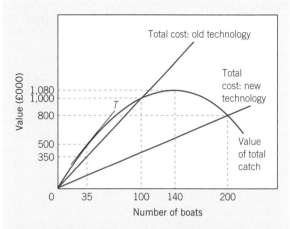

Figure 13.1 Overfishing of a common property fishery

A common property resource is exploited beyond the socially optimal level. Adding boats to the fleet adds to the total catch but at a diminishing rate up to 140 boats, after which additional boats lower the total catch. With the old technology, the cost (capital and current) of running each boat is £10,000, giving the steeper of the two total cost curves. The socially optimal level is 35 boats, where the addition to total catch, as shown by the slope of the tangent to the total catch curve, just equals the addition to the total cost of running one more boat, as shown by the slope of the total cost curve. At that point there is a surplus of revenue over total cost of £150,000. At that fleet size, a new boat expects to catch about £14,300 (i.e. £500,000/35) worth of fish, so entry is profitable from the private point of view. When the fleet reaches 100 boats, a new boat expects to catch £10,000 worth of fish, which just matches its cost. With new technology, each boat costs only £4,000 to run. The fleet expands to 200 boats catching £800,000 worth of fish. This yields revenue of £4,000 per boat, which just matches cost. Production has been pushed beyond the point of negative marginal returns.

This tendency to overexploitation of a common property resource is illustrated by the example in Figure 13.1. Free-market entry proceeds until the cost of the last boat, which is average total cost per boat, equals the revenue it expects, which is the average revenue per boat. This is the same as saying total cost equals total revenue, so there are no economic profits to attract further entrants. The surplus over cost that could be earned with a smaller fleet is dissipated by entry. In this example, the fishing fleet numbers 100 vessels. Each boat costs £10,000 to run and catches £10,000 worth of fish. If the fleet were restricted to 35 boats, each £10,000 boat would catch fish worth just over £14,000. Later, when some new technology reduces the cost of running each boat, entry proceeds well beyond the 140-boat level where each additional boat actually begins to reduce the total catch.

Box 13.4 Buffaloes, cows, and elephants

For centuries North American bison—commonly called buf-faloes—were a common property resource for the Plains Indians, whose populations were small enough that they could kill all they needed without endangering the ability of the herds to reproduce themselves. In a little over a decade following the end of the American Civil War in 1865, white hunters destroyed the herds. Buffalo Bill Cody may have been a folk hero, but he, and those like him, were the buf-falo's executioners.

The buffalo was replaced by cattle, which did not follow the buffalo into extinction. The difference was that cattle were the private property of the ranchers. Rustlers and other predators attacked the herds, but the self-interest of ranch-ers made it worthwhile for them to protect their cattle.

Many people, watching the destruction of wildlife in Africa and Asia, have argued that property rights should be used to turn these animals from the modern equivalent of the buffalo into the modern equivalent of cattle. Wildlife is a common property resource. When it becomes endangered, laws are passed to prevent predatory hunting. But no one has any profit motive in enforcing these laws. Government officials are employed to do this job, but they are often few

in number and poorly paid. Some become corrupted by the large sums poachers are willing to pay to avoid enforcement. Others find the policing job impossible, given the inade-quate resources that their governments devote to enforcement.

Some African governments have dealt with the problem by giving ownership of the wild animals to local villages and allowing them to use the animals as a commercial asset. The animals are the subjects of camera safaris whose organ-izers pay the locals for the privilege. They are also prey for hunters who pay large sums for licences to kill a selected number of animals. Local tribesmen control poachers and keep the licensed kill rate below the reproduction rate because they have a profit motive in protecting what has become their very valuable property.

These schemes have many opponents as well as many supporters. Some opponents object to any permissible 'sports hunting' and other commercial use of wild animals. They argue for more effective public enforcement of anti-poaching laws. Supporters counter that leaving the animals as common property is bound to result in their extinction. Farming them is, they argue, better than presiding over their extinction.

Fishing grounds, common pastures, and other common prop-erty resources often show a pattern of overexploitation.

This is true of almost all of today's fishing grounds, except where the catch is effectively regulated by govern-ments. The third case study at the end of this chapter discusses the issue of fishing further.

One solution to the common property problem is to agree on the optimal level of use and then police the resource to reduce its use to that level. This is done with such items as fishing quotas and hunting licences. The problem here is to enforce the restrictions. It is possible to control the number of fish caught in the high seas, but doing so is difficult and costly, as attested by the frequent international disputes over alleged quota violations.

Another method is for the state to create property rights that make the resource excludable. Its private owners then have an incentive to exploit it efficiently. The English enclosure movement that peaked between 1793 and 1815 did just that. Although those who had previously used the common grazing land were hurt by the measure, the land was much more efficiently used under private ownership. Issuing licences for the use of each particular wavelength can control the airwaves. State forests, which are being destroyed by excessive wood gathering, can be sold to pri-vate owners. Property rights to wildlife can be given to local villages, and so on. This last case is controversial and

is further discussed in Box 13.4. The problem of the tropi-cal rainforests is discussed below in the second case study at the end of this chapter.

All of these cases show the common problem of a trade-off between efficiency and equity. When a common prop-erty resource is 'privatized', the efficiency of its use typically rises but the former users typically suffer some losses. The difficult issue of trading off efficiency of the resource's use against justice for the present users has no easy resolution. What is certain, however, is that if the resource is being exploited to the point of destruction, little is achieved for either equity or efficiency by preserv-ing its common property status.

Public goods: non-excludable and non-rivalrous

Goods that are neither excludable nor rivalrous are called **public goods**, or sometimes **collective consumption goods**. They provide the third reason on our list of causes for market failure. The classic case is national defence. An army of a given size protects all the nation's citizens equally, no matter how many citizens there are and whether or not a particular individual pays taxes to support it. Similarly, a police force that keeps the public streets safe protects all of the street's users, no matter how many there are. If some do not pay their share of the costs, they cannot be denied protection as long as they continue to use the safe street. Information is often a public good. It is clearly non-rivalrous and often non-excludable. Suppose a certain food additive causes cancer. The cost of discovering this has to be paid only once. The information is then of value to everyone who might have used the additive. Once it is in the public domain, no one can be stopped from learning about the information. Other public goods include national parks and publicly available weather forecasts.

Because public goods are non-excludable, private firms will not provide them.

The obvious remedy in these cases is for the government to provide the good and pay for its provision out of general tax revenue.

When should a public good be provided?

To illustrate the basic principle, consider a community composed of just two consumers. The government is considering whether or not to provide a park. Arthur is prepared to pay up to £200 for use of the park, while Julia is willing to pay up to £100. The total value to the two individuals of having the park is £300. If it can be produced for £225, there is a £75 gain on its production since it provides services that the community values at £300 at a cost of only £225.

The optimal quantity of a public good

The above example reveals a key point about public goods. If one person consumes a unit of an ordinary good, another person cannot also consume that unit. Thus, to satisfy all the demand at any given price, the sum of all the quantities demanded must be produced. With a public good, however, everyone can consume any specific unit. A new defence system, for example, protects everyone in the country, and the fact that one person is protected does not reduce the protection received by all others.

The demand for a unit of the good is represented by the sum of the prices that each individual consumer would be willing to pay for that unit. Therefore the community's demand curve for a public good is the vertical sum of the demand curves of the individual consumers.

If the amount of a public good can be varied continuously, the optimal quantity to produce is that quantity for which the marginal cost of the last unit is just equal to the sum of the prices all consumers would be willing to pay for that unit.

This equilibrium, which is analysed in Figure 13.2, guarantees that the last unit of the public good costs as much to produce as the value that it gives to all of its consumers.

Who pays?

One way to pay for a public good is to charge each person the same proportion of the maximum amount he or she would be prepared to pay rather than go without the good, while fixing that proportion so as to cover the total

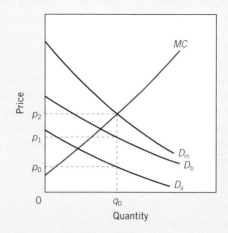

Figure 13.2 A public good

The society's demand curve for a public good is the vertical sum of all the individuals' demand curves. The demand curves D_a and D_b refer to two individuals. Their collective demand is shown by D_m, which is the vertical summation of D_a and D_b. For example, individual *a* would pay p_0 for quantity q_0, while individual *b* would pay p_1 for the same quantity. Together they are willing to pay the sum of p_0 and p_1, which is p_2. The optimal quantity of the good to produce is q_0, where the marginal cost curve *MC* cuts the collective demand curve. At this point the marginal cost of another unit is just equal to the sum of the values that each person places on that unit.

costs of production. In the two-person community discussed above, Arthur is prepared to pay £200 and Julia £100 for the park rather than go without. If it costs £150 to produce, then each person can be charged half of their own maximum, making £100 for Arthur and £50 for Julia. Each of them gets the use of the park for half of what he or she is prepared to pay. Their payments just cover the total costs of production, leaving £150 of total consumers' surplus.

The practical problem in using any formula based on what people are willing to pay for the public good lies in getting people to reveal their preferences. Suppose, for example, that the government is considering building a public park to serve a community of 1,000 people. It asks each of them how much he or she is prepared to pay. If I am one of those 1,000, it is in my interests to understate my true valuation, as long as everyone else does not do the same. Indeed, I might say that I valued the park at zero, while others reported enough value to cover the costs. The public good would then be produced, and I would get the use of it for no payment at all.

The **free-rider problem** refers to each person's motivation to understate the value of a non-rivalrous good in the hope that others will end up paying for it. This motivation makes it difficult to cover the costs of such goods by any formula based on people's individual valuations.

The free-rider problem can be avoided by covering the costs of public goods out of tax revenue.

Goods such as national defence, weather forecasts, navigation aids, police, and fire protection are typically paid for from tax revenue and provided free to all users. This allows the goods to be produced above the levels at which the free market would produce them (often the free market would produce nothing). It also avoids the problem of *inefficient exclusion* that we encountered in the context of discussion of the first source of market failure above. Those who value a particular good higher than the average valuation gain more than those who value it below the average valuation. The hope is that, over a large number of public goods, these individual differences will cancel out. Everyone will then gain on balance as a result of the government's provision of public goods out of tax revenue. However, there is nothing to guarantee that the political process will deliver the socially optimal level of provision of public goods and there is no simple way of determining what that socially optimal provision might be.

Externalities

A perfectly competitive economy allocates resources optimally because price equals marginal cost in all lines of production. For this to be the outcome, it is necessary that all costs are incurred by the producers and all benefits are reaped by their customers. This localization of costs does not occur when there are **externalities**, which are costs or benefits of a transaction that are incurred or received by other members of the society but not taken into account by the parties to the transaction. They are also called *third-party effects*, and sometimes *neighbourhood effects*, because parties other than the primary participants in the transaction (the consumers and the producers) are affected. Externalities are the fourth item on our list of causes of market failure.

Externalities arise in many different ways, and they may be beneficial or harmful. For example, a harmful externality occurs when a factory generates pollution. Individuals who live and work in the neighbourhood bear costs arising from the factory's production, including adverse health effects and clean-up costs. Profit-maximizing factory owners do not take these effects into account when they decide how much to produce. The element of social cost that they ignore is external to their decision-making process as long as they are maximizing their profits.

A beneficial externality occurs, for example, when I paint my house and enhance my neighbours' views and the values of their properties. Other cases arise when some genius—an Einstein, a Mozart, a Van Gogh—gives the world discoveries and works of art whose worth is far in excess of what he or she is paid to create them. A much more important beneficial externality occurs when someone makes an invention that allows many others to make further inventions that use the original one. Externalities create a divergence between the private benefits and costs of economic activity and the social benefits and costs.

Private costs are those costs that are incurred by the parties directly involved in some economic activity. When a good is produced, the private costs are those borne by the producing firm. **Social costs** are the costs incurred by the whole society. These are the private costs *plus* any costs borne by third parties. **Private benefits** are the benefits received by those involved in the activity. In the case of a marketed good these are the utilities obtained by buyers. **Social benefits** are the benefits to the whole society. They are the private benefits *plus* any benefit to third parties.

Society's resources are optimally allocated when social marginal cost equals social marginal benefit.

When this is so, there can be no social benefit in reallocating resources among different lines of production. Free markets will not produce social optimality when there are discrepancies between private and social costs and private and social benefits. The reason is that under perfect competition *private* marginal cost is equated to *private* marginal benefit (the price of the product).

Two important results follow immediately.

1. The outputs of firms that create harmful externalities will exceed the socially optimal levels.

When marginal private cost is equated to price and hence to marginal private benefit, marginal social cost, which is higher because of harmful externalities, will exceed marginal social benefit. Thus, there is social gain from reducing the level of output. The reason for this discrepancy is that the private firm takes no account of the costs imposed on others.

2. The outputs of firms that create beneficial externalities will be less than the socially optimal levels.

When marginal private cost is equated to price and hence to marginal private benefit, the marginal social benefit, which is higher because of beneficial externalities, will exceed marginal social cost. Thus, there is social gain from increasing the level of output. The reason is that the private firm takes no account of the benefits received by others.

Consider a simple example in which an electric power station produces a million units of electricity per day at a marginal cost of 5p per unit and sells power for 5p per unit to consumers. If there are no externalities, this is the socially optimal output, because the 5p valuation that each consumer puts on the last unit consumed is equal to the 5p opportunity cost of producing that unit. Now, let there be 2p of negative externalities created when each unit is produced (perhaps from pollution of the atmosphere from a coal- or gas-fired station). Marginal social cost of 7p exceeds the marginal social benefit of 5p on the last unit produced. To move towards the social optimum, output should be reduced. Alternatively, suppose the externality is beneficial instead of harmful, conferring external benefits valued at 3p a unit on third parties. Now marginal social benefit of 8p exceeds marginal social cost of 5p. To approach a social optimum, output should be increased.

To achieve the optimal allocation of resources in the face of externalities, the production of goods with positive externalities needs to be encouraged and the production of those with negative externalities discouraged, compared with what would be produced under free-market conditions.

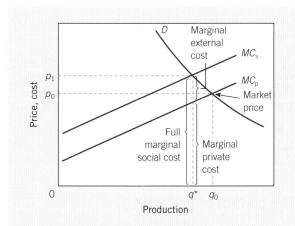

Figure 13.3 Private and social cost

Negative externalities cause marginal social cost to exceed price in competitive equilibrium. Marginal social cost, MC_s, exceeds marginal private cost, MC_p, by the amount of the external cost imposed on others. At the competitive output, q_0, marginal private cost equals price, but marginal social cost exceeds it. The socially optimal output is q^*, where MC_s = price. For every unit between q^* and q_0 marginal social cost exceeds price and hence its production involves a social loss.

Figure 13.3 illustrates the market failures caused by externalities as well as their optimal correction.

Another important case of a beneficial externality is with new technologies. The ideas describing any new invention are non-rivalrous, and so the market provides little incentive to invent and innovate new technologies unless they can be made rivalrous by keeping them secret for long enough or by providing patent protection which creates a temporary property right on the use of the invention. Furthermore, the externalities can be large, and in the case of general-purpose technologies discussed in Chapter 11, they can be very large. For example, the dynamo that permitted the generation of universally available electric power was, and still is, of enormous economic value. A vast array of modern products could not exist without electricity. However, the return to the inventors was minute compared with the social benefits that have already stretched over a century and a half, and that will continue into the indefinite future. Such massive discrepancies between the return to the inventors and innovators of major new technologies and the social benefit that they create is the reason for encouraging invention and innovation through public funds to finance such activities as university research, government laboratories, and tax refunds for, and subsidies on, research and development (R&D). Finally, since no one can foresee the ultimate value of a new technology when it is first being developed, there is no way to decide on an optimal amount of R&D activity. But the judgment of virtually all governments that the social value of major inventions greatly exceeds any private return to inventors and innovators justifies the allocation of a significant amount of public funds to encourage these activities.

Externalities and the Coase theorem

Externalities arise because of a lack of property rights. A factory throws its liquid waste into the river and its smoke into the atmosphere because no one owns them. Both the river and the air are common property resources. If they were in private hands, the owners would have a self-interest in preserving them. Let us see how this might come about.

An example

Say, for example, that a manufacturing plant needs pure water for one of its processes. It gets this from a short mountain stream that then tumbles into the ocean. A chemical plant is established upstream and dumps its waste into the river. The river is a common property resource so in the absence of suitable legislation, the plant cannot be stopped from imposing negative externalities on the downstream user, who must now set up an expensive water purification system.

A downstream owner

Assume that the downstream plant owns the stream. Its owner might say to the chemical plant's managers, 'Do not dump *your* waste into *my* stream'. The managers might counter that they were willing to pay for the privilege. The downstream owner asks, 'How much?' After considering the cost of alternative waste-disposal mechanisms, the chemical plant's managers answer, '£6 per tonne of waste'. The owner of the downstream plant determines that the cost of purifying the water in the stream is £8 per tonne of waste. 'No deal', she says. The upstream chemical plant opens an alternative waste-disposal system at a cost of £6 and thus the least costly method of dealing with the waste is used.

Later, technological improvements in water purification allow the downstream plant to purify its water for only £3 per tonne. The owner calls the upstream managers and says, 'I hear your disposal plant is coming up for renewal next year. I am prepared to let you dump the waste in my stream for a fee of £4 per tonne'. 'Done', say the upstream managers, and next year the waste is disposed of in the river. The water is then cleaned up by the downstream user at a cost of £3 per tonne, instead of at a cost of £6 when the chemical plant treated the waste. Once again, the cheapest method of disposal and use is adopted.

An upstream owner

What would have happened if the river had been owned by the chemical plant instead of the downstream user? The managers of the chemical plant decide to use their stream for disposal of their waste. But the downstream users of water complain and offer to pay for the use of the fresh water. Their costs of making the water usable are £8 per tonne of waste. So they can offer up to that much to dissuade the chemical plant from dumping its waste. That plant can use an alternative waste-disposal method at a cost of £6 per tonne. So the managers say, 'Yes, how about giving us £7 for every tonne of our waste that we do not dump into our river?' A deal is struck and the cheapest method is undertaken.

Later, when the new water purification technology is developed, the downstream users can purify the water at a cost of only £3 per tonne. So they will offer no more than that to prevent the chemical plant from dumping its waste. When the upstream plant's alternative waste-disposal system wears out, it will not be replaced. The waste will be dumped and the downstream plant will purify its water at a cost of £3 per tonne. Once again the cheapest method of dealing with the waste will have been adopted.

The theorem

This example illustrates a remarkable result developed some years ago by the British-born economist Ronald Coase, who received the 1991 Nobel Prize in economics. The result is now called the **Coase theorem**.

If the two sides to an externality—the one causing it and the one suffering from it—can bargain together with zero transactions costs, they will produce the efficient use of resources.

What is needed is that one of the two has a property right that forces the other side to bargain. Surprisingly, however, it does not matter which side has the property right. We saw this in the above example, where the same result was arrived at independently of who owned the river. Property rights will determine who gets most of the consumers' surplus on the bargain, because they determine who has to pay whom. But, given that both sides bargain for their own self-interest, the allocation of resources to deal with the externality will be independent of where the property right resides. It should also be clear that the settlement has to be agreed voluntarily by both sides.

High transaction costs

What makes the Coase theorem work is that (a) someone has a property right over what is causing the externality, (b) both sides can bargain effectively together, *and* (c) nothing can go ahead until they have reached an agreement. The second condition is a matter of transaction costs. It was easy enough for the owners of the two plants to talk on the phone and reach an efficient bargain. It is another matter for all the citizens of the cities of London or São Paulo to bargain with the hundreds of factory owners, car drivers, and other producers of pollution in order to reach an efficient solution to dealing with air and water pollution in and around their cities.

In cases in which property rights cannot be assigned and/or where transaction costs are excessive, there are only two possibilities. We may accept the externality and learn to live with it, or governments may intervene on our behalf to deal with it.

We will see, however, that although governments often do improve matters somewhat, arriving at the most efficient solution is no easy task.

The control of pollution

In this section we illustrate government policies with respect to negative externalities in the context of one of their most important applications—environmental damage caused by pollution. Steel plants produce heat and smoke in addition to steel. Farms produce chemical run-off as well as food. Household consumption produces human waste and refuse. Indeed, there are few human activities that do not produce some negative pollution externalities.

For this reason it is impossible to reduce pollution to zero. Instead, the optimal amount of pollution abatement occurs when the marginal benefit of a unit of abatement is just equal to the marginal cost of abatement.

Unregulated markets tend to produce excessive amounts of environmental damage. However, zero environmental damage is neither technologically possible nor economically efficient.

Pollution of some types is a global problem and requires international agreements to achieve results. Of major current concern is the problem of climate change which is (at least in part) caused by emissions of greenhouse gases, such as carbon dioxide, which result from the burning of fossil fuels, such as coal and oil. One attempt at an international agreement to limit global greenhouse-gas emissions was the Kyoto Protocol of 1997, which was a modification of the United Nations Framework Convention on Climate Change. Signatories to the Kyoto Protocol agreed to cut average greenhouse gas emissions by 2010 by around 5 per cent of the 1990 level (which would amount to more like 30 per cent of the predicted 2010 level). As of January 2009, 183 countries had ratified the Kyoto Protocol but these did not include the United States (the world's biggest emitter of greenhouse gases) and Australia. China and India are signatories, but they have no effective limits under the Protocol even though they are among the fastest-growing economies in the world. The 2009 Copenhagen conference made little headway and by 2010 most of the signatores had not come near to meeting their quotas for reducing greenhouse gas omissions. But progress towards a new global agreement was made at Cancun in December 2010 and again in Warsaw in 2013. The latest target is for a new global agreement on emissions to be signed at the Paris conference in December 2015.

Where greenhouse gas emissions are to be limited, the issue arises as to how this can be achieved.

Pollution control through direct regulation

Direct controls are a common method of environmental regulation. For example, UK car emissions standards must be met by all new cars and by cars over three years of age when they take their annual MOT test. Many cities and towns prohibit the private burning of leaves and other rubbish because of the air pollution problem that the burning would cause. The UK Clean Air Act 1956 obliged people to switch from coal to smokeless fuels with the result, among other things, that the famous and harmful London smogs became a thing of the past. Similarly, the government gradually reduced the amount of lead allowed in petrol and provided tax incentives for drivers to switch to unleaded petrol. Since the mid-1970s, petrol consumption has increased by about 50 per cent while lead emissions have fallen by about 75 per cent.

Problems with direct controls

Although direct controls sometimes work effectively they are often economically inefficient. This is because controls typically mandate the same response from different polluters independently of their costs of pollution abatement. Although these requirements may seem reasonable, they will be inefficient unless the polluters face the same pollution abatement costs. Alternative, more flexible, methods can often provide the same amount of abatement at a lower cost.

Direct pollution controls are usually inefficient because, by mandating the same response from all agents, they do not minimize the cost of any given amount of pollution abatement.

Efficient allocation of pollution abatement between firms with different prevention costs is analysed in Figure 13.4. As long as one firm has a lower abatement cost than another firm, it pays to reallocate a given amount of abatement. The lower-cost firm should abate more and the higher-cost firm less. The general conclusion is that:

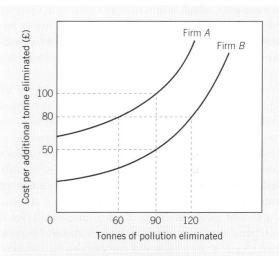

Figure 13.4 Pollution abatement

Efficient methods of abating pollution take account of differences in costs of abatement among firms. The figure shows the different marginal costs of pollution abatement for two firms. For any given amount of abatement, firm *A* has a higher cost of a further unit of abatement than firm *B*. When they are both mandated to reduce pollution by 90 units, *A*'s marginal cost of £100 exceeds *B*'s marginal cost of £50. This is inefficient. *A* could cut its abatement by one unit, saving £100, while *B* increased its abatement by one unit, adding £50 to its costs. Total abatement would then be unchanged, but costs would fall by £50. An emissions tax of £80 per tonne of pollution is now imposed. Low-cost firm *B* now abates pollution by 120 tonnes, while high-cost firm *A* abates by 60 tonnes. This is the efficient way of producing 180 tonnes of abatement since the two firms have the same abatement costs at the margin, thus minimizing the total cost of reducing pollution by 180 tonnes.

Efficient abatement requires that each firm have the same marginal cost of the last unit of abatement undertaken.

Nonetheless, direct controls are effective when it is important not to exceed certain dangerous thresholds. They are also useful in situations where production is undertaken by a very small number of publicly owned natural monopolies. They can also be useful when the cost of measuring each agent's pollution and the costs of inter-agent transactions are prohibitively high, as is the case with automobile emissions. In other cases policies that create economic incentives not to pollute are more effective than those that operate on the command principle.

Control through emissions taxes

The great British economist A. C. Pigou (1877–1959), who did path-breaking work on externalities of all sorts, was a pioneer in developing public policy tools for their control. His name is associated particularly with pollution taxes, which provide an alternative method of directing controls. The advantage of such taxes is that they *internalize the externality*, which means increasing the firm's private cost by the amount of the external cost. This makes private and social costs the same, with the result that efficient outcomes can result from decentralized decisions made by individual producers.

Look again at the example in Figure 13.4. If all firms are required to pay a tax of £80 on each unit of pollution, profit maximization will lead them to reduce emissions to the point at which the marginal cost of further reduction is equal to the tax. This means that firm B will reduce emissions much more than firm A, and that in equilibrium both will have the same marginal cost of further abatement, which is required for efficiency.

A second great advantage of using emissions taxes is that they do not require the regulators to specify how polluters should abate pollution. Firms can be left to find the most efficient abatement techniques. The profit motive will lead them to do so, because they will want to minimize their tax bill.

In principle, emissions taxes can perfectly internalize pollution externalities, so that profit-maximizing behaviour on the part of firms will lead them to produce the efficient amount of pollution abatement at minimum cost.

Emissions taxes in practice

Emissions taxes can work only if it is possible to measure emissions accurately. In some cases this does not pose much of a problem, but in many other cases there are no effective measuring devices that can be installed at reasonable cost. One important example is automotive pollution. Today (but possibly not at some future date) it would be very expensive to attach a reliable monitor to every car and lorry, and then to assess taxes based on readings from the monitor. In this case, as in many others, direct controls are the only cost-effective method.

Another problem involves setting the tax rate. The regulatory agency needs to estimate the marginal social damage caused per unit of each pollutant and set the tax equal to this amount. This would perfectly internalize the pollution externality. However, the required information is often difficult to obtain. If the regulatory agency sets the tax rate too high, too many resources will be devoted to pollution control. If the tax is set too low, there will be too much pollution. Also, if technological change causes the social damage to change, the optimal tax rate is also changed.

For a period in the late 1990s and early 2000s the UK government was increasing taxes on petrol with the deliberate intention of discouraging use of road transport so as to reduce emissions from this source. However, in 2004 there were protests about the high price of petrol and the government postponed its planned tax increases. The subsequent government also postponed fuel tax rises in 2010–14, in part because there had already been rises in world energy prices. Hence, political expediency may conflict with a rational policy of taxing carbon emissions.

Control through tradable emissions permits

Tradable emissions permits can solve many of the problems associated with direct controls and emissions taxes. To use them, the regulator must decide how much pollution to permit. In Figure 13.4 the original regulations required each firm to reduce its total pollution by 90 tonnes. This is exactly the same as permitting the firms to pollute by their original amount of pollution *minus* 90 tonnes. To pose the problem this way, the regulators issue to each firm a right to pollute by that amount. To illustrate, if each firm had been generating 150 tonnes of pollution, exactly the same reduction occurs if firms are ordered to reduce pollution by 90 tonnes or if they are permitted to pollute to a maximum of 60 tonnes.

Tradable permits in theory

Now, however, comes the new twist. A large efficiency gain can be achieved by making these rights to pollute tradable. This allows the firm with the low cost of pollution abatement to sell its right to pollute to the firm with the high abatement cost. Total pollution and total pollution abatement will be unchanged, but more abatement will be done by the firm with the low abatement cost (which sold its rights to pollute to the other firm), thus reducing the total cost of meeting the target for any given amount of pollution reduction.

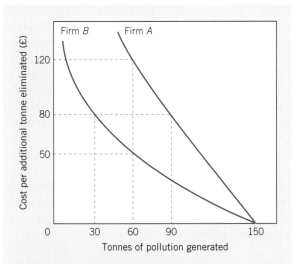

Figure 13.5 Tradable pollution permits

Tradable permits achieve the same results as the most efficient tax. Each firm produces 150 tonnes of pollution when no abatement procedures are followed. Abatement reduces the amount of pollution but at a rising marginal cost. Each firm is originally given an endowment of permits to emit 60 tonnes of pollution. If no trading is allowed, the marginal costs of abatement are £120 for A and £50 for B. With trading, B sells 30 tonnes' worth of permits to A. Firm A then pollutes by 90 tonnes and firm B by 30 tonnes. The price of a permit is £80, which is the same as both firms' marginal cost of abatement at their new levels of pollution.

Figure 13.5 illustrates this case. Where Figure 13.4 showed the amount of abatement, Figure 13.5 shows the amount of emissions. The cost curves now rise to the left instead of to the right as they did in Figure 13.4. Starting from the 150 tonnes of pollutants that each firm is emitting with zero abatement, the abatement cost rises as less and less pollution is allowed. Production with zero pollution is impossible, and so the costs rise rapidly as very low pollution levels are achieved. The government wishes to cut pollution from its existing level of 300 tonnes to 120 tonnes, so it gives each firm 60 tonnes' worth of pollution permits. When they each cut their pollution to 60 tonnes, firm A has a much higher marginal cost than firm B. So B sells A some permits. B abates more and A pollutes more. Total pollution is unchanged but total abatement costs fall. Trade will be profitable as long as A's marginal abatement costs exceed B's. In the final equilibrium, both firms have the same marginal cost of abatement, which equals the price of a permit to abate by one tonne. Now each firm is indifferent between abating by one tonne and buying a permit to avoid abating by one tonne. The cost of abatement is minimized and both firms have gained. A has saved more clean-up costs than the cost of the permits it has bought. The prices of the permits that B sells exceed

the cost of the extra abatement it must incur because of having fewer permits.

Everyone is better off. Society gets its abatement at the least cost in terms of valuable resources. Both firms have more money in their pockets than if each had been ordered to cut pollution by an identical amount.

Notice that the £90 price of a permit to produce one tonne of pollution is the same as the pollution tax required to induce 150 tonnes of abatement at the least cost. The difference is that permits require less information than taxes. The authorities just issue the number of permits they decide upon and let the market fix the price. If taxes are to be used, the government must determine the best tax rate and then impose it.

Tradable emissions permits can be used to achieve the same allocation of resources as would occur with emissions taxes, while reducing the amount of information required by the regulatory authorities.

Tradable emissions permits in practice

A policy that sets a limit on emissions and allows permits to be traded is referred to as 'cap and trade'. The US implemented an Acid Rain Program that started in 1995. This was targeted on reducing sulphur dioxide emissions from around 18 million tons a year, as it was in the 1980s, to a level of just under 9 million tons by 2010. This programme has been successful: '*The US Acid Rain Program has achieved greater emission reductions in such a short time than any other single program to control air pollution*'.[7]

Until recently European governments had shown a preference for 'ecotaxes' over tradable pollution permits. However, a UK Emissions Trading Scheme began in March 2002, and an EU Emissions Trading Scheme commenced on 1 January 2005.

There were teething problems with the EU carbon trading scheme, but many of these had been ironed out by 2014 and the UK scheme had been merged with it. The UK government continued to have ambitious plans to reduce carbon emissions and carbon trading plays an important role in these:

The 2008 Climate Change Act established the world's first legally binding climate change target. We aim to reduce the UK's greenhouse gas emissions by at least 80% (from the 1990 baseline) by 2050 ... To make sure that UK government policies contribute effectively to our greenhouse gas reduction targets, we're:

- *setting carbon budgets to limit the amount of greenhouse gases the UK is allowed to emit over a specified time*

---

[7] See <http://www.epa.gov/airmarkets/trading/basics/>.

- *using statistics on greenhouse gas emissions and further evidence, analysis and research to inform energy and climate change policy*

- *using the EU Emissions Trading Scheme to deliver a significant proportion of the UK's carbon emission reductions between 2013 and 2020*

- *using a set of values for carbon to make sure project and policy appraisals account for their climate change impacts*

(*<https://www.gov.uk/government/policies/reducing-the-uk-s-greenhouse-gas-emissions-by-80-by-2050>*)

Conclusion

Much environmental pollution is caused by the failure of markets to account for externalities. At the same time, market-like mechanisms can be used to internalize the externalities. Pollution is an example of a problem in which, once governments create the right incentives, markets themselves can be used to correct market failures.

The problem of externalities arises because of the absence of property rights. For example, the polluting firm uses the free air to dump its waste. If it owned the air, it would worry about the loss of the value of its property caused by the pollution. If those affected by the pollution owned the air, they would not allow it to be used unless they were paid sufficient compensation.

Since many externalities arise from an absence of property rights, externalities can often be internalized if appropriate property rights can be created.

Asymmetric information

Markets work best when everyone is well informed. People cannot make maximizing decisions if they are poorly informed about the things they are buying or selling. Lack of relevant information is the fifth item on our list of reasons for market failure.

Rules requiring that products and prices be described correctly are meant to improve the efficiency of choices by providing people with correct and relevant information. In many cases where the consequences of errors are not dramatic, consumers can be left to discover, through trial and error, what is in their own best interests. In other cases, however, the results of error can be too drastic to allow consumers to learn from their own experiences which products are reliable and which unreliable. For example, botulism, caused by poorly preserved foods, can cause death, as it did in large numbers up to about 100 years ago. In such cases the state intervenes to impose standards and testing requirements in the consumers' own best interests.

One potential source of market failure is adverse selection, which we first discussed in the context of labour markets in Chapter 10 and then again in the context of insurance contracts in Chapter 12. Adverse selection can arise when there is unequal knowledge of participants in a market about product characteristics. This arises, for example, when some types of insurance are bought mainly by those who know better than the insurers that they are bad risks and are avoided by those who know better than the insurers that they are good risks. Adverse selection can also operate in credit markets where those who are keenest to borrow may be the least likely to repay. In general, adverse selection may cause the market outcome to be less efficient than if all participants were equally well informed.

Missing markets

In the 1950s two American economists, Kenneth Arrow and Gerard Debreu, who were subsequently awarded Nobel Prizes in economics, studied the necessary conditions for optimality in resource allocation. One of the conditions is that there must exist a separate market in which each good and service can be traded to the point where the marginal benefit equals the marginal cost. Missing markets are the sixth item on our list of causes of market failure.

Not only do markets not exist for such prominent things as public goods and common property resources, but they are also absent in a number of less obvious but equally important cases.

One important set of missing markets involves risk. You can insure your house against its burning down. This is because your knowledge of the probability of this occurrence is not much better than your insurance company's, and because the probability of your house burning down is normally independent of the probability of other houses burning down.

If you are a farmer, you cannot usually insure your crop against bad weather. This is because the probabilities of your crop and your neighbour's crop suffering from bad weather are interrelated. If the insurance company has to pay you, the probabilities are that it will also have to pay your neighbour and everyone else in the county—perhaps even throughout the country. An insurance company survives by pooling independent risks. It cannot survive if the same event affects all its clients in the same way. (This is why, although you can insure your house against a fire from ordinary causes, you cannot insure it against fires caused by war.)

If you are in business, you cannot insure against bankruptcy. Here the problem is adverse selection. You know much better than does your would-be insurance company the chances that your business will fail. If insurance were offered against such failure, it would mainly be taken out by people whose businesses had recently developed a high chance of failure.

Another set of missing markets concerns future events. You can buy certain well-established and unchanging products, such as corn or oil, on futures markets. But you cannot do so for most manufactured products, such as cars and TV sets, because no one knows the precise specifications of future models. Futures markets for these products are missing, so there is no way that the costs and benefits of planned future expenditure on these products can be equated by economic transactions made today.

Public policy towards monopoly and competition

The seventh and last item on our list of reasons for market failure concerns market power. For example, cartels and price-fixing agreements among oligopolists, whether explicit or tacit, have long met with public suspicion and official hostility. These, and other non-competitive practices, are collectively referred to as monopoly practices. Note that these are not just what monopolists do. They include non-competitive behaviour of firms that are operating in other market structures, such as oligopoly. The laws and other instruments that are used to encourage competition and discourage monopoly practices make up competition policy and are used to influence both the market structure and the behaviour of individual firms.

The goal of controlling market power provides rationales for both competition policy and economic regulation. It is impossible to achieve perfect competition in most sectors of the economy where product differentiation and scale effects imply market power for most firms. However, competitive behaviour can be encouraged and monopoly practices discouraged by influencing either the *market structure* or the *market behaviour* of individual firms. (See Chapter 6 for the distinction between competitive market structures and competitive behaviour.) By and large UK competition policy has sought to create more competitive market structures where possible. Where such structures could not be established, policy has sought to discourage monopolistic practices and to encourage competitive behaviour. In addition, the government employs economic regulations, which prescribe the rules under which firms can do business, and in some cases determine the prices that businesses can charge for their output.

We study three aspects of these policies: the direct control of natural monopolies, the direct control of oligopolies, and the creation of competitive conditions. The first is a necessary part of any competition policy, the second has been important in the past but is less so now, and the third constitutes the main current thrust of UK competition policy.

Direct control of natural monopolies

The clearest case for public intervention arises with a **natural monopoly**, which is an industry in which economies of scale are so dominant that there is room for only one firm to operate at or near the minimum efficient scale. UK policy-makers have not wanted to insist on the establishment of several smaller, less efficient producers whenever a single firm would be much more efficient; neither have they wanted to give a natural monopolist the opportunity to restrict output, raise prices, and reap monopoly profits.

One response to natural monopoly is for government to assume ownership of the single firm, setting it up as a nationalized industry. Another response has been to allow private ownership but to regulate the monopoly firm's behaviour. Until the 1980s, UK policy favoured public ownership. Recently, such industries have been privatized—that is, sold to members of the public—and then regulated to some extent. Examples are telecommunications, gas, water, and electricity. Whichever choice the government makes, it will seek to influence the behaviour of these industries.

Short-run price and output

What is the correct price–output policy that the government should encourage these industries to adopt?

Marginal cost pricing

Sometimes the government dictates that price should be set equal to short-run marginal cost so as to maximize consumers' plus producers' surpluses. However, marginal cost pricing does create some problems. The natural monopoly may still have unexploited economies of scale and hence be operating on the falling portion of its average total cost curve. In this case marginal cost will be less than average total cost and pricing at marginal cost will lead to losses, as shown in Figure 13.6.

A falling-cost natural monopoly that sets price equal to marginal cost will suffer losses.

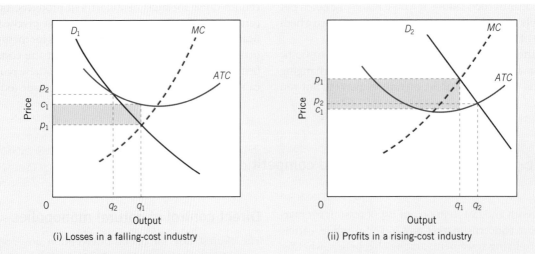

Figure 13.6 Pricing policies for natural monopolies

Marginal cost pricing leads to profits or losses; average cost pricing is inefficient. In each part the output at which marginal cost equals price is q_1 and price is p_1. In part (i) average costs are falling at output q_1, so marginal costs are less than the average cost c_1. There is a loss of $c_1 - p_1$ on each unit, making a total loss equal to the blue area. In part (ii) average cost of c_1 is less than price at output q_1. There is a profit of $p_1 - c_1$ on each unit sold, making a total profit equal to the blue area. In each part of the diagram the output at which average cost equals price is q_2 and the associated price is p_2. In part (i) marginal cost is less than price at q_2, so output is below its optimal level. In part (ii) marginal cost exceeds price at q_2, so output is greater than its optimal level.

Average cost pricing

Sometimes natural monopolies are directed to produce the output that will just cover total costs, thus earning neither profits nor losses. This means that the firm produces to the point where average revenue equals average total cost, which is where the demand curve cuts the average total cost curve. Figure 13.6 shows that for a falling-cost firm this pricing policy requires producing at less than the optimal output in order to avoid the losses that would occur under marginal cost pricing.

Average cost pricing is usually allocatively inefficient.

The very long run

Natural monopoly is a long-run concept, meaning that, given existing technology, there is room for only one firm to operate profitably. In the very long run, however, technology changes. Not only does today's competitive industry sometimes become tomorrow's natural monopoly, but also today's natural monopoly sometimes becomes tomorrow's competitive industry.

A striking example is the telecommunications industry. Not long ago the transmissions of voice and hard-copy messages were natural monopolies. Now technological developments such as satellite transmission, electronic mail, the internet, and fax machines have made these activities highly competitive. Also, new firms can be given access to existing infrastructure, such as cables, thus greatly lowering set-up costs and encouraging

competition from new entrants. As a consequence, in many countries an odd circumstance arose: formerly nationalized industries, such as the UK Royal Mail and BT, sought to maintain their profitability by prohibiting entry into what would otherwise have become a fluid and competitive industry. A public firm may be more successful than a privately owned firm in preserving its monopoly long after technological changes have destroyed its 'naturalness'. This issue arises especially when the government is intending to privatize it and wants to obtain the highest possible price, which will occur if the firm has a monopoly rather than a lot of competitors.

Government policies need to be adjusted frequently to keep them abreast of more or less continuous technological change.

Regulation of natural monopolies

Now that most UK nationalized industries have been privatized, those that are natural monopolies are regulated by public regulatory authorities, such as Ofcom (telecoms and media), Ofgem (gas and electricity), and Ofwat (water). In the United States, such regulatory bodies were often captured by the firms they were supposed to regulate and ended up working against the interests of consumers. Indeed, many large US corporations give hefty bonuses to senior executives to allow them to take lower-paying government jobs regulating the industry in which they are currently employed! An opposite pitfall that some worry about in the United Kingdom is that prices may be pushed so far down in the short-term interests of consumers that the regulated industries will have little incentive to invest in technological innovations. In response to this worry, firms were given the right to appeal if they feel prices are being pushed too low. In today's world of rapid technological change these low prices could work to the long-term disadvantage of consumers.

Direct control of oligopolies

From time to time governments have intervened in industries that were oligopolies, rather than natural monopolies, seeking to enforce the type of price and entry behaviour that was thought to be in the public interest. Such intervention has typically taken two distinct forms. In the United Kingdom from 1945 to 1980 it was primarily nationalization of whole oligopolistic industries such as airlines, railways, steel, and coalmining, which were then run by government-appointed boards. In the United States firms in such oligopolistic industries as airlines, railways, and electric power were left in private hands, but their decisions were regulated by government-appointed bodies that set prices and regulated entry.

Deregulation and privatization

The last two decades of the twentieth century witnessed a movement in virtually all advanced industrial nations, and in the vast majority of less-developed nations as well, to reduce the level of government control over industry.

Causes

A number of forces had been pushing in this direction.

- Expectations that nationalized industries would be superior to private firms in the areas of efficiency, productivity growth, and industrial relations were falsified by experience.

- Falling transportation costs, and the information and communications revolutions, have exposed domestic industries to much more international competition than they had previously experienced. This has lowered concern over high national concentration ratios.

- Regulatory bodies sometimes had the effect of reducing, rather than increasing, competition.

- When largely staffed by former employees of the industry they were supposed to control, the regulatory bodes often worked to the advantage of these industries.

- Despite being allocatively inefficient because price exceeds marginal cost (by virtue of each firm's negatively sloped demand curve), oligopolistic market structures provided much of the economic growth of the twentieth century. New products, and new ways of producing old products, have followed each other in rapid succession, all leading to higher living standards and higher productivity. Many of these innovations have been provided by firms in oligopolistic industries such as automobiles, agricultural implements, steel, petroleum refining, chemicals, and telecommunications. As long as governments can keep oligopolists competing with each other rather than cooperating to produce monopoly profits, most economists see no need to regulate such things as the prices at which they sell their products and the conditions of entry into their industries.

The worldwide movement towards privatization and deregulation was part of a growing belief among policy-makers that private firms operating in free markets are more willing than governments to be efficient producers and to accept the kind of risks that are necessary to become successful innovators.

The call was for a diminished role of government in resource allocation compared with what it had been through most of the second half of the twentieth century—but not for a zero role. Although the belief that government intervention had been excessive is almost worldwide, there are many reasons why the public interest still requires significant intervention. Externalities and other market failures are some of the reasons why it is not necessarily efficient to leave the free market solely to decide all issues of resource allocation.

The natural outcome of these revised views has been the privatization of nationalized industries and the deregulation of privately owned ones. This latter policy was intended, among other things, to return price-setting and entry decisions to market determination.

Privatization has gone a long way in the United Kingdom. The majority of the nationalized industries have been returned to private ownership. Some details are given in Box 13.5.

A setback to these trends emerged in the financial crisis of 2007–8. During this period the UK government was obliged to nationalize two financial institutions and to take a major stake in several others. We discuss this episode in more detail in the first case study at the end of the chapter. However, for present purposes the key point is that these nationalizations were done to halt a financial collapse and not in the belief that state ownership is the best long-term structure. On the contrary, the government planned to sell these institutions back to the private sector at the earliest opportunity. But at the same time, the belief grew that further regulations were required to make the financial sector work on the social interest.

Box 13.5 Privatization in the United Kingdom

Privatization has been a complex development in the United Kingdom. Some nationalized industries were sold outright; in others, the government maintained substantial holdings while selling off the rest of its shares. In yet other cases, profitable parts of unprofitable enterprises were separated off and sold. In still other cases, the government sold shares that it held in private companies that had never been nationalized.

The first step towards UK privatization was the sale of council houses, which began in 1979. Over the succeeding decade there was a major reduction in the stock of publicly owned housing, with almost 700,000 dwellings being sold to their occupiers.

The next phase covered a number of relatively small operations in markets where competition was strong. These included the British Sugar Corporation, British Rail Hotels, Sealink Ferries, British Ports, Jaguar, and British

Aerospace. These companies have operated successfully, under relatively competitive conditions, since their privatization, though some have merged with other firms or been taken over.

The third phase covered the great industrial giants. It began with British Telecom in 1984 and continued with British Gas in 1986, British Airways in 1987, and British Steel in 1988. Sale of shares in the publicly owned electricity industry began in 1990, with water following soon after. Sale of the remaining coal pits was completed in 1994. The privatization of British Rail was completed by 1997, with the track going to Railtrack and the train services going to several private operators (though owing to financial problems Railtrack was temporarily taken back under government control in 2001–2 and reborn as a non-profit organization called Network Rail, though still notionally owned by the state). Royal Mail was privatized in 2013.

Outcomes

The evidence of the effects of privatization is largely encouraging. Prices have fallen markedly in the telecommunications industry, and they fell for some time after privatization in the gas and electricity industries. Some former state-owned companies have become world leaders in a manner that did not occur under state control. The most obvious examples are BT and British Airways. Many have been attractive targets for takeover bids by foreign utilities. All of this is strong evidence that their performance has been improved by being transferred to private ownership. The least successful privatization in the UK has been the railways. Railtrack had to be taken back into state ownership, and some companies had to be deprived of their regional franchises. Several serious accidents also raised safety concerns. To date, however, there have been no serious moves to renationalize the railways. There is strong evidence that the failure of railways to live up to expectations has resulted to a significant extent from the ways in which they were denationalized—for example, leaving providing and maintaining the track and the running of trains in separate companies.

Privatization has also spread to other EU countries. For example, Deutsche Telekom was privatized in 1996. Part of the pressure to privatize has come from stiff competition from efficient foreign firms and part from the Maastricht Treaty, which limits public spending and government borrowing. There has also been a trend towards deregulation of many markets. Major pressure in this direction has been exerted by the Single Market Act, which is discussed in Chapter 27. A notable example is air travel, where state-imposed restrictions, often designed to

protect state-owned national airlines, have been phased out. Many private carriers have entered the industry, such as easyJet and Ryanair based in the United Kingdom. The ensuing competition has pushed many fares down.

Intervention to keep firms competing

The least stringent form of government intervention is designed to create conditions of competition by preventing firms from merging unnecessarily or from engaging in certain anticompetitive practices such as colluding to set monopoly prices. Such policies seek to create the most competitive market structure possible and then to prevent firms from reducing competition by engaging in certain forms of cooperative behaviour. (See Box 13.6 for more details on UK competition policies.)

Why worry?

For some time up until the early 1990s, industrial concentration increased in the United Kingdom, with the percentage of industrial production accounted for by the five largest firms in each industry growing steadily. Two major causes were the growth of large firms at the expense of smaller ones and mergers of existing firms. Although very recent data are difficult to come by, those that exist suggest that recent developments have been mixed. Concentration increased, for example, in pharmaceuticals when Glaxo merged with Wellcome, and then again with SmithKline Beecham to form GlaxoSmithKline; and Zeneca merged with Astra to form AstraZeneca. Concentration also increased in commercial banking when RBS took over NatWest and Lloyds merged with

Box 13.6 UK competition framework

A new framework for policing competition policy in the UK was implemented in April 2014 as a result of the Enterprise and Regulatory Reform Act 2013. It set up the Competition and Markets Authority (CMA) as the UK's primary competition and consumer agency, with a *'vital role to play in helping stimulate economic growth and innovation and ensuring consumers get a good deal'*. At the same time the Financial Conduct Authority (FCA) was set up to monitor competition in (among other things) financial markets.

Bringing together the Competition Commission (CC) with the competition and certain consumer functions of the Office of Fair Trading (OFT), the CMA has a range of new responsibilities and powers to ensure it meets its mission of making markets work well for consumers, businesses and the economy. These include tighter timetables for investigations, a stronger role in ensuring competition in regulated sectors like financial services and energy, and a reformed legal framework for prosecuting individuals involved in criminal cartel activity....

In its first Annual Plan, the CMA sets out its priorities and work programme. These focus on merger control, market studies and investigations, and enforcement of competition and consumer law. The CMA has already taken on a challenging programme of markets work in key strategic areas such as banking, energy, payday lending and higher education. It will now take on from the OFT and CC more than a dozen live competition enforcement and consumer cases, over 30 merger cases and three on-going Phase 2 market investigations.

(<https://www.gov.uk/government/news/new-competition-authority-to-make-markets-work-well-for-consumers-business-and-the-economy>)

The goals set out by the CMA in its early days were:

1. *Deliver effective enforcement*
   - *Deter wrongdoing and prevent consumers losing out from anticompetitive mergers or practices*

   - *Ensure that businesses and individuals understand the law and know that effective sanctions follow if they break it*
   - *Pursue the right cases and manage them well so it makes good, timely decisions that stand up to appeal*

2. *Extend competition frontiers*
   - *Use the markets regime to improve the way competition works where evidence shows it can most benefit consumers*
   - *Ensure the application of competition law and policy in regulated sectors, working alongside and supporting sector regulators*
   - *Act to encourage effective competition where markets and business models are evolving.*

3. *Refocus consumer protection*
   - *Empower consumers to exercise informed choice, using both competition and consumer powers to help markets work well*
   - *Lead policy development and identify and pursue complex, precedent-setting cases where it is best placed to intervene and can have the greatest impact on markets*
   - *Support and work effectively alongside other UK consumer agencies*

4. *Achieve professional excellence*

5. *Develop integrated performance*

('Vision, values and strategy for the CMA', CMA, January 2014)

We have not set out goals 4 and 5 in full as they relate to organizational issues. At the time of writing (April 2014) it is too early to say how well the CMA will perform and whether its behaviour will differ from that of the previous competition authorities.

HBOS. However, in some other industries large firms have been broken up by their owners, reducing concentration ratios. Hanson and Tomkins were both conglomerates that split into their main constituent businesses.

Globalization—the growing internationalization of competition—is one reason why this increasing domestic concentration in production has not necessarily implied less market competition. (Globalization was discussed in detail in Chapter 1.) The size of most markets now extends well beyond the boundaries of a single nation. A firm with an apparent monopoly in the United Kingdom may well

be operating in a highly competitive international market that includes German, French, and Japanese firms. Nonetheless, some intervention to keep firms competing rather than colluding is still thought necessary in most countries.

Unsettled questions: market structure in the very long run

The case against monopoly and monopolistic practices is based on the allocation of resources with a given technology. In the very long run, however, technology is constantly changing as a result of both the discoveries of lower-cost methods of producing old products and the introduction of new and improved products and production processes. Does market structure affect the rate of innovation in the very long run?

The incentive to innovate

Who gets the profits?

Both the monopolist and the perfect competitor have a profit incentive to introduce cost-reducing innovations. A monopoly can always increase its profits if it can reduce costs. Furthermore, since it is able to prevent the entry of new firms into the industry, these additional profits will persist into the long run. Thus, a firm that is either a monopoly or an oligopolist with entry barriers has both a short- and a long-run incentive to reduce its costs.

Firms in perfect competition have the same incentive in the short run, but not in the long run. In the short run a reduction in costs will allow a firm that was just covering costs to earn profits. In the long run other firms will be attracted into the industry by these profits. Existing firms will copy the cost-saving innovation, and new firms will enter the industry using the new techniques. This will go on until the profits of the innovator have been eliminated.

Monopolies and oligopolists with entry barriers have both a short- and a long-run incentive to innovate; perfectly competitive firms have only a short-run incentive.

In industries where entry is easy, competitive firms have little incentive to innovate because the short run is too short in calendar time for them to cover the costs and risks associated with inventing and implementing some new technology.

Funds for research and development

The large profits available to oligopolistic firms provide a ready fund out of which research and development can be financed. However, the typical perfectly competitive firm is earning only enough to cover all its production costs, and will have few funds to spare for research and development. As an empirical illustration, farmers producing under perfect competition developed none of the innovations that have vastly raised agricultural productivity over the past century. Rather, they were developed by a few oligopolistic manufacturers of farm equipment, improved crops, and pesticides, as well as by researchers in universities and in government-financed research institutions.

Schumpeter's defence of oligopoly and monopoly

In Joseph Schumpeter's theory (discussed in Chapter 7), monopolistic and oligopolistic market structures are more conducive to growth than is perfect competition.[8] He claimed that since it is the incentive of profits that leads individuals and firms to take the great risks involved with innovation, market power is much more important than perfect competition in providing the climate under which innovation occurs. The large short-run profits earned by firms with market power provide the incentive for others to try to usurp some of these for themselves. Oligopolistic firms compete for each other's profits, as well as for the new profits that will be generated by major innovations. If they do not compete, or if they have a genuine monopoly, outsiders will seek to enter in order to share in the profits of the sitting firm or firms. If a frontal attack on the major barriers to entry is not possible, then the barriers can be circumvented by such dodges as the development of similar products against which the established firms will not have entry protection. Schumpeter called the replacement of one entrenched position of market power by another through the invention of new products and new production techniques the *process of creative destruction*.

In this respect, perfect competition is not only impossible but inferior, and has no title to being set up as a model of ideal efficiency. It is hence a mistake to base the theory of government regulation of industry on the principle that big business should be made to work as the respective industry would work in perfect competition.

(Joseph Schumpeter, Capitalism, Socialism and Democracy (3rd edn), New York: Harper & Row, 1950, p. 106).

Schumpeter's theory is not easy to test. Nonetheless, business school studies of firm behaviour show that much, probably most, inter-firm competition is in product and process innovation. Firms rarely fail because they set the wrong prices—for one reason, it is easy to alter prices that turn out to be uncompetitive. However, firms do fail when they fall behind their competitors in the constant battle to produce new and better products by ever more cost-efficient methods.

The future of competition policy

Even though governments on the whole are no longer in the business of owning industries or tightly controlling their pricing and output decisions, governments have an important role as both rule-makers and referees of the market economy. Even the strongest advocates of Schumpeter's theory of creative destruction accept that the public interest is better served when oligopolists are induced to compete with each other rather than colluding to avoid aggressive competition.

---

[8] At the time that Schumpeter first wrote, economists only recognized two market structures: perfect competition and monopoly. Thus he applied his arguments about creative destruction to monopolies. Now that oligopoly is seen to be the dominant market form in manufacturing, it is clear that his arguments apply with more force in oligopoly, where the threat of competition is more immediate, than in monopoly.

CASE STUDIES

1. Market failure and the 2007–8 financial crisis

Box 13.1 discusses the swings in the long-running debate about the role of free markets. Here we discuss the 2007–8 financial crisis and the issues that arose from it in the context of the broader debate and the themes of this chapter,

The financial crisis started in the summer of 2007 with the failure of Northern Rock in the United Kingdom and the subprime[9] crisis in the United States. Many banks had participated in the business of issuing mortgage loans, combining them into a bundle and selling them on to other investors (including other banks) in the form of mortgage-backed securities. Many mortgages carried low interest rates for several years and much higher rates thereafter. When the higher rates came due, many subprime borrowers found themselves unable to make their payments. Defaults and foreclosures ensued. As a result, housing prices fell dramatically and many who could just meet their higher interest payments found themselves holding negative equity (the amount of the mortgage debt exceeded the present market value of the house). Mortgage-backed securities then depreciated sharply in value. Many other asset prices also dropped sharply in value and many banks who were holding these securities found themselves in difficulty.

In September 2008, US investment bank Lehman Brothers went bust and in the same year other major US financial institutions, such as Merrill Lynch and Bear Stearns, were forced into mergers, and the US government injected massive funds in supporting several major financial institutions. In the United Kingdom, Northern Rock and Bradford & Bingley were nationalized and the government injected substantial capital into Lloyds (which had taken over loss-making bank HBOS) and the Royal Bank of Scotland.

The financial crisis had wider effects on the real economy. Reductions in asset prices made many people worse off and led to reductions in spending. Companies found it harder to get the bank loans they needed to finance their current production. World trade contracted sharply, as did investment. Unemployment rose, as did personal and corporate insolvencies. In other words, the financial crisis led to a recession.[10]

We explained the general pattern of financial crises in Chapter 12; however, the issue of relevance to this chapter is what this tells us about the failure of markets. Note first that the crisis originated in the financial sector. So far in this half of the book, which concerns microeconomics, we have said almost nothing about banks and other financial institutions. All of the analysis of optimality and market failures so far has referred to sectors that produce goods and (non-financial) services and not to the financial sector. Yet the financial and the production sectors are intimately linked. There are many reasons for this, not the least of which is that many firms cover the gap between paying for inputs and selling the products that they produce through bank loans. Also, new firms almost always require substantial credit to cover their start-up costs. Even in an economy that was perfectly competitive in the production of goods and services, the banking sector could not be perfectly competitive because of large-scale economies in that sector. So, the financial sector would always have the potential to cause trouble in the production sector. Note next that one interpretation of the quote from Gordon Brown in Box 13.1 is that we have tried a free-market economy and it has failed. However, another interpretation is that the failure is on the part of those who have been preaching the dogma of free-market economics. Certainly, governments have had a substantial role in all countries' economies even where the market is the dominant form of interaction and capitalism is the dominant form of production. Indeed, there are no proposals coming out of recent events for a major extension of state ownership of institutions or a bigger role for the state in markets. Even where the state has taken ownership of financial institutions, the presumption is that this direct involvement will not last any longer than is absolutely necessary. What many do argue, however, is that the unregulated market is not acceptable in the financial sector where firms are so large that the failure of any one of them can cause major repercussions throughout the whole economy. The argument then is for significant control over the organization and behaviour of firms in the financial sector. What is not yet clear at the time of writing is how much and what kind of government rules, regulations, and controls are needed in that sector.

We have not listed as a category of market failure the fact that market economies tend to have cycles. Business cycles have been well documented for centuries, but have not always been regarded as a sign of 'failure'. We study these in great depth from Chapter 15 onwards. We will note

---

[9] Subprime mortgages are those that were lent to people who had low incomes and/or had a high loan to value ratio and were thus riskier than many other mortgages.

[10] A recession is generally defined as two successive quarters of negative growth in national output (see Chapter 15).

there that, at least since the Keynesian revolution of the 1930s, it has been regarded by many as the job of governments to use their monetary and fiscal tools to attempt to reduce the cycles in the economy. So you could argue that the recent recession has been an example of government failure rather than market failure, even though it is clear that the recent problems were associated with a financial market boom and bust. We return to this macro debate in later chapters, but note for now that the microeconomic analysis of market failure has focused on the case where economies are on their production-possibility frontier. Any regular tendency to deliver outcomes where there are unemployed resources, and thus productive inefficiency, could be a further category of market failure and a reason for government intervention.

For the present we focus on the microeconomic elements of market failure that are listed in the current chapter and are relevant to understanding the current debate about the causes and lessons of the financial crisis.

What is certainly *not* necessarily a sign of market failure is the occurrence of failing businesses. A key part of the dynamics of a market economy that we discussed in earlier chapters is that successful firms will be profitable and grow while unprofitable firms will fail and close. Resources are thus attracted to their most valuable uses and firms succeed by providing consumers with goods and services that best satisfy their needs. This is what we have referred to as 'creative destruction'. Badly managed businesses or those that produce out-of-date products should disappear, and it is generally a positive thing for the efficiency of the economy that they do.

However, it is problematic to let major retail financial institutions like banks go bust, as this would impose losses on large numbers of individuals and firms who are not at fault in any way. There are two elements to this that are sources of market failure and are discussed above.

First, there are wider social costs to a bank failure other than the direct losses to the bank's shareholders. These are similar to externalities or neighbourhood effects. Banks are involved in transmitting payments, and any collapse of a major bank would affect a large fraction of payments in transit; it would also threaten the viability of other banks with which it transacted, and it could destroy confidence in banks in general. For this reason, major banks are often regarded as 'too big to fail' and are implicitly guaranteed not to fail by the government. Statutory deposit insurance exists in many countries, but the financial crisis revealed that the commitment of governments to support the depositors of failing banks is almost unlimited in the sense that whole banks were supported with government funds, not just depositors up to the deposit insurance limit.[11] Banks are regulated by governments, so widespread bank failures

may also reflect the failure of regulators. After the crisis the discussion was about better regulation and not about more government ownership of banks, though there remained a possibility that large banks may be broken up so that they would not be 'too big to fail'.

Secondly, retail financial markets involve the sale of products to households that have elements of asymmetric information. Many people do not understand the savings and loan products that they are buying, and it may take many years for this information to become evident. If you buy a car you can easily tell if it does not go, but if you buy a savings product it will be many years before you find out how much it is worth. It is easy to promise a high future value, but it is another thing to deliver. Financial scams are common, and even well-intentioned investment schemes frequently disappoint. For this reason, government regulation and monitoring have long been deemed necessary. But this does not stop scams happening. In July 2009, Bernard Madoff was sentenced to 150 years in prison in the United States for conning investors out of close to $65 billion.

Government intervention in financial markets to 'protect consumers' does not always have the intended effect. If failing banks know that they can rely on governments to bail them out, this creates moral hazard. They can adopt riskier loan strategies seeking higher returns, but in the process make failure more likely.

Another aspect of asymmetric information in big banks (and also in some big non-financial companies) relates to the principle–agent problem. Pay structures in banks have provided incentives for short-term risk-taking and not the long-term success of the bank itself. In some high-profile cases a CEO has brought a bank to the point of collapse but has walked away with a substantial pay-off or pension pot. Individual traders have had an incentive to book deals that will boost their current-year bonus, even if there are long-term costs to the bank that eventually materialize.

Inappropriate incentive structures within firms are not normally considered to be a market failure, but they certainly create distortion of economic outcomes and are therefore relevant to this discussion. Financial regulators have already tightened rules on bonuses to ensure that employees have an incentive to consider the longer-term health of the business and not just short-term profit.

Thus the 2007–8 financial crisis has made it clear that banking and finance cannot be left to market forces alone and that a regulatory presence on behalf of government is essential. However, this implies better monitoring of markets and more effective regulation of private companies,

---

[11] At the time of writing (April 2014) the United Kingdom guarantees 100 per cent of each deposit in a bank or building society up to £85,000 per depositor.

and not the abolition of any markets or greater state owner-ship of firms. In short, the market economy is alive and well for most purposes, but financial firms are likely to find much tighter regulation of their activities for the foresee-able future. In the last two centuries at least we have never had anything even approaching a totally free-market econ-omy. The role of government as an actor and as a regulator may be increased somewhat in the short to medium term, but another danger to a productive economy may come from the inefficiencies of an overactive state.

2. Property rights and the destruction of tropical rain forests

A key factor leading to the destruction of tropical rain for-ests has been the lack of property rights assigned to these forests. With lack of ownership nobody has an incentive to plan for the long-term preservation of the trees and sustain-ability of forest industries. Rather, the incentive is to cut down the trees, sell the timber, and then move on—that is, take what money can be made immediately and move on.

The following two extracts from the *World Development Report* give examples of how Brazilian state authorities are creating incentives for preservation of the Amazon forest. In the first, tax rebates on value added tax (ICMS) are related to the areas of protected forest. The second has introduced tradable conservation permits.

The ICMS Ecologico is a unique Brazilian mechanism that uses state-to-municipality transfers to reward the creation and maintenance of protected areas for biodiver-sity conservation and watershed protection. The intent is to counteract the local perceptions that maintenance of protected areas reduces municipal revenue... Since the programs were adopted, about 1 million hectares have been placed under environmental zoning restrictions in Parana, and about 800,000 in Minas Gerais.

The Brazilian state of Parana has created a market for conservation by allowing trade in landholder obligations to maintain forests. A long-standing Brazilian law has required that property owners maintain 20 per cent of each property under native vegetation (50 per cent to 80 per cent in the Amazon region). But noncompliance was common ... A preliminary analysis of a hypothetical similar program for the nearby state of Minas Gerais illustrates how efficiency-enhancing programs such as this might increase biodiver-sity conservation and economic output ... When landholders are free to trade within the biome, compliance costs drop by almost three-quarters, while the proportion of higher-ecological-quality forest reserve increases to 72 per cent.

(World Development Report 2003, World Bank, page 173)

This illustrates the point that socially suboptimal exploi-tation of resources can arise when property rights are not

appropriately assigned. However, incentives can be intro-duced to encourage a socially efficient outcome.

Another case of inappropriate property rights has arisen in Canada. It has been seriously argued that some of the incentives for non-sustainable logging in the vast forests of Western Canada are created by the system of property rights in place there.[12] The government owns the forests and leases them out to the lumber companies for specific periods of time. As a result, the company logging a par-ticular area has little incentive to act in a way that is com-patible with efficient reforestation. Therefore laws are needed to force the companies to behave in the way that they would behave if they owned the land themselves. Once the laws are in place they must be enforced, which is not always easy, particularly in remote areas. If the log-ging companies owned the land they would have a self-interest in preserving the forests for their own future logging. More efficient logging practices and more effect-ive reforestation would be the result.

3. Endangered fish

The fish in the ocean are a common property resource, and theory predicts that such a resource will be overexploited if there is a high enough demand for the product and sup-pliers are able to meet that demand. In past centuries there were neither enough people eating fish nor efficient enough fishing technologies to endanger stocks. Over the last fifty years, however, the population explosion has added to the demand for fish and advances in technology have vastly increased the ability to catch fish. Large boats, radar detection, and more murderous nets have tipped the balance in favour of the predator and against the prey. As a result the overfishing prediction of common property theory has been amply borne out. Today fish are a common property resource; tomorrow they could become no one's resource.

Overfishing

Since 1950 the world's catch has increased fivefold. The increase was only sustained by substituting smaller, less desirable fish for the diminishing stocks of the more desir-able fish and by penetrating ever further into remote oceans. Today, all available stocks are being exploited, and now even the total tonnage is beginning to fall. The United Nations estimates that the total value of the world's catch could be increased by nearly $30 billion if fish stocks were properly managed by governments interested in the total

---

[12] Much of the concern of environmentalists is with another issue—whether or not the remaining first-growth lands should be logged at all. Our concern here is with the efficient management of those areas that it is agreed will be logged.

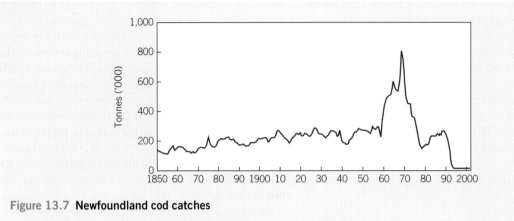

Figure 13.7 **Newfoundland cod catches**

Source: Dr R. Meyers, Canadian Department of Fisheries and Oceans, St John's, Newfoundland.

catch, rather than exploited by individuals interested in their own catch.

The developed countries have so overfished their own stocks that Iceland and the European Union could cut their fleets by 40 per cent and catch as much fish as they do today. This is because more fish would survive to spawn, allowing each boat in a smaller fleet to catch about 40 per cent more than does each boat in today's large fishing fleet.

The problem became so acute that Canada shut down its entire Atlantic cod fishing industry in 1985 and its Pacific salmon industry in 1988. Tens of thousands of Newfoundland residents lost their livelihoods in the demise of what had been the province's largest industry—the catching, freezing, and canning of fish—an industry that had flourished for five centuries (see Figure 13.7). Canada and the European Union have since been in conflict over what Canada claims is predatory overfishing by EU boats just outside Canadian territorial waters. The Canadian cod stocks show no signs of recovery.

The Mediterranean has been so overfished that seafood which was once the staple for the poor is now an expensive luxury eaten mainly by rich tourists.

Policy response

The European Union has a Common Fisheries Policy covering the territorial waters of its member countries. Since 1983, total allowable catches for all main species have been set annually and divided up into catch quotas for each member country. Minimum mesh size on nets and other ways of protecting young fish are also imposed. Inspection and monitoring measures are applied to give force to the regulations. However, measures in place up to 2002 failed to solve the problem. In May 2002, the EU announced a new radical plan.

Dwindling fish stocks, diminishing catches, too many vessels chasing too few fish, steady job losses and a lack of effective control and sanctions ... the Common Fisheries Policy (CFP) needs fundamental change ... The Commission proposes to do away with the annual ritual of setting fishing quotas at too high levels. In future, total admissible catches would be fixed within a multi-annual management plan, on the basis of the most recent scientific advice to ensure that enough fish stay in the sea to replenish stocks ... the necessary cut in fishing effort (between 30 and 60% according to the state of stocks and the regions) under multi-annual plans would result in an estimated withdrawal of some 8,600 vessels which represents 8.5% of the number of EU fishing vessels and about 18% in tonnage ... To achieve sustainable fisheries beyond EU waters on the basis of stronger international co-operation, the reform package includes an action plan against illegal fishing and a strategy for EU fisheries development partnerships with third countries.

(Source: Press release, 28 May 2002. See <http://europa.eu.int/comm/fisheries>)

A review of the Common Fisheries Policy was set up in 2009 but it took until 2013 for reforms to be agreed. Here is the UK government view on the reforms.

The Common Fisheries Policy (CFP) is the EU's instrument for managing fisheries and aquaculture.

The current CFP, which aims for an economically viable fishing industry that minimises impacts on marine ecosystems, has failed. The health of fish stocks has deteriorated, as has the profitability of fishing businesses. Centralised bureaucracy has increased.

A historic deal to reform the broken CFP has been agreed and the new regulation enters into force on 1 January 2014. The ground-breaking new CFP will radically transform fishing practices in Europe and includes the key UK government priorities of:

- *firm dates to ban fish discards*

- *a legally binding commitment to fish at sustainable levels*

- *decentralised decision making, allowing Member States to agree the measures appropriate to their fisheries.*

As a result of the agreement we will see a ban on discarding in 'pelagic' fisheries (such as mackerel and herring) starting on 1 January 2015, with a further ban on discards in other fisheries starting from 1 January 2016.

The CFP also includes, for the first time, a legally binding commitment to fish at sustainable levels, achieving 'maximum sustainable yield' by 2015 where possible, and by 2020 at the latest. This will ensure that annual quotas will be underpinned by scientific advice, to achieve healthy fish stocks and a prosperous fishing industry.

The new laws will also allow countries to work together regionally to implement measures appropriate to their own fisheries, rather than be subject to ineffective micro-management from Brussels. This will replace the over-centralised system that currently hinders progress in our fisheries.

These measures and the work on domestic fisheries management reform will help make the whole EU fishing fleet economically sustainable.

(Source: <https://www.gov.uk/government/policies/reforming-and-managing-marine-fisheries-for-a-prosperous-fishing-industry-and-a-healthy-marine-environment/supporting-pages/reforming-the-common-fisheries-policy>)

The UN World Summit on Sustainable Development, held in Johannesburg in September 2002, agreed that there should be a strategy for restoring fish stocks at the global level. It was agreed to implement an action plan to address illegal fishing, and to set up a network of marine protected areas by 2012. The longer-term target was to restore fisheries to their maximum sustainable yields by 2015. It is not yet clear if any progress has been made towards this target, but it seems unlikely as a UN report in 2012 concluded:

Most of the stocks of the top ten species, which account in total for about 30 per cent of world marine capture fisheries production, are fully exploited and, therefore, have no potential for increases in production, while some stocks are overexploited and increases in their production may be possible if effective rebuilding plans are put in place.

(Source: <http://www.fao.org/docrep/016/i2727e/i2727e.pdf>)

It remains to be seen how many types of fish will be caught to extinction and how many will recover as nations slowly learn the lesson of economic theory. Common property resources need central management if they are not to be overexploited to an extent that risks extinction.

Conclusion

Some see completely free markets as the ideal structure for the economy, and government activity as always inefficient and bureaucratic. Others see a very limited role for government, but would take government activity no further than absolutely necessary. Just provide an effective basis for law and order, they say, and the miracle of Adam Smith's hidden hand will do the rest. Most people, although not quite all, reject this view. The case against the minimalist state lies in what we observed at the outset of this chapter and have illustrated in the above case studies: although markets work—and work very effectively much of the time—markets also fail in many ways—and sometimes fail quite seriously.

We have devoted much space to explaining the *why*, *how*, and *where* of these market failures. We have also explained what might be done to alleviate the most serious of them.

In the next chapter we discuss further the role of government in the economy. The balance between government intervention and the free market is often controversial, and opinions about what is the appropriate balance change over time and from place to place. However, there is no doubt about three points. First, markets do fail in many important ways. Secondly, governments provide the only institutions available to deal with many of these failures. Thirdly, economists have designed many instruments, some of them highly subtle, by which governments can deal with these failures.

As Adam Smith observed long ago (see Chapter 1), altruism, no matter how valuable a motive in many situations, cannot be the basis for the day-to-day functioning of a market economy, which must be based on the pursuit of self-interest. Similarly, altruism, although often a highly effective motive behind locating and publicising market failures, cannot be the basis for a systematic and sustained handling of these failures. Instead, they are often best coped with by creating incentives that direct self-interested behaviour in the direction of alleviating them.

SUMMARY

Basic functions of government

- Effective governments have a legal monopoly of violence. They also define and protect the rights and obligations of property owned by individuals and institutions. They also create other institutions that assist the function of a largely market driven economy, such as laws governing bankruptcy and contracts.

- Key characteristics of market economies are (a) their ability to coordinate decentralized decisions without conscious control, (b) their determination of the distribution of income, and (c), compared with the alternatives, their minimization of arbitrary economic power.

Market efficiency

- A perfectly competitive economy would be allocatively efficient in the static sense because it produces where price, which measures the value consumers place on the last unit produced, equals marginal cost, which measures the value to consumers that the resources used to produce the marginal unit could produce in other uses. Equating price to marginal cost maximizes the sum of producers' and consumers' surpluses.

- Free markets economies fail to achieve optimal static efficiency because of the widespread existence of scale economies that make small price-taking firms inefficient producers, inefficient exclusion of users from facilities with excess capacity, common property resources, public goods, externalities, asymmetric information, missing markets, and market power.

Non-rivalrous and non-excludable goods

- The optimal price for the service of a facility with excess capacity is zero. Since private owners will charge a positive price, their facility will be inefficiently underused.

- The private market will exploit a common property resource to the point where the average revenue per producer equals the production cost of a new entrant instead of to the socially optimal level, where the marginal addition to total product caused by a new entrant equals its production cost.

- The optimal quantity of a public good is provided when the marginal cost of production is equal to the sum of the prices that all its consumers would be willing to pay for the marginal unit produced. This is difficult to attain because of the free-rider problem—the incentive for individuals to understate the true value that they place on a public good.

Externalities

- The Coase theorem shows that if those parties that create an externality and those that are affected by it can bargain together with minimal transaction costs, an optimal solution can be achieved independent of which party owns the property right to the creator of the externality.

- Where private bargaining is impossible or overly expensive, the government can alleviate negative externalities by imposing rules and regulations or, more efficiently, by internalizing externalities through such measures as taxes and tradable permits to pollute.

Public policy towards monopoly and competition

- Government policy with respect to market power is designed to encourage competitive practices and discourage monopolistic ones.

- Direct control of pricing and entry conditions of some key oligopolistic industries has been common in the past, but deregulation is reducing such control.

- An important issue concerns the effect of market structure on economic growth. The allocation of resources which is productively inefficient in the static sense that results whenever firms have market power is typically more conducive to technological change than is the productively efficient allocation (in the static sense) that results from perfect competition.

TOPICS FOR REVIEW

- Government as a monopolist of violence and a protector of property rights
- The efficiency of a perfectly competitive economy
- Rivalrous and non-rivalrous goods
- Excludable and non-excludable goods
- Inefficient exclusion
- Common property resources and the tragedy of the commons
- Rules for providing and pricing public goods

- Harmful and beneficial externalities
- Emissions taxes
- Tradable emissions permits
- Government control of market power
- Marginal and average cost pricing
- Competition policy
- Privatization
- Deregulation

QUESTIONS

1 Your local authority undoubtedly provides a police station, a fire brigade, and a public library.

   a) What are the market imperfections, if any, that each of these seeks to correct?

   b) Which of these are closest to being public goods?

   c) Which are furthest from being public goods?

   d) What would happen if governments were prevented from offering these services?

2 Not counting the ones mentioned in the text, list some goods and services that are:

   a) non-rivalrous but excludable

   b) non-excludable but rivalrous

   c) non-rivalrous and non-excludable.

3 An industry consists of two firms producing the same product but using different technologies. Each emits 50 tonnes of pollution each year. One can clean up the first tonne at a cost of £1,000, and the cost of each additional tonne cleaned up rises by £1,000 per tonne until the last tonne costs £50,000. The second firm's cost for the first tonne cleaned up is £20,000, and the cost rises by £1,000 per tonne until the fiftieth tonne is cleaned up at a cost of £70,000. The government wishes to cut the industry's total emissions from 100 to 50 tonnes a year. It gives each firm 25 tradable permits, each one allowing 1 tonne of pollution.

   a) What will be the equilibrium price of a permit to pollute by 1 tonne?

   b) How many permits will be traded?

   c) By how much will each firm clean up its own pollution?

   d) What would you infer if, in a subsequent year, the price of a pollution permit fell by 50 per cent?

4 Which one of the following is **not** a source of market failure?

   a) Inefficient exclusion

   b) Asymmetric information

   c) Externalities

   d) Diminishing returns

   e) Monopoly power

5 Which two of the following statements are **not** a necessary condition of productive efficiency?

   a) All firms producing the same product should have the same marginal cost.

   b) Production should be on the economy's production-possibility boundary.

   c) It should be possible to produce more of one product without producing less of another product.

   d) Every firm should produce any given output at the lowest possible cost.

   e) It should not be possible to make one person better off without making at least one other person worse off.

6 Why do we worry about the behaviour of natural monopolies and about collusion among oligopolists? What can be done to prevent the undesirable effects of their behaviour without stifling technological advance?

7 'There would be no externalities, harmful or beneficial, if everyone affected was well informed and could bargain with each other with no transactions cost.' Explain why you agree or disagree.

8 What are public goods, and why cannot markets easily provide such goods?

9 Why do common property resources tend to be overexploited and what solutions are available?

10 Why would it be inefficient to exclude people from using a facility that had excess capacity? Is this allocative or productive inefficiency?

11 What market failures have contributed to global warming and climate change?

CHAPTER 14

THE ROLE OF GOVERNMENT

In Chapter 13 we established three important results. First, free markets are effective ways of coordinating decentralized decision-taking. Secondly, although markets work quite well most of the time, they seldom work optimally in the static sense because of the almost universal presence of one type of market failure or another (such as the absence of perfect competition), and they occasionally fail quite dramatically as they did in the worldwide financial crisis of 2007–8 and the subsequent recession in 2008–9. Thirdly, government policy can alleviate some of the most serious market failures, either by imposing more efficient behaviour using rules, regulations, and public production or by internalizing externalities. But, while government interventions may have potential to improve the workings of markets, this does not imply that governments always get it right. What objectives do governments actually have for their economic actions? Do they usually succeed in improving economic outcomes by their interventions, or do they often make outcomes worse? What costs do government interventions impose on the private sector? Do governments sometimes pursue objectives of their own—objectives that do not reflect the interests of the community as a whole?

In particular, you will learn that:

● Governments have objectives for stability, growth, and equity as well as for efficiency.

● Equity, efficiency, and growth objectives may conflict.

● Tools of government policy include taxation and spending, the law and regulation, and the public production of goods and services.

● Government interventions usually involve both direct costs of administration and indirect costs associated with interference with the price mechanism.

● The incentives facing specific governments may deviate from those needed to deliver economic efficiency.

We start by outlining the objectives that governments may have in addition to correcting market failures. We then outline the many tools that are available to the government to achieve its policies, showing how these tools can be applied to areas other than market failure. After that, we allow for the *costs* of government activity. These must be offset against the benefits in order to assess the net value of any proposed government intervention. Finally, we note that governments do not always act in the best interest of society as a whole. Elected politicians often have agendas of their own, or of the section of society that elected them. We discuss potential outcomes when governments in these circumstances act in ways that generate either inefficiency in resource allocation or undesirable inequities in income distribution.

Government objectives

Governments have multiple objectives, only some of which we studied in the previous chapter. The main ones are as follows.

1. To protect life and property by exercising a monopoly of force and establishing property rights.

2. To improve economic efficiency by addressing the various causes of market failure.

3. To protect the environment, including assessing the possibility of human-caused climate change and dealing with its consequences.

4. To achieve some accepted standard of equity.

5. To protect individuals from others and from themselves.

6. To influence the rate of economic growth.

7. To stabilize the economy against income and price-level fluctuations.

The first three of these objectives were considered in the previous chapter. The next three are considered in this chapter (Chapter 26 is also devoted to the third and sixth objectives). The last is a major subject of the second half of this book, which deals with macroeconomic theory and policy. The explicit economic policy goals for the UK government as of 2013 are set out in a case study at the end of this chapter.

Policies for equity

Markets usually generate reasonably efficient allocations of the nation's resources because, most of the time, the information that they need to allow them to perform well, even if not optimally, is derived from agents' desires to improve their private circumstances. Therefore no one should be surprised that markets do not efficiently allocate resources towards achieving such broad social goals as establishing an 'equitable' distribution of income and promoting shared community values. Markets do not directly foster these goals, precisely because individuals do not seek to achieve them when they are purchasing goods and services in markets. Instead, they look to the political system or the many NGOs (non-government organizations, such as Greenpeace or Oxfam) to achieve desired outcomes in this respect.

The distribution of income

An important characteristic of any market economy is the *distribution* of income that it determines. People whose skills, inherent and acquired, are scarce relative to supply tend to earn large incomes, whereas people whose skills are plentiful relative to supply tend to earn much less.

As we have seen in earlier chapters, differentials in earnings serve the important function of motivating people to adapt. The advantage of such a system is that individuals can make their own decisions about how to alter their behaviour when market conditions change. The disadvantage is that temporary rewards and penalties are dealt out as a result of changes in market conditions that are beyond the control of the affected individuals. The resulting differences in incomes will often seem inequitable to many—although they are the incentives that make markets work.

Concerns about equity have two dimensions—horizontal and vertical equity. **Horizontal equity** means that people in similar circumstances should be treated similarly. Although this type of equity appeals to many people as desirable, it is not always a goal of government policies. For example, people who are exposed to similar natural risks are given more government assistance when they are planting crops than when they are mining ore, cutting trees, or extracting oil. This may be because farmers have more political power than others, or it may stem from a gut feeling on the part of the electorate that food production is more basic than any other economic activity. There are also times when agriculture is subsidized for strategic reasons, to ensure that food is available in times of war or economic isolation. **Vertical equity** means treating people in different economic situations differently in order to reduce inequalities between them.

Figure 14.1 shows what is called a **Lorenz curve**. It shows how much of total income is received by various proportions of the nation's income earners. It indicates how total income is *distributed* among individuals or groups. The further the curve bends away from the diagonal, the more unequal are the incomes of the people in society. For example, the curve shows that in 2011–12 the bottom 20 per cent of all UK individuals received only 6 per cent of all taxable income earned, while the bottom 80 per cent received only about 50 per cent of total taxable income. The remaining 50 per cent went to the top 20 per cent of income earners. The top 10 per cent of total income was received by 0.5 per cent (that is, one in every two hundred) of the population. The income shown in the figure is taxable income, measured before taxes and benefits.[1] After the impact of taxes and benefits is included, the share of the bottom 20 per cent

---

[1] The data refer only to income with some tax liability and therefore exclude all income that escapes the notice of the tax authorities or is otherwise exempt from income tax.

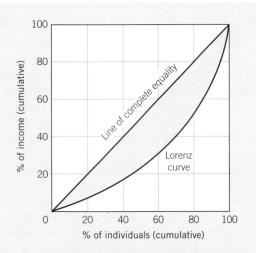

Figure 14.1 A Lorenz curve of individual pre-tax income in the United Kingdom, 2011–12

The size of the shaded area between the Lorenz curve and the diagonal is a measure of the inequality of income distribution. If there were complete income equality, the Lorenz curve would coincide with the diagonal line. The extent of income inequality (e.g. the lower 30 per cent receive only 10 per cent of the income) determines how far the Lorenz curve lies below the diagonal.

Source: ONS, *Annual Abstract of Statistics*, 2013.

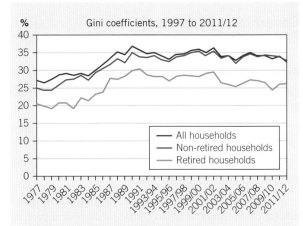

Figure 14.2 UK Gini coefficient, 1977 to 2011/12

The Gini coefficient is measured as the ratio (expressed as a percentage) of the blue shaded area in Figure 14.1 to the whole of the triangle to the southeast of the 45° line of perfect equality. The evolution of the UK Gini coefficient indicates a sharp rise in income inequality in the 1980s but a slight fall since 1990. The calculation uses disposable incomes (after taxes and benefits).

Source: ONS

rises to about 8 per cent and the share of the top 20 per cent falls from 50 per cent to about 44 per cent. The top 10 per cent of post-tax income was received by just under 1 per cent (that is one in every 100) of the population. Thus, the UK tax–benefit system has the effect of narrowing (but not eliminating) the large disparities in the distribution of income between the various income classes.

The Gini coefficient is a summary measure of inequality that is based on the Lorenz curve. It is zero if the distribution of income is perfectly equal and 100 per cent if all the income is received by a single person in the population. It is measured as the ratio (expressed as a percentage) of the blue shaded area in Figure 14.1 to the whole of the triangle to the southeast of the line of perfect equality. Figure 14.2 shows the evolution of the UK Gini coefficient from 1977 to 2011–12. This is based on disposable incomes (after taxes and benefits) and indicates a sharp rise in income inequality in the 1980s but a slight fall since 1990.

Figure 14.3 shows the UK distribution of weekly household disposable income in 2011–12. This is measured after taxes and benefits but before any deduction for housing costs, and the data are adjusted for household structure to give a measure of living standards per person[2]. Each coloured section is a decile of the population (10 per cent). There are

large numbers clustered on relatively low incomes and then a long upper tail of people with higher incomes. There are fewer and fewer people in each income range as the income level gets higher. The full extent of the long upper tail is not shown in the figure owing to space limitations.

Policies that seek to redistribute income among the nation's citizens are of two general types. Some, such as the progressive income tax, are concerned with vertical equity. They seek to alter the size distribution of income in quite general ways. Marginal rates of income tax that rise with income, combined with a neutral spending system that benefits all income groups more or less equally, will narrow income inequalities.

Other policies seek to mitigate the effects of markets on particular individuals. They do not seek to narrow income gaps in general but to deal with specific unfortunate events. Should farmers bear all the losses associated with the destruction of livestock after an outbreak of foot and mouth or mad cow disease? Should heads of households be forced to bear the full burden of their misfortune if they lose their jobs through no fault of their own? Even if they lose their jobs through their own fault, should they and their families have to bear the whole burden, which may include starvation? Should the ill and the aged be thrown on the mercy of their families? What if they have no families? Policies designed to deal with such situations usually seek horizontal equity in treating similarly all those who fall into some group.

---

[2] This process is known as 'equalization'.

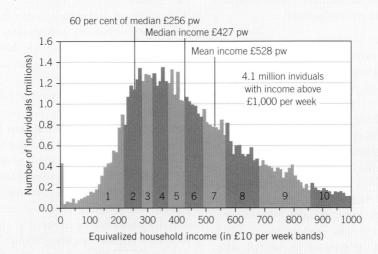

Figure 14.3 Distribution of weekly household disposable income*, 2011–12

Large numbers of people have weekly income that is bunched at a level between about £200 and £600 per week, while there is a long upper tail of people who have income levels above £1,000 per week (not shown). Each numbered section with alternating colours shows 10 per cent of the population. There is a greater concentration of people at the lower levels of weekly income, with nearly two-thirds of individuals living in households with below average (mean) income. The long tail at the upper end of the distribution is in fact considerably longer than shown; there were an estimated additional 4.1 million individuals living in households with disposable income greater than £1,000 per week who are not shown on the chart, but who are included in the calculation of mean and median income. The substantial numbers of individuals living in households with relatively high incomes skews the distribution in the figure, and produces the large difference between the overall mean income of £528 per week and the median of £427 per week.

* Equivalized household disposable income before deduction of housing costs using OECD equivalization scale.
Source: Social Trends 39, 2013, ONS.

Both private charities and a great many government policies are concerned with modifying the distribution of income that results from such things as one's parents' abilities, luck, and how one fares in the labour market.

The distribution of wealth

It is sometimes argued that egalitarian economic policy should devote more attention than it does to the distribution of wealth and less to the distribution of income. Wealth confers economic power, and wealth is more unequally distributed than income. However, in the United Kingdom heavy estate duties caused a gradual reduction in the inequality of wealth distribution during most of the twentieth century. The trend was slowed, if not reversed, over the last two decades of that century, largely because of the build-up of pension wealth in the hands of 50–70-year-olds. Nonetheless, in 2012, the top 1 per cent of people in the United Kingdom held just less than 20 per cent of all marketable wealth, while receiving 12 per cent of current income. Also, the top 50 per cent of UK citizens owned just over 90 per cent of all marketable wealth, while receiving 78 per cent of the total income.

There are two main ways in which inequalities in the distribution of wealth can be reduced. The first is to levy taxes on wealth at the time that wealth is transferred from one owner to another, either by gifts during the lifetime of the owner or by bequest after death. Currently, gifts among individuals during their lifetime are potentially exempt from tax. They only become taxable if made within seven years of the donor's death. The UK inheritance tax rate in 2014–15 was zero on estates up to £325,000 and 40 per cent thereafter, though there was no tax for inheritance by a surviving spouse and a married couple could leave a combined total of £650,000 tax free.

The second method is an annual tax on the value of each person's wealth. A wealth tax of this sort has been considered in the past but it has never been instituted in the United Kingdom and has not been actively debated in the past two decades.

Equity versus efficiency

Problems arise when government measures designed to improve equity seriously inhibit the efficient operation of the price system.

The goal of a more equitable distribution can sometimes conflict with the goal of a more efficient economy.

Suppose that we were so extreme as to believe that equity demanded that everyone should receive the same income. All incentives to work hard and to move from job to job would be eliminated. In the previous century, some command economies came close to this extreme position, and the results were predictably disastrous. To be less extreme, suppose we believed that earnings received by some owners of resources should be controlled and therefore not reflect short-term fluctuations in demand and supply. The UK controls on rented accommodation did just that during much of the twentieth century, as do rent controls in several other countries today. Without controls, a rise in demand creates extra earnings, which attract resources to meet the demand. In contrast, when controls are effective, the incentive system for resource allocation is eliminated, and supply shortages and rationing often result. Remove the price reaction and there is no incentive for the resources to be reallocated.

Policies to protect individuals

Protection from others

People can use and even abuse other people for economic gain in ways that members of society find offensive. Child labour laws and minimum standards of working conditions are responses to such actions. In an unhindered free market, the adults in a household usually decide how much education to buy for their children. Selfish parents might buy no education, while egalitarian parents might buy the same education for all their children, regardless of their abilities. The members of society usually interfere in these choices, both to protect the child of the selfish parent and to ensure that some of the scarce educational resources are distributed according to ability rather than the family's wealth. All households are forced to provide a minimum of education for their children, and a number of inducements are offered—through public universities, scholarships, loans, and other means—for talented children to consume more education than they or their parents might choose if they had to pay the entire cost themselves.

Protection from oneself

Members of society, acting through the government, often seek to protect adult (and presumably responsible) individuals not from others, but from themselves. Laws prohibiting the use of heroin, crack cocaine, and other drugs, and laws prescribing the installation and use of car seat belts are intended primarily to protect individuals from their own ignorance or short-sightedness. This kind of interference in the free choices of individuals is called paternalism. Whether such actions reflect the wishes of the majority in society or whether they reflect the interference of overbearing governments, there is no doubt that the market will not provide this kind of protection. Buyers do not buy what they do not want, and sellers have no motive to provide it.

It is interesting to note that these kinds of paternalism can change people's tastes. For example, many people would now voluntarily use seat belts, having been shown their value by the laws prescribing their use. This is an example of the many ways that education seeks to alter people's tastes, as also does advertising. The strongest case for completely free markets assumes that tastes are given and fully exogenous to economic activity. Once it is realized that tastes can be changed by the activities of both state and private sector agents, and in ways that the majority sometimes approves of and sometimes disapproves of, the case for a completely free market allocation of resources needs modification.

Paternalism is often closely related to **merit goods**. Merit goods are goods that society, operating through the government, deems to be especially important or that those in power feel individuals should be encouraged to consume. Housing, education, health care, and certain cultural activities, such as the opera, are often cited as merit goods. Critics argue that the concept is merely a way of imposing the tastes of an elite group on others.

Policies to promote social obligations

In a free-market system, if you can persuade someone else to clean your house in return for £50, both parties to the transaction are presumed to be better off. You prefer to part with £50 rather than clean the house yourself, and the person you hire prefers to have £50 rather than avoid cleaning your house. Normally society does not interfere with people's ability to negotiate mutually advantageous contracts.

However, most people do not feel this way about activities that are regarded as social obligations. For example, during major wars, when military service is compulsory, contracts similar to the one between you and your housekeeper could also be negotiated. Some people, faced with the obligation to do military service, could no doubt pay enough to persuade others to do their tour of service for them. By exactly the same argument as we just used, we can presume that both parties would be better off if they were allowed to negotiate such a trade. Yet such contracts are usually prohibited as a result of widely held values that cannot be expressed in the marketplace. In times of major wars, of the sort that were experienced twice in the twentieth century, military service by all healthy males in the right age groups is held to be a duty that is independent of an individual's tastes, income, wealth, or social position.

Military service is not the only example of a social obligation. Citizens are not allowed to buy their way out of jury duty or to sell their votes, even though in many cases they could find willing trading partners. Even if the price system did allocate goods and services with complete efficiency, members of a society would still not wish to rely solely on the market for all purposes, since they have other goals that they wish to achieve.

Policies for economic growth

Over the long term, economic growth is the most powerful determinant of living standards (see Chapter 26). Whatever the policies concerning efficiency and equity, people who live in economies with rapid rates of growth find their living standards rising on average faster than those of people who live in countries with low rates of growth. For example, if citizens in two different countries start out with identical per capita incomes but economic growth makes these incomes rise at 1 per cent in one country and 3 per cent in the other, in about thirty years the citizens of the faster-growing country will have incomes that are twice as large as those in the slower-growing country! Clearly, these growth-induced changes tend to have much larger effects on living standards over a few decades than any policy-induced changes in the efficiency of resource allocation or the distribution of income.

For the last half of the twentieth century most economists viewed growth mainly as a macroeconomic phenomenon related to total savings and total investment. Reflecting this view, most textbooks did not even mention growth in their chapters on microeconomic policy.

More recently, there has been a shift back to the perspective of earlier economists, who saw technological change as the engine of growth, with individual entrepreneurs and firms as the agents of innovation. This is a microeconomic perspective that is meant to add to, not replace, the macroeconomic stress on capital accumulation.

Governments are aware of this microeconomic perspective on growth. Today few microeconomic policies escape being exposed to the question 'Even if this policy achieves its main goal, will it have unfavourable effects on growth?' Answering 'yes' is not a sufficient reason to abandon a specific policy. But it is a sufficient reason to think again. Is it possible to redesign the policy so that it can still achieve its main objective, while removing its undesirable side-effects on growth?

Tools and performance

The main sets of tools available to governments to achieve their goals are taxes, spending, rules, and public ownership. In this section we discuss these tools and show how they are used to achieve the specific objectives outlined earlier.

Taxation

Taxes and spending are by far the most important items on this list. Governments spend money to achieve many purposes, and that money must be either borrowed or raised through taxes. We leave borrowing aside as it is only a temporary measure. Interest must be paid on borrowed money and, if that too is borrowed, the total government debt eventually explodes to unmanageable proportions.

So sooner or later all government spending must be paid for out of taxes. Borrowing only postpones the need to tax.

Table 14.1 shows the major sources of tax revenues, along with the major classes of government spending, for the United Kingdom in 2012–13.

As well as providing the revenues needed to finance all of the government's activities, taxes are also used as tools in their own right for a wide range of purposes. For

Table 14.1 Spending and revenue of UK central and local government, 2012–13

Spending	£billion	Revenue	£billion
Health	124	VAT	98
Education	87	Income tax, capital gains tax, National Insurance contributions	253
Defence	42	Corporation tax	42
Pensions	139	Oil tax	28
Welfare	117	Tobacco tax	9
Debt interest	47	Stamp duty	10
Public order and safety	31.5	Alcohol taxes	10
General government	14	Other	18
Transport	17		
Other	54.2		
Total managed spending	675	Total revenue	469

Source: HM Treasury, *Pre-Budget Report*, December 2013.

Box 14.1 The impact of a per-unit tax in a perfectly competitive industry

Many kinds of tax affect the costs of firms. We illustrate here a tax that is levied on each unit produced.

From the firm's point of view the tax on each unit produced is just another cost of production. It shifts each firm's marginal cost curve vertically upwards by the amount of the tax, where marginal cost now refers to the firm's total outlay—costs and taxes—associated with each additional unit of production.

The figure shows a perfectly competitive market in equilibrium with the demand and supply curves D and S intersecting at E_0 to produce an equilibrium price and output of p_0 and q_0. A tax of T per unit is then placed on the product. We show the effect of the tax by adding it to the supply curve. The 'costs' of producers now comprise production costs plus the tax that must be paid to the government. Every point on the supply curve shifts vertically upwards by the amount of the tax. The intersection of the new supply curve S_T and the demand curve D yields the new quantity and market price of q_1 and p_1. Producers' after-tax receipts are read from the original supply curve S and are p_2 ($= p_1 - T$) per unit.

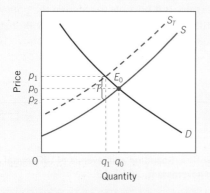

The upward shift in marginal cost curve makes the industry's supply curve shift upward by the amount of the tax. The impact is similar to that of an increase in costs for a firm in perfect competition (see Chapter 6, especially Box 6.4).

A per-unit tax on the output of a perfectly competitive industry will:

(1) raise price in the short run, but by less than the amount of the tax, so that the burden will be shared by consumers, who pay a higher price, and by producers, who do not cover their average total costs;

(2) cause the industry to contract in the long run until the losses disappear, and the whole burden will fall on consumers;

(3) if the cost curves of firms remaining in the industry are unaffected by the contraction in the size of the industry, cause the price to rise in the long run by the full amount of the tax.

The second of the above consequences is an example of a most important general proposition. We have done the analysis for a perfectly competitive industry so that we could draw a unique industry supply curve, but point 2 is more general. In any industry with freedom of entry or exit and where there is room for a large number of firms, profits will always be pushed to zero in the long run. Thus, any temporary advantage or disadvantage given to the industry by any public policy or private action must be dissipated in the long run— free entry and exit always ensures that surviving firms earn zero pure profits. Something similar holds for oligopolies. A tax large enough to reduce profits significantly may lead to the exit of one or more of the weakest of the competitors and allow for a rise in price that increases the profits earned by the survivors. A subsidy large enough to make it profitable for another firm to enter the industry will attract such a firm. Its entry will typically drive prices down somewhat and erode some, if not all, of the advantages conferred by the subsidy.

Government intervention in an industry with a large number of firms and freedom of entry and exit can influence the size of the industry, the total volume of its sales, and the price at which its goods are sold, but intervention cannot influence the long-run profitability of the firms that remain in the industry.

In industries with a small number of firms, small changes in government intervention may affect only the profits of existing firms, but larger changes will cause entry or exit that will to some extent erode the initial effects of the intervention.

Many government policies have started out raising the profitability of a particular industry but ended up increasing the number of firms, each operating at an unchanged level of profits. This illustrates the point that any intervention policy will fail to raise economic profits in the long run unless there are sufficiently strong existing barriers to entry or new barriers create a monopoly.

---

example, they can be used to alter the incentives to which private maximizing agents react, and to alter the distribution of income.

Indirect taxes

Taxes are divided into two broad groups, depending on whether people or transactions are taxed. An **indirect tax** is levied on a transaction and is paid by an individual by virtue of being involved in that transaction. Taxes and stamp duties on the transfer of assets from one owner to another are indirect taxes, since they depend on the assets being transferred. Inheritance taxes, which depend on the size of the estate being inherited and not on the circumstances of the beneficiaries, are also an indirect tax.

The most important indirect taxes in today's world are those on the sale of currently produced products. These taxes are called excise taxes when they are levied on manufacturers, and sales taxes when they are levied on the sale of goods from retailer to consumer. The EU countries levy a comprehensive tax of this sort on transactions involving the production and sale of goods and services, whether at the retail, wholesale, or manufacturer's level, called the **value added tax (VAT)**. Value added is the difference between the value of inputs that the firm purchases from other firms and the value of its output. Therefore it represents the value that a firm adds by virtue of its own activities. VAT is an indirect tax because it depends on the value of what is made and sold, not on the wealth or income of the maker or seller.

Indirect taxes may be levied in two basic ways. An **ad valorem tax** is a percentage of the value of the transaction on which it is levied. The United Kingdom's 20 per cent VAT is an ad valorem tax. A **specific tax** or **per-unit tax** is a tax expressed as so many pence per unit, independent of the commodity's price. Taxes on cinema and theatre tickets, and on each litre of petrol or alcohol, and on each packet of cigarettes are all specific indirect taxes. Box 14.1 outlines the main impact of a per-unit tax on the price and output of firms.

Direct taxes

Taxes in the second broad group are called **direct taxes**. These are levied on people and vary with the status of the taxpayer. The most important direct tax is the income tax. The personal income tax falls sometimes on the income of households and sometimes separately on each member of the household. It varies with the size and source of the taxpayer's income and various other characteristics, such as marital status and number of dependants.

Firms also pay taxes on their incomes. UK companies are subject to corporation tax, which is levied on their profits as defined by accountants (i.e. the return on their capital plus any economic profits that may exist). This is a direct tax, both in the legal sense that the company is an individual in the eyes of the law, and in the economic sense that the company is owned by its shareholders so that a tax on the company is a tax on them. The impact of taxes on profits is discussed in Box 14.2.

Progressivity

It is important for many purposes to distinguish average from marginal rates of any direct tax. The average rate of income tax paid by a person is that person's total tax divided by his or her income. The marginal rate of tax is the rate he or she would pay on the next pound's worth of income.

Box 14.2 **The effect of taxes on profits**

A famous prediction is that a tax levied as a percentage of profits will have no effect on price and output under any market structure. Let us first see how the prediction is derived, and then consider its application to real-world situations.

Given free entry there will be no economic profits in long-run equilibrium. Thus, the firms in an industry that is perfectly or monopolistically competitive will pay no profit tax in the long run (*X* per cent of zero is zero). It follows that the tax does not affect any firm's long-run behaviour and hence has no effect on industry price and output.

A tax on profit, as defined in economics, affects neither price nor output of a competitive industry in equilibrium. Hence, it does not affect the long run allocation of resources.

Does this prediction apply to those taxes on firms' profits that are actually levied in many countries? The answer is no, because profits are defined in tax law according to accountants' rather than economists' usage. In particular, the tax-law definition includes the opportunity cost of capital and the reward for risk-taking. To economists this is a cost; for tax purposes it is profit. (To review economists' definition of profit see Chapter 5.)

A tax on the return to capital will have some effects. First, perfectly competitive firms will pay such taxes even in

long-run equilibrium, since they use capital and must earn enough money to pay a return on it. There will be losses in the short run but these will lead to exit until the remaining firms are just earning zero economic profits. Secondly, the tax will affect costs differently in different industries. To see this, compare two industries. One is very labour intensive, so that 90 per cent of its costs of production go to wages and only 10 per cent to capital and other factors. The other is very capital intensive, so that fully 50 per cent of its costs (in an economists' sense) are a return to capital. The tax on the return to capital will take a small part of the total earnings of the first industry and a large part of those of the second industry. If the industries were equally profitable (in the economists' sense) before the tax, they would not be afterwards, and producers would be attracted into the first industry and out of the second one. This would cause prices to change until both industries became equally profitable (post-tax), after which no further movement would occur.

A tax on profits as they are defined in tax law does affect price and output and hence alters the allocation of resources. It also implies a higher effective tax rate in capital-intensive industries (though an analysis of the impact of real tax systems would have to look at the entire range of taxes, including those on labour).

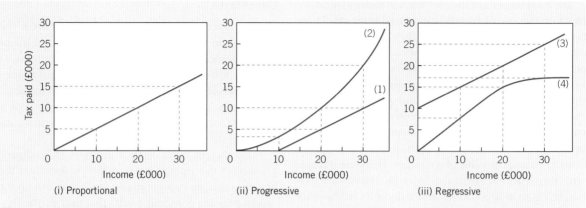

Figure 14.4 Income taxes with different progressivities

Income taxes may be proportional, progressive, or regressive. In part (i) the proportional tax's average and marginal rates remain unchanged at 50 per cent as income changes. In part (ii) tax (1) has a constant marginal rate of 50 per cent, but the average rate rises with income, being zero at income £10,000, 25 per cent at income £20,000, and 33.3 per cent at income £30,000. With tax (2) both the marginal and the average tax rates rise as income rises. In part (iii) tax (3) has a constant marginal rate of 50 per cent. But the average rate falls as income rises, being 150 per cent at £10,000, 100 per cent at £20,000, and 83.3 per cent at £30,000. With tax (4) both the marginal and the average rates fall as income rises.

The general term for the relation between the level of income and the percentage of income paid as a tax is **progressivity**. A **regressive tax** takes a *smaller percentage* of people's incomes the larger is their income. A **progressive tax** takes a *larger percentage* of people's incomes the larger is their income. A **proportional tax** is the boundary case between the two; it takes the *same percentage* of income from everyone. Taxes on food, for example, tend to be regressive, because the proportion of income spent on food tends to fall as income rises. Taxes on wines and spirits tend to be progressive, since the proportion of income spent on wines and spirits tends to rise with income. Taxes on beer, on the other hand, are regressive. Different types of progressivity are shown in Figure 14.4.

Progressivity can be defined for any one tax or for the tax system as a whole. Different taxes have different characteristics. Inevitably, some will be progressive and some regressive. The impact of a tax system as a whole on high-, middle-, and low-income groups is best judged by looking at the progressivity of the whole set of taxes taken together. For example, income taxes are progressive in the United Kingdom, rising to a maximum marginal rate of 45 per cent. The overall tax system is also progressive, but much less so than one would guess from studying only the income tax rates. This is because much revenue is raised by indirect taxes, which are much less progressive than income taxes.

Spending

Some government spending involves the hiring of people and the hiring or purchase of land and capital to produce public services, such as health and education. Clearly,

when the government uses these inputs to produce goods and services in the public sector of the economy, they are unavailable to produce private sector output. A civil servant who works full time for the government cannot also work for a private company. This type of spending is sometimes called *exhaustive spending*. Exhaustive spending is one of the tools available for filling in gaps in what the free market delivers. For example, public goods, such as national defence, the legal system, and coastal navigation aids, must be produced by the government or not at all. In those cases the failure of the free market and the potential for a remedy by government action are obvious.

The remainder of government spending consists of **transfer payments**, which are payments *not* made in return for any contribution to current output. Old-age pensions, unemployment insurance and supplementary benefits, welfare payments, disability payments, and a host of other expenditures made by the modern welfare state are all transfer payments. They do not add to current marketable output; they merely transfer the power to purchase output from those who provide the money (usually

Table 14.2 UK government spending as a percentage of GDP

Spending on	1956	1976	1997	2012
Goods and services	20.7	25.9	20.8	21.8
Transfer payments	13.2	21.0	18.6	18.9
Total spending	33.9	46.9	39.2	40.7

Source: ONS, UK National Accounts.

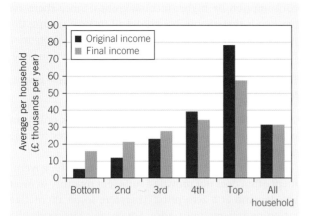

Figure 14.5 The effects of taxes and benefits on household incomes, United Kingdom, 2011–12 (all households)

The distribution of original income is much more unequal than the distribution of final income. Original income is altered by the subtraction of direct and indirect taxes and the addition of cash benefits and benefits in kind to obtain final, or after-tax/benefit, income.

Source: ONS.

taxpayers) to those who receive it. Therefore their main purpose is to alter the *distribution* of income. Tax-induced redistributions are not just from rich to poor. They also make transfers from those working to those retired and unemployed, from the healthy to the sick, and from city-dwellers to farmers (through, for example, agricultural subsidies in the European Union). None of these transfer payments represents a claim by the government on real productive resources. Nonetheless revenue must be raised to finance them. Table 14.2 shows UK government spending expressed as a proportion of national output (GDP).

Figure 14.5 shows the overall redistributive effect of the UK tax–spending system. Although there were some increases in inequality in the 1980s (see Figure 13.2), the UK fiscal system still redistributes incomes from rich to poor. The main benefits to lower-income groups come from cash payments, such as welfare and unemployment benefits, and in-kind benefits, mainly education and the NHS. High income groups contribute to the income redistribution because although they receive many benefits, they pay even higher amounts of both direct and indirect taxes.

Rules and regulations

Rules and regulations pervade economic activities. Governments use rules both to set the framework within which market forces operate and to alter the workings of unhindered markets so as to redress market failures. Shop hours and working conditions are regulated. Rules govern

the circumstances under which various types of union can be formed and operated. Discrimination between labour services provided by males and females is illegal in the United Kingdom and in many other countries. Children cannot be served alcoholic drinks. They must attend school in most countries, and be inoculated against communicable diseases in many. Laws prohibit people from selling or using certain drugs. Prostitution is prohibited in many societies, even though it usually involves a willing buyer and a willing seller. In many countries you are forced to purchase insurance for the damage you might do to others with your private motor car. In some countries people who offer goods for sale cannot refuse to sell them to someone just because they do not like the customer's colour or religion. There are rules against fraudulent advertising and the sale of substandard, adulterated, or poisonous food. In some countries, such as the United States, anyone can purchase a variety of firearms. In other countries, such as the United Kingdom, it is difficult for a private citizen to obtain a handgun and guns must be registered with the police.

As we saw in Chapter 13, most business practices have some control exerted on them by rules and regulations. In many countries agreements between oligopolistic firms to fix prices, or divide up markets, are illegal. The mere existence of monopoly is outlawed in some countries. When large economies of scale create a natural monopoly, the prices that a firm can charge, and the return it can earn on its capital investment, are often regulated. Also, firms in the financial sector such as banks, insurance companies, and investment managers are subject to many rules and regulations.

Public ownership

In the past many governments have used public ownership of nationalized industries as a tool for achieving policy goals. In the United Kingdom today most of these industries have been privatized. The main remaining publicly owned industries in the United Kingdom (as of 2014) are the Post Office, the BBC, Network Rail, state education, and the National Health Service (NHS).[3] We deal briefly with education, and then in more detail with the NHS. The provision of both these services, education and health, has been largely removed from the UK private sector and provided free to consumers.

The inefficiency of free goods

Of course, there is no such thing as a costless good or service. The production of anything requires resources,

---

[3] In 2014, the UK government also owned a bank and was a major shareholder in one other. These were taken into public ownership only to stop them collapsing. It is intended to sell them back to the private sector once market conditions permit.

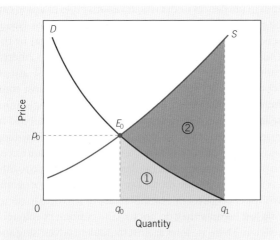

Figure 14.6 The inefficiency of free goods

Consumption of a free good exceeds what it would be at the efficient competitive equilibrium. Competitive equilibrium is at E_0 with price p_0 and quantity q_0. At a zero price q_1 is consumed. Since each extra unit that is produced adds its marginal cost to the total cost of production, total costs rise by the area under the industry's marginal cost curve (its supply curve). The two shaded areas 1 and 2 show this extra cost. The additional consumers' surplus is given by the light blue shaded area 1. So the efficiency loss is the dark blue shaded area 2.

which have opportunity costs. So a 'free good' is not a costless good, only one whose costs are not borne by its users. Instead, the costs of state-provided free goods are borne by taxpayers.

Providing any good or service freely to its users poses efficiency problems. We illustrate with a product that has neither positive nor negative externalities so that private and social costs and benefits coincide. If such a product is provided free and all demand is met, then people will go on consuming it until the last unit has a zero value to them. But that unit will have a positive marginal cost of production that represents the value to consumers that the resources used in its production could create in other lines of activity.

Providing without charge goods and services that are costly to produce is allocatively inefficient because their price (of zero) is less than their marginal cost.

Figure 14.6 shows the resource waste. It is obvious that the size of the waste will depend on the elasticity of the demand curve for the subsidized product. With a highly inelastic demand curve the policy induces only a small increase in output, so only a small quantity of resources are inefficiently allocated. With a highly elastic demand the quantity of misallocated resources is large.

From the point of view of improving equity in income distribution, free goods also have major shortcomings. Much of the money spent goes to subsidize their

consumption by higher-income groups. Since there are few goods that are not bought by all income groups, the policy is much like shooting at a target with a shotgun—the bull's-eye will be hit, but so will almost everything else.

Transfer payments can be targeted at specific income groups; free goods cannot.

This lack of targeting makes the free-goods policy an unnecessarily expensive way of helping low-income groups.

A further problem with free goods is that the government often does not provide a sufficient quantity to meet the demand at a zero price. Therefore some alternative rationing scheme must arise. Sometimes queues do the rationing. At other times, sellers' preferences do the job. This happens, for example, when those considered most worthy by administrators or doctors are given expensive health care, while others receive cheaper alternatives.

Despite all these problems, governments provide many goods and services free of charge, including medical and hospital care and basic education.

Education

Education could be left completely to the private sector. Those who were willing to pay would choose from the many schools at all levels that the private sector would no doubt provide. Most countries leave a substantial amount of education to be provided in this way. In the United Kingdom in 2012, about 7 per cent of 5–16-year-olds were being educated in the private sector. Thus, state schools still account for the vast majority of pupils. This raises three questions that are distinct, although often confused. First, why is education made compulsory? Secondly, who should pay for education? Thirdly, who should provide it?

Why compulsion?

There are three main reasons for making education compulsory up to some allowable education-leaving age, which is 18 in the United Kingdom. The first is protection of children. If selfish parents decided to spend money on themselves and nothing on their children, they would hamper their children's ability to function in the economy when they grew up. The second is income redistribution. It is held that no one should be prevented from gaining some minimum level of education because of lack of parental income. The third reason is externalities. Everyone gains from living in a society where everyone else has some minimum level of education. The type of society in which almost all workers are unskilled is very different for all of its members from one in which there is a range of skills, with most people educated up to their ability. Because of externalities we insist that everyone should remain in education up to some legal leaving age.

Why free?

If an expensive service is made compulsory because it is of benefit to everyone, the obvious way to pay for it is through taxes. This is more acceptable because the proposition that free goods are consumed in inefficient amounts does not apply to any good or service whose consumption is compulsory. Because everyone of school age must attend school, the elasticity of demand for such education is zero. Thus, the amount of resources allocated to compulsory education is independent of who pays for it. The method of payment will affect the distribution of income but will not cause any allocative inefficiency.

Who should provide it?

There is no universal agreement on the question of provision. In the United Kingdom many parents opt out of the system and provide private education for their children. For this they must pay (in addition to the taxes that they already pay to support the state system). Those who go through the state system have little choice. They must go to the local school (possibly choosing between two nearby ones if space is available). They must accept the current curriculum and whatever educational practices are currently being mandated. They cannot purchase an alternative educational experience that does not currently have ministry approval (without opting out of the state sector entirely). In short, as with any other nationalized industry, there is little market choice available and innovation is centralized.

There are several arguments commonly advanced for state provision of education. It creates a desirable uniformity of standards. Pay and working conditions will be the same throughout the system. The state with all its educational experts is presumed to know better than the child and its parents what educational experience is in the child's best interest. Ministries can research new methods and techniques, and institute them efficiently when they seem to be improvements on current practices.

Opponents of the state monopoly in the provision of state-funded education argue for more market determination of who provides state-funded education. The state could give every child education vouchers to the value of what the state is providing. These vouchers could be used to purchase education in any establishment that accepts them. Proponents of this type of system argue several alleged advantages. It would give parents more choice among various schools. Parents and their children usually have a better idea of what kind of education is needed and of whether or not they are getting it at the school currently being attended. This would penalize schools with poor academic and discipline records. Salaries would not be uniform across all schools; instead, the earnings of schools and the salaries of teachers would vary with the success of individual schools in attracting students. Poorer schools

would get fewer vouchers and hence less revenue out of which to pay their staff. The system would also encourage experimentation. Anyone with a new idea could try it out provided only that she could fill one classroom with students. The small amount of current centralized experimentation would be replaced with a large amount of decentralized experimentation. If some new educational idea or fad gained majority acceptance it would not be forced on all students. Anyone that disagreed with it would need only to find a school that was not following the herd.

These are some of the arguments advanced by some for exposing education to market forces, while ensuring that it remains available to everyone. Many others worry about exposing education to market forces and prefer the system of state monopoly.

Although state financing of education is not in dispute in modern countries, the value of a state monopoly in providing free education is debated. Some think it the best system; others wish to inject market competition into the provision of free education.

Health and medical care

The case for providing hospital and medical services at a price below cost (zero in the limit) rests on three considerations. First, private provision is prone to market failure. Secondly, it is alleged that the inefficiencies of free medical care are not large. Thirdly, serious equity issues arise when health care is left to private markets.

Market failure

In the previous chapter we studied the types of market failure that emerge when all sides to a transaction are not equally informed. So, we merely need note how these failures apply to the market for medical and health care. First, doctors are better informed about their patients' needs than are the patients themselves. Therefore doctors are in a position to influence the demand for their services rather than responding to the demands of their patients. As a result of this asymmetric information, elective surgery and other treatments of non-life-threatening medical conditions are observed to vary with the supply of doctors. Secondly, patients are better informed than their medical insurers on the state of their own health. This creates the problem of adverse selection first mentioned in Chapter 10. Thirdly, people who are fully insured may be more careless with their health than those who must pay themselves. This is the problem of moral hazard, also discussed in Chapter 10. It is worth noting that the first problem exists with any fee-for-service health system, no matter who pays the bill. The second exists only when insurance companies pay the bill, while the third exists in all systems where anyone but the patient pays.

With medical care, social and private costs and benefits are thought to diverge substantially. If I do not cure my infectious disease, the effects are not felt by me alone. More generally, everyone gains by living in a healthy rather than a disease-ridden society. Thus, there are arguments for reducing the private costs of these services below the market rate by means of a subsidy.

Insurers can do little to avoid some adverse selection, but they will not insure those whom they know to be already ill or serious risks for other reasons. This means that a considerable number of people just cannot get medical insurance under free-market provision. This group includes those who were born with serious health problems or acquired them while still living at home. It also includes those with serious health problems whose medical coverage runs out when they leave their present employer to change firms or retire. When they try to reinsure themselves in a private plan they often find themselves uninsurable.

Small inefficiencies?

Recall that the magnitude of the resource cost of a free-good policy depends on the slope of the demand curve between the free-market price and the subsidized price. Studies suggest low incidence of unnecessary hospitalization in free-hospital systems. If the demand for services is not much larger than it would be in the free market (where many, perhaps most, people would be privately insured), the magnitude of the waste caused by divergence between the zero price and the positive marginal cost will be small.

Other potential inefficiencies also exist. Governments typically do not provide facilities to meet all the demand for free services, so scarce funds must be allocated within the system. However, bureaucratic decisions are seldom efficient in allocating scarce funds so that their marginal benefits are the same in all uses. In the mid-1990s a controversial internal market mechanism was introduced into the NHS. Patients got treatment free, but doctors had a notional budget that they used to buy services from hospitals. Hospitals priced operations, and these prices varied substantially over the country. This internal market system was abolished by the Labour Government in 1999. A ten-year plan was embarked upon in 2000 to improve health service resources and the efficiency of the internal allocation mechanisms. There was a substantial increase in spending on health, but this addition of resources did not solve the problem created by virtually permanent excess demand at a zero price. The UK coalition government that came to power in 2010 was committed to protecting health service spending in real terms, but it did attempt further reorganization in order to achieve efficiency gains at a time when all other government departments were asked to cut spending (relative to plans) by 25 per cent over four years.

Equity considerations

There are also more subtle arguments about social values. It has been argued that in richer societies decisions about basic medical care should be taken out of the economic arena. It is degrading for a person to have to balance medical care for a child against other family needs. Therefore, it is argued, the inefficiency cost of freely provided basic medical care is worth accepting in order to produce a society where choices about basic medical services are eliminated.

Notice the use of the word 'basic' in the previous paragraph. The above position is arguable if it is confined to basic services for all. Modern medical technology is so expensive that the state could not afford to make all conceivable services freely available to all. The more expensive services must be rationed. This can be done either by prices or by decisions about need taken by medical and hospital authorities.

For all its problems the NHS remains one of the most popular of the government's many activities. Therefore it seems likely to stay in place for a long time to come. As a result, understanding its shortcomings and using economic analysis to alleviate the worst of its inefficiencies is an important social activity.

Economic growth

Economic growth has been the cause of the sustained long-term increase in living standards that began some time early in the nineteenth century (i.e. about 200 years ago). However, the contemporary focus on the interface between microeconomic policies and economic growth is relatively new. As we have already observed, a few decades ago growth policies would have been considered solely a macroeconomic issue relating to aggregate demand and aggregate investment. However, in recent times the focus on growth policies or 'supply-side policies' has concentrated on microeconomic issues, such as flexibility of labour markets, incentives for invention and innovation, and disincentive effects of taxation and red tape. One issue for policy-makers is the unintentional side effects on growth of policies with other primary objectives. Another issue is the effectiveness of micropolicies that are directly focused on encouraging growth. Both are relevant when policy tools are chosen.

Taxation policies for growth

Almost all taxes can affect growth by altering incentives to save, to work, or to take risks.

Taxation of consumption or income

Income taxes apply to income when it is earned; spending taxes (such as VAT) apply only to that part of income that is spent on consumption.

As an example, consider a woman in the 40 per cent marginal tax bracket who earns an extra £1,000 and pays

£400 income tax. If she spends her after-tax income, she will be able to buy £600 worth of goods. If she saves the money, she will be able to buy a £600 bond. If the bond pays, say, a 4 per cent real return, she will earn £24 interest per year. But a 40 per cent tax must then be paid on the interest earnings, leaving only a £14.40 annual income. This is a 2.4 per cent after-tax return on the bond and a 1.44 per cent after-tax return on the original £1,000 income!

This 'double taxation' of savings is a disincentive to save. Some economists who wish to encourage saving, which helps to finance growth-creating investment, argue for taxes on consumption, not on income. Under an expenditure tax any income that is saved is untaxed. Our saver in the previous paragraph would be taxed only when the interest earned on the savings was actually spent on consumption.

Steeply progressive rates of tax

Steeply progressive tax rates are an incentive to emigrate, or at least move one's business abroad. They also penalize people with fluctuating incomes, such as authors, self-employed builders, and small-scale innovators. Consider an innovator who tries to introduce one new product each year. She just covers costs on her first four attempts and then has a success that yields £250,000 over costs in the fifth year. Her income over the five years is the same as a salaried employee who earns £50,000 for each of these five years. Yet under a steeply progressive tax regime she will pay much more tax than he will. This was a really serious problem when the maximum rate of tax in the United Kingdom was 70 per cent. (Immediately after the Second World War, in 1945, it was well over 90 per cent!) In the 1980s the maximum rate was cut to 40 per cent, which greatly reduces the tax penalty paid by someone with a highly fluctuating income. But it is still there. At 2009–10 tax rates, the lady innovator would have paid £92,542 in taxes, while over the same five-year period the salaried man would have paid £62,708 (assuming that each had no dependants). After April 2010 she would pay even more tax, as a higher rate of tax of 45 per cent was applied on incomes over £150,000.

Here we see one of the many possible conflicts between growth and equity. Policy-makers may favour steeply progressive tax rates on grounds of equity but be persuaded to moderate the degree of progressivity in the interest of discouraging emigration of the rich and successful and encouraging the risk-taking that is necessary for promoting growth.

Adjustment policies for growth

The innovations in products and production processes that underlie growth require continual changes and adaptations throughout the economy. If government policies discourage change, growth will be slowed. The realization that many policies designed to improve equity can discourage change has led to some policy re-evaluations.

Labour market policies

When people lose jobs because of economic change, the various measures that constitute the welfare safety net provide them with income support. Although such passive support provides immediate relief, it provides no incentive for recipients to change their situation and can sometimes even discourage such efforts. An alternative is to make some, or all, of the support conditional on adjusting to change, for example by retraining or relocating.

Support of firms and industries

Governments are always tempted to support declining industries. Over the past century both Labour and Conservative governments have done a lot of this. Such policies reduce unemployment in the short run, but if economic forces are leading to a continual decline, the policies are only costly ways of postponing the inevitable. Furthermore, when it finally does come, the adjustment often comes suddenly. This is because government support is withdrawn all at once when the growing cost of the support finally becomes unacceptable.

Patents

If an innovation can easily be copied, new firms may enter an industry so quickly that the innovating firm is not compensated for the costs and risks of innovation. The innovation is, in effect, a public good, and private firms are not motivated to produce it. Patent laws are designed to provide the needed incentives by creating a temporary property right over the invention, allowing the invention's owner to earn profits as a reward for inventing. Once the patent expires, others can legally copy the innovation and production will expand until profits fall to normal. In the modern age of electronics the main cost of producing many goods and services is in the invention and development stages, while direct costs of production are low. In such industries patents became much more important than they were in the past, since much time is required to recoup the large R&D costs through sales revenues once the product has come to market.

Reduction of entry barriers

Schumpeter's theory of *creative destruction* holds that oligopolies and monopolies will be unable to exercise undesirable market power over the very long run because they will be attacked by competitors who will introduce new products and new production processes to get around the established firms' control of the market. An extreme version of this theory holds that anti-monopoly policy and public utility regulations are unnecessary as policies to influence behaviour in the very long run. Advocates worry that state intervention will inadvertently create entry barriers that will protect existing firms from the growth-creating process of creative destruction. They believe that government policies directed at minimizing entry barriers are the only industrial and competition policies that are needed.

Nationalization and regulation

Those who emphasize Schumpeter's theory argue that nationalization and public regulation are likely to defeat their own purposes in the long term by inhibiting the process of creative destruction. A government monopoly provides the most enforceable entry barrier. It may inhibit the introduction of new products, and of new ways to produce old products, that would have occurred when new firms attacked the entrenched positions of existing firms. Supporters of this view point to the former Soviet Union's need to buy technology from Western countries, and argue that the rapid development of new products and processes in the oligopolistic and monopolistic industries operating in market-oriented economies gives support to Schumpeter's view. Box 14.3 deals

---

Box 14.3 The great Microsoft antitrust case

Some of the greatest innovations in information and communications technology have been due to Bill Gates and his firm Microsoft. Gates is one of the world's wealthiest people. He is a classic entrepreneur who entered the PC software industry when it was new, fiercely competitive, and rapidly developing. His Windows operating system achieved instant customer approval and now dominates the industry.

In 1998 the US Department of Justice brought an antitrust suit against Microsoft for alleged monopoly practices. The firm was accused of tactics designed to make entry difficult for smaller firms selling specialized products that competed with some parts of Microsoft's array. In particular, when customers buy any new version of the Windows operating system, they are automatically provided with Microsoft's internet browser. This bundling of Microsoft products undoubtedly makes competition more difficult for smaller firms producing one type of product.

The suit reveals all the conflicting views that can be taken about competition and technical change.

- Technological innovations have transformed the lives of ordinary people several times since the first industrial revolution in the mid-eighteenth century.
- A new industry producing a wholly new range of products typically starts off as highly competitive, as did cars, aircraft, and computers. Soon, however, the winners in the race to expand and improve the range of products eliminate most of the weaker competitors. They emerge as oligopolists in a mature industry.
- The dominant firm in the technological race often establishes something close to a monopoly position. This dominance is partly a result of continued successful innovation—established oligopolies have been the source of much growth-inducing technological change over the past 150 years. It is also partly a result of the firm's ability to suppress competition from smaller upstart firms.
- Over the long haul, even if the oligopolist becomes something close to a monopolist, it cannot perpetuate its position indefinitely—new firms with new products eventually arise to challenge and unseat the established firms.

So how should the US government react? Should it constrain Microsoft in order to create more growth-enhancing competition? Or should it accept Microsoft's dominant position in the industry as the reward for its amazing record as an innovator? Should it accept Schumpeter's argument that, in the very long run, neither Microsoft nor any other dominant firm will be able to maintain its position unless it outperforms actual and potential competitors in the race to provide consumers with more, better, and cheaper products?

Faced with that decision, the US Department of Justice took the line that Microsoft's behaviour was designed to stifle competition. Later, a US appeals court took the opposite line. These early differences in legal opinion illustrate the difficulty in distinguishing successful competitive behaviour from behaviour designed to suppress competition. Later court hearings had found Microsoft guilty in some aspects of anticompetitive behaviour but not in others. The US Justice Department proposed a final judgment that

... will stop recurrence of Microsoft's unlawful conduct, prevent recurrence of similar conduct in the future, and restore competitive conditions in the personal computer operating system market by, among other things, prohibiting actions by Microsoft to prevent computer manufacturers and others from developing, distributing or featuring middleware products that are threats to Microsoft's operating system monopoly; creating the opportunity for independent software vendors to develop products that will be competitive with Microsoft's middleware products; requiring Microsoft to disclose interfaces and license protocols in order to ensure that competing middleware and server operating system products can interoperate with Microsoft's desktop operating systems; and ensuring full compliance with the [final judgment].

(For details of the final judgment and subsequent monitoring of implementation, see <www.usdoj.gov/atr/cases/ms_index.htm>)

European Union antitrust action against Microsoft continued. In 2004, the EU Commission fined Microsoft, and an appeal against this fine was rejected by the courts in 2007. Microsoft paid around €1.7 billion in fines and penalties. In December 2009, the EU competition authorities finally dropped their case after reaching an agreement that the software maker would offer customers a choice of rival web browsers.

with an important court case in which many of the issues relating to monopoly power and creative destruction arose.

Most people now accept this case against nationalisation. But some hold a less extreme version of Schumpeter's theory than that expressed above. They accept the obvious existence of creative destruction over the very long run, but hold that anti-monopoly and public utility regulation policies are needed because market power can be abused for a long time before being curtailed by creative destruction. These people argue that government policies are required to prevent monopolies from earning large profits and otherwise exploiting consumers over quite considerable periods of time.

A short-term/long-term trade-off?

Economists who accept both the force of the argument that monopolistic firms can earn large exploitative profits in the short term *and* Schumpeter's argument about the very long run face a policy dilemma. In the short term firms that gain monopoly power may earn very large profits at the expense of consumers. However, in the very long term attempts to control these monopolies may inhibit the creative destruction that helps to raise living standards through productivity growth.

The policy world is not a simple place, and policies that help to achieve desired goals over one time span must be constantly scrutinized for undesired effects over other time spans.

The costs of government intervention

We have seen that governments have many reasons to take action and many tools that help them to achieve their goals. However, to evaluate government intervention, we need to consider costs as well as benefits.

Large potential benefits do not necessarily justify government intervention, nor do large potential costs necessarily make it unwise. What matters are net benefits—the balance between benefits and costs.

Three types of cost of government intervention are important. These are costs that are internal to the government, costs that are external to the government but directly paid by others in the sector where the intervention occurs, and costs that are external to the government and felt more generally throughout the entire economy.

Internal costs

Everything the government does uses resources that must be paid for. It costs money when government inspectors visit plants to check on compliance with government-imposed health standards, industrial safety, or environmental protection. The inspectors and their support staff must be paid and their offices maintained. The salaries of the judges, clerks, and court reporters who are needed when an anti-monopoly case is heard are costs imposed by the regulation.

Armies of office workers, backed up by computerized information technology, keep track of income tax and VAT receipts. Inspectors take to the field to enforce compliance, and the courts deal with serious offenders. Unemployment and other benefits must be administered. Although the benefit payments themselves are transfer payments and so use no resources, administering their collection and disbursement does use resources.

Direct external costs

External costs are those that the government's action imposes on others; they may be either direct or indirect. Direct external costs fall on agents with whom the government is directly interacting. Regulation and control often add directly to the costs of producing goods. For example, firms must inspect machinery to ensure that it meets government safety standards. Anti-pollution laws often require producing firms to spend large sums on new non-polluting technologies and to incur a range of other smaller but cumulatively significant appliance costs. Much business activity is devoted to understanding, reporting, and contesting regulatory provisions. Occupational safety and environmental control have increased the number of employees not working on the shop floor. The costs of complying with tax laws can run to large sums each year. Firms, and wealthy individuals, spend substantial sums on lawyers and accountants to help them to comply with tax laws and choose tax-minimizing courses of action.

Quite apart from the actual cost to business, government intervention may reduce the incentive for experimentation, innovation, and the introduction of new products. Requiring advance government clearance before introducing a new method or product (on grounds of potential safety hazards or environmental impact) can reduce the incentive to develop it. New lines of investment may be chosen more for their tax implications than for their potential for reducing production costs and so contributing to productivity growth.

Indirect external costs

Indirect external costs are costs of the government's action that spread beyond those immediately affected by it—sometimes to the entire economy. Here is a sample of the many costs of this type.

Externalities

Ironically, government intervention to offset adverse externalities can create new adverse externalities. For example, government regulations designed to ensure the safety of new drugs delay the introduction of all drugs, including those that are safe. The benefits of these regulations are related to the unsafe drugs kept off the market. The cost includes the delayed availability of new safe drugs.

The shifting of taxes often causes major externalities. **Shifting** refers to the passing of the incidence of a tax from the person who initially pays it to someone else. The **incidence** refers to who actually bears the tax. One major problem with the use of taxes to achieve a social goal such as redistributing income is that market forces may shift the burden of the tax from the person who initially pays it to others. In Box 14.1, we studied the effects of a tax levied in a single market and concluded:

If the supply curve is positively sloped, and the demand curve negatively sloped, the burden of a tax is shared between producers and consumers.

This outcome does not depend on who actually makes the tax payment to the government. If producers initially pay the tax, the upward shift in the market supply curve will raise the price and pass some of the tax burden on to consumers. If consumers initially pay the tax, the downward shift in their after-tax demand curve will lower the price received by producers. This passes some of the burden on to producers.

There will also be repercussions in other markets. As the price of one product rises, the demand curves for substitutes will shift to the right, while the demand curves for complements will shift to the left. The resulting changes in their market prices will induce changes in prices charged and incomes earned in other related markets. Thus the effects of a tax on one market will spread throughout the economy, making the final distribution of the burden difficult to ascertain.

Inefficiencies

Many government interventions have some adverse efficiency effects. These have played an important part in the so-called supply-side criticisms of government policy, and we need to look at them in some detail.

First, consider a sales tax on a good produced under perfectly competitive conditions. The tax raises the

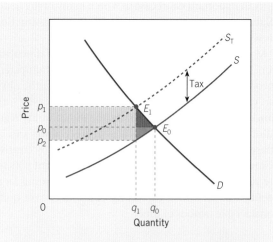

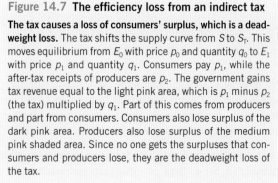

Figure 14.7 The efficiency loss from an indirect tax

The tax causes a loss of consumers' surplus, which is a dead-weight loss. The tax shifts the supply curve from S to S_T. This moves equilibrium from E_0 with price p_0 and quantity q_0 to E_1 with price p_1 and quantity q_1. Consumers pay p_1, while the after-tax receipts of producers are p_2. The government gains tax revenue equal to the light pink area, which is p_1 minus p_2 (the tax) multiplied by q_1. Part of this comes from producers and part from consumers. Consumers also lose surplus of the dark pink area. Producers also lose surplus of the medium pink shaded area. Since no one gets the surpluses that consumers and producers lose, they are the deadweight loss of the tax.

relative price that consumers face for that good, so they will buy less of it and more of other products. Production falls below the competitive equilibrium level, which is the one that maximizes the sum of consumers' and producers' surplus. The result, as shown in Figure 14.7, is a loss of consumers' surplus exactly analogous to the deadweight loss of monopoly.

This result applies to any taxes that affect the prices of products in different proportions and hence change relative prices. Thus it applies to VAT whenever different products are taxed at different rates. The key is that:

Consumers equate their marginal utilities to prices including tax, while producers equate their marginal costs to the price net of the tax. Hence, the tax causes some inefficiency, since the value that consumers place on the last unit consumed exceeds the marginal cost of making it.

Next consider an income tax. It creates some inefficiency by distorting the work–leisure choice. Employers pay one wage (pre-tax) and employees receive another wage (post-tax). Employees, reacting to after-tax wage rates, see a rate of substitution between work and leisure that differs from the rate implied by the pre-tax wage that the employer is prepared to pay.

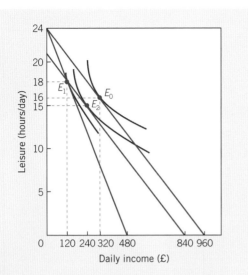

Figure 14.8 An income tax and the work–leisure choice

An income tax results in an inefficient choice between work and leisure. This person earns £40 an hour. His budget line runs from 24 hours (no work) to £960 (no sleep!). He maximizes utility at E_0 with 16 hours of leisure (8 hours of work) and income of £320 per day. An income tax of 50 per cent shifts his after-tax budget line to run from 24 hours to £480 (no sleep). He maximizes utility by moving to E_1 with 18 hours of leisure (6 hours of work) and a gross pay of £240. This yields him an after-tax income of £120. The government could raise its £120 through a tax that did not alter the income–leisure trade-off (say, a poll tax). The after-tax budget line in this case shifts in to 21 hours (the tax is the equivalent of 3 hours' work) and £840. The individual now moves from E_0 to E_2, consuming 15 hours of leisure (working 9 hours) and £240 worth of goods. E_2 is superior to E_1 because it lies on a higher indifference curve.

only tax that does not do so, under normal conditions, is the poll tax. It avoids the income tax's specific negative efficiency effects because the amount paid does not vary with the taxpayer's economic income or wealth or any of his or her economic decisions. It is precisely for this reason that most people find it *unacceptable*, on equity grounds, as anything other than a minor source of revenue. Furthermore, as explained in the footnote, the poll tax has inefficiencies of its own.[4]

Disincentive effects

If we consider a 'closed economy' where there is no possibility of emigration, marginal rates of up to 40 per cent or so do not seem to have strong disincentive effects. Economic theory makes no general prediction about how altering income tax rates in this range will affect the supply of effort. In Box 9.5 we showed that a rise in the wage rate might increase, or decrease, the supply of effort, and, similarly, a fall in the wage rate might have either effect. Now observe that the after-tax wage rate is lowered by a rise in the rate of income tax, and raised by a fall in the rate. It follows immediately that any given change in the rate of income tax may either raise or lower the supply of effort. At some point, however, high marginal tax rates begin to have more serious disincentive effects. As marginal rates approach 100 per cent, the disincentive effect becomes absolute.

In an open society, where emigration is possible, very high marginal rates of tax have major effects. Authors, artists, pop groups, and others who 'strike it rich' are given a strong incentive to emigrate to countries that will allow them to keep a much higher proportion of their incomes. Emigration of successful people of this type from the United Kingdom to the United States was significant between 1945 and 1980, when UK marginal rates of income tax were often double those in the United States.

From the point of view of maximizing tax revenues and reducing tax burdens on middle- and lower-income groups it would be better to have high income people still in the country paying tax rates of 40–50 per cent than out of the country avoiding much higher tax rates.

Governments throughout the world have come to accept that very high marginal rates of tax exert various

To understand the source of the inefficiency, compare the income tax with a **poll tax**, which takes the same lump sum from everyone. Because it is not related to income, a poll tax leaves the marginal rate of substitution between goods and leisure unaffected. The tax exerts no disincentive to work at the margin, and thus in this respect it is more efficient than the income tax.

Figure 14.8 demonstrates the inefficiency of an income tax. It shows that, other things being equal, each individual achieves a higher indifference curve when he or she is forced to pay a given amount of tax revenue through a poll tax, rather than through an income tax. The poll tax is more efficient in this respect because it leaves each person facing a choice at the margin that reflects the wage rate actually paid by employers in the labour market.

The importance of the figure lies in its demonstration that *any practical tax* has some negative efficiency effects, because it distorts relative price signals. Theoretically, the

---

[4] The argument given in the text that the poll tax imposes no inefficiencies requires several questionable assumptions. For example, the economy must be closed and everyone must actually pay the tax. In practice, however, a poll tax will have some negative efficiency effects. A large enough poll tax will cause some people to emigrate. It will also cause some people to choose jobs, and lifestyles, that facilitate evasion. People with no fixed address and no regular job find evasion easier than people who are stuck with one job and own their own house or apartment. Thus at the margin the poll tax will influence some people's job and residence decisions, which implies that it does have adverse efficiency effects.

Table 14.3 UK marginal rates of income tax (tax rate on an extra £1 of income)

Taxable income*	Marginal tax rate (%)	
	1978–9	2014–15
1,500	34	20
6,000	34	20
18,000	45	20
24,000	50	20
30,000	65	20
36,000	70	49
54,000	83	40
150,000	83	45

UK income taxes are less progressive than they used to be. In 2014–15 the 40 per cent tax rate set in at a taxable income of £31,866, and at 45 per cent for taxable incomes over £150,000. This is considerably lower than the high marginal tax rates that were applied after the Second World War, until the 1980s.

*Income after deducting allowances.
Source: ONS *Financial Statistics* and HM Treasury, *Budget Report*.

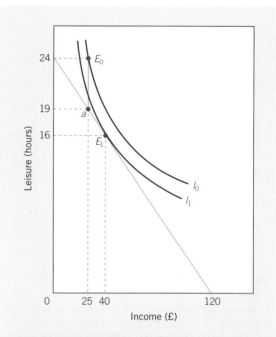

Figure 14.9 Disincentives of welfare schemes

Income-tested benefits provide disincentives to work. The individual is not employed but is receiving benefits of £25 per day from some income-related scheme. This puts him at point E_0, consuming 24 hours of leisure and receiving £25 pounds of income. He is now offered work at £5 per hour, presenting him with a budget line that ends at £120 (for 24 hours' work). In the absence of the benefit he would locate at E_1, consuming 16 hours of leisure (working 8 hours) and earning £40 of income. But for every £1 he earns he loses £1 of benefit, so the budget line starts at E_0 and is vertical to point a, where he is working 5 hours and still getting £25 but now all from work. Further work nets him £5 an hour, so the budget line has its normal slope below a. Since the indifference curve through E_1 is lower than the curve through E_0, his rational choice is not to work.

important disincentive effects. Table 14.3 shows marginal rates of income tax in the United Kingdom for 1978–9 and 2014–15 It is worth noting that the higher rate in 1978 was much lower than the highest marginal rate of 97.5 per cent levied in the United Kingdom in the period shortly after the Second World War. (This enormous rate included a surtax on investment income.) Also, a new higher marginal rate of 50 per cent came into force in April 2010 for taxable incomes of over £150,000 per annum, though this was reduced to 45 per cent in April 2013.

As with taxes, all other government interventions have some disincentive effects. For example, payments designed to help certain low income groups are often means tested. Sometimes, the welfare payments are reduced by £1 for every £1 of income received by welfare recipients. In effect, the person faces a marginal tax rate of 100 per cent on every unit of income earned up to the level of the benefit payments. The effect, called the *poverty trap*, is a severe disincentive to work, and we should not be surprised when people respond rationally to these market signals by avoiding work that pays less than the benefits they are receiving.

Say, for example, benefit payments are £25 a day and are cut by £1 for every £1 of income earned. If the person makes £5 a day, benefits fall to £20; if £10 is earned, benefits fall to £15, and so on. Only when more than £25 per day is earned will the person's disposable income begin to rise. Even if the benefits are reduced at a less sharp rate, say 50p per £1 earned, the disincentive of the high implicit tax rate is strong. Figure 14.9 illustrates this

disincentive effect by showing how such schemes induce many people to reject employment that they would have accepted if the schemes had not existed.

Benefit payments are required to help those in real need. However, if they are income related, they tend to discourage recipients from working.

This does not argue against welfare payments, but it does suggest that welfare schemes should be designed to balance costs and benefits.

Costs versus benefits

It is difficult to estimate the overall direct and indirect costs of general government activity. About the most that can be said is that both are not insignificant. The level of uncertainty is great enough that those who wish to reduce the scope of government activity can argue that these costs are high, while those who wish to maintain or enlarge the present scope of government can argue that the benefits greatly outweigh the costs.

The costs are often clearer when specific government activities are considered, rather than all activities together. For example, when it became generally accepted that high marginal rates of income tax had serious consequences, governments (eventually) moved to lower these rates. When it became accepted that government-run business enterprises were no more efficient than privately run ones, and often much less efficient, many governments moved to privatize the industries that they owned. Currently, a debate rages over the costs of environmental regulation. Although full indirect costs are hard to measure, most estimates do not show these costs to be prohibitive. But the costs and inefficiencies of direct mandates to specific firms have seemed large enough that governments have searched for more efficient, less costly methods. In many cases the best solution seems to be tradable pollution permits. The issue would be easier for governments to deal with in a closed economy. However, the economy is not closed and firms that have major costs of environmental regulation imposed on them by one government can argue, as many firms do argue, that they will lose out to competitors based in countries that do not have such stringent regulations. If that argument fails to convince policy makers, they can threaten to move their operations to such lower-cost countries.

So the lesson is that there is no general lesson about too much or too little government, but that government activity *is* costly and, in some circumstances, can be very costly. So every activity, existing or projected, needs to be assessed on its individual merits. Only if the benefits appear to outweigh the measurable costs, and the best guess about the unmeasurable costs, should the activity be initiated or continued.

Government failure

So far we have dealt with a government that is trying its best to achieve the goals that we laid out at the beginning of this chapter. It may impose costs, some expected and some unexpected, but it is seeking, as best it can, to achieve socially desirable goals.

Is this too naïve a view of government and the political process? Today, many observers of the political scene, including not a few economists, would answer with an emphatic yes.

Without doubt governments are far from perfect. This is not because bureaucrats and politicians are worse than other people—more stupid, more rigid, or more venal. Instead it is because they are like others, with flaws as well as virtues and with motives of their own. So having found potential net benefits from perfect but costly government intervention, the final issue is whether the imperfect governments that we encounter in the real world would achieve all, or even some, of these benefits. Where they do not succeed in achieving potential benefits that exceed the full direct and indirect costs, we speak of **government failure** to distinguish it from market failure.

Governments may sometimes make isolated mistakes, just as private decision-makers do. What is interesting, however, is why governments tend, under certain circumstances, to be more systematically in error than unhindered markets. There are many possible causes of systematic government failure.

Rigidities

Rules and regulations, tax rates, and spending policies are hard to change. However, market conditions change continually and often rapidly. A rule requiring the use of a certain method to reduce pollution may have made sense when the cost of that method was low. It may, however, become a wasteful rule when some alternative becomes a less costly method.

Today's natural monopolies are often made into tomorrow's competitive industries by technological innovations. For example, the near monopoly of the early railways was eliminated by the development of cheap road transport, and the falling cost of air transport is currently providing potent competition for surface transport in the movement of many products.

A centralized decision-taking body has difficulty in reacting to changing conditions as fast as decentralized decision-takers react to market signals.

Governments are often slow to admit mistakes even when they become aware of them. It is often politically easier to go on spending money on a project that has turned sour than to admit fault. A classic example was the development of Concorde, the supersonic airliner. Successive governments realized that it was an enormous money loser, but went on supporting it long after any chance of commercial success was gone.

Markets are much harsher in judging success. When people are investing their own money, the principle that bygones are bygones is usually followed. (See the discussion of *sunk costs* in Chapter 11.) No firm could raise fresh financial capital for what was currently a poor prospect just because the prospects had seemed good in the past. Nor could it do so because much money had already been spent on it, or because those who supported it in the past would lose face if it were now dropped.

Decision-makers' objectives

An important potential cause of government failure arises from the nature of the government's own objectives. Why is economists' advice followed closely in some cases, while it is systematically ignored in others? Governments are not faceless robots doing whatever economic analysis shows to be in the social interest. Instead they have their own objectives, which they may seek to maximize.

Governments undoubtedly do care about the social good to some extent, but public officials have their careers, their families, and their prejudices as well. Elected MPs and local councillors no doubt care about the public good, but they must also worry about being re-elected. The resulting problems are similar to the principal–agent issues mentioned earlier as a source of market failure. In the present case the *principals* are the public; they want governments to do certain things. However, their *agents*— elected and appointed—are motivated by considerations that pull against what the public wishes.

An important advance in understanding economic policy came from modelling governments as maximizers of their own welfare, and then incorporating them into theoretical models of the working of the economy. One of the pioneers of this development was the American economist James Buchanan (1919–2013), who was awarded the 1986 Nobel Prize in economics for his work in this field. The theory that he helped to develop is called *public choice theory*.

The key idea is to view the government as just another economic agent engaging in its own maximizing behaviour. When this view is adopted, there is still room for many competing theories, depending on what variables are in the government's preference or utility function (i.e. what things the government cares about and thus is trying to achieve). Consider the other two main decision-taking bodies in orthodox economics. Firms have only profits in their utility functions, and they seek to maximize these. Consumers have only goods and services in their utility functions, and they seek to maximize their satisfaction from consuming them. An analogous simplistic theory of the government allows only one variable in its utility function, the variable being votes! Such a government would take all its decisions with a view to maximizing its votes at the next election.

Public choice theory

Full-blown public choice theory deals with three maximizing groups. *Elected officials* seek to maximize their votes. *Civil servants* seek to maximize their salaries (and hence their positions in the hierarchy). *Voters* seek to maximize their personal level of satisfaction. To this end, voters look to the government to provide them with goods and services and income transfers that raise their personal utility. No one in this hypothetical world cares about the general public interest!

On the one hand, this is surely not a completely accurate characterization of motives. Elected statesmen have acted in what they perceive to be the public interest, hoping to be vindicated by history even if they know they risk losing the next election. Some civil servants have exposed inside corruption even though it cost them their jobs. And some high income individuals vote for the political party that advocates the most, not the least, income redistribution.

On the other hand, the characterization is close to the mark in many cases. Most of us have read of politicians whose only principle is 'What will get me most votes?' And many voters ask only 'What is in it for me?' This is why the theory can take us a long way in understanding what we see, even though real behaviour is more complex.

Here is one example. Why, despite strong advice from economists, have governments persisted in subsidizing agriculture for decades, until the current situation where many governments face problems from the high cost of farm subsidies and international pressure over the associated protectionist trade policies. Public choice theory looks at the gainers and the losers among the voters.

The gainers from agricultural supports are domestic farmers. They are a politically powerful group, and are aware of what they will lose if farm supports are reduced. They would show their disapproval of such action by voting against any government that even suggests it. The main domestic losers are the entire group of consumers. Although the losers are more numerous than the gainers, and although their total loss is large, each individual loser suffers only a small loss. For example, a policy that gives £50 million a year to British farmers need only cost each citizen £1 per year.[5] Citizens have more important things

---

[5] 'Why worry?' you may ask. 'Isn't the small loss to each consumer a reasonable price to pay?' It may be in this one case. The problem, however, lies not in one such policy, but in the cumulative effects of many. If each of many special-interest groups secures a policy that costs each member of the public a small amount, the total bill over all such policies can be, and in many countries is, very large indeed.

to worry about, and so do not vote against the government just because it supports farmers. As long as the average voters are unconcerned about, and often unaware of, the losses they suffer, the vote-maximizing government will ignore the interests of the many and support the interests of the few. The vote-maximizing government will consider changing the agricultural policy only when the cost of agricultural support becomes so large that ordinary tax-payers begin to count the cost. What is required for a pol-icy change, according to this theory, is that those who lose become sufficiently aware of their losses for this awareness to affect their voting behaviour.

Another group of losers from agricultural protection (which usually accompanies farm subsidies) is foreign farmers in countries that do not provide similar support. They are often excluded from overseas markets by import levies or quantitative import restrictions, or hurt by sub-sidies on foreign exports to their home markets. They are worse off as they are denied market access and thus receive a lower price for their products than they otherwise might. Clearly, foreign farmers do not have a vote and this can explain why domestic politicians do not give them much weight in making their decisions. However, this can change when key foreign countries get together and use their collective negotiating strength to negotiate better access to rich-country markets, perhaps in exchange for other concessions on market access. International organi-zations such as the World Trade Organization (WTO) are designed to provide a means whereby those in countries who suffer from policies adopted by other countries can exert pressure for these to be changed.

The ability of elected officials and civil servants to ignore the domestic public interest is strengthened by a phenomenon called **rational ignorance**. Many policy issues are extremely complex. For example, even the experts are divided when assessing the pros and cons of the United Kingdom's decision to stay out of the first wave of membership in the euro, the common European cur-rency. Much time and effort is required for a layperson even to attempt to understand the issue. Similar com-ments apply to the evidence for and against capital pun-ishment or lowering the age of criminal liability. Yet one person's vote has little influence on which party is elected, or on what they really will do about the issue in question once elected. So the costs of becoming well informed are large, while the benefits from voting on that knowledge are small. Thus, a majority of rational self-interested vot-ers will remain innocent of the complexities involved in most policy issues.

Who will be the informed minority? The answer is those who stand to gain or lose a lot from the policy, those with a strong sense of moral obligation, and those policy junkies who just like this sort of thing.

Inefficient public choices

A major principle of most people's idea of democracy is that each citizen's vote should have the same weight. One of the insights of public choice theory is that resource allocation based on the principle of one-person–one-vote will often be inefficient because it fails to take into account the *intensity of preferences*.

To illustrate this problem, consider three farmers, Al, Bob, and Charles. Farmers Al and Bob want the govern-ment to build an access road to each of their farms, each road to cost £6,000. Charles's farm is on the main road and so requires no new access road. Suppose that the road to Al's farm is worth £7,000 to Al and that the road to Bob's farm is worth £7,000 to Bob. Suppose that, under the current taxing rules, the cost of building each road would be shared equally among the three farmers—£2,000 each. It is efficient to build both roads, since each gener-ates net benefits of £1,000 (£7,000 gross benefits to the farmer helped, less £6,000 total cost). But each would be defeated 2–1 in a simple majority vote. (Bob and Charles would vote against Al's road; Al and Charles would vote against Bob's road.)

Now suppose that we allow Al and Bob to make a deal: 'I will vote for your road if you will vote for mine'. Although political commentators often decry such deals, the deal enhances efficiency. Both roads now get 2–1 majorities, and both roads get built. However, such deals can just as well reduce efficiency. If we make the gross value of each road £5,000 instead of £7,000 and let Al and Bob make their deal, each road will still command a 2–1 majority because the total cost is £4,000 to each farmer, while Al and Bob each gain £5,000 worth of road. However, it is socially inefficient to build the roads, since the gross value of each road is now only £5,000, while the cost is still £6,000. Al and Bob will be using democracy to appro-priate resources from Charles while reducing economic efficiency.

This case can be interpreted in a different way. Instead of being the third farmer, Charles might be all the other voters in the county. Instead of bearing one-third of the costs, Al and Bob might each bear only a small portion of the costs. To the extent that Al and Bob are able to go to the local government and forcefully articulate the ben-efits that they would derive from the roads, they may be able to use democracy to appropriate resources from tax-payers in general. Much of the concern with the power of 'special interests' stems from the fact that the institutions of representative democracy tend to be responsive to ben-efits that focus on particular, identifiable, and articulate groups. Often, the costs are diffused among all taxpayers, who hardly notice them and in any case are rationally ignorant about them.

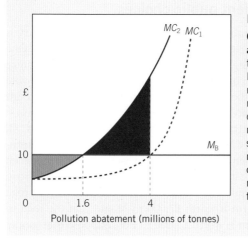

Figure 14.10 Government failure

Choice of an unnecessarily costly method of control reduces the optimal amount of abatement. Each tonne of pollution imposes a social cost of £10, so the marginal social benefit of abatement is £10 per tonne as shown by the M_B line. The most efficient method of control has a marginal cost curve of MC_1, making it socially optimal to prevent 4 million tonnes of pollution. The government misguidedly chooses an abatement procedure that has a marginal cost curve of MC_2. Optimal abatement is now only 1.6 million tonnes. If the government insists on having 4 million tonnes abated, there is a loss of the pink shaded area above marginal benefit curve and below the MC_2 curve. That loss may exceed the benefit, which is given by the blue shaded area between the M_B curve and the MC_2 curve. If so, the programme causes a net social loss. Having no programme would then be better than having the inefficient one imposed at too high a level of abatement.

The effects of government failure

Suppose that, for any of the reasons discussed above, the government makes a mistake in regulation. Say it mistakenly specifies a method of pollution control that is less effective than the best method. If it insists on the level of control appropriate to the best method, but chooses the poorer method, it can convert a social gain from control into a social loss. This possibility is illustrated in Figure 14.10.

If governments pursue their own objectives, such as vote maximizing, they may sometimes fail to act in the voters' interest by design rather than by mistake. If government economists foresee that a politically popular policy will increase the degree of market failure in the long term, while seeming beneficial in the short term, the government may adopt the harmful policy, despite the unfavourable long-run consequences. The government could plead in such cases that it was only being democratic in following the public will. But if governments are to follow exactly where public opinion leads, they do not require experts who are able to foresee consequences that are not obvious to casual observers who are rationally ignorant about complex issues.

CASE STUDIES

1. UK government policy goals

In this chapter we have discussed the goals of governments in rather general terms. In this case study we report the economic policy goals of the UK government as set out explicitly in the December 2013 Autumn Statement. The statement illustrates the complexity of what the government was trying to achieve, especially given the background of a plan to cut the budget deficit largely by cuts in public spending. There are obvious areas in which seemingly desirable goals can create conflicts. For example, redistributive taxes that support the goal of fairness may discourage productivity growth by discouraging enterprise, and desires for a sustainable environment may conflict with the wish to cap fuel prices.

Autumn Statement 2013 sets out the next steps in the government's long-term economic plan:

• *delivering sound public finances by setting out a fiscally-neutral Autumn Statement and further detail on how the government will ensure continued progress on reducing the deficit and debt beyond this Parliament*

• *supporting businesses to grow and create jobs through a major package of support with the cost of business rates and an updated National Infrastructure Plan*

• *equipping all young people to compete in the global economy by abolishing employer National Insurance contributions for most under-21 year olds, removing the cap on university places, reforming apprenticeships, and improving basic skills training*

• *helping hard-working people to keep more of the money they earn by reducing the impact of government policies on energy bills and freezing fuel duty for the rest of the Parliament*

• *increasing the incentives to work and providing a benefit system that is fair to those who need it and those who pay for it*

- *clamping down further on tax evasion, avoidance and aggressive tax planning, ensuring that those with the most in society make a fair contribution to reducing the deficit*

- *taking action to reduce levels of tax debt and to reduce fraud, error and debt in the benefit and tax credit systems*

On specific policies to support growth:

Autumn Statement 2013 announces that the government will:

- *support businesses to expand and create jobs by capping the Retail Prices Index increase in business rates to 2% in 2014–15 and extending the doubling of Small Business Rate Relief to April 2015*

- *provide additional support to the retail sector through a business rates discount of up to £1,000 in 2014–15 and 2015–16 for retail properties (including pubs, cafes, restaurants and charity shops) with a rateable value of up to £50,000, and a 50% discount from business rates for new occupants of previously empty retail premises for 18 months*

- *make it cheaper for businesses to employ young people by abolishing employer National Insurance contributions for under-21 year olds on earnings up to £813 per week, equivalent to the point at which higher rate tax is charged*

- *remove the cap on higher education student numbers to ensure that an estimated 60,000 more young people can go to university every year*

- *announce further reforms to make the most of the UK's science base, including an Emerging Powers Research Fund to promote scientific progress through collaborative research, and a new network of Quantum Technology Centres*

- *introduce a new tax relief for shale gas, and increase support for employee ownership and the creative industries*

- *improve the UK's infrastructure — National Infrastructure Plan 2013 sets out progress on delivery since 2010, a refreshed list of priority investments, a pipeline of public and private infrastructure projects to enable developers and supply chains to plan effectively, and progress on the UK Guarantees Scheme — including towards a Guarantee for a new nuclear power plant at Wylfa; in addition, the UK insurance growth action plan includes a commitment by UK insurers to work with partners to deliver at least £25 billion of investment in UK infrastructure over the next 5 years*

- *take further action to increase housing supply and support home ownership by funding infrastructure to unlock large housing sites; and by increasing the funding available for new affordable homes by raising local authority Housing Revenue Account borrowing limits, allocated on a competitive basis, and from the sale of vacant high-value social housing*

The following sets out the statement of 'fairness' of the policy stance:

The government's plan to build a stronger economy is underpinned by its commitment to delivering a fairer society. From April 2014, the income tax personal allowance will be increased to £10,000, and a typical basic rate taxpayer will pay £705 less income tax per year in cash terms than they would have in 2010–11. Income inequality is at its lowest level since 1986 and the proportion of workless households is at its lowest since 1996.

Autumn Statement 2013 sets out further action to support household incomes, help people into work, and ensure that businesses and individuals contribute their fair share to the consolidation.

Autumn Statement 2013 announces that the government will:

- *freeze fuel duty for the remainder of this Parliament, saving the average motorist £11 every time they fill their tank by 2015–16; by the end of the Parliament, average pump prices will be 20 pence per litre lower than under pre-2010 plans*

- *deliver an average saving of £50 in household bills by reducing the impact of government policies on energy bills, while maintaining support for the poorest families and providing new home owners with incentives worth up to £1,000 to undertake energy efficiency measures*

- *cap the average increase in regulated rail fares for 2014 in line with the Retail Prices Index, complementing the decision by the Mayor of London to cap average fare increases in London for 2014*

- *allow married couples and civil partners to transfer £1,000 of their income tax personal allowance to their spouse where neither is a higher rate taxpayer — worth up to £200 in 2015-16 to benefiting eligible couples*

- *provide free school meals for all infant school pupils in reception, year 1 and year 2*

- *provide more support to the young unemployed and implement a new Help to Work scheme for the long-term unemployed—to encourage work and ensure that the welfare system is fair to those who need it and to those who pay for it*

(*Source:* HM Treasury, *Autumn Statement 2013*, Cm 8747, December 2013)

2. Crash landing for BAA

UK airports used to be owned by the government, but in 1986 they were privatized under the ownership of BAA (formerly known as the British Airports Authority). BAA owned many of the United Kingdom's main airports, including Heathrow, Gatwick, and Stansted. BAA was itself taken over by an international consortium led by Ferrovia of Spain in 2006.

Concerns grew that there was excessive concentration in the provision of airport services, and the case was referred to the UK Competition Commission. Their report[6] gave the following summary of their investigation:

1. *The Competition Commission (CC) has concluded that BAA Limited's (BAA's) common ownership of airports in south-east England and lowland Scotland gives rise to adverse effects on competition (AECs) in connection with the supply of airport services by BAA. It has also concluded that a number of other features of the relevant markets give rise to AECs, namely:*

    (a) Heathrow Airport's position as the only significant hub airport in the South-East or indeed the UK;

    (b) Aberdeen Airport's comparatively isolated geographical position combined with other factors that make it unattractive to serve a catchment area of Aberdeen's size with more than one airport;

    (c) aspects of the planning system;

    (d) aspects of government policy; and

    (e) the current regulatory system for airports.

2. *The CC has concluded that a package of remedies would be effective in remedying the AECs identified:*

    (a) the divestiture of both Stansted Airport and Gatwick Airport to different purchasers;

    (b) the divestiture of either Edinburgh Airport or Glasgow Airport;

    (c) the strengthening of consultation procedures and provisions on quality of service at Heathrow, until a new regulatory system is introduced;

    (d) undertakings in relation to Aberdeen, to require the reporting of relevant information and consultation with stakeholders on capital expenditure; and

    (e) recommendations to the Department for Transport in relation to economic regulation of airports.

The report notes that:

BAA's seven airports together account for over 60 per cent of all passengers using UK airports. More significantly, Heathrow, Gatwick, Stansted and Southampton account for 90 per cent of airport passengers in south-east England (in which for the purpose of our analysis we include Southampton), and Edinburgh, Glasgow and Aberdeen account for 84 per cent of airport passengers in Scotland.

On BAA's performance the report is very critical:

In our view, a number of aspects of the performance of the BAA Scottish airports can be attributed to the AECs we have identified. We found a much slower development of routes at all three Scottish airports than at other regional airports, particularly until the involvement of the

Scottish Government in its *Air Route Development Fund (RDF) in 2002; and a lack of ambition in the development of Aberdeen, through underinvestment, poor facilities, and use of cash generated there elsewhere in BAA. We have also noted that BAA's Scottish airports, particularly Aberdeen, are more profitable than its designated airports, and that their prices are relatively high, even though BAA's stated policy has been to increase prices below changes in the RPI in order, BAA told us, to reduce the risk that the airports might be designated for formal price-cap regulation. Price reductions have been greater at Glasgow, due to competition from Prestwick, than at Edinburgh, which has faced little competition.*

We have found that at the south-east airports BAA currently shows a lack of responsiveness to the interests of airlines and passengers that we would not expect to see in a business competing in a well-functioning market, but which, in our view, is also attributable to weaknesses in the regulatory system. This is evidenced in BAA's approach to planning capital expenditure, including weaknesses in consultation and lack of responsiveness to the differing needs of its airline customers, and hence passengers, and the consequences for the quantity, quality, location and timing of investment. Although the process of Constructive Engagement introduced by the CAA has undoubtedly had some positive effects at Heathrow and Gatwick, it seems to us, from our recent regulatory review of these airports and from significant other evidence, to have been conducted in a way which excludes genuine two-way dialogue and exchange of views. Its weaknesses include asymmetry of information; the scope for BAA to take advantage of the differing requirements of individual airlines; its control over the timetable for releasing information and conducting discussion; and the lack of a dispute resolution mechanism. Although there is evidence of some recent improvements in consultation procedures at Heathrow following the Q5 reviews, we remain concerned about BAA's general processes for consulting on capital expenditure, including on major capital expenditure programmes important to the competitive position of airlines. Our Stansted Q5 inquiry also suggested apparent inadequacies in BAA's consultation processes: before the Stansted Q5 review was referred to us, the process of Constructive Engagement with airlines at Stansted had failed and been terminated by the CAA, and the evidence we received during the course of our Stansted inquiry suggested scope for significant savings in capital expenditure.

Lack of responsiveness to users is also evidenced in the apparent unwillingness to consider options of separate terminal development, co-investment or longer-term contracts; a failure to ensure operating excellence, including a failure to market test some key activities and the likelihood of consequent higher costs than would be expected in a more competitive environment; and deficiencies in the level and quality of service, as shown also by the continued public concern about the effects of

---

[6] BAA *Airports Market Investigation: A Report on the Supply of Airport Services by BAA in the UK*, Competition Commission, 19 March 2009.

shortage of capacity, particularly at Heathrow. BAA also has a financial structure with a dependence on a single highly-geared group parent balance sheet that could constrain the ability of the airports adequately to invest or maintain service standards.

As a direct result of this report, BAA put some of its airports up for sale. It has since sold Gatwick, Stansted, and Edinburgh airports. In October 2012, the company was renamed Heathrow Airport Holdings Limited, though it retains ownership of Southampton, Glasgow, and Aberdeen airports in addition to Heathrow.

What is clear from this case is that the competition authorities have substantial powers to investigate specific industries from a competition perspective and to force through substantial changes when this is perceived to be in the public interest.

Conclusion

Do governments intervene too little, or too much, in response to market failure? This question reflects one aspect of the continuing debate over the role of government in the economy.

Over the last three decades or so in most of the advanced industrial countries the mix of free-market determination and government ownership and regulation has been shifting towards more market determination, but this trend is not universal. No one believes that government intervention can, or should, be reduced to zero. Do we still have a long way to go in reversing the tide of big intrusive government that flowed through most of the twentieth century? Or perhaps we have gone too far and have given some things to the market that governments could do better? These are some of the great social debates of the early decades of the twenty-first century, especially in light of the financial crisis of 2007–8 and the resulting recession in 2008–9, and the increased role of governments that these events triggered.

SUMMARY

Government objectives

- Governments seek to protect life and property, improve economic efficiency, protect individuals from others and (sometimes) from themselves, influence the rate of economic growth, and stabilize the economy against fluctuations in national income and the price level.

- Policies for equity include making the distribution of income and wealth somewhat less unequal.

- Equity, efficiency, and growth often come into conflict. Policies to increase equity may reduce efficiency and/or growth, while policies to increase efficiency or growth may make some situations less equitable.

Tools and performance

- Governments may seek to achieve their policies using the tools of taxes, spending, rules and regulations, and public ownership.

The costs of government intervention

- Government activity incurs many types of cost. Internal costs refer to the government's own costs of administering its policies. Direct external costs refer to the costs imposed on those directly affected by these policies in such terms as extra production costs, costs of compliance, and losses in productivity. Indirect external costs refer to the efficiency losses that spread throughout the whole economy as a result of the alteration in price signals caused by government tax and spending policies.

Government failure

- As well as showing the potential for benefits to exceed costs in a world where the government functioned perfectly, it is necessary to consider the likely outcome in the imperfect world of reality. Government failure—not achieving some possible gains—can arise because of rigidities causing a lack of adequate response of rules and regulations to changing conditions, poorer foresight on the part of government regulators compared with private participants in the market, and government objectives—such as winning the next election—that conflict with such objectives as improving economic efficiency.

TOPICS FOR REVIEW

- The goals of government policy
- Measures of inequality at a point in time and over time
- Pre-tax and post-tax distribution of income
- Direct and indirect taxes
- Exhaustive expenditures and transfer payments

- Progressive, regressive, and proportional taxes
- The benefits and costs of government intervention
- Sources of government failure
- Public choice theory
- Rational ignorance

QUESTIONS

1 What inefficiencies will be caused by (*a*) VAT, (*b*) the personal income tax, (*c*) farm subsidies, (*d*) free health care, (*e*) free elementary school education, (*f*) welfare payments to non-working persons. Explain why such inefficiencies do not provide *sufficient* reasons to end the activity.

2 How many rules, regulations, prohibitions, and other 'command-type' tools of government policy can you think of that could be replaced by market-based incentive schemes?

3 Can you think of government programmes that would have effects on all three goals of *equity*, *efficiency*, and *growth*? Select those programmes that have desirable effects on some and undesirable effects on others of these three goals. (Assume that your equity criterion is to have a less unequal distribution of income.) Discuss the trade-offs involved in these policy conflicts.

4 Discuss the relative efficiency and equity effects of two programmes designed to assist certain needy groups. One programme provides coupons that reduce the purchase price of groceries by 50 per cent. (The shop returns the coupons to the government and gets back the discount that it gave to the coupon holder.) The other programme gives a money income supplement that has the same value as the food coupons.

5 List some things that *only* governments can do and some things that the government can do better than the private sector. Can you think of anything that the British government did forty years ago, or that it does now, that the private sector could probably do better? Can you think of anything that the private sector did forty years ago, or is doing now, that the government could probably do better?

6 Discuss the distinction between the initial incidence of a tax and the ultimate bearer of the tax.

7 Why is a role for government inevitable even in a market economy?

8 What difficulties arise in determining and implementing an optimal government intervention in the economy?

9 What are the arguments for and against government provision of health and education?

10 What government policies might best encourage economic growth?

MACRO
ECONOMICS

PART FIVE

MACROECONOMICS: ISSUES AND FRAMEWORK

CHAPTER 15

MACROECONOMIC ISSUES AND MEASUREMENT

So far in this book we have analysed individual markets or firms. Now we look at the economy as a whole. What caused the major recession in many countries in 2008–9? Why was the recovery so slow? What can governments do to reduce such undesirable events and does it matter that governments may incur large fiscal deficits when trying to stimulate their economies to recover from a recession? Why do some economies grow with steady increases in their total outputs and living standards while others do not? What harm do inflations do? Why do many economies undergo modest inflations while others encounter very rapid ones? What is meant by 'monetary policy'? How do central banks, such as the Bank of England, use their monetary policies to influence economic behaviour and what are their objectives in doing so? All of these are issues addressed by macroeconomics—issues that will be covered in the chapters ahead.

In this chapter we begin our study of the economy as a whole by introducing some key issues and concepts.

In particular, you will learn that:

- Macroeconomics looks at the economy as a whole, dealing with such aggregate phenomena as growth in total output and living standards, commonly called 'economic growth', business cycles, changes in the average level of all prices – which is called inflation when prices rise and deflation when prices fall – unemployment, changes in the productivity of the labour force, and total imports, total exports, and the balance between them.

- The macroeconomics we develop in the next few chapters focuses on cycles in economic activity, whereas growth theory (covered in Chapter 26) focuses on determinants of long-run trends.

- The total output of the economy is called its gross domestic product, or GDP for short.

- GDP refers to the value of what is produced in this country, while gross national income or GNI (formerly called gross national product or GNP) refers to the income accruing to UK residents, including net income from overseas assets.

- GDP can be measured in three ways: as the sum of values added by all producers, as the sum of income claims generated in producing goods and services, or as the spending on all final goods and services produced.

- The GDP gap is the difference between actual real GDP and its potential or trend value.

- GDP is a specific measure of output in the market economy, and is not a measure of welfare or happiness.

In this chapter we explain how macroeconomics differs in approach from the microeconomics of the first half of this book and outline the main issues addressed. We then look in detail at how the production of the economy as a whole, called its GDP, is measured before discussing the interpretation of this and some related measures. In subsequent chapters we are concerned with explaining how GDP is determined, and what government policy can do to influence it. Growth theory, which we discuss in Chapter 26, is about what determines the long-term trend in GDP. The traditional focus of macroeconomic analysis, which we deal with first, is mainly on the short term and the issue of what explains deviations of output from its long term trend level.

We largely use the United Kingdom as an example in this chapter, but the principles involved apply equally to other countries. In later chapters we include more examples from other countries.

What is macroeconomics?

Macroeconomics is the study of how the economy behaves in broad outline without dwelling on much of its interesting, but sometimes confusing, detail. Macroeconomics is largely concerned with the behaviour of economic *aggregates*, such as the entire nation's total output—its GDP, its total investment, and its total exports and its imports. It is also concerned with the average price of all goods and services, rather than the prices of specific products. These aggregates result from activities in many different markets and from the behaviour of different groups of decision-makers such as households, governments, and firms. Note that while microeconomics deals with individual consumers, in macroeconomics the corresponding decision unit is the household defined as all people living under one roof and involved in joint financial decisions. In contrast, *microeconomics* deals with the behaviour of individual markets, such as those for wheat, computer chips, or strawberries, and with the detailed behaviour of many different sets of producers and consumers.

In macroeconomics we add together the value of cornflakes, beer, cars, strawberries, haircuts, and restaurant meals, along with the value of all other goods and services produced, to obtain the nation's aggregate *national product*. We also average the prices of all goods and services and discuss the *general price level* for the entire economy—usually just called the price level. In practice, the averages of several different sets of prices are used. The UK has two standard measures of the price level. One is known as the Retail Price Index (RPI) and the other is the Consumer Price Index (CPI). Other countries mainly use the term CPI for their main price index. An appendix to this chapter discusses how the RPI is calculated.

We know full well that an economy that produces much wheat and few cars differs from one that produces many cars but little wheat. We also know that an economy with cheap wheat and expensive cars differs from one with cheap cars and expensive wheat. When studying aggregates and averages, some valuable detail is lost but the big picture may become clearer.

In macroeconomics we look at the broad range of events affecting the economy as a whole. When national product rises, the outputs of most firms, and the incomes of most people, usually rise with it. When interest rates rise, most borrowers, including firms and homeowners, have to make bigger payments on their debts, while many savers will get a higher return on their savings. When the price level rises, virtually everyone in the economy is forced to make adjustments because of the lower value of money. When the unemployment rate rises, workers are put at increased risk of losing their jobs and suffering losses in their incomes. These movements in economic aggregates are strongly associated with the economic well-being of most households: the health of the sectors in which they work and the prices of the goods that they purchase. These associations between the health of the macro economy and the economic fortunes of many people are one reason why macroeconomic aggregates such as output, inflation, and unemployment are often in the news.

We also study how governments can use what are called their *monetary and fiscal policies* to influence economic activity when they are worried about recessions, and to dampen it down when they are worried about inflationary pressures caused by booms. The experience of the 2008–9 recession and the subsequent very slow recovery makes clear that there may be limits on what policy makers can achieve. Monetary policy-makers found that lowering interest rates nearly to zero did not have the hoped for effect on economic activity, and fiscal policy makers were criticized when deficits ballooned.

Why do we need macroeconomics?

We need a separate subject called macroeconomics because there are forces that affect the economy as a whole that cannot be fully or simply understood by analysing individual markets and individual products. A problem that is affecting all firms, or many workers, in different industries, such as the major recession of 2008–9, may need to be tackled at the level of the whole economy, or indeed by cooperation between several countries. Certainly, if circumstances are common across many sectors of the economy, analysis at the level of the whole economy may help us to understand what is happening.

Box 15.1 sets out a report about the progress of the UK economy. This is typical of the comments that appear

Box 15.1 The UK macroeconomy as seen by a policy-maker

The following is an extract from a statement made by Mark Carney, Governor of the Bank of England, at the Inflation Report press conference in November 2013. By the time you have finished studying macroeconomics you will understand all this much better. For now, just notice that he is referring to what is going on in the UK economy in terms of all the concepts that we discuss in this chapter: growth of GDP, employment, unemployment, consumer spending, investment, real wages, productivity, and inflation. The language is exactly what you will need to understand if you want to follow news reports and other statements by policy-makers or other commentators. The state of the economy will change over time but the ways in which it is discussed and analysed change little, and our goal in this chapter is to help you learn and understand this language.

Inflation is now as low as it has been since 2009. Jobs are being created at a rate of 60,000 per month. The economy is growing at its fastest pace in 6 years. For the first time in a long time, you don't have to be an optimist to see the glass as half full. The recovery has finally taken hold.

It is welcome that the economy is growing again, but a return to growth is not yet a return to normality. Nearly one million more people are out of work than in the years before the financial crisis. Many others in part time work would prefer to be working full time. Real wages are not yet increasing. And the economy remains 2.5% smaller than it was in 2008. A strong and sustained recovery is needed to put people back in work and use up the slack in the economy.

A sustained recovery requires a revival of business investment. So far the upswing in growth has been driven by a modest recovery in consumer spending and a revival in housing investment. That is not surprising—we cannot expect to see strong export demand from the UK's major trading partners, and business investment typically takes time to pick up during recoveries.

The eventual recovery in business investment will be supported by the continuing improvement in credit conditions as our banking system gains in strength, and by reduced uncertainty about future prospects. While recent surveys of investment intentions have been encouraging, the handover from household to business spending may not be smooth.

Quarterly growth rates of GDP are likely to ease back a little next year and, over the forecast horizon, growth is likely to remain modest compared to past recoveries. A sustained recovery requires price stability. CPI inflation has

fallen back unexpectedly sharply, to 2.2% in October. It may tick up slightly in coming months as recently announced utility price increases take effect. But the lower starting point, an appreciation of sterling in recent months, and persistently weak domestic price pressures mean that inflation is projected to be significantly lower than in August. Under the assumption that Bank Rate follows a path implied by market yields, the 2% target is reached a full year earlier and inflation is expected to remain persistently a little below the target in the later part of the forecast period. The MPC assesses the chance of inflation being at or above 2.5% towards the end of next year to be only around one in three—much lower than in August. The MPC also judges that inflation expectations remain sufficiently well anchored. (The monetary policy committee, the MPC, has the task of setting monetary policy for the Bank of England. It was established in 1997 and is discussed in detail in later chapters.)

A sustained recovery requires confidence that exceptionally stimulative monetary policy will be maintained in the face of weak foreign demand and on-going repair of household, bank and government balance sheets...

In line with the unexpected strength of demand, the unemployment rate has fallen a little more rapidly than expected in August. That is to be welcomed: 100,000 more people are in work as a result. The MPC continues to make the conservative assumption that productivity recovers only gradually so that none of the gap relative to its pre-crisis path is closed over the forecast period. As a result, stronger near-term growth causes unemployment to fall faster than expected in August. ... Already, the Bank has revised up its view of the average hours people want to work, which implies somewhat more slack in the labour market than previously assumed. Our views on productivity will also evolve as the recovery progresses.

With the recovery taking hold, our task now is to secure it. The Bank will remain vigilant to risks to financial stability from the housing sector, in particular from rapid increases in house prices and household leverage ... We will continue the process of repairing the financial sector. And we will continue to provide exceptional monetary stimulus so that British households and businesses have, for the first time in a long time, the confidence not just that the glass is half full, but that it will be filled. (Mark Carney, Inflation Report Press Conference Opening Remarks, *November 2013.)*

whenever there are new data, a policy announcement, or a new assessment by some group. Once we have completed our exposition of macroeconomics, you should be able to understand such reports and critically assess their content. The emphasis in the media will change as events

change, but the framework that macroeconomics provides will prepare you to monitor events in the economy as a whole and in the wider world for yourself.

Let us now look at some of the issues that are best studied in a macroeconomic context.

Major macroeconomic issues

Economic growth

Both total and per capita output have risen on average for many decades in most industrial countries. These long-term trends have produced rising living standards for the typical citizen. In the United Kingdom the real value of the average wage doubled in the twenty years between 1953 and 1973. It stagnated for a while in the 1970s, but then grew steadily again from the 1980s until the end of the first decade of the twenty-first century. There was a pause in growth of real wages during the 2008–9 recession, and falls in average real wages continued until at least 2013, but a return to a positive growth rate was expected after that.

Long-term growth is the predominant determinant of living standards and the material constraints facing a society from decade to decade and generation to generation. We discuss some of the influences on long-term growth in Chapter 26. Macroeconomics has traditionally taken the trend in output as given and looked at how to minimize deviations from that trend. However, in recent years there has been discussion of whether the policies used to stabilize activity may also influence the long-term trend. Among the most important issues in macroeconomics is identifying policies that increase the chances that worldwide growth will continue without the type of slowdown that happened in the 1970s or the serious recessions of the early 1980s, early 1990s, and 2008–9. Thus, growth is a clear objective of macroeconomic policy.

Productivity

Economic growth can be achieved either by using more inputs, such as increased capital or numbers of workers, or by getting more output for any given amount of inputs. The latter is known as **productivity growth**. Increasing productivity is a central target of most governments as this is the most obvious way to make per capita real incomes grow. Labour productivity (calculated as either output per worker or output per hour worked) is especially important in this regard, as growth in this is a necessary condition for sustained growth of real wages. Those who do not work do not produce, so the real living standards of the entire population are ultimately determined by the output per head of each of those who are in work. Labour productivity can increase if workers have more capital to work with, but over the long term what most matters is technical progress.

One of the central goals of the UK government in the first decade of the twenty-first century was: 'raising the sustainable rate of productivity growth, through reforms that promote enterprise and competition, enhance flexibility and promote science, innovation, and skills'.[1] None of the policies listed in this quotation would traditionally have been considered part of the macro policy toolbox, which focuses on using monetary and fiscal policy to affect total demand for the nation's output . Rather, these would be considered supply-side policies—policies that seek to influence the nation's overall productivity and thus its ability to produce more output. But a key point to note is that modern governments, at least up to the 2008–9 recession, have put much greater emphasis on supply-side policies to foster economic growth and living standards than they did in the past.

Business cycles

The economy tends to move in a series of ups and downs, called *business cycles*, rather than in a steady pattern. The 1930s saw the greatest worldwide economic depression in the twentieth century, with nearly one-fifth of the UK labour force unemployed for an extended period. In contrast, the twenty-five years following the Second World War were a period of sustained economic growth, with only minor interruptions caused by modest recessions. Then the business cycle returned in more serious form. There have been four major recessions in the United Kingdom during the past four decades (1973–5, 1979–81, 1990–2, 2008–9), and most other major countries have experienced a similar pattern. From 1992 to 2008 there was no UK recession in the technical sense that there were not two successive quarters in which the GDP actually fell, but there were still cyclical variations in the rate of growth of national output. In 2009, however, another recession was experienced as the UK's GDP fell by around 5 per cent.

During recessions many businesses go bust, while profits fall for most of the survivors. In contrast, during a boom demand for most products rises, profits rise, and most businesses find it easy to expand. Governments sometimes claim that their policies will bring stable growth and an end to cycles, but business cycles have been around for a long time, and most economists now believe that some cyclical variation in aggregate activity is inevitable. Nonetheless the government's anti-cyclical policies do matter; for example, the 2008–9 downturn would most likely have been much worse without aggressive interventions from policy-makers. Also, there is a vigorous debate about the best policies for the countries of the EU to adopt to help them recover from the prolonged period of low output and high unemployment

---

[1] *Pre-Budget Report*, HM Treasury, December 2005, p.3.

that began in 2009 after the financial crisis and lasted for several years afterwards.

Macroeconomics as a subject was invented to help produce policies that could ameliorate economic fluctuations. Much of what follows is devoted to explanations of why the economy goes through these ups and downs, and what, if anything, the government can do about them.

Unemployment

A recession in economic activity causes an increase in unemployment. Indeed, it was the great depression of the 1930s with its accompanying high unemployment that led to the establishment of the subject now known as macroeconomics, and unemployment is still a central concern of policy-makers and economists. During that time UK unemployment rose to nearly 20 per cent of the labour force, and even higher levels were reached in some other countries. Although in the 1950s and 1960s unemployment was consistently very low in most industrial countries, higher unemployment returned in the 1980s and 1990s. UK unemployment reached peaks of 12.2 per cent in 1986 and 10.8 per cent in 1993 in the two recessions, while unemployment in France and Germany reached postwar highs of 12.5 per cent and 11.7 per cent, respectively, in 1997. In June 2002 Japanese unemployment reached 5.4 per cent, a level which had not seen there since the Second World War. By the mid-2000s unemployment had fallen to a thirty-year low in Britain, but it was still relatively high in several European countries, such as Spain, Germany, and France. A new bout of high unemployment occurred in many countries from 2008 onwards. Aggregate unemployment is thus back on the agenda as a major policy issue, but even in those countries where it is not such a major problem as in the past, there are still big concerns about youth unemployment.

The main method of reducing aggregate unemployment that economists developed early in the twentieth century was for governments to increase their spending and reduce taxes. Such deliberate use of government spending and taxes to influence the economy is known as **fiscal policy**. We will discuss later why many governments have found it necessary to raise taxes and cut spending even though they have depressed output and high unemployment in their economies.

Inflation

The annual UK inflation rate was over 25 per cent in 1975. Inflation at that rate causes retired people who are living on incomes that are fixed in money terms, and those who have made savings deposits or bought life insurance policies, both of which were fixed in money value, to have their living standards, or their wealth, cut in half every three years! The government of Margaret Thatcher was elected in 1979 on the promise of adopting policies that would eliminate inflation from the British economy. Inflation did fall below 5 per cent by 1984, but it rose again to around 10 per cent before the end of the decade. By the late 1990s active government policies had bought the annual rate of inflation down to around 2–3 per cent, which was the lowest rate seen since the early 1960s.

In May 1997 the incoming Labour government set a target level of inflation of 2.5 per cent and gave the Bank of England the power to set interest rates in order to achieve this target[2]. But the overall power to determine monetary policy was given to the newly formed Monetary Policy Committee (MPC), chaired by the Governor of the Bank and composed of five senior officials of the Bank and four outsiders appointed by the government. The MPC sets monetary policy, while the Bank carries it out by such means as setting interest rates and buying and selling securities on the open market. Since this ability to set and carry out monetary policy is placed in different hands in different countries, it is simplest to use the generic team 'the Bank' to cover all those who set and carry out monetary policy. We adopt this procedure here and refer to the MPC separately from the Bank only when the distinction is relevant. Thus in our coverage:

'the Bank' refers to those who set and carry out monetary policy.

From 1997 to 2002 inflation stayed within one percentage point of the target, as intended. From 2003 onwards, the inflation target was set at 2 per cent inflation using a slightly different measure of inflation. (We discuss the details in Chapter 25.) Between 2007 and 2013 there were several episodes when inflation was more than one percentage point above the official target, but the 2 per cent target remained in place until at least 2015.

Swings in economic activity have usually been accompanied by swings in the inflation rate, with booms being accompanied by increases and recessions by decreases. Conversely, government policies designed to affect the level of economic activity have had effects on inflation. Attempts to reduce a high inflation rate have tended to bring about recessions. Alternatively, attempts to stimulate economic activity have often been accompanied by increases in inflation. The rise in inflation during boom times has often led policy-makers to raise interest rates or taxes in order to bring inflation

---

[2] Before that the official interest rate was set by the Chancellor of the Exchequer.

under control. When inflation falls during and immediately after a recession, policy-makers have often felt that they have the leeway to stimulate the economy again—but not so much as to cause a resurgence of inflationary pressures. Hence, they have to tread carefully to achieve a suitable balance between stimulus and contraction, and we will learn later that timing policy interventions in order to achieve a desired outcome is not a simple matter.

Government budget deficits

The balance of the government's budget is said to be in deficit when it is spending more than it is raising by way of taxes and in surplus when it is spending less than it is raising. This balance can be looked at in two ways. First, what is its long-term average? Second, what is its cyclical behaviour? Because tax revenues fluctuate over the cycle, falling as total incomes earned fall in recessions and rising as total incomes earned rise in recoveries, the budget balance varies cyclically. Deficits tend to rise in recession and fall, and possibly even turn into surpluses, during recoveries.

Whatever their cause, deficits have to be financed by government borrowing. If this is from the public, it raises the national debt as the public lends money to the government that it might otherwise have spent itself. If it is from the Central Bank it is inflationary because the Bank creates new money that it lends to the government (without any necessary expectation of being repaid) while no one else has to reduce spending.

In the UK the long-term average has been a deficit. Indeed, with the exception of three brief periods (1970, 1988–9, and 1999–2001), the government has had a *budget deficit* every year since the Second World War. The deficit continued throughout the 1990s and the early 2000s, although the government was always projecting a return to surplus a few years further ahead. Owing mainly to falling tax revenues and higher unemployment-related benefits caused by the recession, the budget deficit in 2009–10 was above 10 per cent of GDP. The new UK government elected in June 2010 adopted as a major goal the elimination of the budget deficit by 2015–16[3]. Four countries in the EU—Ireland, Portugal, Spain, and Greece—had even more pressing deficit problems. The Greek deficit was so serious that it threatened default on the interest due on government borrowing, and a massive loan from other Eurozone countries had to be arranged.

In a serious recession governments that have already been running a deficit face a cruel dilemma. To stimulate the economy out of its recession more government spending and resulting large deficits are called for, but the effect of rising debt in the face of an already large amount of such debt can be crippling in the long run. In later chapters, we will discuss how the budget deficit affects the economy and the debate over the role of the government budget that is central to macroeconomics.

Interest rates

In addition to fiscal policy, government (or the central bank, where this is independent of government) has available the tools of monetary policy. **Monetary policy** in normal times involves setting a specific interest rate in order to influence the economy. High interest rates are a symptom of a tight monetary policy. When interest rates are high, firms find it more costly to borrow, and this makes them more reluctant to invest. Households with mortgages or bank loans are also hit by high interest rates since it costs more to make their loan repayments. Hence, high interest rates tend to reduce demand in the economy—firms invest less and those with mortgages have less to spend.

Low interest rates tend to stimulate demand, but in the 2008–9 recession interest rates were so low that they could go no lower. Accordingly, central banks looked for other ways to try to stimulate the economy. One new policy they adopted was called **quantitative easing**. This involved the central bank buying large amounts of government debt (and some other assets). We discuss this further in Chapter 25.

Another important channel of monetary policy is via the exchange rate, at least for countries whose exchange rates are flexible. Changes in exchange rate can affect the relative prices, and thereby the competitiveness, of domestic and foreign producers. A significant fall in the cost of buying domestic currency on the foreign exchange market makes domestic goods cheaper relative to foreign goods. This may lead to a shift of demand towards domestic goods and away from foreign goods, thus stimulating the domestic economy. Such shifts have important influences on domestic economic activity.

Targets and instruments

The issues that we have just discussed are of two types. First, there are the things that really matter for their own sake. These are the things that affect living conditions and the state of the economic environment. Living standards, unemployment, business cycles, and inflation are outcomes that matter. Almost everyone wants rising living standards, high employment, and low

---

[3] But by 2015 looked like missing this target by about three years.

unemployment, as well as avoidance of recessions and inflation. These things are known as the **targets** of policy. 'Good' values of these variables are what governments would like to achieve.

Fiscal and monetary policies (government spending, taxes, interest rates, and the money supply) are not so much valued for their own sake. Rather, they are the **instruments** of policy and are valued for the effect they have on the targets. *Instruments* are the variables that the government can change directly, in order to achieve its *targets*.

The macroeconomic policy problem is to choose appropriate values of the policy instruments in order to achieve the best possible combination of the outcomes of the targets. This is a continually changing problem because the targets are perpetually being affected by shocks from various parts of the world.

The GDP gap

We now introduce concepts known as *potential GDP* and the *GDP gap* which are helpful in separating trends from cycles and will be important in the analysis of subsequent chapters. After this we go on to discuss how we measure GDP and other income and output concepts.

Economic growth is about the long-term trend in GDP, and we return to a study of this in Chapter 26. The cycle about this long-term trend is the topic on which much of the rest of macroeconomics focuses, and we study this from the next chapter onwards. In order to facilitate this separation we use the concepts *actual* and *potential GDP*, and we refer to the difference between them as the *GDP gap*.

Actual GDP represents what the economy actually produces. An important related concept is **potential GDP**, which measures what the economy would produce if all resources—land, labour, and productive capacity—were fully employed at their normal levels of utilization. *Actual* GDP—what is produced—is distinguished from *potential* GDP—what could have been produced. We give potential GDP the symbol Y^* to distinguish it from actual GDP, which is indicated by just Y. It is also important to be aware that *real* GDP is distinguished from *nominal* GDP, the latter being measured in current prices and the former in constant prices. Whenever we refer to GDP without qualification it should always be assumed that we are talking about real GDP and the symbols Y and Y^* refer to actual 'real' GDP and potential 'real' GDP.

What is variously called the **output gap** or the **GDP gap** measures the difference between what would have been produced if potential, or full-employment, GDP had

been produced and what is actually produced, as measured by the current GDP. The gap is calculated by subtracting potential GDP from actual GDP (Y - Y^*).

When potential GDP exceeds actual GDP, the gap measures the market value of goods and services that *could have been produced* if the economy's resources had been fully employed, but that actually went unproduced. The goods and services that are not produced when the economy is operating below Y^* are permanently lost to the economy. Because these losses occur when employable resources are unused, they are often called the *deadweight loss* of unemployment. When the economy is operating below its potential level of output—that is, when Y is less than Y^*—the negative output gap is sometimes called a recessionary gap.[4]

In booms actual GDP may *exceed* potential GDP, causing the output gap to become positive. Actual output can exceed potential output because potential GDP is defined for a *normal rate of utilization* of inputs, and these normal rates can be exceeded temporarily. Labour may work longer hours than normal; factories may operate an extra shift or not close for routine repairs and maintenance. Although many of these expedients are only temporary, they are effective in the short term. When actual GDP exceeds potential GDP, there may be upward pressure on prices at some point. For this reason, when Y exceeds Y^*, the positive output gap is often called an **inflationary gap**. We will refer to positive and negative GDP gaps, rather than inflationary and recessionary gaps, as the links between the GDP gap and the rate of inflation seem to have changed in recent years. We expand on this issue in Chapter 22.

Figure 15.1(i) shows one estimate of UK potential GDP for the years 1970–2018.[5] The rising trend reflects the growth in productive capacity of the UK economy over this period. The figure also shows actual real GDP, which has kept approximately in step with potential GDP. The distance between the two, which is the GDP gap, is plotted in Figure 15.1(ii). Fluctuations in economic activity are apparent from fluctuations in the size of the gap.

Growth theory aims to explain the long-term trend in potential GDP, while the short-run macroeconomic model usually focuses on explaining the GDP gap.

---

[4] Note that this is not the way the US President's Council of Economic Advisors defined it when they invented the concept in the early 1960s. For them, a positive GDP gap measured the economic waste of unemployment.

[5] Note that in both parts of Figure 15.1 the data for 2013 to 2018 are IMF projections as of October 2013 rather than actual outcomes. The estimates of UK potential GDP for 1970–1990 are from the IMF *World Economic Outlook* (*WEO*), September 2002, and the estimates from 1990 onwards are from later issues of the *WEO*.

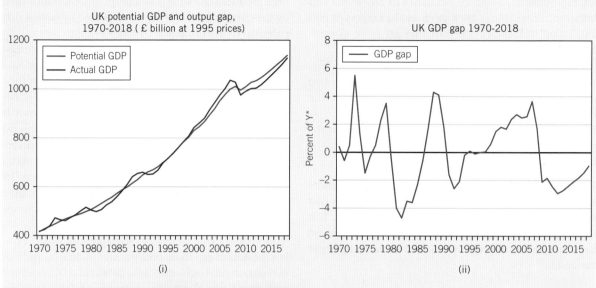

Figure 15.1 Potential and actual GDP: UK 1970 to 2018

Potential and actual GDP have both displayed an upward trend in recent years, but actual GDP fluctuates around its potential level.
(i) Growth in the economy has been such that both potential and actual GDP have more than doubled since 1970. Both series are in real terms and are measured in 1995 pounds sterling. Measurement of potential GDP is controversial and there is no official UK series at present. These figures were calculated by the IMF. The data from 1970 to 1990 are from the *World Economic Outlook* (*WEO*), 2002, while the data for 1990 to 2018 are from various later issues of the *WEO*. The 2013 to 2018 figures are IMF projections as of October 2013. (ii) The cycles in the economy are apparent from the behaviour of the output gap. Slumps in economic activity produce large negative gaps, and booms produce positive gaps. The zero line indicates where actual and potential GDP are the same. The areas below the zero line indicate the deadweight loss that arises from unemployment during periods when there is a negative output gap. Notice the large recessionary gaps in the early 1980s, the early 1990s, and 2009–18.

Source: IMF *World Economic Outlook*, various issues.

Measurement of national output

Macroeconomics has as its central goal the explanation of the determinants of the nation's income and its output. The term 'national income' was used in economics long before anyone tried to measure it. Eventually a series of related measures were defined and are now central to any understanding of the behaviour of the macro economy. Today, national income is often taken as a generic term for all such measures. However, in this book we use it as synonymous with gross domestic product, or GDP.

In the next chapter we start to build an analytical framework that helps us to understand the forces that influence these variables in the short term. In Chapter 26 we discuss the determinants of growth of GDP in the longer term. First, however, we have to understand what it is we are talking about. What do we mean when we refer to GDP, and how does it differ from other related concepts such as GNI and GNP?

We start by discussing the measurement of GDP, and find that by summing the *value added* for each industry or sector we arrive at a standard measure of GDP. We then discuss how we can arrive at the same value of GDP both by adding up the spending on the nation's output and by adding up the incomes generated by producing that output. This discussion will demonstrate the equivalence of the definitions of GDP measured by adding up the incomes generated by its production or adding up the outputs themselves. One note of caution here: in an older usage the nation's productive resources of land, labour, and capital were called 'factors of production'. Therefore the national account often label the income generated by production as 'factor incomes'. In other contexts, this usage is much less common, and when we are discussing the things that firms use to produce their outputs we will talk about 'inputs' rather than 'factors'.

Value added as output

The measured national output or the national product is related to the sum of all the outputs produced in the economy by households, firms, and governmental organizations. To obtain it, however, we cannot just add up all the outputs of individual production units. The reason why getting a total for the nation's output is not quite as straightforward as it may seem at first sight is that one firm's output is often another firm's input. A maker of clothing buys cloth from a textile manufacturer and buttons, zips, thread, pins, hangers, etc. from a range of other producers. Most modern manufactured products have many ready-made inputs. A car or aircraft manufacturer, for example, has hundreds of component suppliers.

Production occurs in stages: some firms produce outputs that are used as inputs by other firms, and these other firms in turn produce outputs that are used as inputs by yet other firms.

If we merely added up the market values of all outputs of all firms, we would obtain a total that was greatly in excess of the value of the economy's actual output. The error that would arise in estimating the nation's output by adding all sales of all firms is called **double counting**. 'Multiple counting' would be a better term, since if we added up the values of all sales, the same output would be counted every time that it was sold from one firm to another.

The problem of double counting is solved by distinguishing between two types of output. **Intermediate goods and services** are the outputs of some firms that are in turn used as inputs for other firms. **Final goods and services** are goods that are not used as inputs by other firms in the period of time under consideration. The term **final demand** refers to the purchase of final goods and services for consumption, for investment (including inventory accumulation), for use by governments, and for export. It does not include goods and services that are purchased by firms and used as inputs for producing other goods and services.

If the sales of firms could be readily separated into sales for final use and sales for further processing by other firms, measuring total output would still be straightforward. Total output would equal the value of all *final goods and services* produced by firms, excluding all intermediate goods and services. However, when a textile manufacturer sells a piece of cloth it does not necessarily know whether it is being purchased by a fashion house that will sell it on in the form of a dress, or by a consumer for use as, say, a sofa cover. Thus, at the point of sale, it is not always obvious if this is a final or intermediate sale. Therefore the problem of double counting must be resolved in some other manner.

To avoid double counting, statisticians use the important concept of **value added**. Each firm's value added is the value of its output minus the value of the inputs that it purchases from other firms (which were in turn the outputs of those other firms). Thus, a steel mill's value added is the value of its output minus the value of the ore that it buys from the mining company, the value of the electricity and other fuel that it uses, and the values of all other inputs that it buys from other firms. A bakery's value added is the value of the bread and cakes it produces minus the value of the flour and other inputs that it buys from other firms.

The total value of a firm's output is the *gross* value of its output. The firm's value added is the *net* value of its output. It is this latter figure that is the firm's contribution to the nation's total output. It is what its own efforts add to the value of what it takes in as inputs.

Value-added measures each firm's own contribution to total output—the amount of market value that is produced by that firm. Its use avoids the statistical problem of double counting.

The concept of value added is further illustrated in Box 15.2. In this simple example, as in all more complex cases, the value of total output of final goods is obtained by summing all the individual values added.

The sum of all values added in an economy is a measure of the economy's total output. This measure of total output is called gross value added. It is a measure of all final output that is produced by all productive activity in the economy.

Table 15.1 gives the gross value added by major industrial sectors for the UK economy in 2011[6]. You will see from this table that gross value added becomes GDP by the addition of a further term (taxes on products minus subsidies). We will explain this step in moving from value added to GDP later.[7]

'Gross' in National Accounts aggregates refers to the fact that we are measuring currently produced outputs or incomes without taking into account the wearing out, or *depreciation*, of capital goods during their production. Thus, gross value added is the value added of the economy as a whole *before* any allowance for depreciation, and gross domestic product is the nation's output before allowing for depreciation.

Notice that we have used 'gross' in two different senses, first in comparing the gross and net values of a

---

[6] More recent data for this table and for Tables 15.2 and 15.3 can be found in the Online Resource Centre.

[7] Gross value added at basic prices is similar to what used to be called GDP at factor cost, but the latter term has not been reported in the National Accounts since 1998.

Box 15.2 Value added through stages of production

Because the output of one firm often becomes the input of other firms, the total value of goods sold by all firms greatly exceeds the value of the output of final goods. This general principle is illustrated by a simple example in which firm R starts from scratch and produces goods (raw materials) valued at £100; the firm's value added is £100. Firm I purchases these raw materials valued at £100 and produces semi-manufactured goods that it sells for £130. Its value added is £30 because the value of the goods is increased by £30 as a result of the firm's activities. Firm F purchases the semi-manufactured goods for £130 and works them into a finished state, selling them for £180. Firm F's value added is £50. The value of final goods, £180, is found either by counting the sales of firm F or by taking the sum of the values added by each firm. This value is less than the £410 that we obtain by adding up the market value of the commodities sold by each firm. The table summarizes the example.

Transactions between firms at three different stages of production

	Firm R	Firm I	Firm F	All firms
A: Purchases from other firms	£0	£100	£130	£230 = total interfirm sales
B: Purchase of inputs in production (wages, rent, interest, profits)	£100	£30	£50	£180 = value added
Total A + B = value of product	£100	£130	£180 = value of final goods and services	£410 = total value of all sales

Table 15.1 **Gross value added at current basic prices by sector, UK, 2011**

Sector	£ million	% of GDP
Agriculture, hunting, forestry, and fisheries	9,438	0.6
Mining and quarrying	31,380	2.0
Manufacturing	140,539	9.1
Electricity, gas, and water supply	33,289	2.2
Construction	86,789	5.6
Distribution, transport, hotels	247,518	16.1
Information and communications	88,035	5.7
Finance, insurance, real estate	260,004	16.9
Professional and support services	158,811	10.3
Government, education, health	258,982	16.9
Other services	46,140	3.0
Gross value added at current basic prices	1,360,925	
Plus adjustment to current basic prices (taxes minus subsidies on products)	176,012	11.5
= GDP at market prices	**1,536,937**	100

The table shows gross value added by industrial sector in the United Kingdom for 2011 at current basic prices. The sector values added combine to make gross value added. Gross value added is equal to the total output of goods and services minus the purchase of intermediate goods. It is also the sum of the factor rewards attributable to each sector. Percentages do not add up to 100 because of rounding.

Source: ONS, *UK National Accounts (The Blue Book),* 2013.

firm's output and then in the term 'gross value added'. The first usage relies on the common meanings of 'gross' and 'net'. The gross value of the firm's output is the total output before making any deductions, while the net value deducts inputs made by other firms. In 'gross value added' the usage is different. Value added is already defined as firms' net output; the word 'gross' is added because of its specific meaning in national accounts statistics. 'Gross' in National Accounts aggregates refers to

the fact that we are measuring currently produced outputs or incomes without taking into account the wearing out, or *depreciation*, of capital goods during their production. Thus, gross value added is the value added of the economy as a whole *before* any allowance for depreciation, and gross domestic product is the nation's output before allowing for depreciation. This latter meaning will be used in many measures considered later, such as *gross domestic product*.

The circular flow of income, output, and spending

Figure 15.2 shows a stylized version of how income and spending interact in what is called **the circular flow of income**. Consider an economy composed of domestic households and domestic firms with neither foreign trade nor government. Households provide factor services to firms receiving incomes in return. This flow is shown by the black line on the left-hand side of the figure. Households spend their incomes on the final output of firms. This flow is shown by the black line on the right-hand side of the figure. GDP can be measured either on the spending side, in terms of the spending on final goods produced, or on the income side in terms of the incomes generated by production.

To complete this model, we allow for two further sets of flows. The first covers all those sources of final spending on firms' output that does not arise from the spending of domestic households. These are the spending on consumption by governments, on investment by firms, and on exports by foreign sources (indicated by the red lines). These are **injections** into the circular flow, defined as spending on final output that do not arise from the spending of domestic households. The second covers that part of household incomes that does not end up as spending on the output of firms. These are taxes paid to the government, savings, and imports (indicated by the green lines). These are called **withdrawals** from the circular flow, defined as those flows that are withdrawn from (or leak out of) the domestic flow between households and firms.

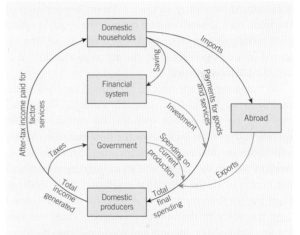

Figure 15.2 **An economy is made up of income and spending flows between firms and households**

For the level of income and output to be constant (neither rising nor falling), the injections of spending into the circular flow must equal the withdrawals (or leakages) going out of the circular flow.

The circular flow shows how domestic incomes earned by households give rise to spending, which gives rise to the output of firms, which creates incomes for households.

Withdrawals are income that are not passed on through spending, while injections are spending that does not arise out of domestic incomes and thus is exogenus.

GDP, GNI, and GNP

The various measures of the nation's income and product that are used in the United Kingdom derive from an accounting system that has been standardized by

international agreement and is thus common to most major countries. It is known as the System of National Accounts (SNA). A more detailed specification of this accounting system applies to all EU member states under the European System of Accounts 1995 (which was applied in all EU countries by April 1999 and was introduced into UK accounts in 1998). These accounts have a logical structure based on the simple yet important idea that all output must be owned by someone. So whenever national output is produced, it must generate an equivalent amount of claims to that output in the form of the nation's income. Thus, corresponding to the two halves of the circular flow in Figure 15.2 are two ways of measuring GDP: by determining the value of what is produced and by determining the value of the income claims generated by production. Because everything that is produced must generate an income claim by some entity, both measured values yield the same total—the GDP. When it is calculated by adding up the total spending for each of the main components of final output, the result is called GDP *spending-based*. When it is calculated by adding up all the incomes generated by the act of production, it is called GDP *income-based*.

All value produced must be accounted for by a claim that someone has to that value. For example, when you buy a TV set that is your spending on output, and the money you spend is income for the firm that sold the set, which can be divided into the incomes earned by those workers who made the set and all of its components and the profits of all the firms that employed these workers. Thus the total amount spent equals the income earned (and the value of the output produced). Thus, the two values calculated on income and spending bases are identical conceptually and differ in practice only because of errors of measurement. Any discrepancy arising from such errors is then reconciled so that one common total is given as *the* measure of GDP. Both calculations are of interest, however, because each gives a different and useful breakdown. Also, having two independent ways of measuring the same quantity provides a useful check on statistical procedures and unavoidable errors in measurement.

GDP spending-based

GDP spending-based for a given year is calculated by adding up the spending going to purchase the final output produced in that year. Total spending on final output is expressed in the National Accounts as the sum of three broad categories of spending: consumption, investment, and net exports. Consumption is further divided into the consumption spending of government and that of private households (and non-profit organizations serving households). So there are four important categories of spending that we will discuss: private consumption, government consumption, investment, and net exports. In Chapter 16 we explain why these particular categories have received more attention in macroeconomics than have the net sector outputs listed in Table 15.1 and the income categories discussed later (Table 15.3). Here, we define what these spending categories are and how they are measured. Remember that they are exhaustive; they are defined in such a way that *all* spending on final output falls into one of the four categories.

Private consumption spending

Private consumption spending includes spending by households on goods and services produced and sold to their final users during the year. It includes services, such as haircuts, telephone calls, meals out, and legal advice, non-durable goods, such as fresh meat, clothing, cut flowers, and fresh vegetables, and durable goods, such as cars, TV sets, and microwave ovens. However, it excludes purchases of newly built houses, as these are counted as investment.[8] Also measured in the National Accounts as part of private consumption is the final consumption spending of non-profit-making institutions serving households (NPISH). These are institutions, such as charities, that are neither firms nor governmental organizations but do contribute some spending and so have to be included somewhere in the National Accounts. We denote private consumption spending by the symbol C.

Government consumption spending

When governments provide goods and services that their citizens want, such as health care and street lighting, it is obvious that they are adding to the sum total of valuable output in the same way as do private firms that produce cars and video cassettes. With other government activities the case may not seem so clear. Should spending by the UK government to negotiate over the political situation in some foreign country, or to pay a civil servant to help draft legislation, be regarded as contributions to the national product? Some people believe that many (or even most) activities in Whitehall and in town halls are wasteful, if not downright harmful. Others point out that governments produce many of the important things of life, such as education, health care, law and order, and pollution control.

National accounts statisticians do not speculate about which government spending is worthwhile. Instead they include all government purchases of goods and services as part of national output. (Government spending on investment goods appears as public-sector capital formation, which is a part of total investment spending.) Just as the national product includes, without distinction,

---

8 Private consumption does not include purchases of existing houses as these are not part of current production. Rather, this involves a transfer of an existing asset.

the outputs of both gin and bibles, it also includes refuse collection and the upkeep of parks, along with the services of judges, members of Parliament, and even Revenue and Customs inspectors.

The UK National Accounts distinguish two different categories of government consumption. When government pays for the goods and services that are consumed by private households, this is referred to as *individual government final consumption*. This applies, among other things, to health spending and education. If, for example, National Health Service doctors perform an operation, it is paid for by the government but the service is received by an identifiable household. In contrast, the government also pays for street lighting, national defence, and law and order, but the benefit is consumed by the population at large rather than some specific household. This is spending on *public goods*, which we discussed in Chapter 13. Spending by the government, but where the consumption cannot be assigned to specific household, is called *collective government final consumption* in the National Accounts. As a simplification, in macroeconomics we lump together individual government final consumption and collective government final consumption into one term—government consumption, sometimes just called government spending. Government consumption spending is denoted by the symbol G.

Government output is typically valued at cost rather than at the market value. In most cases there is really no choice. The output of public services is not (generally) sold in the marketplace, so government output is not observed independently of the spending that produces it. What, for example, is the market value of the services of a court of law? No one knows. However, we do know what it costs the government to provide these services, and so we value them at their cost of production.

Although valuing at cost is the easiest way to measure many government activities, it does have one curious consequence. If, owing to an increase in productivity, one civil servant now does what two used to do, and the displaced worker shifts to the private sector, the government's measured contribution to the national product will register a decline. However, if two workers now do what one worker used to do, the government's measured contribution will rise. Both changes could occur even though the services the government actually provides have not changed. This is an inevitable consequence of measuring the value of the government's output by the cost of the inputs, mainly labour, that are used to produce it, rather than by the value of outputs.[9]

It is important to recognize that only government spending *on currently produced goods and services* is included as part of GDP. A great deal of government spending is not a part of GDP. For example, when the Department for Work and Pensions (DWP) makes a payment to an old-age pensioner, the government is not purchasing any currently produced goods or services from the retired. The payment itself adds neither to employment nor to total output. The same is true of payments on account of unemployment benefit, income support, and interest on the national debt (which transfers income from taxpayers to holders of government bonds). All such payments are examples of **transfer payments**, which is government spending not made in return for currently produced goods and services. It is not a part of spending on the nation's total output, and therefore is not included in GDP.[10]

Thus, when we refer to government spending as part of GDP or use the symbol G, we include all government spending on currently produced goods and services, and we *exclude* all government transfer payments. (The term *total government spending* is often used to describe all government spending, including transfer payments, though the current usage in HM Treasury is the term *total managed expenditure (TME)*.)

Investment spending

Investment spending is defined as spending on the production of goods not for present consumption but rather for future use. The goods that are created by this spending are called **investment goods** (or **capital goods**). Investment spending can be divided into three categories: changes in inventories, **fixed capital formation**, and the net acquisition of valuables.

Changes in inventories

Almost all firms hold stocks of their inputs and their own outputs. These stocks are known as inventories. Inventories of inputs and unfinished materials allow firms to maintain a steady stream of production despite short-term fluctuations in the deliveries of inputs bought from other firms. Inventories of outputs allow firms to meet orders despite temporary fluctuations in the rate of output or sales. Modern 'just-in-time' methods of production, pioneered by the Japanese, aim to reduce inventories held by manufacturing plants to nearly zero by delivering inputs just as they are needed. However, most of the economy does not achieve this level of efficiency and never

[9] UK National Accounts statisticians are developing some new measures of the output of government that will help to improve measurement of productivity, but this exercise is in its infancy.

[10] When the recipients of transfer payments spend these on buying goods and services, their spending is measured as consumption spending, and thus as part of GDP in the same way as any other consumption spending. We do not want to measure it twice, which we would be doing if we included in GDP both the government transfer and the spending by the recipient.

will. Retailing, for example, would certainly not be improved if shops held no stocks.

An accumulation of stocks and unfinished goods in the production process counts as current investment because it represents goods produced (even if only half-finished) but not used for current consumption. A drawing down of inventories, also called *destocking*, counts as negative investment because it represents a reduction in the stocks of finished goods (produced in the current period) that are available for future use. Inventories are valued at what they will be worth on the market, rather than at what they have cost the firm so far. This is because the spending-based measure of GDP includes the value of what final spending on these goods would be if they were sold, even though they have not been sold yet.

Fixed capital formation

All production uses capital goods. These are manufactured aids to production, such as machines, computers, and factory buildings. Creating new capital goods is an act of investment and is called *fixed investment* or **fixed capital formation**. The economy's total quantity of capital goods is called the **capital stock**. Much of the capital stock is in the form of equipment or buildings used by firms or government agencies in the production of goods and services. This includes not just factories and machines, but also hospitals, schools, and offices. A house or a flat is also a durable asset that yields its utility (housing services) over a long period of time. This meets the definition of fixed capital formation, so (as we pointed out above) housing *construction* is counted as investment spending rather than as consumption spending. When a family purchases a house from a builder or another owner, the ownership of an already produced asset is transferred, and that transaction is not a part of current GDP.

Net acquisition of valuables

Some productive activity creates goods that are neither consumed nor used in the production process. Rather, they are held for their intrinsic beauty or for their expected appreciation in value. Examples are jewellery and works of art. Such works are known as *valuables*. Acquisitions less disposals of valuables are treated as investments in the National Accounts.

Gross and net investment

Total investment spending is called **gross investment** or **gross capital formation**. Gross investment is divided into two parts: replacement investment and net investment. **Replacement investment** is the amount of investment that just maintains the level of existing capital stock; in other words it replaces the bits that have worn out or have

been discarded as obsolete[11]. Replacement investment is classified as the **capital consumption allowance**, or simply **depreciation**. Gross investment minus replacement investment is **net investment**. Positive net investment increases the economy's total stock of capital, while replacement investment keeps the existing stock intact by replacing what has been used up, has worn out, or has been discarded as obsolete.

All of gross investment is included in the calculation of GDP. This is because all investment goods are part of the nation's total output, and their production creates income (and employment) whether the goods produced are a part of net investment or are merely replacement investment. Total investment spending is denoted by the symbol I.

Net exports

The fourth category of aggregate spending, one that is very important to the UK economy, arises from foreign trade. How do imports and exports affect the calculation of GDP?

Imports

A country's GDP is the total value of final goods and services produced *in that country*. If you spend £20,000 on a car that was made in Germany, only a small part of that value will represent spending on UK production. Although some of it represents payment for the services of the UK dealer and for transportation within this country, much of the rest is the output of German firms and spending on German products, though there may be component suppliers from several countries. If you take your next vacation in Italy, much of your spending will be on goods and services produced in Italy and thus will contribute to Italian GDP.

Similarly, when a UK firm makes an investment spending on a UK-produced machine tool that was made partly with imported materials, only part of the spending is on British production; the rest is spending on production by the countries supplying the materials. The same is true for government spending on such things as roads and dams; some of the spending is for imported materials, and only part of it is for domestically produced goods and services.

Private consumption, government consumption, and investment all have an import content. To arrive at total spending on UK output, we need to subtract from total UK residents' spending actual spending on imports of goods and services, which is represented by the symbol *IM*.

Exports

If UK firms sell goods or services to German consumers, the goods and services are a part of German consumption

---

[11] Most capital goods that are replaced are discarded as obsolete rather than because they have physically worn out.

spending but also constitute spending on UK output. Indeed, all goods and services that are produced in the United Kingdom and sold to foreigners must be counted as part of UK GDP; they are produced in the United Kingdom, and they create incomes for the UK residents who produce them. However, they are not purchased by UK residents, and so they are not included as part of C, I, or G. Therefore, to arrive at the total value of spending on the domestic product, it is necessary to add in the value of UK exports. Exports of goods and services are denoted by the symbol X.

It is convenient to group imports and actual exports together as **net exports**. Net exports are defined as total exports of goods and services minus total imports of goods and services ($X - IM$), which will also be denoted by NX. When the value of exports exceeds the value of imports, the net export term is positive. When the value of imports exceeds the value of exports, the net export term becomes negative.

Market prices and basic prices

There is one important difference that arises when calculating the level of GDP from the spending side of the economy compared with calculating it by summing the values added in production. This difference arises because the price paid by consumers for many goods and services is not the same as the sales revenue received by the producer. There are taxes that have to be paid that place a wedge between what consumers pay and what producers receive. Taxes attached to transactions are known as *indirect taxes*. Examples of UK indirect taxes include VAT and excise duties.[12] Thus, if you pay £120 for a meal in a restaurant, the restaurateur will receive only £100, and £20 will go to the government in the form of VAT.

In cases where products are subsidized by the government, the producer receives more than the consumer pays. In 2011 subsidies on UK products were small, amounting to less than 1 per cent of GDP.

The term **basic prices** is used in the National Accounts to refer to the prices of products as received by producers. **Market prices** are the prices as paid by consumers. Thus, basic prices are equal to market prices *minus* taxes on products *plus* subsidies on products. In the example of the meal bill above, the market price was £120 but the basic price was £100.

If you look again at Table 15.1, you will see that the sum of sectoral values added that we present there is referred to as gross value added at *basic prices*. You should also notice that by adding to gross value added at basic prices a term labelled 'adjustment to current basic prices' we arrived at the total for

GDP at market prices. This adjustment to current basic prices is made up of taxes minus subsidies on products.

Since our final spending categories are all measured at market prices—as they measure what is spent by purchasers rather than what is received by producers—we can proceed by adding up this final spending to arrive at GDP *at market prices* directly.

Total spending

The spending-based measure of gross domestic product at market prices is the sum of the four spending categories that we have discussed above, or in symbols:

$$\text{GDP} = C + I + G + (X - IM)$$

The actual spending components of GDP for the United Kingdom in 2011 are shown in Table 15.2.

GDP spending-based is the sum of private consumption, government consumption, investment, and net export spending on currently produced goods and services. It is GDP at market prices.

GDP income-based

The production of a nation's output generates income. Labour must be employed, land must be rented, and capital must be used. The calculation of GDP from the income side involves adding up the income claims of owners of resource inputs (land, labour, capital, etc.) so that all of that value is accounted for. In essence we are taking the value added displayed for the economy as a whole in Table 15.1 and dividing this up by types of income rather than by industrial sector. We have already noted that because all value produced must be owned by someone, the value of production must equal the value of income claims generated by that production.

National income accountants distinguish three main categories of income: operating surplus, mixed incomes, and compensation of employees.

Operating surplus

Operating surpluses are net business incomes after payment has been made to hired labour and for material inputs but before *direct taxes* (such as corporation tax) have been paid. Direct taxes are those taxes levied on individuals or firms, usually in relation to their income. Operating surpluses are in large part the profits of firms, but also included is the financial surplus of organizations other than companies, such as universities. Some profits are paid out as **dividends** to owners of firms; the rest are retained for use by firms. The former are called *distributed profits*, and the latter are called *undistributed profits* or *retained earnings*. Both distributed and undistributed profits are included in the calculation of GDP.

---

[12] The rate of VAT was 20 per cent in the UK in 2015 and applied to a wide range of goods and services. Excise duties applied mainly to tobacco, alcohol, and petrol.

Table 15.2 **Spending-based GDP and its components, UK, 2011**

Spending categories	£ million	% of GDP
Individual consumption		
Household final consumption	953,882	62.1
Final consumption of non-profit institutions serving households	38,457	2.5
Individual government final consumption	212,781	13.8
Total actual individual consumption	1,205,120	78.4
Collective government final consumption	124,389	8.1
Total final consumption	1,329,509	86.5
Gross capital formation		
Gross fixed capital formation	220,726	14.4
Change in inventories	8,797	0.6
Acquisition less disposals of valuables	1,166	0.07
Total gross capital formation	230,689	15.0
Exports of goods and services	492,884	32.1
Less imports of goods and services	−516,144	−33.6
External balance of goods and services (net exports)	−23,260	−1.5
Statistical discrepancy	0	0
Gross domestic product at market prices (money GDP)	1,536,937	100

Spending-based GDP is made up of consumption, investment, and net exports. Consumption is by far the largest spending category, equal to about 86 per cent of GDP. Private consumption makes up most of this (around 65 per cent of GDP) and government consumption makes up the rest. Investment accounts for 15 per cent of GDP. Whereas exports and imports are both quite large (each over 30 per cent of GDP), net exports are small; in 2011 they represented (negative) 1.5 per cent of GDP. Government consumption is reported in two parts: that which is paid for by government but is consumed by households, such as health services and education, and that which is consumed collectively, such as defence and the legal system.

Source: ONS, *UK National Accounts* (*The Blue Book*), 2013.

Mixed incomes

This category covers the many people who are earning a living by selling their services or output but who are not employed by any organization. It includes some consultants and those who work on short contracts but are not formally employees of an incorporated business. They are self-employed individuals who are running sole-trader businesses. Also included are some partnerships where the partners own the business. The reason why the incomes of this group are referred to as *mixed incomes* is that it is not clear what proportion of their earnings is equivalent to a wage or salary and what proportion is the profit or surplus of the business. They are a mixture of the two.

Compensation of employees

This is wages and salaries (usually just referred to as *wages*). It is the payment for the services of labour. Wages include take-home pay, taxes withheld, National Insurance

contributions, pension fund contributions, and any other fringe benefits. In other words wages are measured gross. In total, wages represent that part of the value of production that is attributable to hired labour.

The various components of UK income-based GDP in 2011 are shown in Table 15.3. Notice that the three income categories in Table 15.3 add up to gross value added at basic prices, as shown in Table 15.1. These income-based and output- or value-added-based measures are showing the same thing—the sum of factor incomes for the whole economy. In both cases we add taxes on production less subsidies to arrive at GDP at market prices.

Income produced and income received

GDP at market prices provides a measure of total output produced in the United Kingdom and of the total income generated as a result of that production. However, the

Table 15.3 Income-based GDP and its components, UK, 2011

Income type	£ million	% of GDP
Operating surplus, gross (profits)	435,956	28.4
Mixed incomes	85,322	5.6
Compensation of employees	820,157	53.4
Taxes on production and imports	207,746	13.5
Less subsidies	−12,245	−0.8
Statistical discrepancy	0	0.0
GDP at market prices	1,536,937	100
Employees' compensation		
Receipts from rest of world	1,121	
Less payment to rest of world	−1,293	
Total	−172	
Less taxes on production paid to rest of world *plus* subsidies received from rest of world	−5,122	
Other subsidies on production	3,166	
Property and entrepreneurial income		
receipts from rest of world	191,250	
Less payments to rest of world	−168,584	
Total	22,666	
Gross national income (GNI) at market prices	1,557,475	

The income-based measure of GDP is made up of gross operating surplus (profit), mixed incomes, compensation of employees, and net taxes on goods. Mixed incomes are largely the incomes of the self-employed or non-incorporated businesses, where it is hard to distinguish profits from employee compensation. By far the largest income category is compensation of employees, which makes up 53 per cent of GDP. GNI is GDP at market prices plus various net income receipts from the rest of the world. In 2011, UK GNI was 1.3 per cent larger than GDP.

Source: ONS, *UK National Accounts (The Blue Book),* 2013.

total income received by UK residents differs from GDP for two reasons. First, some domestic production creates factor earnings for non-residents who either do some paid work for UK residents or have previously invested in the United Kingdom; on this account, income received by UK residents will be less than UK GDP. Secondly, many UK residents earn income from work for overseas residents or on overseas investments; on this account, income received by UK residents will be greater than GDP.

While GDP measures the output, and hence the income that is *produced in* this country, the **gross national income (GNI)** measures the income that is *received by* this country. To convert GDP into GNI, it is necessary to add three terms that combine to account for the difference between the income received by this country and the income produced in this country. The first term is employees' compensation receipts from the rest of the world minus payments to the rest of the world. Thus, if a London-based consultant sells

her services to a French firm, the income received will contribute to UK GNI but will be part of French GDP.

The second term is (minus) net taxes on production paid to the rest of the world plus subsidies received from the rest of the world. The logic of this is that we are measuring GNI (as with GDP) at market prices. If some element of the market prices paid is an indirect tax that generates revenue for a foreign government, then that tax represents a loss of income for the domestic economy as a whole and reduces domestic gross national income. Equally, if the product is subsidized by a foreign government, then this raises domestic incomes by enabling us to consume a given amount of goods at lower prices.

The third component of the difference between GDP and GNI is property and entrepreneurial income receipts from the rest of the world minus payments to the rest of the world. For example, if you live in Manchester and own a holiday home in Spain that you rent out for part of the year, the revenue earned will count as part of GDP in Spain (as it is produced there), but the income (net of any Spanish taxes and local costs) accrues to a UK resident so it adds to UK GNI. Similarly, many UK firms have subsidiaries located in other countries. The value added of those subsidiaries counts as part of GDP in the host country, but profits remitted to the parent count as part of the UK's GNI. Conversely, a Japanese firm located in the UK contributes all its value added to UK GDP, but profits remitted back to Japan are deducted from GDP in order to arrive at GNI (as they are not part of UK income).

Total output produced in the economy, measured by GDP, differs from total income received, measured by GNI, owing to net income from abroad.

It is important to note that the term gross national income was introduced as recently as 1998 to replace the term gross national product or GNP. GNI and GNP are conceptually identical. However, the latter has been in use for several decades all over the world, so readers will continue to come across it for many years to come even if it is replaced by GNI in many new publications. This minor difference in terminology is not important for understanding macroeconomics, since this is concerned primarily with GDP, but it is important not to be confused when these terms are encountered.

GDP and GNI (or GNP) at market prices are the most commonly used concepts of the nation's output and income. Once we move on to theory in the next chapter, we ignore the small difference between GDP and GNI and refer to GDP at all times unless stated otherwise. This is true even though we sometimes talk about 'GDP' and sometimes about the 'national product', depending on the context. For analytical purposes they are the same thing.

Reconciling GDP with GNI

Table 15.3 shows the reconciliation of GDP with GNI. UK GNI was greater than GDP in 2011, but only by a little over 1 per cent. This reflects slightly greater income from abroad for UK residents than UK-generated income paid out to foreigners. Clearly, GNI could be smaller than GDP if outward payments were greater than income earned from abroad.

Figure 15.3 provides a visual representation of the information in Tables 15.1–15.3. It shows both the relationship between gross value added at basic prices and GDP at market prices, and the difference between GDP and GNI (at market prices). Components of the three possible decompositions of GDP are also displayed.

Other income concepts

Personal income is income that is earned by or paid to members of a household, before allowing for personal income taxes on that income. Some personal income goes for taxes, some goes for savings, and the rest goes for consumption. **Personal disposable income** is the amount of current income that households have available for spending and saving; it is personal income minus personal income taxes and National Insurance contributions.

Personal disposable income is GNI minus any part of it that is not actually paid to members of households (such as retained profits of companies) minus personal income taxes plus transfer payments received by them.

Interpreting income and output measures

The information provided by National Accounts data is useful, but unless it is carefully interpreted, it can be misleading. Furthermore, each of the specific measures gives different information. Each may be the best statistic for studying a particular range of problems, but it is important to understand these differences if you are going to use these data for analytical purposes. Here we discuss some of the caveats to bear in mind.

Real and nominal measures

It is important to distinguish between *real* and *nominal* measures of income and output. When we add up money values of outputs, spending, or incomes, we end up with what are called *nominal values*. Suppose that we found that a measure of nominal GDP had risen by 50 per cent between 2010 and 2020. If we wanted to compare *real GDP* in 2020 with that in 2010, we would need to determine how much of that 50 per cent nominal increase was due to increases in the general level of prices and how much was due to increases in quantities of goods and services produced. Although there are many possible ways of doing this, the basic principle is always the same. It is to compute the value of output, spending, and income in each period by using a common set of *base-period prices*. When this is done, we speak of real output, spending, or income as being measured in *constant prices* or, say, 2005 *prices*.

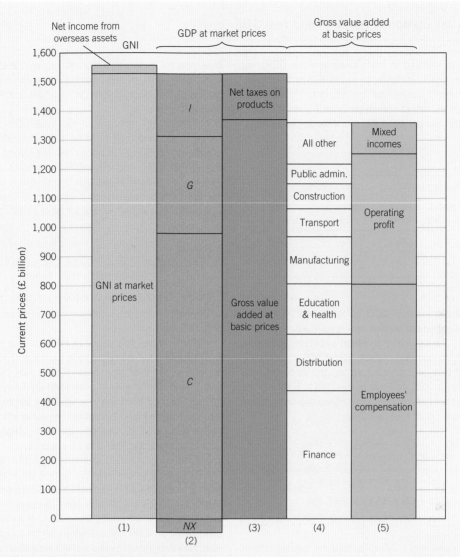

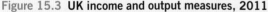

Figure 15.3 UK income and output measures, 2011

Measurement of the nation's income and output can be approached in three different ways, but they are all related. The figure shows the actual UK aggregates GNI at market prices, GDP at market prices, and gross value added at basic prices for 2011. Column (1) is GNI at market prices. Columns (2) and (3) add up to GDP at market prices. Columns (4) and (5) add up to gross value added at basic prices (or what used to be called GDP at factor cost). Column (1) exceeds column (2) by 1.3 per cent. This difference is net income from abroad. In 2011 this was positive but small. Column (2) shows that GDP is made up of the spending components: consumption (*C*), investment (*I*), government spending (*G*), and net exports (*NX*). Notice that in 2011 net exports were negative, so *NX* has to be subtracted from the sum of *C* + *I* + *G* to arrive at GDP. Columns (3) and (4) show that gross value added at basic prices is equal to GDP at market prices minus net taxes on production. Column (4) shows that gross value added is made up of the sum of the values added of each of the production sectors of the economy; for example, manufacturing produces about 10 per cent of gross value added. Column (5) shows that gross value added can also be broken down by income type. Employees' compensation amounts to about 53 per cent of GDP at market prices.

Source: ONS, UK National Accounts (The Blue Book), 2013.

A recent innovation in UK National Accounts is to calculate a *chained-volume measure* of real GDP instead of using the prices from a single base year. This concept is explained in Box 15.3.

GDP valued at current prices (i.e. money GDP) is a nominal measure. GDP valued at base-period prices, or as a chained-volume measure, is a real measure of the volume of the nation's output and income.

Box 15.3 Calculation of nominal and real GDP

To see what is involved in calculating nominal GDP, real GDP, and the implicit deflator, an example may be helpful. Consider a simple hypothetical economy that produces only two commodities, wheat and steel. Table I gives the basic data for output and prices in the economy for two years.

Table I

	Quantity produced		Prices	
	Wheat (bushels)	Steel (tons)	Wheat (£ per bu.)	Steel (£ per ton)
Year 1	100	20	10	50
Year 2	110	16	12	55

Table II shows nominal GDP, calculated by adding the money values of wheat output and steel output for each year. In year 1 the value of both wheat and steel production was £1,000, so nominal income was £2,000. In year 2 wheat output rose, and steel output fell; the value of wheat output rose to £1,320, and that of steel fell to £880. Since the rise in value of wheat was greater than the fall in value of steel, nominal GDP rose by £200.

Table II

Year 1	$(100 \times 10) + (20 \times 50) = £2,000$
Year 2	$(110 \times 12) + (16 \times 55) = £2,200$

Table III shows real GDP, calculated by valuing output in each year by year 2 prices; that is, year 2 becomes the

Table III

Year 1	$(100 \times 12) + (20 \times 55) = £2,300$
Year 2	$(110 \times 12) + (16 \times 55) = £2,200$

base year for weighting purposes. Using year 2 prices, the value of the fall in steel output between years 1 and 2 exceeded the value of the rise in wheat output, and real GDP fell.

In Table IV the ratio of nominal to real GDP is calculated for each year and multiplied by 100. This ratio implicitly measures the change in prices over the period in question and is called the *implicit deflator* or *implicit price index*. The implicit deflator shows that the price level increased by 15 per cent between year 1 and year 2 (calculated as $(13.04/86.96) \times 100$, where 13.04 is $(100 - 86.96)$).

Table IV

Year 1	$(2,000/2,300) \times 100 = 86.96$
Year 2	$(2,200/2,200) \times 100 = 100.00$

In Table IV we used year 2 as the base year for comparison purposes, but we could have used year 1. The implicit deflator would then have been 100 in year 1 and 115 in year 2, and the increase in price level would still have been 15 per cent. Or the base year could be some earlier year. No matter what year is picked as the year in which the index had a value of 100, the change in the implicit deflator between year 1 and year 2 is 15 per cent.

UK national income statisticians used to calculate UK real GDP using prices from the same base year for several years in a row. Thus, in the past, real GDP growth between 2000 and 1999 might have been calculated using 1995 as the base year for prices. They would then have big revisions some time later when they shifted to using a new base year. However, now they use a *chain-weighted* volume index of real output, which means that the price weights are adjusted each year on the basis of an average of prices in the most recent few years. This is similar to the way in which quantity weights are adjusted each year in the construction of the UK Retail Price Index (RPI) (see Case Study 1 at the end of this chapter). Revisions to these data are discussed in Case Study 2.

Any *change* in nominal GDP reflects the combined effects of changes in quantities and changes in prices. However, when real income is measured over different periods by using a common set of base-period prices, changes in real income reflect only changes in real output.

The implicit deflator

If nominal and real GDP change by different amounts over some time period, this must be because prices have changed over that period. Comparing what has happened

to nominal and real GDP over the same period implies the existence of a price index measuring the change in prices over that period. We say 'implies' because no price index was used in calculating real and nominal GDP. However, an index can be inferred by comparing these two values. Such an index is called an *implicit price index* or an *implicit deflator*. It is defined as follows:

$$\text{Implicit deflator} = \frac{\text{GDP at current prices}}{\text{GDP at base-period prices}} \times 100\,\%$$

The implicit GDP deflator is the most comprehensive index of the price level because it covers all the goods and services that are produced by the entire economy. However, it has the limitation that it is subject to revision when the National Accounts are revised. In contrast, RPI and CPI figures are never revised once published. Box 15.3 illustrates the calculation of real and nominal GDP and an implicit deflator for a simple hypothetical economy that produces only wheat and steel. See Case Study 1 at the end of this chapter for a discussion of the construction of the retail price index.

A change in any nominal measure of GDP can be split into a change due to prices and a change due to quantities. For example, UK nominal GDP ('money' GDP) in 2011 was around 3.4 per cent higher than in 2010. This increase was due to a 2.3 per cent increase in prices combined with a 1.1 per cent increase in real GDP. Table 15.4 gives nominal and real GDP and the implicit deflator for selected years since 1900.

Table 15.4 **Nominal and real GDP at market prices, 1900–2013**

	Money GDP (£ billion)	Real GDP (1990 prices) (£ billion)	Implicit GDP deflator (1990 = 100)
1900	1.9	109.5	1.7
1930	4.7	138.6	3.4
1950	13.1	200.4	6.5
1970	51.6	350.9	14.7
1980	231.2	426.8	54.2
2001	988	708	137.9
2013	1,613.4	840.0	183.5

The data in the table are money GDP, real GDP, and the implicit GDP price deflator for selected years. The first column shows that money (nominal) GDP increased nearly 850-fold between 1900 and 2013. However, the second column shows that there was only a 7.7-fold increase in real GDP over the same period. The difference between the two is accounted for by the final column, which shows that the implicit price deflator for GDP rose 108-fold in this period. Since 1950 real GDP has seen a just over 4-fold increase, while the GDP price deflator has increased over 28-fold.

Sources: ONS website (<http://www.ons.gov.uk>) and earlier editions of this book.

International comparisons of GDP

One purpose to which GDP measures are often put is an international comparison of living standards or real income. It is natural to want to know if people have higher living standards in the United Kingdom or in, say,

Germany or France. However, comparisons using measures such as GDP must be conducted with great care. There are many dimensions to living standards which are not measured by GDP or GNI.

For some purposes we may want to compare the absolute size of one economy relative to another, but normally we are interested in how well off the average individual is in each country. For this purpose we want to look at GDP per head or per capita (or perhaps GNI per capita). To get this figure we divide GDP by the total population of the country. This tells us the share of total GDP that is available for the average citizen.

GDP in each country is measured in the local currency. So, to make comparisons, we have to convert different countries' nominal GDP into the same currency. To do this, we have to use an exchange rate. This is problematic because exchange rates fluctuate, sometimes dramatically. Even in normal conditions it is not unusual for exchange rates to move by 10 per cent in a few weeks, and the move could easily be reversed a little later.

To solve the problem of making comparisons using unreliable or atypical exchange rates, economists make comparisons of GDP using the exchange rate that equates the prices of a representative bundle of goods in two countries. This is known as the *purchasing power parity (PPP)* rate. We will discuss this concept more fully in Chapter 24.

Some comparisons of GNI per capita in thirteen different countries (using PPP exchange rates) are given in Table 15.5. Figures are all expressed in US dollars. Several other indicators of material well-being are included in the table. Broadly speaking, they tell the same story as the GNI figures—the inhabitants of the richer countries can purchase more goods and services and tend to have longer life expectancy. However, the rankings would be different for each possible indicator of well-being. The significance of this is that GNI per capita contains some useful information but other important indicators sometimes tell a slightly different story.

What GDP does not measure

GDP measures the flow of economic activity in organized markets in a given year. But much economic activity takes place outside the market economy. Although these activities are not typically included in GDP or GNI, they nevertheless use real resources and satisfy real wants and needs.

Unreported activities

A significant omission from measured GDP is the so-called underground or black economy. The transactions that occur in the underground economy are perfectly legal in themselves; the only illegality involved is that such transactions are not reported for tax purposes. One example of

Table 15.5 **International comparisons of living standards**

	GNI per capita 2012 ($) Using PPP exchange rates	Passenger cars per 1,000 people, 2010	Mobile telephones per 100 people, 2012	Under-5 mortality per 1,000, 2011	Maternal mortality rate per 100,000 live births, 2010	Life expectancy at birth, 2012	Incidence of TB per 100,000 population, 2011	Doctors per 1,000 people, 2011 (or latest year available)
USA	52,610	423	98	7	21	79	4	2
Australia	43,300	556	106	5	7	82	7	4
Germany	43,230	517	131	4	7	81	6	4
Canada	42,530	420	76	5	12	81	5	2
UK	37,340	457	131	5	12	81	15	3
France	36,720	481	98	4	8	82	8	3
Japan	36,300	453	109	3	5	83	19	2
Spain	31,670	58	108	5	6	82	14	4
Russia	22,720	233	184	10	34	68	91	4
Mexico	16,450	191	87	16	50	77	23	2
Brazil	11,530	178	129	14	56	73	46	2
China	9,040	44	81	14	37	75	73	2
India	3,910	12	69	56	200	66	176	1

The table shows eight different indicators of living standards for thirteen countries. Most of the indicators tell the same story—wealthy countries have more goods and better life expectations. However, there are some interesting anomalies. Russia has as many doctors per 1,000 people as any other country in the table, yet life expectancy is lower than in China, which has half as many doctors per person.

Source: World Bank, *World Development Indicators*, 2013.

this is the carpenter who repairs a leak in your roof and takes payment in cash or in kind in order to avoid taxation. Because such transactions go unreported, they may be omitted from GDP.

The growth of the underground economy could be encouraged by high rates of taxation and is facilitated by the rising importance of services in the nation's total output. The higher the tax rates, the more there is to be gained by 'going underground'. It is also much easier for a carpenter or plumber to pass unnoticed by government authorities than it is for a manufacturing establishment. However, when the carpenter who has received an undeclared payment spends it in the shops it will appear in measures of consumer spending, so it will not escape measurement entirely.

Studies of the scale of the underground economy show that its importance has been growing in recent years. Estimates have put the underground economy in the United Kingdom at about 7 per cent of GDP. A Canadian study concluded that 15 per cent of Canadian GDP went unreported because it was in the underground economy.

In other countries the figures are even higher. The Italian underground economy, for example, has been estimated at about 20 per cent of GDP; estimates are close to 25 per cent for Spain and 30 per cent for Greece!

Non-marketed activities

If homeowners hire a firm to do some landscaping, the value of the landscaping enters into GDP; if they do the landscaping themselves, the value of the landscaping is omitted from GDP. Other non-marketed activities include, for example, the services of those who do housework at home, any do-it-yourself activity, and voluntary work such as canvassing for a political party, helping to run a volunteer day-care centre, or coaching an amateur football team.

One important non-marketed activity is leisure itself. If a lawyer voluntarily chooses to work 2,200 hours a year instead of 2,400 hours, measured GDP will fall by the lawyer's hourly wage rate times 200 hours. Yet the value to the lawyer of the 200 hours of new leisure, which is enjoyed outside the marketplace, must exceed the lost wages (because the leisure has been voluntarily chosen in preference to the extra work), so total economic welfare has risen rather than fallen. Until recently one of the most important ways in which economic growth benefited people was by permitting increased amounts of time off work. Because the time off is not marketed, its value does not show up in measures of GDP.

Economic bads

When a coal-fired electricity generator sends sulphur dioxide into the atmosphere, leading to acid rain and environmental damage, the value of the electricity sold is included as part of GDP, but the value of the damage done by the acid rain is not deducted. Similarly, the petrol that we use in our cars is part of GDP, but the damage done by burning that petrol is not deducted. To the extent that economic growth brings with it increases in pollution, congestion, and other disamenities of modern living, GDP measures will overstate the value of the growth. They measure the increased economic output and income, but they fail to deduct the increased 'bads', or negative outputs, that generally accompany economic growth.

Do the omissions matter?

GDP does a reasonable job of measuring the flow of goods and services through the market sector of the economy. This is exactly what the government wants to know when deciding on its fiscal policy and what the central bank

wants to know when deciding on measures designed to keep inflation under control. An increase in GDP also implies greater opportunities for employment for those households that sell their labour services in the market. Unless the importance of unmeasured economic activity changes rapidly, *changes* in GDP will do an excellent job of measuring *changes* in economic activity. However, when the task at hand is measurement of the overall flow of goods and services available to satisfy people's wants, regardless of the source of the goods and services, the omissions that we have just discussed become undesirable and potentially serious. Still, in the relatively short term, changes in GDP will usually be good measures of the direction, if not the exact magnitude, of changes in economic welfare.

The omissions cause serious problems when GDP measures are used to compare living standards in structurally different economies, as was discussed in the previous section. Generally, the non-market sector of the economy is larger in rural than in urban settings and in less developed than in more developed economies. Be cautious, then, when interpreting data from a country with a very different climate and culture. When you hear that the per capita GNI of India is about $3,910 per year, you should not imagine living in Manchester on that income. The average Indian is undoubtedly poorer than the average Briton, but perhaps not one-tenth as well off, as the GNI figures suggest.

CASE STUDIES

1. How the RPI is constructed

Two important questions must be answered when any price index is constructed. First, what group of prices should be used? This depends on what the index is intended to measure. The Retail Price Index (RPI), which is calculated by the Office for National Statistics (ONS), covers prices of goods and services that are commonly bought by households. Changes in the RPI are meant to measure changes in the typical household's *cost of living*. (Other indexes, such as the wholesale price index or the producer price index, cover the prices of different baskets of commodities. The implicit deflator for GDP covers all of the nation's output, not just consumer prices.)

Secondly, how should the movements in consumer prices be added up and summarized in one price index? If all prices changed in the same proportion, this would not matter: a 10 per cent rise in every price would mean a

10 per cent rise in the average of all prices, no matter how the average was constructed. However, different prices usually change in different proportions. It then matters how much importance we give to each price change. Changes in the price of bread, for example, are much more important to the average consumer than changes in the price of caviar. In calculating a price index, each price is given a *weight* that reflects its importance.

Let us see how this is done for the RPI. Government statisticians periodically survey a representative group of households in what is called the Family Expenditure Survey. This shows how consumers spend their incomes. The average bundle of goods that is bought is determined, along with the proportion of spending that is devoted to each good. These proportions become the weights attached to the individual prices in calculating the RPI. As a result, the RPI weights rather heavily the prices of commodities on which consumers spend much of their income, and

Table 15.6 Calculation of weights for a price index

Commodity	Price (£)	Quantity	Spending (£) (price × quantity)	Proportional weight
A	5	60	300	0.50
B	1	200	200	0.33
C	4	25	100	0.17
Total			600	1.00

The weights are the proportions of total spending that are devoted to each commodity. This simple example lists the prices of three commodities and the quantities bought by a typical household. Multiplying price by quantity gives the spending on each, and summing these gives the total spending on all commodities. Dividing spending on each good by total spending gives the proportion of total spending that is devoted to each commodity, as shown in the last column. These proportions become the weights for the price indexes that are calculated in Table 15.7.

weights rather lightly the prices of commodities on which consumers spend only a little of their income. Table 15.6 provides a simple example of how these weights are calculated.

Once the weights are chosen, the price index can be calculated for each period. This can be done, as shown in Table 15.7, by multiplying the price index for each commodity by its weight and summing the resulting figures. Notice that the price index for each commodity is set to 100 in the base year (2000 in this example) and it then changes in proportion to the change in its price compared with the base year. Thus, as the price of commodity B rises from £1 in 2000 to £1.50 in 2005, so its price index rises from 100 to 150. The overall price index, shown in the bottom line of the table, is the weighted average of the index numbers for the component commodities (using the weights calculated in Table 15.6).[13]

We do not normally need to refer to index numbers for prices of individual commodities as we can compare their prices directly. For example, we can say that a litre of petrol now costs £1.20 while a year ago it cost £1.00, and thus its price has risen by 20 per cent. However, for a varied bundle of goods and services we can only compare their price changes using an index number series. By construction, the base-period value in this series equals 100; if prices in the next period average 20 per cent higher, the index number for that period will be 120. A simple example of how these calculations are carried out is given in Table 15.7.

Price indexes are constructed by assigning weights to reflect the importance of the individual items being combined. The value of the index is set equal to 100 in the base period.

Table 15.7 shows the calculation of what is called a *fixed-weight index*. The weights are the proportion of income that is spent on each of the three goods in the base

Table 15.7 Calculation of a price index

Commodity	Weight	Price (£) 2000 (index)	Price (£) 2005	Price index 2005	Weighted price index 2005	Price (£) 2010	Price index 2010	Weighted price index 2010
A	0.50	5 (100)	6.00	120	60	14	280	140
B	0.33	1 (100)	1.50	150	50	2	200	67
C	0.17	4 (100)	8.00	200	34	9	225	38
Price index		100			144			245

A price index can be calculated as the weighted index of the prices of the component commodities, where the weights are derived from the proportion spend on each commodity in the base year. In our example there are three components in the price index: commodities A, B, and C. The weights in the second column are those derived in Table 15.6. The third column shows the prices of each commodity in the base year (2000). The index number for each commodity is set to 100 in the base year, as is the overall price index. The prices of each commodity in 2005 are shown in the fourth column and these are expressed as index numbers in the fifth column. The weighted index numbers (column 2 multiplied by column 5) are in the sixth column, and the overall price index is the sum of those. The remaining three columns take 2010 prices and repeat the same exercise. The overall price index is the weighted sum of its components.

[13] Alternatively, the cost of purchasing the original bundle of goods at the new prices can be calculated and expressed as a ratio of the cost of purchasing the same bundle at the original prices and then multiplied by 100 to express the result as an index number.

year. These weights are then applied to the prices in each subsequent year. The value of the index in each year measures exactly how much the base-year bundle of goods would cost at that year's prices. Fixed-weight indexes are easy to interpret, but problems arise because consumption patterns change over the years; the fixed weights represent with decreasing accuracy the importance that consumers *currently* place on each of the commodities.

The RPI used to be calculated using fixed weights that were only changed every decade or so. Now they are revised annually. This avoids the problem of the fixed-weight index becoming steadily less representative of current spending patterns.

Measuring the rate of inflation

In December 2013 the RPI was 127.5. (The value for January 2005 equals 100.) This means that in December 2013 it cost just over 27 per cent more to buy a representative bundle of goods than it did in the base period, which in this case is January 2005.[14] In other words, there was a 27.5 per cent *increase* in the price level over that period, as measured by the RPI. The *percentage change* in the cost of purchasing the bundle of goods that is covered by any index is thus the level of the index minus 100.

The *inflation rate* between any two periods of time is measured by the percentage increase in the relevant price index from the first period to the second period. In the rare event of a drop in the price level, we speak of a *deflation*. When the amount of the rise in the price level is being measured from the base period, all that needs to be done is to subtract the base-period index (100) from the later index, as we have just done. When two other periods are being compared, we must be careful to express the change as a percentage of the index in the first period.

If we let P_1 indicate the value of the price index in the first period and P_2 its value in the second period, the inflation rate is merely the difference between the two, expressed as a percentage of the value of the index in the first period:

$$\text{Inflation rate} = \frac{(P_2 - P_1) \times 100}{P_1}$$

When P_1 is the base period, its value is 100, and the expression shown above reduces to $P_2 - 100$. In other cases the full calculation must be made. For example, suppose the index increased to 144.7 in June 2012 from 141.0 in June 2011 (using a hypothetical base year earlier than 2005). The rise of 3.7 points in the index is a 2.6 per cent

rise over its initial value of 141.0, indicating a rate of inflation of 2.6 per cent over the year.

If the two values being compared are not a year apart, it is common to convert the result to an *annual rate*. For example, suppose the RPI is 135.2 in January 2012 and 135.6 in February 2012 (on a base of, say, 1998 = 100). This is an increase of 0.296 per cent over the month ((0.4/135.2) × 100). It is also an *annual rate* of approximately 3.55 per cent (0.296 per cent × 12) over the year.[15] This means that if the rate of increase that occurred between January and February 2012 continued for a year, the price level would rise by approximately 3.55 per cent over the year. In practice, inflation rates are usually expressed as the rate of change between the latest month and the same month a year ago. So when we say that inflation was 2.4 per cent in December 2013, this means that the RPI was 2.4 per cent higher in December 2013 than it had been in December 2012. It does not mean that annualized inflation between November 2013 and December 2013 was 2.4 per cent.

Variations on RPI

There are three additional, often quoted, variations on RPI in use in the United Kingdom.

1. CPI is a Consumer Price Index used to form the basis of the inflation target set by the government for the Bank of England's Monetary Policy Committee. (Chapter 21 discusses the Committee in some detail.) This index used to be called HICP (Harmonized Index of Consumer Prices). It is calculated on a different basis from the RPI in order to conform with EU statistical practices. (This includes some differences in components and is calculated as a geometric rather than an arithmetic average. The details of these differences are somewhat arcane and not important to understand at this stage.)

2. RPIX is an index calculated using the same components as RPI except that it excludes mortgage interest payments. This is the index that was used as the basis for the UK inflation target from 1997 to 2003.

3. RPIY is RPIX but with the further modification that it excludes the effects of indirect tax changes on prices. RPIY is sometimes referred to as 'underlying inflation' or 'core inflation' because it excludes the effects on inflation induced by changes in monetary *and* fiscal policies.

---

[14] Notice that the base period relative to which the RPI is calculated could be changed at some time in the future, but the base period in current use in 2014 remained January 2005.

[15] We say *approximately* because a 0.296 per cent rise each month that is *compounded* for twelve months will give rise to an increase over the year that is greater than 3.55 per cent. The appropriate procedure is to increase the index in January by 0.296 per cent twelve times (calculate [(1.00296)^{12} - 1] × 100) rather than just to multiply it by 12. The two results are the difference between simple and compound interest rates. Note, however, that the headline inflation rate is calculated as the percentage change of the price level in a specific month relative to its value twelve months earlier, and not as an annualized change over a single month.

In December 2013 the annual inflation rate according to each of these measures was:

- RPI = 2.7 per cent
- RPIX = 2.8 per cent
- RPIY = 2.8 per cent
- CPI = 2.0 per cent

The European Central Bank uses the CPI for the Euro-zone as a whole to judge whether it is meeting its objective of price stability.

2. Revisions to National Accounts data

In Tables 15.1–15.3 we reported the data for UK GDP in 2011 and its major components. Policy-makers use this type of information in order to assess what is going on in the economy, and to inform decisions about whether, for example, taxes or interest rates need to change. However, National Accounts statistics are frequently revised and sometimes by a large amount, so great caution has to be used in putting too much weight on what any particular statistical release reports.

One example of significant revisions to National Accounts arose in the early 2000s when the volume measures of GDP were converted from a fixed-base-period method of estimation to a chained-index basis. On the old basis, real growth in 1999 and 2000 had been estimated at 2.9 per cent and 3.7 per cent, respectively, but in 2003 these estimates were revised to 2.4 per cent and 3.0 per cent. These changes may not seem large, but changes of this magnitude could have made policy-makers change their perception as to whether the economy was growing at well above its sustainable long-run trend or, as later appeared true, at very close to its long-run trend.

The most dramatic examples of revisions to data arise in the balance of payments figures, which broadly measure the difference between imports and exports of goods and services (for further explanation see Chapter 24). Table 15.8 shows the official data for the UK current account balance of payments deficit for the years 1988–96, as reported first in the 1997 Balance of Payments *Pink Book* and then figures for the same years as reported in 2005. There were substantial revisions to all these figures, but the most dramatic revisions to the figures reported in 1997 were those for the most recent three years 1994–6. Of course, the current account balance is arrived at as the difference between two large numbers (exports and imports), so it requires only small percentage revisions to the measured totals for trade flows to lead to quite large percentage revisions to the deficit or surplus.

In 2014, the ONS announced that it was changing its methodology for calculating GDP and this would result in

Table 15.8 Revisions to UK current account balance of payments deficit between 1997 and 2005

	Data as of 1997 *Pink Book* (£ million)	Data as of 2005 *Pink Book* (£ million)
1988	–16,475	–19,321
1989	–22,398	–26,321
1990	–18,746	–22,281
1991	–7,954	–10,659
1992	–10,133	–12,974
1993	–10,295	–11,919
1994	–1,655	–6,768
1995	–3,672	–9,015
1996	–435	–7,324

substantial revisions to UK growth estimates. These were to be published in the October 2014 *Blue Book*. This will come out after this book has gone to press so we will update readers on the effects of these changes in the Online Resource Centre.[16]

However, some data are not subject to revisions, and it is worth knowing which these are. Most financial market data, such as exchange rates, interest rates, and share prices are not revised. These prices are recorded accurately at a point in time and so there is no reason for revision. Of course, the prices will change over time, sometimes quite significantly, but data for prices at a past point in time will not be revised later.

More surprising, perhaps, is the fact that inflation data are not revised once they have been published. This does not mean that the statisticians could not have made an error. It is just that any such errors will not lead to data revisions. The main reason for this is that RPI data and other inflation measures are used in legal contracts, affecting some wage agreements, pension contracts, and the yield on some inflation-linked securities (such as indexed gilts), and it would cause chaos if the basis on which such payments are made were to be changed repeatedly retrospectively. Hence, an inflation figure, once announced, can be taken as the truth, even if it isn't.

However, the general message of this case study is that formulating economic policy is difficult as some of the key data on which decisions are based can be substantially revised later.

---

[16] <http://www.oxfordtextbooks.co.uk/orc/lipsey13e/>

Conclusion

We now know how to measure and interpret the various concepts related to the nation's income and output, of which the gross domestic product (GDP) is the most commonly used aggregate measure. We are now ready to begin

to develop a theory of how they are determined and the consequences of changes in them due to either natural or policy-induced causes.

SUMMARY

What is macroeconomics

■ Macroeconomics is about the economy as a whole. It studies aggregate phenomena, such as growth, business cycles, living standards, inflation, unemployment, and the balance of payments. It also asks how governments can use their monetary and fiscal policy instruments to help stabilize the economy.

Why do we need macroeconomics?

■ Macroeconomics is useful because it enables us to study events that affect the economy as a whole without going into detail about specific products and sectors.

The GDP gap

■ Potential GDP is the level of national output that would be produced if the economy were operating at its normal capacity, or full-employment, level.

■ The GDP gap is the difference between actual GDP and its potential level.

■ When actual GDP is above potential the positive gap is sometimes called an inflationary gap, and when actual GDP is below potential the negative gap is sometimes called a recessionary gap.

Measurement of national output

■ As national accountants define things, each firm's contribution to total output is equal to its value added, which is the gross value of the firm's output minus the value of all intermediate goods and services—that is, the outputs of other firms—that it uses. Goods that count as part of the economy's output are called final goods; all others are called intermediate goods. The sum of all the values added produced in an economy is called gross value added at basic prices. Basic prices are the prices received by producers net of taxes on products (plus subsidies).

The circular flow of income, output, and spending

■ The determination of GDP can be represented as a circular flow of income and spending.

■ Withdrawals of spending arise when income received is not spent on the domestic economy.

■ Injections of spending are those that are not the result of domestic income receipts, but rather come from sources other than domestic income recipients.

GDP, GNI, and GNP

■ Measured gross domestic product (GDP) can be calculated in three different ways: (1) as the sum of all values added by all producers of both intermediate and final goods; (2) as the income claims generated by the total production of goods and services; and (3) as the spending needed to purchase all final goods and services produced during the period. By standard accounting conventions these three aggregations define the same total, as long as we add taxes on products (minus subsidies) to the first two in order to measure GDP at market prices. Market prices are the prices paid by consumers.

■ From the spending side of the National Accounts, $GDP = C + I + G + (X - IM)$. C comprises private consumption spending. I is investment in fixed capital (including residential construction), inventories, and valuables. Gross investment can be split into replacement investment (necessary to keep the stock of capital intact) and net investment (net additions to the stock of capital). G is government consumption. $(X - IM)$ represents net exports, or exports minus imports; it will be negative if imports exceed exports.

■ GDP income-based adds up all factor rewards in production. The main income categories making up GDP are operating surpluses, mixed incomes, and compensation of employees.

■ UK GDP measures production that is located in the United Kingdom, and UK gross national income (GNI) measures income accruing to UK residents. The difference is due to net income from overseas. GNI is the same thing as was formerly called gross national product (GNP).

- Real GDP is calculated to measure changes in real volumes of output and real income. Nominal GDP measures changes in both prices and quantities. Any change in nominal GDP (or GNI) can be split into a change in real GDP and a change due to prices. Appropriate comparisons of nominal and real measures yield implicit deflators.

- Personal income is income received by households' members before any allowance for personal taxes. Personal disposable income is the amount actually available for households to spend or to save—that is, income minus taxes.

Interpreting income and output measures

- GDP and related measures of the nation's income and output must be interpreted with their limitations in mind. GDP excludes production that takes place in the underground economy or that does not pass through markets. Moreover, GDP does not measure everything that contributes to human welfare.

- GDP is one of the best measures available of the total economic activity within a country. It is particularly valuable when changes in GDP are used to indicate how economic activity has changed over time.

TOPICS FOR REVIEW

- Targets and instruments of macroeconomic policy
- Injections and withdrawals
- Potential GDP
- The GDP gap
- Value added
- Intermediate and final goods
- Spending-based and income-based GDP
- GNI and GNP
- Personal disposable income
- Implicit deflator
- What GDP does and does not measure

QUESTIONS

1 Assuming an economy with no government and no foreign trade, calculate GDP for the following output scenario. There are three firms: firm A is a mining company, firm B is a steel producer, and firm C is a car manufacturer. In a specific year, firm A sells £100 million worth of iron ore to firm B, firm B sells £200 million worth of steel to firm C, and firm C sells £500 million worth of cars to the general public. If there are no changes in inventories, no taxes, and no other producers in the economy, what is GDP?

2 How would the answer to Question 1 change if firm B had increased its inventories of iron ore by £20 million during this year?

3 How would the answer to Question 2 change if firm C had sold £50 million worth of lorries to firm A in addition to its car sales?

4 Suppose again that there are only three companies in an economy. Company A grows crops and extracts minerals from its land with no inputs from other companies. Its sales are £100m per year, half of which goes to consumers and half to companies B and C in equal amounts. Company B buys inputs from A and sells its entire output of £200m to company C. Company C buys inputs from A and B and sells its £450m output directly to consumers (though 20 per cent of this is overseas). What is gross value added at

basic prices? If there is only one indirect tax, value added tax levied at 10 per cent, what is the value of GDP at market prices?

5 If the price index in 2011 is 220 and by 2012 it has risen to 228, what is the annual rate of inflation? If nominal GDP has risen from £1,500 billion to £1,575 billion, what is the growth rate of real GDP?

6 Explain why we cannot calculate the national product simply by adding up the production of all firms.

7 What is the difference between real GDP and nominal GDP and why does this distinction matter? Which measure would be appropriate for judging changes in standard of living?

8 What are the limitations of GDP per head as a measure of the quality of life?

9 What would it mean to be told that a country's GNI was greater than its GDP?

10 Using the spending-based definition ($C + I + G + NX$), explain where each of the following appears in the national income accounts measure of GDP, if at all: state pensions; company pensions; student grants; theatre receipts; judges' salaries; unsold cars in showrooms; receipts from beer sales in a students' union bar; receipts from purchases of new copies of this book; receipts from purchases of second-hand copies of this book.

CHAPTER 16

A BASIC MODEL OF THE DETERMINATION OF GDP IN THE SHORT TERM

For the next several chapters, we are going to build a model that is designed to explain the causes and consequences of deviations of GDP from its potential level. This is the behaviour of what we defined in Chapter 15 as the *GDP gap*. We seek to answer questions such as: 'Why are there sometimes booms in activity and recessions at other times?' 'What happens to GDP when government spending is increased?' and 'Under what conditions do we get inflation?'

In this chapter, you will learn that:

- Macroeconomic theory is designed to explain the deviation of actual from potential GDP—that is, the GDP gap.

In the theory presented here:

- The determination of GDP in the short run depends on the behaviour of key categories of aggregate spending: consumption, investment, government spending, and net exports.
- Consumption spending depends on disposable income and wealth.
- Investment spending depends on real interest rates and business confidence.
- A necessary condition for GDP to be in equilibrium is that desired domestic spending is equal to actual output.

The macro problem: inflation and unemployment

Although the long-term living standard of a nation is determined by the growth of its potential GDP (which we discuss in Chapter 26), short-term deviations from the long-run trend also have important consequences. For example, in the 1930s, when the great UK economist John Maynard Keynes first developed macroeconomics, the actual GDPs of the industrialized countries stayed below their potential levels for almost a decade, with the consequence of massive levels of unemployment. Indeed, macroeconomics as a subject was invented in order to explain why there was mass unemployment in the 1930s and to discover what could be done to eliminate it. In more recent times, the sharp UK recession of 2008–9 took GDP well below its potential level, and the IMF forecast in 2013 was that the negative GDP gap will not be eliminated until 2018. In contrast, GDP has several times stayed above its potential level for several years and in some periods inflation ensued. As a result, much of macroeconomic theory

is devoted to examining the causes and consequences of such deviations. Also as a result, much economic policy is aimed at preventing the onset of the major bouts of unemployment and inflation that are often associated with deviations of actual GDP from its potential and in mitigating these consequences when they do occur.

Actual economies do not expand slowly and steadily as the level of potential GDP grows. Instead, virtually all economies have some periods when actual GDP is growing faster than potential and other periods when it is growing more slowly than potential, or even falling. In other words, actual economies exhibit cycles about the trend growth path. The growth rate of UK GDP since 1886 is shown in Figure 16.1[1] (and the GDP gap since 1970 is shown in Figure 15.1 in the previous chapter). This chart makes clear that, while long-term growth is generally positive, year-to-year changes

---

[1] Data for 2013–18 are IMF forecasts as of October 2013.

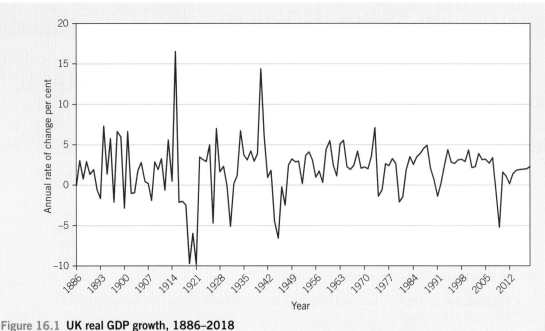

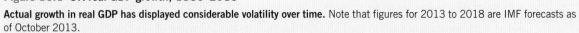

Figure 16.1 UK real GDP growth, 1886–2018

Actual growth in real GDP has displayed considerable volatility over time. Note that figures for 2013 to 2018 are IMF forecasts as of October 2013.

Source: 100 Years of Economic Statistics, The Economist; *UK National Accounts*, ONS, and IMF *World Economic Outlook*.

in actual GDP are quite volatile. There are some periods of very strong positive growth, while there are others when growth is negative (such as 2009 when UK GDP fell by around 5 per cent). The terminology associated with such cycles in economic activity is set out in Box 16.1.

Periods in which actual GDP is below potential GDP are costly because output that could have been produced is lost for ever. This is what we have referred to in Chapter 7 as a *deadweight loss*. Thus, unemployment is undesirable and it is commonly agreed that policy-makers should aim to keep unemployment at a low level. However, economic downturns do not typically cause all citizens to lose an equal amount of income. Rather, some lose their jobs (or their businesses) and thus suffer a loss of income and well-being while others remain employed and do not suffer directly.

A different problem arises when policy-makers try to make their economies grow too fast. This is especially so when governments try to encourage a growth of spending in the economy that is faster than the growth in productive capacity. The outcome of an excessive growth in demand relative to supply is often inflation, and inflation itself is disruptive to the economy (for reasons that we discuss in Chapter 23).

Thus, the central problem for macroeconomic policy-makers is to decide how to manage the economy in such a way that inflation is kept under control while unemployment is also kept to a minimum.

Our job in the next several chapters is to understand how the macroeconomic system works in the short term and what policy-makers can do to help keep the economy stable and close to potential output. This is not a trivial task, and many mistakes have been made in the past. It should be noted, however, that the Keynesian model that we are about to explain has proved very valuable in explaining the 2008–9 recession. So it will help us to explain the causes of this recession and the policy reactions to it.[2]

Macroeconomics as theory

We are now going to build a model of how GDP is determined in relation to its potential level, which we take as given for the next few chapters. This model will help us to understand the forces that drive how actual GDP and the price level are determined from year to year.

We start by setting out some of the conceptual foundations of the short-term analysis of macroeconomic activity. We then build the simplest possible model of GDP determination, under some very special assumptions. Later chapters make our model increasingly realistic. Whenever in the next chapters, we say something will happen or is true, we are referring to the assumptions and the behaviour of the model (often called its predictions).

[2] See, for example, Robert Skidelsky, *Keynes: The Return of the Master*, London: Allen Lane, 2009.

Box 16.1 **The terminology of business cycles**

The red line shows the hypothetical path of national output relative to trend, or potential, over time. Although the phases of business fluctuations are described by a series of commonly used terms, no two cycles are the same.

Trough

A trough is characterized by high unemployment and a level of demand that is low in relation to the economy's capacity to produce. Thus there is a substantial amount of unused productive capacity. Business profits are low; for some individual companies they are negative. Confidence about economic prospects in the immediate future is lacking, and as a result many firms are unwilling to risk making new investments.

Recovery

The characteristics of a recovery, or expansion, are many—rundown equipment is replaced, employment, income, and consumer spending all begin to rise, and expectations become more favourable as a result of increases in production, sales, and profits. Investments that once seemed risky may be undertaken as the climate of business opinion starts to change from one of pessimism to one of optimism. As demand rises, production can be increased with relative ease merely by re-employing the existing unused capacity and unemployed labour.

Peak

A peak is the top of a cycle. When $Y > Y^*$ at the peak, existing capacity is utilized to a high degree, labour shortages may develop, particularly in key skills, and shortages of essential raw materials are likely. As shortages develop in many markets, a situation of general excess demand develops. Costs rise but, since prices also rise, business remains profitable.

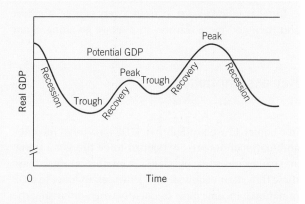

Recession

A recession, or contraction, is a downturn in economic activity. Common usage defines a recession as a fall in real GDP for two quarters in succession. Demand falls off, and as a result production and employment also fall. As employment falls so do personal incomes. Profits drop, and some firms encounter financial difficulties. Investments that looked profitable with the expectation of continually rising demand now appear unprofitable. It may not even be worth replacing capital goods as they wear out because unused capacity is increasing steadily. In historical discussions, a recession that is deep and long-lasting is often called a depression.

Booms and slumps

Two non-technical but descriptive terms are often used. The period at or near the bottom of an abnormally deep recession is called a *slump*, and the period at or near the top of an abnormally strong recovery is called a *boom*.

Whether or not these things are true of the world in which we live cannot, of course, be decided without appealing to factual observations. However, we would not ask you to learn all of this if we did not think that much of the model's behaviour does agree with the facts—and we illustrate how it does in many cases along the way. Some things, however, are still open to debate, either because one or more of the model's assumptions are questioned (e.g. the effect of changes in the price level on wealth) or because it is not certain that the model's behaviour fits the facts fully (e.g. how well the long-run properties of the model describe real behaviour over various actual time periods).

Our task is to understand what *causes* macroeconomic variables to behave as they do in the short term, and how they are interrelated. It is important to realize that we are about to discuss *theory*. In this process we will build up a conceptual model of the economy. This model will be simple. It needs to be simple so that we can understand

how it works. This branch of macroeconomics has been around for well over half a century.[3] It has developed and changed a great deal in this time. It is going to take several

---

[3] It also important to note that the approach we develop below sets out how macroeconomic analysis has traditionally been approached, but students who go on to study economics at a more advanced level will come across a different approach. The traditional approach, which is still the basis of most practical econometric models used for policy purposes by central banks and finance ministries, assumes that there can be disequilibria in the economy, such as unemployment and output gaps, and explains these in terms of aggregate spending flows compared with some hypothetical potential level of production. The newer, but not necessarily better, approach builds models of the economy in which all agents, such as consumers and firms, are continuously optimizing their behaviour and all markets clear continuously, so there are no disequilibria even in the short term, and hence no involuntary unemployment. These models are useful for some purposes, but they are technically more demanding in that they require advanced mathematics, so they will not be discussed here. But students who go further in economics should be alert to a change in approach at some stage, even though courses that adopt this approach may still be called macroeconomics.

chapters before we get close to outlining the complete picture. Hence, the reader should be patient and not rush to draw policy conclusions too soon.[3]

In what follows we start from a very simple structure and then add more features to it as we go along. Some clearly stated *assumptions* will define our macroeconomic model. Some of these assumptions will be relaxed as we go along; others will remain throughout. The permanent or temporary nature of individual assumptions will be indicated as they are introduced.

Key assumptions

In Chapter 15 we learned that 'GDP', 'national income', and 'national output' are defined to be the same thing, and can be measured by 'GDP'. From now on we will use these three terms equivalently. However, we refer to GDP or national income most frequently when discussing the determinants of domestic spending, as incomes are one of the most important determinants of consumers' spending. We refer to national output more commonly when discussing the responses of producers to changes in spending. Remember, though, that the actual measured values of these three concepts are identical, although their components are different.[4]

We also saw in Chapter 15 that we could arrive at a measure of GDP by three different routes. We could add up the incomes of owners of resource inputs, we could add up the values added of each industrial sector, or we could add up total final spending. Now that we want to develop a theory that *explains* the determination of GDP rather than just describing it, we have to decide which of these three classifications we are going to rely on to structure our theories. We will learn very shortly that macroeconomics, as a subject, has developed by attempting to explain the major categories of final spending in the economy. We need to understand why this approach was adopted.

Suppose that we were to start our theory of GDP by trying to explain the net output (value added) of each major industrial sector, such as manufacturing, agriculture, etc., as listed in Table 15.1. We could establish the capital stock and employment in each sector and we could analyse demand forces for the output of each sector. In essence, we would be building a theory around demand and supply forces in each industry in the economy, and then we would add up the results to get total output.

One reason we do not do this in macroeconomics is that such an approach would not really be dealing with the aggregate economy at all. Models that explain output industry by industry do exist, but such microeconomic models require so much detail that they make it difficult to handle many important issues that affect the whole economy simultaneously.

A second reason why we do not apply the tools of demand and supply on an industry-by-industry basis in macroeconomics is that those tools are not appropriate for handling the most important macro problems. In particular, macroeconomics seeks to explain why an economy might have unemployment and excess capacity for some time. In contrast, the microeconomic analysis of markets deals with situations in which prices move to clear markets. Macroeconomists also want to be able to study simultaneous (or near simultaneous) movements in output that are common to all sectors—the business cycle. An important question in macroeconomics is: 'What causes the cycle in GDP and can government policy stabilize it—that is, smooth out the cycles?'

Two other important assumptions are, first, that there exists a macroeconomic equilibrium for the whole economy where output is at its potential level and all resources are employed at their normal levels of activity and, secondly, that there is an automatic adjustment mechanism that tends to move the economy back to that equilibrium whenever it deviates from it. If we assume, as we do in the next few chapters, that potential output is given and that the technology of production is unchanged, such an equilibrium does exist in our model. It is an open question whether or not it is useful to assume that such an equilibrium exists in our world, in which technology is continually altering the structure of the economy and potential output is growing but not necessarily steadily. We postpone considering this question until Chapter 22, but it is important to note now that the existence of an equilibrium and forces that restore it if it is disturbed is an assumption of our model not a statement of obvious empirical fact.

---

[4] As we have seen, there is a small difference between GDP and GNI (in 2011, for example, UK GNI was 1.3 per cent larger than GDP); however, we are now assuming that this difference can be ignored. Recall also that GNI used to be called GNP, but GNI became standard in the UK national accounts in 1998. You will no doubt see references to GNP in the economics literature for many years to come.

Aggregation across industries

In macroeconomics we take the industrial structure of the economy as fixed. When national output expands or contracts, all sectors are assumed to expand and contract together. No consideration is given to relative prices of different goods or services. In this respect the economy of our model is best thought of as being made up of many competitive firms, all producing the same type of product. These firms are all aggregated into a single productive sector. It is the behaviour of this sector that will determine national output and GDP.

In elementary macroeconomics we assume the existence of a single productive sector producing a homogeneous output.

This assumption will remain throughout our study of macroeconomics. We will also analyse the behaviour of this single sector as if it were a manufacturing industry, though this is only a matter of convenience.

The fact that we assume a single production sector explains why we approach the determination of GDP by focusing on spending categories: there are no subdivisions of output by type of product. However, an important implication for final spending is that *in our model* it is all spent on the same final good—the product of 'United Kingdom PLC'. This means that while different categories of spending may be differently motivated, they all have the same effect once implemented.

From time to time we use concrete examples, such as 'suppose the government increases spending on road building' or 'suppose firms decide to buy more machines (invest)'. The point to bear in mind is that all spending in the model has the same effect once it is made because it is assumed to be demand for the output of the single-product industrial sector.

The government sector

Confusion can arise out of the assumption of a single sector when we come to discuss the role of government. In reality, part of government activity involves producing goods and services, such as health and education. However, in order to maintain the simplicity of the assumption that there is only one sector, in macroeconomics we ignore the fact that government is a producer and treat government as a purchaser of the output of the private industrial sector. In other words we make no exceptions to our assumption about the homogeneity of productive activity.

Justification

The extreme assumption that there is only one output is of course not meant as a description of reality. It is a theoretical abstraction, meant to simplify our study without losing the essence of the problem in which we are interested. In this case the one-product model captures the assumption that the similarities between the effects of £1 spent in each sector of the real-world

economy are more important than the differences. Note that it is only similarities with respect to the effects of spending that are in question. Causes of different types of spending are not assumed to be the same. Indeed, much of our effort is directed at developing consumption, investment, and net export functions that explain the *different* motives that determine the various spending flows.

Time-scale

The part of macroeconomics that we are about to study has traditionally been concerned with the short-run behaviour of an economy, while growth theory has been concerned with long-run trends. However, it is important to note that the concepts of 'short run' and 'long run' have a different meaning in macroeconomics from the usage in microeconomics. Indeed, 'long run' itself is used in two different senses even within macroeconomics.

Short run

In microeconomics 'short run' is used to analyse the behaviour of firms during the period in which their capital stock is taken as given and they can only change their variable inputs (labour and materials). In other words the short run is a period during which the capital stock is fixed; nonetheless, firms are in short-run equilibrium because they are producing their optimal output given their capital stock. In macroeconomics the short run is the period during which the economy maintains a deviation of actual from potential output, or a GDP gap. This deviation is associated either with the existence of excess capacity and unemployment, in the case of recession, or unsustainable output and/or inflation, in the case of a boom. In practice, the short run may be measured in terms of several years, so it is not really short in the common-sense meaning of the term.

In its early days as a discipline, macroeconomics concentrated entirely on the short run as we have just defined it. However, recent developments have increasingly emphasized longer-run considerations.

Analysis of the short run in macroeconomics is concerned with explaining why national output can deviate from its potential level. It is about the GDP gap and how to keep both positive and negative gaps as small as possible—that is, how to keep actual GDP as close as possible to potential GDP.

Long run

The long run is a period sufficient to allow time for the automatic adjustment mechanisms (discussed below) to return economic activity to our model's assumed equilibrium after it has been disturbed by an exogenous shock. This equilibrium is reached when the economy returns to producing the level of potential (or full-employment) output. For analytical purposes we will assume that the long-run level of output is constant and is associated with a fixed capital stock and a fixed level of technical knowledge. This contrasts markedly with the usage of 'long run' in microeconomics, where it relates to a period within which the capital stock can vary. Even in macroeconomics there is really a 'long run' and a 'longer run', where the latter permits growth in productive capacity and therefore growth in potential output. For the most part we use the static concept of long run, unless we are explicitly discussing growth, as in Chapter 26.

The long run in macroeconomics is the period it takes the economy to return to the level of potential GDP once it has been disturbed.

Temporary assumptions

In order to get us started in building a theory of macroeconomics, we need to make a few additional assumptions, which will be relaxed later.

The price level

At the outset we will assume that the price level—the money price of the economy's single output good—is fixed. All input prices are also fixed. Permitting the price level to vary simultaneously with output will be the main task addressed in Chapters 21 and 22. In the meantime, while the price level is held constant variations in the money value of all variables represent real changes in these variables. It is important to be aware for the future that all spending (consumption, investment, government spending, and net exports) will continue to be defined in real terms even when the price level is permitted to vary. In order to do this, changes in money values must be corrected for changes in the price level so that they measure real changes.

Excess capacity

Initially, we will assume that the economy has excess capacity. Thus it is not constrained from producing more output by shortages of capital stock or labour.

We start with the twin assumptions of a fixed price level and excess capacity because it is easiest to begin in an environment where all changes in GDP are changes in real GDP. Developing a theory to explain how changes in money GDP are divided between changes in the price level and changes in real GDP requires a more complicated model, which we come to in Chapters 21 and 22.

Closed economy

In this chapter alone we will ignore the possibility that the output of our economy can be sold overseas and that domestic consumers can buy foreign-produced goods. We assume an economy with no foreign trade, so domestic spending and domestic output are equal. This is not an assumption we will need for very long. It will be dropped in the next chapter.

No government

Government enters into macroeconomics in two ways: first, through decisions relating to taxation and spending, and, secondly, through the setting of interest rates or influencing the money supply.

A final simplifying assumption in this chapter is that there is no government sector either demanding goods (spending) or raising money through taxes, but we will drop this assumption in the next chapter.

Interest rates are one of the most important tools by which policymakers seek to control the macroeconomy. Interest rates have their main impact via influencing various categories of private spending and asset prices. In this and subsequent chapters we point out the impact that interest rate changes have on private spending. In Chapters 19 and 20 we provide a detailed analysis of the transmission mechanism of monetary policy—that is, of how changes in interest rates affect GDP and inflation in normal times.

It is worth summarizing all these assumptions:

- **we have a closed economy**
- **with a single industrial sector**
- **producing a homogeneous output**
- **at a fixed price**
- **with no government.**
- **It has a unique equilibrium at potential output, which is characterized by normal rates of utilization of all resources; currently, however, there is excess capacity.**
- **So there are no resource constraints preventing the expansion of national output.**

By now the reader may be wondering: what is left after we have assumed away so many potentially important things? The answer is: final demand or spending on the output of the economy. Developing a theory of final spending will enable us to understand what determines GDP in our model.

In terms of the circular flow model introduced in Chapter 15 this, our simplest model, contains a flow of income from households to firms as spending and from firms to households as incomes ('factor' payments in the form of wages or profits), while there is only one withdrawal or leakage, household savings, and one injection, investment spending. Later, we will add the flows associated with the government and foreign trade.

There is a good reason for starting with an explanation of spending. Many economists believe that variations in spending are the most important causes of variations in the gap between potential and actual GDP that we are seeking to explain.

What determines aggregate spending?

Before we can answer the question posed in the heading we must deal with a few more important preliminaries.

Some important preliminaries

From actual to desired spending

In Chapter 15 we discussed how statisticians divide actual measured GDP, calculated from the spending side, into its components: private consumption, investment, government consumption, and net exports. For any particular year (such as 2011 used in Tables 15.1–15.3) we reported actual values of all those variables for that year. These are the outcome of what actually happened in that year.

When building our theory of GDP determination we are concerned with a different concept. It is variously called *desired*, *planned*, or *intended* spending. Of course, all people would like to spend virtually unlimited amounts, if only they had the resources. However, desired spending does not refer to what people would like to do under imaginary circumstances; it refers to what people want to spend out of the resources that are at their command (i.e. their income or wealth).

Every single agent who has income to spend makes spending decisions. Fortunately, it is unnecessary for our purposes to look at each of the millions of such individual decisions. Instead, it is sufficient to consider four main groups of decision-makers: households, firms, governments, and foreign purchasers of domestic output. The actual purchases made by these four groups account for the four main categories of spending that we studied in the previous chapter: private consumption, investment, government consumption, and net exports. These groups' desired spending—desired private consumption, desired investment, desired government consumption, and desired exports—account for total desired spending. (To allow for the fact that many of the commodities desired by each group have some imported content, we subtract spending on imports to arrive at the value of spending on domestic output.) The result is total desired spending on domestically produced goods and services, called **aggregate spending**, or *AE*:[5]

$$AE = C + I + G + (X - IM).$$

Desired spending need not equal actual spending, either in total or in any individual category. For example, firms may not plan to invest in the accumulation of unsold stock this year but may do so unintentionally. If they produce goods to meet estimated sales but demand is unexpectedly low, the unsold goods that pile up on their shelves are undesired, and unintended, inventory accumulation. In this case actual investment spending exceeds desired investment spending.

The process by which the spending plans are reconciled during an adjustment process is what drives the model. Hence, people may be trying to implement some spending plans that are not consistent with each other, but this will generate economic forces that bring about consistency after the event.[6]

The national accounts measure actual spending in each of the four categories: private consumption, investment, government consumption, and net exports. The theory of GDP determination deals with desired spending in each of these four categories.

Recall, however, that these spending categories differ because different agents are doing the spending and have different motivations for that spending. They are not different in the effects of their spending because in our simple theory they all generate spending on the final output of the single productive sector.

---

[5] We use *AE*, which is short for 'aggregate expenditure', as we reserve *AS* to refer to 'aggregate supply'.

[6] Early macro theorists used a distinction between 'ex ante' (before the event) variables and 'ex post' (after the event) variables. This corresponds to our distinction between desired or planned variables and the actual outcomes.

Box 16.2 Savings make the news

In 2007 UK savings made headlines for being so low. For example:

Savings rate hits 47-year low

A little more than two years later savings were causing headlines again but for very different reasons.

Household savings hit 16-year high

But by 2013 the mood had changed and again the headlines were of the form:

Biggest drop in savings for 40 years, Bank of England figures reveal

Each of these headlines was followed by a story suggesting that the reader should be worried about the latest state of affairs. So how can high savings and low savings both be signs of a worrying state of affairs? The answer is that they can't, but there are positive and negative aspects to each situation, and in both extreme cases the media emphasized the negative aspects.

We reconcile these two views of saving in the first case study at the end of this chapter, but for now we note that swings in saving behaviour are the inverse of swings in consumer spending. So when savings rates are high spending is low, and vice versa. These swings are an important component in the business cycle because high consumer spending is associated with high demand and a boom in output, while high savings rates are associated with lower spending and falling output. In this sense, high savings rates can be linked to slow or negative real growth, as this implies low consumer spending. This outcome is known as the *paradox of thrift* because high savings rates suggest thriftiness, but could also cause weak final demand and hence slow or negative growth, though more likely both high savings and slow growth were being driven by a broader set of influences.

Autonomous and induced spending

In what follows it will be useful to distinguish between *autonomous* and *induced* spending. Components of aggregate spending that *do not* depend on current domestic incomes are called **autonomous**, or sometimes *exogenous*.[7] Autonomous spending can and does change, but such changes do not occur systematically in response to changes in income. Components of aggregate spending that *do* change in response to changes in income are called **induced**, or *endogenous*. As we will see, the induced response of aggregate spending to a change in income plays a key role in the determination of equilibrium GDP in our model.

A simple model

To develop a theory of GDP determination, we need to examine the determinants of each component of desired aggregate spending. In this chapter we focus on desired consumption and desired investment. Private consumption is the largest single component of aggregate spending (about 65 per cent of UK GDP in 2011) and, as we shall see, it provides the single most important link between desired aggregate spending and actual GDP. Investment is national output that is not used either for current consumption or by governments, and it is motivated by firms' desire to increase the capital stock.[8]

Desired private consumption spending

We are now ready to study the determinants of desired spending flows. We start with private consumption.

People can do one of two things with their disposable income: spend it on consumption or save it. **Saving** is defined as all disposable income that is not consumed. Box 16.2 picks up some conflicting views about saving reported in the media, and the first case study at the end of this chapter considers these further.

By definition there are only two possible uses of disposable income, consumption and saving. So when each household decides how much to put to one use, it has automatically decided how much to put to the other use.

What determines the division between the amount that households decide to spend on goods and services for consumption and the amount that they decide to save? The things that influence this decision are summarized in the consumption function and the saving function, which are two ways of showing the single decision of how to divide income between spending and saving.

The consumption function

The **consumption function** relates the total desired consumer spending of households[9] to the variables that affect

---

[7] 'Autonomous' means self-motivated, or independent. 'Exogenous' means determined outside the model, while 'endogenous' means determined inside the model.

[8] In practice, government and consumers do some of the nation's investment, but, for simplicity, we focus mainly on the investment behaviour of firms. The principles involved can be easily generalized.

[9] We refer to households as the basic units here even though this includes single individuals, and we sometimes refer to them as consumers when their spending decisions are being discussed. We shall also refer to the personal sector and the household sector interchangeably.

it. It is one of the central relationships in the kind of macroeconomics that we are studying here.

Although we are ultimately interested in the relationship between consumption and GDP, the underlying behaviour of households is assumed to depend on the income that they actually have to spend—their disposable income. Under the simplifying assumptions that we have made in this chapter, there are no taxes. Households receive all income that is generated.[10] Therefore, disposable income, which we denote by Y_d, is equal to GDP, Y. (Later in our discussion Y and Y_d will diverge, because taxes are a part of GDP that is not at the disposal of households.

Consumption and disposable income

It should not surprise us to hear that a household's spending is related to the amount of income available. However, there is more than one way in which this relationship could work. To see what is involved, consider two quite different types of individual.

The first is an unimaginative rule follower. He puts some of his income aside for the future, but in making this decision he never asks if the future will be different from today. As a result he decides once and for all what proportion of his income he will spend and what he will save. If his income rises, he spends and saves more, while if his income falls, he spends and saves less. Thus, this person's spending each week is directly linked to each week's take-home pay—that is, to his current disposable income.

The second individual is a prudent planner. She thinks about the future as much as the present and makes plans that stretch over her lifetime. She puts money aside for retirement and for the occasional rainy day when disposable income may fall temporarily—she knows that she must expect some hard times as well as good times. She also knows that she will need to spend extra money while her children are being raised and educated, and that her disposable income will probably be highest later in life when the children have left home and she has finally reached the peak of her career. This person may borrow to meet higher expenses earlier in life, paying back out of the higher income that she expects to attain later in life. A temporary, unexpected windfall of income may be saved. Spending the savings that were put aside for just such a rainy day may cushion a temporary unexpected shortfall. In short, this person's current spending will be closely related to her expected average *lifetime income*. Fluctuations in her *current income* will have little effect on her current spending, unless such fluctuations also cause her to change her expectations of lifetime

income, as would be the case, for example, if an unexpected promotion came along.

John Maynard Keynes (1883–1946), the famous English economist who developed the basic theory of macroeconomics—and gave his name to 'Keynesian economics'—populated his theory with the first type of individual. For them, current consumption spending depends only on current income. To this day a consumption function based on this assumption is called a *Keynesian consumption function*.

Later, two US economists, Franco Modigliani and Milton Friedman, both of whom were subsequently awarded the Nobel Prize in economics, analysed the behaviour of prudent consumers who take a longer-term view in determining their consumption. Their theories, which Modigliani called the *life-cycle theory* and Friedman called *the permanent-income theory*, explain some observed consumer behaviour that cannot be explained by the Keynesian consumption function. Most modern approaches to private consumption behaviour are based upon the life-cycle or permanent-income approaches in which rational consumers plan their consumption over a broad time horizon, and may even build in plans to leave money to their children (thus planning consumption *beyond* their own lifetimes).

However, the differences between the modern theories and the Keynesian consumption function are not as great as they might seem at first sight. To see why this is so, let us return to our two imaginary individuals and see why their actual behaviour may not be quite as divergent as we have described it.

Even the prodigal son may be able to do some smoothing of spending in the face of income fluctuations. Most people have some money in the bank and some ability to borrow, even if it is just from friends and relatives. As a result, not every income fluctuation will be matched by an equivalent spending fluctuation.

In contrast, although the prudent person wants to smooth her pattern of consumption completely, she may not have the borrowing capacity to do so. Her bank may not be willing to lend money for consumption when the security consists of nothing more than the expectation that income will be much higher in later years. This may mean that, in practice, her consumption spending fluctuates more with her current income than she would wish.

This suggests that the consumption spending of both types of individual will fluctuate to some extent with their current disposable incomes and to some extent with their expectations of future disposable income. Moreover, in any economy some people will be closer to one of the extremes while others are closer to the other extreme, and a mix of the two types will determine aggregate consumption. As we develop our basic theory, we will often find it

---

[10] We are assuming here that all firms pass on all their profits to the people who own them, so there is no retained profit.

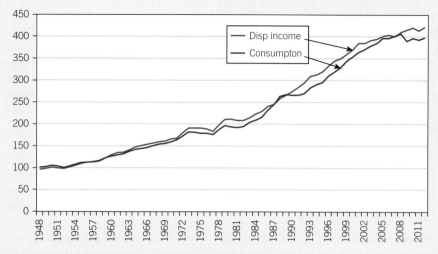

Figure 16.2 Consumption spending and household disposable income, UK, 1948–2012 (Annual data, £ billion at constant 1985 prices)

Consumption spending and disposable income are closely related over time. The two lines show that most of disposable income goes to pay for consumption spending.

Source: ONS online database.

useful to make the simplifying assumption that consumption spending is primarily determined by current disposable income. That is, we will often use a Keynesian consumption function and then indicate how things change if we consider influences on consumer spending other than current income. Figure 16.2 shows real personal disposable income and real consumer spending in the UK from 1948 to 2012. It is clear that the two series are closely related.

The term 'consumption function' describes the relationship between household consumption spending and the variables that influence it. In the simplest theory, consumption spending is primarily determined by current personal disposable income.

When income is zero, a typical household will still (via borrowing, or drawing down savings) consume some minimal amount.[11] This level of consumption

<hr />

[11] Many individuals, such as dependent children or non-working partners, have no income but continue to consume. In this case there is normally at least one earner in a household, and it is the household income that is relevant. The household is the decision unit in that context. Such distinctions are important if we want to study the behaviour of individual spending units, but they are not critical in macroeconomics, which studies the aggregate behaviour of all consumers and relates their total spending to their total income. Hence, we can talk about households and individuals interchangeably.

spending is *autonomous* because it persists even when there is no income. The higher a household's income, the more that household will want to consume. This part of consumption is *induced*—that is, it varies with disposable income and hence, in our simple model, with GDP.

Consider the schedule relating personal disposable income to desired consumption spending for a hypothetical economy that appears in the first two columns of Table 16.1. In this example autonomous consumption spending is £100 million, whereas induced consumption spending is 80 per cent of disposable income. In what follows we use this hypothetical example to illustrate the various properties of the consumption function.

Average and marginal propensities to consume

To discuss the consumption function concisely, economists use two technical expressions.

The **average propensity to consume** (*APC*) is total consumption spending divided by total disposable income: $APC = C/Y_d$. Column (3) of Table 16.1 shows the *APC* calculated from the data in the table. Note that *APC* falls as disposable income rises.

The **marginal propensity to consume** (*MPC*) relates the *change* in consumption to the *change* in disposable income that brought it about. *MPC* is the change in

Table 16.1 The calculation of average and marginal propensity to consume (*APC* and *MPC*) (£ million)

Disposable income (Y_d) (1)	Desired consumption (Y_d) (2)	$APC = C/Y_d$ (3)	Change in Y_d (ΔY_d) (4)	Change in C (ΔC) (5)	$MPC = \Delta C/\Delta Y_d$ (6)
0	100	–			
			100	80	0.80
100	180	1.800			
			300	240	0.80
400	420	1.050			
			100	80	0.80
500	500	1.000			
			500	400	0.80
1,000	900	0.900			
			500	400	0.80
1,500	1,300	0.867			
			250	200	0.80
1,750	1,500	0.857			
			250	200	0.80
2,000	1,700	0.850			
			1,000	800	0.80
3,000	2,500	0.833			

APC measures the proportion of disposable income that households desire to spend on consumption; *MPC* measures the proportion of any increment to disposable income that households desire to spend on consumption. The data are hypothetical. We call the level of income at which desired consumption equals disposable income the break-even level; in this example it is £500 million. *APC*, calculated in column (3), exceeds unity—that is, consumption exceeds income—below the break-even level; above the break-even level *APC* is less than unity. It is negatively related to income at all levels of income. The last three columns are set between the lines of the first three columns to indicate that they refer to *changes* in the levels of income and consumption. *MPC*, calculated in the last column, is constant at 0.80 at all levels of Y_d. This indicates that, in this example, £0.80 of every additional £1.00 of disposable income is spent on consumption, and £0.20 is saved.

disposable income divided into the resulting consumption change: $MPC = \Delta C/\Delta Y_d$ (where the capital Greek letter delta (Δ) means 'a change in'). Column (6) of Table 16.1 shows the *MPC* that corresponds to the data in the table. Note that, because we are dealing with the Keynesian consumption function, *MPC* is constant.

The slope of the consumption function

Figure 16.3(i) shows a graph of the consumption function, derived by plotting consumption against income using data from the first two columns of Table 16.1. The consumption function has a slope $\Delta C/\Delta Y_d$, which is by definition the marginal propensity to consume. The positive slope of the consumption function shows that the *MPC* is positive; increases in income lead to increases in spending.

Using the concepts of the average and marginal propensities to consume, we can summarize the assumed properties of the short-term consumption function as follows.

1. There is a break-even level of income at which *APC* equals unity. Below this level *APC* is greater than unity; above it, *APC* is less than unity. Below the break-even level consumption exceeds income, so households run down savings or borrow. Above the break-even level income exceeds consumption, so there is positive saving.

2. *MPC* is greater than zero, but less than unity, for all levels of income. This implies that for each additional £1 of income, less than £1 is spent on consumption and the rest is saved. For a straight-line consumption function, the *MPC* is constant at all levels of income.

The 45° line

Figure 16.3(i) contains a line that is constructed by connecting all points where desired consumption (measured on the vertical axis) equals disposable income (measured on the horizontal axis). Because both axes are given in the same units, this line has a positive slope of unity; that is, it forms an angle of 45° with the axes. Therefore this line is called the 45° line.

The 45° line makes a handy reference line. In Figure 16.3(i) it helps to locate the break-even level of income at which consumption spending equals disposable income. The consumption function cuts the 45° line at the break-even level of income, in this instance £500 million. (The consumption function is flatter than the 45° line because *MPC* is less than unity.)

The saving function

Households decide how much to consume and how much to save. As we have said, this is a single decision: how to

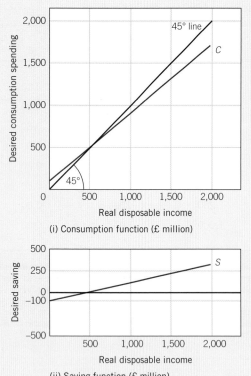

(i) Consumption function (£ million)

(ii) Saving function (£ million)

Figure 16.3 The consumption and saving functions

Both consumption and saving rise as disposable income rises. Line C in part (i) relates desired consumption spending to disposable income by using the hypothetical data from Table 16.1. Its slope, $\Delta C/\Delta Y_d$, is the marginal propensity to consume (MPC). The consumption line cuts the 45° line at the break-even level of disposable income, £500 million in this case. Note that the level of autonomous consumption is £100 million. Saving is all disposable income that is not spent on consumption ($S = Y_d - C$). The relationship between desired saving and disposable income is derived in Table 16.2 and is shown in part (ii) by line S. Its slope, $\Delta S/\Delta Y_d$, is the marginal propensity to save (MPS). The saving line cuts the horizontal axis at the break-even level of income. The vertical distance between C and the 45° line in part (i) is, by definition, the height of the S line in part (ii); that is, any given level of disposable income must be accounted for by the amount consumed plus the amount saved. Note that the level of autonomous saving is –£100 million. This means that at zero income consumers will draw down existing assets by £100 million a year or borrow this amount.

Table 16.2 Consumption and saving schedules (£ million)

Disposable income	Desired consumption	Desired saving
0	100	–100
100	180	–80
400	420	–20
500	500	0
1,000	900	+100
1,500	1,300	+200
1,750	1,500	+250
2,000	1,700	+300
3,000	2,500	+500
4,000	3,300	+700

Saving and consumption account for all household disposable income. The first two columns repeat the data from Table 16.1. The third column, desired saving, is disposable income minus desired consumption. Consumption and saving both increase steadily as disposable income rises. In this example the break-even level of income is £500 million. At this level all income is consumed.

There are two saving concepts that are exactly parallel to the consumption concepts of APC and MPC. The **average propensity to save (APS)** is the proportion of disposable income that households want to save, which is derived by dividing total desired saving by total disposable income: $APS = S/Y_d$. The **marginal propensity to save (MPS)** relates the *change* in total desired saving to the *change* in disposable income that brought it about: $MPS = \Delta S/\Delta Y_d$.

There is a simple relationship between the saving and consumption propensities. APC and APS must sum to unity, and so must MPC and MPS. Because income is either spent or saved, it follows that the fractions of incomes consumed and saved must account for all income ($APC + APS = 1$). It also follows that the fractions of any increment to income consumed and saved must account for all of that increment ($MPC + MPS = 1$). Calculations from Table 16.2 will allow you to confirm these relationships in the case of the example given. MPC is 0.80 and MPS is 0.20 at all levels of income, while, for example, at an income of £2,000 million APC is 0.85 and APS is 0.15.

Figure 16.3(ii) shows the saving schedule given in Table 16.2. At the break-even level of income, where desired consumption equals disposable income, desired

divide disposable income between consumption and saving. It follows that once we know the dependence of consumption on disposable income, we also automatically know the dependence of saving on disposable income. (This is illustrated in Table 16.2.)

saving is zero. The slope of the saving line $\Delta S/\Delta Y_d$ is equal to the MPS.

Wealth and the consumption function

The Keynesian consumption function that we have been analysing can easily be combined with the permanent-income or life-cycle theories of consumption. As we have already noted, according to these theories households save in order, among other reasons, to accumulate wealth that they can use during their retirement (or pass on to their heirs[12]). Suppose that there is an unexpected rise in wealth. This will mean that less of current disposable income needs to be saved for the future, and it will tend to cause a larger fraction of disposable income to be spent on consumption and a smaller fraction to be saved. Thus, the consumption function will be shifted upwards and the saving function downwards, as shown in Figure 16.4. A fall in wealth increases the incentive to save in order to restore wealth. This shifts the consumption function downwards and the saving function upwards.

The interest rate and consumer spending

Higher interest rates will generally lead to lower consumption spending. Higher interest rates encourage saving, as the rewards for saving are increased. Higher interest rates also discourage borrowing, as the cost of credit rises. Many households have purchased houses with borrowed money in the form of a mortgage. Most mortgages in the United Kingdom have a variable interest rate so that monthly mortgage payments will increase as interest rates increase. Higher mortgage payments leave less out of any given income for spending on current consumption. Higher interest rates also tend to lead to lower asset values (for reasons we discuss in Chapter 19), and this then generates a fall in wealth that lowers consumption as discussed above.

When we fully incorporate interest rates into our model in Chapter 20, we will have the main impact running from interest rates to investment. But it is also consistent with our analysis to think of higher interest rates lowering autonomous consumption.[13]

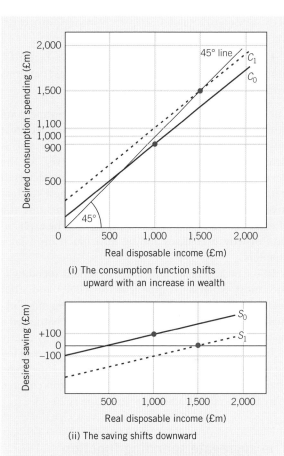

Figure 16.4 Wealth and the consumption function
Changes in wealth shift the consumption function. In part (i) line C_0 reproduces the consumption function from Figure 16.3(i). An increase in the level of wealth raises desired consumption at each level of disposable income, thus shifting the consumption line up to C_1. In the figure the consumption function shifts up by £200 million, so with disposable income of £1,000 million, for example, desired consumption rises from £900 million to £1,100 million. As a result of the rise in wealth the break-even level of income rises to £1,500 million. The saving function in part (ii) shifts down by £200 million from S_0 to S_1. Thus, for example, at a disposable income of £1,000 million, saving *falls* from +£100 million to –£100 million.

Desired investment spending

Three major forms of investment need to be distinguished.

• Investment in *inventories*: changes in the stocks of finished goods, work in progress, and raw materials held by firms.

• Investment in *residential housing construction*: spending on the construction of new houses and the renovation

---

[12] Empirical evidence suggests that there is a significant 'bequest motive' for saving. This means that some people plan even further ahead than their own lifetime, because they want to leave money to their children.

[13] UK monetary policy-makers' own perception of how monetary policy works also includes an effect of interest rates working on consumer spending. See the reference in footnote 2 in Chapter 25 page 622.

of existing ones, but not the transfer of ownership of existing houses from one owner to another.

- Investment in *business fixed capital*: factories, offices, machines and all other durable things that firms own in pursuit of their business activities.

The determinants of all of these types of investment are discussed in some detail in Chapter 19 when we treat investment as an endogenous variable whose size is determined from within our theory. However, for the development of the simplest theory of income determination in this and the next chapter it is best to treat investment as exogenous. This allows us to study the effects of changes investment while leaving the explanation of why it changes and by how much until later chapters.

In the meantime we note that investment spending is the most volatile component of GDP, and that such changes are strongly associated with economic fluctuations. For example, the Great Depression witnessed a major fall in investment. Total investment fell by nearly a quarter between 1929 and 1932. In 2009 investment fell by 15 per cent and GDP fell by 5 per cent. How these changes affect GDP is an important topic in this chapter. Why they occur is studied later in Chapters 20–23.

The aggregate spending function

The aggregate spending function relates the level of desired real spending to the level of real GDP. In our complete model total desired spending on the nation's output is the sum of desired private consumption, investment, government consumption, and net export spending. In the simplified economy of this chapter aggregate spending is just equal to $C + I$:

$$AE = C + I$$

Table 16.3 shows how the AE function is calculated, given the consumption function of Tables 16.1 and 16.2 and a constant level of desired investment of £250 million. In this specific case all investment spending is autonomous, as is the £100 million of consumption that would be desired when GDP is zero (see Table 16.1). Thus, total autonomous spending is £350 million—induced spending is just equal to induced consumption, which is equal to 0.8Y. Thus, desired aggregate spending, whether thought of as $C + I$ or as autonomous plus induced spending, can be written as $AE = $ £350 million + 0.8Y. This aggregate spending function is illustrated in Figure 16.5.

The propensity to spend out of GDP

The fraction of any increment to GDP[14] that will be spent on purchasing domestic output is called the

Table 16.3 The aggregate spending function in a closed economy with no government (£ million)

GDP (Y)	Desired consumption spending ($C = 100 + 0.8Y$)	Desired investment spending ($I = 250$)	Desired aggregate spending ($AE = C + I$)
100	180	250	430
400	420	250	670
500	500	250	750
1,000	900	250	1,150
1,500	1,300	250	1,550
1,750	1,500	250	1,750
2,000	1,700	250	1,950
3,000	2,500	250	2,750
4,000	3,300	250	3,550

The aggregate spending function is the sum of desired consumption, investment, government, and net export spending. In this table government and net exports are assumed to be zero, investment is assumed to be constant at £250 million, and desired consumption is based on the hypothetical data given in Table 16.2. The autonomous components of desired aggregate spending are desired investment and the constant term in desired consumption spending (£100 million). The induced component is the second term in desired consumption spending 0.8Y. The marginal response of consumption to a change in GDP is 0.8, the marginal propensity to consume. The marginal response of desired aggregate spending to a change in GDP, $\Delta AE/\Delta Y$, is also 0.8, because all induced spending in this economy is consumption spending.

economy's **marginal propensity to spend**. It is measured by the change in aggregate spending divided by the change in income, or $\Delta AE/\Delta Y$, the slope of the aggregate spending function. In this book we will denote the marginal propensity to spend by the symbol c, which will typically be a number greater than zero and less than one.

Similarly, the **marginal propensity not to spend** is the fraction of any increment to GDP that does not add to desired aggregate spending. This is denoted $(1 - c)$—if c is the part of any £1 of incremental income that is spent, $(1 - c)$ is the part that is not spent.[15] In the example given in Table 16.3, c, the marginal propensity to spend, is 0.8. If GDP increases by £1, then 80p will go into

....

[14] Recall that any increase in GDP generates an equal amount of additional income.

[15] More fully, these terms would be called the marginal propensity to spend *on the national product* and the marginal propensity not to spend *on the national product*. The marginal propensity not to spend, $(1 - c)$, is sometimes referred to as the *marginal propensity to withdraw*. Not spending some part of income amounts to a *withdrawal* or a *leakage* from the circular flow of income, as illustrated in Figure 15.2 in Chapter 15.

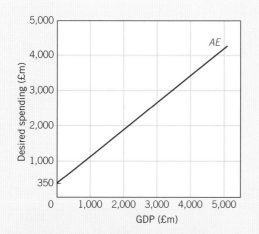

Figure 16.5 An aggregate spending function

The aggregate spending function relates total desired spending to GDP. The *AE* function in the figure plots the data from the first and the last columns of Table 16.3, which are repeated in Table 16.4. Its intercept (which in this case is £350 million) shows autonomous spending, which in the present model is the sum of autonomous consumption of £100 million and investment of £250 million. Its slope (which in this case is 0.8) shows the marginal propensity to spend.

increased spending. Twenty pence (£1 times 0.2, the value of $(1-c)$) will go into increased saving and will not be spent.

The marginal propensity to spend, which we have just defined, should not be confused with the marginal propensity to consume, which we defined earlier in the chapter. The marginal propensity to spend is the amount of extra total spending induced when GDP rises by £1, while the marginal propensity to consume is the amount of extra consumption spending induced when *personal disposable income* rises by £1. In the simple model of this chapter, in which the only element of spending that changes is household consumption spending, the marginal propensity to spend is equal to the marginal propensity to consume, and the marginal propensity not to spend is equal to the marginal propensity to save. In later chapters, when we add spending that comes from the government and the international sector, the marginal propensity to spend differs from the marginal propensity to consume. Both here and in later chapters it is the more general measures c and $(1-c)$ that are important for determining equilibrium GDP.

Equilibrium GDP

We are now ready to see what in our model determines the *equilibrium* level of GDP. When something is in equilibrium, there is no tendency for it to change; forces are acting on it, but they balance out, and the net result is *no change*. Any conditions that are required for something to be in equilibrium are called *equilibrium conditions*.

Table 16.4 illustrates the determination of equilibrium GDP for our simple hypothetical economy. Suppose that firms are producing a final output of £1,000 million, and thus GDP is £1,000 million. According to the table, at this level of GDP aggregate desired spending is £1,150 million. If firms persist in producing a current output of only £1,000 million in the face of an aggregate desired spending of £1,150 million, one of two things must happen.[16]

One possibility is that consumers and investors will be unable to spend the extra £150 million that they would like to spend, so queues and unfulfilled order books will appear. These will send a signal to firms that they can increase their sales if they increase their production. When the firms increase production, GDP rises. Of course, the individual firms are interested only in their own sales

Table 16.4 The determination of equilibrium GDP (£ million)

GDP (Y)	Desired aggregate spending (AE = C + I)	
100	430	
400	670	
500	750	Pressure on Y
1,000	1,150	to rise
1,500	1,550	↓
1,750	**1,750**	**Equilibrium Y**
2,000	1,950	↑
3,000	2,750	Pressure on Y
4,000	3,550	to fall

GDP is in equilibrium where aggregate desired spending equals national output. The data are copied from Table 16.3. When GDP is below its equilibrium level, aggregate desired spending exceeds the value of current output. This creates an incentive for firms to increase output and hence for GDP to rise. When GDP is above its equilibrium level, aggregate desired spending is less than the value of current output. This creates an incentive for firms to reduce output and hence for GDP to fall. Only at the equilibrium level of GDP is aggregate desired spending equal to the value of current output.

---

[16] A third possibility, that prices could rise, is ruled out by assumption in this chapter.

and profits, but their individual actions have as their inevitable consequence an increase in GDP.

The second possibility is that consumers and investors will spend everything that they want to spend. Then, however, spending will exceed current output, which can happen only when some spending plans are fulfilled by purchasing stocks of goods that were produced in the past. In our example, the fulfilment of plans to purchase £1,150 million worth of commodities in the face of a current output of only £1,000 million will reduce inventories by £150 million. As long as stocks last, more goods can be sold than are currently being produced.[17]

Eventually stocks will run out. But before this happens, firms will increase their output as they see their sales increase. Extra sales can then be made without a further depletion of inventories. Once again the consequence of each individual firm's behaviour, in search of its own individual profits, is an increase in the national product and GDP. Thus, the final response to an excess of aggregate desired spending over current output is a rise in GDP.

At any level of GDP at which aggregate desired spending exceeds total output, there will be pressure for GDP to rise.

Next consider the £4,000 million level of GDP in Table 16.4. At this level desired spending on domestically produced goods is only £3,550 million. If firms persist in producing £4,000 million worth of goods, £450 million worth must remain unsold. Therefore stocks of unsold goods must rise. However, firms will not allow unsold goods to accumulate indefinitely; sooner or later they will reduce the level of output to the level of sales. When they do, GDP will fall.

At any level of GDP for which aggregate desired spending is less than total output, there will be pressure for GDP to fall.

Finally, look at the GDP level of £1,750 million in Table 16.4. At this level, and only at this level, aggregate desired spending is equal to national output (GDP). Purchasers can fulfil their spending plans without causing inventories to change. There is no incentive for firms to alter output. Because everyone wishes to purchase an amount equal to what is being produced, output and income will remain steady; GDP is in equilibrium.

The equilibrium level of GDP occurs where aggregate desired spending equals total output.

This conclusion is quite general and does not depend on the numbers that are used in the specific example.

....
[17] Notice that in this example actual GDP is equal to £1,000 million. Desired consumption is £900 million and desired investment is £250 million, but the reduction of inventories by £150 million is unplanned negative investment; thus actual investment is only £100 million.

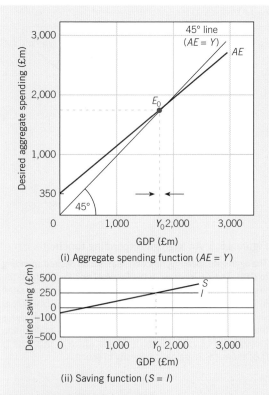

Figure 16.6 Equilibrium GDP

Equilibrium GDP occurs at E_0, where the desired aggregate spending line intersects the 45° line. If real GDP is below Y_0, desired aggregate spending will exceed national output, and production will rise. This is shown in part (i) by the arrow to the left of Y_0. If GDP is above Y_0, desired aggregate spending will be less than national output, and production will fall. This is shown by the arrow to the right of Y_0. Only when real GDP is Y_0 will desired aggregate spending equal real national output. When saving is the only withdrawal and investment is the only injection, the equilibrium Y_0 is also the level of GDP at which saving equals investment, shown in part (ii). At levels of GDP greater than Y_0 saving exceeds investment (withdrawals exceed injections), so aggregate spending is less than output and the economy contracts. At levels of GDP below Y_0, investment exceeds saving (injections exceed withdrawals), so spending exceeds output and the level of GDP increases. Parts (i) and (ii) are just two different ways of looking at the same phenomena.

Figure 16.6 shows the determination of the equilibrium level of GDP. In the figure the line labelled *AE* graphs the aggregate spending function given by the first and last columns of Table 16.3, also shown in Table 16.4. The line labelled 45° line (*AE = Y*) graphs the equilibrium condition that aggregate desired spending equals national output. Since in equilibrium the variables measured on the two axes must be equal, the line showing this equality is a 45° line. Anywhere along that line the value of desired spending, which is measured on the vertical axis, is equal to the value of national output, which is measured on the horizontal axis.[18]

Graphically, equilibrium occurs at the level of GDP at which the aggregate desired spending line intersects the 45° line. This is the level of GDP where desired spending is just equal to total national output and therefore is just sufficient to purchase that output.

Exactly the same equilibrium is illustrated in part (ii), but in terms of the saving–investment balance. The line labelled S is equal to aggregate saving. In an economy without government and without international trade—the case we are studying here—aggregate saving is just equal to Y – C, the difference between GDP and consumption. The line labelled I is investment, in this case assumed to be constant at all levels of income.

Notice that the vertical distance between S and I is just equal to the distance between the 45° line and AE. When desired investment exceeds desired saving, desired aggregate spending exceeds national output by the same amount. When desired investment is less than desired saving, desired aggregate spending is less than national output by the same amount.

Now we have explained the determinants of the equilibrium level of GDP at a *given price level*. A simple analogue, which will help us to understand why it is that equilibrium GDP is associated with equality of desired investment and saving, is set out in Box 16.3. In the next section we will study how equilibrium income may be changed. We will see that shifts in autonomous consumption and investment spending cause changes in equilibrium GDP.

Box 16.3 A hydraulic analogue of GDP determination

The key concept to understand in this chapter is how it is that GDP achieves its equilibrium level (for given values of exogenous spending). This is one of the most important ideas in macroeconomics, because it explains how GDP can be in equilibrium even when there is excess capacity in the economy.

Think of the economy as a water container, say a basin, which has inflows and outflows on a continuous basis—the tap is turned on and there is no plug in the plughole. Although the water is always changing, there is some condition under which the level of water in the basin will remain unchanged. This is when the volume of the inflow and the volume of the outflow are exactly equal.

Call the inflow 'investment', the outflow 'saving', and the level of water in the basin 'GDP'. GDP will stay at one level as long as the volume of investment just equals the volume

of saving. (The same principle can be viewed in terms of the circular flow diagram in Figure 15.2 in Chapter 15 when there is no foreign trade and no government. Only when I = S will the level of the circular flow be stable.)

What happens if the basin fills to overflowing? That is the problem of capacity constraints and full employment that we discuss in later chapters. Realistically, the basin will never run empty, because that would mean GDP and output had fallen to zero—though the problem of the water getting undesirably low is what macroeconomics was invented to study.

Note also that in later chapters we will see that investment is not the only inflow, or injection (government spending and exports will be added), and saving is not the only leakage, or withdrawal (taxes and imports are also leakages).

Changes in GDP

Because the AE function plays a central role in our explanation of the determination of the equilibrium value of GDP, you should not be surprised to hear that shifts in the

[18] Because it turns up in many different guises, the 45° line can cause a bit of confusion until one gets used to it. The main thing about it is that it can be used whenever the variables plotted on the two axes are measured in the same units, such as pounds sterling, and are plotted on the same scale. In that case equal distances on the two axes measure the same amounts. One centimetre may, for example, correspond to £1,000 on each axis. In such circumstances the 45° line joins all points where the values of the two variables are the same. In Figures 16.3 and 16.4 the 45° line shows all points where *desired consumption spending in real terms* equals *real disposable income*, because these are the two variables that are plotted on the two axes. In Figure 16.6 and all those that follow it the 45° line shows all points at which *desired total spending in real terms equals real national output (GDP)*, because those are the variables that are measured on the two axes of these figures.

AE function play a central role in explaining why GDP changes. (Remember that we continue to assume that the price level is constant.) To understand this influence, we must recall an important distinction first encountered in Chapter 2—the distinction between *shifts* in a curve and *movements along* a curve.

Suppose that desired aggregate spending rises. This may be a response to a change in GDP (and therefore in incomes), or it may be the result of an increased desire to spend at each level of GDP. A change in GDP causes a *movement along* the aggregate spending function. An increased desire to spend at each level of GDP causes a *shift* in the aggregate spending function. Figure 16.7 illustrates this important distinction.

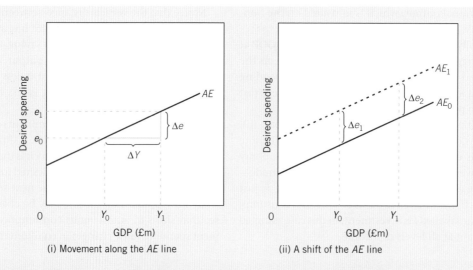

Figure 16.7 Movements along and shifts of the *AE* function

A movement along the aggregate spending function occurs in response to a change in GDP; a shift of the *AE* function indicates a different level of desired spending at each level of GDP. In part (i) a change in income of ΔY, from Y_0 to Y_1, changes desired spending by Δe, from e_0 to e_1. In part (ii) a shift in the spending function from AE_0 to AE_1 raises the amount of spending associated with *each level* of GDP. At Y_0, for example, desired aggregate spending is increased by Δe_1; at Y_1 it is increased by Δe_2. (If the aggregate spending line shifts parallel to itself, $\Delta e_1 = \Delta e_2$.) (Notice that from here on we drop 'aggregate' from the vertical axis label and write 'desired spending'. The term 'aggregate' is always understood, even when we omit it to save space.)

Shifts in the aggregate spending function

For any specific aggregate spending function there is a unique level of equilibrium GDP. If the aggregate spending function shifts, the equilibrium will be disturbed and GDP will change. Thus, if we wish to find the causes of changes in GDP, we must understand the causes of shifts in the *AE* function.

The aggregate spending function shifts when one of its components shifts—that is, when there is a shift in the consumption function, in desired investment spending, in desired government spending on goods and services, or in desired net exports. In this chapter we consider only shifts in the consumption function and in desired investment spending. Both of these are changes in desired aggregate spending at every level of income. Such changes could, for example, be induced by a change in the level of the interest rate set by the central bank.

Upward shifts

What will happen if households permanently increase their levels of desired consumption spending at each level of disposable income, or if a major company desires to invest in more fixed capital because of improved confidence about the future health of the economy? (Recall that an increase in any component of spending has the

same effect, because it is an increase in demand for the output of the single production sector.) In considering these questions, remember that we are dealing with continuous flows measured as so much per period of time. An upward shift in any spending function means that the desired spending associated with each level of GDP rises to and stays at a higher amount.

Because any such increase in desired spending shifts the entire aggregate spending function upwards, the same analysis applies to each of the changes mentioned. Two important types of shift in *AE* need to be distinguished. First, if the same addition to spending occurs at all levels of income, the *AE* function shifts parallel to itself, as shown in Figure 16.8(i). Secondly, if there is a change in the propensity to spend out of GDP, the slope of the *AE* function changes, as shown in Figure 16.8(ii). (Recall that the slope of the *AE* function is *c*, the marginal propensity to spend.) A change such as the one illustrated would occur if consumers decided to spend more of every £1 of disposable income—that is, if *MPC* rose.

Figure 16.8 shows that upward shifts in the aggregate spending function increase equilibrium GDP. After the shift in the *AE* function, output is no longer in equilibrium at its original level, because at that level desired spending exceeds national output. Equilibrium GDP now

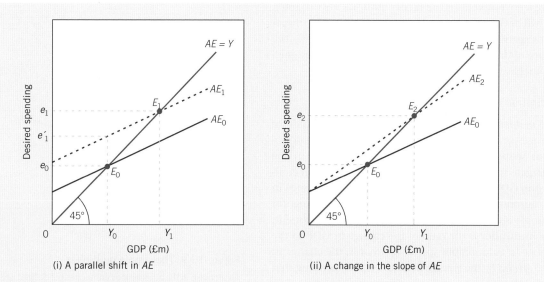

Figure 16.8 Shifts in the *AE* function

Upward shifts in the *AE* function increase equilibrium GDP; downward shifts decrease equilibrium GDP. In parts (i) and (ii) the aggregate spending curve is initially AE_0 with GDP Y_0. In part (i) a parallel upward *shift* in the *AE* function from AE_0 to AE_1 means that desired spending has increased by the same amount at each level of GDP. For example, at Y_0 desired spending rises from e_0 to e_1' and therefore exceeds national output. Equilibrium is reached at E_1, where output is Y_1 and spending is e_1. The increase in desired spending from e_1' to e_1, represented by a *movement along* AE_1, is an induced response to the increase in GDP from Y_0 to Y_1. In part (ii) a non-parallel upward shift in the *AE* function, say from AE_0 to AE_2, means that the marginal propensity to spend at each level of GDP has increased. This leads to an increase in equilibrium GDP. Equilibrium is reached at E_2, where the new level of spending e_2 is equal to output Y_1. Again, the initial *shift* in the *AE* function induces a *movement along* the new *AE* function. Downward shifts in the *AE* function, from AE_1 to AE_0 or from AE_2 to AE_0, lead to a fall in equilibrium GDP to Y_0.

occurs at the higher level indicated by the intersection of the new *AE* function with the 45° line, along which aggregate spending equals national output.

Downward shifts

What happens to GDP if there is a decrease in the amount of consumption or investment spending that is desired at each level of income? These changes shift the aggregate spending function downwards. A constant reduction in desired spending at all levels of income shifts *AE* parallel to itself. A fall in the marginal propensity to spend out of GDP reduces the slope of the *AE* function. When we use the saving–investment relation, we must note that a downward shift in the consumption function causes an upward shift in the saving function, reducing the equilibrium level of income and output, at which saving equals investment.

The multiplier

We have learned how to predict the direction of the changes in GDP that will occur in response to various shifts in the aggregate spending function.

1. A rise in the amount of desired aggregate spending that is associated with each level of GDP will increase equilibrium national output.

2. A fall in the amount of desired aggregate spending that is associated with each level of GDP will lower equilibrium national output.

Now we would like also to predict the *magnitude* of these changes.

During a period of persistent high unemployment the government sometimes seeks to stimulate the economy by injecting new spending. This could, for example, take the form of building new or replacing obsolete infrastructure such as roads, bridges, and sewers. If this action has a larger effect than expected, demand may rise too much and potential GDP may be reached with demand still rising. (We will see in Chapters 21 and 22 that this outcome may have an inflationary impact on the economy.) If the government overestimates the effects of this new spending, the recession will persist longer than is necessary. In this case there is a danger that the policy will be discredited as ineffective, even though the correct diagnosis is that too little of the right thing was done. Since we do not have a government in the model until the next chapter, we will deal here with an autonomous increase in investment spending, but the effects are similar whatever the source of the autonomous increase in spending designed to purchase current output.

Definition

The *multiplier* provides a measure of the magnitude of changes in GDP induced by a given change in autonomous spending. We have just seen that a shift in the aggregate spending function will cause a change in equilibrium GDP. Such a shift could be caused by a change in any autonomous component of aggregate spending, for example an increase or decrease in desired investment. The **multiplier** is the ratio of the change in GDP to the change in autonomous spending—that is, the change in GDP *divided by* the change in autonomous spending that caused the change.

Why the multiplier can be greater than unity

What will happen to GDP if GlaxoSmithKline PLC spends £100 million more per year on new factories? Initially, the construction of the factories will create £100 million worth of new demand for the output of the production sector (recall that there is only one type of output) and £100 million of new GDP, and a corresponding amount of extra wages for workers and profits for firms (the income components of GDP). But this is not the end of the story. The increase in GDP of £100 million will cause an increase in disposable income, which in turn will cause an induced rise in consumption spending.

Workers who gain new income directly from the building of the factory will spend some of it on consumer goods. (In reality they will spend it on many different goods, such as beer and cinema visits. In the simplified world of our model all spending is on the final output of the single industrial sector.) When output and employment expand to meet this demand, further new incomes will be created for workers and firms. When they then spend their newly earned incomes, output and employment will rise further. More income will be created, and more spending will be induced. Indeed, at this stage we might wonder whether the increases in income would ever come to an end. To deal with this concern, we need to consider the multiplier in somewhat more precise terms.

The simple multiplier defined

Consider an increase in autonomous spending of ΔA, which might be, say, £100 million per year. Remember that ΔA stands for any increase in autonomous spending; in our

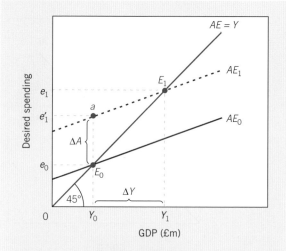

Figure 16.9 The simple multiplier

An increase in the autonomous component of desired aggregate spending increases equilibrium GDP by a multiple of the initial increase. The initial equilibrium is at E_0, where AE_0 intersects the 45° line. At this point desired spending, e_0, is equal to national output, Y_0. An increase in autonomous spending of ΔA then shifts the desired spending function upwards to AE_1. If GDP stays at Y_0, desired spending rises to e'_1. (The coordinates of point a are Y_0 and e'_1.) Because this level of desired spending is greater than national output, GDP will rise. Equilibrium occurs when GDP rises to Y_1. Here, desired spending, e_1, is equal to output, Y_1. The extra spending of e_1 represents the induced increases in spending. It is the amount by which the final increase in income and output, ΔY, exceeds the initial increase in autonomous spending, ΔA. Because ΔY is greater than ΔA, the multiplier is greater than unity.

simple model this must be an increase in either investment or the autonomous component of consumption. The new autonomous spending shifts the aggregate spending function upwards by that amount. GDP is no longer in equilibrium at its original level, because desired aggregate spending now exceeds output. A movement along the new AE function restores equilibrium.

The **simple multiplier** measures the change in equilibrium GDP that occurs in response to a change in autonomous spending *at a constant price level*.[19] We refer to it as 'simple' because we have simplified the situation by assuming that both the price level and the interest rate are fixed. Figure 16.9 illustrates the simple multiplier. Box 16.4 provides a numerical example.

---

[19] Recall that we have assumed that there is excess capacity in the economy, so an increase in spending can lead to extra real activity. The situation is very different when we begin with resources already fully employed. We consider this situation in later chapters.

Box 16.4 **The multiplier: a numerical example**

Consider an economy that has a marginal propensity to spend out of GDP of 0.80. Suppose that autonomous spending increases by £100 million per year because a large company spends an extra £100 million per year on new factories. GDP (and output) initially rises by £100 million, but that is not the end of it. The workers involved in factory building that received the first £100 million spend £80 million. This second round of spending generates £80 million of new income. This new income, in turn, induces £64 million of third-round spending, and so it continues, with each successive round of new income generating 80 per cent as much in new spending. Each additional round of spending creates new income (and output) and yet another round of spending.

The table carries the process through ten rounds. Students with sufficient patience (and no faith in mathematics) may compute as many rounds in the process as they wish;

they will find that the sum of the rounds of spending approaches a limit of £500 million, which is five times the initial increase in spending.

The graph of the cumulative spending increases shows how quickly this limit is approached. Thus, the multiplier is 5, given that the marginal propensity to spend is 0.8. Had the marginal propensity to spend been lower, say 0.667, the process would have been similar, but it would have approached a limit of three, instead of five, times the initial increase in spending. Notice that since our model has only a single productive sector, it makes no difference what the initial spending goes on. That, and all subsequent spending, is on the output of this single industry. In reality, the impact of spending increases may vary slightly depending on the product first demanded.

Round of spending	Increase in spending (£ million)	Cumulative total (£ million)
Initial increase	100.0	100.0
2	80.0	180.0
3	64.0	244.0
4	51.2	295.2
5	41.0	336.2
6	32.8	369.0
7	26.2	395.2
8	21.0	416.2
9	16.8	433.0
10	13.4	446.4
11–20 combined	47.9	494.3
All others	5.7	500.0

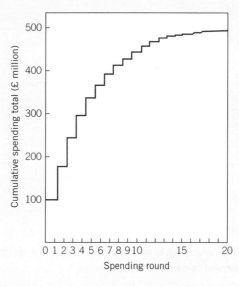

The size of the simple multiplier

The size of the simple multiplier depends on the slope of the AE function—that is, on the marginal propensity to spend, c. This is illustrated in Figure 16.10.

A high marginal propensity to spend means a steep AE function. The spending induced by any initial increase in income is large, with the result that the final rise in GDP is correspondingly large. By contrast, a low marginal propensity to spend means a relatively flat AE function. The spending induced by the initial increase in income is small, and the final rise in GDP is not much larger than the initial rise in autonomous spending that brought it about.

The larger the marginal propensity to spend, the steeper is the aggregate spending function and the larger is the multiplier.

The precise value of the simple multiplier can be derived by using elementary algebra. (The derivation is given in Box 16.5.) The result is that the simple multiplier, which we call K, is

$$K = \frac{\Delta Y}{\Delta A} = \frac{1}{1-c}.$$

where c is the marginal propensity to spend out of GDP. (Recall that c is the slope of the aggregate spending function.)

Box 16.5 The derivation of the multiplier

In models of short-run GDP determination, aggregate spending is divided into autonomous and induced spending. In the simple model of this chapter *autonomous spending* is investment plus autonomous consumption and induced spending is just that part of C that varies with GDP. When we add imports and government in the next chapter, induced spending will include induced imports, and autonomous spending will include government spending and exports. All that matters, however, is that desired aggregate spending can be divided into one class of spending that varies with income and another class that does not. Letting consumption depend on income linearly, we can write $C = a + bY$, where a is the autonomous component of C and b is the marginal propensity to consume ($0 < b < 1$). Letting investment be I we can write

$$E = bY + (a + I). \qquad (16.1)$$

Now, we write the equation of the 45° line:

$$E = Y \qquad (16.2)$$

which states the equilibrium condition that desired aggregate spending equals GDP. Equations (16.1) and (16.2) are two equations with two unknowns, E and Y. To solve them, we substitute eqn (16.1) into eqn (16.2) to obtain

$$Y = bY + (a + I). \qquad (16.3)$$

Subtracting bY from both sides

$$Y - bY = (a + I), \qquad (16.4)$$

factoring out Y

$$Y(1 - b) = (a + I), \qquad (16.5)$$

and dividing through by $1 - b$ yields

$$Y = \frac{(a + I)}{(1 - b)}. \qquad (16.6)$$

To discover how GDP changes when autonomous spending changes, i.e. the multiplier K, we note that a change in $(a + I)$ will lead to a change in Y that is equal to the change in a or I multiplied by $1/(1 - b)$. This is the value of the multiplier K discussed in the text. In this case b is equal to c in the text. The more general case where c and b are not equal is derived in Box 17.2 in the next chapter.

As we saw earlier, the term $(1 - c)$ stands for the marginal propensity not to spend out of GDP. For example, if £0.80 of every £1.00 of new GDP is spent ($c = 0.80$), then £0.20 is the amount not spent. The value of the multiplier is then calculated as $K = 1/(0.20) = 5$.

The simple multiplier equals the reciprocal of the marginal propensity not to spend.

From this we see that if $(1 - c)$ is small (i.e. if c is large), the multiplier will be large (because extra income induces much extra spending). What if $(1 - c)$ is large? The largest possible value of $(1 - c)$ is unity, which arises when c equals zero, indicating that none of any additional GDP is spent. In this case, the multiplier itself has a value of unity; the increase in equilibrium GDP is confined to the initial increase in autonomous spending. There are no induced additional effects on spending, so GDP only increases by the original increase in autonomous spending. The relation between $(1 - c)$ and the size of the multiplier is illustrated in Figure 16.10.

To estimate the size of the multiplier in an actual economy, we need to estimate the value of the marginal propensity not to spend out of GDP in that economy, i.e. $(1 - c)$. Evidence suggests that in the United Kingdom the value of the marginal propensity not to spend is much larger than the 0.2 used in the above example.

This is because there are 'leakages' from the circular flow of income other than saving—income taxes and import spending (which will be added to our model in the next chapter). Allowing for these extra withdrawals leads to a realistic estimate of something around 0.65 for $(1 - c)$.[20] Thus the simple multiplier for the United Kingdom is somewhere just less than 1.5, rather than 5 as in the above example. Furthermore, the multiplier refers to an increasing domestic spending. In fact, most autonomous increases in spending have an import component. For example, many new construction projects use imported materials and components so, strictly, the multiplier refers to that proportion of autonomous spending that is on domestically produced output.

The simple multiplier is a useful starting point for understanding the effects of autonomous spending shifts on GDP. However, as we shall see in subsequent chapters, many qualifications are needed before we can derive any policy significance from its estimated value.

---

[20] This value of 0.65 is calculated using a marginal propensity to save of 0.2, a marginal propensity to import of 0.25, and an income tax rate of 0.25 (25p in the pound).

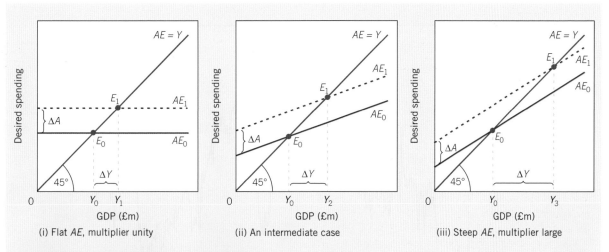

Figure 16.10 The size of the simple multiplier

The larger the marginal propensity to spend out of GDP (c), the steeper is the AE function and the larger is the multiplier. In each part of the figure the initial aggregate spending function is AE_0 and equilibrium is at E_0, with GDP of Y_0. The AE function then shifts upwards to AE_1 as a result of an increase in autonomous spending of ΔA. This ΔA is the same in each part. The new equilibrium is at E_1. In part (i) the AE function is horizontal, indicating a marginal propensity to spend of zero ($c = 0$). The change in GDP, ΔY, is only the increase in autonomous spending because there is no induced spending by those who receive the initial increase in income. The simple multiplier is then unity, its minimum possible value. In part (ii) the AE function slopes upwards but is still relatively flat (c is low). The increase in GDP to Y_2 is only slightly greater than the increase in autonomous spending that brought it about. In part (iii) the AE function is quite steep (c is high). Now the increase in GDP to Y_3 is much larger than the increase in autonomous spending that brought it about. The simple multiplier is quite large.

CASE STUDIES

1. The highs and lows of UK savings

The headlines quoted in Box 16.2 reflected the facts that UK household savings (as a percentage of disposable income) in mid-2007 were the lowest they had been since the 1950s, while by the third quarter of 2009 they had risen sharply to levels not seen since the mid-1990s, but then the savings ratio fell again. The official data on the savings ratio are presented in Figure 16.11 and confirm the broad facts behind these reports, except that the fall in the savings ratio was not as dramatic as that suggested in 2013. However, the implication of these stories seemed to be that both high and low savings rates are bad news. How could this be?

The low savings rates of 2005–7 were worrying for two different reasons. The first is that households did not seem to be saving enough for their old age. This concern led the government to introduce a user-friendly state-backed pension scheme and to encourage people to stay in work longer before they retire.

The second worry about low savings was that this reflected high consumption spending financed in part by increasing household debt. At the time, unemployment was low, house prices and other asset prices were rising, and people felt very confident about their future ability to repay the debt. The household consumption spending boom contributed to rising aggregate demand and as a result GDP kept growing … at least for a while. The worry was that households were making themselves financially vulnerable by taking on too much debt and not saving enough 'for a rainy day'.

The global financial crisis that broke out in 2007, and got much worse in 2008, caused asset prices to fall sharply, and some financial institutions failed while others were bailed out by governments. Financing for firms became much harder to find and aggregate demand fell in many European countries as well as in the United States. In the United Kingdom, unemployment rose sharply and consumers decided to exert caution, which meant cutting back on consumption spending while increasing savings

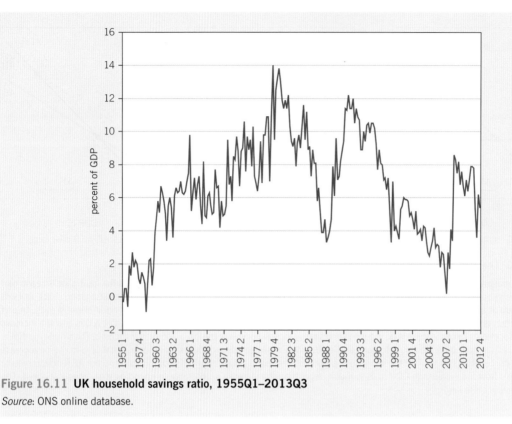

Figure 16.11 UK household savings ratio, 1955Q1–2013Q3
Source: ONS online database.

and reducing borrowing. The sharp rise in the savings ratio in 2009 is evident from Figure 16.11.

It is perfectly sensible for the individual household to cut back on spending when prospects become more uncertain (and their wealth may also have fallen as a result of lower house prices and share prices). The problem for the economy as a whole was that if firms are cutting back their investment spending, then *I* is falling at the same time as *C* is falling. At the same time world trade was falling so *X − IM* was falling. This meant that as *C + I + (X − IM)* are all falling, GDP will inevitably fall unless *G* can rise sufficiently to offset the fall in all other demand components. (We discuss the role of *G* and *X − IM* in the next chapter.) In 2009, UK GDP fell by around 5 per cent as there was not a sufficient rise in *G* to offset the fall in all the other demand components. Thus, the rise in household saving was a contributory factor to the fall in aggregate spending that led directly to a fall in GDP.

The 'paradox of thrift' is the name associated with this effect. High saving in relation to income is the same thing as low consumption, and this means low aggregate demand (other things being equal). This is the sense in which the high savings rate could be holding back economic recovery. For GDP to be growing, some category of spending must be growing. Consumption spending represents about 65 per cent of GDP so it plays a big role in what is happening to GDP. The fall in the savings ratio in the first quarter

of 2013 coincided with some pick-up in consumer confidence and consumer spending that helped deliver some growth in GDP at a time when other components of final demand were all weak.

2. The ups and downs of UK investment

In the current chapter we have treated investment as exogenous, but in later chapters we will see that it is affected by other variables in the economy. Here, we discuss the level of investment as a percentage of GDP.

Figure 16.12 shows the ratio of UK gross domestic fixed capital formation to GDP since 1955. Generally, investment is pro-cyclical. When the economy is booming investment is also high and when the economy is depressed investment tends to fall. There was an investment boom in 1972–3 and in the late 1980s. During both these periods there was also a boom in GDP. In the recessions of 1980–2 and 1990–2, investment fell sharply. Following the 2008–9 recession, investment as a share of GDP fell to its lowest level since the data series started (in 1955) but then fell even lower at the end of 2012, despite signs of recovery elsewhere in the economy.

Clearly a fall in investment will lead to a fall in GDP through the multiplier effects that we have discussed in this chapter. However, there is also causation running from

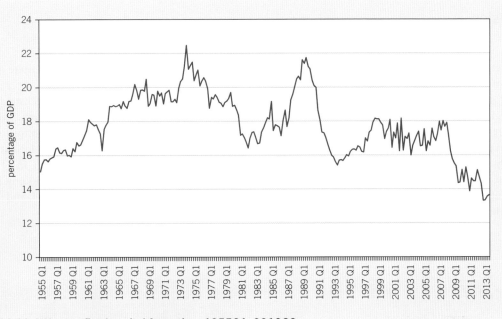

Figure 16.12 UK gross fixed capital formation, 1955Q1–2013Q3
Source: ONS online database.

GDP itself to investment. Firms will want to invest most when demand for their products is buoyant, so it makes sense for them to hold back on investment when demand is expected to be weak—that is, when an economic slowdown is occurring or is anticipated. (We discuss further this important interaction between investment and output (and its role in business cycles) in Chapter 23.

One of the puzzles about the UK investment data is that investment remained relatively weak in the 1990s and 2000s even though the economy had a period of stable growth. Its level at the cyclical peaks in 2000 and 2007 was well below the previous peaks in 1973 and 1989. Indeed, the level of UK investment (as a share of GDP) at all times since 1990 has been consistently below all observations during the period 1964–80. This is despite the fact that most commentators on UK economic policy would say that economic performance in the UK economy was much better in the 1990s and 2000s than it had been in the 1960s and 1970s.

There are at least three possible reasons why measured investment was relatively low during the past 20 years or so. The first is the globalization of production. Many British businesses were highly profitable and expanding their activities in this period, but they were investing in productive capacity outside the UK and this does not show up as part of the UK investment figures even though these investments are owned by UK firms and the earnings on them will contribute to UK incomes.

A second possible reason is that the nature of much investment has changed in recent years. A few decades ago, if a car manufacturer built a new factory or installed a new set of machine tools, it was clear that this was an investment and it would have been measured as such. However, if a bank installs a new software system for its employees or even replaces out-of-date desktop computers, it is not so clear that this is investment spending rather than just a current expense of the business. Many investments in information and communications technologies are harder to identify as investments, and thus the true level of investment may be underestimated.

A third possible reason is that the size of the UK service sector has grown relative to production industries. Service industries are increasingly based on the productive skills of their employees, and investment in skills and training is not counted as investment in the UK data. That is, investment in human capital is not included in the data, as 'investment' only relates to 'fixed capital formation' (plus inventories and housing).

At the time of writing, a major puzzle remains unanswered: why is investment in the UK so low despite many signs that the economy is finally growing again and has got over the worst effects of the 2008–9 recession? The hope and expectation must be that investment will recover soon … but we said the same in the 12th edition of this book (written in early 2010) and this pick-up in investment had still not appeared in the official statistics by early 2014[21].

---

[21] See also first case study in Chapter 20: 'UK business investment: why so weak?'

Conclusion

We can get a long way towards understanding the determinants of GDP in the short term by studying consumption and investment, two of the components of final spending. Household consumption spending and saving, and aggregate investment continue to be topics of major interest to policy-makers.

The key idea that emerges from the approach we have developed in this chapter is that aggregate spending on the output of the economy affects the outcome. The resulting level of GDP may or not be at a desirable level and, in particular, could be one where there are underutilized resources and unemployment.

We make the analysis increasingly realistic in the following three chapters. We begin by introducing the government and then we open the economy to external trade. We then add money to our model. Next we make investment spending endogenous. Then, in Chapters 21 and 22, we add a supply side to the economy and study the interaction of real activity, price level, and inflation.

SUMMARY

The macroeconomic problem: inflation and unemployment

- Models of the short-term determination of GDP seek to explain why actual GDP deviates from potential GDP.

- Actual GDP above potential is often associated with inflation, while actual GDP below potential is typically associated with unemployment and lost output.

Key assumptions

- For simplicity we aggregate all industrial sectors into one, so the economy produces only one type of output. We explain GDP determination through the major spending categories: household consumption, investment, government consumption, and net exports.

What determines aggregate spending?

- Desired aggregate spending includes desired consumption, desired investment, and desired government spending, plus desired net exports. It is the amount that economic agents want to spend on purchasing the national product. In this chapter we consider only consumption and investment.

- A change in household disposable income leads to a change in desired private consumption and saving. The responsiveness of these changes is measured by the marginal propensity to consume (MPC) and the marginal propensity to save (MPS). These are both positive and sum to unity, indicating that, by definition, all disposable income is either spent on consumption or saved.

- A change in wealth tends to cause a change in the allocation of disposable income between consumption and saving. The change in consumption is positively related to the change in wealth, while the change in saving is negatively related to this change.

- The part of consumption that responds to changes in income is called *induced* spending.

- Investment depends, among other things, on real interest rates and business confidence. In our simple theory investment is treated as *autonomous*, or exogenous, which makes it a constant term in the aggregate expenditure function, called *autonomous* investment.

Equilibrium GDP

- At the equilibrium level of GDP, purchasers wish to buy exactly the amount of national output that is being produced. At GDP above equilibrium, desired spending falls short of national output, and output will sooner or later be curtailed. At GDP below equilibrium, desired spending exceeds national output, and output will sooner or later be increased.

- In a closed economy with no government, desired saving equals desired investment at equilibrium GDP.

- Equilibrium GDP is represented graphically by the point at which the aggregate spending curve cuts the 45° line—that is, where total desired spending equals total output. In the present simplified model, this is the same level of GDP at which the saving function intersects the investment function.

Changes in GDP

- With a constant price level, equilibrium GDP is increased by a rise in the desired consumption or investment spending that is associated with each level of GDP. Equilibrium GDP is decreased by a fall in desired spending.

- The magnitude of the effect on GDP of shifts in autonomous spending is given by the multiplier. It is defined as $K = \Delta Y/\Delta A$, where ΔA is the change in autonomous spending and ΔY is the resulting increase in GDP.
- The simple multiplier is the multiplier when the price level is constant. It is equal to $1/(1 - c)$, where c is the marginal propensity to spend out of GDP. Thus, the larger c is, the larger is the multiplier. It is a basic prediction of macroeconomics that the simple multiplier, relating £1 worth of increased spending on domestic output to the resulting increase in GDP, is greater than unity.

TOPICS FOR REVIEW

- Aggregation across sectors
- Actual and potential GDP
- The GDP gap
- Desired spending
- Consumption function
- Average and marginal propensities to consume and to save
- Aggregate spending function
- Marginal propensities to spend and not to spend
- Equilibrium GDP at a given price level
- Saving–investment balance
- Shifts of, and movements along, spending functions
- The effect on GDP of changes in desired spending
- The simple multiplier
- The size of the multiplier and slope of the AE function

QUESTIONS

1. Calculate GDP using the following information (where there is no government and no foreign trade and $C =$ consumption, $I =$ investment, and $Y =$ GDP): $C = 100 + 0.8Y$; $I = 1,000$.

2. How will the answer to Question 1 change if I increases to (a) 2,000, (b) 4,000, and (c) 10,000?

3. How would the answers to Questions 1 and 2 change if the consumption function were (a) $C = 1,000 + 0.6Y$, (b) $C = -200 + 0.9Y$, and (c) $C = -200 + 1Y$.

4. What is the value of the multiplier when the marginal propensity to spend is: (a) 0.6; (b) 0.7; (c) 0.9?

5. Why is there a close relationship between personal disposable income and consumer spending?

6. Explain why an increase of £100 in autonomous spending can lead to an increase in GDP that is greater than £100.

7. What things do you think would put limits on how far increases in spending can lead to increases in real GDP?

8. What do you think are likely to be the main determinants of investment spending by firms?

9. Is it likely that the household's marginal propensities to spend out of disposable income will vary with the age of its members? If so, how would you expect it to vary?

10. Do you think that the marginal propensity to spend out of disposable income would be different at different times of year? If not why not, and if so why?

CHAPTER 17

GDP IN AN OPEN ECONOMY WITH GOVERNMENT

In this chapter we continue building a model of the short-run determination of GDP. Our model in Chapter 16 contained five simplifying, but temporary, assumptions—no government, no foreign trade, an exogenously determined interest rate and level of investment, a fixed price level, and excess productive capacity. The current chapter relaxes the first two of these. Chapters 19 and 20 relax the fixed interest rate and investment assumption, while Chapters 21 and 22 relax the fixed price level and excess capacity assumptions.

In this chapter you will learn that in our model:

- Government consumption contributes to aggregate spending in the same way as any other component of autonomous spending.
- Taxes affect private consumption via their effect on disposable income.
- Net exports are assumed to be negatively related to GDP.
- The addition of government and foreign trade leaves unchanged the condition for GDP to be in equilibrium that desired aggregate domestic spending is equal to national output for GDP.
- The size of the multiplier is negatively related to the income tax rate and the marginal propensity to import.

In what follows we first add government and then a foreign sector to our simple model. Adding the government sector allows us to study **fiscal policy**, which is defined as the use of the government's taxing and spending powers to affect the level of GDP. In an open economy, net foreign demand for domestic output is an important source of final spending, so it has to be included in any complete treatment of the spending components of GDP. After adding the government and the foreign trade sector, we examine how these additions alter both the structure of the model and its behaviour in response to changes in autonomous spending.

As we proceed, it is important to remember that the key elements of our theory of GDP determination in the short run are unchanged. The most important of these that will remain true, even after incorporating government and the foreign sector, are restated here.

1. Aggregate desired spending can be divided into autonomous (or exogenous) spending and induced spending. *Autonomous spending* is determined outside the model and is treated as a constant. We will ask what happens when some component of autonomous spending

changes, but these changes are imposed from outside the system and can be thought of as external 'shocks'. *Induced spending* is spending that is determined within the model, which so far is spending that depends on the level of GDP.

2. The equilibrium level of GDP is the level at which the sum of autonomous and induced desired spending in the domestic economy is equal to the level of output. Graphically, this is where the aggregate spending function intersects the 45° line.

3. The simple multiplier measures the change in equilibrium GDP that takes place in response to a unit change in autonomous domestic spending, with the price level held constant.

Recall that the spending-based measure of GDP is made up of private consumption, investment, government consumption spending, and net exports. We have already built a model of GDP determination that includes private consumption and investment. We are about to extend this model to include government consumption and net exports. Recall also that national output and 'GDP' are equivalent terms for our purposes.

Government spending and taxes

Government spending and taxation policies affect equilibrium GDP in two important ways. First, government spending is part of autonomous spending in our model; that is, it is an exogenous element of spending in the economy. Secondly, as we saw in Chapter 15, to derive disposable income, tax payments must be subtracted from GDP, and government transfer payments must be added. Because disposable income determines private consumption spending, the relationship between desired private consumption and GDP becomes more complicated when a government is added. A government's plans for taxes and spending determine its *fiscal policy*, which has important effects on the level of GDP in both the short and the long runs.

Government spending

In Chapter 15 we distinguished between *government consumption spending on goods and services* and government *transfer payments*. The distinction bears repeating here. Government consumption is part of GDP. When the government hires a civil servant, buys a paper clip, or purchases fuel for the navy, it is directly adding to the demand for the economy's current output of goods and services. Thus, desired government purchases, G, are part of desired aggregate spending. As explained in Chapter 16, in our model we assume that government consumption spending buys the output from the single industrial sector. This makes government spending have the same effect on GDP as any other component of autonomous spending.

The other part of government spending, transfer payments, also affects desired aggregate spending, but only indirectly. Consider, for example, state pensions or unemployment benefit. These are payments (transfers) made by government to households who will spend at least some of the money. Since that spending is recorded as personal consumption, we do not want to count it twice by recording it under G as well. Government transfer payments affect aggregate spending only through the effect that these payments have on personal *disposable* income. Transfer payments increase disposable income, and increases in disposable income increase desired consumption spending via the consumption function.

The distinction between transfers and government consumption is important when it comes to issues such as determining the amount of GDP that is accounted for by government. Measuring the size of government to include transfers makes it look as though government's share of GDP is much bigger than it really is. However,

looking only at G makes the government's revenue needs look smaller than they are, since transfers must be financed by taxes or borrowing, just as spending on goods and services must be. In what follows, government spending always excludes transfers, unless the contrary is stated.

Tax revenues

Tax revenues may be thought of as negative transfer payments in their effect on desired aggregate spending. Tax payments reduce disposable income relative to GDP; transfers raise disposable income relative to GDP. For the purpose of calculating the effect of government policy on desired consumption spending, it is the net effect of the two that matters.

We define **net taxes** to be total tax revenues received by the government minus total transfer payments made by the government, and we denote net taxes as T. (For convenience, when we use the term 'taxes', we will mean *net* taxes unless we explicitly state otherwise.) Since transfer payments are smaller than total taxes, net taxes are positive, and personal disposable income is less than GDP. Household disposable income was almost 70 per cent of GDP at market prices in 2012.

The budget balance

The **budget balance** is the difference between total government revenue and total government spending or, equivalently, net taxes minus government spending, $T - G$. When revenues exceed spending, the government is running a **budget surplus**. The government will then reduce the national debt, since the surplus funds will be used to pay off old debt. When spending exceeds revenues, as it has for much of the period since the Second World War (1969–70, 1988–9, and 1998–2001 were the only exceptions in the United Kingdom between 1945 and 2015), the government is running a **budget deficit**. The government must then add to the national debt, since it must borrow to cover its deficit.[1] When the budget surplus (or deficit) is zero, the government has a **balanced budget**. Since the budget deficit is simply a negative budget surplus, we generally use 'budget surplus' to cover

---

[1] It does this by selling government bonds (known as 'gilts' in the UK). When the government runs a surplus, it uses the excess revenue to purchase outstanding government bonds. The stock of outstanding bonds is termed the *national or public debt* (public debt is the debt of the entire public sector, which includes local authorities and nationalized industries; national debt is the debt of the central government only).

Box 17.1 Deficits in the news

During the worldwide recession of 2008–9 many governments found their finances deteriorating as tax revenues fell and recession-related spending (such as unemployment benefits) rose. Maintaining government demand (*G*) at a time when both private domestic demand (*C* + *I*) and external demand (*X* – *IM*) were falling was a policy designed to prevent what would have been even larger falls in GDP. However, the very large increases in budget deficits and resulting projected increases in public sector debt also caused great concern (see the first case study at the end of this chapter for the UK case).

One European government that found itself in a crisis over its deficit was Greece, as stated in the following headline:

Greece in turmoil over cuts to budget: country brought to standstill by protests

(February 2010)

However, it is worth noting that much of Greece's fiscal problem was not the result of the recession, since it became clear that the government had used various subterfuges to conceal an underlying deficit that had been building up for years before the recession increased an already serious problem. However, only three years later one headline said:

Greece doubles estimate of 2013 budget surplus

(November 2013)

as the cuts in spending (and tax rises) introduced in earlier years created a *primary budget surplus*. This means that there was a surplus on the current budget if debt interest payments are excluded from the calculation.

Greece was not alone in having to make budget cuts:

Ireland braced for swingeing budget cuts

(December 2009)

was a headline linked to the fact that that the Irish government had had budget deficits of the order of 12–16 per cent of GDP in each of the three years 2009–11 and it had to borrow money from the EU to help finance its spending. However, here too the cuts seem to have worked, and the prospects had improved substantially such that by late 2013 the headlines were more like:

Ireland on course to narrow budget deficit

and the story was that the Irish budget deficit would be around 3 per cent of GDP by 2015.

Many other countries, such as Portugal, Iceland, the Baltic States, Hungary, and Ukraine, had similar fiscal crises and not all of these were over at the time of writing (June 2014).

Even the United States saw a big increase in its budget deficit after the 2007–8 financial crisis. The initial budget deficit was the result of major tax cuts early in the decade and the financing of wars in Iraq and Afghanistan with no increase in taxes. This already serious problem was then exaggerated when the recession caused revenues to fall drastically while welfare-based spending rose.

At the time of writing, the United States seemed able to finance its deficit without any major crisis (partly by borrowing from China), but many smaller countries found their credit ratings falling in the face of large deficits, so that, for them, borrowing was both more difficult and more expensive. However, the US administration did have problems of an internal political nature associated with attempts to persuade Congress to increase the limit on the size of the federal government's debt.

The important point to note, however, is that government deficits are big news and likely to remain so for several years to come. The debts built up while running a deficit are also important, and these are likely to be around even longer than the deficits that brought them about.

---

both cases, so bear in mind that the budget surplus can be negative.

The size of budget deficits has been a topic of great importance in many countries since the financial crisis of 2007–8 and the resulting recession of 2008–9. Box 17.1 picks up some media headlines, and the first case study at the end of the chapter looks at the UK budget deficit in more detail.

Tax and spending functions

We treat government spending as exogenous in our model; that is, it does not vary with GDP. The government is assumed to decide how much it wishes to spend in real terms and to hold to these plans whatever the level of

GDP. We also treat *tax rates* as exogenous. The government sets its tax rates and does not vary them as GDP varies. This makes *tax revenues* endogenous. As GDP rises with given tax rates, the tax revenue will rise. For example, when their incomes rise, households and firms pay more total tax, even if tax rates are unchanged. A major contribution to growing budget deficits in 2009 and beyond was the fall in tax revenue that resulted from a combination of lower personal incomes (and thus less income tax revenue), lower profits (and thus lower corporation tax revenue), and lower spending (and thus lower value added tax and excise tax revenue). Note also that transfer payments in terms of such things as job-seekers' allowance and income support payments tend to rise as

Table 17.1 **The budget surplus function (£ million)**

GDP (Y)	Government spending (G)	Net taxes (T = 0.1Y)	Government surplus (T – G)
500	170	50	–120
1,000	170	100	–70
1,750	170	175	5
2,000	170	200	30
3,000	170	300	130
4,000	170	400	230

The budget surplus is negative at low levels of GDP and becomes positive at high levels of GDP. The table shows that the size of the budget surplus increases with GDP, given constant spending and constant tax rates. For example, when GDP rises by £1,000 million, the deficit falls or the surplus rises by £100 million.

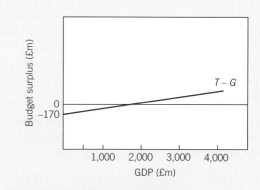

Figure 17.1 **Budget surplus function**

The budget surplus increases as GDP increases. This figure plots the T – G column from Table 17.1. Notice that the slope of the surplus function is equal to the income tax rate of 0.1.

incomes fall during recessions, and fall as incomes rise during periods of rising activity and employment. This is a second reason why net taxes rise as GDP rises: higher tax revenue and lower transfer payments.

Table 17.1 and Figure 17.1 illustrate how tax revenue will rise with GDP using a specific example in which there is one tax on the whole of GDP. The illustration shows the size of the government's surplus when its desired purchases (G) are constant at £170 million and its net tax revenues are equal to 10 per cent of GDP. Notice that the

government budget surplus (or public saving) increases with GDP. This relationship occurs because net tax revenues rise with GDP but, by assumption, government spending does not. The slope of the budget surplus function is just equal to the income tax rate. The *position* of the function is determined by fiscal policy, as we discuss later in this chapter.[2]

For given tax rates, the government budget surplus (public saving) increases as GDP rises and falls as GDP falls.

Net exports

The UK's foreign trade sector is significant in relation to its GDP. Exports of goods and services in 2012 were just under 32 per cent of GDP at market prices. Although the total volume of trade is important for many purposes, such as determining the amount by which a country gains from trade (see Chapter 27), the balance between exports and imports (the current account balance) is particularly important in determining GDP.

The net export function

In macroeconomics we are interested in how the balance of trade responds to changes in GDP, the price level, and the exchange rate. Our theory covers trade in goods *and services*. The effect on GDP of selling a service to a foreigner is identical to that of selling a physical commodity. In our model this is because it contains only one type of product so that all desired spending is treated as a demand

for this product. More generally, however, whether one sells a good or a service this creates GDP and employment for those who produce each of these.

Exports depend on spending decisions made by foreign consumers or overseas firms that purchase domestically produced goods and services. Therefore we assume that exports are determined by influences outside the home economy. This is autonomous, or exogenous, spending from the point of view of the determination of domestic GDP.

Imports, however, depend on the spending decisions of domestic residents. Most categories of spending have an import content; British-made cars, for example, use large

---

2 The numerical example used here is designed only to illustrate the principles of GDP determination developed in this chapter. To avoid the appearance of direct applicability of overly simplified models, we have deliberately chosen not to use 'realistic' numbers. The example produces GDP of £2,000 million, whereas UK money GDP in 2012 was around £1,500,000 million.

quantities of imported components and raw materials in their manufacture. Thus, imports rise when the other categories of spending rise. Because consumption rises when the income of domestic households rises, imports of foreign-produced consumption goods, and of materials that go into the production of domestically produced consumption goods, also rise with GDP.

Desired net exports are negatively related to GDP because of the positive relationship between desired imports and GDP and the assumption that exports are exogenous.

This negative relationship between net exports and GDP is called the *net export function*. Data for a hypothetical economy with constant exports and with imports that are assumed to be 25 per cent of GDP are given in Table 17.2 and illustrated in Figure 17.2. In this example exports are the autonomous component and imports are the induced component of the desired net export function. The formulation in the table implicitly assumes that all imports are for final consumption. Imports rise when GDP rises, but imports do not change when *other* categories of autonomous spending change, so there is no direct import content of G, I, and X. This simplification will prove useful in our development of the determination of equilibrium GDP and does not affect the essentials of the theory.

Shifts in the net export function

We have seen that the net export function relates net exports ($X - IM$), which we also denote by NX, to GDP. It is drawn on the assumption that everything that affects net exports, except domestic GDP, remains constant. The major variables that must be held constant are foreign GDP, relative international price levels, and the exchange rate. A change in any of these will affect the value of net exports at each level of GDP and hence will shift the net export function.

Notice that anything that affects domestic exports will change the values in the 'Exports' column in Table 17.2 and so will shift the net export function parallel to itself (in Figure 17.2(i)), upwards if exports increase and downwards if exports decrease. Also notice that anything that affects the proportion of GDP that home consumers wish to spend on imports will change the values in the 'Imports' column in the table, and thus will change the slope of the net export function by making imports more or less responsive to changes in GDP. What factors will cause such shifts?

Foreign GDP

An increase in foreign GDP, other things being equal, will lead to an increase in the quantity of domestically produced goods demanded by foreign countries—that is, to an increase in our exports. This is because as foreign GDP rises, foreign residents will receive higher incomes and they will buy more of all goods, including imports. But

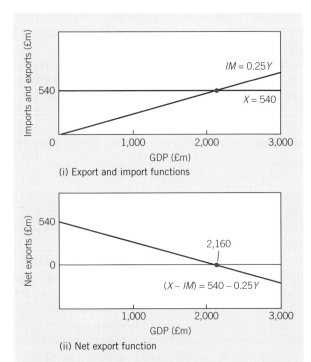

(i) Export and import functions

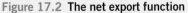

(ii) Net export function

Figure 17.2 The net export function

Net exports, defined as the difference between exports and imports, are negatively related to the level of GDP. The figure is based on the hypothetical data in Table 17.2. In part (i) exports are constant at £540 million, while imports rise with GDP. Therefore net exports, shown in part (ii), decline with GDP. With GDP equal to £2,160 million, imports are equal to exports at £540 million and net exports are zero. For levels of GDP below £2,160 million, imports are less than exports, and hence net exports are positive. For levels of GDP above £2,160 million, imports are greater than exports, and hence net exports are negative.

Table 17.2 The net export function (£ million)

GDP (Y)	Exports (X)	Imports ($IM = 0.25Y$)	Net exports ($X - IM$)
0	540	0	540
1,000	540	250	190
2,160	540	540	0
3,000	540	750	−210
4,000	540	1,000	−460
5,000	540	1,250	−710

Net exports fall as GDP rises. We assume that exports are constant and that imports are 25 per cent of GDP. In this case net exports are positive at low levels of GDP and negative at high levels of GDP.

foreign imports are domestic exports. Because the same additional amount is sold at each level of domestic GDP, the increase is in the constant of the domestic net export function, X. This causes NX to shift upwards, parallel to its original position. A fall in foreign GDP leads to a parallel downward shift in the net export function.

Relative international prices

Any change in the prices of home-produced goods relative to those of foreign goods will cause both imports and exports to change. This will shift the net export function.

Consider first a rise in domestic prices relative to prices in foreign countries. On the one hand, foreigners will now see domestically produced goods as more expensive relative both to goods produced in their own country and to goods imported from other countries. As a result domestic exports will fall. On the other hand, domestic residents will see imports from foreign countries become cheaper relative to the prices of home-produced goods. As a result they will buy more foreign goods, and imports will rise. Both these responses will cause the net export function to shift downwards and change its slope, as shown in Figure 17.3.

Secondly, consider the opposite case of a fall in UK prices relative to prices of foreign-made goods. On the one hand, potential UK exports will now look cheaper in foreign markets relative to both their home-produced goods and goods imported from third countries. As a result UK exports will rise. On the other hand, the same change in relative prices—British-made goods become cheaper relative to foreign-made goods—will cause UK imports to fall. Thus, the net export function will shift upwards, in exactly the opposite way to the movement in Figure 17.3.

What circumstances will cause relative international prices to change? Two important causes of changes in competitiveness, for a country as a whole, are international differences in inflation rates and changes in exchange rates.

Consider inflation rates first, and assume that the United Kingdom is the home country. If the sterling exchange rate remains constant, UK prices will rise relative to foreign prices if the UK inflation rate is higher than the inflation rates in other major trading countries. In contrast, UK prices will fall relative to foreign prices if the UK inflation rate is lower than the rates in other major trading countries.

Now consider the exchange rate. Holding domestic and foreign price levels constant, a depreciation of sterling will make imports more expensive for domestic residents and UK exports cheaper for foreigners. This is because UK residents will get less foreign currency for each pound sterling and foreigners will get more pounds for each unit of their own currency. Both foreigners and domestic

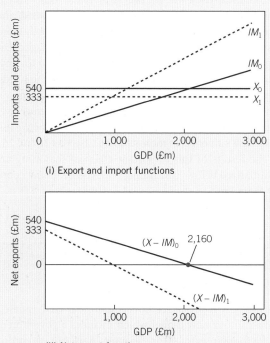

Figure 17.3 Shifts in the net export function

An upward shift in imports and/or a downward shift in exports shifts the net export function downwards. A rise in the domestic price level relative to foreign price levels, or a rise in the exchange rate, lowers exports from X_0 to X_1 and raises the import function from IM_0 to IM_1. This shifts the net export function downwards from $(X - IM)_0$ to $(X - IM)_1$. (In the figure imports are 25 per cent of Y along IM_0 and are assumed to rise to a third of Y when domestic goods become more expensive relative to foreign goods, while exports fall from £540 million to £333 million.)

consumers will shift spending towards the UK-produced goods, which have become cheaper relative to foreign goods. The net export function will thus shift upwards.

An appreciation of sterling (holding price levels constant) has the opposite effect. It makes UK goods relatively expensive, thus shifting the net export function downwards.[3]

Exchange-rate changes may be brought about by changes in interest rates implemented by the central bank. The

---

[3] A depreciation of sterling that is exactly proportional to the excess of UK inflation over foreign inflation will leave the relative price of UK exports and imports unchanged. This would be referred to as a constant *real exchange rate*, or as preserving purchasing power parity (PPP). The real exchange rate is the relative price of home- and foreign-produced goods. It is also referred to as 'competitiveness' or the 'terms of trade'. A rise in the real exchange rate (fall in competitiveness) shifts the net export function down because it lowers exports and increases imports at each level of GDP. These concepts are discussed more fully in Chapter 24.

domestic currency will generally appreciate (other things being equal) when the domestic interest rate is raised, and vice versa. This is because more people will wish to buy assets denominated in the home currency to take advantage of the high domestic interest rates, and a high demand for anything, including currency, tends to push its price upwards. As we shall see, changes in the exchange rate are an important way in which monetary policy can exert leverage over domestic aggregate spending in an open economy. We discuss these influences in more detail in Chapters 24 and 25.

The results of this important chain of reasoning are summarized below (continuing with the UK home country example).

1. UK prices rise relative to foreign prices if either the UK inflation rate exceeds the rate in other major trading countries (with exchange rates fixed) or the pound sterling appreciates (with price levels constant). This discourages exports and encourages imports, causing the net export function to shift downwards.

2. UK prices fall relative to foreign prices if either the UK inflation rate is less than the rates in competitor countries (with exchange rates fixed) or the pound sterling depreciates (with price levels constant). This encourages exports and discourages imports, causing the net export function to shift upwards.

Equilibrium GDP

We are now ready to see how equilibrium GDP is determined in our new model which includes a government and a foreign sector. As in Chapter 16 we can determine the equilibrium in two ways that come to the same thing in the end: by relating output and spending, and by relating saving and investment.

The aggregate spending approach

In Chapter 16 we determined equilibrium GDP by finding the level of GDP where desired aggregate spending is equal to national output. The addition of government and the foreign sector changes the calculations that we must make but does not alter the basic principles that are involved. Our first step is to derive a new aggregate spending function that incorporates the effects of government activity and foreign trade.

Relating desired consumption to GDP

Our theory of GDP determination requires that we relate each of the components of aggregate spending to GDP, Y. Personal income taxes cause personal disposable income to differ from GDP (by the proportion of income taxation net of transfers). For simplicity at this stage, we assume that disposable income is always 90 per cent of GDP.[4] Thus, whatever the relationship between C and Y_d, we can always substitute $0.9Y$ for Y_d. For example, if changes in consumption were always 80 per cent of changes in Y_d, changes in consumption would always be 72 per cent (80 per cent of 90 per cent) of changes in Y.

Table 17.3 illustrates how we can write desired consumption as a function of Y as well as of Y_d. We can then derive the marginal response of consumption to changes in Y by determining the proportion of any change in GDP that goes to a change in desired consumption.

Table 17.3 Consumption as a function of disposable income and GDP (£ million)

GDP (Y)	Disposable income ($Y_d = 0.9Y$)	Desired private consumption ($C = 100 + 0.8Y_d$)
100	90	172
1,000	900	820
2,000	1,800	1,540
3,000	2,700	2,260
4,000	3,600	2,980

If desired private consumption spending depends on disposable income, which in turn depends on GDP, desired consumption can be written as a function of either concept. The second column shows deductions of 10 per cent of any level of GDP to arrive at disposable income. Deductions of 10 per cent of Y imply that the remaining 90 per cent of Y becomes disposable income. The third column shows consumption as £100 million plus 80 per cent of disposable income.

By relating the second and third columns, one sees consumption as a function of disposable income. By relating the first and third columns, one sees the derived relationship between consumption and GDP. In this example the change in consumption in response to a change in disposable income (i.e. *MPC*) is 0.8, and the change in consumption in response to a unit change in GDP is 0.72.

---

[4] In this case desired net taxes, T, would be given by the function $T = 0.1Y$. Recall that for simplicity we ignore indirect taxes.

The marginal response of consumption to changes in GDP ($\Delta C/\Delta Y$) is equal to the marginal propensity to consume out of disposable income ($\Delta C/\Delta Y_d$) multiplied by the fraction of GDP that becomes personal disposable income ($\Delta Y_d/\Delta Y$).

This table shows how desired consumption spending varies as GDP varies, including the effects of taxes and transfer payments ($C = 100 + 0.72Y$; arrived at from $C = 100 + 0.8Y_d$ by substituting $0.9Y$ for Y_d). This equation is part of the aggregate spending function.

The aggregate spending function

In order to determine the equilibrium level of GDP, we start by defining the aggregate spending function:

$$AE = C + I + G + NX.$$

Table 17.4 illustrates the calculation of this function. It shows a schedule of desired spending for each of the components of aggregate spending, and it shows total desired *aggregate* spending at each level of GDP. Figure 17.4 shows this aggregate spending function in graphical form.

The marginal propensity to spend

The slope of the aggregate spending function is the *marginal propensity to spend (c)*. However, with the addition of taxes and net exports, the marginal propensity to spend is no longer equal to the marginal propensity to consume.

Suppose that the economy produces £1 of extra GDP and that the response to this is governed by the relationships in Tables 17.1 and 17.2, as summarized in Table 17.4.

Since £0.10 is collected by the government as net taxes, £0.90 is converted into disposable income, and 80 per cent of this amount (£0.72) becomes consumption spending. However, import spending also rises by £0.25, so spending on domestic goods (i.e. aggregate spending) rises by only £0.47. Thus, *c*, the marginal propensity to spend out of GDP is 0.47. What is not spent on domestic output includes the £0.10 in taxes, the £0.18 of disposable income that is saved, and the £0.25 of import spending, making a total of £0.53. Hence, the marginal propensity not to spend, $(1 - c)$, is $1 - 0.47 = 0.53$.

Determining equilibrium GDP

The logic of GDP determination in our (now more complicated) hypothetical economy is exactly the same as in the closed economy without government discussed in Chapter 16. We have added two new components of aggregate spending, G and $(X - IM)$. We have also made the calculation of desired private consumption spending more complicated; taxes must be subtracted from GDP in order to determine personal disposable income. However, *equilibrium GDP is still the level of GDP at which desired aggregate spending equals national output.*

The aggregate spending function can be used directly to determine equilibrium GDP. In Table 17.4 the equilibrium is £2,000 billion. When GDP is equal to £2,000 billion, it is also equal to desired aggregate spending.

Suppose that GDP is less than its equilibrium amount. The forces leading back to equilibrium are exactly the same as those described in Chapter 16. When domestic

Table 17.4 The aggregate spending function (£ million)

GDP (Y)	Desired private consumption spending ($C = 100 + 0.72Y$)	Desired investment spending ($I = 250$)	Desired government spending ($G = 170$)	Desired net export spending ($IM = 540 - 0.25Y$)	Desired aggregate spending ($AE = C + I + G + (X - IM)$)
0	100	250	170	540	1,060
100	172	250	170	515	1,107
500	460	250	170	315	1,195
1,000	820	250	170	290	1,530
2,000	1,540	250	170	40	**2,000**
3,000	2,260	250	170	−210	2,470
4,000	2,980	250	170	−460	2,940
5,000	3,700	250	170	−710	3,410

The aggregate spending function is the sum of desired private consumption, investment, government, and net export spending. The autonomous components of desired aggregate spending are desired investment, desired government spending, desired export spending, and the constant term in desired consumption (first row). These sum to £1,060 million in the above example. The induced components are the second terms in desired consumption spending (0.72Y) and desired imports (0.25Y).

The marginal response of consumption to a change in GDP is 0.72, calculated as the product of the marginal propensity to consume (0.8) and the fraction of GDP that becomes disposable income (0.9). The marginal response of desired aggregate spending to a change in GDP, $\Delta AE/\Delta Y$, is 0.47.

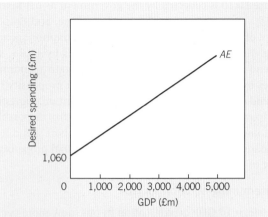

Figure 17.4 An aggregate spending function

The aggregate spending function relates total desired spending to GDP. The *AE* line plots the data from the first and last columns of Table 17.4. Its intercept shows £1,060 million of autonomous spending (£100 million autonomous consumption plus £250 million investment plus £170 million government spending plus £540 million autonomous net exports). Its slope is the marginal propensity to spend (which, following the calculations in Table 17.4, is 0.47).

consumers, firms, foreign consumers, and governments try to spend at their desired amounts, they will try to purchase more goods and services than the economy is currently producing. Thus, some of the desired spending must either be frustrated or take the form of purchases of inventories of goods that were produced in the past. As firms see that they are (or could be) selling more than they are producing, they will increase production, thereby increasing the level of national output (GDP).

The opposite sequence of events occurs when national output is greater than the level of aggregate desired spending at that level of GDP. Now the total of personal consumption, investment, government spending, and net foreign demand for the economy's output is less than the national product. Firms will be unable to sell all of their output. Their unsold stocks will be rising, and they will not let this happen indefinitely. They will seek to reduce the level of output until it equals the level of sales, and GDP will fall.

Finally, when national output is just equal to desired aggregate spending (£2,000 billion in Table 17.4), there is no pressure for output to change. Private consumption, investment, government consumption, and net exports just add up to the national product. Firms are producing exactly the quantity of goods and services that purchasers want to buy, given the level of GDP.

Equilibrium GDP is determined where desired aggregate spending equals national output. In our extended model aggregate spending includes private consumption, investment, government consumption, and net exports.

Graphical exposition

Figure 17.5 illustrates the determination of equilibrium GDP and the behaviour of the economy when it is not in equilibrium. The line labelled *AE* is simply the aggregate spending function shown in Figure 17.4. The slope of *AE* is the marginal propensity to spend out of GDP (0.47 in our example). Recall that *AE* plots the behaviour of desired purchases. It shows demand for the domestic product at each level of GDP. (The *AE* function is sometimes referred to as the 'aggregate demand curve' in this context. However, we reserve this term for another, related construct that we use in Chapter 21, once we have made the price level an endogenous variable.)

The line labelled *AE = Y* (the 45° line) depicts the equilibrium condition that desired aggregate spending be equal to actual national output (GDP). Any point on this line *could* be an equilibrium, but only one is. Equilibrium occurs where behaviour (as depicted by the *AE* function) is consistent with equilibrium (as depicted by *AE = Y*). At the equilibrium level of GDP desired spending is just equal to national output (GDP) and therefore is just sufficient to purchase the total domestic product.

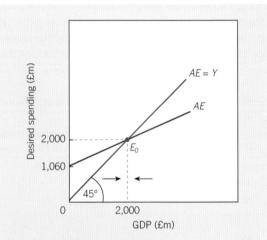

Figure 17.5 Equilibrium GDP

Equilibrium GDP occurs at E_0, where the desired aggregate spending line intersects the 45° line. The aggregate spending line, *AE*, is taken from Table 17.4; autonomous spending is £1,060 million, and its slope is 0.47. If real GDP is below £2,000 million, desired aggregate spending will exceed national output, and production will rise. This is shown by the arrow to the left of *Y* = £2,000 million. If GDP is above £2,000 million, desired aggregate spending will be less than national output, and production will fall. This is shown by the arrow to the right of *Y* = £2,000 million. Only when real GDP is £2,000 million will desired aggregate spending equal real national output.

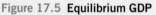

The augmented saving–investment approach

An equivalent way of determining equilibrium GDP is analogous to finding the point where desired saving equals desired investment. Finding the level of GDP where $S = I$ was appropriate in Chapter 16, where we were dealing with a closed economy with no government. Now, we have to take account of government and net exports both of which provide an injection of spending that plays a similar role to investment.

Additional injections and leakages

In Chapter 16, saving and investment had to be equal for GDP to be in equilibrium, as this provided a balance of inflows and outflows (injections and leakages). It may be helpful at this stage to review both the hydraulic analogue in Box 16.3 and the circular flow of income and spending, illustrated in Figure 15.2. The principles involved are unchanged. Now, however, we have two additional sources of leakage and two additional sources of injection.

In Chapter 16, saving was the only leakage of spending from the circular flow. The marginal propensity to save told us how much was not spent out of each additional £1 of income received. Now we add personal income taxes. These are levied on individuals' gross incomes, and so they also represent a proportion of income earned that cannot be spent. The second additional leakage is imports. Imports are a leakage because they create demand for foreign output. This does not generate domestic GDP.

Investment was the only injection in our model in Chapter 16. In this chapter we have added government spending. This is received as income by the private sector, and this extra income leads to further spending as before. Similarly, export demand comes from other countries, but it generates domestic GDP. Hence, export demand is our second new injection.

The condition for GDP to be in equilibrium is now that the sum of desired injections should equal the sum of desired leakages. We can write this condition as an equation, with the sum of all leakages (saving, S, plus net taxes, T, plus imports, IM) equal to the sum of all injections (investment, I, plus government spending, G, plus exports, X):

$$S + T + IM = I + G + X.$$

An equivalent equilibrium condition to $AE = Y$ for the determination of equilibrium GDP is that injections (investment plus government spending plus exports) must equal leakages (saving plus taxes plus imports).

Graphical exposition

In order to illustrate the determination of GDP via the equality of injections and leakages, it is convenient to rearrange the above equation. The graphical expression is then made simpler, and the economic explanation is more intuitive.

Subtracting G and IM from both sides of the above equation gives

$$S + (T - G) = I + (X - IM).$$

The brackets do not change the meaning of anything, but they do identify two terms we are already familiar with. $(T-G)$ is the government budget surplus. In this context it can be thought of as public sector (government) saving. Since S is private saving, $S + (T - G)$ is total domestic saving, or national saving. $(X - IM)$ is our old friend net exports. When there is no net income from abroad—that is, when GNI (or GNP) and GDP are equal, as was approximately true in the United Kingdom in 2011 (GNI was about 1.3 per cent larger than GDP[5])—net exports equal the net accumulation of claims on foreigners. This is because if we sell more to foreigners than we buy from them, we must either

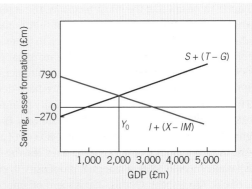

Figure 17.6 National saving and national asset formation

The economy is in equilibrium at Y_0, where desired national saving, $S + (T - G)$, equals desired national asset formation, $I + (X - IM)$. To the left of Y_0 desired national asset formation exceeds desired national saving. This implies that desired aggregate spending exceeds national output. Firms will respond to the imbalance by producing more, moving the economy towards equilibrium. To the right of Y_0 desired national asset formation is less than desired national saving and aggregate spending is less than national output. Firms will cut back on output in order to avoid accumulating excess inventories, and the economy will move towards equilibrium.

---

[5] The initial estimates of UK GDP and GNI for 2012 have GNI about 0.3 per cent smaller than GDP.

acquire a new foreign asset or reduce some foreign liability. Hence net exports cause the net acquisition of foreign assets, or overseas investment. I is domestic investment, so $I + (X - IM)$ is domestic plus overseas investment, or what is called **national asset formation**. Thus, the equation

$$S + (T - G) = I + (X - IM)$$

can be interpreted as a generalization of the condition that saving equals investment, since it says that national saving equals national asset formation.

Figure 17.6 illustrates how GDP is determined by the intersection of the national saving and national asset formation schedules. Notice that this is exactly the same level of GDP at which $AE = Y$.

Changes in aggregate spending

Changes in any of the autonomous components of planned aggregate spending will cause changes in equilibrium GDP. In Chapter 16 we investigated the consequences of shifts in the consumption function and the investment function. Here, we discuss fiscal policy—the effects of government spending and taxes. We also consider shifts in the net export function. First, we show that the simple multiplier is reduced by the presence of taxes and the marginal propensity to import.

The simple multiplier revisited

In Chapter 16 we saw that the *simple multiplier*, the amount by which equilibrium GDP changes when autonomous spending changes by £1, was equal to $1/(1 - c)$. In the example considered throughout Chapter 16, the marginal propensity to spend, c, was equal to 0.8, and the multiplier was equal to 5, or $1/(0.2)$. In the example that we have developed in this chapter, with a marginal propensity to import of 0.25 and a marginal (net) income tax rate of 0.1, the marginal propensity to spend is 0.47. (Ten per cent of a £1 increase in autonomous spending goes to taxes, leaving 90p of disposable income. With a marginal propensity to consume of 0.8, 72p is spent. Of this, 25p is spent on imports, leaving a total of 47p to be spent on domestically produced consumption goods.) Thus, $(1 - c)$ is 0.53, and the simple multiplier is $1/(0.53) = 1.89$. Box 17.2 sets out the full derivation of the multiplier in the presence of taxes and imports.

Fiscal policy

Fiscal policy involves the use of government spending and tax policies to influence total desired spending in order to achieve any specific goal set by the government.

Since government spending increases aggregate desired spending and taxation decreases it, the *directions* of the required changes in spending and taxation are generally easy to determine once we know the direction of the desired change in GDP. But the *timing, magnitude*, and *mixture* of the changes pose more difficult issues.

Any policy that attempts to influence GDP through fiscal measures such as changes in taxes and government spending is called **stabilization policy**. In the extreme such policy may seek to stabilize GDP at or near any desired level (usually potential GDP), or it may seek merely to reduce the magnitude and/or duration of fluctuations, or just to alleviate some persistence of GDP below potential with its accompanying high unemployment. The basic idea of stabilization policy follows from what we have already learned. A reduction in tax rates or an increase in government spending shifts the AE function upwards, causing an increase in equilibrium GDP. An increase in tax rates or a decrease in government spending shifts the AE function downwards, causing a decrease in equilibrium GDP.

If the government has some target level of GDP, it can use its taxation and spending as instruments in an attempt to push the economy towards that target. First, suppose the economy is in a serious recession. The government would like to increase GDP. The appropriate fiscal tools are to raise spending and/or to lower tax rates. Secondly, suppose the economy is 'overheated'. In later chapters we will study what this means in detail. In the meantime we observe that an 'overheated' economy has such a high level of GDP (relative to potential) that shortages have developed and are causing inflation. Without worrying too much about the details, just assume that the current level of GDP is higher than the target level that the government judges to be appropriate. What should the government do? The fiscal tools at its command are to lower government spending and to raise tax rates, both of which have a depressing effect on GDP.

The proposition that governments can alleviate recessions by deliberately stimulating aggregate demand created a major revolution in economic thought. This is still known as the Keynesian Revolution. Box 17.3 gives further background on the origins of this revolution and its impact on policy. We have already done enough macroeconomics to understand what this was all about. According to the theory we have developed so far, an

Box 17.2 The multiplier in an open economy with taxes

In this and the previous chapter we have shown how the size of the multiplier depends on the size of the propensity to spend out of GDP, c. Using this concept the multiplier is always given by $1/(1 - c)$. The derivation of this expression was shown in Box 16.5 for the case where c depends only on the marginal propensity to consume, which was labelled b in that box.

We now wish to show exactly what determines c when we have three forms of leakage: saving, taxes, and imports. In a closed economy with no taxes it depended only on the value of the marginal propensity to consume.

Our full model consists of the desired equilibrium condition that desired spending equals actual output:

$$Y = C + I + G + (X - IM). \qquad (17.1)$$

The consumption function is

$$C = a + b(1 - t)Y, \qquad (17.2)$$

where a is autonomous consumption, b is the marginal propensity to consume out of disposable income, and t is the income tax rate.

Imports are some proportion m of GDP:

$$M = mY. \qquad (17.3)$$

G, I, and X are exogenous variables that are determined outside the model.

To find the solution for Y we substitute eqn (17.2) and eqn (17.3) into eqn (17.1) for C and M. This gives

$$Y = a + b(1 - t)Y + I + G + X - mY.$$

Taking the terms containing Y over to the left-hand side gives

$$Y - b(1 - t)Y + mY = a + I + G + X$$

or

$$Y(1 - b(1 - t) + m) = a + I + G + X.$$

Therefore the solution for Y is

$$Y = \frac{a + I + G + X}{(1 - b(1 - t) + m)}$$

Thus the value of the multiplier is $1/(1 - b(1 - t) + m)$. This shows explicitly what is shown with a numerical example in the text: the multiplier is larger the bigger is the marginal propensity to consume, b, and it is smaller the larger is the income tax rate, t, and the propensity to import, m. The marginal propensity to spend out of GDP, c, is thus now given by $b(1 - t) + m$.

---

economy can reach an equilibrium level of GDP well below its full-employment or potential level. According to Keynesian theory, governments can use fiscal policy to increase aggregate spending by increasing government spending or reducing taxes (or both).

The aggregate spending model of GDP and output determination predicts that GDP can get stuck at a level below its full potential. It also suggests how fiscal policy might be used to return an economy to its potential level of GDP.

Now let us look in a little more detail at how this might work out. Bear in mind, however, that we are still dealing with a special case in which prices are fixed and there is excess capacity, so we are just looking at how our present model works, not yet at how the real world works.

Changes in government spending

Suppose that the government decides to increase its road-building programme by £10 million a year.[6] Desired government spending, G, rises by £10 million at every level of GDP, shifting AE upwards by the same amount. By how much would equilibrium GDP change? This can be calculated, in our simple model, using the multiplier. Government purchases are part of autonomous spending, so a *change* in government consumption of ΔG will lead to a *change* in equilibrium GDP of the multiplier times ΔG. In this numerical example equilibrium GDP would rise by

£10 million times the simple multiplier, or £18.9 million. Figure 17.7 shows the effect on GDP of an increase in government spending. It shows an upward parallel shift of the aggregate spending function, and a resulting increase in GDP. The same analysis could be applied equally to an increase in any other autonomous spending, such as investment or exports.

Reducing government spending has the opposite effect of shifting the AE function downwards, parallel to itself, and reducing equilibrium GDP. For example, if the government were to spend £2 million less on new roads, equilibrium GDP would fall by £2 million times the simple multiplier, or £3.78 million.

A change in government spending, in this model, changes the equilibrium level of GDP by the size of the spending change times the simple multiplier.

Changes in tax rates

If tax rates change, the difference between disposable income and GDP changes. As a result, the relationship between desired consumption spending and GDP also

---

[6] It does not matter what we assume the extra spending goes on, as long as it is domestic output and not imports. In our model it is always spent on the output of the single homogeneous industrial sector. Notice also that the value of the multiplier used in this section is hypothetical and based on the numerical example in Table 17.4.

Box 17.3 The Keynesian Revolution

In the 1930s a major depression affected most of the industrial world. Unemployment in the United Kingdom reached levels around 20 per cent overall, and as high as 50 per cent in some areas. In the United States unemployment reached nearly 25 per cent overall. World trade collapsed and factories lay idle. The economic orthodoxy at the time suggested that the best course for governments was first to let market forces solve the problem and secondly to get their own houses in order by increasing taxes and cutting spending to reduce the budget deficits that usually accompany recessions. Prices would adjust to clear markets and eventually excess supplies would be eliminated and confidence would be restored by seeing the government being financially prudent. Even if it was understood that this would take time, there was thought to be nothing much that governments could do to help the process of recovery other than by setting a good example of financial prudence. John Maynard Keynes challenged this conventional view in his path-breaking book *The General Theory of Employment, Interest and Money* (Macmillan, 1936). This work, and its subsequent interpretations and extensions, marks the beginning of macroeconomics as we are setting it out in Chapters 16–20.

One insight that Keynes expressed that is still considered valid today is that labour markets are not like conventional commodity markets, in that prices do not rapidly adjust to clear the market. This argument was discussed in the context of the 'efficiency wage' in Chapter 10. This 'wage stickiness' implies that unemployment can persist for a long time without the market mechanism doing much to eliminate it.

In the context where there is a general excess supply of productive resources, the question then arises: why is demand not high enough to utilize these resources? Keynes' answer was 'effective demand failure'. What this means in terms of the analysis of this chapter is that the *AE* function is too low. It is leading to an equilibrium level of GDP (such as illustrated in Figure 17.5) that is well below its full-employment or potential level. Thus the cause of the 'great depression' was that one or all of *C* + *I* + *G* + *NX* were too low, perhaps as a result of a collapse of consumer confidence (and the reinforcing effect of unemployment on GDP), a collapse of investor confidence (in the context of low demand for output), and a decline of world demand (as other countries were suffering too).

The analysis suggested not just the cause of the problem but also a potential solution. By increasing *G*, governments would create a positive multiplier effect, shift aggregate spending upwards, and cause GDP to move towards its full-employment or potential level. Thus, the Keynesian Revolution suggested an active role for fiscal policy in helping to stabilize the economy and a promise that mass unemployment could be a thing of the past. We discuss later in Chapter 25 why these lofty ambitions for fiscal policy became tempered, but the idea did have a huge policy impact. It underpinned the New Deal policies of US President Roosevelt in the 1930s and was influential in many other countries, especially the United Kingdom, which in the post-World War II period used fiscal policy actively to manage aggregate demand in an attempt to stabilize activity.

In December 1965, *Time Magazine* famously ran a cover story with the headline: 'We are all Keynesians now'. Paradoxically, when President Nixon even more famously quoted the same statement in 1971, it was almost certainly no longer true. In the 1970s and 1980s the problem most pressingly facing the world was moving on from that of unemployment to inflation and high energy prices. In the inflation story, governments came closer to being villain rather than saviour, and active counter-cyclical fiscal policies went out of fashion. However, in the recession of 2008–9 there was a collapse of private demand on a global scale and governments initially saw fit to let their deficits expand in order to prop up aggregate demand in their home economies. These deficits were partially endogenous, as tax revenues fell and welfare spending rose, and partly policy-induced as governments undertook new spending in order to inject new demand into the economy and so reduce unemployment. In many places Keynes was back in fashion, and fiscal deficits were once again regarded by many as an important policy tool for demand management. Although this change of view was dramatic, it was not held by everyone, and major controversies did occur, particularly in the United States, over the wisdom of using fiscal tools to fight the recession. Also those who thought that the large budget deficits in many EU countries, particularly those in the Mediterranean area, were a more serious problem than unemployment urged governments to rein in their spending and raise taxes in order to reduce their deficits, despite this being a contractionary fiscal policy. We will have more to say about this controversy in Chapter 25.

changes. For any given level of GDP there will be a different level of disposable income and thus a different level of consumption. Consequently, a change in tax rates will also cause a change in *c*, the marginal propensity to spend out of GDP.

Consider a decrease in the tax rate. If the government decreases its rate of income tax so that it collects 5p less out of every £1 of GDP, then disposable income rises in relation to GDP. Thus, consumption, which in our model depends only on disposable income, will also rise at every

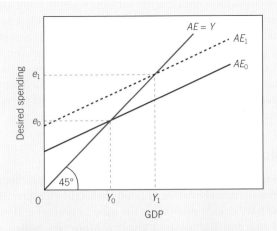

Figure 17.7 The effect of a change in government spending

A change in government spending changes GDP by shifting the *AE* function parallel to its initial position. The figure shows the effect of an increase in government spending. The initial level of aggregate spending is AE_0, and the equilibrium level of GDP is Y_0, with desired and actual spending e_0. An increase in government spending shifts aggregate spending upwards to AE_1. As a result, equilibrium GDP rises to Y_1, where desired and actual spending is e_1. The increase in GDP from Y_0 to Y_1 is equal to the increase in government spending times the multiplier. A reduction in government spending can be analysed in the same figure if we start with aggregate spending function AE_1 and GDP of Y_1. A reduction in government spending shifts the *AE* function downwards from AE_1 to AE_0 and, as a result, equilibrium GDP falls from Y_1 to Y_0. The fall is equal to the change in government spending times the multiplier.

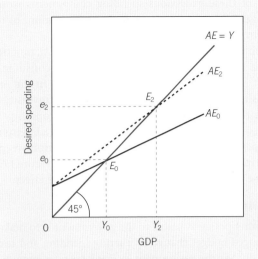

Figure 17.8 The effect of changing the tax rate

Changing the tax rate changes equilibrium GDP by changing the slope of the *AE* function. A reduction in the tax rate pivots the *AE* function from AE_0 to AE_2. The new curve has a steeper slope, because the lower tax rate withdraws a smaller percentage of GDP from the desired consumption flow. Equilibrium GDP rises from Y_0 to Y_2, because at every level of GDP desired consumption, and hence aggregate spending, is higher. If we take AE_2 and Y_2 to be the initial equilibrium, an increase in tax rates will reduce the slope of the *AE* function, thereby reducing equilibrium GDP, as shown by AE_0 and Y_0.

level of GDP. This results in a non-parallel upward shift of the *AE* function—that is, an increase in the slope of the line, as shown in Figure 17.8. The result of this shift will be a rise in equilibrium GDP.

A rise in the tax rate has the opposite effect. It causes a decrease in disposable income, and hence consumption spending, at each level of GDP. This results in a (non-parallel) downward shift of the *AE* function and thus decreases the level of equilibrium GDP.

Tax rates and the multiplier

We have seen that the *simple multiplier* is equal to the reciprocal of one minus the marginal propensity to spend out of GDP. That is, the multiplier equals $1/(1-c)$. The simple multiplier tells us how much equilibrium GDP changes when autonomous spending changes by £1 and there is no change in prices.

When tax rates change, the multiplier also changes. Suppose that *MPC* is 0.8 and the tax rate *falls* by 5p per pound of GDP. This would increase the marginal propensity to spend by 4p per pound of GDP. (Disposable income

would rise by 5p per pound at each level of GDP, and in our simple model consumption would rise by the marginal propensity to consume, 0.8, multiplied by 5p, which is 4p.) The increase in the value of c, the marginal propensity to spend, would cause the multiplier to rise, making equilibrium GDP more responsive to changes in autonomous spending from any source. In our example the multiplier has gone up from 1.89 to 1.96 ($(1-c)$ has fallen from 0.53 to 0.51).

The lower the income tax rate, the larger is the simple multiplier.

This can also be seen from the complete expression for the multiplier as set out in Box 17.2.

GDP may change as a result of a shift in any of the other exogenous components of spending—net exports, investment, and autonomous consumption. An increase in any of these would increase GDP by the shift times the multiplier, as illustrated (for the case of a government spending increase) in Figure 17.7. An increase in any exogenous spending shifts the *AE* function vertically upwards by the amount of the spending increase. The new intersection with the 45° line determines the new level of GDP, and its increase is measured relative to the original position on the horizontal axis. A reduction in any of these exogenous spending components would shift the *AE* function downwards by the amount of the fall in spending.

Changes that would alter the slope of the *AE* function are a shift in the marginal propensity to consume, a shift in the rate of income tax, and a shift in the propensity to import. A fall in the marginal propensity to save (hence a rise in *MPC*, the marginal propensity to consume), a fall in the income tax rate, and a fall in the propensity to import all make the *AE* function steeper and increase the multiplier, as illustrated in Figure 17.8. A rise in any of these three has the opposite effect.

Balanced budget changes

Another policy available to the government is to make a balanced budget change by altering spending and taxes equally. Say the government increases tax rates enough to raise an extra £100 million which it then uses to purchase domestically produced goods and services. Aggregate spending would remain unchanged if, and only if, the £100 million that the government takes from the private sector would otherwise have been spent by that sector. If so, the government's policy would reduce private spending by £100 million and raise its own spending by £100 million. Aggregate demand, and hence GDP and employment, would remain unchanged.

But this is not the case in our model. When an extra £100 million in taxes is taken away from households, they reduce their spending on domestically produced goods by less than £100 million. If the marginal propensity to consume out of disposable income is, say, 0.75, consumption spending will fall by only £75 million. If the government spends the entire £100 million on domestically produced goods, aggregate spending will increase by £25 million. In this case the balanced budget increase in government spending has an expansionary effect because it shifts the aggregate spending function upwards and thus increases GDP.

A balanced budget increase in government spending will have a mild expansionary effect on GDP, and a balanced budget decrease will have a mild contractionary effect.

The **balanced budget multiplier** measures these effects. It is given by the change in GDP divided by the balanced budget change in government spending that brought it about. Thus, if the extra £100 million of spending (combined with the tax increases to finance it) causes GDP to rise by £50 million, the balanced budget multiplier is 0.5; if GDP rises by £100 million, it is 1.0.

When government spending is increased with no corresponding increase in tax rates, we say that it is deficit-financed. Because there is no increase in tax rates, there is

no consequent decrease in consumption to offset the increase in government spending. However, with a balanced budget increase in spending, an offsetting increase in the tax rate and decrease in consumption does occur. Thus, the balanced budget multiplier is much lower than the multiplier that relates the change in GDP to a deficit-financed increase in government spending (with the tax rate constant).

Monetary policy

Monetary policy influences aggregate spending through several channels that we will study in detail in Chapter 25. We have already mentioned the most important of these in this and the previous chapter. **Monetary policy** is defined as the influencing of the economy via the effects on aggregate spending of changes in interest rates and/or the money supply. This works because the central bank can set a specific short-term interest rate (Bank Rate) at any level it thinks appropriate. It can also buy assets with money that it creates.

As we saw in Chapter 16, interest rate changes are known to affect consumption spending. Higher interest rates encourage people to cut their spending in order to save more and discourage borrowing in order to spend more. They also generate wealth effects on consumption via changes in the value of financial assets and property. We also saw that interest rates affect investment, with higher interest rates discouraging firms from borrowing in order to invest in such things as new equipment. Another channel from interest rates to aggregate spending is via the effect on the exchange rate to net exports (discussed further below).

Interest rate changes lead to a shift in spending (whether it be consumption, investment, or net exports) and can be analysed in the same way as a change in government spending shown in Figure 17.7. A rise in interest rates reduces some components of spending and thus shifts the *AE* function downwards. A cut in interest rates raises spending and shifts the *AE* function upwards. Thus, there is a negative relationship between the interest rate and aggregate spending, and between interest rates and GDP from the spending side of the economy.

The central bank will aim to lower aggregate spending if there is a positive GDP gap. It will aim to raise spending if actual GDP is below potential—that is, demand is low compared with supply capacity. For the moment, however, the key point to notice is that monetary policy works through influencing one or more of the categories of aggregate spending that we have studied in this and the previous chapter.

Net exports and equilibrium GDP

As with the other elements of desired aggregate spending, if the net export function shifts upward, equilibrium GDP will rise; if the net export function shifts downward, equilibrium GDP will fall. Again we take the United Kingdom as the home country.

Autonomous net exports

Net exports have both an autonomous component and an induced component. We have assumed that exports themselves are autonomous (exogenous) with respect to domestic GDP. Foreign demand for UK goods and services depends on foreign GDP, on foreign and UK prices, and on the exchange rate, but it does not depend on the United Kingdom's GDP. Export demand could also change because of a change in tastes. Suppose that foreign consumers develop a taste for British-made goods (perhaps in reality Jaguars or Land Rovers, but in the model it is for the output of the single sector) and desire to purchase £500 million more per year of such goods than they had in the past. The net export function (and the aggregate spending function) will shift up by £500 million, and equilibrium GDP will increase by £500 million times the multiplier.

Induced net exports

The domestic demand for imports depends in part on GDP. The greater is domestic GDP, the greater will be UK residents' demand for goods and services in general, including those produced abroad. Because imports are subtracted to obtain net exports (net exports equal $X - IM$), the greater is the marginal propensity to import, the lower will be the marginal propensity to spend on the domestic product, and the lower will be the multiplier, $1/(1 - c)$.

The exchange rate regime

We have noted above that foreign demand for domestic exports will depend upon the exchange rate (and that this can be affected by the interest rate set by the central bank). The way in which the exchange rate interacts with net exports will vary according to the exchange rate regime in operation at the time. For example, the adjustment of net exports will be different if the exchange rate is floating (determined by market forces) rather than pegged (fixed by the government). It may be different again for countries that share a common currency, such as in the Eurozone. For now we assume that there are no endogenous exchange rate changes affecting net exports, so our economy can best be thought of as one with a fixed exchange rate regime.

Lessons and limitations of the income–spending approach

In this and the preceding chapter we have discussed the determination of the four categories of aggregate spending and seen how they simultaneously determine equilibrium GDP and output. The basic approach, which is the same no matter how many categories are considered, was first presented in Chapter 16 and has been restated and extended in this chapter.

Any factor that shifts one or more of the components of desired aggregate spending will change equilibrium GDP, *at a given price level*. Holding the price constant has been necessary because we do not yet have a supply side to our analysis. So the level of GDP that we have been determining is the one that would be determined by demand conditions alone on the assumption that firms will supply everything that is demanded at the going price level. The actual outcome will depend on supply behaviour as well as on demand behaviour, so what we have done so far is only part of the story.

In later chapters we augment the income–spending model by allowing the price level to change in both the short and the long run. That is, we explicitly add a relationship that determines aggregate supply. When prices change, real GDP will change by amounts different from those predicted by the simple multiplier. We will see that changes in desired aggregate spending sometimes change both prices *and* real GDP. This is why the simple multiplier, derived under the assumption that prices do not change, is too simple.

However, there are three ways in which the simple income–aggregate spending model developed here remains useful, even when prices are incorporated. First, the simple multiplier will continue to be a valuable starting place in calculating actual changes in GDP in response to changes in autonomous spending. Secondly, no matter what happens to the price level, equilibrium requires that desired aggregate spending must equal output (GDP) in equilibrium, or equivalently that injections equal leakages.

CASE STUDIES

1. The UK budget deficit: going, going, ...?

During the recession of 2008–9, the UK government permitted its budget deficit to grow well above its levels of recent decades. It was considered necessary to do this in order to offset the falls in aggregate spending that were coming from a decline in consumption spending (and an accompanying rise in household saving (see the first case study in Chapter 16)), a fall in investment (see the second case study in Chapter 16), and weakness in world demand. The coalition government that was elected in May 2010 was committed to reducing the budget deficit. The tax rises and spending cuts announced by George Osborne, the Chancellor of the Exchequer, in June 2010 had the aim of eliminating the budget deficit by 2014–15. This goal was not accomplished, and by April 2014 the achievement of a balanced budget had been put back to 2018–19.

One major reason why the budget deficit did not fall as planned was that GDP grew much more slowly than expected. It remains an issue of great controversy as to what extent the slow growth was caused by the fiscal tightening, as tax rises and spending cuts were introduced as intended. We discuss the uses of fiscal policy further in Chapter 25. Here, we simply present some data on the UK government budget.

Figure 17.9(i) shows the total spending of the UK government since 1900 as a percentage of GDP. The level of government spending rose sharply during each of the two World Wars, but it is notable that after each war it stayed

higher than it had been before the war. Since the 1950s it has fluctuated around 40 per cent of GDP. This figure tends to rise during recessions and fall during booms, as spending is more stable than GDP (so when GDP falls the ratio of government spending to GDP tends to rise).

Figure 17.9(ii) shows the government budget surplus as a percentage of GDP since 1980. Data for 2014 onwards are the IMF forecast, and negative values indicate a deficit. This is the forecast that has the budget deficit eliminated by 2018–19, and so that is when borrowing is forecast to fall to zero. The out-turn will almost certainly be different from this forecast even with no change in fiscal policy, as the underlying forecast for GDP growth will not be exactly what happens. So the budget deficit may be eliminated faster or more slowly than this.

2. Government consumption

The data for UK government spending shown in Figure 17.9(i) include a significant proportion of transfer payments, such as state pensions and unemployment-related benefits. These transfers are not included in what we are representing by G in our model. This is because total government spending includes transfer payments. Transfer payments are (largely, as some subsidies are received by firms) received by households and will be measured as part of their disposable incomes, and thus finance some of their consumption spending or saving. We exclude this from G as we do not want to measure it twice in valuing the GDP and output.

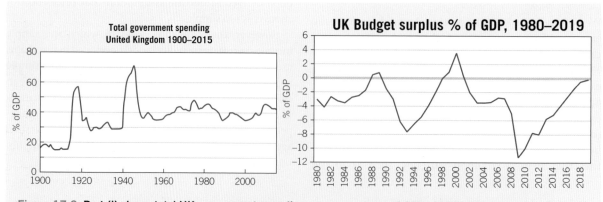

Figure 17.9 Part (i) shows total UK government spending as a percentage of GDP, 1900–2015; part (ii) shows the UK government budget surplus, 1980–2019 (values for 2014 onwards are IMF forecasts)

Sources: part (i) <ukpublicspending.co.uk>; part (ii) IMF, *World Economic Outlook data base,* April 2014

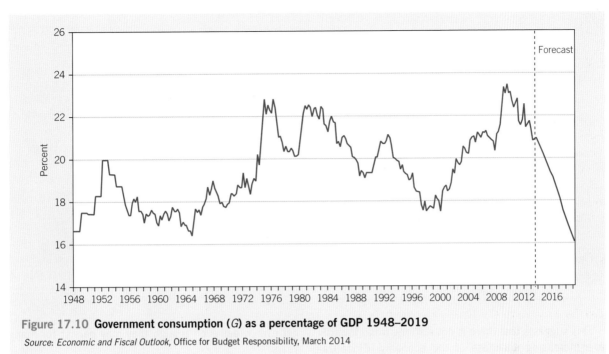

Figure 17.10 Government consumption (*G*) as a percentage of GDP 1948–2019

Source: Economic and Fiscal Outlook, Office for Budget Responsibility, March 2014

Figure 17.10 shows the data for government consumption spending since 1948 as a percentage of GDP. This is what we are calling *G* in our model. The peak of this series is at around 23 per cent of GDP in 2009, while total government spending in the same year was about 47 per cent of GDP. This implies that just over half of all government spending goes on transfer payments (equivalent to 24 per cent of GDP), but only just under half of the total is government consumption. The transfers to households are sometime called *welfare payments*.

Recall from Table 15.3 that the National Accounts report government consumption in two parts: collective and individual government consumption. The former includes activities paid for by the government, but where the benefit accrues to society as a whole and not to specific households. This includes defence spending and law and order. The latter includes health and education where the benefit of the government spending accrues to identifiable households.

Notice again that *G* tends to be at its highest in relation to GDP when the economy is in recession, such as in the mid-1970s, the early 1980s, the early 1990s, and 2009–10. It might be thought that this is a result of governments trying to increase *G* to stimulate demand. In reality, it is mainly due to the fact that government spending plans take a long time to change and *G* is generally planned to be at a stable proportion of GDP. However, when GDP falls, as in a recession, the ratio of *G* to GDP

tends to rise just because *G* stays more or less constant while GDP falls.

3. The openness of the economy

The UK is an open economy, and in many ways it has become more open in recent years owing to falling transport costs, cheaper communication technology, and lower barriers to international trade. 'Globalization' has become the buzz word for the process that is alleged to be affecting us all. However, media hype and political agitation can create a mistaken impression of what has actually been happening.

Figure 17.11 shows the exports and imports of goods and services as a percentage of GDP for the UK economy from 1955 to 2013. There has clearly been a slight upward trend. Imports and exports in the 1950s and 1960s were around 20 per cent of GDP, and in the mid-2000s they seemed to be fluctuating in the 25–35 per cent range. However, most of this upward movement happened in the early 1970s. This may be a result of the fact that the United Kingdom joined the EU in 1973. If we had drawn the chart just since 1974, no clear upward trend would be evident. It is true that the all-time high for imports (as a percentage of GDP) was in 2012 Q2 and for exports it was in 2011 Q4, but these levels were only a fraction higher than the previous peaks (in 1974 Q2 for imports and 1977 Q3 for exports).

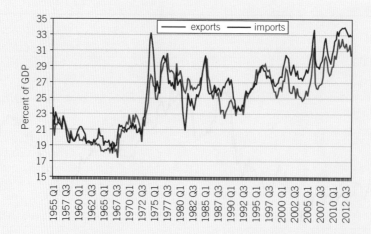

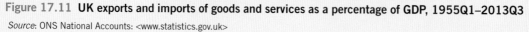

Figure 17.11 UK exports and imports of goods and services as a percentage of GDP, 1955Q1–2013Q3

Source: ONS National Accounts: <www.statistics.gov.uk>

This suggests that there is not a strong trend towards ever-increasing openness of the economy. Globalization of trade in some products, such as manufactured goods and food products (e.g. fresh fruit), is perhaps being offset by a growing proportion of services in GDP, and many services are provided locally rather than being traded in a global marketplace. What is also apparent from the chart is that imports and exports tend to move together in the long run. There are periods when the gap (the balance of trade in goods and services) tends to widen, but these deviations do not get ever wider even though they may persist for many years.

Both exports and imports have been fluctuating around about 30 per cent of GDP and this looks to be their normal level for the foreseeable future. This level of imports and exports makes the United Kingdom much more open than some industrial countries, such as Japan and the United States, which have exports and imports at around 15 per cent of GDP. Germany in contrast has imports and exports of around 50 per cent of GDP. France and Canada are similar to the United Kingdom in this respect.

Conclusion

We have now looked at all the main components of final demand in the economy, and seen that whatever determines aggregate spending also determines GDP. We next have to add a monetary sector to our model before adding a supply side and making the price level an endogenous variable. We can then discuss in more detail the policy choices available. However, it is worth bearing in mind that C, I, G, and NX remain the key determinants of final demand in the economy, and any aggregate demand policy that influences GDP must work through one of those variables. Thus what we add in subsequent chapters complicates the linkages but does not change the make-up of GDP itself.

SUMMARY

Government spending and taxes

■ Government consumption is part of autonomous aggregate spending. Taxes minus transfer payments are called net taxes and affect aggregate spending indirectly. Taxes reduce disposable income, whereas transfers increase disposable income. Disposable income, in turn, determines desired private consumption, according to the consumption function.

- The budget balance is defined as government revenues minus government spending. When this difference is positive, the budget is in surplus; when it is negative, the budget is in deficit.

- When the budget is in surplus, there is positive public saving because the government is spending less on the national product than the amount of income that it is withdrawing from the circular flow of income and spending. When the government budget is in deficit, public saving is negative.

Net exports

- Since desired imports increase as GDP increases, desired net exports decrease as GDP increases, other things being equal. Hence the net export function is negatively sloped (net exports fall as GDP rises).

Equilibrium GDP

- GDP is in equilibrium when desired aggregate spending, $C + I + G + (X - IM)$, equals national output.

- The sum of investment and net exports is called national asset formation because investment is the increase in the domestic capital stock and net exports result in investment in foreign assets. At the equilibrium level of GDP, desired national saving, $S + T - G$, is just equal to national asset formation, $I + X - IM$.

Changes in aggregate spending

- The size of the multiplier is negatively related to the income tax rate.

- A shift in exogenous spending changes GDP by the value of the shift times the simple multiplier.

- A shift in aggregate spending can be brought about by fiscal policy changes or by a change in the official interest rate.

TOPICS FOR REVIEW

- Taxes and net taxes
- The budget balance
- Public saving
- The net export function
- The marginal propensity to spend

- National asset formation
- National saving
- Calculation of the simple multiplier
- Fiscal policy and equilibrium GDP
- Monetary policy

QUESTIONS

1. Using the same notation as in the text, solve for the value of GDP, given the following relationships and values of exogenous variables: $C = 100 + 0.8(Y - T)$; $IM = 0.25Y$; $I = 1,000$; $G = 100$; $T = 100$; $X = 500$ (where T is a lump sum income tax).

2. Repeat Question 1 where income tax is a proportion of GDP so the consumption function can be written $C = 100 + 0.8 (1 - t)Y$, where t is the income tax rate that can be taken as 0.2 (i.e. 20%).

3. How does the answer to Question 1 change if a) G rises to 200, b) X rises to 600, c) I rises to 1,100? (Take all other exogenous variables to be at their initial value in each case.)

4. Using the relationships in Question 1 calculate a) the impact on GDP of an equal increase in G and T, b) the impact of an equal increase in X and IM. (Hint: increase each by the same number, say 100. In the case of IM, add the chosen number as an intercept to its equation.)

5 What is the value of the simple multiplier in an open economy with taxes, where the marginal propensity to consume is 0.8, the income tax rate is 0.2, and the import propensity is 0.14? Choose one.

   a) 1.55
   b) 2.4
   c) 5.56
   d) 2.0
   e) 1.0

6 Explain how governments might try to use their fiscal policy instruments to end a recession. What practical difficulties might be encountered in implementing such a policy?

7 Why does the trade balance deteriorate as domestic GDP increases?

8 How is the size of the multiplier related to a) the income tax rate, b) the marginal propensity to import, c) the marginal propensity to consume?

9 Explain how a change in foreign demand for UK goods will affect the level of UK GDP.

10 For the model of GDP determination set out above to be adequate, what must be assumed about the supply side of the economy? Are the necessary assumptions plausible?

CHAPTER 18

MONEY AND MONETARY INSTITUTIONS

In the previous chapters we developed a model of the determination of the GDP under the assumptions of a constant interest rate and price level. The interest rate is the price of borrowing money for a period of time. Changes in the price level—called inflations and deflations—have long been thought to be related to the amount of money in the economy. Certainly a change in the price level *is* a change in the value of money, but the direction of causation is not always clear. In order to make interest rates and the price level endogenous, we must now make a significant digression to study the nature of money and the monetary system.

What role does money play in the economy and how did it evolve? How does money get into the economy and how is the total amount of money determined? What role do banks play in the creation of money? These are some of the questions that we address in this chapter. In the following chapters we add a monetary sector to our macro model and analyse how monetary policy works, before going on to incorporate links between the monetary system and final spending and endogenizing the price level.

In this chapter you will learn that:

- Money acts as a medium of exchange, unit of account, and store of value.
- Money facilitates a wider range of transactions than would otherwise be feasible.
- Money was originally composed of commodities such as gold and silver.
- Paper currency was originally convertible into gold or silver, but now has nothing backing it except its acceptability in payment.
- The money multiplier is the ratio of broad money to high-powered money.
- Bank deposits are now the biggest part of the total amount of money in the economy, so the behaviour of the banking system is central to determining that total.
- In a competitive banking system, where banks charge interest for loans and pay interest on deposits, banks' behaviour is best understood in terms of demand and supply curves for loans and deposits. Banks must compete to attract deposit and loan business.

If you obtain more money you are better off because you can buy more things with it. But if a fully employed society obtains more money, everyone is not made better off, because the attempt to spend the additional money when output cannot be expanded will merely cause all prices to rise. Thus, although money allows those who have it to buy someone else's output, the total amount of goods and services available for everyone to buy depends on the total output produced, not on the total amount of money circulating in the economy. In the terminology of Chapter 15, an increase in the total quantity of money will not increase Y^*, the level of potential GDP. Although this much is generally agreed, the link between money and real activity has been a source of considerable debate among economists over the centuries, and we will discuss such debates later in this book. Here we start by discussing the nature of money, its historical origins, and the links between money and the banking system.

The nature of money

There is probably more widespread misunderstanding of money and the monetary system than of any other aspect of the economy. In this section we describe the functions of money and briefly outline its history.

At the outset it is important to note that the amount of money in an economy is a *stock* (in the United Kingdom it is so many billions of pounds), not a *flow* of so many pounds per month or per year. Previously, we have been talking about flows of output or spending *per period*. It is also important to notice that the money supply is a nominal variable measured in money units, whereas the other variables in our macro model are real variables measured in purchasing power units; that is, they are measured holding the price level constant.

What is money?

Money is defined as any generally accepted medium of exchange. A *medium of exchange* is anything that will be widely accepted in a society in exchange for goods and services. Although being a medium of exchange is usually regarded as money's defining function, money can also serve other roles:

Money acts as a medium of exchange and can also serve as a store of value and a unit of account.

A medium of exchange

As we saw in Chapter 1, if there were no money, goods would have to be exchanged by barter (one good being swapped directly for another). The major difficulty with barter is that each transaction requires a double coincidence of wants: I can only buy from someone who wants what I can offer in exchange. Anyone who specialized in producing one commodity would have to spend a great deal of time searching for suitable trading partners. Thus, a thirsty economics lecturer would have to find a brewer who wanted to learn economics before he could swap a lesson in economics for a pint of beer.

The use of money as a medium of exchange alleviates this problem. People can sell their output or services for money and subsequently use the money to buy what they want from others. So a monetary economy typically involves exchanges of goods and services for money and of money for goods and services, but not of goods and services for other goods and services.

The double coincidence of wants, which is required for barter, is unnecessary when a medium of exchange is used.

By facilitating transactions, money makes possible the benefits of specialization and the division of labour, which in turn contribute to the efficiency of the economic system. It is not without justification that money has been called one of the great inventions contributing to human freedom and well-being.

To serve as an efficient medium of exchange, money must have a number of characteristics. It must be readily acceptable and therefore of known value. It must have a high value relative to its weight (otherwise it would be a nuisance to carry around). It must be divisible, because money that comes only in large denominations is useless for transactions having only a small value. Finally, it must be difficult, if not impossible, to counterfeit.

A store of value

Money is a convenient way to store purchasing power; goods may be sold today, and the money taken in exchange for them may be stored until it is needed. However, to be a satisfactory store of value, money must have a relatively stable value. A rise in the price level leads to a decrease in the purchasing power of money, because more money is required to buy a typical basket of goods. When the price level is stable, the purchasing power of a given sum of money is also stable; when the price level is highly variable, this is not so, and the usefulness of money as a store of value is undermined.

Although in a non-inflationary environment money can serve as a satisfactory store of accumulated purchasing power for a single individual, even in those circumstances it cannot do so for society as a whole. A single individual can accumulate money and, when the time comes to spend it, can command the current output of some other individual. However, if everyone in a society were to save their money and then retire simultaneously to live on their savings, there would be no current production to purchase and consume. Society's ability to satisfy wants depends on goods and services being available. Money may be accumulated as savings to help individuals buy goods and services at some future date, but that money will be useless unless real goods and services are available at that future date—either because they are produced by the economy's real resources at that date or because they have been carried over from earlier production. Money and real income and wealth should not be confused.

Money is a store of value for individuals but not for society as a whole.

A unit of account

Money may also be used purely for accounting purposes, without having a physical existence of its own. For instance, a government store in an imaginary centrally planned society might say that everyone had so many 'pounds' to spend or save each month. Goods could then be assigned prices and each consumer's purchases recorded, the consumer being allowed to buy until his or her allocated supply of pounds was exhausted. These pounds need have no existence other than as entries in the store's books, yet they would serve as a perfectly satisfactory unit of account. Whether they could also serve as a medium of exchange between individuals depends on whether the store would agree to transfer credits from one customer to another at the customer's request. Banks will transfer pounds credited to current account deposits in this way, and so a bank deposit serves as both a unit of account and a medium of exchange[1].

In the (UK) horseracing world, guineas are still used as a unit of account even though there is no currency[2] in that form. The 2000 Guineas is a famous horse race at Newmarket. The world record price paid (also at Newmarket) in October 2013 for a one-year-old racehorse was 5 million guineas. Payments will not actually be made in guineas, but rather in pounds. By convention a guinea is worth £1.05.

A related function of money is that it can be used as a standard of deferred payment. Payments that are to be made in the future, for repayment of debts for example, are specified in money. Money's ability to serve as a unit of account over time in this manner can be harmed if there is significant inflation. Serbia had a major inflation in 1993 and thereafter a foreign currency, the euro, was used to denominate loan contracts, such as mortgages, in that country.

The origins of money

The origins of money go back at least 4,000 years and probably earlier. Examples of Roman coins circulating in Britain around 2,000 years ago can be seen in the British Museum and other regional museums.

Metallic money

All sorts of commodities have been used as money at one time or another, but gold and silver proved to have great advantages. They were precious because their supplies were relatively limited, and they were in constant demand by the wealthy for ornament and decoration. Thus, these metals tended to have a high and stable price. Further, they were easily recognized, they were divisible into extremely small units, and they did not easily wear out.

Before the invention of coins, it would have been necessary to carry the metal itself. When a purchase was made, the requisite quantity of the metal was carefully weighed on a scale. The invention of coinage eliminated the need to weigh the metal at each transaction, but it created an important role for an authority, usually a monarch, who made the coins by mixing gold or silver with base metals to create convenient size and durability, and stamped his or her seal on the coin, guaranteeing the amount of

precious metal that the coin contained. This was clearly a great convenience, as long as traders knew that they could accept the coin at its 'face value'. The face value was nothing more than a statement that each coin contained a certain weight of gold or silver.[3] Box 18.1 discusses some phrases linked to the coinage and the maker of the UK coinage.

However, coins often could not be taken at their face value. A form of counterfeiting—clipping a thin slice off the edge of the coin and keeping the valuable metal—became common. This, of course, served to undermine the acceptability of coins, even if they were stamped. To get around this problem, the idea arose of minting the coins with a rough edge; the absence of the rough edge would immediately indicate that the coin had been clipped. This practice, called milling, survives on some coins (such as the current UK 5p, 10p, £1, and £2 coins) as an interesting anachronism to remind us that there were days when the market value of the metal in the coin was equal to the face value of the coin.[4]

Not to be outdone by the cunning of their subjects, some rulers were quick to seize the chance of getting something for nothing. The power to mint coins placed rulers

---

[1] Bitcoin is a privately created unit that exists as a computer entry but is accepted in some places as a means of payment. It has no intrinsic value other than what people will pay for it.

[2] 'Currency' means that it is in general circulation.

[3] This is why the unit for weight, a pound, is also the unit for money.

[4] The tradition of using precious metals is also reflected in current UK coinage. The small change, 1p and 2p coins, look like copper, the 5p, 10p, 20p, and 50p coins look like silver, and the £1 coin looks like gold, while the £2 coin is part gold and part silver. However, they are all made of much cheaper materials.

Box 18.1 In mint condition ... to coin a phrase!

Money has been around in Britain for over two millennia and thus it is not surprising that common expressions have arisen that relate to the form of the money used, especially coins, or the metal that was originally used to form the coinage. You have all heard someone being described as having a 'heart of gold' or as being 'as good as gold'. Someone who expresses an opinion without it necessarily being called for is having their 'two pence worth' or 'two cents worth', and similar points of view are 'opposite sides of the same coin'. A very poor person is 'on his or her bottom dollar' or 'penniless'. Going to the toilet is still frequently called: 'spending a penny' even though it may cost very much more than the old UK penny, which would be equivalent to a little less than half of one penny in today's money (as before the pound's decimalization in the 1970s, there were 240 pence in one pound).

Phrases such as 'in mint condition' for something brand new and 'he or she is minting it' for someone who has a high income come from the fact that the places that manufacture coins are known as mints. The website of the Royal Mint explains.

Minting began in Britain around the end of the second century BC. The earliest coins were cast in moulds, but later coins were struck by hand in much the same way as they were to be made for the next 1,500 years.

The coinage of Iron Age Britain ceased with the Roman conquest and thereafter Roman coins, the universal currency in the Western Empire, circulated in Britain. For a time at the end of the third century Roman coins were actually struck at a mint in London. This London mint set up by the Romans is the earliest recorded mint in the capital, but it functioned for no more than 40 years.

For some 200 years or so after the withdrawal of the Romans no coins appear to have been struck in Britain. Following the consolidation of the English Kingdoms a London mint was in operation again from soon after 650. At first its existence was somewhat precarious but from about the time

of Alfred the Great, king of Wessex from 871 to 899, its history became continuous and increasingly important [... and this is when the connection with the sovereign began and some of the coins were stamped with the head of the king or queen].

At that time London was merely one of many mints. There were by then about 30 mints and by the reign of Ethelred II (978–1016) the number had grown to more than 70. These were mostly in the southern half of the country and there can have been few market towns of any consequence where coins were not struck. By the Norman Conquest their number had begun to decline and from the early part of the 13th century minting was mainly confined to London and Canterbury. The precise location of the London mint at that time is doubtful but it is placed by one account in Old Change, conveniently close to the goldsmiths' quarter in Cheapside. By about 1279 the mint had moved to more secure quarters within the Tower of London.

For the next 500 years the Royal Mint remained in the Tower of London, but it was the 16th century before the Royal Mint had a monopoly of coin production for the whole country. Minting processes were finally mechanised in the 17th century. The installation of mills and presses, while improving the appearance of the coins and making them more difficult to clip and to counterfeit, served also to aggravate the cramped conditions in the Tower. Occasional disputes with the garrison caused further tension, and in the first decade of the 19th century the Royal Mint was moved to a new building on Tower Hill.

<http://www.royalmint.com>

It remained in this building until it was moved to new premises in Llantrisant, South Wales, in 1980, where it continues to operate today. The Royal Mint is a company that is wholly owned by the UK Treasury. It makes coins not just for the United Kingdom but also for many other countries in the world ... it must make a mint!

---

in a position to work a really profitable fraud. They often used some suitable occasion—a marriage, an anniversary, an alliance—to re-mint the coinage. Subjects would be ordered to bring their coins into the mint to be melted down and coined afresh with a new stamp. However, between the melting down and the re-coining, the rulers had only to toss some further inexpensive base metal in with the molten coins. This debasing of the coinage allowed the ruler to earn a handsome profit by minting more new coins than the number of old ones collected, and putting the extras in the royal vault.

The result of debasement was inflation. The subjects had the same number of coins as before, and hence could demand the same quantity of goods. However, when rulers paid their bills, the recipients of the extra coins could be expected to spend them. This caused an increase in demand, which in turn bid up prices.

Debasing the coinage was a common cause of increases in prices.

It was the experience of such inflations that led early economists to stress the link between the quantity of

Box 18.2 Gresham's law

The early experience of currency debasement led to the observation known as Gresham's law, after Sir Thomas Gresham, an adviser to the court of Elizabeth I, who stated that 'bad money drives out good'.

When the queen came to the throne of England in the middle of the sixteenth century, the coinage had been severely debased. Seeking to help trade, Elizabeth minted new coins that contained their full face value in gold. However, as fast as she fed these new coins into circulation, they disappeared. Why?

Suppose that you possessed one new and one old coin, each with the same face value, and had a bill to pay. What would you do? Clearly, you would use the debased coin to pay the bill and keep the undebased one. (You part with less gold that way.) Again, suppose that you wanted to obtain a certain amount of gold bullion by melting down the gold coins (as was frequently done). Which coins would you use? Clearly, you would use new undebased coins because you would part with less 'face value' that way. For these reasons, the debased coins would remain in circulation, and the undebased coins would disappear.

Gresham's insights have proved helpful in explaining the experience of a number of twentieth century high inflation economies. For example, in the 1970s, inflation in Chile raised the value of the metallic content in coins above their face value. Coins quickly disappeared from circulation as private citizens sold them to entrepreneurs who melted them down for their metal. Only paper currency remained in circulation and was used even for tiny transactions such as purchasing a box of matches. Gresham's law is one reason why modern coins, unlike their historical counterparts, are merely tokens that contain a metallic value that is only a minute fraction of their face value.

Gresham's law has had another modern interpretation in regimes of pegged exchange rates, where the values of two currencies are pegged together artificially. If one currency is overvalued and widely expected to have to be devalued, this causes people to spend it fast (the bad money), while building up their holdings of the undervalued currency (the good money). The combination of hoarding one currency and running down balances of the other often brings about the devaluation that was feared—as when the pound sterling was forced to leave the European Exchange Rate Mechanism (ERM) in September 1992, and when Argentina was forced to break the link of its currency to the US dollar in January 2002.

---

money and the price level. The relationship, known as the 'quantity theory of money', will be discussed later. A famous law in economics that owes its origins to the era of metallic money is set out in Box 18.2.

To this day the revenue generated from the power to create currency is known as *seigniorage*. Today, the possibility of debasement does not apply to this term. Instead the term applies to the revenue that accrues from the monetary authority's power to create money by such means as printing banknotes.

The benefits of seigniorage could arise simply because the government usual acting through its central bank prints money and spends it, so its value would be equal to the increase in note issue each period. In practice, the relevant monetary authority is the **central bank**, which is a government-owned institution. It is the sole money-issuing authority and it also acts as banker to the commercial banking system.[5] The UK central bank is known as the Bank of England, for the United States it is the Federal Reserve System, and for the euro area it is the European Central Bank (ECB).

When the central bank provides banknotes to the private sector it typically buys interest-bearing bonds with each new issue of notes. Thus the seigniorage from the notes in circulation is equal to the interest per period on those bonds. So, for example, if the note issue was £100 and the central bank had bought £100 worth of bonds in issuing those notes, and the yield on the bonds was 5 per cent, then seigniorage would be £5 per year. In the United Kingdom the Bank of England returns all the revenue from seigniorage to HM Treasury.[6]

Paper money

The next important step in the history of money was the evolution of paper currency, one source of which was goldsmiths. Since goldsmiths had secure safes, the public began to deposit their gold with them for safekeeping. Goldsmiths would give their depositors receipts that promised to hand over the gold on demand. When any depositor wished to make a large purchase, she could go to her goldsmith, reclaim some of her gold, and hand it over to the seller of the goods. If the seller had no immediate need for the gold, he would carry it back to the goldsmith for safekeeping on his behalf.

---

[5] 'Commercial banks' are the private sector banks that provide deposit and loans services to personal and corporate customers, such as Barclays, NatWest, and HSBC.

[6] The Bank of England's 2014 Annual Report shows that the Issue Department paid £443 million to HM Treasury from this source in the year to end February 2014.

If people knew the goldsmith to be reliable, there was no need to go through the cumbersome and risky business of physically transferring the gold. The buyer needed only to transfer the goldsmith's receipt to the seller, who would accept it as long as he was confident that the goldsmith would pay over the gold whenever it was needed. If the seller wished to buy something from a third party who also knew the goldsmith to be reliable, passing the goldsmith's receipt from the buyer to the seller could also effect this transaction. The deposit receipt was 'as good as gold'. The convenience of using pieces of paper instead of gold is obvious.

When it came into being in this way, paper money represented a promise to pay so much gold on demand. In this case the promise was made first by goldsmiths and later by banks.[7] Such paper money, which became banknotes, was backed by precious metal and was convertible on demand into this metal.[8]

Fractionally backed paper money

Early on, many goldsmiths and banks discovered that it was not necessary to keep a full ounce of gold in the vaults for every claim to an ounce circulating as paper money. At any one time, some of the bank's customers would be withdrawing gold, others would be depositing it, and most would be trading in the bank's paper notes without indicating any need or desire to convert them into gold.

As a result, the goldsmiths and later the commercial banks were able to issue more money (initially notes, but later deposits) redeemable in gold than the amount of gold that they held in their vaults. This was good business, because the money could be invested profitably in interest-earning loans (often called advances) to individuals and firms. The demand for loans arose, as it does today, because some customers wanted credit to help them over hard times, to finance the gap between purchases of labour and materials and selling the products that they produced, and to buy capital equipment. To this day banks have many more claims outstanding against them than they actually have in reserves available to pay those claims. We say that the currency issued in such a situation is *fractionally backed* by the reserves.

The major problem with a fractionally backed convertible currency was maintaining its convertibility into the precious metal by which it was backed. The imprudent bank that issued too much paper money would find itself unable to redeem its currency in gold when the demand for gold was even slightly higher than usual. It would then have to suspend payments, and all holders of its notes would suddenly find that the notes were worthless. Although the prudent bank that kept a reasonable relationship between its note issue and its gold reserve would find that it could meet a normal range of demand for gold without any trouble, if the public lost confidence and demanded redemption of its currency en masse, the banks would be unable to honour their pledges. The history of nineteenth- and early-twentieth-century banking around the world is full of examples of otherwise sound banks that were ruined by 'panics', or sudden runs on their gold reserves. When this happened, the banks' depositors and the holders of their notes would find themselves with worthless pieces of paper.[9]

Fiat money

As time went on, note issue by private banks became less common, and central banks, which are (usually) state-owned institutions, took control of the currency. Over time central banks have assumed a monopoly in the provision of legal tender to the economy.[10] As a result, they have the job of controlling monetary conditions and are ultimately responsible for determining the value of a nation's (or group of nations') currency.

Originally central banks issued paper currency that was fully convertible into gold. In those days gold would be brought to the central bank, which would issue currency in the form of 'gold certificates' that asserted that the gold was available on demand. Thus, the gold supply set some upper limit on the amount of paper money in circulation. However, central banks, like private banks before them, could issue more paper money than they had in gold, because in normal times only a small fraction of that money was presented for payment in gold at any one time. Thus, even though the need to maintain convertibility under a **gold standard** put an upper limit on note issue, central banks had substantial discretionary control over the quantity that was outstanding.

---

[7] Banks grew out of at least two other trades in addition to goldsmiths. There were scriveners, who had writing skills and sold their services managing other people's financial affairs, and there were also merchant bankers, who started trading in commodities but ended up specializing in trade finance—Barings and Rothschilds started this way, and are still referred to as 'merchant banks' today. (In US terminology they are called 'investment banks'.)

[8] One of the earliest issuers of formal banknotes was the Riksbank of Sweden, established in 1668. It is thus twenty-six years older than the Bank of England, which was established in 1694. The Riksbank, which is now the central bank of Sweden, instituted the Nobel Prize for economics in 1968 to commemorate its tercentenary.

[9] In the early 1930s about 10,000 banks, or a third of the total, went bust in the United States. The personal and corporate losses involved were a major contributor to the Great Depression.

[10] In England and Wales no new banks have been permitted to issue notes since the 1844 Bank Charter Act, though in Scotland banks such as the Bank of Scotland, the Royal Bank of Scotland, and the Clydesdale Bank still issue the main notes in circulation. (Since 1845, however, the Scottish note issue has had 100 per cent backing with Bank of England liabilities, and hence has been fully under Bank of England direction.) In 2002 euro notes were issued by the European Central Bank to replace the previous currencies of the eleven member states of the Eurozone. In 2014 the Eurozone had eighteen members.

During the first half of the twentieth century almost all of the countries of the world abandoned the gold standard; thus, their money was no longer convertible into gold. Money that is not convertible by law into anything else derives its value from its acceptability in exchange. *Fiat money* is widely acceptable because government order, or fiat,[11] declares it to be legal tender. Legal tender is anything that by law must be accepted when offered either for the purchase of goods or services or to discharge a debt. Bank of England notes have been legal tender in England and Wales since 1833.

Today almost all currency is fiat money.

Bank of England notes still say on them 'I promise to pay the bearer on demand the sum of *x* pounds', and they are signed by the chief cashier. Until 1931 (apart from occasional temporary suspensions of convertibility) you could take these notes into the Bank of England and demand gold of equivalent value in return for your notes.

Today, however, the promise is a quaint tradition rather than a real contract. The pound sterling, like all major currencies, is a fiat currency that is not backed by gold or any other commodity (though some people still argue for the return to a gold standard).

Fiat money is valuable because it is accepted by convention and in law in payment for the purchase of goods or services and for the discharge of debts.

Many people are disturbed to learn that present-day paper money is neither backed by, nor convertible into, anything more valuable—that it consists of nothing but pieces of paper whose value derives from general acceptance. Many people believe that their money should be more substantial than this.

If fiat money is always acceptable in payment, it is a medium of exchange, and, if its purchasing power remains stable, it is a satisfactory store of value. If both of these things are true, it will also serve as a satisfactory unit of account.

How does money get into the economy?

When gold was the basis of money, it was not too difficult to see how more gold got into circulation in any one country. It was produced from local gold mines, converted from non-monetary uses (such as jewellery), or imported from other countries. In effect, it was received in payment for some transaction from the owners of gold mines, or from the previous owner of the gold, wherever in the world they happened to be. The holders of the gold would soon take it to a bank and receive banknotes in return because of the obvious convenience of notes or gold bullion. The bank could then issue more notes than the gold it received because, as already noted, most holders of notes did not want to convert them into gold. Eventually, central banks took over the role of note issuance from private banks.

The central bank and high-powered money

Once countries left the gold standard (at various times in the twentieth century), central banks no longer put money into circulation in return for gold received. Neither do they just drop money from the sky, or even just give it to the government to spend. Instead they buy bonds from the government and pay with money in the form of government deposits, which are put into circulation when the government pays its bills with these deposits. What the central bank has direct control over is referred to by three terms, all of which refer to the same thing: **high-powered money**, the **cash base**, and the **monetary base**. This consists of currency (banknotes and coin) held by the public and the banks, and deposits held by the commercial banks with the central bank which are called bankers' deposits.[12] The monetary base is referred to as high-powered money because it is the basis upon which a much bigger stock of monetary assets is built (including the biggest component of the money stock, bank deposits). High-powered money is an asset to anyone in the private sector who holds it, but it is a liability to the central bank.

Any country's central bank, including the Bank of England, gets high-powered money into the economy simply by buying securities (usually government debt instruments). It pays for these purchases with newly issued high-powered money.

The result of these purchases depends on who sells them. In the first case, the Bank buys them from a member of the public. Here it is allowing the public to alter the proportion in which it holds its wealth in money and

---

[11] *Fiat* means 'let there be' in Latin, and hence 'by decree'.

[12] The monetary base includes bankers working balances at the Bank of England but it excludes compulsory cash ratio deposits. The latter are a form of tax on the banks that finance the Bank of England, making it non-reliant on government funding. This is because the cash ratio deposits are not interest bearing while other bankers' deposits at the Bank of England (their reserves) pay interest at bank rate.

Table 18.1 **Bank of England balance sheet, 22 January 2014**

Assets	(£m)	Liabilities	(£m)
(i) Balance sheet of issue department			
Repo and bonds acquired via market	4,872	Notes in circulation	59,438
Other securities	54,565		
Total assets	59,438	Total liabilities	59,438
(ii) Balance sheet of banking department			
Reverse repo	70	Foreign currency secs	3,624
Bonds acquired via market transacts.	11,909	Cash-ratio deposits	4,078
Other assets	385,015	Reserves and other acs.	300,583
		Other liabilities	88,710
Total assets	396,995		396,995

The Bank of England is divided into the Issue Department and the Banking Department. The table shows the balance sheets of these two departments at 22 January 2014. The only function of the issue department is to issue currency (banknotes). It does this in exchange for purchases of securities, normally through a transaction with the banking department. The Banking Department acts as banker to the government and also holds deposits from the banks.

Source: Bank of England, *Monetary and Financial Statistics*.

securities. When the Bank buys the securities it is taking them out of the hands of the public and putting in an equivalent amount of money. In the second case, the Bank buys the securities from the government. Here the government creates new securities which it sells to the Bank and the Bank pays for them with newly created high-powered money in the form of a deposit credited to the government. When the government uses this deposit to finance its spending, it is putting new money into the economy without any decrease in the number of securities in the hands of the public.

When the Bank buys securities from the public, it is allowing the public to alter the ratio of securities to money in their hands but not changing the total. When the Bank buys securities from the government, it is increasing the total supply of money in circulation without reducing the total of securities in the hands of the public.

In creating new high-powered money, the central bank is expanding both sides of its own balance sheet. At the same time as it increases its liabilities, it purchases assets of equal value. In the UK case, of the two components of high-powered money, bankers' deposits are the liability of the Banking Department of the Bank of England and currency is the liability of the Issue Department. The balance sheets of these two departments are shown in Table 18.1.

It is simplest to think of the process of high-powered money creation in two steps. First, we will discuss, using the UK example, how the purchase of securities by the

Bank of England creates bankers' deposits. Then, we shall see how currency gets into circulation.

Bankers' deposits

Consider a situation in which there are initially no net transactions between the Bank of England and the rest of the economy. The Bank now buys £1 million worth of securities from an agent in the private sector. The seller receives a cheque for £1 million from the Bank of England that is paid into the recipient's bank account at, say, Barclays Bank. Barclays' deposits rise by £1 million, but at the same time Barclays receives an increase of £1 million in its deposits at the Bank of England. The balance in Barclays' account at the Bank of England is an example of what are called *bankers' deposits*. This increase in its bankers' deposits at the Bank of England arises when Barclays clears the cheque drawn on the Bank of England. (A cheque deposited in Barclays drawn on HSBC Bank would simply transfer bankers' deposits from HSBC to Barclays, but a cheque drawn on the Bank of England creates new bankers' deposits at the central bank.)

This is not the end of the story as far as Barclays is concerned, because as we shall see bankers' deposits constitute reserves against which the commercial banks can create new deposits. These reserves are often called 'cash reserves' because, although they are merely book entries at the central bank, they can be turned into cash any time the commercial banks require it. We will soon explain how the banks do create new deposits. In the meantime, this is most of what we need to know about how the Bank of England expands the monetary base, though in Chapter 25 we will look more closely at how the Bank of England uses its money market operations to set interest rates in normal times and we will also explain the special monetary measures, known as **quantitative easing**, that were introduced in 2009. Contraction of the monetary base simply reverses the process—the Bank sells securities. A member of the public then writes a cheque drawn on, say, NatWest Bank, payable to the Bank of England, and NatWest transfers bankers' deposits of an equivalent amount to the Bank. The monetary base falls.

Currency

The above discussion explains how central banks, such as the Bank of England, create or destroy high-powered money. The division of high-powered money between bankers' deposits and currency is determined by the demand for currency on the part of the general public. If private individuals (or firms) choose to increase their currency holdings, relative to bank deposits, they simply go to their bank and withdraw deposits in cash. The bank (if it did not have enough cash in its tills) would go to the Bank of England and withdraw some bankers' deposits in cash from the Banking Department. The Banking Department, in turn, would replenish its own stock of cash by selling securities to the Issue Department. The Issue Department prints the new currency. Currency is made available on demand to the economy in this way and is not restricted in supply by the Bank of England.

The stock of currency in circulation is determined entirely by the demands of the public and is not set by any policy-makers. Policy-makers are concerned with the overall supply of high-powered money but not with how that total is divided between bankers' deposits and currency.

Modern money

The total amount of money in the economy is called the **money supply** or the **money stock**.[13] The creation of high-powered money is only part of the story of how the money supply is created, because most measures of the money supply include a wider range of assets than just the monetary base. In particular, money is usually defined to include bank deposits.

Deposit money

Today's bank customers frequently deposit coins and paper money with the banks for safekeeping, just as in former times they deposited gold. Such a deposit is recorded as a credit to the customer's account. A customer who wishes to pay a debt may come to the bank, claim the money in currency, and then pay the money to someone else, who may themselves redeposit the money in a bank.

As with gold transfers, this is a tedious procedure. It is more convenient to have the bank transfer claims to money on deposit. As soon as cheques, which are written instructions to the bank to make a transfer, became widely accepted in payment for commodities and debts, bank deposits became a form of money called 'deposit money'. Deposit money is defined as money held by the public in the form of deposits in commercial banks that can be withdrawn on demand. Cheques, unlike banknotes, do not circulate freely from hand to hand; thus cheques themselves are not currency. However, a balance in a current account deposit is money; the cheque simply transfers that money from one person to another. Because cheques are easily drawn and deposited, and because they are relatively safe from theft, they have been widely used in the past. However, technology has replaced many cheque transactions by computer transfers. Plastic cards, such as Visa, MasterCard, and Maestro, enable holders of bank accounts to transfer money to another person's account in new ways.[14] The principle is the same, however: the balance in the bank account is the money that is to be transferred between customers, not the cheque or the plastic card.

When commercial banks lost the right to issue notes of their own, the form of bank money changed, but the substance did not. Today banks have money in their vaults (or on deposit with the central bank) just as they always did. Once it was gold; today it is the legal tender of the times—fiat money. It is true today, just as in the past, that most of the banks' customers are content to pay their bills by passing among themselves the banks' promises to pay money on demand. Only a small proportion of the value of the transactions made by the banks' customers involves the use of cash.

Bank deposits are money. Today, just as in the past, banks can create money by issuing more promises to pay (deposits) than they have cash reserves available to pay out.

The main reason that we are interested in the money stock is that if the amount of money is increased too quickly inflation will result. Here, 'too fast' roughly means faster than real GDP is growing. For this purpose, it is the broad measure of the money stock that includes bank deposits that is most relevant, as bank deposits can be

---

[13] Those who have studied microeconomics should note that the concept of a money supply is different from the concept of the supply of some commodity. In microeconomics, supply refers to a desired quantity: how much a producer would like to make and sell per period. In macroeconomics, the money supply is the actual amount of money that is in existence at a point in time.

[14] With credit cards such as Visa or MasterCard, if you buy, say, petrol today, the petrol company will receive a credit in its bank account after a few days and you will have to settle with the credit card company once a month. With so-called EFTPOS (electronic funds transfer at the point of sale) cards like Maestro, however, the funds are transferred directly from your account to the account of the petrol company very quickly. The technology is likely to keep changing, but it does not fundamentally alter the nature of the bank account transfer that is involved.

Box 18.3 Definitions of UK monetary aggregates

The way in which 'money' is defined has changed a great deal over time and is likely to change again in the future. In 1750 money would almost certainly have been defined as the stock of gold in circulation (specie). By 1850 it would probably have been defined as gold in the hands of the non-bank public plus banknotes in circulation. In 1950 the most likely definition would have been currency held by the public plus current account bank deposits. In 1998 money was usually defined to include currency held by the public plus all deposits (current and savings) in banks and building societies. By 2050, who knows? Perhaps money on the internet will be included.

There have been many changes in the definition of money even in the last few decades. Many of these are the result of the financial innovations of the 1980s. We should not expect this to be the end of the story. UK money measures such as M1 and £M3 (sterling M3), which were at the centre of monetary policy debates into the first half of the 1980s, have disappeared. These had to be dropped after 1989, when the Abbey National Building Society converted into a bank (and other conversions followed later). Thereafter, any monetary aggregate that contained bank deposits but not building society deposits became distorted. M0, which includes notes and coin in circulation and bankers' working deposits at the Bank of England, used to be used as a narrow money measure, but this has been dropped since the rules affecting banks' reserves were changed in 2006. Banks' reserve holdings have been even more distorted by quantitative easing in the period from 2009 to 2012, the effects of which may remain for many years yet to come.

The money measures current in 2014 were as follows:

• **Notes and coin.** This measure refers to all the currency in circulation outside the Bank of England.

• **Retail M4.** This encompasses UK non-bank and non-building-society holdings of notes and coins, plus sterling retail deposits with UK banks and building societies.

• **M4.** M4 is retail M4 plus all other private sector sterling interest-bearing deposits at banks and building societies, plus sterling certificates of deposit (and other paper issued by banks and building societies of not more than five years' original maturity).

• **M3.** This is a harmonized measure created to have standard money definitions throughout the EU. It is equal to M4 plus residents' foreign currency deposits in UK banks and building societies plus public corporations' sterling and foreign currency deposits in UK banks and building societies.

The accompanying table presents data for these monetary aggregates for December 2013.

UK money supply, December 2013 (£ million, SA)

Notes and coin in circulation	59,370
Retail deposits	1,348,121
Wholesale deposits	694,275
M4	2,108,213
M3	2,374,527

Note: Data for components of M4 do not add up to the whole owing to separate seasonal adjustments.

Source: Bank of England, *Monetary and Financial Statistics*.

used in payment for goods, and it is often said that 'too much money chasing too few goods' is the source of inflation. Which specific measure of broad money we choose to use is of second-order importance.

Box 18.3 shows the various measures of the money stock that were in use in the United Kingdom in 2014. The main aggregate is M4, a broad measure that includes all retail and wholesale bank and building society deposits. Notes and coin in circulation are also available, as is retail M4.[15] Notice that there is also an EU harmonized measure of broad money known in the United Kingdom as M3. This is slightly larger than M4 because it adds residents' foreign currency deposits (and some public sector deposits) to M4.

We now turn to a discussion of the role of banks in determining the broad money supply and in transmitting policy-determined interest rate changes to the economy.

Two models of banking

We now present two models of the creation of deposit money. The first shows how banks can create a large volume of deposit money on the basis of a given amount of reserves. It is called the ratios approach to the creation of money and is best suited for showing the relation between reserves and deposit money. The second shows how banks

work in a competitive environment to attract the reserves they need in order to create deposit money. This model is

---

[15] Notes and coin plus bankers' deposits at the Bank of England used to be known as M0, but big changes in the Bank's reserve operations and quantitative easing have caused major distortions in M0 so this is no longer used as a monetary aggregate. Retail M4 used to be known as M2.

better suited to understanding both the forces of competition between banks themselves and the competition between banks and other channels of **financial intermediation** (such as securities markets). *Financial intermediation* occurs when some institutions or markets channel funds from savers to borrowers.

The ratios approach to the creation of deposit money

If you deposit cash with a bank, that deposit is an asset to you and a liability to the bank—because the bank owes that amount to you. Because the bank has the cash as an asset, its assets equal its liabilities. If a bank gives you a loan, it writes an extra balance into your account. This creates a deposit for you, but it is also a loan that you have to repay. So the process of overdraft or loan creation creates both deposits and loans simultaneously. In general, banks' deposits are their liabilities, and whatever loans they make or securities they purchase constitute their assets. We shall see below how banks can create deposits (and loans) that are some multiple of their cash reserves. This *fractional reserve* banking is analogous to the fractional backing of the note issue discussed above. Notice two slightly different meanings of the term cash. 'Cash' held by the banks can be currency in their tills or deposits at the central bank; 'cash' for the public means currency.

Suppose that, in a system with many banks, each bank obtains new deposits in cash. Say, for example, that there are ten banks of equal size and that each receives a new deposit of £100 in cash. Each bank now has on its books the new entries shown in Table 18.2. The banks are on what is called a fractional reserve system, which means that they do not need to hold reserves equal to 100 per cent of their deposit liabilities. We assume for purposes of this illustration that they wish to hold 10 per cent cash reserves against all deposits. The new deposits put the banks into disequilibrium, since they each have 100 per cent reserves against these new deposits.

First, suppose that only one of the ten banks begins to expand deposits by making new loans (advances). When a bank makes a loan to a customer, it simply writes a larger balance into the customer's account, thereby increasing the size of its deposits. Now, when cheques are

Table 18.3 Deposit expansion in expectation of a cash drain

Liabilities	(£)	Assets	(£)
Deposit	190	Cash	100
	___	Loans	90
	190		190

If a bank expands deposits in the expectation of a cash drain, it will end up with excess reserves. The table shows the position if a bank expands deposits on the basis of receiving £100 in new cash deposits and in the expectation that 90 per cent of any new deposits will drain out of the bank in a cash flow. The bank obtains new assets of loans and bonds of £90 by creating new deposits of that amount. It expects £81 of these to be withdrawn in cash, leaving it with £19 to provide a 10 per cent reserve against £190 of deposits.

written on these deposits, the majority will be deposited in other banks. If, for example, this one bank has only 10 per cent of the total deposits held by the community, then, on average, 90 per cent of any new deposits it creates for its customers—and thus much of its £100 in cash—will drain away to other banks. On this basis the bank will make loans of £90, expecting that it will suffer a cash drain of £81 on account of these loans, leaving it with a £19 cash reserve (£100 new deposit minus the £81 cash drain). This is the position shown in Table 18.3.

One bank in a multi-bank system cannot produce a large multiple expansion of deposits based on an original accretion of cash when other banks do not also expand their deposits.

Now assume, that all ten banks begin to expand their deposits based on the £100 of new reserves that each received. On the one hand, since each bank does one-tenth of the total banking business, 90 per cent of the value of any newly created deposits will find its way into other banks as customers make payments by cheque or electronic transfers to others in the community. This is a cash drain to these other banks. On the other hand, 10 per cent of the new deposits created by each other bank should find its way into this bank. Thus, if all banks receive new cash, and all start creating deposits simultaneously, no bank should suffer a significant cash drain to any other bank. Instead of finding itself with its surplus cash drained away, a bank with the balance sheet shown in Table 18.3 would have cash reserves of close to 53 per cent (£100 reserves against £190 deposits) rather than only 10 per cent as desired.

When all banks can go on expanding deposits without losing cash to each other, they need only worry about keeping enough cash to satisfy those depositors who occasionally require cash. Thus, the expansion can go on, with each bank watching its own ratio of cash reserves to deposits, expanding its deposits as long as the ratio exceeds 1:10 and ceasing to do so when it reaches that figure. Assuming no cash drain

Table 18.2 A new cash deposit

Liabilities	(£)	Assets	(£)
Deposit	100	Cash	100

A new cash deposit has 100 per cent backing. The balance sheet shows the changes in assets and liabilities resulting from a new cash deposit. Both cash assets and deposit liabilities rise by the same amount.

Table 18.4 **Restoration of a 10 per cent reserve ratio**

Liabilities	(£)	Assets	(£)
Deposit	1,000	Cash	100
		Loans	900
	1,000		1,000

With no cash drain, a new cash deposit will support a multiple expansion of deposit liabilities. The table shows the changes in assets and liabilities when all banks engage in deposit expansion after each has received a new cash deposit of £100. New assets are £900 and new deposits are £900. The accretion of £100 in cash now supports £1,000 in deposits, thus restoring the 10 per cent reserve ratio.

to the public, the process will not come to a halt until each bank has created £900 in additional deposits, so that, for each initial £100 cash deposit, there is now £1,000 in deposits backed by £100 in cash. Now each of the banks will have new entries in its books similar to those shown in Table 18.4.

A multi-bank system creates a multiple increase in deposit money when all banks with excess reserves expand their deposits in step with each other.

A complication: cash drain to the public

So far we have ignored the fact that the public actually divides its money holdings in a fairly stable proportion between cash and deposits. This means that when the banking system as a whole creates significant amounts of new deposit money, the system will suffer a cash drain as the public withdraws enough cash from the banks to maintain its desired ratio of cash to deposits.

An example

Assume that the public wishes to hold a proportion of cash equal to 10 per cent of the size of its bank deposits. This means that for a given stock of cash in the system, the amount that will be held in bank reserves is reduced, so the maximum amount of deposit creation is also reduced. In this special case in which banks have a reserve ratio of 10 per cent and the public holds cash to the value of 10 per cent of the size of its bank deposits, the outcome will be as in Table 18.5. Half of the cash in existence (assumed to be £100 in total) will be held in banks' reserves, and the public will hold the other half. On the basis of their £50 reserves, banks will extend £450 of loans, so total deposits will be £500. This is only half of the value of deposits that were created when the entire £100 of cash was held in bank reserves (as shown in Table 18.3).

A cash drain to the public reduces the expansion of deposit money that can be supported by the banking system.

Table 18.5 **Deposit creation with a cash drain to the public**

Liabilities	(£)	Assets	(£)
Deposit	500	Cash	50
		Loans	450
	500		500

A cash drain to the public greatly reduces the amount of new deposits that can be created on the basis of a given amount of cash. The table shows the balance sheet of the banking system on the assumption that there is £100 of cash in the system but the public desires cash holdings equal to 10 per cent of their bank deposits. The outcome that satisfies both the banks' desired reserve ratio and the public's cash to deposit ratio is such that the banks hold £50 in reserves and issue £450 worth of loans. Total deposits are £500, and £50 is held in cash by the public. The total money stock is £550 (deposits plus cash held by the public). An example in which the banks' reserve ratio differs from the public's cash to deposits ratio is given in Table 18.6.

The general case of deposit creation

The two ratios that we have discussed (the banks' reserve ratio and public's ratio of cash to deposits) can now be used to determine the total level of deposit creation in a formal way. Let R be the cash held in bank reserves, C be the cash held by the non-bank public, H (for high-powered money) be the total cash in the economy, and D be the size of bank deposits. Thus

$$C + R = H. \tag{18.1}$$

This says that the total cash in the economy is held either by the banks or by the public. Let the desired reserve ratio of banks be x. This allows us to write

$$R = xD. \tag{18.2}$$

Finally, let the public hold a fraction, b, of its bank deposits in cash:

$$C = bD. \tag{18.3}$$

Substituting the second and third equations into the first gives

$$bD + xD = H$$

and solving for D yields

$$D = \frac{H}{(b+x)}. \tag{18.4}$$

Equation (18.4) shows that if the public's desired cash ratio is zero, deposits rise by the reciprocal of the cash reserve ratio. (If the banks' reserve ratio were 0.1 (10 per cent), then deposits would be ten times the cash in the economy.) However, a positive value of b means that the resulting cash drain lowers the increase in deposits since it raises the value of the denominator in eqn (18.4).

The money multiplier

The total money supply in an economy with a banking system is defined as $D + C$. (It does not include R because the deposit that created the original bank reserves is already counted in with deposits, D, and should not be counted twice.) Hence the money supply, M, is

$$M = C + D. \tag{18.5}$$

We can arrive at an expression that links M and H by substituting eqn (18.2) into eqn (18.5) for C and then eqn (18.4) into eqn (18.5) for D. This gives

$$M = \frac{(b+1)}{(b+x)} H. \tag{18.6}$$

Expression (18.6) is known as the money multiplier, because it tells us how much bigger the money supply is than the cash base of the system. In the UK banking system, prior to the financial crisis of 2007–8, reserve ratios and cash ratios were small and the money multiplier was of the order of 40, since M4 was 40 times greater than notes and coin in circulation plus bankers' deposits at the Bank of England.[16] However, as a result of the special monetary operations called quantitative easing in 2009–12, bankers' deposits at the Bank of England rose enormously and the money multiplier shrank to about 6. We discuss quantitative easing in more detail in Chapter 25.

The money multiplier should not be confused with the multiplier that links changes in exogenous spending with changes in GDP. The same term is used for two different concepts.

The size of the money multiplier is greater, the smaller is the banks' desired reserve ratio x and the smaller is the public's desired cash ratio b.

A diagrammatic exposition of the preceding algebra is given in Figure 18.1. It shows that the two ratios, combined with a given cash base, can be used to determine the level of deposits that result and also the money supply. A numerical example of the same ideas is given in Table 18.6.

A competitive banking system

The ratios approach to bank behaviour gives us important insights into how deposit money is created as some multiple of high-powered money, but it does not provide an accurate picture of how modern banks work. They do not just sit around waiting for cash deposits to be made and then lend some multiple of the deposit (though it is

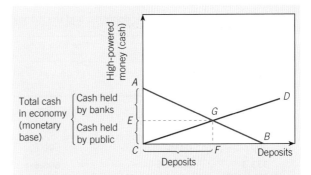

Figure 18.1 The ratios approach to the determination of the money supply

The money supply is determined by the stock of high-powered money (monetary base), the reserve ratio of the banks, and the cash–deposit ratio of the non-bank public. The diagram illustrates the size of deposit creation, given the banks' reserve ratio $x (= AC/CB)$, the public's cash–deposit ratio $b (= EC/CF)$, and the total cash in the economy AC. Deposits plus cash held by the public make up the total money supply. The total stock of high-powered money, or cash, in the economy has to be held by either the banks or the public. At point A the public holds all the cash available so there are no bank deposits, and the total money supply is just AC, which is all cash. At point C the banks hold all the cash and on that reserve base they create deposits of CB. Thus the line AB plots the level of deposit creation resulting from each level of cash reserves (where point A represents the point where banks have no cash or deposits and point C represents the point where all the cash in the economy is held in bank reserves, and CB is the value of bank deposits created on that reserve base). Thus the banks' reserve ratio AC/CB is equal to (minus) the slope of AB.

The line CD represents the cash–deposit ratio for the non-bank public. Its slope, measured by EC/CF, is equal to that cash–deposit ratio. For a given base of high-powered money (cash), deposit creation will be determined at the point where these two ratios are both satisfied. This will be where CD and AB intersect. So the actual outcome is at point G, where banks have AE cash in reserves and create CF of deposits. The public holds EC of cash and CF of deposits. The total money supply at G is given by CF plus EC.

certainly true that their deposits are some multiple of their reserves). Instead, modern banks usually start from the other end. They wait until they have found a profitable lending opportunity, and then they take steps to make sure that funds are available to make the loan. They can do this either by offering higher interest on deposits, or by borrowing from other banks.

In the ratios world, banks passively receive deposits and then use these to make loans. In the modern world, however, banks are trading in highly competitive markets for both deposits and loans. In a competitive market there will be a market-clearing interest rate for both deposit money and loans. Banks cannot expand their activity in either of these markets without taking into account the supply curve of deposits and the demand curve for loans that they face.

---

[16] This was the figure in 2006, for example.

Table 18.6 **High-powered money, deposits, and the money supply**

Banks		Non-bank public		High-powered money ($H = C + R$)	Money supply ($M = C + D$)
Reserves (R)	Deposits (D) ($R \times 20$)	Cash (C) ($1,000 - R$)	Deposits (D) ($C \times 10$)		
(1)	(2)	(3)	(4)	(5)	(6)
1,000	20,000	0	0	1,000	
600	12,000	400	4,000	1,000	
400	8,000	600	6,000	1,000	
333.3	**6,666.6**	**666.6**	**6,666.6**	**1,000**	**7,333.3**
200	4,000	800	8,000	1,000	
100	2,000	900	9,000	1,000	
0	0	1,000	10,000	1,000	

For a given stock of high-powered money, the amount of bank deposits created will be the amount that is consistent with the banks' reserve ratio and the non-bank public's cash–deposit ratio. The table sets out a range of desired positions for banks and the non-bank public independently. Only one of these positions satisfies the desired positions for both the banks and the public, such that the deposits the banks wish to create are the same as the deposits the public wishes to hold.

The example assumes that high-powered money (the cash base or monetary base) is fixed at £1,000. This can be held in some proportion between the banks and the public, but it cannot be changed other than by the central bank. Commercial banks are assumed to have a reserve ratio of 5 per cent, and the non-bank public is assumed to wish to hold cash at a level 10 per cent of their holding of bank deposits. Column (1) shows a range of possible levels of reserve holding for the banks, ranging from all of the £1,000 to none of it. Column (2) shows the level of deposits they would like to create (by making loans) in order to satisfy their desired reserve ratio for each level of reserve holding in column (1). Column (3) shows the cash holding by the public that is implied for each level of banks' reserves in column (1), so it is equal to £1,000 minus the number in column (1). Column (4) shows the level of deposits that the public would like to hold given their cash holdings in column (3). Column (5) reminds us that the stock of high-powered money is fixed at £1,000 throughout. Column (6) shows the value of the money supply for the unique position that satisfies the desires of both the banks and the public.

The actual outcome is the single position where the deposits that the banks wish to create are exactly equal to the deposits that the public wishes to hold. This is where the level of deposits is £6,666.6. At this point the banks hold £333.3 in reserves and the public holds £666.6 in cash. The money supply is £7,333.3 (deposits plus cash held by the public) and the money multiplier (M/H) is 7.333. We could also calculate this from equation (18.6): $(b + 1)/(b + x)$ is 1.1/0.15 (where $b = 0.1$ and $x = 0.05$); this is 7.333.

The market for bank loans is illustrated in Figure 18.2. This shows a positively sloped supply curve for the loans that banks are willing to make to the public and a negatively sloped demand curve for the loans that the public is willing to take out. The supply curve of loans is determined by two factors: the supply curve of deposits and the spread. The **spread** is the difference between what the banks have to pay to borrow money and what they get by lending it (which has to provide a margin to cover staff costs, return on capital employed, and default risk). Remember that banks have to take in deposits in order to make loans. They borrow from one set of people or firms and lend to another.

The supply curve of deposits is positively sloped because for given interest rates elsewhere in the economy, banks can attract more deposits by offering higher interest rates. (Not all deposits in banks pay interest, but the deposits that banks can increase by offering high interest rates—their marginal deposits—do.) To make the explanation easier, we assume that the spread is a constant absolute size, so that the supply curve of loans is drawn parallel to

the supply curve of deposits, but above it by the constant amount of the spread.[17]

The public's demand curve for loans is negatively sloped because the higher the interest rate being charged, the less will customers wish to borrow. Equilibrium in the market for bank loans occurs where the demand and supply curves intersect—the amount customers wish to borrow is equal to the amount banks wish to lend.

Money supply and competitive banking

The ratios approach to money supply creation and the competitive model of banking present two rather different ways of looking at the banking system, but they are compatible. Indeed, each helps us understand the other better, and both are necessary for a complete understanding of modern monetary control techniques.

_____

[17] Although the spread may vary from loan to loan depending, among other things, on the size of the loan and the creditworthiness of the customer, on average the spread over all loans is driven down by competition among banks to an amount that will just cover costs with no pure profits. Hence, its average value can be reasonably assumed to be constant.

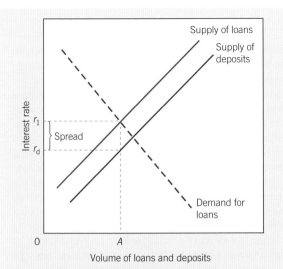

Figure 18.2 Competitive banking: supply of and demand for loans

The volume of bank loans is determined by the intersection of the supply curve of loans and the demand curve for loans. The diagram shows the positively sloped supply curve of loans and the negatively sloped demand curve for loans. The supply curve of loans is determined by the supply curve of deposits and the spread, or the interest margin that banks require to cover costs and risk. For given interest rates elsewhere in the economy, the supply curve of deposits is positively sloped because higher interest will attract more savings. The demand curve for loans is negatively sloped—high interest rates discourage borrowing and low rates encourage borrowing. Competition in banking drives the margin between deposit and loan rates to a level such as $r_1 - r_d$, where the spread is just enough to allow banks to cover costs and make a normal return on capital. With the demand and supply curves shown there will be OA deposits and loans, and depositors will receive an interest rate of r_d while borrowers pay the loan rate r_1.

The ratios approach tells us that the total money supply is related to the stock of high-powered money, this relationship being determined by the reserve ratio of banks and the cash–deposits ratio of the public. For given reserve ratios the total money supply would be determined if the central bank fixed the supply of high-powered money. However, the UK central bank (and most other central banks, including the European Central Bank which is the central bank for all the countries that use the euro as their currency.) do not normally operate this way. Rather, they aim to control total deposits via the demand for bank loans. If they wish to lower deposits (and loans), they force up short-term interest rates, as shown in Figure 18.2. In other words, the central bank uses its knowledge of the market demand curve for loans in order to influence the total stock of deposits and, therefore, the money supply. Box 18.4 discusses whether the evolution of electronic money, sometimes called e-money, will have an impact on the way that the monetary system works.

Having chosen what they think is the correct interest rate to generate the desired demand for loans, the UK central bank supplies whatever high-powered money is demanded at that going interest rate. So, the Bank does not fix the supply of high-powered money; rather, this is demand determined at the interest rate that the Bank has set. The competitive model of banking helps us to see how this can be done by moving up or down the market demand curve for bank loans. We shall return to this issue in more detail later.

Before moving on, however, there are two other important insights provided by the competitive model of banking. First, in the absence of reserve requirements

Box 18.4 **The implications of electronic money for the monetary system**

Some people have argued that electronic money will fundamentally change the nature of the monetary system, and perhaps even eliminate the power of central banks to either control the stock of high-powered money or set the short-term interest rate in money markets. Is this likely?

Our answer is that this is possible, but unlikely. There are two main forms of electronic money.

First, what is sometimes called an 'electronic purse' involves loading some prepaid credits onto a plastic card (which either has a magnetic strip or a computer chip recording information). The carrier of the card can then use this to make retail payments in various shops where some

of the balance on the card can be transferred to the retailer. Such cards are just a more general form of pre-paid telephone cards which carry some credit paid for in advance. They are certainly feasible methods of facilitating some payments. But whether they catch on remains to be seen. The key thing to note is that they offer no difference in principle from earlier payment methods. In effect, they are just a new way of transferring ownership of bank deposits from one person to another. They may lead to the general public needing to hold less cash, but they do not change the reality that bank deposits are the main component of money. The

(*continued*)

Box 18.4 *continued*

amount of cash loaded onto one of these cards is in effect a bank deposit and this is transferred to the retailer when a purchase is made. This is just a new way of ordering your bank to transfer money from your account to that of someone from whom you buy goods.

Secondly, there are some forms of money that are transferred via the internet. Here the answer depends on the nature of the transaction involved. If all you are doing is using an internet message to transfer funds from your bank account to someone else's, then again this is just a new way of writing a cheque and no new principles are involved. However, if new types of institution become able to issue tokens that become widely accepted in payment, this would be a new departure and these new forms of money could provide a substitute for existing moneys. However, if such new moneys did emerge, it is most likely that governments would regulate them. The money issuers would be regulated like

banks, and as banks they would have to hold deposits with the central bank, in which case, again, no new principles would be involved. Indeed, most large payments, both in the domestic economy and in the international economy, have been made electronically for many years. This trend started with the invention of the telegraph in the 1830s and continued with the opening of the transatlantic telegraph cable in the 1880s. The internet is a new technology for authorizing payments, but the monetary principles involved are not new.

This all suggests that e-money is not going to break the monopoly of central banks to issue high-powered money and so it is not going to weaken their ability to set interest rates in wholesale money markets. Neither is e-money going to affect the ability of central banks to control inflation, as that depends largely on the impact of interest rates on spending decisions which is not affected in any obvious way by the nature of the payments technology.

---

imposed on the banking system by the central bank ,[18] we can see that the reserve ratio that banks will choose will be the outcome of an internal optimization process. Banks will try to keep the level of reserves as low as possible, subject to the need to supply cash on demand when customers wish to withdraw deposits. This is because reserves earn a relatively low interest rate, and so banks would like to devote as much as possible of the funds that are available to them to more profitable uses. Thus, in the absence of high legal reserve requirements (and aside from the crisis conditions of recent years), banks' chosen reserve ratios tend to be very small, especially when, as in normal market conditions, they can access liquid funds very quickly by borrowing in the interbank market.

Secondly, the competitive model helps us to understand that the banking system as a whole is in competition with other financial channels in the economy for the available amount of borrowing and lending (intermediation) business at any point in time. The real size of the banking sector, relative to other channels of finance (and, indeed, other industries), is determined by how efficient it is in channelling funds from savers to borrowers in the economy. Issues relating to the nominal size of bank deposits and the money supply should be kept separate from the question of the real relative size of the banking system compared with other channels of borrowing and lending flows (such as through securities markets).

CASE STUDIES

1. Cash makes a comeback

One of the key trends in payments methods that has been evident for the past several decades is the growing use of new technologies, as we discussed earlier in

---

[18] In the United Kingdom in January 2014 a specific part of reserves (known as the cash–ratio deposit, or CRD) held with the Bank of England was required to be 0.18 per cent of deposits above £600 million for big banks and zero for smaller deposit-taking institutions (with deposits less than £600 million). These are non-interest-bearing (while the bulk of reserves pay interest at bank rate) and the Bank of England buys interest-bearing assets with these funds, the earnings from which pay the Bank's operating costs.

this chapter. Growing numbers of ATMs in multiple locations have made it easier to get cash at any time of the day or night. Bank cards, such as debit and credit cards, have made it increasingly easy to make payment without the use of cash or cheques. Online retail and online banking have grown rapidly, so that the internet plays an expanding role in purchases and in payments.

One might think that these innovations would reduce the role in the economy of conventional cash in the form of notes and coins. Indeed, this role was shrinking up to the end of the 1980s. Figure 18.3 shows the ratio of

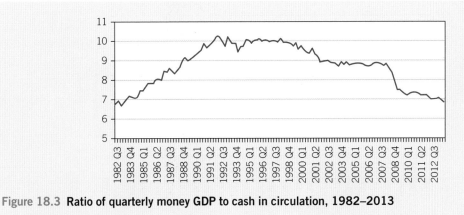

Figure 18.3 Ratio of quarterly money GDP to cash in circulation, 1982–2013

Source: ONS and Bank of England

money GDP to notes and coin in circulation from 1982. This ratio was rising in the 1980s (and before). This ratio is often referred to as the *velocity of circulation* as it measures how many times the stock of cash would have to turn over if it were used in each final transaction that is measured in GDP. When velocity is rising the amount of cash per pound of GDP is falling. So when the role of cash in transaction is falling and more transaction are using other means of payment, you would observe the ratio of GDP to money rising. As we can see from the figure, this is what was happening up to about 1990. However, since then the ratio of money GDP to cash has fallen, especially since the start of the twenty-first century. There was a sharp fall in this ratio during the 2008–9 recession, and further falls have taken place since then.

The amount of cash in circulation is entirely determined by what people choose to hold, so there is nothing driving this trend other than what is demanded. Clearly, cash remains a popular form of money. In 2012, something like 55 per cent of all transactions by volume were in cash, even though cash was first overtaken by debit cards as a payment method (by value) in 2010. However, cash is dominantly used in small transaction with an average value of around £11. Cheques are now used in only 2 per cent of transactions (by volume) but the average value of payments made by this method is close to £1,000.

So why has the amount of cash in circulation been growing relative to money GDP? The answer is that we do not know for sure. However, there are a number of possibilities. The first is that the pace of innovation in payments technology has slowed down, at least to the extent of failing to dent the role of cash further. Secondly, the era of very low interest rates on saving deposits that has been especially evident since 2009 has made it attractive for people to hold more of their savings in cash.

No interest is paid on cash, but the lower the interest available on bank deposits, the more attractive cash becomes. Thirdly, cash transactions are popular in the so-called *black economy* which involves illegal activities and those which although legal are deliberately avoiding taxes. The reason for this popularity is that cash transactions leave no recorded evidence behind, whereas all other forms of payment, such as credit and debit cards, cheques, and bank transfers, leave a trail.

Whatever the true explanation of these trends, it is clear that the role of cash in our economy has a very long history and it also seems to have a very bright future.

2. Money, money, money …

Notes and coin play an important role in the transactions of the economy, but the amount in circulation only made up just under 3 per cent of the UK money supply, M4, at the end of 2013 (see Box 18.3). The rest of the money stock is in the form of deposits in banks and building societies. These fulfil the functions of money in much the same ways as cash—they are transferred to someone else in exchange for goods or services. With cash you hand over the notes or coin in making payment, but with bank deposits you transfer the ownership of the deposit by means of cheque, debit card, credit card, or an order to your bank (possibly by phone or internet).

Many people have their wages or pensions paid directly into a bank account and only withdraw cash for convenience to use in regular small transactions. Current accounts at banks and building societies allow you to withdraw cash instantly and are linked to your payment cards or cheque book. These accounts may also pay some interest on outstanding balances, but a higher rate of interest is usually available in a savings account which may have some

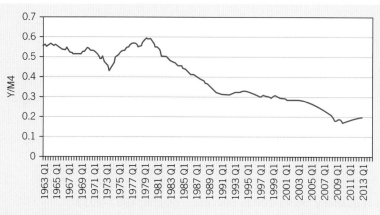

Figure 18.4 **M4 velocity, 1963–2013**

Source: ONS and Bank of England

restrictions on withdrawal of funds or payments out. Savings accounts are also included in the standard M4 measure of the money stock even though they are not normally used for transactions. Rather, people hold them as a store of value and for the interest they receive. Thus, this form of bank account is commonly held as a place to store savings and not just for transactions purposes as a short-term bridge between income and spending.

Figure 18.4 shows the ratio of quarterly money GDP to the M4 measure of the money stock from 1963 to 2013. As discussed in the first case study, this ratio is known as the velocity of circulation of M4 as it tells us the value of GDP each quarter per pound of the money stock. In other words, this tells us how many times the average unit of money turns over within the quarter in the final spending that makes up GDP. Clearly, the velocity of M4 is much smaller than that of notes and coins, as M4 is a much larger number than notes and coin, while the GDP values are the same in both Figure 18.3 and Figure 18.4.

The velocity of M4 cycled around a flat trend in the 1960s and 1970s but has fallen steadily since around 1980. This contrasts with the velocity of cash, which was rising in the 1980s and did not fall significantly until the 2000s. These patterns may be connected. In the 1980s there was substantial financial innovation and banks became more aggressive in trying to attract deposits by paying higher interest rates. This could explain both the rising velocity of cash and the falling velocity of M4, as people held more of their wealth in bank accounts but less in cash (in relation to incomes and spending).

Changes in banking technology linked to plastic cards and internet banking may also help to explain why bank deposits continued to grow in relation to GDP in the 1990s and into the 2000s. However, this does not seem to be connected in any obvious way to the growth in cash holding at the same time. The sharp (relative) rise in the role of cash after the 2007–8 financial crisis does seem to be connected to the rise in M4 velocity over this same period, as very low interest rates since 2009 have made savings accounts at banks (and building societies) much less attractive than they had been previously.

Starting in the next chapter, we look at the theoretical underpinnings of money demand and then link this all to our macroeconomic model.

Conclusion

The role of money and the monetary sector is vital in any market economy as its permits the specialization of function that is fundamental to any modern economy. Banks play an important role in the payments system and in providing credit for households and firms. However, when financial crises occur, as a result of over-expansion of credit and asset price inflation, the ensuing collapses of banks and firms can have a major impact on the real economy that can be severe and long-lasting.

SUMMARY

The nature of money

- Money is a medium of exchange, a unit of account, and a store of value.
- Money avoids the need for a double coincidence of wants and thus facilitates a wider range of transactions.

The origins of money

- Money has evolved from being based primarily on a precious metal to being mainly in the form of bank deposits.
- Early money was based on commodities, and especially precious metals like gold and silver.
- Paper currency started as a claim to a deposit of precious metal.
- Bank deposits comprise most of modern money.

How does money get in the economy?

- Central banks create the monetary base or high-powered money, which is made up of notes and coins and bankers' deposits at the central bank.
- Banks create deposit money by expanding loans and deposits.

Two models of banking

- Banks create deposits to some multiple of their cash reserves.
- In a competitive market in which banks pay interest on deposits and charge interest on loans, banks' behaviour is best understood in terms of demand and supply curves of deposits and loans. Banks must pay competitive interest rates to attract deposits, and they must charge competitive rates on their loans.

TOPICS FOR REVIEW

- Medium of exchange
- Unit of account
- Store of value
- Gold standard
- Reserve ratio

- Fiat money
- Money multiplier
- Competitive banking systems
- Interest rate spread

QUESTIONS

1 Suppose that the monetary base is £20 billion, that the general public wish to hold 20 per cent of their money in cash and the remaining 80 per cent in bank deposits, and that banks wish to hold a 5 per cent cash reserve. What will be the size of the broad money stock, according to the ratios approach?

2 How does the answer to Question 1 change for bank reserve ratios of a) 0 per cent, b) 1 per cent, and c) 10 per cent?

3 How does the answer to Question 1 change for general public cash holdings of a) 0 per cent, b) 5 per cent, c) 100 per cent?

4 How would the answers to Questions 2 and 3 change if the monetary base were £40 billion?

5 How is the broad money stock determined in a system where the monetary base is demand determined, the central bank sets an interest rate, and the banking system is competitive?

6 Why do people hold money when there is normally a higher yielding asset available?

7 What role does money play in a market economy?

8 What difference would it make to the economy if there were no modern money? What types of commodity might serve as money instead?

9 What is the difference between the money multiplier and the multiplier that we discussed in Chapters 16 and 17?

10 How is the UK money measure M4 defined?

CHAPTER 19

MONEY, INTEREST, AND GDP: THE *LM* CURVE

In the previous chapter we discussed the nature of money and saw how the quantity of money was determined by the joint actions of the central bank and the commercial banks. In this chapter we take the first step in integrating money into the model of the determination of GDP that we started building in Chapters 16 and 17. The key to this link is that the interaction of money demand and supply determines an interest rate, and this affects a component of final spending—investment. Investment then affects GDP. However, GDP also influences the amount of money demanded so we need to be able to handle these connections in an integrated way.

In this chapter we concentrate on the money market in which money demand and supply interact to determine the interest rate. The following chapter studies how the interest rate determined in the money market affects final spending via investment. We then put all this together in the enhanced model.

In this chapter you will learn that:

- There is an important distinction between nominal money values and real (or relative) values.
- Money and other assets are stocks while GDP and all the final spending variables are flows.
- We simplify the asset structure in the economy to just two assets: money and bonds.
- The real interest rate is (approximately) the nominal rate minus the inflation rate.
- The market price of a bond is inversely related to its interest yield.
- The demand for money is positively related to GDP and wealth and negatively related to the rate of interest.
- The *LM* curve shows combinations of GDP and the interest rate for which money demand and supply are equal when the money stock is held constant.
- The *LM* curve is positively sloped.
- Monetary policy normally works by setting the interest rate and letting the money supply be determined by demand.

The reason we are adding a monetary sector to our model may be obvious but it is still worth a reminder. The purpose of macroeconomics is to understand what determines real GDP and why it can deviate from its potential, or normal capacity, level for significant periods of time. We also want to understand why sometimes we get periods of high inflation, which is costly in itself but also costly to eradicate once it takes hold. Policymakers, in the form of elected governments or their agents, use the instruments available to them in an attempt to ensure both that economic activity stays at as high a level as is sustainable and that unacceptably high inflation rates are avoided. The tools that can be used for this purpose are monetary and fiscal policies. Fiscal policy works mainly through changes in government spending and taxation, and we already have a model that allows us to analyse these. However, since monetary policy works via interest rates and the money supply, we need to add a monetary sector to our model. Hence our goal in this chapter is to add this sector and then in subsequent chapters to use the augmented model to obtain a fuller understanding of the monetary and fiscal policy issues that face the United Kingdom and other major economies at the present time.

Box 19.1 highlights some of the ways in which monetary policy has been hitting the headlines.

Box 19.1 Money matters

Monetary policy is in the headlines on a regular basis. Before the 2007–8 financial crisis the story was usually about rises or falls in interest rates and the success or failure of monetary policy to control inflation. Since the crisis, interest rates have fallen to such low levels that monetary policy-makers have looked for new ways to influence the economy. The latest, which is known as 'quantitative easing', involves the central bank buying large quantities of government bonds (and other securities) with newly created money. We look in detail at how all these policies work later in this book. The point for now is that adding a monetary sector into our macro model is not just a dry and boring analytical exercise. On the contrary, it is allows us to use the model we develop to provide you with a framework that will aid the understanding of policy issues not just now but also for the rest of your careers. Building the model may seem abstract and unreal, but the issues it will help throw light on are real and tangible. The understanding developed will be of use not just to economics students but to anyone working in business or government.

Examples of recent media headlines about monetary policy are:

The central bank money-printing party (January 2013)

Yellen's [The Chair of the Board of Governors of the American central bank called the Federal Reserve System]

tapering of quantitative easing disruptive at home and abroad (February 2014)

Bank of England confirms interest rates and quantitative easing to remain unchanged in show of confidence in the economy (February 2014)

Bank of England rewrites forward guidance signalling no rate rise until 2015 (February 2014)

The first two of these are from the United States and the latter two are from the United Kingdom, but they all relate to the latest policy scenarios at the time of writing. Some of the media comments are critical of policy and others are more supportive. 'Tapering' refers to the fact that the US Federal Reserve had been continuing to buy bonds with new money right through to 2013–14, having started its first purchases in 2009, but had just announced that the size of the purchases was to be reduced in steps. The term 'forward guidance' refers to a policy change that was introduced by UK monetary policy-makers for the first time in August 2013. Instead of announcing the policy on a month-by-month basis, they gave a commitment that interest rates would not rise in future until certain conditions had been met. We will come back to a more detailed discussion of monetary policy in Chapter 25.

Money values and relative values

Money is our measuring rod for most economic activity. We value our wealth, our incomes, what we buy, and what we sell, all in money terms. When we think of a commodity's market value we usually think of its money price. 'What', we might ask, 'is the value of this refrigerator?' 'It costs £X' might be the reply. 'Is this refrigerator worth more than this TV set?' is another type of value question we frequently ask. Assuming the TV set costs £200, the answer is 'yes' if the refrigerator is priced at more than £200 and 'no' if it is priced at less. 'Have I saved enough money this winter to afford a week's holiday in Spain next summer?' is another common type of question. The answer depends on comparing the amount you have saved now with what you expect the Spanish trip to cost you.

Money prices are our measure of economic value. Money prices allow us to compare different values at any point in time, as with the refrigerator and the TV set. They also allow us to compare values over time, as with the amount saved now and the package holiday to be taken later.

Money as a veil

Suppose you tell a man, newly arrived from Patagonia, that the price of a refrigerator is £200. If he knows no other sterling values, this would convey no useful information to him.

But let us say that he entered Britain with £2,000. Now he knows that his funds are sufficient to buy 10 refrigerators. He has compared two money values: the market value of the refrigerator and the value of the funds he has brought in with him. But is the £2,000 he has with him a little or a lot? Now he needs to know the prices of all the things he might want to buy, either individually or expressed as an average. This requires that he relate the amount of his funds to the *general level* of prices.

Consider a further example. How much meat, beer, and travel can we buy for a day's wages? Such 'exchange rates'—between the labour that we sell and the goods that we buy—are what determine our living standards. If a worker sells his labour for £40 a day and buys a suit for £120, then what matters is that it costs him three days' work to buy the suit. If instead he only received £20 a day while a suit only cost him £60, the *real* exchange rate would be unchanged at three days' work to obtain the suit.

Adam Smith, writing in 1776, saw what the above examples illustrate, that individual sums of money and individual money prices, each looked at in isolation, convey no useful information. Instead, the comparison of two or more monetary values is what conveys significant information. Such comparisons allow us to look behind individual money prices to find real opportunity costs: how much of one thing must be given up to obtain a stated amount of something else.

The important insight is that value is *relative*; the monetary unit in which values are expressed is irrelevant. For example, if wheat is worth twice as much per bushel as barley, it does not matter, as far as their exchange rate is concerned, whether wheat is £2 and barley £1, or wheat £4 and barley £2, or wheat £100 and barley £50. Thus early economists talked of money as a veil behind which real economic relations occurred and were reacted to.

The point to take away from this discussion is that the production and consumption of real goods and services are what matters in the economy, while nominal values and the stock of money are conceptually different. They have a role, but they are a means to an end not the end itself.

The classical dichotomy

What is, perhaps misleadingly, called the classical dichotomy asserts a separation between the real side of the economy and its monetary side. In the 'real part', *relative* prices, quantities, and the allocation of resources are determined by such things as consumers' tastes, production technology, and the degrees of competition among buyers and sellers. In the 'monetary part', the *absolute level of prices* is determined by monetary forces. Thus, for example, the relative price of wheat and barley might be determined in the real part of the economy at one bushel of wheat equals two bushels of barley, their outputs at 1 and 5 million tonnes, and the resources of land and labour allocated to each at 1 and 2.5 million hectares and 10,000 and 20,000 person-hours, respectively. These are determined by the real forces of tastes and production possibilities operating through the markets for commodities and for productive inputs. The monetary part of the economy would then set the price level at which transactions would take place. For example, wheat might be priced at £4 and barley at £2 a bushel, and agricultural wages at £3 an hour; or wheat at £8 and barley at £4 and wages at £6. Both these levels of absolute prices yield the same *price relatives*.

It is one thing to say correctly that money is a veil behind which relative prices are what matters and quite another to say that the real and the money side of the economy are functionally separate, the real side determining what matters and the money side only determining the level of prices at which the real transactions are made. For this separation to be valid, what happens in the monetary part of the economy must have no effects on the real part, a proposition that is referred to as the *neutrality of money*. But, as noted later, money and credit play an important part in influencing the flow of production that takes place over time and the flow of investment designed to introduce new technologies. Thus what happens in the 'money part' of the economy has important effects on the 'real part', and vice versa. So, although considering only the real part of the economy has its uses, as in the micro theory in the first half of this book, it is profoundly misleading to think that what goes on in either part has no significant effects in the other part.

Furthermore, the banks that we studied in the previous chapter are institutions that operate in the real part of the economy in that they employ workers and produce services that others consume, and they channel funds from savers to borrowers and thus help finance real investment. Indeed, the financial services industry is one of the biggest sectors of the UK economy. Yet these institutions are also central to the monetary sector of the economy.

The neutrality of money

The classical dichotomy gives rise to what is called the doctrine of the **neutrality of money**. It can be stated in different forms.

Neutrality with respect to the level of prices

In its least controversial form, the doctrine of neutrality states that the *level* of money prices has no effect on the real economy. What matters for the real economy are relative prices not absolute prices. If the money prices of absolutely everything, all goods, all services, all pensions, all bank balances, all contracts, and everything else, were multiplied by ten, or a hundred, or any other number, there would be no effect on the real side of the economy where goods and services are produced, sold, and consumed. Everyone would have twice as much money to spend but everything would cost twice as much to buy, and so on.

This version of neutrality is relevant when, after undergoing a major inflation, a country decides on a currency reform that takes two or three zeros off its currency. Everything set in money terms is altered in the same proportion so that nothing real is changed. This was done in many European countries over the last half of the twentieth century.

According to a generally accepted version of the neutrality of money, the absolute values of a country's prices have no real effects; all prices can be changed in equal proportion with no real effects.

A slightly stronger version of neutrality states that when an economy is operating with either a stable price level or a fully anticipated modest positive rate of inflation, say 2 per cent, all real relations will be unchanged. Say, for example, that firm *A* wishes to raise its price by 2 per cent relative to ten other competitors who do not wish to alter their positions relative to each other. When the price level is stable, *A* just raises its price by 2 per cent and then leaves it there. If there is a general 2 per cent inflation all firms will be raising their prices by 2 per cent each year. Now what *A* must do is to raise its price by 4 per cent and then return to a general rise of 2 per cent each year. In both cases, the same relative price adjustment occurs with *A*'s price rising above those of its competitors by 2 per cent and staying there.

Money is neutral in the sense that an economy can function in exactly the same way if it has a steady price level or if it has a fully anticipated inflation of a modest rate.

Notice the two caveats. The inflation rate must be fully anticipated and occur at a modest rate. An unexpected inflation has real consequences, as the impact depends on how fast various actors learn about the inflation and adjust to it. Since not all adjustments take place at the same rate, there will be relative price changes and hence real consequences. The inflation rate must be modest. Inflation rates of over 10 per cent, such as were experienced in the developed countries from time to time in the 1970s and 1980s, were regarded as undesirable and downright harmful— and even more so when they reached as high as 50 per cent or more in some developing nations. No one can say for sure just what is the maximum modest rate that would have no real effects, but anything from 0 to 4 per cent would have few if any real effects once it was fully adjusted to. As we shall see in later chapters, an inflation rate around 2 per cent has been accepted as a modest target rate in many of the advanced countries since the early 1990s.

This is all that we need for the subsequent development of our model of the determination of GDP. However, the doctrine of neutrality does come in some stronger versions, some of which are currently still subject to debate. These are considered in Chapter 25 when we discuss monetary policy.

Money illusion

A person who understands the real choices facing her will be unaffected by changes that merely add or subtract the number of zeros on *all* prices and all money values. If that person's money income, and money wealth, is multiplied by 10, and all the prices she faces are also multiplied by 10, she will recognize that no real change has occurred. Thus, her economic behaviour will be unaffected. Such a person has penetrated the veil of money and is responding to the real choices that lie behind it.

Economists use the term **money illusion** to refer to behaviour that responds to purely nominal changes in money prices and values in either direction. Say, for example, that, faced with a tenfold increase in all prices, a second person felt poorer and increased his savings in response, even though his money income and money wealth had also been increased tenfold. That person is experiencing money illusion, altering his behaviour in response to changes in money values that leave all real choices unaffected.

Some people may suffer from money illusion in the short term, feeling harmed by inflation even though their incomes, and the values of all their wealth, rise in step with the rise in prices. However, over longer periods of time money illusion seems less common. People may not at first realize that an inflation that leaves unchanged the relation between the incomes they earn and the prices they pay leaves them unaffected, but they will realize eventually. This implies that, over the long run, real spending decisions are affected relatively little by purely nominal changes in all money prices (and wages).

We now want to start the process of building a monetary sector that fits into the model of the economy that we developed in Chapters 16 and 17. The aim is to investigate linkages between events in the 'monetary sector' and in the sector that delivers real outputs and incomes. The monetary sector that we build will not just consist of the money stock; it includes other financial assets that have a rate of return and whose market values can change. In order to understand the linkages between the monetary sector and the rest of the economy, we first need to understand some important characteristics of financial assets and interest rates.

Kinds of asset

Stocks and flows

It is important at this stage to recall the important distinction between *stocks* and *flows* that we made in Box 2.2 near the start of this book. The variables we have studied so far in our macro model have all been flows: consumption, investment, government spending, imports, exports, and GDP. These are all measured as amounts produced or purchased *per period*. So the amount measured over a month would be different from that over a quarter and again over a year. Roughly speaking, all of these variables will be four times bigger if measured over a year rather than over a quarter.

Money and other financial assets are not flows; they are stocks. They are just so many pounds sterling worth and they are measured at a point in time and not over a time period. So if you have £100 in cash it is just £100, with no time dimension. Therefore when we add assets to our model of the economy we are adding a new type of variable and we have to think carefully about the links between the stocks and the flows. With monetary assets such as bonds, this link generally comes from the interest yield on the asset stock which is a flow in the form of some percentage of the value of the asset *per period*. Money held in the form of cash does not pay interest, though some bank accounts do, but the interest rate that matters most is that on the assets other than money, which we will call bonds.

Money and bonds

At any moment in time, households have a given stock of wealth. This wealth is held in many forms. Some of it is held as money in the bank or in the wallet; some is held as short-term securities such as certificates of deposit and treasury bills; some is held as long-term bonds; and some as real capital, which may be held directly, in such forms as farms, houses and family businesses, or indirectly, in the form of equities (shares) that indicate part ownership of a company's assets. Although not too many households carry such a diverse portfolio of individual assets, many hold shares directly in mutual funds in which, depending on the degree of risk desired, there will be a mixture of bonds and shares carrying different degrees of risk. They also own, indirectly, their pension funds which will be invested in a broad range of assets, including many types of bonds and shares.

The ease with which any asset can be turned into money is called its liquidity. Liquidity has two aspects: (1) uncertainty about how much money can be obtained by selling it and (2) how easy it is to make a sale. Money is perfectly liquid on both counts since it requires no transaction to turn it into itself! Other financial assets are liquid in the second sense since they can normally be sold at any time on organized markets, such as the stock exchange. But they are not perfectly liquid in the sense that the prices at which they can be sold are uncertain. In this respect a short-term treasury bill is more liquid that a 20-year bond since its price will not fluctuate much from day to day and it can be turned into money either by selling it today or waiting to its maturity date, at which time the amount of money that one can get for it is determined by the bill's face value. The 20-year bond is less liquid because the amount that can be obtained by selling it on an organized market, such as the stock exchange, will vary considerably as the interest rate changes. In contrast, a house is less liquid in both senses in that it takes time to sell it, time measured in months and sometimes even in years, and the price that can be obtained for it varies over time.

All ways of holding wealth can be grouped into three main categories.

• Assets that serve as a medium of exchange—that is, paper money, coins and bank deposits.

• Other financial assets, such as bonds earning a fixed rate of interest, that will yield a specific money value at some future maturity date. Some of these assets, such as deposits in building societies, have a fixed money value at all times; others, such as government bonds, can be converted into currency before their maturity date by selling them at a price that fluctuates on the open market.

• Claims on real capital, such as shares that are claims to some of the profit stream generated by a company and physical objects such as factories, machines, and houses.

To simplify our discussion at the outset, it is helpful to assume that all wealth can be held in only two kinds of financial asset: money, which is perfectly liquid but earns no interest, and bonds, which are less liquid but earn an interest return. Thus in our present theory *bonds* stand for all interest-earning financial assets plus claims on real capital such as equities, while *the interest rate* stands for the whole *structure of different rates* that are earned by various financial assets with different liquidities. This assumption amounts to assuming that all these rates vary together, rising or falling by the same percentage. This is not an unreasonable first approximation, but in later chapters we will need to study what happens when rates move in ways that differ from each other.

The rate of interest and the price of bonds

The rate of interest and present value

A bond is a document that promises to pay a stated sum of money as interest each year, and to repay the face value of the bond, called the 'principal' at some future 'redemption date', often many years distant. The time until the redemption date is called the term to maturity, or, more simply, the term of the bond. Some bonds, called perpetuities, pay interest for ever but never repay the principal.

The **present value (***PV***)** of a bond, or of any asset, refers to the value now of the future payment or payments to which ownership of the asset gives a claim. Present value depends on the rate of interest, because when we calculate present value, the interest rate is used to discount the future payments. Two extreme examples help to illustrate this relationship between the rate of interest and present value.

A single payment one year hence

We start with the simplest case. How much would someone be prepared to pay now to purchase a bond that will produce a single payment of £100 in one year's time?

Suppose that the interest rate is 5 per cent, which means that £1.00 invested today will be worth £1.05 in one year's time. Now ask how much someone would have to lend out in order to have £100 a year from now. If we use *PV* to stand for this unknown amount, we can write *PV* (1.05) (which means *PV* multiplied by 1.05) = £100. Thus, *PV* = £100/1.05 = £95.24.[1] This tells us that the present value of £100 receivable in one year's time is £95.24; anyone who lends out £95.24 for one year at 5 per cent interest will get back the £95.24 plus £4.76 in interest, which makes £100.

What if the interest rate had been 7 per cent? At that interest rate the present value of the £100 receivable in a year's time would be £100/1.07 = £93.46, which is less than the present value when the interest rate was 5 per cent.

A perpetuity

Now consider another extreme case—a perpetuity that promises to pay £100 per year to its holder for ever but has no redemption date or redemption value. The present value of the perpetuity depends on how much £100 per year is worth, and this again depends on the rate of interest. At 10 per cent interest it is worth £1,000, because

£1,000 invested at 10 per cent per year will yield £100 interest per year for ever. However, the same bond is worth £2,000 when the interest rate is 5 per cent per year, because it takes £2,000 invested at 5 per cent per year to yield £100 interest per year. The lower the rate of interest obtainable on the market, the more valuable is an existing bond paying a fixed amount of interest.

Similar relations apply to bonds that are more complicated than single payments but are not perpetuities. Although in such cases the calculation of present value is more complicated, the same negative relationship between the interest rate and present value still holds.

The present value of any asset that yields a given stream of money over time is negatively related to the current market interest rate.

Present value and market price

Present value is important because it establishes the market price for an asset. To see this, return to our example of a bond that promises to pay £100 one year hence. When the interest rate is 5 per cent, the present value is £95.24. To see why this is the maximum that anyone would pay for this bond, suppose that some sellers offer to sell the bond at some other price, say £98. If, instead of paying this amount for the bond, a potential buyer lends her £98 out at 5 per cent interest, at the end of one year she would have more than the £100 that the bond will produce; at 5 per cent interest, £98 yields £4.90 in interest, which when added to the principal makes £102.90. Clearly, no well-informed individual would pay £98—or by the same reasoning any sum in excess of £95.24—for the bond.

Now suppose that the bond is offered for sale at a price less than £95.24, say £90. A potential buyer could borrow £90 to buy the bond and would pay £4.50 in interest on the loan. At the end of the year the bond yields £100. When this is used to repay the £90 loan and the £4.50 in interest, £5.50 is left as profit. Clearly, it would be worthwhile for someone to buy the bond at the price of £90—or by the same argument at any price less than £95.24. But at £90 no holder would want to sell the bond. If she needed £90 she could borrow it for a year and then cash in the bond at the end of the year, pay back the £90 plus £4.50 interest, and be £5.50 better off than if she had sold the bond for £90 at the beginning of the year.

Thus, *all* bondholders would want to sell at any price over £95.24 but no one would want to buy at those prices, while no bond holder would want to sell at any price

---

[1] Notice that in this type of formula the interest rate, *r*, is expressed as a decimal fraction. For example, 5 per cent is expressed as 0.05, so (1 + *r*) = 1.05.

below £95.24 while all potential buyers would want to buy. Thus £95.24 is the only price at which there will be both willing buyers and willing sellers; £95.24 is the price that will rule for that asset on the market.

In a free market the equilibrium price of any asset is the present value of the income stream that it produces.

Box 19.2 shows the market prices of some real UK government bonds.

The rate of interest and market price

The discussion above leads us to three important propositions. The first two stress the negative relationship between interest rates and asset prices:

1. If the current market rate of interest falls, the value of an asset producing a given income stream will rise.

2. A rise in the market price of an asset producing a given income stream is equivalent to a decrease in the rate of interest earned by the asset.

Thus a promise to pay £100 one year from now is worth £92.59 when the interest rate is 8 per cent and only £89.29 when the interest rate is 12 per cent: £92.59 at 8 per cent interest (£92.59 × 1.08) and £89.29 at 12 per cent interest (£89.29 × 1.12) are both worth £100 in one year's time.

The third proposition focuses on the term to maturity of the bond:

3. The nearer the maturity date of a bond, the less the bond's value will change with a change in the market rate of interest.

To illustrate the third proposition consider an extreme case. The present value of a bond that is redeemable for £1,000 in one week's time will be very close to £1,000 no

---

Box 19.2 UK government bonds or 'gilts'

There are many different government bonds that are held by the general public, but the biggest holders are pension funds and life assurance companies. The table lists some of the UK government bonds that are available at the time of writing. It is helpful to understand some of their features and what the numbers mean. The prices are those ruling on 24 January 2014, but you can look at latest figures in the financial press.

Maturity date	Coupon	Price	Yield
2016	2%	102.6	0.68
2020	4.75%	115.19	2.09
2025	5%	120.14	2.87
2052	3.75%	105.41	3.49
War loan	3.5%	82.59	4.24

The maturity date is the time at which the face value of the bond (typically £100 in the UK) will be paid back. Each will have a specific date and time when this will happen. The last bond labelled 'war loan' is a *perpetuity*, which means that it has no redemption date so could continue in existence for ever, though the issuer (the UK Treasury) could buy it back at any time that it wants. These bonds were issued during the Second World War and were still being held by some investors in 2014 (though they are likely to have changed hands many times since 1945).

The coupon on a bond is the amount of interest that a bond pays out each year (typically in two equal half-yearly slices). The coupon is fixed at the time of issue of the bond

and does not change throughout its life. So the first bond with a coupon of 2 per cent pays to the holder £2 per year in two equal payments of £1 each. When bonds were all in paper form, the coupon was printed on the bond and it would be cut off and presented to the issuer (or a specific agent acting for the issuer) on the date and time specified on the coupon. Nowadays, most bonds are registered on a computer system and never exist in paper form. The coupon payment is transferred electronically to the holder's bank account.

The price of the bond is what it is selling for on the day these prices were quoted. So the price of the first bond listed was £102.60. The yield is the yield to maturity which tells us that if you pay £102.60 for the first bond then the combination of the redemption value and the coupon payments still to be delivered would represent an annual interest rate of 0.68 per cent to the holder. In other words, if you pay £102.60 for this bond you will get back £100 when the bond matures at some date in 2016 and you will get the coupon payments still due until then.

Notice that the current price of a bond with a high coupon is greater than that of a bond with a low coupon. Notice also that the yield tends to increase as the term to maturity increases. This does not always have to be true, but it has been a characteristic of bond yields in recent times when short-term interest rates have been low. The line plotting the full range of yields against the term to maturity is known as the 'yield curve'. In 2014, the yield curve was positively sloped, as indicated by the yields in the table above and in Figure 19.8 later in this chapter.

matter what the interest rate may be. After all, the bond will be redeemed for £1,000 in one week whatever the rate of interest, and there is only a negligible difference between what £1,000 will earn at 5 per cent and at 10 per cent for only one week. Thus, its value will not change much even if the rate of interest leaps from 5 to 10 per cent during that week. Note what this implies for any interest-earning components of *money* such as interest-bearing bank deposits; they are so short term that their values remain unchanged when the interest rate changes.

As a second example consider two bonds, one that promises to pay £100 next year and one that promises to pay £100 in 10 years. A rise in the interest rate from 8 to 12 per cent will lower the value of £100 payable in one year's time by 3.6 per cent, but it will lower the value of £100 payable in ten years' time by 37.9 per cent.[2]

The real and the nominal interest rate

The rate of interest that we have considered so far is called the nominal rate of interest or money rate of interest, the two terms referring to the same thing. They express the money return on an asset. These are the rates that are quoted in the media and that you pay on a student loan.

Given what people expect to happen to the price level, a second interest rate, called the **real rate of interest** is implied. It expresses the return on any asset in terms of the purchasing power that the asset is expected to earn. If people expect the price level to remain unchanged over the period being considered, the real and nominal rates of interest are the same. For example, £100 invested at a nominal interest rate of 10 per cent for one year will earn £10 in money and the principal of £100 will be returned. Since £110 will buy 10 per cent more goods than the £100 that was invested one year ago, the real rate is also 10 per cent. But now suppose that the price level is expected to rise by 10 per cent over the year. Then when the £110 is paid at the end of the year, it will buy exactly the same amount of goods as the £100 principal would have bought at the beginning of the year. In this case the real rate of interest is zero.

The real rate of interest is approximated by the nominal rate minus the expected inflation rate.

This approximation is good enough for our purposes and we will use it throughout.[3]

For the time being we will assume that the price level is expected to remain constant so that the real and nominal rates are the same.

Money demand and supply

The supply of money

In Chapter 18 we discussed the variety of definitions of the money stock. For present purposes we use the UK broad definition of money, M4. This includes notes and coins in circulation outside the banks, plus all sterling deposits with UK banks and building societies.[4] M4 is a nominal amount measured in monetary units—so many pounds sterling in the United Kingdom, or dollars in the

United States. The real money supply measures money in purchasing power units. To do this we divide the nominal quantity by the price level. (Letting M be the nominal quantity of money and P the price level, the real quantity is given by M/P.) Although this is an arbitrary number, depending on the specific index used to measure P, changes in it do adequately measure the real quantities of money—that is, changes in its purchasing power. For example, if the price level doubles with the nominal quantity of money being constant, the real quantity of money has halved. It will buy half as much as before. Throughout most of the rest of this chapter the price level is assumed to be constant, so real and nominal quantities are the same.

The nominal quantity of money is determined by the interaction between the monetary policy-makers (the central bank), the banking system, and the general public. However, for much of what follows we will make one of two alternative simplifying assumptions. The first is that

---

[2] The example assumes annual compounding. The first case is calculated from the numbers of the previous example: (92.58 – 89.29)/92.58. The 10-year case uses the formula

Present value = principal/$(1 + r)^n$

which gives £46.30 at 8 per cent and £28.75 at 12 per cent. Thus, the percentage fall in value is (46.30 – 28.75)/46.30 = 0.379, or 37.9 per cent.

[3] The correct formula is as follows:

(1+nominal interest rate)/(1+inflation rate) = (1+real interest rate).

For example, if the nominal interest rate is 10 per cent and the inflation rate is 5 per cent, the formula gives 1.10/1.05 = 1.04762, which is a real rate of a bit less than a 5 per cent. So the approximation

real interest rate = nominal interest rate – inflation rate

slightly overstates the real rate, but this is of no consequence for any analysis in this book.

[4] Also included are sterling certificates of deposit (and other paper issued by banks and building societies of not more than five years' original maturity).

the nominal money supply is set by the makers of monetary policy, and the second is that the makers of monetary policy set the nominal interest rate and let the money stock be determined by whatever is demanded at that interest rate. To see how this works we need to study the determinants of the demand for money.

The demand for money

Recall our assumption that all wealth must be held in either money or bonds. The amount of wealth that everyone in the economy wishes to hold in the form of money balances is called the demand for money. Because people are choosing how to divide their given stock of wealth between money and bonds, it follows that if we know the demand for money, we also know the demand for bonds. With a given level of wealth, a rise in the demand for money necessarily implies a fall in the demand for bonds; if people wish to hold £1 million more money, they must wish to hold £1 million less of bonds. It also follows that if the public is in equilibrium with respect to its money holdings, it is also in equilibrium with respect to its bond holdings.

You may say at this point: 'Hang on, if I have more money than I want to hold then I will just spend it on a holiday or a good night out, and I certainly would not be buying bonds with it'. However, the thing to bear in mind is that we are not just talking about the choices of single individuals but rather of the whole economy, and spending money just passes it on to someone else in the same economy, it does not get rid of it. So in the aggregate we focus on the forces that work if people are trying to hold more or less money in total. Collectively they cannot do this if the supply of money is fixed. But by attempting to adjust their mix of assets between money and bonds, they can change the price of bonds and thus the interest rate on bonds, and they will continue to do so until the existing money stock is willingly held.

Real and nominal money demand

The nominal demand for money is measured in money units: the amount of pounds sterling that the British public wishes to hold, or the amount of US dollars that the American public wishes to hold. The real demand for money is the number of units of purchasing power that the public wishes to hold in the form of money balances. For example, in an imaginary one-product (wheat) economy, the number of bushels of wheat that could be purchased with the money balances held would be the measure of their real value. In a more complex economy it could be measured in terms of the number of 'baskets of goods', represented by a price index such as the RPI or

CPI, that could be purchased with the money balances held. When we speak of the demand for money in real terms, we speak of the amount demanded in constant pounds.

The real demand for money (or the demand for real money balances) is the nominal quantity demanded divided by the price level.

In the fifty years from January 1964 to December 2013, on the M4 definition, the nominal quantity of money balances held in the United Kingdom increased nearly 150-fold, from around £14,104 million to around £2,108,000 million. However, over the same period the price level, as measured by the RPI, increased nearly 19-fold. This tells us that the real quantity of money held by the public rose from £14,104 million to about £112,700 million, measured in constant 1964 prices, an eightfold increase.

Because we are holding the price level constant in most of this chapter, the real demand can be measured in current monetary units. Any percentage change in the nominal amount of money demanded implies the same percentage change in the real amount demanded. For example, if 10 per cent more nominal money is held, this also represents a 10 per cent increase in the real amount being held as long as the price level remains unchanged.

Earlier we distinguished between the real and the nominal or money rates of interest. For the decision concerning the holding of money balances it is the money rate that matters. To see this consider an example in which the nominal rate is 10 per cent and the expected inflation rate is also 10 per cent, making the real rate zero. Anyone who holds money over the period will be 10 per cent worse off than if she had invested in a bond, in which case her purchasing power would at least have been unchanged over the year. So the opportunity cost of holding money in this case is expressed by the 10 per cent nominal rate, not the zero per cent real rate.

Money demand depends on the nominal rate of interest

In our simplified model of the financial system there are only two assets to choose from: money and bonds. Money pays no interest but bonds do. So what you give up by holding money rather than bonds is the interest yield on those bonds. The higher that interest yield, the more likely it is that people will want to hold more bonds and less money, and vice versa.

The opportunity cost of holding any money balance is the extra interest that could have been earned if the money had

been used instead to purchase bonds (i.e. the nominal rate of interest).[5]

Motive for holding money

Since there is a cost of holding money, you may wonder why the public holds any money at all. Clearly, money will be held only when it provides services that are valued at least as highly as the opportunity cost of holding it—that is, the interest foregone. Three important services that are provided by money balances give rise to three motives for holding money: the transactions, precautionary, and speculative motives.

The transactions motive

Most transactions in a market economy require money as the form of payment. Money passes from consumers to firms to pay for the goods and services produced by firms; money passes from firms to employees to pay the wages and salaries of those employees. Money balances that are held on average to make such payments are called **transactions balances**.

In an imaginary world in which the incomes and spending of all consumers and firms were perfectly synchronized, it would be unnecessary to hold transactions balances. If every time a consumer spent £10 she received £10 as part payment of her wages, no transactions balances would be needed. In the real world, however, receipts and payments are not perfectly synchronized.

Some money balances are held because of the timing of wage payments. Suppose, for example, that firms pay wages every Friday and that employees spend all their wages purchasing goods and services evenly over the week. Thus, on Friday morning firms must hold balances equal to the weekly wage bill; on Friday afternoon the employees will hold these balances. Over the week employee's balances will be drawn down as a result of purchasing goods and services. Over the same period the balances held by firms will build up as a result of selling goods and services until, on the following Friday morning, firms will again have built up balances equal to the wage bill that must be met on that day. Although the ownership of the money balance changes over the week, the total held by firms and households combined is constant.

The transactions motive arises because payments and receipts are not synchronized.

What determines the size of the transactions balances to be held? It is clear that in our example total transactions balances vary with the amount of the wage bill. If the wage bill rises by 10 per cent because 10 per cent more workers have been employed, or existing workers have had a 10 per cent pay rise, the transactions balances held by firms and households for this purpose will also double on average. As it is with wages, so it is with all other transactions: the size of the balances held is positively related to the amount of the transactions.

For our purposes we need to know how money demand relates to GDP rather than to total transactions. As we saw in Chapter 15, the value of all transactions greatly exceeds the value of the economy's final output. When the miller buys wheat from the farmer and the baker buys flour from the miller, both are transactions against which money balances must be held, although only the value added at each stage is part of GDP.

Normally it is safe to assume that there is a stable positive relationship between transactions and GDP. A rise in GDP also leads to a rise in transactions and hence to an associated rise in the demand for transactions balances. This allows us to relate transactions balances to GDP.

The larger is GDP, the larger are the transactions balances that will be held.

The precautionary motive

Many reasons for spending arise unexpectedly, such as when your car breaks down, or when you have to make an unplanned journey to visit a sick relative. As a precaution against cash crises, when receipts are abnormally low or disbursements are abnormally high, firms and households carry money balances. These are called **precautionary balances** and they provide a cushion against uncertainty about the timing of cash flows. The larger such balances are, the greater is the protection against running out of money because of temporary fluctuations in cash flows.

The seriousness of the risk of a cash crisis depends on the penalties that are inflicted for being caught without sufficient money balances. A firm is unlikely to be pushed into insolvency, but it may incur considerable costs if it is forced to borrow money at high interest rates in order to meet a temporary cash crisis.

---

[5] Many of the bank and building society deposits that are included in M4 now yield interest. This complicates, but does not fundamentally alter, the analysis of the demand for money. In particular, it means that the opportunity cost of holding those interest-bearing components of money is not the *level* of interest rates paid on bonds but the *difference* between that rate and the rate paid on money. Because the interest earned on deposits tends to fluctuate less than rates on marketable securities, the difference tends to move with the level of interest rates in the economy, rising when rates rise and falling when rates fall. For simplicity, we talk of the demand for money responding to the *level* of interest rates. In reality it is the *difference* between the rates in money and in bonds that is the opportunity cost of holding money.

The precautionary motive arises because households and firms are uncertain about the degree to which payments and receipts will be synchronized.

The protection provided by a given quantity of precautionary balances depends on the volume of payments and receipts. A £100 precautionary balance provides a large cushion for a person whose volume of payments per month is £800 and a small cushion for a firm whose monthly volume is £250,000. To provide the same degree of protection as the value of transactions rises, more money is necessary.

The precautionary motive, like the transactions motive, causes the quantity of money demanded to vary positively with the GDP.

For most purposes the transactions and precautionary motives can be merged, as they both show that desired money holdings are positively related to the GDP.

The speculative motive

Money can also be held for its characteristics as an asset. Firms and households may hold some money in order to provide a hedge against the uncertainty inherent in fluctuating prices of other financial assets. Money balances held for this purpose are called **speculative balances**. This motive was first analysed by Keynes, while Professor James Tobin, the 1981 Nobel Laureate in economics, developed the modern analysis.

Any holder of money balances forgoes the extra interest income that could be earned if bonds were held instead. However, market interest rates fluctuate, and so do the market prices of existing bonds, since their present values depend on the interest rate. Thus bonds are risky assets, because their prices fluctuate. Many individuals and firms do not like risk; they are said to be *risk-averse*.[6]

In choosing between holding money and holding bonds, wealth-holders must balance the extra interest income that they could earn by holding bonds against the risk that bonds carry. At one extreme, if households hold all their wealth in the form of bonds, they earn extra interest on their entire wealth, but they also expose their entire wealth to the risk of changes in the price of bonds. At the other extreme, if people hold all their wealth in the form of money, they earn less interest

income, but they do not face the risk of unexpected changes in the price of bonds. Wealth-holders do not usually take either extreme position. They hold part of their wealth as money and part of it as bonds; that is, they diversify their holdings. The fact that some proportion of wealth is held in money and some in bonds suggests that, as wealth rises, desired money holdings will also rise.

The speculative motive implies that the quantity of money demanded varies positively with wealth.

Although one household's wealth may rise or fall rapidly, the total wealth of a society changes only slowly. For the analysis of short-term fluctuations in GDP, the effects of changes in wealth are fairly small, and we will ignore them for the present. Specific households may undergo large wealth changes in response to bond price changes, but with inside wealth the total effect is small.[7] When lenders gain, borrowers lose, and when lenders lose, borrowers gain. Over the long term, however, variations in aggregate wealth can have a major effect on the demand for money.

Wealth that is held in cash or deposits earns less interest than could be earned by holding bonds; hence the reduction in risk involved in holding money carries an opportunity cost in terms of forgone interest earnings. The speculative motive leads households and firms to add to their money holdings until the reduction in risk obtained by the last pound added is just balanced (in each wealth-holder's view) by the cost in terms of the interest forgone on that pound. A fall in the rate of return on bonds with an unchanged amount of risk will encourage people to hold more of their wealth as money and less in bonds. A rise in their rate of return for a given level of risk will cause people to hold more bonds and less money.

Because of the speculative motive, the quantity of money demanded is negatively related to the rate of interest.

The precautionary and transactions motives may also be negatively related to interest rates at the margin, because higher returns on bonds encourage people to economize on their money holding. However, in practice we only observe total money holdings, so we cannot distinguish the components held for different motives. Hence:

---

[6] A person is risk-averse when he or she prefers a certain sum of money to an uncertain outcome for which the expected value is the same. For example, a person is risk-averse if he would definitely prefer having £100 for certain over a 50/50 chance of winning either £200 or nothing. See Chapter 12 for a discussion of risk-aversion.

[7] An inside asset is one for which both the issuer and holder are in the domestic economy. Thus a change in the asset's value affects issuer and holder in opposite directions and so has no net effect on total domestic wealth. The distinction between inside and outside assets is discussed in detail in Box 21.2.

The demand for money, as a whole, is positively related to GDP and wealth, and negatively related to the nominal interest rate.

The demand for money and the price level.

So far, because we have held the price level constant, we have identified the determinants of the demand for real money balances. These are real GDP, real wealth, and the nominal interest rate. Now suppose that, with the interest rate, real wealth, and real GDP held constant, the price level doubles. Because the demand for real money balances will be unchanged, the demand for nominal balances must double. If the public previously demanded £300 billion in nominal money balances, it will now demand £600 billion. This keeps the real demand unchanged at £600/2 = £300 billion. The money balances of £600 billion at the new higher price level represent exactly the same purchasing power as £300 billion at the old price level.

Because the real demand for money balances is independent of the price level, the nominal demand varies in direct proportion to the price level; when the price level doubles, desired nominal money balances also double.

This is a key proposition that drives a famous economic theory called the quantity theory of money, which is discussed in Box 19.3.

Total demand for money

Parts (i) and (ii) of Figure 19.1 summarize the influences of the nominal rate of interest and real GDP on the real demand for money. If we wish to get the nominal demand, we must multiply the real demand by an index of the price level. Thus, as shown in Figure 19.1(iii), the nominal money demand rises in direct proportion to the price level. These three variables account for most of the short-term variations in the nominal quantity of money demanded.

The function relating money demanded to the rate of interest is often called the **demand for money function**, even though the demand for real money balances also depends on GDP and wealth, while the demand for nominal balances depends on these variables and the price level.

We have seen that the public has a fixed stock of wealth at any point in time. When it decides how much money to hold, for the reasons studied above, it is also deciding how many bonds to hold. So the public can be seen as adjusting the balance of its portfolio of wealth between the two assets, money and bonds. When it is in disequilibrium, it is trying to alter that balance either by selling bonds and getting money, or by buying bonds and giving up money. When it is in equilibrium, it has the desired balance between the two assets.

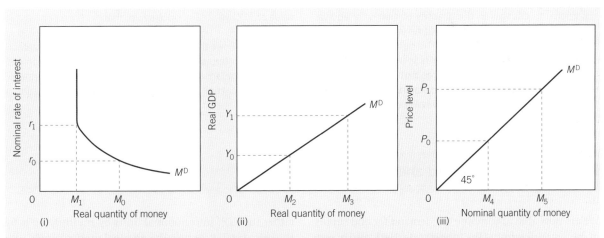

Figure 19.1 The demand for money as a function of the nominal interest rate, the GDP, and the price level

The real quantity of money demanded varies negatively with the nominal rate of interest and positively with real GDP while the nominal quantity demanded varies positively with the price level. In part (i) the real quantity of money demanded is shown as negatively related to the interest rate. When the interest rate rises from r_0 to r_1, the quantity of money demanded falls from M_0 to M_1. In part (ii) the real quantity of money demanded is shown as positively related to real GDP. When real GDP rises from Y_0 to Y_1, the quantity demanded rises from M_2 to M_3. In part (iii) the nominal quantity of money demanded is shown as positively related to the price level. When the price level doubles from P_0 to P_1, the quantity demanded doubles from M_4 to M_5. In the text we refer to the M^D curve in (i) as the money demand function. It is drawn for given values of real GDP and wealth.

Box 19.3 The quantity theory of money

The quantity theory of money is a famous theory that relates the quantity of nominal money in an economy to its price level. The theory can be set out in the following equations. Equation (1) states that the demand for nominal money balances, D^M, depends on the value of transactions as measured by nominal GDP, which is real GDP, Y, multiplied by the price level, P:

$$D^M = kPY \qquad (1)$$

Equation (2) states that the supply of nominal money, M, is exogenously determined by the central bank (or under the gold standard by past gold flows from abroad) at some given level M^S:

$$M = M^S. \qquad (2)$$

Equation (3) states the equilibrium condition that the demand for money must equal the supply:

$$D^M = M^S. \qquad (3)$$

Substitution from eqns (2) and (3) into eqn (1) yields

$$M^S = kPY. \qquad (4)$$

Rearranging (4) gives

$$P = M^S/kY \qquad (5)$$

The original classical quantity theory assumes that k is a constant given by the transactions demand for money and that Y is constant because potential GDP is maintained. Letting $(1/kY) = \alpha$ we can write:

$$P = \alpha M^S. \qquad (6)$$

In words, the price level is determined by the quantity of money. By taking first differences ($\Delta P = \alpha \Delta M$), we derive the prediction that changes in the price level will be proportional to changes in the quantity of money, or equivalently that the rate of inflation will be equal to the rate of growth of the money supply if Y remains constant at its potential level. Alternatively, if Y is growing at a constant rate, a constant price level requires that the money supply grows at the same rate. Although we know that GDP does not stay constant at its potential level, but instead cycles

around it, the theory can be interpreted as showing what will happen when GDP is at potential.

The quantity theory is often presented using the *equation of exchange*:

$$M^S V = PY, \qquad (7)$$

where V is the velocity of circulation of money. From equation (5), V is just the reciprocal of k. Thus it makes no difference whether we choose to work with k or V. So if k is assumed to be constant, V must also be constant.

Velocity can be interpreted as showing the average amount of 'work' done by a unit of money. If annual money GDP is £600 billion and the stock of money is £200 billion, on average each pound's worth of money is used three times to create the values added that compose GDP.

An example may help to illustrate the interpretation of each. Suppose that the stock of money that people wish to hold equals one-fifth of the value of total transactions. Thus k is 0.2, and V, the reciprocal of k, is 5. If the money supply is to be one-fifth of the value of annual transactions, each pound must be 'used' on average five times.

The modern version of the quantity theory does not assume that k and V are exogenously fixed. However, it does argue that they will not change in response to a change in the quantity of money. Considering only potential GDP and dividing (7) by Y we obtain

$$P = MV/Y. \qquad (8)$$

If we assume that V is constant and use α for the constant value of V/Y, we obtain, once again, that

$$P = \alpha M \qquad (9)$$

which only shows that it does not matter whether we state the theory in terms of k, the fraction of GDP that people wish to hold as money balances or V, the amount of times that the typical unit of money must change hands to create the existing level of Y.

Equating money demand and supply

We are now able to combine the demand for and supply of money to determine the interest rate. Here, and in everything else that follows, we must be clear whether we are dealing in real or nominal units. The quantity of money is measured in nominal units but our theory of the demand for money was developed in real purchasing power units, although, as we have just seen, it can also be expressed in nominal units by multiplying it by the price level. If we let D^M stand for the demand for money expressed in real purchasing power units and M for the supply of money measured in nominal units, we can

either turn D^M into nominal units by multiplying it by the price level, P, or turn the nominal money supply into real units but dividing it by the price level, P. We can see that these are equivalent by writing the equilibrium condition that the demand for money should equal its supply in two ways. First, with everything in nominal units, we have

$$PD^M = M \qquad (19.1)$$

and then, with everything expressed in real units, we have

$$D^M = M/P. \qquad (19.2)$$

These are clearly equivalents since dividing the first expression through by P yields the second expression. Therefore we can use whichever expression that is most convenient for any particular purpose.

Monetary equilibrium and the interest rate

Monetary equilibrium occurs when the demand for money equals the supply of money. In Chapter 2 we saw that in competitive markets the price will adjust so as to ensure equilibrium. The rate of interest is the relevant price in the money markets. The easiest way to understand how this works is to start by showing how interest rates would adjust to clear the money market (i.e. equate demand and supply) if there was a fixed money supply. We then show how the money supply adjusts to equate demand and supply when the Bank of England[8] chooses to fix the interest rate and let the money supply adjust to demand. To study all this it is convenient to define everything in nominal units, using eqn (19.1) as our equilibrium condition.

Equilibrium interest rate

Figure 19.2 shows supply and demand curves for nominal money. The supply of money that is in existence at the initial point in time is shown as a vertical line, indicating that the money supply is a given nominal quantity. The money demand curve is based upon the speculative demand illustrated in Figure 19.1(i) with the real quantity in that figure now multiplied by the price level to turn it into a demand for nominal balances. It is negatively sloped because people wish to hold less money as interest rates rise. The nominal money demand curve is drawn for given levels of real GDP, the price level, and wealth, and will shift to the right if any of these variables increase.

Figure 19.2 also shows how the interest rate would move in order to equate the demand for money with its supply, given the initial money stock and the existing stock of bonds. When a few people find that they have less money than they wish to hold, they can sell some bonds and add the proceeds to their money holdings. This transaction simply redistributes given supplies of bonds and money among households it does not change the total supply of either money or bonds.

Now suppose that all of the firms and households in the economy have excess demands for money balances. They all try to sell bonds to add to their money balances, but what one person can do, all cannot necessarily do. At any moment the economy's total supply of money and bonds

is fixed—there is just so much money and there are just so many bonds in existence. If everyone tries to sell bonds, there will be no one to buy them, and the price of bonds will fall.

We saw earlier in this chapter that a fall in the price of bonds means a rise in the rate of interest, which is the yield on bonds. As the interest rate rises, people economize on money balances because the opportunity cost of holding such balances is rising. Eventually the interest rate will rise enough that people will no longer be trying to add to their money balances by selling bonds. At that point there is no longer an excess supply of bonds, and the interest rate stops rising. The demand for money again equals the supply.

Suppose now that all firms and households hold larger money balances than they would like. A single household or firm would purchase bonds with its excess balances, achieving monetary equilibrium by reducing its money

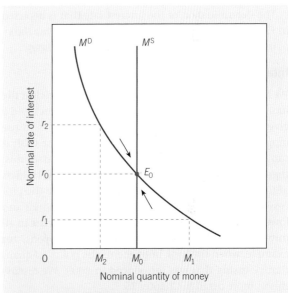

Figure 19.2 The equilibrium interest rate

The equilibrium interest rate arises where the demand for money equals the supply of money. A given quantity of money, M_0, is shown by the vertical supply curve M^S. The demand for money curve is M^D; its negative slope indicates that a fall in the rate of interest causes the quantity of money demanded to increase. Equilibrium is at E_0, with a rate of interest r_0. If the interest rate is r_1, there will be an excess demand for money of $M_1 - M_0$. Bonds will be offered for sale in an attempt to increase money holdings. This will force the rate of interest up to r_0 (the price of bonds falls), at which point the quantity of money demanded is equal to the fixed supply, M_0. If the interest rate is r_2, there will be an excess supply of money $M_0 - M_2$. Bonds will be demanded in return for the excess money balances. This will force the rate of interest down to r_0 (the price of bonds rises), at which point the quantity of money demanded has risen to equal the fixed money supply, M_0.

---

[8] We will refer to the 'Bank of England' as 'the Bank' from now on. We will also refer to the Monetary Policy Committee of the Bank of England, which actually takes UK monetary policy decisions, as 'the MPC'. Its workings are explained in Chapter 25.

holdings and increasing its bond holdings. However, just as in the previous example, what one household can do, all cannot do. At any moment the total quantity of bonds is fixed, so not everyone can simultaneously add to personal bond-holdings. When all agents enter the bond market and try to purchase bonds with unwanted money balances, they bid up the price of existing bonds, and the interest rate falls. Households and firms then become willing to hold larger quantities of money; that is, the quantity of money demanded increases along the money demand curve in response to a fall in the rate of interest. The rise in the price of bonds continues until firms and households stop trying to convert bonds into money. In other words, it continues until everyone is content to hold the existing supply of money and bonds.

Monetary equilibrium occurs when the rate of interest is such that the demand to hold money equals the supply available to be held, and hence the demand to hold bonds equals the supply available to be held.

The determination of the interest rate that is depicted in Figure 19.2 is often called the *liquidity preference theory* of interest and sometimes the *portfolio balance theory*.

Interest rates and monetary policy

We have just seen how the interest rate adjusts to clear the money market for a given level of the money stock and a given money demand curve. If the Bank wishes to use monetary policy to exert upward pressure on the GDP, it can do so by increasing the money supply. If it does this, there will initially be an excess supply of money. Holders of this money will demand more bonds, and via the process discussed above this will raise the price of bonds and lower the interest rate. This in turn will induce a rise in all interest-sensitive spending. This is what happens, for example, when the Bank implements the policy of quantitative easing that was introduced in 2009. We discuss this in more detail in Chapter 25.

However, this is not what happens in the normal times that existed before the financial crisis of 2007–8. Rather than setting the quantity of money, the Bank sets the level of the interest rate. When it decides to increase demand in the economy and thus exert upward pressure on GDP, it lowers the interest rate. At this lower interest rate, the public wishes to hold more money as the yield on the alternative asset, bonds, has gone down. So there is excess demand for money. In order to achieve portfolio balance (that is, the desired composition of asset holding), the public tries to sell bonds for money. If the monetary authority did nothing, the sales of bonds would raise the interest rate. However, the monetary authority is setting the interest rate, so in order to maintain that rate it accommodates the public's desire to switch from bonds to money by buying bonds and supplying newly created money. Thus the money supply increases to whatever is demanded at the new interest rate.

Conversely, if the Bank wishes to exert downward pressure on the GDP it seeks to raise interest rates and thus discourage interest-sensitive spending. To do this it may raise the interest rate. The public now wishes to reduce its holdings of money balances, which it does by buying bonds. The Bank sells the bonds to the public, retiring the money it receives from circulation. Or it could reduce the money supply directly and let the market determine a higher interest rate as the public seeks to replenish its holdings of money balances by selling bonds. Figure 19.3 illustrates how all of this works. The really important result is as follows.

The outcome is exactly the same when the Bank fixes interest rates and lets the money supply adjust as it is when it fixes the money supply and lets the interest rate adjust.

It makes no difference to the equilibrium of our macro model which way it is done. However, as discussed in Chapter 25, the different policies of fixing the interest rate or fixing the quantity of money each have different difficulties associated with them, and each will cause the economy to respond differently when it is hit by various exogenous shocks.

In normal times, the central banks in most industrial countries (or currency zones) set the interest rate and let the money stock adjust to demand.

The *LM* curve

We can now use our theory of how the demand for money is related to GDP and the interest rate to develop a new concept called the *LM* curve. In expressing this relation, we choose to express everything in real terms. We do this because we are going to use it in our model of the determination of the GDP, which is expressed in real terms. Thus our equilibrium condition that the demand for money equals its supply is expressed by equation (19.2).

The LM curve shows all of the combinations of GDP and interest rate for which the real *demand for money equals the* real *supply.*

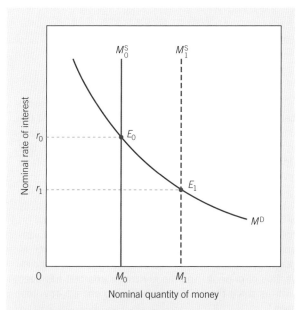

Figure 19.3 Interest rates and money supply changes

An exogenous change in the money supply leads to a change in the equilibrium interest rate while a policy-determined change in the interest rate requires the money supply to change. In the figure the initial money supply is shown by the vertical line M_0^S and the demand for money is shown by the negatively sloped curve M^D. The initial equilibrium is at E_0, with interest rate r_0. If the Bank wishes to lower the interest rate from r_0 to r_1 it has two ways of doing this.

1. It can generate an increase in the money supply, from M_0^S to M_1^S. At the original interest rate of r_0 there is now an excess supply of money of $M_1 - M_0$. The public then seeks to purchase bonds with their excess money balances. This raises the price of bonds and lowers the interest rate. This continues until the rate reaches r_1, at which point the public is willing to hold the increased supply of money.

2. It can lower the interest rate that it sets to r_1. At the initial money supply M_0 and the new interest rate r_1 there is an excess demand for money of $M_1 - M_0$. In order to add to their money balances, the public sells bonds which the Bank purchases with newly created money. This continues until the money supply has been increased to M_1, leaving the market in equilibrium at the new interest rate r_1. In both cases the interest rate falls and the money supply increases.

Alternatively, if we start from an equilibrium at E_1 the Bank can raise the equilibrium interest rate either by lowering the quantity of money to M_0 and letting the market determine the new interest rate of r_0 or by setting the rate at r_0 and selling bonds to the public until the public has reduced its money holdings to M_0.

Figure 19.4 plots the two variables that determine the demand for money—GDP on the horizontal axis and the rate of interest on the vertical axis. Now choose any value of GDP and determine the interest rate that will

equate the demand for money with its supply at that level of GDP. This is plotted as point E_0 in the figure, with GDP Y_0 and interest r_0. Next let GDP increase to Y_1. More money will now be demanded for transactions and precautionary purposes. People and firms will attempt to sell bonds to add to their money balances. But as we have seen, what one person can do, everyone cannot do. Thus this collective effort to turn bonds into money drives down the price of bonds and hence drives up the rate of interest until everyone is content to hold the money and bonds that currently exist. Assume that this occurs at interest rate r_1. This gives us point E_1 in the figure. If we repeat this process for every level of GDP and corresponding interest rate, we will trace out the positively sloped curve labelled *LM* in the figure. The equilibrium condition $D^M = M/P$ is also shown to remind us that the *LM* curve shows all those combinations of Y and r for which the real quantity of money demanded equals its real supply.

Note that this is a new type of figure. It does not just describe the behaviour of those who demand money. Instead, it shows all the combinations of GDP and interest rate that will equate the demand for money with its fixed supply. In technical terms this is locus of equilibrium values for Y and r not a simple behavioural relation.

The LM curve is positively sloped because a rise in GDP increases the quantity of money demanded (transactions *and* precautionary demand) and so must be accompanied by a rise in the interest rate that decreases the quantity of money demanded (speculative demand) by the same amount if equilibrium is to be maintained with total quantity demanded equal to the total supply.

For those who would like to see it, an algebraic derivation of the *LM* curve is given in Box 19.4.

As noted in Figure 19.4, all points above the *LM* curve represent combinations of GDP and interest rate for which the demand for money, D^M, is less than the real supply of money, M/P. This can be seen by starting at any one point on the *LM* curve at which, as with all such points on that curve, the quantity of money demanded equals its supply. Then reduce GDP arbitrarily. This lowers the quantity of money demanded which is now less than the supply.

As also shown in Figure 19.4, all points below the *LM* curve represent combinations of GDP and interest rate for which the quantity of money demanded exceeds it supply. To see this, start once again from any point on the *LM* curve and increase GDP arbitrarily. This increases the quantity of money demanded, which must now exceed its supply.

Box 19.4 The derivation of the *LM* curve

Figure 19.4 shows the graph of the *LM* curve, but it may be helpful to see how this is derived from the underlying behavioural equations, the key one being the demand for money function. Using our present model and assuming that the relations are linear, the monetary sector is expressed by two equations:

$$M = M^S \qquad (1)$$
$$M^D/P = aY - br. \qquad (2)$$

Equation (1) states that the money supply is some fixed value, M^S, determined by the central bank. Equation (2) states that demand for real money balances is positively related to real GDP (transactions and precautionary demand) and negatively to the nominal interest rate (speculative demand). We rearrange equation (2) as follows:

$$M^D = P(aY - br)$$

Setting money demand equal to money supply we get

$$M^S = P(aY - br)$$

and rearranging with *Y* on the left-hand side gives

$$Y = M^S/aP + br/a \qquad (3).$$

This is the *LM* curve, which shows a positive relationship between GDP, *Y*, and the interest rate, *r*. Notice that the intercept with respect to the *Y* axis is M^S/aP so an increase in the nominal money supply shifts the *LM* curve to the right (for a given *P*) and an increase in *P* shifts it to the left for a given M^S.

The slope of the *LM* curve is *b/a* which is the ratio of the interest sensitivity of money demand to the GDP-sensitivity of money demand. Note also that in writing *LM* with *Y* on the left-hand side we are treating it as the dependent variable and should draw it on the vertical axis. However, in reality both *r* and *Y* are endogenous variables and the convention of drawing *Y* on the horizontal axis that has been with us since the 1930s is unlikely to change any time soon.

Stability of monetary equilibrium

Suppose that the variables whose equilibria we are considering, GDP and interest rate in this case, depart from their equilibrium values. If forces exist to push them back towards their equilibrium values, the equilibrium is said to be stable. If forces exist that drive the variables further away, the equilibrium is said to be unstable. Figure 19.5 presents an analysis of the stability of the equilibria represented by the *LM* curve. Above the curve, the demand for money is less than its supply and that will put downward pressure on the interest rate, driving the economy back towards the *LM* curve. In contrast, at all points below the *LM* curve the demand from money exceeds its supply and that puts upward pressure on the interest rate, again driving the economy upwards towards the curve.

Shifts in the *LM* curve

Finally, we ask what can cause the *LM* curve to shift its position. First, anything that changes the relation between the demand for money and either the interest rate or GDP will shift the curve. For example, the growth in the use of credit cards that has occurred over the past half-century has lowered the precautionary demand for money. If this had happened all at once instead of gradually, the restoration of equilibrium would have required a rise in GDP or a lowering of the interest rate to restore the quantity of money demanded to its original amount so that it would once again equal the unchanged money supply. This shifts the *LM* curve downwards and to the right. This is shown as a shift from LM_0 to LM_2 in Figure 19.6.

Secondly, anything that alters the real supply of money will shift the *LM* curve. An increase in the nominal money supply or a fall in the price level will increase the real money supply. There will now be an excess supply of money, and attempts to turn the excess into bonds will

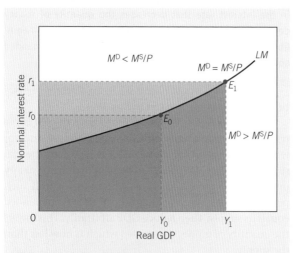

Figure 19.4 The *LM* curve

Everywhere on the *LM* curve the demand for money equals its supply. The *LM* curve is the locus of equilibrium positions where the demand for money M^D is equal to its constant real supply, M^S/P. At all points above and to the left of the curve the demand for money is less than the supply as indicated by $M^D < M^S/P$. At all points below and to the right of the curve the demand for money exceeds its supply as indicated by $M^D > M^S/P$.

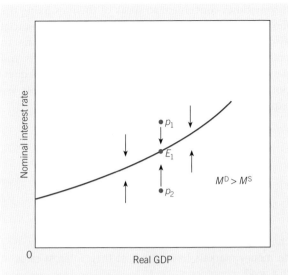

Figure 19.5 Stability of the *LM* equilibrium

Forces exist to push the economy from any point off the *LM* curve to some point on the curve. At any point above the *LM* curve, such as p_1, the demand for money is less than its supply. Attempts to substitute the excess money for bonds will push bond prices up and hence push the interest rate down. This downward pressure on the interest rate is shown by the downward pointing arrows above the curve. At any point below the *LM* curve, such as p_2 the demand for money exceeds its supply. The attempt to substitute bonds for money will lower the price of bonds, which raises the interest rate. This upward pressure on interest rates is shown by the upward pointing arrows below the *LM* curve.

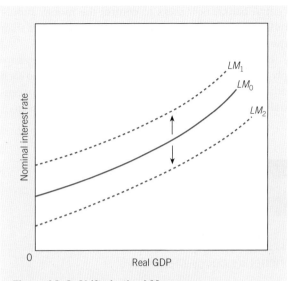

Figure 19.6 Shifts in the *LM* curve

Shifts in the *LM* curve show that at each level of income a new higher or lower interest rate is required to restore equilibrium between the quantity of money demanded and the quantity supplied. The *LM* curve is shifted upwards and to the left from LM_0 to LM_1 by (1) anything that increases the real demand for money, such as a rise in wealth, and (2) anything that reduces the real supply of money, such as a reduction in the nominal money supply, M_S, or an increase in the price level, P. The resulting money shortage implies that at each level of GDP there is a higher equilibrium rate of interest. The *LM* curve is shifted downwards from LM_0 to LM_2 by (1) anything that decreases the real demand for money, such as a fall in wealth, and (2) anything that increases the real supply, such as an increase in the nominal money supply, M_S, or a decrease in the price level, P. The resulting money surplus implies that at each level of GDP there is a lower equilibrium rate of interest.

raise the price of bonds and lower interest rate. So, for any level of GDP, the new equilibrium will require a lower interest rate. This again shifts the *LM* curve downwards and to the right. In contrast, a fall in the nominal quantity of money or a rise in the price level will lower the real money supply and lead to an excess demand for money at the original equilibrium. The attempt to replenish money balances will lead to an attempt to sell bonds, which will lower their price and raise the interest rate. Thus to restore equilibrium at any given level of GDP the interest rate must rise, shifting the *LM* curve upwards and to the left. This is shown as a shift from LM_0 to LM_1 in Figure 19.6.

The central bank and the *LM* curve

We have just seen that changes in the money supply shift the *LM* curve. We saw earlier how the quantity of money is determined by the interaction of the central bank, the banking system, and the non-bank private sector. We also saw two ways in which the central bank could seek to control that quantity. In the UK case the central bank concerned is the Bank of England, referred to here as the Bank. On the one hand, if the Bank fixed the supply of high-powered money, then, for given reserve ratios by the commercial banks, the total money supply would be determined. On the other hand, if it fixed the short-term interest rate through its open-market operations, it could influence the amount of money demanded and thus the amount created by the banking system.

Some time ago there was heated debate among economists as to whether, in pursuit of its monetary policy, the Bank should seek to determine the money supply or the interest rate. In practice, it is much easier for the Bank to set the interest rate than to set the money supply since much of the latter is not under its direct control. It can control the high-powered money supply, which is the base of the total money supply, but it cannot control how the commercial banks will react to a change in this supply. So in practice the Bank of England, and most other major central banks, now seeks to control the money supply indirectly by controlling the rate of interest rather than the supply of high-powered money.

However, as we saw earlier, controlling the money supply and controlling the interest rate are equivalent to each other. Although the Bank of England and most major central banks operate by the latter policy as we have seen, it is sometimes convenient to speak of them as fixing the money supply. So far we have assumed a single financial asset called a 'bond' and hence a single interest rate. In practice, however, there are many different assets and hence many different interest rates. This raises the question of which interest rate the Bank actually controls. We expand on this question in the first case study.

CASE STUDIES

1. Bank rate or bond yield? What do the monetary policy-makers set?

As we have noted in the text, the monetary policy-maker in the United Kingdom is the Bank of England. It started life as a privately owned joint-stock company, but in 1946 it was nationalized. From 1946 to 1997 the Bank had a key role in implementing monetary policy, but the decisions about policy were all taken by the elected government of the day, in the person of the Chancellor of the Exchequer. However, in May 1997 the incoming Labour government decided to delegate the power to set interest rates to the Bank of England with effect from June 1997, and the new arrangements were embodied in the Bank of England Act of 1998. This formally established the Monetary Policy Committee (MPC) and the framework within which it operates. We discuss the make-up of the MPC and its mode of operation further in Chapter 25. For now, what matters is that, as we briefly noted in Chapter 15, the MPC was charged with setting monetary policy in order to hit an inflation target. From 1997 until 2009 the MPC implemented monetary policy by setting a specific interest rate. The interest rate set by the MPC is known as bank rate. This is the rate of interest that the Bank pays on commercial banks' reserve balances at the Bank of England.[9] A chart showing the recent history of bank rate and it predecessors is shown as Figure 25.4 in Chapter 25.

Suppose that the MPC has decided to change bank rate. How does it act in order to make this change stick? In practice it announces the new rate to the media and it appears on Reuters and Bloomberg screens around the City at noon on the announcement day. Banks then change their base rates[10] more or less immediately. Why do money markets have to adjust their interest rates in this way?

The reason is that they know that the Bank of England has changed the interest rate at which it will lend high-powered money to the banks as this rate is set just above bank rate. And they also know that *the Bank of England can force them to borrow from it on a regular basis.* Banks will not wish to lend to their customers at a rate lower than one at which they might have to borrow. So the general level of money market rates is set by the rate at which the central bank will provide base money (cash plus bankers' deposits at the Bank of England in the UK case) to the participants in the money markets.

The Bank of England can force other banks to borrow from it because it is the monopoly supplier of high-powered money and it can conduct security sales (open-market operations) to ensure that the banks are short of cash. Thus, suppose the Bank wishes to raise its official interest rate. It announces that this is the rate at which it will lend to the private banks, and the banks know that they may be forced to borrow from the Bank at this new rate. Very quickly the banks raise the rates at which they will lend to their customers (and borrow and lend between each other, the inter-bank rate). Any subsequent borrowings by the banks from the Bank of England are then at the new higher interest rate. So the Bank of England official interest rate, bank rate, has been passed on into other money market rates.

The interest rate decisions of the MPC are implemented in normal times by the Bank of England fixing the interest rate it pays on commercial banks' operational deposits at the Bank. This determines the interest rate at which the Bank will lend

---

[9] The rate set is a very short-term rate (see next case study) as it is an 'overnight rate'. In effect, this is a one-day rate of interest which is 1/365 times the annual rate. At the time of writing, bank rate is 0.5 per cent per annum, so the interest paid per day on reserve deposits is one 365th of that.

[10] The base rate is an interest rate set by each bank as a reference point for the loan rates charged to customers. For example, a large corporate client may be charged interest at the base rate plus 1 per cent, while a (more risky) smaller business may be charged base rate plus 4 per cent.

high-powered money to commercial banks, and in turn what commercial banks will charge their customers.

Since the 2007–8 financial crisis, times have been far from normal and monetary policy has had to adapt. By March 2009 bank rate had been reduced to 0.5 per cent, and for operational reasons it was considered that it could go no lower. The economy was still in a recession and the MPC wished to stimulate demand further. Therefore it introduced the policy of **quantitative easing (QE)**. This means buying bonds on a massive scale with newly created money. In effect, the Bank wrote a cheque on itself to buy these bonds. The vast majority of the bonds bought were UK government bonds, as the amounts of corporate bonds in existence were small.

Between March 2009 and October 2012 the Bank of England bought £375 billion worth of bonds with newly created money. The effect of this is exactly as represented by a rightward shift of the *LM* curve that we derived earlier. The bond purchases raise the price of bonds and this lowers the yield on existing bonds, so the rate of interest falls for each level of GDP and the *LM* shifts down to the right. Figure 19.7 shows the cumulative size of Bank of England purchases of government bonds.

In this case, the MPC is not actually setting the bond yield but it is undoubtedly affecting it. How this is transmitted through the economy and other effects on the

economy are discussed further in Chapter 25. However, to answer the question posed in this case study title: the MPC still sets bank rate but it has been fixed at 0.5 per cent from March 2009 until at least mid-2014. The policy of QE must have an effect on longer-term interest rates in the form of the yield on government bonds, but these rates are still partly determined in the market. So the MPC influences these rates without actually setting them.

Note that, as we said in Chapter 15, since this ability to set and to carry out monetary policy is placed in different hands in different countries it is simplest to use the generic team 'the Bank' to cover all those who set and carry out monetary policy. We adopt this procedure in this book and refer to the MPC separately from the Bank only when the distinction is relevant, as it is in this case study and in Chapter 25. Thus usually in our coverage:

'the Bank' refers to those who set and carry out monetary policy.

2. The UK yield curve before and after the financial crisis

Box 19.2 gives some information for a few specific UK government bonds. We mentioned the concept of the yield curve in that box. This shows the range of yields on

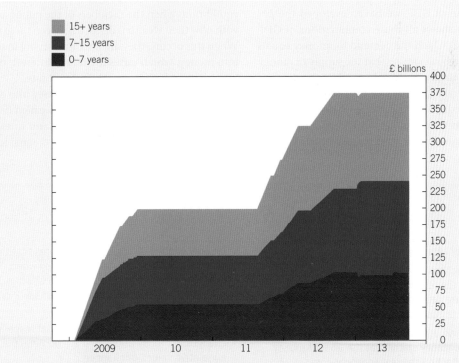

Figure 19.7 **Bank of England bond purchases, 2009–2013, by maturity of bonds purchased**

bonds of different maturities at the same point in time. Figure 19.8 reports the UK yield curve for two different dates: December 2006 and December 2013. The first of these dates was before the 2007–8 financial crisis when policy rates (which are short-term rates) were between 5 and 6 per cent. In 2013, the policy rate had been at 0.5 per cent for over four years, and this explains why short-term rates on government bonds were also low at this point in time. When bank rate is low this influences all other short-term interest rates, particularly those on very safe assets such as government bonds.

While the short end of the government bond yield curve in 2013 was being held down by short-term policy rates, the same could not be said for long rates. However, these have been influenced by quantitative easing. Substantial purchases of bonds by the Bank of England will have raised their price and lowered the yield.

The lesson here is that, while the textbook model has just one specific interest rate in it, the real financial markets are more complex. There are a whole range of different interest rates that apply for different terms to maturity, even for virtually risk-free government bonds. There is an

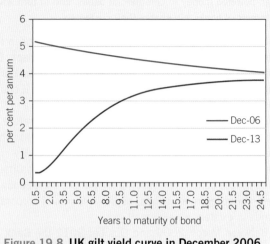

Figure 19.8 UK gilt yield curve in December 2006 and December 2013

even wider range of interest rates on private sector assets as the holders need to be compensated for wide variations in the riskiness of the borrowers.

Conclusion

As the first step in integrating money into our theory of the determination of GDP, we have developed the *LM* curve. This curve shows all those combinations of GDP and interest rate at which the demand for money equals its supply. We start by assuming that the supply of money is determined by the Bank of England while the demand is determined by the public's need for money. This, in turn, is determined by how the public wishes to divide its wealth holdings between money, which satisfies various needs but earns no interest, and bonds, which do earn

interest but cannot act as money. The rate of interest is in equilibrium when the members of the public are content with how their wealth is divided between these two assets. When this occurs, they are no longer trying to turn bonds into money, which raises the rate of interest, nor money into bonds, which lowers the interest rate.

As a second step in integrating money into our theory, we develop in the next chapter the so-called *IS* curve that shows all the combinations of GDP and interest rate at which aggregate desired expenditure is equal to GDP.

SUMMARY

The classical dichotomy and the neutrality of money

■ The classical dichotomy asserts a separation between the real side of the economy, where quantities and relative prices are determined, and the monetary side, where absolute prices are determined .

■ In its mildest, and uncontroversial, version the theory of the neutrality of money states that the *level* of money prices has no effect on the real economy.

■ An only slightly stronger version states that the economy will behave in the same way when the price level is constant over time or when it is rising at a modest annual rate of say 2 or 3 per cent.

■ Money illusion refers to behaviour that responds to changes in money prices that are nominal but that leave all relative values unchanged.

Stocks and flows

- All spending variables are flows (so much per period of time), while money and other financial assets are stocks that do not require a time dimension to give them meaning.

Money and bonds

- The liquidity of an asset refers both to any uncertainty about how much money can be obtained by selling it and to how easy it is to make a sale.

- Money is perfectly liquid on both counts since it requires no transaction to turn it into itself!

- To simplify things at the outset, we assume that all wealth can be held in only two kinds of financial assets: money, which is perfectly liquid but earns no interest, and bonds, which are less liquid but earn an interest return.

The rate of interest and the price of bonds

- The present value (PV) of any asset is the value now of the future payment or payments to which ownership of the asset gives a claim.

- The present value of any asset that yields a given stream of money over time is negatively related to the current market interest rate.

- In a free market the equilibrium price of any asset is the present value of the stream of money that it produces.

- Thus the market price of bonds and the rate of interest are negatively related to each other.

The real and the nominal interest rate

- The nominal or money rate of interest expresses the money return on an asset.

- The real rate of interest expresses the return on any asset in terms of the purchasing power of that return

- The real rate of interest is approximately the nominal rate *minus* the expected inflation rate.

The supply of money

- The money supply as measured by M4 is a nominal amount measured in monetary units.

- The real money supply measures money in purchasing power units: the nominal quantity *divided by* the price level.

- We consider two cases: (1) the nominal money supply is set by the makers of monetary policy, and (2) the monetary policy-makers set the interest rate and let the money supply be whatever is demanded at that interest rate.

The demand for money

- The amount of wealth that everyone wishes to hold in the form of money balances is called the demand for money.

- Since the supply of money and bonds is fixed at any one time, attempts by the public to alter the proportion of their total wealth held in these assets (more money and fewer bonds or more bonds and less money) causes the price of bonds and hence the interest rate to change until the public is willing to hold these two assets in the proportion in which they exist.

- The real demand for money (or the demand for real money balances) is the nominal quantity demanded divided by the price level.

- Money demand depends on the nominal (not the real) rate of interest

- Although holding money carries an opportunity cost (the interest that could be earned by holding bonds instead), money is held for three main reasons: (1) the transactions motive and (2) the precautionary motive, both of which are related to the GDP, and (3) the speculative motive, which is related to the interest rate.

- Because the real demand for money balances is independent of the price level, the nominal demand varies in direct proportion to the price level.

- The demand for money function relates money demand to the rate of interest, all other influences being held constant.

Monetary equilibrium

- Monetary equilibrium occurs when the demand for money equals the supply of money, which also implies that the demand for bonds equals their supply.

Interest rates and monetary policy

- If the Bank wishes to use monetary policy to exert an upward pressure on GDP, it can increase the money supply which lowers the interest rate and increases interest-sensitive spending.

- In normal times, the central banks in most industrial countries that wish to put upward pressure on GDP, lower the interest rate directly and then provide all the money that is demanded at that rate.

The *LM* curve

- The *LM* curve shows all of the combinations of GDP and interest rate for which the real demand for money equals the real supply.

- The *LM* curve does not just describe the behaviour of those who demand or supply money. Instead, it is the locus of equilibrium values for Y and r.

- The *LM* curve is positively sloped because a rise in GDP increases the quantity of money demanded, so that the interest rate must rise sufficiently to decrease demand to equal the unchanged total supply.

- The *LM* curve is shifted to the right by (1) by a reduction in the amount of money demanded at each

level of GDP or at each interest rate, or (2) an increase in the nominal money supply or a fall in the price level, both of which increase the real money supply. The opposite changes shift the curve to the left.

TOPICS FOR REVIEW

- The classical dichotomy
- Theories of the neutrality of money
- Money illusion
- Stocks and flows
- Various forms in which wealth can be held in reality and in the present model
- The present value of a financial asset
- The relation between the price of a financial asset and its present value.

- The relation between the interest rate and the price of bonds
- The real and the nominal interest rate
- The real and nominal supply of money
- The real and nominal demand for money
- Monetary equilibrium
- The *LM* curve: definition, slope, and shifts

QUESTIONS

1 Suppose a bond is issued that is a perpetuity, which pays £5 per year and is issued for £100. What will this bond be worth if the current interest rate is a) 2 per cent, b) 10 per cent, and c) 20 per cent?

2 At an interest rate of 5 per cent, what is the present value of £1,000 in a) one year's time, b) five years' time, and c) ten years' time?

3 Describe the sequence of events following a large purchase of bonds by the central bank.

4 Describe the sequence of events that would follow if an increase in political uncertainty led households and firms to wish to increase their stocks of money balances held for precautionary purposes.

5 Assume that there is a large cyclical increase in the GDP. What would be the effects on the interest rate and the GDP if the bank decided to hold the money supply constant? What would be the effects on the

GDP and the money supply if the Bank decided to hold the interest rate constant?

6 What is the neutrality of money? Does it mean that monetary policy can have no real effects?

7 What is the classical dichotomy? Is it the same as neutrality of money?

8 Which of the following are stocks and which flows: a) UK imports, b) London restaurant receipts, c) the UK official foreign exchange reserves, d) the government budget deficit, and e) the national debt?

9 What is money illusion? Give an example. Do you think that it exists in economic decision-making?

10 What happens to the *LM* curve when a) real GDP rises due to some exogenous increase in final demand, b) the Bank increases the money supply, and c) the Bank lowers the money supply?

CHAPTER 20

INVESTMENT, THE INTEREST RATE, AND GDP: THE *IS–LM* MODEL

We have seen how the nominal rate of interest adjusts to produce asset equilibrium, which means that all households and firms are holding the quantities of money and bonds that they wish to hold, given their income, wealth, and the current yield on bonds. We now come to the critical link between the financial asset markets and real spending: not only does the nominal rate of interest influence people's portfolio-balance decisions—that is, their demands for money and bonds—but also the real interest rate affects aggregate spending through its impact on investment. Since we are assuming a constant price level until the next chapter, the real and nominal rates are the same.

To understand the link between real GDP and spending on the one hand, and money and bonds on the other, we need to expand our model of the determination of GDP that we developed in Chapters 16 and 17. Up to now we have treated investment as an exogenous constant. In this chapter we make that important component of aggregate spending endogenous.

In this chapter you will learn that:

- Investment can affect the level of potential GDP, but we ignore this supply-side effect in the short-run analysis, and focus on the demand effects.
- Investment in our model is negatively related to the real rate of interest.
- The *IS* curve plots the combinations of the interest rate and real GDP for which desired spending equals actual output or, equivalently, for which injections equal withdrawals.
- When the price level is fixed and the economy has excess capacity, equilibrium in the *IS–LM* model, which is where the *IS* and *LM* curves intersect, shows the combination of interest rate and real GDP for which there is equilibrium in the money market (*LM*) and in the output–spending relationship (*IS*).
- A positive demand shock in the form of an increase in any component of exogenous spending shifts the *IS* curve to the right, raising GDP and the interest rate, while a negative demand shock does the reverse.
- In a process called the monetary transmission mechanism, an increase in the nominal money stock shifts the *LM* curve to the right, raising equilibrium GDP and lowering the interest rate, while a reduction in the nominal money stock shifts the *LM* to the left, lowering equilibrium GDP and raising the interest rate.

In short, we are now extending our model of the determination of GDP by combining the determinants of final spending ($C + I + G + NX$) with the determinants of the demand and supply of money. Throughout this chapter we continue to hold the price level constant. Then in the following chapter we add a supply side to our model economy, which allows us to make the price level endogenous. In this chapter we start by taking a brief look at the effect of investment on both the demand and supply sides of the economy.

Investment in the economy

Recall from Chapter 16 that investment is composed of purchases of capital equipment, a build-up of inventories, and new housing construction. Recall also that our theory of GDP determination is a short-run theory. It takes the economy's technology, supplies of factors of production, and hence potential GDP, Y^*, all as given. In these circumstances fluctuations in aggregate desired spending determine the degree to which resources are utilized and hence, also, the size of GDP and the GDP gap. A rise in any type of investment spending increases aggregate spending and this raises GDP, and so reduces any GDP gap (assuming, as we have done so far, that the economy starts with excess capacity). In the long run, investment increases the capital stock, and thus it also raises potential GDP. Investment sometimes embodies existing technologies and

sometimes those new technologies that are a major driving force of long-term growth.

In the long run, investment increases the capital stock and hence the size of potential GDP. In the short run, changes in investment affect aggregate spending and hence the employment of existing resources and thus the size of the GDP gap.

The effect of investment on growth of potential GDP will be discussed in a later chapter. In the meantime, we continue to study investment as a major component of aggregate spending. Box 20.1 sets out some comments on business investment by one of the United Kingdom's current monetary policy-makers, and we expand further on the issue of explaining UK investment in the first case study at the end of this chapter.

Box 20.1 Some views from a policy-maker on UK business investment

UK business investment was extremely weak in the years after the 2007–8 financial crisis and the subsequent recession. This weakness lasted until at least 2013. We discuss this further in the first case study at the end of this chapter. The following is an extract from a speech made in January 2014 by UK Monetary Policy Committee member Ian McCafferty.

What exactly does business investment encompass? Over the past thirty years, we have seen a wholesale restructuring of the UK economy, away from manufacturing towards service activities, and this significantly changes the way we need to think about business investment and its contribution to the economy.

According to the Office for National Statistics (ONS), business investment accounts for about eight percent of GDP and consists of spending on machinery and plant, transport equipment, commercial property and software. Yet it is important to recognise that other types of spending, which you and I might think of as business investment in a modern economy, are not treated as such in the national accounts. For example, spending by companies on business services, such as advertising, falls under the category of intermediate consumption, and the contribution of such spending to final demand (what is captured in GDP) primarily shows up as household consumption and exports rather than investment. Some consulting services appear as investment, but others are recorded as final consumption. And spending on Research and Development (R&D) has been treated as intermediate consumption in the national accounts, rather than as

business investment. So it is welcome news that in the next Blue Book, to be published later this year (2014), the ONS will for the first time record R&D as investment spending, allowing it to contribute directly to GDP. It is also worth pointing out that spending on intangible assets, an increasingly important part of companies' capital expenditure which is included in the official definition of business investment, is believed to be under recorded in the national accounts.

Even after setting aside these measurement issues, business investment remains one of the most difficult output components to analyse and forecast. Ten years at the Confederation of British Industry taught me that investment models based on profit maximisation and the cost of capital only explain a small part of investment dynamics. Of course investment decisions will be affected by expected profits, marginal tax rates, the relative price of investment goods, the cost (and availability) of external funding, and internal funds. But I believe that neoclassical-type models miss an important factor, which has played a substantial role in driving the current investment cycle—uncertainty. Changes in uncertainty and 'animal spirits' are a critical determinant of how businesses themselves think and behave, and, more importantly, provide a better understanding of the likely outlook for investment.

(*Source:*<http://www.bankofengland.co.uk/publications/Documents/speeches/2014/speech703.pdf>)

Intangible assets, mentioned in this extract, include things like brands (discussed in Chapter 11), inventions, patents, designs, and other intellectual property such as manuscripts, art works and recorded music.

The financing of investment

To see the effects of making investment endogenous, we must now look at how it is financed. There are two ultimate sources of funds for this. These are domestic savings in the form of (1) firms' retained profits and households' savings, and (2) borrowing of savings that have been made abroad. Both domestic and overseas savings may be channelled into investment directly via the purchase of shares or bonds issued by firms, or indirectly via financial intermediaries such as banks who borrow the savings from the private sector and make loans to firms to fund their investments.

The determinants of investment

The expectation of profits provides the basic motive determining the investment decisions of private sector firms. Firms will buy new plant and equipment if they expect the investment to add value to the firm. (This is equivalent to saying that the present value of the extra revenue generated by the investment must be greater than the present value of the extra costs incurred, as we explained in Chapter 11.) The factors that affect expected profitability determine the amount of planned investment spending in the economy as a whole. We first list them, and then discuss how each influences investment decisions:

- the price and the productivity of capital goods;

- expectations about the future demand for the output to be produced by the capital goods, and about the costs of producing that output;

- the development of new techniques of production and of new products;

- profits previously earned by firms and available for reinvestment;

- the real rate of interest.

The price and productivity of capital goods

The price and the productivity of capital equipment influence the profitability of investing in that equipment. Anything that reduces the price of capital goods will make investment more profitable. For example, if the price of a machine falls from £10,000 to £8,000, the machine is more likely to yield a profit, other things being equal.

Also, any new invention that makes capital equipment more productive will make investment more attractive. For example, if the machine that costs £10,000 can be made to produce a larger output, the income that can be earned by operating it will rise.

Expectations of the future

Expectations of future demand conditions and future cost conditions exert a strong effect on current investment decisions. Expected demand conditions matter because the profitability of any investment depends on being able to sell the future output of the capital goods at favourable prices. Expected cost conditions also matter because the expected profits that motivate investment depend on market prices for output and the costs of producing that output. When a machine is bought now, the cost of the machine is known now. But the cost of the labour that will operate the machine and the cost of the materials that will be used over the lifetime of the machine depend on prices that will rule in the future. If firms have favourable expectations about the future prices of their products and the costs of their inputs, they will be inclined to invest more in new capital equipment than if they have unfavourable expectations about future prices.

On occasion, these expectations about the future can change dramatically and suddenly as a result of what Keynes called the 'animal spirits' of business-people. A sudden swing from pessimism to optimism about the future can lead to a large increase in planned investment spending, while the opposite swing from optimism to pessimism can lead to a drastic curtailment or postponement of investment plans.

Innovations

The economy changes constantly as new inventions are put into commercial use in a procedure that is called *innovation*. Process innovations—new ways of producing old products—are usually embodied in new equipment, which means new investment. Product innovations, creating the capacity to produce new products, require investment spending either to modify existing equipment or to create wholly new equipment.

Profits

Some investment is financed by borrowed funds, but much is financed by the firm's own revenues. Significant amounts of the profits earned on past sales are retained by firms to be reinvested in new capital equipment instead of being paid out to their owners as dividends. Thus, one determinant of investment spending is current profits. Higher profits provide a larger flow of funds available for reinvestment.

The rate of interest

We have seen that the demand for money depends on the nominal rate of interest. In contrast, desired investment spending depends on the real rate of interest. To see this, compare two situations in which a person is considering investing £100 for one year. In the first situation the price level is expected to remain unchanged over the year and the interest rate he is offered is 3 per cent. At the end of the year he will have £103, 3 per cent more purchasing power that he had at the beginning of the year. In the second situation the price level is expect to rise by 5 per cent over the year and he is offered a nominal interest rate of just over 8 per cent. At the end of the year he will also have 3 per cent more purchasing power than he had at the beginning of the year. Since both situations have the same real interest rate and thus the same real outcome, we would expect him to react in the same way to both. We would not expect a rational investor to decide not to invest in the first because the nominal interest rate was so low, while deciding to invest in the second because the nominal interest rate was so high. In general then:

Desired investment spending depends on the real not the nominal interest rate.

This rate exerts an influence on all three of the major components of investment spending that we mentioned above: capital equipment, inventories, and new housing.

The rate of interest paid by different firms is not always the same, as some firms are considered riskier than others and this means that they cannot all borrow at the same interest rates as governments (which have powers of taxation) can borrow. This means that the cost of capital to firms may be higher than the market yield on government bonds.[1] However, in macroeconomics we assume that there is a constant margin between the market interest rate and the cost of capital, and so these all move together. Thus, when we talk about the interest rate rising or falling in this context, we mean that the whole range of borrowing costs available to firms is rising or falling in more or less the same way

Capital equipment

The real rate of interest measures the opportunity cost of capital to the firm. If the firm borrows to spend on investment, it must pay interest to its creditors. If the firm uses its own funds, it must forgo the revenue that it could have obtained by lending those funds to others. The lower is the rate of interest, the lower is the cost of capital, and so the more new investment firms will tend to make. To see this, consider a simple example. Let there be four investment opportunities for new capital equipment, each involving spending £10,000 now and obtaining a single sum one year hence. The most profitable pays £12,000, the next £11,500, the next £11,000, and the least profitable only £10,500. At interest rates in excess of 20 per cent, none of these four will be profitable. At rates between 15 and 20 per cent, only the first will be profitable. For example, if the rate were 17 per cent, then the £10,000 could be borrowed at a cost of £1,700. In a year's time the

investment would yield £12,000, allowing a profit of £300 after repaying the £10,000 borrowed and paying interest of £1,700. At rates between 10 and 15 per cent, the two best opportunities will be profitable. A rate below 10 per cent makes the third one profitable, while any rate below 5 per cent makes even the fourth opportunity profitable. Thus, as the rate of interest falls, first one, then two, then three, then all four opportunities become profitable. As this happens, desired investment spending rises from £10,000 to £20,000 to £30,000 to £40,000.

Other things being equal, the lower is the rate of interest, the greater the number of investment opportunities that will be profitable and therefore the greater the investment spending that firms will wish to undertake.

Inventories

The opportunity cost of holding inventories (also known as *stocks*) of finished goods or raw materials is what the firm could earn by selling the inventories and investing their value in something else. A measure of this is the interest rate, since the firm could certainly lend out its funds and earn the market rate of interest. Thus, a rise in the rate of interest raises the cost of holding inventories. This induces firms to reduce their inventories until the present value to the firm of holding the inventories is just equal to the present value of the costs incurred. Thus the desired holding of inventories tends to be negatively related to the rate of interest.

Note, however, that the flow of investment spending on inventories occurs when the size of the stock is being changed. If inventories are being added to, the addition is current investment; if inventories are being reduced, the amount of the reduction is disinvestment.

A fall in the rate of interest leads to a temporary spurt of inventory investment while the inventories are being increased; a rise in the rate of interest leads to a temporary spurt of inventory disinvestment while the inventories are being decreased.

New housing construction

Interest payments are a large part of total mortgage payments. At an interest rate of 8 per cent, about half of the repayments on a 20-year mortgage is interest, and only half is for repayment of the principal sum borrowed. Because interest is such a large part of the total payments on a mortgage, small changes in the rate of interest cause relatively large changes in annual mortgage payments. For instance, a rise in the rate of interest by two percentage points from 8 to 10 per cent increases the monthly payments on a 20-year mortgage by over 15 per cent (from £8.37 to £9.66 per thousand pounds borrowed). Therefore changes in interest rates can have large effects on the demand for new housing. They also have significant effects on demand for

---

[1] See the discussion in Chapter 11.

old houses, but only new housing production is part of GDP, so this is what is relevant for aggregate investment. Transfers of ownership of existing houses do not affect GDP as they are not part of current production.

A fall in the rate of interest will lead to a rise in investment in building new housing. A rise in interest rates will reduce the demand for building new housing.

Therefore it is not surprising that most econometric studies show a significant negative relation between the rate of interest and total investment spending.

The investment demand function

In what follows, we isolate the relation between investment and the rate of interest by assuming that all the other influences are held constant. This relation is called the investment demand function: it relates the quantity of desired investment spending to the cost of capital, as proxied by the real interest rate. It is negatively sloped, as shown in Figure 20.1. A rise in the interest rate leads to a fall in investment, while a fall in the interest rate leads to a rise in investment. The investment demand curve shifts to the right if any of the influences being held constant change to improve investment prospects—for example, if firms become more optimistic that demand will increase

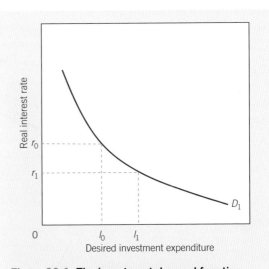

Figure 20.1 The investment demand function

Curve D_i **shows the relation between desired investment spending and the real interest rate, with all of other influences held constant.** When the real interest rate is r_0, desired investment spending is I_0; when the interest rate falls to r_1 desired investment rises to I_1.

in the future. However, if they become more pessimistic (or other factors look adverse for investment prospects), the investment demand curve shifts to the left.

The *IS* curve

Making investment endogenous

We are now ready to drop the assumption used in our models so far that investment is an exogenous constant. We now make it endogenous, something that is determined within the model. To do this, we recall from Chapter 17 that the aggregate spending function in our basic model was

$$AE = C + I + G + NX. \qquad (20.1)$$

where consumption, C, and net exports, NX, varied with GDP and I was an exogenously determined constant as was government spending, G. Equilibrium occurred when aggregate desired spending, AE, equalled actual output, Y:

$$AE = Y. \qquad (20.2)$$

We now wish to derive a new relationship called the *IS* curve.

The *IS* curve shows all those combinations of GDP and interest rate for which aggregate desired spending equals actual output.

The reason that the curve was originally called the *IS* curve is that in a closed economy with no government it represents the combinations of GDP and the interest rate for which investment and saving are equal. More generally it is the combination of GDP and the interest rate for which the sum of all injections equals the sum of all leakages, or, alternatively, the sum of all elements of desired spending equal actual total output, which gives the same result.

The geometrical derivation of this curve is shown in Figure 20.2. An alternative algebraic derivation for those who would like to study it is given in Box 20.2, which can be ignored by those who do not find algebra helpful.

The intuition of the *IS* curve can be expressed as follows. Start with any level of GDP, say Y_0, and assume for simplicity that G and NX are zero. If the interest rate is raised high enough (say 2 million per cent!) investment will be eliminated. Equilibrium will then be where the consumption function cuts the 45° line, since investment is zero. Now lower the interest rate until there is some positive investment spending. Say at 100 per cent rate of interest there is some significant but small amount of

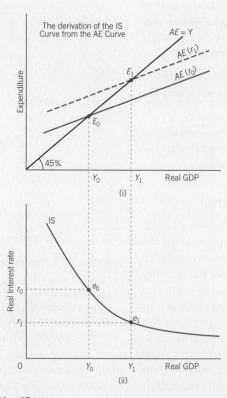

Figure 20.2 The derivation of the *IS* curve

The *IS* curve plots combinations of GDP and the interest rate that yield equilibrium between desired spending and actual output. The two parts of the diagram plot GDP on their horizontal axes and so can be related to each other. The type of equilibrium analysed in Chapter 16 is shown as E_0 in part (i) of the figure. It occurs where the 45° line labelled $AE = Y$, which graphs the equilibrium condition that desired spending equals actual GDP, intersects the solid line labelled $AE(r_0)$. This latter line shows how desired spending varies as GDP varies with investment held constant at the amount determined by the interest rate r_0. The equilibrium GDP of Y_0 can now be plotted in part (ii) of the figure, which has GDP on the horizontal axis and the interest rate on the vertical axis. The point e_0 in the figure plots GDP Y_0 against the interest rate r_0. If we now let the interest rate fall to r_1, the AE curve in part (i) shifts upwards to $AE(r_1)$ taking GDP to Y_1. Plotting the GDP of Y_1 against interest rate r_1 in part (ii) of the figure yields a second point, e_1. Repeating this procedure for every possible interest rate traces out the negatively sloped curve in part (ii), which is the called the *IS* curve.

Box 20.2 **Algebraic derivation of the *IS* curve**

In our model, consumption is positively associated with GDP while investment is negatively associated with the real interest rate. For simplicity we omit government spending and net exports. If we assume that all relationships are linear, these can be expressed in following equation:

$$AE = d + cY - fr \qquad (1)$$

The parameter d is the positive constant on the consumption function, c is the propensity to consume and hence is a positive fraction, $0 < c < 1$, and f is a positive parameter relating the interest rate and desired investment spending, and since that relationship is negative, f appears with a minus sign. The equilibrium condition that desired aggregate spending equals actual output is expressed as

$$AE = Y. \qquad (2)$$

Substituting (1) into (2) gives

$$d + cY - fr = Y$$

Rearranging gives

$$Y - cY = d - fr$$

Factoring out the Y and dividing through by $(1 - c)$ *gives*

$$Y = d/(1 - c) - f/(1-c)r$$

which is the equation of the *IS* curve in linear form. The constant $d/(1 - c)$ is a positive shift parameter, changes in which shift the entire curve. The slope of the curve is given by the sign of the constant attached to r. Since in that constant, $1 - c$, is positive when f is positive but has a minus sign in front of it, the whole constant has a negative value. Hence, the *IS* curve is negatively sloped.

investment. This will shift the *AE* function upwards and lead to a new higher level of GDP. Plot this point on a graph with GDP on the horizontal axis and the interest rate on the vertical axis to give one point on the new *IS* curve. Now cut the interest rate again, say to 50 per cent this time. Plotting this new level of GDP against the new interest rate in our figure will yield a second point on the *IS* curve. If we go through all possible interest rates and the corresponding equilibrium levels of GDP, we can trace out the whole *IS* curve, each point on which gives the level of GDP and a corresponding interest rate (and hence volume of investment spending) that will yield equilibrium with desired total spending equal to actual GDP. The curve is negatively sloped because lower interest rates are associated with higher equilibrium levels of GDP, and vice versa.

Note that this is the second case of a new type of figure—the *LM* curve was the first. It does not just describe directly the behaviour of those who wish to spend on the nation's output. Instead, it shows all the combinations of GDP and interest rate that will equate the desired level of spending to actual output. In technical terms this is a locus of equilibrium values for *Y* and *r*, not a simple behavioural relation.

The *IS* curve is negatively sloped because a fall in the interest rate increases investment spending and hence increases equilibrium GDP.

We call the points on the *IS* curve points of *spending equilibrium* to distinguish them from points on the *LM* curve, which we have called points of *monetary equilibrium*.

Stability and shifts

An equilibrium is stable if forces exist to restore that equilibrium if it is disturbed. The stability of *IS* equilibria is shown in Figure 20.3. At all levels of GDP to the left of the curve desired spending is less than actual output. This excess of demand over existing output will put pressure on output to rise, as shown in the figure by the arrow pointing towards the curve from all points to its left. At all levels of GDP to the right of the curve, desired spending is less than output. This deficiency of demand for the nation's output will put pressure on GDP to fall, which shown by the arrows pointing back towards the curve from all points to the right of it.

Shifts in the *IS* curve are shown in Figure 20.4. The cause of a rightward shift of the *IS* curve is any increase in an exogenous spending variable, such as government spending or exports or a fall in tax rates. It is also caused by any *shift* in the consumption function such as would be caused by an increase in household wealth. This could occur when there was a rise in the price of assets owned by households, such as houses and company shares. Such shifts were discussed in Chapter 16 and occurred in practice when there was a large rise in house prices leading up to the crash of 2008. When the *IS* curve is shifted to the

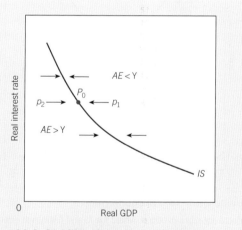

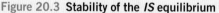

Figure 20.3 Stability of the *IS* equilibrium

When the economy is at any point off the *IS* curve, forces push it back towards the curve. At all points to the left of the *IS* curve, aggregate desired spending is greater than current GDP (*AE* > *Y*), while for all points to the right of the curve aggregate desired spending is less than GDP (*AE*<*Y*). Now, starting from point p_0 on the *IS* curve, lower GDP to take the economy to point p_2. Since aggregate desired spending is now greater than GDP, GDP will rise as shown by the arrows pointing towards the curve from the left. Next raise GDP to point p_1. Aggregate desired spending is now less than GDP, so GDP will fall, pushing the economy back towards the IS curve as shown by the arrows pointing towards the curve from the right.

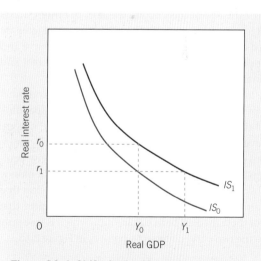

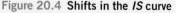

Figure 20.4 Shifts in the *IS* curve

A rise in autonomous spending shifts the *IS* curve to the right. An increase in autonomous spending shifts the *IS* curve to the right, from IS_0 to IS_1. Now any given interest rate will be associated with a higher level of equilibrium GDP, as is r_1 with Y_1 instead of Y_0. Any given GDP will be associated with a higher equilibrium interest rate, as is Y_0 with r_0 instead of r_1. A fall in autonomous spending has the opposite effect, as can be seen by shifting the curve from IS_1 to IS_0.

right, this indicates that a higher level of GDP is associated with any given interest rate. A fall in any of these sources of spending will shift the *IS* curve to the left.

It is important to note that the change in GDP caused by the rightward shift in the *IS* curve when an exogenous spending component rises is equal to that given by the multiplier times the change in exogenous spending, just as we found in the analysis in Chapter 16. When we compare the points on the two curves at the same interest rate, as with Y_0 and Y_1 in Figure 20.4, we are looking at the change in GDP (when investment is held constant as it was in Chapters 16 and 17) after there has been a change in some component of exogenous spending, such as government spending or exports.

The *IS–LM* model

We are now ready to combine the two curves *IS*, which we have developed in this chapter, and *LM*, which we developed in Chapter 19, and use them to develop a theory of the determination of the GDP and the interest rate. This theory is an extension of the one we developed in Chapters 16 and 17 in that it changes the interest rate and desired investment spending from being exogenous (determined outside the model as they were in Chapters 16 and 17) to being endogenous (determined within the new model).

IS–LM equilibrium

Figure 20.5 plots the *IS* and the *LM* curves on the same diagram. Because the price level is constant, the real and nominal interest rates are the same. This allows us to plot the *IS* and *LM* curves on the same chart, even though *IS* depends on the real rate of interest and *LM* on the money rate. For the rest of this chapter we label the interest axis as just 'interest rate', since both real and nominal rates are plotted on the same figure, nominal for the *LM* curve and real for the *IS* curve, but as there is no inflation real and nominal interest rates are identical.

We have seen that the *IS* curve plots all those combinations of GDP and the real interest rate that give spending equilibrium where desired spending equals actual output. We have also seen that the *LM* curve plots all those combinations of GDP and the nominal interest rate that give equilibrium in the asset market because the demand for money (and hence for bonds) equals the supply. It is now clear that equilibrium of the macroeconomic system requires that both of these markets be in equilibrium, which is true only where the two curves intersect—point e_0 in Figure 20.5.

Stability of *IS–LM*

The arrows in the figure show the stability of the *IS-LM* equilibrium. The curves in the figure divide the space into four parts. If we combine what we saw in Figures 20.3 and 19.3, we obtain the inequalities shown in Figure 20.5. If this figure looks complicated, return to Figures 20.3 and 19.3, make sure you understand each, and then plot the arrows from each

onto a fresh figure starting with only the *IS* and *LM* curves. You will then have constructed Figure 20.5 for yourself.

In each of the four spaces there is disequilibrium in both the spending and the asset markets. In part (1) both the interest rate and GDP exceed their full equilibrium values because the points in that space lie above both curves. People will seek to substitute money for bonds, which puts upward pressure on the price of bonds and hence downward pressure on interest rate. People will not be willing to buy all the output that is produced, which puts downward

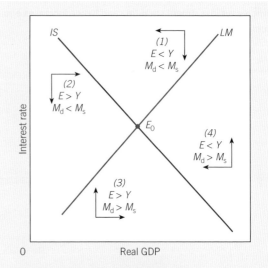

Figure 20.5 *IS–LM* equilibrium

Macro equilibrium occurs where the *IS* and *LM* curves intersect, indicating that both the goods and the money market are in equilibrium. The intersection of the *IS* and *LM* curves produces equilibrium at E_0 and divides the diagram into four parts. In part (1) both GDP and the interest rate exceed their full equilibrium values so there is downward pressure on the interest rate and GDP as shown by the arrows. In part (3), both GDP and the interest rate are below their equilibrium values so there is upward pressure on both to rise as shown by the arrows. In part (2), GDP is below while the interest rate is above their equilibrium values. This puts pressure on GDP to rise and interest rate to fall as shown by the arrows. Finally, in part (4), GDP is above and interest rate is below their equilibrium values, putting pressure on GDP to fall and interest rates to rise, as shown by the arrows.

pressure on GDP. These pressures are shown by the arrows in part (1). In part (3), both the interest rate and GDP are below their full equilibrium values because points in this space lie below both curves. People will seek to substitute bonds for money, which puts downward pressure on the price of bonds and upward pressure on the interest rate. People will want to purchase more than is being produced, which puts pressure on output to increase. These pressures are shown by the arrows in that section. In part (2) the interest rate is above its equilibrium value (all points lie above the *LM* curve) while GDP is below its equilibrium value (all points lie below the *IS* curve). When people seek to substitute money for bonds, this puts upward pressure on the price of bonds and hence downward pressure on the interest rate. People will seek to buy more output than is being produced, which puts upward pressure on GDP. This is shown by the arrows in part (2). Finally, in part (4) the interest rate is below and GDP is above their equilibrium values (all points lie below the *LM* curve and above the *IS* curve). The attempt to substitute bonds for money puts downward pressure on the price of bonds and hence upward pressure on the interest rates. People will want to buy less than is being produced, which puts downward pressure on GDP. This is shown by the arrows in section (4).

Shifts in the *IS* and *LM* curves

We saw earlier in this chapter that changes in any component of exogenous spending shift the *IS* curve (see Figure 20.4), while we saw in Chapter 19 that any change in the real money supply shifts the *LM* curve (see Figure 19.4). The effects on GDP and the interest rate of each of these shifts are shown in Figures 20.6 and 20.7. Several conclusions follow from the analysis in these figures, the first of which is:

An increase in autonomous spending shifts the *IS* curve to the right and raises the equilibrium values of both GDP and the interest rate. A decrease does the reverse.

We know from our earlier chapters that an increase in any autonomous spending flow increases equilibrium GDP. We now also know that it increases the interest rate. The reason is that an increase in GDP increases the amount of money that people wish to hold for transactions and precautionary purposes. In an attempt to add to their money holdings, people seek to sell bonds. But if the stocks of money and bonds are fixed, as they are at any moment in time, all they succeed in doing is forcing up the interest rate until they are satisfied with their existing stocks. The rise in the amount of money demanded that

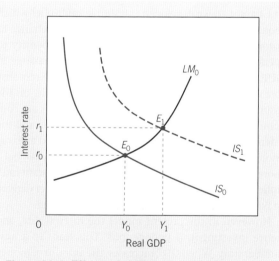

Figure 20.6 Effects of shifts in the *IS* curve

A rightward shift in the *IS* curve raises the equilibrium values of both GDP and the interest rate. The initial curves are IS_0 and LM_0, yielding equilibrium at E_0, with values of Y_0 and r_0 for GDP and the interest rate. An increase in autonomous spending now shifts the *IS* curve to IS_1. At the original equilibrium values, there is now an excess of desired spending over actual GDP. This causes GDP to rise. This increases the quantity of money demanded, and the attempt to sell bonds to replenish money balances forces down the price of bonds which implies a rise in the interest rate. At the new equilibrium, E_1, the values for GDP and interest rate are Y_1 and r_1. A reduction in autonomous spending reverses the process.

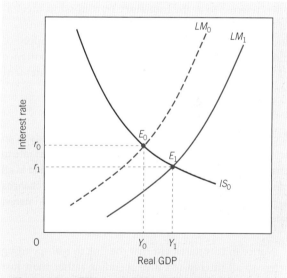

Figure 20.7 Effects of shifts in the *LM* curve

A rightward shift in the *LM* curve increases GDP and deceases the interest rate. An increase in the real money supply or a fall in money demand shifts the *LM* curve from LM_0 to LM_1. At the original equilibrium values of Y_0 and r_0, there is now an excess supply of money. In an effort to turn the extra money balances into bonds, the price of bonds is bid up which mean a fall in the rate of interest. The new equilibrium is at E_1, with GDP Y_1 and interest rate r_1. A reduction in the real money supply, or a rise in money demand, is analysed by letting the *LM* curve shift from LM_1 to LM_0, thus reversing the process.

is caused by the increase in GDP is just balanced by the decrease in the amount of money demanded that is caused by the rise in the interest rates.

The second main result is:

An increase in the real money supply or a reduction in real money demand shifts the *LM* curve rightwards, lowering the equilibrium interest rate while raising equilibrium GDP. A decrease in real money supply or an increase in real money demand does the reverse.

Do not forget that the real money supply can be changed by a change in either the nominal money supply, *M*, or the price level, *P*. For the moment, we concentrate on changes in the nominal money supply with the price level constant. When that money supply is increased, people find themselves with more money than they wish to hold at the given level of GDP and interest rate. They seek to buy bonds with their surplus funds. This forces the price of bonds up, which is the same thing as a fall in the rate of interest. The fall in the interest rate leads to more investment spending, which increases GDP. Conversely, when the money supply is decreased, people have less money than they wish to hold at the given levels of GDP and the interest rate. They seek to replenish their cash balances by selling bonds. This forces the price of bonds down, which means an increase in the interest rate. The rise in the interest rate reduces desired investment, which in turn reduces equilibrium GDP.

These two conclusions lead to an interesting result.

Fluctuations in exogenous spending flows cause changes in GDP and interest rates to be positively associated with each other, rising and falling together. Fluctuations in the real money supply cause changes in GDP and changes in the interest rates to be negatively associated with each other, one rising while the other falls.

The monetary transmission mechanism

The shifts in the *LM* curve just studied integrate the monetary and spending sides of the economy. The linkage is often referred to as the **monetary transmission mechanism**, which means the transmission of a monetary shock, such as change in the demand for or supply of money, into an effect on real spending. The importance of the mechanism makes a further summary statement worthwhile.

The basic linkage is through the interest rate:

A change in the demand for or supply of money leads to an attempt to buy or sell bonds, which causes the interest rate to change. This in turn causes a change in investment, and in all other interest-sensitive spending. This in its turn changes aggregate spending. In the new equilibrium, both the interest rate and GDP are changed.

Notice in this statement that the link to real spending refers to all interest-sensitive spending rather than just investment. In our model investment is the only spending flow that responds to interest rates. In practice, other flows may also respond. For example, consumer spending may fall off when interest rates rise because credit is more expensive, or because households have increased mortgage payments and thus have less disposable income to spend on discretionary items once they have made their mortgage payments. To allow for such possibilities, the reference is to interest-sensitive spending which, of course, includes investment.

The *IS–LM* multiplier

In Chapter 16 we developed the simple multiplier which took the form $\Delta Y = \Delta A/(1 - c)$, where ΔA is the change in autonomous spending, c is the marginal propensity to spend out of income, and ΔY is the resulting change in GDP. This multiplier tells us how GDP changes in response to a change in any exogenous spending variable, on the assumption that the only endogenous variables are consumption and GDP. (In particular, the price level and the interest rate, and hence investment, were treated as exogenous variables.) We called this the simple multiplier, but a more descriptive term would be the interest-constant multiplier. The more specific version of this multiplier derived in Box 17.2 is also an interest-constant multiplier.

However, in the present model the interest rate, and hence investment, is endogenous. This leads to a now familiar story. When GDP increases, the amount of money demanded also increases. Given a constant money supply, this forces up the rate of interest. This in turn reduces investment spending and chokes off some of the expansion that would otherwise have occurred. The resulting change in GDP is due to what may be called the interest-variable multiplier. The reasoning behind this conclusion is laid out in the caption to Figure 20.8.

The interest-constant multiplier is shown by the horizontal shift in the *IS* curve in response to a shift in some component of exogenous spending. The interest-variable *IS–LM* multiplier is always smaller than the interest-constant multiplier.

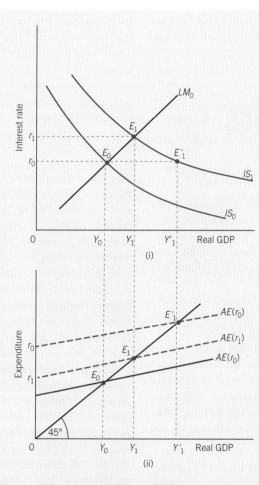

Figure 20.8 The interest-constant and interest-variable multipliers

The rise in the interest rate that accompanies a rise in GDP with a constant real money supply reduces the value of the multiplier. In part (i), the initial curves are IS_0 and LM_0, which intersect at E_0 to give equilibrium values of Y_0 and r_0. The IS curve then shifts to IS_1. If the interest rate had remained constant at r_0, equilibrium GDP would be at E_1' with GDP rising to Y_1'. This is the result given by the interest-constant multiplier. If the LM curve is held constant, the actual new equilibrium is at E_1, with GDP of Y_1 and interest rate of r_1. GDP rises to Y_1 rather than Y_1' because the rise in the interest rate from r_0 to r_1 chokes off some investment spending. This is the result predicted by the interest-variable multiplier. The crowding-out effect is $Y_1' - Y_1$. This reduction in the multiplier effect can be prevented if the Bank allows the quantity of money to increase enough to shift the LM curve to intersect the IS curve at E_1'.

Part (ii) shows what is happening in terms of the 45° diagram. Initially the aggregate spending curve is $AE(r_0)$. Equilibrium is at E_0, with GDP Y_0 and interest rate r_0. Now a rise in autonomous spending shifts the aggregate spending curve to $AE'(r_0)$. With a constant interest rate at r_0, equilibrium shifts to E_1' with GDP at Y_1'. This is the result predicted by the interest-constant multiplier. However, the increase in GDP increases the interest rate and lowers desired investment spending, shown as a downward shift in the AE function to $AE(r_1)$, creating equilibrium at E_1 and GDP Y_1. The increase from Y_0 to Y_1 is the result predicted by the interest-variable multiplier.

The term **crowding-out effect** refers to the lowering of investment spending whenever a rise in GDP is accompanied by a rise in the interest rate; spending is crowded out by the rise in the interest rate that occurs when the quantity of money demanded rises because GDP rises.

Assume, for example, that during a period of recession the government increases its spending, G, in an attempt to expand the economy back towards potential GDP. If the central bank adopts a policy that holds the nominal money supply constant, interest rates will rise as GDP rises. This will crowd out some private investment spending, offsetting some of the expansionary effect of the initial increase in G. Thus, although the expansionary fiscal policy does succeed in increasing total spending and total GDP, it will also lead to the crowding out of some private interest-sensitive spending, and in our model this is investment. Therefore the increase in G leads to some reduction in I as a result of the consequent rise in the interest rate.

Of course, the central bank does have other options available if it wants to avoid the crowding out of investment. It can hold the interest rate constant and allow the money supply to expand as the demand for money increases with the increase in GDP. Then the interest-constant multiplier holds and there is no crowding out. These two possibilities for Bank policy are shown in Figure 20.8

CASE STUDIES

1. UK business investment: why so weak?

In the second case study at the end of Chapter 16 we examined the level of investment in the United Kingdom and saw that it was at historically low levels. We now look more closely at a major part of total investment: business investment. (Total investment also includes government and household investment.)

Figure 20.9 shows the path of business investment before and after the peaks of the past three business cycles. It is very clear that, following the 2007–8 financial crisis, business investment fell further and stayed low for longer than in the previous two recessions. Figure 20.10 shows the annual rate of change of business investment and a range of survey measures of investment intentions. So why was business investment so weak? Plausible reasons for this have been offered by Ian McCafferty in the speech referred to in Box 20.1.

So why has business investment been so weak? To answer that question and get a handle on what the recovery might look like, we need to look at what happened during the crisis and its aftermath.

The financial crisis of 2008–2009 is best characterised as a large negative demand shock—a shock to the level of activity. A number of factors have been identified as the

root cause: the mispricing of risk, financial innovation coupled with lax regulation and excessive leverage ['leverage' is the amount of money borrowed by a firm relative to the owners' capital]. *Balance-sheet repair by households, businesses and banks, together with fiscal consolidation, has weighed on activity here and in other advanced economies in recent years. But it is the proximate triggers of the crisis that precipitated the negative demand shock: the failure of several banks, and the associated seizing up of money and credit markets, brought about a collapse of business and consumer confidence—so-called 'animal spirits'—and with it private spending and world trade.*

Yet it is not just the level of activity that was hit—firms, consumers and investors did not just become more pessimistic about the future and cut down their spending. They also became much more uncertain about it, facing a wider range of possible outcomes. The heightened degree of uncertainty caused by the banking crisis was then compounded in 2011–12 by the escalation of the sovereign debt crisis within the Eurozone. This combination of pessimism and heightened uncertainty represented a major shock to animal spirits, causing companies and households to retrench sharply...

For business investment, the mechanism by which a rise in uncertainty operates is simple. Because investment is costly to reverse, when a firm decides to undertake a project, it gives up the option of waiting to gather more information. But that option has a value, which increases with the level of uncertainty about future conditions. So to give up this 'option to wait', a firm will require a higher rate of return from investment, net of costs, as compensation. In other words, uncertainty reduces the incentive to invest by pushing up on the opportunity cost of undertaking an investment project. So it is not surprising that, in business surveys, when firms are asked which factors are restraining capital spending, 'uncertainty about future demand' is quoted by the greatest number of firms.

Another important factor highlighted by McCafferty is finance.

The credit crunch resulted in a sharp decline in finance raised by UK private non-financial companies (PNFCs), reflecting both lower demand for funds and constraints on the supply of bank lending. With commercial banks, under pressure to repair their own balance sheets, less willing to extend loans,

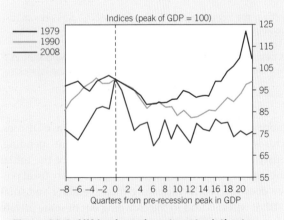

Figure 20.9 UK business investment relative to cyclical peaks

Source: ONS and Bank calculations

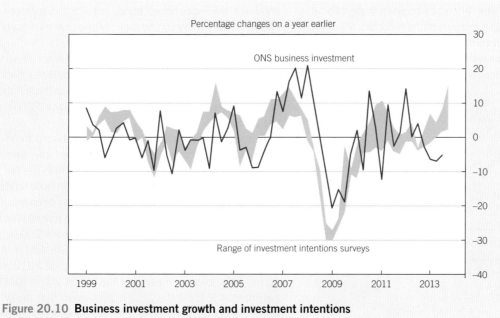

Figure 20.10 Business investment growth and investment intentions

Source: Bank of England, Inflation Report, February 2014

the relative importance of corporate loans on UK PNFCs' balance sheets has declined since the onset of the recession.

This dearth of bank lending has no doubt been a factor holding back business investment. But the relationship between bank financing and investment is more subtle than the aggregate numbers suggest. Different firms tend to rely on different forms of finance, so the link between bank finance and business investment may not be as direct as sometimes perceived...

Internal funds, generated through retained earnings, are an important, and often overlooked, source of funding for investment for all firms. A simple accounting of ONS net financing flows over the past ten years shows that long-term funding raised by UK PNFCs from external sources has not been sufficient to fund aggregate business investment. While the exact matching of sources and uses of financing is uncertain, this seems to imply that, in an average year, firms have relied on internal funds for at least 60% of UK business investment, particularly so following the crisis. And, in my experience from talking to businesses, these retained funds are likely to be even more important for those firms with limited sources of external finance. Evidence from micro data on listed firms supports this—there is a strong correlation between the cash profits and investing cash flows of these 'middle-tier' firms without bond market access. And over the last twenty years, the median listed firm without bond market access has on average generated sufficient cash from its operations in an average year to cover more than 80% of its capital expenditure.

The important role of retained earnings is consistent with the so-called pecking order theory of corporate finance, where internal financing is preferred as it is cheaper than raising funds externally. It is also consistent with how companies appear to operate in practice. From my conversations with company finance directors, it is apparent that most firms do not consider investment decisions in the way that economists describe—that is that investment will be undertaken as soon as the marginal return exceeds the marginal cost of capital, and that borrowing levels are subordinate to that. In practice, for most companies, the total amount of external debt raised (the level of 'gearing') is strategically set at some pre-determined level—trading off the benefits of extra debt with the risk of going insolvent—leaving investment decisions more dependent on the amount of internal funds available.

(Source: <http://www.bankofengland.co.uk/publications/Documents/speeches/2014/speech703.pdf>)

The good news in this story is that, at the time of writing, credit conditions were improving, the cash flow of companies was healthy, and investment intentions surveys had picked up sharply. Readers can check for themselves if this led to a sharp pick-up in business investment, as seemed likely in the Spring of 2014.

2. Real and nominal interest rates

Figure 20.11 shows real and nominal interest rates for the United Kingdom between 1985 and 2014. The nominal rate is measured by the yield on ten year government bonds, while the real rate comes from the yield on ten year indexed government debt. In addition, to this yield, the holder receives a sum to compensate for the annual increase in the retail price index. The difference between these two rates can be thought of as a measure of the expected rate of inflation that is known as the *break-even* inflation rate. The reason for this name is that it is the inflation rate that would make an investor indifferent between holding the nominal

bond and the index-linked bond. Indeed, this measure is often used as a proxy for the expectations of market participants of the inflation rate in the future.

The narrowing of the difference between real and nominal interest rates over time reflects the fact that inflation fell after the 1980s and settled very close to the inflation target (2 per cent inflation of the CPI since 2003) by the 2000s.

It is also notable that there was a downward trend in both real and nominal interest rates over the sample period. The fall in nominal rates partly reflects the fall in inflation, but the general downward trend in both reflects the worldwide fall in interest rates that has been associated with the tendency for world savings to rise relative to demand for investment finance since the early 2000s.

A surprising feature of the real interest rate data is that real rates are recorded as negative in parts of 2012 and 2013. This does not mean that the holder would have to pay interest to the issuer, but it does mean that the pricing of the bonds is such that a holder would lose purchasing power by buying a bond and holding it to redemption. For example, if the nominal rate of interest is 1.5 per cent while the inflation rate is 2.5 per cent, the real interest rate is −1 per cent.

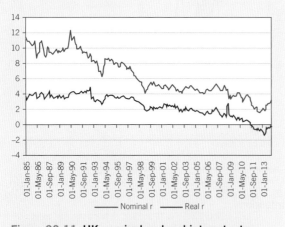

Figure 20.11 UK nominal and real interest rates, 1985–2014

Source: Bank of England online data base.

Conclusion

Of the various factors that influence the level of investment, we have concentrated here on the negative relation between investment and the interest rate. We know from earlier chapters that any exogenously determined level of investment is associated with an equilibrium level of GDP at which desired expenditure equals *actual* output. Since investment is now assumed to vary with the interest rate, it follows that for every interest rate there will be a particular level of investment and hence a particular level of equilibrium GDP. The *IS* curve shows that relation by plotting the interest rate and *equilibrium* GDP against each other.

Since the *LM* curve is influenced by both the demand for and the supply of money, we have now integrated money into the theory of the determination of GDP. We can now show how monetary changes work through the transmission mechanism to alter equilibrium GDP.

Our next step is taken in Chapter 21 where we make the price level endogenous. We do this by combining the *IS* and *LM* curves into a new curve called the aggregate demand curve and then developing a new concept called the aggregate supply curve.

SUMMARY

Investment in the economy

■ In the long run investment increases the capital stock and hence the size of potential GDP.

■ In the short run changes in investment affect aggregate spending and hence the level of GDP and the size of the GDP gap.

- The amount of planned investment spending on capital goods is influenced by (1) the price and the productivity of capital goods, (2) expectations about the future demand for the output to be produced by the capital goods and about the costs of producing that output, (3) the development of new techniques of production and new products, (4) profits previously earned by firms and available for reinvestment, and (5) the *real* (not the nominal) rate of interest.

- A fall in the rate of interest leads to a temporary spurt of inventory investment while the inventories are being increased; a rise in the rate of interest leads to a temporary spurt of inventory disinvestment while the inventories are being decreased.

- A fall in the rate of interest causes a rise in investment in building new housing while a rise in the rate reduces new building.

- The investment-demand function shows a negative relation between the quantity of desired investment spending to the real interest rate, assuming that everything else that influences investment is held constant.

The *IS* curve

- The *IS* curve shows all those combinations of GDP and the real interest rate for which aggregate desired spending equals actual GDP.

- The *IS* curve is not a simple behavioural relation but rather a *locus of equilibrium values* for *Y* and *r*.

- The *IS* curve is negatively sloped because a rise in the real interest rate lowers desired spending and hence lowers equilibrium GDP.

- An increase in exogenous spending shifts the *IS* curve to the right, indicating that a higher level of GDP is associated with any given interest rate. A decrease does the reverse.

The *IS–LM* model

- Macroeconomic equilibrium occurs where the *IS* and *LM* curves intersect, indicating that both the money and goods markets are in equilibrium (demand for money equals its supply and desired spending equals actual GDP).

- An increase in autonomous spending shifts the *IS* curve to the right and raises the equilibrium values of both GDP and the interest rate—changes in the GDP and the interest rate are positively related.

- An increase in the real money supply or a reduction in real money demand shifts the *LM* curve to the right, lowering the interest rate and raising GDP—changes in the GDP and the interest rate are negatively related.

The monetary transmission mechanism

- A change in the demand for or the supply of money causes a change in the interest rate, which causes a change in interest-sensitive spending, which changes GDP.

- Because of the transmission mechanism money cannot be neutral in the short run.

The *IS-LM* multiplier

- The interest-constant multiplier of earlier chapters is shown by the horizontal shift in the *IS* curve in response to a shift in some component of exogenous spending.

- The interest-variable, or *IS-LM,* multiplier is always smaller than the interest-constant multiplier.

- Whenever some increase in autonomous spending causes a rise in GDP and the interest rate, interest-sensitive spending is reduced, thus lowering the multiplier effect of the original impulse.

- The central bank can avoid the crowding-out effect by holding the interest rate constant, which requires that it allows the money supply to expand as the demand for money increases because of the increase in GDP.

TOPICS FOR REVIEW

- Effects of investment in the short and long runs
- Determinants of investment in the capital stock, inventories, and housing
- The investment-demand function
- The *IS* curve, definition, reasons for its slope and shifts
- Macroeconomic equilibrium

- Effects of shifts in the *IS* curve
- Effects of shifts in the *LM* curve
- The *IS–LM* and the interest-constant multipliers
- The monetary transmission mechanism
- Crowding out

QUESTIONS

1 An investment costs £2,000 today and will return £2,150 in one year's time. What is the minimum rate of interest at which this investment will be profitable? What if the investment only returned £2,050?

2 What are the predicted effects on the *IS* and *LM* curves and equilibrium GDP of each of the following headlines:

   a) Unemployment rises as recession takes hold.
   b) Bank of England signals a rise in interest rates.
   c) New oil discoveries lead to an investment boom.
   d) Money supply shrinks as banks add dramatically to the cash reserves.

3 Use *IS* and *LM* curves to examine what would happen in the following circumstances.

   a) There is a large fall in investment spending in county *X* whose central bank is committed to a policy of maintaining a constant nominal money supply.
   b) Compare this with the outcome if the central banks had been committed to a policy of maintaining the interest rate constant and allowing the market to determine the money supply.

4 The slope of the *IS* curve in a closed economy is determined by both (choose one):

   a) the income elasticity of money demand and the multiplier;
   b) the interest elasticity of investment and the rate of inflation;
   c) the interest elasticity of investment and the multiplier;
   d) the interest elasticity of money demand and the marginal propensity to consume';
   e) the money multiplier and reserve ratio of banks.

5 In the *IS/LM* model a relaxation of monetary policy will (choose one):

   a) shift the *IS*, and *LM* curves to the right;
   b) shift the *IS* curve to the left and the *LM* curve to the right;

   c) shift the *IS* curve to the right and leave *LM* unchanged;
   d) shift the *LM* curve to the right and leave the *IS* curve unchanged;
   e) shift the *LM* curve to the left and leave the *IS* curve unchanged.

6 In the *IS/LM* model at less than full employment, an increase in government spending will (choose one):

   a) shift the *LM* curve to the right, leading to a lower interest rate and higher real GDP;
   b) shift the *IS* curve to the right leading to a higher interest rate and higher real GDP;
   c) shift the *IS* curve to the left leading to a lower interest rate and lower real GDP;
   d) shift the *IS* curve to the right leading to a higher interest rate and lower real GDP;
   e) shift the *IS* curve to the right leading to a lower interest rate and higher real GDP.

7 Suppose it is known that investment is volatile so that the *IS* curve shifts left and right in a cyclical fashion. What would be the best monetary policy to stabilize GDP:

   a) peg the interest rate and let the money stock vary in line with demand;
   b) hold the money stock constant and let the market interest rate vary.
   c) Would your answers to a) and b) change if the volatility was due to instability in the demand for money?

8 Explain why an increase in government spending might 'crowd out' some interest-sensitive spending.

9 Use the *IS–LM* model to explain what would happen if the government chose to reduce its spending at the same time as monetary policy was loosened.

10 Use the *IS–LM* model to explain what would happen if government spending is increased at the same time as there is a monetary policy loosening. Is there any limit to how far monetary and fiscal policies can be relaxed?

CHAPTER 21

GDP AND THE PRICE LEVEL: AGGREGATE DEMAND AND AGGREGATE SUPPLY

So far we have studied the effects of shocks to the economy stemming from changes in the components of spending that cause the *IS* curve to shift, and from the changes in the monetary sector that cause the *LM* curve to shift. We did this under two key assumptions: (1) the price level was constant, and (2) firms had excess capacity and so were willing to provide all that was demanded at the going prices. Thus only GDP and the interest rate were free to react to such shocks. To go further we need to allow the price level to be determined within the model and to consider the behaviour of firms when their outputs are near or even above normal capacity. Among other things, this will add a third type of shock to our model: supply-side shocks which occur when costs rise exogenously due to increases in such things as the prices of imported components or energy prices, causing firms to want to raise their output prices irrespective of what is happening to demand.

We make the transition to a variable price level in two steps. First, we study the consequences for GDP of *exogenous* changes in the price level—changes that happen for reasons that are not explained by our present model of the economy. This allows us to develop the so-called aggregate demand curve. Then we develop a theory of aggregate supply which, when combined with aggregate demand, provides a theory that simultaneously determines both GDP *and* the price level. We then develop a theory of how an economy behaves when it is below, at, or above potential GDP.[1]

We do this for three different situations called *regimes*. In the first regime, everyone expects the price level to remain constant over time. Prices may rise in boom times but they will fall in times of slump. Thus, although the inflation rate will vary cyclically, the trend rate is expected to be zero. In the second regime, everyone expects that the average inflation rate will not only be positive but will vary considerably over time. In the third regime, everyone expects the inflation rate to be positive but close to constant over time.

The major part of this chapter serves two purposes. It develops those elements of the theory that are common to a study of all three regimes and also the specific aspects that are needed to study the first regime. Then the latter part of the chapter amends the theory so that it covers the second regime. The third regime is the subject of Chapter 22. We stress that there are many common elements to the theories that cover all three regimes. Indeed, all three theories are best understood as variations of a macroeconomic theory with an endogenous price level.

The very important first case study at the end of this chapter shows that these three regimes existed successively in the developed countries, including the UK, over the last 200 years. The first for well over a century, the second for a mere 25 troubled years, and the third from the early 1990s until today. The second case study shows that the third regime is not confined to the UK but spreads over at least all of the G7 countries (US, UK, Canada, France, Germany, Italy, and Japan).

In this chapter you will learn that:

● The aggregate demand (*AD*) curve shows a negative relationship between the price level and real GDP.

---

[1] Recall that potential GDP may sometimes be referred to as full-employment or normal capacity output.

- The slope of *AD* is negative because a rise in the price level reduces GDP for three main reasons: (i) it reduces the real money supply and this raises the interest rate which in turn lowers investment, (ii) it reduces the competitiveness of the home economy and thus reduces net exports, (iii) it reduces consumption because it reduces the real value of households' stock of wealth and current savings.

- GDP is assumed to diverge from its potential level because changes in input prices lag behind changes in output prices when the price level changes.

- The short run aggregate supply curve, which relates short-run variations in GDP to the price level, is assumed to have a positive slope because unit costs rise as output rises above potential.

- Starting with GDP at its potential level, an aggregate demand shock will cause GDP and the price level to rise together.

- Starting with GDP at its potential level, an aggregate supply shock will cause GDP and the price level to move in opposite directions; an adverse supply shock raises input prices causing GDP to fall and the price level to rise.

- The Phillips curve shows a negative relation between the rate of change of money wage rates and the level of unemployment, and hence a positive relation between wage changes and the GDP gap. This helps to explain the shifts in the *SRAS* curve in the face of positive and negative GDP gaps.

- The long-run aggregate supply curve is assumed to be vertical at the level of potential GDP and this is the level of GDP to which the economy will return when all prices have fully adjusted to a demand shock.

- According to the model in this chapter a stable rate of inflation (including a zero rate) can only be achieved when GDP is at its potential level and unemployment is at the rate that occurs at potential GDP and is called the NAIRU.

- The long-run aggregate supply curve moves rightwards in line with long-term economic growth which results from rising productive capacity and technical progress.

Aggregate demand

We now wish to incorporate the price level into our model.[2] We proceed by asking: What happens to real GDP when the price level changes for some exogenous reason? We first look at this question from the demand side of the economy, then at the production or supply side, and finally put the two together to make both the price level and GDP endogenous.

The main graphical representation of the model we have developed from Chapter 16 onwards is now going to be called the **aggregate demand curve (AD)**. Do not be put off by the change in terminology. *AD* still

represents the sum of the variables that make up total spending on the domestic product (GDP), so it is determined by $C + I + G + (X - IM)$. In this respect it is very similar to the *AE* function of Chapters 16 and 17. However, what has changed is that we want to plot the effects of changes in the domestic price level on GDP, and this is what the AD curve achieves. We thus proceed by asking: How does a change in the price level affect GDP? We analyse this by asking how a price level change affects the components of GDP. Box 21.1 shows that assessments of what is happening to the growth of components of aggregate demand are central to policy-makers' analyses of the economy.

There is one key result that we need to establish: an exogenous rise in the price level shifts both the *LM* and the *IS* curves to the left, thus reducing the equilibrium level of GDP. In other words, the equilibrium level of GDP established by the intersection of the *IS* and *LM* curves is negatively related to the price level. This is the result of

---

[2] Once we have a variable price level there can be differences between real and nominal magnitudes, so it is important to recall that all our spending variables (*C, I, G,* and *NX*) and GDP itself are real (i.e. constant price) variables throughout. The main nominal variable is the money stock, *M*. However, in all cases that follow in this chapter we are dealing with equilibria in which the price level is constant and hence the real and nominal interest rates are the same. So we can continue to draw the *IS* and *LM* curves on the same diagram.

Box 21.1 *AD* and macro policy

Just in case you are thinking that our discussion of macroeconomics is far too theoretical and abstract, the following extract might help to convince you that the analysis of aggregate demand really is at the heart of macroeconomic policy-making, so the framework we are building here will help you to understand the macroeconomic environment throughout your careers, irrespective of whether we are going through good times or bad. What follows is an extract from the February 2014 *Inflation Report*, published by the Bank of England and written on behalf of the Monetary Policy Committee (MPC), which sets UK monetary policy.

The UK economy grew by 1.9% in 2013, the strongest annual growth rate for six years. Much of that expansion was driven by consumer spending, as lifting uncertainty and easing credit conditions prompted households to reduce their rate of saving. That brightening in the economic environment also prompted a revival of the housing market, with housing transactions in 2013Q4 up more than 25% on a year earlier, accompanied by a pickup in house price inflation. This revival helped support strong growth in housing investment. In contrast, business investment has remained

subdued, although surveys of investment intentions suggest that it is likely to gather pace this year. Despite stronger activity in the United Kingdom's main overseas markets, export performance continued to disappoint...

(*Source*: Bank of England, *Inflation Report*, February, 2014, page 4)

Notice that this paragraph is talking about consumption, then investment, and then exports, so it is focusing on $C + I + (X - IM)$ which are the private sector components of aggregate demand. You may ask what happened to G. This was not mentioned in this particular *Inflation Report* (at least not at this point in the assessment), but other *Inflation Reports* often contain a statement such as 'The Committee's projections are conditioned on the tax and spending plans set out in the ... Budget'.[3] This means that the MPC does not try to forecast (or influence) government policy, but rather takes the announced fiscal plans as a given that is then built into its own projections of the likely future course of GDP and inflation.

---

[3] This is quoted from the August 2012 Inflation Report (page 6) where the dots can be replaced with 'March 2012'.

---

three separate effects, the first of which shifts the *LM* curve, while the other two shift the *IS* curve.

The real money effect

We already know from Chapter 20 that a rise in the price level lowers the real quantity of money and hence shifts the *LM* curve upwards and to the left (as shown in Figure 19.6). If you are in any doubt about this, you should review the discussion around that figure now. This *LM* shift lowers equilibrium GDP as shown in Figure 20.7, and if nothing else happened, it would raise the equilibrium rate of interest. This in turn would lower investment spending and all other interest-sensitive spending. We call this the *real money effect* because it is caused by a decline in the real money supply. (It is also sometimes called the *real balance effect*.) To find the reasons for the shift in the *IS* curve we need to develop what are called the *wealth effect* and the *balance-of-payments effect*.

The wealth effect

We saw in Chapter 16 that a rise in wealth is predicted to causes a rise in consumption spending, while a fall in wealth has the opposite effect. What remains to be established is the effect of a rise in the price level on the wealth held by households. A rise in the price level reduces the real value of any asset that is denominated in money terms,

such as a bank deposit or a bond. Say, for example, that I lend you £100 and you promise to pay me £110 a year from now. If the price level doubles unexpectedly over the year, you gain because the £110 you pay me will buy much less than the £100 you borrowed. To see this, assume that you bought some real asset whose price rose by the amount of the inflation. Now you can sell the asset for £200, pay me the £110, and pocket £90 profit just because there was an inflation. From my point of view, I lose because of the same alteration in the purchasing power of money. For example, if I put off buying something for £100 in order to lend you the money, when I get my £110 a year from now it will cost me £200 to make the same purchase. So I will be worse off by £90. These two effects are offsetting: you are £90 better off and I am £90 worse off. The lesson is clear:

Unexpected increases in the price level bring real purchasing power gains to borrowers and real purchasing power losses to lenders.

However, there is at least one important case in which this is not true. If I hold a bank deposit, I lose by a rise in the price level but the bank does not necessarily gain because both its liabilities (e.g. deposits held by the public) and its assets (e.g. loans to the public and to the government in the form of government bonds and bills) are denominated in nominal money terms. So, on balance, a rise in the price level lowers

Box 21.2 The wealth effect

Much wealth is held in the form of assets with a fixed nominal money value, such as bank deposits and government bonds and bills. The case of bank deposits has been discussed in the text, and we explicitly ignore them in what follows. When a bill or a bond matures, the owner is repaid a specific sum of nominal money whose real value—the amount it can buy—depends on the price level. Thus an unexpected rise in the domestic price level lowers the real value of all assets that are denominated in nominal monetary units, reducing the wealth of the holders of such assets. However, the real wealth of the issuers of the assets is increased when the price level rises unexpectedly. This is because the issuers will part with less purchasing power when they redeem the assets and so they have more wealth. Thus an unexpected change in the price level affects the wealth of holders of assets denominated in money terms in exactly the opposite way to how it affects the wealth of those who issued the assets. The qualification 'unexpected' is important, because if everyone expects some specific rise in the price level, the nominal interest rate determined by the market will alter to account for this.

An *inside asset* is one that is issued by an individual or a firm in the domestic private sector and held by someone else in the domestic private sector. It follows that, for inside assets, a rise in the price level lowers the real wealth of the asset-holders but raises the real wealth of the asset-issuers. So with inside assets a change in the price level has no net effect on total private sector wealth.

An *outside asset* is one that is held by someone in the domestic private sector but issued by some agent outside that sector. In practice, bank deposits excluded, this usually means the domestic government or any foreign issuer. In these cases, the only private sector wealth-holders to experience wealth changes when the price level changes are the holders of the outside assets. There are no offsetting private sector wealth changes for the issuers of these assets since they are not in the private sector. It follows that a rise in the price level lowers the real wealth of domestic private sector holders of these assets. (The opposite is true when the issuers are in the domestic private sector and the holders are in other countries. But we are assuming that on balance there are more domestic holders of foreign-issued assets than foreign holders of domestic-issued assets.)

If the assets were issued by foreigners, that is the end of the story. Real domestic wealth is reduced when the price level rises and desired consumption decreases. However, if the assets were issued by the domestic government in the form of bonds or treasury bills, there is a possible offsetting effect, which is called the **Ricardo effect**. When the government redeems the bonds in the future, it will part with less purchasing power than if the price level had not risen. This implies that the real purchasing power value of the taxes it will have to raise to redeem the bonds will be lower than it would have been if the price level had not risen. (Taxpayers will have to make the same amount of nominal tax payments, but the real value of those payments will be less because of the rise in the price level.) This in turn implies that the future real tax liability of taxpayers is reduced by the same amount as the real wealth of bondholders has increased in the present. If taxpayers understand this, and look into the future when making spending plans, the overall effect of the rise in the price level on wealth held in the form of government debt is zero. However, the balance of evidence is that many members of the public are not so farsighted, in which case a rise in the price level causes a perceived reduction in private sector wealth and hence a reduction in desired spending. This issue is still debated, and there is some disagreement as to how far the Ricardo effect does offset the apparent reduction in wealth perceived by the private sector and hence the effect on their current spending.

---

the real wealth of households that is held in bank deposits with no offsetting rise in the real wealth of the banks (which are, in the final analysis, owned by households). The opposite is true of a fall in the price level. The public is better off while the banks are not made significantly worse off.[4] Thus:

A decrease in household wealth caused by a rise in the price level will in turn cause consumption spending to decrease— the *IS* curve will shift to the left.

---

[4] There is a partial offset to this effect that arises from any debts that households owe to banks. As prices rise, the real value of that nominal debt falls and indebted households are better off. However, we assume that the net effect is that households' financial wealth falls in real value as the price level rises.

This wealth effect is called *the Pigou effect* after the British economist A.C. Pigou (1857–1959) who first pointed it out. It applies to any asset in which the gains and losses from an unexpected inflation are not fully offsetting. It applies, for example, to foreign bonds that are held by domestic households and firms. An unexpected rise in the price level decreases the real wealth of the domestic holders and increases the real wealth of the foreign issuers. So there is a net decrease in domestic wealth and an induced decrease in consumption—a shift of the *IS* curve to the left. The case of non-bank financial assets that are both issued and held domestically is considered further in Box 21.2.

How important is this wealth effect? Much of the wealth of UK households is held in the form of assets that will rise in nominal value as the price level rises, such as housing (about 50 per cent of all household wealth) and shares in companies (about 6 per cent). If these rise in price by the same amount as the general price level rises, households suffer no change in the real wealth as a result. However, about 16 per cent of household wealth is held in the form of bank deposits or cash.[5] This is sufficient to provide a significant wealth effect and lead to a reduction in consumption spending when the price level rises.

The balance of payments effect

When we consider the effects of a rise in the price level on domestic GDP that works through the effect on foreign trade, we need to distinguish two cases depending on what caused the price level to rise. First, consider the case in which the cause is domestic, such as an overall rise in money wages with no corresponding rise in labour productivity. Then when the domestic price level rises, domestically produced goods become more expensive relative to foreign goods. This change in relative prices tends to cause domestic consumers to reduce their purchases of domestically produced goods and to increase their purchases of foreign goods. At the same time, consumers in other countries tend to reduce their purchases of the now relatively expensive goods that are exported from the domestic country. We make the usual assumption that the changes in quantities are sufficient to cause the amount spent on these categories to change in the same direction as the quantity changes (i.e. the elasticities of demand for imports and exports exceed unity). Thus the value of exports falls and the value of imports rises. These changes can be thought of as substitution effects; consumers substitute cheaper foreign goods for the now more expensive domestic ones. As we saw in Chapter 17, the changes can be summarized as a downward shift in the net export function. This causes a decrease in total desired spending and hence a leftward shift in the *IS* curve.

A rise in the domestic price level with domestic causes, and elastic demands for foreign-traded goods, reduces net exports and hence shifts the *IS* curve to the left.

This balance of payments effect would not be important if the exchange rate changed in line with changes in the price level. For example, if UK domestic prices all rise by 10 per cent and the value of sterling on the foreign exchange market falls by 10 per cent, there will be no changes in any relevant relative price. To a foreigner, UK goods now cost 10 per cent more in sterling, but each

unit of sterling can be bought with 10 per cent less of the foreigner's domestic currency. So foreigners see no change in the price of UK exports in their domestic market. Similarly, although UK prices have risen by 10 per cent and foreign imports have unchanged prices in foreign currency, it now costs 10 per cent more sterling to buy a unit of foreign currency. Thus the cost of imported goods rises by 10 per cent, equalling the rise in the price of home-produced goods. In practice, however, as shall will see at length in Chapter 24, the exchange rate does not alter in the short run to offset exactly, or even approximately, changes in the domestic price level. Thus the balance of payments effect can be significant in causing a reduction in net exports when the domestic price level rises.[6]

Now consider the second case in which the cause of the rise in the domestic price level is external to the home economy. If this was a general rise in all import prices, we would get the reverse of the case just considered. Consumers would reduce their consumption of foreign goods and increase that of domestic goods, causing domestic spending to increase, thus shifting the *IS* curve to the right. But there is an important special cases in which the demand for the imported good whose price has risen is highly inelastic (i.e. the quantity purchased does not fall much as price rises, causing more to be spent on the imported good). This would be the case, for example, if there was a major increase in the price of imported energy (e.g. oil and gas), such as has happened more than once in the recent past. If the prices of imported energy rise, there are few close substitutes so domestic residents will have to spend more of their incomes on imported energy and will have less to spend on consuming domestic goods. Aggregate demand falls when the rise in imported energy prices increases the domestic price level. This can be thought of an income effect. Domestic consumers spend less on domestic goods because they have lower real incomes due to spending more on foreign imports.

A rise in the domestic price level caused by a rise in the prices of imports that have few, if any, domestic substitutes (the demand for them is inelastic) causes the *IS* curve to shift to the left.

So far we have discussed the effect of a rise in the price level. The effect of a fall is just the reverse. A fall in the

---

[5] The remaining 28 per cent of household wealth is largely in pension funds or life assurance policies, for which the wealth effect of price level changes is harder to estimate.

[6] A fourth effect is sometimes mentioned: the rise in the price level may lower the real value of government spending. This may happen, but since most tax revenues, especially those from income taxes and VAT, rise as prices and incomes rise, a government can keep its real spending constant by raising its money spending along with the increase in the money value of its tax revenues.

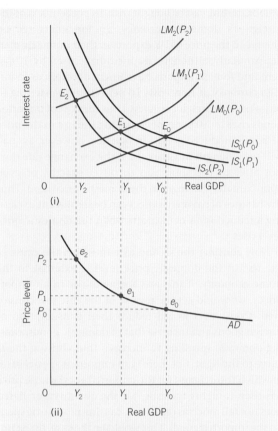

Figure 21.1 Derivation of the *AD* curve

The *AD* curve shows how the equilibrium level of GDP produced by the *IS–LM* model changes as the price level changes. The nominal money supply is constant, and when the price level is P_0 the curves are $LM_0(P_0)$ and $IS_0(P_0)$, with the Ps showing the price level to which the IS and LM curves refer. Equilibrium is at E_0 with GDP of Y_0. Plotting Y_0 against P_0 in part (ii) of the figure gives the point e_0. A rise in the price level to P_1 shifts the LM curve to $LM_1(P_1)$ and the IS curve to $IS_1(P_1)$. Equilibrium shifts to E_1 with GDP of Y_1. Plotting Y_1 against P_1 in part (ii) gives the point e_1. A further rise in the price level to P_2 shifts the LM curve to $LM_2(P_2)$ and the IS curve to $IS_2(P_2)$. This takes equilibrium GDP to Y_2. Plotting Y_2 against P_2 in part (ii) yields the point e_2. Joining up all the equilibrium points in part (ii) for every possible price level traces out the AD curve.

price level increases equilibrium GDP because the real money supply falls, household wealth associated with outside assets rises (which raises consumption[7]), and net exports rise, all of which lead once again to a negative relation between GDP and the price level.

---

[7] The income effect mentioned in the previous footnote may also contribute if there is a fall in world energy prices which increases domestic real incomes.

The derivation of the *AD* curve

Now let us see how the *AD* curve can be derived. Figure 21.1(i) plots the familiar *IS–LM* diagram with the interest rate and real GDP on the axes. In Figure 21.1(ii) we plot real GDP on the horizontal axes and the price level on the vertical axis. Because real GDP is plotted on the horizontal axes of both parts (i) and (ii), we can stack one part over the other and relate them easily. Given a value of the price level, the equilibrium value of GDP and the interest rate are determined in part (i), while in part (ii) we plot that GDP against the given price level, which gives one point on the *AD* curve.

When the price level is increased exogenously to some new level, the real money supply is reduced, causing the *LM* curve to shift upwards and to the left. This causes the interest rate to rise and all interest-sensitive spending to fall in response. Also, households' wealth falls while exports become more expensive in foreign markets and imports become cheaper domestically, all of which cause the *IS* curve to shift to the left as desired spending on consumption and net exports both fall. Both the *LM* and *IS* curve shifts lead to a fall in equilibrium GDP. (What happens to the interest rate depends on which curve shifts more—*IS* or *LM*.) The new lower equilibrium level of GDP is then plotted in part (ii) against the new higher price level that brought it about. Repeating this procedure for many alternative price levels allows us to derive the negatively sloped aggregate demand curve shown in part (ii).

A rise in the price level shifts both the *LM* curve and the *IS* curve to the left and hence produces a new lower equilibrium level of GDP. Each combination of GDP and its associated price level defines a particular point on a negatively sloped *AD* curve.

Because each point on the aggregate demand curve is derived from an *IS–LM* equilibrium for a given nominal money supply, each point represents a position at which (1) desired spending is equal to actual GDP (as is true of all points on the *IS* curve) and (2) the demand for money equals its supply (as is true for all points on the *LM* curve).

Note that because the *AD* curve relates real GDP to the price level, changes in the price level that cause *shifts in* the *LM* and *IS* curves cause *movements along* the *AD* curve. Thus a movement along the *AD* curve shows how exogenous changes in the price level cause real equilibrium GDP to change in such a way that desired spending equals actual output and the demand for money (and hence for bonds) equals the supply. Notice also that the only exogenous change we are permitting at present is a change in the price level.

The nature of the *AD* curve

In Chapter 2 we saw that demand curves for individual goods such as carrots and cars are also negatively sloped. However, the reasons for the negative slope of the *AD* curve are different from the reasons for the negative slopes of the individual demand curves that are used in microeconomics. Microeconomic demand curves refer to the consequences of a change in one price relative to all other prices. Say for example, that the price of oranges rises while all other prices remain constant. This causes consumers to alter the pattern of their purchases, buying fewer oranges and more of substitutes whose prices have fallen relative to oranges. In contrast, the *AD* curve refers to the consequences of a change in all money prices. The consequent fall in the real quantity of money causes the interest rate to rise and investment spending to fall while the wealth and balance of payments effects cause consumption and net-export spending to fall.[8]

Notice that the level of GDP determined by the *IS* and *LM* curves for a given nominal money supply and price level is called the 'equilibrium' level of GDP. This is the equilibrium for GDP in a theory that deals mainly with demand-side forces on the assumption that firms will produce enough to supply everything that is demanded at the going price level. But when we alter that assumption concerning the behaviour of firms, we will find a different equilibrium level of GDP and price level.

Points off the *AD* curve

The *AD* curve depicts combinations of GDP and the price level at which aggregate desired spending is equal to actual output and the demand for money equals its supply. These points are said to be *consistent* with spending and asset-holding decisions.

The level of GDP given by any point on the aggregate demand curve is such that if that level of output is produced, aggregate desired spending at the given price level will exactly equal total output and the demand for money (and hence for bonds) will equal the supply.

---

[8] The balance of payments effect is the only one that is similar to the micro demand curve. A domestically generated rise in the price level entails a rise in all domestic prices while holding foreign prices constant. Although this provides no incentive to substitute among domestic goods and services, it does give rise to some substitution between domestic and foreign goods and services. Domestic products rise in price relative to imported products, and the switch in spending lowers desired aggregate spending on domestic output and hence contributes to the reduction in the equilibrium level of GDP. If the price level rise is driven from abroad, such as from a rise in the price of energy which lacks close substitutes, domestic residents are worse off as their real incomes have fallen and their consumption spending will, fall leading to a fall in domestic GDP.

Points to the left of the *AD* curve show combinations of GDP and the price level for which aggregate desired spending exceeds output. Thus there is pressure for output to rise because firms could sell more than their current output. Points to the right of the *AD* curve show combinations of GDP and the price level for which aggregate desired spending is less than current output. Thus there is pressure for output to fall because firms will not be able to sell all of their current output.

Shifts in the *AD* curve

Anything that alters the equilibrium GDP that is associated with each given price level will cause the *AD* curve to shift. If it increases that equilibrium, the *AD* curve shifts to the right. If it decreases it, the *AD* curve shifts to the left. Such shifts are called *aggregate demand shocks*.

Anything other than a change in the price level that causes either the *IS* or the *LM* curve to shift will also shift the *AD* curve and thus create a demand shock. In Chapter 19 we saw that an increase in the nominal money supply or a decrease in the amount of money demanded for transactions or precautionary purposes would shift the *LM* curve to the right, and thus do the same to the *AD* curve. In Chapter 20 we saw that an increase in any exogenous spending component, such as government spending, an increase in the propensity to consume, or a decrease in taxes that causes disposable income to rise, will shift the *IS* curve to the right and so shift the *AD* curve similarly to the right. Also, a shift in the investment function indicating an increase in the amount of desired investment associated with each interest rate will also shift the *IS* and *AD* curves to the right. These important shifts shown in Figures 21.2 and 21.3.

We summarize the factors that shift the *AD* curve as follows:

The *AD* curve is shifted to the right, indicating a positive demand shock by:

- **an increase in the propensity to consume;**
- **an increasing the amount of investment spending associated with each interest rate;**
- **a rise in net exports;**
- **an increase in the nominal money supply;**
- **a decrease in the amount of money that the public wishes to hold at each level of GDP.**

The *AD* curve is shifted to the left, indicating a negative demand shock by the reverse of each of the above forces.

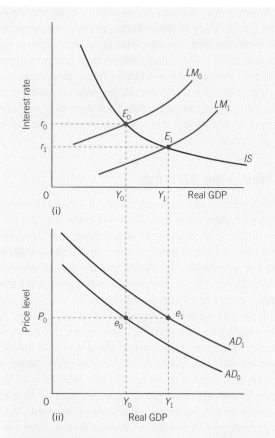

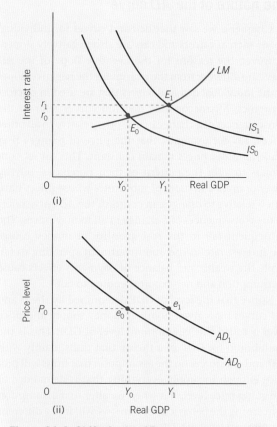

Figure 21.2 Shifts in the *AD* curve caused by shift in the *LM* curve

Anything other than a change in the price level that causes the *LM* curve to shift also causes the *AD* curve to shift. The original curves *IS* and LM_0 in part (i) are drawn for price level P_0. This gives rise to the equilibrium at E_0, with interest rate r_0 and GDP Y_0. Plotting Y_0 against the price level P_0 gives one point, e_0, on the aggregate demand curve AD_0 in part (ii). As shown in Figure 21.1, varying the price level causes the *LM* curve to shift (shifts not shown in this figure) in such a way as to trace out the whole curve AD_0. *With the price level constant at P_0,* anything that causes the *LM* curve to shift to LM_1, such as an increase in the nominal quantity of money, moves the equilibrium to E_1 with interest rate r_1 and GDP of Y_1. Plotting Y_1 against the unchanged price level P_0 produces the new point e_1 on a new aggregate demand curve. Changes in the price level will then shift the LM_1 curve (not shown in the diagram), tracing out a new aggregate demand curve shown by the line AD_1.

Figure 21.3 Shifts in the *AD* curve caused by shifts in the *IS* curve

Anything other than a change in the price level that causes the *IS* curve to shift also shifts the *AD* curve. The original curves IS_0 and *LM* in part (i) are drawn for price level P_0. This gives rise to the equilibrium at E_0 in part (i), with interest rate r_0 and GDP Y_0. Plotting Y_0 against the price level P_0 gives one point, e_0, on the aggregate demand curve AD_0 in part (ii). Varying the price level causes the *LM* curve to shift in the manner shown in Figure 21.1 (not shown in this figure) in such a way as to trace out the whole curve AD_0. *With the price level constant at P_0,* anything that causes the *IS* curve to shift to IS_1 moves the equilibrium to E_1 with interest rate r_1 and GDP Y_1. Plotting Y_1 against the unchanged price level P_0 produces the point e_1 on a new aggregate demand curve. Changes in the price level will then shift the *LM* curve (shifts not shown in the figure), tracing out a new aggregate demand curve, AD_1.

Aggregate supply

So far in this chapter, we have developed a theory of how the equilibrium level of GDP is determined and how that equilibrium changes as the price level is changed exogenously on the assumption that firms are willing to supply everything that is demanded at the prevailing prices. Before we make the price level endogenous we need to say more about the supply decisions of firms.

Basic assumptions

We now make some simplifying assumptions about the equilibrium in our model, assumptions that we will modify in important ways in the next chapter.

1. The economy is assumed to have a unique long-run macro equilibrium that occurs when GDP is at its potential level.

2. The market prices of all goods and services and all inputs are assumed to be flexible so that they rise whenever there is excess demand and fall whenever there is excess supply. Thus when the economy is in equilibrium from a macroeconomic viewpoint all individual markets will be in equilibrium from a microeconomic viewpoint, giving rise to a unique equilibrium set of relative prices.

3. Technology and potential GDP are assumed to be constant. (Although these do change continually in line with trend growth, the changes are assumed to be slow enough that they can be ignored for purposes of short-run analysis.)

The aggregate supply curve

Aggregate supply (AS) refers to the total of all the outputs of goods and services that firms wish to produce and sell over a specific period of time, such as a month or a year—that is, the economy's GDP. Aggregate supply is the outcome of the decisions of all producers in the economy to hire workers and buy other inputs in order to produce goods (and services) to sell to households, governments, and other producers, as well as for export.

The **aggregate supply curve** relates GDP to the price level. Two such curves are defined: a **short-run aggregate supply (SRAS) curve** shows the relationship between the price level and GDP (total output) over a short period of time, and a **long-run aggregate supply (LRAS) curve** shows combinations of the price level and GDP that can arise when the economy is in full equilibrium. The LRAS curve is vertical at potential GDP, Y*, because of the first of the above assumptions that there is a unique general equilibrium level of GDP. In contrast, the SRAS curve is assumed to have a positive slope, indicating that a rise in the price level is associated with a rise in GDP. There are now two separate issues that need to be considered with respect to the SRAS curve. First, if the economy has a unique macro equilibrium in which all individual markets are also in equilibrium, why does it ever diverge from that equilibrium, which it does when it undergoes fluctuations over the business cycle? Secondly, what is the relation between these divergences from the long-run equilibrium level of GDP and the price level?

These are not easy questions to answer and economists have given several different answers over the years. In the text we present the most common explanation. In Box 21.3 we outline some other explanations and discuss why finding the 'correct one' is so difficult.

Box 21.3 More on the *SRAS* curve

Why is there a problem?

The theory developed in this chapter integrates the price level into the model developed so far. To do this, a constant price level is assumed and then one change is introduced. Initially, we did this to develop the AD and SRAS curves. Later we will shift the AD or SRAS curve, which will cause the price level to change from one constant level to another.

When the theory is used to analyse the behaviour of economies since the end of the World War II in 1945, it covers a period of sustained inflation. Between 1945 and 1970 the inflation rate oscillated between 1 and 9 per cent and never stayed constant from one year to the next. Then from 1970 to the early 1990s, the inflation rate varied between 5 and over 25 per cent, with the exception of only two years when it fell slightly below 5 per cent! This experience is what the Swedish monetary economist Axel Leijonhufvud has termed 'ragged inflation'. The rate never varied systematically enough for observers to be able to form reliable expectations about what it would be in the near future.

The key point for us is that from 1945 until early in the 1990s, there was never a period when the price level was constant for any length of time and then, disturbed by a single event, increased to a new constant level. As a result, there has never been a period of time in which the SRAS curve could be observed directly or estimated reliably from observed data. As we shall see later in this chapter, a relation between the inflation rate and the GDP gap can be estimated with more or less reliability, but one between the price level and GDP itself cannot.

This helps to explain why there is more than one competing explanation of the SRAS curve. Being unable to observe it directly or estimate it empirically, does not rule out its usefulness as long as it can be used to make predictions that can be tested against data. But it does make it difficult to judge among alternative and sometimes conflicting explanations.

Alternative explanations of the *SRAS* curve

In the text we rely on the most common explanation that wages lag behind the prices of final output and this provides the profit incentive for firms to alter output in the same direction as prices are changing. The problem with this explanation is that it implies that real wages should fall on the

(continued)

Box 21.3 *continued*

upswing of the business cycle and rise on the downswing. But this is the opposite of what is observed, with real wages being weakly pro-cyclical rather than counter-cyclical.

Wage rates and GDP

One alternative explanation starts by assuming a negative relation between unemployment, *U*, and the wage rate, *W*. Stated linearly, this is

$$W = -aU \qquad (1)$$

Next, relate *U* negatively to GDP, *Y*:

$$U = -bY \qquad (2)$$

Substituting (2) into (1) gives:

$$W = abY \qquad (3)$$

Now assume, as a first approximation, that prices, *P*, are a constant mark-up over wages:

$$P = cW \qquad (4)$$

Substituting (3) into (4) gives:

$$P = cabY \qquad (5)$$

This is the desired positive relation between the price level and the GDP. It is stated linearly for simplicity, but if non-linear relations are used, the curve shown in Figure 21.4 can be derived.

The problem with this explanation is that there is no evidence that the money wage rate is related in any simple way to the level of GDP or the level of unemployment.

Misunderstood price signals

In selling their products or services firms and workers are assumed to care about the price of what they are selling *relative* to all other prices. If the price of a firm's output rises relative to all other prices, it is assumed to be willing to supply more, and if the wages of workers rise relative to the prices of all goods and services, they are assumed to be willing to supply more labour. When the price level rises,

firms are assumed to be unaware of what is happening else-where in the economy and so misinterpret this general rise in prices as a rise in the relative price of their product and so they produce more output. Similarly, perceiving a rise in their money wage rates, labourers confuse this with a rise in their real wages and are willing to work more. As a result, a rise in the price level causes total output and employment to rise above their long-run equilibrium values. Sooner or later, however, firms and workers realize that *all* prices have risen and their relative prices have not changed so they then restore the original levels of output and employment.

This explanation is open to a number of criticisms. First, it assumes that what motivates firms is the prices of their products relative to the prices of all other products. Yet the standard theory of the firm, as outlined in the microeconomics part of this book, shows that to maximize its profits all that the firm needs to know is the demand for its own product and its production costs. Secondly, it assumes that workers are unable to discriminate between a rise in their own wage relative to the prices of the things that they buy and a rise in their own wage accompanied by a rise in the prices of what they buy. Yet they are offered that knowledge every time they make a purchase. Third it assumes that unemployment is all voluntary. Workers are deciding to work less in a recession because they think the real wage they are offered is too low. (They do not realize that the prices of everything they buy have fallen along with their money wages so that their real wage is unchanged.)

The surprises-only SRAS curve

A specific version of the above explanation adds the assumption that agents have rational expectations of future values of the price level so they do not make persistent mistakes in estimating what the inflation rate will be. Thus output only increases in response to an unexpected rise in the price level and not at all to one that was fully anticipated. With ragged inflation, this explanation is not unlikely at some times but it has problems when the changes are more systematic, as they have been at times when a rising GDP gap was associated over several years with a rising inflation rate, which should be rationally expected.

Why the economy diverges from its long-run equilibrium

The most common explanation for this divergence relies on lags in input price adjustments. Output prices are assumed to react to shocks faster than input prices. Most important, labour contracts usually settle wage rates for one or more years, while most product prices can be changed whenever the producer wishes. To capture this assumed lag in a stylized fashion, the short-run aggregate supply (*SRAS*) curve shows the quantity of output that firms would like to produce and sell at each price level under the assumption that the prices of all inputs are held constant. Now, a rise in the prices of final output with input prices held constant will lead firms

to increase production, while a fall in output prices with input prices constant will lead firms to decrease production.

Deviations from long-run equilibrium are assumed to occur because the prices of final goods rise relative to input prices when aggregate demand rises, leading firms to wish to increase production; they fall relative to input prices when aggregate demand falls, leading firms to wish to contract production.

Reasons for a positive slope to *SRAS*

We assume that the typical firm's real costs per unit of output (i.e. the physical units of inputs required per

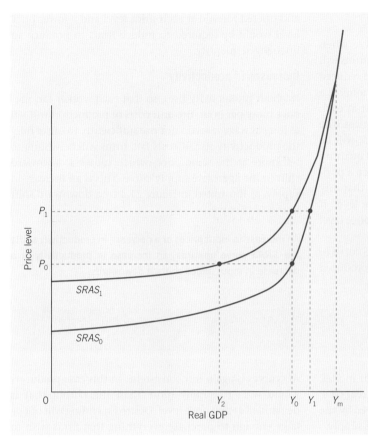

Figure 21.4 A short-run aggregate supply curve

The *SRAS* curve is positively sloped over its whole length. In this theory, with all input prices constant, total desired output and the price level are positively associated. For example, on $SRAS_0$, a rise in the price level from P_0 to P_1 will be associated with a rise in the quantity of total output supplied from Y_0 to Y_1. Although in this theory the slope of the *SRAS* curve is relatively flat at low levels of output and very steep at higher levels, it is positively sloped throughout and eventually, at a very high level of real GDP, becomes vertical. A shift of the *SRAS* curve upwards and to the left indicates a decrease in supply; a shift downwards and to the right indicates an increase in supply. Starting from (P_0, Y_0) on $SRAS_0$, suppose that there is an increase in input prices that shifts the *SRAS* curve to $SRAS_1$, which is above and to the left of $SRAS_0$. At price level P_0 only Y_2 would now be produced. Alternatively, to get output Y_0 would require the price level to rise to P_1. An increase in supply caused, say, by a decrease in input prices would shift the *SRAS* curve downwards and to the right, from $SRAS_1$ to $SRAS_0$.

unit of output) vary directly with the volume of its output. If the price that the firm can charge rises and at the same time the money costs of all of its inputs rise, nothing real has changed and the firm will not be motivated to change its output. But because of the assumed lag between input and output prices, a rise in the price that the firm can charge (input prices being constant) implies a higher profit per unit of output and an incentive to increase production. Similarly, a fall in the price that the firm can charge for its output, input prices being constant, implies a fall in per unit profits and an incentive to reduce production. Aggregation over all firms gives a short-run aggregate supply curve that shows a positive relation between the price level and desired output.[9]

....
[9] The text sets out all you need to know to proceed. But if you are wondering how much more or less the firm will want to produce and sell when the price it can charge varies by some specific amount, the answer is to be found in the microeconomic theory of the firm. The key is that the cost of producing one more or one less units of output, what is called marginal cost in microeconomics, is assumed to be positively associated with the volume of output. So as the price that the firm can charge rises, the profit on the last unit produced also rises and the firm will be motivated to increase its output until the cost of the last unit of output just equals the extra revenue that can be obtained from selling it. Similarly a decrease in the price that the firm can charge will motivate it to reduce output until the cost of the last unit produced falls enough to be equal to the amount that can be gained from selling that unit.

The *SRAS* curve shows a positive relation between the price level and GDP because the higher are the prices that firms can charge (input prices being constant), the higher are the outputs that firms will be willing to produce and offer for sale.

Figure 21.4 shows two *SRAS* curves whose shape agrees with the description just given. Note that at some high level of GDP, Y_m in the figure, the *SRAS* curve becomes vertical. This represents the absolute maximum amount of output that can be a squeezed out of the economy by such measures as working all facilities 24 hours a day, ignoring all but minimum necessary maintenance, and bringing all able-bodied persons into the work force. These are the kinds of measures only adopted in times of extreme crisis, such as an all-out war effort. Since such extreme behaviour is seldom seen in peace time, we do not need to show this vertical portion of the *SRAS* curve in subsequent diagrams.

Shifts in the *SRAS* curve

Shifts in the SRAS curve from one position, such as $SRAS_0$ in Figure 21.4 to another, such as $SRAS_1$, are called aggregate supply shocks. Two sources of aggregate supply shocks are of particular importance: changes in the price of inputs and increases in productivity.

Changes in input prices

Input prices are held constant along the *SRAS* curve; when they change, the curve shifts. If input prices rise, firms will find the profitability of their current production reduced and react by decreasing production. For the economy as a whole this means that there will be less output at each price level than before the increase in input prices (the *SRAS* curve shifts to the left) and a higher price will be required to induce firms to supply an unchanged quantity (the *SRAS* curve shifts upwards). Notice that when a positively sloped curve shifts upwards, indicating that any given quantity is associated with a higher price level, it also shifts to the left, indicating that any given price level is associated with a lower quantity.[10]

Similarly, a fall in input prices causes the *SRAS* curve to shift downwards and to the right. More will be produced and offered for sale at each price level and a lower price level would be required to induce firms to produce an unchanged quantity.

Increases in productivity

If labour productivity rises, so that each worker can produce more per hour, the unit costs of production will fall as long as wage rates do not rise sufficiently to offset fully the productivity rise. If costs fall, firms will be willing to sell more at the same price, which causes a downward shift in the aggregate supply curve. This is an increase in supply, as illustrated in Figure 21.4 by a downward shift in the *SRAS* curve.

An increase in input prices or a decrease in productivity shifts the *SRAS* curve upwards; an increase in productivity or a decrease in input prices shifts it downwards.

Macroeconomic equilibrium

Now that we have added the *SRAS* curve to our model, we are ready to develop a theory of how both real GDP and the price level are simultaneously determined by the interaction of aggregate demand and aggregate supply.

The equilibrium values of real GDP and the price level occur at the intersection of the *AD* and *SRAS* curves, as shown by the pair Y_0 and P_0 at point E_0 in Figure 21.5. This combination of real GDP and price level at the intersection of the *AD* and *SRAS* curves is called a **macroeconomic equilibrium**.

To see why the pair of values (Y_0, P_0) is the only possible macroeconomic equilibrium (for the given values of all exogenous variable that lie behind these specific *AD* and *SRAS* curves), first consider what Figure 21.5 shows would happen if the price level were below the intersection of the *AD* and *SRAS* curves. At this lower price level the desired output of firms, as given by the *SRAS* curve, is less than desired aggregate spending. The excess desired aggregate spending will cause prices to be bid up, and as this happens output will increase along the *SRAS* curve. Hence there can be no macroeconomic equilibrium when the price level is below the intersection.

Similarly, if the price level were above the intersection of the two curves, the behaviour underlying the *SRAS* and *AD* curves is again not consistent. In this case producers would wish to supply more than the output that is demanded at that price level. Desired spending will not be large enough to purchase everything that firms wish to produce at that price level. This excess aggregate supply will cause prices to fall so that output will contract along the *SRAS* curve.

Only at the combination of GDP and price level given by the intersection of the *SRAS* and *AD* curves are desired spending (aggregate demand) and desired production (aggregate supply) activities consistent.

Notice that macroeconomic equilibrium requires that three conditions are satisfied.

1. From Chapters 16 and 17: at the prevailing price level, desired aggregate spending must be equal to GDP, which means that purchasers are just willing to buy all that is produced.

2. From Chapter 20: the levels of GDP and the interest rate must be such that the demand for money is equal to its supply. The *AD* curve is constructed in such a way that the two conditions hold everywhere on it since it is the locus of *IS–LM* equilibrium positions for alternative price levels.

3. From this chapter: at the prevailing price level, firms must be willing to produce the prevailing level of GDP. This condition is fulfilled everywhere on the *SRAS* curve.

Only where the two curves *SRAS* and *AD* intersect are all three conditions fulfilled simultaneously At that point

---

[10] There is some ambiguity over whether this should be called a 'positive' or 'negative' supply shock, as the shock moves the supply curve up but also to the left. However, it is clearly an 'adverse' supply shock as it raises prices for each level of output. We will generally refer to a supply shock as 'positive' if it increases output at each price level and thus moves the supply curve to the right, and vice versa for a 'negative' supply shock. So negative and adverse are the same in our terminology.

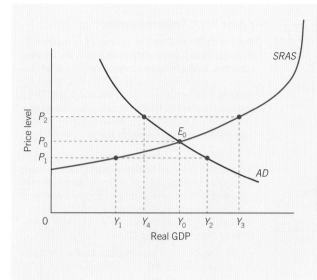

Figure 21.5 Macroeconomic equilibrium

Macroeconomic equilibrium occurs at the intersection of the *AD* and *SRAS* curves. Given the *AD* and *SRAS* curves in the figure, macroeconomic equilibrium occurs at E_0, with GDP equal to Y_0 and the price level equal to P_0. At P_0 the desired output of firms, as given by the *SRAS* curve, is equal to the level of GDP that is consistent with spending and money-holding decisions, as given by the *AD* curve. If the price level was P_1, the desired output of firms would be Y_1. However, at P_1 the level of output that is consistent with spending and money-holding decisions given by the *AD* curve is Y_2, which is greater than Y_1. Hence, when the price level is P_1, or any other level below P_0, the desired output of firms will be less than the level of output that is consistent with spending and money-holding decisions. At price level P_2, firms would like to supply Y_3 while purchasers would only be willing to buy Y_4. Hence when the price level is P_2, or any other price level above P_0, the desired output of firms, given by the *SRAS* curve, exceeds the level of output that is consistent with spending and money-holding decisions, given by the *AD* curve.

firms are not willing to produce either more or less than the equilibrium output at the prevailing price level.

Also notice two important points about this model—points that will be contrasted with the approach to be developed in the next chapter.

1. It is the price level that does the adjusting. If there is excess aggregate supply, the price level falls, more is demanded, and less is supplied until equilibrium is reached. If there is excess aggregate demand, the price level rises causing more to be produced and less demanded until equilibrium is again reached.

2. Each equilibrium that occurs when any of the curves shift has its own unique combination of price level and GDP.

Changes in GDP and the price level

The aggregate demand and aggregate supply curves can now be used to show how in this theory various shocks to the economy affect both GDP and the price level.

Aggregate demand shocks

Figure 21.6 shows the effects of an aggregate demand shock. An increase in aggregate demand causes both the price level and real GDP to rise, while a decrease causes both to fall. Adjustment to the new equilibrium following such a shock involves a movement along the *SRAS* curve.

Aggregate demand shocks cause the price level and real GDP to change in the same direction; both rise with an increase in aggregate demand, and both fall with a decrease in aggregate demand.

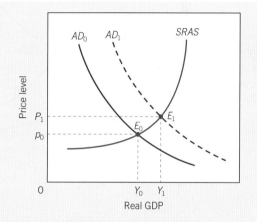

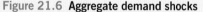

Figure 21.6 Aggregate demand shocks

Shifts in aggregate demand cause the price level and real GDP to move in the same direction. An increase in aggregate demand shifts the *AD* curve upwards and to the right—say, from AD_0 to AD_1. Macroeconomic equilibrium moves from E_0 to E_1. The price level rises from P_0 to P_1 and real GDP rises from Y_0 to Y_1. A decrease in aggregate demand shifts the *AD* curve to the left—say, from AD_1 to AD_0. Equilibrium moves from E_1 to E_0. Then price level falls from P_1 to P_0, and real GDP falls from Y_1 to Y_0.

The multiplier

In Chapters 16 and 17 we developed the simple multiplier on the assumption that investment was constant and that firms would supply all that was demanded at the going price level (i.e. the *SRAS* curve was horizontal). In Chapter 20, when we made investment endogenous, we saw that assuming a constant supply of nominal money reduced the multiplier because a positive demand

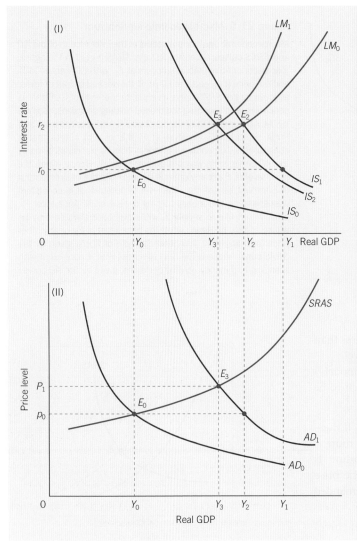

Figure 21.7 Three multipliers

The multiplier of Chapters 16 and 17 is reduced if, in response to a positive demand shock, the interest rate rises, and is reduced further if the price level also rises. The original equilibrium is at point E_0 where IS_0 and LM_0 intersect in part (i) and where AD_0 and $SRAS$ intersect in part (ii). Real GDP is Y_0, the interest rate is r_0, and price level is P_0. An increase in desired aggregate spending then shifts the IS curve to IS_1.

(1) *The interest-constant multiplier of Chapters 16 and 17* If the Bank holds the interest rate constant at r_0, thus making the LM curve horizontal at that rate, and if firms were willing to supply everything that was demanded, GDP would rise to Y_1. This rise from Y_0 to Y_1 is the simple interest-constant multiplier of Chapters 16 and 17.

(2) *The IS–LM multiplier* Because the LM curve is positively sloped, the IS–LM equilibrium is at E_2 with GDP of Y_2 and interest rate r_2. The rise in GDP from Y_0 to Y_2 is the IS–LM multiplier for a horizontal $SRAS$ curve (not shown on the figure) and thus a constant price level. It also gives the vertical shift in the AD curve in response to the demand side shock.

(3) *The AD–AS multiplier* Since the $SRAS$ curve is assumed to be positively sloped, the shift in the AD curve raises the price level to P_1 and shifts the LM curve to LM_1 and the IS curve to IS_2. GDP is then Y_3, the price level is P_1 and interest rate is r_2. (Whether the interest rate for this multiplier is higher or lower than the one for the IS–LM multiplier, or unchanged as drawn here, depends on the relative shifts of the IS and LM curves when the price level rises.) The change from Y_0 to Y_3 is the multiplier when the interest rate and the price level are both free to change and the $SRAS$ curve is positively sloped.

shock tends to raise the interest rate, thus reducing desired investment spending. Now we can see that if the $SRAS$ curve is positively sloped the multiplier is even smaller. This is shown in Figure 21.7.

When the *SRAS* curve is positively sloped throughout its whole range, the multiplier is smaller than the *IS–LM* multiplier, which in turn (assuming a constant nominal money supply) is smaller than the interest-constant multiplier.

When output rises following a positive demand shock and the nominal money supply is assumed to be constant, two forces are set in motion that limit the size of the expansion. First, the interest rate will rise, causing investment and hence equilibrium GDP to fall back according to the *IS–LM* multiplier (relative to where it would go if interest rates did not rise). Secondly, the positive slope of the *SRAS* curve causes the price level to rise,

which reduces the real money supply and shifts the *LM* curve to the left, thus lowering the expansion of equilibrium GDP still further. Therefore adding the monetary sector makes the multiplier smaller and adding the aggregate supply curve makes it even smaller, but still positive.

Aggregate supply shocks

Figure 21.8 illustrates the effects on the price level and real GDP of aggregate supply shocks. Following an upward shift in the *SRAS* curve, the price level rises and real GDP falls.[11] The figure also shows that a downward shift in the

---

[11] This combination of events has been called a *stagflation*, a rather inelegant word that has been derived by combining *stagnation* (a term that is sometimes used to mean slow growth or even falling output) and *inflation*.

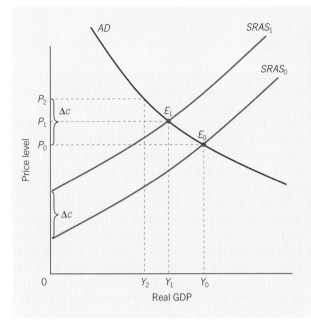

Figure 21.8 Aggregate supply shocks

Shifts in aggregate supply cause the price level and real GDP to move in opposite directions. The original equilibrium is at E_0 with GDP of Y_0 and price level P_0. An increase in input costs shifts the $SRAS$ curve upwards by Δc, taking the new equilibrium to E_1, raising the price level to P_1, and lowering GDP to Y_1. At the new equilibrium of E_1 the rise in the price level from P_0 to P_1 is less than the rise in costs of Δc. Although the $SRAS$ curve shifts upwards by Δc, as output falls unit costs fall and so firms will reduce output by less than they would if costs had remained constant as output fell. This can be seen by assuming that firms' unit costs do not change as output falls, making the $SRAS$ curve horizontal. Its initial position would have been given by a horizontal line starting at P_0 and it new position after the supply-side shock would be a horizontal line starting at P_2, which is higher than P_0 by Δc. The price level then rises to P_2 (i.e. by the whole amount of the cost increase) and GDP falls to Y_2, which is less than Y_1.

$SRAS$ curve leads to an increase in real GDP and a decrease in the price level.

Note that the slope of the $SRAS$ curve affects the magnitude of the changes. The flatter the $SRAS$ curve, the bigger is both the rise in price and the fall in output following from the supply shock. The reason lies in the assumed effect on firms' unit costs of changes in their outputs. If the $SRAS$ curve was horizontal so that unit costs were unchanged as output falls, all the adjustment would come from a fall in the quantity of output that can be sold at the new higher price level. However, with the positively

sloped $SRAS$ curve, firms' unit costs fall when output falls and this reduces the changes—a reduction in output and a rise in the price level—needed to restore equilibrium.

Aggregate supply shocks cause the price level and real GDP to change in opposite directions: with an increase in supply ($SRAS$ shifts rightwards and downwards) the price level falls and output rises; with a decrease in supply ($SRAS$ shifts leftwards and upwards) the price level rises and output falls.

Box 21.4 give examples of some supply shocks that have significantly affected the UK economy.

Box 21.4 Supply shocks

Oil prices have provided three major examples of sustained aggregate supply shocks in recent decades. The major industrial economies have been greatly affected by changes in the market for oil because, in addition to being used to produce energy, it is an input into many materials that are widely used in production and consumption, from plastics to cosmetics to fertilizer. Massive increases in oil prices during 1973–4 and 1979–80 caused leftward shifts in the $SRAS$ curve for virtually all major economies. GDP fell while the price level rose, causing stagflation (a combination of high inflation and falling output). During the mid-1980s oil prices fell substantially and stayed low for most of the 1990s (except for a blip after Iraq invaded Kuwait in 1990). This shifted

the $SRAS$ curve to the right, increasing GDP and putting downward pressure on the price level. However, oil prices rose sharply again after 1999, reversing some of the earlier positive supply shock, and remained on an upward trend during the 2000s as the world economy grew steadily. Oil prices reached very high levels in 2008 (over $150 per barrel compared with around $70 per barrel in March 2010) but then fell sharply when the world economy slowed after the financial crisis. They rose again to around $110 in the spring of 2014 as major economies slowly recovered, but not close to the levels seen in 2008. Then later in that year they began a rapid tumble that took them to levels lower than anything experienced in recent decades.

The long run

In the theory of the short-run behaviour of the economy that we just outlined, goods prices are allowed to react to shocks from the demand and supply side but input prices are assumed to be constant. This is a simplification designed to capture the assumption that input prices are assumed to react to such shocks more slowly than the prices of final goods and services. We now need to set out the implications of the assumptions that we made earlier in this chapter: (1) the macro economy has a unique long-run equilibrium; (2) flexible prices of all goods and services and all inputs ensure that when the economy is in equilibrium from a macroeconomic viewpoint, a unique microeconomic equilibrium set of relative prices will also obtain; (3) technology and potential GDP are constant. To this we now add a fourth assumption: (4) the period of time under consideration is long enough for all prices and wages to adjust to any shock that has hit the economy.

The long-run aggregate supply (*LRAS*) curve

What is called the long-run aggregate supply (*LRAS*) curve shows the relationship between the price level and real GDP after wage rates and all other input prices have been fully adjusted so that equilibrium obtains in all markets for both inputs, including labour, and outputs. This does not mean, as we shall see in Chapter 23, that recorded unemployment is zero, only that all existing unemployment is associated with normal frictions as young workers enter the labour market and old ones retire, while others are in the process of moving between jobs. In the terms that we shall define more closely later, all existing unemployment is due to frictional or structural causes and not to a deficiency of aggregate demand. Output is at its potential level so that there are neither positive nor negative GDP gaps. It follows from the assumptions in the previous paragraph that the long-run aggregate supply curve is vertical at potential GDP.

In the theory presented in this chapter, equilibrium GDP is determined in the long run by the *LRAS* curve while the aggregate demand curve determines only the price level.

Notice that the vertical *LRAS* curve does not represent the same thing as the vertical portion of the *SRAS* curve shown in Figure 21.4. Over the vertical range of the *SRAS* curve, the economy is at the utmost limit of its existing productive capacity, as might occur in an all-out war effort. No more can be squeezed out. The vertical shape of the *LRAS* curve is due to the workings of an assumed

adjustment mechanism that brings the economy back to potential GDP, even though actual output may differ from its potential level for considerable periods of time. It is called the long-run aggregate supply curve because it arises as a result of adjustments that take a significant amount of time. However, it is not long run in the sense of allowing for economic growth that increases potential GDP over time.

Figures 21.9 and 21.10 illustrate the result stated in the above bold-faced passage. Assume that GDP is initially at its potential level, Y^*. The impact effect of a positive aggregate demand shock raises output prices while input prices remain constant. So, as shown in Figure 21.9, real GDP and the price level rise. Then, when input prices start to adjust, this shifts the *SRAS* curve upwards, pushing the economy back along its aggregate demand curve, raising the price level further, and lowering GDP. Eventually, the economy returns to its position of long-run equilibrium at the initial level of potential GDP but a higher price level. This adjustment occurs because the higher price level brings into play the three effects outlined earlier: the real money effect, the wealth effect, and the balance of payments effect.

Although its total is unchanged from the initial pre-demand-shock position, the composition of GDP will usually be altered. Assume, for example, that the original demand shock was caused by an increase in government spending. This has an expansionary effect in the short run, but in the long run, when GDP has returned to potential, the rise in the interest rate due to the real money effect will have crowded out an equivalent amount of interest-sensitive spending.[12]

Figure 21.10 shows the short- and long-run effects of a negative aggregate demand shock. Again starting from long-run equilibrium, the leftward shift in the *AD* curve lowers both real GDP and the price level. But this leads to excess supplies in input markets, including the labour market. This is because prices have fallen but money wages have not, so real wages rise. Workers are happy to offer more labour at the higher real wage, but firms wish to hire less, so supply exceeds demand. This excess supply is assumed eventually to lead to a reduction in input prices, including money wages, shifting the *SRAS* curve downwards and to the right until GDP returns to its potential level but at a lower price level.

---

[12] There may also be an effect working through net exports if the higher price level raises the relative price of home exports, and there may be an effect on consumption of changes in the real value of savings. All these effects work in the same direction.

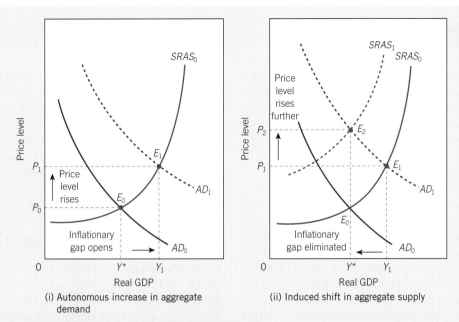

(i) Autonomous increase in aggregate demand

(ii) Induced shift in aggregate supply

Figure 21.9 Positive demand shocks in the short and long runs

A rightward shift of the *AD* curve first raises prices and output along the *SRAS* curve, and then induces a shift of the *SRAS* curve that further raises prices but lowers output. In part (i) the economy is in equilibrium at E_0 with GDP at its potential level indicated by Y^* with a price level P_0. The *AD* curve then shifts to AD_1. This moves equilibrium to E_1 with GDP Y_1 and price level P_1, and opens up a positive GDP gap of $Y_1 - Y^*$. In part (ii) the GDP gap results in an increase in input prices, shifting the *SRAS* curve upwards and to the left. GDP falls and the price level rises along AD_1. When the curve has shifted to $SRAS_1$, output is back to Y^* and the GDP gap has been eliminated, but the price level has risen to P_2.

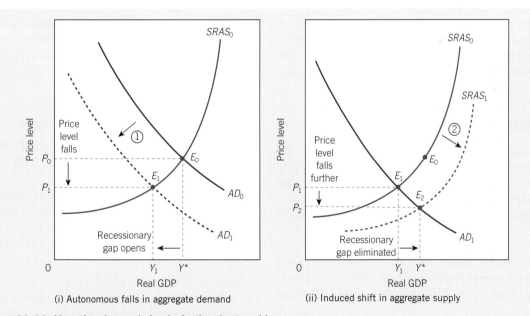

(i) Autonomous falls in aggregate demand

(ii) Induced shift in aggregate supply

Figure 21.10 Negative demand shocks in the short and long runs.

A leftward shift of the *AD* curve first lowers prices and output along the *SRAS* curve and then induces a (slow) shift of that curve which lowers prices further but raises output along the *AD* curve. In part (i) the economy is in equilibrium at E_0 at its level of potential output Y^* and price level P_0. The *AD* curve then shifts to AD_1 moving equilibrium to E_1 with output Y_1 and price level P_1. This opens up a negative GDP gap of $Y_1 - Y^*$. Part (ii) shows the adjustment back to full employment that occurs from the supply side of the economy. The fall in input prices shifts the *SRAS* curve downwards and to the right. Real GDP rises, and the price level falls further along the *AD* curve. Eventually the *SRAS* curve reaches $SRAS_1$, with equilibrium at E_2. The price level stabilizes at P_2 when GDP returns to Y^*, eliminating the recessionary gap.

The Phillips curve

Up to now it has been enough to say that a positive GDP gap puts upward pressure on input prices to rise and that this shifts the *SRAS* curve upwards. Now we focus on an important component of input prices—wages. To do this, we make use of a famous relation called the Phillips curve.

The theory of the Phillips curve

The **Phillips curve** is named after the New Zealand economist A.W. Phillips who, while a professor at the London School of Economics, was studying stabilization policy in the context of dynamic models of the economy.[13] The original Phillips curve relates the percentage rate of change of money wage rates (measured at an annual rate) to the level of unemployment (measured as the percentage of the labour force unemployed). Unemployment is plotted on the horizontal axis and wage changes on the vertical axis. Thus, any point on the curve relates a particular level of unemployment to a particular rate of change of money wages. Phillips showed that this curve was a fairly close fit to the UK data from 1861 to 1957.

An example of such a curve is shown in Figure 21.11(i). Note that this is a new kind of curve. Up to now we have related GDP to the level of prices. Now we relate unemployment to *the rate of change* of wage rates, and soon we will relate GDP to *the rate of change* of prices. In studying the Phillips curve, we continue with the assumption maintained throughout this chapter so far that the price level is expected to remain unchanged.

The shape of the Phillips curve

The Phillips curve has a negative slope, showing that the lower the level of unemployment, the higher is the rate of change of money wages. This should not surprise us. Low rates of unemployment are associated with boom conditions, when excess demand for labour will be causing money wages to rise rapidly. High rates of unemployment, on the other hand, are associated with slump conditions, when the slack demand for labour will lead to low increases in money wages, or possibly even to decreases. Moving along the Phillips curve from right to left, the curve gets steeper, showing that wage rates rise more rapidly the higher is GDP.

Box 21.5 gives an alternative derivation of the Phillips curve that is often encountered. It starts from an *SRAS* curve that relates the price level to GDP rather than from Phillips' more direct observation of a relation between wage changes and unemployment (and thus also to GDP). Since this derivation gives the same results as derived in the text, the alternative is shown in an optional box.

The Phillips curve and the *SRAS* curve

To see what is happening to unit costs of production, we need to relate the increase in wage rates to the increase in labour productivity. For simplicity, in the rest of the discussion we will assume that labour is the only variable factor used by firms. This allows us to associate the labour costs of each unit of output with total variable costs per unit of output. (We could equally well have assumed that all input prices change at the same rate as does the price of labour.)[14]

What happens to unit costs of production now depends on the differences between what labour costs the firm and what labour produces for the firm. To illustrate we add to the curve in Figure 21.11(i) a horizontal line labelled *g* which shows the rate at which labour productivity is growing year by year. The intersection of the Phillips curve and the productivity line at the point *x* now divides the graph into an inflationary and a deflationary range described in the following numbered points.

1. At unemployment rates less than at the intersection point, wages are rising faster than productivity and thus unit costs of production (input costs per unit of output) are rising. If unit costs are rising, the *SRAS* curve must be shifting upwards.

2. At unemployment rates greater than at the intersection point, money wage rates are rising more slowly than productivity is rising. Thus, unit costs are falling. If unit costs are falling, the *SRAS* curve must be shifting downwards.

Given the assumptions set out in the first paragraph of the section entitled 'The long run', the unemployment associated with point *x* must be the unemployment that exists at potential GDP (all unemployment is either frictional or structural).

---

[13] The curve that Phillips used in his original papers on stabilization policy related the rate of change of the price level to the GDP gap (although he did not use that gap terminology since it had not been invented). Later he looked behind the price–GDP curve to study how wage changes would drive price changes. To do this he related the rate of change of money wage rates to the level of unemployment, which is the form in which the curve became famous.

[14] Or we could allow a given percentage change in wage rates to alter the *SRAS* curve by a smaller percentage determined by the percentage of total unit cost made up of wage costs.

Box 21.5 An alternative derivation of the Phillips curve

In the text we derive the Phillips curve directly as Phillips did from a relation between unemployment and the *rate of change* of money wage rates. An alternative derivation starts from the AS curve in Box 21.3 that relates unemployment to the *level* of wage rates. It is more complicated and arrives at the same end point but since it is often used, we repeat it here for those who are interested.

We start by repeating the price determination given in eqn (4) of Box 21.3

$$P = (1 + m)W \qquad (1)$$

where we have replaced the *c* of the earlier box with its equivalent, *1 + m*, where $\underline{m}$ is the mark up of price over wage cost. For example if the mark up is 10 per cent, *m* is 0.1 and *c* is 1.1.

We then use our subsequent discussion of the role of price expectations in wage setting to give us a relation in which wages are positively related to the expected price level and negatively related to unemployment. The specific form is:

$$W = P^e(1 - aU) \qquad (2)$$

This equation is similar to equation (1) in Box 21.3 but has the addition of the expected price level. We then substitute (2) into (1) to get:

$$P = P^e(1 + m)(1 - aU) \qquad (3)$$

We now add time subscripts to the variables.

$$P_t = P_t^e(1 + m)(1 - aU_t) \qquad (4)$$

In order to go from levels to inflation rates we divide both sides of (4) by last year's price level:

$$P_t/P_{t-1} = (P_t^e/P_{t-1})(1 + m)(1 - aU_t) \qquad (5)$$

Next note that the fraction on the left-hand side of (5) is 1 plus the inflation rate expressed as a decimal fraction. For example if *P* was 100 last year and 110 this year, the fraction P_t/P_{t-1} equals 1.10, which is one plus the inflation rate of 10 per cent. Writing the inflation rate as π, which is commonly done, we get

$$(1 + \pi_t) = (1 + \pi_t^e)(1 + m)(1 - aU_t) \qquad (6)$$

Divide (6) through by $(1 + \pi_t^e)(1 + m)$ to get

$$(1 + \pi_t)/(1 + \pi_t^e)(1 + m) = 1 - aU_t \qquad (7)$$

Next then note that, provided the πs and *b* are not too large, a good approximation to the LHS of the new equation is $1 + \pi_t - \pi_t^e - m$. Substituting this for the LHS of (7) gives

$$1 + \pi_t - \pi_t^e - m = 1 - aU_t \qquad (8)$$

and simplifying:

$$\pi_t = \pi_t^e + m - aU_{t1} \qquad (9)$$

which is our Phillips curve.

This derivation follows that of Olivier Blanchard, Alessia Amighini, and Francesco Giavazzi, *Macroeconomics: A European Perspective*, Harlow: Pearson, 2013, p. 235.

Notice that although we have drawn the Phillips curve to show complete downward inflexibility of money wages, this does not imply complete downward inflexibility of unit costs. As long as money wages rise less than productivity rises, unit costs of production will be falling, and the SRAS curve will be shifting downwards. Complete downward inflexibility of unit costs—and thus the total absence of the equilibrating mechanism that comes from downward shifts in the SRAS curve—requires more than the downward inflexibility of money wages; it requires that money wages never rise by less than the increase in productivity.

Figure 21.11(ii) shows a new curve that relates the rate of unemployment to the change in unit costs, rather than to the change in money wage rates. This curve still has unemployment on the horizontal axis, but it is now plotted against the rate of increase in unit costs as shown on the vertical axis. Since this is merely the rate of increase in money wage rates minus the rate of increase of productivity, the new diagram is the same as part (i) of the figure, except that the origin on the vertical axis has been shifted by the rate of productivity growth.

The new curve tells us the rate at which unit costs of production are changing—and thus the rate at which the SRAS curve is shifting upwards or downwards—at each level of unemployment. To distinguish these two curves we call the first a wage Phillips curve and the second a unit-cost Phillips curve.

We can now transform the curve in Figure 21.11(ii) into a new relationship using the fact that unemployment is negatively related to the level of GDP; as GDP rises, unemployment tends to fall. (Continuing with our assumption that potential GDP is constant at Y*, all changes in GDP represent changes in the GDP gap.) The new curve is shown in Figure 21.11(iii). It shows the same rate of change in unit costs of production, but plots it against the level of GDP. Since GDP and unemployment vary negatively with each other, the curve in part (iii) has the opposite slope to the curve in part (ii). We call this new curve the transformed Phillips curve since it has been transformed from a relation between wage rates and unemployment to one between unit costs and GDP.

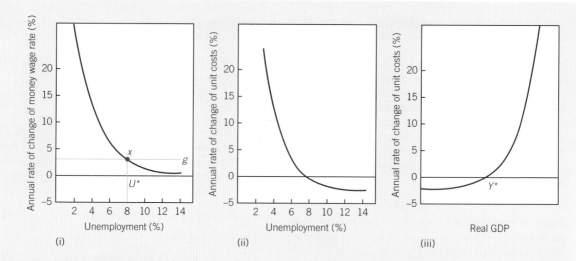

Figure 21.11 Three Phillips curves

The figure shows (i) the original Phillips curve with unemployment related to wage inflation, (ii) the curve adjusted for growth, and (iii) the curve transformed to show GDP related to wage inflation. Part (i) shows an example of a Phillips curve that relates unemployment *negatively* to the rate of wage inflation. We can call this the wage Phillips curve. The horizontal line *g* indicates the assumed exogenous rate of growth of productivity. The point *x* shows the level of unemployment (8 per cent in the figure) at which wage rates rise at the same rate as productivity is rising, implying that the *SRAS* curve is not shifting. This is the amount of unemployment that occurs when there is no GDP gap indicated by U^* in the figure. (Later we will see that U^* is called the *NAIRU* and sometimes the natural rate of unemployment.) The curve in part (ii) can be called the unit-cost Phillips curve. It shows the rise in money wages *minus* the rise in productivity and hence what is happening to unit costs. The point *x* in part (i) is the same as where the new curve cuts the axis, indicating wage changes equal to productivity changes. Part (iii) can be called the transformed Phillips curve because the variable in the horizontal axis has been changed from unemployment to GDP. This is done by making use of the negative relation between GDP and unemployment. Thus it shows unit cost inflation *positively related* to the GDP. The point at which unit costs are constant, and hence so is the price level, is indicated by Y^* to show that it occurs at potential GDP.

Shifts in the *SRAS* curve explained

Figure 21.12(i) shows the familiar *AD–AS* diagram. Figure 21.12(ii) shows the transformed curve, relating the rate of change of unit costs to GDP. Both parts have GDP on their horizontal axes, and by lining these up we can compare one with the other. The *AD* and *SRAS* curves in part (i) determine the short-run levels of prices and GDP. Given the GDP so determined, the transformed Phillips curve tells us the rate at which the *SRAS* curve is shifting. Since from now on we will always be working with the transformed curve, we will just call it a Phillips curve.

The long-run equilibrium of the economy is at potential GDP. All that the curve in part (ii) tells us is how fast the *SRAS* curve in part (i) is shifting, moving the economy towards its long-run equilibrium. The steepness of the curve for *Y* greater than Y^* (i.e. a positive GDP gap) shows the rapid adjustment towards equilibrium after a single expansionary shock. The relative flatness of the curve below equilibrium shows the slowness of adjustment towards equilibrium after a single contractionary shock.

The non-linearity of the transformed Phillips curve expresses the assumption that costs, and hence prices, rise rapidly in the face of a positive GDP gap, but fall only slowly in the face of an equivalent negative GDP gap.

Expectations of a positive inflation rate

Up to now we have been considering the behaviour of the economy when the public expects that the price level will stay more or less constant so that there is no expectation of a continuing positive inflation rate. This is the first of the three regimes that we defined at the beginning of the chapter. Now we need to consider the second of the three

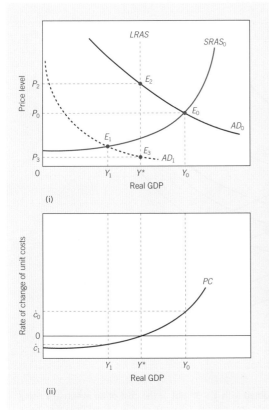

(i)

(ii)

Figure 21.12 The Phillips curve and the *AS–AD* relationship

The automatic adjustment mechanism pushes GDP to its potential level in the long run.

(1) *Removing a positive GDP gap* When the curves are AD_0 and $SRAS_0$ in part (i), they intersect at E_0 to produce equilibrium GDP of Y_0. Part (ii) is similar to the transformed Phillips curve from part Figure 21.11(iii) of the previous figure. It shows that when GDP is Y_0, the rate of change of unit costs is $\dot{c}_0$ per year (a dot over a variable indicates its percentage rate of change). Thus the *SRAS* curve is shifting upwards at that rate. This moves the GDP towards Y^* as the point of macroeconomic equilibrium moves up the fixed *AD* curve towards the long-run equilibrium at E_2, which is reached when the *SRAS* curve has shifted enough to intersect the AD_0 curve at E_2. The conclusion is the same as we reached in Figure 21.9(i), except that the Phillips curve now shows the speed at which the movement from the short-run to the long-run equilibrium takes place.

(2) *Removing a negative GDP gap* When the curves are AD_1 and $SRAS_0$ in part (i), equilibrium is at E_1, with GDP of Y_1. Part (ii) shows that when GDP is Y_1, unit costs will be declining at the rate of $\dot{c}_1$ per year. Hence the *SRAS* curve will be shifting downwards at that rate. Thus the point of equilibrium is moving slowly downwards along AD_1 towards a long-run equilibrium at E_3. This is reached when *SRAS* has shifted downwards sufficiently to intersect AD_1 at E_3. Both the long-run equilibria have the same level of GDP but a different price level. The conclusion is the same as we reached in Figure 21.9(ii), except that the Phillips curve now shows the speed at which the movement from the short-run to the long-run equilibrium takes place.

regimes, one in which inflations last long enough that the public comes to expect them to continue, but at a rate that will vary over time. All of the properties of the model that deal with the first regime also apply here, with the major exception that we change the assumption concerning inflation expectations.

Repeated demand shocks and sustained inflation

The easiest way to study this new issue of sustained inflation is to deal with repeated demand shocks. These shocks could originate from the private sector or from public policy. The case in which the sustained shock was generated by changes in public policy is the case that is most relevant to the actual transition from the first to the second regime that occurred in the 1970s. But we stress that this is only one of the possible scenarios we could study for the generation of sustained inflation.

Consider the rise in the price level shown in Figure 21.9. It comes to a halt when aggregate input costs have risen as much as output prices, shifting the *SRAS* curve upwards and pushing equilibrium back along the *AD* curve until the positive GDP gap is eliminated as GDP returns to its potential level Y^*. However, now assume that the Bank, using its monetary policy tools, wishes to maintain the higher level of GDP (Y_1 in Figure 21.9). To do this it must adopt a policy that shifts the *AD* curve upwards and to the right as fast as the *SRAS* curve is shifting upwards and towards to left. This requires that it causes the money supply to grow at the same rate at which prices are rising so that the real money supply stays constant. The Bank does this by buying bonds, paying for them with new high-powered money. This adds to the reserves of the commercial banks who can then make new loans, expanding the supply of deposit money. Thus the *LM* curve does not shift backwards despite the rise in the price level. This holds equilibrium GDP at its higher level by allowing the *AD* curve to shift outwards as the nominal money supply increases. The inflation is then said to have been **accommodated**. The rise in the price level continues, as does the positive GDP gap. This is shown in Figure 21.13.

But this is not the end of the story. Sooner or later the providers of inputs will realize what is happening—that is, they will come to expect the inflation to continue. This requires that we drop our assumption that people expect that the price level will remain relatively stable in order to consider the effect of expectations of inflation.

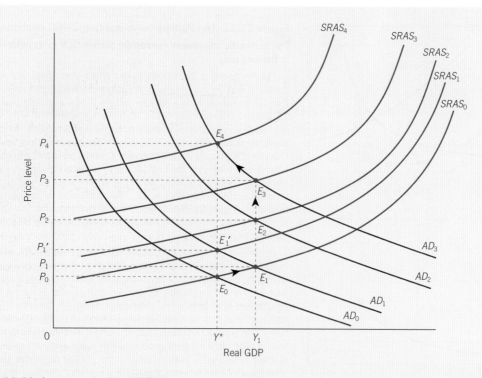

Figure 21.13 An accommodated inflation

If a demand inflation is fully accommodated, the GDP gap can be maintained with $Y > Y^*$ but at the cost of an eventually rising inflation rate. An initial increase in aggregate demand from AD_0 to AD_1 opens up a positive GDP gap of $Y_1 - Y^*$ and raises the price level from P_0 to P_1. When input prices start to adjust, the $SRAS$ curve starts to shift upwards and to the left. If nothing else is done, the curve will eventually rise to $SRAS_1$, taking GDP back to Y^* with equilibrium at E_1' and price level P_1'. But if the inflation is fully accommodated by increasing the nominal money supply at the same rate as the price level is rising, the AD curve will shift upwards at same rate as the $SRAS$ curve. This makes the equilibrium follow the track of the arrow heads with a rising price level and a constant GDP gap. We have shown two intermediate equilibrium points E_2 and E_3 with price levels P_2 and P_3. If the $SRAS$ curve begins to rise faster because input costs are adjusted to the rising price level with a shorter lag, the AD curve must be shifted upward faster as well if GDP is to be held at Y^*. This increases the rate at which the price level is rising. When the Bank finally decides to stop the inflation, it holds the nominal money supply constant, letting the real money supply fall. The $SRAS$ curve continues to shift upwards with equilibrium following the arrow head moving upwards along the now fixed AD curve until a point such as E_4 is reached at the intersection of AD_3 and $SRAS_4$. Now the GDP gap has been eliminated and the price level holds constant at P_4.

Suppose, for example, that both employers and employees have come to expect a 4 per cent inflation rate to continue into next year. Unions will start negotiations from a base of a 4 per cent increase in money wages, which would hold their real wages constant. Firms also may be inclined to begin bargaining by conceding at least a 4 per cent increase in money wages, since they expect that the prices at which they sell their products will rise by 4 per cent. Starting from that base, unions will attempt to obtain some desired increase in their real wages, while employers may attempt to shade real wages downwards. Now such factors as profits, productivity, and bargaining power become important.

Box 21.6 discusses some theories of how expectations of inflation are determined. All we need for the text, however, is the fairly simple assumption that if a given inflation rate continues for long enough, people will come to expect that inflation rate to continue and take actions that are appropriate to that rate.

The general expectation of an x per cent inflation rate creates pressures for money wages to rise by x per cent more than productivity, thus holding real wages constant while shifting the $SRAS$ curve upwards by x per cent.

As a result, suppliers of labour services may seek to have their wage rates rise along with, rather than lag behind, the rise in final goods prices. (When we allow for other inputs, the same considerations will apply to their suppliers.) As the lag between output and input prices is reduced, the speed at which the two curves are rising must increase, and therefore so does the rate of inflation. For example if the $SRAS$ shift lags the AD shift by one year, each of the

Box 21.6 The formation of inflation expectations

We have already discussed expectations in Chapter 20 in the context of investment behaviour, since firms invest in the expectation of earning future profits. We will also discuss them in Chapter 24 in the context of the determination of exchange rates. Here, we consider expectations of inflation in the context of the Phillips curve.

Backward-looking theories

Keynesian theories of expectations assume that expectations are slow to change. The theory of *extrapolative expectations* says that expectations depend on extrapolations of past behaviour and respond only slowly to what is currently happening to prices. In one simple form of the theory the expected future inflation rate is merely a moving average of past actual rates. The rationale is that unless a deviation from past trends persists, firms and workers will dismiss the deviation as transitory. They do not let it influence their wage- and price-setting behaviour.

The theory of *adaptive expectations* states that the expectation of future inflation rates adjusts to the error in predicting the current rate. Thus, if you thought the current rate was going to be 6 per cent and it turned out to be 10 per cent, you might revise your estimate of the next period's inflation rate upwards by, say, half of your error, making the new expectation 8 per cent. More generally, next year's expected rate is equal to this year's actual rate *minus* the rate expected for this year multiplied by some constant between zero and one that shows the extent to which the current prediction error influences expectations about next year.

In an obvious sense, these two theories are backward-looking, since the expectations about the future can be calculated using data on what has happened already.

Forward-looking theories

Rational expectations are forward-looking. The rational expectations hypothesis assumes that people do not continue to make persistent systematic errors in forming their expectations. More important, if the economic system about which they are forming expectations remains stable, their expectations are assumed to be correct *on average*. Thus, any individual's expectations at any time about next year's price level can be thought of as the actual price level that will occur next year plus a random error term that has a mean of zero.

Rational expectations have the effect of speeding up the adjustment of expectations. Instead of being based on past inflation rates, expected inflation is based on an informed forecast of the future behaviour of the economy as influenced by existing (and expected future) policies.

Backward-looking expectations are overly naïve. People do look ahead to the future and assess future possibilities rather than just blindly reacting to what has gone before. Yet the assumption of unbiased forward-looking expectations requires that workers and firms have a degree of understanding of inflation forecasting that few economists would claim to have. For example, there was a great debate among economists as to whether or not the large amounts of liquidity injected into the economy by the policy of 'quantitative easing' instituted by many central banks after the downturn of 2008 would be inflationary despite the existence of large negative GDP gaps (see Chapter 25 for a discussion of quantitative easing). If economists were so divided on their expectations of future inflation, the general public could hardly be assumed to make the right prediction.

It is possible that in reality inflationary expectations in general and wage-setting in particular are influenced by a mixture of rational forward-looking considerations and expectations based on the experience of the recent past. Depending on the circumstances, expectations will sometimes tend to rely more on past experience, and at other times to rely more on present events whose effects are expected to influence the future.

As we shall see in detail in the next chapter, in recent decades central banks in many countries have sought to establish *credible* regimes for the control of inflation. Central banks have been made independent of day-to-day political influence and allowed independence to establish and maintain clearly defined low-inflation targets. These are meant not just to control inflation directly but also to *make people believe that inflation really will be kept under control*. Once such a regime of a constant inflation rate and a creditable policy to maintain that rate has been established, both forward- and backward-looking theories predict that expectations will be for that rate to continue into the future. In the next chapter we will alter this chapter's model to take account of the new regime of a stable and fully expected inflation rate.

---

offsetting upward shifts in *SRAS* and *AD* would happen once a year, while if the lag fell to six months they would happen every six months, thus doubling the annual inflation rate.

No matter how inflation expectations are formed, as long as people come to expect the inflation to continue,

input prices will begin to rise faster and faster, chasing the expected inflation rate upwards. As a result, the Bank will, sooner or later, have to give up on its policy of expanding the nominal money supply at the rate of inflation because the rising rate of inflation will become unacceptable. The Bank must then slow the rate of monetary expansion, letting the real money supply fall. This stops the *AD* curve from shifting upwards in step with the *SRAS* curve. As the *SRAS* curve continues to shift upwards, equilibrium moves up along the now fixed *AD* curve until the GDP gap is removed and the price level reaches the much higher level shown in Figure 21.13. This whole sequence follows the arrow heads in the figure, first rising along the fixed *SRAS* curve in response to the initial demand shock. Then, as the *SRAS* curve starts to shift upwards and the Bank causes the *AD* curve to shift upwards in parallel, the economy follows the vertical path upwards; once the Bank stops validating the inflation, the economy follows the path shown by the fixed *AD* curve until the GDP gap is eliminated and equilibrium is reached at Y^*.

According to this theory, if the Bank takes steps to maintain the positive GDP gap, the inflation rate will rise continually.

Also note that once the GDP falls back to its potential level, the GDP gap disappears and there is no demand pressure for the prices of final goods and inputs to rise. This gives rise to a second important prediction of this theory.

Inflations, whether short- or long-lived, are caused by a GDP gap and cannot be stopped unless the gap is removed.

But this is still not the end of the story. There has been an ongoing demand-driven inflation right until the GDP gap is eliminated. Unless expectations adjust instantaneously, the price level will continue to rise because the public expects it to rise. Prices of final output and wages will now rise in expectation of further increases in the price level, thus causing such increases. The economy now moves from a demand inflation to what can be called an expectational inflation. Because we do not have inflation explicitly shown in Figure 23.13, what comes next is best left to be studied after we have introduced a variation on the Phillips curve.

The argument concerning a rising inflation rate can be applied in reverse if there is a negative GDP gap. Output falls below potential because the reduction in input prices lags the reduction in output prices, leading firms to cut production. If the Bank were to reduce the money supply as fast as the price level was falling, the gap could be maintained. But sooner or later the lag between the adjustment of input and output prices would shorten as people came to expect the deflation to continue. Then the rate of deflation would increase until the Bank stopped reducing the money supply in line with the fall in the price level.

Negative GDP gaps will be associated with falling and then negative inflation rates, which will become more negative if the gap persists over a long time.

From this there follows another key prediction of the model in this chapter.

The only level of GDP that is compatible with a constant, fully expected, and fully accommodated rate of inflation is potential GDP, as indicated by the position of the *LRAS* curve.

The Phillips curve as a trade-off between inflation and unemployment

After Phillips published his original curve, some economists interpreted it as showing a permanent trade-off between inflation and unemployment. If the economy developed a positive GDP gap and a positive inflation rate, the adjustment mechanism that would push the economy back to potential GDP could be frustrated by the central bank. If the Bank increased the money supply at the same rate as prices were rising, this would hold the economy at a point on the curve at which there was a positive inflation rate and a lower unemployment rate than would occur at potential GDP. This erroneous assumption ignored the important effect of changes in inflation expectations. We saw in the previous section that the inflation rate would accelerate if the Bank tried to hold GDP above potential for any length of time. We now show this in an amended Phillips curve analysis that will allow us to take the argument a step further than before.

The expectations-augmented Phillips curve

We can now add expectations to the Phillips curve. The Phillips curve in Figure 21.12(ii) shows the effects only of demand pressures since it was drawn on the assumption that everyone expected the price level to remain constant. Thus it will predict actual inflation only if the expected inflation rate is zero. We can now add inflation expectations to the Phillips curve in the following way by writing

$$\dot{W} = F(Y - Y^*) + \dot{P}^e$$

where a dot over a variable indicates its annual percentage rate of change so that $\dot{P}_e$ is the expected rate of inflation. The term $F(Y - Y^*)$ tells us that the demand pressure on wage rates will be positive when the GDP gap is positive and negative when the gap is negative. The second term tells us that any expected rise in the price level will tend to cause an equivalent rise in the level of money wage rates so as to hold real wages constant.

Figure 21.14 shows this curve from Figure 21.12(ii), this time with $(\dot{P}_e = 0)$ attached to it to indicate that the curve shows the demand pressure on wage rates at various levels of GDP on the assumption that the expected inflation rate is zero. We start at Y^* and a stable price level and impose a demand shock that raises GDP above Y^* to, say, Y_1 in the figure. Demand pressure then causes

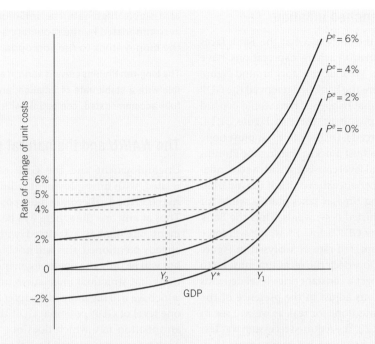

Figure 21.14 Accelerating inflation and the Phillips curve

If the Bank takes steps to hold GDP above potential, the inflation rate will rise continually. This figure uses the transformed Phillips curve from Figure 21.12(ii). Originally, GDP is at Y^*, the actual and expected rate of inflation is zero, and the transformed-Phillips curve is that labelled $\dot{P}^e = 0$. A demand shock then raises GDP to Y_1 and the wage costs rise at 2 per cent, taking the price level with them. The Bank then allows the nominal money supply to expand, thus holding the real money supply constant and allowing GDP to remain at Y_1. When expectations adjust to this new inflation rate, the Phillips curve shifts upwards to the curve labelled $\dot{P}^e = 2\%$. Wage and price inflation now rises to 4 per cent, of which 2 per cent is due to demand pressures and 2 per cent to the expectations of a continued 2 per cent inflation. Once again, expectations will adjust to the new 4 per cent rate, shifting the Phillips curve upwards to the curve labelled $\dot{P}^e = 4\%$. Inflation now rises to 6 per cent, of which 2 per cent is due to demand pressure and 4 per cent to expectations of a 4 per cent inflation. As long as the Bank holds GDP at Y_1, the inflation rate will continue to accelerate.

To consider a contractionary monetary policy assume that the Bank has lowered GDP to Y^* while expected inflation is 6 per cent. If GDP is reduced further to Y_2 while a 6 per cent rate of inflation is expected, inflation will be below expectations at 5 per cent. Expectations can then be assumed to be revised downwards. The induced slump with GDP below Y^* will have to be maintained for as long as it takes for expectations to be adjusted downwards, shifting the transformed Phillips curve down once again to the curve labelled ($\dot{P}^e = 0$).

wage rates to rise—at 2 per cent per year in the example shown in the figure. But after a while, expectations of a zero inflation will be abandoned and people will begin to assume that the 2 per cent rate is here to stay. As a result wages will begin to rise by an additional 2 per cent to cover the expected inflation. This is shown by the new Phillips curve with ($\dot{P}^e = 2\%$) attached to it. Now the inflation rate becomes 4 per cent (2 per cent because of demand pressures and 2 per cent because of the expectations of a 2 per cent inflation). This will persist as long as the Bank accommodates the inflation by causing the nominal money supply to rise as fast as the price level is rising. After a while people will come to expect that the 4 per cent inflation is here to stay. The curve will then shift upwards again to reflect the continuing 2 per cent inflation because of demand pressures and now 4 per cent because of the expected inflation rate. As long as the

Bank takes steps to maintain the GDP gap, the inflation rate will accelerate in this way.

The same argument holds in reverse if there is a negative GDP gap, as also shown in the figure. Now because of negative demand pressures the rise in the wage rates and hence in the price level will be less than the expected rate of inflation. If the gap persists, the expected rate of inflation will continue to be revised downwards. If the Bank does not accommodate this deflation by reducing the nominal money supply along with the fall the price level (and there is no reason why is would do this), the fall in the price level will raise the real quantity of money, which shifts the *AD* curve to the right pushing GDP back towards potential.

According to the expectations-augmented Phillips curve shows that the only level of GDP that is compatible with a stable inflation rate is potential GDP and its corresponding level of unemployment, the *NAIRU*.

Breaking an entrenched inflation

Now we can take up the story of what the Bank faces when breaking an inflation where expectations have adjusted to a high rate. We took the story around Figure 21.13 to the point where the Bank had removed the GDP gap and then we said what happened next would depend on expectations. We pick it up there in Figure 21.14. When the Bank has forced GDP back to Y^*, it must hope that expectations will adjust quickly, shifting the Phillips curve back to its original level consistent with a zero inflation rate. However, experience shows that if the inflation has persisted for a long time, it takes quite a while for expectations to be adjusted downwards. Thus the Bank must take steps to lower GDP below Y^*, which will force inflation below the expected rate as analysed in Figure 21.14. How long and how deep the recession must be to cause the public to expect a constant price level depends on how fast expectations adjust in the presence of the recession. When this was done for real, as we will see in more detail in Chapter 22, the required recession was less severe than pessimists predicted but more severe than optimists expected.

The long-run Phillips curve

We have argued earlier that only at potential GDP can the inflation rate be constant, neither accelerating as with a positive GDP gap nor decelerating as with a negative gap. The same point can be made with the Phillips curve. When GDP is at Y^*, the demand component of inflation is zero, as shown by the equilibrium points E_0 and E_4 in Figure 21.13. Or, if we look at Figure 21.14, we see that when $Y > Y^*$ the actual inflation rate exceeds the expected rate while when $Y < Y^*$ actual inflation is less than expected. Only at Y^* on each of the expectations-augmented Phillips curves is actual inflation equal to expected inflation. Then there are no surprises. Inflation is what everyone expects it to be and to which everyone is adjusted. No one's plans are upset, so no one has any incentive to alter plans as a result of what actually happens to inflation.

According to the theory in this chapter, provided that the inflation rate is fully accommodated, any rate of inflation can persist indefinitely if and only if GDP is held at its potential level.

We now define the **long-run Phillips curve (*LRPC*)** as the relationship between GDP and stable rates of inflation that neither rise nor fall. This occurs when the expected and actual inflation rates are equal. On the theory just described, the long-run Phillips curve is vertical, because only at Y^* can the expected and actual rates of inflation be equal. Of course, to remain at a stable high rate the inflation would have to be accommodated by the monetary authority's permitting the money stock to rise appropriately.

The long-run Phillips curve is vertical at Y^*, only Y^* is compatible with a stable rate of inflation, and any stable rate is, if fully accommodated, compatible with Y^*.

The *NAIRU* and the natural rate

Unemployment and the GDP gap are quite closely related, with unemployment falling when the GDP gap rises (i.e. the gap becomes more positive or less negative). Thus at any one time there will be a specific unemployment rate that is associated with potential GDP. As already mentioned, this will not be zero unemployment but will be only the unemployment associated with frictions and structural imbalances in the economy, about which we will say more in Chapter 23. So, if there is only one level of GDP, potential GDP, that is consistent with an inflation rate which does not become increasingly positive over time (when $Y > Y^*$) or increasingly negative over time (when $Y < Y^*$), there is only one unemployment rate that is consistent with the rate of change of wage costs not becoming increasingly positive over time (when $Y > Y^*$) or increasingly negative over time (when $Y < Y^*$). That rate is called the *non-accelerating inflation rate of unemployment*. That mouthful is, thankfully, shortened to its initials *NAIRU*, by which it is universally known.

The unemployment rate that is associated with potential GDP is also often referred to as the **natural rate of unemployment**. The problem with this designation is that there is really nothing natural about this particular unemployment rate. After all, potential GDP is a statistical estimate which, like all such estimates, is subject to some margin of error—and no one can be quite sure how large that error may be. Also, the amount of unemployment that exists when the estimated GDP gap is zero is itself subject to change for natural and policy-created reasons (as we shall see in Chapter 25).

We have now reached two conclusions with respect to this model. Starting from potential GDP, Y^*:

1. a single demand shock raises GDP but when input costs catch up with the rise in output prices, the *SRAS* curve shifts upwards causing GDP to return to its original level;

2. if the Bank takes steps to maintain the positive GDP gap, GDP will remain above potential for a while but sooner or later the inflation rate will accelerate as input prices begin to adjust faster and faster to the persistent disequilibrium in the labour market and the rising inflation rate.

Short- versus long-run effects

In the theory developed so far we have been concerned with the cyclical or short-run behaviour of such macroeconomic variables as GDP and the price level. When we added a *LRAS* curve just now, we were only allowing for delayed adjustments of input prices to demand and supply shocks but not for long-term shifts in the *LRAS* curve. However, another sense in which we could talk about the long-run behaviour of the economy relates to economic growth, which involves rightward shifts in the long-run aggregate supply curve. These two meanings of long term can be seen in Figure 21.15 which distinguishes three ways in which GDP can be increased according to the theory we have developed so far.

As shown in Figure 21.15(i), an increase in aggregate demand will yield a one-time increase in real GDP. If that increase occurs when there is a negative GDP gap, it pushes GDP towards its potential level. Thus it short-circuits the

working of the automatic adjustment mechanism that would eventually have achieved the same outcome by depressing input prices, as just discussed. If the demand shock pushes GDP above its potential level, the rise in GDP will be only temporary. The positive GDP gap will cause wages and other input prices to rise, shifting the *SRAS* curve to the left. This drives GDP back towards its potential level, so that the only lasting effect is on the price level.

Increases in aggregate supply will also lead to increases in GDP. Here, it is useful to distinguish between two possible kinds of increase that might occur—those that leave the *LRAS* curve unchanged and those that shift it.

Figure 21.15(ii) shows the effects of a positive shock (downward shift) to short-run aggregate supply that leaves potential GDP unchanged, such as would be caused by a fall in the prices of imported oil. This will shift the *SRAS* curve to the right but will have no effect on the *LRAS*

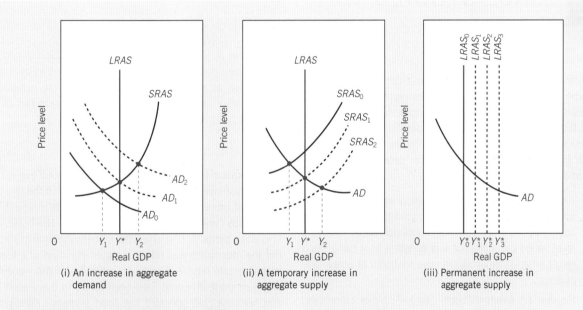

Figure 21.15 Three ways of increasing GDP

GDP will increase in response to an increase in aggregate demand or an increase in aggregate supply. In parts (i) and (ii) the *LRAS* is constant. Part (i) covers two cases. If aggregate demand was initially at AD_0 with GDP at Y_1, the increase in aggregate demand to AD_1 would raise GDP to Y^* without setting in motion any forces to lower it again. However, if aggregate demand was initially at AD_1 with GDP at Y^*, the rise to AD_2 would raise GDP to Y_2, but this would be temporary. A positive GDP gap would have been opened up, putting upward pressure on input prices causing the *SRAS* curve to shift upwards until GDP was returned to Y^*. Part (ii) also covers two cases. If the initial level of output is Y_1, the shift from $SRAS_0$ to $SRAS_1$ increases GDP to Y^* without setting in motion any forces to reduce it again. However, if the initial GDP was Y^*, the increase in aggregate supply from $SRAS_1$ to $SRAS_2$ would raise GDP to Y_2 and thereby open up a positive GDP gap. This causes input prices to rise until GDP is returned to Y^*. In part (iii) the *LRAS* curve shifts to the right, causing potential GDP to increase. Whether or not actual output increases immediately depends on what happens to the *AD* and *SRAS* curves. Since, in the absence of other shocks, actual GDP eventually converges to potential GDP, a rightward shift in the *LRAS* curve leads to an increase in actual GDP. If the shift in the *LRAS* curve is recurring, GDP will grow continually. There will also be downward pressure on the price level unless the *AD* curve is also shifted outwards.

curve. Thus the shock will cause GDP to rise towards potential if it begins below potential. But a shock that takes GDP beyond potential will eventually be reversed.

Figure 21.15(iii) shows the effects of permanent increases in aggregate supply that shift the *LRAS* curve. A once-and-for-all increase due, say, to an increase in the total supply of labour due to immigration will lead to a one-time increase in potential GDP. A recurring increase that is due, say, to population growth, capital accumulation, or ongoing improvements in productivity causes a continual rightward shift in the *LRAS* curve, giving rise to a continual increase in potential GDP. If the aggregate demand curve remains unchanged, the rise in potential output will be accompanied by a fall in the price level. If the *AD* curve shifts outward along with the *LRAS* curve, as would happen, for example, if the money supply was increased along with the rise in GDP, the expansion in output can take place at a constant price level.

Eliminating a severe negative GDP gap could cause a once-and-for-all increase in GDP of, say, 4 per cent. However, a modest GDP growth rate of 2 per cent per year raises GDP by 10 per cent in just under 5 years, *doubles* it in 34 years, and *quadruples* it in 72 years.

Economic growth, a gradual rise in potential GDP, is the main source of improvements in the standard of living over the long term.

We will discuss cyclical variations in some detail in Chapter 23 and economic growth in Chapter 26. Before we address any of these matters, our next step is to alter our theory of the endogenous price level to accommodate the third regime listed at the outset of this chapter—a regime in which there is an ongoing steady inflation rate that is fully accommodated by the Bank's monetary policy, that everyone expects to continue, and to which everyone is fully adjusted.

CASE STUDIES

1. Three monetary regimes

Over the past two centuries, the developed countries have experienced three major monetary regimes with varying results concerning inflation and business cycles. First, we outline them and then give some pertinent details. Everyone needs to know the outline, while the details are helpful in understanding the differences between the regimes but are not critical.

Regime 1a, the gold standard, early eighteenth century to 1931 Because it was tied to gold the money supply could not be altered at will by any central bank. The price level varied cyclically but was constant as a trend. As a result inflation expectations were anchored at an average of zero.

Regime 1b, Bretton Woods, 1945–72 Major currencies, including sterling, were convertible into US dollars at a fixed rate, while the dollar was convertible into gold. Maintaining a fixed exchange rate required that the central banks controlled the money supply with the object of keeping inflation no higher than the very low rate that ruled in the United States. Expectations of inflation were low, but not zero.

Regime 2, Floating exchange rates, 1972 to early 1990s The world's central banks were now free to vary the money supply in pursuit of domestic goals and a period of high and variable inflation ensued.

Regime 3, inflation targeting, early 1990s to date Monetary policy was successfully directed at holding inflation at a very low target rate. Inflation expectations were once again anchored, not at zero but at a target typically around 2 per cent.

The regimes and the Phillips curve

In his famous 1958 study A.W. Phillips provided evidence for the existence of a stable relationship between the rate of change of money wages and the level of unemployment— the Phillips curve. The period of his study was 1861–1957. This was a period during which the monetary regime in place (for the most part) was either the gold standard or a fixed exchange rate regime. The key to why the inflation–unemployment trade-off could have been stable in that period is that both the gold standard and fixed exchange rates provided a 'nominal anchor' that tied down inflation expectations—the former because the value of home currency was fixed in terms of a real commodity, gold, and the latter because in the Bretton Woods system (introduced after World War II) the home currency was pegged to a foreign currency (the US dollar) which itself was pegged to gold.

With the end of the Bretton Woods system in 1972 the currencies were no longer pegged to anything. The world's economy's entered the next regime of high and variable inflation. At that time the expectations-augmented Phillips curve came into play.

We show in Chapter 22 that inflation targeting has proved itself to be a new type of regime that has once again successfully tied down inflation expectations and, in effect, flattened out the Phillips curve.

Experience under the gold standard

Figure 21.16 shows the inflation and unemployment data for the UK from 1885 to 1957 (thus covering much of the period of the original Phillips study, but excluding 1861–84 for reasons of data availability, and focusing on price inflation rather than wage inflation). The path of inflation is shown by the continuous line and the direction is made clear by comparing any two dates.

The cluster of data in the oval labelled 'gold standard years' shows the behaviour of inflation and unemployment during the gold standard regime. This cluster contains all the data from 1885 to 1913 and the data from 1925 to 1929, a period when the UK was explicitly on the gold standard. Inflation in these years appears to be symmetrical around zero and the short-run trade-off between inflation and unemployment looks weak, but slightly negative. This is consistent with inflation expectation being anchored at zero, while inflation rises slightly at low levels of unemployment and falls slightly at high levels.

The outliers from this central cluster of data points are also instructive. The high inflation rates around the point labelled 1917 are during World War I and its aftermath.

Clearly, there was a high pressure of demand and very low unemployment. The gold standard was not abandoned formally but it was in practice, as gold coins were removed from circulation and (more than) replaced by paper currency. The money supply was increased substantially, which helps to explain the high war-time inflation rate. The war was followed by a very sharp and severe deflation as the government cut spending substantially, exports fell, and prices declined. A comparable deflation occurred in the United States for similar reasons. It is not entirely clear why prices fell so much in 1921 and 1922, but one possible explanation is what has been called 'gold standard expectations'. Under the gold standard prices fell back to a 'normal level' after any rise, so it is possible that people expected the price level to return to its pre-war value and this helped drive the price level down. Another contributory factor is that during the war new cost-of-living clauses had linked wages to prices (initially to head off industrial disputes when inflation was high), and these were still in place after the war but kicked in a reverse direction as prices fell, wages followed, and a downward wage–price spiral resulted.

In the Great Depression of the 1930s it took very high levels of unemployment to lead to even modest reductions in the price level, and it is this period that led many Keynesians to argue that prices and wages had become sticky downwards, even though most of them would also have experienced the rapid price and wage falls of 1921 and 1922. However, by the 1930s cost-of-living clauses

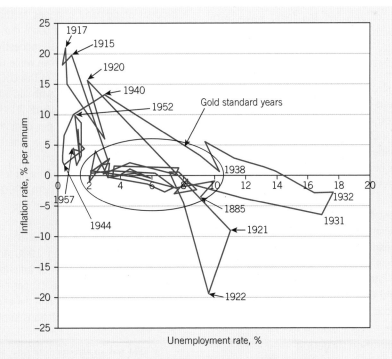

Figure 21.16 UK inflation, unemployment, and monetary regimes, 1885–1957

had been removed from wage contracts, so there was no automatic link from price level reductions to reductions in wage rates, and therefore the scale of the deflation was much more modest even though unemployment was much higher than it had ever been in recorded history. Although the experience of this period was extreme, it did nothing to upset the expectation that the long-run trend was for the price level to stay constant.

Experience under Bretton Woods

World War II and its aftermath were handled rather better than World War I from an inflation and unemployment perspective. Inflation did reach around 13 per cent in 1940, but price controls and rationing then took effect and inflation fell even though unemployment also fell. The end of the war saw the introduction of the Bretton Woods system in which exchange rates were pegged to the US dollar and the dollar was convertible into gold. This provided an anchor once again, although less strong than under the gold standard since there was always the possibility of altering the exchange rate if the price level got out of line with that of the United States. The data for this period are seen in the small cluster of very low unemployment with an inflation rate that varies between 2 and 10 per cent, averaging slightly less than 5 per cent. The higher rates approaching 10 per cent were associated with high US demand and government stockpiling associated with the Korean War in the early 1950s. This was regarded as exceptional and so not setting any high inflation trend. Therefore the price level was not rising uncontrollably but the trend was clearly upwards, in contrast with the gold standard.

Experience under floating exchange rates

All of this contrasts strongly with the behaviour of inflation and unemployment from 1972 to 1992, as shown in Figure 22.2 in the next chapter. In 1972 the pound was floated, which means that its value was not tied to anything but rather was determined by supply and demand in a free market. The Bank was now free to vary the money supply in pursuit of purely domestic objectives. A significant monetary and fiscal stimulus was soon introduced (the Barber Boom). Unemployment fell slightly but inflation soared, and this is when inflation expectations started to rise and the expectations-augmented Phillips curve came into play. High inflation became endemic, and thus expected, although the precise rate varied and was hard to predict with any accuracy, and only high unemployment seemed able to bring down those expectations.

Experience under inflation targeting

After various failed attempts with anti-inflation policies that included wage and price controls, then often called incomes

policy, money growth targeting, direct controls on banks, exchange rate targeting, and joining the European Exchange Rate Mechanism (ERM)[15], a new regime of inflation targeting was introduced in the UK in 1993 (announced in 1992). The effect was dramatic. Unemployment fell, but inflation remained anchored close to the target inflation rate. Indeed, the negative relationship between inflation and unemployment disappeared. Chapter 22 develops a model that applies to this period and looks at the experience in more detail. Of course, the period of high and variable inflation could return, but that will happen only if the inflation targeting regime has failed or been abandoned.

2. Inflation and unemployment in the G7 countries, 1980–2019

The previous case study reported data for the UK. We now show that the experience of the other major economies of the world has been similar. Figure 21.17 shows the course of inflation and unemployment for a weighted average of the G7 major countries since 1980. Inflation was over 12 per cent on average in 1980 and contractionary policies designed to reduce inflation succeeded, but only at the price of high unemployment. Such was the slack in most economies in the early 1980s that some recovery was possible without generating any inflationary pressure. Between 1983 and 1986 unemployment fell at the same time as inflation fell (a contributory factor here was falling world energy prices which can be thought of as a negative supply shock for each country on its own, even though it is partly a product of demand changes at the world level). From 1986 to 1990 there was a boom during which unemployment fell while inflation rose modestly. In the subsequent recession, unemployment rose while inflation fell slightly.

From 1993 onwards, as in the UK, unemployment fell in a steady recovery but with no increase in inflation. Indeed, from that point onwards it looks as if inflation has been anchored close to 2 per cent and has been largely unaffected by any changes in unemployment and thus also changes in the GDP gap.

The cyclical peak in 2007 had a level of unemployment that was below the level in both 1990 and 1980, but with a significantly lower rate of inflation. Indeed, it could be argued that this chart shows three separate Phillips curves for three different levels of inflation expectations. The first is the one running between 1980 and 1985 which was associated with a high level of inflation expectations, possibly of the order of around 10 per cent. The high unemployment and falling inflation of the early 1980s succeeded in reducing inflation expectations such that it was around

---

[15] The ERM was an agreement to limit the range of fluctuation between values of the member currencies. It was set up in 1979, but the UK was only a member of the exchange rate setting arrangement for a short time between 1990 and 1992.

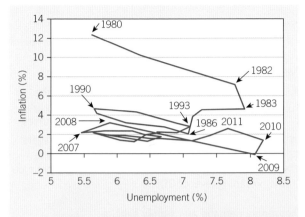

Figure 21.17 The path of inflation and unemployment in the G7 countries from 1980 to 2019

The data are a weighted average of the values for each of seven countries, using GDP as weights. The seven countries are: the United States, the United Kingdom, Canada, France, Germany, Italy, and Japan. Data for 2014–2019 are IMF forecasts as of April 2014.

Source: IMF, *World Economic Outlook* database, April 2014

varied between just under 5.5 per cent to around 8.2 per cent, but inflation stayed close to 2 per cent. Critics could say that even here there is a negatively sloped Phillips curve, for which there is some evidence, but this is entirely dependent on the two observations for 2008 and 2009 which were very abnormal years. The negatively sloped line joining these two years is the product of the global financial crisis and resulting worldwide recession. In 2008 inflation had nudged up in most countries, not due to domestic wage and price pressure but rather due to high world prices of energy, and some other commodity prices. The crisis and resulting global recession caused substantial reductions in output and a sharp rise in unemployment. The associated collapse of world trade also led to large reductions in commodity prices, including oil. These price reductions led to a sharp fall in inflation in 2009. Therefore the key events of 2008 and 2009 were an upward supply shock in 2008, which raised prices, followed by a substantial negative demand shock, which lowered output and raised unemployment, combined with a downward supply shock which lowered prices. The two supply shocks were temporary and quickly reversed, so that by 2010 inflation was rising even as unemployment continued to rise. After 2010, unemployment fell steadily even though inflation remained around 2 per cent.

3–4 per cent by the second half of the 1980s, and the data from 1986 to 1990 trace out the associated Phillips curve.

The third Phillips curve is essentially flat, based on inflation expectations around 2 per cent and encompasses all the data from 1993 onwards. Unemployment

Conclusion

In this and the next chapter we develop variations of our basic theory of GDP determination that are applicable to various historical periods. However, these variations are not just relevant to ancient history because the model that is appropriate to each successive period builds on the model appropriate to the earlier period. Thus the earlier version is needed to understand the variations that are introduced to deal with the later models.

The version of the theory developed in the first part of this chapter fits well the world from the early 1800s to the 1970s, during which time the average price level was fairly constant and was expected to remain so. It did change over the cycle, rising in booms and falling in slumps. But it did not change significantly from cycle to cycle.

The aggregate demand curve shows the equilibrium level of GDP as determed by the *IS* and *LM* curves for each endogenously determined price level. The short-run aggregate supply curve shows the desired level of aggregate production that is associated with each price level. Combining the two produces a theory of the determination of equilibrium GDP and the price level, showing how each changes when either demand or supply shocks impinge on the economy (but where price level is assumed to be constant over the long term).

The long-run aggregate supply curve is assumed here to be vertical at potential GDP and the Phillips curve shows the speed at which long-run GDP is re-established after a shock that moves it away from its potential level.

The latter part of the chapter deals with a situation in which the price level is not expected to hold constant over the long term. This requires that we consider how expectations about the future price level are formed and how they affect the behaviour of our model when it is hit by various demand or supply shocks. This version of the theory best fits the period of ragged inflation that persisted from about 1970 to the early 1990s. In the next chapter, we introduce those variations that are required to deal with the present situation in which the price level, although not constant, is rising at a slow and fully expected rate.

SUMMARY

The aggregate demand curve

- An exogenous rise in the price level shifts the *LM* curve to the left due to the real money effect; the real money supply is diminished, causing the *LM* curve to shift upwards and to the left.

- An exogenous rise in the price level shifts the *IS* curve downwards and to the left because of the wealth and balance-of-payments effects.

- An exogenous rise in the price level reduces equilibrium GDP because of both the *IS* and *LM* curve shifts that it causes.

- The aggregate demand curve, *AD*, is derived by plotting each exogenous price level against the equilibrium GDP that results from the *IS–LM* equilibrium that is consistent with each given price level.

- Any point on the *AD* curve is such that *if* that level of output is produced, (1) aggregate desired spending will exactly equal total output and (2) the demand for money will equal the supply.

- Shifts in the *AD* curve.

- A rightward shift in the *AD* curve, called a demand shock, is caused by anything that increases aggregate spending and hence shifts the *IS* curve to the right, or anything that increases the real money supply and hence shifts the *LM* curve to the right.

The aggregate supply curve

- The short-run aggregate supply curve, *SRAS,* shows the relation between the price level and GDP over a short period of time. It is assumed to have a positive slope indicating that a rise in the price level is associated with a rise in GDP.

- Deviations from long-run equilibrium are assumed to occur because the fast adjusting prices of goods rise relative to slow adjusting input prices when aggregate demand rises, leading firm to wish to increase production; while they fall relative to input prices when aggregate demand falls, leading firms to wish to contract production. Hence the *SRAS* curve is not vertical.

- In the circumstances assumed in this model firms' costs rise as their outputs rise, so that they need a higher price to induce them to raise output. Hence the *SRAS* curve has a positive slope.

Shifts in the *SRAS* curve

- Increases in input prices shift the *SRAS* curve upwards and to the left while increases in productivity do the opposite.

Macroeconomic equilibrium

- Macroeconomic equilibrium, which determines the equilibrium values of real GDP and the price level, occurs at the intersection of the *AD* and *SRAS* curves.

- At macroeconomic equilibrium, (1) desired aggregate spending equals GDP, (2) the demand for money is equal to its supply, and (3) firms are willing to produce the prevailing level of GDP.

Aggregate demand and supply shocks

- Aggregate demand shocks cause the price level and real GDP to change in the same direction, rising when aggregate demand is increased and falling when aggregate demand is reduced.

- Because the *SRAS* curve has a positive slope, the *AD–AS* multiplier is smaller than the *IS–LM* multiplier, which in turn is smaller than the interest-rate-constant multiplier.

- Aggregate supply shocks cause the price level and real GDP to change in opposite directions. Importantly, with a decrease in supply (the *SRAS* shifts to the left and upwards) the price level rises and output falls.

The *LRAS* curve

- The long-run aggregate supply (*LRAS*) curve shows the relation between the price level and real GDP after wage rates and all other input prices have been fully adjusted.

- The *LRAS* curve is vertical at potential output.

- Equilibrium GDP is determined in the long run by the *LRAS* curve, while the aggregate demand curve determines only the price level.

Demand shocks and sustained inflation

- If the Bank takes steps to maintain an existing positive GDP gap, the inflation rate will rise continually.

- If the Bank takes steps to maintain a negative GDP gap, the price level will fall ever faster.

- Inflations, whether short- or long-lived, are caused by a GDP gap and cannot be stopped unless the gap is removed.

- According to the theory in this chapter, the only level of GDP that is compatible with a constant, fully expected and fully accommodated rate of inflation is potential GDP, as indicated by the position of the *LRAS* curve. It is located at Y^* and the *NAIRU*.

The Phillips curve

- The Phillips curve relates the percentage of the labour force unemployed to the rate of increase of money wage rates (often called wage inflation).

- By subtracting the rate of increase of labour productivity, the curve can be turned into a unit-cost Phillips curve.
- By substituting GDP for unemployment the curve can be transformed into a relation between GDP and the rate of wage inflation.
- The transformed curve shows how fast the *SRAS* curve is shifting, upwards in the face of a positive GDP gap, or downwards in the face of a negative GDP gap.

Short- versus long-run effects

- A rightward shift in the *AD* curve (positive demand shock) or in the *SRAS* curve will increase GDP permanently if it occurs when there is a positive GDP gap, but only temporarily if it occurs when GDP is already at its potential.
- A rightward shift in the *LRAS* curve will raise potential GDP permanently.

TOPICS FOR REVIEW

- Effect of a rise in the price level on the *IS* and *LM* curves
- The real money effect
- The wealth effect
- The balance-of-payments effect
- The derivation of the *AD* curve
- Causes of demand shocks
- The *SRAS* curve, definition and slope
- What causes the *SRAS* curve to shift

- Macroeconomic equilibrium
- The effects of aggregate demand shocks on macroeconomic equilibrium
- The effects of aggregate supply shocks on macroeconomic equilibrium
- The three multipliers
- The *NAIRU*
- The Phillips curve

QUESTIONS

1 Explain what happens to the UK *AD* curve in response to each of the following exogenous changes: (a) a rise in optimism leads to higher investment, (b) the government decides to build many new schools, (c) there is a recession in the United States, (d) consumers become cautious about the future and decide to save more, (e) GDP in France and Germany rises, and (f) new computer technology increases productivity in manufacturing industry. Answer these questions first for an economy that starts at Y^* and then for one that starts with a negative GDP gap $(Y < Y^*)$.

2 Show what would happen to the *SRAS* curve if (a) investment in transport infrastructure lowers costs of shipping goods and raw materials, (b) oil prices rise, (c) workers agree to work for lower wages, (d) there is an increase in export demand, and (e) there is a technical innovation that drastically lowers costs in the manufacturing industry.

3 Look at Figure 21.14. What would the actual rate of wage and price inflation be if the expected rate was 4 per cent and GDP was Y_2? What if the expected rate

was 2 per cent and GDP still at Y_2? What is the relation between the actual and the expected rate when actual Y is less that Y^*?

4 Outline how the interaction of the *AD* and *SRAS* curves determines the course of GDP and the price level in response to (a) a rise in wage rates, (b) an increase in investment, (c) a reduction in government consumption, and (d) a boom in demand in neighbouring economies.

5 Explain why it is that changes in the price level lead to changes in desired aggregate spending for each level of GDP.

6 Explain why the change in real GDP in response to an increase in export demand is smaller than that suggested by the simple multiplier. What happens to the size of this effect as GDP rises above its potential level?

7 Explain how it is that the shifts in *AD* set out in Question 1 are consistent with the condition that injections equal leakages.

8 How do you think changes in interest rates would affect aggregate demand?

9 Starting with the economy below Y^*, (a) explain how the economy will eventually adjust back to Y^* through the automatic adjustment mechanism, and (b) explain how fiscal and monetary policy could help return the economy to Y^*.

10 Repeat Question 8, but starting from a position where current GDP is above Y^*.

11 Explain carefully the differences between the adjustment of the economy in a negative GDP gap and a positive GDP gap.

12 Why is the *LRAS* curve assumed to be vertical? What does this imply about the impact of aggregate demand shifts on equilibrium real GDP?

CHAPTER 22

THE DETERMINATION OF GDP WITH STEADY INFLATION

In the previous chapter we presented two versions of a standard model of the macroeconomy which assumes a unique equilibrium level of real GDP to which the economy returns if disturbed and at which the price level is constant. The two versions were distinguished by the assumption concerning inflation expectations. In the first version, the price level was expected to remain constant on average. In the second version, the price level was expected to change over time. Both of these versions offer many useful insights but they do not handle well the behaviour of the economy in recent times in which the central bank has established a credible commitment to a low inflation policy. As a result, the actual inflation rate has been low, relatively steady, and fully anticipated, while GDP has varied over a significant range. In this chapter we alter the model of Chapter 21 to make it apply to this recent experience.

In what follows you will learn that:

- Over the past more than two decades the Bank of England has successfully held the inflation rate to about one percentage point on either side of its target rate of 2 per cent per annum.
- Variations outside of the target range for inflation have been due to supply-side rather than demand-side shocks.
- There no longer appears to be a connection between the GDP gap and changes in the price level, at least for both positive and negative GDP gaps of moderate size.
- A version of the *AD* curve called *AD** shows a negative relationship between real GDP and unexpected inflation.
- A version of the aggregate supply curve called *AS** shows that GDP can vary over a wide range while the inflation rates stays close to the rate that is targeted by the Bank and fully expected by the public.
- A demand shock that takes GDP well above its potential level will cause the inflation rate to rise above target, but unless that inflation is accommodated by a corresponding monetary expansion, the rate will soon return to the target range.
- A supply shock due to exogenous increases in input prices will cause the inflation rate to rise temporarily while GDP falls.
- If the Bank adopts a monetary policy that maintains a positive GDP gap the inflation rate will rise continually, the speed of increase depending on how fast expectations adjust to the rising inflation rate.

Three price level regimes

Over the past two centuries there have been three different monetary regimes affecting the behaviour of the price level and inflation expectations. These regimes were spelled out in detail in the first case study of Chapter 21. Here we first briefly mention the first regime. We then devote more space to experience under the second regime, since that

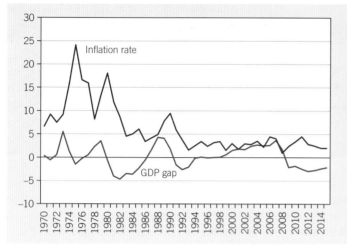

Figure 22.1 Inflation and the GDP gap

The GDP gap and inflation were closely related until the early 1990s but not thereafter. The figure shows one estimate of the GDP gap and the inflation rate for the UK from 1990 to 2015. The peaks in the inflation rate follow the peaks in the GDP gap by about a year, which, given the lags in the system, is about what would be expected on the basis of the theory presented in Chapter 21. However, after the early 1990s the inflation rate stayed close to 2 per cent while the GDP gap varied considerably.

Source: CPI data from ONS; GDP gap estimates from IMF *World Economic Outlook*, various issues. Data for 2014 and 2015 are IMF forecasts.

experience provided the motivation for establishing the third regime. Then the rest of the chapter describes the third regime and develops a theory that deals with it.

The gold standard and Bretton Woods

The first regime was one in which there was an anchor to the *price level* so that both average inflation and inflation expectations were effectively zero. This came in two versions, the gold standard, which worked exactly like that, and the Bretton Woods system, which followed World War II and provided considerable, but somewhat weaker, incentives and constraints that kept inflation low. But because there was always the option of occasional devaluations of the exchange rate, inflation was somewhat higher than under the gold standard. The first sections of Chapter 21 provide the theory needed to study this regime. The *AD* and *SRAS* curves explained the reaction of the economy to macro disturbances, and the simple Phillips curve showed how the inflation rate responded to cyclical variations in the GDP gap, although that rate was more or less constant over the long term.

Floating exchange rates

The second regime began with the abandonment of the Bretton Woods System in 1972. When this happened, exchange rates were free to fluctuate, a situation often referred to as one of floating exchange rates. Now there was no constraint that tended to anchor the price level or the inflation rate. Inflation soared in response to expansionary monetary and fiscal policies, but there was uncertainty among economists and policy-makers about its causes. Some argued that inflation was driven by demand, while others argued that it was driven by cost push forces, particularly strong unions who forced wage rates up, causing prices to rise, and oil prices that had been forced up by

the Organization of Petroleum Exporting Countries (OPEC). These 'cost push' and 'demand pull' theories were strenuously advocated by different groups. This led to uncertainty as to the course of inflation, since even the experts were not sure what was causing it to vary, and even more uncertainty about what to do about it.

What followed in the United Kingdom were three 'boom–bust cycles during which the economy first reached a high level of activity associated with a positive GDP gap that was soon followed by a rise in the inflation rate. When the boom turned to recession (often in response to policy tightening using the fiscal and monetary tools that we will study in detail in Chapter 25), a negative GDP gap emerged, which was soon followed by a decline in the inflation rate.

Figure 22.1 shows an estimate[1] of the UK GDP gap (the blue line) and the inflation rate (the red line). There was a boom in 1972–3 that created a positive GDP gap, and high inflation followed. Policy tightening lowered GDP and eventually brought down inflation. There was a further boom in GDP in the late 1970s and, once more, a positive GDP gap led to higher inflation.[2] Policy was again tightened and the recession of the early 1980s resulted, bringing inflation down with it. In the late 1980s there was another boom in activity leading to a positive GDP gap and another pick-up in inflation, both of which collapsed in the early 1990s recession. During that time most governments had no explicit inflation targets, but were mostly altering their policies in response to developing situations that they wished to change. In the United Kingdom, a succession of monetary targets, quantitative controls, and exchange rate targets were tried with little success.

---

[1] There are no UK official measures of the GDP gap, so we use here an estimate taken from various issues of the IMF World Economic Outlook.

[2] Both the early 1970s inflation and that of 1979–80 were complicated by the combination of a demand boom and a supply shock due to higher oil prices.

Understanding the behaviour of the economy under the second regime required that the theory set out in the first part of Chapter 21 be altered to allow for the influence of positive inflation expectations. At the time there was much debate about how these expectations were formed and how they influenced macroeconomic behaviour. Whatever the precise theory of expectation formation that was used, it was agreed that expectations had to be added to the simple Phillips curve. This expectations-augmented version provides a series of Phillips curves, as shown in Figure 21.14, each one applying to some specific expected inflation rate. The implication is that if the Bank attempts to maintain a positive GDP gap by expanding the nominal money supply at the same rate as the price level is rising, the inflation rate will increase continually.

Why was inflation a problem?

In a market economy money is our measure of value, but as we saw in Chapter 18 it is relative monetary values that matter. Is this product expensive? To answer meaningfully, you need to relate its price to your money income and to the prices of other substitute products. Is this new product worth producing? To answer this, the firm needs to relate the price that it expects to be able to charge to the production costs it expects to encounter. Have I saved enough for my retirement? Here I need to compare the money income that my retirement investments and pension are expected to bring in with my expected money spending. These and myriad other similar questions are answered by comparing different money values, both as they exist today and as we expect them to be at some future date.

These comparisons are easiest when the price level is constant or when it is changing at a modest and predictably constant rate. But the inflations of the 1970s and 1980s were not modest, were not constant, and were not easily predictable. Instead, they were what the Swedish economist Axel Leijonhufvud called 'ragged'. If you saved money for your retirement, you did not know what it would buy when you retired, possibly many decades into the future. If I invested money in bonds or life insurance, the contracts were usually specified in money units. So, with ragged inflation I do not know what these contracts would yield me in terms of purchasing power when I, or my heirs, need it later. When firms undertook to produce some product in the future, they did not know what its price or production costs would be. If both changed evenly, it might not matter how much they changed, as this would keep the margin between them equal. But this was not the usual case. Price adjustments were ragged in the sense that some adjusted rapidly and more or less continually, while others adjusted in occasional discontinuous jumps. In such circumstances, it was hard, if not impossible, to distinguish genuine changes in equilibrium relative prices

and costs from temporary changes due to lags in the adjustment of various prices to inflationary pressures.

More generally, as we saw in Chapter 21, unanticipated inflation leads to a redistribution of wealth from lenders to borrowers. The qualification 'unanticipated' is important because many of the effects of a predictable inflation can be prevented by setting the nominal interest rate above the desired real rate by the expected inflation rate. But with ragged and unpredictable inflation, there will inevitably be redistributions of wealth. If the actual rate turns out to be below the expected rate, the nominal rate would have been set too high, so that lenders would gain at the expense of borrowers. But if the actual rate turns out to exceed the expected rate, the nominal rate would have been set too low and borrowers would gain while lenders would lose.

There were other fears based on some disastrous experiences of the past. These concerned the hyperinflations associated with what is popularly called the printing-press financing of large and uncontrollable government budget deficits. Although these were not a significant worry for the world's major economies at the beginning of the 1990s, they do account for some serious underlying concerns about inflation in general. Box 22.1 explains the mechanism of printing press financing of government deficits as well as the experience of hyperinflations to which they sometimes lead.

For these and many other similar reasons, the high and ragged inflation rates of the 1970s and 1980s came to be regarded as extremely undesirable. As a result, a major policy change occurred in most of the world's developed countries early in the 1990s.

Inflation targeting

Restrictive monetary policy initiated in 1990 succeeded in driving the inflation rate down from its local high of about 10 per cent, but at the cost of a growing negative GDP gap. At first this appeared to be yet another reaction to the successive periods of high inflation that had been the rule since the 1970s. But then early in the 1990s a new macro policy regime was established—the third one in our sequence of regimes. It was based upon an inflation target. The target was first officially announced in the United Kingdom in 1992 when it was put in the hands of the Bank of England.[3]

---

[3] The initial target was set in 1992 as a band from one to four per cent inflation. It was changed in 1997 to 2.5 per cent with a one percentage point band on either side, and finally altered to two per cent with the same one percentage point band in 2003. Inflation was originally measured as the annual percentage change in the RPIX which is the full retail price index but excluding mortgage interest payments and then later to the CPI, which has a common definition throughout the EU. It is similar to the RPIX in that it does not include the effects of interest rates on housing costs but it uses a geometric weighting method while RPIX uses arithmetic averaging.

Box 22.1 Printing press finance and hyperinflations

If a government's spending exceeds its current revenues from taxes and other revenue sources, it can finance the deficit by borrowing from domestic firms and households, by borrowing from foreign sources, or by selling bonds to the central bank. The last case is what is called 'printing press finance'. The government prints bonds and sells them to the central bank. The Bank buys them by giving the government a credit on the Bank's books. When the government pays its bills by writing cheques on its newly created deposits, the cheques will be deposited in commercial banks which then find themselves with new deposits of cash on which they can expand deposits by making new loans. Where the printing press comes in is that when the banks expands the amount of deposit money, the public will want to hold some proportion of that new money in cash balances for the reasons we have discussed earlier. To meet that demand the Bank must print new money.

We have already seen that an increase in the nominal money supply shifts the *LM* curve to the right and expands the economy. Once the economy reaches full employment of resources, the extra demand causes prices to rise. If the budget deficit is modest, a modest inflation will ensue, possibly of the order or 5–10 per cent. For those who dislike inflation this is bad enough. But if the deficit is large, so that the accompanying printing press finance is large, the inflation can rise exponentially. Say that the government has a deficit equal to 10 per cent of GDP each period of time, a deficit that it must finance by selling bonds to the central bank. If the money value of GDP is currently £1 billion, it must create £100 million of new money to finance the deficit. If the ensuing inflation raises the money value of GDP to £1.2 billion next period, it must now create £120 billion of new money. By the time the inflation has doubled the money value of GDP to £2 billion, the Bank needs to create £200 million to finance the deficit. And so it goes on with ever larger and larger amounts of new money being created each period.

When inflation becomes so rapid that people lose confidence in the purchasing power of their currency, they rush to spend it. People who have goods become increasingly reluctant to accept the rapidly depreciating money in exchange. The rush to spend money accelerates the increase in prices until people finally become unwilling to accept money on any terms. The price system can then be restored only by repudiation of the old monetary unit and its replacement by a new unit. This destroys the value of monetary savings and of all contracts specified in terms of the old monetary unit.

There have been a number of cases in which the printing press financing of government deficits have had such an effect. A classic case occurred in Germany shortly after the end of World War I. Although Germany had experienced substantial inflation during the war, averaging more than 30 per cent per year, the immediate postwar years of 1920 and 1921 gave no sign of an explosive inflation; indeed, price stability was experienced during 1920. However, in 1922 and 1923 the price level exploded. The index of wholesale prices in Germany shows that a product purchased with one 100 mark note in July 1923 would have required ten million 100 mark notes for its purchase only four months later! On 15 November 1923 the mark was officially repudiated, its value wholly destroyed.

There are about a dozen documented hyperinflations in world history, among them the collapses of the continental (this is the name given to the notes issued by the American Continental Congress at that time) during the American War of Independence, the rouble during the Russian Revolution, the drachma during and after the German occupation of Greece in World War II, and the Chinese national currency during 1946–8. The all-time record goes to Hungary, where inflation reached 4.19 quintillion per cent just after the end of World War II.

Every one of these hyperinflations was accompanied by huge increases in the money supply; new money was printed to give governments the purchasing power that they could not or would not obtain by taxation. Further, every one occurred in the midst of a major political upheaval in which grave doubts existed about the stability and the future of the government itself.

Do not assume that hyperinflation is a curiosity only to be found in ancient history books. In Serbia between July and December of 1993 and the end of the year inflation went from 500 per cent per month to 500,000 per cent and more. By January, prices were rising faster than 100 per cent per hour! Nor is this the only modern case. In 2008–9 Zimbabwe's inflation rose to 231 million per cent according to official figures. Just a bit later, an independent expert estimated that country's inflation rate was 2 trillion per cent a year!

(The change over from the old reactive regime to one of inflation targeting is detailed in Chapter 25). The object of monetary policy was to keep the inflation rate within a narrow band of one percentage point on either side of what became the 2 per cent target. Thus the acceptable rate was anything within the target range defined by the upper bound of 3 per cent and the lower bound of 1 per cent. This policy regime succeeded in stabilizing first the inflation rate

and then, importantly, expectations concerning that rate. Ever since the early 1990s, the correlation between the GDP gap and inflation has disappeared. In other words the Phillips curve has been flattened or, put another way, the Phillips curve has pretty well disappeared.

One of the most important developments in macroeconomic management in recent decades has been the adoption of

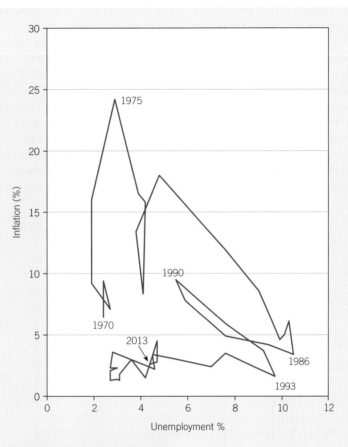

Figure 22.2 Inflation and unemployment in the UK

Except for several deviations due to supply-side shocks, the UK inflation rate has stayed within a band of one percentage point on either side of the 2 per cent target since the early 1990s. Restrictive government policies in the late 1980s and early 1990s drove the inflation rate down from high levels until it fell below 3 per cent in 1993. Since then, it has stayed within the acceptable band of one percentage point on either side of the target rate of 2 per cent, while unemployment has varied over the range from just over 10 per cent to just over 4 per cent. The upward deviations in 2008, 2010, and 2011 were due to observable positive supply-side shocks and a rise in VAT, while the one major downward deviation in 2000 was due to a negative supply-side shock.

Source: ONS online database

explicit inflation targets by many of the world's central banks, including the Bank of England, and making these targets credible by strong action to maintain the target rate by appropriate monetary policy.

Figure 22.2 offers a slightly different perspective in showing the course of UK inflation from 1970 to the present plotted against the rate of unemployment. For reasons of availability we use unemployment rather than the GDP gap. Since the two are closely related—the higher is the unemployment rate the more negative is the GDP gap— high unemployment is associated with negative GDP gaps and low unemployment with positive GDP gaps.

Figure 22.2 shows that there was a very high cost in term of unemployment that resulted from attempts to

eliminate the high inflation of the 1970s, but since the adoption of inflation targeting in the early 1990s inflation has stayed low while unemployment fell consistently up to the 2008–9 recession and then rose for several years. Although inflation has deviated somewhat from target three times during this period, these deviations have not been linked to the GDP gap. Instead, they were due to supply-side shocks that were beyond the control of monetary policy, which must work by altering aggregate demand and hence the GDP gap. The rise in the inflation rate in 2008 was related to a rise in world prices of oil, gas, and other basic commodities. The low inflation rate of 2009 was caused by a cut in VAT and a collapse of world commodity prices following the 2007–8 financial crisis. Inflation was close to 5 per cent in 2011 even though the GDP gap was negative at the time. Much of this price rise was due to a sharp increase in the rate of value added tax (VAT) and an increase in world energy prices. So each time inflation has breached the target range, supply-side shocks were the culprit—in the first and third cases inputs prices rose so the aggregate supply curve shifted up to the left, and in the second case input prices fell so the aggregate supply curve shifted down to the right.

These conclusions are strengthened by examining what is called **core inflation**. This is the rate of inflation as measured by the consumer price index but excluding such volatile items as the price of oil, which is set on world markets,

and the prices of food products, which are subject to seasonal and other climatic factors such as droughts and floods. Although the core rate is not the rate that is used as the formal target, it is still instructive since it excludes most of the items that cannot be controlled by monetary policy.

Figure 22.3 shows the UK inflation rate as measured by the CPI and the core rate. The data are for each month calculated as a percentage change over the same month of the previous year. As already noted, since the establishment of the regime of inflation targeting the upper bound of the target range has only been breached for two periods by the CPI rate and only once by the core rate. The rise in

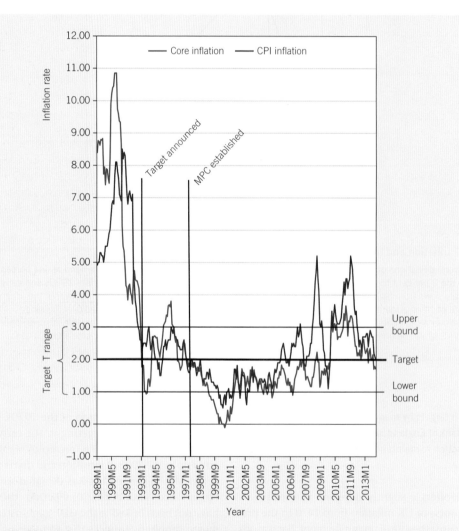

Figure 22.3 **UK, CPI, and core inflation, monthly, 1989–2013**

Core inflation, which excludes the volatile prices of energy and food, has almost always been less than CPI inflation since the establishment of the inflation targeting regime. The data give the monthly inflation rates calculated as the percentage change of the price level in a specific month compared with the same month of the previous year. The exceptions since the foundation of the Monetary Policy Committee in 1997 have been the low inflation around 2000, which was due to a negative supply shock due to falling world prices, and the high inflation in 2010–11 due to a rise in VAT. (Inflation based on CPI; core inflation is CPI excluding food and energy.)

Source: CPI from ONS database; core inflation from Federal Reserve Bank of St Louis FRED database.

both rates was to a great extent due to a sharp increase in VAT, which is included in the core rate but is clearly beyond the control of the Bank. Indeed, if the VAT change had been excluded, the core rate would have stayed within the upper bound at all times since the announcement of inflation targeting in 1993.

This behaviour is not what would have been predicted by the theory of the previous chapter where positive GDP gaps were associated with a rising price level and negative gaps with a falling price level, both of which had the effect of pushing the economy back towards potential GDP.

Over the past two and a half decades the experience of the United Kingdom and many other countries which have also adopted inflation targets, either officially or unofficially, strongly suggests two important conclusions.

1. As long as the central bank has established a credible inflation target, the economy can function over a wide range of unemployment and GDP gaps with no related tendency for the inflation rate either to rise or to fall.

Instead, inflation remains broadly constant, at least on average over several years, with short-term variations in the rate being associated mainly with aggregate supply rather than aggregate demand shocks.

2. Economies can function just as well with a fully expected low rate of inflation as with a fully expected constant price level (a zero rate of inflation).

In Chapter 18 we discussed a theory called the **neutrality of money**. A fairly uncontroversial version of this theory predicts that this second conclusion is correct. More controversial versions are discussed in Chapter 25.

The target rate

Here is how the Bank of England currently states its commitment to the target rate of inflation.

The inflation target of 2% is expressed in terms of an annual rate of inflation based on the Consumer Prices Index (CPI). The remit is not to achieve the lowest possible inflation rate. Inflation below the target of 2% is judged to be just as bad as inflation above the target. The inflation target is therefore symmetrical.

If the target is missed by more than 1 percentage point on either side—i.e. if the annual rate of CPI inflation is more than 3% or less than 1%—the Governor of the Bank must write an open letter to the Chancellor explaining the reasons why inflation has increased or fallen to such an extent and what the Bank proposes to do to ensure inflation comes back to the target.

The European System of Central Banks (ESCB), which manages the euro, has a similar commitment as laid down

in the Treaty on the Functioning of The European Union, Article 127(1). It states that the 'the primary objective of the European System of Central Banks […] shall be to maintain price stability'. It goes on to say that: 'Without prejudice to the objective of price stability, the ESCB shall support the general economic policies in the Union with a view to contributing to the achievement of the objectives of the Union as laid down in Article 3 of the Treaty on European Union'. These other objectives are '… the sustainable development of Europe based on balanced economic growth and price stability, and a highly competitive social market economy, aiming at full employment and social progress'. Thus, the Treaty establishes several objectives but makes it clear that price stability is the most important contribution that monetary policy can make to achieving a favourable economic environment and a high level of employment.

A similar but not identical set of targets is set out in the so-called **Taylor rule**, which states that changes in monetary policy should be made in relation to deviations of both inflation from its target rate and GDP from its potential level. Professor John B. Taylor of Stanford University argued that his rule was a generalization derived from the actual behavior of the US central bank (which is called the Federal Reserve System). According to this rule the Bank should tighten monetary policy by raising interest rates when inflation rose above target and when a positive GDP gap developed. In its simplest form, this rule can be expressed in the following equation:

$$i_t = 2 + p_t + g_p(p_t - p^\star) + g_x(Y_t - Y^\star)$$

where i_t the nominal short-term interest rate that monetary policymakers set, p_t is the latest annual inflation rate, $p^\star$ is the target inflation rate, Y_t is actual GDP, $Y^\star$ is potential GDP, and g_p and g_x are weights attached to the inflation target and GDP gap, respectively. The constant, 2, in the equation is the long-run average real interest rate. So, if GDP is at potential and inflation is on target, the nominal interest rate will be set to equal the long-run real rate plus the current inflation rate.

Although this rule is popular in theoretical treatments and captures the general interest of central banks in both inflation and the GDP gap, it does not capture the ordering of priorities between these two objectives. According to the rule the central bank has a given reaction to each specific GDP gap whatever the inflation rate may be. For example, if the inflation rate was a bit above the upper target band while GDP was quite a bit below its potential level, the rule says to lower interest rate in order to expand the economy. In contrast, it is clear that the central banks that have embraced the regime of inflation targeting are primarily concerned to keep inflation within their target band. Only if the inflation rate stays within that band will they take action to expand the economy to reduce a negative GDP gap. Faced with such a gap and an inflation rate that was on target, the Bank might lower interest rates to reduce the gap. But as soon as the inflation rate rose above the upper limit of the target band, a contractionary monetary policy would be put in place by raising the interest rate until inflation fell back inside the target band. The technical term for this behaviour with respect to the two targets of controlling inflation and the GDP gap is that the objects are ordered lexicographically. The first target of keeping inflation within the band is paramount, and only when that

objective is being fulfilled will action be taken with respect to the second objective of reducing any GDP gap.

What matters is that the Bank's low inflation target is credible; the actual rule, if any, that is followed is less important than that the public believes that the Bank is fully committed to holding inflation within the target band.

Indeed, the best results may come when the Bank reacts to deviations of the rate that it forecasts for the forthcoming period from its target rate rather than to actual inflation data (which become available with a lag).

IS–LM in a world of steady inflation

We now need to see how our *IS-LM* model is affected by being transferred from the initial part of Chapter 21's world of zero inflation in equilibrium to this chapter's world of a steady 2 per cent inflation in equilibrium—an inflation that is fully expected and adjusted to by everyone and is being fully accommodated by the central bank which produces the appropriate amount of monetary expansion. First we see what does not need to be changed and then what does. No new behavioural assumptions are needed on the demand side of our model.

No change needed

In Chapter 21 (at the beginning of the section entitled 'Aggregate demand' on page 498) we saw three main effects of a rise in the price level, assuming that the nominal money supply was held constant. The first two effects shift the *IS* curve to the left. The *wealth effect* lowers consumption spending because of a fall in the domestic wealth to the extent that the public holds outside assets. We also saw that the wealth effect can be offset by setting the nominal interest rate above the desired real rate by the amount of the expected inflation. However, this does not work well when, as in the past, the inflation rate is high and volatile and hence not fully predictable—what we called a ragged rate. The *balance-of-payments effect* works though a rise in the relative price of domestic goods relative to imported goods. The third effect, *the real money effect*, works by shifting the *LM* curve to the left as the rising price level lowers the real money supply. So the net effect of these changes is to shift the *AD* curve to the left.

In this chapter we are now dealing with a regime of stable and fully anticipated inflation in which case none of these effects will be operating. First, there will be no significant wealth effect because a fully anticipated inflation can be offset by setting the nominal interest rate

above the real rate by the amount of the expected inflation. What about the balance-of-payments effect? Our earlier analysis referred to a local inflation. But if the country's major trading partners are also on a regime of low and predicable targeted inflation, as are both the United States and the European Union, there will be no significant changes in international relative prices that would occur if there were different national inflation rates.[4] (As we shall see in Chapter 24, changes in the UK price level relative to the price levels of its major trading partners are measured by what is called the real exchange rate, and the stability of this rate through most of the last two decades shows that the assumption of no significant balance-of-payments effect is close to reality.) Finally, if the Bank sets the interest rate such that the nominal money supply increases at the same rate as the price level is rising, the *LM* curve will be stable so that there will be no real money effect.

Thus the position of the *IS* curve is unchanged by the fully expected 2 per cent target rate of inflation from what it would be if inflation were zero. The position of the *LM* curve is similarly unaffected, provided that the Bank accommodates the inflation with the appropriate rate of monetary expansion, thus holding the real money supply constant.

A distinction needed

Because we have an ongoing inflation, the real and the nominal interest rates have to be distinguished in a way that was not necessary when we were studying an economy with a constant actual and expected price level.

---

[4] One effect that may be important, even if it is anticipated, is the income effect associated with a terms-of-trade loss, such as would arise from an exogenous rise in world energy prices.

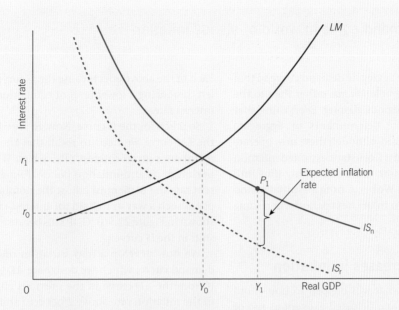

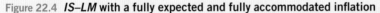

Figure 22.4 *IS–LM* with a fully expected and fully accommodated inflation

A fully expected inflation shifts the *IS* curve plotted against the real interest rate upwards by the amount of that inflation to yield an *IS* curve plotted against the nominal interest rate. The Bank is expanding the nominal money supply at the inflation rate, thus holding the real money supply and the *LM* curve constant. IS_r is the *IS* curve related to the real interest rate, which is the rate that influences investment spending. IS_n is the IS_r curve shifted vertically upwards by the expected rate of inflation. For any point on the IS_n curve, such as the point p_1, the IS_n curve shows the nominal market interest rate needed to establish spending equilibrium for GDP corresponding to that point, Y_1 in this case. Equilibrium is at the intersection of the *LM* and the IS_n curves. Here GDP is Y_0, the nominal interest rate is r_1, and the real rate is r_0, which is below the nominal rate by the expected rate of inflation.

If the expected rate of inflation rises, the IS_n curve will shift upwards by that amount. If the Bank fully accommodates that new rate, the *LM* curve will shift upwards by the same amount, leaving real GDP and the real interest rate constant while the nominal rate rises by the same amount that expectations of inflation have risen.

Figure 22.4 shows the now familiar *IS–LM* diagram. The vertical axis measures interest rates and the subscripts *n*, for nominal, and *r*, for real, are added to each curve to tell us which interest rate is relevant to that curve. The *IS* curve is drawn as a dashed line and labelled IS_r to remind us that investment responds to the real not the nominal interest rate. We wish to relate the *IS* curve to the nominal rate so that we can compare it directly with the *LM* curve, which does relate to the nominal rate. To do this, the *IS* curve must be shifted upwards everywhere by 2 per cent to the solid curve labelled IS_n. This indicates that any given *IS* equilibrium requires a 2 per cent higher nominal rate than the required real rate. More generally, the IS_n curve must be above the IS_r curve by the expected infla- tion rate, reflecting the approximate relation

nominal interest rate = real interest rate + inflation rate.[5]

If the Bank wishes to maintain an unchanged real GDP at Y_0 in Figure 22.4 and a 2 per cent inflation rate, it must engineer a nominal increase in the money supply of 2 per cent per year. This keeps the real money supply constant, thus holding the *LM* curve steady. We say that the Bank is *accommodating* the 2 per cent inflation rate by increasing the nominal money supply to allow the inflation to continue without itself affecting the level of the real money supply and hence of real GDP. At the new equilibrium, GDP remains at Y_0 and the real interest rate at r_0 while the nominal rate is r_1, which is 2 per cent higher than r_0. In everything that follows we will plot the *IS* curve against the nominal interest rate, but the exist- ence of another *IS* curve vertically below the plotted curve by the expected rate of inflation is always under- stood. Only when it is relevant will we show the curve relating *IS* to the real interest rate. Curves without a sub- script refer to the nominal interest rates, while if we wish to show a curve that is related to the real interest rate we give it the subscript *r*.

[5] This expression is discussed and the exact formula developed in Chapter 19 footnote 3.

The aggregate demand curve in world of steady inflation

We now wish to alter the aggregate demand curve so that it relates real GDP to the *inflation rate* rather than to the price level, as in the previous chapter. Everything that was assumed about the determinants of aggregate demand remain unchanged, although these now operate in a world in which there is a constant expected inflation rate. To study this situation, think of dividing time into periods of, say, one year. We begin from an initial period and ask what will happen in the next period when some change occurs.

Unanticipated increases in inflation

The first step is to ask what will happen to household spending if there is an unanticipated exogenous rise of the inflation rate—say it rises by one percentage point, going from 2 to 3 per cent due to an increase in energy prices that are determined on world oil markets. Although, as we saw above, the anticipated rate of 2 per cent does not affect the *IS* curve, an *unexpected* rise will shift the curve to the left for reasons discussed earlier in the section entitled 'No change needed'. There the effects were shown not to be operative with a fully anticipated inflation. Now we see them in operation when there is an *unanticipated* inflation.

1. *The wealth effect* As we saw in Chapter 21, the importance of the wealth effect is debatable. In so far as it does exist, however, the unexpected lowering of the wealth of holders of outside assets will serve to lower their consumption spending.

2. *The balance-of-payments effect* The unexpected rise in the price level (assuming that the cause is domestic in origin) makes imports unexpectedly less expensive in the home market and exports unexpectedly more expensive in foreign markets. Both of these lead to a substitution of foreign for domestic goods in both the domestic and foreign markets, thus shifting the net export function downwards which lowers domestic spending. If people do not expect these low prices to continue once inflation reverts to its expected rate of 2 per cent, they may increase their purchases of imported goods more than if they expected the relative price change to be long-lasting. If the rise originates from an increase in the price of some imported goods that have inelastic demands at home, such as imported energy, domestic consumers will suffer a loss of real income because more must be paid to foreigners for energy imports. This income effect lowers domestic spending.

Each of the above effects cause the *IS* curve to shift to the left, producing a lower level of equilibrium GDP at each interest rate.

So much for the *IS* curve. Now, to see what happens to the *LM* curve we need to recall that the Bank seeks to maintain a given interest rate, which it only varies in pursuit of its anti-inflation policy. To maintain the current rate the Bank must adjust the nominal money supply in such a way as to hold the interest rate constant, as shown in Figure 22.5(i). GDP falls because of the leftward shift in the *IS* curve.

We now develop a new variation on the aggregate demand curve, which we designate *AD** to distinguish it from the *AD* curve in the previous chapter. The rise in the inflation rate above 2 per cent shifts the *IS* curve to the left for the two reasons outlined above. As also mentioned in the previous paragraph, the Bank must now take appropriate action to hold the nominal interest rate constant. In doing this it lowers the real money supply until the *LM* curve shifts to the left to intersect the *IS* curve at an unchanged interest rate but a lower level of GDP as shown in Figure 22.5(i). Plotting this new lower equilibrium level of GDP against the higher inflation rate of 3 per cent gives a second point on the new *AD** curve.

Now assume that instead of a one percentage point unexpected rise in the inflation rate, the rise is two percentage points, taking the inflation rate from 2 to 4 per cent. The *IS* and *LM* curves are shifted further to the left, creating a lower equilibrium GDP and a new point on the *AD** curve, indicating a lower GDP and a higher inflation rate. By considering many alternative unanticipated rises in the inflation rate and the consequent larger and larger reductions in equilibrium GDP, we can trace out a negatively sloped aggregate demand curve that plots real GDP against the realized inflation rate.

Points on this new ad* curve are not sequential in time but are alternatives showing the impact effect over one time period of various alternative realized inflation rates when the rate had been expected to remain constant at some given rate.

We have developed the *AD** curve on the assumption that the Bank holds to its usual policy of maintaining the interest rate. An alternative is often considered in the literature, although it does not conform to current Bank policy. In this alternative, the Bank holds to a target of a 2 per cent increase in the nominal money supply rather

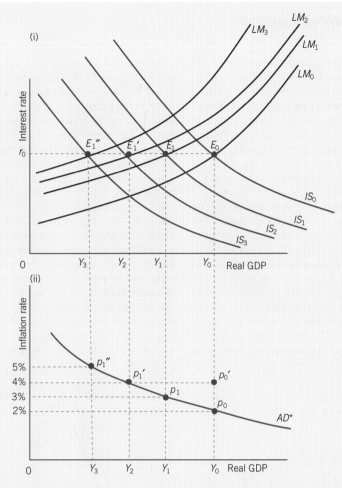

Figure 22.5 **Derivation of the *AD** curve for a constant expected inflation rate and a constant nominal interest rate**

This *AD** curve shows the effects of alternative realized inflation rates for a given expected rate of inflation and a fixed nominal interest rate. The Bank is following a policy of pegging the interest rate at r_0. It is also accommodating the actual and expected inflation rate of 2 per cent by expanding the nominal money supply by 2 per cent so as to hold the real quantity of money, and hence the *LM* curve, constant. The original equilibrium in part (i) is E_0 with GDP of Y_0 and interest rate r_0 determined by the intersection of the curves IS_0 and LM_0. Plotting this GDP against the actual and expected rate of 2 per cent gives the point p_0 on the *AD** diagram. If the inflation rate rises unexpectedly to 3 per cent household behaviour shifts the *IS* curve to IS_1. To hold the interest rate constant, the Bank must allow the *LM* curve to shift to LM_1, which it does by sticking to its 2 per cent rate of monetary expansion which is now below the inflation rate of 3 per cent. Equilibrium shifts to E_1 with real GDP at Y_1. Plotting Y_1 against an inflation rate of 3 per cent gives a new point p_1 on the *AD** curve. If the inflation rate had instead risen to 4 per cent, the *IS* and *LM* curves would have shifted more, to IS_2 and LM_2, yielding equilibrium at E_1' with GDP of Y_2. Plotting this GDP against a 4 per cent inflation rate gives another alternative point p_1' on the *AD** curve. Similarly, if the inflation rate had risen to 5 per cent, equilibrium would have been at E_1'' where the *IS* and *LM* curves have shifted more, this time to IS_3 and LM_3 so that equilibrium GDP is Y_3. This yields a new alternative of p_1'' on the *AD** curve. These equilibria are distinguished with prime marks rather than higher and higher numbers to indicate that they are alternative outcomes in the first period after different unexpected accelerations in the inflation rate.

As shown in the last paragraph of the caption to Figure 22.4, if in the initial position the fully expected and fully accommodated inflation rate had been 4 per cent, the initial point on the *AD** curve would have been p_0' with the GDP of Y_0 plotted this time against a 4 per cent inflation rate. The *AD** curve would then be negatively sloped through that point, with each GDP being related to an inflation rate two percentage points above its original point which referred to a 2 per cent inflation rate.

than holding the nominal interest rate constant. For completeness this is analysed in Box 22.2. However, since it is not the usual case in practice, and since it leads to the same conclusion that the *AD** curve is negatively sloped, the box is optional.

Shifts in the *AD** curve

This new variation of the aggregate demand curve is drawn for some specific fully expected and fully accommodated inflation rate. So far we have assumed that to

Box 22.2 A nominal money supply policy

In the text we assume that the Bank holds the interest rate constant in the face of an unexpected rise in the inflation rate. An alternative policy would be to stick to its policy of expanding the nominal money supply at a 2 per cent rate in order to accommodate the expected inflation rate of 2 per cent. In this case the real money supply falls, causing the LM curve to shift left along with the IS curve.

This case is shown in the figure in which the curves are drawn as straight lines to facilitate comparisons, but relative slopes are all that matters. The original IS curve is IS_0. There are two alternative sets of LM curves labelled LM^e for 'relatively elastic' and LM^i for 'relatively inelastic'. The original equilibrium is at E_0 where IS_0 and both alternative LM_0 curves intersect. GDP is Y_0 and the interest rate is r_0. The IS curve then shifts to IS_1 as a result of an unexpected rise in the inflation rate. The elastic LM curve shifts from its initial position at LM_0^e to LM_1^e, causing the interest rate to rise to r_1^e and GDP to fall by a relatively large amount to Y_2. Alternatively, if the LM curve was the relatively inelastic curve LM_0^i, it would shift to LM_1^i. (Both e and i curves shift by the same vertical amount.) The interest rate then falls to r_1^i while GDP falls by the relatively small amount to Y_1.

What this analysis tell us is that what happens to the interest rate and GDP depends on the relative slopes of the IS and the LM curves, and the size of their respective shifts. As far as the slopes are concerned, if the LM curve is steep relative to the IS curve, the interest rate falls. If the LM curve is flat relative to the IS curve, the interest rate rises. In the case of the steep LM curve, the reduction in the interest rate induces an increase in some interest-sensitive spending and this mitigates the reduction in GDP caused by the initial reduction in consumption spending. In the case of a relatively flat LM curve, the interest rate rises, inducing some reduction in interest-sensitive spending which leads to a much larger reduction in GDP.

Both Bank policies of a constant interest rate, studied in the text, and a constant rate of monetary expansion, studied here, lead to a fall in GDP. Thus the AD^* curve that we derived in Figure 22.5 for the case of the constant interest rate applies to the case of a constant rate of monetary expansion—a negatively sloped AD^* curve, the only difference being in the magnitude of its negative slope which is determined by how much GDP falls as a result of the unexpected rise in inflation.

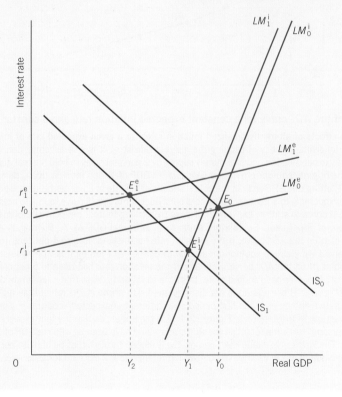

be 2 per cent. But what if the rate had been, say, 4 per cent, and everyone was fully adjusted to that rate and the Bank was accommodating it? The AD^* curve would then show the same real GDP at 4 per cent inflation as it

did previously at 2 per cent when that rate was fully expected and fully accommodated. In other words, a rise in the fully expected and accommodated inflation rate, at least over some modest range, shifts this AD^* curve vertically upwards by the amount of that increase. (This was also argued in the last paragraph of the caption to Figure 22.4. It was shown there that a rise in the fully expected and fully accommodated inflation rate would shift both the *IS* and *LM* curves upwards by the same amount, raising the nominal interest rate by 2 per cent but leaving equilibrium real GDP and the real rate of interest unchanged.)

Now let us consider shifts in the *AD** curve that are caused by an exogenous shift in either some real spending or some monetary variable.[6] Exactly the same forces as shift the *AD* curve that relates real GDP to the price level will shift the *AD** curve that relates real GDP to the inflation rate. This should be clear from a comparison of Figures 21.1 and 22.5. In Figure 22.1 the *AD* curve is derived from various *IS–LM* equilibrium positions, and the same is true for the *AD** curve in Figure 22.5. In Figure 22.5 the equilibrium is at E_0 in part (i) and point p_0 in part (ii). Therefore anything that shifts either the *IS* or the *LM* curve to the right will raise the equilibrium level of GDP that is associated with a constant 2 per cent inflation rate and hence will also shift the *AD** curve. It follows that the *AD** curve will be shifted to the right by:

1. An increase in consumption spending due to either an increase in autonomous consumption or a rise in the marginal propensity to consume.

2. An increase in investment resulting from a shift upwards of the investment function or a change in its slope.

3. An increase in net exports due to either an exogenous increase in export demand or a fall in propensity to import.

4. An increase in government spending or a cut in taxes that increases households' disposable income.

5. An increase in the fully expected and fully accommodated inflation rate, as noted earlier. (This is the only force that we did not include in the previous chapter where the price level was constant in equilibrium.)

6. An increase in the real supply of money (i.e. the nominal money supply increases faster than the price level rises).

7. A decrease in the quantity of money demanded that is associated with each given level of GDP and the interest rate.[7]

Points 6 and 7 both have the effect of increasing the demand for bonds, driving up their price and hence driving down the interest rate and so increasing all interest-sensitive spending.

The opposite changes shift the *AD** curve to the left. For example, the real money supply might be reduced because the Bank lowers the rate of expansion of the nominal money supply below the inflation rate This drives the interest rate up and induces a reduction in interest-sensitive spending, which in turn reduces the equilibrium level of GDP that is associated with the 2 per cent inflation rate.

To complete the analysis of the economy as a whole we need to construct a new aggregate supply curve suitable for studying a sustained, fully anticipated, and fully accommodated inflation rate.

The aggregate supply curve

In the previous chapter we developed two aggregate supply curves: the short-run curve, which was defined for a situation in which final goods prices rise as result of a demand shock while input prices remain constant, and a 'long-run' curve, which was defined for a situation in which all prices and costs have fully adjusted to that shock. But this distinction is not relevant to the current situation. Now GDP is varying while the current inflation rate of 2 per cent is being fully accommodated by the Bank, and the public expects that rate to continue. So, output and input prices are both rising on average at the same 2 per cent rate. Thus the derivation of the *SRAS* curve based on lags that applied to the first two of our

regimes cannot be used here. (Nor can any other derivation that relies on surprises—unexpected changes in the price level.)

We call the aggregate supply curve that relates output to the inflation rate in this new situation the *AS** curve. We plot it on a figure that has GDP on the horizontal axis and the *rate of inflation* (instead of the price level as in Chapter 21) on the vertical axis. We must now investigate the specific shape of this new curve.

To see how the inflation rate and the output of firms react to short-term variations in demand under these circumstances, we need, first, to consider the pricing and output choices of firms operating in two different market structures and, secondly, how costs vary with output.

---

[6] In the case of money supply, this would need to be some shift in the rate of monetary expansion relative to the level that would accommodate the expected rate of inflation, thus changing the real money supply.

[7] The effect of these changes in shifting the AD curve were also analysed in Figures 21.2 and 21.3 in Chapter 21.

Pricing and output decisions

Pricing and output decisions taken by firms are studied in detail in microeconomics courses and were covered in the first half of this book. In microeconomics the price level is assumed to be constant, and therefore a rise in either the input or the output price that the firm faces is a rise in the relative price of that input or output. In the present context, in which there is an ongoing fully expected inflation of 2 per cent, a rise in the relative price of a firm's input or output refers to a rise in the price of more than 2 per cent in the year under consideration.

We distinguish between two types of market structure. In the first there are many small firms, no one of which is large enough to affect the market price of its product by altering its output. This is the case, for example, with many farmers, some of the smaller oil companies, many mining companies, and some other producers, mainly of primary products. These firms must accept whatever price is determined by the market for their products, producing and selling all they wish at that price. In order to induce them to produce and sell more, the market price of their products must rise (or their costs fall). So, for them, we expect to find a positive relationship between market price and output. We call them price-taking firms. An economy composed wholly of this market structure, which we saw in Chapter 6 is called perfect competition, would have a short-run aggregate supply curve that was positively sloped throughout, similar to the one we set out in Chapter 21.

The second type of market structure is the dominant one in developed economies. Here, all firms face negatively sloped demand curves for their products. This is clearly true of a monopoly firm. Because such a firm is the only producer, it faces the market demand curve for that product. It is also true of firms that sell differentiated products that are similar to each other but not identical, such as different brands of clothing, TV sets, computers, refrigerators, motor cars, and telephones, as well as many modern services such as those provided by restaurants, computer programmers, and entertainers. There is no aggregate market that sets an industry price for some generic version of each of these products. Instead, every producer must set a price for each version of its various products and then let market demand determine how much is sold. (Of course, the firm may seek to influence that demand through advertising and other selling techniques, but this does not change the fact that the producer sets the price and purchasers have the final say as to how much is sold.) This is true of the many industries in which there are only a few sellers, so-called oligopolies. It is also true of industries in which there are many sellers as long as each firm's product is differentiated in some way, such as by brand, design, or quality——so-called monopolistically competitive industries. We call all firms of this type price-setting firms.

Cost factors

Because we start with a steady fully expected 2 per cent rate of inflation, the money prices of both firms' inputs and outputs will be increasing on average at that rate (but any other relatively low fully expected rate is also possible). To study how unit costs vary as output is varied, it is best to deal with real costs, the ratio of input prices to output prices. If a firm's output is unchanged, its real costs per unit of output will be unchanged, although its money costs per unit will be rising at 2 per cent per year along with the prices of the products it sells.

The $SRAS$ curve that we encountered in the previous chapter was positively sloped throughout its entire range, indicating that, starting from any output, firms require an increase in the price of their product to induce them to produce and sell more of it. As we observed above, this would be so if all firms were price takers, able to sell all they wished at the going market price. But, as we just noted, most firms are price setters and what they require to induce them to increase their production depends to a great extent on how their unit costs vary with their outputs. If their unit costs are positively related to their volume of output, they would not typically be willing to produce more unless they could raise their prices. This is what we assumed in the previous chapter when constructing the $SRAS$ curve.

One of the many possible reasons for making this assumption relies on the famous law of diminishing returns that is encountered in microeconomics. In Chapter 21 we did not rely explicitly on this law in making the assumption that unit costs rose as output rose, but since it is often quoted to support such an assumption, we consider it further in Box 22.3. In contrast with this assumption about the behaviour of unit costs in the short run, there is considerable evidence that many firms typically have *real unit costs* that are relatively insensitive to changes in outputs over a wide range of outputs. The real cost of producing one more automobile or one more refrigerator of a specified type is much the same if the plant is operating at 90 per cent of normal capacity or at 95 per cent. This empirical observation of constant real unit cost over a wide range of output is also discussed in Box 22.3, and we elaborate on it further below.

The AS^* curve over a perfectly elastic intermediate range

Faced with such cost conditions and a fully expected 2 per cent inflation rate, price-setting firms that are currently operating at or below normal capacity output will raise their prices by more than 2 per cent per year in response

Box 22.3 Short-run costs in a modern firm

In microeconomics firms are usually assumed to have a positively sloped unit cost curve in the short run, which is a period of time long enough to vary the amount of labour and materials used but not long enough to alter fixed capital equipment. When the firm varies its output with the fixed input constant, the outcome is predicted by the famous law of diminishing returns, which says that the increments to the flow of output generated by combining additional units of a variable input with a given amount of a fixed input must eventually diminish. If so, unit costs must rise as output rises. But this derivation assumes that the firm must use all of its fixed capital all of the time and so must vary the proportion in which the fixed and variable inputs are used. We say the fixed input is *indivisible*. But the fixed input may be *divisible* in the sense that although more than is available cannot be used, some that is available need not be used. This allows the firm to maintain a fixed ratio among all of its inputs. For firms with divisible capital the law of diminishing returns need not apply when output is increased until all of the fixed input is fully employed. Only then will expansions of output necessitate varying the ratio of variable inputs to the fixed inputs.

In most modern manufacturing processes there is virtually no room to vary the ratio of labour to capital. The machinery is there and must be operated by the specified number of workers. Adding one more worker to the existing employed equipment would make little sense in these processes. Therefore output is varied by altering the amount of time that the company's factories are operated. 'Auto workers put on short time' is a common headline in the business section of the press when a cyclical downswing hits the industry.

In many traditional service industries there is also little opportunity to alter the ratio of employed labour to employed capital. Go into a barber shop at busy times and you will see customers waiting to be served. But never will you see two barbers trying to cut two customers' hair while both customers sit in one chair. Go in at slack times and you will see some barbers sitting around chatting with each other or reading magazines, while the chairs and clippers stay unused. The situation is a little different with restaurants. At peak times more workers can be employed to speed up the service in a given establishment (given capital). But at slack times waiters and tables will both be idle. So up to full capacity the ratio of labour to capital tends to be constant, although at or near full capacity it can be altered as more waiters are used to speed up the service: constant marginal cost up to at or near full capacity and rising thereafter.

Most of their costs of many industries in the new electronic economy are associated with developing new products and improving old ones, while the marginal cost of producing another unit of current output is at, or close to, zero and so does not vary significantly with output. For any firm that provides its product online, costs are independent of how many users there are. Facebook, Twitter, and YouTube, for example, make their money by selling advertising, and the more users they have the more they can charge for advertising. But adding another user adds nothing to their costs, and similarly for newspapers, magazines, and books that have gone online. TV shows cost a great deal to make, but the marginal costs of another viewer is again zero. Aeroplanes and cruise ships require the same crew whether they are full to capacity or only three-quarters occupied, so once more the ratio of labour to capital does not vary as numbers of passengers served varies. London buses need one driver for each bus whether the bus is full or nearly empty.

So the case of varying the amount of labour applied to a fixed amount of employed capital as output varies over the short run is closer to being a rare exception than the general rule. The more general case is that labour and capital are varied in equal proportions as output varies, making marginal and average variable costs constant, at least up to full capacity. Furthermore, compared with the average fixed cost associated with developing and marketing the product, the variable unit cost is often small and frequently close to zero.

to changes of more than 2 per cent in input prices, including labour costs. They may also do so in response to changes in their competitive positions relative to other firms in their industry. But they will not normally do so in response to cyclical variations in demand that affect all competing firms more or less equally and do not have major effects on input prices. So output can vary over a significant range without requiring a change in prices. Instead, price-setting firms set their price and then sell all that is demanded at that price, and variations in demand are met with variations in output without necessarily causing any change in product prices.

(Remember that in this context a fixed price means one that actually rises at 2 per cent along with the average of all other prices.) So over this range the *AS** curve has a horizontal portion, as shown the Figure 22.6. Box 22.4 discusses whether or not the behaviour of the firms being assumed here is consistent with profit-maximizing behaviour.

The *AS** curve at its extremes

We do not expect this curve to stay horizontal over its entire range, which would indicate that the inflation rate was insensitive to all levels of GDP. First, consider what

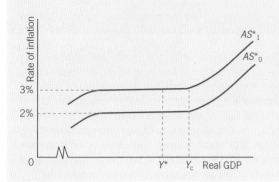

Figure 22.6 The new aggregate supply curve for constant costs and a constant rate of inflation

This new aggregate supply curve, *AS**, is positively sloped at low levels of GDP and, horizontal at the expected rate of inflation in its mid-range up to a GDP of Y_c, but positively sloped beyond that. The curve AS^*_0 applies to an expected inflation rate of 2 per cent. It is positively sloped for levels of GDP far below potential and then horizontal for a significant range up to GDP of Y_c, which is slightly above the normal capacity output of Y^*, but positively sloped after that. The curve is shifted permanently upwards to AS^*_1 by a rise in the expected rate of inflation to 3 per cent, and temporarily upwards by a rise in input prices.

Box 22.4 Are cyclically constant prices compatible with profit maximization?

Do firms hold their prices constant as they vary their outputs over a wide range? If so, why would they do that? To consider the first question, several years ago a group of economists at Oxford University quizzed business managers at great length to find out many things about their behaviour. One thing that constantly stood out came to be called 'full-cost pricing'. Managers said that they did not try to find the profit-maximizing price every time the demand for their product changed cyclically. Instead, they calculated full unit cost of production and then added a mark up to that cost, selling whatever the market demanded at that price.

The second question was subject to a great debate following the publication of these results. Some economists argued that they showed the erroneous nature of the assumption used in most micro theories that firms maximized their profits. Others argued that it was not useful to ask managers what they did, as they did not understand what they were doing instinctively while economists

did—whatever managers thought they were doing, they were really maximizing their profits.

Holding price constant as demand varied cyclically seemed inconsistent with profit maximization as long as firms had positively sloped marginal cost curves. These should cause unit costs to vary positively with output. If so, profit-maximizing firms would surely have to raise prices to cover the extra costs when output rose cyclically.

However, full-cost pricing over the cycle may not be far off profit-maximizing behaviour if, as we have pointed out in this chapter, unit costs are constant as production varies cyclically up to some upper limit. Consistency with profit-maximizing behaviour then only requires two things. First, the mark-up at normal capacity must be at, or at least near, the profit-maximizing mark-up. Secondly, either the elasticity of demand does not change significantly as demand varies cyclically or the benefit gained from constantly changing price by small amounts as the profit-maximizing mark-up changes cyclically is less than the cost of making these changes.

---

might happen if there was a large negative GDP gap such as is associated with a severe slump in economic activity. The evidence is that it takes a very large and persistent slump—such as was experienced by some of the countries of southern Europe in the aftermath of the 2008 financial crisis—to cause the overall level of money wages actually to fall. But what does sometimes happen is that money wages rise by less than productivity is rising. In this case unit costs of production will be falling. For a while, this may be taken up by a rise in profits, but it also usually causes prices to rise by less that the target rate of inflation and, in the extreme, actually to fall (a situation called disinflation). This is shown by the positively sloped section of the *AS** curve to the left of its horizontal middle section.

A large enough negative GDP gap may cause the inflation rate to fall below target, and in extreme cases, even become negative (a disinflation).

This possibility is illustrated by the downward-sloping portion of the *AS** curve to the left of its flat portion. In modern times the average level of wages has occasionally risen slower than productivity in the face of large negative GDP gaps, but this has not been sufficient to force the inflation rate to breach the lower target bound. Furthermore, inflation has never become negative in the UK or most other developed countries in modern times[8].

----

[8] Japan is the obvious exception, and a few other countries did have temporarily negative inflation rates in 2008-9, but it has not happened in the UK since the 1930s.

Because we have had no real experience with this portion of the AS^* curve, no one has much idea of how large the GDP gap would have to be for it to become relevant. Possibly a gap of 20–25 per cent of potential GDP would be sufficient, but it might also depend on how long the gap persisted. So, in the absence of such experience, we cannot be sure. In any case nothing like a gap of 90 per cent of GDP would be necessary. But to prevent implying that GDP would have to fall by that amount, which is inconceivable, we show a break in the GDP axis in Figure 22.6. Also, to avoid this complication, we do not draw the downward portion in later figures, although it is there at some level of GDP gap and could be restored if ever we needed to study an economy undergoing such a severe recession with its very large accompanying GDP gap.

Of course, at any level of GDP negative supply-side shocks and other random events can cause the AS^* curve to shift downwards temporarily. Inflation would then fall temporarily below target. But what we are concerned with here is a case in which the deviation of inflation below its target range is directly caused from the demand side—that is, by a negative GDP gap. This would be the result of substantial excess capacity, high levels of unemployment, and very weak final demand for goods and services. Figure 21.16 shows that this is what happened in the United Kingdom in the early 1930s during the Great Depression, but it has not happened since, even after the recession of 2008–9.

Now consider what happens when output reaches a level at which firms are operating at or just above normal capacity. Now additional output can typically only be produced with rising real unit costs. On the production side, as output increases beyond that amount, less efficient standby plants may have to be used and less efficient workers may have to be hired, while existing workers may have to be paid overtime rates for additional work. On the input side, shortages of material and specific types of labour may cause wages and other input prices to begin to rise faster than 2 per cent. Both of these changes, rising real costs of production and rising money costs of inputs, will cause firms to raise prices by more than 2 per cent per year. This is shown by the positively sloped right-hand portion of the AS^* curve in Figure 22.6.

Consider the point, Y_c, in Figure 22.6, where the AS^* curve starts to slope upwards indicating that further increases in output will be associated with an inflation rate that begins to rise above the expected rate, which is 2 per cent in our present case. This critical level of GDP is of great interest to policy-makers, as we shall see in later chapters. Unfortunately, it is not a clear cut-point that is easily established empirically. There are many reasons for this ambiguity. First, the economy's individual markets for inputs and outputs are never all in equilibrium at the same time. The technological changes that drive economic growth are occurring continually. They alter the cost conditions of firms, the products they sell, and their demands for various inputs. Markets typically adjust to these changes with lags, so that at any one time there will be excess demands in some markets and excess supplies in others, even though these may sum to zero over the entire economy. Thus at each cyclical expansion there may be a different levels of GDP at which the inflation rate will begin to accelerate because relative price increases in some markets (prices rising faster than 2 per cent) begin to outweigh the relative price decreases in other markets (prices rising by less than 2 per cent). Secondly, many firms like to hold in reserve a little capacity above their normal expected production and sales so that they can easily meet transitory increases in demand. For these and other similar reasons, the critical Y_c—the level of GDP at which the inflation rate starts to rise above the expected rate—is a little above what we have called potential output in previous chapters. It might be 3 per cent more or 5 per cent more. No one is quite sure exactly where it is and how it is changing over time. In the figure we indicate Y^* as what we have called potential output in previous chapters. This is the level of output that the economy would be producing if all firms were operating at what they regarded as their normal level of output, and all unemployment of labour is due to frictions and structural imbalances but not to a deficiency of aggregate demand. (The technical meaning of full employment of labour is discussed in the next chapter, but for now it can be taken as occurring when the number of unemployed workers is not zero but is at an equilibrium level consistent with normal turnover in labour markets.) As shown in the Figure 22.6:

The critical value of GDP, Y_c, at which inflation starts to rise above the expected rate is a small but uncertain amount in excess of normal capacity output, Y^*.

Shifts in aggregate supply

An increase in the expected rate of inflation shifts the AS^* curve permanently upwards, as shown in Figure 22.6. ('Permanently' as long as the higher inflation expectation is maintained.) If the Bank is instructed by the government to raise the inflation target to, say, 4 per cent and adopts a rate of monetary expansion sufficient to accommodate that rate, sellers of outputs and inputs will tend to raise their prices by that amount as a routine matter. Although they will shade these prices upwards or downwards depending on local market conditions, on average the prices of outputs and inputs will tend to rise by 4 per cent. This important point is worth emphasizing.

The perfectly elastic portion of the *AS** curve occurs at the expected inflation rate. A rise in that rate shifts the curve upwards by the same amount, while a fall shifts the curve downwards by the amount of the fall.

The *AS** curve is also shifted upwards *temporarily* by an exogenously induced rise of more than 2 per cent in the price of any important input, including labour, raw materials, and imported components. If all input prices had been rising at 2 per cent but suddenly they all rise by 4 per cent

for one year, goods prices, and hence the rate of inflation, will have to rise by a similar amount to allow firms to pass on the higher input prices. If the rise is in only some input prices, output prices will have to rise by an amount equal to the proportion of those inputs in the total of all input costs.[9] The adjustment of output prices could be accomplished by a 4 per cent rise in their prices for one year, or a 3 per cent rise for two years, or any other combination that cumulates to a rise in prices equal to the unexpected rise in input prices.

AD–AS** equilibrium

Figure 22.7 puts the *AD** curve together with an *AS**curve drawn for a fully expected and accommodated inflation rate of 2 per cent. Variations in output up to Y_c cause GDP and employment to vary but leave the inflation rate unchanged. This is in line with the data in Figures 22.1–22.3, which show GDP fluctuating over a wide range with no rise or fall in the average inflation rate.

Demand shock

If an exogenous rise in some component of final spending takes the *AD** curve above Y_c, the inflation rate starts to rise above 2 per cent. If the Bank holds publically to its inflation target by only allowing the nominal money supply to expand at 2 per cent, the real money supply will begin to fall. This shifts the *AD** curve to the left, a shift that will continue until the inflation rate falls once again to 2 per cent. (The Bank could also raise the interest rate, which would shift *AD** to the left moving GDP towards a point below Y_c.)

For this policy of holding the inflation rate at 2 per cent to succeed, the Bank must act quickly and decisively to reaffirm its commitment to the 2 per cent target. Also, the adjustment back to that lower rate must be fast enough so that people do not come to expect the higher rate to be maintained. If the leftward shift of the *AD** curve does not happen fast enough just through the reduction in the real money supply brought about by the rise in the price level at over 2 per cent per year, the Bank always has the option of lowering the nominal money supply or raising its policy interest rate as well. The former will hasten the reduction in the real supply of money and the latter will reduce

---

[9] In this case the rise in just some input prices, if it persists, is a rise in their price relative to other input prices and this may induce substitutions between them and other, now cheaper, inputs that mitigate the amount by which output prices may have to rise. But these adjustments typically take much time to accomplish, so that the initial impact is for overall input costs to rise according to the present proportion of the cost of that input in total production costs.

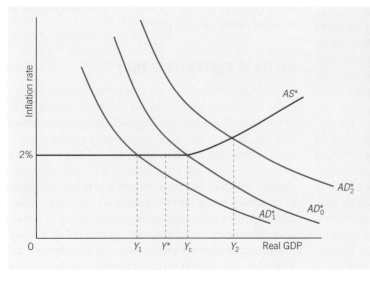

Figure 22.7 ***AD*–AS**** **equilibrium with a constant expected inflation rate**

Below Y_c, GDP can fluctuate at a stable inflation rate but above Y_c the inflation rate starts to rise. Fluctuations in the aggregate demand curve between AD_0^* and AD_1^* cause GDP to fluctuate between Y_c and Y_1 while the inflation rate remains constant at 2 per cent. But if the *AD** curve shifts to AD_2^*, taking GDP to Y_2, the inflation rate starts to rise. To maintain its 2 per cent inflation target, the Bank must allow the real money supply to decline sufficiently to shift the *AD** curve back to AD_0^*, or a little below it to yield a GDP of Y^*.

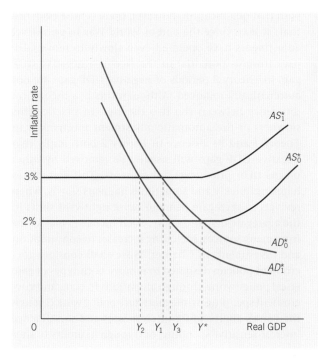

Figure 22.8 A supply-side shock

An upward shift in the aggregate supply curve causes GDP to fall while the inflation rate rises. The original curves are AD_0^* and AS_0^* with GDP of Y^* and 2 per cent inflation. An exogenous increase in the rate at which input prices are rising causes the AS^* curve to shift upward to AS_1^*. This moves the economy upwards along AD_0^* to a 3 per cent inflation rate and a lower GDP of Y_1. If the Bank continues to expand the nominal money supply at 2 per cent, the real money supply falls, causing the AD^* curve to shift to AD_1^* in the next period, combining the 3 per cent inflation with an even smaller GDP of Y_2. If costs stop rising by more than 2 per cent after two periods, the inflation rate falls to 2 per cent and the AS^* curve shifts back to AS_0^*. However, GDP rises only to Y_3 because the reduction in the real money supply caused by the 3 per cent inflation has shifted the AD^* curve to AD_1^*. To return to a GDP of Y^* the Bank must increase the nominal money supply so as to return the real money supply to its original amount and so shift the AD^* curve back from AD_1^* to AD_0^*.

interest-sensitive spending, both of which lead to a leftward shift in the AD^* curve.

Supply shock

Consider the effects of an exogenous increase in the cost of some important input above 2 per cent per year, such as an increase in world oil prices. This case is shown in Figure 22.8. If overall input costs rise by, say, 3 per cent during one period of time, this will shift the horizontal portion of the aggregate supply curve upwards to 3 per cent.[10] The economy is then moved upwards along the negatively sloped AD^* curve, indicating a reduced output associated with a higher inflation rate, something that could not happen as a result of demand-side changes alone.

If the Bank holds to its 2 per cent rate of monetary expansion for another period, the AD^* curve is shifted to

the left, causing a lower level of GDP to be associated with the 3 per cent inflation, and so on, until either the Bank starts to accommodate the 3 per cent inflation rate or the costs stop rising at that rate. Let us say that after two periods the rise in costs returns to 2 per cent. The AS^* curve now shifts back down. The inflation rate returns to 2 per cent and GDP stops falling. The return of inflation to its target level could equivalently be achieved by the Bank setting a higher interest rate which would have a similar effect in moving AD^* to the left and lowering GDP. In either case, because of the decline in the real money supply over the period of above-target inflation, real GDP is well below potential.

The problems involved in returning the economy to its potential GDP, Y^*, without causing the inflation rate to rise above 2 per cent once again are discussed in the next chapter where we consider inflation in more detail.

Comparisons and contrasts between two macro models

Chapter 21 first presented a theory that was applied to a situation in which expectations were for zero inflation, and then a theory designed to be applied when

---

[10] If the inputs whose prices rise account for only a subset of production costs, the upward shift in the supply curve will be smaller.

expectations were for a positive, often ragged, inflation. Although they apply to quite different real-world regimes, they can be regarded as a single theory with zero inflation expectations being a special case of the theory that explicitly incorporates inflation expectations. For purposes of comparison, we call this Theory 1. The theory presented in this chapter, which we call Theory 2, has some significant properties in common with Theory 1 but also some important differences. Therefore it may be helpful if we compare the two. Not only will this help you to appreciate the differences between them, it will also serve as a review of both theories.

The similarities

Both theories predict the following.

1. Positive aggregate demand shocks raise GDP while negative shocks lower it.

2. Supply shocks in the form of exogenous increases in input prices above the current established inflation rate cause that rate to increase temporarily while GDP falls.

3. Inflations due to a high level of aggregate demand which results from a positive GDP gap (in Chapter 21) or GDP above Y_c (in Chapter 22) will eventually be brought to an end if the Bank forces the real money supply to decline by expanding the nominal money supply more slowly than prices are rising, or equivalently by raising interest rates to reduce aggregate demand sufficiently to eliminate the inflationary pressure.

The differences

1. Theory 1 explains deviations from potential GDP as being short run in duration and caused by lags in adjustment between goods prices (fast) and input prices (slow). In today's world, in which the inflation rate is steady around a target rate of 2 per cent, the observed large variations in GDP gaps cannot be explained by lags between the prices of goods and inputs. However, they are consistent with Theory 2's horizontal AS^* curve below a GDP level of Y_c.

2. Theory 1 assumes that an increase in prices is needed to call forth an increase in national output (GDP); hence its *SRAS* curve is positively sloped over its whole range. Theory 2 allows national output to vary over a wide range with no consequent change in the inflation rate (which could be positive or zero), and hence no positive relation between changes in prices and changes in output. The evidence of the sort shown in Figures 22.1–22.3 favours Theory 1 in earlier periods but Theory 2 in the more recent period starting in the early 1990s.

3. In Theory 1 there is an automatic adjustment mechanism that moves GDP back towards potential GDP whenever there is either a positive or a negative GDP gap. When there is a negative GDP gap the adjustment mechanism is assumed to operate slowly. Even

with that qualification, however, there is little evidence that, at least since the end of World War II, price level adjustments have operated even slowly to move GDP back towards potential in the face of a negative GDP gap. In Theory 2 periods of negative GDP gaps are not automatically removed. Although this is a theoretical difference between the two theories, in practice this slowness of the automatic adjustment mechanism in Theory 1 and its absence in Theory 2 both imply that negative GDP gaps will usually be removed by other means than price level adjustments. This sometimes happens quickly and sometimes happens slowly, when revivals of aggregate demand cause rightward shifts in the aggregate demand curve. Such increases may come from many sources, including increases in consumption and investment. In Chapter 25 we shall consider government policies designed to remove both types of gap. Fiscal policy works through alterations in taxes and government spending, while monetary policy work through the Bank's ability to fix interest rates and so influence interest-sensitive spending, or through its ability to alter the money supply by such means as quantitative easing.

4. Theory 1 predicts that the only levels of GDP and its associated level of unemployment that are compatible with a stable inflation rate are potential GDP and the NAIRU. Theory 2 predicts that any level of GDP, at or below Y_c, is compatible with a stable inflation rate, provided that the Bank adopts a credible target for that inflation rate and supports it with the appropriate rate of monetary expansion, which it can do by manipulating the interest rate to produce that result. The evidence given at the beginning of this chapter clearly favours Theory 2 over Theory 1 in this respect.

5. More generally, Theory 1 assumes the existence of a unique macroeconomic equilibrium, plus an adjustment mechanism that pushes the economy back towards that equilibrium whenever it is moved away from it by various shocks. In contrast, although Theory 2 accepts the existence of a range of GDP above Y_c that is incompatible with a steady rate of inflation, it assumes no unique macro equilibrium for the economy. Although there is major disagreement among economists about this point, the path of UK GDP since the 2007–8 financial crisis has raised serious doubts about whether it will ever return to the previous trend. This is consistent with the view that there is no unique level (or trend growth path) of GDP to which the economy will inevitably return. Major shocks can and often do have permanent effects. Box 22.5 gives an introduction to some of the issues involved in this debate.

Box 22.5 How relevant is the concept of a long-run equilibrium?

The theory in Chapter 21 is based on the concept of a static long-run equilibrium (or, in more sophisticated versions, an equilibrium growth path) to which the economy returns after any disturbance. In contrast, evolutionary economics builds on the observation that the economy is subject to continual and uneven technological changes. These are generated endogenously mainly by profit-seeking firms in the private sector competing with each other by developing new products, new production processes, and new forms of organization. These are continually altering, and over time transforming, our economic, social, and political structures, while driving economic growth. Over the past few decades, for example, computers and the internet have transformed the products we make and the way we make them, as well as how we interact with others.

A unique long-term equilibrium to which the economy returns after a transitory disturbance is a concept that has no counterpart in the evolutionary view of an evolving economy that generates a continuous flow of surprises due to technological changes made under conditions of uncertainty. The equilibrium condition that aggregate desired spending equals the total production is still regarded as useful for analysing how the economy reacts initially to demand and supply shocks, but there is no unique positively sloped *SRAS* curve because firms can, and do, alter outputs over wide ranges as the demand for their products varies without having their unit costs or their prices vary. Thus, the economy can exist within a wide range of output and employment without any tendency to converge on a unique equilibrium.

Indeed, evolutionary economists argue that the concept of a long-run equilibrium to which the economy returns after being disturbed (as shown by a vertical *LRAS* curve) has no operational meaning in a rapidly evolving world. To determine the long-run equilibrium after some shock hits the economy, everything—tastes, technologies, and all other exogenous variables—must be held constant as the economy is allowed to converge on its equilibrium. But if it takes considerable time for the real economy to adjust to some shock and if technologies are changing continually and endogenously, the results of a long-run equilibrium exercise that holds these variables constant is no guide to what actually happens as the economy adjusts over time. What actually happens will depend on the path by which the economy changes after being hit by some external shock, and that path itself will influence the course of future behaviour. Say, for example, that the shock that hits the economy is one that temporarily discourages domestic R&D relative to what is happening in other countries. Over time, the economy's firms will be disadvantaged relative to those in other countries, and what would have happened if everything, including technology, had remained unchanged while the economy was adjusting to the shock will be irrelevant to what actually happens.

The figure showing the level of real GDP before and after the last great demand-side shock of 2008 suggests that the economy shows no signs of returning to an equilibrium growth path from which it diverged in that year.

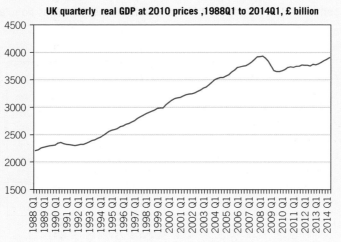

UK quarterly real GDP at 2010 prices, 1988Q1 to 2014Q1, £ billion

Source: ONS online database.

CASE STUDIES

1. Inflation convergence in the G7 countries

In the second case study at the end of Chapter 21 we showed that the inflation behaviour of the G7 countries on average was similar to that of the United Kingdom. Figure 22.9 shows the data for each of the G7 countries separately. They all had high but widely varying inflation rates in 1980, but all fell during the early 1980s. All then rose again between 1986 and 1990 during a global expansion and subsequently fell during the slowdown of the early 1990s.

Up to this point inflation could be explained as following the normal business cycle, rising in a boom and falling in the subsequent recession. However, from around the mid-1990s onwards the cycle in inflation that corresponded to the cycle in real activity disappeared. Inflation for almost all settled at around 2–3 per cent and stayed there.

All these countries showed a slight uptick in inflation in 2008 and a fall in 2009, but this is not well explained by the cycle in real activity. Rather, it is consistent with each country suffering from the same supply shock that raised United Kingdom prices in 2008 (energy and commodity prices) and benefiting from similar price falls in 2009. Inflation rates returned to their 'normal' range in 2010, even though activity in most countries remained depressed and unemployment continued to rise in many. It is notable that the IMF in 2014 was forecasting that all these countries would have inflation rates of around 2 per cent throughout their forecast period.

The one country that looks rather different from the others in inflation performance is Japan. We look at their experience in more detail in a case study at the end of Chapter 25.

2. Inflation convergence in the Eurozone

The phenomenon that we have just seen of convergence of inflation rates to levels around 2 per cent is nowhere more strongly evident than in the Eurozone, which has three countries (France, Germany, and Italy) in common with the G7 group discussed above. Figure 22.10 shows inflation rates for fourteen members of the Eurozone from 1981 to 2019. The key date for convergence in the case of these countries is clearly 1999, which is the year when the common currency came into being. Before that point in time inflation rates were high and divergent, but the convergence process was working from around 1991 onwards.

Clearly this convergence was not due to the independent adoption of inflation targeting, but rather to the adoption of a common currency and a single monetary policy. With free movement of goods and people as well as a common currency, it is not surprising that inflation rates converged. However, what is worth noting is that, while inflation rates converged, unemployment behaviour did not. In June 2014, the latest reported unemployment figures for Greece and Spain were 26.6 per cent and 25.1 per cent, respectively, while the comparable figures for Austria and Germany were 4.9 per cent and 6.7 per cent. This means that, on a cross-country basis, there was no relationship between inflation

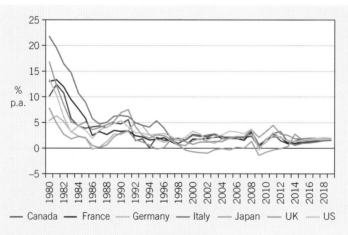

Figure 22.9 Inflation rate in seven major countries, 1980–2019

Source: IMF WEO database, April 2014. Data for 2014–19 are IMF forecasts

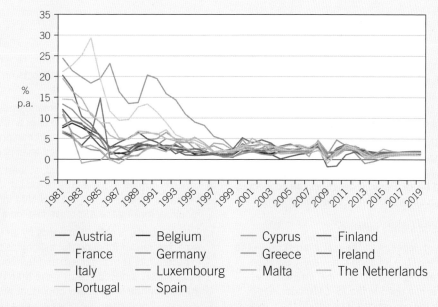

Figure 22.10 Inflation in fourteen Eurozone countries, 1981–2019

Four members of the Eurozone (Estonia, Latvia, Slovakia, and Slovenia) are not included in the chart because of data availability and different times of joining the Eurozone

Source: IMF *World Economic Outlook* database, April 2014. Data for 2014 onwards are IMF forecasts.

and unemployment. All members of the Eurozone had similar inflation rates, but there were widely divergent unemployment levels and GDP gaps. Thus the inflation performance in these countries could not be explained by the size of unemployment or of the GDP gap, since all had a very similar inflation rate after 1999. It follows that it would not help to understand the economies of any of these countries to apply a model in which the domestic price level was presumed to adjust in response to the GDP gap (or the level of unemployment). Neither would it be sensible to think of the Eurozone as a whole as being an economy in which the price level responds to positive or negative GDP gaps in order to return the Eurozone GDP to its potential level. In short, the rate of inflation and inflation expectations are anchored at around 2 per cent, and variations in real activity and employment require a different explanation.

Conclusion

In this chapter we have considered a situation in which the Bank of England has established an inflation rate that is fully accommodated by the appropriate rate of monetary expansion and is fully expected to continue. The new aggregate demand curve, AD^*, relates GDP to the actual inflation rate for some given expected rate. The new aggregate supply curve, AS^*, is perfectly elastic at the actual and expected inflation rate up to and a little beyond capacity GDP, at a point labelled Y_c; after that, it is positively sloped when the inflation rate rises above the expected rate. In this model, demand shocks cause variations in income but at a constant inflation rate up to a GDP of Y_c.

The version of the theory that covers this situation has many similarities to the earlier versions. However, there are important differences, the most obvious one being that there is no unique equilibrium level of GDP towards which the economy is inevitably propelled. Instead, GDP can vary over a wide range with no change in the price level acting to push the economy back to potential GDP. Equally important is the characteristic that variations in output below Y_c are caused by changes in aggregate demand and do not need to be induced by changes in prices. The absence of a unique self-sustaining equilibrium for the whole economy has important implications that we consider in the next chapter.

SUMMARY

Recent experience of inflation and output

■ The theory of Chapter 21, with both zero and positive inflation expectations, associates changes in the price level with changes in the GDP gap. It describes the economy's macro behaviour fairly well until the early 1990s.

■ The theory of Chapter 22 predicts that GDP can vary over a wide range, while the inflation rate stays within a narrow target band set by the government and accommodated by the Bank. It describes the economy's macro behaviour since the early 1990s fairly well.

IS–LM in a world of steady inflation

■ Since investment depends on the real interest rate—the nominal rate *minus* the inflation rate—every point on the *IS* curve drawn against the nominal interest rate, IS_n, which is the one used in the *IS–LM* model, lies vertically above the corresponding point on the curve plotted against the real rate, IS_r, by an amount equal to the expected inflation rate.

■ If the Bank wishes to maintain an unchanged real GDP and a 2 per cent target inflation rate, the rate must be accommodated by allowing a nominal increase in the money supply of 2 per cent per year, thus holding the real money supply and the *LM* curve constant.

The aggregate demand curve in world of steady inflation

■ A fully expected and accommodated inflation has no effect on the *IS* curve because the wealth, balance-of-payment and income effects do not operate in such a situation, nor does it affect the *LM* curve as long as the money supply is increasing at the same rate as prices are rising.

■ An unanticipated exogenous rise of the inflation rate reduces spending and thus shifts the *IS* curve to the left because of the wealth effect, the balance-of-payments effect, and the real income effect. Equilibrium real GDP falls as a result.

■ Points on the negatively sloped AD^* curve are alternatives showing the impact effect on equilibrium real GDP over one time period of various alternative actual inflation rates when the rate had been expected to remain constant at some target rate.

■ The AD^* curve is shifted to the right by an increase in consumption, investment, net exports, government spending, the real money supply, or the fully expected inflation rate, and a decrease in either the tax rate or the demand to hold money balances.

Pricing and output decisions and the AS^* curve

■ In the modern economy most firms sell differentiated products and hence must set their own prices and let consumer demand determine their sales.

■ In the modern economy most firms face constant marginal and average (i.e. unit) costs up to, or a little above, normal capacity output.

■ In response to variations in demand, most firms are willing to vary their outputs up to or a little beyond their normal capacity outputs without changing their prices at a different rate than the price level is changing.

■ Thus the AS^* curve is horizontal, at least up to normal capacity output, Y^*, or a little beyond it, Y_c. Above Y_c increases in prices above the expected inflation rate are required, making the AS^* curve take on a positive slope.

■ The AS^* curve is shifted upwards by an increase in the expected rate of inflation (for as long as the new expected rate is maintained) and temporarily by an exogenously induced rise by more than the target rate of inflation in the price of any important input.

$AD^*–AS^*$ equilibrium

■ Variations in output up to Y_c cause GDP and employment to vary but leave the inflation rate unchanged.

■ An exogenous rise in final spending that takes the AD^* curve above Y_c raises the inflation rate.

■ Unless that rate is accommodated by an increased rate of monetary expansion, the real money supply is reduced by the increased inflation which shifts the AD^* curve back until inflation returns to its target rate.

■ To succeed in returning inflation to its target, the Bank must act quickly and decisively to reaffirm its commitment to its target.

■ An exogenous increase in the cost of some important input above the target inflation rate shifts the AS^* curve upwards, causing GDP to fall and the inflation rate to rise.

Comparisons and contrasts

■ Theory 1 in Chapter 21 and Theory 2 in Chapter 22 are similar in predicting that (1) positive aggregate demand shocks raise GDP while negative shocks lower it, (2) aggregate supply shocks increase the inflation rate while reducing GDP, and (3) inflations due to a positive GDP gaps will be eliminated if the real money supply is allowed to decline, thus raising the interest rate and reducing aggregate spending sufficiently to eliminate the gap.

■ The two theories differ in that: (1) Theory 1 explains deviations from potential GDP as being the short-run effects of lags in adjustment between goods prices (fast) and input prices (slow), while Theory 2 explains these deviations by variations in demand interacting with a horizontal AS^* curve. (2) Theory 1 assumes that increases in prices are needed to call forth increases in national output, while Theory 2 assumes that firms are willing to sell more at the existing prices if the demand is forthcoming up to a GDP of Y_c. (3) Theory 1 has an automatic adjustment mechanism that moves GDP back to potential GDP when there is a GDP gap of either sign, while in Theory 2 periods of negative GDP gaps are not automatically removed. (4) Theory 1 predicts that the only level of GDP that is compatible with a stable inflation rate is potential GDP and its corresponding NAIRU, while Theory 2 predicts that any level of GDP, at or below Y_c, is compatible with a stable inflation rate.

TOPICS FOR REVIEW

- Historical experience of the relation (if any) between GDP gaps and inflation
- The AD^* curve, how it is derived and why it shifts
- The behaviour of firms' costs and prices that underlie the AS^* curve
- The effects on GDP and inflation of aggregate demand shocks
- The effects on GDP and inflation of aggregate supply shocks
- Comparisons and contrasts of Theories 1 and 2

QUESTIONS

1 Describe the course of GDP and the inflation rate if the economy starts at potential GDP and then suffers a recession that opens up a large negative GDP gap, then a recovery that eventually opens up a positive GDP gap, and then returns to potential GDP.

2 Outline all the changes that could cause the AS^* curve to shift upwards (i) temporarily and (ii) permanently.

3 What could cause the inflation rate to rise above the upper limit of the target band and (i) lead the Bank to make no change in the interest rate or (ii) lead the Bank to raise the interest rate? Would there be any causes of this breaching of the upper limit that would lead the Bank to lower the interest rate?

4 What determines the size of the multiplier effect in the middle section of the AS^* curve, assuming an exogenous rightward shift of AD coming, for example, from an increase in export demand? Is it larger or smaller that it would be in the model of Chapter 21?

5 What forces might return GDP to Y^* if the inflation rate remains close to target, but GDP is below Y^*?

6 What factors will determine whether the target inflation rate is credible and thus able to tie down inflation expectations?

7 Using the IS–LM model and AD^*, and starting at an inflation rate of 2 per cent that is fully expected, show what happens to GDP (starting at Y^*) in the short and long run if the monetary authorities increase the rate of growth of the money stock to 4 per cent permanently.

8 What role might fiscal policy have in maintaining the credibility of the inflation target?

9 Why might the adoption of a common currency, the euro, lead to the convergence of inflation rates in member countries of the Eurozone?

10 Why might Y_c be different from Y^*?

PART **SIX**

MACROECONOMICS OF THE GLOBAL ECONOMY

CHAPTER 23

BUSINESS CYCLES, UNEMPLOYMENT, AND INFLATION

In earlier chapters we saw that the economy tends to move in a series of ups and downs, called *business cycles*, rather than along a steady path of economic growth, and it would be a good idea to review now the section entitled 'The macro problem: inflation and unemployment' at the beginning of Chapter 16. Indeed, the discussion that follows makes use of the material introduced there. In Chapter 21 we developed a theory that applied well to the period before the 1990s. In this theory there is a unique equilibrium level of GDP, called potential GDP and designated Y^*, that has two key characteristics: first, it is the only level of GDP that is compatible with stable rate of inflation, and, secondly, there is an adjustment mechanism that automatically propels the economy back to that equilibrium whenever actual GDP deviates from it, as it does over the business cycle, with the price level rising in the face of a positive GDP gap ($Y > Y^*$) and falling in the face of a negative one ($Y < Y^*$). In Chapter 22 we saw that there is no evidence that, since the beginning of the 1990s, the economy has such a unique equilibrium level of GDP with the characteristics just described. We then went on to develop a theory explaining why the economy can have a stable rate of inflation while GDP varies cyclically. This raises several questions.

1. Why does the economy shows cyclical fluctuations rather than just growing along a stable growth path?

2. Are there limits to the fluctuations in GDP?

3. Might GDP become stalled at a level substantially below its potential and show little or no tendency to rise toward it?

4. What are the characteristics of the labour market that contribute to the economy's cyclical behaviour?

5. Why is the possibility of inflation above the target rate a matter of concern?

We deal with the first three questions in the first part of this chapter when we consider the business cycle in more detail. Then in the second part, we deal with the fourth question while studying the unemployment that accompanies cyclical downswings. Finally, in the third part we deal with the last question by elaborating on the analysis of inflation that we began in the previous two chapters.

In this chapter you will learn that:

- The economy tends to fluctuate over a range that varies from negative GDP gaps, with anything from 10–15 per cent of its workforce unemployed in a typical trough, to positive GDP gaps in which all unemployment is either frictional or structural.

- Each business cycle has its own special characteristics, while the turning points have several different explanations.

- Aggregate demand shocks are a major cause of cyclical fluctuations.

- The accelerator theory emphasizes that a significant part of investment is a disequilibrium phenomenon occurring when the actual stock of capital goods differs from the desired stock.

- Unemployment is composed of cyclical, frictional, and structural unemployment, with the last two making up equilibrium unemployment.

- Wage stickiness helps to explain why business cycles cause cycles in unemployment.

- Equilibrium unemployment arises from frictions in the economy and structural changes in economic activity.

- It is neither possible nor desirable to reduce unemployment to zero.

- A cyclical expansion that is rapid and strong can open up a large positive GDP gap and initiate an inflation above the target rate.

- If the Bank does not accommodate the inflation with an expansive monetary policy, the rising price level will raise interest rates, curtail spending, and push GDP back to its potential level.

- If the Bank accommodates the inflation, thus maintaining the GDP gap, the inflation rate will tend to rise.

- If the Bank seeks to break an entrenched inflation, a negative GDP gap will ensue until expectations fall to the desired level.

- A supply shock that raises input prices will initiate a stagflation: GDP falls while the price level rises.

The business cycle

Output, employment, and living standards have all shown an upward trend in advanced countries over the past two centuries. If you compare the GDP of any year in the first part of this century with the GDP of the corresponding year in the first part of the previous century, your overwhelming impression will be one of growth, even if you choose a recent year of low activity and compare it with a boom year from the early 1900s. However, if you take the GDP of each year of the twenty-first century and compare it with that of the previous year, you will find that economic activity proceeds in an irregular path, with forward spurts being followed by pauses and even relapses. These short-term fluctuations are commonly known as business cycles. Sometimes the year-to-year patterns have been remarkably regular, but at other times less so.

In the past, investigators have identified several types of cycle in economic activity. One type, which is clearly observable in the nineteenth-century British data, had a duration of about nine years from peak to peak. This was the one usually called the trade cycle. A second type of cycle lasted anywhere from eighteen to forty months, and was associated with variations in inventories—something that is much less likely to occur with the modern development of computer-based, just-in-time inventories. Finally, some economists argue for a third, very long, cycle of about fifty years' duration that is associated with major fluctuations of investment activity due to a group of related innovations. This type of cycle and its

technological explanation was popularized by the Austrian-born, and later American, economist Joseph Schumpeter, and more recently by the late British economist Christopher Freeman writing with the Portuguese economist Francisco Louçá. Although the existence of a regular fifty-year cycle is much debated, Freeman and Louçá have made a strong case for the existence of long cycles peaking every fifty or so years and associated with the exploitation of major new technologies. We will return to these long cycles in Chapter 26 when we discuss economic growth. In this chapter we confine ourselves to the shorter-term fluctuations, typically lasting on average less than ten years from peak to peak.

In Chapter 15 we introduced some terminology of the cycle, which we now summarize, although a more detailed description is given in the earlier chapter. The *trough* is characterized by high unemployment and a large negative GDP gap. During the *recovery* the GDP gap is narrowed, unemployment falls, profits rise, and business and consumer confidence returns—all of which may happen quickly in some cycles and slowly in others. In the *peak*, which may be sharp or more like an extended plateau, the negative GDP gap has usually disappeared and, in some cases, a positive GDP gap has developed, often accompanied by a rise in the inflation rate. The *downturn* typically has various causes and may be sudden or more gradual. This is followed by a period of either actual or relative decline. A *recession* is defined as a fall in real GDP for two quarters in succession, but the actual *slump* may last much longer and take the form of a GDP that grows much more slowly than average and a persistent negative GDP gap. When the slump is prolonged and deep, it is referred to as a *depression*.

Most cycles do not see a formal recession and even when they do, it is usually of short duration. During most of its time the slump takes the form of GDP rising less than its trend value. There is still a large GDP gap with its accompanying unemployment of both labour and capital, with GDP rising too slowly to eliminate the gap. At the same time some sectors of the economy are producing at or near capacity and are still investing in the innovation of new products and new processes. But there are enough depressed sectors to create a significant GDP gap.

When we talk about cycles and slumps it is important to realize that most of the economy stays employed all of the time. For example, in the depression of the 1930s, the worst depression (in employment terms) since the beginning of the Industrial Revolution, unemployment peaked at between 20 and 25 per cent in most industrialized countries. This means that 75–80 per cent of the labour force remained employed. In more typical cycles, unemployment reaches around 8–12 per cent, which implies that 88–92 per cent of the labour force is still in employment. Unemployment may actually be somewhat worse than these figures suggest because many potential workers become discouraged and cease looking for a job during a prolonged slump. Since they are not counted as being in the labour force, they are not included in the unemployment data.

An important implication of the fact that cycles differ is that we are unlikely to find a single explanation of the cycle that covers all cases all of the time. There are such theories, two of which are the multiplier–accelerator theory and the real business cycle theory. The former unites the multiplier that we know from earlier chapters and the accelerator that we will study briefly in this chapter, while the latter explains cycles as deviations from a steady long-term growth path caused by random fluctuations in tastes and technology.

Nonetheless the evidence suggests that although there are some common characteristics of cycles, each cycle has its own special characteristics while each turning point may have a different explanation including, at one time or another, changes in private or public sector real spending and changes in financial conditions.

Explaining business cycles

An explanation of the business cycle must answer two questions: (1) What are the factors that cause GDP and other key macro variables to fluctuate? (2) What causes those fluctuations to form a cyclical pattern? These two questions are considered in the two main sections that follow.

Why do GDP and employment fluctuate?

Over the course of economic history, the business cycle has been driven mainly by fluctuations in aggregate demand, although the causes of these demand fluctuations are various, running from variations in technologically driven investments, through speculative bubbles, to financial crashes. Also, some particular cycles can be explained in part by aggregate supply shocks. Indeed, events of the mid-1970s made the citizens of advanced countries acutely aware of supply-side causes.

Aggregate demand shocks are a major historical source of fluctuations in GDP; aggregate supply shocks are a secondary source.

Sources of aggregate demand shocks

Aggregate demand shocks that cause GDP and employment to rise or fall have numerous sources. Occasionally, shifts in the consumption function that raise or lower aggregate spending alter GDP significantly. Increases in exports or decreases in imports that increase domestic production can give a major upward push to aggregate demand and employment. Major shifts in government spending and tax policies can raise or lower aggregate demand. Monetary policy can also have a major influence. A contractionary monetary policy that shifts the *LM* curve to the left and forces interest rates to rise can reduce interest-sensitive spending, lowering GDP. An expansionary monetary policy that lowers interest rates can do the reverse. All of these forces can result in significant demand shocks to the economy. Probably the most important factor from the demand side, however, is investment and we will look at this in more detail in the next section. The first case study at the end of this chapter gives the anatomy of the latest worldwide recession, the aftermath of which was still being felt in the middle of the present decade. This recession originated in the financial sector and then caused major decreases in aggregate demand.

Changes in investment

In Chapter 16 we discussed the main determinants of investment and that discussion should be re-read now. The theory of aggregate demand already takes account of the response of investment (and other types of interest-sensitive spending) to variations in interest rates. That responsiveness is a major determinant of the slope of the *IS* curve and hence of the slope of the *AD* and *AD** curves. Shifts in the *AD* and *AD** curves (recall that the same things shift both curves) caused by investment must arise from changes in determinants of investment other than the interest rate.

Here, we consider the major source of investment spending—investment in the capital equipment that provides capacity for future production of both existing and new products and existing and new production processes. The expected profitability of such investments depends on expected future market conditions. Expectations are uncertain at the best of times and may occasionally be influenced by waves of optimism or pessimism that sweep over the community.

Such investment also depends critically on, and varies with, the amount of newly invented products and processes that currently exist and that are the basis for innovations that are expected to be profitable. (Economists distinguish between the *invention* of new products and processes and *innovation*, which is producing and marketing them, both of which activities may require many subsidiary inventions and refinements.) Product and process innovations are not developed at an even pace. Key new technologies, often called general purpose technologies (see Chapter 11), give rise to a host of opportunities for the development of myriad new products and new processes, and often require a heavy investment in infrastructure. For example, the invention of the dynamo made possible the widespread use of electricity. Think of all the products, from your refrigerator to your computer to your Facebook entry, that use electricity and could not have been invented when the major power source was the steam engine. The electrification of factories made possible the development of mass production techniques. The spreading use of electricity required the development of a massive infrastructure of dams, water- and coal-powered generation plants, and electric transmission cables. More recently, the understanding of the genetic code and the ability to manoeuvre and alter genes has given rise to a massive growth of products and processes that utilize the techniques of biotechnology. Another key development that is just beginning to give rise to myriad investment opportunities is nanotechnology—the manipulation of materials one atom at a time. These, and many other major new technologies that have a wide range of potential applications, give rise to profitable new investments in order to create new products that derive from them and the facilities to produce and market these products. They have also sometimes given rise to speculative bubbles, such as the internet bubble of the late 1990s, which have increased the value of companies far beyond their earning capacity and then burst, destroying much paper wealth, and in turn leading to declines in spending and a fall in either GDP itself or its growth rate.

Although a smaller part of aggregate spending than consumption, investment is more volatile and hence a major source of fluctuations in aggregate demand.

Cumulative processes

Starting from a trough in the business cycle, let there be some exogenous shift in spending that begins an expansion. (We will discuss reasons for such a shift later.) Why does a period of expansion, once begun, tend to develop its own momentum? First, the multiplier process tends to cause cumulative movements. As soon as a revival begins, some unemployed labourers are re-employed. With their newly acquired incomes, these people can afford to increase their consumption spending. This new demand causes an increase in production and creates new jobs for other previously unemployed workers. As incomes rise demand rises, and as demand rises incomes rise.

According to multiplier theory, some sustained increase in new investment spending will raise GDP, but only by a finite amount. GDP will stop growing when it has given rise to an equivalent amount of new savings and other withdrawals, so that the total of new withdrawals and new injections are equal. Assume, for example, that there is £100 of new investment spending that continues in future periods and that the marginal propensity not to spend (which is one *minus* the marginal propensity to spend of Chapter 16) is 0.4. Then those who receive £100 of new income as a result of the new investment spending will spend £60, while £40 will leak out in savings, imports, and taxes. Those who receive the £60 of new income will spend £36 while £14 will be withdrawn, and so on. At the end of this process, income while stop rising when it, and hence GDP, have risen by £250 (£100/0.4) and total withdrawals by £100.

But this calculation assumes that there is only a single permanent increase in investment spending. If, instead, investment spending were to rise as income rose, the upward movement could go on for a long time. There are at least three reasons why this may be so. These are provided by the accelerator theory, increased availability of funds for investment, and changes in expectations. We consider each below.

The accelerator

The need for plant and equipment is obviously derived from the demand for the goods and services that the plant and equipment are designed to produce. If there is a once-and-for-all rise in demand that is expected to persist, and that cannot be met with existing capacity, new plant and equipment will be needed. This increases the desired stock of capital goods, and there will be a rise in investment spending while the new capital is being produced. But if nothing else changes, and even though business conditions continue to look rosy enough to justify the increased stock of capital, investment in new plant and equipment will cease once the larger capital stock is achieved. This motivation for new investment lasts as long as demand is

Box 23.1 The accelerator theory of investment

Let there be a simple relationship between GDP and the amount of capital needed to produce it:

$$K = \alpha Y \qquad (1)$$

where Y is GDP and K is the required capital stock. The coefficient α is the amount of capital needed per unit of GDP, which is called the capital–output ratio and given by $\alpha = K/Y$. This is also called the accelerator coefficient. From eqn (1) we know that the change in K is equal to α multiplied by the change in Y, or in symbols:

$$\Delta K = \alpha \Delta Y \qquad (2)$$

Since the change in the capital stock is equal to the amount of investment, we have

$$I = \alpha \Delta Y \qquad (3)$$

which states that investment is a constant proportion of the *change* in GDP. This is called the 'simple', or sometimes the 'naïve', accelerator.

Taken literally, the accelerator posits a mechanical and rigid response of investment to changes in sales (and thus by aggregation to changes in GDP). It does this by not allowing for the existence of unused capital (excess capacity) at the trough of a cycle, by assuming a proportional relationship between changes in GDP and the size of the desired capital stock, and by assuming a fixed capital–output ratio. The issue of unused capacity is discussed in the text. Here we consider the other two assumptions.

Even when there is little unused capacity, changes in sales that are thought to be temporary will not necessarily lead to new investment. It is usually possible to increase the level of output from a given capital stock by working overtime or extra shifts. While this would usually be more expensive per unit of output in the long run, it will usually be preferable to making investments in the new capital equipment that would lie idle after a temporary spurt of demand had subsided. Thus expectations about what is the required stock may lead to a much less mechanistic response of investment to income than the accelerator suggests.

Different lines of production require very differ amounts of capital per unit of output. Therefore the total amount of capacity that is required to meet a cyclical rise in demand depends on how that demand is distributed among the economy's various industries. There is no evidence that this distribution is the same for each recovery, so there is no evidence that the I required for each increase in Y will be the same in each cyclical upturn.

A further limitation of the accelerator theory is its view of what constitutes investment. The fixed capital–output ratio emphasizes investment in 'capital widening', which is investment in additional capacity that uses the same ratio of capital to labour as does existing capacity. It does not explain 'capital deepening', which is the kind of increase in the amount, of capital per unit of labour that occurs in response to a fall in the rate of interest. Nor does the theory say anything about investments stimulated by new processes or products. Furthermore, it does not allow for the fact that investment in any period is likely to be limited by the capacity of the capital-goods industry so that the I associated with a single ΔY might be spread over many time periods. (The so-called flexible accelerator takes account of this last objection by allowing for lags in the adjustment of K to ΔY.)

Despite all these limitations, the accelerator theory does provide the very valuable insight of showing how some part of investment is related to changes in GDP rather than to its level.

---

increasing but stops once demand levels off, even if at a high level.

This dependence of some investment on changes in, rather than the level of, GDP is called the **accelerator**. Although, as discussed in Box 23.1, the theory of the accelerator has many limitations, it does provide an important insight:

Accelerator theory emphasizes that a significant part of investment is a disequilibrium phenomenon, something that occurs when the stock of capital goods differs from what firms and households would like it to be.

This gives the accelerator its particular importance in connection with fluctuations in GDP.

One problem with accelerator theory is that firms typically have excess capacity at the bottom of the cyclical trough. So when demand increases, they are more interested in putting unused capacity back into production than creating new capacity. However, the longer the trough persists, the more old capital will fall into disrepair and/or become obsolete and so the more likely is it that there will be some accelerator effect even in the early stages of the upswing. Then, later in the upswing when firms get closer to capacity output, they will need new capacity so there is likely to be a spurt of accelerator-type investment near the top of the cycle, and this will give the expansion an extra boost. Box 23.1 outlines the theory of the accelerator and some criticisms in more detail.

Availability of funds

Firms often have many opportunities to innovate new products and new production processes but are restrained by lack of funds. This is particularly so when there are major opportunities for making innovations based on new applications of general purpose technologies that have recently been developed. Think, for example, of all the new products and processes that were enabled by the invention of the computer or the internet. If new savings that are initially a leakage from the circular flow of income find their way into financial institutions, they are potentially available to be lent to firms to make their desired new investments. In this case, the expansion can go on for much longer than simple multiplier theory would suggest because much of what is withdrawn by way of savings finds its way back onto the income stream by way of loans to finance new investment spending. In effect, the innovations in information technology have made the financial system more efficient and thus lowered the cost of finance to firms as well as increased its availability (for any given level of income) as well as opening up more investment opportunities in IT-related sectors.

Also, as we have seen earlier, much investment in existing products and techniques, as well as much R&D to develop new ones, is financed from the profits of firms. Such profits are typically low or non-existent at the trough of the cycle. Therefore firm-financed spending on investment and R&D tends to be low. Then, as a recovery proceeds, profit rises and with it so does firm-financed investment and R&D spending.

Expectations

A third major reason for cumulative movements is expectations. All production plans take time to fulfil. Current decisions to produce consumer goods and investment goods are strongly influenced by business expectations. Such expectations can sometimes be volatile, and sometimes self-fulfilling. For example, if enough people think, that prices of shares are going to rise, they will all buy these in anticipation of the price rise, and these purchases will themselves cause prices to rise. If, on the other hand, enough people think share prices are going to fall, they will sell quickly at what they regard as a high price and thereby actually cause prices to fall. This is the phenomenon of *self-realizing expectations*. It applies to many parts of the economy. If enough CEOs think the future looks rosy and so begin to invest in increasing their firms' productive capacity, this will create new employment and income in the capital-goods industries. The resulting increase in demand will help to create the rosy conditions whose expectations started the whole process. One cannot lay down simple universal rules about such a complicated psychological phenomenon as the formation of expectations, but there is often a bandwagon effect. Once things begin to improve, people expect further improvements, and their actions, based on this expectation, help to cause further improvements.

Another reason for the importance of expectations is the attitude of banks and other financial institutions.

Often after a financial collapse, such as happened in 2008, these institutions become very risk averse. They worry so much about their balance sheets and past failed loans that they are reluctant to make new loans to all but the most secure of their customers. This group seldom includes those with untested ideas for new products and new processes. Once a recovery goes on long enough for the managers of these institutions to become more optimistic about the future course of the economy, they become more willing to make loans to a wider range of customers. This change helps to fuel the expansion.

Downswings

All of the discussion so far has related to cumulative upswings. However, all of the forces seen there happen in reverse, tending to make downswings cumulative once they begin. The multiplier tends to accentuate any reduction in GDP as those who lose their jobs and incomes cut their spending, which causes others to lose their jobs and incomes, and so on. Again, this process would not be cumulative if it was in response to a once-and-for-all reduction in some element of spending such as investment. But the other forces just analysed also work in reverse. In so far as new investment depends on increases in GDP, as GDP stops rising and starts to fall, such investment will come to halt. (Even if the output of some parts of the economy does not fall, demand will fall in the industries that are most affected by the downturn and, for them, the accelerator will act in reverse.) In so far as an investment is financed by the savings of households and firms, such investment will be curtailed as incomes and profits fall in the downswing. Expectations about future sales and profits are also likely to become pessimistic as current sales fall in the downswing.

What halts cumulative swings?

The next question is: Given that upswings and downswings tend to be cumulative, why do they stop and eventually reverse themselves, downswings turning into upswing and upswings into downswings, sometimes after short periods at the trough or peak and sometimes after prolonged periods at either end of the cycle? We deal with this in two stages, asking: What would eventually bring expansions and contractions to a halt if nothing else intervenes before then? Why do cycles sometimes stop before reaching the extreme bottom and peak that is possible?

Floors and ceilings

The most obvious force slowing an expansion is the capacity of plant, equipment, and other resources. In the slump many firms have excess capacity and the expansion can be fast while that capacity is being put back in work. But once full capacity is reached, further expansion of output requires new capital equipment. However, if this new investment causes a scarcity of investment funds, interest rates will rise. Firms will now find new investments more expensive than anticipated, and some will now appear unprofitable. A similar story applies to labour. Early in the expansion unemployed labour is being put back to work. But once most of the pool of unemployed is exhausted, any sustained rapid growth of GDP and employment will be slowed. As shortages of labour and other inputs grow, wages and other input prices will begin to rise faster than before. The resulting rise in the inflation rate will tend to cut real spending for all the reasons discussed in the previous chapter. Since the Bank has an inflation target, it will tend to raise its interest rate in order to head off the rise in inflation, and this will reduce interest-sensitive spending as well as generating expectations of a slow-down in the growth of demand.

As full capacity is reached, rises in wages, interest rates, and material costs due to shortages of labour, capital, and raw materials may slow the expansion of production and even stop it. The accelerator implies that even a slowing of GDP may cause a fall of investment spending. The shortages and increases in costs may lead to a fall of business confidence that induces a further reduction in investment spending, bringing an expansion to a halt.

A rapid contraction is also eventually brought to an end. Think of the worst sort of depression imaginable—one in which all postponable spending of households, firms, and governments has been postponed. Even then, aggregate demand will not fall to zero. Households can use up savings, or go into debt, to buy necessities of life. This creates employment and income for people to spend. Moreover, payments to households in the forms of unemployment benefits and welfare payments provide the funds to support minimum consumption spending. Also, much government spending is committed by statute and so sustained. Civil service salaries and defence spending will continue, as will spending on health and education. Even business investment, in many ways the most easily postponable component of aggregate demand, will not fall to zero. In the industries providing food, clothing, and shelter, demand may remain high despite quite large reductions in incomes. These industries will certainly be carrying out some investment to replace equipment as it wears out, and they may even undertake some new investment. Furthermore, technological innovations may provide opportunities for new investment even in the midst of a serious slump. For example, in the depths of the Great Depression of the 1930s, when unemployment was pushing 50 per cent in the north of England, the new electronics industries, based on such newly popular products as radios and gramophones, underwent a boom that held unemployment low and investment high in southeast England.

Taken together, the minimum levels of consumption, investment, and government spending will assure a minimum equilibrium level of GDP which, although well below the potential level, will not be zero.

This is the floor.

The preceding discussion has raised a point that will be discussed at more length in Chapter 25. This concerns the so-called built-in stabilizers that tend to dampen both upswings and downswings. Much government revenue, including that raised by income tax and VAT, varies directly with GDP. So also does spending associated with the welfare safety net. Although the latter does not count as *G* in our model of the determination of GDP, it does affect final demand by increasing disposable incomes through increased unemployment benefits and welfare payments just as the employment incomes of many households fall. So, on the downswing, these government activities withdraw less from the income stream through taxes and inject more through transfer payments, both of which tend to mitigate the fall in GDP. On the upswing, the growing withdrawals through rising tax revenue and the falling injections through transfer payments all tend to mitigate the cumulative forces on the upswing.

Finally, as will be discussed in Chapter 25, discretionary counter-cyclical variations in government spending can mitigate both the upswings and the downswings in GDP brought about by changing spending on the part of the private sector.

Turning points

Many different forces can stop an expansion and sometimes turn it into a downswing. Often the collapse of a speculative bubble, such as accompanied the building of railways in the mid-nineteenth century, or the end of the stock market bubble in 1929, or the collapse of the dot. com bubble in the early twenty-first century, can do the trick. Also, as we explain in the first case study at the end of this chapter, a financial crisis such as accompanied the end of the subprime mortgage debacle, can halt an upswing and turn it into a downswing by severely curtailing the credit that finances so much spending by both firms and households. Also, if the expansion is strong enough to open up a large positive GDP gap, the resulting forecast of inflation may cause the central bank to apply a restrictive monetary policy quickly and strongly. This can initiate a downswing which, once begun, is hard to stop quickly. We saw earlier that according to the accelerator theory, a slackening in the speed at which GDP is rising, due, say, to resource limitations, can cause some types of investment to decline. This implies that a levelling off in GDP at the top of a cycle may lead to a decline in the level of investment, which can itself initiate a downswing.

What about the upturn from the trough? Investment theory predicts that, sooner or later, an upturn will begin. If nothing else causes an expansion of business activity, there will eventually be a revival of replacement investment. As existing capital wears out, the capital stock will eventually fall to the level required to produce current output. After that, new machines will be bought to replace those that subsequently wear out. The rise in the level of activity in the capital-goods industries will then cause, by way of the multiplier, a further rise in GDP. Also, do not forget that in a typical trough 80–90 per cent of labour and productive capacities are still employed and there are reasons why some investment may pick up, not least being new inventions that provide possibilities for major new innovations, particularly in those industries that have not been hard hit by the recession.

Avoiding extreme floors and ceilings

Finally we note that many, indeed most, cycles stop their downswings well before reaching the most extreme floor, and some stop their upswing before they reach full capacity output and full employment of labour. A temporary decline in investment opportunities due to the exhaustion of the most obvious ways of exploiting a long-established general purpose technology, a rise in the price of imported materials and components, a loss of wealth due to some financial problems, a change in government policy, and many other things can be strong enough to stop an expansion before it reaches a ceiling.

A new set of investment opportunities due to some new technological breakthrough that opens up many new avenues for developing new products and processes, a favourable change in the cost of imported materials and components, a revival of consumer and producer confidence, and many other favourable developments can be enough to stop a downturn at any stage and turn it into an expansion.

Finally, as we shall study in more detail in Chapter 25, government fiscal and monetary policies provide some tools both to help start an upswing and prevent it from coming to a halt well short of full employment of labour and capital and to halt a contraction well before it hits a floor.

Anatomy of a financial boom and bust

The financial sector has often been a major cause of an unsustainable boom and then the inevitable downturn into recession.

Optimism in the upturn

Many financial crises have their roots in a sustained period of economic growth and rising optimism. This may have started as a slow recovery after a previous slowdown or recession. We have noted that as activity increases, consumer confidence rises and demand in the economy expands. Firms invest to provide more capacity with which to supply their products and this enhances job prospects, which further enhances consumer confidence.

In the financial sector, banks see firms and consumers with growing incomes and feel confident about lending to finance further industrial expansion or property purchases. The prices of houses, company shares, and other assets rise in value, and this makes lenders even more confident as they see the collateral of borrowers increasing in value. Worries about risks of default tend to shrink as economic prospects generally improve and a sustained period of growth continues. This makes finance even cheaper for those who wish to borrow to finance investment or asset acquisition.

As asset prices rise, speculative purchases can lead to even further rises. In stock markets, investors buy in expectation of being able to sell at higher prices later. In housing markets, potential buyers see prices rising and rush to buy now in case prices rise even higher in future. Those with spare cash feel that property would be a good investment, so they buy in order to let rather than occupy. All of these forces cause prices to continue rising for some time. Many feel encouraged to borrow as much as they can in order to buy assets whose values are rising. Consumers feel confident in borrowing to finance further spending as their incomes are rising and their jobs seem secure.

The build-up phase prior to a financial crisis has the same pattern as a boom in the business cycle. Rising demand and employment lead to greater optimism, and this in turn leads to higher asset prices, easier finance, and reduced worries about risk. Higher asset prices encourage further buying by those seeking capital gains, and some of these speculative purchases are funded by increasing debt.

Often, specific stories circulate to reinforce people's optimism during the upturn. Sometimes it is a belief that a new technology is underpinning a sustainable surge in growth. This happened when the introduction of railways was revolutionizing the UK transport system in the 1840s, it happened in the 1920s when electricity was the new technology, and it happened again during the internet boom of the late 1990s. At other times it may be the belief in the wisdom of a specific regulator or government policy regime that sustains optimism. This played some role in the run-up to the financial crisis in 2008. Indeed, the period from the early 1990s to 2007 was called then by some 'the great moderation' owing to the apparent success of policy-makers in keeping GDP close to potential and inflation under control.

Optimism turns to fear

The boom in activity and asset prices can go on for many years and the forces working in the upturn tend to reinforce each other. The longer it goes on, the more likely are firms and financial institutions to have borrowed heavily to invest on the assumption of even more profits to come in future. However, at some point some event makes people question their belief that the boom will continue for ever. Many factors could trigger the end of the boom, but once households and firms suddenly become very cautious about their prospects, the forces of contraction can set in quite quickly. The first visible sign of the downturn is often a sharp fall in prices on the stock market. This leads those who have been speculating on rising share prices to want to sell as quickly as possible. Selling pressure can lead to very large percentage falls in values. Losses in wealth lead households to cut back on spending and firms to become more cautious about investment. Some firms that have been relying on assets as collateral against loans may go bust, while others find demand for their products shrinking. Loan defaults may follow, and this will lead to losses for banks so that they become very cautious about further lending.

The downturn becomes a financial crisis when banks themselves get into difficulty. Defaults on loans they have made, and insolvency of firms to which they have lent money, can lead to losses. Reductions in the market value of banks' shares can erode their capital. Rumours of financial difficulties in a specific bank can cause depositors to seek to withdraw their funds and make other banks unwilling to lend in the wholesale inter-bank market.

Bank failures can be triggered by an insolvency in which a bank's assets become worth less than its liabilities, or by a liquidity shortage in which a bank is unable to borrow even though it may still strictly be solvent. In some cases the bank may be closed down, in others the authorities may organise a takeover by a stronger bank, and in still others the government may step in and take over the bank or inject substantial public loans.

The collapse of any bank and the fear that this induces in many households and firms (as well as other banks) make credit hard to find as other banks become much more cautious about lending. This is what leads to such crises becoming known as 'credit crunches'. These reveal an intimate relation between the real and monetary sectors that is often not appreciated. This is that since all production takes time, firms must pay out to buy or hire all of their inputs of labour and materials long before they can sell their products to recoup their production costs and reap any profits. Much of this gap between payments to inputs and sales revenue from outputs is filled by credit. So, if credit becomes hard to get, firms are often forced to cease normal production activities for lack of funds to pay

for their inputs. The result is falling employment and output. Then, as consumers cut back on spending and firms cut back on investments, aggregate demand falls. Firms lay off workers which reduces confidence even further and asset prices continue to fall. As asset prices and demand continue to fall, other firms and financial institutions find themselves in difficulty. Some big institutions may then fail and things get even worse.

The possibility that what we have just described is endemic to market systems was argued many years ago by US economist Hyman Minsky (1919–1996). His central idea was that modern financial systems are inherently unstable, even if they appear to be stable for long periods. Indeed, Minsky argued that the longer stability persists, the more dangerous this becomes because the public becomes overconfident about the upturn continuing and they underestimate risk. The turning point comes when the bubble bursts and asset prices start to collapse. Because he argued that the collapse was inevitable, the turning point has come to be known as a 'Minsky moment'. Minsky called the subsequent downward spiral *debt deflation*.

Minsky described what he called his financial instability hypothesis in the following words.

The essence of the financial instability hypothesis is that financial traumas, even into debt deflations, occur as a normal functioning result in a capitalist economy. This does not mean that a capitalist economy is always tottering on the brink of disaster. There are situations where the short term debt financing of business and households is modest, this leads to robust financial markets which are not susceptible to debt deflation processes. … The normal functioning of an economy with a robust financial situation is both tranquil and, on the whole, successful. Tranquillity and success are not self-sustaining states, they induce increases in capital asset prices relative to current output prices and a rise in (1) acceptable debts for any prospective income flow, (2) investment and (3) profit. These concurrent increases lead to a transformation over time of an initially robust financial structure into a fragile structure.

(*Source:* H. Minsky, 'The financial instability hypothesis: a restatement', *Thames Papers in Political Economy*, 1978)

Conclusion

Although there may not be a unique equilibrium level of GDP towards which the economy is inevitably driven when it deviates from it, there are good reasons why:

The economy tends to fluctuate over a finite range that varies from negative GDP gaps, with anything from 85 to over 90 per cent of its resources still employed in a typical trough, to positive GDP gaps which, in some cases, could initiate a rising inflation rate if not restrained by the monetary policy needed to keep inflation close to target.

Unemployment

Unemployment of labour is observed to vary with the cycle, rising on downswings and falling in upswings. Here, we are interested in the causes and effects of this cyclical behaviour of unemployment, and we will also briefly look at other types of unemployment.

Measurement and definitions

The unemployed can be classified in various ways: personal characteristics, such as age, sex, degree of skill or education, geographical location, occupation, duration, or reasons for their unemployment. Although it is usually impossible to say why a particular person is unemployed, it is usually possible to understand the several causes of aggregate unemployment.

The ways in which unemployment is measured have changed many times over the years. UK figures used to include only those people actively looking for work and registered for benefits. This is referred to as the *claimant count*. The claimant count is still published, but it is more common to use a measure of unemployment based upon a survey of the labour force. These two measures of unemployment are explained in Box 23.2.

The recorded figures for unemployment may significantly understate or overstate the numbers who are actually willing to work at the existing set of wage rates. Overstatement arises because measured unemployment includes people who are not interested in work but who say they are in order to collect unemployment benefits. Understatement arises because of the voluntary withdrawal from the labour force of people, termed *discouraged workers*, who would like to work but have voluntarily withdrawn from the labour force because they believe that they cannot find a job under current labour market conditions. It is generally accepted that the understatement due to discouraged workers greatly exceeds the overestimate due to cheating.

Box 23.2 How is unemployment measured?

Two measures of unemployment are available in the UK today, the UK *claimant count* and what is called *ILO unemployment* as defined by United Nations International Labour Office. The European Union and the OECD have adopted the ILO unemployment definition.

The claimant count

The UK claimant count is all those people claiming unemployment-related benefits at Employment Service offices. Percentage unemployment is then expressed as follows:

$$\left(\frac{\text{number of claimants}}{\text{number employed in full–time or part–time jobs} + \text{number of claimants}} \right) \times 100$$

Three big problems with this measure are as follows: as the benefits system changes, so the numbers able to claim benefits change; it does not measure anyone who is unemployed but does not claim benefits; it counts anyone with two jobs twice. Therefore the percentage of persons who are not employed but would take work if it were available is underestimated. Nonetheless, the series is useful because it is the longest available series for UK unemployment. Figure 23.1 shows this series, starting in 1885!

ILO unemployment

Under the ILO approach all people aged 16 and under 65 are put into one of three classes:

1. ILO employed—those who have at least one hour's paid work a week, or who are on a government-supported training scheme, or who do unpaid work for a family business, or are away temporarily from a job (such as on vacation)
2. unemployed—those who are either out of work and have sought work in the last four weeks, or are out of work but have found a job that will start in the next two weeks
3. economically inactive—everyone else.

The unemployment percentage expresses numbers of ILO unemployed, group (2), as a percentage of the total numbers in groups (1) and (2). ILO unemployment is measured by a monthly survey, which in the United Kingdom is called the Labour Force Survey (LFS). Hence ILO unemployment is sometimes also referred to in the UK as *LFS unemployment*. About 40,000 individuals are interviewed each month, and the unemployment figure announced is the average of data for the previous three months.

The advantage of the ILO measure of unemployment is that it measures those who say they are unemployed and not just those claiming benefits. One disadvantage is that it lumps together as 'employed' anyone who takes even one hour's paid work with those who work much longer hours.

In January–March 2014 the UK unemployment percentage was 6.8 per cent by the ILO definition and 3.4 per cent by the claimant count definition. Figure 23.2 shows the data for ILO unemployment for eleven countries.

Three main types of unemployment are often distinguished. **Cyclical unemployment** or **demand-deficient unemployment** occurs because the economy is currently operating significantly below its potential GDP. It is zero when the GDP gap is zero or positive. **Frictional unemployment** is unemployment that arises as part of the normal turnover of labour. Firms and products are continually changing, and workers are moving from one job to another or from work to training and from training to work. Since such movements take time, there will always be some workers who are between jobs, or just entering the labour force looking for their first job, who are classified as unemployed. **Structural unemployment** occurs when there is a **mismatch** between the characteristics and skills of the people looking for work and those desired by potential employers. Jobs may exist in London while the available workers are in Liverpool, or there may be plenty of opportunities for computer programmers while many construction workers are looking for jobs. Frictional and structural unemployment make up **equilibrium unemployment**, which is defined as the unemployment that exists when GDP is at its potential level, a condition that is also described as **full employment**. Our main concern here is with cyclical unemployment, although we will also deal briefly with equilibrium unemployment.

Some economists have attempted to explain unemployment as a voluntary choice made by workers. However, the evidence shows that people become unemployed through redundancy rather than voluntary job leaving. Hence, most economists believe that:

The majority of the unemployed are involuntarily unemployed in the sense that they would willingly accept an offer of work in a job for which they are trained at the going wage rate.

Experience of employment and unemployment

The caption to Figure 23.1 describes the course of UK unemployment over time. Since 1945, unemployment has varied between business cycles more than within business cycles. For example, in the 1920s and 1930s unemployment cycled about a high average level, but in the period from 1945 to the early 1970s it cycled about a low level.

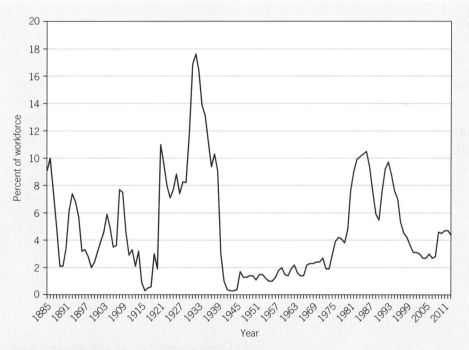

Figure 23.1 UK claimant count unemployment 1885–2013

UK unemployment has varied considerably over the past century and a quarter. The sequence of peaks and troughs that characterized UK unemployment for most of the nineteenth century are clearly visible up to the start of World War I. Then came the massive unprecedented unemployment of the Great Depression of the 1930s. Unemployment was extremely low at the end of World War II in 1945, and the next two decades saw small fluctuations around a slowly rising trend. Then came two peaks of very high unemployment followed by a gradual decrease until the recession that started in 2008 once again caused a rise in unemployment, followed by a fall after 2012. Although claimant count is always lower than the ILO unemployment rate based upon the Labour Force Survey, the movements in the two series over the business cycle are highly correlated.

Source: 100 years of economic statistics, The Economist, and the ONS database.

Then, from the mid-1970s to the early 1990s, the average rate was quite high, only to fall again from that time until the onset of the recession in 2008 when the rate rose, but not as much as it had done in the 1980s and early 1990s even though the GDP fall was greater. Unemployment fell again from 2012 to the time of writing (May 2014).

The trend of total employment in the United Kingdom has been slowly rising over the post-war period. The number of people who were economically active rose from 25.5 million in 1971 to around 31 million in 2010 and 32.6 million in 2014. The numbers in employment rose from 24.5 million in 1971 to 28.9 million in 2010 and 30.4 million in 2014. This steady but fairly slow growth is partly explained by population growth. However, there have also been some major structural changes in the pattern of employment. There were, for example, large shifts between sectors, such as a decline in manufacturing employment and a rise in services. Also, there have been changes in the composition of the labour force. Declining male employment has been offset by increased female participation rates. The **participation rate** is the proportion of any group that is in the labour force. For example, the participation rate of males over the age of sixteen declined from 84 per cent in 1971 to 70 per cent in 2014, while the female rate rose from 45 per cent in 1971 to 58 per cent in 2014.

Unemployment has not been a uniquely UK problem; hence, international comparisons are instructive. Figure 23.2 shows unemployment in major EU countries, as well as the United States and Japan, since 1980. One of the many facts that can be seen from the figure is that most European countries experienced high unemployment in the 1980s, but by the 2000s they had divided into two groups—one that still had high unemployment and one which had relatively low unemployment. Then, after 2008, the division was between those with high unemployment rates and those with even higher rates!

Characteristics of the unemployed

Unemployment is a pool (or stock). It is raised by a flow of potential workers who leave jobs but seek new work and those joining the labour force and looking for jobs. It is lowered by the flow of workers out of unemployment because either they have found jobs or they have given up looking for them.

In EU countries the flows into and out of unemployment have been quite small. As a result, a high proportion of the unemployed have been unemployed for a long time. For example, in Belgium, Ireland, and Italy around 60 per cent of the unemployed (at the peak of the unemployment upturn in the 1990s) had been unemployed for more than twelve months, which is defined as long-term unemployment. The figures for Germany, France, and the United Kingdom were all around 35 per cent. This contrasts with Canada and the United States, where only just over 10 per cent of the unemployed had been without jobs for more than twelve months. In the United States, in particular, flows into unemployment have typically been high but flows out were just as high, so the level of long-term unemployment was low. All this changed in the recession that began in 2008 when the percentage of American unemployed who had been out of work for more than a year rose to over 30 per cent and remained stubbornly high over several subsequent years.

The pre-2008 transatlantic differences may provide an important clue to the reasons for the higher persistence of unemployment in several EU countries. First, during long periods of employment, human capital tends to deteriorate. (Human capital is the present value of all the knowledge and skills that people have acquired from both formal education and on-the-job experience.) As a result, the long-term unemployed are perceived (rightly or wrongly) as being less employable than those who have recently been in work. Secondly, the North American labour force may adapt more quickly than the European force to shifts in the regional and occupational patterns of the demand for labour.

A common pattern across countries is that low-skilled workers are four or five times more likely to be unemployed than skilled or professional workers. About 75 per cent of unemployed men are manual workers.

In most EU countries female unemployment is greater than male unemployment. The United Kingdom is the exception, with 6.4 per cent female unemployment compared with around 7.0 per cent for males in March 2014 (although a higher proportion of UK female employment is part-time).

Older workers are less likely to be unemployed than young workers. Youth unemployment is universally higher than adult unemployment. Figure 23.3 shows this for the United Kingdom from 1992 where the gap has grown over the last slump that began in 2008. The rates were even higher after the recession that began in 2008. As shown in Figure 23.4, UK youth unemployment was close to the European Union's high average of just over 20 per cent, while it was distressingly high in Greece at 43 per cent and Spain at 45 per cent.

Consequences of unemployment

Unemployment causes harm in terms of both the output lost by the whole economy and what it does to unemployed individuals. Unemployed workers are valuable resources whose potential output is wasted. The material counterpart of unemployment is the negative GDP gap—potential GDP that is not produced. The cumulative loss of UK output in the six years 2009–14 was £230 billion (at

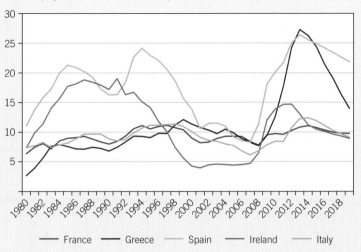

(i) Unemployment in France, Greece, Spain, Ireland and Italy, 1980-2019

— France — Greece — Spain — Ireland — Italy

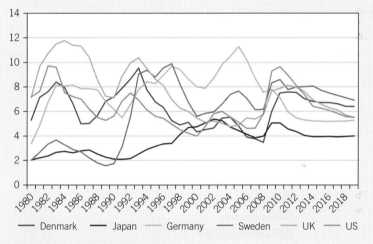

(ii) Unemployment in Denmark, Japan, Germany, Sweden, UK, and US, 1980-2019

— Denmark — Japan — Germany — Sweden — UK — US

Figure 23.2 Unemployment in eleven countries, 1980–2019

The behaviour of unemployment has varied considerably within the industrialized world. Part (i) shows that unemployment was very high in Spain and Ireland in the 1980s and early 1990s, but fell to relatively normal levels in the 2000s. Unemployment in all countries except Germany (shown in part (ii)) rose sharply after the financial crisis of 2007-8, but worst affected in this selection of countries were Spain and Greece. Japan had among the lowest levels of unemployment throughout this period, even though it suffered a major slowdown of activity in the 1990s and early 2000s. It was less affected by the recent crisis that other countries.

Source: IMF, *World Economic Outlook*, April 2014. Data for 2014 onwards are IMF forecasts.

2014 prices).[1] This is nearly £4,000 for every member of the population, or about £7,200 for each member of the labour force. In a world of scarcity with many unsatisfied wants, this loss is serious. It represents goods and services that could have been produced but are gone for ever.

[1] This figure is calculated using the IMF estimates of actual and potential GDP shown in Figure 15.1. The loss is just the sum of the gaps between actual and potential output in each of these seven years.

Because of the social welfare system, being unemployed in the United Kingdom is no longer quite the personal disaster that it once was. But the longer-term effects of high unemployment rates for the disillusioned who have given up trying to make it within the system and who contribute to social unrest should be a matter of serious concern to the haves as well as the have-nots. As UK economists Richard Layard, Stephen Nickell, and Richard Jackman put it:

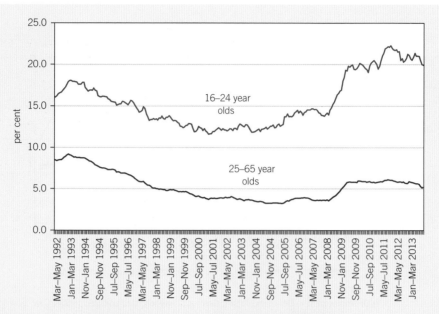

Figure 23.3 Youth and general unemployment in the United Kingdom, 1992–2013

Youth unemployment in the United Kingdom has always been higher than overall unemployment. Youth unemployment follows approximately the same pattern as general unemployment. It was extremely high in the early 1990s, fell steadily, and then rose to even higher levels in the recession that began in 2008. The gap between youth unemployment and general unemployment has widened over recent years. Youth unemployment is defined as the unemployment rate of those aged 16–24, while general unemployment is those aged 25–65. Data are based upon the ONS Labour Force Survey which uses a rolling three-month average of a sample survey.

Source: ONS, *Young People in the Labour Market*, 2014.

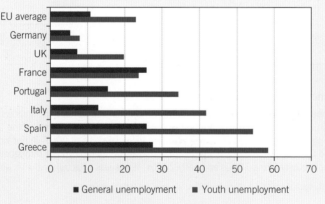

Figure 23.4 Youth unemployment in the European Union

Always high, youth unemployment rose dramatically in the recession that began in 2008. In December 2013, many EU counties had distressingly high levels of youth unemployment, in particular Spain and Greece where over half of young people were without jobs.

Source: Eurostat, *News Release, Euro Indicators*, April 2014.

Unemployment matters. It generally reduces output and aggregate income. It increases inequality, since the unemployed lose more than the employed. It erodes human capital. And, finally, it involves psychic costs. People need to be needed. Though unemployment increases leisure, the value of this is largely offset by the pain of rejection.

(*Source:* R. Layard, S. Nickell and R. Jackman, *The Unemployment Crisis*, Oxford: Oxford University Press, 1994)

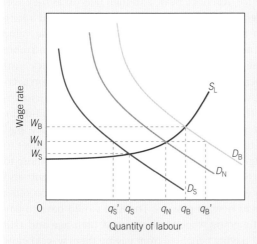

Figure 23.5 Employment and wages in a competitive labour market
There is cyclical involuntary unemployment when the wage rate is fixed but none when it is free to vary so as to equate demand and supply. S_L is the supply curve of labour to this market. Demand is varying cyclically from D_B in the boom period through D_N when the GDP gap is zero to D_S in a slump. When the wage rate is free to vary so as to equate demand and supply, it varies between w_B and w_S, while employment varies between q_B and q_S over the cycle. Since all points of equilibrium are on the supply curve of labour, there is no involuntary unemployment. In contrast, when the wage rate is fixed cyclically at w_N, employment varies between q_N and q_S'. Since the number wanting to work at the fixed wage rate w_N is given by q_N at all times, there is involuntary unemployment whenever demand is less than D_N. When it is D_S, involuntary unemployment is $q_N - q_S'$. In booms there will be an excess demand for labour. When demand is D_B, excess demand is $q_B' - q_N$. Employers may find ways of raising wages above the fixed rate, in which case employment goes to q_B and the wage rate to w_B as in the free market. If not, the labour shortage will persist. In either case there is no involuntary unemployment when demand is at or above D_N.

Causes of cyclical unemployment

Cyclical or demand-deficient unemployment occurs whenever there is a negative GDP gap. It is the number of people who would be employed if the economy were at potential GDP *minus* the number of people currently employed. When the GDP gap is zero or positive, cyclical unemployment is zero and all existing unemployment is equilibrium unemployment, either structural or frictional.

Although, as we shall see below, cyclical unemployment and equilibrium unemployment are not unrelated, it is useful to analyse them separately. This is because the cyclical variety is the unemployment that can be reduced by monetary and fiscal policies via their effect in shifting aggregate demand.

Fluctuations in GDP are not sufficient to create fluctuations in demand-deficient unemployment. Something else is needed. These fluctuations will, indeed, cause the demand for labour to fluctuate, rising in booms and falling in slumps. However, if the labour market had fully flexible wage rates, wages would fluctuate to keep the quantity demanded equal to the quantity supplied. We would observe pro-cyclical fluctuations in employment, the participation rate, and the wage rate, but there would be no cyclical unemployment.

Figure 23.5 contrasts the effects of cyclical fluctuations in demand on employment and wages when the wage rate is free to vary and when it is fixed. If either of these are the typical case in most markets, the same results will be observed over the whole economy.

The case of competitive wage determination is not what we actually observe. Although some pro-cyclical changes in wage rates do occur, they are insufficient to equate demand and supply. As a result, we see cyclical fluctuations not only in employment, but also in demand-deficient unemployment. Note also that there is

involuntary unemployment in the sense that there are unemployed workers who would be willing to accept jobs at the going wage rate if such jobs were available. We call this situation in which wages do not fluctuate sufficiently to clear the market over the cycle *wage stickiness*.

Causes of wage stickiness

Early Keynesian economists merely assumed that it was obvious that wages did not fluctuate freely so as to equate labour demand and supply. However, a later generation of economists sought to explain why wages would have this observed stickiness in the face of significant amounts of involuntary unemployment. They examined the forces that determine wage-setting and hiring decisions in what were considered to be more realistic labour market institutions than perfectly competitive markets. They sought reasons that are consistent with rational optimizing behaviour by participants in the market but still allow wage rates to be largely unresponsive to cyclical fluctuations.[2] This would explain the rational existence of wage stickiness and so explain why labour markets displayed unemployment during recessions and excess demand during booms.

These theories start with some everyday observations. When unemployed workers are looking for jobs, they do not knock on employers' doors and offer to work at lower wages than are being paid to current workers. Instead, they answer job advertisements and hope to get the jobs that are offered, but are often disappointed. Similarly, employers, seeing an excess of applicants for the few jobs that are available, do not go to their current workers and

---

[2] In Chapter 10 we discuss many reasons why employers may not in general set wages to clear the labour market. Here we concentrate on those that are relevant for cyclical stickiness.

reduce their wages until there is no one who is looking for a job. Instead, when demands for their products vary cyclically, employers lay off workers while holding the wages of the remaining employees more or less constant. Then when demand recovers, they rehire the workers at the prevailing wage rates.

These observations refer to cyclical variations in the demand for labour and changes in the overall level of wages. They do not conflict with the different observation that when firms get into long-term competitive trouble, workers sometimes renegotiate contracts and agree to wage cuts in order to save the firm—and their jobs. Also over the long term, the relative wages of different types of worker tend to change in response to demand and supply. When new technologies require workers of a different sort, often with more or different education, wages for those who meet the new specifications will drift upwards while the wages for those who are not now in such heavy demand tend to drift downwards. For example, the robotization and automation of assembly lines greatly reduced the demand for semi-skilled workers in many manufacturing industries and their relative wages fell quite dramatically over a decade or so, as did the demand for their services. (These are the kinds of changes in relative wages that are studied in microeconomics under the topic of the determinants of relative wages.)

One important reason for the stickiness of the general level of wages is that in many industries both workers and employers find it advantageous to have relatively long-term stable employment relationships. Workers want job security in the face of fluctuating demand; employers want workers who understand the firm's organization, production, and marketing plans. Under these circumstances both parties care about things in addition to the wage rate, and wages become relatively insensitive to cyclical fluctuations. Given this situation, the tendency is for employers to 'smooth out' the income of employees by paying a steady money wage and letting profits and employment fluctuate to absorb the effects of temporary increases and decreases in demand for the firm's product.

In many cases, wages are in effect regular payments to workers over an extended employment relationship, rather than a device for fine-tuning the current supplies and demands for labour.

Several labour market institutional arrangements work to achieve these results. Employment contracts often provide for a schedule of money wages over a period of several years. Fringe benefits, such as membership of the company pension scheme, a company car, and perhaps private health insurance, tend to bind workers to their employers. A worker's pay tends to rise with years of service, despite the known fact that in many industries the output attributable to workers rises rapidly as they gain

experience, reaches a peak, and then falls off as they age. Under gradually rising wages, workers who spend a long time in the same firm tend to get less than the value of their marginal products when they are young and more than the value of their marginal products as they near retirement. But over the long haul they are paid, on average, the value of their marginal products, just as microeconomic theory predicts. Such features help to bind the employee to the company, whereas redundancy pay, related to years of service, tends to bind the employer to the long-term worker, who would cost the firm more to dismiss than to keep employed. These arrangements also help to explain why firms are reluctant to take on older workers as new employees. The firm would have to pay them the going wage for workers of their age and skill without having benefited from paying them wages below their marginal products when they were young. For this reason, when older workers become redundant in their current job, perhaps because the industry in which they worked is in long-term decline, they find it much more difficult to find new jobs than those who are younger.

In labour markets characterized by long-term relationships, the wage rate does not fluctuate to clear the market. Wages are written over what has been called the long-term 'economic climate' rather than the short-term 'economic weather'.

In such an environment optimizing firms will adjust employment rather than wages during the cycle. Although redundant employees might prefer to accept a lower wage rather than be laid off, in many work environments seniority rules imply that it is those most recently hired who are most at risk of being laid off when demand is low. So the majority of long-term employees will not see any disadvantage to cyclically sticky wages and the cyclical variations in employment that they imply.

There are several other factors that work in the same direction. Workers who are inside the company and know its work practices are worth retaining. New workers will be costly to train. Thus the more firm-specific human capital workers have, the more reluctant will firms be to lay them off during a downswing that is thought to be temporary. If they do, they risk not being able to rehire them later. In many industries loyalty to the firm is an important motivating factor leading to high employee performance. Such loyalty is eroded if the firm is known to be willing to cut wages in face of temporary fluctuations in sales. This can be avoided over the cycle by holding wages firm.

Although some employees are better workers than others, large firms often do not know the characteristics of individual employees, at least until after they have sunk costs into hiring and training them. Good workers know who they are and are likely to have a higher reservation wage (the wage at which they are prepared to stay in their present job) than poor workers. By lowering the wage that firms offer during a downturn, the best workers may be more willing to leave than the poorer workers, since they know that their skills make them employable elsewhere. This will lower the average productivity of the firm's remaining workforce.

If firms are reluctant to cut the wages of all their workers, it is possible for firms to pay lower wages to new workers? But tiered wage structures, in which several people doing the same job get different rates of pay, are observed to cause serious morale problems. This does not prevent firms from paying experienced workers more than inexperienced ones. But it does restrain firms from responding to job queues by offering new workers a lower lifetime earnings profile than that enjoyed by existing workers doing the same job.

Some industries, such as construction, fast food and those that provide other basic services, hire many unskilled, often temporary, workers. Here behaviour is often much closer to that described by competitive market theory—at least for non-unionized firms. But for the majority of manufacturing firms and those in the service sectors that have semi-skilled and skilled employees, wage stickiness is the rule rather than the exception.

The basic message of these theories of wage stickiness is that labour markets cannot be relied upon to eliminate involuntary unemployment by equating current demand for labour with current supply.

Equilibrium unemployment

Equilibrium unemployment—unemployment that occurs when there is no GDP gap—is composed of *frictional* and *structural* unemployment. As we observed in Chapter 21, this is also called either the NAIRU or the natural rate of unemployment. It is called the NAIRU because, according to the theory of Chapter 21, it is the only rate of unemployment consistent with a stable inflation rate. But as we saw in Chapter 22, this does not hold under a regime of successful inflation targeting because the inflation rate stays roughly constant despite wide variations in the unemployment rate. Also, as we observed in that chapter, there is nothing natural about this rate. It can vary from time to time because of causes that are endogenous to the economy and it can be altered by public policy as discussed in the fifth case study at the end of this chapter.

Frictional unemployment

Frictional unemployment results from the normal turnover of labour: young people who enter the labour force and take time looking for first-time jobs, and others who are currently between one job and the next. Such people are said to be frictionally unemployed or, alternatively, in *search unemployment*.

The normal turnover of labour causes some frictional unemployment to persist, even when the economy is at potential GDP and the structure of jobs in terms of skills, industries, occupations, and location is unchanging.

Structural unemployment

Structural adjustments can cause unemployment. Shifts in demand for existing products and the development of new products and new processes typically cause the pattern of the demand for labour to change. Also, as the geographical distribution of world production changes under the impact of technological change and international competition, so does the composition of production and of labour demand change in any one country. Labour adapts to such shifts by changing jobs, skills, and locations, but until the transition is complete, structural unemployment exists.

Lags in adjusting the supplies of various types and locations of labour to the continually changing pattern of the demand for labour cause structural unemployment to persist even when there is no GDP gap

One of the more dramatic recent structural changes combines the effects of new technologies and new international competition. This is the decline in manufacturing employment and the rise in service employment in the United Kingdom and most of the other developed nations. Employment in UK manufacturing had been declining since the late 1950s. The UK shift was accentuated when the exchange rate appreciated in the late 1970s and early 1980s (partly associated with another structural change, the emergence of North Sea oil production). Then the strongest factor came with the rise of low-cost manufacturing in the developing countries, most notably China. Those manufacturing firms that did remain in the developed nations changed their production processes from being labour-intensive to being capital-intensive with the advent of robotic processes. Although the total of jobs available over the whole economy did not change much, the structure of demand changed dramatically. It was not always easy for a newly unemployed factory worker to find employment in the expanding service sector, particularly when many of the new jobs required new skills.

Why does the equilibrium unemployment change?

Structural unemployment can increase because the pace of change accelerates or the pace of adjustment to change slows down. An increase in the rate of growth, for example, usually speeds up the rate at which the structure of the demand for labour is changing. The adaptation of labour to the changing structure of demand may be slowed by such diverse factors as a decline in educational achievement, regulations that make it harder for workers in a given occupation to take new jobs in other areas or occupations, and income support programmes that reduce incentives to do the same. Any of these changes cause equilibrium unemployment to rise. Changes in the opposite direction cause it to fall.

Structural unemployment increases if there is either an increase in the speed at which the structure of the demand for labour is changing or a decrease in the speed at which labour is adapting to these changes.

The size of equilibrium unemployment can be influenced by what is called the **hysteresis effect** from the Greek word *hysteresis*, meaning 'coming late'. In economics it means that the current equilibrium is not independent of what has gone before—it is path-dependent. In the case of unemployment, equilibrium unemployment may be higher after periods of high unemployment associated with large negative GDP gaps than after periods of low unemployment.

During periods of high unemployment young people find it hard to get their first jobs and thus miss the important experience that such jobs give to new workers. Older workers who are laid off for considerable periods of time find that some of their acquired human capital erodes with lack of use. They will also miss out on acquiring from on-the-job

experience some of the new human capital suitable to the rapidly changing nature of firms. Hysteresis effects show that cyclical and equilibrium unemployment are not always unrelated. A large and persistent negative GDP gap with its accompanying high unemployment, much of which is long-term, can cause the equilibrium level of unemployed to rise.

When the GDP gap is eliminated by a recovery from the slump, hysteresis suggests that equilibrium unemployment will often be higher than at its previous cyclical peak.

Evidence suggests that such hysteresis effects are part of the explanation of the high levels of persistent unemployment in many EU countries, including the United Kingdom.

Conclusion

There are many reasons why wages tend to be sticky over the business cycle, and this stickiness accounts for fluctuations in involuntary unemployment as the GDP gap fluctuates. This deficient-demand unemployment is augmented by frictional and structural unemployment that persists even when the GDP gap is non-existent.

Non-targeted inflation

Cyclical unemployment is eliminated when GDP reaches potential during the expansion phase of the cycle, thus eliminating the GDP gap. However, the expansion may not stop there. If it continues strongly, GDP may rise into the range (denoted by Y_c in Chapter 22) where the inflation rate begins to breach the upper limit of the target band, which we have seen is currently 3 per cent. In Chapter 22 we studied the effect of a single demand shock that took the GDP into the inflationary range. As shown in Figure 22.7, if the Bank holds to its 2 per cent target by not allowing the rate of monetary expansion to rise along with the inflation rate, the rising price level will lower the real money supply. This shifts the AD^* curve to the left and this continues until the inflation rate returns to target.

Now consider what would happen if, as has happened many times in the past (before there was a Monetary Policy Committee), the Bank accommodates the higher inflation rate by increasing the rate of monetary expansion. For example, it might decide that it is worth having a bit more inflation as the price of having the extra GDP when GDP rises above potential. The analysis is essentially the same as we saw in Chapter 21 using the AD–AS model. But it is worthwhile checking how it works out with our new AD^*–AS^* model.

First, look at Figure 23.6. The curve labelled $AS^*(\dot{P}^e = 2\%)$ is the aggregate supply curve for an expected inflation

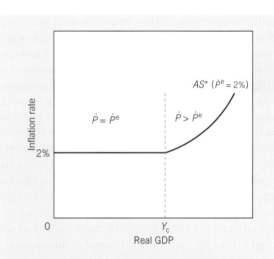

Figure 23.6 The AS^* curve and expectations of inflation

The GDP of Y_c divides the AS^* curve between a stable and an unstable inflation. On the horizontal portion of the AS^* curve to the left of Y_c, the actual inflation rate is equal to the expected rate and so the actual rate will show no tendency to increase. On the positively sloped portion to the right of Y_c the actual inflation rate is above the expected rate and so, sooner or later, the expected rate will increase.

rate of 2 per cent. Like all AS^* curves, it is horizontal up to a GDP of Y_c but positively sloped after that. The point at which the AS^* curve begins to take on a positive slope divides the figure into two parts. For any equilibrium on the AS^* curve at or below Y_c the actual inflation rate is equal to the expected rate. But for any GDP above Y_c the actual inflation rate exceeds the expected rate. Whatever their differences, all theories of the formation of expectations agree that the economy cannot long remain settled in a situation in which the actual inflation rate stays persistently above the expected rate. (It would be a good idea at this time to review Box 21.6 on expectations.) As people revise their expectation of future inflation to come into line with the actual rate, the AS^* curve will begin to shift upwards and will continue to do so as long as the expected rate of inflation falls short of the actual rate. Figure 23.7 takes up the story from this point.

Let the Bank try to maintain GDP significantly above Y_c by accommodating the higher inflation rate that the resulting gap initially causes. To do this, the Bank must increase the rate of monetary expansion. It can do this directly or by setting a low enough interest rate and then creating all the new money that is demanded at that rate. This policy of holding GDP significantly above Y_c may work for a while. Sooner or later, however, the public will realize that the higher rate is being maintained and expectations will be revised upwards to that new

rate. But, as shown in Figure 23.7, this will cause the rate to rise again. This is because the continuing positive GDP gap acting on the positively sloped AS^* curve will cause the actual rate to remain above the expected rate even as the expected rate is revised upwards. If the Bank then accommodates this new rate, once again expectations will sooner or later rise to equal the new rate. Once this happens, the actual rate will rise above the expected rate again. This process will go on with the rate of inflation rising as long as the Bank accommodates whatever rate of inflation is needed to maintain the positive GDP gap.

The rate at which a fully accommodated inflation is proceeding will increase as long as the rate is being accommodated so as to maintain Y in excess of Y_c, with the increase being as rapid as expectations adjust.

This last point is important: the faster expectations of future inflation catch up with the current inflation rate, the faster will the current rate rise.

Breaking an entrenched inflation

Now assume that after a period of rising inflation, the Bank has taken steps to hold the rate of monetary expansion consistent with a 6 per cent inflation rate. GDP has stabilized at Y^* and the 6 per cent rate has come to be the expected rate.

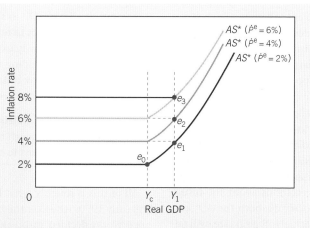

Figure 23.7 Accelerating inflation

The positive slope of the AS^* curve ensures that as long as Y exceeds Y_c, the actual inflation rate will rise continually. To avoid cluttering the figure unnecessarily, the AD^* curves are not shown. Let the original equilibrium be a GDP of Y_c and an actual and expected inflation rate of 2 per cent. This is at e_0 on the $AS^*(\dot{P}^e = 2\%)$ curve. (A dot over a variable indicates that it is a percentage rate of change.) A rise in aggregate demand now shifts the equilibrium to e_1, opening up a positive gap of $Y_1 - Y_c$ and taking inflation to 4 per cent. Once people come to expect the 4 per cent rate to continue, expectations are revised to that rate, which shifts the AS^* curve upwards to $AS^*(\dot{P}^e = 4\%)$. The Bank now increases the rate of monetary expansion to accommodate that 4 per cent inflation rate, thus holding GDP at Y_1 and the gap at $Y_1 - Y_c$. Equilibrium is now at e_2 with an actual inflation rate of 6 per cent and a persistent gap. Once expectations adjust to that 6 per cent rate, the AS^* curve shifts up again to $AS^*(\dot{P}^e = 6\%)$ Equilibrium now shifts to e_3, with an 8 per cent inflation. As long as the Bank accommodates whatever inflation rate that ensues so as to maintain the positive gap of $Y_1 - Y_c$, the inflation rate will go on rising as expectation continues to chase the actual rate upwards. The faster these expectations adjust to the actual rate, the faster will the actual rate rise.

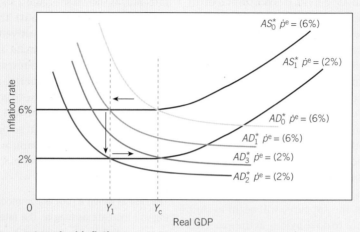

Figure 23.8 Breaking an entrenched inflation

Breaking an entrenched inflation requires inducing a recession large enough to cause expectations of inflation to be revised downwards. Originally the Bank has stabilized the actual and expected inflation rate at 6 per cent with curves $AD_0^*(\dot{P}^e = 6\%)$ and $AS_0^*(\dot{P}^e = 6\%)$ and GDP at Y_c. The Bank now stops accommodating this rate. It raises the interest rate sufficiently to slow the rate of monetary expansion below 6 per cent. This shifts the AD^* curve to the left as shown by the leftward pointing arrow. If inflationary expectations remain at 6 per cent, GDP declines. At a GDP of Y_1 with AD^* at $AD_1^*(\dot{P}^e = 6\%)$ expectations of future inflation begin to decline. This shifts both the AD^* and AS^* curves downwards as shown by the downward pointing arrow. Once they reach $AD_2^*(\dot{P}^e = 2\%)$ and $AS_1^*(\dot{P}^e = 2\%)$, the economy comes to rest with a GDP of Y_1 and a fully accommodated inflation of 2 per cent. The Bank now engages in some monetary expansion by lowering the interest rate sufficiently to expand the money supply faster than 2 per cent. This causes the AD^* curve to shift rightwards raising GDP as shown by the rightward pointing arrow leaving the inflation rate unchanged. The Bank will want stop to the expansion at Y^*, which is just short of Y_c but not shown here. It will know if Y passes Y_c but must estimate the location of Y^*.

Now let the Bank wish to drive the inflation rate down to 2 per cent. To do this it cuts the rate of monetary expansion to a rate consistent with 2 per cent inflation, which it can do by setting a high enough interest rate. (Of course it can do this in stages rather than all at once, which we assume only to simplify the figure showing what is happening.)

Figure 23.8 shows what happens next. As long as the 6 per cent expected inflation rate remains fixed in people's beliefs—colloquially this is called an 'entrenched inflation'—the AD^* curve will shift to the left as the real money supply diminishes, and GDP will fall while inflation stays high. Eventually, the public will realize that the Bank is serious about accepting a recession as the price of breaking the entrenched inflation. Expectations about the future course of inflation will fall. As they do, both the AD^* and the AS^* curves, and hence the actual inflation rate, will fall as well. (Recall that a change in the expected inflation rate shifts both the AD^* and the AS^* curves.) Eventually, the rate will reach 2 per cent. Once the public comes to believe that the 2 per cent rate will be maintained, expectations will fall to that level. The AD^* curve will stop shifting to the left and the horizontal portion of the AS^* curve will come to rest at the 2 per cent level. The GDP will then stabilize with a large negative GDP gap and a 2 per cent inflation.

To return to full employment, the Bank must expand the money supply to shift the AD^* curve rightwards until potential GDP is reached while the inflation rate remains at 2 per cent. This is the so-called re-entry phase and, if done right, it allows GDP to slowly approach Y^*. But the Bank must be careful not to rekindle inflationary expectations. The art lies in slowly expanding the economy back towards Y^* while persuading the public that it is serious about holding to its new inflation target and that it will induce another recession if needed to maintain the target.

Breaking an entrenched inflation usually requires that the Bank engineer a large enough recession to cause the public to revise their expectations to conform with the Bank's new target rate.

All of this is roughly what happened in the late 1980s and early 1990s when central banks throughout the developed world decided to break their high inflation rates. Each central bank lowered its rate of monetary expansion, usually by raising interest rates high enough to accomplish this. Initially the short-term interest rate rose to a range approaching 20 per cent in many countries. This was a startling figure since this rate is normally well below 5 per cent. GDP fell first, and eventually the inflation rate fell to the newly established target. Once the public finally came to expect that this target would be maintained, central banks slowly expanded their economies back toward potential GDP while inflation remained around 2 per cent.

However, some commentators worried that this re-entry policy would be inflationary. They based their worries on a naïve version of the quantity theory of money, which predicted that any monetary expansion at a rate faster than the current inflation rate would cause that rate to rise. The problem with such a theory is that it does not allow for different effects of a monetary expansion when the economy is operating at or above potential GDP and when there is a large negative GDP gap. What ensued was what our theory predicts: the main effect of a cautious expansion of the real money supply in the presence of a large negative GDP gap is for GDP to rise, reducing the gap without kindling a rise in the actual or expected inflation rates.

The key to this success in growing the economy while keeping inflation in check was the credible inflation target which successfully tied down inflation expectations.

Stagflation

Finally, we consider the effects of an autonomous increase in the cost of inputs above 2 per cent per year. This case has already been shown in Figure 22.8. If all input costs begin to rise by, say, 3 per cent, this will shift the horizontal portion of the aggregate supply curve upward to 3 per cent. If the Bank maintains its current rate of monetary expansion at 2 per cent, the AD^* curve will shift to the left, causing GDP to fall and thus opening up a negative GDP gap. The economy will experience what is called a stagflation with GDP falling and inflation and unemployment rising, something that could not happen as a result of any demand shock.

If there is an increase in the rate at which costs are rising, a further fall in GDP combined with a further rise in the inflation rate will ensue. Once costs stop rising for external reasons, and expectations return to a 2 per cent inflation rate, the AS^* curve shifts down as shown in the figure but GDP will not return to potential because of the large reduction in the real money supply caused by the period during which the inflation rate exceeded 2 per cent. The Bank must then adjust in the same way as it did after a demand inflation was stopped. It must engineer a monetary expansion that will allow the AD^* curve to shift rightwards until potential GDP is restored.

This sequence is roughly what happened after 1972 when the Organization of Petroleum Exporting Countries (OPEC) engineered a large increase in the price of petroleum. Since oil is a critical source of energy and its refining produces many widely used by-products such as plastics and fertilizers, this caused costs of production to rise worldwide. Because it took several years for all the effects of this increase in petroleum prices to work through the economy, the resulting stagflation lasted for several years.

This phenomenon of rising inflation and falling GDP and employment had not been seen before, and there was much confusion as to its causes. Up to then, bouts of inflation has been associated with demand and monetary causes. Rightward shifts in the IS curve could cause a temporary inflation when there was no change in aggregate supply as prices rose for a while. Increases in the real money supply could cause an inflation as the LM curve shifted to take GDP into the inflationary range of the AS curve. When held there by constant expansions in the nominal money supply, inflations could continue for quite some time, but at an accelerating rate. (This is the process we studied in Figure 23.7.)

It took years before stagflation was understood. Indeed, many economists argued that stagflation provided a decisive refutation of the kind of Keynesian model for the determination of the GDP that you are studying in this book! What was finally understood was that the source of the problem lay in the supply side of the economy—something that had been given little attention in macro models before that time. But once the supply side of the theory was developed, as we have done in this chapter, the explanation became clear. As is often true after an initially confusing event is finally understood, it is hard for those who did not live through the period to understand the years of confusion and debate that the stagflation of the 1970s caused at the time.

More recently, there have been one or two episodes since the Bank's low inflation target came to be accepted by the public in which supply-side changes, such as the 2010 and 2011 increase in VAT combined with higher energy prices, caused a temporary rise in the inflation rate. This episode squeezed real incomes and reduced spending. This in turn slowed the recovery in demand that might otherwise have occurred, contributing to the weakest recovery from a recession since records began (and this includes the Great Depression of the 1930s).

Conclusion

Temporary increases of the inflation rate due to demand-side shocks beyond the control of the Bank need not lead to further acceleration in the rate as long as the Bank makes it clear that it is willing to accept any reduction in GDP that is needed to return inflation to target. Temporary increases due to supply-side shocks cause stagflations, with GDP falling and inflation rising. Again, if the Bank determines that the shocks are temporary, it can wait for them to end, allowing the inflation rate then to return to target. However, if the Banks seeks to hold income at or above potential in the face of recurring demand or supply shocks, it risks having the inflation rate accelerate and then having to induce a major recession to get the rate back to target

CASE STUDIES

1. The great recession of 2008

In 2008 the developed world experienced the largest slump in economic activity since the Great Depression of the 1930s. It started in the United States but quickly spread to all of the developed countries. Although the technical recession, defined by two successive periods of negative GDP changes, lasted only a short time, the slump with a large negative GDP gap and high unemployment persisted. By 2014 the GDP gap and high unemployment had still not totally disappeared in most of the affected countries.

Where did it all begin? Starting in the mid-2000s there was a boom in new US housing construction financed by credit creation through mortgages. As house prices rose, existing owners were able to re-mortgage their homes and spend the proceeds. High consumer spending combined with high incomes in the housing industry caused high and rising levels of GDP and employment. The housing boom was partly sustained by the unrealistic expectations of homeowners that their prices would go on rising indefinitely and partly by overly zealous and sometimes dishonest mortgage brokers. Many of the mortgages had low or non-existent payments for several initial years, followed by relatively high ones. Some mortgages, called 'subprimes', were sold to people who had poor credit ratings and little possibility of meeting their mortgage payments once the initial low payment period ended.

The mortgages were bundled into packages called mortgage-backed securities (MBS), each one of which gave part ownership, possibly only 1 per cent, of each of a large number of mortgages. This arrangement was supposed to make the MBS carry a low risk, which it would have done if so many mortgages had not failed at the same time. The rating agencies classified them as low risk, often without even knowing the precise content of each MBS. They were then sold both domestically and internationally to investors and banks.

When the higher interest payments kicked in, defaults rose dramatically and the building boom came to an abrupt halt. Many lost their homes while others, even though they could sustain their mortgage payments, had to cut other spending. The resulting collapse in demand was followed by a major recession. The recession spread worldwide because many foreign banks, including some important ones in the United Kingdom, had invested heavily in these

MBSs. Also many other countries, most notably Ireland, had followed the United States in this subprime mortgage binge. Many banks were bailed out by government loans or even nationalized, some were taken over and one, Lehman Brothers, failed. When the banks got into such trouble they cut back severely on their loans to households and to firms. This contributed significantly to the decline in spending by firms and households, adding further pressure to the general decline in economic activity.

Although there is some debate among economists about interpreting the 2008 recession, the explanation that is consistent with the models in this book runs as follows.

- The recession was caused by a collapse of demand following the bursting of the housing boom, a boom that had been caused partly by the 'animal spirits' of buyers and over-eagerness and sometimes downright deception on the part of lenders.

- The rise in unemployment was caused by a fall in demand for housing, leading to a more general fall in other asset prices and in the demand for goods and services, leading to a fall in the demand for labour services.

- Those who lost their homes and those who had increased their mortgages to sustain consumption spending did not have rational expectations about the future housing prices nor about their ability to handle the mortgage payments when the higher rates kicked in.

- The markets for subprime mortgages and MBSs were not efficient markets. Fraud, pervasive ignorance, and bandwagon effects played an important role in them.

One lesson that many economists have drawn from this experience is that modern macro models need a much fuller treatment of the financial sector than they typically now have. Possibly by the 14th edition of this book, economists will have done this job so well that we can incorporate some of this new financial sector modelling into our macro chapters!

2. Asset price bubbles and how long they take to deflate

Monetary policy-makers in the Bank of England and the European Central Bank (and some other central banks) are charged with keeping prices under control. However,

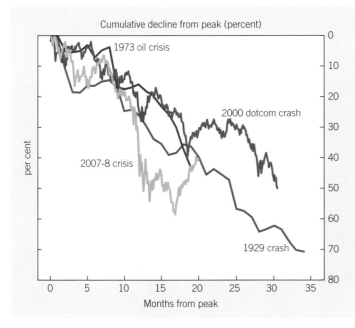

Figure 23.9 FTSE world equity index during crises

The data show the course of the world's stock markets following specific financial crises. The peaks were: 1929 crash, 31 October 1929; 1973 oil crisis, 28 February 1973; 2000 dotcom crash, 27 March 2000; 2007–8 financial crisis, 11 October 2007.

Source: Bank of England, *Financial Stability Report*, June 2009; data from Global Financial Data Inc. and Bank calculations.

the targets that are used for this purpose are based upon consumer prices—that is, prices of currently produced retail goods and services. In recent years, consumer price inflation has generally been under control, and in this respect monetary policy has been very successful. However, there have been other prices, notably asset prices, that have been very volatile, and the boom and bust in these prices has been associated with considerable disruption to the economy as a whole. The question then arises: should monetary policy-makers try to influence asset prices as well as consumer prices? Notice that asset prices are partly the prices of physical assets, such as houses and factories produced in the past, and partly the prices of securities, such as company shares, the values of which are determined by the profit streams that are expected in the future.

The conventional view until recently has been that monetary policy should stick to targeting consumer price inflation—that is, the prices of currently produced goods and services. If it succeeds in controlling them, it cannot achieve much more. Some go further and argue that, because asset prices are so volatile, any attempt to target them would make monetary policy too unstable and would induce policy cycles that caused unnecessary volatility in real activity. It is also hard to see how any central bank could decide what is an appropriate level of asset prices and what weight they should give to different classes of assets, such as housing and shares.

The counter-argument is that if bubbles in asset prices are ignored, they can cause significant disruption

to real activity that might have been avoided by timely policy interventions. Following the financial crisis of 2008–9, many have argued that the central banks should have done more in advance and that steps should be taken to ensure that policy-makers take stronger preventative action in future to moderate asset price bubbles. What that action might be is still under discussion.

What is clear is that, when major asset bubbles burst, asset prices can fall a long way and the downward adjustments that follow can take many months to reach their nadir. Figure 23.9 compares the declines in world equity prices during four major crashes. It is clear that the fall in prices takes many months to work through, and that after about eighteen months all four episodes involved decreases of about 40 per cent. The 1929 Great Crash went on to bring asset prices down by around 70 per cent.

It is unlikely that inflation targets will be changed to include asset prices. But it is very likely that policy-makers (including regulators) will be very careful in future in assessing the significance of asset price movements and in deciding if there is anything that policy should be doing to avoid a bubble overinflating or possibly to help deflate it gently. The monitoring and regulation of asset price bubbles may not be in the hands of monetary policy-makers but rather those responsible for financial stability such as the UK Financial Policy Committee (which also operates inside the Bank of England).

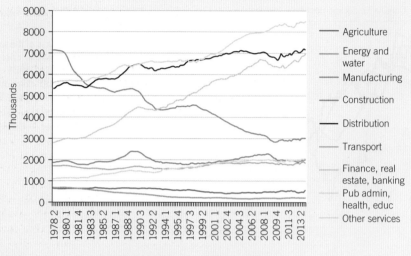

Figure 23.10 Employment by sector, United Kingdom, 1978Q2–2013

Source: <http://www.statistics.gov.uk>

3. Changing patterns of employment

Changes in the pattern of employment have been rapid in the past few decades. Figure 23.10 shows the changing industrial structure of UK employment between 1978 and 2014. The figures quoted include self-employment as well as employee jobs. There is high and rising employment in three main sectors: (i) public administration, education, and health; (ii) distribution, hotels, and restaurants; (iii) finance, real estate, and banking. These three sectors combined provided around 70 per cent of UK employment in 2014, up from 51 per cent in 1978. Over the same period, the manufacturing sector fell from providing just over 7 million jobs to around 3 million. Significant numbers were also employed in three other sectors: construction (2.0 million in 2014), transport and communications (1.8 million), and other services (2 million). But the UK primary industries were small employers and continued to decline still further. Agriculture, hunting and fishing, and energy and water combined employed less than 2.0 per cent of the working population.

The trend over time for rising employment in services and declining employment in agriculture is a not unique to the UK; in fact, it is a global phenomenon. Employment in services is universally rising, while employment in agriculture is declining. The picture for industrial employment is different, as this has tended to rise in developing countries but decline in the richer ones.

Figure 23.11 shows the employment shares in three major sectors for 139 countries between 1980 and 2012.

Each blue dot is one country in one year. The decline in the share of agricultural employment is clearly shown, as is the rise in the employment share of services. Industrial employment rises when per capita GDP rises up to a point, but then falls.

Three specific countries are highlighted in the charts. China shows a sharp fall in the share of agricultural employment from around 75 per cent in 1980 to just under 40 per cent in 2011; over the same period employment in services rose from around 15 per cent to around 35 per cent. Perhaps surprisingly, China's employment share in industry rose only modestly from just under 20 per cent to almost 30 per cent. Brazil and the United States both experienced rising employment shares in services and declining employment shares in agriculture. US industrial employment fell steadily, while the trend in Brazil was less clear. Overall it fell slightly as a share of employment, but there were some years when it rose and others when it fell. Brazil is a middle-income country for which the global trends suggest that its industrial employment share might have continued to rise, but this was not the case over the period covered.

4. Male and female employment

The rates of male and female employment have evolved quite differently in the United Kingdom over the past half century[3] as shown in Figure 23.12. Female employment

---

[3] Again, data refer to total employment, which includes self-employment as well as employee jobs.

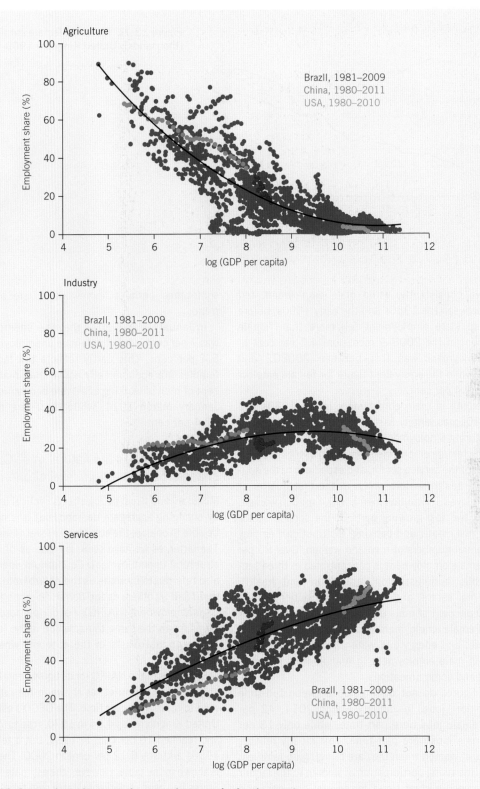

Figure 23.11 Sectoral employment shares and economic development

Source: ILO, *Global Employment Trends*, 2014.

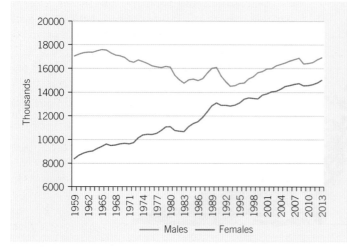

Figure 23.12 **Male and female employment (thousands), United Kingdom 1959–2013.**

Source:<http://www.statistics.gov.uk>

has grown consistently, while male employment fell sharply between the 1960s and the early 1990s, before recovering. Male employment fell more than female employment in the 2008–9 recession: 4.2 per cent of male employment was lost between 2008Q2 and 2009Q4, while the equivalent figure for female employment was 1.4 per cent.

The decline in male employment in the 1980s and early 1990s was largely associated with the decline in manufacturing employment, and to a lesser extent mining. Rising female employment has been associated with expansion of the service sector, and especially of the education and health sectors which in the first quarter of 2014 employed 1.7 million men and 5.4 million women. The other two fast-growing parts of the service sector (finance, real estate, and banking; distribution)[4] employ roughly equal numbers of men and women. Over 80 per cent of female employment is concentrated in three sectors (public administration, education and health; finance, real estate, and banking; distribution), while under 60 per cent of male employment is in these three sectors. Female employment is minimal in construction, agriculture, and energy and water, and it is also much lower than male employment in manufacturing and in transport and communications.

These figures do not distinguish between full-time and part-time jobs. In January–March 2014, 42 per cent of female jobs were part-time, while only 13 per cent of male jobs were part-time. This clearly reflects the needs of women when they are bringing up families. However, the rising participation of women in the labour force has been a clear trend for several decades, and increased job flexibility and changing technology, which

sometimes permits homeworking, are assisting this trend.

In January–March 2014 the male unemployment rate was 7 per cent, while the female unemployment rate was 6.4 per cent. This partly reflects the fact that fewer females are economically active than males: 83.8 per cent of men of working age[5] were economically active in January–March 2014, while the figure for women is 72.4 per cent.

5. How natural is the natural rate? Can policy change the equilibrium level of unemployment?

Monetary and fiscal policy affects cyclical unemployment by changing aggregate demand, but it is not thought to be able to change the equilibrium level of unemployment. The latter, as we have seen, is made up of frictional and structural unemployment. Equilibrium unemployment is also referred to by some as the *natural rate of unemployment* and by others as the *non-accelerating inflation rate of unemployment* (NAIRU). For our purposes these three terms mean the same thing, which is the level of unemployment that exists in the economy when GDP is at potential.

Estimates of the NAIRU (or its equivalent) vary considerably between countries, as shown in the table. They also tend to move a lot over time. The OECD's estimate for the United Kingdom was 4.54 in 1970, rose to 7.56 in 1980, and reached 10 per cent in 1986, but it fell back in the 1990s and was 6.12 per cent in 2000. The 2014 figure is shown in the table. However, the estimate for the United States has been remarkably stable over time, as it has only varied between 5.5 and 6.5 in the 44 years between 1970

---

[4] 'Distribution' includes shops, hotels, and restaurants.

[5] Working age 16–64.

Estimates of the NAIRU in 2014 (per cent of the workforce)

Denmark	5.67
France	9.19
Germany	6.33
Ireland	10.56
Italy	9.9
Japan	4.3
Spain	21.5
Sweden	7.01
United Kingdom	6.68
United States	6.08

Source: OECD *Economic Outlook*, No. 95, May 2014.

and 2014. In reality, the estimates of the NAIRU are affected by the severity and persistence of the business cycle in a particular country and over a specific period, even though the theoretical concept of equilibrium unemployment is independent of the business cycle.

So can government policy affect the size of the NAIRU? The answer is almost certainly yes, but policy can work to increase it as well as to lower it, and the policies concerned are not macro policies.

Government interventions that can increase the NAIRU are those that increase rigidities in the labour market or lower incentives for those out of work to find employment. For example, in the past some countries have adopted policies that discourage movement among regions, industries, and occupations. These policies tend to raise structural unemployment, though state subsidies may disguise it for a while. Policies that discourage firms from replacing labour with machines may protect employment over the short term. However, if such policies lead to the decline of an industry because it cannot compete effectively with innovative foreign competitors, serious structural unemployment can result in the long run.

High minimum-wage laws may cause structural unemployment by pricing low-skilled labour out of the market. As explained in Chapter 10, minimum-wage laws have two effects when they are imposed on competitive markets: they may reduce employment of the unskilled, and they raise the wages of the unskilled who retain their jobs.

Workers who lose their jobs receive unemployment benefit. The size of the benefits paid, relative to pay levels in work, is known as the **replacement ratio**. A high replacement ratio raises the NAIRU. It affects the willingness of the unemployed to accept job offers and it affects the intensity with which they search for work. Differences in unemployment benefit systems between countries do seem to play an important role in explaining international differences in unemployment. It is not just the replacement ratio faced by newly unemployed workers that matters; the duration for which that benefit is provided (if it is for a short period, the worker has an incentive to find work quickly) and the degree to which the benefit is conditional on job-seeking activity are also important. Countries with only temporary benefits and both incentives for and assistance with finding work tend to have low equilibrium unemployment rates.

Those who are unemployed for a long time find it hardest to get a job, so the reduction of persistence is a major challenge. It probably requires both a reform of the benefits system and active policies to ensure that those in danger of long-term unemployment get work experience and training. The feature of the benefits system that seems to be most harmful (in the sense of creating long-term unemployment) is an indefinite period of benefit payments. This reduces the incentive of the recently unemployed to seek work urgently. Some commentators advocate compulsory public sector work for the unemployed after some period of time; others advocate state subsidies of private sector employment as ways of getting people back into the labour market. However, the general point is that policies need to be targeted directly on the unemployed.

Another cause of persistence of unemployment is mismatch. Policies to reduce mismatch seek to make it easier for workers to change occupations by assisting retraining and relocation. Some argue that it is the responsibility of individuals and firms to finance mobility and retraining. However, individuals may be financially constrained, and firms may feel that it is not worth training a worker who may go elsewhere. The state funds education for the young, so there is no reason, in principle, why older people who need retraining should be treated differently.

6. Inflation and the price level in the long run

Figure 23.13 shows the UK price level and inflation rates since 1661. The vertical axis in part (i) plots the price level on a logarithmic scale in which equal vertical distances show equal percentage changes. Looking first at the price level in part (i), it is obvious that there was no upward trend to the price level from 1661 until the 1930s. Indeed the UK[6] price level in 1699 was the same as in 1906, a period of just over 200 years. However, while the price level had no upward (or downward) trend (and was thus what we would now call 'mean reverting') it was certainly not constant. Part (ii) of the figure shows that prices were quite volatile, going up and down frequently. However, whenever

---

[6] Of course the United Kingdom did not exist in 1661. Price indexes for this time are generally based on prices in England and were constructed much later.

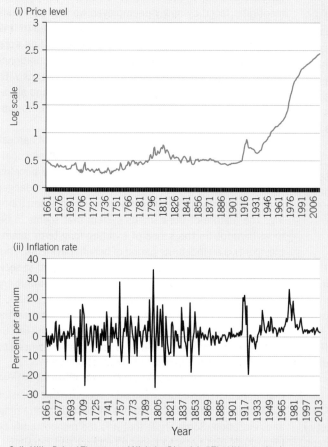

(i) Price level

Figure 23.13 UK price level and inflation rate, 1661–2015

Part (i) shows the log of the price level since 1661, and part (ii) shows the rate of inflation over the same period. The price level was about the same in 1900 as it had been in 1661, but it has risen continuously since the 1930s. Inflation was more volatile in earlier time as it was linked mainly to food prices, but it was often negative as well as positive. Since the Second World War it has never been negative.

(ii) Inflation rate

Year

Sally Hills, Ryland Thomas, and Nicholas Dimsdale "*The UK recession in context—what do three centuries of data tell us?*" Bank of England Quarterly Bulletin, 2010 Q4 (database available with article online). (Recent years from ONS online database)

they went up, sooner or later, they came back down again, and generally this was sooner rather later.

The main reason for the mean reversion of prices up to the early 1930s was that the value of sterling was tied to a physical commodity—gold. Thus the quantity of money could not be increased by policy-makers in an attempt to hold interest rates below their market value and thereby stimulate the economy. This is the period of the so-called 'gold standard'. Prices were volatile under the gold standard because most of the products that are counted in the price indexes of that time were agricultural and subject to variations in supply due to weather. It is still true today that many agricultural prices are highly variable, for the same reasons, but they now have a much smaller weight in the consumer price index. Many of the goods and services we now buy did not exist 20 years ago, let alone 200 years ago.

After the abandonment of the gold standard in 1931, sterling floated for a while, but after World War II it was then pegged to the US dollar until 1972. From then on there was no 'nominal anchor' and the UK price level rose rapidly. In

the 1990s an inflation target was adopted to keep inflation under control. While this has clearly helped to keep inflation low and stable, it is nonetheless positive. Hence, the price level keeps rising, and has risen in every year since the 1930s (with the one exception[7] of 1960 when inflation was zero). Thus, the price level is no longer mean reverting. Even at an inflation rate of only 2 per cent, the price level doubles every 35 years or so. Thus, unless there is another regime change, there is little chance that prices in 2115 will be on average the same as those in 2015.

Why then does the government not ask the Bank of England to target a constant price level, thus duplicating the experience of the earlier centuries? One reason is that the prices of most of the commodities that we buy today are not as volatile as the basic goods providing food and shelter that took up most of the public's spending in earlier centuries.

---

[7] RPI inflation was negative for parts of 2009, but this was mainly due to a temporary cut in VAT. The fall in prices was reversed once the tax rate returned to its original level, and in any event would have dropped out of the annual inflation rate after twelve months.

The prices of manufactured goods and labour inputs tend to be rather inflexible downwards. Given a long and severe enough slump, wages and prices will come down, but they tend to do so only slowly. To hold the average level of prices constant, an upward shock to the price level, such as is often caused by a rise in the prices of energy or raw materials would have to be accompanied by a fall in wage costs and other goods prices. Since this would not happen quickly, the transition effect would be a recession of the sort caused by an adverse shock to input prices as shown in Figure 22.9. Since the transition would sometimes be spread over years rather than months, holding the price level constant in the face of periodic upward price shocks would require periodic and often persistent recessions. Most of us would probably agree that the preferred alternative to such a situation is a mild inflationary trend that accommodates occasional upward shocks in some prices by allowing all other prices to rise to restore equilibrium relative prices.

SUMMARY

The business cycle

- Over the past two centuries, economic activity has proceeded on a rising trend, but irregularly with forward spurts being followed by pauses and even relapses.

- Even in the deepest recession, the great majority of the nation's workers and other productive resources remain employed.

- Although there are some common characteristics of cycles, each business cycle has its own special characteristics, while the turning points have various explanations, including at one time or another changes in real spending and changes in financial conditions.

Why do GDP and employment fluctuate?

- Aggregate demand shocks are a major source of fluctuations in GDP; aggregate supply shocks are a secondary source.

- The causes of fluctuations in aggregate demand are various, ranging from variations in technologically driven investments, through speculative bubbles, to financial crashes

- Although a smaller part of aggregate spending than consumption, investment is more volatile and hence is a major source of fluctuations in aggregate demand.

Cumulative processes

- A period of expansion, once begun, tends to develop its own momentum.

- According to multiplier theory, a continued injection of a given amount of new investment spending will raise GDP, but only by a finite amount.

- Investment spending usually rises on upswings of the cycle because (i) the accelerator theory makes (some) new investment depend on changes in GDP not on its level, (ii) much new investment is financed from firms' profits, which rise on the upswing, and (iii) investment depends partly on expectations about future business conditions, which usually turn favourable on the upswing.

- All these forces—the multiplier, the accelerator, profits, and expectations—also tend to make downswings cumulative once they have started.

Floors and ceilings

- As potential GDP is reached and exceeded, rises in wages, interest rates, and material costs due to shortages of labour, capital, and raw materials may slow the expansion of production and even stop it. The accelerator implies that even a slowing of expansion may cause a fall of investment spending.

- The minimum levels of consumption, investment, and government spending assure a minimum equilibrium level of GDP which, although well below the full employment level, is well above zero.

Avoiding extreme floors and ceilings

- Most cycles stop their downswings well before reaching the most extreme floor and some stop their upswings before they reach full capacity output and full employment of labour. This may happen because of natural causes or government fiscal and monetary policies which provide powerful tools that are often capable of starting and stopping upswings.

Unemployment

- Two main measures of unemployment are the *claimant count* of those people actively looking for work and registered for benefits and *ILO unemployment,* which counts as unemployed those who are either out of work and have sought work in the last four weeks, or are out of work but have found a job that will start in the next two weeks.

- Recorded unemployment understates actual unemployment because it omits *discouraged workers,* who would like to work but have ceased looking because they believe that they cannot find a job given current labour market conditions.

- Cyclical or demand-deficient unemployment occurs because the economy is currently operating significantly below its potential GDP.
- Frictional unemployment occurs because of the normal turnover of labour.
- Structural unemployment occurs when there is a mismatch between the characteristics of the people looking for work and those desired by potential employers.
- Frictional and structural unemployment make up equilibrium unemployment, which is all that exists when GDP is at its potential level.
- Unemployment is highest among youth and older workers.

Causes of cyclical unemployment

- Fluctuations in GDP cause the demand for labour to fluctuate.
- If wage rates were fully flexible, we would observe pro-cyclical fluctuations in employment, the participation rate, and the wage rate but not in involuntary unemployment.
- Involuntary cyclical unemployment requires that wage rates do not fluctuate sufficiently to clear the labour market over the cycle.

Causes of wage stickiness

- Early Keynesian economists merely found it obvious that wages did not fluctuate freely so as to equate labour demand and supply. Later economists have provided reasons for this observation.
- A number of labour market institutions ensure that, in many cases, wages are regular payments to workers over an extended employment relationship, rather than a device for equating the current supplies and demands for labour.
- In labour markets characterized by long-term relationships, the wage rate does not fluctuate to clear the market. Wages are written over what has been

called the long-term 'economic climate' rather than the short-term 'economic weather'.
- Thus labour markets cannot be relied upon to eliminate involuntary unemployment by equating current demand for labour with current supply.

Equilibrium unemployment

- The normal turnover of labour causes some frictional unemployment to persist, even when there is no GDP gap.
- Lags in adjusting the supplies of various types and locations of labour to the continually changing pattern of the demand for labour cause structural unemployment to persist even when there is no GDP gap.
- Structural unemployment can increase because either the pace of change accelerates or the pace of adjustment to change slows down.
- The size of equilibrium unemployment can be influenced by hysteresis effects due to youth missing out on first-job training experience and older workers losing human capital during extended periods of being unemployed.

Non-targeted inflation

- If a cyclical expansion opens up a significant positive GDP gap, the inflation rate will begin to rise above target. If the Bank does not validate this extra inflation, the rising price level will lower the real money supply and push GDP back to Y_c.
- If the Bank accommodates the higher inflation rate by increasing the rate of monetary expansion, the inflation rate will begin to rise, and will continue to do so until the Bank ceases validating the inflation.
- Once validation ceases, a temporary slump may ensue whose length will depend on how long it takes for expectations of future inflation to revert to the target rate.
- An autonomous increase in the cost of inputs above the target rate of inflation will cause a stagflation with inflation and unemployment rising at the same time, and hence GDP falling.

TOPICS FOR REVIEW

QUESTIONS

1 Look up the GDP data for the last several years and consider what phase of the cycle we are now in.

2 Without looking back, list as many causes as you can of frictional and structural unemployment. Can you think of any that are not listed in the text?

3 The Beveridge curve plots the number of job seekers on one axis and the number of unfilled vacancies on the other. What would you expect the phase of the business cycle to be in each of the following circumstances: (i) the number of job seekers greatly exceeds the number of unfilled vacancies; (ii) the number of job seekers is substantially less than the number of unfilled vacancies; (iii) the number of job seekers equals the number of unfilled vacancies? Why is anyone unemployed when in situation (iii) there are as many available jobs as there are people seeking jobs?

4 Explain why, according to hysteresis theory, the amount of equilibrium unemployment found when a current negative GDP gap disappears may be higher the longer that the gap has persisted.

5 Look up the rate of inflation over the last four quarters and determine how close it has come in each quarter to the target rate and the upper and lower target bands.

6 What would be the effects on the price level, the inflation rate, and the GDP of a once-and-for-all very large rise in input costs? Would this require any reaction from a central bank interested in meeting a 2 per cent inflation target while minimizing any negative GDP gaps.

7 Why do you think that youth unemployment rose more following the 2007–8 financial crisis than did the unemployment of those aged over 25? What policies would best help reduce it?

8 What policies could help reduce (a) equilibrium unemployment and (b) cyclical unemployment?

9 What factors lie behind the turning points of business cycles? In other words, explain what factors tend to turn a boom into a bust, and a recession into a recovery.

10 Is it desirable for policymakers to try to eliminate the business cycle? What are the costs and benefits?

CHAPTER 24

EXCHANGE RATES AND THE BALANCE OF PAYMENTS

What determines exchange rates and why are floating exchange rates volatile? Is a balance-of-payments deficit a sign of economic failure? These are two of the questions we address in this chapter.

In particular, you will learn that:

- The exchange rate is determined by the demand and supply of domestic currency in a floating exchange rate regime.

- Exchange rates often overshoot the long-run equilibrium and they can be volatile as they react to 'news'.

- The exchange rate is an essential element of the transmission mechanism that turns monetary policy shocks into real shocks in an open economy under flexible exchange rates.

- Balance-of-payment accounts measure the net transactions between domestic residents and the rest of the world over a specific period.

- The current account balance is identically equal and opposite to the capital and financial account balance.

- There is nothing inherently 'good' or 'bad' about a current account deficit or surplus.

- International payments imbalances played an important role in the build up to the recent global financial crisis.

The focus in this chapter is on the linkages between an economy and the rest of the world. We have mentioned some of these linkages before, but here they are the main concern. There are financial (or monetary) linkages through the international money and capital markets, and there are 'real' linkages through international trade and travel. The real and the monetary links are not independent of each other. Real transactions cannot take place without money and finance, and are influenced by monetary forces; equally, money markets are influenced by the fundamentals of the real economy.

The discussion of these issues will bring together much material from elsewhere in this book: the theory of supply and demand (Chapter 3), the nature of money (Chapter 18), international trade (yet to come in Chapter 27), and short-run macroeconomics (Chapters 16–22). Indeed, we have had exports and imports (in the form of net exports, *NX*) explicitly in our macroeconomic model since Chapter 17. We now need to look at these issues in much greater detail to prepare the ground for our policy discussions in the next chapter.

In the first part of this chapter we discuss the exchange rate—what role it plays in connecting the domestic economy with foreign economies, and what economic forces determine its value. In the second part of this chapter we discuss the balance of payments. This is an important concept concerned with net transactions between one country and the rest of the world. We ask what the 'balance of payments' means, how it is measured, and why it matters.

We have seen that exports (*X*) are a part of aggregate spending on domestic production—an injection into the domestic circular flow of income that contributes to the GDP. So far we have treated exports as exogenous to the system. We have also seen that imports (*IM*) are spending that contributes to the GDPs of other countries—a leakage from the domestic circular flow of income. So far we have made imports dependent on domestic GDP in a relationship called the import function. In our theory of the determination of GDP we linked these two flows together and dealt only with net exports *X – IM*. Since exports add to spending on domestic output and imports subtract from it, only the difference between the two matters as far as GDP is concerned.

So far in this book we have studied many types of market—markets for such things as wheat, motor cars, labour, and bonds. Now we need to study the market where the national currencies of various countries are bought and sold—the foreign exchange market. The exchange rate—the rate at which one nation's currency can be exchanged for another's in the foreign exchange market—influences the prices of both a country's imports and its exports. Thus it makes exports partially endogenous and provides an additional reason why imports are endogenous.

The foreign exchange market

Markets where one country's currency is exchanged for another's can be analysed with the tools of demand and supply just like any other market. However, before doing this, it is helpful to remind ourselves why we need such markets.

Money is central to the efficient working of any modern economy, which must rely on specialization and exchange. Yet modern fiat money is a *national* matter, one that is closely controlled by national governments. Until recently each nation-state had its own currency, though in 1999 twelve[1] EU nations adopted a common currency, the euro. For the purposes of the following discussion we treat the Eurozone countries as if they were a single country, as the euro commands a single price in terms of any one other national currency. Other nation-states each have their own currency. If you live in Sweden, you earn kronor and spend kronor; if you run a business in Australia, you get revenue in Australian dollars and meet your wage bill with Australian dollars. The currency of a country is acceptable within the bounds of that country, but usually it will not be accepted by people and firms in another country. The Stockholm buses will accept kronor for a fare, but not Australian dollars; the Australian worker will not take Swedish kronor for wages, but expects to be paid in Australian dollars.

UK producers require payment in pounds sterling for their products. They need pounds to meet their wage bills, to pay for their raw materials, and to reinvest or distribute their profits. There is no problem when they sell to UK-based purchasers. However, if they sell their goods to, say, residents of India, either the Indians must exchange their rupees to acquire pounds to pay for the goods, or the UK producers must accept rupees[2] and then exchange them for pounds. The same holds true for producers in all countries; they must eventually receive payment in the currency of their own country.

Trade between nations typically requires the exchange of one nation's currency for that of another. The major exception is the Eurozone, where member states have a common currency.

International payments involve the exchange of currencies between people who have one currency and require another. Suppose that a UK firm wishes to acquire ¥3 million for some purpose. (¥ is the currency symbol for the Japanese yen.) The firm can go to its bank and buy a cheque, or money order, that will be accepted in Japan as ¥3 million. How many *pounds* the firm must pay to purchase this cheque will depend on the value of the yen in terms of pounds.

The exchange of one currency for another is a *foreign exchange transaction*. The term 'foreign exchange' refers to the actual foreign currency or various claims on it, such as bank deposits or promises to pay that are traded for each other. The UK *exchange rate* is the value of the domestic currency in terms of foreign currency; it is the amount of foreign currency that can be obtained with one unit of the domestic currency or, what is the same thing, the amount of foreign currency that must be given up to get one unit of domestic currency. For example, if £1 will buy ¥100, the yen–pound exchange rate is 100 and it will take ¥100 to buy £1. However, most other countries express their exchange rate the other way round—that is, the number of units of domestic currency that it takes to buy one unit of foreign currency. In the above example, it would take 1p to buy ¥1 or, what is the same thing, ¥1 will buy £0.01 In this chapter we stick with UK practice, although in economic theory the exchange rate is usually expressed as a quantity of domestic currency it takes to buy a unit of foreign currency. If this sounds confusing, and exchange rates do often confuse people, think of the rate as the price, or value, of sterling; it is how much £1 is worth in terms of some foreign currency—that is, how many units of foreign currency you will get for £1.[3]

A rise in the external value of the pound (i.e. a rise in the exchange rate) is called an **appreciation** of the pound; for example, if one can now obtain ¥110 for £1, the pound has *appreciated*. A fall in the external value of the pound (i.e. a fall in the exchange rate) is called a **depreciation** of the pound; for example, if one can now obtain only ¥90 for £1, the pound has *depreciated*.[4]

Because the exchange rate expresses the value of one currency in terms of another, when one currency appreciates, the other must depreciate.

Box 24.1 shows a measure of the UK exchange rate from 1964 to 2014 and discusses alternative ways of measuring it.

---

[1] There were 18 Eurozone members in June 2014.

[2] Some trade, especially in primary commodities such as wheat and oil, is conducted in US dollars, even when US residents are not involved. In this respect the US dollar has a special role as an international medium of exchange or unit of account.

[3] At the time of writing, May 2014, £1 actually buys about ¥171.

[4] When the external value of the currency changes as a result of an explicit policy of the central bank, it is often said to have been *devalued* when it falls and *revalued* when it rises.

Box 24.1 The UK exchange rate

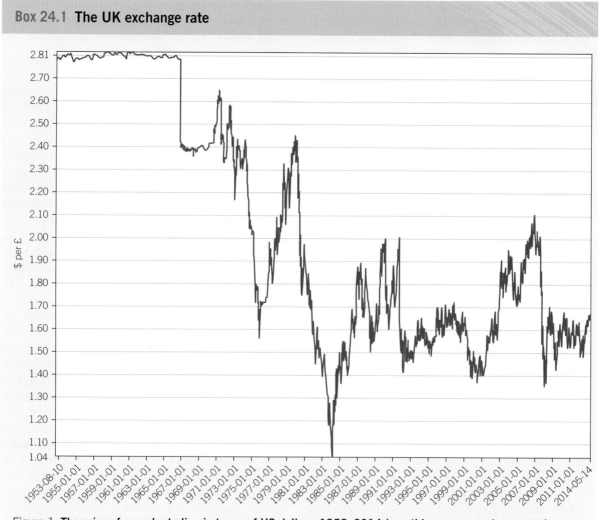

Figure 1 The price of pounds sterling in terms of US dollars, 1953–2014 (monthly average exchange rate)

Source: <http://fxtop.com>

There are two main ways of measuring the nominal exchange rate. The first is the price of a currency in terms of one other currency, such as the US dollar. Thus the exchange rate for the pound sterling is often expressed as the number of dollars per pound. Figure 1 shows the monthly value of the pound sterling in terms of the US dollar from August 1953 until May 2014. From 1948 until 1967, the value of the pound was pegged at around $2.80 by the UK government (see Box 24.3 on how this was done), but it was devalued in November 1967 to around $2.40. From June 1972 the price of the pound has been floating, which means that its price is determined by market forces, and this price changes minute by minute while the foreign exchange markets are open. Its value against the dollar has fluctuated a great deal since 1972 between a high of around $2.60 and a low of around $1.04.

In the early 1990s, the UK was a member of the European Exchange Rate Mechanism (ERM) which involved pegging the exchange rates between member currencies within the ERM,

but not against the US dollar. However, there was a sharp devaluation of the pound against the dollar in September 1992 when the UK adopted free floating again. The exchange rate of the pound has floated freely ever since 1992.

The second way of expressing a nominal exchange rate is as an index number where the value is calibrated against a basket of other currencies. This is called the *nominal effective exchange rate*. This index takes account of the fact that the pound also has exchange rates against the euro, the yen, and all other tradable currencies. It is a price index rather like the RPI or the CPI (see Chapter 15) that uses weights based upon the relative importance of each currency to UK trade. Figure 2 shows an index of the UK nominal effective exchange rate from 1964 to 2014, where the index is given a value of 100 in 2010. A third important way of measuring exchange rates is the *real exchange rate index*. This measures the relative prices of domestic and foreign goods and services. This is illustrated in Figure 24.3 and explained in the accompanying text.

(continued)

Box 24.1 *continued*

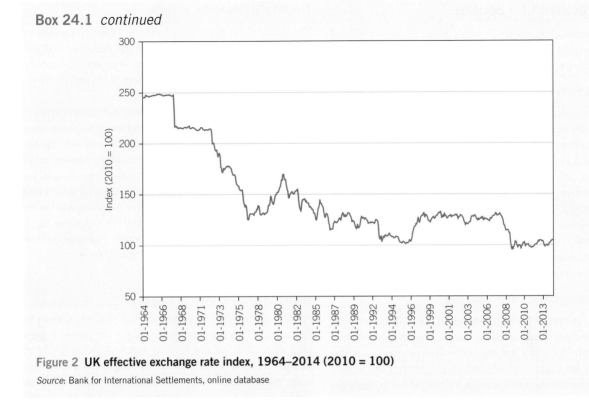

Figure 2 **UK effective exchange rate index, 1964–2014 (2010 = 100)**

Source: Bank for International Settlements, online database

The determination of the exchange rate

The exchange rate is just a price, albeit a very important price. Since it is determined in a competitive market in which there are many buyers and many sellers, we can analyse its behaviour using the demand and supply analysis that we first encountered Chapter 2. To do so, we need only recall that *in the market for foreign exchange*, transactions that generate a receipt of foreign exchange represent a demand for pounds, and transactions that require a purchase of foreign exchange represent a supply of pounds. We focus on the demand and supply of pounds arising from transactions both in the import and export of goods and services and in movements of capital. Later, we turn to the important role of official intervention by the domestic authorities.

For simplicity we use an example involving trade between the United Kingdom and the United States and the determination of the exchange rate between their two currencies, the pound sterling and the US dollar, for which we use the shorthand forms 'pound' and 'dollar'. The two-country example simplifies things, but the principles apply to all foreign transactions. Thus, 'dollar' stands for foreign exchange in general, and the value of the pound in terms of dollars stands for the foreign exchange rate in general.[5]

When £1 = $1.50, a US importer who offers to buy £1 million with dollars must be offering to sell $1.5 million. Similarly, a UK importer who offers to sell £1 million for dollars must be offering to buy $1.5 million.

Because one currency is traded for another in the foreign exchange market, it follows that a demand for foreign exchange (dollars) implies a supply of pounds, while a supply of foreign exchange (dollars) implies a demand for pounds.

For this reason a theory of the exchange rate between the pound and the dollar can deal either with the demand for and the supply of pounds or with the supply of and the demand for dollars. One implies the other, so we do not need both. We will concentrate on the demand, supply, and price of the pound (quoted in dollars).

---

[5] The foreign exchange market between the pound and the dollar is still often referred to as 'cable', because trades used to be conducted, using Morse code, via transatlantic telegraph cables.

The demand for pounds

The demand for pounds arises from all international transactions that generate a receipt of foreign exchange. We deal with each of these below.

UK exports

One important source of demand for pounds in foreign exchange markets is foreigners who do not currently hold pounds but who wish to buy UK-made goods and services. A German importer of Scotch whisky is such a purchaser; an Austrian couple planning to take a holiday in Cornwall is another; the Chinese national airline seeking to buy Rolls Royce engines for its passenger aircraft is yet another. All are sources of demand for pounds, arising out of international trade. Each potential buyer wants to sell their own currency and buy pounds for the purpose of purchasing UK exports.

Income payments and transfers

A UK resident who owns shares in, say, Apple receives dividend payments on those shares. The dividend is paid by Apple in dollars. But the UK resident wants to use the money for a meal out in London, so converts the dollars into pounds, thereby creating a demand for pounds on the foreign exchange market.

Capital inflows

A third source of demand for pounds comes from foreigners who wish to purchase UK assets. In order to buy UK assets, holders of foreign currencies must first buy pounds in foreign exchange markets.[6]

Reserve currency

Governments often accumulate and hold foreign exchange reserves, just as individuals maintain savings accounts. For example, the government of Nigeria may decide to increase its reserve holdings of pounds and reduce its reserve holdings of dollars; if it does so, it will be a demander of pounds (and a supplier of dollars) in foreign exchange markets. The pound sterling used to be a very important reserve currency, particularly for countries that were formerly British colonies. This role has been greatly reduced (relative to the US dollar and euro), but it still creates a significant overseas demand for pounds. Currency reserves are often held in an interest-bearing asset, so it is the expected return on these assets that is likely to influence the choice, just as with private sector capital flows.

---

[6] Capital inflows also arise when UK citizens sell foreign assets because they enter the foreign exchange market and sell the foreign currency received for the assets and buy pounds.

The total demand for pounds

The demand for pounds by holders of foreign currencies is the sum of the demands for all the purposes just discussed—for purchases of UK exports of goods and services, for income payments and transfers, for capital movements, or for adding to currency reserves.

Furthermore, because people, firms, and governments in all countries purchase goods from, and invest in, many other countries, the demand for any one currency will be the aggregate demand of individuals, firms, and governments in a number of different countries. Thus the total demand for pounds, for example, may include Germans who are offering euro, Japanese who are offering yen, Australians who are offering Australian dollars, and so on. For simplicity, however, we continue with our two-country example and use only the United Kingdom and the United States.

The demand curve for pounds

The demand for pounds in terms of dollars is represented by a negatively sloped curve, such as the one shown in Figure 24.1. This figure plots the price of the pound (measured in dollars) on the vertical axis and the quantity of pounds on the horizontal axis. Moving down the vertical scale, the pound is worth fewer dollars and hence is depreciating in the foreign exchange market. Moving up the scale, the pound is appreciating.

Why is the demand curve for pounds negatively sloped? Consider the demand for pounds from foreigners who wish to purchase UK exports. If the pound depreciates, the dollar price of UK exports will fall because holders of dollars require fewer of them to buy each pound. As long as demand for exports is elastic, US citizens will buy more of the cheaper UK goods and will require more pounds for this purpose. Thus the quantity of pounds demanded will rise. In the opposite case, when the pound appreciates, more dollars are required to buy each pound, and so the price of UK exports rises in terms of dollars. US citizens will buy fewer UK goods and thus will demand fewer pounds.

Similar considerations affect other sources of demand for pounds. When the pound is cheaper, UK assets become cheaper to buy and hence more attractive, and the quantity purchased will rise. As it does, the quantity of pounds demanded to pay for the purchases will increase.

The demand curve for pounds in the foreign exchange market is negatively sloped when it is plotted against the dollar price of £1.

The supply of pounds

The sources of supply of pounds in the foreign exchange market are merely the opposite side of the demand for dollars. (Recall that the *supply* of pounds by people who

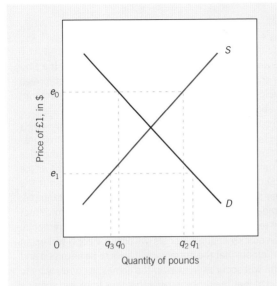

Figure 24.1 The market for foreign exchange.

The demand curve for pounds, *D*, is negatively sloped, and the *supply* curve of pounds, *S*, is positively sloped. The demand curve represents the sum of transactions giving rise to receipts of foreign exchange. When the exchange rate is e_0, the quantity of pounds demanded is q_0. A depreciation of the pound is indicated by a fall in the exchange rate to e_1; foreign demand for UK goods and assets rises, and hence the quantity of pounds demanded also rises, from q_0 to q_1. An appreciation has the opposite effect; a rise in the exchange rate from e_1 to e_0 causes the quantity of pounds demanded to fall from q_1 to q_0.

The supply of pounds represents the sum of transactions that require payments of foreign exchange. When the exchange rate is e_0, the quantity of pounds supplied is q_2. If the exchange rate falls to e_1, UK demand for foreign goods and assets falls, and hence the quantity of pounds supplied also falls, from q_2 to q_3. An appreciation has the opposite effect; a rise in the exchange rate from e_1 to e_0 causes the quantity of pounds supplied to rise.

The exchange rate is in equilibrium where the two curves intersect.

are seeking dollars is the same as the *demand* for dollars by holders of pounds.)

Who wants to sell pounds? UK residents seeking to purchase foreign goods and services or assets will be supplying pounds and purchasing foreign exchange for this purpose. In addition, holders of UK assets may decide to sell their UK holdings and shift them into foreign assets, and if they do they will sell pounds; that is, they will be supplying pounds to the foreign exchange market. Similarly, a country with some sterling reserves of foreign exchange may decide that the sterling-denominated assets offer a poor return and that it should sell pounds in order to buy another currency.

The supply curve of pounds

When the pound depreciates, the sterling price of US exports to the UK rises. It takes more pounds to buy the

same US goods, so UK residents will buy fewer of the now more expensive US goods. Therefore the quantity of pounds being offered in exchange for dollars in order to pay for US exports to the United Kingdom (UK imports) will fall.[7]

In the opposite case, when the pound appreciates, US exports to the United Kingdom become cheaper, more are sold, and a greater quantity of pounds is spent on them. Thus, more pounds will be offered in exchange for dollars to obtain the foreign exchange that is needed to pay for the extra imports. The argument also applies to purchases and sales of assets.

The supply curve of pounds in the foreign exchange market is positively sloped when it is plotted against the dollar price of £1.

This is also illustrated in Figure 24.1.

The equilibrium rate

The demand and supply curves in Figure 24.1 do not include official foreign exchange market intervention by the domestic government (or by the monetary authorities, depending on the institutional arrangements in the country concerned), though they do include any transactions in pounds by foreign monetary authorities. Under what was called the Bretton Woods[8] regime, governments, including the that of the United Kingdom, intervened in the foreign exchange market to fix their exchange rates within a narrow band. This system, which is discussed further in Box 24.2, came to an end early in the 1970s, although some governments still fix their exchange rates.

[7] As long as the demand for imports is elastic (price elasticity greater than 1 (in absolute terms)), the fall in the volume of imports will swamp the rise in price, and hence fewer pounds will be spent on imports. If the elasticity of demand for imports is less than 1 (in absolute terms), the volume of imports will fall but the amount of domestic money spent on them will still rise. A similar issue arises with exports. A fall in the foreign price of British exports will cause more of them to be bought, but more will be spent on them only if the foreign demand for these products is elastic. In what follows, we adopt the case of elastic demand for both imports and exports, which is usual in this area. In a more general form this is called the *Marshall–Lerner condition*, after two famous British economists who first studied the problem.

[8] At a conference held in Bretton Woods, New Hampshire, in 1944 the re-design of international monetary institutions was agreed and the International Monetary Fund (IMF) was established.

Box 24.2 Fixed exchange rates

When there is official intervention in the foreign exchange market to maintain a particular exchange rate, this prevents the rate from adjusting sufficiently to guarantee that the demand for foreign exchange just equals the supply. The authorities must then satisfy any private sector excess demand or supply of pounds. In the process of intervention the authorities will be building up or running down their foreign exchange reserves. The exchange rate is normally set within some range, typically the official 'pegged' rate plus or minus one per cent.

Consider a simplified analysis of how such pegged exchange rate regimes operate. Assume for simplicity that the domestic authorities peg the UK exchange rate between, say, $1.50 and $1.60. The authorities then enter the market to prevent the rate from going outside this range. At the price of $1.50 the authorities offer to buy pounds (in exchange for dollars) in unlimited amounts. At the price of $1.60 the authorities offer to sell pounds (in exchange for dollars) in unlimited amounts. When the authorities buy dollars (sell pounds) their foreign exchange reserves rise, but when they sell dollars (buy pounds) their exchange reserves fall.

If, on average, the demand and supply curves intersect in the range $1.50–$1.60, exchange reserves will be relatively stable. If the demand curve for pounds intersects the supply curve above $1.60, the authorities will find themselves acquiring reserves each period. Such a situation can be sustained indefinitely, provided that the authorities are willing to acquire foreign currency and other assets that they purchase with that currency. This has been the case with China during recent decades. Its currency has been

held well below its market equilibrium value and the Chinese authorities have acquired growing amounts of foreign currency reserves that have reached a massive total amount well above $3 trillion in 2014.

In contrast, if demand for pounds intersects the supply curve below $1.50, the authorities will find themselves losing reserves each period, and sooner or later the authorities will run out of reserves. They must then either move the bands of fluctuation (devalue), or take action to shift the demand or supply curves. This could be done, for example, by trade restrictions or by raising interest rates to attract short-term capital inflows. If they do not take remedial action quickly enough, a crisis will ensue. People will begin to anticipate that the currency will have to be devalued and a flight will occur as holders of the domestic currency try to get rid of it at the present value that they think will soon be reduced. This flight of the currency exacerbates the problem, forcing the authorities to devalue immediately rather than waiting for a preferred time.

With fixed exchange rates and an undervalued currency, the monetary authorities will be acquiring reserves. With fixed exchange rates and an overvalued currency, the monetary authorities will be losing reserves. If nothing is done to alter the situation, the currency will have to be devalued sooner or later, and if a flight from the currency occurs devaluation may be forced on the authorities sooner rather than later.

The problems associated with fixing the exchange rate provide a good example of the difficulties that governments often have in trying to manage market prices.

In most countries today the exchange rate is free to fluctuate to equate demand and supply, although governments sometimes intervene in that market to buy or sell foreign exchange in order to influence that rate. To do this they hold stocks of foreign exchange reserves which are added to when they buy foreign exchange and subtracted from when they sell it.[9] When they do this, they act as just one more demander or supplier of foreign exchange. Such a regime is called a *floating rate regime* or a *managed float regime* depending on how much and how seriously the government intervenes to influence or 'manage' the rate.

Consider an exchange rate that is set in a freely competitive market, with no intervention by the authorities. Like any competitive price, this rate fluctuates according to the conditions of demand and supply.

Suppose that the current price of the pound is so low (say, at e_1 in Figure 24.1) that the quantity of pounds demanded exceeds the quantity supplied. Pounds will be in short supply in the foreign exchange market, some people who require pounds to make payments to the United Kingdom will be unable to obtain them, and the price of the pound will be bid up. The value of the pound vis-à-vis the dollar will appreciate. As the price of the pound rises, the dollar price of UK exports to the United States and UK assets rises and the quantity of pounds demanded to buy UK goods and UK assets decreases. At the same time as the sterling price of imports from the United States falls so do the UK prices for US assets; a larger quantity of US goods and assets will be purchased and the quantity of pounds supplied will rise. Thus, a rise in the price of the pound reduces the quantity demanded and increases

---

[9] In the United Kingdom the official reserves used to be entirely owned by the government but managed by the Bank of England. However, following the Bank of England Act 1998, the Bank was given some of the UK reserves, so that foreign exchange market intervention could be performed with either the Treasury's or the Bank's reserves, though neither has attempted to use its reserves to influence the exchange rate in any significant way in recent decades. The European Central Bank can also intervene in foreign exchange markets as it has its own foreign exchange reserves.

the quantity supplied. Where the two curves intersect, quantity demanded equals quantity supplied and the exchange rate is in equilibrium.

What happens when the price of the pound is above its equilibrium value? The quantity of pounds demanded will be less than the quantity supplied. With pounds in excess supply, some people who wish to convert pounds into dollars will be unable to do so. (Equivalently, we could say that there is an excess demand for dollars.) The price of the pound will fall, fewer pounds will be supplied, more will be demanded, and an equilibrium will be re-established.

A foreign exchange market is like other competitive markets. The forces of demand and supply lead to an equilibrium price at which quantity demanded equals quantity supplied.

In a floating exchange rate regime it is exchange rate adjustment that determines the transactions in both goods and services and capital movements, even though planned, or desired, trade and investment decisions may have been inconsistent. Suppose that at the beginning of some period importers and exporters had plans that would have created an excess demand for dollars and domestic investors had plans to demand dollars to

buy foreign securities (while foreigners had no such plans). The attempt to implement these plans would create an excess supply of pounds (demand for dollars). This would force a sterling depreciation, which would continue until it had induced changes in the plans. Indeed, sterling would depreciate far enough so that any supply of pounds generated by an excess of imports over exports was just balanced by a demand for pounds to pay for a capital inflow (or any excess of exports over imports was just balanced by a capital outflow).

Changes in exchange rates

What causes flexible exchange rates to move? The simplest answer to this question is changes in demand or supply in the foreign exchange market. Anything that shifts the demand curve for pounds to the right or the supply curve of pounds to the left leads to an appreciation of the pound. Anything that shifts the demand curve for pounds to the left or the supply curve of pounds to the right leads to a depreciation of the pound. This is nothing more than a restatement of the laws of supply and demand, applied now to the market for foreign currencies; it is illustrated in Figure 24.2.

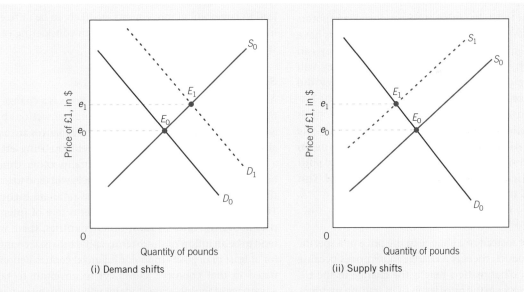

(i) Demand shifts   (ii) Supply shifts

Figure 24.2 Changes in exchange rates

An increase in the demand for pounds or a decrease in the supply will cause the pound to appreciate; a decrease in the demand or an increase in the supply will cause it to depreciate. The initial demand and supply curves, D_0 and S_0, are shown as solid lines. Equilibrium is at E_0 with an exchange rate of e_0. An increase in the demand for pounds, shown by a rightward shift in the demand curve from D_0 to D_1 in part (i), or a decrease in the supply of pounds, shown by a leftward shift in the supply curve from S_0 to S_1 in part (ii), will cause the pound to appreciate. In both parts the new equilibrium is at E_1, and the appreciation is shown by the rise in the exchange rate from e_0 to e_1.

A decrease in the demand for pounds, as shown by a leftward shift in the demand curve from D_1 to D_0 in part (i), or an increase in the supply of pounds, as shown by a rightward shift in the supply curve from S_1 to S_0 in part (ii), will cause the pound to depreciate. The equilibrium will shift from E_1 to E_0, and the depreciation is shown by the fall in the exchange rate from e_1 to e_0 in both parts.

What causes the shifts in demand and supply that lead to changes in exchange rates? There are many causes, some of which are transitory and some of which are persistent. We will discuss some of the most important ones.

A rise in the domestic price of exports

Suppose that the sterling price of UK-produced telephone equipment rises. The effect on the demand for pounds depends on the price elasticity of foreign demand for the UK products.

If the demand is inelastic (say, because the United Kingdom is uniquely able to supply the product for which there are no close substitutes), then more will be spent; the demand for pounds to pay the bigger bill will shift the demand curve to the right, and the pound will appreciate. This is illustrated in Figure 24.2(i).

If the demand is elastic, perhaps because other countries supply the same product to competitive world markets, the total amount spent will decrease and thus fewer pounds will be demanded; that is, the demand curve for pounds will shift to the left, and the pound will depreciate. This is also illustrated in Figure 24.2(i), by a reverse of the previous shift.

A rise in the foreign price of imports

Suppose that the dollar price of US-produced computers increases sharply. Suppose also that UK consumers have an elastic demand for US computers because they can easily switch to UK substitutes. In this case they will spend fewer dollars for US computers than they did before. Hence, they will supply fewer pounds to the foreign exchange market. The supply curve of pounds shifts to the left, and the pound will appreciate. If the demand for US computers were inelastic, spending on them would rise and the supply of pounds would shift to the right, leading to a depreciation of the pound. This is illustrated in Figure 24.2(ii).

Changes in price levels

Suppose that instead of a change in the price of a specific exported product, there is a change in *all* prices because of inflation. What matters here is the change in the UK price level *relative to* the price levels of its trading partners. (Recall that in our two-country example the United States stands for the rest of the world.)

If UK inflation is higher than that in the United States, UK exports are becoming relatively expensive in US markets while imports from the United States are becoming relatively cheap in the United Kingdom. This will shift the demand curve for pounds to the left and the supply curve to the right. Each change causes the dollar price of £1 to fall; that is, it causes the pound to depreciate.

If the price level of one country is rising relative to that of another country, the equilibrium value of its currency will be falling relative to that of the other country.

Indeed, the price level and the exchange rate are both measures of a currency's value. The price level is the value of a currency measured against a typical basket of goods, while the exchange rate values a currency against other currencies.

Capital movements

Major capital flows can exert a strong influence on exchange rates, especially as, on any particular day, the size of capital flows (in the modern globalized financial system) can swamp payments made with respect to imports and exports of goods and services. An increased desire by UK residents to invest in US assets will shift the supply curve for pounds to the right, and the pound will depreciate. This is illustrated in Figure 24.2(ii) by the shift from curve S_1 to curve S_0.

A significant movement of investment funds has the effect of appreciating the currency of the capital-importing country and depreciating the currency of the capital-exporting country.

This statement is true for all capital movements—short-term and long-term. However, because the motives that lead to large capital movements are likely to be different in the short and long terms, it is worth considering each separately.

Short-term capital movements

A major motive for short-term capital flows is a change in interest rates. International traders hold transactions balances just as domestic traders do. These balances are usually lent out on a short-term basis rather than being left in a non-interest-bearing deposit. Naturally, other things being equal, the holders of these balances will tend to lend them in those markets where interest rates are highest. Thus, if one major country's short-term rate of interest rises above the rates in most other countries, there will tend to be an inflow of short-term capital into that country (or at least of deposits in major financial centres denominated in that country's currency) in an effort to take advantage of the high rate, and this will add to the demand for the country's currency on the foreign exchange market and tend to appreciate its value. If these short-term interest rates should fall, there will most likely be a sudden shift away from that country as a location for short-term funds, and its currency will tend to depreciate.

A second motive for short-term capital movements is speculation about a country's exchange rate. If foreigners expect the pound to appreciate, they will rush to buy assets denominated in pounds; if they expect the pound to depreciate, they will be reluctant to buy or to hold UK financial assets.

Long-term capital movements

Long-term capital movements are largely influenced by long-term expectations about another country's profit opportunities and the long-run value of its currency. A US firm would be more willing to purchase a UK firm if it expected that the profits in pounds would buy more dollars in future years than the profits from investment in a US factory. This could happen if the UK business earned greater profits than the US alternative, with exchange rates remaining unchanged. It could also happen if the profits were the same, but the US firm expected the pound to appreciate relative to the dollar.

Structural changes

An economy can undergo structural changes that alter its equilibrium exchange rate. 'Structural change' is an all-purpose term for a change in technology, the invention of new products, or anything else that affects the pattern of comparative advantage. For example, when a country's products do not improve in quality as rapidly as those of some other countries, two changes will slowly occur. First, that country's consumers' will slowly shift their purchases away from domestic products and towards those of its foreign competitors. Secondly, foreigners will find that country's exports less attractive and will buy fewer of them. The first change will increase the supply of the country's currency on the foreign exchange market, while the second change will reduce the demand for it. Thus the currency will slowly lose value on that market.

An important example of a structural change in recent UK history was the production of oil and gas from the North Sea that began in the 1970s. This reduced UK demand for imported oil, leading to a reduced supply of pounds in the foreign exchange market and an appreciation of the UK exchange rate. It also put exporters of UK manufactured goods under heavy pressure as the foreign price of these goods rose. As a result, a large number of UK manufacturing firms went out of business.

Exchange rate experience

The degree of exchange rate variability experienced since the advent of floating in the early 1970s has been bigger than was expected.

Why have exchange rates been volatile? This question remains at the centre of debate and controversy among researchers and policy commentators. In this section we provide only a cursory view of this and related questions about the behaviour of exchange rates.

First, we look at one measure of the value that the exchange rate would take on if it were subject to the influence of what might be called the underlying, or fundamental, market determinants. We can then compare this with the actual value of the exchange rate. Secondly, we provide one explanation for the divergence of the exchange rate from the path determined by these fundamentals.

Purchasing power parity

Purchasing power parity (PPP) theory holds that over the long term the average value of the exchange rate between two currencies depends on their relative purchasing power. The theory holds that a currency will tend to have the same purchasing power when it is spent in its home country as it would have if it were converted to foreign exchange and spent in the foreign country.

If at existing relative price levels and the existing exchange rate, a currency has a higher purchasing power in its own country, it is said to be undervalued. There is then an incentive to sell foreign exchange and buy the domestic currency in order to take advantage of this higher purchasing power (that is, the fact that goods seem cheaper) in the domestic economy. This will put upward pressure on the domestic currency.

Similarly, if a currency has a lower purchasing power in its own country, it is said to be overvalued; there is then an incentive to sell the domestic currency and buy foreign exchange in order to take advantage of the higher purchasing power (cheaper goods) abroad. This will put downward pressure on the domestic currency.

In estimating whether a currency is currently over- or undervalued on the exchange market, international agencies calculate what is called a PPP index, which is determined by relative price levels in the two countries compared with some base period. It is calculated by dividing one country's price index by a corresponding price index of another country.[10] For example, assume that the UK price level rises by 20 per cent, while the US price level rises by only 5 per cent over the same period. The PPP value of the dollar then appreciates by approximately 15 per cent against sterling.

---

[10] This calculation can use one of several alternative price indexes, so there is no unique measure of this concept.

A related concept to PPP is the real exchange rate. While the actual (also called the nominal) exchange rate tells how much foreign currency can be exchanged for a unit of domestic currency, the real exchange rate tells how much of the goods and services in the domestic country can be exchanged for the goods and services in a foreign country. The real exchange rate is represented by the following equation:

$$\text{real exchange rate} = \text{nominal exchange rate} \left(\frac{\text{domestic price index}}{\text{foreign price index}} \right)$$

or, what is the same thing,

$$\text{real exchange rate} = (\text{nominal exchange rate}) \times (\text{PPP index}).$$

If the nominal exchange rate always adjusted to changes in purchasing power, the real rate would be constant. For example, if the domestic price level rose by 10 per cent with foreign prices constant and the nominal rate depreciated by 10 per cent, the real rate would be constant. But the real exchange rate does vary considerably. One of the main reasons is that inflation rates in most major countries do not differ by much and yet nominal exchange rates are quite volatile, so the real exchange rate is highly correlated with the nominal rate in the short term. One reason why nominal exchange rates are volatile is that they respond quickly to new information; this is discussed in Box 24.3. This also means that real exchange rates move in a similar way in the short term (as price level are slow to adjust). However, over the long haul there is evidence that real exchange rates return to some average level, and this implies that PPP holds in the long run.

PPP exerts a strong influence on exchange rates in the long term, but there are often significant deviations from PPP in the short to medium term.

Figure 24.3 shows an index of the real exchange rate for the United Kingdom, the United States, Japan, and Germany for 1975–2013. The United Kingdom had a high real

Box 24.3 'News' and the exchange rate

Foreign exchange markets are different from markets for consumer goods in that the vast bulk of trading takes place between professional foreign exchange dealers of banks. These dealers do not meet each other face to face. Rather, they conduct their transactions over the telephone or via computers, and the other party to the deal can be anywhere in the world. The structure of this market has one interesting implication: exchange rates respond to news. Let us see why this is and what it means.

Deals done by the professional dealers are all on a large scale, typically involving sums no smaller than £1 million and often very much larger. Each dealer tends to specialize in deals between a small number of currencies, say the pound sterling and the euro. But the dealers in all currencies for each bank sit close together in a dealing room, so that they can hear what is going on in other markets. When a big news event breaks, anywhere in the world, this will be shouted out to all dealers in the room simultaneously.

Each dealer is also faced with several computer screens and many buttons which will connect him or her very quickly by telephone to other dealers. Speed of transaction can be very important if you are dealing with large volumes of money in a market that is continuously changing the prices quoted. Latest price quotes from around the world appear on the screens. However, contracts are agreed over the telephone (and nowadays are recorded in case of disagreement) or via an online trading system and the paperwork follows within two days.

As exchange rates are closely related to expectations and to interest rates, the foreign exchange dealers have to keep an eye on all major news events affecting the economic environment. Since all the players in the foreign exchange markets are professionals, they are all well informed—not just about what has happened, but also about forecasts of what is likely to happen. Accordingly, the exchange rate, at any point in time, reflects not just history but also current expectations of what is going to happen in the future.

Expectations of future events will change as new information becomes available, but the only component in today's news that will cause the exchange rate to change is what was not expected to happen. Economists attribute the unforecastable component of news to a random error. It is random in the sense that it has no detectable pattern to it and is unrelated to the information available before it happened.

Some events, such as an earthquake in Japan or a head of state having a heart attack, are clearly unforecastable. Others are the production of economic statistics for which forecasts have generally been published. In the latter case it is the deviation of announced figures from their forecast value that, if large, tends to move exchange rates.

Exchange rates are moved by news. Since news is random and unpredictable, changes in exchange rates will tend to be random.

Some people, observing the volatility of exchange rates, conclude that foreign exchange markets are inefficient. However, with well-informed professional players who have forward-looking expectations, new information is rapidly transmitted into prices. Therefore volatility of exchange rates may reflect the volatility of relevant, but unexpected, events around the world.

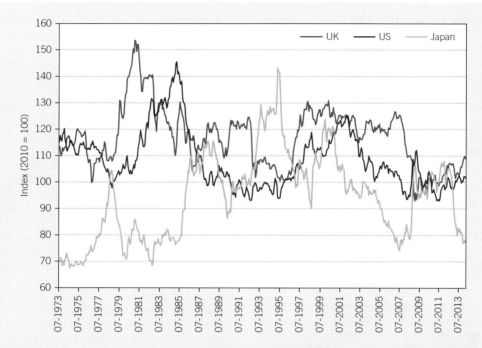

Figure 24.3 Real exchange rates for the United Kingdom, the United States, and Japan, 1973–2014

Deviations from PPP can be substantial in the short run, but over the long run exchange rates tend to converge to their PPP values.
At the PPP exchange rate the real exchange rate would be constant. The figure shows real exchange rates for three countries, calculated by adjusting actual exchange rates by indexes of consumer prices and set to a value of 100 in 2010. The UK real exchange rate rose strongly between 1978 and early 1981. It then fell in stages. It rose again at the end of the 1980s, but fell sharply after September 1992 when Britain left the ERM. It rose again in 1996 and stayed high up to 2007, but fell during the financial crisis. The United States experienced a dramatic appreciation of its real exchange rate from 1980 to 1985, after which time it fell back sharply. The dollar was strong again in real terms during the internet boom of the late 1990s but fell after 2001. The Japanese real exchange rate was strong in the mid-1990s, but in the early 2000s Japan suffered a major depression and its currency weakened in real terms, only to recover sharply in 2008–9. It fell again in 2012–13.

Source: Bank for International Settlements, online database.

exchange rate in the early 1980s, associated with its emergence as an oil producer. This led to a sharp loss of competitiveness of the non-oil sectors of the economy (especially manufacturing), causing a sharp decline in UK manufacturing output that in turn contributed to the 1979–81 recession. The UK real exchange rate fell significantly between 1981 and 1986. The UK real exchange was high again at the end of the 1990s and in the early years of the twenty-first century, but it fell after the financial crisis of 2007–8. However, the most dramatic swing in the 1980s was in the US real exchange rate, which increased by 50 per cent between 1980 and 1985, and then fell back to its 1980 level by 1987.

A simple model of the exchange rate implied by the quantity theory of money and PPP is set out in Box 24.4.

Exchange rate policies

Today's exchange rate regime is generally one of free floating, which means that demand and supply forces are free to determine the exchange rate. However, some central banks do intervene in the market from time to time to try to influence their country's exchange rate. To do this they use their foreign currency reserves, often held in the form of US dollars but sometimes in other major currencies such as sterling.

On the one hand, if they seek to lower their current exchange rate they must buy foreign exchange, adding it to their reserves, and sell domestic currency in exchange. Since they can create domestic money in unlimited amounts, there is no limit to their ability to follow a policy of undervaluing their currency on the foreign exchange market.[11] On the other hand, if they seek to support the rate, they must sell foreign exchange, taking in domestic currency in exchange. Since they hold a finite amount of reserves, they cannot follow a policy of overvaluing their currency indefinitely.

---

[11] But they will then have to manage the potential inflationary consequences of the increase in the money supply.

Box 24.4 Exchange rates and the quantity theory of money

A simple expression for the exchange rate can be derived from the quantity theory of money (as set out in Box 19.3) when there are two countries and an exchange rate that follows its PPP value.

Let the foreign country be denoted by an asterisk (*), so that it has an equation linking the money supply (M), velocity (V), price level (P), and GDP (Y):

$$M^* V^* = P^* Y^* \qquad (1)$$

Using values for home money supply, velocity, price level, and GDP, we already have

$$MV = PY \qquad (2)$$

All we need to add is the relationship implied by PPP. This is that prices will be the same in both economies when converted at the current exchange rate:

$$PE = P^* \qquad (3)$$

where E is the exchange rate (expressed as the number of units of foreign currency required to buy a unit of home currency). Now all we do is rearrange equations (1) and (2) as expressions for P and P^*, and then substitute into (3) and arrange as an expression for E. This gives[†]

$$E = M^* YV^*/(MY^* V). \qquad (4)$$

This equation gives us some new insights into the exchange rate. The first term is the ratio of the home and foreign money supplies. E falls in proportion to the home money supply and rises in proportion to the foreign money supply. This means that when the home money supply rises, the exchange rate depreciates in the same proportion. The logic of this has two steps. First, a rise in home money supply leads to a proportional increase in the home price level (for given levels of Y and V). Secondly, a rise in the home price level leads to a proportional depreciation of the home currency to preserve PPP.

The second term in equation (4) has an important implication. Domestic real GDP is positively related to E. This means that, other things being equal, a rise in domestic GDP leads to an appreciation of the home currency. The reason for this is that an increase in Y leads to an increased transactions demand for the home currency. As we have learned in this chapter, anything that increases demand for the home currency will tend to appreciate its exchange rate.

Although this simple model of exchange rates gives important insights, it is only a beginning. Many other factors affecting interest rates and expectations can easily be incorporated by a more detailed specification of the determinants of V. However, the main elements of (4) are recognizable in many of the empirical exchange rate models of the last two decades.

[†] The steps are as follows.

1. $P^* = M^* V^*/Y^*$ and $P = MV/Y$.
2. Substituting into equation (3), $E(MV/Y) = M^* V^*/Y^*$.
3. Rearranging gives equation (4).

Most governments that intervene in the foreign exchange market do so to iron out what they believe to be temporary fluctuations in the exchange rate. For example, if they feel that a fall in the exchange rate is due to temporary factors, they can support the rate by selling foreign exchange from their reserves and then replacing it when the rate returns to its more normal value. Many developing countries do this, as their foreign exchange markets are relatively illiquid and so their exchange rate could be volatile if the central bank did not participate in the market. However, the major countries have found that it is hard to affect their exchange rate when acting alone as those markets have very large turnover. Occasionally there have been coordinated interventions by several major central banks acting together, and this has more chance of moving the markets.

In contrast, some countries, of which China is the prime example, seek to undervalue their currency for long periods of time. This has several effects. The government accumulates large and growing stocks of foreign exchange. The prices of imported goods appear high compared with the prices of locally produced goods, while the prices of the country's exports appear cheap in foreign markets.

The resulting high value of net exports ($X - IM$) adds stimulus to the domestic market and, in China's case, helps to provide manufacturing jobs for workers who are leaving farms to migrate to the city.

Exchange rate overshooting

Differences in interest rates between countries, arising from differences in monetary and fiscal policies among other factors, can trigger large capital flows as investors seek to place their funds where returns are highest. These capital flows will in turn result in swings in the exchange rate between the two countries. Some economists argue that this is the fundamental reason for the wide fluctuations in exchange rates that have been observed.

To illustrate, suppose that an exogenous change in monetary policy causes UK interest rates to rise four percentage points above those in New York. The interest rate differential will lead to a capital inflow into the United Kingdom. UK and foreign investors alike will sell assets denominated in US dollars and will buy UK assets that earn higher interest. These capital inflows will lead to an increased demand for pounds on the foreign exchange market as investors exchange dollars for pounds to buy UK assets. The increased demand will in turn lead to an appreciation of sterling.

A relative rise in domestic interest rates will cause a capital inflow and an appreciation of the home currency.

When will the process stop? It will stop only when expected returns on UK and foreign assets are again roughly equalized; as long as the return on UK assets is above that on foreign assets, the capital inflows, and the upward pressure on the pound, will continue. The key is that the expected return includes not only the interest earnings, but also the expected gains or losses that might arise because of changes in the exchange rate during the period of the investment. A foreign investor holding a UK asset will receive pounds when the asset is sold, and will at that time want to exchange pounds for foreign exchange. If the value of the pound has fallen, that will be a source of loss that has to be balanced against the interest income in assessing the net return on holding the asset.

When UK interest rates rise above foreign rates, equilibrium occurs when the rise in value of the pound sterling in foreign exchange markets is large enough that investors will expect a future depreciation that just offsets the interest premium from investing funds in sterling-denominated assets.

Suppose investors believe that the long-run equilibrium exchange rate is £1 = $1.50, but as they rush to buy pounds to take advantage of the 4 per cent UK interest differential, they drive the rate to, say, £1 = $1.75. (Because £1 now buys more dollars, the pound has appreciated, and because it takes more dollars to buy £1, the dollar has depreciated.) They do not believe that this rate will be sustained and instead expect the pound to lose value in future periods. If foreign investors expect the pound to depreciate by 4 per cent per year, they will be indifferent between lending money in London and doing so in New York. The extra 4 per cent per year of interest that they earn in London is exactly offset by the 4 per cent that they expect to lose when they turn their money back into their own currency.

A policy that raises domestic interest rates above world levels will cause the external value of the domestic currency to appreciate enough to create an expected future depreciation that will be sufficient to offset the interest differential.

While interest differentials persist, the exchange rate must deviate from its longer-term equilibrium value; this is often referred to as exchange rate overshooting because, at the time interest rates are raised, the exchange rate will jump beyond its long-run equilibrium level. This is illustrated in Figure 24.4.

The argument that a rise in domestic interest rates will cause an appreciation of the home currency requires an

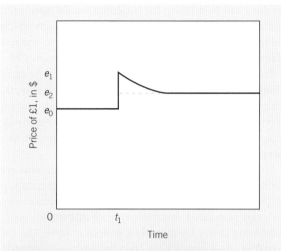

Figure 24.4 Exchange rate overshooting
The adjustment of exchange rates to policy changes often involves overshooting the long-run equilibrium. The figure illustrates how the exchange rate may move over time after a monetary policy tightening. The initial exchange rate is e_0. At time t_1 the central bank raises domestic interest rates and the exchange rate appreciates to e_1. Over time it then depreciates back towards the new long-run equilibrium level of e_2.

important proviso. The interest rate rise has to occur with all other factors, especially long-run inflation expectations, held constant. For example, if a rise in expectations of future inflation had triggered events, the story would be quite different. In this case the interest rate rise would be responding to these expectations and to the consequent expectation of a long-run *depreciation* in the home currency. Now the change in the exchange rate would depend upon the size of the interest rate rise relative to the size of the expected long-run depreciation. In short, we need to be careful when applying economic analysis that works *holding other things constant* to a world where many things are changing simultaneously.

Implications of overshooting

One policy implication of exchange rate theory is that a central bank that is seeking to use its monetary policy to attain its domestic policy targets may have to put up with large fluctuations in the exchange rate. Indeed, overshooting of the exchange rate in response to interest rate changes may be one of the most important elements of the monetary transmission mechanism.

In the case of a tightening of monetary policy, which raises interest rates, the overshooting (appreciation) of the pound beyond its PPP rate would put export- and import-competing industries under temporary but severe pressure from foreign competition because UK goods would become expensive relative to imported goods. The resulting fall in demand for UK goods would open up a recessionary gap, and this is one channel through which the restrictive monetary policy is transmitted to the rest of the economy. This is discussed further in Chapter 25.

The two recessions in the United Kingdom in the early 1980s and early 1990s illustrate this mechanism at work. Both were associated with tight monetary policy and an overvalued exchange rate, although, as there were worldwide recessions at roughly the same time, domestic factors cannot be the whole story.

More recent episodes of exchange rate movements are less easy to fit with the overshooting story, and it is important to realize the overshooting is not the only reason why exchange rates can deviate from the rate that would equate purchasing power for quite long periods of time. The UK exchange rate experienced another period of overvaluation from mid-1996 until 2007. Initially, it is likely that the strength of sterling was due to the uncertainty affecting other EU currencies (especially the Deutschmark) over prospects for the creation of a single currency. Sterling was regarded as something of a 'safe haven' for investors of funds. This was reinforced by the extra credibility attached to the UK monetary policy regime once the Bank of England was given monetary policy independence in May 1997 (see Chapter 25). The strength of the pound in this period made UK exporters (and producers of import-competing goods) less competitive, and resulted in a trade deficit.

Sterling did weaken by about 20 per cent in the summer of 2007 at about the time when the financial crisis first became evident. This was probably not to do with domestic monetary policy but rather to the problems hitting the world banking system and the fact that London was a major financial centre. Indeed, it is notable that the United Kingdom, the United States, and the Eurozone were all affected substantially by the financial crisis and so there is no reason for big shifts in their relative exchange rates, though the euro was weak during the Eurozone debt crisis of 2011–12. Japan did experience a real exchange rate appreciation in 2008–9 and this may be because it had its own banking crisis much earlier.

One thing we have learned in this chapter is that the exchange rate is an essential element of the transmission mechanism that turns monetary policy shocks into real shocks in an open economy under flexible exchange rates.

The balance of payments

So far we have seen how the demands for and supplies of foreign exchange determine the exchange rate. We now look in much more detail at the reasons why agents wish to buy and sell foreign exchange. Briefly, the transactions that give rise to demand and supply on the market for foreign exchange fall into two main categories: *current account transactions*—payments and receipts on account of the imports and exports of goods and services, income earned abroad by domestic residents, and transfers (such as when a foreign worker in the UK sends money back home)—and *capital and financial account transactions*—payments and receipts on account of the sales and purchases of financial and other assets. The difference between the value of purchases and sales on each of these accounts, taken individually or collectively, is referred to as the **balance of payments**. Therefore this balance can be calculated on the current account, or on the capital and financial account.

The balance-of-payments accounts had a high profile in political arguments over economic policy throughout the past century in countries such as the United Kingdom. The United Kingdom had recurring balance-of-payments problems—a tendency for payments to exceed receipts on the current and capital accounts. In the past decade or two, balance-of-payments issues have been of most concern for developing economies, though in the 2000s there was considerable concern about global imbalances, especially the deficit in the United States and China's large surplus. We discuss this further in the first case study at the end of this chapter.

We will first explain how the balance of payments is recorded, using the United Kingdom as an example, and we will then ask in what ways the balance of payments matters.

Balance-of-payments accounts

In order to know what is happening to international payments, governments keep track of the transactions between countries. The *balance-of-payments accounts* records these transactions . Each transaction, such as a shipment of exports or the arrival of imported goods, is classified according to the payments or receipts that would typically arise from it.

Transactions that lead to a receipt of payment from foreigners, such as a commodity export or a sale of a domestic asset to foreign residents, are recorded in the balance-of-payments accounts as a *credit*. As we have seen, these transactions lead to a supply of foreign exchange and a demand for sterling on the foreign exchange market. Transactions that lead to payment to foreigners, such as a commodity

Table 24.1 **The UK balance of payments, 2012 (£ million)**

	Credits	Debits	Balances
1. Current account	**672,309**	**731,519**	**−59,210**
A. Goods and services	492,810	526,111	−33,901
1 Goods	299,457	407,350	−107,893
2 Services	193,353	119,361	73,992
B Income	161,980	164,234	−2,254
1 Compensation of employees	1,124	1,272	−148
2 Investment income	160,856	162,962	−2,106
C Current transfers	17,519	40,574	−23,055
1 Central government	3,715	20,086	−16,371
2 Other sectors	13,804	20,488	−6,684
2 Capital and financial accounts	**−20,839**	**−72,831**	**51,992**
A Capital account	6,140	2,352	3,788
1 Capital transfers	4,450	1,023	3,427
2 Acquisition/disposal of non-produced, non-financial assets	1,690	1,329	361
B Financial account	−26,970	−75,183	48,213
1 Direct investment	39,365	48,250	−8,885
2 Portfolio investment	−92,489	118,756	−211,245
3 Financial derivatives (net)		−26,757	26,757
4 Other investment	26,154	-223,074	249,228
5 Reserve assets		7,642	−7,642
Total (1 + 2)	**651,479**	**658,688**	**−7,209**
Net errors and omissions			7,209

Source: *UK Balance of payments Pink Book*, ONS, 2013

import or the purchase of a foreign asset by domestic residents, are recorded as a *debit*. As we have seen, these transactions give rise to a demand for foreign exchange and a supply of sterling on the foreign exchange market.[12] In calculating the *balance*, credits are positive and debits are negative, so the overall balance is simply credits minus debits. A summary of the balance-of-payments accounts of the United Kingdom for 2012 is given in Table 24.1. Please visit the Online Resource Centre to see the latest data.

Current account

The current account is divided into three main sections. The first of these is the *goods and services* account, which has two parts. The first part relates to 'goods' trade and is often called

the **visible account**, the **trade account**, or the **merchandise account**. It records payments and receipts arising from the import and export of tangible goods, such as computers, cars, wheat, and shoes. UK imports require payments to be made to foreign residents in foreign exchange, and hence are entered as debit items on the visible account. In 2012 UK residents spent over £407 billion on buying goods imported from overseas. UK exporters earn payments in the form of either sterling that the purchaser has bought with foreign currency on the foreign exchange market or foreign exchange that the exporter must then convert into sterling on that market. Hence exports are recorded as credit items. In 2012 UK exports amounted to about £251 billion. We can see from Table 24.1 that in 2012 there was a goods trade deficit of just under £108 billion, which is the difference between the value of exports and imports.

The second part of the goods and services account is services. Trade in services covers transactions that do not involve a physical commodity (or asset) changing hands, such as insurance, banking, consulting, shipping, and

---

[12] In the Eurozone it is the payments for the Eurozone as whole vis-à-vis the rest of the world that matter for the exchange market of the euro. In this chapter we assume that external payments or receipts generate demands or supplies of foreign exchange. However, this would not be true for countries within a single currency area or for regions of a single country.

tourism.[13] Trade in services showed a surplus of around £74 billion in 2012; however, this was smaller than the deficit in goods trade, so that trade in goods and services had a (negative) balance of just under £34 billion.

The second element of the current account is the *income account*. This again has two components. The first is employee compensation. Credit items involve UK residents being paid for working for non-residents, while the debit items result from UK residents employing non-residents. The second component is investment income. Credit items involve interest and dividend income received by UK residents from assets overseas, while debits reflect similar payments to non-resident owners of assets in the UK. The income component of the current account showed a deficit of just over £2 billion in 2012.

The third element in the current account is *current transfers*. This is subdivided into central government and other transfers. An example of a central government transfer is payment of a UK old-age pension to a former UK resident now living in Spain. An Italian restaurant owner in London sending money to his mother in Milan is an example of an 'other' transfer. Current transfers contributed a deficit of around £23 billion to the UK current account in 2012, which means that the UK government and UK residents transferred more abroad than they received from abroad.

All components of the current account *other than trade in goods* are sometimes referred to as **invisibles** because you can see goods entering the country but you cannot see, for example, the services of a consultant crossing borders.

Overall, the current account of the UK balance of payments showed a negative balance (or deficit) of around £59 billion in 2012.

Capital and financial accounts

The other major component in the balance of payments is the capital and financial accounts, which record transactions related to international movements of ownership of financial assets. It is important to notice right away that the 'capital' and financial accounts do not relate to imports and exports of physical capital: trade in such things as machine tools and construction equipment is part of the *goods trade account*. Rather, the capital and financial accounts of the balance of payments relate only to cross-border movements in ownership of assets, a large part of which involves financial instruments such as ownership of company shares, bank loans, or government securities.

The entire capital and financial accounts used to be referred to just as the 'capital account', and we will continue this usage below. However, in the UK accounts shown in Table 24.1, the 'capital account' and 'financial account' are itemized separately. In the accounting conventions used today the item labelled 'capital account' is relatively insignificant.[14] The second component of the capital and financial accounts is the financial account. This is made up of four elements: direct investment, portfolio investment, other investment, and reserve assets. **Direct investment** relates to changes in non-resident ownership of domestic firms and resident ownership of foreign firms. One form of direct investment, called greenfield investment, is the building of a factory in the United Kingdom by a foreign firm—for example, the Toyota car factory near Derby. Another form of direct investment, called brownfield investment,[15] is a takeover in which a controlling interest in a firm previously controlled by residents is acquired by foreigners—such as when the American firm Ford acquired Jaguar from its domestic owners. In contrast, **portfolio investment** is investment in bonds or a minority holding of shares that does not involve legal control. Direct and portfolio investment combined is sometimes referred to as the *long-term capital* element of the capital and financial accounts.

'Other investments' is made up mainly of what are called *short-term capital flows*. These include deposits and loans intermediated by UK-based banks, and sales or purchases of short-term financial instruments, such as Treasury Bills or commercial bills. In a normal year these other investment inflows and outflows in the UK balance-of-payments accounts are large and positive, reflecting the role of the City of London as an international financial centre. 'Reserve assets' reflect changes in the official foreign exchange reserves that are held by the Bank of England.

From now on we adopt the convention that the terms 'capital flows' and 'capital account' refer to all items in the 'capital and financial accounts' of the balance of payments. UK purchases of foreign investments (which then become assets to the UK) are called a *capital outflow*. They must supply domestic currency and purchase foreign

---

[13] The symbols *X* and *IM* as used in this book refer to exports and imports of both tangible goods *and* services, but do not include payments of interest, dividends, and profits, or transfers.

[14] It is made up of 'capital transfers' and 'acquisition/disposal of non-produced, non-financial assets'. Included in the former are items such as a government investment grant to build a hospital overseas, and debt forgiveness between the UK government and an overseas government. The latter includes overseas sales or purchases of art works, patents, trademarks, or copyrights.

[15] The terms are used slightly differently in the context of, for example, house building. Here 'greenfield' building means building on what used to be agricultural or park land, while 'brownfield' means building on land that had previously had an industrial or commercial use.

exchange in order to buy the foreign investment, and so they are entered as a debit item in the UK payments accounts.[16] Foreign investment in the United Kingdom (which thereby increases UK liabilities to foreigners) is called a *capital inflow*. Because the foreign investors must sell foreign exchange and buy domestic currency it is entered as a credit (positive) item.

As shown in Table 24.1, in 2012 UK residents reduced their investments abroad by just under £74 billion, while foreigners reduced their investments in the United Kingdom by just under £21 billion. Overall there was a net capital inflow, resulting in a surplus in the capital and financial accounts of about £52 billion. This means that there was a net decrease in foreign assets (or increase in borrowing from foreigners) of £52 billion.[17]

The meaning of payments balances and imbalances

We have seen that the payments accounts show the total of receipts of foreign exchange (implying demands for sterling and supplies of foreign exchange and hence credit items) and payments of foreign exchange (implying supplies of sterling and demands for foreign exchange and hence debit items) on account of each category of payment. It is also common to calculate the *balance* on separate items or groups of items. Interest in 'the balance of payments' and its interpretation has a number of aspects, so we approach this issue in a series of steps.

The balance of payments must balance overall

The notion that the balance-of-payments accounts must balance should present no great mystery. The accounts are constructed so that this has to be true. The idea behind this proposition is quite general. Take your own personal income and spending. Suppose that you earn £100 by selling your services (labour) and you buy £90 worth of clothing. You have exports (of services/labour) worth £100 and imports (of clothing) worth £90. Your current account surplus is £10. However, that £10 surplus must be invested

in holding a financial claim on someone else. If you hold cash, it is a claim on the Bank of England; if you deposit the money in a bank, it becomes a claim on the bank, and so on.

Whichever way you look at it, the £10 you have acquired is the acquisition of an asset. It represents a capital outflow from your personal economy that is the inevitable consequence of your current account surplus. So you have a current account surplus of £10 and a capital account deficit (outflow) of £10. The main difference between your accounts and those for the UK economy as a whole is that, with the latter, payments across the foreign exchange markets are involved.[18] A country with a current account surplus in its balance of payments must, at the same time, have acquired net claims on foreigners to the same value, and this is measured as a capital outflow.

The current and capital account balances are necessarily of equal and opposite size. When added together, they equal zero.

There is one important caveat to the above statement with regard to actual official accounts. This is that while conceptually the current and capital account are defined to be equal and opposite, in practice the national income statisticians are not able to keep totally accurate records of all transactions, and hence there are always errors in measurement. This means that a balancing item, called 'net errors and omissions', is included in the balance-of-payments table. This balancing item stands for all unrecorded transactions and is defined to be equal to the difference between the measured current account and the measured capital and financial account. Therefore, in practice, it is the sum of the current account, the capital and financial accounts, and net errors and omissions that is always zero by construction.

Does the balance of payments matter?

The *balance of payments on current account* is the sum of the balances on the visible and invisible accounts. As a carryover from a long-discredited eighteenth-century economic doctrine called *mercantilism*, a credit balance on current account (where receipts exceed payments) is often called a *favourable balance*, and a debit balance (where payments exceed receipts) is often called an *unfavourable balance*. Mercantilists, both ancient and modern, hold that the gains from trade arise only from having a favourable balance of trade. This misses the point of the doctrine of comparative advantage that is explained in detail in

---

[16] Capital outflows are sometimes also referred to as *capital exports*. It may seem odd that whereas a merchandise export is a credit item on current account, a capital export is a debit item on capital account. To understand this terminology, consider the export of UK funds for investment in a German bond. The capital transaction involves the purchase, and hence the *import*, of a German bond, and this has the same effect on the foreign exchange market and the balance of payments as the purchase, and hence the import, of a German good. Both items involve payments to foreigners, and both use foreign exchange. Thus both are debit items in UK balance-of-payments accounts.

[17] Note that this figure relates only to transactions in assets. It does not account for capital gains or losses resulting from valuation changes of existing asset holdings. Thus the capital and financial accounts balance is *not* a measure of the total change in indebtedness between the United Kingdom and the rest of the world.

[18] Areas that do not have their own currency still have a balance of payments. For example, the member countries of the Eurozone have balance-of-payments accounts even though they share a common currency. We could in principle also construct balance-of-payment accounts for Wales or Scotland.

Box 24.5 Trade and modern mercantilism

Media commentators, political figures, and much of the general public often judge the national balance of payments as they would the accounts of a single firm. Just as a firm is supposed to show a profit, the nation is supposed to secure a balance-of-payments surplus on current account, with the benefits derived from international trade measured by the size of that surplus.

This view is related to the exploitation doctrine of international trade: one country's surplus is another country's deficit. Thus, one country's gain, judged by its surplus, must be another country's loss, judged by its deficit.

People who hold such views today are echoing an ancient economic doctrine called *mercantilism*. The mercantilists were a group of economists who preceded Adam Smith. They judged the success of trade by the size of the trade balance. In many cases, this doctrine made sense in terms of their objective, which was to use international trade as a means of building up the political and military power of the state, rather than as a means of raising the living standards of its citizens. A balance-of-payments surplus allowed the nation (then and now) to acquire foreign exchange reserves. (In those days the reserves took the form of gold. Today they are a mixture of gold and claims on the currencies of other countries.) These reserves could then be used to pay armies, to purchase weapons from abroad, and generally to finance colonial expansion.

People who advocate this view in modern times are called *neo-mercantilists*. In so far as their object is to increase the military power of the state, they are choosing means that could achieve their ends. In so far as they are drawing an analogy between what is a sensible objective for a business, interested in its own material welfare, and what is a sensible objective for a society, interested in the material welfare of its citizens, their views are erroneous, because their analogy is false.

If the object of economic activity is to promote the welfare and living standards of ordinary citizens, rather than the power of governments, the mercantilist focus on the balance of trade makes no sense. The law of comparative advantage shows that average living standards are maximized by having individuals, regions, and countries specialize in the things that they can produce comparatively best and then trading to obtain the things that they can produce comparatively worst. The more specialization there is, the more trade occurs.

On this view the gains from trade are to be judged by the volume of trade. A situation in which there is a *large volume* of trade but in which each country has a *zero balance* of trade can thus be regarded as quite satisfactory. Furthermore, a change in commercial policy that results in a balanced increase in trade between two countries will bring gain, because it allows for specialization according to comparative advantage, even though it causes no change in either country's trade balance.

To the business interested in private profit, and to the government interested in the power of the state, it is the *balance* of trade that matters. To the person interested in the welfare of ordinary citizens, it is the *volume* of trade that matters.

Chapter 27. It states that countries can gain from a *balanced increase* in trade because this allows each country to specialize according to its comparative advantage. The modern version of mercantilism is discussed in Box 24.5.

It would be tempting to refer to a deficit on capital account as an unfavourable balance as well. However, by now it should be clear that this would be nonsense, because a current account surplus is the same thing as a capital account deficit. Hence, it is impossible for one to be 'good' and the other 'bad'. However, this discussion does have one important implication.

The terms balance-of-payments *deficit* and balance-of-payments *surplus* must refer to the balance on some part of the payments accounts. In the United Kingdom these terms almost always apply to the current account.

A current account deficit is just as likely to be the product of a healthy growing economy as it is of an unhealthy economy. Suppose, for example, that an economy has rapidly growing domestic industries that offer a high rate of

return on domestic investment. Such an economy would be attracting investment from the rest of the world, and as a result it would have a capital account surplus (capital inflows) and a current account deficit. Far from being a sign of weakness, the current account deficit would indicate economic health. True, the economy is acquiring external debt; but if this debt is being used to finance rapid real growth, it can be repaid out of higher future output.[19]

Our study of exchange rate determination in the first part of this chapter shows how this will come about. Foreigners wish to invest in UK industries and hence demand sterling on the foreign exchange market. This bids up the price of sterling until exports fall and imports rise, or other current account changes occur, until there is a current account deficit exactly equal to the capital account surplus. Otherwise, since demand must equal supply on the foreign exchange

---

[19] 'Debt' is used here in its general sense to refer to foreign liabilities rather than in the context of debt versus equity. These external debts could be in any specific form, including equity, bonds, or bank loans.

market, the investors could not obtain the sterling they needed on that market to make their investments.

In contrast, in another economy the government may be borrowing abroad to finance foreign wars that it is unwilling to pay for by taxing its citizens. These wars produce no future increment to GDP in the way that productive investment does. Thus the foreign borrowing, and the current account deficit that is its inevitable consequence, represents a real burden on future domestic tax payers who will have to be taxed to pay interest on the foreign loans and eventually repay the principal. The import of foreign funds comes about by offering attractive interest rates to foreign lenders who buy domestic currency to invest in the home country. This demand increases the exchange rate, which reduces exports and increases imports until a current account deficit opens up equal to that capital account surplus. The excess of imports over exports provides the domestic supply of local currency in the foreign exchange market just sufficient to allow foreign investors to buy that currency to make their investment.

The existence of a current account balance-of-payments deficit tells us only that an economy's total spending on current account items exceeds its total receipts on that account and that it has a capital inflow. The existence of such a deficit is consistent both with both productive borrowing by healthy growing economies, and with unproductive borrowing to finance spending that does not add to future productive capacity.

There are some times when balance-of-payments problems are associated with crises. The causes of these differ from place to place and time to time. Some of the issues that arise are discussed in Box 24.6.

Actual and desired transactions

The discussion in this section has focused on *actual* transactions as measured in the balance-of-payments accounts. It is the actual capital inflow that must equal the actual current account deficit. However, there is no reason at all, why *desired* (or planned) current account transactions should equal desired capital account transactions. In practice, it is

---

Box 24.6 Balance-of-payments crises

Many countries have experienced crises in recent decades that have been linked to external payments problems. The Mexican crisis of 1994, the Asian crisis of 1997, the Russian crisis of 1998, the Argentinian crisis of 2001–2, and the Icelandic crisis of 2008 are but a few examples. Here, we summarize some common features of these crises and discuss who bears the costs of the adjustments necessary to deal with them.

We argued in the text that a current account deficit could be a healthy sign when it indicates that a country is borrowing from abroad to finance investment in real economic growth. But a current account deficit could be unhealthy if it involves borrowing to finance current wars or current consumption so that debts build up but there is no investment in real assets that can help repay the debt.

The most common reason for balance-of-payments crises is that potential investors in a specific economy revise their analysis of an economy's prospects and come to believe that the level of international borrowing is unsustainable. At this point, capital inflows turn into outflows as foreigners try to get their money out, and domestic residents also try to move their funds abroad. If the exchange rate is pegged by the domestic government (see Box 24.2 for a discussion of how this is done), there will be a run on official foreign exchange reserves and this will put pressure on the domestic authorities to change their monetary and/or fiscal policies. If the currency is floating, the exchange rate will fall sharply and this will lead to a sharp increase in domestic inflation.

There could be many reasons for the change in assessment of an economy that triggers a crisis. It could be political instability or the introduction of profligate government spending plans. It could be a sharp fall in the market price of the country's main export commodity. It could be a general rise in world interest rates that sharply increases the costs of servicing foreign debts.

Countries hit by such crises generally seek loans from the International Monetary Fund (IMF) that are intended to help provide finance while policies are put in place to correct the underlying problem. As a condition of the loan the IMF usually requires a significant tightening of domestic monetary and fiscal policies, which takes the form of higher interest rates, cuts in spending, and higher taxes.

Two main groups suffer from the after-effects of such crises. International banks and other investors who have lent to the country may find that the value of their investment has fallen sharply or in some cases that there is a debt default. However, the main sufferers are typically domestic residents who often suffer sharp falls in their income and wealth and may lose their jobs or their businesses. Critics of IMF policies have argued that IMF loans and the conditions attached help to bail out international investors but do little to help the adjustment pains felt by domestic residents. This is controversial, but it seems unlikely that countries suffering such crises could be better off with no source of international financial support, even if it is conceded that the handling of such crises by the IMF could be improved.

movements in the exchange rate that play a key role in reconciling actual and desired transactions (at least for a country that has its own currency and a flexible exchange rate). This is the same as in any market: what is bought must equal what is sold, which is what the balance-of-payment statistics record. But what people want to buy may not equal what others want to sell, which is what demand and supply curves tell us. When these two desires are not equal, the price—in this case the exchange rate—changes until there two are brought into equilibrium.

CASE STUDIES

1. Global imbalances and the financial crisis of 2007–8

The 2007–8 financial crisis had a huge impact on the world economy which will last at least a further decade. The causes of this crisis have been linked to big balance-of-payments deficits and surpluses that are known as *global imbalances*. Here, we use an extract from the 2009 Turner Review[20] to set out explicitly what those links are.

The global story: macro trends meet financial innovation
At the core of the crisis lay an interplay between macro-imbalances which had grown rapidly in the last ten years, and financial market developments and innovations which have been underway for about thirty years but which accelerated over the last ten to fifteen, partly under the stimulus of the macro-imbalances.

Macro-imbalances
The last decade has seen an explosion of world macro-imbalances [Figure 24.5]. Oil exporting countries, Japan, China, and some other east Asian emerging developing nations have accumulated large current account surpluses, while large current account deficits have emerged in the USA, but also in the UK, in Ireland, Spain, and some other countries.

A key driver of those imbalances has been very high savings rates in countries like China; since these high

[20] <http:// www.fsa.gov.uk/pubs/other/turner_review.pdf>

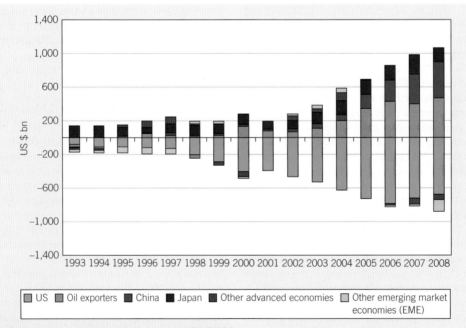

Figure 24.5 **Global current account balances, 1993-2008**
Global imbalances have grown steadily over recent decades. Virtually all of the global deficit is accounted for by the United States. Most of the global surplus is due to China, Japan, and the oil exporting countries.
Source: The Turner Review, data from IMF, FSA calculations.

savings exceed domestic investment, China and other countries must accumulate claims on the rest of the world. But since, in addition, China and several other surplus countries are committed to fixed or significantly managed exchange rates, these rising claims take the form of central bank reserves. These are typically invested not in a wide array of equity, property, or fixed income assets—but almost exclusively in apparently risk-free or close to risk-free government bonds or government guaranteed bonds.

This in turn has driven a reduction in real risk-free rates of interest to historically low levels. In 1990 an investor could invest in the UK or the US in risk-free index-linked government bonds at a yield to maturity of over 3% real; for the last five years the yield has been less than 2% and at times as low as 1%.

These very low medium- and long-term real interest rates have in turn driven two effects:

- *First, they have helped drive rapid growth of credit extension in some developed countries, particularly in the US and the UK—and particularly but not exclusively for residential mortgages—with this growth accompanied by a degradation of credit standards, and fuelling property price booms which for a time made those lower credit standards appear costless.*

- *And secondly, they have driven among investors a ferocious search for yield—a desire among investors who wish to invest in bond-like instruments to gain as much as possible spread above the risk-free rate, to offset at least partially the declining risk-free rate. Twenty years ago a pension fund or insurance company selling annuities could invest at 3.5% real yield to maturity on an entirely risk-free basis; now it would be only 1.5%. So any products which appear to add 10, 20, or 30 basis points to that yield, without adding too much risk, have looked very attractive.*

Financial market innovation

The demand for yield uplift, stimulated by macro-imbalances, has been met by a wave of financial innovation, focused on the origination, packaging, trading, and distribution of securitised credit instruments. Simple forms of securitised credit—corporate bonds— have existed for almost as long as modern banking. In the US, securitised credit has played a major role in mortgage lending since the creation of Fannie Mae in the 1930s and had been playing a steadily increasing role in the global financial system and in particular in the American financial system for a decade and a half before the mid-1990s. But from the mid-1990s the system entered explosive growth in both scale and complexity:

- *with huge growth in the value of the total stock of credit securities;*
- *an explosion in the complexity of the securities sold, with the growth of the alphabet soup of structured credit products; and*
- *with the related explosion of the volume of credit derivatives, enabling investors and traders to hedge underlying credit exposures, or to create synthetic credit exposures.*

This financial innovation sought to satisfy the demand for yield uplift. It was predicated on the belief that by slicing, structuring, and hedging, it was possible to 'create value', offering investors combinations of risk, return, and liquidity which were more attractive than those available from the direct purchase of the underlying credit exposures. It resulted not only in massive growth in the importance of securitised credit, but also in a profound change in the nature of the securitised credit model.

As securitisation grew in importance from the 1980s on, its development was lauded by many industry commentators as a means to reduce banking system risks and to cut the total costs of credit intermediation, with credit risk passed through to end investors, reducing the need for unnecessary and expensive bank capital. Rather than, for instance, a regional bank in the US holding a dangerously undiversified holding of credit exposures in its own region, which created the danger of a self-reinforcing cycle between decline in a regional economy and decline in the capital capacity of regional banks, securitisation allowed loans to be packaged up and sold to a diversified set of end investors. Securitised credit intermediation would reduce risks for the whole banking system. Credit losses would be less likely to produce banking system failure. But when the crisis broke it became apparent that this diversification of risk holding had not actually been achieved. Instead most of the holdings of the securitised credit, and the vast majority of the losses which arose, were not in the books of end investors intending to hold the assets to maturity, but on the books of highly leveraged banks and bank-like institutions.

(Source: *The Turner Review: A Regulatory Response to the Global Banking Crisis*, FSA, March 2009, Chapter 1.)

2. Asymmetric adjustment: who takes responsibility for correcting imbalances?

It has long been understood that there was an asymmetry in the pegged exchange rate system that most countries (outside the communist world) adopted after World War II. Box 24.2 discusses how a surplus country can maintain its exchange rate peg by buying foreign currency with its home currency. It builds up foreign exchange reserves in the process but there is no effective limit on how much home currency it can create. Hence, it has no constraint on maintaining its surplus if it so wishes and if the underlying economic position persists.

A deficit country, however, has no such leeway. It maintains its peg by buying up the home currency with foreign currency that comes out of its reserves. However big the reserves balances were to start with, at some point they will run out, and speculators will make them run out very fast if they think that devaluation is possible. Thus the pressure on deficit countries to adjust was much greater than that on surplus countries.

Some observers thought that the general adoption of floating exchange rates would change all this, but this is far from the case. First, some major countries, such as China have continued to peg their currency and have resisted pressure from others to let their currency appreciate, or adjust in other ways (such as stimulating domestic demand). Secondly, many small countries have found themselves under severe pressure to adjust when they had current account deficits or budget deficits or both. Greece, Ireland, Spain, and Portugal are all members of the Eurozone who found themselves under massive external pressure in 2009–10 to cut budget deficits (and/or current account deficits) as the price for obtaining external finance (or support from other Eurozone countries). Hungary, Ukraine, and the Baltic States were under similar pressure and sought assistance from the IMF. Iceland had a major crisis in 2008 as its banking system collapsed with foreign currency debts that greatly exceeded its government's foreign exchange reserves. Thirdly, some countries which had large surpluses, such as Middle East oil exporters,

received all their revenue in dollars and this would not be affected by changes in the domestic exchange rate. Fourthly, the biggest deficit country for some time was the United States and it could finance both its current account and budget deficits easily by borrowing in global markets as it was regarded as a safe haven. Hence, adjustment pressures were felt by small and weak countries but not by the major players.

There is now a new type of asymmetry in the present situation. When all countries were on fixed exchange rates, one country's surplus was another country's deficit and the deficit country had to adjust one way or another. Under the present situation some countries, such as China, can operate a fixed rate in which their currency is undervalued and hence accumulate large surpluses, while the deficit countries, such as the United States, are not on a fixed exchange rate and hence under no pressure to adjust as long as they can borrow on international markets.

The asymmetry of adjustment pressure does not just apply to current account deficits. It also applies to fiscal deficits (see Chapter 25). The 2007–8 financial crisis left many countries with large fiscal deficits at the same time as the economies concerned had high unemployment and negative GDP gaps. Worries about the size of the deficit and growing debt led many governments to raise taxes and cut spending, thus reducing demand further and increasing unemployment and the negative GDP gap. The situation could have been eased if some countries with strong fiscal positions had boosted demand and thus increased world aggregate demand. This might have raised demand even in those countries where fiscal consolidation (reducing G and/or raising T) could not have been avoided and thus helped to ameliorate the recession to some extent.

Conclusion

In our theory of the determination of GDP, net exports are a component of aggregate demand. The exchange rate (along with incomes) is a major determinant of both exports and imports. If sterling is expensive (other currencies are cheap in relation to sterling), this will reduce UK exports and increase UK imports. If sterling is cheap (other currencies expensive), this will increase UK exports and reduce UK imports. If imports and exports were the only reason for demanding and supplying sterling on the foreign exchange market, the exchange rate would tend to

its purchasing power level and trade would be in balance, with imports equal to exports. However, there are major capital flows in our globalized world and these can hold exchange rate well away from its purchasing power level. As a result, major imbalances can occur from time to time with imports either well in excess of, or well short of, exports. Some of the major problems that face policymakers as a result of these exchange rate movements are discussed in the section on stabilization policy in the Online Resource Centre.

SUMMARY

- International trade normally requires the exchange of the currency of one country for that of another. The major exception is trade within the eurozone. The exchange rate between two currencies is the amount of one currency that must be paid in order to obtain one unit of another currency.

The market for foreign exchange

- The demand for pounds arises from UK exports of goods and services, income payments from overseas, capital inflows, and the desire of foreign governments to use sterling assets as part of their reserves.

- The supply of pounds to purchase foreign currencies arises from UK imports of goods and services, income payments to overseas, capital outflows, and the desire of holders of sterling assets to decrease the size of their holdings.

- The demand curve for pounds is negatively sloped and the supply curve of pounds is positively sloped when the quantities demanded and supplied are plotted against the price of pounds, measured in terms of a foreign currency.

The determination of exchange rates

- When the authorities do not intervene in the foreign exchange market, there is a flexible exchange rate. Under fixed exchange rates the authorities intervene in the foreign exchange market to maintain the exchange rate within a specified range. To do this, they must hold sufficient stocks of foreign exchange reserves.

- Under a flexible (or floating) exchange rate regime the exchange rate is market-determined by supply and demand for the currency.

- Fluctuations in exchange rates can be understood as fluctuations around a trend value that is determined by the purchasing power parity (PPP) rate. The PPP rate adjusts in response to differences in national inflation rates. Deviations from the PPP rate are related, among other things, to international differences in interest rates.

- Exchange rates tend to overshoot their long-run equilibrium in response to shocks. A relaxation of monetary policy, which lowers domestic interest rates, will cause the exchange rate to depreciate. However, it will tend to depreciate to a point from which it can then appreciate at a rate sufficient to compensate for the interest rate fall. A rise in domestic interest rates will tend to make the exchange rate overshoot in the opposite direction (upwards).

The balance of payments

- Actual transactions among the firms, consumers, and governments of various countries are recorded in the balance-of-payments accounts. In these accounts any transaction that uses foreign exchange is recorded as a debit item, and any transaction that produces foreign exchange is recorded as a credit item. If all transactions are recorded, the sum of all credit items necessarily equals the sum of all debit items, because the foreign exchange that is bought must also have been sold.

- The two major categories in the balance-of-payments accounts are the current account and the capital and financial accounts. When we talk about a balance-of-payments surplus or deficit, we are normally referring to the current account balance alone. A balance on the current account must be matched by a balance on the capital and financial accounts of equal magnitude but opposite sign.

- There is nothing inherently good or bad about deficits or surpluses in the current account. Persistent deficits or surpluses involve a build-up or run-down of a country's net foreign assets.

TOPICS FOR REVIEW

- Foreign exchange and exchange rates
- Appreciation and depreciation
- Sources of the demand for and supply of foreign exchange
- Effects on exchange rates of capital flows, inflation, interest rates, and expectations about exchange rates
- Fixed and flexible exchange rates
- Adjustable pegs and managed floats

- Purchasing power parity
- Exchange rate overshooting.
- Balance of trade in goods and services
- Balance of income payments and transfers
- Current and capital accounts
- Mercantilist views of the balance of trade and volume of trade

QUESTIONS

1 If PPP holds and the same basket of goods that is priced at $100 in the United States costs £80 in the United Kingdom, what should be the exchange rate between the pound and the dollar?

2 Starting from the position in Question 1, if UK prices now rise by 10 per cent while US prices rise by 5 per cent, what will the new PPP exchange rate be?

3 Suppose that a camera costs $280 in the United States and £200 in the United Kingdom Ignoring travel costs, taxes, etc., where would you want to buy your camera at the following exchange rates? a) $1.5 per £, b) $1.2 per £, c) $1.60 per £, and d) $1.4 per £?

4 What is the PPP exchange rate in Question 3?

5 Where (if at all) do each of the following appear in the balance-of-payments accounts?

   a) Money earned by an Italian waiter in London that is sent to his family in Italy.

   b) A purchase by a UK resident of a house in France financed entirely by a loan from a French bank.

   c) A purchase of shares in an American company by a UK pension fund.

   d) The amount paid for an airline flight from the United Kingdom to the United States on a US airline (would it change if it were a UK airline).

6 Why is it not always true that a current account deficit indicates a weak economy?

7 What are the pros and cons of a country having a strong currency?

8 When and why do floating exchange rates tend to overshoot?

9 'Capital outflows are a bad thing for the home economy as they mean that we are investing in jobs overseas'. Critically evaluate this statement.

10 Why doesn't PPP hold in the short run?

CHAPTER 25

FISCAL AND MONETARY POLICIES

Macroeconomics was partly developed to explain why economies could experience periods of recession or high inflation and partly to explain what policies could be adopted by governments to deal with these unwanted situations. The main policy tools available are fiscal and monetary policies. The former involves the use of government spending and taxes to influence the economy, and the latter involves influencing interest rates, the exchange rate, and the money supply by the central bank. Fiscal and monetary policies can be conceived of in macroeconomics as ways of shifting the aggregate demand curve. If this was all there was to it, we would not need a whole chapter on this topic. But there are limitations and complications that need to be spelled out in both cases.

In this chapter you will learn that:

- Fiscal policy affects total government spending and taxes and not just the *G* and *T* of our macro model.

- In the past fiscal stabilization policy was focused on fine-tuning aggregate demand in order to keep the economy close to potential GDP, often referred to as full employment GDP.

- The ambitions of fiscal fine-tuning were moderated many years ago because of many difficulties associated with managing both government spending and taxes and timing their impact.

- Fiscal policy still plays some role in stabilizing the economy, but the overall goal is to balance the budget on average over the business cycle which implies having what is called a zero structural budget deficit.

- The cornerstone of monetary policy is the inflation targeting framework introduced in 1993 and reinforced in 1997 with the setting up of the independent Monetary Policy Committee which has been discussed in earlier chapters.

- Monetary policy in normal times works via the setting of a specific interest rate, known as bank rate in the United Kingdom.

- From 2009 until (at least) 2014 bank rate was set at a lower bound of 0.5 per cent and monetary policy-makers resorted to a policy of quantitative easing to try to affect aggregate demand.

- UK monetary policy decisions were for some time announced monthly without any advance warning of future intentions, but in August 2013 the Bank started to give 'forward guidance' about what changes might be coming.

Fiscal policy

Central to the Keynesian revolution in economic policy-making in the 1930s was the idea that government spending and taxation policy could be used in a counter-cyclical manner to minimize fluctuations of GDP around its potential level. The Keynesian approach continued to dominate for at least three decades after World War II. Accordingly, we discuss how changes in government taxing and spending policies might be used as tools of what

Box 25.1 UK government spending and revenue

We have had government spending and taxation in our model since Chapter 17. However the *G* and the *T* in that model are different from the concept of government spending and taxation generally used in the analysis of actual fiscal policy. *G* in the macro model includes just those elements of government spending that directly involve demand for current output. This is sometimes referred to as government consumption spending or resource-consuming government spending. *T* in the macro model is net taxes—that is, total tax revenue minus transfer payments to the private sector.

However, the fiscal position of the government normally focuses on total current spending and total receipts. Total current spending includes government consumption spending and transfer payments such as unemployment benefits and pensions. Tax revenue is the total of tax receipts and is not net of the transfers paid back to individuals. In the United Kingdom total government spending is called total managed expenditure (TME). Neither TME nor total tax revenue should be thought of as indicators of the share of the nation's output consumed by the government. The reason is that about half of TME is given to the private sector in transfer payments and thus involves, in so far as they are financed by taxes, redistribution from some citizens to others, and

so leads to either private consumption or saving on the part of the recipients .

The figure shows total managed expenditure and total tax revenue as a percentage of GDP over time between 1978–9 and 2018–19 (where the data for 2014–15 onwards are projections from the Office for Budget Responsibility (OBR) made in March 2014).

Tax revenue as a percentage of GDP has been remarkably stable since the mid-1990s but TME has swung from about 34 per cent of GDP in 2000–1 to about 47 per cent of GDP in 2009–10. The very sharp rise in TME as a percentage of GDP in 2008–9 and 2009–10 was largely due to a fall in GDP at that time, though there were some increases in spending resulting from the recession (such as higher unemployment-related benefits). This is consistent with a more general pattern that TME tends to rise (as a percentage of GDP) in recessions and fall in booms. Given the relative stability of tax revenue as a percentage of GDP, this also implies that the overall government budget deficit tends to rise during recessions and shrink during booms. The budget deficit in 2009–10 was around 11 per cent of GDP. There were also budget deficits associated with the recessions in the early 1980s and early 1990s. In contrast, there was a small budget surplus in 1988–9 and also in 1999–2000 and 2000–1.

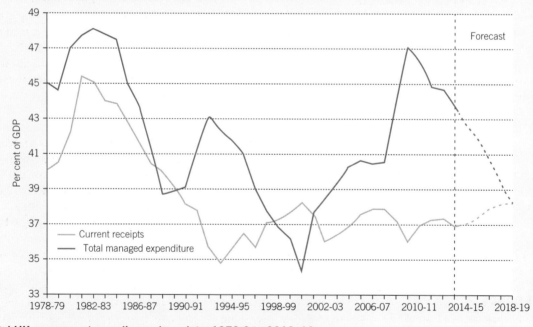

Total UK government spending and receipts, 1978-9 to 2018–19

Source: Economic and fiscal outlook, OBR, March 2014. (excludes Royal Mail and APF transfers)

is known as *fiscal stabilization policy*. Box 25.1 discusses an important measurement issue, and shows data for UK government spending and tax revenues. We discuss monetary policy later in this chapter.

Since increases in government spending raise aggregate demand and increases in taxation reduce it, the *directions* of the required changes in spending and taxation are easy to determine, once we know the direction of the desired change in GDP—cutting taxes and raising spending will tend to increase GDP, reducing any negative GDP gap, while the opposite policy changes will tend to lower it, reducing any positive GDP gap. However, the *timing*, *magnitude*, and *mixture* of the changes pose more difficult issues.

There is no doubt that the government can exert a major influence on GDP. Prime examples are the massive increases in military spending during major wars. British government spending during World War II rose from 13.4 per cent of GDP in 1938 to 49.2 per cent of GDP in 1944. At the same time the unemployment rate fell from 9.2 per cent to 0.3 per cent. Most observers agree that the increase in government spending was the major cause of the rise in GDP and the associated fall in unemployment. Similar experiences occurred during the rearmament of most European countries before, or just after, the outbreak of World War II in 1939 and in the United States during the Vietnam War in the late 1960s and early 1970s.

In the heyday of fiscal policy activism, from about 1945 to about 1970, many economists were convinced that the economy could be stabilized adequately just by varying the size of the government's taxes and spending. That day is past. Today, most economists are aware of the many limitations of fiscal policy, even though fiscal tools were used proactively in order to offset the worst effects of the 2007–8 financial crisis.

The basic theory of fiscal stabilization

A quick survey of how fiscal stabilization works will provide a useful review. The various possibilities are illustrated in Figure 25.1

A negative GDP gap

A fall in aggregate demand can open up a negative GDP gap. This gap might be removed by the normal corrective forces discussed in the section on the business cycle in Chapter 23. However, if the gap persists for some time, fiscal policy may be used instead. Government spending may be increased. Cutting the rate of VAT or personal income tax will increase the disposable incomes of households and lead to an increase in their spending. Either of these policy changes will shift the AD^* curve to the right, thus reducing or eliminating the gap.

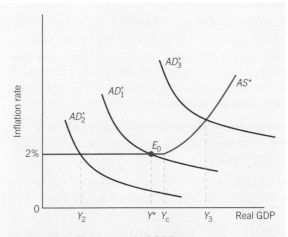

Figure 25.1 The removal of GDP gaps

Positive and negative GDP gaps may be removed by a fiscal-policy-induced shift in aggregate demand. If the initial curves are AD_2^* and AS^*, there is a negative GDP gap of $Y_2 - Y^*$. This gap can be removed by an expansionary fiscal policy that shifts the AD^* curve to AD_1^*. If the initial curves are AD_3^* and AS^* there is a positive GDP gap of $Y_3 - Y^*$. The gap can be removed by a contractionary fiscal policy that shifts the AD^* curve to AD_1^*.

A positive GDP gap

If an increase in aggregate demand pushes the economy far enough beyond potential GDP, the inflation rate will begin to rise above target. If it breaches the upper target bound, the government must act quickly to bring the rate down before inflation expectations began to rise above the 2 per cent anchor. On the fiscal side it can cut spending or raise tax rates to shift the AD^* curve to the left to interest AS^* at or near potential GDP.

The danger of over reaction

If the government underestimates the actions needed, or if the actions have less effect that expected, the gaps will persist longer than intended. If the gap is negative, the slump will last longer than hoped—a serious but not disastrous outcome. But if the gap is positive, doing too little too late risks having inflation stay above the upper target bound long enough for expectations of a continued 2 per cent inflation rate to be threatened—a very serious matter indeed.

What if the government overestimates the actions needed, or if the actions have greater effect than expected? If the GDP gap had been negative, this over-reaction risks pushing the economy into the range where the inflation rate begins to rise above target. A quick reversal will then be required for the reason discussed in the previous paragraph. If the gap had been positive, over-reaction risks turning the boom with inflationary pressure into a slump as a negative GDP gap opens up.

A key proposition

This discussion suggests that when the economy fails to adjust quickly enough on its own, or gives rise to undesirable side effects such as rising prices, there is at least a potential stabilizing role for fiscal policy. Because the actions require conscious decisions on the government's part, the policy is referred to as *discretionary fiscal policy*.

Changes in government taxes and spending shift the *AD** curve and hence can be used to remove both positive and negative persistent GDP gaps.

Furthermore, if the government is well enough informed about what is happening and can act very quickly, it might stop a contraction before it opens up a significant negative GDP gap and stop an expansion before it opens up a significant positive GDP gap.

Automatic stabilizers

The government budget surplus increases as GDP increases. This is because tax revenues rise, some transfer payments, especially unemployment-related benefits, fall, and government consumption is generally unaffected by cyclical fluctuations. Thus the budget surplus moves in the same direction as GDP. This implies that there are automatic increases in leakages as the economy expands and reductions in leakages as the economy contracts—automatic in the sense that no new government decision is needed to bring them into play .

For example, in Chapter 17 we assumed that the net income tax rate was 10 per cent. This implies that a £1 rise in autonomous spending would increase disposable income by only 90p, dampening the multiplier effect of the initial increase. Generally, the wedge that income tax places between GDP and disposable income reduces the marginal propensity to spend out of GDP, thereby reducing the size of the multiplier. The lower the multiplier, the less will equilibrium GDP tend to change for a given change in autonomous spending. The effect is to stabilize the economy, reducing the fluctuations in GDP that are caused by changes in autonomous spending. Because no policies need to be changed in order to achieve this result, the properties of the government budget that cause the multiplier to be reduced are called **automatic fiscal stabilizers.**

Many transfer payments are pro-cyclical, varying in the opposite direction as GDP varies. For example, unemployment benefits and welfare payments rise during a cyclical downswing and fall during an upswing. If every new transfer payment was made from new taxes, there would be no effect (except for a small one if the marginal propensity to spend of the those who paid the taxes was lower than the marginal propensity of those who received the transfers). However, in fact, when transfer payments rise in the downswing tax receipts tend to fall. Thus more and more of new spending by the recipients of transfer payments are injections into the circular flow of income with no offsetting withdrawals through taxes.

Even when the government does not undertake stabilization of the economy via discretionary fiscal policy, the fact that the budget deficit varies in the opposite direction to GDP means that there are fiscal effects that cause the government budget to act as an *automatic stabilizer* for the economy.

Of course, a government might try to follow a balanced budget policy, which means tying its spending in each year to the tax revenue it raises in that year. This would change the impact of fiscal policy in a major way by making it *pro-cyclical*. With a pro-cyclical fiscal policy the government restricts its spending during a recession because its tax revenue is low, and it increases its spending during a recovery when its tax revenue is rising. In other words, it moves with the economy, raising and lowering its spending in step with everyone else, exactly counter to the theory of fiscal stabilization that we have just discussed. Some politicians have proposed changing the law so that governments must balance their budget every year. However, only the most extreme fiscal conservatives call for anything more restrictive than a policy aimed at balancing the budget on average over the course of the business cycle. A budget that is balanced on average over several years, but not in any one year, will still permit the automatic stabilizer properties of the fiscal system to work.

Limitations of discretionary fiscal policy

The previous discussion might suggest that returning the economy to potential when the automatic stabilizers do not do the whole job, as they typically do not, is simply a matter of making discretionary changes in tax rates and government spending. However, many economists argue that such policies would be likely to do as much harm as good. Part of their reasoning is that the execution of successful discretionary fiscal policy is anything but simple.

Changing fiscal policy in response to GDP gaps requires changing tax rates and government spending, and this can take much time for several reasons. First, statistical data take time to collect and process, so some time passes before the size of the current gap can be discerned. This reason for delay, which implies that the government is reacting to what has happened rather than to what is happening, is known as an **information lag**.

There is a much more serious delay caused by the policy-making process itself. In the UK case the changes must be agreed upon by the Cabinet and passed by Parliament. Major changes in taxes are normally announced only once a year, in the spring Budget Statement, although 'mini-budgets' are possible if 'crisis' measures need to be taken at other times of year. In the 'Autumn Statement', usually in December, the Chancellor of the Exchequer normally announces spending plans for the succeeding three years. In the United States and most European countries, the budgetary process involves an annual round of policy proposals and legislation, though many spending programmes are for much longer horizons.

The political stakes in such changes are usually very large. Taxes and spending are called 'bread-and-butter issues' precisely because they affect the economic well-being of almost everyone. Thus, even if experts agree that the economy would be helped by a tax cut, politicians may spend a good deal of time debating *whose* taxes should be cut and *by how much*. The delay between the initial recognition of a significant positive or negative GDP gap and the enactment of legislation to change fiscal policy is called a **decision lag**.

Once policy changes are agreed upon, it may take some time before the changes are made. If it is for changes in tax rates, these can be instituted immediately once they are agreed on. But if it is for an increase in government spending, the planning and preparation for new spending, such as building roads or schools, typically takes many months. These delays are called **execution lags**.

Finally, once taxes or spending have been changed, it will usually take still more time for their economic consequences to be felt.

Because of these lags, it is quite possible that by the time a given fiscal policy decision has any impact on the economy, circumstances may have changed so that the policy is no longer appropriate.

The two main possibilities are shown in Figure 25.2. Let the original problem be caused by a persistent negative GDP gap. Let the government adopt an expansionary fiscal policy sufficient to eliminate the gap. But now assume that private sector spending recovers at the same time. This risks turning a negative GDP gap into a positive one, pushing the economy into the range where the inflation rate threatens to breach the upper target bound.

In the opposite case, there is an initial positive GDP gap. The government now alters its fiscal policy sufficiently to eliminate that gap. But assume that at the same time a reduction in private spending occurs that would have been sufficient to remove the gap on its own. Now a positive gap is turned into a negative gap and a recession results.

Note in conclusion that all these changes have been studied in a situation in which there were equilibrium positions for the economy—positions that are disturbed by single shifts in AD^*. But in fact the economy is continually changing under the types of dynamic cumulative process that we studied in the business cycle section of

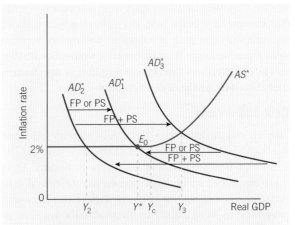

Figure 25.2 Possible perverse results of fiscal policy

Fiscal policies that are initially appropriate may become inappropriate if reinforced by unexpected shifts in private sector spending. As in Figure 25.1, if the initial curves are AD_2^* and AS^*, there is with a negative GDP gap of $Y_2 - Y^*$. As shown by the arrow labelled 'FP or PS', this gap can be removed by either an expansionary fiscal policy (FP) or a revival of private sector spending (PS) that shifts the AD^* curve to AD_1^*. But if there is a revival of private sector spending that was not anticipated by the policy-makers, both may happen at the same time, as shown by the right-pointing arrow labelled 'FP + PS'. Now the economy overshoots, opening up a positive gap of $Y_3 - Y^*$. Inflation rises above target as the economy enters the inflationary range of GDP. Also, as shown in Figure 25.1, if the initial curves are AD_3^* and AS^* there is a positive GDP gap of $Y_3 - Y^*$. The gap can be removed by either a contractionary fiscal policy or a decline in private sector spending that shifts the AD^* curve to AD_1^*. But if there is a decline in private sector spending that was not anticipated by the policy-makers, both may happen at the same time, as shown by the left-pointing arrow labelled 'FP + PS'. Now the economy overshoots, opening up a negative gap of $Y_2 - Y^*$ as the economy experiences a recession.

Chapter 23. This makes the problem of getting stabilization policy right even more complex than it must seem in the light of the difficult issues studied above.

To make matters even more frustrating, tax changes that are instituted for stabilization purposes are typically thought of as temporary measures. If there is a cut in tax rates to combat an economic slump, many tax payers will understand that tax rates will probably be returned to their pre-slump level once the negative GDP gap has been eliminated. But tax changes that are known to be temporary may be less effective than measures that are expected to be permanent. As we saw in Chapter 16, in the section entitled 'Consumption and disposable income', the permanent income and life-cycle hypotheses predict that if consumers know that a given tax cut will only last for a year or so, they may recognize that the effect on their long-run consumption possibilities is small and may adjust their short-run consumption relatively little. Instead, they may save most of what they regard as a temporary windfall or use it to retire debt accumulated in the past. The more closely household consumption spending is related to lifetime (or 'permanent') income rather than to current income, the smaller will be the effects on current consumption of tax changes that are assumed to be of short duration.

Debt and deficits

The original theory of fiscal stabilization policy held that the budget should be balanced over the cycle with deficits in slumps being covered by surpluses in booms. Thus there would be no long-term increase in total debt due to such policies. But experience showed that although many governments were willing to allow deficits to occur in slumps, they were less willing to raise taxes or cut spending in boom periods in order to produce a cyclically balanced budget. The fear that this behaviour would become habitual served to dim the willingness of many to accept the deficit half of fiscal stabilization policy.

Governments that run deficits for long periods build up substantial debts. These debts require significant tax revenues just to pay the interest, and this limits the ability of governments to spend on other programmes. As the debt rises over time, financial markets may become worried about its size and require higher interest rates before extending further credit to the government. If so, the rising interest bill further restricts the government's ability to spend on current programs. Although there is little real worry that a major country such as the United Kingdom or the United States would actually default on its debt, there is another more realistic worry. This is that the government would inflate its way out of the debt burden. As we saw in Chapter 22, if the government resorts to printing press finance to cover its spending, a major inflation will ensue. This has the effect of lowering the real burden of the government's debt at the expense of those who hold it. For example, if the price level doubles, the real purchasing power value of the debt, and hence the burden of repaying it, is halved. In the past, many governments have escaped from a seemingly impossible mountain of debt by devaluing their currency through inflation.

Box 25.2 presents data on UK public debt and debt interest for over three centuries. We look at further aspects of the UK budget position in the first case study at the end of this chapter and at the Eurozone debt crisis in the second case study.

Open economy

It used to be thought that an expansionary fiscal policy would be ineffective when the exchange rate was floating because induced exchange rate movements would cause offsetting changes in net exports. A fiscal expansion that raises GDP puts upward pressure on the home interest rate as the public tries to convert bonds into money to add to their transactions balances. Higher interest rates attract foreign capital, putting upward pressure on the exchange rate, which raises imports and lowers exports. The fall in net exports is contractionary and so offsets the original fiscal stimulus at least to some extent.[1] However, this sequence of events only occurs if the Bank holds the money supply constant and allows the interest rate to be determined by market forces. But today the Bank sets the interest rate and allows the money supply to be determined endogenously. When the increase in GDP causes the public to wish to turn bonds into money for transactions purposes, the Bank meets this demand by creating new money. There are now no offsetting international capital movements because the interest rate does not rise to attract them.

The current role of discretionary policy

In today's regime of successful inflation targeting the main role of fiscal policy is seen as contributing to the credibility of monetary policy by keeping the budget and the public debt of manageable size. If this is done, there need be no serious concern that the government will resort to printing press finance to meet a growing interest bill. This removes worry about one major cause of many past inflations and thus contributes to public confidence that the Bank will be able to maintain its low inflation target.

Fiscal gross-tuning

Although fine-tuning is no longer seriously advocated by anyone, many argue that when a negative GDP gap is large enough and persists for long enough, as did the gap that developed beginning in 2008, deliberate countercyclical fiscal policies can be effective. **Gross-tuning** refers to the occasional use of fiscal policy to remove such large and persistent GDP gaps. Policy-makers who advocate gross-tuning hold that fiscal policy can be used to push the economy towards its potential GDP when there exists a negative GDP gap that is large and persistent. The persistence of a gap allows time to overcome most or all of the lags described earlier which prevent fine-tuning from being successful. Other policy-makers argue that fiscal policy should not be used for economic stabilization under any circumstances. They argue that tax and spending behaviour should be the outcome of public choices regarding the long-term size and financing of the public sector, and should not be altered for short-term considerations. Be that as it may, most governments did resort to some discretionary gross-tuning in response to the major slump that ensued after the financial crisis of 2007–8.

---

[1] For a detailed analysis of this argument see Chapter 23 of the 12th edition which is available in the Online Resource Centre.

Box 25.2 UK government debt and debt interest

One of the main reasons why governments worry about the size of their debt is that they have to service it out of current tax revenues, and the higher the total interest bill, the more spending has to be diverted from other public services or the more taxes have to rise. This implies that governments generally wish to keep debt at manageable levels and hence they would not wish to run deficits that necessarily lead to a build-up of debt for very long periods. The Labour government of 1997–2010 initially had a target maximum ratio of public net debt to GDP of 40 per cent and managed to keep below that until the 2007–8 financial crisis.

Part (i) of the figure shows the UK public sector debt (sometimes called the national debt which is actually the debt of the central government) since the end of the seventeenth century. It is clear from the timing of big rises in debt that the main driver is wars. Debt rose to around 250 per cent of GDP after the Napoleonic Wars, over 160 per cent

of GDP at the end of World War I, and almost 240 per cent of GDP at the end of World War II.

It is not surprising that debt should rise in wartime as governments have to do whatever is necessary to avoid defeat by some foreign power. What is not so obvious from this figure is that most of this debt is owed by the central government to its own citizens, as people regard it as their patriotic duty to lend to their own government to help the war effort. The UK government was in debt to the US government at the end of the World War II, but this was a small part of the total debt.

Part (ii) shows the debt interest payments as a percentage of GDP. This had a short spike at the time of the 1715 Jacobite Rebellion. At the end of the Napoleonic Wars it amounted to 10 per cent of GDP and reached about 9 per cent of GDP after World War I, but was kept below 6 per cent of GDP after World War II. Debt interest payments were under 2 per cent of GDP in the early 2000s but had risen to around 3 per cent in 2014–15.

(i)

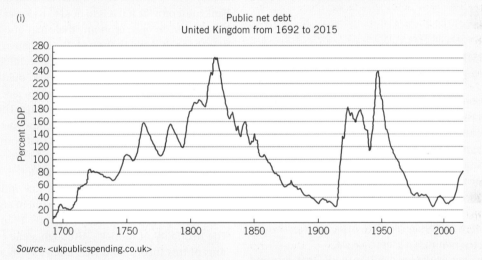

Source: <ukpublicspending.co.uk>

(ii)

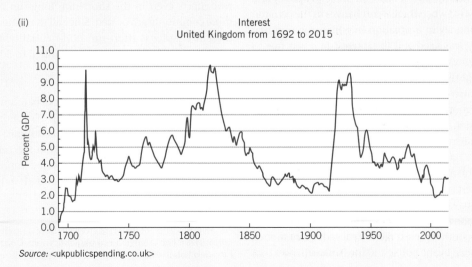

Source: <ukpublicspending.co.uk>

Monetary gross-tuning

We discuss monetary policy in detail in the next section. However, it is worth noting at this point that gross-tuning that uses the tools of monetary policy is very much with us today. As we saw in Chapter 22, central banks have typically been told to concern themselves with negative GDP gaps in so far as the measures adopted to deal with these do not cause the inflation rate to rise above the target band. This amounts to advocating qualified monetary gross-tuning. Monetary, because it uses monetary rather than fiscal tools. Qualified, in the sense that it is to be followed only when inflation is within the target band. Gross rather than fine, because it will be used only in the face of persistent negative GDP gaps. We shall see later that in the case of the persistent negative GDP gap that emerged following the financial crash of 2007–8, the Bank has not only been using its traditional method of interest rate control in an attempt to reduce the gap, but has also used the relatively novel tool of quantitative easing.

Monetary policy

In discussing monetary policy, we start from a fully expected and fully accommodated 2 per cent inflation. The Bank is expanding the money supply at 2 per cent and a monetary shock consists of changing that rate temporarily, increasing it for a positive shock and decreasing it for a negative shock.

The transmission mechanism of monetary policy

The link between the monetary and the real part of the economy is the basic channel by which monetary policy affects GDP and the price level. In Chapter 20 we termed this link the monetary transmission mechanism (MTM) and stated it as follows: *A change in the demand for or the supply of money leads to an attempt to buy or sell bonds, which causes the interest rate to change. This in turn causes a change in investment, and in all other interest-sensitive spending. This in its turn changes aggregate spending. In the new equilibrium, both the interest rate and GDP are changed.*

In that chapter, we did not mention monetary policy and analysed the MTM when there were changes in the demand or supply of money in a situation in which the nominal money supply was fixed and the interest rate was free to vary. But although monetary policy relies on the MTM, it does so in a slightly different way than described above. The method of control used by central banks is to set the interest rate. (For the moment we continue with the assumption made in Chapter 19 that all interest rates move together, so that when the Bank sets its rate longer-term rates follow, see the section in Chapter 19 entitled 'Money and bonds', later we will relax this assumption and consider the links among different interest rates in more detail.) Assume that the Bank lowers the interest rate. We saw in Chapter 19 that the demand for money depends on both the interest rate and GDP. Thus when the interest rate is reduced, more money will be demanded by the public and the Bank will meet that need by buying bonds and supplying new high-powered money. The lower interest rate affects some investment and other interest-sensitive spending, and this in turn affects aggregate demand. Then when GDP starts to rise, more money will be demanded on that account and again the Bank must provide it if it is to hold to its lower interest rate. Note that in an open economy there may also be transmission channels working through the exchange rate and net exports. Because of the lower interest rate, foreign investors will find sterling assets less attractive to hold. The movement of funds out of the United Kingdom raises the supply of sterling on the foreign exchange market. This lowers the UK real exchange rate, which in turn raises net exports.[2]

The existence of the MTM implies that both a change in the quantity of money in a world a stable price level and a change in the rate of monetary expansion in a world of a fully expected and accommodated low inflation, have effects on real variables such as investment and GDP. This raises an issue first discussed in Chapter 19 in the section 'The neutrality of money'. Although some extreme versions of this theory hold that monetary shocks have no real effects even in the short run, long-run neutrality is more commonly advocated. Since all that is needed for the present chapter is short-run non-neutrality, the debates about longer-run neutrality are confined to Box 25.3.

Targets and instruments

Some decades ago there was a major debate among economists over monetary policy. A group of economists called monetarists, led by the American economist and Nobel laureate Milton Friedman, argued that the central banks should use the high-powered money supply as their instrument of monetary policy, and that their target

---

[2] An explanation of the MTM given by the MPC itself is available at <http://www.bankofengland.co.uk/publications/Documents/other/monetary/montrans.pdf>

Box 25.3 **More on the neutrality of money**

Are there real effects when the economy is hit by a temporary monetary shock? Given a fully anticipated, fully accommodated two percent inflation, this means temporary increases in the rates of monetary expansion and inflation above 2 per cent. However, when considering neutrality theories it is simpler to study an economy with a stable price level, in which case a monetary shock means a once-and-for-all injection of new money and a temporary inflation that causes a once-and-for-all increase in the price level.

Short-run neutrality

An extreme version of neutrality states that anticipated monetary shocks have no real short-run effects. Assume a monetary shock that would raise the price level by 10 per cent. If it is perfectly foreseen, everyone will alter their prices when the shock occurs. Hence there will be no changes in relative prices and no real effects. In practice, because monetary impulses cannot be generated instantaneously, it takes real time for money to be injected into the economy, and for the effects to work out. Although these transition effects are not included in the equilibrium theories of micro economics, they are important in practice.

An increment to the money supply is typically fed into the system by the central bank buying short-term securities to drive down the short-term interest rate and increase the high-powered money supply in the hands of the commercial banks. These banks then increase lending to their customers. This increases demand in the first instance on the part of those who sell to the recipients of the new loans. Profit maximization requires that those who first gain an increase in the demand for their products should raise output (and possibly prices) even if they know that eventually the prices of everything else will rise and they will be induced to go back to their original level of output at the higher price that will be determined by the increase in the quantity of money. So all that is needed for short-run non-neutrality is that the monetary impulse is injected over a period of time, that not all agents receive the injection initially, and that it takes time to work through the economy—no one has ever identified a real economy where this is not so. Indeed, if money was neutral in the short run, the sort of monetary policy that is practised by the central banks of many countries, including the Bank of England, would be ineffective.

Long-run neutrality

A more controversial version of the doctrine of neutrality states that the monetary shocks have no real effects over the long run. Note that the effects of changes in the price level are typically only studied in macro models. Virtually all micro theory texts deal with real quantities and relative prices, while saying nothing about absolute prices or other monetary effects. Because they do not include the monetary side of the economy, they are not set up to consider the question of the possible interactions between the real and monetary sides over any run. In many major macro models money is neutral. For example, in Chapter 21 we considered a model in which there is a unique long-run equilibrium level of real GDP that is independent of the path by which that level is restored if it is departed from temporarily. Thus the amount of money determines only the level of money prices and has no effect on real equilibrium GDP. Although there is a monetary sector in these models, it is only specified in terms of macro variables. The real micro relations that, when disturbed in the short run might have long-run effects, are not included in the model.

Both of these equilibrium types of model, micro and macro, omit some key behaviour in the real economy that blurs the division between the real and the monetary sectors. The structure of the economy is continually being altered by endogenously generated changes in product, process, and organizational technologies. New products, new production processes, and new firms are to a great extent financed by credit. Thus credit conditions can alter the flow of production based on new technologies. So a once-and-for-all bout of credit contraction designed to reduce the quantity of money (or reduce its rate of growth), not matched in other countries, can restrict the flow of funds to the local firms innovating some new technology. This can give a first-entry advantage to firms in other countries and thus affect the future course of technological evolution, and hence the nature of employment, GDP, and economic growth over the foreseeable future.

There are other possible long-lasting effects of a monetary disturbance. For example, since contracts set in monetary units have various lengths to run, from weeks to many years, monetary disturbances have real effects on the distribution of income and wealth. Such effects can be long-lasting and profound. Also a phenomenon called hysteresis that we studied in Chapter 23 shows that the persistence of large negative GDP gaps, such as occur in a recession and can be induced by restrictive monetary policy, can have long-lasting effects on the labour force that can in turn affect the level of potential GDP.

For these reasons some economists, while admitting that money is neutral in the long term in many economic models, hold that it is not neutral in the real economy. They argue that the short-run behaviour that occurs over the business cycle or when the economy is hit by a monetary shock, can have long-term effects on such real macro values as potential GDP and the growth rate.

should be to keep the rate of monetary expansion equal to the rate of growth of GDP. Modern monetary policy rejects both these contentions. The main target of monetary policy is now set as keeping the inflation rate within bounds, typically as in the United Kingdom within a band of one percentage point around the target rate of 2 per cent. As to instruments, it is generally agreed that the interest rate is, and for the most part always has been, the main instrument of monetary policy.

One problem with using the money supply as the main tool of monetary policy is that although central banks can control the high-powered money supply, they cannot directly control any larger concept of the money supply such as M4. But it is that larger concept that is relevant to the *LM* curve and hence to how monetary policy is transmitted to the economy's real sector.

Note that if the Bank could control the relevant money supply, the transmission mechanism would work as it does when the interest rate is controlled. An increase in the money supply when the price level is constant, or in the rate of monetary expansion when the price level is rising at a fully expected and accommodated rate, creates an excess supply of money. The resulting purchases of bonds increases their price and lowers the interest rate. The interest rate change then does the work. The only difference between the two procedures is that generally monetary policy-makers set a short-term money market interest rate, the overnight rate in the UK, but changes in the money supply would affect the bond yield, which is a long-term rate. As mentioned earlier in this section, we assumed in Chapter 19 that the whole structure of interest rates changes in the same way. In this case changes in the short-term rate will change all other rates. But this link between the rate that the bank can set and the rate that affects investment and other interest-sensitive spending is not as mechanical as we assumed there. This difference will later help us understand both some of the limitations of modern monetary policy in affecting the real sector and also what happens with quantitative easing, as this works, in part, by expanding the money supply and affecting the yield on long-term bonds.

From stabilization to inflation targeting

By the 1980s the discrediting of fiscal fine-tuning had made monetary policy the main tool of stabilization policy. Interest rates were lowered in the face of negative GDP gaps and raised in the face of positive gaps. Then, as we have seen, under the regime of inflation targeting the Bank's main concern became to control inflation and only in so far as this was done to worry about GDP gaps. Negative GDP gaps cause no problem as they are typically associated with low inflation rates. So the Bank is free most of the time to lower interest rates in an attempt to shift the aggregate demand curve outwards, thus reducing the gap. Positive GDP gaps are typically associated with high and often rising inflation rates. So there is no conflict between the policies for lowering inflation and reducing the gap. Both call for policies that shift the aggregate demand curve to the left, lowering the positive gap and reducing inflationary pressure. However, deciding how to respond to positive supply shocks is more difficult, as a shock that raises prices will lower output and vice versa. Tightening monetary policy by raising interest rates in an attempt to control the price rise would make the output loss even worse and, in so far as supply shocks are beyond the control of the Bank, it would not help to alleviate the inflationary pressures.

Any fiscal gross tuning by government in the face of a large and persistent gap will assist monetary policy because it will also work in the direction of reducing both kinds of gap. On the one hand, monetary policy has some advantages over fiscal policy. Although the information lag is the same, the other two lags are much shorter. Policy can be changed frequently. Today the UK Monetary Policy Committee, which sets monetary policy for the Bank, meets every month, the ECB meets every two weeks, and the US Federal Open Market Committee meets every six weeks (but can react more quickly if necessary via a video conference). The execution lag is even shorter. Once a policy decision has been made, interest rates can be changed within minutes of the decision being taken. On the other hand, monetary policy is subject to another time lag due to slow reactions of interest-sensitive spending. The full effects of any policy-induced change in interest rates takes a long time to be felt. The traditional rule of thumb was that a change in monetary policy today takes about a year to have its maximum impact on output and a further year to have its maximum impact on the inflation rate. Lags of this magnitude are still considered by monetary policy-makers to be plausible today.

Also, as we saw in Chapter 22, there is some uncertainty about the level of GDP at which inflationary pressures will begin to mount, forcing the Bank to adopt a contractionary monetary policy. In the model of Chapter 21, this occurs at potential GDP. In the model of Chapter 22 it occurs at a somewhat higher GDP, denoted there by Y_c. Since the establishment of the regime of inflation targeting there has been no experience of rising inflation due to a positive GDP gap (as opposed to being due to external supply-side shocks which have occurred). Thus, no one quite knows when an expansion will begin to generate such pressures. This uncertainty calls for a cautious expansion as GDP approaches or even slightly exceeds potential. Then it will be a matter of feeling one's way into the area between a stable and a rising inflation rate.

Implementation of monetary policy

How is monetary policy implemented by the Bank of England in the United Kingdom? Here, we discuss the arrangements in normal times and then discuss the special measures adopted in response to the recent financial crisis and recession. To repeat: in the United Kingdom the main objective of monetary policy is to control inflation, and this is done in normal times by setting a specific short-term interest rate that then influences other sterling interest rates. The same is also generally true of other central banks in the major industrial countries. The institutional details vary from place to place, and they are also likely to change in small ways from time to time. Indeed, the arrangements we describe were only introduced in the United Kingdom in 1997.

The Bank of England

The Bank of England started life as a privately owned joint-stock company, but in 1946 it was nationalized. From 1946 to 1997 the Bank had a key role in implementing monetary policy, but the decisions about policy were all taken by the elected government of the day in the person of the Chancellor of the Exchequer. However, in May 1997 the incoming Labour government decided to delegate the power to set interest rates to the Bank of England with effect from June 1997, and the new arrangements were embodied in the Bank of England Act of 1998. This formally established the Monetary Policy Committee and the framework within which it operates. First, we outline the make-up and procedures of this committee, then we explain what it tries to achieve, and finally we describe how its interest rate decisions are transmitted to financial markets.

The Monetary Policy Committee

Up until now we have not separated the body that sets monetary policy and the body that carries it out, referring to them jointly as 'the Bank'. To consider monetary policy in detail we need to distinguish the two. The Monetary Policy Committee (MPC) that sets policy for the bank to carry out is made up of nine members. Five of these are senior Bank of England officials and four are outsiders appointed by the Chancellor of the Exchequer. The Governor of the Bank of England chairs the committee. The outside members are each appointed for a three-year period, while the term of the Bank insiders depends upon the length of their Bank contract.[3]

The MPC meets formally to set interest rates once every month, with announcements coming at noon on the first Thursday after the first Monday of each month. Decisions are made by a simple majority vote, with the Governor

having a casting vote in the event of a tie. Prior to making this decision, the MPC has three days of meetings to evaluate the latest data on the state of the economy and debate among themselves the appropriate course of action. A record of the debate is published two weeks later in the form of the minutes of the meeting.

Four times a year, the Bank also publishes its *Inflation Report*, which gives an in-depth assessment of the state of the economy. It contains the Bank's forecast of inflation and GDP growth over the succeeding three-year period. Members of the MPC are also summoned from time to time by the Treasury Select Committee of the House of Commons to answer questions about how and why they reached the decisions they did on monetary policy in the past.

The monetary policy set-up in the United States and the Eurozone is outlined in Box 25.4.

Policy goals

The government sets the target for inflation that the MPC is meant to achieve. The target set in 1997 was to keep inflation at 2.5 per cent using RPIX as the measure of inflation targeted. RPIX is constructed by removing mortgage interest payments from the standard retail price index, the RPI. The logic of using this measure was that if inflation was expected to rise and the MPC tightened monetary policy in order to control it, this rise in interest rates would itself raise RPI but not RPIX. However, since November 2003 the target has been specified in terms of the CPI index and the target inflation rate from this time until at least 2015 was set at 2 per cent. The CPI excludes costs of owner-occupied housing and so is not affected directly by interest rate changes.

The actual inflation rate is calculated as this month's CPI divided by the CPI for the same month of the previous year minus one to make it a percentage change expressed as a decimal fraction. For example if the CPI is 110 this January and was 100 in January of last year, the inflation rate is $(110/100) - 1 = (1.1) - 1 = 0.10$, which is an inflation rate of 10 per cent expressed as a decimal fraction. This method has the advantage of eliminating seasonal factors since it compares the CPI this year with the CPI for the corresponding month of last year. However, it has the disadvantage that a single cost push that raises the CPI for one month will show up in the inflation rate for the next twelve monthly calculations. For example, let the CPI be 100 for the last twelve months. Then in January of this year let an increase in the VAT and some other cost push elements raise the CPI to 105, where it stays for the rest of the year. Now the inflation rate in January will be calculated at $(105/100) - 1 = 0.05$. This 5 per cent inflation is actually what did occur in January. But in February the calculated inflation rate will be the same since the CPI this year is still 105 while it was 100

---

[3] The Governor and two Deputy Governors have five-year contracts that are renewable.

Box 25.4 The ECB and the Fed

The European Central Bank (ECB)

The ECB runs monetary policy for the eighteen EU countries that adopted the euro in place of their former currencies.[4] The ECB is at the centre of the European System of Central Banks (ESCB), which also includes the central banks of other EU member countries but only central banks of Eurozone members have a say in ECB monetary policy. The ECB has an Executive Board of six members responsible for implementation of monetary policy decisions. The Governing Council of the ECB is responsible for taking monetary policy decisions, and it is made up of the Executive Board plus the governors of the member central banks (of the Eurozone). From its inception until January 2015, all central bank governors on the Governing Council had a vote on monetary policy decisions, but with the likely accession of Lithuania in 2015, votes will rotate. Votes will be allocated according to the size of the economy represented. The Governors from the five largest economies—currently, Germany, France, Italy, Spain, and the Netherlands—share four voting rights. The other fourteen (if Lithuania joins) share eleven voting rights. The Governors take turns to vote on a monthly rotation, but they will all be able to attend and speak at all meetings.

The Maastricht Treaty defined the primary objective of the ESCB to be 'to maintain price stability'. But 'without prejudice to the primary objective of price stability' the ESCB has to support the general economic policies of the European Union, which include a 'high level of employment' and 'sustainable and non-inflationary growth'. In October 1998 the Governing Council of the ECB decided that 'price stability shall be defined as a year-on-year increase in the Harmonized Index of Consumer Prices (HICP) for the euro area of below 2 per cent' and that the goal would be to maintain price stability according to this criterion over the medium term. The Governing Council later clarified that, in the pursuit of price stability, it aims to maintain inflation rates below, but close to, 2 per cent over the medium term. This goal has remained unchanged

through to 2014 (at least). The target of maintaining Eurozone inflation at a fraction less than 2 per cent over the medium term is likely to endure for the foreseeable future.

The ECB has both target and instrument independence but with a general objective to maintain price stability imposed by an EU treaty.

The Federal Reserve System (the Fed)

The Fed has some clear similarities with the ECB but also some differences. The Federal Reserve System is made up of twelve regional Federal Reserve Banks and the Board of Governors of the Federal Reserve System (which has seven members) located in Washington, DC. The committee that sets monetary policy is the Federal Open Market Committee (FOMC). The FOMC has twelve voting members, seven of whom are the members of the Board of Governors and hold permanent voting rights, rather like the ECB's Executive Board members on the Governing Council. The President of the New York Fed has a permanent voting right, the Presidents of the Federal Reserve Banks of Chicago and Cleveland vote every other year, and the Presidents of the other nine Federal Reserve Districts vote every third year.

The US Congress established the statutory objectives for monetary policy—maximum employment, stable prices, and moderate long-term interest rates—in a 1977 amendment to the Federal Reserve Act 1913. The FOMC does not have a formal inflation target, but inflation has clearly been an implicit target for many years and

Following its meeting in January 2012, the FOMC issued a statement regarding its longer-run goals and monetary policy strategy. The FOMC noted in its statement that the Committee judges that inflation at the rate of 2 per cent (as measured by the annual change in the price index for personal consumption expenditures, or PCE) is most consistent over the longer run with the Federal Reserve's statutory mandate. Communicating this inflation goal clearly helps keep longer-term inflation expectations firmly anchored, thereby fostering price stability and moderate long-term interest rates and enhancing the FOMC's ability to promote maximum employment.

(*Source*: <http://www.federalreserve.gov/faqs/money_12848.htm>)

---

[4] The twelve original members are France, Germany, Italy, Spain, Portugal, Belgium, the Netherlands, Luxembourg, Austria, Finland, Greece, and the Republic of Ireland. Estonia, Latvia, Slovenia, Slovakia, Malta, and Cyprus joined subsequently. Monaco, San Marino, and the Vatican have formal agreements that permit them to use the euro as their currency, and Andorra, Kosovo, and Montenegro have adopted the euro as their home currency without agreement.

---

in February last year. And so it will go, with the 5 per cent inflation rate reported for every month of this year. Then next January, the inflation rate will finally fall back to zero since the CPI for this January and for the previous January will both be 105.

The MPC has been given a target band of plus or minus 1 per cent, because it is impossible to hit an inflation target exactly. If CPI inflation turns out at more than 3.0 per cent or less than 1.0 per cent, the Governor of the Bank of England, on behalf of the MPC, has to

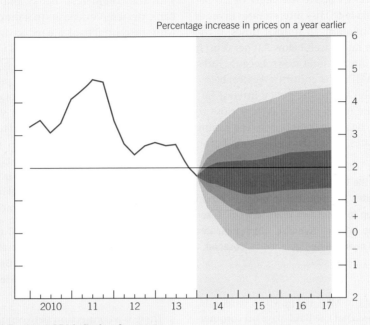

Percentage increase in prices on a year earlier

Figure 25.3 Bank of England CPI inflation forecast

The Bank of England forecasts the probability distribution of inflation for three years ahead, but aims to target inflation at the two year horizon. Each level of shading represents 30 per cent of the probability distribution. There are three bands, so the bank is 90 per cent sure that inflation will lie somewhere in the shaded area. The mean of the forecast is in the dark area at the centre of the distribution. The target inflation rate is 2.0 per cent. CPI inflation projections are based on market interest rate expectations and £375 billion purchased assets.

Source: Bank of England, *Inflation Report*, May 2014.

write an open letter to the Chancellor of the Exchequer explaining why this deviation has happened and setting out what the MPC intends to do about it. This covers the possibility that there will be unavoidable external shocks, for example a rise in the price of oil, which affect inflation in such a way that the return to low inflation will have to be managed over some time. The MPC was set up in May 1997 but the first open letter was written in April 2007, as inflation breeched its target bands for the first time. Between April 2007 and May 2014 thirteen subsequent open letters were written.[5] Because of the way that the MPC calculates the inflation rate, this does not mean that there have been thirteen separate instances in which actual inflation exceeded the bands.[6]

<hr>

[5] These are all available at <http://www.bankofengland.co.uk/monetarypolicy/Pages/inflation.aspx>

[6] Actually the MPC only make a new forecast every three months as GDP data only come out quarterly, so they also use a quarterly measure of inflation in their projections. However, letter writing (when the target is exceeded) does refer to the headline monthly inflation rate But letters are only written every three months if the target is exceeded. Thus a single price shock that caused recorded inflation to exceed target for one year would cause four letters to be written.

The MPC has been given instrument independence in that it can set the official interest rate at whatever level it thinks appropriate, but it does not have goal independence as the government determines that control of inflation will be its main goal and then sets the target rate.

Choosing an interest rate to achieve an inflation target is not a simple matter. It requires a detailed quantitative understanding of the economy's transmission mechanism. Because of time lags, the full effect of any policy change is spread over many months. This means that policy has to be forward looking. In effect, policy-makers are targeting an inflation forecast rather than current inflation, because there is nothing they can do about inflation already reported, but they can take actions that will influence inflation in the future.

Figure 25.3 shows a 'fan chart' for inflation as published in the Bank of England *Inflation Report*. This shows the Bank's estimated probability distribution of future inflation over a two-year period looking forward. The Bank estimates this range of probabilities on the basis of previous variability of inflation. Clearly, an important piece of information in the policy process is the mean of this probability distribution, which expresses the most likely outcome for the inflation rate. If the mean forecast inflation rate is significantly above the target of 2.0 per cent, the MPC will be likely to raise interest rates in order to curb the expected inflation. In normal times, if the mean forecast inflation rate is well below 2.0 per cent, it will be likely to bring interest rates down because inflation is expected to be well under control. (We deal below with the recent situation where the policy interest rate can go no lower.) If the mean forecast is very close to target, there is likely to be a fine balance between raising and lowering interest rates, with a strong likelihood of an unchanged rate.

The monetary regime in the United Kingdom is one where in normal times interest rates are adjusted in order to hit an inflation target looking up to about two years forward. A key intermediate target is the inflation forecast, which indicates whether monetary policy needs to be tightened or loosened.

Implementation

The interest rate set by the MPC is known as bank rate. This is the rate of interest that the Bank pays on commercial banks' reserve balances at the Bank of England (see the discussion of the role of bank reserves in Chapter 18).

Suppose that the MPC has decided to change bank rate. How does it act in order to make this change stick? In practice it announces the new rate to the media and it appears on Reuters and Bloomberg screens around the City at noon on the announcement day. Banks then change their base rates more or less immediately. The base rate is an interest rate set by each bank as a reference point for the loan rates charged to customers. For example, a large corporate client may be charged interest at the base rate plus 1 per cent, while a (more risky) smaller business may be charged base rate plus 4 per cent.

Why do money markets have to adjust their interest rates in this way? The reason is that they know that the Bank of England has changed the interest rate at which it will lend high-powered money to the banks as this rate is set *just above* bank rate. And they also know that *the Bank can force them to borrow from it on a regular basis*. Commercial banks will not wish to lend to their customers at a rate lower than they themselves might have to borrow. So the general level of money market rates is set by the rate at which the central bank will provide base money (cash plus bankers' deposits at the Bank of England in the UK case) to the participants in the money markets.

The Bank of England can force other banks to borrow from it because it is the monopoly supplier of high-powered money and it can conduct security sales (open-market operations) to ensure that the banks are short of cash reserves. It does this by selling treasury bills or bonds. When the public pays in cheques drawn on their accounts with the commercial banks and made payable to the Bank, the reserve deposits that the commercial banks hold with the central bank are reduced.

Suppose that the MPC wishes to raise interest rates. It announces that it will raises its official interest rate, the rate at which it will lend to the private banks. The commercial banks know that they may be forced to borrow from the Bank at this new rate. Very quickly they raise the rates at which they will lend to their customers (and borrow and lend among each other—the interbank rate). Any subsequent borrowings by the banks from the Bank of England are then at the new higher interest rate. So, the Bank of England's official interest rate, bank rate, has been passed on into other money market rates.

Interest rate decisions of the MPC are implemented by the Bank of England fixing the interest rate it pays on commercial banks' operational deposits at the Bank. This determines the interest rate at which the Bank will lend high-powered money to commercial banks.

There is a connection between the setting of bank rate and the money supply. When bank rate is high, commercial banks will be reluctant to increase their lending (and so increase the money supply) because they do not want to risk having to borrow reserves from the Bank of England. Also, there will be a lower demand for loans from the banks when loan rates are higher. When bank rate is low, banks will be more inclined to increase lending (and hence the money supply) because the penalty for having to borrow reserves from the Bank is low and demand for borrowing from the banks is high.

Monetary policy in times of crisis

In 2007–8 there was a major crisis in the financial system that began in the United States but spread to affect the United Kingdom and much of Europe. We have explained earlier that this led to a collapse of aggregate demand and the emergence of a negative GDP gap; GDP fell sharply relative to potential and unemployment rose. Since the inflation rate was well within target, the MPC was free to follow its secondary objective of reducing negative GDP gaps whenever that was consistent with meeting their primary objective of controlling inflation. In all the affected countries, monetary policy-makers responded by lowering their official interest rates.

Figure 25.4 shows the UK official bank rate (or its earlier equivalent) from 1973 to April 2014. In September 2008 bank rate was 5 per cent, but it was lowered in successive months to reach 0.5 per cent in March 2009. Once it reached this low level, the MPC did not find it practical or useful to lower it any further because some small amount above zero is a lower bound for the interest rate that the Bank can charge. The ECB and the Federal Reserve also

Changes in bank rate, minimum lending rate, minimum band 1 dealing rate, repo rate and official bank rate [1,2,3,4]

- Min lending rate
- Min band 1 dealing rate
- Repo rate
- Official bank rate

1 - Bank rate, minimum lending rate, repo rate and official bank rate are interest rates. The minimum band 1 dealing rates are discount rates.
2 - Data refer to the minimum published rate the bank discounted bills to relieve money market shortages (excludes late assistance and repurchase and sale agreements).
3 - 16.9.92, UK leaves the european exchange rate mechanism MLR set at 12%, raised to 15% (with effect from 17.9.92; never implemented).
4 - The official bank rate paid on commercial bank reserves.

Figure 25.4 UK official policy rate, 1973–2014

The institutional details of interest rate setting have changed over time and the names of the rates set have also changed, but the broad principles have not changed. Since 2006, the policy rate has been the official bank rate. This was lowered sharply at the onset of the 2008–9 recession and remained at an all-time low of 0.5 per cent until at least 2015.

Source: Bank of England

reached an effective lower bound to their policy interest rates at around the same time, but at slightly different levels of their respective rates.

Policy-makers then faced the problem that they wanted to stimulate aggregate demand further. Clearly, they could not do more by lowering their official interest rate. So what else could they do? The answer was to initiate a policy of **quantitative easing (QE)**. This involves the central bank buying large amounts of assets with money created for this purpose by the central bank itself. The vast majority of the assets purchased were UK government bonds. Such an operation is not unusual, as it is a form of open market operation that we have discussed earlier. However, what is unusual, in fact unprecedented, is that this was done on a massive scale.

QE and aggregate demand

We look at this operation in the UK context in more detail later. First, we ask how this policy might affect aggregate demand?

There are four main channels through which QE might affect aggregate demand.

Interest rates

The *IS–LM* model developed in Chapter 20 had only one interest rate—the yield on bonds. As we have seen, however, there are many different interest rates depending on the term and the riskiness of the loan. Monetary policy normally affects short-term interest rates—that is, rates on borrowing and lending in the wholesale money markets from overnight loans up to about three months. The UK policy of QE that involved mainly buying large amounts of government bonds was intended to affect the prices of these bonds and hence their yield. Thus, while policy-makers could not lower short-term rates any further than they already had done, they could lower long-term rates. Lower long-term rates would make it cheaper for companies to borrow to finance investment spending which, as we have seen, is a major component of aggregate demand.

Money supply

The central bank's purchases of bonds directly increased the money supply. When the sellers of the bonds deposited their Bank of England cheques in the commercial banks, they got an increase in their bank balances, and when the commercial banks presented these cheques to the Bank of England they received an increase in their reserve balances at the Bank. Former holders of bonds would then want to use their bank deposits to buy other assets.

Asset prices and spending

When investment institutions purchase assets such as company shares, this boosts stock market prices. Purchases of corporate bonds raise the price and lower the yields, and this will reduce the cost of capital for companies. Holders of shares and bonds feel better off as the value of their wealth will rise. This will encourage consumer spending, as consumption is positively related to household wealth.

Confidence

The fourth channel is through the confidence of both firms and households. Some of the fall in aggregate demand in a downturn comes from the uncertainty that makes both firms and households postpone spending until they are surer about how the economy is developing. Firms will not invest if they think that demand for their product may be weak. Households will hold back on spending if they are worried about their income falling or even losing their job. The proactive behaviour of the monetary authorities in implementing QE and the accompanying projections of economic recovery can increase confidence and thus encourage spending.

Quantitative easing in the United Kingdom

The first wave of quantitative easing was implemented when the Bank of England purchased £200 billion worth of bonds between March 2009 and February 2010.[7] It announced a pause at that point, but started further asset purchases in October 2011 to a total value of an additional £175 billion. The bonds purchased were mainly UK government bonds which had maturities varying from three years to over twenty-five years. There were also a small amount of corporate bond purchases in the first wave, but these only amounted to about £1.5 billion out of the £200 billion total. Figure 25.5 shows the path of the total amount purchased.

----

[7] Similar policies of substantial asset purchases were adopted in 2008–9 by the Federal Reserve for the United States and by the ECB for the Eurozone. The latest information about policy statements can be found via the internet at <http://www.bankofengland.co.uk> for the Bank of England, at <http://www.ecb.int> for the ECB, and at <http://www.federalreserve.gov> for the US Federal Reserve.

We have already discussed how quantitative easing might work to affect aggregate demand. However, it is very clear that the initiation of QE coincided with the start of a major stock market recovery. The market had fallen sharply in late 2008 and early 2009, but from March 2009, when QE started, share prices rose steadily for the next nine months or so (though with some later setbacks).

This recovery in the stock market cannot be entirely attributed to the UK policy. The Federal Reserve started a major asset purchase programme at about the same time and this helped US stock markets to recover. This alone might have had an impact on UK sentiment. However, the effects of both UK and US policies were more effective because they both acted at the same time and global stock markets generally recovered soon after. The ECB had also initiated a similar policy after reaching what it considered to be its lower bound of interest rate moves.

The global nature of the stock market recovery does not detract from the value of UK policy. We will never know what would have happened if the United Kingdom had not introduced QE when others did. What we do know is that other indicators also suggested that from March 2009 the worst of the recession was over. Consumer confidence started to stabilize and then rise, house prices stopped falling and edged up in some areas, business confidence stopped falling, and the rise in unemployment that had started early in 2008 came to a halt. Interest rates in the UK interbank market (relative to bank rate) fell steadily for the following six months, suggesting an improvement in liquidity in the wholesale money markets and a decline in worries about further bank collapses.

Thus the first wave of QE appeared to have a positive effect on the UK economy during 2009 and 2010. However, the rise in GDP came to a standstill in 2011–12, prompting the MPC to initiate a second wave of QE (often called QE2) in October 2011. The external environment was seriously affected in 2011–12 by the Eurozone debt crisis which lowered demand in Europe and dented confidence. Against this background, it is generally agreed that QE2 had less of an impact than QE1.

Forward guidance

The UK economy was still afflicted by slow growth and excess capacity in 2013, and there were estimates that GDP was still 1 or 2 per cent below potential. Up to this point in time the MPC had always announced its policy decision month by month, with no information about future intentions. However, in August 2013 when the

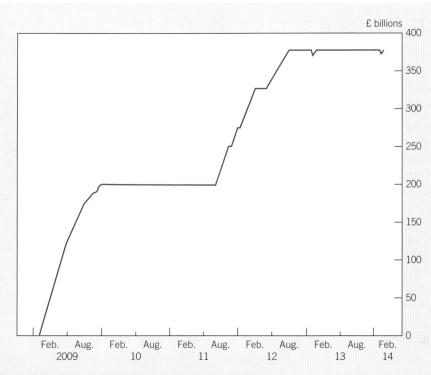

Figure 25.5 Bank of England cumulative asset purchases

The UK policy of quantitative easing started in March 2009 and largely consisted of purchases of government bonds (gilts). Between March and November 2009 the Bank bought £200 billion worth of gilts. There was then a pause. In October 2011 purchases resumed to a total value of a further £175 billion. There were no further purchases after October 2012 (at least until December 2014).

Source: Bank of England

unemployment rate was around 8 per cent, the Governor of the Bank of England, Mark Carney, introduced forward guidance by stating that the bank rate will not be raised until unemployment has fallen below 7 per cent. In line with inflation control being the Bank's prime policy, this projected policy was subject to an escape clause that would kick in if there were a sharp rise in inflation prospects.

In subsequent months, the UK economy did pick up sharply with a rise in consumer spending and business investment. Unemployment also fell to just above 7 per cent in February 2014. At this time the 7 per cent unemployment figure was dropped from the forward guidance and replaced by a statement to the effect that bank rate would not be raised while the economy continued to have excess capacity. Indeed, unemployment fell below 7 per cent in the spring of 2014 without any immediate rise in bank rate. At the time of writing (May 2014), the first rise in bank rate for several years still seemed some time ahead as the economy had yet to reveal at what level of GDP the inflation rate would begin to rise above target. Was it Y^* as in Chapter 21,

or Y_c as in Chapter 22, or some other higher level of GDP?

So how might this forward guidance help monetary policy? Clearly the intention is that it should help boost aggregate demand. We do not know for sure, but the likely channels would include: an increase in investment resulting from a boost to confidence of firms and investors who could be sure that interest rates were not about to rise; a rise in consumption spending from households who could be sure their mortgage interest rates were not about to increase; a weakening of the exchange rate as international investors realized that sterling rates of return would not be rising in the near future, thus helping net exports; and a lowering of yields on longer-term bonds as expectations of higher nominal interest rates were revised downwards. All of these factor could be expected to boost the confidence of private sector agents, causing them to increase spending and so help the recovery. How much it actually did do this will be studied for years to come, but what is obvious is that the UK economy did pick up soon after (or even before) forward guidance was first used.

CASE STUDIES

1. The UK cyclically adjusted budget deficit and fiscal policy

We have seen that the government budget deficit tends to rise in recessions and fall in booms, but we have also seen that this happens because of built-in stabilizers that respond to changes in GDP and not necessarily from discretionary changes in fiscal policy. So how are we to decide whether discretionary fiscal policy is tight or loose? The answer is by looking at the cyclically adjusted budget deficit (or surplus) which tells us what the budget deficit would be if the economy was at potential GDP. Changes in the cyclically adjusted budget balance must be due to fiscal policy stance rather than to deviations of actual GDP from potential.

The cyclically adjusted budget balance is sometimes called the *structural budget* balance, as this is what it would be if the economy was at its normal trend capacity level so that temporary cyclical influences have been removed from the measure.

Another important concept is the *primary* budget balance. This is the difference between total current spending less debt interest and total tax revenue. This includes everything that is in the actual budget balance except for payments of debt interest.

Figure 25.6 shows the projected decline of the UK cyclically adjusted budget deficit (as reported in the 2014 Budget Statement) from an actual figure in excess of 5 per cent of GDP in 2009–10 to a projected figure of cyclically adjusted budget balance by 2016–17. This does not necessarily mean a balanced budget in that year, as the economy may still be operating with a negative GDP gap. The figure also shows the *fiscal consolidation* in each financial year from 2010–11 onwards. This is the planned reduction in the budget deficit in that year as a

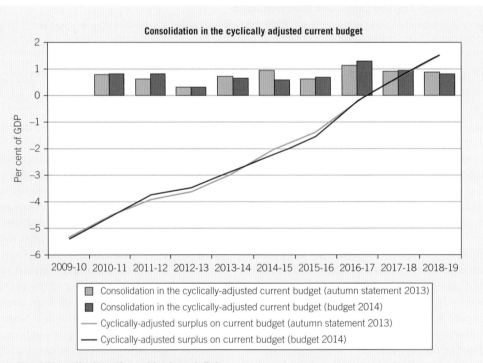

Figure 25.6 The UK cyclically adjusted budget deficit.
The cyclically adjusted budget deficit is what the deficit would be if the economy were at potential GDP. It is sometimes called the *structural budget deficit*. The lines on the chart show the cyclically adjusted budget deficit for the UK government as estimated at two different dates: the grey line is as of the Autumn Statement in December 2013 and the black line is as of the Budget in March 2014. The bars show the consolidation of this budget in specific financial years: the light green bar is as estimated in December 2013 and the dark green bar is as estimated in March 2014. According to these estimates the structural budget deficit will be eliminated in 2016–17.

Source: OBR and HM Treasury.

percentage of GDP. The two different bars for each year are the estimates in the December 2013 Autumn Statement and in the March 2014 Budget. Both show a steady tightening of fiscal policy up to at least 2018–19. What is not shown in the figure is the fact that discretionary fiscal policy had increased the budget deficit by about 2 per cent of GDP in 2008–9 and by about 3 per cent of GDP in 2009–10 in an attempt to offset some of the decline in private sector demand in those years. So discretionary fiscal policy was used to try to stabilize the economy after the financial crisis.

2. UK public sector debt

A major concern in UK fiscal policy in recent years has been the size of the public sector net debt (*net debt* is gross debt minus assets owned by the government). According to forecasts presented in the March 2014 Budget Report, the level of UK public sector net debt looks likely to peak at around 80 per cent of GDP in 2015–16 and then start to fall after that time. Chart (i) in Box 25.2 shows that this is not a very high level of debt by the United Kingdom's own historical standards, even though it is well above the 40 per cent level that the 1997–2010 Labour government set as their target (though in reality exceeded once the financial crisis hit in 2007–8).

So what level of public debt is too much? Indeed, there is no single critical number for 'too much' that applies to all countries at all times. Greece found itself in severe difficulty with a public (gross and net) debt level of around 150 per cent of GDP in 2011–12 (see the next case

study), but Japan had a gross debt of around 230 per cent of GDP in the same period without any financing problems (though its net debt was rather smaller at around 135 per cent of GDP).

A clear difference between Greece and Japan is that the latter could finance its debt at a very low interest rate while the former could not. Part of the reason for this is that Japan had very high private savings rates, so the Japanese government could borrow cheaply from its own citizens while Greece had to borrow extensively and expensively abroad. The large UK debt at the end of World War II (around 250 per cent of GDP) was also financed at low interest rates and mainly borrowed from domestic residents. Thus the proportion of the debt financed externally is also an important dimension to be considered when asking how much debt is too much.

Figure 25.7 shows projections of the net UK public debt level up to 2035–6 on the basis of two alternative assumptions. The first is an overall budget surplus of 1 per cent of GDP and the second assumes a balance on current spending but a small budget deficit that finances government investment spending (such as on roads and hospitals). Critical to these forecasts is an assumption about the future growth of GDP. Even a small budget deficit is consistent with falling net public debt as long as GDP grows faster than the deficit. Thus, a deficit of 1.4 per cent of GDP (as assumed) will be consistent with a falling debt ratio as long as GDP growth is faster than this, as it would be if it grew at its long-run trend rate of around 2.5 per cent (in constant price terms). A 1 per cent surplus on the overall budget combined with the same trend

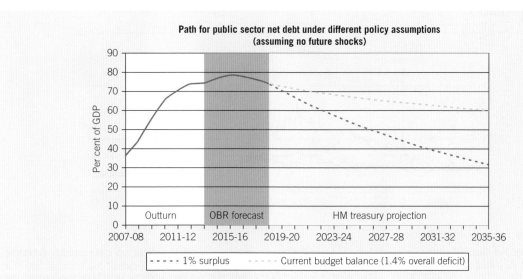

Figure 25.7 **A forecast of UK public sector debt**

The figure shows actual public sector net debt as a percentage of GDP (labelled out-turn) from 2007–8 to 2013–14, the forecasts by the Office for Budget Responsibility for 2014–15 to 2018–19, and projections by HM Treasury on two alternative assumptions up to 2035–6.

Source: HM Treasury, *Budget Report 2014*

growth of GDP brings the level of public debt back to about 40 per cent of GDP (the level in 2007–8) by 2030–1.

3. The Eurozone debt crisis

Several countries in the Eurozone experienced serious problems in financing their public debt levels in 2011–12. They had to seek loans from other Eurozone member states in order to avoid major defaults, though Greece did restructure its debt in a way that amounted to writing off some of it. This episode is relevant to the question posed in the preceding case study about how much debt is too much. It gives an example of what can happen when public debt gets so large that financing on the world markets becomes impossible. This is the type of problem that many politicians fear and, as a result, adopt a more cautious fiscal stance than may be absolutely necessary.

Prior to the 2007–8 financial crisis the debt of all Eurozone governments was regarded as equally safe (at least in the five years preceding the crisis), and so the interest rate on government debt was very similar in all member countries despite the fact that some countries, such as

Greece, had high deficits and debt levels. Low interest rates on government debt made the situation manageable even for countries with high debt levels.

The 2007–8 financial crisis made the finances of all governments deteriorate. As the GDPs declined their deficits rose and debt levels started to climb. Financial market investors started to worry about the viability of some countries' finances and the interest rate on their debt started to rise (Figure 25.8). Some governments realized that they could no longer afford to borrow in the markets as the cost of debt service would be too high. In May 2010, the IMF and EU agreed a loan to Greece. Later the same year Ireland also needed a loan, and Portugal followed in early 2011.

The initial loan to Greece turned out to be inadequate as the Greek public finances turned out to be in much worse shape than original realized and political instability affected the whole Greek economy adversely. Yields on Greek government bonds went upwards towards a peak of nearly 50 per cent as there was talk of debt default and of Greece leaving the Eurozone. With public debt of around 150 per cent of GDP, an interest rate of 50 per cent would require debt service alone of around 75 per cent of GDP, which vastly exceeds the total public spending level of any major government! So something had to give. Greece was

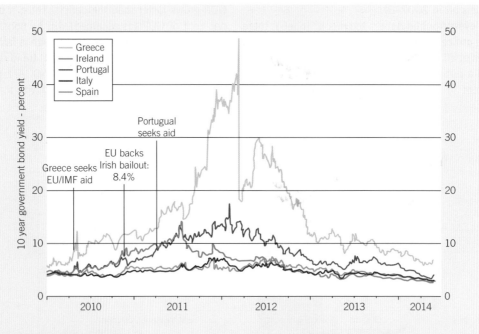

Figure 25.8 Eurozone bond yields
Before the 2007–8 financial crisis government bond yields of Eurozone member governments were all very close together, reflecting the fact that they were all denominated in the same currency and were considered equally safe. However, the financial crisis hit some countries worse than others and perceptions grew that some governments had unsustainable finances. The figure shows the course of bond yields for five countries: Greece, Ireland, Portugal, Italy and Spain. Clearly Greek yields were worst affected, followed by Portugal and Ireland.

Source: <http://graphics.thomsonreuters.com/F/09/EUROZONE_REPORT2.html>

granted a further loan by the IMF and EU on condition that drastic measures to restructure the public finances were introduced. Holders of Greek debt were also to accept a cut of over 50 per cent in the face value of their holdings of Greek government bonds, which was tantamount to a default on 50 per cent of the debt. The ratification of the loan package in February 2012 led to a sharp fall in Greek government bond yields. The financial crisis was over, though much work remained to be done to get the Greek public finances and the Greek economy back on a sustainable course.

The crises in Ireland and Portugal were of a similar nature even though their bond yields did not go quite so high. In both cases, loans from the EU and IMF bought time for fiscal policy tightening. The corrections implemented worked especially well in Ireland, which appeared to be back in a sustainable financial position by late 2012, but doubts remain about the prospects for Portugal and even more so for Greece, at least as reflected in their market bond yields.

4. You heard it here first: monetary policy in Japan

Japan was the first country in the modern era to experience the problem of wishing to stimulate aggregate demand but hitting the zero lower bound of interest rates. It took the Japanese some time to figure out what could be done in this situation; indeed, they came up with a solution similar to quantitative easing. This example helped the United States, the United Kingdom and the Eurozone monetary authorities to decide what to do when they hit the same constraint.

Japan was one of the most successful economies of the post World War II period. It experienced spectacular growth rates of real GDP in the 1950s and 1960s, which averaged nearly 10 per cent. This rapid growth moderated somewhat in the 1970s, but in the ten-year period 1979–88 Japan still had the highest average growth rate of all the major industrial countries at 3.8 per cent, compared with an average for the seven major industrial countries (the G7) of 2.9 per cent. However, in the next ten years, 1989–98, Japanese economic growth at 2.4 per cent had fallen very close to the G7 average of 2.2 per cent, as shown in Figure 25.9. Then in the period 1998–2004 Japan had the *lowest* rate of economic growth of all the major economies, and it exhibited a negative GDP gap and rising unemployment for much of this period. It also had inflation very close to zero and at some times negative. Its GDP returned to potential in 2006 and 2007, but then it was hit by the global slowdown in 2008–9.

The problems of the Japanese economy in the second half of the 1990s and early 2000s were to an important extent a product of the extreme success of the Japanese economy in the previous four decades. Rapid real growth became the norm, and expectations of continued rapid growth were built into market prices. In 1991 the Japanese stock market index peaked at around 38,000, but in

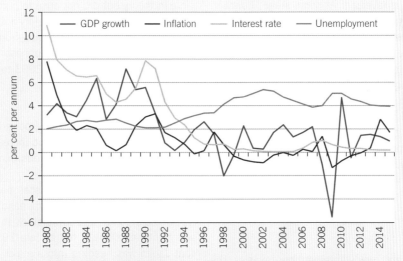

Figure 25.9 Japan 1980–2015: GDP growth, inflation, interest rate, and unemployment.
The figure shows four key indicators of the Japanese economy: GDP growth, inflation, interest rates, and unemployment. Note that the interest rate reported here is the six month Yen LIBOR and not the official discount rate. This is why this rate rises a little during the financial crisis as it is an unsecured private sector rate which includes a risk premium.

Source: IMF, *World Economic Outlook*, April 2014.

August 1998 it stood at around 15,000 and in October 2002 it was around 8,500—less than a quarter of its peak value. This collapse of share prices was mirrored in property prices, which also fell dramatically in the second half of the 1990s and early 2000s.

Asset prices are an important influence on spending decisions. We discussed the importance of wealth effects on consumer spending in Chapter 16. As wealth rose in the 1980s, Japanese consumers felt very well off, and they increased their spending on both consumer goods and property. However, a collapse of wealth had the reverse effect, causing them to cut their spending and feel increasingly cautious about the future.

Asset prices are also very important in spending decisions by companies and lending decisions by banks. Companies with high stock market values find it easier to raise more capital, and banks are happy to lend on the basis of high property values or share holdings. Banks in Japan also hold shares in companies directly, so a fall in share values affects the capital of the banks, and thereby their ability to make further loans.

Thus falling asset prices, falling spending, and loss of confidence create a process that can spiral downwards for some time. Some elements of this downward spiral are evident in any recession. However, the situation was worse than a normal cyclical recession in Japan in the late 1990s because of the abnormally large falls in asset prices. This experience was labelled by American economist Irving Fisher (1867–1947) as a situation of **debt deflation.**

The process of debt deflation will not go on for ever, but it may take the economy into a very deep or persistent recession before it is reversed. At some stage, however, goods and asset prices fall to a level so low that they appear cheap. Consumers start spending again, and firms want to invest. Once confidence returns, the interaction of the multiplier and the accelerator help to run any initial increase in spending into an upturn as the spiral starts in an upward direction.

Given the overall scenario of an economy exhibiting a large negative GDP gap, what could the Japanese authorities do to help improve the situation? The main policy tools at their disposal were the monetary and fiscal policy instruments that we have discussed earlier in this chapter.

Monetary policy

A standard monetary policy intervention involves the authorities changing the interest rate at which they will lend to the money markets. In Japan this is the official discount rate. For an economy in recession, a monetary policy reaction intended to stimulate the economy would involve lowering the interest rate.

Figure 25.9 shows that the Japanese monetary authorities did indeed lower their interest rate steadily from 1991. This was almost certainly an attempt to moderate the rise in the exchange rate, rather than to stimulate output directly, as at that time the Japanese economy was above potential GDP. However, in the late 1990s and early 2000s, when the economy was running well below potential, there was no room to lower interest rates further. At this stage the problem became a novel one, but now all too familiar. *When interest rates have already been pushed down as low as they can go, what can the monetary authorities do then in order to stimulate aggregate demand?* The answer is: not much with interest rates.

This problem was encountered during the recession of the early 1930s in the US and UK economies, and it was extensively discussed in debates associated with the Keynesian revolution. The problem was known as the **liquidity trap**. It arises when interest rates are so low that nothing else can be done to stimulate spending via even lower rates. If investors cannot be encouraged to invest when interest rates are close to zero, it is not clear what else the monetary authorities can do to increase aggregate demand.

Even if the government were simply to print more money and give it to people,[8] in a genuine liquidity trap this does not necessarily increase spending, as people can simply save the money (because of lack of confidence in the future). Keynes described this powerlessness of monetary policy in a liquidity trap as being the same as trying to move an object by 'pushing on a string'. In the post-war period most economists in the major economies had dismissed the liquidity trap as a phenomenon that was possible in theory but did not arise in practice.

However, the Japanese monetary authorities did embark on a policy of quantitative easing from March 2001 and this may have helped the Japanese recovery. Certainly there was steady growth from 2003 to 2007.

Fiscal policy

When monetary policy becomes powerless, fiscal policy is an alternative. Cuts in taxes and increases in spending by the government can create public demand where private demand is lacking.

In the 1980s Japanese fiscal policy was generally designed to reduce aggregate demand, but from 1992 to 1996 fiscal policy was stimulatory. In 1997 fiscal policy was tightened sharply, but by late 1997 it became clear that Japan was heading into a major slowdown. In April

---

[8] In practice the monetary authorities would not usually literally print money and spend it; rather, as we explained in this chapter, they would buy long-term government debt with high-powered money. This increases the liquidity of both the public and the banks with possible positive effects on spending.

1998 the Japanese government announced a package of fiscal stimuli in addition to some financial support for weak financial institutions. The net effect of the fiscal package was claimed to be a boost to demand by about 2–3 per cent of GDP, though some commentators thought that the effect would be less and the net effect did little more than reverse the tightening of the previous year. In any event the fiscal stimulus was insufficient to keep Japan from recession. The budget deficit rose to 8 per cent of GDP in 2002 but much of this was the product of lower tax revenues as output growth slowed. By 2002, government debt had reached 140 per cent of GDP, well above what is often considered prudent. So there seemed to be limited scope for further fiscal stimulus.[9]

---

[9] By 2014 this figure had reached 240 per cent of GDP, though this is the gross figure and Japan does at least have funded state pension schemes (in contrast with the UK and many other countries) so its net debt is more like 140 per cent of GDP.

The recovery of domestic and world demand that helped Japan recover in 2005 also helped bring down its budget deficit from over 8 per cent of GDP in 2003 to 5.8 per cent of GDP in 2005, but concerns remained that it would have to reduce its budget deficit much further if its government debt was to be stabilized at sustainable levels.

The 2007–8 financial crisis hit Japan hard and GDP fell while unemployment rose. It bounced back somewhat in 2010, but then settled into a further period of very slow growth and relatively high unemployment (by Japan's own historical standards). In 2013, Prime Minister Shinzo Abe launched a dramatic attempt to stimulate the Japanese economy with a further fiscal stimulus and another round of quantitative easing. He also introduced a series of structural reforms that were designed to improve the flexibility of the economy. Readers can check for themselves to see if these measures achieved the intended outcome.

Conclusion

Fiscal and monetary policies are the standard tools available for stabilizing the macroeconomy. However, worries about debt and deficits combined with practical issues of timing have limited the ambition of successive governments. Rather, the focus has shifted towards elimination of the structural budget deficit and limiting the size of public debt to manageable levels. Since the early 1990s monetary policy has successfully focused on targeting the inflation rate. In normal times monetary policy was implemented by changes in the official interest rate, now known as the official bank rate. However, after 2009 the MPC wished to raise aggregate demand but could not set bank rate any lower, so they introduced a policy of quantitative easing supported more recently by forward guidance.

SUMMARY

1. Fiscal policy

- In principle, fiscal policy can be used to stabilize the position of the AD^* curve at or near potential GDP. To remove a negative GDP gap, governments can shift AD^* to the right by cutting taxes and increasing spending. To remove a positive GDP gap, governments can pursue the opposite policies.

- Because government tax and transfer programmes tend to reduce the size of the multiplier, they act as automatic stabilizers. When GDP changes, in either direction, disposable income changes by less because of taxes and transfers.

- Discretionary fiscal policy is subject to information, decision, and execution lags that limit its ability to stabilize the economy at or near potential GDP.

Monetary policy

- Monetary policy can also be used to shift the AD^* curve.

- Monetary policy-makers can react quickly, but the impact of interest rates changes is also subject to a lag.

- Central banks are the ultimate suppliers of cash to the monetary system, and they have the power to set short-term interest rates in the money markets.

- In normal times the Bank of England uses the official bank rate as its policy instrument.

- The UK inflation target is set by the government, and the Monetary Policy Committee has been delegated the responsibility of setting monetary policy in order to keep inflation close to target.

- Quantitative easing involves the central bank buying assets and increasing the money supply.

- Forward guidance involves announcements by the MPC of the likely future course of monetary policy.

TOPICS FOR REVIEW

- Economic stabilization
- Information, decision, and execution lags
- Automatic stabilizers
- Fiscal policy
- Cyclically adjusted budget deficit
- Monetary policy
- The transmission mechanism

- Targets and instruments
- From stabilization to inflation targeting
- Bank rate
- The MPC
- Quantitative easing
- Forward guidance
- Debt deflation

QUESTIONS

1 Set out the reasons why fiscal policy was once thought to be able to offset shocks to the economy. Why is the effectiveness of fiscal policy now thought to be much more limited?

2 Explain what is meant by 'automatic stabilizers'. How do these help to reduce the amplitude of the business cycle?

3 What is the difference between $G - T$ in our macro model of Chapters 16–22 and the actual budget deficit?

4 What is the difference between: the actual budget deficit, the cyclically adjusted budget deficit, the structural budget deficit, and the primary budget deficit?

5 Explain how changes in bank rate will work to change aggregate demand.

6 How might 'forward guidance' by the Bank help to change aggregate demand?

7 Critically assess the case for monetary policy decisions being delegated to an independent committee of experts (the MPC) rather than being in the hands of elected governments. Could fiscal policy be made in the same way? If not why not?

8 Why do you think we have an inflation target of 2 per cent rather than of zero per cent?

9 Why do we not target the price level instead of the inflation rate?

10 Explain the channels through which quantitative easing might affect aggregate demand.

CHAPTER 26

ECONOMIC GROWTH AND SUSTAINABILITY

Why are some countries getting richer while others seem mired in persistent poverty? Why are we so much better off materially than our grandparents? Will our children be better off than us? Will they and their children have to face the consequences of resource exhaustion and climate change? Does growth destroy jobs? Does it make the rich richer and the poor poorer? Does it increase human happiness? These are questions about economic growth: what determines it, and its consequences. This is one of the most important topics in economics as it affects how well off people are, and how this changes over time. It also relates to the long-run sustainability of living standards.

In particular, you will learn that:

- Economic growth theory studies the determinants of the long-run trend in GDP, while macroeconomics studies fluctuations about this trend.

- Even small differences in growth rate can lead to big differences in material living standards between generations.

- The long-term growth of output depends primarily on changes in technology, which raise productivity (i.e. output per unit of input), and also on growth in inputs such as capital and labour.

- While growth has many benefits, it also brings with it significant costs and serious risks.

- Continued growth puts pressure on supplies of non-renewable resources and the environment.

- Sustainability of growth has become an important policy issue.

In this chapter we first discuss the distinction between long-term growth in the productive capacity of the economy and the cycles about that long-term trend. We then emphasize the importance of growth, and discuss the costs and benefits of economic growth. After that we outline some of the theories that economists use to understand the growth process. We deal with these first at a highly aggregated (or macro) level, and then at a more disaggregated (or micro) level. We end with a discussion of sustainability.

Background issues

We first need to consider some important background issues concerning economic growth.

Two kinds of growth

It is important to distinguish between *extensive growth* and *intensive growth*. Extensive growth relates to the growth of total GDP, whereas intensive growth is about GDP per head. Thus the former is relevant to discussions of total market size, military power, and income of the economy as a whole. The latter is relevant to understanding the real living standard of average individuals in the economy. The former tells us about the size of the cake, while the latter tells us how much cake is available for each citizen.

Trends and cycles

In Chapters 16–22 we built a model of the macroeconomy. The emphasis in that model was on explaining the deviations of actual GDP (*Y*) from potential GDP (*Y**). For all of that analysis we took the current level of *Y** as exogenously given. The macroeconomic policy we have considered so far is aimed at keeping the economy as close to potential as possible, mitigating cycles and avoiding both positive and negative GDP gaps. In this chapter we study changes in potential GDP. Indeed, the growth of GDP over the long term is the most important determinant of how our material living standards and welfare change over time and thus is one of the most important topics in economics.

The theory of economic growth seeks to explain the determinants of the long-term trend in potential GDP.

The study of fluctuations around *Y** and the study of the growth of *Y** itself are usually treated as separate subjects. This is because growth and fluctuations are to a great extent driven by different forces. The main causes of long-term growth in *Y** are such long-term supply-side factors as technical change and the growth of inputs, in particular the capital stock and the labour supply. In contrast, deviations around *Y** are to a great extent driven by short-term demand and supply shocks, the latter stemming from changes in input costs.

However, we saw in Chapter 23 that short-term fluctuations can have a significant effect on long-term growth, particularly because of hysteresis effects. The opposite is also true: long-term growth can have a significant effect on short-term cycles. This latter view was pioneered by the Austrian, and later American, economist Joseph Schumpeter. We first met his views in the macro half of this book at the outset of Chapter 23[1] and they are developed in Box 26.1. Schumpeter emphasized that long-term growth is primarily driven by periodic bursts of innovations that exploit the possibilities created by the invention of some major new technology that has widespread potential applications. According to Schumpeter, the irregular occurrence of these

---

[1] Schumpeter's views about monopoly were discussed in Chapter 7.

Box 26.1 Are economic growth and cycles related?

Economic theory is not a body of revealed truth. It is instead a set of theories, some of which are widely agreed to have strong supporting evidence and some of which are still highly controversial. The latter is the case with the theories of growth and cycles. Standard growth models assume that technological change, and the growth that it drives, proceeds at a more or less regular rate along what is called a steady-state growth path. In contrast, Schumpeterian evolutionary economics sees growth coming in spurts. First, come booms associated with the exploitation of the possibilities created by a major new technology (or small set of related technologies). Then come recessions as the advances are consolidated and obsolete technologies discarded.

Major new technologies, often called general-purpose technologies (as discussed in Chapter 11), typically begin as single-purpose technologies but eventually spread their influence over much, or even all, of the economy. A few of the many examples are the factory system, railroads, electricity, the electronic computer, and biotechnology. Computers, for example, started as single-purpose technologies to solve limited military problems during World War II (1939–1945). Over the next few decades, they were improved vastly in efficiency. This allowed their range of application to grow continually until today there are few manufactured products that are not made with the assistance of, and/or incorporate in their finished form, some type of electronic computing power. Similarly, many modern service industries make heavy use of computers and other modern information and communication technologies.

According to these theories the development of such major new technologies is associated with booms in economic activity, often financed by major expansions of credit extended by financing institutions to innovating firms and those speculating on their success. Investors become optimistic, often resulting in stock market upsurges. Eventually the major applications of these new sets of technologies are exploited and a fall-off in new investment occurs. This can trigger a downward revision of expectations, leading to a stock market decline, or even a crash and a calling in of loans. A recession is the typical result. Although undesirable on many counts, the recession has positive effects because when the economy is booming the older technologies that have been rendered obsolete by the newer ones can coexist alongside their more modern competitors. But when the downturn begins the older technologies are seen to be outmoded and are discarded in a burst. This necessary 'housecleaning' further exaggerates the downturn. Unemployment and falling output occur as major parts of the economy go into permanent decline, eventually to be fully replaced by the new rising sectors. We studied such speculative booms in the chapter on business cycles (Chapter 23).

Schumpeterian theory links the technological changes that are the major source of long-term growth with the shorter-term fluctuations of the business cycle.

major inventions is the cause of long-term cycles in the economy and of shorter-term ones as well.

In this chapter we follow the more usual procedure of looking at what can learn about long-term growth by treating it separately from shorter-term cycles. Box 26.1 gives a short introduction to the alternative view that economic growth and cycles are intimately related—a view that is developed in the branch of the subject called evolutionary economics that originated in Schumpeter's path-breaking work.

Continued long-term impact of growth[2]

Since 1885 the annual average growth rate of real output (GDP) per head of population in the UK has been around 2 per cent. Two per cent per year may not sound like much, and may not seem much from one year to the next but it has very big effects over the average person's lifetime. A 2 per cent growth rate doubles real incomes every 36 years and quadruples it every 72 years. This means that each generation has, on average, been more than twice as well off materially as its parents, and there has been, on average, a fourfold increase in material living standards during most people's lifetimes! Specifically, people living in 1965 were on average four times better off materially than those living in 1895, and those living in 2015 were four times better off than those living in 1965.

What look like quite modest annual growth rates have a powerful effect in raising material living standards over the decades because growth can go on indefinitely and its effects accumulate.

Table 26.1 illustrates the cumulative effect of what seem to be very small differences in growth rates. For simplicity, we assume that population is constant in each of these countries so that we can concentrate on per capita growth. Notice that if one country grows faster than another, the gap in their respective living standards will widen progressively. For example, if two countries start from the same level of GDP, and the first country grows at 2 per cent per year while the second grows at 1 per cent, the first country's per capita GDP will be twice that of the second country's in about 70 years. Having started from equality, the citizens of the second country will come within one lifetime to look poor and backward to the citizens of the first country.

Figure 26.1 shows the level of UK real GDP since 1885. The steady upward trend throughout this period is clearly evident. Real GDP increased more than eleven-fold between 1885 and 2018, while the population only increased by

---

[2] The concern in this chapter is mainly about growth in the established industrial countries. Growth in developing countries is discussed in the Online Resource Centre <www.oxfordtextbooks.co.uk/orc/lipsey13e>

Table 26.1 How GDP changes when growth rates differ

Year	Country (rate of growth per year)				
	A (1%)	B (2%)	C (3%)	D (5%)	E (7%)
2015	100	100	100	100	100
2025	110	122	135	165	201
2025	135	182	246	448	817
2045	165	272	448	1,218	3,312
2085	201	406	817	3,312	13,429
2115	272	739	2,009	14,841	109,660

Small differences in growth rates cause enormous differences in GDPs over even a few decades. In the year 2015 all five countries in the table have the same level of GDP (equal to 100) but they have different growth rates. Within even ten years there are large differences between the GDPs of the various countries, and by 2085, the span of one lifetime, there are massive differences. By 2085 even the country with a 2 per cent growth rate has twice the income of the country with the 1 per cent rate, while the others have vastly more.

about 75 per cent over the same time, which means that real incomes per head rose by over sixfold. The figure uses a logarithmic scale on which the long-term trend is close to a straight line. This indicates a constant long-term rate of growth, though there appears to have been a shift in trend after World War I and also after the 2007–8 financial crisis.

Shown in terms of levels of real GDP, the strong upward trend has only a few small blips around an otherwise relentless upward drift. There were periods of faster growth during the two world wars as national resources were mobilized for the war effort, and these periods were both followed by post-war recessions (periods of negative growth). Since World War II, however, growth has always been positive except for four short periods of negative growth (1974–5, 1980–2, 1991–2, and 2008–9).

While growth throughout the past 130 years has been generally positive, and this is what generates the upward drift in incomes, the annual growth rates have been quite variable. Figure 16.1 shows the same data as those that lie behind Figure 26.1 but expressed as annual growth rates. UK economic growth was extremely volatile in the interwar period. Growth has generally been positive since 1950 and has been much less variable, with most annual growth rates falling in the range of 0–5 per cent.

Catch-up growth versus growth at the technological frontier

So far we have disused the UK's growth performance, which is typical of countries that were at or near the technological frontier. This means that their production

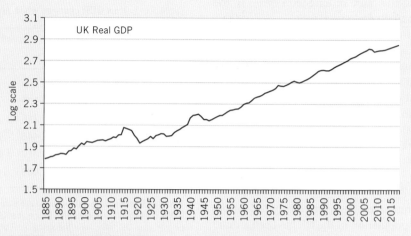

Figure 26.1 UK real GDP growth, 1885–2018

Real GDP, which measures the total production of goods and services for the whole economy over a year, has grown steadily over the past century. Long-term growth is reflected in the upward trend of real GDP. There were significant declines in real GDP after each of the world wars, there was a recession in the 1930s, and there have been four notable recessions since 1970. Otherwise the trend dominates the cycle in the long term. Data from 2014 to 2018 are IMF projections as of April 2014.

Source: 100 Years of Economic Statistics, The Economist, UK National Accounts, and IMF *World Economic Outlook*.

processes were installed using close to the most advanced techniques available, and that they were producing a bundle of goods that included some that were close to the most advanced of their type. (We stress when the processes were *installed* because, given the long life of much capital equipment, that equipment could be well within the efficiency frontier at the end of its life, even if it had been state-of-the-art when installed.) As a result, further long-term growth depends on the invention and innovation of new products, new production processes, and new forms of organization. These countries did not each have to invent the new technologies on its own. What mattered was that each had access to them when they were invented and innovated elsewhere, and adopted them with a fairly short time lag. The evidence of the last few centuries is that when growth depends on advancing the technological frontier, it proceeds at somewhere between 1 and 2.5, or at the very most, 3 per cent per year.

The second half of the twentieth century saw much higher growth rates achieved by a series of so-called catch-up countries. The four Asian tigers—Singapore, Hong Kong, South Korea, and Taiwan—were the first, followed by many others such as Brazil, Indonesia, India, and, most notably, China. These all had at one time or another sustained annual growth rates of over 5 per cent and at times close to 10 percent. As Table 26.1 shows, a growth rate of even 7 per cent doubles GDP every ten years and increases it eightfold in thirty years. Since the population was also growing in most of these countries, particularly at the

early stages of their rapid growth spurt, per capita income grew by somewhat smaller figures. Nonetheless the rise in per capita real incomes was spectacular. As can be guessed from these figures, all of these countries underwent profound social and economic changes when their GDPs grew so rapidly. In particular, there was a massive movement of people from the agricultural sector, where production was often at subsistence levels, to the industrial sector, which typically implied a move from rural to urban settings. In smaller countries the transition was more or less complete with only a small proportion of the population left on the land, while in big countries, such as China and India, the movement to the cities was large but many were still left on the land.

The important point about this experience is that such high growth rates can only be sustained while the population is abandoning old, outdated, and inefficient production methods in either manufacturing or agriculture, and adopting state-of-the-art techniques often in agriculture and manufacturing, but also in services. Such high catch-up growth rates can go on long enough to transform whole societies but they cannot be sustained once state-of-the-art techniques are being used everywhere in the country to produce state-of-the-art products. Once that happens, growth is limited by the invention and innovation of new techniques and new products, either created locally or diffused from elsewhere. As the evidence shows, this limits growth to around the 2 per cent level.

Determinants of growth

The four most important determinants of growth of the GDP are as follows.

1. *Growth in the labour force*, such as occurs when the population grows or participation rates rise.

2. *Investment in human capital*, such as formal education and on-the-job experience.

3. *Investment in physical capital*, such as factories, machines, transportation, and communications facilities.

4. *Technological change*, brought about by innovation that introduces new products, new ways of producing existing products, and new forms of organization both on the factory floor and in management.

Each of these is discussed in some detail later in this chapter.

Benefits and costs of growth

We now look at the benefits of growth, and we then consider the costs.

Benefits of growth

Growth and living standards

For those who share in it, growth is a powerful weapon against poverty. A family that is earning £25,000 a year today can expect an income of about £30,500 within ten years (in constant pounds and with no promotion) if it shares in a 2 per cent growth rate, and £37,000 if that rate is 4 per cent.

The transformation of the lifestyle of ordinary workers in advanced industrial nations over the last two centuries shows the massive improvements in living standards and quality of life that growth makes possible. In the two decades that followed the end of World War II in 1945 growth rates in advanced countries were at historically high levels of around 3–3.5 per cent. Table 26.1 shows that it makes quite a difference over 20 year whether your economy grows at 2 or 3 per cent, let alone at 3.5 per cent. When, during the late 1970s, growth fell back to its long term historical rate of around 2 per cent, at first policy-makers who had become used to the high rates thought that this was a negative deviation from what could be expected, rather than a return to the historical norm. Thus much of the recent concern over economic problems facing Europeans stems from this decline of growth in the mid-1970s and in the recessions of the early 1980s, early 1990s, and 2008–9. The real incomes of many working families grew little in the 1970s and only modestly in the 1980s, 1990s, and 2000s, partly because growth slowed in those periods and partly because the distribution of income was changing unfavourably for them. Several European countries continued to grow slowly in the 2000s and exhibited high levels of unemployment, as we saw in Chapter 23.

Growth and lifestyle

A household often finds that a big increase in its income can lead to a major change in the pattern of its consumption— that extra money buys important amenities of life. In the same way, members of society typically change their consumption patterns as their average income rises. Not only do markets in a country that is growing rapidly make it profitable to produce more cars, but also the government is led to construct more roads and to provide more recreational areas for its newly affluent and mobile citizens. At yet a higher level of income, concern about litter, pollution, and congestion may become important, and their correction may then begin to account for a significant fraction of GDP. Such 'amenities' usually become matters of social concern only when growth has ensured the provision of the basic requirements for food, clothing, and housing of a substantial majority of the population.

More subtle, but in the long term more important, are the effects of the technological changes that drive growth on the whole nation's lifestyle. Today's real incomes are five to ten times those of Victorians who lived in the second half of the nineteenth century. But we do not spend this higher purchasing power on more of what Victorians consumed; instead we buy new and better products made in new and better ways. We will return to this point later (see also Chapter 11).

The new products and production processes created by technological change transform our entire ways of living.

As a check it would be interesting to find out how many of the goods and services that you consume or use today were unknown, probably to your parents and certainly to your grandparents, when they were your age.

Growth and income redistribution

Not everyone benefits equally from growth. Many of the poorest are not even in the labour force and thus are unlikely to share in the higher wages that, along with higher profits, are the primary means by which the gains from growth are distributed. Others lose their jobs as a result of technical change, and the older ones may find it difficult to retrain for anything like as good a job as they lost. For this reason, even in a growing economy, redistribution policies will be needed if poverty and extreme hardship are to be averted.

If a constant total of GDP is redistributed, someone's standard of living will actually have to be lowered. However, when there is economic growth, and when only part of the increment in income is redistributed by the government, it is possible to reduce income inequalities while lowering everyone's real income. Since, with constant tax rates, tax revenues rise as GDP rises, when economic growth raises the incomes of households and firms, it also produces some of the extra tax revenues that governments need for redistributive purposes.

It is much easier for a rapidly growing economy to be generous towards its less fortunate citizens—or a neighbour—than it is for a static economy.

Costs of growth

Other things being equal, most people would probably regard a fast rate of growth as preferable to a slow one, but other things are seldom equal.

Opportunity costs

In a world of scarcity almost nothing is free. Growth requires heavy investment of resources in research and development, education, and capital goods. Often these investments yield no immediate return in terms of goods and services for current consumption; thus they imply that sacrifices have been made by the current generation of consumers.

Growth, which promises more goods tomorrow, is achieved by consuming fewer goods today. For the economy as a whole, this sacrifice of current consumption is an important cost of growth.

But the sacrifice is not in the form of a reduction of actual current consumption, only in what that consumption might have been. To see this, start from a zero growth position and then divert some resources to growth-creating activities. These resources will have to come from production for current use and so represent a reduction in

current living standards. But now start from an already growing economy, which is the actual case we all face. Say that this economy directs some fraction of its resources to growth-creating activities that do not produce for current consumption. Also assume that, owing to technological advances, the economy is growing at some constant rate. If growth rates are spread evenly through the economy, the outputs of goods for current consumption and of those for growth-creating activities will both be rising at the economy's growth rate. Now the sacrifice is only that production for consumption could have been higher if some of the resources directed to growth-creating activities had been transferred to production for current consumption (but at the cost of lower future growth rate).

Social and personal costs

A growing economy is a changing economy. Innovation renders some machines obsolete and also leaves some people partly obsolete. No matter how well trained workers are at age 25, in another 25 years many will find that their skills are at least partly obsolete. A rapid growth rate requires rapid adjustments, which can cause much upset and misery to the people who are affected by them. It is often argued that costs of this kind are a small price to pay for the great benefits that growth can bring. Even if this is true in the aggregate, these personal costs are very unevenly borne. Many of those for whom growth is most costly (in terms of lost jobs) share least in the fruits that growth brings. For example, the early Industrial Revolution destroyed the jobs of many skilled textile workers and created jobs for unskilled factory workers. The introduction of mass production in the early 1900s created many well-paying jobs for semi-skilled factory workers. The introduction of robots into factory assembly lines destroyed these jobs and forced many to take much lower paying jobs in the service industries, while creating jobs for a smaller number of skilled persons who handled the new robotized factories.

So growth destroys old jobs and creates new ones. Box 26.2 deals with a worry that has been expressed since the early days of the Industrial Revolution that growth may destroy more jobs than it creates, leading to long-term high unemployment for a growing body of structurally unemployed workers. So far that worry has not materialized. But nearly 250 years later it is still heard, and often in newly persuasive arguments.

Time distribution of costs and benefits

The costs of technological change tend to be borne immediately. Jobs are lost, and people trained in the old technologies lose their jobs and find their skills obsolete. The forgone consumption needed to finance the investment

Box 26.2 The end of work?

From time immemorial, people have observed that technological change destroys particular jobs and have worried that it will destroy jobs in general. Two points are important in assessing this issue.

First, technological change does destroy particular jobs. When waterwheels were used to automate the fulling of cloth in twelfth-century Europe, there were riots and protests among the fullers who lost their jobs. In 1900, half the labour force in North America and Europe was required to produce the food needed to feed the population. (The figure was a little lower in the United Kingdom because British manufactured goods were exported in return for imported foodstuffs.) Today, less than 3 per cent of the labour force is needed in the high-income countries to feed all their citizens. In other words, out of every 100 jobs that existed in 1900, 50 were in agriculture and 47 of those have been destroyed by technological progress over the course of the last century.

The second point is that new technologies create new jobs just as they destroy old ones. The displaced agricultural workers did not join the ranks of the permanently unemployed—although some of the older ones may have done, their children did not. Instead they, and their children, took jobs in manufacturing and service industries and helped to produce the mass of new goods and services that raised living standards over the century—such as cars, refrigerators, computers, foreign travel, and so on, covering a vast list of new things that did not exist in 1900.

New technologies usually require new skills. Those who are unable to retrain may suffer but their children can train appropriately from the outset.

Technological change raises living standards by destroying jobs in existing lines of production and freeing labour to produce new commodities as well as more of some existing commodities.

Modern technologies have two new characteristics that worry some observers. First, they tend to be knowledge intensive. A fairly high degree of literacy and numeracy, as well as familiarity with computers, is needed to work with many, but not all, of these new technologies. Secondly, owing to the globalizing of world markets—through falling costs of transporting goods and the new ability to coordinate their production worldwide—unskilled and semi-skilled workers in advanced countries have come into competition with similar workers everywhere else in the world. Both of these forces are decreasing the relative demand for unskilled and semi-skilled workers in developed countries. This has led to falling relative wages for the unskilled and, where

labour markets are insufficiently flexible, to some structural unemployment. From the world's point of view this globalization of the market for unskilled and semi-skilled labour has been a great benefit. It has raised billions in the less developed world from agricultural poverty to urban living standards which, although they are still low by our standards, are high by the standards of anything available to them in the past. But from the standpoint of the much smaller group of such workers in the developed nations, globalization has brought only downward pressure on wages and the reduction of relatively high paying jobs, particularly in manufacturing.

For these reasons some people blame the high unemployment rates in Europe on the new technologies. However, this is hard to reconcile with the fact that until recently the lowest unemployment rates in the industrialized countries were recorded in the United States, which is the most technologically dynamic of all countries and the one where policy-makers have worried least about the unemployment effects of new technologies. This suggests that the cause of high European unemployment rates may be not enough technological change and too much government interference in labour markets rather than too much technological change.

Over all of recorded history so far, technological change has created more jobs than it has destroyed.

Current worries centre, as to some extent they always have done, on the effect of modern technologies on future jobs. Robots have already displaced myriad workers on factory assembly lines. (Just compare a picture of a modern automobile assembly line with one taken in the 1960s.) But robots are beginning to spread into many other areas, including warfare at one extreme and the home at another. 3-D printing is beginning to do many things that workers used to do. Artificial intelligence is just beginning to come out of the science laboratory and make its impact on the commercial world. Many of these technologies threaten to replace white collar jobs of a clerical and other routine nature. That these and other similar technologies will destroy many jobs is beyond doubt. But two related questions are still subject to debate. Will sufficient new jobs become available to employ all those who are displaced? Will these jobs offer anything like the same incomes that are currently being earned by those who will be displaced? If we look only at the past, we would worry more about the second question than the first. But although extrapolating past behaviour into the future can be enlightening, there are all too many counter examples where the future surprised us all.

that embodies the new technologies happens right away. In contrast, the benefits are felt by many in the present generation and by almost everyone in the future. We are all better off for having most of the new products that were created by past technological changes, even though those who made the older competing products probably suffered when the new ones were first introduced. As a result, everyone is a beneficiary of past growth-inducing technological change—the costs have been paid and the benefits are still with us. But not everyone is a beneficiary of current change. Most benefit, but some suffer, and some of those would have been better off if the change that affected them adversely had never happened.

Negative externalities

One of the greatest recent concerns about growth has been the worry about growing greenhouse gas emissions and the resulting effect on climate change. This is not a concern about growth itself but rather about the burning of fossil fuels (such as coal and oil), which release carbon into the atmosphere, that has accompanied the industrial growth of the past century or so. Growth in some countries has also led to cutting down of forests which can no longer fulfil their natural function of absorbing carbon dioxide and releasing oxygen.

We return to this negative aspect of growth later in the chapter but for the present it is worth noting that for growth to be beneficial it must be **sustainable**, a concept that was made popular by the influential 1987 UN report on growth entitled *Our Common Future*, commonly known as the Brundtland Report. Sustainability may well require the incorporation of strategies to limit carbon emissions and preserve the environment from other negative externalities of growth.[3] It will also inevitably require the development of alternative technologies that generate energy without both the burning of fossil fuels and the release of carbon dioxide. Such alternative energy sources ... es. But ... many ... remain

Growth and happiness

Even though growth does not appear to make us any happier once we have reached a certain standard of living.[4] In the United States, for example, surveys show that the percentage of the population feeling 'very happy' was no higher

in u ... blin ... sure ... to in ... Soci ... gle ... fami ... inclu ... fami ... rivation associated with not working can be even worse.

We discussed happiness research in the first case study at the end of Chapter 4 and in Box 4.1. There, the emphasis was mainly on the links between happiness and the microeconomic concept of utility or satisfaction. Here, we want to revisit the issue of whether there is a conflict between the happiness research result that growth does not necessarily make us happier and the conclusion that growth makes us better off in definable ways.

It is clear that in many ways we are better off objectively than our ancestors. Consider just a few measurable examples. People living at the beginning of the 20th century did not have modern dental and medical equipment, penicillin, bypass operations, organ transplants, safe births, control of genetically transmitted diseases, opportunities for fast and cheap worldwide travel, affordable universities, central heating, air conditioning, computers, the internet, and social media, as well as food free from ptomaine and botulism. Detergents, washing machines, electric stoves, vacuum cleaners, refrigerators, dishwashers, and a host of other labour-saving household products have eliminated the endless drudgery that was the lot of most housewives until well into the twentieth century. Also, robot-operated, computer-controlled, modern factories have largely replaced the noisy dangerous factories that spewed coal smoke over the surrounding countryside a hundred years ago. The technological changes that drive economic growth in the long run have also eliminated or controlled the terrible diseases that maimed, crippled, and killed—plague, tuberculosis, cholera, dysentery, smallpox, and leprosy, to mention only the most common—and it has done much to control, if not yet to eradicate, AIDS and cancer. In 1700, average European life expectancy was about thirty years. In 1900, death from botulism and ptomaine poisoning from contaminated food was common. Chemical additives have virtually eliminated these killers and allow us to live long enough to worry about the long-run cancer-causing effects of some of these additives. Now they are being replaced by safer preservatives.

It is clear from this partial list that the technological changes that drive long-run economic growth have made people better off in many measurable ways.

---

[3] Some of these issues were discussed in the context of market failure and the role of government in Chapter 13.

[4] See Richard Layard *Happiness: Lessons from a New Science*, Harmondsworth: Penguin, 2005.

Nonetheless, it has not necessarily made people happier. The key here is that being better off than previous generations is different from being happier than previous generations. One of the main reasons is that people have no direct experience of what it would have been like to live 100 years ago. There is little doubt that if we were transferred back to 1900 in the same relative income position we would become less happy and would eagerly accept being transferred back to the present. But this is not a comparison that we actually make. Instead, we are more likely to judge our happiness relative to our neighbours' living standards or our own situation in the recent past, accepting without thought all the technological advances that have made us better off than our ancestors.

Before returning later in this chapter to the problems potentially caused by growth we turn now to explanations of what drives growth in the first place.

Theories of economic growth

In this section we study some of the theories of growth. One main line of theorizing uses a concept called the aggregate production function. Another line seeks to go behind that function to look at the causes of growth in a more disaggregated way. We consider those that use an aggregate function first.

The aggregate production function

The aggregate production function expresses an assumed relation between the total amounts of labour (*L*), physical capital (*K*), and human capital (*H*) that are employed[5] and the nation's total output—its GDP. Since in standard growth theory we ignore short-term fluctuations of output around its trend, the GDP in the aggregate function is to be interpreted as potential GDP. The function is written as follows:

$$\text{GDP} = f(L, K, H) \qquad (26.1)$$

This is an aggregate function because it relates the economy's total output, its GDP, to the total amount of the three main inputs that are used to produce that output. (A micro production function, such as is discussed in Chapter 5, relates the output of one firm to the inputs employed by that firm.) The function, indicated by the letter f, shows the relation between the inputs of *L*, *K*, and *H* and the output of GDP. The production function tells us how much GDP will be produced for given amounts of labour and human and physical capital that is employed. For example, the function may tell us that when 200 million units of labour per period of time, 400 million units of physical capital per period, and 100 million units of human capital per period are used, the GDP will be 4,000 million units of output per period.[6]

Two important characteristics of this aggregate function relate to what happens when a single input is varied on its own and what happens when all of them are varied in equal proportion.

Returns to a single input

To start with, suppose that the population of the country grows while the stocks of physical and human capital remain constant. More and more people go to work using the same fixed quantity of physical capital and knowledge. The amount that each new unit of input adds to total output is called its *marginal product*. The operation of the famous **law of diminishing returns** tells us that the successive employment of equal additional units of labour will eventually add less to total output than the immediately previous unit of labour. In other words, sooner or later each additional unit of labour will produce a diminishing marginal product. This is referred to as **diminishing returns to a single input**. We first met it in Chapter 5 and it is illustrated in Figure 26.2.

The law of diminishing returns applies to any input that is varied while the other inputs are held constant. Thus successive amounts of physical capital added to *a fixed supply of labour and human capital* will also eventually add less and less to GDP.

---

[5] Growth theory focuses on the production of manufactured goods and services, where, in contrast with agriculture, land is rarely a limiting factor. All the relatively small amounts of land that are needed can be obtained, and hence nothing significant is lost by ignoring land in the analysis of an industrialized economy—although this cannot be done for an agricultural economy. Of course, a service-based economy needs even less land than does manufacturing.

[6] A simple example of a production function is GDP = $z(LKH)^{1/3}$. This equation states that to find the amount of GDP produced, multiply the amount of labour by the amount of physical capital and by the amount of human capital, take the cube root, and multiply the result by the constant z. This production function has positive but diminishing returns to each factor. This can be shown, using calculus, by evaluating the first and second partial derivatives with respect to *L*, *K*, and *H* and showing that the first derivatives are positive while the second derivatives are negative. In the numerical example in the text z is taken as 20, making $20[200 \times 400 \times 100)]^{1/3} = 4,000$.

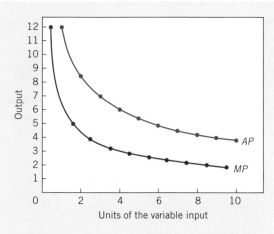

Figure 26.2 The average and marginal products of a variable input

The average and marginal products of any variable input decline as successive units of that input are added to a fixed amount of another input. This figure shows the marginal and average products of the variable input declining as more and more units of that input are used. The marginal products are plotted between the units of the variable input since they apply to a change from one amount to the next.

According to the law of diminishing returns, the increment to total production will eventually fall whenever equal increases of one variable input are combined with one or more other inputs whose quantities are fixed.[7]

Returns to scale

The three logical possibilities when all inputs are varied in equal proportion are that the output varies (i) in the same proportion (called constant returns to scale), (ii) in a larger proportion (called increasing returns to scale), and (iii) less than in that proportion (called decreasing returns to scale). For example, if all inputs are increased by 20 per cent, constant returns means that the output also increases by 20 per cent, increasing returns means that it increases by more than 20 per cent, and decreasing returns means that it increases by less than 20 per cent. We first met these scale effects in Chapter 5.

All theories that use the aggregate production function assume decreasing returns to a single input, but they vary in the assumption they make about returns to scale.

Classical growth theory

The theories of the early classical economists were important starting points in economists' thinking about growth. Although they did not explicitly use the aggregate production function, their theories were at that level of aggregation and so can be expressed in terms of aggregate functions. Also, although their theories have long been superseded, they used one important assumption that is still much heard about today—the Malthusian theory of population. Box 26.3 gives a brief outline of classical thinking about growth and Malthus' theory.

Neoclassical growth theory

What is called neoclassical growth theory was begun in a path-breaking article in 1956 by the Nobel Prize winning American economist, Robert Solow. At the time there was concern that the growth process might be unstable, easily degenerating into a cumulative slump or an explosive expansion. Using an aggregate production function that had standard properties—diminishing returns to each input on its own and constant returns to scale—Solow showed that growth could proceed along a stable path to which it would return if forced to deviate from it temporarily.

Sources of growth in the neoclassical model

Now consider each of the four main sources of growth that were listed earlier in this chapter. To begin with, we let each source operate with the others held constant.

Labour force growth

In the long term we can associate labour force growth with population growth (although in the short term the labour force can grow if participation rates rise, even though the population remains constant). As more labour is used, there will be more output and, consequently, a growth in total GDP. The law of diminishing returns tells us that, whatever the precise nature of the production function, sooner or later both the marginal and average product of labour will begin to decline. In other words, each additional unit of labour will add less and less to total output and the output per worker will also fall.[8] Although economic growth continues in the sense that total output is growing, living standards are falling in the sense that average GDP per head of population is falling. If we are interested in the growth in living standards, we are concerned with increasing GDP *per person*.

---

[7] In some production functions marginal product may rise at first and begin to decline only after a certain critical amount of the variable input is used. However, in the neoclassical constant-returns production function marginal product declines from the outset, as shown in Figure 26.2.

[8] In any production function that has constant returns to scale diminishing returns set in from the outset, so that there is no range over which population increases cause rising marginal or average product of labour. The issue of when diminishing returns set in need not concern us here, since all that matters for the text discussion is that increases in any one input, other things held constant, must eventually encounter diminishing returns.

Box 26.3 Malthus and the classical theory of growth

The early classical economists such as Adam Smith, David Ricardo, and the Reverend Thomas Malthus saw economic growth mainly in terms of capital accumulation and population growth. Since they were not concerned with what we now call human capital, we can think of their theory in terms of a production function that omits the H in eqn (26.1). Also, they considered a less aggregated version of the economy, which they divided into two sectors: agriculture, which was the predominant activity at the time, and manufacturing, which was beginning to become important. They assumed constant returns to scale in manufacturing, where land was not an important input, but diminishing returns in agriculture where land, which was fixed in supply, was an important and necessary input. These different assumptions about the production functions in agriculture and manufacturing had some interesting implications that need not concern us here since we are mainly interested in the Malthusian part of their growth theory.

Malthus's *An Essay on the Principle of Population* was published in 1798 and had an immediate impact on the thinking of many of his contemporaries (as well as on many today). Malthus argued that, left unchecked, population would grow exponentially. For example, if every couple had four children who survived to childbearing age, and if each generation was on average 25 years apart, the population would double every 25 years. This implies a sixteen-fold increase is just in one century! Malthus believed that there was no way that the food supply could keep up with such an increase in the number of mouths to feed. Thus population would be constantly pressing on the food supply and forcing living standards in agriculture to be pushed down to the subsistence level. But population would not stop growing even then. So he argued that population growth had to be checked. He distinguished two sorts of checks. *Preventative checks* were voluntary checks on births, such as late marriages (a common occurrence in Ireland in his time) and abstinence from sexual activity outside marriage. Although the checks could do something to reduce the problem of overpopulation, he was pessimistic about their full efficacy and therefore held that what he called *positive checks* would come into play—plague, famine, and pestilence.

The other classical economists accepted Malthus's analysis and incorporated it into their growth theories. The figure illustrates this. The *AP* curves show how the output of agricultural goods per worker varies as the number of workers employed in agriculture varies. Because of diminishing returns in agriculture, the curve must eventually take on a negative slope, falling as the number employed rises. The output of q_s is the subsistence output for a family. Below it, families cannot survive for long. Above it, they enjoy a living standard above subsistence.

Let the original curve be AP_0. As long as the agricultural work force is less than n_0, people are living above the subsistence level. But now Malthus's theory comes into play and the rural population expands inexorably. As the number employed increases, the average output per worker falls until it reaches the subsistence level at n_0.

Now let there be an increase in agricultural productivity due to some new invention that shifts average product curve to AP_1. For a while, living standards rise as output per head increases to q_1. But now Malthusian pressures come into play again and the population expands until it reaches n_1, the new subsistence level of employment. If it goes beyond that, the positive checks of famine and pestilence come into play, holding the employed population at n_1.

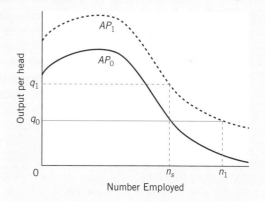

All that is now needed is to assume that the rate of technical progress in agriculture is less that the rate at which the population can increase. Then the only equilibrium is when living standards are at the subsistence level.

Classical growth theory, combined with Malthus's views on population, led to the prediction that growth could not raise living standards above subsistence except for short bursts associated with innovations. But then the inevitable population expansion would force living standards back to subsistence. This prediction contributed to the label of nineteenth-century economics as the 'dismal science' (although Carlyle, who introduced this term, first used it in a different context).

What went wrong with this pessimistic prediction? Why did the dismal science label cease to apply as the nineteenth century wore on, and become totally obsolete by the beginning of the twentieth century? Malthus and his contemporaries missed out on two key developments. First, they did not foresee that the voluntary control of births due to the growing use of contraceptive devices would limit the population growth that was

(continued)

Box 26.3 *continued*

predicted to happen every time living standards rose above subsistence. Secondly, they all underestimated the power of economic growth to be exponential rather than episodic or at best linear. We have already noted how exponential growth has raised living standards greatly over the centuries since the Industrial Revolution. However, that growth was so slow that it was not until early in the twentieth century that people saw for certain that the benefits of growth were indeed trickling down to all levels of society.

Whenever diminishing average returns apply, increases in population on their own are sooner or later accompanied by falling living standards.

Physical capital

Increases in the amount of physical capital on their own affect GDP in a manner similar to population growth alone. Eventually, each successive unit of physical capital will add less to total output than each previous unit of physical capital.

However, there is a major contrast with the case of labour growth, because it is output per person that determines living standards, not output per unit of capital. Thus, as physical capital increases, living standards increase because output is rising while the population is constant. Indeed, per capita output can be increased by adding more physical capital as long as its marginal product exceeds zero. However, since the increases in output are subject to diminishing returns, successive additions to the economy's capital stock bring smaller and smaller increases in both total and per capita output.

In the neoclassical model, the operation of diminishing returns implies that equal increases in physical capital on their own bring smaller and smaller increases in per capita GDP.

Human capital

Human capital has several aspects. One involves improvements in the health and longevity of the population. Of course, these are desired as ends in themselves, but they also have consequences for both the size and the productivity of the labour force. There is no doubt that improvements in the health of workers have increased productivity per worker-hour by cutting down on illness, accidents, and absenteeism.

A second aspect of the quality of human capital concerns technical training—from learning to operate a machine to learning how to be a scientist. This training depends on the current state of knowledge, and advances in knowledge allow us not only to build more productive physical capital, but also to create more effective human capital. Training is clearly required if a person is to operate, repair, manage, or invent complex machines. More subtly, there may be general social advantages to an educated population. Productivity improves with literacy. The longer a person has been educated, the more adaptable, and thus the more productive in the long run, that person tends to be in the face of new and changing challenges.

A third aspect of human capital, but one that takes us beyond the neoclassical production function, is its contribution to growth and innovation.

Not only can human capital embody in people the best current technological knowledge, but, by training potential innovators, it leads to advances in knowledge and hence contributes to growth.

Balanced growth

Now consider what happens if labour, physical, and human capital all grow at the same rate. In this case, the neoclassical assumption of constant returns to scale means that GDP grows at the same rate. As a result, per capita output (GDP/L) remains constant.[9] This is called a **balanced growth path**. It is one in which all inputs and outputs are growing at the same constant rate. However, per capita GDP is unchanged.

This is not the kind of growth that concerns those interested in living standards. It is just more of the same: larger and larger economies, with more capital and more labour, doing exactly what the existing capital and the existing labour were already doing. There is nothing new. This is the kind of steady-state growth path illustrated in Box 26.4.

Growth and living standards

In this constant technology neoclassical model the only way for growth to add to living standards is for the per capita stocks of physical and human capital to increase. However, the law of diminishing returns dictates that the rise in living standards brought about by successive equal increases in capital will inexorably diminish. Raising living standards becomes more and more difficult as capital accumulation continues.

---

[9] In all of these models a constant fraction of the population is assumed to be in the labour force, so that output per employed person and output per head of population always change in the same direction.

Box 26.4 The Solow–Swan growth model

This basic neoclassical growth model is named after its two main originators, Robert Solow, whom we have already mentioned, and the Australian economist Trevor Swan. The assumptions of the Solow–Swan model are as outlined in the text, except that the aggregate production function expresses national output as a function of inputs of only two factors, labour and capital. As in the text, this function exhibits constant returns to scale. So, if both capital and labour inputs are increased in the same proportion, output will also increase in that proportion: a 10 per cent increase in capital and labour will lead to a 10 per cent increase in output. But there are diminishing returns to each individual input. So, if we hold the labour input constant, each successive unit of capital will produce a declining increase in units of output.

The figure illustrates the working of the model. The vertical axis measures output per worker and the horizontal axis measures capital per worker. With a given labour force, the accumulation of capital increases the amount of capital per head as well as income per head. But because of diminishing returns to any one input, output per head increases at a diminishing rate as capital, and hence capital per head, increases. Labour saves a constant fraction of its income that is always invested. So, as capital increases, so does output (and income) per head and, as a result, so does saving and investment. This is shown by the line labelled saving and investment. As one moves out along this line, income is rising, as is saving and investment, but at a diminishing rate.

The straight line labelled 'Capital replacement requirement' shows the investment in capital per worker needed to keep the capital–labour ratio at its current level in the face of a constant growth rate of the labour force and a constant depreciation rate of capital. This is a straight line because it represents points for which capital and labour are increasing in the same proportion and there are constant returns to scale (so an equal percentage increase in both inputs leads to the same percentage increase in output).

There are two possible cases depending on what we assume about technical progress.

In the first case we assume that the technology is given, so there is no productivity growth. The 'steady state' in the model is at point A. The economy will be attracted towards point A because to the left of A investment is greater than is needed to keep the capital–labour ratio constant so capital per worker is rising; while to the right of A investment is too low to keep the capital–labour ratio constant so the capital–labour ratio is falling. At point A saving (and therefore investment) is just sufficient to generate a rate of growth of the capital stock which just keeps up with the growth of the labour force and compensates for any depreciation of capital. So, at point A capital per worker is constant and output grows at the rate of growth of the workforce. But there is no growth in real living standards as the expanding labour force delivers 'more of the same' in the sense that output per worker is constant so real wages are also constant.

In the second case there is technical progress so that labour productivity grows over time at some exogenous rate. In this world total output grows at the rate of population growth plus the rate of productivity growth, but the rate of growth of output per head depends entirely on the rate of technical progress. Thus, in this second case, the rate of growth of real incomes depends entirely on the rate of technical change, but this is not explained within the model. More recent theories have focused on trying to explain technical change as an endogenous variable, as discussed in the text.

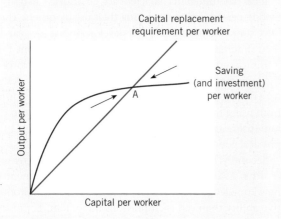

Technological change in the neoclassical growth model

So far we have held technology constant. In fact, over the centuries (and even decades) economic growth is dominated by technological changes. As we have already observed, we are not better off than our Victorian ancestors because we have more Victorian factories making more Victorian commodities. We are better off because technological change has provided us with new commodities often made in radically new ways. In the neoclassical model technological change can be shown as shifting the production function so that the same amount of labour, physical capital, and human capital produces more GDP. This result is depicted in Figure 26.3 by rightward shifts in the *MP* curves of each input—the same amount of input produces more output. This change is exogenous to the model. It just happens. It is unexplained and

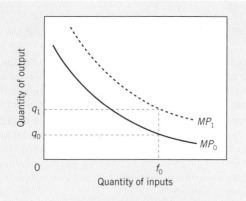

Figure 26.3 Shifts in marginal product curves

Technological change shifts the marginal product curve of each input so that any given amount will produce more. In this example technological change shifts the marginal product curve of the input from MP_0 to MP_1. The amount f_0 of the input formerly produced a marginal product of q_0, but after the change it produces the larger amount q_1.

the issue of how resources are allocated to bringing about such changes by R&D activities is not considered.

The neoclassical growth model can accommodate such exogenous technological change along balanced growth paths if physical and human capital are growing at a constant rate and technological change increases the efficiency of labour at the same rate, making labour grow at a constant rate when measured in *efficiency units*. This is called labour-augmenting, or Harrod-neutral, technical change. The result is that there is no increase in output per efficiency unit of labour, but there is an increase in output per worker. Along such a balanced growth path labour is constant, measured in number of workers employed, while human and physical capital, the efficiency of labour, and total and per capita output are all growing at a constant rate. All that has been done here is that instead of having labour grow at a constant rate in terms of physical numbers, leading to balanced growth with constant living standards, labour is growing at a constant rate measured in efficiency units (with the number of workers constant) so that per capita output is growing at the balanced growth rate.

Endogenous growth

As we have just seen, in the neoclassical model, technological change shifts the production function but is itself unexplained. In other words, technological change is treated as *exogenous*. It has profound effects on economic variables, such as GDP, but it is not influenced by economic causes. It just happens.

However, microeconomic research by many scholars over the past several decades has established that technological change *is* responsive to such economic 'signals' as prices and profits. In other words, technological change is *endogenous*

to the economic system. The modern understanding that technological change is at the heart of the growth process has led to two important developments in many economists' views on growth. The first is that technological change is largely endogenous to the economic system. The second is that the investment that increases the capital stock may encounter increasing rather than diminishing returns.

This understanding has led to two different lines of research. The first seeks to embody endogenous technical change in growth models that use an aggregate production function, while the second looks to much more detailed evidence gathered at the microeconomic level by students of technology and economic history. We look at each of these in turn.

Endogenous growth in macro models

The American economist Paul Romer who, along with another American economist Robert Lucas, developed the first macroeconomic models of endogenous growth stressed the important difference between goods and ideas.

Physical goods, such as factories and machines, exist in one place at one time. The nature of this existence has two consequences. First, when physical goods are used by someone, they cannot be used by someone else. Secondly, if a given labour force is provided with more and more physical objects to use in production, sooner or later diminishing returns will be encountered.

Ideas have different characteristics. First, ideas can be used by one person without reducing their use by others. Thus, once someone has an idea and develops it, the idea can be used simultaneously by everyone. For example, if one firm is using a certain lorry, another firm cannot use that lorry at the same time; but one firm's use of a revolutionary design for a new suspension on a lorry does not prevent other firms from using that design as well. Ideas are not subject to the same use restrictions as goods. (In the language of Table 13.1, physical goods are rivalrous; ideas are non-rivalrous.)

Secondly, ideas are not necessarily subject to decreasing returns. As our knowledge increases, each increment of new knowledge does *not* inevitably add less to our productive ability than did each previous increment. For example, a year spent improving the operation of semiconductors may be more productive than a year spent improving the operation of vacuum tubes, the technology used before semiconductors.

Modern growth theories stress the importance of ideas in producing what can be called knowledge-driven growth. New knowledge provides the input that allows investment to produce constant or increasing rather than diminishing returns. Furthermore, the evidence from modern research is that new technologies are usually absolutely input-saving—they typically use less of all inputs per unit of output. Since there are no practical boundaries to human knowledge, there need be no immediate boundaries to

Box 26.5 Endogenous growth and the aggregate production function

If we are to deal with endogenous growth, we need to allow explicitly for research and development (R&D). This covers the activities that develop the new technologies that, as we have seen, are the major cause of long-term growth. Although technological change is a very complicated process, a very simplified version of it can illustrate some of the key issues.

Let all inputs—human and physical capital, labour, and land—be bundled into a single composite input called K. Let the amount of K devoted to R&D be labelled K_R, while K_C stands for the amount going to produce everything else—that is, goods and services for consumption, investment, and government.

Let our first pass at an aggregate production function be

$$GDP = Af(K_R, K_C) \qquad (1)$$

where A is a very simplified representation of the technology that determines how much is produced by a given amount of resources. As technical progress proceeds, A increases in value, indicating a growing output for the same amount of input.

Now note that these two Ks have different effects on output. K_C is producing goods and services while K_R is producing ideas that can be thought of as blueprints for new and improved goods and services and production processes. If we reduce K_C, we reduce the production of goods and services for consumption, investment, and government. However, if we reduce K_R, the amount of resources devoted to R&D, we do not affect the current output of goods and services. Indeed, we could reduce K_R to zero and go on indefinitely producing a constant flow of goods and services using our unchanged technology.

To show how these are related in the production process, we need to have a separate production function for ideas:

$$Y = Af(K_C) \qquad (2)$$
$$\dot{A} = G(K_R) \qquad (3)$$

where the dot over the A indicates its percentage rate of change. This now shows explicitly that resources devoted to R&D increase the efficiency of the resources devoted to all other lines of production.

If we increase K_C for one period and then return it to its original level, GDP will correspondingly increase for one period and then fall back to its original level. However, if we increase K_R for one period and then let it fall back to its original level, we will alter the rate of growth of A for that period and those effects will last long after K_R has returned to its original level. For all subsequent periods A, and hence GDP, will be higher than it would have been if the one-period extra burst of R&D had not occurred.

If we are going to develop a full-blown theory of growth driven by endogenous technological change, we need a theory of how resources are allocated between K_C and K_R, but that would take us well beyond the scope of an introductory chapter on economic growth.

---

finding new ways to produce more output using less of all inputs. Box 26.5 looks briefly at some of the issues involved in allowing for endogenous technological change in growth models that use an aggregate production function.

Classical and neoclassical growth theories gave economics the name 'dismal science' by emphasizing that diminishing returns under conditions of given technology put a cap on growth based on capital accumulation. Modern growth theories are more optimistic because they emphasize the unlimited potential of knowledge-driven technological change to economize on all resource inputs, and because they display increasing or constant returns to investment that embodies new technology.

These theories refer to long-term trends, and over the long haul there seems no reason to believe that equal increments of human inventive effort must inevitably be rewarded by ever-diminishing increments to real GDP.

Increasing returns theories

Theories that deal with increasing returns span both the macro and micro approaches to understanding technological change. We saw earlier that neoclassical theories assume that investment is always subject to diminishing returns.

Some new growth theories emphasize the possibility of *historical increasing returns to investment*. This means that as investments in some new areas—products, power sources, or production technologies—proceed through time, each new increment of investment is more productive than previous increments. A number of sources of increasing returns have been noted. These fall under the general categories of once-and-for-all or fixed costs and ideas.

Fixed costs

Here are three ways in which once-and-for-all costs can cause increasing returns to investment:

1. Investment in the early stages of development of a country or region may create new skills and attitudes in the workforce that are then available to all subsequent investors, whose costs are therefore lower than those encountered by the initial investors. In the language of Chapter 13 the early firms are conferring an externality on those who follow them.

2. Each new investor may find the environment increasingly favourable to its investment because of the necessary infrastructure that has been created by those who came before.

3. The first investment in a new product will encounter countless problems, both technical problems of production and problems of product acceptance among customers. Once the technical problems are overcome, they do not exist for subsequent investors. When a new product is developed, customers will often resist adopting it, partly because they may be conservative and partly because they know that new products often have teething troubles. Customers also need time to learn how best to use the new product. The first firms in the field with a truly new idea, such as personal computers, usually meet strong customer resistance, but this resistance is eroded over time.

All of these cases, and many more that could be mentioned, are examples of a single phenomenon:

Many investments require fixed costs, the advantages of which are then available to subsequent investors; hence the investment costs for 'followers' can be substantially less than the investment costs for 'pioneers'.

More generally, many of the sources of increasing returns are variations on the following theme:

Doing something really new is difficult, both technically and in terms of customer acceptance, whereas making further variations on an accepted and developed new idea becomes progressively easier.

Ideas

Romer's endogenous growth models also yield increasing returns even if the production of goods and services obeys constant returns. If you increase the allocation of resources to current production, you will increase output in proportion. But if you increase the allocation of resources to R&D you are producing ideas that can be thought of as blueprints for new products and production processes. When these raise industrial efficiency, they raise the flow of production not just now, but for a long time into the future. Thus the total value of return to these ideas is often a large multiple of the value of the resources that went into developing them. Also, the productivity of a pound's worth of the capital that embodies these new ideas may be larger than the value of a pound's worth of the capital that embodied the older technologies, creating historical increasing returns to capital investment.

If R&D creates so much value, why then do firms not devote much more of their resources to R&D and less to the creation of physical capital? The reason is that only a small fraction of the social value of these new ideas is captured by those that create them, whether a firm or an individual. Because ideas can be used by everyone, the overall value of a really good new idea is greatly in excess of the value of that idea to the firm that created it. Patent laws allow the firm to capture more of the total value than they would otherwise get, but even then they get only a small fraction of the value that accrues to the whole of society. Think, for example, of the vast and unmeasurable amount of social value created by the R&D that went into the invention of the means to generate and distribute electricity—the electricity that is essential for all of the modern world's vast array of electronics.

Endogenous growth at the microeconomic level

Much of the earliest work devoted to understanding the existence and complexity of endogenous technological change was done in the UK by scholars, such as Christopher Freeman, who were associated with the Science Policy Research Unit (SPRU) at Sussex University. However, the most influential overall single study was by the American professor Nathan Rosenberg, whose path-breaking book *Inside the Black Box* dealt with this issue in great detail.[10]

Technological change stems from R&D and from innovating activities that put the results of R&D into practice. These are costly and highly risky activities, undertaken largely by firms and usually in pursuit of profit. It is not surprising, therefore, that these activities respond to economic incentives.

Rosenberg established two key relations. First, R&D designed to apply known basic principles to new problems is responsive to economic signals. For example, if the price of some particular input such as petrol or skilled labour goes up, R&D and innovating activities will be directed to altering the production function to economize on these inputs. This process does not involve substituting less expensive for more expensive inputs within the confines of known technologies that is stressed in microeconomic theory; rather, it is the development of new technologies in response to changes in relative prices. Secondly, *basic research* itself is also responsive to economic incentives. One reason for this is that the basic

[10] N. Rosenberg, *Inside the Black Box: Technology and Economics*, Cambridge: Cambridge University Press, 1982. See also N. Rosenberg, *Exploring the Black Box: Technology, Economics, and History*, Cambridge: Cambridge University Press, 1994.

research agenda is strongly influenced by practical issues of the day. For example, university-based research in solid state physics became popular, and was heavily funded, only after the development of the transistor, which is the basic component of the modern computer.

There are many important implications of this understanding that growth is achieved through costly, risky, innovative activity that occurs to a significant extent in response to economic signals. We will discuss a few of these below.

Kinds of technological change

Increases in productive capacity that are created by installing new and better capital goods are called **embodied technical change**. The historical importance of embodied technical change is clear: the assembly line and automation transformed most manufacturing industries, the aeroplane revolutionized transportation, and electronic devices now dominate the information and communications industries. These innovations, plus lesser known but no less profound ones—for example, improvements in the strength of metals, the productivity of seeds, and the techniques for recovering basic raw materials from the earth—create new investment opportunities.

Less obvious, but nonetheless important, changes occur through **disembodied technical change**—that is, changes in the organization of production that are not embodied in particular capital goods. Examples are improved techniques of management, design, marketing, and organization of business activity, and feedback from user experience to product improvement. One of the most interesting and powerful examples of disembodied technological change occurred when factories changed their power source from the steam engine to the electric motor in the late nineteenth century. Steam power was created by a large engine located outside the factory which drove a central drive shift suspended from the factory ceiling. Each machine was driven by a belt transferring power from the drive shaft. Because of the high friction loss in belt transmission, the machines that used most power were located close to the drive shaft and those that needed least power furthest away. This led to an almost random movement of each product as it was moved from one machine to another to complete various parts of its construction. With electricity, a separate motor was attached to each machine. It then occurred to some genius that the machines could be rearranged according to the flow of production, with the machine needed first at the front door and one needed last at the rear door. This, in itself, led to a large increase in efficiency as the product moved steadily from one machine to the next without undue effort or loss of time. Also,

without that new arrangement, the assembly line and mass production with its vast increase in efficiency could not have been invented.

The complexity of the innovation process

The pioneering theorist of innovation Joseph Schumpeter developed a model in which innovation flowed in one direction, starting from a pure discovery 'upstream', to more applied R&D, then to working machines, and finally to output 'downstream'.

In contrast, modern research shows that innovation involves a large amount of what are called 'learning by doing' and 'learning by using' at all of its stages. 'Doing' refers here to making the good in question. It is usual that costs per unit of output fall steadily over time as firms learn how to manage the production of products that embody new technologies. (This was discussed in more detail in Chapter 11.) 'Using' here refers to those who first use the product. Although everything possible to make a good product is done at the design stage, problems are often not obvious until the product is put into use. First users often find defects and, more often, places where the product's performance could be improved. What is learned 'downstream' in production and use is then used to modify what needs to be done 'upstream' at the design stage. The best innovation-managing systems encourage this sort of feedback from the more applied phases to designers.

The location of innovation

Innovation typically takes place in different parts of the producer–user chain in different industries—as shown, for example, by the research of American economist Eric von Hippel in his book *The Sources of Innovation*. von Hippel shows that in some industries manufacturers make most of the product innovations, in others the users make most of them, and in yet others the innovating is done by those who supply components or materials to the manufacturer.

von Hippel provided examples of cases where, because policy-makers failed to appreciate these differences, public policy designed to encourage innovation in specific industries went seriously astray. For example, one programme that was intended to encourage innovation in a particular industry gave assistance to the main producers when almost all innovations were coming from the independent parts producers. The message for economists and policy-makers is important: an understanding of the details of the innovating process in each industry is needed if successful innovation-encouraging policies are to be developed.

Costly diffusion

The *diffusion* of technological knowledge from those who have it to those who want it is not costless (as it was assumed to be in Schumpeter's model). Firms need research capacity just to adopt the technologies developed by others. Some of the knowledge needed to use a new technology can be learned only through experience by plant managers, technicians, and operators. (Such knowledge is called *tacit knowledge*.) We often tend to think that once a production process is developed, it can easily be copied by others. Indeed, some advanced economic theories use the hypothesis of replication, which holds that any known process can be replicated in any new location by using the same factor inputs and management as are used in the old location. In practice, however, the diffusion of new technological knowledge is not so simple.

For example, US economists Richard Nelson and Sidney Winter have argued that most industrial technologies require technology-specific organizational skills that can be 'embodied' neither in the machines themselves, nor in instruction books, nor in blueprints. Acquiring tacit knowledge requires a deliberate process of building up new skills, work practices, knowledge, and experience.

The fact that diffusion is a costly, risky, and time-consuming business explains why new technologies take considerable time to diffuse, first through the economy of the originating country and then through the rest of the world. If diffusion were simple and virtually costless, the puzzle would be why technological knowledge and best industrial practices do not diffuse very quickly. As it is, decades can pass before a new technological process is diffused everywhere that it could be employed. Costly and difficult diffusion also explains two important observations about the early stages of development of currently rural economies. It is often difficult to establish state-of-the-art production processes in such poor countries whose labour force lacks the experience needed to operate modern production processes efficiently. This is why it is often necessary to start the development of a backward economy with the production of very simple parts so as to begin the tacit learning by a labour force that may one day rise to world standards.

Market structure and innovation

Because it is highly risky, innovation is encouraged by a strongly competitive environment and is discouraged by monopoly practices. Competition among three or four large firms often produces much innovation, but a single firm, especially if it serves a secure home market protected by trade barriers, often seems much less inclined to innovate.[11]

Although the ideas of Joseph Schumpeter lie behind much of modern growth theory, on the surface this emphasis on competition seems to conflict with his ideas. The apparent conflict arises because the theories available to Schumpeter in his time offered only two market structures: perfect competition and monopoly. He chose monopoly as the structure more conducive to growth on the grounds that monopoly profits would provide the incentive to innovate, and innovation itself would provide the mechanism whereby new entrants could compete with established monopolies. (He called this latter process 'creative destruction'.) Modern economists, faced with a richer variety of theoretical market structures, find that competition among oligopolists is usually more conducive to growth-enhancing technological change than either monopoly or perfect competition.

Government assistance designed to encourage innovation often allows the firms in an industry to work together as one. Unless great care is exercised, and sufficient foreign competition exists, the result may be a national monopoly that will discourage risk-taking rather than encourage it in the way that the policy intended.

The UK provides many examples of this mistaken view of policy. For example, Michael Porter observes in his book *The Competitive Advantage of Nations* that: 'UK policy in the 1960s operated under the faulty theory that encouraging British companies to merge would create world-class competitors. Consolidation of steel, automobiles, machine tools, and computers all led to notable failures'.

Shocks and innovation

One interesting consequence of endogenous technical change is that shocks that would be unambiguously adverse to an economy operating with fixed technology can sometimes provide a spur to innovation that proves a blessing in disguise. A sharp rise in the price of one input can raise costs and lower the value of output per person for some time. But it may lead to a wave of innovations that reduce the need for this expensive input and, as a side effect, greatly raise the productivity of labour.[12]

---

[11] This is supported by evidence from such authors as Alfred D. Chandler, Jr, *Scale and Scope: The Dynamics of Industrial Capitalism*, Cambridge, MA: Harvard University Press, 1990, and David Mowrey and Nathan Rosenberg, *Technology and the Pursuit of Economic Growth*, Cambridge: Cambridge University Press, 1989.

[12] This is why in microeconomics we study three runs: the short run, the long run, and the very long run. Often the very long run response to a change in relative prices is much more important than either the short-run response, limited by fixed capital, or the long-run response, limited by existing technology.

Sometimes individual firms will respond differently to the same economic signal. Those who respond by altering technology may do better than those who concentrate their efforts on substituting within the confines of known technology. For example, in *The Competitive Advantage of Nations*, Michael Porter tells of how US consumer electronics firms decided to move their operations abroad to avoid high, and rigid, labour costs. They continued to use their existing technology and went where labour costs were low enough to make that technology pay. However, their Japanese competitors stayed at home. They innovated away most of their labour costs—and then built factories in the United States to replace the factories of US firms that had gone abroad!

Innovation as a competitive strategy

Managing innovation better than one's competitors is one of the most important objectives of any modern firm that wishes to survive. Firms often fail because they do not keep up with their competitors in the race to develop new and improved products and techniques of production and distribution. Success in real-world competition often depends more on success in managing innovation than on success in adopting the right pricing policies or in making the right capacity decisions from technological possibilities that are already known.

Further causes of growth

So far we have looked at increases in labour and capital and at technological change as causes of growth. Contemporary studies suggest that other causes of growth are also important. The effects of these other causes appear as shifts in the production function, so that any given number of hours of labour operating with a given amount of capital produces more and more output as time passes.

Institutions

Almost all aspects of a country's institutions can foster or deter the efficient use of a society's natural and human resources. Social and religious habits, legal institutions, and traditional patterns of national and international trade are all important. So, too, is the political climate.

Historians of economic growth, such as Paul David, Nathan Rosenberg, and Nobel Prize winner Douglas North, attribute much of the growth of Western economies in the post-medieval world to the development of *new institutions*, such as the joint-stock company, limited liability, efficient forms of insurance, effective patent laws, and double-entry book-keeping. Many students of modern growth suggest that institutions are as important today as they were in the past. They suggest that the

societies that are most successful in developing the new institutions that are needed in today's knowledge-intensive world of globalized competition will be those that are at the forefront of economic growth.

The role of the government

Governments play an important role in the growth process.

First, the government needs to provide the framework for the market economy that is given by such things as well-defined property rights secure from arbitrary confiscation, security and enforcement of contracts, law and order, sound money, and the basic rights of the individual to locate, sell, and invest where and how he or she decides.

Secondly, governments need to provide infrastructure. For example, transportation and communications networks are critical to growth in the modern globalized economy. Some of these facilities, such as roads, bridges, and harbours, are usually provided directly by governments; others, such as telecommunications, rail, and air services, can be provided by private firms, but government regulations and competition policy may be needed to prevent the emergence of growth-inhibiting monopolies in these areas.

Education and health (especially for the disadvantaged) are important forms of government spending. Creating the appropriate inputs to production is critical to creating comparative advantages in products that can be exported. This requires general education, trade schools, and other appropriate institutions for formal education, as well as policies to increase on-the-job training within firms. These activities are even more important today than they were in the past because so much of a nation's capacity to grow, and to compete in a world of rapidly developing ideas, lies in the quality of its human capital—in both those who produce goods and services and in those involved in R&D.

Other possible government policies include favourable tax treatment of saving, investment, and capital gains, R&D tax incentives and funding assistance, and policies to encourage some fraction of the large pools of financial capital held by pension funds and insurance companies to be used to finance innovation.

Finally, emphasis can be placed on poverty reduction for at least two reasons. First, poverty can exert powerful anti-growth effects. People living in poverty will not develop the skills to provide a productive labour force, and they may not even respond to incentives that are provided. Malnutrition in early childhood can affect a person's capacities for life. Secondly, although economic growth tends to reduce the incidence of poverty, it does not eliminate it.

What governments can do in addition to encourage the development of specific new technologies is much debated. Some argue that governments should never seek to interfere at the micro level in the development of new technologies. Certainly, there have been some spectacular and costly failures of this type, including the British government's failure to develop a gas-cooled nuclear reactor and to support a UK challenger to IBM in the field of computers. Others, however, point out that many of the most important modern technologies have received substantial government support in the early stages of their development. For example, the vastly successful Japanese automobile industry was largely dependent in its early stages on tariff protection of the post-World War II Japanese market and the prohibition of US investment in that market. Within this protected environment the Toyota Motor Company developed new techniques that allowed it to create new products faster and then produce them more cheaply than their US competitors.

The massively successful Taiwanese electronics industry was largely the creation of the Taiwanese government. It built up the industry and brokered cooperative relations with US firms from which the Taiwanese firms learned. They then went on to become world leaders, no longer dependent on government support. The United States, which purports to rely exclusively on private initiative, has given government assistance to several of its most successful new technologies. In the 1950s, the US Bureau of Standards encouraged the development of an American software industry primarily to assist in the Cold War. Two major spin-offs were an infrastructure of academic experts created largely with government funding and high industry standards that were set by the rigorous demands of the Department of Defence. Military procurement also supported the growth of the US semiconductor industry, providing for the incubation of innovations that were not yet commercially viable. Firms supplying that market, often on a cost-plus basis, refined their innovations and often reduced their costs sufficiently to achieve commercial

viability. The airframe of the Boeing 707, the first successful long-haul passenger jet aircraft, was developed on a cost-plus basis in a military version before it was put into civilian production. So were the engines of the Boeing 747, the first successful jumbo aircraft. So there have been spectacular government success and failures in attempts to assist new technologies in their early phases of development and debate continues on the advisability of this type of assistance.

So the issue is not do governments always succeed or always fail when picking technological winners, but what are the conditions that make government support of particular new technologies more likely to succeed than to fail.

Growth and economic historians

Although this is not a book about economic history, it must be noted that a vast amount of insightful work on growth, its causes, processes, and consequences, has been done by economic historians. Much of the material in the previous section on other causes of growth comes from the writings of such economic historians as Douglas North, Joel Mokyr, Eric Jones, and David Landes. Although they do not deny the usefulness of growth models that use an aggregate production function, they argue that to understand the growth process as it really unfolds, a great deal more detail is needed than can be incorporated in such aggregate models.

There is space here just to illustrate some of this work by referring to the book *As Time Goes By* by Christopher Freeman and Francisco Louçã. They seek to substantiate Schumpeter's theory that growth proceeds in a series of long waves, each associated with a set of new technologies that some call general purpose. Box 26.6 describes the waves that they identify in British economic growth since the First Industrial Revolution.

Box 26.6 Long waves in British economic growth?

In their book, *As Time Goes By*, Christopher Freeman and Francisco Louçã look at waves of economic activity to answer Schumpeter's question: 'How can economics help to explain history, and how can history help to explain economics?'. They discern six waves that occurred in the course of British economic growth since the First Industrial Revolution

 • *The first wave: the British Industrial Revolution.* The age of cotton, iron, and water power. It started in the 1780s, peaked in 1815, and the downturn lasted until to 1848.

The first wave was mostly confined to Britain where the rate of growth of production was double from the period prior to 1780. However, the growth was uneven with cotton and iron outpacing all other industries. In 1830, the percentage of total world exports that were British exports were: textiles 72 per cent; cottons 48 per cent; iron and steel 12 per cent.

 • *The second wave: the age of iron railways, steam power, and mechanization.* This wave started in 1848, peaked in 1873, and the downturn lasted until 1895. Coal

(continued)

Box 26.6 *continued*

and iron were the key primary materials facilitating the development of railway transportation and steam engines. Britain went from less than 2 per cent of the world manufacturing output in 1750 to approximately 23 per cent in 1880. Germany and the United States also showed huge gains over this time period, while China and India declined significantly. The second wave's technologies started in Britain but spread to Germany and the United States.

- *The third wave: the age of steel, heavy engineering, and electrification.* This wave had an upswing from 1895 to 1918 followed by a downswing to 1940. The US industries dominated the third wave with Germany, Britain, and Japan contributing to the growth but to a lesser degree. By 1913 US GDP per hour surpassed Britain's and was double that of France and Germany. In 1914 the United States accounted for 56 per cent of world manufacturing, Germany was 16 per cent, and Britain dropped to 14 per cent. Britain dropped behind the others because it failed to invest sufficiently in large-scale domestic capital projects such as electricity and steel production. Britain's education system was also failing to produce the technical workers needed for the developing industries. During this time period growth among all countries was uneven and a noticeable gap between rich and poor countries developed.

- *The fourth wave: The Great Depression and the age of oil, automobiles, motorization and mass production.* This wave started in 1941, peaked in 1973 and entered a downswing that lasted until at least the end of the century.

- *The fifth wave: the emergence of a new techno-economic paradigm—the age of information and communication technology (ICT).* This wave had roots that went back to World War II but it was only really felt in the late 1970s. It has yet to reach its peak. This wave is also referred to as the ICT (Information Communication Technology) Revolution. This wave is carried mainly by computers and software, while new infrastructure is the internet and communications. The major structural change has been the internet. Paralleling the 'physical' presence of the internet, the social structure has also moved to a less hierarchical system. The organization of ICT firms moved away from the 'Fordist' style of management to horizontal structures built on networking. Networks have increased the speed and access to information and changed how firms make decisions. The mergers between mega companies have resulted in communication–internet firms so big and global that governments cannot control them—ICT is not land-bound to one country and is difficult to subject to effective regulations.

For a much fuller description of each of these waves, their technologies, and their effects see the Online Resource Centre[13].

[13] <www.oxfordtextbooks.co.uk/orc/lipsey13e>

Growth and sustainability

Most of what we have written in this chapter so far assumes that, on balance, growth is a 'good thing' as it improves the living standards of ordinary people. It has transformed lives in the developed world since the Industrial Revolution and it has had dramatic positive impacts on significant sectors of the population of many developing countries in the past few decades. But the effects of growth are not all good and we have already discussed some costs in the earlier section entitled 'costs of growth'.

In the terminology of Chapter 13, there are significant negative externalities from growth in its current form and these may get much worse in the future. Indeed, there are many opponents of growth who argue that continued world growth is undesirable and some who argue that it will become impossible. Of course, all terrestrial things have an ultimate limit. After all, astronomers predict that the solar system itself will die when the sun burns out in another five billion or so years. However, there are some more pressing problems that will affect the human race over the current century. The most important of these concern climate change. Although there are some dissenters, the broad consensus among scientists who have studied the problem is that if the world is to avoid some of the worst predicted outcomes of environmental degradation, some major changes in our current behaviour are urgently required now.

The more general issue is that of *sustainability*. Will future generations have higher living standards than those attained by those of us alive today? Or will their lives be much harder or lower quality than ours because the sea level has risen to inundate large parts of the world's coastal areas, or because we have used up all the non-renewable resources and have seriously harmed the environment with our pollution? We could even have exploited to extinction those resources that are in principle renewable, such as the fish in the ocean and the native rain forests. These issues are sometimes labelled by the media as the 'green agenda', but they are now getting attention from politicians in most political parties and in many countries. Box 26.7 looks at the question of whether economic policy-makers should attempt to solve resource

Box 26.7 To eliminate growth or control it?

The effects of climate change are all around us, from melting Arctic ice and tundra to dead pine forests, rising sea levels, and storm surges that are already threatening Bangladesh and low-lying Pacific islands. The balance of scientific opinion is that we are a major cause, although there are intellectually respectable dissenters. Two main responses are advocated in the public discussion:

Option 1: halt, or at least drastically restrict, further growth.

Option 2: accept further growth and deal with its undesirable side effects.

Many regard Option 1 as impossible for several reasons. First, the world's major powerhouse economies would never accept such a goal politically—the United States because of the nature of its political system, and India and China (and other developing nations) because stopping growth would condemn to perpetual poverty the more than 50 per cent of their citizens who have so far benefited little from their country's spectacular growth. Secondly, we humans are an inventive species. Faced with a challenge that threatens to worsen our situation or perceiving an opportunity to better it, we will typically seek solutions that involve invention and innovation. Nothing short of a massively repressive regime, or one that was in a state of social and economic chaos, would stop individuals from inventing and innovating their way around their problems—and such activity is the main driver of economic growth.

So, if Option 1 is unachievable what about Option 2?

• New green technologies (which are themselves sources of further economic growth) need to be invented and innovated. Using only existing technologies to raise the average citizen of India and China, to say nothing of Africa, to living standards achieved by even the poorest of the developed nations would be impossible. Climate change, environmental degradation, and pollution would soon reach disastrous levels. So, the only way to achieve the aspirations of these developing nations is through the invention of new greener technologies that use less resources per unit of output (as have almost all new technologies over the last 300 years) and that pollute less in all definable ways. Here, both private initiative and government assistance, in the form of tax relief and subsidization, at early stages of development are needed to do a full job. Developing and marketing these new technologies will produce many new industries and bring commercial success to those who do it first.

• Alternatives to fossil fuels need to be improved in efficiency and reduced cost.

• Pollution-reducing policies, of which cap and trade is a good example, need to be instituted quickly.

• The tax system needs to be used to discourage those production and consumption activities that are most 'polluting' and to encourage those that are most green.

• Although we do not need to adopt zero growth as a policy goal for all of the reasons mentioned above, we can downgrade growth as a policy goal. We can accept that protection of the environment in the broadest sense is a policy goal that is placed above growth. Given any trade-off, the environment could come before growth. Then we could accept whatever growth follows when good environmental measures are adopted (and there will be much of it).

Some argue that we can do away with growth because the industrialized countries are rich enough already. But stopping growth and the technological change that drives it would condemn all the poorer countries to perpetual poverty. It would leave us with existing technologies, many of which are harmful to the well-being of people, other animals, and the environment. It would deny us all the new technologies that are already visible on the horizon. We would not get the really efficient non-fossil-fuel sources that are being researched today. We would not cure Parkinson's disease and many other ailments that are a current scourge. We would not get the ability to regenerate failing organs and artificial limbs that respond to our thoughts rather than mechanically. We would not learn to better predict, prevent, and clean up after natural disasters. We would not learn to develop new synthetics that reduce our dependence on scarce natural resources. And so on, and on, and on. We would also do without many of the things that future generations will come to take for granted but that are unimaginable today, as were most of the things we now take for granted but were unimaginable to our Victorian ancestors.

So, as those who would accept growth but deal with its consequences argue: growth is here to stay. Eliminating it for the world, or a large part of it, is a romantic dream on a par with the nineteenth century romantic dream that socialism would eliminate poverty and end human conflict by issuing in an era of universal peace and brotherhood. Spending time and energy thinking about, and planning for, a no-growth society is, they argue, seriously counterproductive because it deflects attention from the pressing task of trying to eliminate, or at least alleviate, the most serious of the undoubtedly many harmful effects that growth is having now, and will have in the future. This is not an easy task and it may prove an impossible one. If so, real economic and social disaster will be the lot of future generations. We must, they argue, try to prevent this unhappy outcome and to do so will take all of our practical energies that should not be diverted into dreaming about achieving the impossible: a no-growth society.

and environmental pressures by adopting a 'no-growth' strategy, rather than always seeking faster growth as they have until now.

Resource exhaustion

The years since the World War II have seen a rapid acceleration in the consumption of the world's resources, particularly fossil fuels and basic minerals. World population has increased from under 2.5 billion to over seven billion in that period; this increase alone has intensified the demand for the world's resources. Furthermore, as economic development spreads to more and more countries, living standards are rising, in some cases at a rapid rate. As people attain higher incomes, they consume more resources. So, not only are there more people in the world, but many of those people are consuming increasing quantities of resources.

Most economists believe that the technology and resources available at present could not possibly support the whole world's population at a standard of living equal to that currently enjoyed by the average European family. To do so, for example, the annual consumption of oil would have to increase more than tenfold. It seems evident that resources and our present capacity to cope with pollution and environmental degradation are insufficient to accomplish this rise in living standards with our present technology.

However, most economists agree that *absolute* limits to growth, based on the assumptions of constant technology and fixed resources, are not relevant. As modern growth theory stresses, technology changes continually, as do stocks of resources. For example, sixty years ago few would have thought that the world could produce enough food to feed its present population of over seven billion people, let alone the 10 billion at which the population is projected to stabilize sometime in the mid-twenty-first century. Yet this task now seems feasible, and major famines are associated not with our inability to produce enough but often with political upheavals that reduce food production (or distribution) in some areas well below what could be achieved by existing technology.

Although globally there is enough food for everyone, severe problems arise when primarily agricultural economies suffer drought and other natural disasters, or wars and other man-made disasters. Indeed the climate change that is predicted to bring droughts to some areas which are now productive may cause very serious but localized famines in some of the world's most environmentally sensitive areas, such as the Sahel belt in sub-Saharan Africa. The problem, then, is not to produce more food worldwide, but to be sure that it is available where it is needed

and to move populations from areas of permanent drought to more productive areas—a massively difficult exercise for social and political reasons.

It is possible that 50 years from now the global energy problem will be as much a thing of the past as the global food shortage problem is today. By then, technology could have produced a cheap non-polluting energy source to replace our present reliance on fossil fuels. There are many candidates, most of which are used somewhere today and require only further R&D to reduce their costs to competitive levels. These include solar energy, geothermal heat, wind power, hydrogen-based fuel cells, and possibly nuclear fusion.

Yet there is surely also cause for concern. Although many barriers can be overcome by technological advances, such achievements are not instantaneous and are certainly not automatic. There is a critical problem of timing. How soon can we discover and put into practice the knowledge required to solve the problems that are made ever more imminent by the growth in the population, the affluence of the rich nations, and the aspirations of the billions who now live in poverty? There is no guarantee that a whole generation will not be caught in transition between technologies, with enormous social and political consequences.

Market forces do help to some degree in dealing with the problem of exhaustible resources. As a particular fossil fuel or raw material becomes scarcer, its price will be driven up. This is how it will be rationed between competing uses, and the high price will create an incentive for explorers or inventors to discover more or to develop substitutes. Economics is all about how to allocate scarce resources between competing uses.

One important new technology that is just beginning to make its presence felt is nanotechnology, the building of new materials from the bottom up, atom by atom. The promise here is that any required material can be constructed from its plentiful atomic components provided only that it does not violate the laws of nature. Such a revolution, still only just visible on the distant horizon, would alleviate most of our fears of running out of exhaustible materials.

The second case study at the end of this chapter deals with some evidence concerning current resource shortages.

Renewable resources

One possible limitation to growth relates to renewable resources. We discussed the general problem of over-exploitation of common property resources in Chapter 13. The demands placed on them threaten to destroy their natural recuperative cycle. Throughout history, for example, fishermen were a small part of the predatory process. Now the demands of over seven billion people have made fish a scarce resource, threatening to destroy the fish-generating capacity of many oceans, as we saw in the third case study in Chapter 13. The destruction of tropical rain forests is another example. Not all renewable resources are common-property resources and thus liable to over-exploitation, but clearly some are.

The problem here is not growth itself but rather the lack of management of the resources because of undefined property rights or a lack of government jurisdiction. In principle, a growing economy could afford to manage its renewable resources better. Indeed, it is precisely because they are renewable that these resources could be of increasing importance in the future.

Pollution

A major problem is how to cope with pollution. Air, water, and earth are polluted by a variety of natural activities, and through billions of years the environment has coped with these. The Earth's natural processes had little trouble dealing with the pollution generated by its one billion inhabitants in 1800. But the over seven billion people who now exist put demands on pollution-abatement systems that threaten to become unsustainable. Smoke, sewage, chemical waste, hydrocarbon emissions, spent nuclear fuel, and a host of other pollutants threaten to overwhelm the Earth's natural regenerative processes. Detailed analysis of some ways in which these problems may be dealt with was given in Chapters 13 and 14.

Conscious management of pollution and renewable resources was unnecessary when the world's population was one billion people, but such management has become a pressing matter of survival now that over seven billion people are seeking to live in the same space and off the world's limited resources.

Global warming

There is no doubt that global temperatures are rising. This is already having serious consequences, such as the melting of Arctic ice, the migration of sea life to different locations, threats to coral reefs worldwide, increasing infestations of tree-killing beetles whose larvae used to be controlled by winter frosts that are no longer severe enough to do the job, and rising sea levels that so far are measured in centimetres but could reach metres within a few decades or less.

There is debate about how much of this climate change is due to human activity in the form of greenhouse gas emissions and how much to natural causes. But the majority of those who have studied it believe that humans are a major cause, possibly the major cause. There is also uncertainty about what the consequences will be if no steps are taken to curtail the emissions of greenhouse gases over the next decade or two. Many feel that the consequences could be catastrophic and would include such things as the possible diversion of the Gulf Stream, which has happened several times in prehistory. Since the stream is what makes much of the British Isles and Northern Europe habitable, the consequences would be disastrous. Another possibility is a rise in sea level sufficient to flood much of the world's coastal regions, including most of such low-lying countries as Bangladesh and the non-volcanic Pacific islands, and many of its port cities such as London, New York, and Sidney. The social consequences of millions of displaced people desperately searching for food and shelter are hard to imagine, and one must wonder if civil authority could be maintained in the face of such dislocations. These are now only possibilities but enough researchers take them seriously that we need to be aware of them.

While almost everyone agrees that the problem is large, there is some disagreement as to how much harm will be done by any given change in temperature and therefore how many resources it is worth investing now in alleviating the warming. These disagreements matter because they create political room for those who wish not to burden industry with more regulations.

If enough of the public become willing to make the effort, technology is available, or could be developed, to eliminate most of these causes within decades rather than centuries, although the short-run problems could still be formidable. Therefore the problem is not with technology but with human assessment of the costs and benefits of doing nothing versus adopting various costly prevention programmes now. We discuss some of the issues raised by global warming in the first case study at the end of this chapter.

It is conceivable that we will so mismanage these problems as to destroy growth for a long time to come and even reduce living standards by large amounts. But if we do so, it will not be because the problems are technologically insoluble. Humans are technological animals and there are no practical limits to new technological knowledge. If we do create environmental disasters, it will more likely be because we are unwilling to face up to our problems, or to create the institutions necessary to deal with them, or any number of other social, political, and psychological reasons—but not because solving them is technically impossible. (Note that a 'solution' might include abandoning the use of a particular technology because its harmful side effects cannot be eliminated.)

CASE STUDIES

1. Economics of climate change: some big questions

The consensus among the many scientists who have studied this question is that climate change is one of the most important issues facing the human race today. Here we briefly set out, first, the view of the UN scientists who have been studying this issue for some time, and then some economic issues that are raised by the climate change problem.

In 1988 the UN established the Intergovernmental Panel on Climate Change (IPCC). In 2014 it published its fifth assessment report written and reviewed by several hundred experts from around the world. The report defines climate change as follows: 'Climate change refers to a change in the state of the climate that can be identified (e.g., by using statistical tests) by changes in the mean and/or the variability of its properties, and that persists for an extended period, typically decades or longer'.

Here are a few of its important conclusions. Stated after each is the degree of confidence that the report attaches to each on the basis of the best available evidence.

In recent decades, changes in climate have caused impacts on natural and human systems on all continents and across the oceans.

In many regions, changing precipitation or melting snow and ice are altering hydrological systems, affecting water resources in terms of quantity and quality (medium confidence).

Many terrestrial, freshwater, and marine species have shifted their geographic ranges, seasonal activities, migration patterns, abundances, and species interactions in response to ongoing climate change (high confidence).

Based on many studies covering a wide range of regions and crops, negative impacts of climate change on crop yields have been more common than positive impacts (high confidence).

Impacts from recent climate-related extremes, such as heat waves, droughts, floods, cyclones, and wildfires, reveal significant vulnerability and exposure of some ecosystems and many human systems to current climate variability (very high confidence).

Climate-related hazards exacerbate other stressors, often with negative outcomes for livelihoods, especially for people living in poverty (high confidence).

Responding to climate-related risks involves decision making in a changing world, with continuing uncertainty about the severity and timing of climate-change impacts and with limits to the effectiveness of adaptation (high confidence).

Climate change over the 21st century is projected to reduce renewable surface water and groundwater resources significantly in most dry subtropical regions (robust evidence, high agreement), intensifying competition for water among sectors (limited evidence, medium agreement).

Due to sea level rise projected throughout the 21st century and beyond, coastal systems and low-lying areas will increasingly experience adverse impacts such as submergence, coastal flooding, and coastal erosion (very high confidence).

Climate change over the 21st century is projected to increase displacement of people (medium evidence, high agreement).

Throughout the 21st century, climate-change impacts are projected to slow down economic growth, make poverty reduction more difficult, further erode food security, and prolong existing and create new poverty traps, the latter particularly in urban areas and emerging hotspots of hunger (medium confidence).

Scientific rather than economic expertise is needed to establish these and most of the other issues dealt with in the report. However, there are some issues whose assessment does involve the expertise of economists. Here we focus on four of them.

Intergenerational equity and discounting

Determining an optimal anti-global warming policy is fraught with difficulty and can never be done with any precision. Yet it is worth looking at how we would do so if we had all the evidence because this may help to clarify what is at issue.

We first need an objective. Let us say it is to reduce the causes of climate change to levels that are estimated to hold the global rise in temperature to no more than 2°C, which is regarded by many as the tipping point beyond which too many effects will become irreversible.

Next we must take account of the fact that costs incurred today will have benefits that are felt over a long time in the future. How do we weigh the interests of those who are alive in the future against those who are alive today? In standard investment appraisal we discount future costs and revenues in order to calculate their present value. (See the section entitled 'The rate of interest and present value' in Chapter 19.) This calculation requires the use of a discount rate that for firms making profit-maximizing decisions may be approximated by the market rate of interest. For society we require what is called the social discount rate, which takes account of effects on society that are omitted when firms and households make decisions about present consumption and investment.[14]

Next look at a single payment made now to achieve some future gain. If the economies of the industrialized nations grow at 2 per cent per annum over the next 50 years, the typical country's GDP will be about 3.2 times as high as it is now. Thus, £1 billion spent today represents the same percentage of GDP as will £3.2 billion spent in 50 years. So even without any time discounting, spending, say, £1 billion today to prevent £2 billion of damage 50 years from now is a poor bargain because those living 50 years from now could do the same job for a much smaller proportion of their incomes. If we take the social rate of discount to be 3 per cent per annum, £1 billion spent today is the equivalent of about £4.4 billion spent 50 years from now. So to spend £1 billion today to get any 50-year distant benefit of less than £4.4 billion (a return of 440 per cent!) would, on these calculations, be a bad bargain.

Now look at the real case in which costs will start now and spread well into the future, while benefits will start soon and also extend well into the future. The costs will be higher than the benefits in the near future but, further along, the flow of benefits will greatly exceed the costs. Because of the point made in the previous paragraph, each year's costs and benefits need to be expressed as a percentage of that year's estimated GDP. If both flows had the same time profile, this deflation would not be necessary, but since there will be different profiles of costs (high now falling later) and benefits (lower now and much higher later) the deflation is needed.

Now we need to take each year's deflated costs and benefits and calculate their present values by discounting them by the social discount rate. The further into the future are the costs and benefits, the lower will be their present value. We then sum the present values of the expected costs and then the benefits, and subtract the former from the latter. If the result is positive, it is socially valuable to undertake the exercise now. If it is negative, the exercise needs to be redone each year because, as time goes by, the high points in the flow of benefits will get closer to the present and therefore have a higher present value.

As already emphasized, making the cost and benefit estimates on which these calculations would be based cannot be done with any precision. Nevertheless, the exercise does have some value. First, it shows us what is implied in deciding that it is desirable to adopt a climate-mitigation policy now. Secondly, it is a reminder that when any policy is being considered, we must be careful about accepting current sacrifices to help further generations who will in any case be much richer that we are (if the post-Industrial Revolution growth experience continues). But these calculations ignore one important possibility that we take up in the next section.

Uncertainty

The analysis in the previous section is typical of what is found in much of microeconomics. It assumes that marginal costs and marginal benefits vary smoothly, rising or falling along continuous curves which can be compared and suitably discounted when they range over time. In doing so, it ignores one important possibility. Environmental damage may not be smooth and continuous, with a little more cause resulting in a little more harm. Instead, one of the many possible tipping points may be passed, after which the damage becomes cumulative and uncontrollable. For example, the Greenland and South Pole ice packs are already melting at an accelerating rate. If a tipping point is passed, the melting will become uncontrollable, causing, among other things, the ocean to rise by many tens of metres, flooding coastal areas and rich highly populated delta lands throughout the world, as well as most of the world's port cities including much of London. It would be hard to put a price on the resulting disaster, with civil authority possibly breaking down in the face of literally billions of starving displaced persons migrating in search of dry land and food. Such tipping point disasters are not mere figments of imagination because geological evidence tells us that the climate has undergone such abrupt changes several times in the past. So, although it might not make sense from the purely accounting point of view given the previous section, according to those who worry about tipping points controlling climate change now has much to recommend it as an insurance against the possibility of calamitous and irreversible climate changes in the future.

Even if the cost of mitigating the causes of climate change were as high as 3 or 4 per cent of GDP, those who take the above case seriously argue that it is a small price to pay to insure against the possibility of such a disaster. As an analogy, they argue that if you were living below a dam and were told that the leaks in it were very likely to

---

[14] Use of a social discount rate is not universally accepted. For example, Sir Nicolas Stern, in his report published some years ago, argues that we should '... treat the welfare of future generations on a par with our own' (Stern Review: *The Economics of Climate Change*, HM Treasury, 2006, page 35).

cause you serious flooding over the next few decades and might cause the dam to fail totally, it would be folly to reject paying 3 or 4 per cent of your income as your contribution to the community's effort to repair the dam. To those who argue that we cannot be sure that the dam will fail, others reply that even if that is only a small possibility, it is surely worth a small amount of your income to ensure against that possibility of disaster.

Public goods and unequal effects

Some of the countries most at risk are also countries that are least able to do anything to combat climate change. Also, the biggest generators of greenhouse gases will not be the only countries affected, or even those most affected. This means that there are global public good aspects of climate change (see the section entitled 'Public goods' in Chapter 13). All will benefit from greenhouse gas reductions even if they do not contribute to the cost, so all have an incentive not to pay. Within a single country the government can pass laws to control pollution and manage common property resources, but at the global level this can only be achieved by international agreements. These are hard to achieve and even harder to enforce. Developing countries feel that they have the right to grow their economies to catch up with the industrial countries, while the industrial countries feel that they should not have to bear all the costs of emissions reduction. In any event, a stabilization of greenhouse gas concentration can only be achieved if all countries cooperate and not if just a few do. Unfortunately, although every country has much to gain from accepting some costs of mitigating climate change, every country has even more to gain if it becomes what is called a *free rider*, sitting aside and letting all the others do the job so that it obtains the benefits while avoiding the costs.

Effective measures

If the emission of greenhouse gases is to be limited, measures will have to be implemented to achieve the required reductions. Economists have tended to support either cap-and-trade schemes or carbon taxes over attempts at direct controls or blanket limits (for reasons discussed in Chapter 13). Although achieving comprehensive schemes is difficult, the Europe Emissions Tradings System, started in 2005, has shown that a market in pollution permits can be made to work. In such a system the government sets an overall limit on the amount of pollution it allows and distributes saleable permits to emit that much pollution. Those with high costs buy the permits from those with low costs, while these reduce their pollution. This guarantees that the total amount of pollution reduction will be achieved but at the lowest total cost

to firms. Initially, in setting the global quotas, the government accepted the statements of firms about how much they were currently polluting. This gave the firms the incentive to overstate their emissions so that whatever reductions they had to make on paper would be much higher than they would have to make in practice. As a result the overall quota was set too high and the market price of the quotas fell while little overall reduction in pollution was achieved. Then when the global recession hit in 2008–9 industrial output fell dramatically and, with it, so did pollution. So there was a further glut of permits, causing their price to fall even more. Nonetheless the market is there and it does work. What is now needed is more agreement among the EU countries as to how much and how quickly the global quota for emissions should be reduced.

There has been considerable success in developing energy sources that are alternatives to fossil fuels. Wind and solar power generators are now being used in significant numbers, as discussed in the first case study of Chapter 9. But there is still a long way to go. Such sources accounted for 5 per cent of UK electricity generation in 2008 and 15 per cent in 2013. One encouraging fact is that China, having neglected any pollution-reducing activities for years, has now become worried about the air pollution that is making life very difficult in its industrial cities. Solar power is now being adopted in a big way, and, as a result of its R&D, the cost of solar panels has fallen dramatically over the last few years.

In addition to schemes that discourage carbon emissions, there will almost certainly have to be strengthened environmental legislation and incentives (possibly subsidies) for 'green' energy use and development. These are evident in many countries already, but they will have to become universal if the global scale of the problem is to be contained.

The central problems are political and social rather than economic. Technologies exist today that could make a much larger impact on climate change than is now occurring. We also know from past experience that when new technologies are innovated, their initially high costs of production and operation typically fall over time as learning by doing and by using accumulates. No doubt, people care about the environment, but they also care about being able to drive to work and fly abroad for a vacation. Agreeing a course of action is difficult enough in democracies, but it is even harder in other countries where ruling elites are more interested in staying in power or enriching themselves than they are in saving the planet.

However, the current consensus is that climate change is happening, that we are the main cause, and that something can be done to stabilize the problem at manageable levels. Let us hope that containment is possible and that appropriate action is taken to achieve this outcome.

2. Resource scarcity: any signs so far?

We discussed earlier the possibility that some natural resources might become increasingly scarce and that this could put a brake on economic growth as we have experienced it since the Industrial Revolution. It is hard to judge what increasing scarcity might mean in a volume sense for a variety of different types of raw materials, but if it does start to be an issue, this should be reflected in rising prices as current demand outstrips current supply, both evaluated at existing prices. What we can do now is to see if there are any signs of general rises in commodity prices compared with prices of consumer goods and services.

Figure 26.4 shows the prices of four categories of commodities relative to US CPI for the period 1960–2014. These price ratios are all set to unity in 2010 (when the underlying price indexes are all set to 100). These are all dollar price indexes, so the figure is showing the price of this specific commodity group relative to US consumer prices in general. Therefore a relative price that stays at unity means that the nominal commodity price is moving exactly in line with the US CPI.

The commodity groups presented are energy (which includes oil, coal and natural gas), food (which includes cereals, vegetable oil, meat, seafood, sugar, bananas, and oranges), agricultural raw materials (which includes timber, cotton, wool, rubber, and hides), and metals (which includes copper, aluminium, iron ore, nickel, zinc, lead, and uranium). Energy prices were very low in the 1960s, but had two sharp upward spikes in 1973 and 1979 associated with the first and second oil crises. However, after 1980 they declined steadily in relative terms until the early 2000s. There was a sharp spike in energy prices in 2008 which took them to a post-World War II high, but they fell off sharply during the subsequent recession. They subsequently recovered and in 2014 remained at a relative high level compared with most of the past five decades.

Food and agricultural raw materials have generally had a downward trend relative to consumer prices since the early 1970s. Food prices had a major spike in 1973, at the time of the first oil crisis, and they stayed relatively high through the 1970s but then fell steadily until the end of the 1990s. They rose in the 2000s, especially in 2007–8, but they have since fallen back and are still well below the levels of the 1970s in real terms. (Some of the temporary factors affecting prices of specific foods were discussed in the case studies at the end of Chapters 2, 3, and 6). Agricultural raw material prices declined in the 1960s but spiked upwards in 1973 and then cycled for a while around a historically high level before trending downwards in the 1980s and 1990s. They also rose in the 2000s but fell after the 2007–8 financial crisis and in 2014 were at a (relative) level well below that of the 1960s and 1970s.

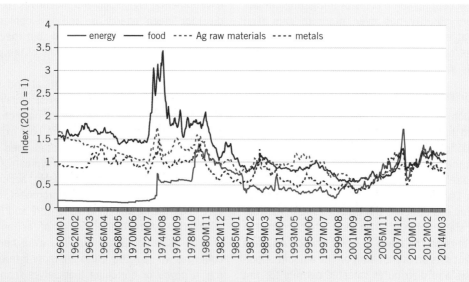

Figure 26.4 Commodity prices relative to US CPI, 1960M1–2014M5

Source: World Bank Commodity Price Data (the Pink Sheet) online database; US CPI from Federal Reserve Bank of St Louis (FRED) online database.

Metal prices have generally moved pro-cyclically, rising during booms and falling during recessions or slowdowns, but there is no strong upward or downward trend in the long term. Indeed, metal prices relative to CPI were about the same in 2014 as they had been in 1962. Food and agricultural raw materials are renewable resources. Metals and energy (at least in the form of oil, coal, and natural gas) are non-renewable. If exhaustion of non-renewables was becoming a problem, we would expect to see metal prices and energy prices rising relative to the others, and relative to consumer prices. However, there has been no upward trend in metal prices relative to either other commodities or consumer prices in general. In contrast the prices of energy products, particularly those that are petroleum based, have had irregular price trajectories. They rose sharply in the 1960s and 1970s then fell for the next two decades, only to rise again in the early 2000s. Then, just as many observers were predicting sharp further price increases based on the expectation that petroleum reserves were approaching exhaustion, the new technique of fraking brought about such major increases in production that prices fell to lows not seen for decades.

Supplies of renewable resources need not be exhausted if they are properly managed, but they could become relatively more expensive if climate change affects production conditions adversely and more generally if demand increases relative to supply capacity. The surge in food prices in 2007–8 is interesting in this respect as it is almost certainly linked to the fact that some crops, such as corn and sugar, can be used in the production of bio-fuels. High energy prices at this time caused a rise in demand for these crops for fuel production (as discussed in the case study at the end of Chapter 3). The positive side of this is that there clearly are some renewable close substitutes for fossil fuels.

In short, the exhaustion of some selected resources may become a problem at some time in the future but it is not yet showing up in commodity price trends. There are also some more general considerations suggesting that fear of an overall exhaustion of materials is unwarranted. First, the principle of substitution suggests that it is usually possible to substitute one material for another as relative costs change. Many individual materials have become scarce in supply in the past only to be replaced by cheaper substitutes. Secondly, the amount of resources and energy per unit of GDP have fallen steadily over the past 200 or so years. More resources are being used now because output has risen so much, not because we need more per unit of output. Thirdly, new sources of energy are already available to replace fossil fuels if they become scarce and hence overly expensive. Fourthly, a new general-purpose technology, nanotechnology, offers relief from any material shortage. Within this century, creating materials from the bottom up, atom by atom, will allow us to produce any material, existing or not yet imagined, from plentiful atoms, provided only that it obeys the laws of physics.

Conclusion

Growth has raised the average citizen of advanced countries from poverty to plenty in the course of two centuries—a short time in terms of human history. Yet the world still faces many problems. Starvation and poverty are the common lot of citizens in many countries and are not unknown in the European Union and the United States, where average living standards are high. Further growth is needed if people in less developed countries are to escape material poverty, and further growth would help advanced countries to deal with many of their pressing economic problems.

Rising population and rising per capita consumption put pressure on the world's natural ecosystems, especially through pollution and overuse. For growth to continue it must be sustainable growth, which in turn must be based on idea-driven technological change. Past experience suggests that new technologies will use less of all resources per unit of output. However, if they are to reduce dramatically the demands placed on the Earth's ecosystems, price and policy incentives will be needed to direct technological change in more 'environmentally friendly' ways. Just as present technologies are much less polluting than the technologies of 100 years ago, the technologies of the twenty-first century need to be made much less polluting than today's.

There is no guarantee that the world will solve the problems of sustainable growth, but there is nothing in modern growth theory and existing evidence to suggest that such an achievement is impossible.

SUMMARY

Growth and cycles

■ Growth theory studies the long-term trend in real output and living standards, while macroeconomics studies cycles about the trend.

■ Growth is the most important determinant of changes in living standards over time.

Benefits and costs of growth

■ The most important benefit of growth lies in its contribution to the long-run struggle to raise living standards and to escape poverty.

■ Small differences in national growth rates can cumulate into large national differences in living standards over a few decades.

■ It is easier to redistribute income in a growing society than in a static one.

■ The opportunity cost of growth to society as a whole is the use of resources for R&D and capital formation that could have been used to produce goods for current consumption

■ The social costs of growth are felt in such things as individuals who are left behind in a rapidly changing world, and for whom the costs can be high and more personal. Such effects can be alleviated by public policy but cannot be avoided. Others, such as pollution and environmental degradation, are important but can be avoided by public policy.

Theories of economic growth

■ The aggregate neoclassical model displays diminishing returns when one input is increased on its own and constant returns when all inputs are increased together. In a balanced growth path, labour, capital, and national output all increase at a constant rate, leaving living standards unchanged. When labour-augmenting productivity growth occurs, a balanced growth path is consistent with rising per capita output and income.

■ In the long term, technological change is the major cause of growth, together with the capital investment that is needed to embody new technologies. Modern growth theory treats technological change as an endogenous variable that responds to market signals. The diffusion of technology is also endogenous. It is costly and often proceeds at a relatively slow pace.

■ Some modern growth theories display increasing returns as investment increases. This is because investment that embodies new technologies creates externalities so that successive increments may add successive amounts to total output that are constant or even *increasing*.

■ The critical importance of increasing knowledge and new technology to the goal of sustaining growth is highlighted by the great drain on existing natural resources that has resulted from the explosive growth of population and output in recent decades. Without continuing technological change, the present needs and aspirations of the world's population cannot come anywhere close to being met.

Growth and sustainability

■ Rising population and rising real incomes place pressure on resources. Although resources in general will not be exhausted, particular resources, such as petroleum, may be. Furthermore, resources that renewed themselves without help from humans when the world's population was one billion people will be exhausted unless they are consciously conserved now that the world's population exceeds seven billion.

■ The enormous increase in population also creates severe problems of pollution. The Earth's environment could cope naturally with most of the pollution caused by humans 200 years ago, but the present population is so large that pollution has outstripped nature's coping mechanisms in many cases. Technological advance is needed to reduce the amount of pollution created by each unit of output.

■ Global warming is one of the biggest potential threats to sustainable economic growth.

TOPICS FOR REVIEW

■ Short-run and long-run effects of investment and saving
■ The cumulative nature of growth
■ Benefits and costs of growth
■ The neoclassical aggregate production function
■ Balanced growth
■ Endogenous technical change

■ Increasing returns to investment
■ Embodied and disembodied technical change
■ The economics of goods and of ideas
■ Resource depletion and pollution.
■ Climate change

QUESTIONS

1 GDP per head of population in the UK in 2013 was about £25,610. Supposing that there is no inflation and zero population growth, what will GDP per head be in 2015, 2025, and 2035 if the rate of economic growth continues at its long-term trend rate of 2 per cent per annum?

2 How would your answers to Question 1 change if the average rate of growth over these periods rose to: a) 3 per cent; b) 4 per cent; c) 5 per cent?

3 Using the actual data for GDP growth in Table 15.4 and the GDP per head figure for 2013 given in Question 1, and assuming the same population as today, calculate the real GDP per head in 1900 (at 2013 prices). In reality the UK population was about 41 million in 1900, while it had grown to about 63 million in 2013. Recalculate your figure for real GDP per head in 1900 using this information.

4 Outline some of the important costs and benefits of economic growth. Can you think of some that are not mentioned in the text?

5 What actions could a) governments, b) firms, and c) individuals take to increase the rate of economic growth?

6 What are the main determinants of economic growth?

7 List products that you use regularly that were not available when a) your parents and b) your grandparents were born. What does the process of product innovation tell us about the nature of economic growth?

8 Must economic growth inevitably come to an end when various non-renewable energy (and commodity) sources are depleted?

9 What weight should be given to future generations who are not yet born in environmental decisions that have a current cost of alleviation but a possibly greater cost imposed in the future?

10 Should positive economic growth continue to be an aim of government policy?

CHAPTER 27

INTERNATIONAL TRADE

Do imports of goods made with cheap foreign labour destroy jobs at home? Is globalization making us better or worse off? Should our government subsidize domestic industries to help them compete internationally? Should we restrict imports of goods made in countries where working conditions are worse than our own? These are some of the questions we address in this chapter.

In particular, you will learn that:

- Gains from trade result from specialization based on comparative advantage, which arises whenever there are international differences in opportunity costs of production.

- Terms of trade determine how the gains from trade are distributed.

- For any given pattern of comparative costs, free trade tends to maximize world GDP.

- For a given world pattern of comparative advantages, protectionism may make one country better off, but it tends to make the world as a whole worse off.

- One valid reason for departing from full free trade, especially during the early stages of economic development, is to alter comparative advantages through government policy and was done successfully in Singapore, Taiwan, South Korea, and Hong Kong.

- The World Trade Organization polices world trade rules and the commercial policies of member governments.

- Regional free-trade areas and common markets bring efficiency gains through trade creation and efficiency losses through trade diversion.

Sales and purchases of goods and services that take place across international boundaries are *international trade*. For example, the British buy BMWs made in Germany, Germans take holidays in Italy, Italians buy spices from Tanzania, Belgians import oil from Kuwait, Egyptians buy Japanese cameras, the Japanese depend heavily on American soybeans as a source of food, and the Taiwanese make many electronic goods whose parts are manufactured throughout Southeast Asia.

There is substantial evidence to show that international trade and economic growth are positively linked. In this chapter we explain why trade increases output and GDP. We then ask why, if trade is generally beneficial, governments have often attempted to restrict the freedom to trade. Finally, we discuss some of the institutional arrangements that affect world trade.[1]

Sources of the gains from trade

An economy that engages in international trade is an **open economy**. One that does not is a **closed economy**. A situation in which a country does not engage in foreign trade is called **autarky**. The advantages realized as a result of trade are called the **gains from trade**. Although politicians often regard foreign trade as being different from domestic

trade, economists from Adam Smith on have argued that the causes and consequences of international trade are

---

[1] In this chapter we focus on the general issue of trade, but we provide a more detailed discussion of how trade affects developing countries in the Online Resource Centre (http://www.oxfordtextbooks.co.uk/orc/lipsey13e).

simply an extension of the principles governing domestic trade. What is the benefit from trade among individuals, among groups, among regions, or among countries?

Interpersonal, inter-regional, and international trade

Let us start by thinking about trade between individuals. Without trade, each person would have to be self-sufficient; each would have to produce all the food, clothing, shelter, medical services, entertainment, and luxuries that he or she consumed. A world of individual self-sufficiency would be a world with extremely low living standards.

Trade between individuals allows people to specialize in those activities that they can do relatively well and to buy from others the goods and services that they themselves cannot easily produce. A good doctor who is a bad carpenter can provide medical services not only for his or her own family, but also for an excellent carpenter who lacks the training or the ability to practice medicine. Thus, trade and specialization are intimately connected. Without trade, everyone must be self-sufficient. With trade, everyone can specialize in what he or she does well and satisfy other needs by trading.

The same principles apply to regions. Without inter-regional trade, each region would be forced to be self-sufficient. With trade, each region can specialize in producing goods or services for which it has some natural or acquired advantage. Plains regions can specialize in growing grain, mountain regions can specialize in mining and forest products, and regions with appropriate skills can specialize in manufacturing. Cool regions can produce dairy products and wool along with crops that thrive in temperate climates, and hot regions can grow such tropical crops as rice, cotton, bananas, sugar, and coffee. Places with lots of sunshine and sandy beaches can specialize in the tourist trade. The living standards of the inhabitants of all regions will be higher when each region specializes in products in which it has some natural or acquired advantage and obtains other products by trade than when all regions seek to be self-sufficient.

The same principle also applies to nations. Nations, like regions or persons, can gain from specialization. Almost all countries produce more of some goods than residents wish to consume. At the same time they consume more than they produce of some other goods.

International trade is necessary to achieve the gains that international specialization makes possible. Trade allows each individual, region, or nation to concentrate on producing those goods and services that it produces relatively efficiently while trading to obtain goods and services that it would produce less efficiently than is done by others.

Specialization and trade go hand in hand because there is no motivation to achieve the gains from specialization without being able to trade the goods produced for the different goods desired. The term 'gains from trade' encompasses the results of both.

There are three main sources of gains from trade. The first is differences between regions of the world in climate and resource endowment that lead to advantages in producing certain goods and disadvantages in producing others. These gains would occur even if each country's costs of production were unchanged by the existence of trade. The second source is the reduction in each country's costs of production that results from the greater production that specialization brings. The third is the international competition that usually promotes more rapid technological change and economic growth than would occur if domestic firms produced solely for a protected home market.

The gains from specialization with given costs

In order to focus on differences in countries' conditions of production, suppose that each country's average costs of production are constant. We will use an example below involving only two countries and two products, but the general principles apply as well to the real-world case of many countries and many products.

Absolute advantage

One region is said to have an **absolute advantage** over another in the production of any good when an equal quantity of resources can produce more of that good in the first region than in the second. When two countries have absolute advantages in the production of different products, it is obvious that world production can be increased if each specializes in producing the commodity in which it has an absolute advantage. If it then trades with the other country it will be able to consume both commodities. Say, for example, that one unit of resources can produce either two units of X or five units of Y in country A while the same amount of resources can produce six units of X and three units of Y in country B. Without trade, both commodities would be produced in both countries. But A has an absolute advantage in Y while B has one in X. If A transfers one unit of resources from producing X to producing Y, the production of X falls by two units and that of Y rises by five units. Now let B make the reverse movement. Transferring one unit of resources from Y reduces its production by three units and employing these resources in Y increases its production by six units. As a result of these two reallocations of resources, total production of X has gone up by 4 (6 – 2) units and production of Y by 2 (5 – 3) units.

How many resources will be transferred in this way depends on the demands for the two products. But for every transfer of this type there is an increase in the production of both products. To satisfy their demands for both products, A will need to export Y to B while B will export X to A in return. So we see that in this case of absolute advantage there are gains in total output from specialization and gains from trade when countries export goods in which they have an absolute advantage and import those in which others have that advantage.

Comparative advantage

When each country has an absolute advantage over others in a product, the gains from specialization and trade are obvious. But what if one country can produce all commodities more efficiently than other countries? In essence this was the question that English economist David Ricardo (1772–1823) posed 200 years ago. His answer underlies the *theory of comparative advantage* and is still accepted by economists today as a valid statement of the potential gains from trade. According to this theory, the gains from specialization and trade depend on the pattern of comparative, not absolute, advantage.

To illustrate, assume that there are two countries, the United States and the European Union. Both countries produce the same two goods, wheat and cloth, but the opportunity costs of producing these two products differ between them. Recall from Chapter 1 that the *opportunity cost* in production is given by the slope of the production-possibility frontier, and it tells us how much of one good we have to give up in order to produce one more unit of the other. For the moment we assume that this opportunity cost is constant in each country at all combinations of outputs.

For the purposes of our example we assume that the opportunity cost of producing 1 kilogram of wheat is 0.60 metres of cloth in the United States, while in the European Union it is 2 metres of cloth. These data are summarized in Table 27.1. The second column of this table gives the same information again, but expressed as the opportunity cost of 1 metre of cloth (so the numbers there are the reciprocals of the numbers in the first column).

The sacrifice of cloth involved in producing wheat is much lower in the United States than it is in the European Union. World wheat production can be increased if the United States rather than the European Union produces it. Looking at cloth production, we can see that the loss of

Table 27.1 Opportunity cost of wheat and cloth in the United States and the European Union

	Wheat (kg) (1)	Cloth (m) (2)
United States	0.60 m cloth	1.67 kg wheat
European Union	2.00 m cloth	0.50 kg wheat

Comparative advantages reflect opportunity costs that differ between countries. Column (1) expresses opportunity cost per kilogram of wheat. Column (2) expresses the same information in terms of a metre of cloth. In this example, the United States has a comparative advantage in wheat production, the European Union in cloth.

wheat involved in producing one unit of cloth is lower in the European Union than in the United States. World cloth production can be increased if the European Union rather than the United States produces it. The gains from a US shift towards wheat production and an EU shift towards cloth production are shown in Table 27.2.

The gains from specialization arise from differing opportunity costs in different countries the gains from trade are realized when countries export goods for which they have a comparative advantage and import goods for which other countries have a comparative advantage.

The slope of the production-possibility boundary indicates the opportunity costs, and the existence of different opportunity costs implies comparative advantages and disadvantages that can lead to gains from trade. Figure 27.1

Table 27.2 Gains from specialization with differing opportunity costs

	Changes from each producing one more unit of the product in which it has the lower opportunity cost	
	Wheat (kg)	Cloth (metres)
United States	+1.0	–0.6
European Union	–0.5	+1.0
Total	+0.5	+0.4

Whenever opportunity costs differ between countries, specialization can increase the production of both products. These calculations show that there are gains from specialization given the opportunity costs of Table 27.1. To produce one more kilogram of wheat, the United States must sacrifice 0.6 m of cloth. To produce one more metre of cloth, the European Union must sacrifice 0.5 kg of wheat. Making both changes raises world production of both wheat and cloth. Since countries will tend to specialize in the production of those commodities in which it has a comparative advantage, reaping these gains from specialization requires that the countries trade with each other so that their consumption patterns can be less specialized than their production patterns

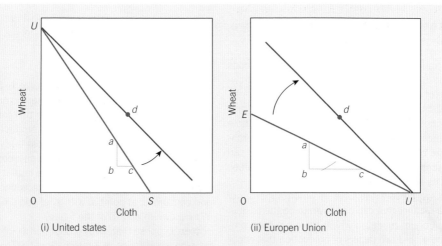

Figure 27.1 Gains from trade with constant opportunity costs

International trade leads to specialization in production and increased consumption possibilities. The dark blue lines in parts (i) and (ii) represent the production-possibility boundary for the United States and the European Union, respectively. In the absence of any international trade these also represent each country's consumption possibilities.

The difference in the slopes of the production-possibility boundaries reflects differences in comparative advantage, as shown in Table 27.1. In each part the opportunity cost of increasing production of wheat by the same amount (measured by the distance *ba*) is the amount by which the production of cloth must be reduced (measured by the distance *bc*). Thus the relatively steep production-possibility boundary for the United States indicates that the opportunity cost of producing wheat in the United States is less than that in the European Union.

If trade is possible at some terms of trade between the two countries' opportunity costs of production, each country will specialize in the production of the good in which it has a comparative advantage. In each part of the figure production occurs at *U*; the United States produces only wheat, and the European Union produces only cloth.

Consumption possibilities are given by the red line that passes through the two *U* points and has a slope equal to the terms of trade. Consumption possibilities are increased in both countries; consumption may occur at some point such as *d* in each part. This involves a combination of wheat and cloth that was not obtainable by either country in the absence of trade.

illustrates how two countries can both gain from trade when they have different opportunity costs in production and the opportunity costs are independent of the level of production. An alternative diagrammatic illustration of the gains from trade appears in Box 27.1, where the production-possibility frontier is curved which means that opportunity cost varies with the composition of output.

The conclusions about the gains from trade arising from international differences in opportunity costs are summarized as follows

1. Country *A* has a *comparative advantage* over country *B* in producing a product when the opportunity cost (in terms of some other product) of production in country *A* is lower. However, this implies that it has a comparative disadvantage in the other product.

2. Opportunity costs depend on the relative costs of producing two products, not on absolute costs.

3. When opportunity costs are the same in all countries, there is no comparative advantage and there is no possibility of gains from specialization and trade.

4. When opportunity costs differ in any two countries, and both countries are producing both products, it is always possible to increase production of both products by a suitable reallocation of resources within each country.

In Question 1 at the end of this chapter you will have the chance of illustrating for yourself that even when a country has an absolute advantage over another in all commodities there are still gains from specialization and trade as long as the margin of this advantage as not the same in all products.

Gains from specialization with variable costs

So far, apart from in Box 27.1, we have assumed that unit costs are the same whatever the scale of output, and we have seen that there are gains from specialization and trade as long as there are inter-regional differences in opportunity costs. If costs vary with the level of output, or as experience is acquired via specialization, *additional* sources of gain are possible.

Box 27.1 The gains from trade with varying opportunity costs

International trade leads to an expansion of the set of goods that can be consumed in the economy in two ways: by allowing the bundle of goods consumed to differ from the bundle produced, and by permitting a profitable change in the pattern of production. Without international trade the bundle of goods produced is the bundle consumed. With international trade the consumption and production bundles can be altered independently to reflect the relative values placed on goods by international markets.

In this box we present the case in which opportunity costs vary in a manner that can be shown to be the case in a general equilibrium model in which there are two commodities, X and Y, and two factors of production that occur in different proportions in the two countries. The demonstration of this so-called Heckscher–Ohlin case (named after the two Swedish economists who first developed it) is beyond the scope of this introductory treatment. Therefore we just note that in this case the opportunity cost of producing a commodity *rises* as output is increased from zero. The country's production possibility curve is shown by the red curve in the figure. Note that where the curve starts on the horizontal axis only X is being produced. Here the opportunity cost of producing some Y is very low as only a small reduction in X produces a large increase in Y. Because of the shape of the curve, the opportunity cost increases as the production of Y increases (and X decreases). By the time the production of X approaches zero, the curve has become very flat, indicating that a very large reduction in X produces only a small increase in the production of Y. We also assume that we are dealing with a country that is not large enough to affect international prices by altering its own production.

The graphical demonstration of the gains from trade in this situation now proceeds in two stages.

Stage 1: fixed production

In each part of the figure the red curve is the economy's production-possibility boundary. If there is no international trade, the economy must consume the same bundle of goods that it produces. Thus, the red production-possibility boundary is also the consumption-possibility boundary. (In contrast with Figure 27.1, opportunity cost here varies along the boundary, increasing as the output of either commodity increases.) Suppose that the economy produces, and consumes, at point a, with x_1 of good X and y_1 of good Y, as shown in part (i) of the figure.

Next suppose that, with production point a, good Y can be exchanged for good X internationally. The consumption possibilities are now shown by the line tt drawn through point a. The slope of tt indicates the quantity of Y that exchanged for a unit of X on the international market.

Although production is fixed at a, consumption can now be anywhere on the line tt. For example, the consumption point could be at b. This could be achieved by exporting $y_1 - y_2$ units of Y and importing $x_2 - x_1$ units of X. Since point b (and all others online tt to the right of a) lies outside the production-possibility boundary, there are potential gains from trade. Consumers are no longer limited by their country's production possibilities. Let us suppose they prefer point b to point a. They have achieved a gain from trade by being allowed to exchange some of their production of good Y for some quantity of good X and thus to consume more of good X than is produced at home.

Stage 2: variable production

There is a further opportunity for the expansion of the country's consumption possibilities: with trade, the production bundle may be profitably altered in response to international prices. The country may produce the bundle of goods that is

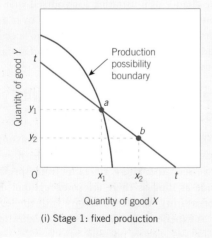

(i) Stage 1: fixed production

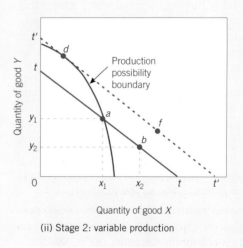

(ii) Stage 2: variable production

Box 27.1 *continued*

most valuable in world markets. This is represented by the bundle *d* in part (ii) of the figure. The consumption-possibility set is shifted to the line *t't'* by changing production from *a* to *d* and thereby increasing the country's degree of specialization in good *Y*. (Note that the slope of *t't'* is the same as that of *tt*, indicating that there is a fixed relative price at with the two goods can be traded internationally independent of this country's output.) For every point on the original consumption-possibility set *tt*, there are points on the new set *t't'* which allow more consumption of both goods; compare points *b* and *f*, for example. Notice also that, except at the zero-trade point *d*, the new consumption-possibility set lies everywhere above the production-possibility curve.

The benefits of moving from a no-trade position, such as *a*, to a trading position, such as *b* or *f*, are the gains from trade to the country. When the production of good *Y* is increased and the production of good *X* is decreased, the country is able to move to a point such as *f* by producing more of good *Y*, in which the country has a comparative advantage, and trading the additional production for good *X*.

In this box we have considered the case in which for general equilibrium reasons costs increase with output. In the text we consider the opposite case in which costs fall as output rises due to scale economies located in firm's own production function.

Gains from scale economies

Real production costs, measured in terms of resources used, often fall as the scale of output increases. The larger the scale of operations, the more can efficient large-scale machinery be used and the more efficient can be the division of labour. Figure 27.2(i) shows a firm with a declining long-run average cost curve due to scale economies. If these are to be exploited, the firm's production must be close to that shown at the right-hand side of the curve. But this may imply more output than the domestic market can take up. So if there is international trade, the country can specialize in such a product, reaping the scale economies while exporting its surplus production in return for other products in which it does not have a comparative advantage. This is especially important, because smaller countries such as Switzerland, Belgium, and Israel, whose domestic markets are not large enough to exploit economies of scale, would find it prohibitively expensive to become self-sufficient by producing a little bit of everything at very great cost.

Trade allows smaller countries to specialize and produce a few products at high enough levels of output to reap the available economies of scale and then export these in return for all the other commodities that its citizens wish to consume.

Gains from learning by doing

The discussion so far has assumed that costs vary only with the level of output. But in the previous chapter we saw a phenomenon called learning by doing—the cost of making a new product typically falls over time as the experience of producing it accumulates. This is something that may be experienced when a country begins production of a new line of goods whose production techniques are more sophisticated than those currently in use. As experience in the particular tasks required accumulates, workers and managers may become more efficient in performing them.

As people acquire expertise, costs tend to fall. There is substantial evidence that such learning by doing does occur, giving rise to a learning curve such as that illustrated in Figure 27.2(iii). The distinction between this phenomenon and the gains from economies of scale is illustrated in the figure. This is one more example of the difference between a movement along a curve, which occurs when existing scale economies are exploited, and a shift of the curve such as can be caused by learning by doing.

Recognition of the opportunities for learning by doing leads to an important implication: policy-makers need not accept *current* comparative advantages as given. Through such means as training and tax incentives, they can seek to develop new comparative advantages. Moreover, countries cannot complacently assume that their existing comparative advantages will persist. Misguided tax incentives and subsidies, or policies that discourage risk-taking, can lead to the rapid erosion of a country's comparative advantage in particular products. So, too, can developments in other countries. We return to this issue later in the chapter.

Gains from encouraging technological change and economic growth

When countries protect their home markets with high tariffs they reduce the amount of international competition faced by their domestic firms. This is particularly important when the countries are small so that there is room for only a few, or possibly even just one, domestic firm to serve the local market. In these circumstances, freeing their international trade can increase competitive pressures that face domestic firms. This in turn may lead to more product and process innovation than occurred under protection. Also, because firms throughout the world are innovating in both product and production

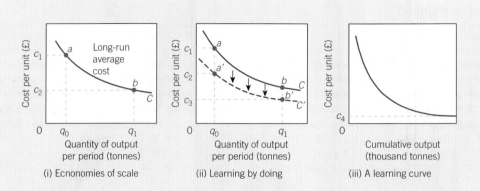

Figure 27.2 Gains from moving along and from shifting cost curves

Exploitation of scale economies implies moving along a given negatively sloped average cost curve while such dynamic forces as learning by doing can cause the whole curve to shift downwards. If a country's home market is only sufficient to absorb q_0 of the commodity whose long-run average cost curve is C in part (i) of the figure, production will be at the high unit cost of c_1. With trade, the country can produce output q_1 at the much lower unit cost t of c_2 This exploits an economy of scale. If it then exports the quantity $q_1 - q_0$ it will still have q_0 available for home consumption but at the much lower resource cost of c_2. This may lead to cost savings in two ways: (i) the increased level of production of q_1 compared with q_0 permits it to *move along* its cost curve, C, from a to b, thus reducing costs per unit to c_2. Trade may also lead to several dynamic effects that shift the whole cost curve down as shown in part (ii) of the figure when the long-run average cost curve shifts from C to C'. Output q_0 is now associated with a unit cost of c_2, while output q_1 is associated with a cost of c_3. Learning by doing or increased invention and innovation due to selling in highly competitive foreign markets may have this effect. Part (iii) shows the typical shape of a learning curve. This shows the relation between the costs of producing a given output per period and the total output over the whole time during which production has taken place. When all learning possibilities have been exploited, costs reach a minimum level, shown by c_4 in the figure. Curves of this shape have been measured for many new industries.

processes, an open trading regime allows consumers to benefit from the many technological changes that occur in other countries as well as locally.

Gains from product differentiation

One of the important lessons learned from patterns of world trade since World War II results from imperfect competition and product differentiation. Virtually all of today's manufactured consumer goods are produced in multiple differentiated product lines. In some industries many firms produce this range; in others only a few firms produce the entire product range. In both cases firms are not price-takers, and they do not exhaust all available economies of scale, as a perfectly competitive firm would do. This means that an increase in the size of the market, even in an economy as large as the United States or the European Union, may allow the exploitation of some previously unexploited scale economies in individual product lines.

These possibilities were first dramatically illustrated when the European Common Market (now called the European Union) was set up in the late 1950s. Economists had expected that specialization would occur according to the classical theory of comparative advantage, with

one country specializing in cars, another in refrigerators, another in fashion clothes, another in shoes, and so on. This is not the way it worked out. Instead, much of the vast growth of trade was in intra-industry trade. Today one can buy French, English, Italian, and German fashion goods, cars, shoes, appliances, and a host of other goods in the shops of London, Paris, Berlin, and Rome. Ships loaded with Swedish furniture bound for London pass ships loaded with English furniture bound for Stockholm, and so on.

What tariff-free European trade did was to allow a proliferation of differentiated products, with different countries each specializing in differentiated product lines. Consumers have shown by their spending patterns that they value this enormous increase in the range of choice among differentiated products. The same phenomenon was later observed as Asian countries expanded exports into European and American markets with textiles, cars, and electronic goods, while European and American manufacturers increasingly specialized their production on particular product lines. They now export textiles, cars, and electronic equipment to Japan, even while importing similar but differentiated products from Japan.

The terms of trade

So far we have seen that world production can be increased when countries specialize in the production of the goods and services in which they have a comparative advantage, and then trade with one another. We now ask how these gains from specialization and trade will be shared between countries. The division of the gain depends on the **terms of trade**, which measure the quantity of imported goods that can be obtained per unit of goods exported.

A rise in the price of imported goods, with the price of exports unchanged, indicates a fall in the terms of trade; it will now take more exports to buy the same quantity of imports. Similarly, a rise in the price of exported goods, with the price of imports unchanged, indicates a rise in terms of trade; it will now take fewer exports to buy the same quantity of imports. Thus, the ratio of these prices measures the amount of imports that can be obtained per unit of goods exported.

Because actual international trade involves many countries and many products, a country's terms of trade are computed as an index number:

$$\text{Terms of trade} = \frac{\text{Index of export prices}}{\text{Index of import prices}} \times 100.$$

A rise in the index is referred to as a *favourable* change in a country's terms of trade. A favourable change means that more can be imported per unit of goods exported than previously. For example, if the export price index rises from 100 to 120 while the import price index rises from 100 to 110, the terms of trade index rises from 100 to 109. At the new terms of trade, a unit of exports will buy 9 per cent more imports than at the old terms.

A decrease in the index of the terms of trade, called an *unfavourable* change, means that the country can import less in return for any given amount of exports or, equivalently, that it must export more to pay for any given amount of imports. For example, the sharp rise in oil prices in the 1970s led to large unfavourable shifts in the terms of trade of oil-importing countries. When oil prices fell sharply in the mid-1980s, the terms of trade of oil-importing countries changed favourably. The converse was true for oil-exporting countries. Oil prices rose again in the mid-2000s. While they had been as low as $40 per barrel in 1998, they reached over $150 per barrel in 2008. Figure 26.4 in Chapter 26 shows the changing terms of trade for the exporters of various commodity groups, as it gives these commodity prices relative to the price of a typical (United States) consumer bundle.

There are two other concepts closely related to the terms of trade that we have come across before, especially in Chapter 24. These are the *real exchange rate* and *competitiveness*. They are also indexes of the relative prices of domestic and foreign goods. However, both competitiveness and the real exchange rate normally relate to the prices of domestic production relative to foreign production, while terms of trade apply just to the subset of outputs that are imported and exported.

Notice, however, an interesting ambiguity in terminology. We have said previously that an improvement in the terms of trade is 'favourable', but a rise in domestic prices relative to foreign prices could also be described as a *loss of competitiveness*. This would normally be considered 'unfavourable'. Clearly, the same event cannot switch from good to bad just because of what we call it. The reality is that whether a relative rise in domestic prices is good or bad depends upon why it came about. If the prices of the things we produce and sell in world markets rise because they are in high demand, this is a good thing and we are better off for it (even though it could be described as a loss of competitiveness). However, if our prices rise because of domestic inefficiency or higher domestic wages bills, *for a given level of world demand for total output*, we will lose sales to foreign competitors and we will be worse off.

We now turn to a discussion of the arguments for and against government intervention in international trade.

The theory of commercial policy

Government policy towards international trade is known as **commercial policy**. Complete freedom from interference with trade is known as a **free trade** policy. Any departure from free trade designed to give some protection to domestic industries from foreign competition is called **protectionism**. Such protection may be achieved either by **tariffs**, which are taxes designed to raise the price of foreign goods, or by **non-tariff barriers**, which are devices other than tariffs that are designed to reduce the flow of imports. Examples of the latter include quotas and customs procedures deliberately made more cumbersome than is necessary.

The case for free trade

The case for free trade is based on the analysis presented above. We saw that *for any given set of real resource costs* whenever *opportunity costs* differ among countries, specialization and trade will raise world living standards. Free trade allows all countries to specialize in producing products in which they have a comparative advantage.

Free trade allows the maximization of world production for any given set of world costs, thus making it possible for each consumer in the world to consume more goods than he or she could without free trade.

This does not necessarily mean that everyone will be better off with free trade than without it. Protectionism could allow some people to obtain a larger share of a smaller world output so that they would benefit even though the average person would lose. If we ask whether it is possible for free trade to improve everyone's living standards, the answer is 'yes'. But if we ask whether free trade does in fact always do so, the answer is 'not necessarily'.

There is abundant evidence that significant differences in opportunity costs exist and that large gains are realized from international trade because of these differences. What needs explanation is the fact that trade is not wholly free. Why do tariffs and non-tariff barriers to trade continue to exist two centuries after Adam Smith and David Ricardo stated the case for free trade? Is there a valid case for protectionism?

The case for protectionism

Two kinds of argument for protection are commonly offered. The first concerns national objectives other than maximizing a country's GDP; the second concerns the desire to increase one country's GDP sometimes, but not always, at the expense of world GDP.

Objectives other than maximizing GDP as reasons for protectionism

It is possible to accept the proposition that GDP is higher with free trade, and yet rationally to oppose free trade because of a concern with policy objectives other than maximizing GDP.

Non-economic advantages of diversification

Comparative advantage might dictate that a country should specialize in producing a narrow range of products. However, the government might decide that there are distinct social advantages in encouraging a more diverse economy. Citizens would be given a wider range of occupations, and the social and psychological advantages of diversification would more than compensate for a reduction in living standards to, say, 5 per cent below what they could be with complete specialization of production according to comparative advantage.

For a very small country, specializing in the production of only a few products—though dictated by comparative advantage—may involve risks that the country does not wish to take. One such risk is that technological advances may render its major product obsolete. Everyone understands this risk, but there is debate over what governments can do about it. The pro-tariff argument is that the government can encourage a more diversified economy by protecting industries that otherwise could not compete. Opponents argue, among other things, that governments, being naturally influenced by political motives, are in the final analysis poor judges of which industries can be protected in order to produce diversification at a reasonable cost.

National defence

Another non-economic reason for protectionism concerns national defence. It used to be argued, for example, that the United Kingdom needed an experienced merchant navy in case of war, and that this industry should be fostered by protectionist policies even though it was less efficient than the foreign competition. The same argument is sometimes made for the aircraft industry. Agriculture has also been protected for strategic reasons in the past—we would need to feed ourselves if trade were disrupted by war. The United States does not allow foreign ships to transport cargo between its domestic ports on the argument that a strong merchant navy, which would not exist without protection, is needed for times of war.

Protection of specific groups

Although free trade will tend to maximize per capita GDP over the whole economy, some specific groups may have higher GDPs under protection than under free trade. An obvious example is a firm or industry that is given monopoly power when tariffs are used to restrict foreign competition. If a small group of firms, and possibly their employees, find their incomes increased by, say, 25 per cent when they get tariff protection, they may not be concerned that everyone else's incomes fall by, say, 2 per cent. They get a much larger share of a slightly smaller total income and end up better off. If they gain from the tariff, they will lose from free trade.

By increasing the production of the protected good and reducing that of others, tariffs tend to raise the incomes of those who work in the industry that is protected and lower the incomes of those who work in unprotected industries.

Conclusion

Other things being equal, most people prefer more income to less. Economists cannot say that it is irrational for a society to sacrifice some income in order to achieve other goals. However, economists can do three things when faced with such reasons for adopting protectionist measures. First, they can ask if the proposed measures really do achieve the ends suggested. Secondly, they can calculate the cost of the measures in terms of lowered living standards. Thirdly, they can see if there are alternative means of achieving the stated goals at lower cost in terms of lost output.

Maximizing GDP as a reason for protectionism

Next, we consider five important arguments for the use of tariffs when the objective is to make GDP as large as possible.

Protection of infant industries

The oldest valid argument for protectionism as a means of raising living standards concerns economies of scale. It is usually called the **infant industry argument**.

It comes in a static and dynamic form. The static form assumes that world technology is given and constant. If an industry has large economies of scale, costs will be high when the industry is small, but will fall as the industry grows. In such industries the country first in the field has a tremendous advantage. A newly developing country may find that in the early stages of development its industries are unable to compete with established foreign rivals. A trade restriction may protect these industries from foreign competition while they grow up. When they are large enough to exploit existing scale economies, they will be able to produce as cheaply as foreign rivals and thus will be able to compete without protection.

The dynamic form emphasizes that technology is constantly changing endogenously and that those countries that are at the frontier of technological advance have an enormous advantage of experience and acquired ability in inventing and innovating over those who seek to industrialize later on. To develop these abilities, so goes the argument, a country needs to protect its domestic industries during the early stages of development. The object is not to move along a given falling long-run cost curve. Instead, it is to develop industries that will have cost curves that fall over time as fast as the similar cost curves are falling in the competing countries due to invention and innovation. To prevent the new industries from becoming stagnant under the protection that shields them from foreign competition, protection must, so goes the argument, be contingent on achieving success in foreign markets within a stated period of time. Once they have developed the skills needed to hold their own in the intense international competition associated with new technologies, the protection can be removed.

The advocates of this argument for early protection point out that virtually all the economically advanced countries developed their early industries under tariff protection. This was true of Germany and France (and to some extent also of the early English industries in the Industrial Revolution, which were helped by the prohibition of imports of Indian cotton goods), the United States, Canada, Australia, and New Zealand, as well as the most successful of the Asian economies, such as Taiwan, South Korea, and Singapore. Those who support such policies argue that the assumption of fixed technology that is implicit in the major arguments for completely free trade is misleading in a world in which most competition is in terms of the technological change. They also point out that the argument does not deny the importance of trade; it just holds that to take part in globalized trade as a fully developed country, early protection may be needed for reasons found both in the theory of endogenous technological change and in the evidence of what most developed countries actually did in the early stages of their development. In so far as there is any validity in this argument, it provides a possible qualification to the proposition that free trade maximizes world GDP. If some limited protection actually raises the level of world innovation in new products and processes, world GDP may be higher with some protection than with pure free trade. What this possibility shows is that, just like all propositions that follow from economic theory, the proposition that free trade maximizes world GDP is open to empirical testing. It is not something that can be shown to be necessarily true in the real world by virtue of theoretical propositions alone.

Encouragement of learning by doing

The dynamic version of the infant industry argument is supported by the argument based on learning by doing. Skills and other things that help to create comparative advantages are not fixed for ever; they can be learned by producing the new products if enough time is allowed for the learning to take place. Thus learning by doing suggests that the pattern of comparative advantage can be changed. If a country learns enough through producing products in which it currently is at a comparative disadvantage, it may gain in the long run by specializing in those products and could develop a comparative advantage as the learning process lowers their costs.

The successes of such newly industrializing countries (NICs) as Brazil, Hong Kong, South Korea, Singapore, and Taiwan are largely based on acquired skills. For example, nothing in Singapore or Taiwan in 1960, in terms of natural resources, capital, or skills, suggested that they would become major producers of state-of-the-art electronic products well before the end of the twentieth century. This type of experience provides evidence that comparative advantages can change, and that they can be developed by suitable government policies. Also, government policies created favourable business conditions and encouraged the development of specific industries that went on to develop comparative advantages—although the importance of such policies in contributing to these developments is subject to debate.

Another major example is the post-World War II Japanese car industry. The Japanese government protected the local market against imports and prevented foreign firms from establishing production facilities in Japan. But fierce competition among the local Japanese firms led to the development of the methods of 'lean production' which, after twenty years of internal development, allowed Japanese firms to challenge foreign automobile industries and become world leaders in the industry. Another exception is the Taiwanese electronics industry. This was created by government policy that protected new local firms, some of which were government owned, and encouraged them to form knowledge-sharing partnerships with highly developed foreign firms, particularly in the United States. When the industry had grown to a viable size, the firms were all turned over to private hands and the protection slowly removed. Eventually, the Taiwanese electronics industry became a world leader that managed among other things to outcompete many of the US firms from which it had originally learned. These are both examples of the successful use of infant industry trade restrictions—restrictions which were removed when the industries had achieved sufficient scale and efficiency to allow them to compete successfully in international markets where continual innovation is a necessary condition for long-term survival.

Protecting a domestic industry from foreign competition may give its management time to learn to be efficient in acquiring all of the skills needed for success in international competition, and its labour force time to acquire the needed skills.

If this is so, it may pay in the very long run to protect the industry against foreign competition while a dynamic comparative advantage is being developed.

Some countries have succeeded in developing strong comparative advantages in targeted industries, but others have failed. One reason such policies sometimes fail is that protecting local industries from foreign competition may make the industries rigid and complacent. Another reason is the difficulty of identifying the industries that will be able to succeed in the long run. All too often the protected infant grows up to be a weakling, requiring permanent tariff protection for its continued existence, or else the rate of learning is slower than for similar industries in countries that do not provide protection from the chill winds of international competition. In these instances the anticipated comparative advantage never materializes. Where such a 'picking of winners' has succeeded it has almost always been the result of cooperation between government bodies and private sector firms, rather than civil servants picking and fostering potential winners on their own initiatives. Examples are Japan's auto industry, Taiwan's electronics industry, Singapore's software industry, and the software and semi-conductor industries in the United States.

Creation or exploitation of a strategic trade advantage

Another argument for tariffs or other trade restrictions is to create a strategic advantage in producing or marketing some new product that is expected to generate profits. To the extent that all lines of production earn normal profits, there is no reason to produce goods other than ones for which a country has a comparative advantage. However, some goods are produced in industries containing a few large firms where large-scale economies provide a natural barrier to further entry. Firms in these industries can earn extra-high profits over long periods of time. Where such industries are already well established, there is little chance that a new firm will replace one of the existing giants.

However, the situation is more fluid with new products. The first firm to develop and market a new product successfully may earn a substantial pure profit over all of its opportunity costs and become one of the few established firms in the industry. If protection of the domestic market can increase the chance that one of the protected domestic firms will become one of the established firms in the international market, the protection may pay off.

Many of today's high-tech industries have declining average total cost curves because of their large fixed costs of product development. For a new generation of civilian aircraft, silicon chips, computers, software, and pharmaceuticals, a very high proportion of each producer's total costs goes to product development. These are fixed costs of entering the market with that product, and they must be incurred before a single unit of output can be sold. In such industries there may be room for only a few firms.

The production of full-sized commercial jet aeroplanes provides an example of an industry that possesses many of these characteristics. The development costs of a new generation of jet aircraft have risen with each new generation.

If the aircraft manufacturers are to recover these costs, each of them must have large sales. Thus the number of firms that the market can support has diminished steadily, until today there is room in the world aircraft industry for only two firms producing a full range of commercial jets, while there are a few more smaller firms that specialize in a few lines such as commuter aircraft and float planes.

The characteristics just described are sometimes used to provide arguments for subsidizing the development of such industries and/or protecting their home markets with a tariff. Suppose, for example, that there is room in the aircraft industry for only three major producers of the next round of passenger jets. If a government assists a domestic firm, this firm may become one of the three that succeed and the profits that are subsequently earned may more than repay the cost of the subsidy. Furthermore, another country's firm, which was not subsidized, may have been just as good as the three that succeeded. However, without a subsidy this firm may lose out in the battle to establish itself as one of the three surviving firms in the market.

This example is not unlike the story of the European Airbus. The European producers received many direct subsidies (and they charge that their main competitor, Boeing, received many indirect ones). Whatever the merits of the argument, several things are clear: the civilian jet aircraft industry remains profitable, there is room for only two producers of a full range of such aircraft, and one of these would not have been the European consortium if it had not been for substantial government assistance.

Generalizing from this and similar cases, some economists advocate that their governments should adopt *strategic trade policies* more broadly than they do currently. This means, for high-tech industries, government protection of the home market and government subsidization (either openly or by more subtle back-door methods) of the product development stage. These economists say that if their country does not follow their advice, it will lose out in industry after industry to the more aggressive Japanese and North American competition—a competition that is adept at combining private innovative activity with government assistance.

Opponents argue that once all countries try to be strategic, they will all waste vast sums trying to break into industries in which there is no room for most of them. Advocates of strategic trade policy reply that a country cannot afford to stand by while others play the strategic game.

Advocates also argue that there are key industries that have major 'spillovers' into the rest of the economy. If a country wants to have a high living standard, it must, they argue, compete with the best. If a country allows all of its key industries to migrate to other countries, many of the others will follow. The country then risks being reduced to the status of a less developed nation.

Opponents argue that strategic trade policy is just the modern version of mercantilism—a policy of trying to enrich oneself at the expense of one's neighbours rather than looking for mutually beneficial gains from trade. They point to the rising world prosperity of the entire period following World War II, which has been built largely on a rising volume of relatively free international trade. There are real doubts that such prosperity could be maintained if the volume of trade were to shrink steadily because of growing trade barriers.

Protection against 'unfair' actions by foreign firms and governments

Tariffs may be used to prevent foreign industries from gaining an advantage over domestic industries by using predatory practices that will harm domestic industries and hence lower GDP. Two common practices are subsidies paid by foreign governments to their exporters and price discrimination by foreign firms, which is called *dumping* when it is done across international borders. These practices are typically countered by two trade policies. Countervailing duties seek to offset the advantage given to foreign producers by government subsidies. The duty is meant to raise the price of foreign imports by as much as the foreign government's subsidy lowers it. Anti-dumping duties are meant to offset predatory price discrimination whereby a foreign firm lowers its price in the importing country's market below its cost of production, often with the intention of eliminating domestic competition. The duty is meant to raise the price of the imported good to a level that would be required to cover all the firm's costs

Alteration of the terms of trade

Trade restrictions can be used to turn the terms of trade in favour of countries that produce, and export, a large fraction of the world's supply of some product. They can also be used to turn the terms of trade in favour of countries that constitute a large fraction of the world demand for some product that they import.

When the OPEC countries restricted their output of oil in the 1970s, they were able to drive up the price of oil relative to the prices of other traded goods. This turned the terms of trade in their favour; for every barrel of oil exported, they were able to obtain a larger quantity of imports. When the output of oil grew greatly in the mid-1980s, the relative price of oil fell dramatically, and the terms of trade became unfavourable for the oil-exploring companies. These are illustrations of how changes in the quantities of exports can affect the terms of trade.

Now consider a country that provides a large fraction of the total demand for some product that it imports. By restricting its demand for that product through tariffs, it can force the price of that product down. This turns the terms of trade in its favour because it can now get more units of imports per unit of exports.

Both these techniques lower world output. However, they can make it possible for a small group of countries to gain because they get a sufficiently larger share of the smaller world output. However, if foreign countries retaliate by raising their tariffs, the ensuing tariff war can easily leave every country with a lowered GDP.

Conclusion

In today's world a country's products must stand up to international competition if they are to survive. Over time this requires that they hold their own in competition for successful innovations. Protection that is high enough to confer a national monopoly reduces the incentive for firms to fight to hold their own internationally. If any one country adopts high tariffs unilaterally, the protected industries, secure in their home market because of the tariff wall, may become less and less competitive in the

international market. As the gap between domestic and foreign industries widens, any tariff wall will provide less and less protection. Eventually, the domestic industries will succumb to the foreign competition.

Although restrictive policies have sometimes been pursued following a rational assessment of the approximate cost, such policies have often been pursued for political objectives, or on fallacious economic grounds, with little appreciation of the actual costs involved.

Methods of protection

We have now studied some of the many reasons why governments may wish to provide some protection for some of their domestic industries. The next task is to see how they do it. What are the tools that provide protection?

The two main types of protectionist policy are illustrated in Figure 27.3. Both cause the price of the imported

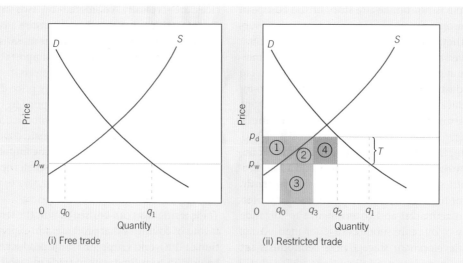

(i) Free trade   (ii) Restricted trade

Figure 27.3 Methods of protecting domestic producers

The same reduction in imports can be achieved by using either a tariff or a quantity restriction. In both parts of the figure D and S are the domestic demand and supply curves, respectively, and p_w is the world price.

Part (i) shows the situation under free trade. At the world price, p_w, domestic consumption is q_1, domestic production is q_0, and imports are $q_1 - q_0$.

Part (ii) shows what happens when protectionist policies restrict imports to the amount $q_2 - q_3$. When this is done by levying a tariff of T per unit, the price in the domestic market rises by the full amount of the tariff to p_d. Consumers reduce consumption from q_1 to q_2 and pay an extra amount, shown by the coloured areas 1, 2, and 4, for the q_2 that they now purchase. Domestic production rises from q_0 to q_3. Since domestic producers receive the domestic price, their receipts rise by the three pink areas, labelled 1, 2, and 3. Area 3 is revenue that was earned by foreign producers under free trade, while areas 1 and 2 are paid by domestic consumers because of the higher prices that they now face. Foreign suppliers of the imported good continue to receive the world price, so the government receives as tariff revenue the extra amount paid by consumers for the $q_2 - q_3$ units that are still imported (shown by the blue area labelled 4).

When the same result is accomplished by a quantity restriction, the government—through either a quota or a *voluntary export restraint (VER)*—reduces imports to $q_2 - q_3$. This drives the domestic market price up to p_d and has the same effect on domestic producers and consumers as the tariff. Since the government has merely restricted the quantity of imports, both foreign and domestic suppliers get the higher price in the domestic market. Thus foreign suppliers now receive the extra amount paid by domestic consumers (represented by the blue area labelled 4) for the units that are still imported.

good to rise and its quantity to fall. However, they differ in how they achieve these results. The caption to the figure analyses these two types of policy.

Policies that directly raise prices

The first type of protectionist policy directly raises the *price* of the imported product. A tariff, also often called an *import duty*, is the most common policy of this type. Other such policies include any rules or regulations that fulfil three conditions: they are costly to comply with, they do not apply to competing domestically produced products, and they are more than is required to meet any purpose other than restricting trade.

As shown in Figure 27.3(ii), tariffs affect both foreign and domestic producers, as well as domestic consumers. The initial effect is to raise the domestic price of the imported product above its world price by the amount of the tariff. Imports fall, and as a result foreign producers sell less and so must transfer resources to other lines of production. The price received on domestically produced units rises, as does the quantity produced domestically. On both counts domestic producers earn more. However, the cost of producing the extra output at home exceeds the price at which it could be purchased on the world market. Thus the benefit to domestic producers comes at the expense of domestic consumers. Indeed, domestic consumers lose on two counts: first, they consume less of the product because of its price rises; secondly, they pay a higher price for the amount that they do consume. This extra spending ends up in two places: the extra that is paid on all units produced at home goes to domestic producers (partly in the resource costs of extra production and partly in profit), and the extra that is paid on units still imported goes to the government as tariff revenue.

Policies that directly lower quantities

The second type of protectionist policy directly restricts the quantity of an imported product. Any implicit or explicit restriction on trade that does not involve a tariff is known as a **non-tariff barrier**. These can take various subtle forms including quality standards that are complicated for foreign firms to interpret or customs forms that take weeks to be approved. However, many non-tariff barriers are more obvious and easy to understand. A common example is the **import quota**, by which the importing country sets a maximum on the quantity of some product that may be imported each year. Popular in the recent past, but less so now has been the **voluntary export restraint (VER)**, an agreement by an exporting country to limit the amount of a good that it sells to the importing country.

The European Union and the United States have used VERs extensively, and the European Union still makes use of import quotas. In the past Japan has been pressured into negotiating several VERs with the European Union and the United States in order to limit sales of some of the Japanese goods that had the most success in international competition. For example, in 1983 the United States and Canada negotiated VERs whereby the Japanese government agreed to restrict total sales of Japanese cars to these two countries for three years. When the agreements ran out in 1986, the Japanese continued to restrain their car sales by unilateral voluntary action; however, they substituted bigger cars that are more profitable to make, as the VER applied to car numbers and not to values. In 2005, the European Union negotiated a voluntary export restriction for exports of textiles from China. This ended in January 2009.

One major difference between tariffs and quotas lies in who get the money. With tariffs the domestic government collects the tariff revenue. With quotas or VERs, the price is held high by the quantity restriction and the benefit of the higher price than would rule in a free market goes to the foreign producers.

Fallacious trade-policy arguments

We saw earlier that there are potential gains from trade and specialization. We have also seen that there are some valid arguments for a moderate degree of protectionism for some specific countries, particularly in the early stages of their development. We conclude our discussion of trade policy by noting that there are also many fallacious arguments that are heard on both sides of debates about such policies. Most of these arguments have been around for a long time, but their survival does not make them true. We examine them now to see where their fallacies lie.

Fallacious arguments for free trade

Free trade always benefits everyone

This is not necessarily so. For example, we saw above that a small group of countries may gain by restricting trade in order to get a sufficiently favourable shift in their terms of trade. Such countries would lose if they gave up these tariffs and adopted free trade unilaterally.

More importantly, some specific labour groups can lose from trade if it makes them more open to foreign competition. The prime example of this is unskilled and semi-skilled workers in advanced countries over the last few decades. Before the advent of globalized trade in manufactured goods and components, most manufactured goods were produced in the advanced industrialized countries such as the United States, the United Kingdom, Japan, and members of the European Union. Unskilled and semi-skilled workers were relatively scarce in these countries and so commanded relatively high wage rates. The globalization of trade (discussed in the section entitled 'Globalization' in Chapter 1 and in Box 8.1) which followed from the development of sophisticated methods of communication and the great reduction in transportation costs in the latter part of the twentieth century changed all that. It now became possible for parts to be produced anywhere in the world where costs were lowest and then shipped to arrive exactly when they were needed. As a result, unskilled and semi-skilled labour came into competition everywhere in the world as production went where it was cheapest. Although this growth of trade was a great benefit to workers in less developed countries, it harmed those in developed countries when they lost their privileged position due to relative scarcity. Many well-paying jobs in manufacturing disappeared, and wages for those that remained stagnated. From the world's point of view this was beneficial, but from the point of view of the unskilled and semi-skilled workers in the developed world it implied loss of job opportunities and stagnating living standards.

Infant industries never abandon their tariff protection

It is often argued that granting protection to infant industries is a mistake because these industries seldom admit to growing up, and will cling to their protection even when fully grown. Note that this is not an argument about economic relations but about political processes. Be that as it may, infant industry tariffs are a mistake only if these industries never grow up, as many have failed to do. In this case, permanent tariff protection would be required to protect a weak industry which was never able to compete on an equal footing in the international market. But if the industries do grow up and achieve the expected scale and learning economies, as many others have succeed in doing, the real costs of production are reduced and resources are freed for other uses. Whether or not the trade barriers remain, a cost saving has been effected by the scale economies. We have already given examples of industries that did 'grow up' to become world leaders in countries such as Japan, Taiwan, and Singapore. Examples of those that did not, despite substantial government protection and assistance, include the Irish steel industry, the UK computer industry, and the Japanese commercial aircraft industry.

Fallacious arguments for protectionism

It prevents exploitation

According to the exploitation theory, trade can never be mutually advantageous; one trading partner must always reap a gain at the other's expense. Thus the weaker trading partner must protect itself by restricting its trade with the stronger partner. By showing that both parties can gain from trade, the principle of comparative advantage refutes this exploitation doctrine of trade. When opportunity-cost ratios differ in two countries, specialization and the accompanying trade make it possible to produce more of all products. This makes it possible for both parties to consume more as a result of trade than they could get in its absence.

It protects against low-wage foreign labour

This argument holds that the products of low-wage countries will drive domestic products in high-wage industrialized nations from the market, and the high domestic standard of living will be dragged down to that of its poorer trading partners. Arguments of this sort have swayed many voters through the years.

As a prelude to considering them, stop and think what the argument would imply if taken out of the international context and put into a local one, where the same principles govern the gains from trade. Is it really impossible for a rich person to gain from trading with a poor person? Would the CEO of a high-street retail chain be better off if she did all her own typing, gardening, and cooking? No one believes that a rich (and busy) person cannot gain from trading with those who are less rich (and less busy).

Why then must a rich group of people lose from trading with a poor group? 'Well,' some may say, 'the poor group will price their goods too cheaply'. Does anyone believe that consumers lose from buying in supermarkets just because the prices are lower there than at the old-fashioned corner shop? Consumers gain when they can buy the same goods at a lower price. If the Koreans pay low wages and sell their goods cheaply, Korean labour may suffer, but the European Union will gain by obtaining imports at a low cost in terms of the goods that must be exported in return. The cheaper our imports are, the better off we are in terms of the goods and services available for domestic consumption.

Stated in more formal terms, the gains from trade depend on comparative, not absolute, advantages. World production is higher when any two areas, say the European Union and Japan, specialize in the production of the goods for which they have a comparative advantage than when they both try to be self-sufficient.

Might it not be possible, however, that Japan will undersell the European Union in all lines of production

and thus appropriate all, or more than all, the gains for itself, leaving the European Union no better off, or even worse off, than if it had no trade with Japan? The answer is 'no'. The reason for this depends on the behaviour of exchange rates, which were discussed in Chapter 24. As we saw in that chapter, equality of demand and supply in foreign exchange markets ensures that trade flows in both directions. The reason that a country cannot import for long without exporting can also be stated as follows.

Imports can be obtained only by spending the currency of the country that produces the imports. Claims to this currency can be obtained only by exporting goods and services, or by borrowing. Thus, lending and borrowing aside, imports must equal exports. If we ignore capital transactions, the supply of pounds on the foreign exchange market arises from UK imports into the United Kingdom, from holders of sterling wanting to purchase other currencies in order to buy foreign goods. The demand for pounds on the foreign exchange market comes from UK exports, as holders of foreign currencies must supply them and demand pounds to pay for their purchases. Equilibrium on the foreign exchange market requires that the quantity demanded must equal the quantity supplied. This is another way of saying that the value of imports must equal the value of exports. If there is a significantly large imbalance the exchange rate will change, altering the price of imports relative to exports until the balance is restored. All trade must be in two directions; we can buy only if we can also sell.

In the long run trade cannot hurt a country by causing it to import without exporting.

Trade, then, always provides scope for international specialization, with each country producing and exporting those goods for which it has a comparative advantage and importing those goods for which it does not. Nonetheless, as we saw earlier, opening international trade can hurt a group within the country which now comes into competition with many similar groups elsewhere and so loses the high GDPs that scarcity had given it.

Exports raise living standards; imports lower them

Exports create domestic income and employment; imports create income and employment for foreigners. Thus, other things being equal, exports tend to increase our total GDP and imports reduce it. Surely, then, it is desirable to encourage exports by subsidizing them and to discourage imports by taxing them.

This is an appealing argument, often heard at times when unemployment is high, but it is incorrect. Exports raise GDP by adding to the value of domestic output, but they do not add to the value of domestic consumption. In

fact, exports are goods produced at home and consumed abroad, while imports are goods produced abroad and consumed at home. The standard of living in a country depends on the goods and services available for consumption, not on what is produced. Also, since trade must balance, imports can only be paid for by selling exports. By producing the goods for which we have a comparative advantage and importing those for which we do not, we allow our real incomes to be higher than if we refused to engage in this two-way trade of exporting and importing.[2]

The living standards of a country depend on the goods and services consumed in that country. The importance of exports is that they permit imports to be made. This two-way international exchange is valuable because more goods can be imported than could be obtained if the same goods were produced at home.

Reducing imports creates domestic jobs and reduces unemployment

An exception to the case for freer trade is provided by an economy with substantial unemployment, such as the European Union in the slump that followed the crisis of 2008–9. Suppose that tariffs or import quotas cut the imports of Japanese cars, Korean textiles, US computers, and Polish vodka. Surely, the argument maintains, this will create more employment in local industries producing similar products. The answer is that it will—initially. But the Japanese, Koreans, Americans, and Poles can buy from the European Union only if they earn euros by selling things to (or by borrowing euros from) the European Union. The decline in their sales of cars, textiles, computers, and vodka will decrease their purchases of Spanish vegetables, French fruit and wine, and holidays in Greece. Jobs will be lost in EU export industries and gained in those industries that formerly faced competition from imports. The likely long-term effect is that overall employment will not be increased but merely redistributed among industries. In the process, living standards will be reduced because employment will expand in inefficient import-competing industries and contract in efficient exporting industries.

Industries and unions that compete with imports often favour protectionism, while those with large exports usually favour more trade. Protection is an ineffective means of reducing unemployment.

---

[2] If we allow for capital transactions. the statements in the text must be amended slightly. The gross flows of capital do not affect what is said, but if there is an excess of either demand or supply on account of capital transactions, there must be an equal offsetting difference between purchases and sales for current transactions.

Global commercial policy

We now discuss supranational influences on commercial policy in the world today. We start by considering some of the many international agreements that govern current commercial policies and then look in a little more detail at the European Union.

Before 1947 most countries were free to impose any tariffs on their imports. However, when one country increased its tariffs, the action often triggered retaliatory actions by its trading partners. The Great Depression of the 1930s saw a high water mark of world protectionism, as each country sought to raise its employment by raising its tariffs. The end result was lowered efficiency and less trade, but no increase in employment. Since that time, much effort has been devoted to reducing tariff barriers on both a multilateral and a regional basis.

The GATT and the WTO

One of the most notable achievements of the post-war era was the creation of the General Agreement on Tariffs and Trade (GATT). There were eight 'rounds' of global trade talks under the GATT, beginning in 1948 and ending in 1993. The three most recently completed rounds of GATT agreements, the Kennedy Round (completed 1967), the Tokyo Round (completed 1979), and the Uruguay Round (completed 1993), each reduced world tariffs substantially, the first two by about one-third each, and the last by about 40 per cent. Figure 27.4 shows that world trade

has grown faster than world GDP in most years since 1980. Since 1950 the level of real GDP has grown around tenfold while world export volumes have grown around thirty-fold. This could not have occurred without the liberalization of international trade brought about through successive rounds of tariff negotiation.

The Uruguay Round created a new body, the World Trade Organization (WTO), which superseded the GATT in 1995. It also created a new legal structure for multilateral trading. Under this new structure all members have equal mutual rights and obligations. Until the WTO was formed, developing countries who were in GATT enjoyed all the GATT rights but were exempt from most of its obligations to liberalize trade—obligations that applied only to the developed countries. However, all such special treatments were phased out over seven years starting in 1995. There is also a new dispute settlement mechanism with much more power to enforce rulings over non-tariff barriers than existed in the past. In its first eight years the WTO dealt with around 300 disputes; while the GATT only heard 300 in forty-seven years!

In 1997 three strands of negotiation that had been left incomplete in the Uruguay Round were completed, involving agreements to lower trade barriers in telecommunications, financial services, and information technology. These agreements were important because they greatly increased the amount of trade covered by WTO rules and dispute settlement procedures, and they led to

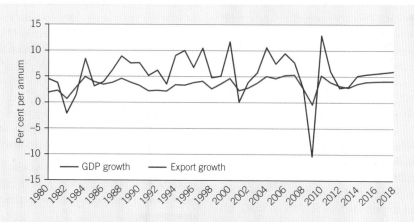

Figure 27.4 World real GDP and export volume growth, 1980–2018

Trade has grown faster than GDP for much of the past three decades. World real GDP growth has averaged around 4 per cent per year over the past three decades while world export growth has averaged around 6 per cent per year. Exports fell sharply in 2009 after the financial crisis, but recovered in 2010. Note that exports here refer to merchandise exports and exclude trade in services. Data for 2014 to 2018 are IMF forecasts as of April 2014.

Source: IMF, *World Economic Outlook* (online database) April 2014.

larger increases in trade volume than did the entire Uruguay Round They also completed most of the unfinished business from Uruguay, clearing the way for a new global trade round. This was started in 2001 at the Qatar capital, Doha, and hence is known as the Doha Round.

One of the most notable achievements was the phasing out of the regime of textile and clothing quotas that had severely restricted trade in these commodities for decades. It was phased out over a ten-year period ending in 2005. From that time on, the developing countries developed large textile industries. Lack of adequate domestic regulation has led to some dramatic disasters, such as the 2013 factory collapse in Bangladesh that killed over 1,000 workers. Nonetheless, this is a domestic problem that international pressure is helping to fix, albeit very slowly. In the meantime, employment opportunities have been created for large numbers in the developing countries at wages that seem low to us but are high relative to the alternative, which is often to stay on the farm and earn nothing other than a bare subsistence.

Because the GATT had already reduced the trade barriers for which there was least resistance, the WTO has faced a tougher job. The powerful developed nations, who were the majority of the charter members, had, albeit often reluctantly, accepted the reductions of the trade barriers on manufactured goods for which they typically had comparative advantages. But they were reluctant to do the same in areas where they lacked such advantages, particularly agricultural commodities and textiles. So the tougher issues—trade in services, intellectual property protection, and agricultural subsidies—had yet to be settled by an ever-growing membership that made the WTO rule of proceeding by consensus increasingly cumbersome. Despite biannual meetings of the WTO countries since 2001, by the end of 2014 agreement had still not been reached on the issues addressed in the new round of multilateral trade negotiations in the Doha Round. Box 27.2 gives some of the reasons for this long and possibly indefinite delay in satisfactorily ending this, the first complete round of negotiations under the WTO.

Box 27.2 Problems with the Doha Round

Although the WTO has achieved a significant degree of liberalization of trade in goods and services since its inception, much of the liberalization that has occurred has resulted from the accession of new members, such as China, from the implementation of WTO obligations and commitments from the Uruguay Round, and from services negotiations associated with unfinished business from the Uruguay Round. As far as new commitments are concerned, there have been substantial difficulties in bringing the Doha multilateral negotiations to a successful conclusion. So far, the only example of a successful multilateral tariff negotiation in the WTO is the International Technology Agreement (ITA) in 1996.

There are many reasons why it has been so difficult to complete the Doha Round compared with the successful completion of previous rounds under the WTO's predecessor, the GATT. Possibly surprisingly, some of the most important of these reasons are associated with the successes that the WTO has already had. One of these is the ITA, which was mentioned above. The spread of the global supply chain for production of computer and telecommunications products is such that a significant number of WTO members were able to reach a consensus on eliminating tariffs on products at various stages of the supply chain for computer and telecommunications products. Although this was a remarkable success in the WTO, it is probable that it has contributed to subsequent difficulties in the Doha negotiations because it removed a major industry group from support of further trade liberalization in a significant number of countries.

Another reason results from the successive rounds of negotiations in the GATT/WTO, where the developed countries made greater tariff reductions than other members. As

a result, the large emerging markets such as Brazil, China, India, Indonesia, Pakistan, Russia, and South Africa have higher tariffs on average and more tariff lines above 15 per cent rates than do the European Union, Canada, Japan, and the United States. Thus it is more difficult to engage in bargaining because of the asymmetry in tariff structures—the latter countries have little more to offer by way of tariff concession to persuade the others to cut their tariffs.

A third reason lies in the success of the earlier Doha negotiations in the granting by developed countries of unilateral duty free and quota free trade to the least developed countries. This remarkable concession gave these countries completely free access to the markets of the developed countries and requested no concessions in return. Unfortunately, this implies that these poor countries now have little to gain from further successful negotiations in the Doha Round, while they stand to lose from erosion of their preferences if these tariffs and quotas are reduced on a wider geographical basis.

There is also another set of reasons that has little to do with previous GATT/WTO successes. India is concerned about protecting agriculture. Countries such as Brazil and India are reluctant to cut their high tariffs, many of which come under the infant industry category. China has lowered tariffs but takes the position that it made enough reductions in its trade barriers in the WTO accession negotiations to relieve it from further obligations to make reductions in trade barriers comparable to other countries in the Doha negotiations. Many developing countries, especially in Africa, do not want the Doha Round to succeed because they have tariff preferences in the markets of the industrial

Box 27.2 *continued*

countries, especially against China. Canada is protecting its agricultural marketing boards and the United States is protecting agricultural subsidies, both of which are exempt from the NAFTA. The European Union is protecting agriculture in multilateral negotiations; its Common Agricultural Policy (CAP) is permitted by European Union rules.

Since the conclusion of the Tokyo Round in 1979 there has been only one successful conclusion of a broad multilateral negotiation, the Uruguay Round in 1993. The expansion of the number of countries engaged in trade negotiations, and the asymmetries in trade policies and negotiating interests just mentioned, to say nothing of the sheer difficulty in

reaching unanimous agreement among the now over 150 WTO members compared with the much smaller group that completed the earlier GATT agreements, have made it increasingly difficult to conclude major multilateral negotiations. As a result, it is possible that the Uruguay Round will turn out to be the last successful round of multilateral trade liberalization under the GATT/WTO. This raises two important questions. Is there any reason for the continued existence of the WTO? And is there any trade liberalizing alternative to multilateral negotiations under the WTO? The first question is dealt with briefly in the text while the second is discussed in the second case study at the end of the text.

If the WTO is unable to complete any further rounds of multilateral trade liberalizing policies, does it have any other reason for continued existence? The answer is a clear 'yes'. By the end of 2014 the WTO had 160 member countries including China and the Russian Federation, with a several others at various stages of negotiation to join.[3] Thus it has become a truly global forum for the regulation of government involvement in world trade. Indeed, the WTO provides protection for those small and weak countries who would be most oppressed in a lawless trading world where the powerful, particularly the United States and the European Union, could behave as they wished. In contrast with such a lawless regime, the WTO has a reasonably effective dispute settlement mechanism. Furthermore, having the developed world listen to the less developed countries' complaints at the Cancun meeting of the WTO, and then agreeing to international negotiations to address them, would have been inconceivable without the WTO.

Some argue, however, that the enforcement of dispute settlements is hindered by the disparities in economic power? Nations with large economies can use trade sanctions against small nations, but the small nation that tries the same sanctions against a large nation often inflicts most harm on its own economy. This is a major defect. But the dispute settlement mechanism has accomplished much, and to discard it because of imperfect enforcement would not seem appropriate, especially when there is no better alternative in sight.

Others argue that the WTO is a failure because it does not permit trade sanctions on those who pollute their environments or exploit their labourers. In fact, the poorer countries oppose such sanctions because they fear that advanced countries would use environmental and labour standards written into the body of trade

agreements, with trade sanctions for non-performers, as concealed non-tariff barriers. This is not to argue against WTO efforts to end slave labour and eliminate forms of pollution with worldwide effects. But it is policy imperialism to argue that the poor must accept the standards of environmental and labour protection that the rich countries can only now afford.

Yet others argue that the rich countries exert too much power over WTO negotiations. No doubt they do exert much influence on the behind-the-scenes negotiations needed to achieve unanimity, often ignoring the poorer countries. But at least the meetings provide a forum for poor nations to speak out, to broker alliances, and to use them to exert influence on the developed nations. The alternative—no voice in a no-rules system—would be much worse for them.

The WTO is undoubtedly a flawed institution—one that needs reform not abolition. Its bureaucracy is probably too small to handle the job. Decision-making by unanimous agreement is cumbersome, encouraging blocking coalitions. One reform would be a system of representation by countries selected according to such criteria as regions, level of development, and trading interests, with a mechanism for rotation. In the meantime, until a better rules-based system for governing trade relations is developed most trade experts agree that we should support the one we have, not abolish it, leaving trade anarchy in its place.

Types of regional agreement

Regional agreements seek to liberalize trade over a much smaller set of countries than in the multilateral agreements undertaken through the WTO. Four standard forms of regional trade liberalizing agreement are free-trade areas, customs unions, common markets, and economic unions.

A **free-trade area** (FTA) is the least comprehensive of the four. It allows for tariff-free trade among the member

---

[3] The latest information about the WTO can be found at <http://www.wto.org>

countries, but it leaves each member free to impose its own trade restrictions on imports from other countries. As a result, members must maintain customs points at their common borders to make sure that imports into the FTA do not all enter through the member that is levying the lowest tariff on each item. They must also agree on rules of origin to establish when a good is made in a member country, and hence is able to pass duty-free across their borders, and when it is imported from outside the FTA, and hence is liable to pay duties when it crosses borders within the FTA. Establishing if a good was made inside or outside an FTA is no easy matter in today's world where the typical manufactured product is composed of parts made in many different countries.

A **customs union** is a free-trade area plus an agreement to establish common barriers to trade with the rest of the world. Because they have a common tariff against the outside world, the members need neither customs controls on goods moving among themselves nor rules of origin.

A **common market** is a customs union that also allows free movement of labour and capital among its members.

An **economic union** takes things still further and creates an area that shares many other aspects of economic policy and harmonized legal structures, such as in the European Union today.

Trade creation and trade diversion

A major effect of regional trade liberalization is on resource reallocation. Economic theory divides these effects on production into two categories.

Trade creation occurs when producers in one member country find that they can undersell producers in another member country because the latter lose their tariff protection. For example, when the North American Free Trade Agreement (NAFTA) came into force, some Mexican firms found that, once tariffs were eliminated, they could undersell their US competitors in some product lines, while some US firms found that they could undersell their Mexican competitors in others. As a result specialization occurred and new international trade developed.

Trade diversion occurs when exporters in one member country replace foreign exporters as suppliers to another member country as a result of preferential tariff treatment. For example, US trade diversion occurred when Mexican firms found that they could undersell competitors from the European Union in the US market, not because they were the cheapest source of supply, but because their tariff-free prices were lower than the tariff-burdened prices of imports from Europe. This effect was a gain to Mexican firms but a cost to the United States, which now has to pay more for any given amount of imports of that commodity than before the trade diversion occurred.

From the global perspective trade creation represents a movement towards a more efficient use of resources, while trade diversion represents a movement towards an inefficient use of resources.

However, from the narrower national points of view of the trading partners, trade diversion brings some gain as well as some loss. In so far as there is a shared desire to increase domestic manufacturing production, trade diversion brings mutual benefit to both countries. It gives producers within the two countries an advantage over producers in the rest of the world, which has the effect of increasing the total amount of production and trade that occurs among the member countries while reducing what comes in from third countries.

EFTA, NAFTA, and other FTAs

The first important free-trade area in the modern era was the European Free Trade Association (EFTA). It was formed in 1960 by a group of European countries that were unwilling to join the European Economic Community, as the European Union was then called, because of its all-embracing character. Not wanting to be left out of the gains from trade, they formed an association whose sole purpose was tariff removal. First, they removed all tariffs on trade among themselves. Then each country signed an FTA agreement with the EEC. This made the EEC–EFTA market one of the largest tariff-free markets in the world. Three of the EFTA countries, Austria, Finland, and Sweden, switched to full membership of the European Union in 1995, and in 2014 the only remaining members were Iceland, Liechtenstein, Norway, and Switzerland.

In 1988 a sweeping agreement was signed between Canada and the United States, instituting free trade on all goods and most non-government services, and covering what was then and still is the world's largest flow of international trade between any two countries. In 1993 this agreement was extended into the North American Free Trade Agreement (NAFTA) by renegotiating the Canada–United States agreement to include Mexico. This phased out trade restrictions between these three countries, and all remaining duties and quantitative restrictions were eliminated, as scheduled, on 1 January 2008. Australia and New Zealand have also entered into an association that removes restrictions on trade in goods and services between their two countries, and a group of countries in Southeast Asia have formed the ASEAN trade group.

The countries of Latin America have been experimenting with free-trade areas for many decades. Most earlier attempts failed, but later a more durable free-trade area, known as Mercosur, has been formed. In 1994 an initiative was started to put in place a free-trade area for the whole of the Americas. Negotiations started in 1998 and were scheduled to be concluded by January 2005, but this deadline was not met. The new free-trade area planned was to create the Free Trade Area of the Americas (FTAA), but at the time of writing (2014) there is considerable doubt as to whether this will come about in the foreseeable future.

Common markets: the European Union

By far the most successful common market, which is now referred to as a single market, is the European Union. Its origins go back to the period immediately following World War II in 1945. After the war there was a strong belief throughout Europe that the way to avoid future military conflict was to create a high level of economic integration between the existing nation-states. Later, the motivation switched to creating a powerful economic bloc that could be competitive with Japan and the United States.

In 1952, as a first step towards economic union, France, Belgium, West Germany, Italy, Luxembourg, and Holland formed the European Coal and Steel Community. This removed trade restrictions on coal, steel, and iron ore among these six countries. In 1957 the same six countries signed the Treaty of Rome. This created the European Economic Community (EEC), which later became the European Community (EC), and after 1993 the European Union (EU). In 1973 the United Kingdom, Denmark, and Ireland joined, and they were followed in 1981 by Greece and in 1986 by Spain and Portugal. Austria, Sweden, and Finland entered in 1995. The European Union welcomed ten new countries in 2004: Cyprus, the Czech Republic, Estonia, Hungary, Latvia, Lithuania, Malta, Poland, Slovakia, and Slovenia. Bulgaria and Romania followed in 2007 and Croatia in 2013. As of 2014 there were five candidates (Iceland, Montenegro, Serbia, Macedonia, and Turkey) and three potential candidates (Albania, Kosovo, and Bosnia-Herzegovina).

In the first two decades of its existence the main economic achievements of the EEC were the elimination of internal tariff barriers and the establishment of common external tariffs (in other words the establishment of a customs union), and the establishment of the Common Agricultural Policy which guarantees farm prices by means of intervention and an import levy. There were other significant EEC policies, such as regional aid and protection of competition, but they did not have great economic impacts early on.

By the mid-1980s it was clear that the intended 'Common Market' had not been achieved. There remained many non-tariff barriers to trade and the mobility of labour. These included quality standards, licensing requirements, and a lack of recognition of qualifications. In financial services there were explicit exchange controls and other regulatory restrictions on cross-border trade. In response, a new push to turn the customs union into a genuine common market began in 1985.

The Single Market Programme

The Single Market Act was signed in 1986. Its intention was to remove all remaining barriers to the creation of a fully integrated single market by the end of 1992. The Single Market Act did not in itself create the single market. Rather, it was a statement (or treaty) of intent that instituted a simplified administrative procedure whereby most of the single market legislation needed only 'weighted majority' support, rather than unanimity. The single market itself was created by a large number of Directives, which were drafted by the European Commission, the European Union's civil service. These become Community law after they had been 'adopted' by the European Council (a committee of the heads of state or other ministers of member states). They then had to be ratified in the law of each member state. Once in force, they have precedence over the domestic laws of member states if there is a conflict.

Eliminating non-tariff barriers was approached on a product-by-product basis. Only in this way could minimum quality standards be created that would permit cross-border trade without the threat of quality checks as a prerequisite to entry (a problem that plagues some branches of Canada–United States trade). This required a complicated set of negotiations on quality standards relating to everything from condoms to sausages and from toys to telecommunications. There is even a quality standard for the bacterial content of aqueous toys—transparent plastic souvenirs containing, perhaps, a model of Big Ben or the Eiffel Tower which, when shaken, create a snow scene.

All countries have such safety or quality standards for their products, and what happened was the harmonization of these standards, which is something that Canada and the United States have also been trying to do since their Agreement was put into force in 1989.

The Single Market Programme is an ongoing process, not a discrete jump. Some of the intended measures have been implemented, but many are still in the pipeline. The process will continue well into the twenty-first century.

The single market in financial services

Perhaps the most significant achievements of the Single Market Programme to date have been in the area of trade in financial services. Although the Treaty of Rome called for free movement of capital as well as goods, this was ignored until the mid-1980s. Most member countries had exchange controls on capital movements. These controls prohibited residents of each country from investing in any other country.

The Capital Liberalization Directive required all member states to abolish exchange controls by June 1990. Some member states, such as the United Kingdom and Germany, had already abolished controls. France and Italy, which had not, were forced to do so by the Directive. Spain, Portugal, Ireland, and Greece were given longer to comply. All except Greece had fully abolished their controls by the end of 1992, and Greece abolished most of its controls by 1994.

Once exchange controls were abolished, it could be argued that nothing else had to be done to create a single market in financial services. Certainly, wholesale financial markets rapidly integrated with the global financial system, once they were free to do so. Indeed, this is one of the key elements of the globalization that we discussed in the section entitled 'Globalization' in Chapter 1 and Box 8.1.

However, agreement was still needed on how to facilitate greater cross-border competition in retail financial markets. Each country in isolation had already created a domestic regulatory regime designed, in part, to protect the consumer. How was the European Union to encourage competition but maintain a sensible regime of consumer protection? Financial services are particularly prone to fraud because the profit margin for a crook is 100 per cent—even a used-car salesman has to show you a car, but the seller of an investment product may offer only future promises!

The European Union adopted a pragmatic approach based upon assuming the competence of existing regulators. Firms in each sector were to be authorized as 'fit and proper' by their home country regulator, and they would then be presumed to be fit and proper to trade in any member state. In effect, the home country gave a driving licence which then permitted an authorized company to 'drive' anywhere in the Union. This mutual recognition of regulators has been wrongly interpreted as permitting financial services firms to trade anywhere in the European Union on the basis of their home country's rules. A moment's thought will tell you why it has to be wrong. Imagine, for example, British drivers being permitted to drive on the left in France just because that is the law in Britain. It is just as disastrous to have banks in any one location trading under fifteen different legal structures.

The single market in financial services is built on a dual set of principles: home country authorization, and host country conduct of business rules. This means that a firm can be authorized to trade throughout the Union by the home regulator, but the trade itself must obey the local laws in the country concerned.

Allowing home countries to regulate entry and host countries to regulate performance is a simple application of the principle of *national treatment* that was developed in the context of the Uruguay Round. It means that foreign firms are treated just the same as local firms.

The Cecchini Report of 1989 estimated that the completion of the Single Market Programme may increase the GDP of the European Union by up to 6 per cent. However, a well-known American economist, Richard Baldwin, has challenged that figure, suggesting that the gains could be at least twice as large (owing to economies of scale external to firms). And this is only the gain in one year. Similar gains will continue to flow in future years. Thus, while politically tortuous, the process of reducing trade barriers, even within groups of countries, is capable of creating considerable gains in economic efficiency.

The Lisbon Agenda

In 2000 a renewed agenda for economic progress in the European Union up to 2010 was adopted at a European Council meeting in Lisbon, Portugal, and hence is known as the Lisbon Agenda. It aimed at making 'the EU the world's most dynamic and competitive economy' by the 2010 deadline. Little progress towards this goal had been made by 2005 so it was relaunched.

In 2008 a second Lisbon initiative called The EU 2020 was launched. Its main areas of focus were (i) 'creating value by basing growth on knowledge' by such measures as improving education at all levels, modernizing the European Union's intellectual property rights system, and creating a real on-line single market, (ii) 'empowering people in inclusive societies' by such measures as making markets work better and anticipating skill needs, and (iii) 'creation of a competitive, connected and greener economy'. All of these are worthy goals, but only time will tell if effective measures for achieving them can be designed and instituted.

The future of the multilateral trading system

At the end of World War II the United States took the lead in forming GATT and in pressing for reductions in world tariffs through successive rounds of negotiations. Largely as a result of this US initiative, the world's tariff barriers have been greatly reduced, while the volume of world trade has risen steadily (see Figure 27.4).

The next few years will be critical for the future of the multilateral trading system which has served the world so well since the end of World War II. If the WTO fails to broker agreement in its first real round of trade liberalizing negotiations, the Doha Round, is the movement for trade liberalization dead? One answer is that regional agreements may fill the gap. Although many economists have been hostile to such agreements, arguing that they would reduce the incentive for further multilateral agreements, others are beginning to argue that they may be the best available alternative in the face of continued impasse at the WTO. This is taken up further in the second case study. If progress towards traded liberalization does halt, some worry that trade barriers will begin to rise. Here, the 1920s and 1930s provide a cautionary tale. Arguments for major trade restrictions always have a superficial appeal and sometimes have real short-term pay-offs. In the long term, however, a major worldwide escalation of tariffs would lower efficiency and GDPs and restrict trade worldwide, while doing nothing to raise employment. Both economic theory and the evidence of history support this proposition. Although most agree that pressure should be put on countries that restrict trade, the preceding analysis suggests that these pressures are best applied using the multilateral institution, the WTO. Unilateral imposition of restrictions in response to the perceived restrictions in other countries can all too easily degenerate into a round of mutually escalating trade barriers.

Since the beginning of the twenty-first century, the United States has been more protectionist than at any other time during the last half of the previous century. New heavy anti-dumping duties on steel and softwood lumber and big new protectionist measures for its agricultural industry are causing worrying ripples internationally. If the United States abandons the position it established over the last sixty years as the leader of the movement for trade liberalization, there is no obvious successor.

The European Union, although it has achieved something close to free trade within the Union, has been equivocal on free trade with the rest of the world. Anti-dumping duties, voluntary export agreements, and other non-tariff barriers have been used with effect against successful importers—particularly the Japanese. Although these measures may bring short-term gains, both economic theory and historical experience suggest that they will bring losses in the long term. Protectionism reduces GDPs because low-priced goods are excluded to the detriment of current consumers, particularly those with lower incomes. It also reduces employment because restrictions on imports are sooner or later balanced by restrictions on exports as other countries retaliate. It also inhibits the technological dynamism that is the source of long-term growth by shielding domestic producers from the need that free international competition forces on them—to keep up with all foreign competitors.

The second case study discusses the future of regional and multilateral trade agreements in more detail.

CASE STUDIES

1. Changing shares of world trade

Figure 27.5 shows the percentage shares of world merchandise exports of six major countries between 1957 and 2013. For most of this period, the United States has been the world's biggest exporter, though it was briefly exceeded by Germany in the late 1980s and then again for a short period in the early 2000s. The United Kingdom was the second biggest exporter in the late 1950s but it was overtaken by Germany in about 1960 and by Japan and France in the early 1970s. Japan's exports grew to rival those of the United States and Germany by the mid-1980s, but then declined in relative importance. China's share of world exports grew slowly from low relative levels during the 1980s and 1990s but then surged very rapidly in the first decade of the twenty-first century. It became the world's largest exporter in 2009 and then moved further ahead. China's growth as an exporter was even more rapid than that of Japan, but the trend of Japanese export growth did not continue in the same vein after 1986. There is no sign yet of China's share of world exports reaching a peak. Note, however, that these data relate to trade in goods, so exports of services (which are especially important for the United Kingdom) are not included.

It would also be a mistake to think that those countries whose relative share of world exports has declined are in any sense failures—far from it. All of these countries showed upward trends of volumes of exports of goods and services and an upward trend in real living standards for almost all of this period. Hence, it is not a 'bad thing' for other countries that China has become so successful. Rather, a wealthier China provides an expanded market for goods and services produced by other countries, and so its rapid growth does not provide any threat to living standards in other countries. Just remember that trade benefits both parties to the transaction, so growing trade is good for world real incomes in general. As shown in Figure 27.4,

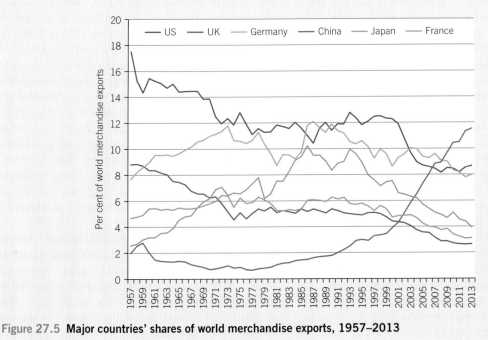

Figure 27.5 **Major countries' shares of world merchandise exports, 1957–2013**

Source: IMF, *International Financial Statistics Yearbook*.

world trade volumes did fall in 2009 but they returned to rapid growth in 2010 and more modest growth after that.

2. Can regional agreements substitute for multilateral agreements under the WTO?

Compared with the early post-war period, multilateral trade negotiations have become much more difficult to conclude because of the factors discussed in Box 27.2. The last successful major multilateral negotiation was the completion of the Uruguay Round in 1993 and there have only been two major successful rounds in the past four decades.

Regional trade agreements (RTAs), both customs unions (CUs) and free-trade agreements (FTAs), are a fact of today's trading system. Several hundred such agreements are in force today and several potentially important ones, involving the United States with both the European Union and many Asian countries, are currently being negotiated. Of these, free-trade agreements accounted for the vast majority, while customs unions accounted for fewer than 10 per cent.

Many economists, in particular Anne Krueger and Jagdish Bhagwati, argue that the political economy effects of regional trade agreements, whether customs unions or free-trade agreements, tend to inhibit further global trade liberation through the WTO by weakening the interest of individuals, firms, and government bodies in subsequent multilateral trade liberalization efforts. The reason they

give is that the political economy of trade negotiations relies to a great extent on bargaining to mobilize export-oriented producer groups to counteract protectionist import competing interests. Thus any successful regional trade negotiation can cause erosion of the political support for future multilateral negotiations because it has already achieved some of industry's goals of assuring better access to its main export markets.

In contrast with such concerns there are several reasons why RTAs may not inhibit or may even encourage further trade liberalization on a wider basis. It is true that most of the recent FTAs have been confined mainly to trade in manufactured goods, with some additional measures affecting investment and services that tend either to incorporate or make very modest additions to the commitments under the WTO. However, both the European Union and NAFTA show that when a small number of countries with relatively common interests are determined to do so they can create arrangements that go deeper than existing multilateral arrangements. When these are shown to work, they can act as templates for subsequent multilateral agreements.

Internal pressures within an FTA often work towards more trade liberalization among the members than was established by the original agreement. This is because the rationalization of production and trade that follows from the creation of an FTA leads to a lowering of the cost structure of industries, through both their expansion and the 'restructuring' of imperfectly competitive industries. As they become more confident in their ability to compete due to falling costs and expanding intra-industry trade, there can be a dynamic favouring deeper integration within the RTA.

The evolution of the EEC into the European Community and now the European Union provides an excellent example of this dynamic. The European Union has deepened through development of common standards, liberalization of trade in services, investment, and labour mobility. The ASEAN Free Trade Area (AFTA) provides another example, as it gradually evolves from a limited covering of some industries into a more comprehensive FTA with agreements also covering services and investment. Over time, multilateral liberalization through unilateral tariff reductions and gradual development of AFTA has led to the expansion of regional production networks that have reinforced the integration process.

A protected industry's original belief that its continued existence depended on high tariffs will be eroded as it finds that it can stand up to competition from firms in other countries. In some cases where the restructuring of an industry is particularly successful, the industry will see new opportunities to expand exports through reciprocal negotiations with third countries, either in subsequent FTAs or through multilateral negotiations. An example is the Canadian wine industry, which feared elimination in the original Canada–United States FTA. Instead, with some transitional government assistance, it restructured to improve quality and became so successful that it now not only competes well in Canada with wine from California and other US sources, but exports many wines, some of which have won prizes in Europe.

Another example of gradual liberalization in protected sectors after the formation of an RTA is AFTA in Southeast Asia. Initially, AFTA was not a full FTA as it had many exceptions for the most protected sectors. Yet over time, through seven rounds of AFTA negotiations, these product exceptions have gradually been brought into the AFTA coverage. At the fourteenth ASEAN summit in 2009, there was a commitment to eliminate the remaining exceptions by 2015. In a number of cases, the AFTA partners have negotiated additional FTAs with third countries, including China, Korea, Japan, Australia, and New Zealand, which have led to a widening of the number of countries whose producers

are eligible for the lower duties and that aim for elimination of most duties. Thus there has been a step by step dynamic in ASEAN to widen the coverage of the AFTA and considerable willingness to negotiate FTAs with third countries.

There are also several reasons why membership in RTAs can lead to greater willingness to participate in multilateral negotiations. For example, smaller countries that negotiate FTAs with large developed countries will lock in a more comprehensive liberalization of their trade regime. Since small countries often retain considerable latitude for trade restrictions in the WTO, the 'lock-in' effect of FTA disciplines commits them more firmly to an open trade regime through subsequent negotiations and reduces the likelihood of volatile domestic politics reversing the liberalization.

The large number of cross-region RTAs that have been negotiated in recent years suggests that the WTO member countries continue to be willing to engage in more open commerce and that the restructuring of production and trade that occurs as a result of RTAs may on balance have a positive influence on further trade liberalization. Although this might well lead to a greater willingness to engage in multilateral trade liberalization by some industries, others may lose interest in further negotiations. Thus it is impossible to predict conclusively the net effects of this rapidly evolving process. However, given the number of political economy pressures pulling in both directions, the pessimistic view that existing RTAs will definitely inhibit further trade liberalization in general, and MTAs in particular, seems unwarranted.

Since the Doha negotiations have remained blocked, more RTAs have become what appears to be the best alternative to doing nothing. The further proliferation of RTAs in this scenario is already spawning a movement for simplification by subsuming many of the overlapping RTAs in more general MTAs. After all, the more countries that have RTAs with their major trading partners, the less they have to worry about negative effects from MTAs and the more they have to gain from removing the administrative costs associated with rules of origin in multiple overlapping RTAs. Thus, over the long term, the proliferation of RTAs that seems so messy in the short term could prove to be the only realistic road to comprehensive MTAs.

Conclusion

The UK is a trading nation and an important part of its GDP is generated by foreign trade. The gains from trade are not measured by the balance between imports and exports, but by the opportunity to concentrate production

on lines in which the country has comparative advantages, exporting these in return for commodities in which other countries have comparative advantages. Thus if trade is in balance, with imports equal to exports, there is a large efficiency gain as a result of specialization according to comparative advantage.

The world has gained greatly from the reductions in tariffs that have followed successive rounds of GATT negotiations over the last half of the twentieth century. Although low tariffs have brought gains to all countries, it does not follow that completely free trade is the best policy for all. One reason for this is that developing countries who need to develop viable industries that can hold their own in the fierce world of international competition do gain from temporary assistance for these industries in the early stages of their development, as has been the case for many trading countries which are now highly successful.

Negotiations for further multilateral tariff reductions have been stalled for some years and most recent tariff reductions have been accomplished by an interlacing set of free-trade agreements that reduce trade barriers between partners but not with the rest of the world. Opinion differs as to the best way to continue trade liberalization—through a revival of multilateral negotiations through the World Trade Organization (the successor to the highly successful GATT), or by negotiating new and more extensive free-trade areas.

SUMMARY

Sources of the gains from trade

- Potential gains from trade exist whenever one country, region, firm, or individual has a comparative advantage in the production of some good or service.

- Comparative advantage occurs whenever countries have different opportunity costs of producing particular goods. World production of all products can be increased if each country transfers resources into the production of the products in which it has a comparative advantage, which means those in which it has the lower opportunity cost.

- The most important proposition in the theory of the gains from trade is that trade allows all countries to obtain the goods in which they do not have a comparative advantage at a lower opportunity cost than they would face if they were to produce all products for themselves. This allows all countries to have more of all products than they could have if they tried to be self-sufficient.

- As well as gaining the advantages of specialization arising from comparative advantage, a nation that engages in trade and specialization may realize the benefits of economies of large-scale production and of learning by doing.

- Classical theory regarded comparative advantage as being determined largely by natural resource endowments, and thus as being difficult to change. Economists now believe that many comparative advantages are acquired and thus can be changed. In today's world acquired knowledge is often more important than natural resource endowments. In this view, a country may influence its role in world production and trade to its advantage. Successful intervention leads to a country acquiring a comparative advantage; unsuccessful intervention fails to develop such an advantage.

The terms of trade

- The terms of trade is the ratio of the prices of goods exported to those imported, which determines the quantity of imports that can be obtained per unit of exports. The terms of trade determine how the gains from trade are shared. A favourable change in the terms of trade (i.e. a rise in export prices relative to import prices) means that a country can acquire more imports per unit of exports.

The theory of commercial policy

- Protection can be a means to ends other than maximizing world living standards. It is also sometimes justified on the grounds that it may lead to higher living standards for the protectionist country than a policy of free trade would. Such a result might come about by developing a dynamic comparative advantage allowing inexperienced or uneconomically small industries to become efficient enough to compete with foreign industries. A recent argument for protection is to operate a strategic trade policy whereby a country attracts firms in oligopolistic industries which, because of scale economies, can earn large profits even in equilibrium.

- Domestic industries may be protected from foreign competition by tariffs, which operate on the prices of imports, or by non-tariff barriers, which operate on the quantities of imports.

- Some fallacious free-trade arguments are that (a) because free trade maximizes world GDP, it will maximize the GDP of every individual country, and (b) because infant industries seldom admit to growing up and thus try to retain their protection indefinitely, the whole country necessarily loses by protecting its infant industries.

- Some fallacious protectionist arguments are that (a) mutually advantageous trade is impossible because one trader's gain must always be the other's loss, (b) our high-paid workers must be protected against the competition from low-paid foreign workers, and (c) imports are to be discouraged because they lower GDP and cause unemployment.

Global commercial policy

■ The World Trade Organization (WTO) has taken over from GATT the role of policing world trade rules relating to government commercial policies and providing a

forum for further international cooperation in evolving the global trade regime.

■ Regional trade liberalizing agreements such as free-trade areas and common markets bring efficiency gains through trade creation and efficiency losses through trade diversion. The North American Free Trade Agreement (NAFTA) is the world's largest and most successful free-trade area, while the European Union is the world's largest and most successful common market (now called a single market).

TOPICS FOR REVIEW

■ Comparative advantage
■ Gains from trade
■ Terms of trade
■ Free trade and protectionism
■ Tariff and non-tariff barriers to trade
■ General Agreement on Tariffs and Trade (GATT)

■ World Trade Organization (WTO)
■ Common markets, customs unions, and free-trade associations
■ North American Free Trade Agreement (NAFTA)
■ European Union (EU)

QUESTIONS

1 The table gives the outputs of two goods X and Y that can be obtained using the same amount of resources in two counties A and B.

Commodity	Country A	Country B
X	10	8
Y	20	12

(i) Which country has an absolute advantage in both commodities?
(ii) Construct a table similar to Table 27.1 showing the opportunity cost of each commodity in terms of the other commodity in each country.
(iii) Who has a comparative advantage in which commodity?
(iv) Construct a table similar to Table 27.2 showing the changes in the outputs if each country moves one unit of resources into the production of the commodity in which it has a comparative advantage.
(v) Now alter one entry in the above table by changing county's B's production of Y with one unit of

resources from 12 to 16 and then answer questions (i)–(iv) again.
(vi) State what is illustrated by a comparison of the results for questions (i)–(iv) with the two different sets of costs, those in the original table and those with the single alteration asked for in (v).

2 It is quite common for governments from time to time to encourage their citizens to buy home-produced goods in preference to foreign-produced goods. (For example, in the United Kingdom a 'buy British' policy has been encouraged in the past.) In what ways, if any, could such encouragement be good for the domestic economy?

3 Outline the arguments for and against free trade.

4 Compare and contrast tariffs and quotas as methods of restricting trade.

5 Why does trading with countries where workers have lower real incomes not make us worse off?

6 Why is it that openness to foreign competition seems to be good for economic growth?

7 What are some of the costs and benefits of globalization?

GLOSSARY

45° line Used in macroeconomics to indicate points where planned spending and actual output are equal, so that what firms produce is just equal to what agents wish to buy.

absolute advantage The advantage that one region is said to have over another in the production of some commodity when an equal quantity of resources can produce more of that commodity in the first region than in the second. Compare *comparative advantage*.

absolute price The price of a good or a service expressed in monetary units. Also called a *money price*.

accelerator theory of investment The theory that the level of investment depends on the rate of change of output.

accommodation An accommodation of inflation is said to occur when the monetary authorities increase the nominal money supply at the same rate as the price level is rising so holding the real money supply constant, which in turn prevents the *LM* and the *AD* curves from shifting left to lower equilibrium GDP.

actual GDP The level of GDP actually produced over a given period.

AD curve See *aggregate demand curve*.

AD* curve A version of the aggregate demand curve showing a negative relationship between real GDP and an unexpected increase in the rate of inflation drawn for a specific expected rate of inflation.

AD-AS multiplier The multiplier when the interest rate and the price level are both endogenous variables. See also *multiplier*.

ad valorem tax A tax levied as a percentage of the value of some transaction.

adaptive expectations The expectation of the future value of a variable formed on the basis of an adjustment that is some proportion of the error in expectations made last period. The error is the difference between what was expected last period and what actually happened.

administered price A price that is set by the decisions of the sellers of products rather than by impersonal market forces.

adverse selection The tendency for people most at risk to insure, while people least at risk do not, so that the insurers get an unrepresentative sample of clients within any one fee category.

agents All decision-makers, including consumers, workers, firms, and government bodies.

aggregate (desired) expenditure (AE) The total volume of purchases of currently produced goods and services that is made within a specific period of time.

aggregate demand(AD) The total desired purchases of final output.

aggregate demand curve A curve that plots all combinations of the price level and GDP that yield equilibrium in the goods and the asset markets—i.e. that yield *IS–LM* equilibrium.

aggregate demand shock A shift in the *aggregate demand curve*. This may result from an autonomous change in either exogenous expenditures or the demand for money or a policy-induced change in interest rates.

aggregate production function The technical relation that expresses the maximum national output that can be produced with each possible combination of capital, labour, and other resource inputs. See also *production function*.

aggregate spending See *aggregate expenditure*.

aggregate supply (AS) The total desired output of all the nation's producers.

aggregate supply curve A curve relating the economy's producers' total desired output, GDP, to the price level, *P*.

aggregate supply shock A shift in the *aggregate supply curve*. This may result from an exogenous change in input prices or from technical change.

allocative efficiency Situation in which total production cannot be reallocated in order to make someone made better off without at the same time making someone else worse off.

allocative inefficiency Situation in which production *can* be reallocated to make someone better off while making no one else worse off.

appreciation When a change in the free market exchange rate raises the value of one currency relative to others.

arbitrage Trading activity based on buying where a product is cheap and selling where it has a higher price (from the French word *arbitrer*: to referee or arbitrate). Arbitrage activity helps to bring prices closer in different segments of the market.

arc elasticity A measure of the average responsiveness of quantity to price over an interval of the demand curve: $(\Delta q/q) \times (p/\Delta p)$. See also *point elasticity*.

AS curve See *aggregate supply curve*

AS* curve A version of the aggregate supply curve that relates desired output of firms to the inflation rate. Its horizontal portion shows that GDP can vary over a wide range while the inflation rate stays close to the rate that is targeted by the Bank and fully expected by the public.

Asset equilibrium The demands for both money and bonds equals their supplies, which is true at any point on the *LM* curve.

asymmetric information A situation in which some economic agents have more relevant information than others and this affects the outcome of a bargain between them.

auction prices Prices that are set by the bidding of buyers, often against each other.

autarky Situation existing when a country does no foreign trade.

automatic fiscal stabilizers Forces that tend to stabilise GDP and that arise because the values of some tax revenues and benefits change with the level of economic activity. For example, income tax revenue rises as personal incomes rise, corporation tax revenue rises as company profits rise, and unemployment benefits fall as employment rises.

autonomous expenditures Expenditures that are determined outside of the model. In the simplest macro model with only consumers and producers, these are expenditures that are independent of the current level of GDP. In the *IS-LM* and *AD-AS* models these are expenditures that are independent of the current levels of the GDP and the interest rate.

autonomous variable See *exogenous variable*.

average fixed costs (AFC) *Total fixed costs* divided by the number of units produced.

average product (AP) Total output divided by the number of units of the *variable factor* used in its production.

average propensity to consume (APC) Total consumption expenditure divided by disposable income, C/Y_d.

average propensity to import Total imports divided by GDP, IM/Y.

average propensity to save (APS) Total saving divided by total disposable income, S/Y_d. Also known as the savings ratio.

average revenue (AR) *Total revenue* divided by the number of units sold.

average total cost (ATC) The total cost of producing any given output divided by the number of units produced, i.e. the cost per unit.

average variable cost (AVC) *Total variable cost* divided by the number of units produced. Also called unit cost.

balance of payments accounts A summary record of a country's transactions that involve payments and receipts of foreign exchange.

balance of trade The difference between the value of imports and exports of goods and services.

balanced budget A situation in which current revenue is exactly equal to current expenditure (usually applied to the finances of the government).

balanced budget multiplier The change in GDP divided by the increase in government spending that brought it about when taxes are raised sufficiently to keep the budget balanced ($\Delta T = \Delta G$).

balanced growth In macroeconomics this occurs when all of the model's real endogenous variables grow at the same rate.

bank rate The rate of interest that the Bank of England pays on commercial banks' reserve balances held at the Bank of England. It is set by the Monetary Policy Committee (*MPC*) and changes in it are one of the main ways in which monetary policy is implemented.

barriers to entry Anything that prevents new firms from entering an industry.

barter The trading of goods directly for other goods rather than for money.

base period A time period chosen for comparison purposes in order to express or compute index numbers. Values in all other periods can be expressed as percentages of the base-period value.

base rate The interest rate quoted by UK banks as the reference rate for much of their loan business. For example, a company may be given a loan at 'base plus 2 per cent'. The base rate changes periodically when the Monetary Policy Committee changes the *bank rate* signalling that it wants changes in money market rates in general. The equivalent term used by US banks is 'prime rate'.

base year A *base period* that is a year.

basic prices Used in National Accounts to refer to prices received by producers that exclude taxes on products, as in 'gross value added at basic prices'.

beta The relationship between the price of a share and the prices in the share market in general. A beta of 1 implies a perfect correlation between the price of the share in question and the general level of prices in the market as a whole.

bill A tradable security, usually with an initial maturity of up to six months, which pays no explicit interest and so trades at a discount to its maturity value.

black market A market in which goods are sold at prices that violate some legally imposed pricing or trading restriction.

bond A debt security carrying a legal obligation to pay interest and repay the principal at some stated future time. This term is used in this book to cover the many different types of debt instrument that exist in practice.

boom Period of high output and high employment usually associated with a positive GDP gap. See also *slump*.

break-even price The price at which a firm is just able to cover all of its costs, including the opportunity cost of capital. See also *shutdown price*.

budget balance The difference between the government's revenues and its expenditures. See also *balanced budget*.

budget deficit The shortfall of current revenue below current expenditure, usually with reference to the government.

budget line Line showing all those combinations of commodities that are just obtainable, given a household's income and the prices of all commodities.

budget surplus The excess of current revenue over current expenditure, usually with reference to the government.

built-in stabilizer Anything that reduces the economy's cyclical fluctuations and is activated without a conscious government decision. See also *automatic fiscal stabilizers*.

business cycles Fluctuations in the general level of activity in an economy that affect many sectors at roughly the same time, though not necessarily to the same extent. In recent times, the period from the peak of one cycle to the peak of the next has varied in the range of five to ten years. Formerly known as trade cycles.

buyout When an investor or group of investors buys up a controlling interest in a firm.

capacity output This output is also called *normal capacity output*. In micro economics it refers to output at which short-run *average total cost* reaches a minimum. In macroeconomics it refers to the level of output at which firms plan to produce under normal conditions. Where firms have horizontal short run unit cost curves, it occurs a bit below the output at which the curves begin to take on a positive slope. See also Y_c

capital All those man-made aids to further production, such as tools, machinery, and factories, which are used in the process of making other goods and services rather than being consumed for their own sake.

capital and financial account Part of the balance of payments accounts that records international transactions in assets and liabilities.

capital consumption allowance An estimate of the amount by which the capital stock is depleted through wear and tear. Also called *depreciation*.

capital deepening Increases in the amount of capital per unit of labour (and other inputs) that can occur, for example, in response to a fall in the rate of interest.

capital goods See *investment goods*.

capital inflow This arises when overseas residents buy assets denominated in the domestic currency or domestic residents sell assets denominated in some foreign currency.

capital outflow This arises when overseas residents sell assets denominated in the domestic currency or domestic residents buy assets denominated in some foreign currency.

capital stock The total quantity of physical capital in existence.

capital widening Investment in additional capacity that uses the same ratio of capital to labour as does existing capacity.

capital–labour ratio The ratio of the amount of capital to the amount of labour used in production.

cartel A group of firms that agree among themselves to act as if they were a single seller.

cash base See *high-powered money* and M0.

central authorities See *government*.

central bank A bank that acts as banker to the commercial banking system and often to the government as well. In the modern world it is usually a government-owned institution that is the sole money-issuing authority and has a key role in the setting and implementation of *monetary policy*. In the UK the central bank is the Bank of England. See also *monetary authorities*

centrally planned economy See *command economy*.

ceteris paribus 'Other things being equal': commonly used to describe a situation in which all but one of the *independent variables* are held constant in order to study the effects of changes in the remaining independent variable on the dependent variables.

change in demand A shift in the whole demand curve, i.e. a change in the amount that will be bought at each price.

change in the quantity demanded An increase or decrease in the specific quantity bought at a specified price, represented by a movement along a demand curve in response to a change in price.

circular flow of income The flow of domestic spending on output and factor services passing between domestic (as opposed to foreign) firms and domestic households.

classical dichotomy Concept in *classical economics* that monetary forces influence the general price level but have no effect on any real variable. Related to the concept of *neutrality of money*.

classical economics A term often loosely used to refer to all mainline economics up to the 1950s. More precisely, it refers to the economics that existed up to the late-1800s before the introduction of marginal theory (often called the marginal revolution). From that time on, the main stream of economics is called Neo-Classical. This body of theory was criticized by Keynes, although he called it Classical. Neoclassical economics still exists today and in some ways is an alternative to Keynesian theory and in other way compliments it.

closed economy An economy that does not engage in international trade (*autarky*).

closed shop A firm in which only union members can be employed. Closed shops may be either 'pre-entry', where the worker must be a member of the union before being employed, or 'post-entry', where the worker must join the union on becoming employed.

Coase theorem The proposition that if those creating an externality and those affected by it can bargain together with zero transaction costs, the externality will be *internalized* independently of whether it is the creators of or the sufferers from the externality who have the related property rights.

collective consumption goods See *public goods*.

command economy An economy in which the decisions of the government (as distinct from households and firms) exert the major influence over the allocation of resources and the distribution of income. Also called a centrally planned economy.

commercial policy The government's policy towards international trade, international investment flow, and related international economic relations.

commodities A term often used to refer to basic goods, such as wheat and iron ore, that are produced by the primary sector of the economy. Also often used by economists to refer to all goods and services.

common market An agreement among a group of countries to have free trade among themselves, a common set of barriers to trade with other countries, and free movement of labour and capital among themselves.

common property resource A resource that is owned by no one and may be used by anyone.

comparative advantage The ability of one nation (or region or individual) to produce a commodity at a lower opportunity cost in terms of other products forgone than another nation (or region or individual). Compare *absolute advantage*.

comparative statics Short for 'comparative-static equilibrium analysis': studying the effect of a change in some variable by comparing the positions of static equilibrium before and after the change.

compensating variation The amount of income that has to be taken away from a consumer following a price fall in one good in order to return the consumer to the original indifference curve and thereby leave the consumer feeling equally well off.

competition policy Policy designed to prohibit the acquisition and exercise of excessive market power by business firms. It is designed to prevent monopolies from arising, or abusing their power where they do exist, and also to prohibit non-competitive behaviour by oligopolistic firms.

complements Two goods for which the quantity demanded of one is negatively related to the price of the other.

concentration ratio The fraction of total market sales (or some other measure of market occupancy) accounted for by a specific number of the industry's largest firms, four-firm and eight-firm concentration ratios being the most frequently used.

constant returns to scale When all of a firm's inputs and its outputs increase at the same rate. For example, when a doubling of all inputs leads to a doubling of all outputs.

consumer An agent who purchases goods or services for his or her own use.

consumers' surplus The difference between the total value that consumers place on all units consumed of a commodity and the payment they must make to purchase that amount of the commodity.

consumption The act of using goods and services to satisfy wants.

consumption function The relationship between personal planned consumption spending and the variables that affect it, such as *disposable income* and wealth.

consumption spending (or expenditure) The amount that individuals spend on purchasing goods and services for consumption within a specific period of time.

contestable market A market in which there are no *sunk costs* of entry or exit, so that potential entry, even with no actual entry, may hold the profits of existing firms to low levels—zero in the case of perfect contestability.

cooperative solution A situation in which existing agents cooperate to maximize their joint profits.

core inflation The inflation rate as measured by the CPI after removing some of the volatile prices that are beyond the control of the Bank's monetary policy, particularly those for energy and agricultural commodities.

corporation See *joint stock company*

cost minimization An implication of profit maximization that the firm will choose the method that produces any specific output at the lowest attainable cost.

creative destruction Schumpeter's theory that high profits and wages earned by monopolistic or oligopolistic firms and unions are the spur for others to invent cheaper or better substitute products and techniques that allow their suppliers to gain some of these profits thus eroding the previously existing market power.

credibility The extent to which actors in the private sector of the economy believe that the government will carry out the policy it promises in the future. Important in policy analysis in macro models that assume *rational expectations*, since expectations of future policy action influence current behaviour.

cross-elasticity of demand The responsiveness of demand for one commodity to changes in the price of another, defined as the percentage change in quantity demanded of one commodity divided by the percentage change in the price of another commodity that brought it about.

cross-sectional data A number of observations on the same variable, such as individuals' savings or the price of eggs, all taken at the same time but in different places or for different agents.

current account An account recording all international transactions between one country and the rest of the world related to goods and services and income payments and receipts.

customs union A group of countries that agree to have free trade among themselves and a common set of barriers against imports from the rest of the world.

cyclical unemployment See *demand-deficient unemployment*.

debt Anything that is owed by one agent to another. In the context of corporate finance this applies to bonds or bank loans, but not equity.

debt instruments Any written documents that record the terms of a debt, often providing legal proof of the conditions under which interest will be paid and the principal repaid.

decision lag The time it takes to assess a situation and decide what corrective action should be taken.

decreasing returns to scale A situation in which output increases less than proportionately to inputs as the scale of production increases in the long run.

deflation A decrease in the general price level.

degree of risk A measurement of the amount of risk associated with some action such as lending money or innovating. When the nature of the risk is known, the degree can be measured by the variance (or standard deviation) of the probability distribution describing the possible outcomes.

demand The entire relationship between the quantity of a commodity that buyers would like to purchase per period of time and the price of that commodity, other things being equal.

demand curve A graphical relation showing the quantity of some commodity that households would like to buy at each possible price.

demand for money The amount of wealth that agents in the economy wish to hold in the form of money balances.

demand for money function The relation between the quantity of money demanded and its principle determinants such as income, wealth, and interest rates. In the *IS-LM* model the term is also used to describe the relation between the quantity of money demanded and the interest rate for a given level of income.

demand management Policies that seek to shift the aggregate demand (*AD*) curve by shifting either the *IS* curve (fiscal policy) or the *LM* curve (monetary policy).

demand schedule A numerical tabulation showing the quantities that are demanded at selected prices.

demand shock See *aggregate demand shock*

demand-deficient unemployment Unemployment that occurs because aggregate desired expenditure is insufficient to purchase all of the output when firms at operating at normal capacity Also called cyclical unemployment.

dependent variable The variable that is determined by the *independent variables*; e.g., in the simple consumption function, consumption is the dependent variable and disposable income is the independent variable.

depreciation (1) The loss in value of an asset over a period of time owing to physical wear and tear and obsolescence. (2) A fall in the free-market value of domestic currency in terms of foreign currencies. See also *capital consumption allowance.*

depression A prolonged period of a large positive GDP gap with high unemployment.

derived demand The demand for an input (factor of production) that results from the demand for the products that it helps to make.

developed countries Usually refers to the rich industrial countries of North America, Western Europe, Japan, and Australasia.

developing countries See *less-developed countries*.

development gap The per capita income gap between *less-developed countries* and *developed countries*.

differentiated product A product that is produced in several distinct varieties, or brands, all of which are sufficiently similar to distinguish them, as a group, from other products (e.g. cars and cell phones).

diminishing marginal rate of substitution The hypothesis that the less of one commodity is presently being consumed, the less willing the consumer will be to give up a unit of that commodity to obtain an additional unit of a second commodity; its geometrical expression is the decreasing absolute slope of an indifference curve as one moves along it to the right.

direct investment See *foreign direct investment*.

direct taxes Taxes levied on persons that can vary with the person's situation such as income or marital status.

discount rate The difference between the current price of a bill and its maturity value expressed as an annualized interest rate.

discouraged worker Someone of working age who has ceased looking for employment and hence has withdrawn from the labour force because of the poor prospects of employment.

diseconomies of scale See *decreasing returns to scale*.

disembodied technical change Technical change that is the result of changes in the organization of production that are not embodied in specific capital goods, e.g. improved management techniques.

disequilibrium A state of imbalance between opposing forces so that there is a tendency to change, as when quantity demanded does not equal quantity supplied at the prevailing price.

disposable income The after-tax income that households have at their disposal to spend or to save. It is usually indicted by the symbol Y_d.

distortions Anything that creates a deviation from some optimality condition, and thereby induces some inefficiency.

distribution of income The division of total GDP among various groups. See also *functional* and *size distribution of income*.

distribution theory The theory of what determines how the nation's total GDP is divided among various groups. See also *functional* and *size distribution of income*.

dividends Profits that are paid out to shareholders.

division of labour The breaking-up of a production process into a series of repetitive tasks, each done by a different worker.

dominant strategy A strategy that offers the best choices for one player independent of what the other players do.

double counting In national income accounting, adding up the total outputs of all the sectors in the economy so that the value of intermediate goods is counted both in the sector that produces them and in the sector that purchases them.

dumping The selling of a commodity in a foreign country at a price below its domestic sale price, for reasons not related to costs.

duopoly An industry containing exactly two firms.

economic growth The positive trend in the nation's total real GDP over the long term.

economic models A term used in several related ways: sometimes as a synonym for theory, sometimes for a specific quantification of a general theory, sometimes for the application of a general theory to a specific context, and sometimes for an abstraction designed to illustrate some point but not meant as a full theory on its own.

economic profits The difference between the revenues received from the sale of an output and the full opportunity cost of the inputs used to make the output. The cost includes the *opportunity cost* of the owners' capital. Also called *pure profits* or simply *profits*.

economic rent Any excess that a factor is paid above what is needed to keep it in its present use.

economic union A group of countries that have a *customs union* and a *common market* and common policies on product regulation, plus freedom of movement of goods, services, capital and labour.

economies of scale See *increasing returns to scale*.

economies of scope Economies achieved by a multi-product firm owing to its overall size rather than its amount of production of any one product; typically associated with large-scale distribution, advertising, and purchasing and lower cost of borrowing money. With modern multipurpose machinery, scope economies can also be achieved when such machines are used to produce a range of commodities the demand for no one of which could keep the machine occupied full time.

economy Any specified collection of interrelated marketed and non-marketed productive activities.

effective exchange rate An index number of the value of a nation's currency relative to a weighted basket of other currencies. Whereas an *exchange rate* measures the rate of exchange of one currency for another specific currency, changes in the effective exchange rate indicate movements in a single currency's value against other currencies in general.

efficiency wage A wage rate above the market-clearing level that enables employers to attract and keep the best workers as well as to provide their employees with an incentive to perform well so as to avoid being sacked.

elastic A percentage change in quantity that is greater than the percentage change in price (elasticity is greater than 1 in absolute value).

elasticity of demand See *price elasticity of demand*.

elasticity of supply See *price elasticity of supply*.

embodied technical change A technical change that is the result of new or improved tangible things such as machines and equipment

endogenous variable A variable that is explained within a theory. Also called an induced variable.

entrepreneur One who innovates, i.e. takes risks by introducing new products and/or new ways of making old products.

entrepreneurship The skill required to be an *entrepreneur*.

entry barrier Barriers to the entry of new firms into an industry. These can be natural, such as occurs with economies of large scale production, or created, such as when firms engage in excessive advertising to make it difficult for a new firm to enter the industry.

envelope curve Any curve that encloses, by being tangent to, a series of other curves. In particular, the envelope cost curve is the *LRAC* curve, which encloses the *SRAC* curves by being tangent to each without cutting any of them.

equation of exchange $MV = PT$, where M is the money stock, V is the velocity of circulation, P is the average price of transactions, and T is the number of transactions. As usually defined, it is an identity that says that the value of money spent is equal to the value of goods and services sold. However, with additional assumptions it provides a basis for the *quantity theory of money*.

equilibrium A state of balance between opposing forces so that there is no tendency to change.

equilibrium differentials Differentials in the prices of inputs, such as in wages, that persist in equilibrium without generating forces to eliminate them.

equilibrium employment The level of employment achieved when GDP is at its potential level. Traditionally referred to as full employment.

equilibrium price The price at which quantity demanded equals quantity supplied.

equilibrium quantity The amount that is bought and sold at the *equilibrium price*.

equilibrium unemployment The level of unemployment achieved when GDP is at its potential level. It is composed of *frictional* and *structural unemployment*.

equities Certificates indicating part ownership of a joint-stock company.

equivalent variation The change in income that leaves a consumer just as well off as some specific change in the price of a good.

excess demand The amount by which quantity demanded exceeds quantity supplied at some price; negative *excess supply*.

excess supply The amount by which quantity supplied exceeds quantity demanded at some price; negative *excess demand*.

excess-capacity theorem The prediction that each firm in a monopolistically competitive industry will be producing below its minimum efficient scale and hence at an average cost that is higher than it could achieve by producing its capacity output.

exchange rate The price at which two national currencies exchange for each other. Often expressed as the amount of domestic currency needed to buy one unit of foreign currency.

excludable good Goods whose owners can prevent others from consuming it or its services.

execution lag The time it takes, once as policy has been decided on, to initiate it and for its full effects to be felt.

exhaustible resource See *non-renewable resource*.

exhaustive expenditures Government purchases of currently produced goods and services. Also called government direct expenditures.

exogenous variable A variable that influences other variables within a theory but is itself determined by factors outside the theory. Also called an autonomous variable.

expectations-augmented Phillips curve A curve created by adding a variable for the expected inflation rate as a second cause to the curve that shows wage changes related to the level of unemployment. The higher the expected rate of inflation, the higher will wage changes be for any given level of unemployment. It follows that there is a separate short-run Phillips curve for each expected inflation rate, the higher the expected rate, the higher the Phillips curve relating wage inflation to unemployment. See also the *short-run Phillips curve* and the *long-run Phillips cuve*.

expected value The most likely outcome of some procedure that is repeated over and over again; the mean of the probability distribution expressing the possible outcomes.

explicit collusion This occurs when firms explicitly agree to cooperate rather than compete. See also *tacit collusion*.

extensive form game Game in which players make moves in some order over time.

external economies Economies of scale that arise from sources outside the firm.

externalities Costs or benefits of a transaction that fall on agents not involved in that transaction.

extrapolative expectations Expectation formation based on the assumption that a past trend will continue into the future. The simplest form of extrapolation would be to assume that the next period's value of a variable will be the same as this period's.

factor markets Markets where factor services are bought and sold. Markets for inputs into the productive process such as land, labour and capital.

factor price theory The theory of the determination of the prices of factors of production (inputs).

factors of production Resources used to produce goods and services; frequently divided into the basic categories of land, labour, and capital. Sometimes entrepreneurship is distinguished as a fourth factor; sometimes it is included in the category of labour.

fair game Any game, or other activity, for which the expected value of the outcome is zero, neither gain nor loss. For example, betting a given sum of money on a head in a series tosses of a fair coin.

fiat money Inconvertible paper money that is issued by government order (or fiat).

final demand Demand for the *final goods and services* produced in the economy.

final goods and services The outputs of the economy after eliminating all *double counting*, i.e. excluding all intermediate goods.

financial capital The funds used to finance a firm, including both equity capital and debt. Also called money capital, as opposed to plant and machinery that is physical capital.

financial innovation Occurs when new products are introduced into the financial system, or when existing suppliers behave in new ways. Changes are often a complex interaction of regulatory changes, changing technology, and competitive pressures.

financial intermediaries Financial institutions that borrow from one lot of agents (often taking deposits of money) and make loans to others.

fine-tuning The attempt to maintain GDP at, or near, its full-employment level by means of frequent changes in fiscal and/or monetary policy. Compare *gross-tuning*.

firm A business unit that employs factors of production (inputs) to produce goods or services that it sells to other firms, to households, or to the government.

fiscal consolidation A situation in which governments that have been running substantial budget deficits decide to aim for a sustainable budgetary position, usually by getting their spending under control or raising taxes.

fiscal policy Policies designed to influence aggregate demand by altering government spending and/or taxes, thereby shifting the *IS* curve, and the *AD* curves.

fixed capital formation See *fixed investment*.

fixed cost A cost that does not change with output. Also called overhead cost, unavoidable cost, or indirect cost.

fixed exchange rate An exchange rate that is held within a narrow band around some pre-announced par value by intervention of the country's central bank in the foreign-exchange market.

fixed factors Inputs whose available amount is fixed in the short run.

fixed investment Investment in plant and equipment.

fixed prices See *administered prices*.

flexible prices See *auction prices*.

floating exchange rate An exchange rate that is left free to be determined on the foreign-exchange market by the forces of demand and supply.

flow variable A variable expressing a rate per period of time and whose value will thus change when it is measured over different time periods. For example, a typical consumer's whose rate of spending was £10 per day is also spending at the rate of £70 per week or £7,300 per year. See *stock variable*.

foreign direct investment (FDI) Non-resident investment in the form of a takeover or capital investment in a domestic branch, plant, or subsidiary corporation in which the investor has voting control. See also *portfolio investment*.

foreign exchange Foreign currencies and claims to them in such forms as bank deposits, cheques, and promissory notes payable in that currency.

foreign-exchange market The market where foreign exchange is traded—at a price that is expressed by the *exchange rate*.

free trade An absence of any form of government interference with the free flow of international trade.

free-market economy An economy in which the decisions of individuals and firms (as distinct from the central authorities) exert the major influence over the allocation of resources.

free-rider problem The problem that arises because people have a self-interest in not revealing the strength of their own preferences for a *public good* in the hope that others will pay for it.

free-trade area (FTA) An agreement between two or more countries to abolish trade restrictions such as tariffs and import quotas on all, or most, of the trade among themselves, while each remains free to set its own trade restrictions against other countries.

frictional unemployment Unemployment that is associated with the normal turnover of labour in a dynamic economy.

function Loosely, an expression of a relationship between two or more variables. Precisely, Y is a function of the variables $X_1, \ldots, X_n$ if, for every set of values of the variables $X_1, \ldots, X_n$, there is associated a unique value of the variable Y. Also referred to as a functional relation.

functional distribution of income The distribution of income among major classes of factors of production such as between owners of land, owners of capital and owners of labour.

functional relation see *function*.

gains from trade Advantages realized as a result of specialization made possible by trade.

game theory The study of the strategic choices between agents, applicable when the outcome for one asgent depends on the behaviour of the others.

GDP See *gross domestic product*.

GDP gap See *output gap*.

general price level Average level of the prices of all goods and services produced in the economy. Usually just called the price level.

Giffen good A good with a positively sloped demand curve.

gilt-edged securities UK government bonds; so called because they are considered to carry lower risk than private sector debt.

given period Any particular period that is being compared with a *base period* by an index number.

globalization The increased world-wide interdependence of most economies. Integrated financial markets, the sourcing of the production of components throughout the world, the growing importance of transnational firms, and the linking of many service activities through the new information and communications technologies are some of its many manifestations.

GNI See *gross national income*.

GNP See *gross national product*.

gold standard Currency standard whereby a country's money is convertible into gold, usually at a fixed price.

Goodhart's law The view that many statistical relations cannot be used for policy purposes because they do not depend on causal relations and are, therefore, unstable.

goods Tangible production, such as cars or shoes. Sometimes all goods and services are loosely referred to as goods.

goods markets Markets where goods and services are bought and sold.

government In economics, all public agencies, government bodies, and other organizations belonging to, or under the control of, the government; sometimes called the central authorities.

government direct expenditures See *exhaustive expenditures*.

government failure Where government intervention imposes costs that would not have been accrued if it had acted differently.

Gresham's law That bad money (i.e. money whose intrinsic value is less than its face value) drives good money (i.e. money whose intrinsic value exceeds its face value) out of circulation.

gross capital formation See *gross investment*.

gross domestic product (GDP) The value of total output actually produced in the whole economy over some period, usually a year (although quarterly data are also available). Money GDP is in current money terms while real GDP is a volume measure that removes the effects of inflation relative to some base period or reference year. GDP is often referred to as national income and is usually given the symbol Y.

gross investment The total value of all investment goods produced in the economy during a stated period of time.

gross national income (GNI) A measure of what a nation earns from all its economic activity throughout the world. It differs from *gross domestic product*, which measures only what is produced in the domestic economy (some of which may generate income for non-residents). Used to be known as *gross national product*.

gross national product (GNP) A National Accounts concept equivalent to *gross national income* used prior to 1998. It measures income earned by domestic residents in return for contributions to current production, whether production is located at home or abroad, and is equal to GDP plus net property income from abroad.

gross return on capital The market value of output minus all non-capital costs: made up of depreciation, the pure return on capital, any risk premium, and the residual, which is *pure profit*.

gross-tuning Use of monetary and fiscal policies to attempt to correct only large deviations from potential GDP. It is contrasted with *fine-tuning*, which aims to adjust aggregate demand frequently in order to keep GDP close to its potential level at all times.

high-powered money The monetary magnitude that is under the direct control of the central bank. In the UK, it is composed of cash in the hands of the public, commercial bank reserves of currency, and deposit balances held by the commercial banks with the Bank of England. Formerly called M0.

homogeneous product A product for which, as far as purchasers are concerned, every unit is identical to every other unit.

horizontal equity Treating similar groups equitably, which usually means treating them similarly. Compare *vertical equity*.

household All people living under one roof and taking, or subject to others taking for them, joint financial decisions.

human capital The capitalized value of productive investments in persons. Usually refers to value derived from expenditures on education, training, and health improvements.

hyperinflation Episodes of very rapid inflation.

hysteresis Literally the lagging of effects behind their causes. In economics the term has come to relate to persistence or irreversibility of behaviour when an economy is moving from one equilibrium to another Its existence implies path-dependency, so that the ultimate equilibrium is not independent of how the economy gets there (i.e. the equilibrium is not unique). For example, if the duration of a period of unemployment affects the amount of the loss of the unemployed's human capital, the magnitude of equilibrium employment will be affeteted by the duration of any period of positive GDP gap.

identification problem The problem, for example, of how to estimate both demand and supply curves from observed market data on prices and quantities actually traded.

import quota A maximum amount set by the government of some product that may be imported each time period.

imputed costs The costs of using factors of production (inputs) already owned by the firm, measured by the earnings they could have received in their best alternative employment.

incentives Motivational influences that drive the behaviour of economic agents. Workers are motivated by the wage rate and working conditions, firms by the profits that can earn by producing and selling goods and services, consumers by the prices that they face for the goods and services they wish to purchase.

incidence In tax theory, where the burden of a tax finally falls.

income effect The effect on quantity demanded of a change in real income, relative prices held constant.

income elasticity of demand The responsiveness of quantity demanded to a change in income as measured by the percentage change in quantity demanded divided by the percentage change in income that brought it about.

income–consumption line On an indifference-curve diagram, a line showing how consumption bundles change as income changes, with prices held constant.

income-elastic The percentage change in quantity demanded exceeds the percentage change in income that brought it about.

income-inelastic The percentage change in quantity demanded is smaller than the percentage change in income that brought it about.

increasing returns industry One in which all firms operate under *increasing returns to scale*.

increasing returns to scale A situation in which long-run average total cost falls as output increases, enabling large firms to produce at lower unit cost than small firms. Arises when output rises more than in proportion to the change in all inputs.

incremental ratio When Y is a function of X, the incremental ratio is the change in Y divided by the change in X that brought it about, $\Delta Y/\Delta X$. The limit of this ratio as ΔX approaches 0 is the derivative of Y with respect to X, dY/dX.

independent variable A variable that can take on any value in some specified range; it influences the value of the dependent variable(s), but is not itself affected by changes in the dependent variable(s) so causation runs from the independent to the dependent variable(s).

index number An observation in a given time period expressed as a ratio to the observation in a *base period* and then multiplied by 100.

index of retail prices See *retail price index*.

indexation Generally, the term applies to any contingent contract tied to an index number. When the contract's value changes with changes in an index of the price level, the contract is then specified in real terms.

indicators Variables that policymakers monitor for the information they yield about the state of the economy.

indifference curve A curve showing all combinations of two specific products that yield equal satisfaction to the consumer and hence among which the consumer is indifferent.

indifference map A set of indifference curves in which curves further away from the origin indicate higher levels of satisfaction than curves closer to the origin. The map represents a continuous surface analogous to the contour map of a mountain in geography.

indirect tax A tax levied on a transaction that is paid by an agent by virtue of the agent's association with some activity and that does not vary with the circumstances of the agent who pays it, e.g. the VAT.

induced Anything that is determined from within a theory. The opposite of autonomous or exogenous; also called endogenous.

induced spending (expenditure) Any spending flow that is related to GDP or to any other endogeneous variable.

induced variable See *endogenous variable*.

industrial union A single union representing all workers in a given industry, whatever their trade.

industry A group of firms that sell a well-defined product or closely related set of products.

inefficient exclusion Situation in which sellers with excess capacity set positive prices, which exclude potential users who put a value on the product or activity that is positive but less than the price.

inelastic The percentage change in quantity is less than the percentage change in price that brought it about (elasticity is less than 1 in absolute value).

infant-industry argument The argument that new domestic industries with potential economies of scale need to be protected from competition from established low-cost foreign producers so that they can grow large enough to achieve costs as low as those of foreign producers.

inferior good A commodity with a negative *income elasticity*; demand for it diminishes when income increases.

inflation A positive rate of increase of the general price level.

inflationary gap A positive GDP gap, i.e. when actual GDP exceeds *potential GDP*.

information lag The time between an event happening and policymakers learning about it. For example, National Accounts data for any quarter do not arrive until six weeks or so after that quarter ends and are revised several times subsequently.

infrastructure The basic facilities (especially transportation and communications systems) on which the commerce of an economy depends. Often used to refer to all publicly created physical capital.

injections Exogenous spending flows into the circular flow of income between domestic households and firms. In the simple macro model the injections are government spending, exports, and investment (the latter when the interest rate is exogenous but not when it becomes endogenous as in the *IS-LM* model).

innovation The commercialisation of something new, a new product, a new way of making an old product or of organising the production process. See also *entrepreneur* and *invention*.

innovators Those who introduce *innovations*. Also called *entrepreneurs*.

inputs The materials and factor services used in the process of production, such as land, labour, capital and raw materials.

Insider-outsider model An analysis that gives more influence over labour market outcomes to those already in employment (usually via trade-union representation) than to the unemployed.

instruments In macro theory the variables that policymakers can control directly. (In econometrics, instruments are proxy variables used in regression equations because of their desirable statistical properties—usually independence from the equation error.)

interest The amount paid each year on a loan, usually expressed as a percentage (e.g. 5 per cent per annum) or as a ratio (e.g. 0.05) of the principal of the loan.

Interest-constant multiplier The multiplier when the interest rate, and hence investment, are exogenous variables. Also called the *simple multiplier*. See also *multiplier*.

Interest variable multiplier See *IS-LM multiplier*

intermediate goods and services All goods and services used as inputs into a further stage of production.

internal economies *Economies of scale* that arise from sources within the firm.

internal labour market The market inside the firm in which employees compete against each other, particularly for promotion.

internalizing an externality Doing something that makes an *externality* enter into the firm's own calculations of its private costs and benefits such as putting a price on carbon emissions.

Invention The discovery and/or development of something new. In economics this is a new product, process or form of organisation. Distinguished from innovation, which is the commercialisation of new inventions.

inventories Goods and materials that are held during the production or distribution process. See also *stocks*.

investment The act of producing or purchasing goods that are not for immediate consumption. These are durable goods that will form part of the physical capital stock, housing and additions to inventories of goods.

investment demand function A negative relationship between the quantity of investment per period and the interest rate, holding other things constant. Sometimes called the *marginal efficiency of investment*.

investment goods Goods produced not for present consumption, i.e. capital goods, inventories, and residential housing.

investment spending Spending on investment goods.

invisibles Services, especially in the context of the balance of payments accounts, that we cannot see physically, such as insurance, freight haulage, and tourist expenditures.

involuntary unemployment Unemployment that occurs when a person is willing to accept a job at the going wage rate but cannot find such a job.

IS curve The locus of combinations of the interest rate and the level of real GDP for which desired aggregate expenditure equals actual national output, GDP. So-called because, in a closed economy with no government, it also reflects the combinations of the interest rate and GDP for which investment equals saving, $I = S$. In general, it reflects combinations for which *injections* equal *withdrawals*.

IS-LM model A diagrammatic representation of a model of aggregate demand determination based upon the locus of equilibrium points in the aggregate spending sector (*IS*) and the monetary sector (*LM*). It is incomplete as a model of GDP determination because in it the price level is exogenous.

IS-LM multiplier The multiplier when the interest rate and thus investment is an endogenous variable (but the price level is exogenous). Also called the *interest-variable multiplier*.

isocost line A line showing all combinations of inputs that have the same total cost to the firm.

isoquant A curve showing all efficient factor combinations for producing a given level of output.

isoquant map A series of *isoquants* from the same production function, each isoquant relating to a specific level of output.

J-curve Pattern usually followed by the *balance of trade* after a devaluation of the domestic currency. Initially the trade balance deteriorates, and then after a lag it improves.

joint-stock company A firm regarded in law as having an identity of its own. Its owners, who are its shareholders, are not personally responsible for anything that is done in the name of the firm. Called a *corporation* in North America.

Keynesian economics Economic theories based on *AE*, *IS*, *LM*, *AD*, and *AS* curves and assuming enough short-run price inflexibility that *AD* and *AS* shocks cause substantial deviations of real GDP from its potential level.

Keynesian revolution Adoption of the idea that government could use monetary and fiscal policy to control aggregate demand and thereby influence the level of GDP and unemployment. For a while it was believed that Keynesian economics had found ways in which policymakers could smooth business cycles and eliminate unemployment.

Kondratieff cycles Long cycles in economic activity of around fifty years' duration. Sometimes referred to as long waves.

labour All productive human resources, mental and physical, both inherited and acquired.

labour force See *workforce*.

labour force participation rate The percentage of the population of working age that is actually in the labour force (i.e. either working or seeking work). The labour force is also called the *workforce*.

labour productivity Total output divided by the labour used in producing it, i.e. output per unit of labour.

Laffer curve A curve relating total tax revenue to the tax rate, showing zero tax revenue when the tax rate is either zero or 100 percent and a single maximum tax yield somewhere between these extreme points.

land All free gifts of nature, such as land, forests, minerals, etc. Sometimes called natural resources.

law of demand A prediction consistent with much evidence that (with rare exceptions) a reduction in a product's price will increase the quantity demanded and vice versa; that is, demand curves have a negative slope.

law of diminishing returns Law stating that, if increasing quantities of a variable input are applied to a given quantity of a fixed input, the *marginal product*, and the *average product*, of the variable input will eventually decrease.

law of price adjustment Law stating that, if there is an excess demand in a competitive market, price will rise, and if there is an excess supply, price will fall.

leakages See *withdrawals*.

learning by doing The increase in output per worker that often results as workers learn on the job through repeatedly performing the same tasks. In the case of a newly introduced product, it causes a downward shift over time in that product's average variable cost curve.

legal tender Currency that is recognized in law as the acceptable medium for any transaction such as a repayment of a debt or the purchase of a good. Bank of England notes became legal tender in England and Wales in 1833. Euro notes became legal tender for members of the eurozone in 2002.

less-developed countries (LDCs) The lower-income countries of the world, most of which are in Asia, Africa, and South and Central America. Also called underdeveloped countries, developing countries or emerging economies.

life-cycle theory A theory that relates a household's current consumption spending to its expected lifetime income or wealth.

limited partnership A form of business organization in which the firm has two classes of owner: general partners, who take part in managing the firm and who are personally liable for all of the firm's actions and debts; and limited partners, who take no part in the management of the firm and who risk only the money that they have invested.

liquidity The ease with which an asset can be converted into money.

liquidity preference The demand to hold wealth as money rather than as interest-earning assets. Also called the *demand for money*.

liquidity trap A situation that may arise when interest rates are so low that further reductions either are not possible or do not stimulate spending. In such situations the monetary authorities cannot stimulate aggregate demand by interest-rate changes alone. In a liquidity trap, money and bonds become perfect substitutes.

LM curve The locus of combinations of the interest rate and real GDP for which money demand equals money supply and hence, in a two-asset model, where the demand for bonds equals their supply. So-called because when it was developed, liquidity preference then referred to the demand for money and M (as it does now) to the money supply.

logarithmic scale A scale on which equal proportional changes are shown as equal absolute distances (e.g. 1 cm may always represent doubling of a variable, whether from 3 to 6 or 50 to 100). Also called log scale or ratio scale.

long run A period of time in which all inputs may be varied but the basic technology of production is unchanged.

long wave See *Kondratieff cycles*.

long-run aggregate supply (LRAS) curve A curve that relates the price level to equilibrium real GDP after all input costs, including wage rates, have been fully adjusted to eliminate any excess demand or supply.

long-run average cost (LRAC) curve Curve showing the least-cost method of producing each level of output when all inputs can be varied. Also sometimes called the long-run average total cost curve.

long-run industry supply (LRS) curve Curve showing the relation between equilibrium price and the output that the firms in an industry will be willing to supply after all desired entry or exit has occurred.

long-run Phillips curve (LRPC) Curve showing the relation between unemployment and the rate of change of money wage rates when all markets are in equilibrium and the actual and expected rates of inflation are equal (no one is surprised by the existing inflation rate). In many macro theories this curve is vertical at the *natural rate of unemployment* or *NAIRU*. The curve is often shown as plotting the inflation rate against GDP on the assumption of stable relations between (i) unemployment and the GDP and (ii) wage and price level changes. See also the expectations-augmented Phillips curve and the short run Phillips curve

Lorenz curve A curve showing the extent of departure from equality in the distribution of income. It graphs the proportion of total income earned by all people up to each stated point in the income distribution, such as the proportion earned by the bottom quarter, the bottom half, and the bottom three-quarters.

Lucas aggregate supply curve An aggregate supply curve that is positively sloped for unexpected increases in the price level but vertical for anticipated increases in the price level. Also known as the 'surprises only' aggregate supply curve.

Lucas critique The proposition that empirical macro models will be inaccurate when used to predict the effects of changes in policy because the behaviour of agents will be different under different policy regimes.

M0 Currency held by the non-bank public plus commercial banks' deposits with the central bank. Also known as the monetary base, the cash base, or *high-powered money*. No longer widely used as an indicator in the UK.

M1 A measure of the money stock that includes currency plus current account bank deposits. This measure is no longer reported by the Bank of England.

M2 Currency held by the public plus retail current and savings accounts in banks and building societies. Also known as 'retail M4', but no longer reported as M2.

M3 Measure of broad money no longer used as an indicator in the UK. It was equal to M1 plus all savings deposits in banks. A harmonized measure of M3, called M3H, is in use in the euro area as a monetary indicator; however, this has a different definition, as it is equal to M4 plus foreign currency and some other deposits.

M4 Currency in circulation plus all sterling deposits in banks and building societies. This is the standard measure of the money stock in current use in the UK.

macroeconomic equilibrium Aggregate demand equals aggregate supply, which implies that desired expenditure equals the actual output which is willingly supplied by producers and that the demand for money and bonds also equal their supplies.

macroeconomic policy Any measure directed at influencing such macroeconomic variables as the overall levels of employment, unemployment, GDP, and the price level.

macroeconomics The study of the determination of economic aggregates and averages, such as total output, total employment, the general price level, and the rate of economic growth.

marginal cost (MC) The increase in total cost resulting from raising the rate of production by one unit. Technically this is incremental cost, $\Delta C/\Delta P$ (where where P indicates production), while marginal cost is the derivative of cost with respect to production dC/dP

marginal cost pricing A policy of setting the price of a product equal to its marginal cost.

marginal efficiency of capital The rate at which the value of the stream of output of a marginal unit of capital must be discounted to make it equal to £1. In effect, it is the interest rate at which one more unit of capital would be just worth buying.

marginal efficiency of capital schedule A schedule that relates the marginal efficiency of each additional £1 worth of capital to the size of the capital stock. It represents the demand curve for capital and is negatively sloped with respect to the interest rate.

marginal efficiency of investment The relation between desired investment and the rate of interest, assuming all other things are equal.

marginal physical product (MPP) See *marginal product*.

marginal product (MP) The change in total product resulting from using one more (or less) unit of the variable factor. Also called marginal physical product. Technically this is incremental product, $\Delta P/\Delta F$, where P denotes product and F the variable factor, while marginal product is the partial derivative of total product with respect to the variable input $\partial P/\partial F$.

marginal productivity theory The demand half of the *neoclassical theory* of income distribution, in which the demand for any variable input is determined by the value of that input's *marginal revenue product*.

marginal propensity not to spend The proportion of any new increment of disposable income that is not passed on in spending, and instead leaks out of (i.e. is withdrawn from) the circular flow of income. Also called the marginal propensity to withdraw and the marginal propensity to leak. Technically this can be expressed as an incremental ratio $\Delta W/\Delta Y_d$, or as the derivative of not spending (withdrawing) with respect to disposable income, dW/dY_d. This can also be expressed in either form as a relation between withdrawals and total GDP rather than disposable income.

marginal propensity to consume (MPC) The proportion of any new increment of disposible income that is spent on consumption, $\Delta C/\Delta Y_d$. Technically this is incremental ratio while marginal propensity is the derivative of consumption with respect to disposable income dC/Y_d.

marginal propensity to import The proportion of any new increment of GDP that is spent on imports, $\Delta IM/\Delta Y$. Technically this is the incremental propensity while the marginal propensity is the derivative of imports with respect to GDP, dC/Y.

marginal propensity to leak See *marginal propensity not to spend*.

marginal propensity to save (MPS) The proportion of any new increment of disposable income that is saved, $\Delta S/\Delta Y_d$. Technically this is the incremental ratio, while the marginal propensity is the derivative of savings with respect to disposable income dS/dY_d.

marginal propensity to spend The ratio of any increment of qaggregate induced expenditure (E) to the increment in total GDP (Y) that brought it about. Technically this can be expressed as an incremental ratio $\Delta E/\Delta Y$, or as the derivative of expenditure with respect to GDP, dC/Y.

marginal propensity to tax The proportion of any increment in GDP that is taxed away by the government, $\Delta T/\Delta Y$. Technically this can be expressed as an incremental ratio $\Delta T/\Delta Y$, or as the derivative of tax revenue with respect to GDP, dT/Y.

marginal propensity to withdraw See *marginal propensity not to spend*.

marginal rate of substitution (MRS) The rate at which one input is substituted for another with output held constant. Graphically, the slope of the *isoquant*.

marginal rate of transformation The slope of the *production possibility boundary*, indicating the rate of substitution of production of one good for that of another.

marginal revenue The change in total revenue (R) resulting from a unit change in the sales (S) per period of time. Technically this can be expressed as an incremental ratio $\Delta R/\Delta S$, or as the derivative of revenue with respect to sales, dR/dS.

marginal revenue product (MRP) The addition to a firm's revenue (R) resulting from the sale of the output produced by an additional unit of the variable input (V). Technically this can be expressed as an incremental ratio $\Delta R/\Delta V$, or as the derivative of revenue with respect to the variable input, dR/dV.

marginal utility The change in satisfaction resulting from consuming one unit more or one unit less of a good or service. Technically this can be expressed as an incremental ratio $\Delta S/\Delta G$, where S is satisfaction and G is a good being consumed or as the derivative of satisfaction with respect to the good consumed, dS/dG.

market An area in either geographical or cyber space over which buyers and sellers negotiate the exchange of a well-defined product.

market economy A society in which agents specialize in productive activities and meet most of their material wants through exchanges voluntarily agreed upon by the contracting parties.

market failure Any market performance that is less than the most efficient possible (the optimal) performance.

market for corporate control Where potential buyers and sellers (both willing and unwilling) bargain about buying or selling the ownership of firms.

market prices In National Accounts, refers to the fact that spending is measured in the prices actually paid by consumers and so include taxes on products. See also *basic prices*.

market sector That portion of an economy in which producers must cover their costs by selling their output to consumers in exchange for money. Non-market sectors include those where goods or services are provided free of charge, such as parts of health and education and the activities of such non-government organisations (NGOs) as Doctors Without Borders and Greenpeace.

market structure The characteristics of a market that influence the behaviour and performance of firms that sell in the market. The four main market structures are *perfect competition, monopolistic competition, oligopoly,* and *monopoly*.

maturity The length of time until the redemption date of a security such as a bond.

medium of exchange A commodity or token that is widely accepted in payment for goods and services.

menu costs Costs associated with changing prices, such as the costs of reprinting catalogues or menus. These costs make it rational for producers to keep output prices fixed until input prices have changed significantly, or to respond to such price changes only periodically.

mercantilism The doctrine that the gains from trade depend on the balance of trade, in contrast with the accepted theory, in which the gains from trade are associated with the volume of trade.

merchandise account The part of the balance of payments accounts relating to trade in goods (but not services).

merchandise trade Trade in physical products. Same as *visible trade*.

merger The uniting of two or more formerly independent firms.

merit goods Goods that the government decides have sufficient merit that more should be produced and consumed than people would choose to do if left to themselves.

microeconomics The study of the allocation of resources to the production of specific goods and services and the distribution of income as they are affected by the working of the price system and by the policies of the central authorities.

minimum efficient scale (MES) The smallest level of output at which long-run average cost is at a minimum; the smallest output required to achieve all economies of scale in production.

mismatch See *structural unemployment*.

mixed economy An economy in which a significant number of decisions about the allocation of resources are made by firms and households and others by the government.

monetarism The doctrine that monetary aggregates (the money supply) exert powerful influences in the economy and that control of these magnitudes is a potent means of affecting the economy's macroeconomic behaviour.

monetary authorities A general term that covers all those who are responsible for the setting and execution of monetary policy, including the generation of high powered money and the setting of interest rates. In the UK, these authorities are the Bank of England and the Monetary Policy Committee.

monetary base See *high-powered money* and *M0*.

monetary equilibrium A situation in which there is no excess demand for or supply of money. In two-asset model this also implies equilibrium between the demand for and the supply of bonds.

monetary policy Policy of seeking to control aggregate demand, and ultimately the GDP and the inflation rate, by setting short-term interest rates, and more recently, by *quantitative easing* which means buying large amounts of government debt (and some other assets) in order to inject liquidity into the system.

Monetary Policy Committee In May 1997 the overall power to determine monetary policy was given to the newly formed Monetary Policy Committee (MPC), chaired by the Governor of the Bank of England and composed of five senior officials of the Bank and four outsiders appointed by the government. The MPC sets monetary policy, while a department of the Bank carries it out.

monetary transmission mechanism The mechanism that turns a monetary shock induced by a change in either the private or the government sector into a real spending shock (as shift of the *IS*, *AD* and *AD* curves*) and thus links the monetary and the real sides of the economy.

money Any generally accepted medium of exchange, i.e. anything that will be accepted in exchange for goods and services.

money illusion Refers to behaviour that responds to purely nominal changes in money prices and incomes in either direction, even though real incomes or relative prices have not changed.

money income Income measured in terms of some monetary unit such as current pounds or dollars, but not taking account of inflation. See also *real income*.

money multiplier The ratio of changes in the money stock to changes in the monetary base (i.e. in, *high-powered money*).

money price See *absolute price*.

money rate of interest The rate of interest as measured in monetary units. See *real rate of interest*.

money stock See *supply of money*.

money supply See *supply of money*.

money-demand function The function that determines the demand to hold money balances in relation to other variables such as income, wealth and interest rates.

monopolist The sole seller of a product.

monopolistic competition A market structure in which there are many sellers and freedom of entry but in which each firm sells a differentiated version of some generic product and, as a result, faces a negatively sloped demand curve for its own product.

monopoly A market structure in which the industry contains only one firm.

monopsonist The sole purchaser of a product.

moral hazard Any change in behaviour resulting from the fact that a contract has been agreed. Examples are motorists who drive more recklessly because they have accident insurance and householders who are careless about home security because they have theft insurance.

multinational enterprises (MNEs) See *transnational corporations*.

multiplier The ratio of the change in GDP (or some other endogenous variable) to the change in autonomous spending (or other exogenous variable) that brought it about. Several different multipliers are distinguished: the simple or interest-constant multiplier; the interest-variable or IS-LM multiplier, when the interest rate and hence investment becomes exogenous, and the AD-AS multiplier when the price level becomes endogenous.

NAIRU The acronym stands for 'non-accelerating-inflation rate of unemployment' – the level of unemployment compatible with a constant rate of inflation – one that neither accelerates nor decelerates. In the long run, when the economy is in competitive equilibrium, the NAIRU is equivalent to the *natural rate of unemployment*.

Nash equilibrium An equilibrium that results when each player in a game (it might be a firm in an industry) is currently doing the best that it can, given the current behaviour of all other players (who might be the other firms in that industry).

Nash theorem That every game with a finite number of players and a finite number of strategies has at least one Nash equilibrium (so long as some random element to strategies is possible).

national asset formation Positive net exports (*X –IM*) (which causes the net acquisition of foreign assets) plus domestic investment, *I*.

national debt The debt of the central government.

national income A generic term for the value of the nation's total output, and the value of the income generated by the production of that output. Measured in practice by *gross national product,* GDP, which is equal to the GNI in a closed economy.

national product A generic term for the nation's total output, typically measured by GDP. See *gross national product*.

natural monopoly An industry whose market demand is insufficient to allow two firms to cover their total costs at any positive level of output.

natural rate of unemployment The level of unemployment in a competitive economy that exists when GDP is at its potential.

For most purposes it is equivalent to the *NAIRU*, but the latter may differ when the economy is adjusting slowly back to full equilibrium following some large shock.

natural scale A scale on which equal absolute amounts are represented by equal distances. Compare *logarithmic scale*.

negatively related Refers to the relationship where an increase in one variable is associated with a decrease in another.

neoclassical theory In general, a theory based on the maximizing choices of well-informed agents pursuing their own self-interest in competitive markets. In *distribution* it is a theory that factor incomes are determined by demand and supply, where demand depends on the value of the factor's marginal product and supply depends on the maximizing decisions of those who own the factors.

net exports Total exports minus total imports of goods and services ($X - IM$).

net investment Gross investment minus replacement investment, which is new capital that represents net additions to the capital stock.

net present value The difference between the present value of revenues and the present value of costs.

net taxes Total tax receipts net of *transfer payments*.

neutrality of money money This theory takes several forms: (1) a change in the money supply that instantaneously changes all monetary values in the same proportion, such as when a monetary reform takes several zeros off all forms of money and money contracts, will have no real effects; (2) there will be no perceptible differences between the real behaviour of an economy that operates with a fully expected zero inflation rate and a fully expected (and fully accommodated) small positive inflation rate, say 2 percent. (3) changes in the money stock as they occur in reality – taking a significant amount of time to occur and to have their full effects felt – do not have real effects in long run (4) such changes do not have real effects in the short run. Version (1) is accepted by virtually all economists; version (2) is shown to be probably correct by the behaviour of those economies that have adapted the regime of successful inflation targeting over the last 20 or so years, Version (3) is accepted by many economists and is a property of many economic models, however, if there are transitional effects that have long-lasting consequences (*hysteresis effects*), it may not hold. Version (4) is a property of a few models but is not accepted by the majority of economists as being true in reality.

New Classical theory A theory that assumes that the economy behaves as if it were perfectly competitive, with all markets always clearing; where deviations from full employment can occur only if people make mistakes and where, given rational expectations, these mistakes will not be systematic.

New Keynesian economics Recent research agenda that has focused on explaining why prices do not adjust to clear markets, especially the labour market. It differs from the traditional Keynesian approach in its concern for *equilibrium unemployment* as well as *demand-deficient unemployment*.

newly industrialized countries (NICs) Formerly *less-developed countries* that have become major industrial producers and exporters in recent times. Sometimes called newly industrialized economies (NIEs).

nominal interest rate Actual interest rate in money terms. It is contrasted with the *real rate of interest*

nominal money supply The money supply measured in monetary units.

nominal national product Total output valued at current prices and usually measured by 'money GDP'.

non-cooperative equilibrium The equilibrium reached when firms calculate their own best policy without considering competitors' reactions and without explicit collusion.

non-excludable A good or service is non-excludable if its owners cannot dictate who will consume it.

non-market sector That portion of an economy in which producers must cover their costs from some source other than sales revenue.

non-renewable (or exhaustible) resource Any productive resource that exists as a fixed stock that cannot be replaced once it is used, such as natural petroleum.

non-rivalrous A good or a service is non-rivalrous if a given unit of it can be consumed by everyone. Thus, one person's consumption of it does not reduce the ability of another person to consume it—as with knowledge, national defence, police protection, and navigational aids.

non-strategic behaviour Behaviour that does not take account of the reactions of others, as when a firm acts in perfect or monopolistic competition.

non-tariff barriers Devices other than tariffs that are designed to reduce the flow of imports.

non-tradables Goods and services that are produced and sold domestically but do not enter into international trade.

normal form game Players make choices based on expected pay-offs simultaneously.

normal good A commodity whose demand increases when income increases. Compare *inferior good*.

normative Things that concern what ought to be and thus depend on value judgments. Compare *positive*.

oligopoly An industry that contains only a few firms that interact strategically. The outcome for each is affected by what the others do.

OPEC Organisation of Petroleum Exporting Countries a permanent, intergovernmental Organization to regulate petroleum production, which was created in 1960, by Iran, Iraq, Kuwait, Saudi Arabia and Venezuela, later joined by nine other members: Qatar, Indonesia, Libya, United Arab Emirates, Algeria, Nigeria, Ecuador, Angola, and Gabon, some of which have subsequently dropped out.

open economy An economy that engages in international trade.

open shop A place of employment in which a union represents its members but does not necessarily have bargaining jurisdiction for all workers, and where membership of the union is not a condition of getting or keeping a job.

open-market operations Sales or purchases of securities by the central bank aimed at influencing monetary conditions.

opportunity cost Measurement of cost by reference to the alternatives forgone.

optimum output See *profit-maximizing output*.

option Options come in two varieties. A *call option* is the right (but not the obligation) to buy some commodity or security in the future at a specific price called the exercise price that is set now. A *put option* is the right (but not the obligation) to sell some commodity or security in the future at a specific price that is set now.

ordinary partnership An enterprise composed of a group of individuals who are all jointly liable for the debts and other obligations of that enterprise.

output The goods and services that result from the process of production.

output gap The difference between actual output and potential output ($Y - Y^*$); negative output gaps are sometimes called *recessionary gaps*; positive output gaps are sometimes called *inflationary gaps*. Also called the *GDP gap*.

overshooting Occurs when the impact effect of a shock takes a variable beyond its ultimate equilibrium level. Most widely applied to the exchange rate. A characteristic of a wide class of exchange-rate models under rational expectations is that when monetary policy is, say, tightened, the exchange rate initially appreciates to a point from which it will later depreciate towards its long-run equilibrium level.

paradox of value The observation that the necessities of life, such as water, often have low prices while dispensable luxuries, such as diamonds, often have high prices. This seemed a paradox to early economists but was explained later by the observation that a product's price is related to its marginal utility not its total utility.

Pareto optimality A situation in which it is impossible to reallocate production activities to produce more of one good without producing less of some other good, and in which it is impossible to reallocate consumption activities to make at least one person better off without making anyone worse off. Also called Pareto efficiency.

participation rate This is the proportion of the population of working age that is economically active and so working or actively seeking work.

partnership An enterprise with two or more joint owners, each of whom is personally responsible for all of the partnership's debts and other obligations.

paternalism The belief that the individual is not the best judge of his or her own self-interest; i.e. the belief that someone else knows better, such as a government official or a politician.

path-dependence The final outcome of a process depends on the path taken to reach that outcome. If a market has path dependence, the nature of the final equilibrium reached after any disturbance will depend on the path taken to reach equilibrium, thus the equilibrium is not unique. In Macroeconomics, one important case of path dependence that is believed to exist is that a long period of positive GDP gap and its resulting unemployment typically affects the stock of physical and human capital for a long time after the gap has been eliminated. This case is sometimes referred to as showing *hysteresis*.

per capita economic growth The growth of per capita GDP or GNI divided by the population.

perfect competition A market structure in which the large number of firms in an industry are price takers and in which there is freedom of entry into, and exit from, the industry.

permanent income The maximum amount that a person can consume per year into the indefinite future without reducing his or her wealth.

permanent income theory A theory that relates actual consumption to *permanent income*.

perpetuity A bond that pays a fixed sum of money each year for ever and has no redemption date. Sometimes called a consol in the UK.

personal disposable income (*PDI*) The gross income of the personal sector less all direct taxes and national insurance contributions. Also called household disposable income and indicated by the symbol Y_d.

personal income Income earned by or paid to individuals before personal income taxes are deducted.

per-unit tax See *specific tax*.

Phillips curve Curve that relates the percentage rate of change of money wages (measured at an annual rate) to the level of unemployment (measured as the percentage of the *working population* unemployed). The curve is often amended to relate the percentage change in money prices (the inflation rate) to the level of the GDP on the assumption of stable relations between (i) unemployment and the GDP and (ii) changes in money wages and changes in the price level. When the two curves are both in use, they are often distinguished by naming them the wage-Phillips curve and the price-Phillips curve. See *short-run Phillips curve, long-run Phillips curve,* and *expectations-augmented Phillips curve*.

point elasticity of demand Measures demand elasticity by using the derivative of quantity demanded with respect to price, $(dq/dp) \times (p/q)$, as opposed to the arc elasticity that uses the ratio $\Delta q/\Delta p$ taken over a small range.

point elasticity of supply Measures supply elasticity by using the derivative of quantity supplied (s) with respect to price, $(ds/dp) \times (p/s)$, as opposed to the arc elasticity that uses the ratio $\Delta s/\Delta p$ taken over a small range.

poll tax A tax that takes the same lump sum from everyone.

portfolio investment Investment in bonds and other debt instruments that do not imply ownership, and in minority holdings of shares that do not establish legal control.

positive Statements concerning what is, was, or will be; they assert alleged facts about the universe in which we live. Compare *normative*.

positively related An increase in one variable is associated with an increase in another.

potential GDP, The level of output at which there is no *demand-deficient unemployment* and firms are producing at their normal rates of output. This is usually indicated by the symbol Y^*

precautionary balances The amount of money people wish to hold because of the possibility of having to make unexpected future payments. Because both these and speculative balances respond to changes in the interest rate, they are often lumped together treated as a single set of balances that change in response to the interest rate.

precautionary motive The motive for holding money balances to meet unexpected future payments.

predatory pricing A pricing strategy that is intended to drive a competitor out of business.

present value The value now of a sum to be received in the future. Also called discounted present value.

price control Anything that influences prices by law rather than by market forces.

price discrimination Situation arising when firms sell different units of their output at different prices for reasons not associated with differences in costs.

price elasticity of demand The percentage change in quantity demanded divided by the percentage change in price that brought it about. Usually just called elasticity of demand.

price elasticity of supply The percentage change in quantity supplied divided by the percentage change in price that brought it about. usually just called elasticity of supply.

price index A statistical measure of the average level some group of prices relative to some base period. The value in the base period is set to 100.

price level See *general price level*.

price system An economic system in which market-determined prices play a key role in determining the allocation of resources to various productive activities and the distribution of the GDP among various groups.

price taker A firm that can alter its rate of production and sales within any feasible range without having any effect on the prices of its products that are determined by impersonal market forces.

price–consumption line A line on an indifference curve diagram showing how consumption changes as the price of one commodity changes, *ceteris paribus*.

price-makers Firms that administer their prices. See *administered price*.

principal (1) The amount of a loan, (2) the agents who employ others to work on their behalf.

principal–agent problem The problem of resource allocation that arises because contracts that will induce agents to act in their principals' best interests are often impossible to write or too costly to monitor.

principle of substitution The prediction that methods of production will change if the relative prices of inputs change. Relatively more of the cheaper input and relatively less of the more expensive input will be used.

prisoner's dilemma A term in game theory for a game in which the *Nash equilibrium* leaves both players less well off than if they cooperated with each other.

private benefits The benefits of some activity that accrue to the parties in that activity.

private consumption spending Spending on the goods *consumed by* private individuals, even where *payment for the goods* may have been made by some other organisation such as the government, as with health services.

private cost The value of the best alternative use of the resources used in production as valued by the producer.

private sector That portion of an economy in which the organizations that produce goods and services are owned and operated by private units such as households and firms. Compare *public sector*.

pro-cyclical Anything that is positively correlated with the business cycle. For example, employment increases when GDP increases.

producer Any unit that makes goods or services.

producers' surplus Total revenue minus total variable cost; the market value that the firm creates by producing goods, net of the value of the resources currently used to create these goods but not counting any contribution to fixed (sunk) costs.

production The act of making goods and services.

production function A mathematical relation showing the maximum output that can be produced by each and every combination of inputs.

production possibility boundary A curve that shows the alternative combinations of commodities that can just be attained if all available productive resources are fully employed and used efficiently; the boundary between attainable and unattainable output combinations.

productive efficiency Production of any output at the lowest attainable cost for that level of output, so that it is impossible to reallocate resources and produce more of one output without simultaneously producing less of some other output.

productivity Output per unit of input employed. Can be expressed in many alternates by dividing output by different inputs such as labour or capital.

products A general term referring to all goods and services. Sometimes also referred to as *commodities*.

profit (1) In ordinary usage, the difference between the value of outputs and the value of inputs. (2) In microeconomics, the difference between revenues received from the sale of goods and the value of inputs, which includes all imputed costs for the services of inputs owned by the firm, the most important of which is the opportunity cost of capital. Also called *pure profit* or *economic profit*. (3) In macroeconomics, a component of factor incomes (and thus income-based measures of national product) which is measured as trading surpluses plus a component of mixed incomes.

profit-maximizing output The level of output that maximizes a firm's profits. Sometimes also called the optimum output.

progressive tax A tax that takes a larger percentage of people's income the larger their income is. Compare *regressive tax* and *proportional tax*.

progressivity The general term for the relation between income and the percentage of income paid in taxes.

proportional tax A tax that takes the same percentage of people's income whatever the level of their income.

protectionism Any departure from free trade designed to give some protection to domestic industries from foreign competition.

public corporation A body set up to run a nationalized industry. It is owned by the state but is usually under the direction of a more or less independent, state-appointed board.

public goods Goods and services that, once produced, can be consumed by everyone in the society such as police protection and parks. Also called collective consumption goods.

public sector That portion of an economy in which production is owned and operated by the government or by bodies created and controlled by it, such as nationalized industries. Compare *private sector*.

purchasing power parity theory Theory that the equilibrium exchange rate between two national currencies will be the one that equates their purchasing powers.

purchasing power parity (PPP) exchange rate The exchange rate between two currencies that equates their purchasing powers and hence adjusts over time for relative inflation rates.

pure market economy An economy in which all decisions, without exception, are made by individuals and firms acting through unhindered markets.

pure profit Any excess of a firm's revenue over all opportunity costs including those of capital. Also called economic profit.

pure rate of interest See *pure return on capital*.

pure return on capital The amount that capital can earn in a riskless investment. Also called the pure rate of interest.

quantitative easing The purchase of government and corporate bonds by the central bank on a large scale intended to raise the money supply, influence assets prices and affect long term interest rates. Used by the Bank of England in 2009–10 when it wanted to stimulate *aggregate demand* but could not lower *bank rate* any further.

quantity actually bought and sold The amount of a commodity that consumers and firms actually succeed in purchasing and selling.

quantity actually purchased See *quantity actually bought and sold*.

quantity demanded The amount of a commodity that households wish to purchase in some time period.

quantity supplied The amount of a commodity that firms offer for sale in some time period.

quantity theory of money Theory predicting that the price level and the quantity of money vary in exact proportion to each other; e.g., changing M by X per cent changes P by X per cent.

ratio scale See *logarithmic scale*.

rational expectations The theory that people fully understand how the economy works and learn quickly from their mistakes, so that, while random errors may be made, systematic and persistent errors are not made.

rational ignorance This occurs when agents have no rational incentive to inform themselves about some government action because the costs of so doing greatly exceed the potential benefits of any action the agent could take as a result of having the correct information.

real business cycles An approach to the explanation of business cycles that uses dynamic equilibrium market-clearing models and relies on productivity and taste shocks as a trigger. In such models all cycles are an optimal response to the real shock and there are no deviations from potential output: rather, it is the full equilibrium that fluctuates over time.

real capital Physical assets, including factories, machinery, and stocks of material and finished goods. Also called *physical capital*.

real exchange rate An index of the relative prices of domestic and foreign goods.

real income The purchasing power of *money income*, measured by deflating nominal income by an index of the price level.

real money supply The money supply measured in purchasing power units, measured as the nominal money supply divided by an index of the price index.

real national product Total output valued at *base-year* or reference year prices, measured for example by GDP at 1999 prices. A volume measure of real activity that removes the effects of inflation.

real product wage The proportion of the sale value of each unit of output that is accounted for by labour costs (including the pre-tax nominal wage rate, benefits, and the firm's national insurance contributions).

real interest rate The return on any investment measured in real terms. It is approximated by the money rate of interest *minus* the inflation rate (or expected inflation rate) and measured precisely by the equation (1+ nominal rate of interest)/(rate of inflation) = (1 + real rate of interest). See also *nominal interest rate*.

real wage The money wage deflated by a price index to measure the wage's purchasing power.

reallocation of resources Some change in the uses to which the economy's resources are put.

recession A sustained drop in the level of aggregate economic activity officially defined to occur when the GDP drops for two successive periods.

recessionary gap A negative output gap, when actual GDP falls short of potential GDP.

redemption date The time at which the principal of a loan is to be repaid.

regressive tax A tax that takes a smaller percentage of people's incomes the larger their income is. Compare *progressive tax*.

relative price Any price expressed as a ratio of another price or of all prices as measured by a price index.

renewable resources Productive resources that can be replaced as they are used up, as with *real capital* or forests; distinguished from *non-renewable resources*, which are available in a fixed stock that when depleted cannot be replaced, such as natural oil and coal.

replacement investment Investment that replaces capital as it wears out but does not increase the capital stock.

replacement ratio Benefits received by those out of work as a proportion of the wage of those in employment.

repo Short for a 'sale and repurchase agreement', whereby a firm sells a security (such as a gilt) to a bank and agrees to buy it back at some future time. The difference in price between sale and repurchase reflects the ruling rate of interest. The deal is a loan (usually short-term) secured on the security involved. Central banks typically set the rate of interest in repo transactions for a specific term. In the UK the Bank of England sets the two-week repo rate.

reservation price The price below which some action will not be taken, such as selling a commodity or accepting a job.

resource allocation The allocation of the economy's scarce resources among alternative uses.

retail price index (RPI) An index of the general price level based on the consumption pattern of typical consumers.

reverse repo Similar to a *repo*, but here the bank sells the security to the firm and agrees to buy it back at some future date.

Ricardo effect The theory that foresighted agents will understand that an increases in current government spending financed by new public debt will require new taxes in the future to service that debt and so will have little current expansionary effect because agents will increase their savings to cover their future tax liabilities by an amount that will just offset the effect of the increase in government spending.

risk premium The return on capital necessary to compensate owners of capital for the risk of loss of their capital.

risk-averse Description of agents who wish to avoid risks and so will play only those games that are sufficiently biased in their favour to overcome their aversion to risk; they will be unwilling to play mathematically fair games, let alone games those that are biased against them.

risk-loving Description of agents who are willing to play some games that are biased against them, the extent of the love of risk being measured by the degree of bias that they are willing to accept.

risk-neutral Description of agents who are indifferent about playing a mathematically fair game and are willing to play games that are biased in their favour but not games that are biased against them.

rivalrous A good or service is rivalrous if, when one person consumes a unit of it, no other person can also consume that unit, as with all ordinary goods and services, such as apples or haircuts.

saving Income received by individuals that they do not spend on *consumption*.

savings ratio See *average propensity to save*.

scatter diagram Plots of a series of observations each made on two variables, e.g. the price and quantity of eggs sold in 20 different cities.

seigniorage The revenue that accrues to the issuer of money.

self-employed Those people who work for themselves.

sellers' preferences Allocation of a commodity by the decisions of sellers when the commodity is in excess demand.

services Intangible production that does not generate a physical product, such as haircuts and medical services.

share option See *option*.

shares See *equities*.

shifting The passing of tax incidence from the person who initially pays it to someone else.

short run The period of time over which some inputs, such as physical capital, cannot be varied.

short-run aggregate supply (*SRAS*) curve The total amount that will be produced and offered for sale at each price level on the assumption that all input prices and technology are fixed.

short-run equilibrium Generally, equilibrium subject to fixed inputs or other things that cannot change over the time period being considered.

short-run Phillips curve Any particular *Phillips curve* drawn for a given expected rate of inflation. See also the expectations-augmented Phillips curve and the long-run Phillips curve.

short-run supply curve A curve showing the relation of quantity supplied to price when one or more factors is fixed; under perfect competition, the horizontal sum of marginal cost curves (above the level of average variable costs) of all firms in an industry.

shutdown price The price that is equal to a firm's average variable costs, below which a profit-maximising firm will produce no output. See also *break-even price*.

simple multiplier Usually applies to the value of the *multiplier* in the aggregate expenditure (*AE*) system when the interest rate is an exogenous variable and firm are willing to supply all that is demanded at existing prices (the aggregate supply curve is horizontal). Also called the *interest-constant multiplier*

single proprietorship An enterprise with one owner who is personally responsible for everything that is done. More commonly called a *sole trader*.

size distribution of income A classification of the amount of income received by income earners who fall within each of a series of income ranges, irrespective of the sources of that income. For example, the amount of income received by those in the bottom 10 percent of the income distribution, the amount received by those in the second 10 percent, right up to amount received by those in the top 10 percent of all income earners.

slump A large and long-lasting positive GDP gap and thus a period of low output and low employment. See also *boom*.

small open economy (SOE) An economy that is a price taker for both its imports and its exports. It must buy and sell at world prices, irrespective of the quantities that it buys and sells.

social benefits The value of an activity to the whole society, which includes the internal effects on those who are involved in deciding on it and the external effects on those who are not involved in the activity.

social cost The value to the whole society rather than to a specific individual or firm.

sole trader A non-incorporated business operated by a single owner. Modern UK terminology for a *single proprietorship*.

specialization When applied to countries, it refers to producing at home products for which the country has comparative advantage and importing those for which it has a comparative disadvantage. When applied to labour within a country, it refers to specialisation in particular tasks rather than producing a wider range of things, and in the extreme case producing everything that a person consumes. It is a continuous variable so that one can speak of 'increasing amounts of specialisation' as for example when one labourer produces everything she consumes, as might have happened in the days of hunter gatherers; producing the whole of just one product, as happens under craft production; or producing a small part of one product, as is typical today. See also *division of labour*

specific tax A tax expressed as so much per unit, independent of its price. Also called a per-unit tax.

speculation Taking a financial position based on expectations of the future that will yield gain if things turn out as, or better than, expected or losses if expectations are not fulfilled.

speculative balances Money held to take advantage of unexpected changes in asset prices (these are only bonds in the simple two-asset macro model). Because both these and precautionary balances respond to changes in the interest rate, they are often lumped together and treated as a single set of balances that change in response to the interest rate.

speculative motive The motive that leads agents to hold money in response to the risks inherent in fluctuating asset prices (these are only bonds in the simple two-asset macro model).

spread The difference between the prices or interest rates on specific assets or loans, such as the spread between deposit and loan rates offered by banks.

***SRAS* curve** See *short-run aggregate supply curve*.

stabilization policy The attempt to reduce fluctuations in GDP, employment, and the price level by use of *monetary* and *fiscal policies*.

stagflation The simultaneous occurrence of a positive GDP gap (with its accompanying high unemployment) and rising inflation.

stock See *equities*.

stock variable A variable that does not have a time dimension. It is contrasted with a flow variable, which does.

stockbuilding The process of building *stocks* or inventories more commonly called inventory accumulation.

stocks Accumulation of inputs and outputs held by firms to facilitate a smooth flow of production in spite of variations in delivery of inputs and sales of outputs. Now called inventories in National Accounts. In US terminology, stocks are ordinary company shares or equities.

strategic Behaviour that takes into account the reactions of others to one's own actions, as when an oligopolistic firm makes decisions that take account of its competitors' reactions.

strategic form game See *normal form game.*

structural unemployment Unemployment that exists because of a *mismatch* between the characteristics of the unemployed and the characteristics of the available jobs in terms of region, occupation, or industry.

substitutes Two goods are substitutes if the quantity demanded of one is positively related to the price of the other.

substitution effect The change in quantity demanded of a good resulting from a change in the commodity's relative price, eliminating the effect of the price change on real income.

sunk costs of entry Those costs that must be incurred for a firm to enter a market and cannot be recouped when the firm leaves.

supergame A game that is repeated an infinite number of times.

supply The whole relation between the quantity supplied of some commodity and its own price.

supply curve The graphical representation of the relation between the quantity of some commodity that producers wish to make and sell per period of time and the price of that commodity, *ceteris paribus.*

supply function A mathematical relation between the quantity supplied and all the variables that influence it.

supply of effort The total number of hours people in the labour force are willing to work. Also called supply of labour.

supply of labour See *supply of effort.*

supply of money The total amount of money circulating in the economy. Also called the money supply or the money stock.

supply schedule A numerical tabulation showing the quantity supplied at a number of alternative prices.

supply shock See *aggregate supply shock.*

supply-side policies Policies that seek to shift either the short-run or the long-run aggregate supply curve.

surprise aggregate supply curve See *Lucas aggregate supply curve.*

sustainable growth A concept introduced by the UN's Bruntland Commission and referring to growth that can continue without causing side effects such as deforestation and climate warming that will slow or stop future growth.

tacit collusion Occurs when firms arrive at the cooperative solution (which maximizes their joint profit) even though they may not have formed an explicit agreement to cooperate.

takeover When one firm buys another firm.

targets The variables in the economy that policymakers wish to influence. Typical policy targets might be inflation, unemployment, or real growth.

tariffs Taxes on imported goods.

term The amount of time between a bond's issue date and its redemption date.

terms of trade The ratio of the average price of a country's exports to the average price of its imports.

theory of games The study of rational decision-making in situations in which each player must anticipate the reactions of competitors to the moves that she makes. It can be applied to analysis of the strategic interaction of firms in oligopolistic markets.

third-party effects See *externalities.*

time-inconsistency Problem that arises in rational expectations models when policymakers have an incentive to abandon their commitments at a later time. The existence of this incentive is generally understood by private sector agents, and it may influence their current behaviour.

time-series data Data on some variable taken at different, usually regularly spaced, points in time, such as consumer spending in each quarter for the last 10 years.

total cost (*TC*) The total of all costs of producing a firm's output, usually divided into *fixed* and *variable costs.*

total final expenditure The total expenditure required to purchase all the goods and services that are produced domestically when these are valued at market prices.

total fixed costs The total of a firm's costs that do not vary in the short run.

total product (*TP*) Total amount produced by a firm during some time period.

total revenue (*TR*) Total amount of money that a firm receives from the sale of its output over some period of time.

total utility The total satisfaction derived from consuming some amount of a commodity.

total variable costs The total of those of the firm's costs that vary in the short run.

tradables Goods and services that potentially enter into international trade.

trade account The part of the balance of payments accounts relating to trade in goods and services. Merchandise trade relates only to goods.

trade creation The increase in trade between the members of a customs union or free-trade area where previously protected industries had served only their own home markets.

trade cycles See *business cycles.*

trade diversion The diversion of a member country's imports or exports from other countries to union members as a result of the preferential removal of tariffs following the formation of a customs union or a free-trade area.

trade or craft union A union covering workers with a common set of skills, no matter where, or for whom, they work.

trade-weighted exchange rate An index of the average of the exchange rates between a particular country's currency and those of its major trading partners, with each rate being weighted by the amount of trade with the country in question. Also called the *effective exchange rate.*

traditional economic system Economic system in which behaviour is based primarily on tradition, custom, and habit.

transaction costs Costs involved in making a trade in addition to the price of the product itself, such as the time involved or the cost of transport.

transactions balances Money balances held because of the non-synchronisation of every day payments and receipts. For example, wages may be paid weekly while spending occurs daily.

transactions motive The motive for holding cash because purchases occur regularly while income is received only periodically–the non-synchronisation of payments and receipts.

transfer earnings The amount that a factor or input must earn in its present use to prevent it from moving (i.e. transferring) to another use.

transfer payments Payments not made in return for any contribution to current output, such as unemployment benefits. Unrelated to retransfer earnings

transmission mechanism See *monetary transmission mechanism*.

transnational corporations (TNCs) Firms that have operations in more than one country. Also called transnationals or multinational enterprises (MNEs).

underdeveloped countries See *less-developed countries*.

unit cost See *average variable cost*.

unit elasticity An elasticity with a numerical measure of 1, indicating that the percentage change in quantity is equal to the percentage change in price (so that total expenditure remains constant).

utility See *marginal utility* and *total utility*.

utils An imaginary measure of utility used in the exposition of marginal utility theory, which assumes that utility is cardinally measurable.

validation When the authorities sustain an ongoing inflation by increasing the money supply at the same rate as the price level is rising.

value added The value of a firm's output minus the value of the inputs that it purchases from other firms.

value added tax (VAT) Tax charged as a proportion of a firm's *value added*.

value of money See *purchasing power of money*.

variable Any well-defined item, such as the price of a commodity or its quantity, that can take on various specific values. *Endogenous variables* are determined from with the theory while *exogenous variables* are determined from without.

variable cost A cost that varies directly with changes in output. Also called direct cost or avoidable cost.

variable factors Inputs whose amount can be varied over the time period being considered, usually the short run.

velocity of circulation The number of times an average unit of money is used in transactions within a specific period. Defined as the ratio of nominal GDP to the money stock.

vertical equity Equitable treatment of people in different income brackets. Compare *horizontal equity*.

very long run A period of time over which the technological possibilities open to a firm or the economy as a whole are subject to change.

visible account The part of the balance of payments accounts relating to trade in goods.

visible trade Trade in physical products. Same as *merchandise trade*.

visibles Tangible goods such as cars, aluminium, coffee, and iron ore, which we can see when they cross international borders.

voluntary export restriction (VER) Restriction whereby an exporting country agrees to limit the amount it sells to a second country.

voluntary unemployment Unemployment that occurs when there is a job available but the unemployed person is not willing to accept it at the existing wage rate.

winner's curse The possibility that the agent who wins the bidding on a contested takeover may pay more than the target firm is really worth because the winner is the one with the highest valuation of all bidders.

withdrawals (also called leakages) Spending that leaves the domestic economy and does not create further incomes for domestic residents. Import spending, for example, creates incomes overseas. Also called *leakages*. The main withdrawals from the circular flow between households and firms are savings, taxes, and imports.

workforce (or working population) The total of the employed, the self-employed, and the unemployed, i.e. those of working age who have a job plus those who are looking for work. Also known as labour force.

X-inefficiency Failure to use resources efficiently within the firm so that firms are producing above their relevant cost curves and the economy is inside its production possibility boundary.

Y_c the level of GDP at which the inflation rate starts to rise above the expected rate. This is a little above potential or normal capacity GDP, Y^*, because firms like to hold a bit of capacity in reserve to meet unexpected temporary increases in demand without having to raise prices.

yield curve A line on a graph plotting the yield on securities against the term to maturity. It illustrates, for example, the differences between three month, six month, one year, five year and twenty years interest rates being quoted at the same point in time.

INDEX